C0-ATR-978

DISCARDED

COMPARATIVE CORPORATE
GOVERNANCE

Comparative Corporate Governance
– The State of the Art and Emerging Research –

Edited by

Klaus J. Hopt, Hideki Kanda, Mark J. Roe, Eddy Wymeersch,
and Stefan Prigge

CLARENDON PRESS · OXFORD
1998

Oxford University Press, Great Clarendon Street, Oxford OX2 6DP
Oxford New York
Athens Auckland Bangkok Bogotá Buenos Aires Calcutta
Cape Town Chennai Dar es Salaam Delhi Florence Hong Kong Istanbul
Karachi Kuala Lumpur Madrid Melbourne Mexico City Mumbai
Nairobi Paris São Paulo Singapore Taipei Tokyo Toronto Warsaw
and associated companies in
Berlin Ibadan

Oxford is a registered trade mark of Oxford University Press

Published in the United States
by Oxford University Press Inc., New York

© K. Hopt, H. Kanda, M. Roe, E. Wymeersch, and S. Prigge 1998

The moral rights of the authors have been asserted

First published 1998

All rights reserved. No part of this publication may be reproduced,
stored in a retrieval system, or transmitted, in any form or by any means,
without the prior permission in writing of Oxford University Press.
Within the UK, exceptions are allowed in respect of any fair dealing for the
purpose of research or private study, or criticism or review, as permitted
under the Copyright, Designs and Patents Act 1988, or in the case of
reprographic reproduction in accordance with the terms of the licences
issued by the Copyright Licensing Agency. Enquiries concerning
reproduction outside these terms and in other countries should be
sent to the Rights Department, Oxford University Press,
at the address above

British Library Cataloguing in Publication Data
Data available

Library of Congress Cataloguing-in-Publication Data
Data available
ISBN 0–19–826888–2

Printed in Great Britain,
on acid-free paper by
Biddles Ltd.,
Guildford and King's Lynn

Preface

This book goes back to a symposium held at the Max Planck Institute for Foreign Private and Private International Law in Hamburg on May 15-17, 1997, with the generous help of the Schwartzkoppen-Stiftung in the Stifterverband für die deutsche Wissenschaft e.V., Essen, the Sloan Foundation, New York, and the Max Planck Society. However, this book is intended to be more than just another conference volume. Instead, it tries to give a comprehensive survey of the state of the art and the most recent research being done on corporate governance in the triad, i.e., Europe (with particular emphasis on Germany and the U.K.), the U.S., and, as far as possible, Japan. The title, *"Comparative Corporate Governance – The State of the Art and Emerging Research –"*, reflects this multinational approach and could be specified further as *"Current Research in Law, Economics, and Economic History in Europe, the U.S., and Japan."*

Corporate governance relates to the internal organization and power structure of the firm, the functioning of the board of directors both in the one-tier and the two-tier system, the ownership structure of the firm, and the interrelationships among management board, shareholders, and other stakeholders, in particular the company's workforce and its creditors. Provided that—as is most probably the case—current corporate governance systems in industrial countries have contributed to the economic success of these economies, they are examples of more or less well-performing systems. Despite their apparent differences, somehow they all seem to achieve a certain degree of punishment for managers who waste resources. So one can draw the important conclusion that there are alternative ways to reach the common goal of efficient resource allocation. Turning from a static to a dynamic perspective, however, further fascinating questions emerge as to the significance of circumstances for the efficiency of a corporate governance system. It is by no means certain that a system that has proved its efficiency in the past will remain efficient when conditions change. Moreover, most probably an economy's adaptability to change will be affected by its corporate governance system. A better understanding of these relations could also serve as a basis for better-founded policy recommendations that could yield significant welfare improvements. Yet so far we have only little knowledge of how such complex systems actually work. Consequently, the ability to give welfare-enhancing recommendations is still poor and needs substantial improvement.

Comparative corporate governance research may bring forth new insights that research conducted only within one system may fail to produce. Analysis of the most successful economies—the U.S., Europe, and Japan—seems to be a natural starting point for such research. Accordingly, we felt it was essential to assemble a unique sample of scholars from the triad countries, and—though an apparent rarity, especially in Europe—a strictly interdisciplinary approach was of the utmost importance. The complexity of corporate governance as an object of research is partly due to the fact that two disciplines, law and economics, each address it within their own sphere, while other disciplines such as the political and social sciences touch it as well. Moreover, the insight is spreading that the analysis of institutions must also consider the roots, which may prove to be revealing and even decisive for current issues and the future (path dependence). The book therefore blends contributions from historians, economists, and law professors, and adds the experience of a few practitioners serving in outstanding positions, such as Allen, former Chancellor of the Court of Chancery of the State of Delaware, the most important U.S. court for corporate law; Baumann, the chairman of the supervisory board of Siemens; Breuer, the CEO of Deutsche Bank; Schmidt, president of the German Auditors' Institute; and Semler, who has been a member of the supervisory board of Daimler-Benz and other major companies.

This volume has three parts: the opening section deals with the roots and perspectives of corporate governance; the different building blocks of a corporate governance system are then each analyzed in a chapter of the second part; and the final segment presents studies that treat corporate governance systems in toto, with a special focus on making or facilitating comparative corporate governance research.

Part I starts with a look at some aspects of historical roots in Europe and the U.S. *Dunlavy* investigates the development of shareholder voting rights and *Hertner* looks at early multinational enterprises from a corporate governance perspective. In Chapter 2 on emerging markets, *Coffee* analyzes the new, just evolving roots in transitional economies, in particular in the Czech Republic and in Poland. The securities market is an important component within the fabric of corporate governance forces; consequently, changes in securities regulation most probably affect corporate governance. *Romano*, in Chapter 3, addresses this aspect and puts it into perspective. She proposes the adoption of the competitive approach in U.S. corporate law to important aspects of U.S. securities regulation. This line of reasoning, as controversial as it was at the symposium, is intellectually challenging; if adopted, it would have far-reaching consequences in other systems as well, such as that of the European Union and its harmonization of corporate law and securities regulation.

Partitioned into seven chapters, *Part II* contains analyses of the various building blocks of a corporate governance system. This starts in Chapter 4 with five papers that deal with the central organ of the corporation, the board. First, *Hopt* reviews the roots, experience, theories, and reform proposals regarding the German two-tier system, which is under acute scrutiny both in academia and politics. *Theisen*, taking a more economic perspective, comments on empirical evidence with a critical résumé as to the current efficiency of the German two-tier system. And *Semler*, drawing from his experience of serving on numerous boards, describes the actual practice of German supervisory boards. Two further contributions in this chapter investigate the U.S. board. *Bhagat* and *Black* first survey previous evidence on the influence of board composition on performance, and secondly present an empirical investigation of their own that casts some doubt on the current enthusiasm for independent directors. Finally, the reader can share in *Allen*'s inside knowledge of the Court of Chancery of Delaware as he investigates the duties of directors and the rationale and legal extent of the business judgment rule.

Labor as a force in corporate governance is one distinguishing feature of the several corporate governance systems. As labor representation on the board is one of the most controversial aspects—attested to, for example, by the uneasy development of European corporate law harmonization—it is dealt with in Chapter 5 immediately after the board. *Gerum* and *Wagner* apply a number of economic theories to the analysis of labor co-determination and build a bridge to corporate governance in Germany and the EU. For the latter, they strongly favor system competition as regards co-determination, thus following *Romano*'s approach in Chapter 3. *Roe* presents an interesting hypothesis which claims that the co-determination rules in the German stock corporation are a major explanatory factor for the low activity in the IPO market and, consequently, in the secondary stock market. *Davies* reports on the present and future role of labor in corporate governance in the U.K., a country with a tradition entirely different from that of Germany. Finally, *Gordon* presents an American case study of the role of labor during the restructuring at United Airlines, suggesting that the corporate governance role of labor might be different in crisis situations and company failures.

Another prominent feature, especially of the German corporate governance system, is the outstanding position of financial intermediaries—in particular banks—both on the board and otherwise. Chapter 6 joins four papers on the different strands of bank influence on corporations. *Mülbert* analyzes German universal banks' motives for holding equity participations in non-financial firms, and the consequences these holdings may have for corporate governance. Moreover, he presents recent data on banks' equity holdings. *Wenger* and *Kaserer* empirically investigate the currently hotly debated question as to the connection between the equity participations of banks and the performance of the respective companies. In addition, they provide an innovative analysis of the relation between recent stock option plans of German companies and their ownership structures. *Breuer* describes his experience with the role of financial intermediaries in Germany and outlines the reforms necessary for improvement of the deficient equity culture in Germany. Finally, *Baums* presents first results of a comparative study of shareholder representation and proxy voting in the EU.

Capital markets, often considered to be in a substitution relation to strong financial intermediaries, are the subject of Chapter 7. To be more precise, venture capital and primary markets as preconditions for a forceful secondary market stand at the center of the two papers. *Bessler, Kaen, and Sherman* present an empirical inquiry into the relation between ownership structure and post-IPO performance in Germany. *Gerke* investigates the reason for the weakness of German IPO activity and proposes a European Information Exchange which could help to solve this market failure.

The importance of the capital market in corporate governance is partly due to the fact that it is also the place of the market for corporate control. This is the subject of Chapter 8. *Franks* and *Mayer* present a comparative study of three cases of hostile takeovers in Germany and develop tentative thoughts on the influence of regulation on takeovers. *Baumann*, chairman of the *Börsensachverständigenkommission* at the German Ministry of Finance, reports first experiences with the voluntary takeover code, effective since October 1, 1995 and reformed as of January 1998, and discusses the connection with pending EU regulation in this field. Two appendices provide details of the cases reviewed so far by the *Übernahmekommission* and present a selected case in greater detail. Turning to the U.S., *Kahan* analyzes the latest development in the Delaware Supreme Court's takeover jurisprudence and the consequences this may have for takeover activity in the U.S.

Disclosure and auditing are indispensable preconditions for the effective functioning of both internal control mechanisms, such as the board, and external forces, e.g., the market for corporate control. In light of this substantial significance, coverage of this field in the corporate governance discussion is surprisingly low. A reason for this may be that research in accounting tends to be a segregated field in economics. The three papers in Chapter 9 address this widely ignored subject. *Fox* delivers a general approach to the connection of disclosure requirements and corporate governance from a U.S. perspective. The forefront of Germany's accounting research is presented by *Baetge* and *Thiele,* who render some results of their unique data base and draw some conclusions with respect to corporate governance, focusing in particular on the currently debated degree of information provided by various accounting standards, and the auditor's task. The latter is more extensively dealt with by *P.J. Schmidt,* who delivers input from the practitioner's side, discussing the auditor's work in relation to both the current and the expected legal framework.

American corporate governance research seems to almost neglect the role of lenders, although companies usually have more debt outstanding than equity, and the potential agency conflicts between management and shareholders on the one side and lenders on the other side are well-known. The existence of this gap is only gradually being recognized. The three papers on lenders as a force in corporate governance in Chapter 10 deliver contributions to this emerging field. *Drukarczyk* and *H. Schmidt* present a general view and a corporate-governance-oriented analysis of covenants, and a comparison of the bankruptcy laws in Germany, France, and the U.S. *Berglöf* and *Sjögren* as well as *Hertig* investigate lenders as a force in corporate governance in Sweden and Switzerland respectively. *Berglöf* and *Sjögren* base their inquiry into whether the Swedish bank-borrower relationship is better characterized as arm's-length or control-oriented finance on an exceptional database consisting of data on individual credits. *Hertig* develops criteria for detecting and measuring the role of lenders and applies these criteria to four categories of representative firms.

Whereas each chapter in the central part of the book is devoted to a particular component of a corporate governance system, *Part III* again widens the perspective and offers analyses of corporate governance in a comparative and systemic sense. This begins with Chapter 11, which assembles three general papers on Japanese corporate governance by *Hoshi*, *Miwa*, and *Kanda*. Although similar at first sight, the papers focus on different main issues and put forward contrasting views on the theory of corporate governance in Japan. *Miwa* in particular is not in the mainstream, regarding employees as the dominating group of stakeholders in Japan with a far greater influence than stockholders. Taking the agency problems immanent in the relationships between the various corporate governance players and the institutions employed to solve them, *Hoshi* applies a systematic approach to derive his characterization of Japanese corporate governance. A key aspect of *Kanda*'s contribution is the spate of recent business scandals, which he comments on from a corporate governance perspective. Thus Chapter 11 gives an impression of the wide range of rather different possible interpretations of corporate governance in Japan.

As the final chapter, Chapter 12 provides more extensive comparative corporate governance analyses. It starts with a general paper by *Macey*, who proposes three measures to characterize corporate governance systems. The following three articles actually pursue comparative corporate governance research. The papers by *Kanda* and *Prigge* on Japan and Germany share a common structure agreed upon in advance. Thus, while they are not comparative when read in isolation, they are written to enable the readers to compare these two systems, which share some components while differing fundamentally in others. Finally, *Wymeersch*, in a contribution paralleling the two previous papers, delivers an extensive comparative inquiry into the corporate governance structures in various continental European countries; this analysis is comparative both as such and in connection with the articles by *Kanda* and *Prigge*. These papers supply a pool of up-to-date, corporate-governance-related facts presented in a manner conducive to comparative research.

The editors have consciously chosen to refrain from going beyond this introduction and trying to extract a general theory of comparative corporate governance. While the contributions to this book yield important parts of such a theory and offer many new insights into both the different systems and their parts, they also show that there are many different approaches to the problems, both from one discipline to another and internally, and that our understanding of how each single system works and how they compare to each other is still at an early stage of research and understanding. Presenting the state of the art of comparative corporate governance at the turn of the century may help to see where we stand, what we know and what we do not know, and, most important, what questions to pursue. International research in this field is going on at a breathtaking pace. This is fortunate—and absolutely necessary—in view of the systemic problems globalized economies face today.

We would like to thank all those colleagues and friends who attended the symposium and, by their contributions and participation, helped to produce this book. We thank the Schwartzkoppen-Stiftung in the Stifterverband für die deutsche Wissenschaft e.V., Essen, the Sloan Foundation, New York, and the Max Planck Society for generous moral and financial assistance. We would also like to mention and thank the research associates and assistants of the Max Planck Institute who helped to organize the symposium and prepared the discussion reports: *Baum, Bliesener, Haar, Merkt, Peddinghaus, Roth, and Voigt*. Finally we are most grateful to *Ingeborg Stahl* at the Max Planck Institute who converted the manuscripts and documents into a print-ready format, *Kristen Zetzsche*, Lynden, Washington, who polished the English language, and *Ingeburg Saldanha*, Klaus J. Hopt's secretary and right hand.

May 1998   *Klaus J. Hopt* and *Stefan Prigge*, Hamburg

Contents

Figures

Tables

E. Wenger and C. Kaserer (Chapter 6)

R.-E. Breuer (Chapter 6)

W. Bessler, F.R. Kaen, and H.C. Sherman (Chapter 7)

J. Franks and C. Mayer (Chapter 8)

K.-H. Baumann (Chapter 8)

E. Wymeersch (Chapter 12)

Abbreviations

A., A.2d	Atlantic Reporter (Second Series)
ABA-Report	American Bar Association-Report
ABl. EG	Amtsblatt der Europäischen Gemeinschaften (Official Journal of the European Communities)
Abs.	Absatz (Paragraph)
ACCL	Australian Company Case Law
ACSR	Australian Corporations and Securities Reporter
aff'd	affirmed
AG	Aktiengesellschaft (Stock Corporation, Germany)
AGM	Annual General Meeting
AICPA	American Institute of Certified Public Accountants
AktG	Aktiengesetz (German Stock Corporations Act)
ALI	American Law Institute
Am. B. Found. Res. J.	American Bar Foundation Research Journal
Am. Bankr. L.J.	American Bankruptcy Law Journal
Am. J. Comp. L.	American Journal of Comparative Law
Am.Rep.	American Reports
ann.	annotation
approx.	approximately
APR	Absolute Priority Rule
Art./art.	Article
Atk.	Atkinson
BALO	Bulletin des annonces légales obligatoires (France)
BAWe	Bundesaufsichtsamt für den Wertpapierhandel (German Federal Authority for Securities Trading)
BDI	Bundesverband der deutschen Industrie (Federation of German Industry)
BFC	Banking and Finance Commission (Belgium), see also CBF
BGBl.	Bundesgesetzblatt (Official Federal Gazette, Germany)
BIS	Bank for International Settlement
Brook. J. Int'l L.	Brooklyn Journal of International Law
Brook. L. Rev.	Brooklyn Law Review
Bus. Law.	Business Lawyer
BV	Besloten Vennootschap (The Netherlands)
BVK	Bundesverband deutscher Kapitalbeteiligungsgesellschaften (German Venture Capital Association)
C.A.	Court of Appeals
CAC 40	Compagnie des agents de change 40 index (French Stock Index)
Cal.	California
Cal. 3d	California Reports (Third Series)
Cal. App. 3d	California Appellate Reports (Third Series)
Cal. Ct. App.	California Court of Appeals
Cal. L. Rev.	California Law Review
CalPERS	California Public Employee Retirement System
CAPM	Capital Asset Pricing Model
CAR	Cumulated Abnormal Return
Cardozo L. Rev.	Cardozo Law Review
Cass.	Cour de cassation (France)

Cass. Com.	Cour de cassation, chambre commerciale et financière (France)
Cass. Crim.	Cour de cassation, chambre criminelle (France)
CBF	Commission bancaire et financière (Belgium)
c.c.	Codice Civile (Italian Civil Code)
CEO	Chief Executive Officer
cf.	confer
CFTC	Commodity Futures Trading Commission
Ch(s).	Chapter(s)
Ch.App.	Chancery Appellate Division
Ch.D.	Chancery Division
Chi.-Kent L. Rev.	Chicago-Kent Law Review
Chicano L. Rev.	Chicano Law Review
Cir.	Circuit
Cm, Cmnd	Command Paper
cmt.	comment(s)
CMVM	Comissão do Mercado de Valores Mobiliários (Portugal)
Cnmv	Comisión Nacional del Mercado de Valores (Spain)
COB	Commission des opérations de bourse (France)
col.	column
Colum. Bus. L. Rev.	Columbia Business Law Review
Colum. L. Rev.	Columbia Law Review
COM	Commission of the European Communities Documents
Comm. L.J.	Commercial Law Journal
Comm. Trib.	Commercial Tribunal (Belgium)
Consob	Commissione Nazionale per le Società e la Borsa (Italy)
Consol.	Consolidated
COO	Chief Operating Officer
Cornell Int'l L.J.	Cornell International Law Journal
Cornell L. Rev.	Cornell Law Review
CPA	Certified Public Accountant (Japan)
CSK	Czech Crown
Ct.	Court
Ct. App.	Court of Appeals
DAX	Deutscher Aktienindex (German Stock Index)
D.D.C.	District Court, District of Columbia
Del.	Delaware Reports
Del. Ch.	Delaware Chancery Reports
Del. J. Corp. L.	Delaware Journal of Corporate Law
Del. Supr.	Delaware Supreme Court
DGB	Deutscher Gewerkschaftsbund (German Trade Union Federation)
Duke L.J.	Duke Law Journal
EASDAQ	European Association of Securities Dealers Automated Quotation (System)
EC	European Community, European Communities
ECT	European Community Treaty
ed(s).	editor(s)
edn.	edition
EEC	European Economic Community
EG	Europäische Gemeinschaft (European Community)
EGM	Extraordinary General Meeting
Emory L.J.	Emory Law Journal
Eng. Rpts.	England Reports

ERISA	Employee Retirement Income Schemes Act
ESOP	Employee Stock Ownership Program
ESOT	Employee Stock Ownership Transaction
EU	European Union
EWC	European Works Council
F.2d	Federal Reporter (Second Series)
F. Supp.	Federal Supplement
FASB	Financial Accounting Standards Board
Fed.	Federal
Fed. Reg.	Federal Register
ff.	folgende (and the following ones)
Fin. Times	Financial Times
Fordham Int'l L.J.	Fordham International Law Journal
Fordham L. Rev.	Fordham Law Review
FSA	Financial Services Act (U.K.)
FTSE	Financial Times Stock Exchange (Index) (U.K.)
GAS	Groupes d'actionnaires stables (France)
GDP	Gross Domestic Product
Geo. L.J.	Georgetown Law Journal
GmbH	Gesellschaft mit beschränkter Haftung (Limited Liability Company, Germany)
GmbHG	Gesetz betreffend die Gesellschaften mit beschränkter Haftung (Limited Liability Companies Act, Germany)
Golden Gate U. L. Rev.	Golden Gate University Law Review
Harv. L. Rev.	Harvard Law Review
HGB	Handelsgesetzbuch (German Commercial Code)
HMSO	Her Majesty's Stationary Office
H.R.	House of Representatives
HR	Hoge Raad (Dutch Supreme Court)
IAS	International Accounting Standards
IASC	International Accounting Standards Committee
IDW	Institut der Wirtschaftsprüfer in Deutschland (Institute of Certified Public Accountants, Germany)
IML	Institut Monétaire Luxembourgeois
Int'l Bus. Law.	International Business Lawyer
Iowa L. Rev.	Iowa Law Review
IPF	Investment Privatization Fund
IPO	Initial Public Offering
IRRC	Investor Responsibility Research Center
ISD	Investment Services Directive
ISSA	International Society of Securities Administrators
JASD	Japan Securities Dealers Association
J. Comp. Corp. L. & Sec. Reg.	Journal of Comparative Corporate Law & Securities Regulation
J. Corp. L.	Journal of Corporation Law
JCP	Juriclasseur périodique (France)
J.L. Econ. & Org.	Journal of Law, Economics & Organization
J. Leg. Stud.	Journal of Legal Studies

KG	Kommanditgesellschaft (Limited Commercial Partnership, Germany)
KGaA	Kommanditgesellschaft auf Aktien (Commercial Partnership Limited by Shares, Germany)
KOM	Commission of the European Communities Documents
KonTraG	Gesetz zur Kontrolle und Transparenz im Unternehmensbereich (Act Concerning Control and Transparency in Companies, Germany)
L.	Law
L.Ed.	Lawyer's Edition
Law & Contemp. Probs.	Law & Contemporary Problems
LBO	Leveraged Buy-Out
LSE	London Stock Exchange
M&A	Merger & Acquisition
MBO	Management Buy-Out
McGill L.J.	McGill Law Journal
MDAX	Deutscher Midcap Aktienindex (Midcap DAX, Germany)
Mich. L. Rev.	Michigan Law Review
MitbestG	Mitbestimmungsgesetz (German Co-Determination Act)
MITI	Ministry of International Trade and Industry (Japan)
MNE	Multinational Enterprise
Mod. Bus. Corp. Act Annot.	Model Business Corporation Act Annotated
MOF	Ministry of Finance (Japan)
MOU	Memorandum of Understanding
n.	note
n.a.	not available
NASD	National Association of Securities Dealers
NASDAQ	National Association of Securities Dealers Automated Quotation (System)
Nat'l L. J.	National Law Journal
NBER	National Bureau of Economic Research
NBW	Nederlands Burgerlijk Wetboek (Dutch Civil Code), Book 2
N.C. L. Rev.	North Carolina Law Review
N.D. Cal.	Northern District of California
N.E. 2d	North Eastern Reporter (Second Series)
N.F.	Neue Folge (New Series)
NIF	National Investment Fund
NJ	Nederlandse Jurisprudentie (The Netherlands)
no(s).	number(s)
NPF	National Property Fund
Nr.	Nummer (number)
NTBF	New Technology-Based Firm
NV	Naamloze Vennootschap (The Netherlands)
Nw. J. Int'l L. & Bus.	Northwestern Journal of International Law and Business
Nw. U. L. Rev.	Northwestern University Law Review
NYSE	New York Stock Exchange
N.Y.U. J. Int'l L. & Pol.	New York University Journal of International Law & Policy
N.Y.U. L. Rev.	New York University Law Review
ÖAktG	Österreichisches Aktiengesetz (Austrian Stock Corporations Act)

OHG	Offene Handelsgesellschaft (General Commercial Partnership, Germany)
Ohio St. L.J.	Ohio State Law Journal
OJEC 'C' series	Official Journal of the European Communities, Information Series
OJEC 'L' series	Official Journal of the European Communities, Legislation Series
OK	Ondernemingskamer (The Netherlands)
OPA	Offre publique d'acquisition (France)
OR	Schweizerisches Obligationenrecht (Switzerland)
OTC	Over the Counter
p.	page
Pa.	Pennsylvania
Pas.	Pasicrisie (Belgium)
PDG	Président-directeur général (France)
PEP	Personal Equity Plan
Proc. Nat'l Acad. Sci.	Proceedings of the National Academy of Sciences
PRR	Pennsylvania Railroad
PSE	Prague Stock Exchange
pt(s)	part(s)
Pub.	Public
RA	Règlement amiable (France)
R.D.	Royal Decree (Belgium)
rev.	revised
Rev. Mod. Bus. Corp. Act	Revised Model Business Corporation Act
REXP	Deutscher Rentenindex (Performance) (German Bond Performance Index)
RLJ	Redressement et liquidation judiciaire (France)
s.	section
SA	Société anonyme (France)
SARL	Société à responsabilité limitée (France)
S.Ct.	Supreme Court Reporter
S.D. Cal.	Southern District of California
S.D.N.Y.	Southern District of New York
SEC	Securities and Exchange Commission
Sec.	Section
SECA	Swiss Private Equity & Corporate Finance Association
Sec. Reg. & L. Rep. (BNA)	Securities Regulation & and Law Reporter (Bureau of National Affairs)
SEL	Securities and Exchange Law (Japan)
SFAC	Statement of Financial Accounting Concepts
SIA	Securities Industry Association
SIB	Securities and Investments Board (U.K.)
So. Cal. L. Rev.	Southern California Law Review
SOE	State-Owned Enterprise
SPA	Società per azioni (Italy)
SPRL-BVBA	(equivalent to SARL)
Stan. J.L. Bus. & Fin.	Stanford Journal of Law, Business & Finance
Stan. L. Rev.	Stanford Law Review
Stat.	Statute(s)
STE	Stichting Toezicht Effectenverkeer (The Netherlands)
Sup. Ct.	Supreme Court/Superior Court

Supp.	Supplement
Tex. L. Rev.	Texas Law Review
Tul. L. Rev.	Tulane Law Review
Tz.	Textziffer (Numbered Subparagraph)
UAL	United Airlines
U. Cin. L. Rev.	University of Cincinnati Law Review
UCLA L. Rev.	University of California at Los Angeles Law Review
U.K.	United Kingdom
U. Mich. J.L. Ref.	University of Michigan Journal of Law Reform
U. Mich. L. Rev.	University of Michigan Law Review
U. Pa. L. Rev.	University of Pennsylvania Law Review
U.S.	United States of America, United States Reporter
U.S. GAAP	United States Generally Accepted Accounting Principles
U. Toronto L.J.	University of Toronto Law Journal
v/v.	versus
Va. L. Rev.	Virginia Law Review
VAG	Versicherungsaufsichtsgesetz (Supervision of Insurance Companies Act, Germany)
Vand. L. Rev.	Vanderbilt Law Review
VAT	Value Added Tax
VBO-FEB	Verbond van Belgische Ondernemingen - Fédération des entreprises de Belgique (Association of Belgian Enterprises)
VEB	Dutch Shareholders' Association
vgl.	vergleiche (confer)
vol.	volume
Wall St. J.	Wall Street Journal
Wash. U. L.Q.	Washington University Law Quarterly
Wis. L. Rev.	Wisconsin Law Review
W.L.R.	Western Law Review
WpHG	Wertpapierhandelsgesetz (Securities Trading Act, Germany)
Yale J. on Reg.	Yale Journal on Regulation
Yale L.J.	Yale Law Journal

The Contributors

William T. Allen

Professor of Law and Clinical Professor of Business, New York University, and Director of the NYU Center for Law & Business, a joint undertaking of the School of Law and the Stern School of Business. B.S. New York University, 1969; J.D. University of Texas, 1972; LL.D. (hon.) Dickinson Law School, 1992. Chairman, Independent Standards Board (board designated by the U.S. Securities & Exchange Commission to establish standards for auditor independence under U.S. securities law). Of counsel, Wachtell, Lipton, Rosen & Katz in New York City. Served as Chancellor of the Court of Chancery of the State of Delaware from 1985-97. Author of numerous judicial opinions on corporate directors' fiduciary duties under U.S. law.

Jörg Baetge

Professor of Business Administration, University of Münster (Germany), and Honorary Professor at the University of Vienna (Austria). Born 1937; Dipl.-Kfm. (MBA) University of Frankfurt/Main (Germany), 1964; Dr. rer. pol., University of Münster, 1968; Habilitation, University of Münster, 1972; Dr. rer. pol. honoris causa, European Business School, Oestrich-Winkel (Germany), 1997. Professor of Business Administration at the University of Frankfurt (1971-77) and at the University of Vienna (1977-79); member, Advisory Council of the Schmalenbach Society for Business Economics; President, Advisory Council of the Society for Economic and Social Cybernetics; Vice President, Association of Academics in Business Administration (1995-96); member, Academy of Science of North Rhine-Westphalia; member, Board of the German Accounting Standards Organization; "Kausch Award" of the University of Sankt Gallen (Switzerland) for Research in Accounting (1998). Over 300 publications on the subjects of cybernetic theory, business strategy, accounting (incl. group accounts), accounting theory, financial statement analysis, business valuation; author of *Bilanzen* 4th edn. (Düsseldorf 1996), *Konzernbilanzen* 3rd edn. (Düsseldorf 1997), *Bilanzanalyse* (1998); co-editor of *Rechnungslegung nach den International Accounting Standards* (Stuttgart 1998).

Harald Baum

Senior Research Associate, Head of Japanese Department, Max Planck Institute for Foreign Private and Private International Law, Hamburg, Germany. Dr. iur., Hamburg, 1985. Vice President, German-Japanese Lawyers Association. Editor of *Zeitschrift für Japanisches Recht* [*Journal for Japanese Law*]; author of *Marktzugang und Unternehmenserwerb in Japan* [*Market Access and Acquisitions of Companies in Japan*] (Heidelberg 1995); editor of *Japan: Economic Success and Legal System* (Berlin 1997); co-editor of *Japanisches Handels- und Wirtschaftsrecht* [*Japanese Economic and Business Law*] (with U. Drobnig) (Berlin 1994), *Börsenreform: Eine ökonomische, rechtsvergleichende und rechtspolitische Untersuchung* [*Stock Exchange Reform: Economics, Comparison of Law, Legal Policies*] (with K.J. Hopt & B. Rudolph) (Stuttgart 1997); various articles in professional journals on business law, corporate governance, and takeovers in Japan.

Karl-Hermann Baumann

Dr. Karl-Hermann Baumann is chairman of the supervisory board, and until February 19, 1998, was Head of Corporate Finance, Chief Financial Officer and Controller, and a member of the executive committee of the managing board of Siemens AG. Dr. Baumann joined Siemens in 1970. After holding several finance positions, he came to the U.S. in 1978 to serve as Senior Vice President of Siemens Capital Corporation. In 1983 he returned to Germany, becoming Vice President in 1984 and a member of the managing board in 1987. He assumed his current responsibilities in 1988. Dr. Baumann studied German, History, and Business Administration at universities in Freiburg, Berlin, Münster, Munich, and Saarbrücken.

Theodor Baums

Professor of Civil Law, Commercial and Economic Law, University of Osnabrück, Germany. Born 1947; Dr. iur. and Habilitation, University of Bonn. Professor, University of Münster, 1985-1987; Director, Institute for Commercial and Economic Law, University of Osnabrück; member, Steering Committee, International Corporate Law Group; European Corporate Governance Network; consultant to the World Bank, 1992-1995. Co-editor of various professional journals; author of numerous articles and books in national and international company, capital market, and antitrust law.

Erik Berglöf

Erik Berglöf directs the Stockholm Institute of Transition Economics and East European Economies (SITE) at Stockholm School of Economics. He has written extensively on financial contracting and corporate governance. In particular, he has applied theoretical insights to the study of differences between financial systems, and specific ownership and control arrangements in these countries. Recent work of his has also analyzed financing problems in the transition economies. He has published in academic journals such as *Quarterly Journal of Economics*, *Journal of Financial Economics*, *Journal of Law, Economics and Organization*, and *Economic Policy* and contributed to several monographs. He is a Research Fellow of the Centre of Economic Policy Research (CEPR) and the William Davidson Institute at the University of Michigan. He was previously Assistant Professor at ECARE, Université Libre de Bruxelles, and has held a visiting position at Stanford University. He has served on various EC-related panels and is currently project director of the Russian-European Centre for Economic Policy (RECEP), an EU-financed think tank/research institute in Moscow.

Wolfgang Bessler

Professor of Finance, University of Gießen, Germany. Dipl.-Kfm., Hamburg University, 1981; Dipl.-Hdl., Hamburg University, 1981; M.B.A. McGill University, 1983; Ph.D. Hamburg University, 1987. Previously taught at the University of Hamburg, Germany; Crouse-Hinds School of Management, Syracuse University, U.S.A.; Lally School of Management and Technology, Rensselaer Polytechnic Institute, U.S.A.; Hamburg School of Economics and Politics, Germany; Ayres Fellowship, American Bankers Association, 1990. Associate editor of *European Journal of Finance*; publications on subjects of commercial bank interest rate risk management, bank dividend policy, theory of the banking firm, and multi-factor-asset-pricing models; author of *Zinsrisikomanagement in Kreditinstituten* (Wiesbaden 1989).

Sanjai Bhagat

Professor of Finance, University of Colorado at Boulder. Previously taught at Princeton University and University of Chicago. Associate editor of *Journal of Financial and Quantitative Analysis*. Has published and consulted extensively on corporate governance, capital budgeting, and project valuation. Recent publications include: 'Shareholder Litigation: Share Price Movements, News Releases, and Settlement Amounts' (with J.D. Beck) *Managerial & Decision Economics* 19 (forthcoming 1998); *The Impact of Corporate Ownership, Performance, and Governance on Takeovers and Managerial Turnover* (with R.H. Jefferis) (Cambridge, MA, forthcoming 1998); 'Corporate Performance and Blockholdings of Investment Professionals' (with B.S. Black and M. Blair) (Association for Investment and Research [AIMR], December 1997); 'Corporate Research & Development Investments: International Comparisons' (with I. Welch) *Journal of Accounting and Economics* 19 (1995) 443-70; 'The Costs of Inefficient Bargaining and Financial Distress:

Evidence from Corporate Lawsuits' (with J.A. Brickley and J.L. Coles) *Journal of Financial Economics* 35 (1994) 221-47.

Bernard Black

Professor of Law, Stanford Law School. Previously Associate Professor of Law (1988-91) and Professor of Law (1992-98), Columbia Law School. A.B. Princeton University, 1975; M.A. (Physics) University of California at Berkeley, 1977; J.D. Stanford Law School, 1982. Law clerk to Judge Patricia Wald, United States Court of Appeals, 1982-83; Associate Attorney at Skadden, Arps, Slate, Meagher & Flom, New York City, 1983-87; Counsel of Commissioner Joseph Grundfest, U.S. Securities and Exchange Commission, 1987-88; Senior Legal Advisor, Harvard Institute for International Development Legal Reform Project, Moscow, Russia, 1994-95. Subjects: corporate acquisitions; corporate finance; foundations of regulatory state; law & economics; securities regulations. Books: *(Some of) The Essentials of Finance* (with Ronald Gilson) (Westbury, NY 1993); *The Law and Finance of Corporate Acquisitions* (with Ronald Gilson) 2nd edn. (Westbury, NY 1995); *A Guide to the Russian Law on Joint Stock Companies* (with Reinier Kraakman and Anna Tarassova) (1998).

Dirk H. Bliesener

Rechtsanwalt, Hengeler Mueller Weitzel Wirtz, Frankfurt am Main, Germany. Born 1967; Maître en Droit, Panthéon-Sorbonne, 1990; C.E.P., Institut d'Etudes Politiques de Paris, 1990; First State Exam (Law), University of Bonn, 1992; LL.M. Yale Law School, 1993; Second State Exam (Law), Hamburg 1997; Dr. iur., University of Hamburg, 1998. Admitted to the New York Bar, 1995; admitted to the Frankfurt am Main (Germany) Bar, 1998. Co-editor of *Yale Journal of International Law* 1992-93. Author of *Aufsichtsrechtliche Verhaltenspflichten beim Wertpapierhandel* [*Rules of Conduct for Securities Firms*] (1998); several articles in professional journals.

Rolf-E. Breuer

Chairman of the Board of Managing Directors of Deutsche Bank AG, Frankfurt am Main. Born 1937. Membership of the Supervisory Board of the Deutsche Börse AG, Deutsche Lufthansa AG, DLW AG, Münchener Rückversicherung AG, Siemens AG, Veba AG. Non-executive directorships: Euroclear Clearance Systems SC, Compagnie de Saint-Gobain S.A. Author of diverse publications, mainly on topics relating to banking, capital markets, and stock exchanges.

John. C. Coffee, Jr.

Adold Berle Professor of Law at Columbia University, New York, U.S.A. Reporter to the American Law Institute's Corporate Governance Project. Co-author of *Business Organization and Finance* (with W. Klein) 6th edn. (Westbury, NY 1996), and of *Knights, Raiders and Targets: The Impact of the Hostile Takeover* (with L. Lowenstein and S. Rose-Ackerman) (New York 1988); various articles in professional journals.

Paul Davies

Cassel Professor of Commercial Law at the London School of Economics and Political Science. B.A. University of Oxford, 1966; LL.M. University of London, 1968; LL.M. Yale Law School, 1969. Formerly Professor of Law of the Enterprise, University of Oxford, and Fellow of Balliol College, Oxford. General editor of *Industrial Law Journal*; author of *Labour Legislation and Public Policy* (with Mark Freedland) (Oxford 1993) and of *Gower's Principles of Modern Company Law* 6th edn. (London 1997); editor of *Palmer's Company Law* 23rd edn. onwards (London); has written widely in journals on the subjects of labor law and securities market law, dealing with both domestic and European Community aspects. Member of the board of the European Law Faculties Association, 1995-98.

Jochen Drukarczyk

Professor of Finance at Regensburg University. He has published many articles in professional journals and books related to theory of finance, valuation of firms, pension systems, bankruptcy, restructuring of firms, and different law and economics issues. He consulted with the Ministry of Justice and firms. He was Guest Professor at Insead (Fontaineblau), ESC Bordeaux, ESC Le Havre, ESC Nantes, Aston University (Birmingham), and Johann Kepler University (Linz, Austria). Author of *Unternehmen und Insolvenz* [*Firms and Bankruptcy*] (Wiesbaden 1987); *Theorie und Politik der Finanzierung* [*Principles of Corporate Finance*] 2nd edn. (Munich 1993); *Unternehmensbewertung* [*Valuation of Firms*] 2nd edn. (Munich forthcoming).

Colleen A. Dunlavy

Associate Professor of History, University of Wisconsin-Madison, U.S.A. B.A. University of California, Berkeley, 1980; Ph.D. Massachusetts Institute of Technology, 1988. Member: Board of Trustees, Business History Conference; Executive Council, Society for the History of Technology; Board of Advisory Editors of *Technology and Culture*; German Marshall Fund Research Fellow and Alfred P. Sloan Foundation grantee, 1997-98; Russell Sage Foundation Visiting Scholar, 1998-99. Author of *Politics and Industrialization: Early Railroads in the United States and Prussia* (Princeton 1994); publications on nineteenth-century comparative industrial history and comparative political economy; various articles in edited collections and professional journals.

Merritt B. Fox

Professor of Law, University of Michigan Law School, U.S.A. B.A. 1968; J.D. 1971; Ph.D. (Economics) Yale University, 1980. Admitted: New York Bar, 1975. Formerly: Acting Instructor in Economics, Yale, 1973; Associate, Cleary, Gottlieb, Steen & Hamilton, New York City, 1974-80; Visiting Lecturer in Economics, Yale, 1976; Associate Professor, Indiana University-Bloomington, 1980-86; Professor and Ira C. Batman Faculty Fellow, 1986-88. Author of *The Signature of Power* (with H.D. Lasswell) (New Brunswick 1979); *Finance and Industrial Performance in a Dynamic Economy* (New York 1987); various articles concerning corporate and securities law and international finance in professional journals.

Julian Franks

City Corporation Professor of Finance, London Business School. Born 1946; B.A. Sheffield, 1968; M.B.A. Columbia University, 1969; Ph.D. London University, 1979. Previously Visiting Professor at the University of North Carolina at Chapel Chill, and the University of California at both Berkeley and Los Angeles. Publications on takeovers, European corporate restructuring, financial regulation, corporate bankruptcy, and ownership and control; consultant to U.K. government regulator of telecommunications industry, and advisor to various private companies; associate editor of *Journal of Empirical Finance, European Journal of Financial Management, Journal of Corporate Finance, Journal of Banking and Finance*, and the *Journal of Financial Services Research*.

Wolfgang Gerke

Professor of Banking and Stock Exchange Issues at the University of Erlangen-Nuremberg (Germany). Born in 1944. Research Professor of the Mannheim-based ZEW: Zentrum für Europäische Wirtschaftsforschung [Central Institute for European Economic Research]; Full

Professor of Banking and Finance at the universities of Passau (1978-81) and Mannheim (1981-92); offered full professorships at the universities of Saarbrücken, Linz (Austria), Münster, and Frankfurt. Co-editor of the German Economic Journal *Die Betriebswirtschaft*; research focuses on issues relating to capital market, banking, stock exchange, set-up financing and financing of small caps, as is also evidenced in his publications.

Elmar Gerum

Professor of Business Administration, Organization Theory, and Human Resource Management, Philipps University of Marburg, Germany. Born 1946; Dr. rer. pol., University of Erlangen-Nuremberg, 1979. Taught in Erlangen-Nuremberg (1980-82), Hamburg (1982-89), and Düsseldorf (1989-94). Author of *Reform der Unternehmensverfassung* (with H. Steinmann) (Cologne 1978); *Grundfragen der Arbeitsgestaltungspolitik* (Stuttgart 1981); *Unternehmensordnung und tarifvertragliche Mitbestimmung* (Berlin 1984); *Der mitbestimmte Aufsichtsrat* (with H. Steinmann and W. Fees) (Stuttgart 1988); *Mitbestimmung und Corporate Governance* (1998). Editor of *Betriebswirtschaftslehre und Theorie der Verfügungsrechte* (with D. Budäus and G. Zimmermann) (Wiesbaden 1988); *Handbuch Unternehmung und Europäisches Recht* (Stuttgart 1993); various articles in professional journals.

Jeffrey N. Gordon

Alfred W. Bressler Professor of Law and Co-Director, Center for Law and Economic Studies, Columbia Law School. B.A. Yale, 1971; J.D. Harvard, 1975. Private practice, 1976-79, NYC; U.S. Treasury, 1979-82, Washington; NYU Law School, 1982-88; Columbia Law School, 1988-present. Past chair, Business Associations section, American Association of Law Schools; Advisor, Restatement (Third) of Trusts: Prudent Investor Rule; Visiting Committee, Harvard Law School. Scholarly publications on capital and securities markets, regulation of fiduciary investment, corporate governance, and the "transition costs of capitalism."

Brigitte Haar

Research Associate, Max Planck Institute for Foreign Private and Private International Law, Hamburg, Germany. LL.M. University of Chicago, 1992; Dr. iur., University of Hamburg, 1995; Visiting Scholar, Yale Law School, 1997/98. Author of *Marktöffnung in der Telekommunikation* (Baden-Baden 1995); various articles on the role of regulation and antitrust in American, European, British, and German telecommunications.

Gérard Hertig

Professor of Law, Swiss Federal Institute of Technology, Zurich. Professor of Law and Director, Centre d'Etudes Juridiques Européenes, University of Geneva (1987-95); Visiting Professor at the Catholic University of Louvain, ULB (Brussels), College of Europe (Bruges), and at the University of Tokyo. Author of 'La diligence des banques: les règles de conduite vis-à-vis des clients, Aspects de droit public' *Zeitschrift für schweizerisches Recht* II 113 (1994) 249; 'Imperfect Mutual Recognition for EC Financial Services' *International Review of Law and Economics* 14 (1994) 177; 'Innovation and Law, A Framework' in: Knapp, Blaise and Charles-André Junot (eds.) *Problèmes actuels de droit économique* 155 (Basle 1997). Editor of *European Business Law* (with Buxbaum et al.) (Berlin 1991); *European Economic and Business Law* (with Buxbaum et al.) (Berlin 1996).

Peter Hertner

Professor of Economic and Social History, University of Halle-Wittenberg, Germany. Born 1942; Diplomvolkswirt, University of Marburg, 1968; Ph.D. in Economics, University of

Marburg, 1971; Habilitation in Modern History, Technische Hochschule Darmstadt, 1985. Previously taught at the Technische Hochschule Darmstadt and at the European University Institute, Florence. Current fields of research: the history of multinational business and the history of European banking; German business history; Italian economic history (19th and 20th centuries). Author among others of *Stadtwirtschaft zwischen Reich und Frankreich. Wirtschaft und Gesellschaft Straßburgs, 1650-1715* (Cologne 1974); *Il capitale tedesco in Italia dall' Unità alla Prima Guerra Mondiale* (Bologna 1984); *Multinationals. Theory and History* (with Geoffrey Jones) (Aldershot 1986). Co-editor of *Società e Storia* (Milano).

Klaus J. Hopt

Director, Max Planck Institute for Foreign Private and Private International Law, Hamburg, Germany. 1974-95 Professor of Law in Tübingen (Dean, 1982-83), Florence (EUI, Head Law Dep't., 1979-80), Bern, Munich; Judge, Court of Appeals, Stuttgart, 1981-85; Member, International Faculty of Corporate & Capital Market Law; Visiting Professor: U. of Pennsylvania 1979, Paris I (Sorbonne) 1987, Kyoto U. 1988, U. Libre de Bruxelles 1990, Geneva 1991, Tokyo U. 1991, U. of Chicago 1994. Honors: Dres. iur. h.c., U. Libre de Bruxelles 1997, U. Catholique de Louvain 1997. Author of *Kapitalanlegerschutz im Recht der Banken* (Munich 1975); *Legal Harmonization and the Business Enterprise* (with Buxbaum) (Berlin et al. 1988); *Kreditrecht* (with Mülbert) (Berlin 1989); Baumbach-Hopt *Kommentar zum Handelsgesetzbuch* 29th edn. (Munich 1995). (Co-)Editor of *Corporate Governance and Directors' Liabilities* (Berlin et al. 1985); *European Business Law* (Berlin et al. 1991); *European Insider Dealing* (London 1991); *European Takeovers—Law and Practice* (London 1992); *Großkomm. AktG* (Berlin et al. since 1992); *Institutional Investors and Corporate Governance* (Berlin et al. 1994); *European Economic and Business Law* (Berlin et al. 1996); *Comparative Corporate Governance—Essays and Materials* (Berlin et al. 1997); *Börsenreform* (Stuttgart 1997); *Rabels Zeitschrift*; *Zeitschrift für Unternehmens- und Gesellschaftsrecht (ZGR)*.

Takeo Hoshi

Associate Professor at Graduate School of International Relations and Pacific Studies at University of California, San Diego since July 1994. B.A. University of Tokyo, 1983; Ph.D. Massachusetts Institute of Technology, 1988. Major research area is the study of the financial aspects of the Japanese economy, especially corporate finance. Currently preparing a book tentatively titled *Keiretsu Financing*, co-authored with Anil Kashyap (University of Chicago). Publications include 'The Impact of Financial Deregulation on Corporate Financing' in: Sheard, Paul (ed.) *Japanese Firms, Finance and Markets* (Melbourne 1996); 'Heterogeneous Beliefs, Wealth Accumulation, and Asset Price Dynamics' (with A. Cabrales) *Journal of Economic Dynamics and Control* 20 (1996); 'Back to the Future: Universal Banking in Japan' in: Saunders, Anthony and Ingo Walters (eds.) *Universal Banking: Financial System Design Reconsidered* (Chicago 1996); and 'Corporate Structure, Liquidity, and Investment: Evidence from Japanese Industrial Groups' (with A. Kashyap and D. Scharfstein) *Quarterly Journal of Economics* 106 (1991).

Fred R. Kaen

Professor of Finance and Co-Director of the Center for International Private Sector Development and Public Policy, Whittemore School of Business and Economics, University of New Hampshire, U.S.A. B.S. Lehigh University, 1963; M.B.A. University of Michigan, 1967; Ph.D. University of Michigan, 1972. Selected publications: *Corporate Finance* (Cambridge, Mass. 1995); co-author: 'The Effects of the Norwegian Banking Crisis on Bank and Non-Bank Stocks' *Journal of Multinational Financial Management* 7 (1997); 'The Effects of Bundesbank Discount and Lombard Rate Changes on German Bank Stocks' *Journal of Multinational Financial Management* 7 (1997); 'Information Effects in Financial Distress: The Case of Seabrook Station' *Journal of Financial Economics* 26 (1990); 'Predictable Behavior in Financial Markets'

American Economic Review 76 (1986). Visiting professorships: University of Hamburg, Norwegian School of Management, Norwegian School of Economics and Business.

Marcel Kahan

Professor of Law, New York University School of Law, U.S.A. B.A. Brandeis University, 1984; M.S. Sloan School of Management (MIT), 1988; J.D. Harvard Law School, 1988. Representative publications include 'Investment Opportunities and the Design of Debt Securities' (with D. Yermack) 14 *J.L. Econ. & Org.* 136 (1998); 'Lockups and the Market for Corporate Control' (with M. Klausner) 48 *Stan. L. Rev.* 1539 (1996); and 'The Qualified Case against Mandatory Terms in Bonds' 89 *Nw. U.L. Rev.* 565 (1995).

Hideki Kanda

Professor of Law at the University of Tokyo. LL.B. University of Tokyo, 1977. Main areas of specialization: commercial law, corporate law, banking regulation, and securities regulation. Taught as Visiting Professor of Law at the University of Chicago Law School in 1989, 1991, and 1993, and at Harvard Law School in 1996. Author of several English language articles including: 'Explaining Creditor Priorities' (with S. Levmore) 80 *Va. L. Rev.* 2103 (1994); 'Debtholders and Equityholders' 21 *Journal of Legal Studies* 431 (1992); 'Politics, Formalism, and the Elusive Goal of Investor Protection: Regulation of Structured Investment Funds in Japan' 12 *U. Pa. J. Int'l Bus. L* 569 (1991); 'Taxes, Agency Costs, and the Price of Incorporation' (with S. Levmore) 77 *Va. L. Rev.* 211 (1991); 'The Stock Exchange as a Firm: The Emergence of Close Substitutes for the New York and Tokyo Stock Exchanges' (with J.R. Macey) 75 *Cornell L. Rev.* 1007 (1990).

Christoph Kaserer

Assistant at the Chair of Banking and Finance, University of Würzburg, Germany. Born 1963; Economics, Vienna, 1988; Dr. rer. pol., Würzburg, 1992. Publications on subjects of corporate governance, banking regulation, capital markets, and derivatives. Member, German Finance Association.

Jonathan R. Macey

J. DuPratt White Professor of Law and Director of the John M. Olin Program in Law and Economics, Cornell Law School. B.A. Harvard, 1977; J.D. Yale Law School, 1982; Ph.D. honoris causa, Stockholm School of Economics, 1996. Member, Scientific Advisory Panel (Comitato Scientifico), International Centre for Economic Research (ICER), Turin, Italy; member, board of directors, American Law and Economics Association; Academic Advisory Board, *Brookings-Wharton Papers on Financial Policy*; advisory board, Centre for the Study of State and Market, Faculty of Law, the University of Toronto; board of editors, *Journal of Financial Crime*; board of editors, *Corporate Practice Commentator*; consultant editor, *Journal of European Financial Services Law*; Academic Advisory Board, Social Philosophy and Policy Center, Bowling Green University; reporter, American Bar Association Committee on Corporate Laws' Model Business Corporation Act Revision Project, 1984-95. Publications in corporate governance, corporate finance, securities regulation, banking law, and public choice.

Colin Mayer

Peter Moores Professor of Management Studies (Finance), Deputy Director (Research), Said Business School, University of Oxford. Born 1953; M.A., M.Phil., D.Phil. (Oxon); Professor of Corporate Finance, City University Business School, 1986-92; Professor of Economics and Finance, Warwick University, 1992-94. Research topics include corporate finance and regulation, and regulation of utilities. Associate editor of the *Oxford Review of Economic Policy*, the *Journal of Corporate Finance*, and the *European Financial Management Journal*; editorial board of the *Journal of International Financial Management and Accounting* and *Fiscal Studies*; associate editor of the *Journal of Industrial Economics*, 1983-95; member of the Panel of Economic Policy, 1988-89; editorial board of the *Review of Economic Studies*, 1986-89; associate editor of the *Review of Economics and Statistics*, 1991-96.

Hanno Merkt

Scholar of Deutsche Forschungsgemeinschaft, Lecturer in Law, University of Hamburg, Germany. First State Exam, University of Bonn, 1987; Dr. iur., University of Münster i. Westf., 1989; LL.M. University of Chicago, 1989. Attorney-at-Law, N.Y., 1990; Stagiaire, EC Commission, General Direction XV (harmonization of corporate law), Brussels, 1991; Second State Exam, Court of Appeals, Hamburg, 1993; Research Associate, Max Planck Institute for Foreign Private and Private International Law, Hamburg, 1990-1996. Various books and articles on German and U.S. corporate law, international business law, international mergers and acquisitions, e.g., *Investitionsschutz durch Stabilisierungsklauseln* (Heidelberg 1989); *US-Amerikanisches Gesellschaftsrecht* (Heidelberg 1991); *Abwehr der Zustellung von Punitive Damages-Klagen* (Heidelberg 1995); *Internationaler Unternehmenskauf* (Cologne 1997).

Yoshiro Miwa

Professor of Economics, University of Tokyo. B.A., M.A., and Ph.D. degrees from the University of Tokyo. On the faculty of Shinshu University from 1976 to 1986. His books include *The Economic Analysis of Antimonopoly Law* (in Japanese) (Tokyo 1982), *Firms and Industrial Organization in Japan* (in Japanese) (Tokyo 1990), and a new enlarged English book with the same title (London 1996), *Financial Administration Reform* (in Japanese) (Tokyo 1993), and *Is Deregulation a Nightmare?* (in Japanese) (Tokyo 1997). He is a co-editor of four books (all in Japanese): *Japanese Small Business* (with M. Tsuchiya) (Tokyo 1989), *Stock- and Land-Prices in Japan* (with K.G. Nishimura) (Tokyo 1990), *Japanese Distribution System* (with K.G. Nishimura) (Tokyo 1991), and *Economics of Corporate Law* (with H. Kanda and N. Yanagawa) (Tokyo 1998).

Peter Otto Mülbert

Professor for Commercial Law, University of Trier, Germany. Born 1957; Dr. iur., University of Tübingen, 1985; Habilitation, University of Munich, 1994. Previously taught at the University of Heidelberg; reporter to the 61st biannual meeting of the association of German jurists. Author: *Bankgarantien und Einstweiliger Rechtsschutz* (Tübingen 1985); *Kreditrecht* (with Klaus J. Hopt) (Berlin 1989); *Aktiengesellschaft, Unternehmensgruppe und Kapitalmarkt* 2nd edn. (Munich 1996); *Empfehlen sich gesetzliche Regelungen zur Einschränkung des Einflusses der Kreditinstitute auf Aktiengesellschaften?* (Munich 1996); various articles in professional journals on corporate law, banking law, and commercial law.

Andrea Peddinghaus

Research Associate, Max Planck Institute for Foreign Private and Private International Law, Hamburg, Germany. First State Exam, University of Hamburg, 1992; Stagiaire, German Embassy in Tokyo, 1991; Lecturer in Law, Hochschule für Wirtschaft und Politik, Hamburg, 1992; Second State Exam, Court of Appeals, Hamburg, 1995.

Stefan Prigge

Research and Teaching Assistant, Chair of Banking and Finance, University of Hamburg, Germany. Born 1966; Economics, Hamburg, 1992; Dr. rer. pol., Hamburg, 1996. Research Associate, Max Planck Institute for Foreign Private and Private International Law, Hamburg, 1996-98. Author: *Zentralbank, Aktienkurssturz und Systemkrise* [*Central Bank, Stock Market Crash, and Systemic Crisis*] (Wiesbaden 1997); co-author: *Corporate Governance in Germany* (with H. Schmidt, J. Drukarczyk et al.) (Baden-Baden 1997); some shorter articles in encyclopaedias (with H. Schmidt).

Mark J. Roe

Milton Handler Professor of Business Regulation, Columbia Law School, and Director of the Columbia Law School Sloan Project on Corporate Governance. Publications include: *Strong Managers, Weak Owners: The Political Roots of Amercian Corporate Finance* (Princeton 1994); 'Backlash' 98 *Colum. L. Rev.* 217 (1998); 'Chaos and Evolution in Law and Economics' 109 *Harv. L. Rev.* 641 (1996); 'From Antitrust to Corporate Governance: The Corporation and the Law, 1959-1995' in: Kaysen, Carl (ed.) *The American Corporation Today* 102 (New York 1996); 'Some Differences in Corporate Structure in Germany, Japan, and the United States' 102 *Yale L.J.* 1927 (1993); 'Takeover Politics' in: Blair, Margaret M. and Uppal Girish (eds.) *The Deal Decade* 321 (Washington 1993); 'Understanding the Japanese Keiretsu: Overlaps Between Corporate Governance and Industrial Organization' (with Ronald Gilson) 102 *Yale L.J.* 871 (1993); 'A Political Theory of American Corporate Finance' 91 *Colum. L. Rev.* 10 (1991); 'Political and Legal Restraints on Corporate Control' *Journal of Financial Economics* 27 (1990) 7; 'The Voting Prohibition in Bond Work-Outs' 97 *Yale L.J.* 232 (1987).

Roberta Romano

Allen Duffy/Class of 1960 Professor of Law, Yale Law School. Fellow, American Academy of Arts and Sciences; Vice President-President Elect, American Law and Economics Association. Past chair: Law and Economics and Business Associations sections, Association of American Law Schools. Co-editor: *Journal of Law, Economics, and Organization* 1988-92; associate editor: *Journal of Corporate Finance* and *The Financial Review*; editorial board: *Journal of Law, Economics, and Organization* and *The Supreme Court Economic Review*; advisory board: *The New Palgrave Dictionary of Economics and the Law* and *Corporate, Securities and Finance Law Abstracts* (Legal Scholarship Network); author: *The Genius of American Corporate Law* (Washington, D.C. 1993); editor: *Foundations of Corporate Law* (Oxford 1993); series editor: Oxford University Press interdisciplinary readers in law.

Markus Roth

Research Assistant, Max Planck Institute for Foreign Private and Private International Law, Hamburg, Germany. Born 1968; First State Exam, University of Konstanz, 1994; Stagiaire at German Embassy in Jakarta, two German law firms, and Hamburg High Court; Second State Exam, Hamburg, 1997.

Hartmut Schmidt

Professor of Banking and Finance at Hamburg University. He studied in Freiburg, Cologne, and Saarbrücken, taught five years at Syracuse University, New York, returned to Germany in 1974 and has headed the Institut für Geld- und Kapitalverkehr der Universität Hamburg since 1978. He has published various articles in professional journals and books related to securities markets in Europe and overseas, and co-edits the *Zeitschrift für Bankrecht und Bankwirtschaft*. He consulted with the Commission of the European Communities, the Office of Fair Trading in

London prior to Big Bang, with major German exchanges, and with the World Bank. Since 1982 he has served on the board of the Hanseatische Wertpapierbörse Hamburg. From 1989-95 he was on the board of the Deutsche Terminbörse. Currently, he is a member of the executive board of the Deutsche Gesellschaft für Finanzwirtschaft [German Finance Association] and chairman of the Wissenschaftliche Kommission Bankbetriebslehre/Finanzierung im Verband der Hochschullehrer für Betriebswirtschaft.

Peter-J. Schmidt

Partner, Wollert-Elmendorff Deutsche Industrie-Treuhand GmbH/Deloitte & Touche GmbH Wirtschaftsprüfungsgesellschaften, Hanover. Born 1936; University of Hanover and University of Hamburg, degree in business administration (Dipl.-Kfm.), 1959. President of Institut der Wirtschaftsprüfer (Institute of Certified Public Accountants), 1995-97; Lecturer in International Taxation at University of Hanover; various articles in professional journals and co-author of textbooks on taxation.

Johannes Semler

Johannes Semler has been of counsel in the office of Pünder, Volhard, Weber & Axster in Frankfurt am Main since July 1, 1996. He works in the area of corporate law, banking, and capital markets, as well as in the field of M&A. He has worked as a member of the board of management in large industrial corporations, mainly as Chief Financial Officer. He was and is a member of several supervisory boards, i.a., at Daimler-Benz, where he intends to retire this summer, Hugo Boss, and Axel Springer Verlag. He studied law at the Universities of Hamburg and Bochum. He passed his German law examination in 1953 and became a Doctor of Law in 1980. He was appointed Honorary Professor at the University of Economics in Vienna in 1989. Johannes Semler advises clients in all aspects of domestic European and international corporate law. He specializes in publication of corporate law and is a member of the Commercial Law Committee of the German Lawyer's Association.

Heidemarie C. Sherman

Senior Economist, ifo Institute for Economic Research, Munich, Germany, since 1980. Ph.D. Wayne State University, Detroit, 1970. Previously taught at the University of New Hampshire (1970-79); seconded as Chief Economist, Group Planning, to Shell International Petroleum Company, London (1993-95). Co-author and co-editor: *Monetary Implications of the 1992 Process* (New York 1990); author: 'The Economics of German Unification' in: Heitger, Bernhard and Leonard Waverman (eds.) *German Unification and the International Economy* (London 1993); co-author with Fred Kaen 'The Behaviour and Thinking of the Bundesbank' in: Cobham, David (ed.) *European Monetary Upheavals* (Manchester 1994); co-author with Fred Kaen 'German Banking and German Corporate Governance' *Tokyo Club Papers* No. 7 (1994); co-author 'Intra-EU Multi-Currency Management Costs' *Single Market Review: Dismantling of Barriers* (1996) (EU GD XV); co-author with Fred Kaen and Hassan Tehranian 'The Effects of Bundsbank Discount and Lombard Rate Changes on German Bank Stocks' *Journal of Multinational Financial Management* 7 (1997).

Hans Sjögren

Hans Sjögren holds a position as Assistant Professor in the Department of Technology and Social Change, University of Linköping, Sweden. He defended his Ph.D. thesis at Uppsala University in 1991, entitled 'Bank and Industry: Cross-Section Analysis and Longitudinal Studies of the Relation Between Swedish Firms and Commercial Banks within the Bank-Oriented Financial System 1916-1947'. He received his Fil. kand. degree (History, Economic History, Economics, Statistics) in Uppsala in 1986. From 1991 to 1993 he worked as an analyst of the Swedish Bond

Promotion (Obligationsfrämjan-det) in Stockholm. In 1993 he was appointed Assistant Professor in Economic History at the University of Stockholm. His research has included works on financial systems (bank-industry relationships, financial distress, bank crises, bond markets, small firm financing), institutional theory, European and Scandinavian integration, and financial and industrial policy. He was awarded a docent degree (Habilitation) in Economic History in 1996.

Manuel R. Theisen

Professor for Business Administration, Tax Management, and Tax Law, Ludwig-Maximilians-University, Munich. Born 1953; Dr. iur., Free University of Berlin, 1980; Dr. rer. pol. habil., University of Regensburg, 1987. Previously taught at the University of Oldenburg (1987-91) and Mannheim (1991-98). Publication on subjects of national and international taxation of different legal forms, including groups of companies and mixed legal forms and also of supervision of corporate governance. Chief editor of *Die Betriebswirtschaft* (Stuttgart). Chief officer of the supervisory board of Central Revision AG, Munich. Author: *Überwachung der Unternehmungsführung* (Stuttgart 1987); *Der Konzern* (Stuttgart 1991); *Informationsversorgung des Aufsichtsrats* 2nd edn. (Stuttgart 1996); *Tax Treatment of Financial Instruments: Germany* (together with M. Wenz) (The Hague et al. 1996); *Wissenschaftliches Arbeiten* 9th edn. (Munich 1998); editor: *Der Konzern im Umbruch* (Stuttgart 1998).

Stefan Thiele

Research and Teaching Assistant, Institute of Accounting and Auditing at the University of Münster (Germany). Studies in Law and in Business Administration at the University of Gießen (Germany) and at the University of Münster (1987-92); Dipl.-Kfm., University of Münster, 1992; Dr. rer. pol., University of Münster, 1996. Author: *Das Eigenkapital im handelsrechtlichen Jahresabschluß* (Düsseldorf 1998).

Hans-Christoph Voigt

Research Assistant, Max Planck Institute for Foreign Private and Private International Law, Hamburg, Germany, Lecturer in Criminal Law, University of Hamburg. Born 1970; First State Exam, 1996; Scholar, Studienstiftung des deutschen Volkes, 1991-96.

Helmut Wagner

Professor of Economics, University of Hagen (Fernuniversität), Germany. Born 1951; Diploma in Economics, 1974; Diploma in Sociology, 1975; Dr. rer. pol., University of Regensburg, 1976; Habilitation, University of Aachen (RWTH), 1981. Professor of Economics, University of Hamburg (HWP), 1982-95; Visiting Professor/Scholar at the University of California from 1982-83, at MIT in 1987, at Princeton University from 1991 to 1992, at the Bank of Japan's Institute for Monetary and Economic Studies in 1988, at IMF Research Department, and at the American Institute for Contemporary German Studies (Johns Hopkins University), Washington, D.C., in 1997. Author of numerous books and articles in professional journals.

Ekkehard Wenger

Professor of Banking and Finance, University of Würzburg, Germany. Born 1952; Business Economics, Munich, 1975; Physics, Stuttgart, 1980; Dr. rer. pol., Munich, 1978; Dr. rer. pol. habil., Munich, 1986. Previously taught at the University of Frankfurt am Main. Publications on subjects of corporate governance, company law, banking regulation, capital markets, capital income taxation, and labor markets. Member, Mont Pelerin Society, German Finance Association; advisor to the Ministries of Finance in several countries of Eastern Europe.

Eddy Wymeersch

Professor for Commercial Law, University of Ghent, Belgium. Publications on subjects of securities regulation, companies law, especially groups of companies, and corporate governance. Consultant to EC Commission, World Bank, and IFC; member of the corporate governance commission of the Brussels Stock Exchange. Publications: *Groups of Companies in the EEC* (ed. with K.J. Hopt) (Berlin 1993), *European Insider Dealing* (ed. with K.J. Hopt) (London 1991), *European Takeovers—Law and Practice* (ed. with K.J. Hopt) (London 1992), *European Company and Financial Law* 2nd edn. (ed. with K.J. Hopt) (Berlin 1994), *Comparative Corporate Governance—Essays and Materials* (ed. with K.J. Hopt) (Berlin 1997); 'Elements of Comparative Corporate Governance' in: Isaksson, Mats and Rolf Skog (eds.) *Aspects of Corporate Governance* (Stockholm 1994); 'Corporate Governance after the Investment Services Directive' *European Financial Services Law* 3 (1996); 'The Implementation of ISD and CAD in National Legal Systems' in: Ferrarini, Guido (ed.) *European Securities Markets. The Investment Services Directive and Beyond* (London 1998).

Part I:

Roots and Perspectives of Corporate Governance

Chapter 1: Historical Roots

Corporate Governance in Late 19th-Century Europe and the U.S.
The Case of Shareholder Voting Rights

COLLEEN A. DUNLAVY, Madison

A century ago, American business found itself amidst the "great merger movement." In Britain, France, and Germany, in contrast, firms tended to eschew consolidation for cooperation, forming looser combinations such as cartels. At the same time, a remarkable concentration of corporate control emerged in the U.S. but not in Europe.

This essay presents preliminary research on the distribution of power among shareholders and the choice of corporate strategies at the turn of the century. It raises new questions about the capacity of firms to consolidate. What enabled American firms to merge with such ease? Did their European counterparts turn to cartels when they would otherwise have preferred to merge, because they lacked a similar capacity to merge?

The evidence presented here concerns nineteenth-century shareholder voting rights in the four countries. Traditional constraints on the power of large investors initially made corporate governance relatively democratic in all four, but such constraints—e.g., graduated voting scales—disappeared earlier in the U.S. Future research will consider whether this made mergers more feasible there and less so in Europe.

Contents

Figures

[Epigraph]

"[I]t is noteworthy that the constitution of the joint-stock corporation and the position of shareholders in Germany are extraordinarily democratic. Every shareholder is entitled to vote and almost all the more important decisions . . .depend on the consent of the general assembly [of shareholders]. In England and—what is most peculiar—especially in America, the joint-stock corporation is much less democratically organized."

—Robert Liefmann (1912)

A. Introduction

Just a century ago, the increasing popularity of incorporation in the United States culminated in a giant wave of consolidation known as the "great merger movement." This startling development, which attracted widespread notice at home and abroad, resulted in the absorption of more than 1,800 firms into horizontal combinations in less than a decade (Lamoreaux 1985: 1-6). Though consolidation was not unknown in Britain, France, or Germany, the intensity of the movement was far less in those countries at the turn of the century (Cornish 1979; Chandler/Daems 1980: 3-7; Chandler 1990). Instead, traditional family firms or at least family control tended to persist longer, and, to differing degrees by country, European firms eschewed consolidation for cooperation, forming a variety of looser combinations. In Leslie Hannah's phrase, these constituted a "third hand" between markets and hierarchies (Hannah 1987: 32) that preserved the independent existence of larger numbers of smaller firms.

Meanwhile, a remarkable—and equally distinctive—concentration of control in the hands of a few individuals within the firm was also evident in the U.S. by the turn of the century. The earliest and in many ways most extreme case was that of the Pennsylvania Railroad (PRR), chartered in 1846 to connect Philadelphia with Pittsburgh. By the mid-1860s, its chief engineer and later president J. Edgar Thomson had wrested control from the PRR's board of directors—hence, from its shareholders. A few years later Thomson undertook a dramatic expansion of the company via consolidation or leasing of adjacent lines and by taking a stake in more distant, connecting lines. Between 1869 and 1873, the PRR expanded from a system of less than 500 miles to one of nearly 6,000 miles. The company's shareholders had little to say about this strategy of rapid expansion; the results were simply presented to them in local newspapers and in the company's annual reports. In the 1870s and 1880s, the PRR's strategy of expansion served as a model for the other trunkline railroads, which built similar "systems" on a regional and interregional scale (Ward 1975; Chandler 1977).

By the turn of the century, an extraordinary concentration of control marked American railroads generally. Two German officials, touring American railroads in 1905 or 1906, compared U.S. corporate practice with what they knew at home and remarked especially on the degree of power wielded by the largest shareholders.[1] Control within a given corporation was achieved by "single persons, families or groups of financiers," they reported, who "hold in their hands, more or less, the actual conduct of business of a railroad or at least of its policies on the strength of their ownership of shares." Such a concentration of power in the hands of a wealthy few they regarded as quite extraordinary, and the consequences for corporate governance did not escape them: "It is evident that by these means the importance of the general meeting in comparison with the board of directors is reduced to a still lower degree than is sometimes apparent with us." Citing as an example the Vanderbilt family's control over the New York Central Railroad, they concluded that its shareholders' meeting were a sham, "reduced to a mere formality." It was only for the sake of "mere appearance," they declared, that "the form of joint-stock companies is maintained" (Hoff/Schwabach 1907: 139-40).

By this time concentration of control in U.S. corporations extended far beyond the railroads. Reflecting on the concentration of wealth and power that seemed to typify American corporations in 1909, Robert Liefmann, a widely published and cited German expert on cartels and trusts, reached very similar conclusions. He attributed the pervasiveness of trusts in the U.S. principally to the influence of "large-capitalist and speculative finance people." It was they who pushed the level of concentration beyond what was desirable on technical grounds. The result in the U.S. was a concentration of capital unlike anything seen in Germany, where cartels predominated. Moreover, since cartels "keep alive" smaller enterprises, Liefmann maintained, they embodied a more "democratic principle." "It is not too much to say," he wrote, "that . . . it is possible for such finance people to control two hundred times as much capital as they possess" (Liefmann 1910: 140, 173). Thinking specifically of the extensive wealth controlled by the J. P. Morgan *Konzern*, Liefmann wondered "how Americans, in those circumstances, can speak of their country as a true democracy." Corporate practice in Germany was, in Liefmann's words, a good deal "more democratic," and this, in his view, made it much harder to carry out mergers and consolidations (Liefmann 1918: 173, 197).

---

[1] Since the vast majority of German railroads were state-owned (literally, *Länder*-owned) by this time, one must assume that the two observers, Senior Privy Councillor W. Hoff and his companion, Privy Councillor F. Schwabach, were comparing corporate governance on American railroads to the general practices of industrial corporations in Germany. They also found exceptional the interlocking forms of control that some large corporations exerted over others, citing the PRR's control of the Baltimore and Ohio Railroad as a prime example.

Why did such large, consolidated, tightly controlled enterprises emerge in the U.S.? James Ward's answer for the extreme case of the Pennsylvania Railroad provides a sample of the conventional thinking. Citing accelerating economic change and "the imperative need for rapid decision making, particularly in the emerging large corporations," he maintains that

> the concept of the authoritative board of directors was rapidly becoming obsolete. Practical considerations involving the volume and complexity of managerial decision *dictated* that power and authority within the corporation would become so highly centralized as to destroy the [state legislature's] carefully constructed lines of internal and ultimately external accountability (Ward 1975: 39, italics added).

This is essentially the understanding of American corporate history that one of its critics, legal scholar Mark J. Roe, terms the "economic paradigm" (Roe 1994: 1-17). Roe examines the historical origins of the distinctively American style of large-scale corporation that became dominant somewhat later: the large public corporation with "distant shareholders, a board of directors that has historically deferred to the CEO, and powerful, centralized management"—very much the model that Thomson crafted on the Pennsylvania Railroad, though it became common only after the turn of the century. Its emergence, Roe notes, is generally taken to have been the natural result of economic evolution. According to this view, technological and market changes at the turn of the century created unprecedented demand for capital. Some of it could be generated internally, but "[e]ventually these new large-scale enterprises had to draw capital from many dispersed shareholders, who demanded [portfolio] diversification"—hence, smaller holdings in larger numbers of corporations, which resulted in shareholder fragmentation (Roe 1994: ix, 3-4). This is a view of the corporation from the outside, so to speak, but Ward reaches a similar conclusion from the interior: the technological and organizational challenges thrown up by the large-scale corporation simply demanded tight administrative control.

This imperative to control—whether in its technical, organizational, or economic variant—certainly made its presence felt early on: a German authority expressed similar sentiments about railroads, especially regarding the need for rapid decision-making, as early as 1860 (Koch 1860: Anlage 1, p. 3). But, as Roe notes in the twentieth-century context, the case of Germany, in particular, raises serious doubts about the compulsion to centralize control implicit in the "economic paradigm." In Germany, control was generally less concentrated, yet industrial enterprise developed along remarkably similar lines during the last half of the nineteenth century. "In Germany as in the United States, but much more than in Britain," Alfred Chandler writes, "entrepreneurs did make the investment in production facilities and personnel large enough to exploit economies of scale and scope, did build the product-specific international marketing and distribution facilities, and did recruit the essential managerial hierarchies." In both the U.S. and Germany, they were willing to share power with salaried managers, became first-movers in the new, capital-intensive industries, expanded abroad, and diversified into related industries. In both, he concludes, "the technologically advanced, capital-intensive industries of the Second Industrial Revolution came to be managed through a system of managerial capitalism and so were driven by the same dynamics of growth" (Chandler 1990: 393). Indeed, the two economies had been so thoroughly transformed on the eve of the Great War that a German author wondered which was *Das Land der Monopole: Amerika oder Deutschland?* (Singer 1913). Yet, despite all this, German corporations generally did not consolidate and centralize administrative control to nearly the same degree. Thus neither demand for capital nor operational imperatives explain the American tendency toward consolidation and concentration of control in any straightforward way.

Beyond the economic paradigm, conventional understanding of consolidation and concentration of control at the turn of the century points to the distinctive incentives for consolidation or cartellization created by the way that courts and legislatures treated interfirm cooperation. From this perspective, industrialists faced a choice in the late nineteenth century between consolidation in giant enterprises and the voluntary cartellization of independent firms, and their decision was ultimately shaped by legal differences in the treatment of combinations. In a nutshell, courts and legislatures made cartellization a more viable strategy in European countries—above all, in Germany—but not in the U.S. Therefore, American firms, unable to cooperate, consolidated via merger instead (Chandler 1990: 395; Freyer 1992).

Yet, despite the apparent coherence of this explanation, it leaves unasked important questions about corporate governance and thus masks a large indeterminacy in our understanding of the impact of antitrust law on corporate strategies. The unasked questions concern the *underlying capacity* of American businesses to consolidate at the turn of the century when other options were foreclosed. Once American courts and legislatures made the formation of looser combinations a risky strategy, American firms turned to outright mergers instead. And it is this, their ability to merge without further ado, that has gone unquestioned.

What if American firms in the 1890s, facing courts and legislatures hostile to cartels, had not had the organizational wherewithal to pursue mergers instead? Or, to put the question the other way around, what was it that *enabled* them to merge with such ease? Would J. Edgar Thomson, for example, have been able to carry out such a rapid expansion of the Pennsylvania Railroad if he had not already seized control of the board? Posing such questions about the American experience raises fresh ones in the European context as well. Cooperation in cartels or similar arrangements was certainly a more available strategy in Britain, France, or Germany, but, if European courts or legislatures had proven as hostile to cooperation as their American counterparts, would European firms have been able to merge with comparable ease? Or, conversely, did they in fact turn more often to cartels, when they would otherwise have preferred to merge, because they lacked the underlying capacity to merge as readily?

Answers to these questions ultimately depend upon how power was distributed among shareholders in the firm. If one assumes that not all investors thought alike—for example, that their interests differed because they held shares for different reasons, that they had different time horizons or a differential tolerance for risk—then it follows that opposition to merger plans might have arisen within the ranks of the investors.[2] Who won out depended on who was more powerful, and who was more powerful depended, in turn, on the finer details of corporate governance—how voting rights were distributed, how boards of directors were chosen, how power was divided between the board and the assembly of shareholders.

Pursuing this line of thinking,[3] my current research submits the power of shareholders not to economic but to political analysis. That is, in an effort to sharpen our understanding of the impact of the law of combinations on corporate strategies, it places corporate governance front and center. In doing so, it:

- regards incorporation not only as a response to economic demand but also as the result of distinctive national *political conditions and processes*;
- conceives of the firm not merely as an economic institution but also as *legally-constructed polity* that is peopled by "citizens" (its investors);
- looks inside the "black box" of shareholders' and directors' meetings to understand how *power relations among investors* were structured; and
- explores the *impact* of these distinctive configurations of power *on the firm's choice of strategies of growth*.

---

[2] This understanding is formulated historically, rather than on the basis of economic theory. One could imagine, for example, that an industrialist who purposefully bought a controlling interest in a railroad in order to control the transportation of raw materials to his factory had very different ideas about appropriate corporate strategy than did, say, a smaller investor who bought shares in the same company purely for the immediate return on his or her investment. I am grateful to several conference participants, especially Jeffrey Gordon and Roberta Romano, for challenging me (ever so cordially) to make this explicit.

[3] The literature on the evolution of power relations in the firm is remarkably thin. The best comparative work is Horn/Kocka (1979), but it does not treat all topics as systematically or fully comparatively as one would like and the authors generally approach their subjects from the standpoint of formal law; as a result, one learns very little about the law in action. Among historically minded legal scholars, Mark Roe, as noted above, issues a powerful call for a political theory of the corporation, but he does not go far enough—or, more specifically, not far enough backward in time. His starting point is anchored fairly firmly in the early 20th century, and what he actually explores is a political *backlash* against precisely the phenomenon that he argues has historically been lacking: the deep involvement of very powerful financial intermediaries in American corporate management. Best known, of course, was J.P. Morgan, the kingpin in the so-called "Money Trust" at the turn of the century, whose men sat on numerous boards of directors.

The larger project, only a piece of which is presented here, traces changes in two measures of "democratic practice" in the firm: *suffrage* (i.e., shareholder voting rights, including proxy rights) and the *constitutional structure of the firm* (i.e., the distribution of power between the assembly of shareholders and representative institutions such as the board of directors—who has the power to make which decisions, by what majority motions must be passed, etc.).

Comparing the U.S., Britain, France, and Germany from the 1830s to the 1910s, the core question is how changes in shareholder voting rights and the power of boards of directors shaped the choice of corporate strategies during the great wave of consolidation and cartellization at the turn of the century. The hypothesis under scrutiny has two parts: 1) the characteristic American style of corporate governance on the eve of the great merger movement was the least democratic, while corporate governance was somewhat more democratic in Britain and even more so in France and Germany; and 2) more democratic styles of corporate governance made mergers more difficult to carry out and therefore increased the attractiveness of cartellization at the turn of the century; less democratic styles, conversely, made mergers easier to achieve. At stake is a new, politically grounded interpretation of the dramatic, turn-of-the-century changes in industrial organization in the U.S. and Europe.

This essay outlines the first results of the research on shareholder voting rights. To set the stage, the next section sketches out the early history of corporate suffrage, when what I call plutocratic voting rights—one vote per share, which now seems somehow so natural—were regarded as a dangerous innovation. It then suggests a conceptual framework for thinking about corporate governance in explicitly political terms. Sections C and D argue that early corporations in the United States as well as in Europe were initially governed in very similar—that is, comparably democratic—fashion. But by mid-century, as Section E shows, a rapid movement toward plutocracy had begun in the U.S. In Europe, in contrast, a more democratic mode of corporate governance persisted considerably longer (Section F), while American corporations continued their head-long movement toward plutocracy (Section G) in the last decades of the century.

B. Thinking About Corporate Suffrage: History and Theory

History. The concept of "corporate suffrage" links two spheres—the economy and the polity—that are, at least in liberal thinking, usually regarded as quite distinct from one another. But a moment's reflection on the average citizen's voting rights in the early nineteenth century makes clear that an intertangling of polity and economy was once taken for granted, where matters of suffrage were concerned. The voting rights of white, male citizens in the U.S., for example, were routinely constrained by property qualifications; a white man enjoyed the right to vote only if he also enjoyed property rights (as slaves and married women did not). The concept of "one man, one vote"—that is, the right of the white male to vote simply because of his humanity—was not at all taken for granted (Porter 1918; Williamson 1960; Smith 1990: 120-3).

In mirror-like fashion, the voting rights of investors in early corporations—the suffrage of capitalists, so to speak—were routinely constrained by political restrictions written into corporate charters or company law. This was true even in the U.S., as legal historian Lawrence Friedman observes, where "[e]arly [corporate] charters did not necessarily adhere to the principle that one share of stock was entitled to only one vote" (Friedman 1973: 168). Indeed, the Bank of North America's Congressional charter of 1781 generated enormous controversy when it did *not* follow tradition: among its offenses, it permitted shareholders one vote per share and allowed the use of proxies. The bank's many and vocal critics, as historian Pauline Maier writes, preferred "that all shareholders have equal votes and be allowed to vote only in person, not by proxy. Alternatively, they suggested that corporate voting rights be distributed under a system that favored small shareholders over large" (Maier 1993: 77).

In the revolutionary American context, aversion to plutocratic voting rights, in which a shareholder's votes are directly proportional to the number of shares owned, reflected two considerations. First of all, British tradition, as Maier explains, regarded the shareholder not as the owner of a portion of capital but as a "member" of the corporation and therefore as an equal among equals. The model here was the English trading company: "Voting in early English profit-seeking corporations such as the East India company," Maier writes, "allowed all shareholders single votes since 'the units of which the corporation was composed were still considered to be the members, as is the case in municipal corporations and guilds,' not shares." Indeed, as late as 1818, the shareholders of the Bank of England who were entitled to vote (those who had invested £500 or more) enjoyed one vote each: "no one Member of the said Corporation," read its charter, "shall . . . have, or give any more than one Vote, whatever his Share or Interest in the said Capital Stock shall be" (*Copy of the Charter* . . . 1818: 17). The flavor of this conception comes through in the language of early American charters as well (though they did not limit votes to one per person).[4] A railroad charter issued by the Rhode Island legislature in 1836, for example, likewise regarded "each proprietor or owner of one share" to be "a member of the corporation" ('An Act to Incorporate . . .' 1836: 10).

This practice—safeguarding the individuality of shareholders as members of a corporation, rather than as owners of a portion of its capital—was well supported by Anglo-American common law. In the absence of explicit arrangements to the

---

[4] A convenient collection of early railroad charters and other laws may be found in Gregg/Pond (1851), which, despite its title, deals only with New England.

contrary in the company's charter or by-laws, the common law regarded share-holders to be entitled to one vote each and it did not allow the use of proxies. As an expert in British corporation law reported in the early twentieth century, moreover, the common law (if the by-laws were silent on the matter) also stipu-lated that "questions arising at a general meeting are to be decided, in the first instance, by a show of hands." In this practice as well, the default was obviously one vote per person. Only if a "poll" was specifically requested did the share-holders vote according to their voting rights as specified in the company's articles of association (Palmer 1909: 167).[5]

The second consideration, alluded to above, was what Lawrence Friedman has described as a "typical, American fear . . . . of unbridled power, as possessed by large landholders and dynastic wealth, as well as by government" (Friedman 1973: 168). As shareholder voting rights evolved in Britain, the practice emerged in the eighteenth century of giving the larger shareholders additional votes, but only up to some maximum that was less than proportional to their share of the capital. As Maier notes, "Such checks on the power of large shareholders were designed, as a 1766 act of Parliament explained, to protect 'the permanent welfare of companies' from being 'sacrificed to the partial and interested views of a few'" (Maier 1993: 77 et seq.)

This practice, too, was put to use in the U.S. in the late 18th century, where graduated voting scales served democratic ends. Critics of the plutocratic alter-native—one vote per share—sought to limit the power of capital, Maier argues, in order to secure a greater degree of democracy:

> By allowing small shareholders at least one vote and capping those of large shareholders, charters might not only limit 'aristocratic' power but build into the very structure of corpo-rations a check on their 'vast influence and magnitude,' a democratic 'counterpoise' to corporate power such as other societies found, as William Findley observed in Pennsylva-nia legislative debates of 1785, in kings, nobles, and great landed families (Maier 1993: 77).

Secretary of the Treasury Alexander Hamilton made a similar argument, though for different reasons, when he laid out in 1790 his thoughts about the proper organization of a national bank. On the question of shareholder voting rights, he turned to the Bank of North America as an example of what should *not* be done. The original plan for that institution, he noted, called for "a vote for each share," while in the final charter there was "the want of a rule." This omission might have been interpreted to mean "that every stockholder is to have an equal and a single vote," Hamilton observed, but this "would be a rule in a different extreme, not less erroneous." The "rule" to govern voting rights "should be a proper one," he declared, and it should be spelled out in the bank's charter, not left to the

---

[5] For other references to the common law, see Morawetz (1886: 450) and Lindley (1889: 342).

company's by-laws. He then went on to discuss and reject the two extremes, reasoning on the following lines:

> A vote for each share renders a combination between a few principal stockholders, to monopolize the power and benefits of the bank, too easy. An equal vote to each stockholder, however great or small his interest in the institution, allows not that degree of weight to large stockholders which it is reasonable they should have, and which, perhaps, their security and that of the bank require. A prudent mean is to be preferred (Hamilton 1790: 73).

Although he sought to protect minority interests, in other words, he seemed to recognize that large investors might not find the shares attractive if their interests did not have at least some "degree of weight." As a compromise, he recommended that shareholder voting rights be ordered in an elaborate, graduated voting scale:

> The number of votes to which each stockholder shall be entitled, shall be according to the number of shares he shall hold, in the proportions following, that is to say: For one share, and not more than two shares, one vote; for every two shares above two, and not exceeding ten, one vote; for every four shares above ten, and not exceeding thirty, one vote; for every six shares above thirty, and not exceeding sixty, one vote; for every eight shares above sixty, and not exceeding one hundred, one vote; and for every ten shares above one hundred, one vote; but no person, co-partnership, or body politic, shall be entitled to a greater number than thirty votes (Hamilton 1790: 75).

(For good measure, he suggested that only those shareholders who actually lived in the United States be allowed to vote by proxy.) When Congress chartered the first Bank of the United States on February 25, 1791, its charter contained identical language (Peters 1848: Ch. X, Sec. 7, I).

Such restrictions on the power of capital in the corporation persisted well into the antebellum years. Indeed, it speaks volumes that Congress, given an opportunity in 1816 to substitute a one-share, one-vote provision for a graduated voting scale when it chartered the Second Bank of the United States, declined to do so. On the contrary, the charter of the Second B.U.S. not only retained the graduated voting scale but restricted its use explicitly to "voting for directors" (Peters 1848: Ch. XLIV, Sec. 11, I).[6] Barring other provisions in the by-laws, this meant that Congress reverted to earlier practice: other votes, e.g., regarding policy matters, proceeded according to the common-law default, one vote per person.

Theory. Regarded in political terms, graduated voting scales sought to implement a relatively democratic form of corporate governance that, as Hamilton indicated, would balance power among investors in the firm. A knowledgeable German observer, the Prussian David Hansemann, formulated the question of shareholder voting rights in more explicitly political terms in 1837:

> The manner in which the voting rights of shareholders are fixed has a most fundamental influence on the organization of [the corporation's] management, because its members are

---

[6] In the only other change of language in this provision, the "he" of 1791 became "he, she, or they, respectively" in 1816.

elected in the general assembly by a majority of votes of the shareholders. The two extremes, giving each shareholder one vote and giving each share one vote, stand in relation to one another like democracy and aristocracy (Hansemann 1837: 116).

He had his own preferences, about which more will be said later, but the question here is not the normative one—which system of voting rights is better—but merely a pragmatic one: how to construct an analytical framework that will enable comparison across companies and countries. Hansemann's dichotomy offers a useful starting point, but the contrast might be more precisely defined as one between democracy and *plutocracy*, for "aristocracy" can include systems of hereditary power while "plutocracy" is linked exclusively to wealth.

At the uppermost levels of the corporation in the nineteenth and early twentieth centuries, three groups contended for power, their membership often overlapping: the owners of the firms (i.e., its shareholders); the members of the board of directors (or, in Germany, members of the supervisory board [*Aufsichtsrat*] as well as the managing board of directors [*Vorstand*]); and the professional managers (Roe 1994: vii). In theory, then, the distribution of power among these groups could take one of three forms:

- more *democratic* power relations obtained when voting rights were relatively broadly distributed and the *mass of shareholders*, voting in assembly, retained important powers of approval over company strategy;
- more *plutocratic* power relations obtained when voting rights were more narrowly distributed (e.g., only some stocks carried voting rights) and weighted in favor of the largest shareholders (e.g., one vote per share) and when the *largest shareholders*, as a result, were able to control the board of directors without the support of a majority of the individual shareholders;
- more *technocratic* power relations obtained when the third group, *professional managers*, were able to control the board of directors and determine company strategy without significant input from the shareholders (possibly even in opposition to the wishes of a majority of the individual shareholders).

These, in turn, may be taken to define a spectrum running from the more democratic to the less democratic (plutocratic) to the least democratic (technocratic). In the nineteenth century in all four countries, the general direction of change was from the more democratic alternative (in the most extreme cases, one vote per *person*) toward plutocratic power relations in which each *share* carried a vote (in the most extreme cases, the smallest shareholders had no votes and the largest stockholders were entitled to vote their wealth). At the turn of the century, corporate governance in the U.S. moved even further in the plutocratic direction, towards a kind of oligarchic plutocracy with the introduction of non-voting stock and cumulative voting (see Section G). For purposes of comparison across companies and countries, it is enough simply to situate different styles of corporate governance relative to one another along this continuum to judge which distributed power more broadly among shareholders and which did not. Figure 1 presents graphically the two extremes at issue in this essay—plutocratic and democratic voting rights—and shows how one example, the graduated voting scale of the South Carolina Canal and Railroad Company ca. 1828, compared with the two extremes.

Figure 1:   Shareholder Voting Rights: Plutocratic vs. Democratic

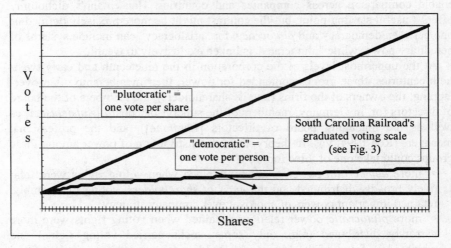

The historical starting point for this comparison is a time when constraints were the norm: when corporate charters began to be issued in large numbers in the 1820s and 1830s, suffrage was routinely and substantially constrained, though in different ways, in both the political and economic spheres. In the political sphere, voting rights were generally restricted to those white males who could meet certain property qualifications (though, as usual, these varied by state in the U.S. and were gone by the early 1840s); in this way, *property rights were used to constrain suffrage*. In the economic sphere, as we will see, shareholders' voting rights were frequently restricted by graduated voting scales or a cap on maximum votes that effectively increased the relative power of small shareholders and diminished that of the larger shareholders; here, *suffrage was used to constrain property rights*. By the end of the century, as the sections below suggest, practice in the two spheres had diverged considerably more in the U.S. than in Britain, France, or Germany.

C. Early Democratic Practice in the U.S.

Before the advent of general incorporation in the U.S., the vast majority of corporate charters were granted by the state legislatures via special legislation,[7] and, because of the common-law default of one vote per person, these acts almost always contained some provision regarding voting rights. By the 1830s and 1840s, the state legislatures' special acts frequently subordinated newly created corporations to generic laws. Unlike general incorporation laws, these generic laws merely allowed a streamlining of legislative charters. Only in the 1850s did general incorporation begin to become important, though the details of the transition varied considerably by state. Provisions regarding voting rights could appear in any of these documents—or in none of them, in which case the common law or the company's by-laws came into play.

The railroad charters issued by the state of Massachusetts in the year 1829 offer a good sense of the diversity of early practice in charters granted via special legislation (though the grounds for the diversity found here and elsewhere are difficult to fathom). In that year the Massachusetts legislature granted four railroad charters. One contained no explicit provision regarding voting rights; barring by-laws to the contrary, this would have meant that shareholders voted as individuals. The second specified one vote for the first share, then one vote for every two additional shares, up to a maximum of ten votes; the member who held more than nineteen shares, in other words, did not gain additional voting power when total votes were capped in this way. The third charter prescribed a slightly more extensive gradation: one vote for the first share; one vote for every two additional shares under ten; and one vote for every four additional shares over ten, up to a maximum of thirty votes. The fourth charter, finally, specified one vote per share but with a proportional cap: no shareholder could cast more than one-quarter of the total votes. Through 1835 Massachusetts railroad charters that bore a restriction on voting rights (many did not) followed the latter model, though the maximum share was reduced from one-fourth to one-tenth. Then in 1836 the Revised Statutes (Ch. 39, Sec. 50) codified a limitation of one-tenth on an individual's voting power, though not on an individual's share of total investment (Gregg/Pond 1851: vol. 2, 30).

---

[7] The charters issued to the first and second Bank of the United States constituted two major exceptions. Another occurred in New York state, which made general incorporation—i.e., incorporation via an administrative process—available to manufacturing corporations in 1811. That legislation, unique at that early date, was also unusual in providing that "each stockholder shall be entitled to as many votes as he owns shares of the stock." *Revised Statutes of the State of New York* (1836), Ch. 67. One of the few modern works on the history of American corporations is Ronald Seavoy's (1982) study of incorporation, which is based solely on the New York experience. To the extent that present-day understanding relies on his study, it would seem to be seriously flawed, since New York's incorporation policy—at least with respect to general incorporation and voting rights—was quite unlike that in other states.

Meanwhile, the Massachusetts Revised Statutes of 1836 also distinguished among types of corporations, some of which were regulated like railroads and others, not. The shareholders of banks, however, could hold one vote per share but only up to a maximum of ten votes, while those who held shares in insurance companies were limited to thirty votes at one vote per share (Mass. *Revised Statutes* 1836: Chs. 311, 324, 329, 343; 1861: Chs. 304, 325, 350). These provisions remained in place until much later in the century.

But manufacturing corporations constituted the big exception, in Massachusetts as elsewhere, for the 1836 Revised Statutes allowed their shareholders to determine their own voting rights via their by-laws. In this, Massachusetts followed a precedent set by New York state a quarter-century earlier. In 1811, in an act extending the privilege of general incorporation to all manufacturing corporations, the New York legislature had taken the unprecedented step of providing that "each stockholder shall be entitled to as many votes as he owns shares of the stock" (*Revised Statutes of the State of New York* (1836), Ch. 67). Through the 1830s, a grant of incorporation implied that a company had passed a test of public usefulness. This loosening of restrictions on manufacturing corporations, which fit the test of public usefulness much less comfortably than did companies that provided transportation or some other public service, may have constituted an essential step in the transformation of corporations from public to private entities over the nineteenth century.

In Virginia, meanwhile, the general thrust of chartering policy during the antebellum period was to limit the power of the largest investors by means of graduated voting scales. A Virginia law of 1836 regulating all manufacturing corporations specified a fairly flat (i.e., democratic) voting scale: one vote for each share up to 15, one vote for every five shares from 15 to 100, and one vote for each increment of 20 shares above 100 shares. Under legislation passed in 1837, railroad shareholders in Virginia were allowed one vote for each share up to ten shares and then one vote for every ten additional shares. (*Laws of Virginia* 1836-37: 108; *Charter for the Richmond . . .* : 19). A dozen years later, the state legislature, in a much debated measure, approved a revised voting structure for all joint-stock companies that standardized voting on the following scale (*Code of Virginia* 1849: Tit. 18, Ch. 57, Sec. 10):

> one vote for each share from 1 to 20;
> one vote for every two shares from 21 to 200;
> one vote for every five shares from 201 to 500; and
> one vote for every ten shares above 500.

This scale remained in place until the eve of the Civil War.

How such schemes played out in practice remains a subject to be explored in company archives, but a published list of shareholdings in a Virginia company in 1834 offers a tantalizing glimpse. The shareholders of an internal improvements company, the James River and Kanawha Company, had one vote for each share

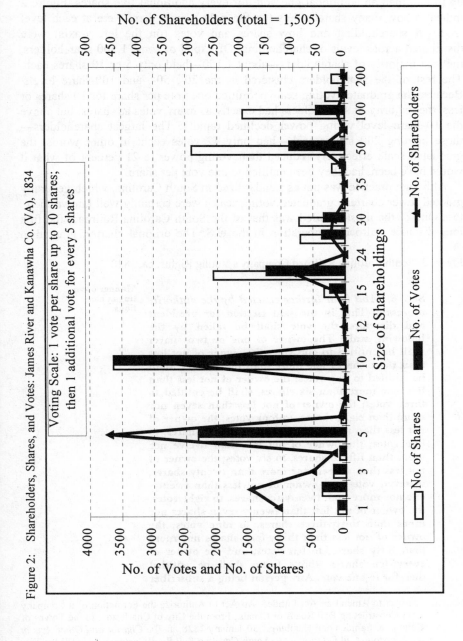

Figure 2: Shareholders, Shares, and Votes: James River and Kanawha Co. (VA), 1834

up to ten, then an additional one vote for every additional five shares. Figure 2 indicates how many shareholders (on the right y-axis) there were at each level (size) of shareholding and how shares and votes (on the left y-axis) were distributed across levels of shareholding. Of a total of some 1,500 shareholders, the vast majority of shareholders—about 1,150—held only 5 or 10 shares each. The rest of the shareholders clustered at the 20-, 50-, and 100-share levels. Because the graduated voting scale permitted one vote per share for 10 shares or less, the majority of shareholders had exactly as many votes as shares, but above the 10-share level voting power declined rapidly. The largest shareholders—those holding 200 shares each—had only 42 votes each; in other words, the graduated scale effectively reduced their voting power to 21 percent of what it would have been, had they been entitled to one vote per share.

Although practice was not as standardized in South Carolina, which generally granted fewer charters, graduated voting scales were certainly well known there, too. One of the most detailed was that of the South Carolina Railroad, the first long-distance railroad in operation in the U.S. The original charter, granted in

Figure 3: South Carolina Railroad Company's Voting Rights, ca. 1828

SEC. 6. *And be it further enacted by the authority aforesaid*, That in the said election for president and directors, the vote shall be taken by the following scale: The owner of one or two shares shall be entitled to one vote; the owner of not less than three shares nor more than four shares, shall be entitled to two votes; the owner of not less than five nor more than six shares, shall be entitled to three votes; the owner of not less than seven nor more than eight shares, to four votes; the owner of not less than nine nor more than eleven shares, to five votes; the owner of not less than twelve nor more than fifteen shares, to six votes; the owner of not less than sixteen nor more than twenty shares, to seven votes; the owner of not less than twenty-one nor more than twenty-six shares, to eight votes; the owner of not less than twenty-seven shares nor more than thirty-three shares, to nine votes; the owner of not less than thirty-four shares nor more than forty shares, to ten votes; and the owner of every ten shares above forty, shall be entitled therefor to one vote. Any person being a subscriber

Manner of voting at elections.

Source: "An Act to Amend an Act Entitled 'An Act to Authorize the Formation of a Company from Constructing Rail Roads or Canals', From the City of Charleston, to the Towns of Columbia, Camden and Hamburg," 30 January 1828, in *The Charter and Other Acts of the Legislature, in Relation to the South-Carolina Rail Road Company*, . . . (1851: 67).

1827, and an amendment the following year both spelled out a graduated voting scale with eleven steps to be used in electing the company's president and directors (see Figure 3). It began with one vote for one or two shares and specified gradually widening increments up to 10 votes for 34 to 40 shares. Thereafter, shareholders received one additional vote for every ten shares above forty. As Figure 1 indicated, this put in place a relatively democratic form of governance, a tendency enhanced by the fact that the scale came into play only in elections. Policy matters that were put to a vote of the shareholders would therefore have been decided on a one-vote-per-person basis (barring by-laws to the contrary). Archival research will help to clarify actual practice, but it is worth noting at least anecdotal evidence that some southern railroads in the U.S. as late as the late 1840s were using graduated scales in the election of directors but otherwise conducted votes by "acclamation" (see, for example, *A Convention . . .* 1847).

Not all South Carolina corporations had as elaborate a voting scale as the South Carolina Railroad, and the general pattern in the state was one of great diversity. Of 61 charters granted by the South Carolina legislature from 1825 through 1838, nearly half did not specify a system of voting rights, which meant that their shareholders had one vote per person if the by-laws specified nothing different. Only 5 of the 31 that did spell out voting rights mandated the modern system of one vote per share; none of these companies, it might be noted, had a capital higher than $500,000. The other 26 specified graduated scales, the authorized capitalization of these firms running the gamut from $6,000 to $6 million. In line with emerging practice in New York and Massachusetts, graduated scales were also more likely to be found among public-service corporations such as turnpike companies and railroads. Indeed, South Carolina legislation passed in 1827 mandated a graduated voting scale for all incorporated turnpike, bridge, and ferry companies, unless the charter explicitly provided otherwise (South Carolina *Statutes at Large* 1825-1838). Two decades later, South Carolina passed legislation mandating one vote for every share, but this applied only to manufacturing corporations (South Carolina *Statutes at Large* 1847: no. 3028). With this step, the state brought itself in line with northern practice, though at a significantly later time.

In short, the practice of placing political restrictions on the power of capital within the corporation carried over from Alexander Hamilton's time well into the nineteenth century. At mid-century, graduated voting scales were the norm only in certain states or only in certain industries in certain states. New York, moreover, was most exceptional, having granted general incorporation with one vote per share to manufacturing corporations as early as 1811. It reaffirmed its exceptional status in 1850, when it passed a general railroad law that explicitly endorsed one-share, one-vote suffrage for the election of directors (*Laws of the State of New York* 1850: Ch. 140, § 5). Nonetheless, given the overall evidence, it seems reasonable to conclude that anyone who set out to incorporate a company in the United States in the 1830s or even the 1840s would surely have recognized graduated voting scales or a cap on total votes as widely practiced techniques of corporate governance.

D. Early Democratic Practice in Europe

Efforts to limit the power of the largest investors were by no means a purely American phenomenon. As suggested above, the practice was widely known in eighteenth-century Britain, and there, too, it carried over into the nineteenth century.[8] As in the U.S., however, practice was mixed. Figure 4 offers an example of a graduated voting scale from the charter of the Great Western Railway, one of the first generation of British railroads. Its charter received official sanction in 1835, and its moderately democratic graduated scale gave shareholders one vote each for the first twenty shares and then one vote for each additional five shares. More systematic evidence regarding railroad corporations may be gleaned from Bradshaw's guide to "All the Railways in the United Kingdom,"

Figure 4: Great Western Railway's Voting Rights, 1835

And be it further Enacted, That at all general and special general meetings held by virtue of this Act, all persons and corporations who shall have duly subscribed for or bedome entitled to any share or shares (not exceeding Twenty) in the said Undertaking, and their respective successors, executors, administrators and assigns, shall have a vote for each such share; and all such persons and corporations as aforesaid, as shall have subscribed for or become entitled to more than Twenty shares in the said Undertaking, their respective successors, executors, administrators and assigns, shall, over and above the Twenty votes which they shall respectively have for or in respect of the first Twenty shares, have an additional vote for every Five shares which they shall have subscribed for or shall have become entitled to in the said Undertaking beyond the number of Twenty shares; and such vote or votes may be given by such

Directing how Subscribers shall vote at meetings.

Source: *An Act for Making a Railway from Bristol to join the London and Birmingham Railway near London, to be called "The Great Western Railway" with Branches therefrom to the Towns of Bradford and Trowbridge, in the County of Wilts*, 31 August 1835, Acts of Parliament 5. Will. IV, Sess. 1835.

---

[8] The research on Britain is the least advanced at present and only the sketchiest of details can be presented here.

which began publication in 1851 and included "Scale of Voting" in its description of many (though not all) railroads. This source indicates that one vote per share was a well-known alternative to the common law by mid-century, as it was in the U.S.. A preliminary survey indicates, however, that many companies—perhaps the preponderance—had graduated scales that resembled the Great Western Railway's, though they differed in the details (Bradshaw's 1851).

On the Continent, meanwhile, graduated voting scales and caps on total votes seem to have been more widely in practice than was the case in either the U.S. or Britain.[9] As noted earlier, the Prussian railroad promoter David Hansemann commented in print on methods of voting in corporations. He himself favored a compromise between what he termed the democratic and aristocratic modes of governance. The compromise included a lower threshold or floor, below which a shareholder would have no votes; an upper threshold or a ceiling, beyond which a shareholder would gain no additional votes; and between the two, a graduated scale (Hansemann 1837: 116). In an appendix to the book in which he expressed these views, he reprinted the Prussian statute of the Rhenish Railroad, approved in 1835, and that of the Prussian-Rhenish Railroad from 1836. Both followed very closely the scheme that he favored. The Prussian-Rhenish Railroad's charter (see Figure 5) set a lower threshold for suffrage at three shares; the Rhenish Railroad put it at four shares. Both also set a maximum number of votes that any shareholder could cast: the Prussian-Rhenish Railroad put it at 40 votes for 1,000 or more shares, while the Rhenish Railroad granted representation only up to 100 shares, for which the shareholder was entitled to 5 votes. The Prussian-Rhenish Railroad's charter specified fourteen gradations between the two extremes; the Rhenish Railroad's statute called for four (Hansemann 1837: 141-2, 157-8).

Five years later, a German authority on the law of joint-stock corporations indicated that such scales were standard practice. First, however, Dr. Meno Pöhls explained in an 1842 legal handbook how joint-stock companies worked in theory, setting up an opposition between theory and practice that would echo through German handbooks on incorporation for the remainder of the century. "Votes [in a joint-stock corporation] are counted not according to heads but according to shares," he began, as if oblivious to current practice; "in an association of capitalists, in which the personages [of the shareholders] necessarily lie outside [the organization], the total capital specified in the charter (the total of the shares) is actually more the *socius* than the proprietor of the share. Whoever possesses more shares, therefore, is so many times *socius* as the total number of

---

[9] Whether limitations on the power of capital in German corporations had their origins in British practice, as they did in the U.S., or perhaps in Dutch or French practice, remains to be explored. For brief comments on the Dutch and French background of the German corporation, see Lehmann (1898: 62-3).

his shares." For this reason, he continued, one share is entitled to one vote and "every member has as many votes as he possesses shares" (Pöhls 1842: 198).

Figure 5: Prussian-Rhenish Railroad's Voting Rights, 1836

Art. 32. Die Eigenthümer von weniger als drei Aktien sind nicht stimmberechtigt. Das Stimmrecht wird in folgendem Verhältniß ausgeübt: (R. §. 12.)

für	3	Aktien und weniger als	6	Aktien	1	Stimme
'	6	' ' ' '	10	'	2	'
'	10	' ' ' '	15	'	3	'
'	15	' ' ' '	20	'	4	'
'	20	' ' ' '	25	'	5	'
'	25	' ' ' '	35	'	6	'
'	35	' ' ' '	50	'	8	'
'	50	' ' ' '	100	'	10	'
'	100	' ' ' '	150	'	15	'
'	150	' ' ' '	250	'	18	'
für	250	Aktien und weniger als	375	Aktien	22	Stimmen
'	375	' ' ' '	500	'	25	'
'	500	' ' ' '	750	'	30	'
'	750	' ' ' '	1000	'	35	'
'	1000	' ' darüber			40	'

Source: Hansemann (1837: 141-2).

But this, it turned out, was mere theory, for Pöhls quickly acknowledged that practice differed substantially. In particular, he noted that individual companies set a limit on the total number of votes that individual shareholders could cast. This was intended in part, he explained, to head off the disadvantages that would accrue if too great a number of votes accumulated in the hands of an individual and "especially to secure for every single share the possibility of participating in the [shareholders'] deliberations" (Pöhls 1842: 198-200). A cap on maximum votes, in other words, would both head off the dangers inherent in an accumulation of power and help to ensure a measure of representation for all shareholders (though not, of course, if a lower threshold were in place).

Other evidence indicates that graduated voting scales were widely used among Prussian railroads and banks at mid-century. In "a handbook for businesspeople, private individuals, capitalists, and speculators" published in 1853, Dr. Julius Michaelis reported in minute detail on all German railroads then in operation. Of the eleven earliest and largest Prussian railroads, eight had graduated voting scales similar to those that David Hansemann showcased in the appendix to his book.[10] Among German banks, the practice was even more wide-spread at this time. Constituting what might be described as a "democracy of plutocrats," the general assembly of shareholders of the Prussian Bank, founded in 1765 and opened to private shareholders in 1846, was limited to the 200 largest shareholders, each of whom was entitled to one vote only "without consideration of the number of his shares" (Hübner 1854: 2/4). The *Disconto-Gesellschaft* in Berlin, similarly, allowed only shareholders of at least 1,000 Thaler (about $700) to vote in the general assembly and each had one vote only (Hübner 1854: 2/98).

More common among German banks, however, were voting scales like those in use on the railroads. The 1850 Prussian charter of the *Bank des Berliner Kassen-Vereins* gave shareholders one vote for every five shares up to 45, then capped total votes at 10 each for those who held more than 45 shares (Hübner 1854: 2/15). The *Leipziger Bank*, originally chartered by Saxony in 1839 and rechartered at ten-year intervals, employed a similar scale, capped at 10 votes, though much less compressed; it specified eleven levels of share ownership, the last yielding 10 votes for 201 or more shares. Other examples among joint-stock banks included the *A. Schaafhausen'sche Bankverein* in Cologne, the *Bank für Handel und Industrie* in Darmstadt, the *Rostocker Bank*, and the *Disconto-Kasse* in Bremen (Hübner 1854: 2/69, 2/100, 2/107, 2/119).

Both railroad corporations and banks in Germany sometimes adopted a lower threshold on voting rights, as Hansemann had recommended, though this was found more often in railroad companies than in banks. Nine of the eleven Prussian railroad charters mentioned earlier, for example, set lower thresholds that ranged from three to ten votes (see note 10). According to Pöhls, writing in 1842, this practice was developed by the larger companies in response to the "inconvenience" (*Unbequemlichkeit*) in voting occasioned by the division of their capital into many small shares; as he duly noted, however, this left the smallest shareholders without any representation in company affairs (Pöhls 1842: 198-9). Two German banks—the *Anhalt-Dessauische Landesbank* and the *Ritterschaftliche Privat-Bank* in Pomerania—seem to have been the only ones to impose a lower threshold (of five and four shares respectively; Hübner 1854: 2/18, 2/86). In this respect, Continental practice departed from the American, for no corporate charter in the antebellum United States, to my knowledge, ever failed to give the smallest shareholder one vote.

In neighboring France, meanwhile, a practice similar to the German prevailed in the middle decades of the nineteenth century. Indeed, charters often specified

---

[10] Michaelis (1854: 30, 34, 39, 49, 76, 87, 141, 189, 220, 241, 252). The eleven lines were the Berg-Mark, Berlin-Anhalt, Berlin-Hamburg, Berlin-Stettin, Cologne-Minden, Düsseldorf-Elberfeld, Magdeburg-Leipzig, Upper Silesian, Rhenish, Stargard-Posener, and Thuringian railroads. Although this book reported on conditions ca. 1853, the author was careful to note changes since the companies had first incorporated.

both a lower threshold in share ownership and an upper threshold on the number of votes a shareholder could cast (Freedeman 1979: 43). Of thirteen railroad charters issued between 1823 and 1845, all required voting members of the general assembly to hold at least three shares and most allowed a shareholder to cast no more than three or five votes (the only exception was a company that set an upper threshold of ten votes). The charters of two major lines, the Paris à Orleans (see Figure 6) and Paris à Rouen railroads, capitalized at 40 million francs and 36 million francs respectively, allowed one vote for every twenty shares (500 francs each), effectively disenfranchising those who held less than twenty shares, and set the upper threshold at five votes total (Cerclet, *passim*). At mid-century this general approach to voting rights was still actively practiced and not confined to railroad corporations. Voting rights in the *Société générale de Crédit mobilier*, chartered in 1852 and an important model of modern banking at mid-century (Kindleberger 1993: 111), were restricted to the largest 200 share-holders, and they received one vote for each forty shares up to a maximum of five votes (or ten votes, including proxies). In a moderately democratizing departure from railroad practice, however, anyone who counted among the largest 200 shareholders but owned less than forty shares also received one vote (Hübner 1854: 199).

Figure 6: Paris à Orleans Railroad's Voting Rights, 1838

46. Les délibérations de l'assemblée générale sont prises à la majorité des voix des membres présent.

47. Vingt actions donnent droit à une voix, le même actionnaire ne peut réunir plus de sinq voix. — En cas de partage, la voix du président est prépondérante.

48. Le nombre d'actions de chaque actionnaire est con-staté par sa carte d'admission.

Source: Cerclet (1845: 437).

On a spectrum running from democratic to plutocratic, then, American and European methods of granting corporate suffrage seem to have been relatively democratic at mid-century. To be sure, at least two significant differences obtained between Continental and Anglo-American practice. On the one hand, the use of graduated scales seems to have been more widespread in France and Germany than in the U.S. or Britain during these years; on these grounds, Continental practice qualified as more democratic. But, on the other hand, even the smallest American shareholders routinely had the right to vote, whereas in France and Prussia the smallest shareholders were frequently disenfranchised. In this respect, American practice might be judged more democratic. Overall, it seems pretty much a draw.

E. The Remarkably Rapid Turn Toward Plutocracy in the U.S.

From these beginnings, founded on long tradition, graduated voting scales virtually disappeared in the United States between the 1840s and the 1880s. In fact, by mid-century, practice had already begun to shift perceptibly toward the modern one-share, one-vote rule in many states. The last Connecticut charter to cap the votes of individual railroad shareholders at one-tenth of the total votes was granted in 1841; thereafter one vote per share become the rule (Gregg/Pond 1851). New Jersey passed legislation in 1846 that spelled out general guidelines for incorporation: "unless otherwise provided in their prospective charters," it read, each share would count for one vote. An observer writing in *Hunt's Merchants Magazine* (New York) in 1850, moreover, regarded the situation in which one individual owned the majority of a corporation's stock and, as a consequence, controlled the corporation to be a relatively new one. Traditional practice, he suggested, had prevented such a concentration of control: "The early corporations of our State attempted to guard against the dangers of so alarming a power, by according to large shareholders a smaller ratio of elective efficiency than was accorded to smaller stockholders," he reported. "[B]ut the guard is abandoned in modern corporations from indifference to the consequences on the part of Legislatures, or from an opinion that every guard can be easily evaded, and that stockholders had better be presented with a known evil, than deluded with a fallacious remedy" (*Hunt's Merchants Magazine* 1850: 630). Indeed, New York, as we have seen, was the earliest to abandon traditional constraints on the power of large capitalists, and such constraints were well gone before the Civil War.

Elsewhere, however, strong vestiges remained, and the movement that made one vote per share the norm continued apace during the Civil War and accelerated afterwards. At the federal level, corporate charters granted to the transcontinental railroads in the 1860s and early 1870s uniformly specified one vote per share.[11] So, too, did the Congressional legislation creating a national currency and nationally chartered banks. In elections of directors and at all their meetings, shareholders of the national banks were to have one vote per share (*U.S. Statutes* 1863: Ch. 58, § 38; 1854: Ch. 106, § 11).

---

[11] The charters for the Union Pacific, Atlantic and Pacific, and Texas Pacific railroads are found, respectively, in *U.S. Statutes* (1862), Ch. 120, Sec. 1; (1866), Ch. 278, Sec. 1; (1871), Ch. 122, Sec. 2. The 1862 charter for the Union Pacific Railroad initially limited shares to two hundred per person, but this provision was repealed two years later.

In the decades after the Civil War, almost all other states followed suit in adopting one vote per share as the rule. Virginia took a significant step away from graduated scales in 1871. In 1860, it had simplified, though not yet eliminated, the 1849 voting scale that applied to all corporations; under the revised code of 1860, each share up to ten received one vote and shareholders received one additional vote for every four shares above ten (*Code of Virginia* 1860: Tit. 18, Ch. 57, § 10). In 1871, however, it abolished graduated voting scales for corporations chartered via a judicial process (a form of general incorporation that it had established in the mid-1850s). Still, the formal requirement that corporations created via special legislation adhere to the state's standardized voting scale was not removed until the 1880s (*Laws of Virginia* 1870-71: Ch. 277). About that time, South Carolina also moved to what was rapidly emerging as the plutocratic norm, passing legislation that mandated one vote per share for railroads in 1882, for manufacturing corporations in 1886, and for most other corporations in 1891 (*General Statutes of So. Car.* 1891: Ch. 46).

To be sure, traces of the traditional practice remained throughout the nineteenth century. One of the very last states to come around was Massachusetts, which had been an early and energetic incorporator. Its manufacturing corporations, as we have seen, were allowed to determine their own voting rights from the 1830s, but the state continued to restrict the voting power of individual railroad investors to one-tenth of the total votes. This restriction was carried forward in the Revised Statutes of 1860 (Ch. 63, Sec. 5), and a general revision in 1882 also left it intact. Now, however, municipalities, the Commonwealth, and other railroad corporations were allowed to vote the whole number of shares that they owned (*Mass. Public Statutes* 1862: 611), suggesting pretty clearly that the intent was to restrict the power of large *individual* investors. Only after the turn of the century, apparently, did the one-tenth restriction disappear altogether in Massachusetts.

Massachusetts was the outlier in this regard, however, for elsewhere in the United States a remarkable revolution in corporate governance had taken place as democratic constraints on the power of large capitalists in the corporation gave way by the 1880s to a plutocratic system in which the power of individual shareholders was weighted according to their investment. In some sense, this now seems "normal" to us—even more democratic, if one does not think too deeply about it. But in the nineteenth-century context, this revolution was remarkable in two ways. Stepping back to take the larger American political economy in view, we see that the removal of suffrage constraints on property rights in the corporation—that is, increasing *plutocracy*—proceeded apace with a quite opposite movement in the political sphere to remove property constraints on popular suffrage—that is, a movement toward increasing *democracy* (though still limited in law or practice to white males). Thus during the last half of the century, suffrage in the two spheres had evolved in radically different directions in the

U.S. In this sense, the revolution in shareholder control may be seen as part of a larger transformation by which the modern—distinctively American?—bifurcation of polity and economy came into being, the normative bifurcation that allowed Henry Ford to declare in the early twentieth century that "democracy stops at the factory gates." In the evolution of power at the uppermost levels of the American corporation, the shift from relatively democratic to more plutocratic forms of governance constituted an integral step in the process by which, as remarked earlier, American corporations came to be regarded as "private" and the space of the "public" in the U.S., accordingly, shrunk (cf. Mitchell 1991).

F. Persistence of Democratic Practice in Europe

The extent to which shareholder voting rights had been transformed in the U.S. seems doubly remarkable when placed in comparative perspective, for events did not progress nearly so fast or so far in Europe during these years.[12] In France, charters were initially issued individually, and an upper threshold on the number of votes that a shareholder could cast was the norm (Cellérier 1905: 98). In 1867 France shifted to a system of general incorporation, and under this legislation, according to an 1870 legal handbook aimed at a practical audience, the number of votes to which each shareholder was entitled could simply be specified in the statutes of joint-stock companies (*société anonymes*)—but with a crucial qualification: in important deliberations in the general assembly of shareholders (including the election of top administrators), no shareholder could cast more than ten votes (de Nancy 1870: 325d). An 1898 treatise on French commercial law and judicial practice, published in English, affirmed that this upper threshold remained in place (Goirand 1898: 85), while just after the turn of the century a student of joint-stock corporations in France and other European countries indicated that lower thresholds remained the rule in France. This author was less clear, however, about the extent to which upper thresholds remained the practice, though he did take the time to argue against them (Cellérier 1905: 90-1, 98).

In Britain, too, graduated scales certainly remained a familiar practice from the 1860s through the end of the century, but, interestingly, the common-law rule of one vote per person was often used in practice. Thomas Tapping published "a little Handbook on Joint Stock enterprise" in 1866, in order, as he explained, to give his readers "an accurate knowledge of 'What to do,' and 'How to do it,' in

---

[12] The challenging question of *why* this transformation took place in the U.S. will be pursued elsewhere; central elements of an explanation will surely be the heightened competition for capital after the Civil War as well as the "shopping around" of corporate attorneys for favorable charter provisions, both artifacts of the regulatory fragmentation inherent in the chartering of corporations by a multiplicity of state governments. On antebellum manifestations of these phenomena, see Dunlavy (1994).

order to establish a Joint Stock Company" (Tapping 1866: 2-3). Legislation recently passed by Parliament, he informed his readers, had repealed all previous acts affecting corporations and his book thus summarized the provisions of the "Companies Act 1862." The act permitted the establishment of three kinds of companies, two well known and one new: familiar were the *limited* company, in which shareholders enjoyed limited liability (i.e., limited to the amount invested or subscribed), and the *unlimited* company, in which the investors were personally liable; new under the 1862 act was the *guarantee* company, in which each investor's liability in the event of bankruptcy was specified individually in the chartering documents. In each case, the company could be formed with or without a capital divided into shares. The joint-stock corporation, then, was a limited company on a share basis. To charter any of the three forms required the company's initial subscribers to file two legal documents, a memorandum of association and articles of association. For the guidance of all companies formed on a share basis, the law carried forward from previous legislation the famous "Table A," which provided ten pages of model provisions (Tapping 1866: 63-74).

Voting rights were to be specified in the articles of association, and Table A suggested a graduated scale (see Figure 7). This entitled the shareholder to one vote per share for the first ten shares, then reduced proportionally the voting power of those who held 11 to 100 shares and reduced even further that of shareholders with more than 100 shares.

According to Tapping, the graduated scale in Table A was mandatory for unlimited companies and for guarantee companies, but optional for limited companies. If the articles of association failed to specify voting rights, however, the scale in Table A took force by default (Tapping 1866: 7, 18, 63-74). To what extent or how long such constraints actually remained in use among limited companies are questions that will yield only to archival research, but it is certainly noteworthy that the mandatory default was a graduated scale through the remainder of the century.

British practice also retained a strongly democratic thrust by other means, however. Although firms could override the common-law default easily enough by specifying something different in their articles of association, the practice described earlier of deciding resolutions in shareholders' meetings first by a show of hands—perforce, one vote per person—reportedly continued in practice. According to the 1862 law, a "poll" or vote according to actual voting rights had to be demanded by at least five members of the assembly (see Fig. 7). Several handbooks on incorporation indicate that conducting votes by a show of hands remained accepted practice through the end of the century (Chadwyck-Healey 1886: 2, 239-40; Lindley 1889: 342; Chadwyck-Healey 1894: 992-3; Palmer 1905: 145-6).

Figure 7: Model Voting Rights in "Table A," 1862-1906

(42). At any General Meeting, unless a Poll is demanded by at least Five Members, a Declaration by the Chairman that a Resolution has been carried, and an Entry to that Effect in the Book of Proceedings of the Company, shall be sufficient Evidence of the Fact, without Proof of the Number or Proportion of the Votes recorded in favour of or against such Resolution.

(43). If a Poll is demanded by Five or more Members it shall be taken in such a Manner as the Chairman directs, and the Result of such Poll shall be deemed to be the Resolution of the Company in General Meeting. In the Case of an Equality of Votes at any General Meeting the Chairman shall be entitled to a Second or Casting Vote.

Votes of Members.

(44). Every Member shall have One Vote for every Share up to Ten: He shall have an additional Vote for every Five Shares beyond the First Ten Shares up to One hundred, and an additional Vote for every Ten Shares beyond the first Hundred Shares.

(45). If any Member is a Lunatic or Idiot he may vote by his Committee, Curator bonis, or other legal Curator.

Source: Tapping (1866).

Meanwhile, the use of graduated voting scales persisted to some measure as well. Handbooks on the law and practice of incorporation in Britain continued to include graduated voting scales among the options available to prospective incorporators. For example, the second edition of C.E.H. Chadwyck-Healey's *A Treatise on the Law and Practice Relating to Joint Stock Companies Under the Acts of 1862-1890: With Forms and Precedents*, published in 1886, suggested a graduated voting scale, though it also provided a model for companies that preferred one vote per share (Chadwyck-Healey 1886: 239-40). The third edition, published in 1894, still offered the graduated scale but this time explicitly noted that the one-vote-per-share system should be used if incorporators wanted to give power to the "largest proprietors" (Chadwyck-Healey 1894: 272).

Only after the turn of the century does there seem to have been a concerted movement away from the graduated scale. The author of a French study published in 1905 acknowledged that the English law of 1862 remained in force, but he maintained that graduated voting scales had fallen out of use in England because they did not meet a "practical need" (Cellérier 1905: 99). The same year, Francis Beaufort Palmer, in *Company Law: A Practical Handbook for Lawyers and Business Men . . .*, reported that it was very common for members to receive one vote per share, though even then it was not exclusively the rule (Palmer 1905: 144). The following year—1906—the Board of Trade, which had authority over company law, finally published a new Table A, this one specifying one vote per share for the first time, though the practice of voting initially by a show of hands apparently remained the norm (Smith/Stiebel 1907: 70-1). Even as late as 1916, Palmer acknowledged in the tenth edition of *Company Law* that graduated scales were still used (Palmer 1916: 170).

In Germany, too, graduated voting scales persisted much longer than in the U.S. An expert on German railroad law, Julius Herrmann Beschorner, confirmed that the practice continued in a legal handbook published in 1858. He opened a discussion of voting rights with words practically identical to Pöhls' more than a decade earlier: "The votes are counted not according to heads"—*nach Köpfen* was the phrase that both used—"but according to shares." Then he repeated the same argument—that the basic units (*Einheiten*) of an association were bundles of capital, not individuals, that the share was the *socius*, and so on. Therefore, he concluded, each share warranted a vote "and every member [*Mitglied*] must have as many votes as he or she possesses shares." Then, like Pöhls, he promptly left theory behind and turned to practice: "Nevertheless, on the grounds of expediency and fairness, a thoroughgoing enforcement of this principle in the charters had to be forsaken." In particular, he cited the problems that arose when a single shareholder accumulated a large number of votes. "Also," he observed, "the interest of the proprietor of many shares often collides with that of the proprietor of one or only a few." For this reason, railroad companies used graduated voting scales, and he offered the reader an example of a ten-step scale that "many joint-stock corporations" used. This began with 1 vote for 1 share, then 2 votes for 2 to 5 shares, and so on through seven more steps to 9 votes for 151 to 200 shares; for 201 or more shares, the shareholder was entitled to 10 votes and no more. Beschorner also noted that a number of railroad corporations retained a lower threshold on the right to vote (Beschorner 1858: 76-7). To this date, at least, nothing had changed.

Although much research remains to be done on the years from the 1860s to the early 1880s, it is clear that a significant change came in 1884 when the German *Reichstag* passed an extensive revision of corporation law.[13] The result—in formal terms, at least—was to reinforce the more democratic thrust of governance in German corporations. The legislation did away with the threshold required to attain the right to vote: "*Jede Aktie gewährt das Stimmrecht*"—Every

---

[13] The legislation is reprinted, among other places, in Weyl (1896: pt. 2, 217-21).

share affords the right to vote—declared *Artikel 190* (Ring 1893: 93, 450-1).[14] At the same time, the law endorsed the one-vote, one-share rule in principle, as earlier commentators had, but it still preserved the option for incorporators to choose to limit suffrage in various ways: "In the event that a shareholder owns several shares," it read, "the corporation statutes can limit the exercise of his voting right by setting a maximum amount or in gradations [*Abstufungen*] or by type of share." As an expert on trusts and cartels pointed out some years later, this meant that a corporation could, if it wanted, even allow only one vote per shareholder (Ring 1893: 450-1). Practice did not likely go so far, but the author of a 1905 German handbook on stocks and joint-stock corporations did note explicitly that the law's provisions allowed voting rights that diminished (*sich mindert*) in a fixed manner as the amount of capital increased. This constituted a safeguard, he explained, so that the "fate of the corporation" would not easily fall "into the hands of large shareholders" (Siemens 1905: 52).

And in 1904, remarkably, the author of a German treatise on the law of joint-stock corporations repeated practically word for word the explanation of theory, then practice, that Pöhls and Beschorner had expressed in 1842 and 1858, respectively. The practice of granting votes according to the number of shares owned, Dr. Karl Lehmann explained, reflected "the nature of the joint-stock corporation as a distinctive association of property [*ausgeprägter Realassozia-tion*], in which the person of the shareholder takes second place to the share." Thus the appropriate form of suffrage: "So many shares, so many votes." But Lehmann then proceeded to repeat just what Pöhls and Beschorner had empha-sized a half century earlier: "Since the ruthless enforcement [*radikale Durch-führung*] of this principle would give too much power to the largest shareholders, laws and charters frequently limited the voting rights as shareholdings increased." Whether German firms continued to use graduated scales can only be answered with firm-level research, but Lehmann noted, as others did, too, that German law left open the possibility of limiting the power of large shareholders (Lehmann 1904: 162-3).

In all three European countries, then, limitations on the power of large inves-tors disappeared more slowly than in the U.S.. As the century drew to a close, they were becoming less and less common, but in neither Britain nor France nor Germany, unlike the U.S., had they disappeared altogether when the great debates about cartellization and trustification got underway in the 1880s and 1890s (Maschke 1969).

---

[14] Ring noted that this represented a real change and that it meant, among other things, that statute provisions that allowed certain, otherwise capable shareholders (*verfügungsfähige Personen*) to cast votes only by means of a proxy would no longer be permissible. Ring (1893: 450). This elliptical statement must have referred to female shareholders, who were traditionally not allowed to attend the shareholders' meetings. Weyl (1896: pt. 2, 107, 160) makes this explicit.

G. Further Movement Toward Plutocracy in the U.S.

In the U.S., meanwhile, voting rights continued to move further toward the plutocratic end of the spectrum during the last decades of the nineteenth century. Corporations began to divide their shares into classes of stocks, the most familiar division being between common and preferred stock, the latter generally claiming prior rights with regard to corporate profits or property. But, as Thomas Conyngton, author of several early twentieth-century handbooks on American incorporation, explained to prospective incorporators in 1908, there were other ways of classifying stock, and "[m]ost of these other classifications relate to the voting right. The simplest is a division of the stock into two classes, one class voting, the other not exercising this right" (Conyngton 1908: 67). In two publications after the turn of the century, Robert Liefmann, a recognized German authority on cartels and trusts, noted the emergence of this "very widespread practice" (Liefmann 1912: 71) in the U.S. and pondered its implications for corporate governance as well as the choice of corporate strategies. An "oligarchic condition" had become the norm with American corporations, he noted in 1912: "[A]lmost routinely a corporation is dominated, 'controlled'—as the technical expression goes—by a small group of powerful shareholders" (Liefmann 1912: 71). "[B]y possessing half of [only] the voting shares," he observed a few years later, "one controls the entire enterprise" (Liefmann 1918: 168). Concerned as he was to understand why so many mergers had taken place in the U.S. at the turn of the century, he thought that the contrary movement in Germany that ensured the right of every shareholder to vote had made the mass of small shareholders relatively more powerful and made takeovers more difficult.[15]

During the same years, another legal change, according to Conyngton, enhanced the rights of minority shareholders in ways that—quite unintentionally—made it easier for a minority to gain control. This was the practice of cumulative voting, which yielded a kind of proportional representation for shareholders (Conyngton 1905: 86-96; 1908: 253-5; Gordon 1994). New York statutes defined it in the following way:

> The certificate of incorporation of any stock company may provide that at all elections of directors of such corporation, each stockholder shall be entitled to as many votes as shall equal the number of his shares of stock multiplied by the number of directors to be elected, and that he may cast all of such votes for a single director or may distribute them among the number to be voted, or any two or more of them as he may see fit, which right, when exercised, shall be termed cumulative voting (Conyngton 1908: 253-4).

[15] The difference was one of degree, not kind, for the German legislation (*Novelle*) did allow special kinds of stock to have enlarged voting rights, but it still meant that one had to contend with more shareholders and therefore that the obstacles to collective action were that much greater.

The first state to adopt cumulative voting was Illinois. Out of a major political battle at the Illinois constitutional convention in 1870 came a system of proportional representation for the Illinois House of Representatives, and this concept was then promptly extended from the political to the economic sphere. As Jeffrey Gordon explains, "The principle having prevailed [with respect to state representatives], the constitutional convention also required cumulative voting in the election of directors of private corporations." Within ten years, seven states had, like Illinois, made cumulative voting mandatory; by 1900 the group totaled eighteen and additional states explicitly permitted the practice (Gordon 1994: 142-5).[16]

The intention behind cumulative voting, as Conyngton explained, was "to secure minority representation on the board." But the practice, as Liefmann suggested, could also make it easier for a minority interest to gain control of the board of directors, which did not necessarily protect the small shareholder and could result in an outcome even less desirable than majority control. Indeed, Conyngton warned as much in a 1908 manual on incorporation. He touted cumulative voting as "one of the most effectual means of securing minority representation on the board of directors," *provided* that minority interests organized themselves before the election. Cumulative voting "must . . . be used with intelligence," he cautioned, "or the results are sometimes surprising. On occasion, an unsuspecting majority has so scattered its votes that a compact, well-handled minority has actually gained control of the board. . . . Such an election, though somewhat unexpected in its results, is legal and would be upheld wherever cumulative voting is employed" (Conyngton 1908: 253-5).

The practical effect of these developments as the twentieth century opened was that Americans—paradoxically, for a people so proud of their democracy—enjoyed a lesser degree of what William N. Parker has termed "shareholder democracy" in the corporate world than their European counterparts (Parker 1991: 961 et seq.). It was this condition—and the sharp contrast with conditions in Germany—that led Liefmann to declare the German style of corporate governance to be "extraordinarily democratic" and American corporations, by comparison, to be "much less democratically organized" (Liefmann 1912: 71). From a vantage point during the war, he returned to the German-American comparison to ponder its implications for the choice of corporate strategy. Plutocratic suffrage inside the American corporation had facilitated a concentration of wealth that astounded him and left him not only puzzled over the American concept of democracy but also convinced that the more democratic style of corporate governance that prevailed in Germany made it much harder to carry out mergers and consolidations (Liefmann 1918: 173, 197). In the plutocratic

---

[16] Gordon (1994: 145) thinks "the high water mark of mandatory cumulative voting was probably the late 1940s."

United States, in contrast, they certainly proved much easier to achieve. Whether the plutocratic form of corporate governance was indeed a vital, though overlooked, precondition of the great merger movement, as Liefmann thought, is the subject of ongoing research.

References

'An Act to Incorporate the New-York, Providence, and Boston Rail Road Company, Passed at the June Session, 1832' (Providence: B. Cranston & Co., 1836).

Beschorner, Julius Herrmann *Das deutsche Eisenbahnrecht mit besonderer Berücksichtigung des Actien- und Expropriationsrechtes* (Erlangen: Verlag von Ferdinand Enke, 1858).

Bradshaw's General Railway Directory, Shareholders' Guide, Manual, and Almanack for 1851 . . . . (London: W. J. Adams; Manchester: Bradshaw and Blacklock, 1851)

Cellérier, Lucien *Étude sur les société anonymes en France et dans les pays voisins* (Paris: Librairie de la société du recueil J.-B. Sirey & du journal du palais, 1905).

Cerclet, A. *Code des chemins de fer ou recueil complet des lois, ordonnances, cahiers de charges, status, actes de société; réglements et arretés* (Paris: Librairie scientifique-industrielle de L. Mathias, 1845).

Chadwyck-Healey, C.E.H., Percy F. Wheeler, and Charles Burney *A Treatise on the Law and Practice Relating to Joint Stock Companies Under the Acts of 1862-1890: With Forms and Precedents* 2nd enl. edn. (London: W. Maxwell & Son, 1886).

Chadwyck-Healey, C.E.H., Percy F. Wheeler, and Charles Burney *A Treatise on the Law and Practice Relating to Joint Stock Companies Under the Acts of 1862-1890: With Forms and Precedents* 3rd enl. edn. (London: Sweet and Maxwell, 1894).

Chandler, Alfred D., Jr. *The Visible Hand: The Managerial Revolution in American Business* (Cambridge, Mass. 1977).

Chandler, Alfred D., Jr. *Scale and Scope: The Dynamics of Industrial Capitalism* (Cambridge, Mass. 1990).

Chandler, Alfred D., Jr. and Herman Daems (eds.) *Managerial Hierarchies: Comparative Perspectives on the Rise of the Modern Industrial Enterprise* (Cambridge, Mass. 1980).

The Charter and Other Acts of the Legislature, in Relation to the South-Carolina Rail Road Company, . . . (Charleston: Steam Power-Press of Walker and James, 1851).

A Convention of the Stockholders of the Greenville and Columbia Rail Road, for the Purpose of Organization, Held at Carolina Hall, Columbia, Tuesday and Wednesday, May 11, 12, 1847 (Columbia, S.C.: South Carolinian Office, 1847).

Conyngton, Thomas *The Modern Corporation, Its Mechanism, Methods, Formation and Management: A Practical Work on the Corporate Form as Used for Private Enterprises* 2nd edn. (New York: Ronald Press, 1905).

Conyngton, Thomas *A Manual of Corporate Organization Containing Information, Directions and Suggestions Relating to the Incorportion of Enterprises* Enl. edn. (New York: Ronald Press, 1908).

A Copy of the Charter of the Bank of England and Also the By-Laws for the Good Government of the Said Corporation (London: H. Teape, 1818).

Cornish, William R. 'Legal Control over Cartels and Monopolization 1880-1914. A Comparison' in: Horn, Norbert and Jürgen Kocka (eds.) *Recht und Entwicklung der Großunternehmen im 19. und frühen 20. Jahrhundert: Wirtschafts-, sozial- und rechtshistorische Untersuchungen zur Industrialisierung in Deutschland, Frankreich, England und den USA* (Göttingen 1979) 280-305.

Dunlavy, Colleen A. *Politics and Industrialization: Early Railroads in the United States and Prussia* (Princeton 1994).

Freedeman, Charles E. *Joint-Stock Enterprise in France, 1807-1867: From Privileged Company to Modern Corporation* (Chapel Hill, N.C. 1979).

Freyer, Tony *Regulating Big Business: Antitrust in Great Britain and America, 1880-1990* (Cambridge, Mass. 1992).

Friedman, Lawrence M. *A History of American Law* (New York 1973).

Goirand, Leopold *A Treatise upon French Commercial Law and the Practice of all the Courts, with a Theoretical and Practical Commentary and the Text of the Laws Relating Thereto, Including the Entire Code of Commerce with a Dictionary of French Judicial Terms* 2nd edn. (London: Stevens and Sons, 1898).

Gordon, Jeffrey N. 'Institutions as Relational Investors: A New Look at Cumulative Voting' 94 *Colum. L. Rev.* 124-92 (1994).

Gregg, W.P. and Benjamin Pond *The Railroad Laws and Charters of the United States . . .* 2 vols. (Boston: Charles C. Little and James Brown, 1851).

Hamilton, Alexander 'National Bank. Communicated to the House of Representatives, Dec. 14, 1790' *American State Papers* vol. 5, 1st Cong., 3rd sess., no. 18 (1790).

Hannah, Leslie 'The Historical Problem of the Growth of Large-Scale Enterpise' in: *Piccola e grande impresa: un problema storico* 29-34 (Istituto per la storia dell' Umbria contemporanea, Milan 1987).

Hansemann, David *Die Eisenbahnen und deren Aktionäre in ihrem Verhältniß zum Staat* (Leipzig and Halle: Renger'sche Verlagsbuchhandlung, 1837).

Hoff, W. and F. Schwabach *Official German Report on American Railroads: North American Railroads, Their Administration and Economic Policy* (New York: Germania Press, 1907).

Horn, Norbert, and Jürgen Kocka (eds.) *Recht und Entwicklung der Großunternehmen im 19. und frühen 20. Jahrhundert: Wirtschafts-, sozial- und rechtshistorische Untersuchungen zur Industrialisierung in Deutschland, Frankreich, England und den USA = Law and the Formation of the Big Enterprises in the 19th and Early 20th Centuries: Studies in the History of Industrialization in Germany, France, Great Britain and the United States* (Göttingen 1979).

Hübner, Otto *Die Banken* (in two parts, separately paginated) (Leipzig: Heinrich Hübner, 1854).

Hunt's Merchants Magazine and Commercial Review Vol. 23 (New York, December 1850).

Kindleberger, Charles P. *A Financial History of Western Europe* 2nd edn. (New York and Oxford 1993).

Koch, Wilhelm *Deutschlands Eisenbahnen. Versuch einer systematischen Darstellung der Rechtsverhältnisse aus der Anlage und dem Betriebe Derselben* (Marburg and Leipzig: N. G. Elwert'sche Universitäts-Buchhandlung 1860).

Lamoreaux, Naomi R. *The Great Merger Movement in American Business, 1895-1904* (Cambridge, Mass. 1985).

Lehmann, Karl *Das Recht der Aktiengesellschaften* vol. 1 (Berlin Carl Heymanns Verlag 1898).

Lehmann, Karl *Das Recht der Aktiengesellschaften* vol. 2 (Berlin Carl Heymanns Verlag 1904).

Liefmann, Robert *Kartelle und Trusts und die Weiterbildung der volkswirtschaftlichen Organisation* 2nd enl. edn. (Stuttgart: Verlag von Ernst Heinrich Moritz, 1910).

Liefmann, Robert *Die Unternehmungsformen* (Stuttgart: Ernst Heinrich Moritz, 1912).

Liefmann, Robert *Kartelle und Trusts und die Weiterbildung der volkswirtschaftlichen Organisation* 3rd edn. (Stuttgart: Verlag von Ernst Heinrich Moritz, 1918).

Lindley, Nathaniel *A Treatise on the Law of Companies Considered as a Branch of the Law of Partnership* 5th edn. (London: Sweet and Maxwell, 1889).

Maier, Pauline 'The Revolutionary Origins of the American Corporation' *William and Mary Quarterly* 3rd ser., 50 (1993) 51-84.

Maschke, Erich 'Outline of the History of German Cartels, 1873-1914' in: Crouzet, François, W.H. Chaloner, and W.M. Stern *Essays in European Economic History* 226-58 (London 1969).

Michaelis, Julius *Deutschlands Eisenbahnen. Ein Handbuch für Geschäftsleute, Privatpersonen, Capitalisten und Speculanten, enthaltend Geschichte und Beschreibung der Eisenbahnen, deren Verfassung, Anlagecapital, Frequenz, Einnahme, Rentabilität und Reservefonds, . . .* (Leipzig: C. F. Amelang's Verlag, 1854).

Mitchell, Timothy 'The Limits of the State: Beyond Statist Approaches and Their Critics' *American Political Science Review* 85 (1991) 77-96.

Morawetz, Victor *A Treatise on the Law of Private Corporations Other Than Charitable* 2nd edn. (Boston: Little, Brown and Company, 1886).

de Nancy, Durand *Le droit usuel pour l'avocat de soi-même: Nouveau guide en affaires contenant toutes les notions de droit et tous les modèles d'actes dont on a besoin pour gérer ses affaires soit en matière civile, soit en matière commerciale* 5ᵗʰ edn. (Paris: Garnier Frères, Libraires-Éditeurs, 1870).

Palmer, Francis Beaufort *Company Law: A Practical Handbook for Lawyers and Business Men. With an Appendix Containing the Companies Act, 1862-1900, and Rules, etc.* 5ᵗʰ edn. (London: Stevens and Sons, 1905).

Palmer, Francis Beaufort *Company Law: A Practical Handbook for Lawyers and Business Men. With an Appendix Containing the Companies (Consolidation) Act, 1908, and Other Acts and Rules* 6ᵗʰ edn. (London: Stevens and Sons, 1909).

Palmer, Francis Beaufort *Company Law: A Practical Handbook for Lawyers and Business Men with an Appendix Containing the Companies (Consolidation) Act, 1908; Companies Act, 1913, and Other Acts and Rules* 10ᵗʰ edn. (London: Stevens and Sons, Ltd., 1916).

Parker, William N. 'The Scale and Scope of Alfred D. Chandler, Jr. *Journal of Economic History* 51 (1991) 958-63.

Peters, Richard (ed.) *The Public Statutes at Large of the United States of America . . .* vol. 1. (Boston: Charles C. Little and James Brown, 1848).

Pöhls, Meno *Das Recht der Actiengesellschaften mit besonderer Rücksicht auf Eisenbahn-gesellschaften* (Hamburg: Hoffman und Campe, 1842).

Porter, Kirk H. *A History of Suffrage* (Chicago: University of Chicago Press, 1918).

Ring, Viktor *Das Reichsgesetz betreffend die Kommanditgesellschaften auf Aktien und die Aktiengesellschaften. Vom 18. Juli 1884* 2ⁿᵈ rev. edn. (Berlin: Carl Heymanns Verlag, 1893).

Roe, Mark J. *Strong Managers, Weak Owners: The Political Roots of American Corporate Finance* (Princeton 1994).

Seavoy, Ronald E. *The Origins of the American Business Corporation, 1784-1855: Broadening the Concept of Public Service During Industrialization* (Westport, Conn. 1982).

Siemens, H. *Das Aktienwesen und die Aktiengesellschaften. Eine übersichtliche Darstellung des Wissenswerten für Bankiers, Kapitalisten, Aktienbesitzer usw.* (Berlin: S. Mode's Verlag, 1905).

Singer, J. *Das Land der Monopole: Amerika oder Deutschland?* (Berlin: Franz Siemenroth, 1913).

Smith, Rogers *Liberalism and American Constitutional Law* (Cambridge, Mass. and London 1990).

Smith, T. Eustace and Arthur Stiebel *A Summary of the Law of Companies* 9ᵗʰ edn. (London: Stevens and Haynes, 1907).

Tapping, Thomas *Joint Stock Companies, How to Form Them; Being the Second Edition of the Handy Book on Public Companies. Designed as a Practical Guide for Projectors, Promoters, Directors, Shareholders, Creditors, Solicitors, Secretaries, and Other Officers* (London: Mining Journal Office, 1866).

Walker, Francis 'The Law Concerning Monopolistic Combinations in Continental Europe in: *Trusts in Foreign Countries: Laws and References Concerning Industrial Combinations in Australia, Canada, New Zealand, and Continental Europe* comp. by Johnson, Fred A. 62-80 (Washington: Government Printing Office, 1912).

Ward, James A. 'Power and Accountability on the Pennsylvania Railroad, 1846-1878' *Business History Review* 49/Spring (1975) 48-9.

Weyl, Ludwig *Hand-Kommentar zu den Bestimmungen des deutschen Handelsgesetzbuchs über die Aktiengesellschaft* (Freiburg i. B. and Leipzig: Akademische Verlagsbuchhandlung von J.C.B. Mohr, 1896).

Williamson, Chilton *American Suffrage: From Property to Democracy, 1760-1860* (Princeton 1960).

Corporate Governance and Multinational Enterprise in Historical Perspective

PETER HERTNER, Halle-Wittenberg

Historical research on the development of international business and the origins of multinational enterprise (MNE) has shown that, in spite of completely different conditions as far as information transfer and transaction costs are concerned, 19th-century firms active in the international field behaved in a way that was quite comparable to the conduct of modern MNEs.

In order to guarantee a sufficient level of monitoring and control, new instruments were developed such as the free-standing company in the case of overseas investment or the financial holding companies which supported the multinational expansion of the electrotechnical industry. Creating these new tools meant that new problems of corporate governance also had to be solved. By looking at the international scene during the second half of the 19th century, this analysis tries to demonstrate if and to what degree such attempts were successful.

Contents

A. Multinational Business Activities and Historical Research

"A multinational or transnational enterprise" is, according to John H. Dunning's "working definition", "an enterprise that engages in foreign direct investment . . . and owns or controls value-adding activities in more than one country."[1] Multinational enterprise (MNE)[2] is different from international trading firms as well as

---

[1] Dunning, John H. *Multinational Enterprises and the Global Economy* 3 (Wokingham 1992).

[2] The adjective "multinational" will be preferred to "transnational" since this essay deals primarily with historical development. The "transnational" concept could at best be applied to quite recent phenomena in this field.

from domestic firms insofar as it "engages in *both* cross-border production and transactions."[3]

Business historians have been able to demonstrate that multinational activities of firms are not a recent phenomenon but can be traced back well into the 19th century, and in some cases even further.[4] It is obvious that these activities have enormously increased over the last few decades, and that therefore their quantity—if not quality—has changed.

Whereas it seems to be widely accepted that so far "no consensus amongst economists concerning the theory of the MNE" has been reached,[5] empirical research looking into the structure and strategies of MNE could indeed profit from the work of business historians. As a matter of fact, some historians have obtained access to internal company records and have thus been able to find out more about motives and concrete elements of success or failure of multinational firms. This information is normally historical in the sense that it is several decades old before it can become an object of research. Despite their historical nature, these new sources can become a welcome addition to the field of empirical studies on the MNE. Such an approach can thus help to develop the evolutionary aspects of the concept of MNE and of its concrete contents.

In spite of some shortcomings, Dunning's "eclectic paradigm" of international production still seems to be the most practical tool for analyzing multinational activities. Particularly to business historians, Dunning's concept of "ownership, location and internalization advantages"[6] offers a workable approach to the empirical phenomena which form the base of their research. One could even say that the 19th and early 20th centuries—with their clearly defined nation states, their nationally distinct legal systems, and their on average fairly competitive trade policies—offer an ideal playground for such theoretical approaches. Ownership advantages and locational factors were perhaps more easily distinguishable then than today, and, generally speaking, firms had more time to undertake one step of internalization after the other.

B. Corporate Governance and the Multinational Enterprise

Among the various definitions employed to describe corporate governance, the one proposed by Shleifer and Vishny seems useful: "Corporate governance deals

---

[3] Dunning, supra n. 1, 4.

[4] Hertner, Peter and Geoffrey Jones (eds.) *Multinationals. Theory and History* 1 et seq. (introduction) (Aldershot 1986).

[5] Hertner and Jones, supra n. 4, 4-5; cf. also Casson, Mark 'General Theories of the Multinational Enterprise: Their Relevance to Business History' in: Hertner and Jones (eds.), supra n. 4, 42-63, 42.

[6] Dunning, John H. *The Globalization of Business* 81-2 (London and New York 1993).

with the ways in which suppliers of finance to corporations assure themselves of getting a return on their investment." The same two authors underline that their "perspective on corporate governance is a straightforward agency perspective, sometimes referred to as separations of ownership and control."[7] There seems in any case to be general agreement that "corporate government has been tradition-ally associated with a principal-agent relationship problem" based on the fact that, according to general experience, "the interests and objectives of investors and managers differ. Corporate governance is concerned with ways of bringing the interests of the two parties into line and ensuring that firms are run for the benefit of investors."[8]

How does the MNE come into this picture? One could say that it is first of all "simply one subspecies of multiplant firm."[9] As such it is of course affected by problems of principal-agent relationship and can thus become an object of research on corporate governance. There are, however, additional features of governance and organization which arise as soon as a firm extends its operations to other national environments. Governance and organizational problems *beyond* the original firm itself become important when arms-length transactions are substituted by cooperation or, alternatively, by internalization. Cooperative schemes are not easy to organize and to monitor, particularly over a long period during which original conditions and the interests involved will have changed. The history of joint-ventures and cartels would be a good case in kind. Internali-zation on the other hand is the paradigm that is particularly linked with the actual and the historical development of MNE. The way from arms-length trading to agency contracts, then further to the establishment of sales affiliates, and finally to the construction or the acquisition of a manufacturing unit, has been theoreti-cally described by economists and empirically researched by business historians over and over again. There was, however, no obligatory route to perfect inter-nalization. Much depended on the general political and economic framework and on eventual technological constraints. The individual character of branches and general circumstances permitting multinational business expansion could also be quite successful in the form of family or non-family networks as an alternative to the creation of integrated international groups.[10]

[7] Shleifer, Andrei and Robert W. Vishny 'A Survey of Corporate Governance' *Journal of Finance* 52 (1997) 737-83, 737-8.

[8] Mayer, Colin 'Corporate Governance, Competition and Performance' 4 (OECD Working Paper no. 164, Paris 1996).

[9] Caves, Richard E. *Multinational Enterprise and Economic Analysis* 1 (Cambridge 1982).

[10] Cf. Casson, Mark and Howard Cox 'Firms, Networks and International Business Enter-prises' (University of Reading, Department of Economics, Discussion Papers in International Investment and Business Studies no. 167, Reading 1993).

C. Early Examples of Multinational Business Activities

According to the established theoretical approach, control problems arise as soon as pure arms-length transactions are abandoned or complemented by more internalized solutions. The fact that agents who are not employees of the exporting firm may act in their own interest can lead to the appointment of employed representatives and ultimately to the establishment of a sales, or buying, subsidiary. Medieval and early modern trading and finance companies grew out of the need to internalize a growing number of transactions for reasons of trust or for simple practicality when recurrent and similar transactions had to be organized. In such cases a hierarchy of managers was established who, for their part, had to be controlled by the companies' owners.[11] In an age of extremely slow and difficult communications, control of agents established at faraway places was notoriously difficult. It is therefore not astonishing that family firms—and apart from the few chartered companies practically all firms were family enterprises until the first decades of the 19th century—normally preferred the solution which in their eyes was most trustworthy and used family members as their agents. Steady control could thus be substituted by authority structures and trust typical of family networks. Besides, distinct religious and ethnic communities like Huguenot immigrants in Britain, the Netherlands, Germany and Switzerland, Jews all over Western and Southern Europe, and Chinese in Southeast Asia offered trust and solidarity also beyond the family proper, and this fact certainly explains part of their success story.[12]

In this respect and for most of its duration, the 19th century presents itself as a typical transition period: besides the traditional small family firms there were also big and internationally expanding family firms—the Rothschilds or the Siemens family, for instance—that used family members as agents or managers abroad, but non-family firms that decided to go abroad naturally sent employees to their foreign subsidiaries who were not relatives of their top managers. Closer control and comparatively intensive monitoring of agents and subsidiaries placed abroad had by now become possible thanks to greatly improved communication systems: railways and steamships linked regions and continents together and information exchange experienced a veritable revolution through the introduction of an international and intercontinental telegraph network between the 1850s and the 1870s.[13]

[11] Carlos, Ann M. and Stephen Nicholas '"Giants of an Earlier Capitalism": The Chartered Trading Companies as Modern Multinationals' *Business History Review* 62 (1988) 389-419.

[12] Cf., for example, Chapman, Stanley D. 'The International Houses: The Continental Contribution to British Commerce, 1800-1860' *Journal of European Economic History* 6 (1977) 5-48.

[13] Cf. Jones, Charles A. *International Business in the Nineteenth Century: The Rise and Fall of a Cosmopolitan Bourgeoisie* 101 et seq. (Brighton 1987).

At that stage of development one could for the first time talk of MNEs *in statu nascendi*: these still quite primitive MNEs were companies that often behaved in a way typical of the much more developed multinational businesses of today, and this is quite remarkable. On the other hand, one must of course admit that they were still rather small firms and not very complex as to their internal organization. At first sight, governance does not seem to have been a major problem in the majority of these early cases. The mother company very often owned one hundred percent of the subsidiary or was at least the majority shareholder. Frequently the mother company was also the major debtholder, either because the host country could not offer the required financial services or because the mother company did not want to disclose its debt status to foreign creditors. In most cases, the reason for such strategies aimed at "safe" control must be sought—if we exclude typical raw material ventures—in the proprietary character of technology. One could naturally give away information on products or technical processes by selling patents, but patents very often covered only part of the necessary know-how. Licensing almost inevitably comprised also a transfer of nonpatentable technology. Firms very often hesitated to hand all this over to a partner who could eventually become a fearsome competitor. "Given the tacit, fungible, and nonpatentable nature of the internal organizational knowledge of technology and markets,"[14] it is understandable that firms preferred in so many cases to maintain control of their foreign offspring.

Things changed when and where technology was accompanied by a growing need for finance. Joint-ventures with competing firms became clearly more attractive in these cases. Another possibility—we shall come back to it further ahead—lay in the participation of the mother company's bank or of special finance companies in the MNE's foreign subsidiaries and their operations.

The choice of the appropriate legal form was an integral part of the decision in favor of a particular foreign direct investment. The host country's legal system and the degree of effective legal protection it could offer to foreign investment were normally not the most important motive for creating a subsidiary in that particular place. The "legal factor", however, became important for the long-run success of the foreign subsidiary since the choice of the legal form could quite often influence the level of taxation the subsidiary was exposed to, and that meant concretely the level of profitability. It could also decide on possibilities of access to the foreign capital market, and it therefore became important for the subsidiary's chances of "independent" growth. Under the legal system of continental Europe, a foreign subsidiary could either remain, legally speaking, a branch of the mother company (which then had to declare officially, mostly for

---

[14] Hikino, Takashi 'Managerial Control, Capital Markets, and the Wealth of Nations' in: Chandler, Alfred D., Franco Amatori, and Takashi Hikino (eds.) *Big Business and the Wealth of Nations* 480-96, 484-5 (Cambridge 1997).

fiscal reasons, the amount of capital invested in that specific subsidiary), or it could choose to become a legally independent company according to the legal provisions of its host country. As long as the mother company controlled the second type of subsidiary, the legally independent one, governance problems were not different from those of the first type. Potentially the independent company solution was much more flexible. This type of company had relatively easy access to equity capital, especially if it was organized as a joint-stock company. It could also become a joint-venture without too many problems because its shares could be traded and thus exchanged between the future partners. Theoretically at least, discrimination against foreign capital coming from the host country's government should have spared this type of foreign direct investment since these companies had the status of "national" ones. Practically speaking and looking at concrete historical experience, it is not difficult to find discriminatory practices; one of these, for instance, consisted in allowing only nationals of the host country to sit on the board of such a company.

The criteria for the choice of a particular legal system by a foreign investor have so far been based on the assumption of a relatively strong mother company able and willing to deliver organization, finance, and technology to its subsidiary. Quite a different type of organization is represented by the so-called *free-standing company*, a term created by Mira Wilkins. She applies it to companies which in most cases were registered in Britain between the mid-19th century and 1914, "to conduct business overseas, most of which . . . did *not* grow out of the domestic operations of existing enterprises that had headquarters in Britain."[15] These free-standing companies normally developed only in those branches where there was no need for the backing of a technologically and organizationally strong mother company. They had a legally established head office in the mother country, but all their business operations, with the exception of their own long-term financing, were done overseas. In this quite specific case, the rather lax British company laws—as they were valid during the period after 1856 and until about 1900—combined with the attractiveness and efficiency of the London capital market, could compensate for the lack of a strong technical and managerial center which otherwise would have had to be created in the home country.[16] Only the home country could offer the comparative advantages in both the intermediation of information as well as the intermediation of finance. Its markets were "supported by a large amount of face-to-face contact between

[15] Wilkins, Mira 'The Free-Standing Company, 1870-1914: an Important Type of British Foreign Direct Investment' *Economic History Review* 2nd ser. 61 (1988) 259-82, 261.

[16] Apart from Britain—and to a much lesser degree also from France—Belgium seems to have produced the major figure of these free-standing companies. The highly permissive Belgian company law between 1873 and 1913 was probably one—if not the—decisive factor which favored this development (cf. Hertner, Peter 'Foreign Capital in the Italian Economy, 1883-1912: The Example of the Free-Standing Companies' (forthcoming)).

merchants;" those were the advantages of the "economies of agglomeration in a metropolitan area."[17]

Thus one might say that the establishment of these free-standing companies was a flexible response to the specific needs of foreign investment under the conditions of the late 19th century when market integration on an international level was still in its infancy and when certain metropolitan markets, above all London, offered a whole range of advantages in intermediation which could not be found overseas. Under these circumstances, the quality of corporate governance depended above all on the intensity of control exercised by investors on operations done overseas by the free-standing firm. Flows of information, technology, and finance which went back and forth between the metropolitan head office and the manufacturing unit abroad could be used for control by investors. The extent to which this was then really done depended on the legal provisions of the company statutes, on investors' shares of capital, and on their willingness to exercise their tasks of monitoring.

D. Corporate Governance and Multinational Enterprise: The Example of the International Electrotechnical Industry From the 1890s Until 1914

I. The Road to Multinational Business

Electricity was an essential—if not *the* essential—part of what has been called the *Second Industrial Revolution*. Concretely speaking, this meant the introduction and the use of the electric telegraph and later on of the telephone, both parts of the so-called low-voltage sector. The high-voltage sector comprised the production and distribution of electric energy and its application to transport, to illumination, as well as to the production of heat and power. The first private and public power stations, built in New York, Milan, and Berlin in 1882/83, were very small direct current producers that supplied electric lighting to a few blocks in the heart of these cities.[18] Growing demand and the subsequent increase in the size of generators created a load problem since illumination peak hours occurred only twice a day in the early morning and during the evening hours. The electri-

---

[17] Casson, Mark 'The Economic Theory of the Free-Standing Company: An Integrated Approach' 37 (University of Reading, Department of Economics, Discussion Papers in International Investment and Business Studies no. 198, Reading 1995).

[18] Cf. Hughes, Thomas P. *Networks of Power: Electrification in Western Society, 1880-1930* 41 et seq. (Baltimore and London 1983); Pavese, Claudio 'Le origini della Società Edison e il suo sviluppo fino alla costituzione del "gruppo" (1881-1919)' in: Bezza, Bruno (ed.) *Energia e sviluppo. L' industria elettrica italiana e la Società Edison* 23-169, 48 (Torino 1986); Matschoss, Conrad, Erich Schulz, and Arnold Theodor Gross *50 Jahre Berliner Elektrizitätswerke* 11 et seq. (Berlin 1934).

fication of public transport seemed to offer a solution to this problem because it could help to increase electricity sales during day hours and could thus help to improve the power plants' efficiency. Thus by the middle of 1890 one-sixth of United States tramways had already switched to electric traction; three years later it was 60%, and by the end of 1903, 98% of U.S. tramways had been electrified. These changes took more time in Europe: by the end of 1895 a quarter of the German tramway network had adopted electric traction; by the end of 1902 practically all German tramways were electrified, whereas in Britain only 38% of the network had been converted by that time.[19]

A second element that helped to improve the load factor was the supply of power to machines in artisan workshops and factories. This process, however, took much more time to develop: it started in the mid-1890s and was concluded only at the end of the 1920s. By 1909, barely a quarter of industrial power had been electrified in the United States; two years later, the share was 19.5% in Germany.[20] A decisive technological breakthrough stood at the beginning of these developments: the first successful demonstration of long-distance transport of high-voltage alternating current achieved in 1891 between Lauffen on the Neckar River in Southwestern Germany and Frankfurt/Main over a distance of no less than 179 kilometers.[21] As a consequence and with subsequent technological development, energy production and consumption could take place at sites which lay hundreds of kilometers apart from each other. Financing the power plants of ever-increasing size as well as the rapidly expanding regional grids of distribution required a steadily increasing share of national income which, in the case of Britain during the first decade of the 20th century, has been estimated at about 10% of gross domestic capital formation.[22]

The swift growth of electrification was, at least in the most industrialized countries of Europe and North America, accompanied—in part, as we will see, also caused—by an equally dynamic development of the electrotechnical industry that produced the necessary equipment for the exploitation of this new source of energy. The 1880s and the following decade were still characterized by a

[19] Jackson, Kenneth T. 'The Impact of Technological Change on Urban Form' in: Colton, Joel and Stuart Bruchey (eds.) *Technology, Economy, and Society. The American Experience* 150-61, 156 (New York 1987); McKay, John P. *Tramways and Trolleys. The Rise of Urban Mass Transport in Europe* 50, 73 (Princeton 1976).

[20] Cf. Devine, Warren D. 'From Shafts to Wires: Historical Perspective on Electrification' *Journal of Economic History* 33 (1983) 347-72, 354; Saul, Samuel Berrick 'The American Impact on British Industry 1895-1914' *Business History* 3 (1963) 129-38, 136, n. 1.

[21] Cf. Hughes, supra n. 18, 129 et seq.; Behrend, Bernard Arthur 'The Debt of Electrical Engineering to C.E.L. Brown' *Electrical World and Engineer* 38/II (1901) part IV 932-4, part V 1015-8.

[22] Byatt, Ian C.R. *British Electrical Industry 1875-1914: The Economic Returns to a New Technology* 5 (Oxford 1979).

relatively large number of small and medium-sized electrotechnical firms active in many industrialized countries. By the end of the 1890s, however, conditions had changed profoundly everywhere. By now, and above all in the high-voltage sector, most of the products had reached a certain level of technical maturity. Thus a premium was awarded to those firms that managed to switch over to standardized mass production. This was especially the case for goods such as light bulbs, cables, or small electric motors which found a rapidly growing market among small enterprises and the mass of urban consumers. On the contrary, the erection of power plants, which constantly grew in scale and sophistication from the middle of the 1880s, favored "full-line" producers who were able to offer solutions for entire systems, as Harold C. Passer has explained it with great clarity:

> "Electrical products had to be part of a system—a lighting system, a power system, or a transportation system. To ensure that the component parts would operate together in a satisfactory manner, manufacturers found it advantageous to produce all, or nearly all, of the components of any system they chose to market. They also found it advantageous to sell and install the complete system."[23]

Standardized mass production of certain components and machines on the one hand and the advantages connected with full-line manufacturing on the other thus created the conditions for a rapid concentration process in this branch.

Finance was another factor that accelerated this movement versus mergers and acquisitions. Fast growth of this branch during the 1890s required increasing amounts of capital which could be mobilized either via direct access to the capital market or with the help of the banking system. Actually, these two ways were interdependent since the banks—at least in the United States and Germany—provided credit and acted as intermediaries for eventual debt consolidation by placing equity and debt titles on the capital market. Concretely speaking, there were firms such as General Electric or Allgemeine Elektricitäts-Gesellschaft (AEG) which were "public companies" with widespread ownership by shareholders and with close links to banks right from their foundation.[24] There was, on the other hand, a typical family enterprise such as Siemens & Halske, founded already in 1847, which, as a result of pressure originating from Deutsche Bank, became a joint-stock company in 1897; the Siemens family, however,

[23] Passer, Harold C. 'Development of Large-Scale Organization: Electrical Manufacturing Around 1900' *Journal of Economic History* 12 (1952) 378-95, 392.

[24] Cf. Carlson, W. Bernard *Innovation as a Social Process: Elihu Thomson and the Rise of General Electric, 1870-1900* 271 et seq. (Cambridge 1991); David, Paul A. 'The Hero and the Herd in Technological History: Reflections on Thomas Edison and the Battle of the Systems' in: Higonnet, Patrice, David S. Landes, and Henry Rosovsky (eds.) *Favorites of Fortune: Technology, Growth, and Economic Development Since the Industrial Revolution* 72-119, 94 et seq. (Cambridge, Mass. and London 1991); Allgemeine Elektricitäts-Gesellschaft '50 Jahre AEG' 21 et seq. (Berlin 1956).

remained in safe possession of the majority of voting stock during the following decades. And there was finally a figure like George Westinghouse, founder of the second largest U.S. company in the high-voltage sector, who equally needed bank support on several occasions and who also got it, but who never really collaborated with these credit institutions in a way which those would have judged to be satisfactory. The result of all this was the recurrent financial instability of the Westinghouse company that went on for decades.[25] If we only look at the German scene, there were finally a number of smaller but still very important firms such as Schuckert of Nuremberg or medium-sized companies like Helios or Kummer which did not have sufficient backing from banks. This was certainly the main reason why, after their rapid expansion during the 1890s, the latter two firms disappeared from the market in the wake of the 1901/02 economic crisis. On that occasion, other producers were forced to merge, as Schuckert did in 1903 when it had to join its high-voltage business with the corresponding part of Siemens.[26]

By 1902/03, when the concentration process had reached its first climax, a worldwide oligopoly had been safely installed in the high-voltage sector: on the U.S. side there was General Electric, founded in 1892 through a merger of Edison General Electric Company with Thomson-Houston Electric Company and Thomson-Houston International Electric Company. The second American firm was the Westinghouse Electric and Manufacturing Company, created in 1891 by the merger of the Westinghouse Electric Company (founded in 1886) with two smaller firms. Around 1900 these two firms, General Electric and Westinghouse, were the only "full-line" manufacturers of high-voltage equipment in the United States.[27] As we have already seen, Siemens, one of the two big German firms, was founded in 1847 and merged, for its high-voltage business, with Schuckert in 1903, with the Siemens family also in control of the new Siemens-Schuckert company. The other "giant" was AEG, created in 1883 as Deutsche Edison-Gesellschaft by the industrialist Emil Rathenau and a group of Frankfurt and Berlin banks. In 1887 the firm changed its name to AEG and

[25] Cf. Kocka, Jürgen *Unternehmensverwaltung und Angestelltenschaft am Beispiel Siemens 1847-1914* 319 et seq. (Stuttgart 1969); Passer, Harold C. *The Electrical Manufacturers 1875-1900* 279 (Cambridge, Mass. 1953).

[26] Cf. Kocka, supra n. 25, 327 et seq.; Feldenkirchen, Wilfried 'Die Rolle der Banken bei der Sanierung von Industrieunternehmen (1850-1914)' in: *Die Rolle der Banken bei der Unternehmenssanierung* 14-39, 30 et seq. (5. Wissenschaftliches Kolloquium zur Bankengeschichte, 7 November 1991, Thun/Switzerland) (*Bankhistorisches Archiv* Supplement 22, Frankfurt am Main 1993).

[27] Cf. the detailed description in U.S. Senate 'Electric Power Industry: Supply of Electrical Equipment and Competitive Conditions' 15 et seq. (70th Congress, 1st Session, Document no. 46, Washington 1928).

managed gradually to free itself from its original technical dependence on the Edison and Siemens companies. This was definitely achieved by 1894.[28]

As to the size of these four oligopolists, we could have a look at their sales in 1913, converted for the sake of comparison into German marks: the Siemens group had sales of 472 million marks, 23% of which, however, stemmed from its low-voltage branch. AEG reached 453 million and General Electric 447, with Westinghouse coming last with sales of about 160 million marks.[29] Siemens and AEG dominated their German home market: there the share of their total sales amounted to about 58% in 1913; the remaining part was produced by a group of about 350 small and medium-sized firms.[30] General Electric's share of total U.S. electrotechnical production in 1914 has been indicated by a figure of 24.8%.[31]

On a worldwide scale, the German electrotechnical industry's part of world production in 1913 has been estimated with a figure of 35%, compared to the United States' 29% in the same year.[32] Another estimate concedes 31% to the Germans and 35% to their American competitors.[33] On the other hand, German industry with its comparatively limited home market dominated world exports of electrotechnical goods with a share of 46% before the outbreak of the First World War; it was followed by the British and the U.S. industries with shares of 22% and 16% respectively.[34] According to contemporary estimates, German electrotechnical industry exported 22% of its production in 1913, whereas the Americans with their huge home market remained at a level of about 7%.[35]

As to their role in the world market, the two German firms could easily be called prototypes of MNE.[36] Both of them maintained so-called "technical offices" at home and abroad. These branch offices were responsible for most of the sales in their specific region or country, as well as for after-sale service which was particularly important in this branch, given the technical complexity of these

---

[28] For a brief description of these developments, cf. Hertner, Peter 'Financial Strategies and Adaptation to Foreign Markets: The German Electro-Technical Industry and its Multinational Activities, 1890s to 1939' in: Teichova, Alice, Maurice Lévy-Leboyer, and Helga Nussbaum (eds.) *Multinational Enterprise in Historical Perspective* 145-59 (Cambridge and Paris 1986).

[29] Byatt, supra n. 22, 166; for General Electric in 1913, cf. U.S. Senate, supra n. 27, 46.

[30] Homburg, Heidrun *Rationalisierung und Industriearbeit. Arbeitsmarkt—Management—Arbeiterschaft im Siemens-Konzern Berlin, 1900-1939* 350 (Berlin 1991).

[31] U.S. Senate, supra n. 27, 66.

[32] Czada, Peter *Die Berliner Elektroindustrie in der Weimarer Zeit* 139 (Berlin 1969).

[33] Jacob-Wendler, Gerhart *Deutsche Elektroindustrie in Lateinamerika: Siemens und AEG (1890-1914)* 11 (Stuttgart 1982); 'Die Elektrizität auf dem Weltmarkt' *Elektrotechnische Zeitschrift* (1913) 1016.

[34] Czada, supra n. 32, 137 et seq.; Jacob-Wendler, supra n. 33, 11.

[35] 'Die Elektrizität auf dem Weltmarkt', supra n. 33.

[36] Cf. Hertner, Peter 'German Multinational Enterprise Before 1914: Some Case Studies' in: Hertner and Jones (eds.), supra n. 4, 113-34.

types of investment goods and the necessity of keeping power plants running around the clock. Exports amounted to 33% of total sales done by Siemens-Schuckert in 1913/14, to 35% in the case of Siemens & Halske (the Siemens low-voltage branch), and to about 40% in the case of AEG.[37] Various reasons, the most important ones being increasing tariff levels and mounting non-tariff protectionism, induced these two companies to establish manufacturing subsidiaries abroad. This was done for the principal European markets: Siemens employed 82,900 persons in 1913, of which almost 17,000 worked in its factories set up in France, Britain, Spain, Russia, and in both parts of the Austro-Hungarian Empire. AEG had 70,162 persons on its payroll in 1912; 6,551 of them belonged to its factories at Vienna, Milan, and Riga.[38]

For the U.S. companies, there are no data available on the share of exports in their total sales before World War I. In 1923, this share amounted to 6% for General Electric and to 6.9% for Westinghouse, compared to a figure of 4.7% for the entire U.S. electrotechnical industry.[39] The corresponding percentage was probably not higher before 1914. As their German counterparts, the American firms had established manufacturing subsidiaries abroad: General Electric, via its subsidiary British Thomson-Houston that was founded in 1894, dominated the market for the electrification of British tramways. It also had a relatively strong position in the market for the equipment of new power plants in Britain, to which it had supplied 16% of the capacity installed between 1909 and 1913.[40] In France, General Electric held a participation—even if its size shrank rapidly after 1894—in the Compagnie Française Thomson-Houston, the largest electrotechnical producer in that country.[41] Westinghouse's international expansion took a quite different path because of the mother company's chronic undercapitalization. This created recurrent difficulties which also left the foreign subsidiaries too often with urgent liquidity problems. When the U.S. mother firm went into receivership in 1907, Westinghouse could count on manufacturing subsidiaries in Canada, Britain, France, Russia, and Italy.[42]

[37] Homburg, supra n. 30, 362.

[38] Cf. Hertner, supra n. 28, 145.

[39] U.S. Senate, supra n. 27, 78.

[40] Byatt, supra n. 22, 33 et seq., 138; cf. also Price-Hughes, H.A. *B.T.H. Reminiscences: Sixty Years of Progress* 9 et seq. (Leicester and London 1946); Wilkins, Mira *The Emergence of Multinational Enterprise: American Business Abroad From the Colonial Era to 1914* 94 (Cambridge, Mass. 1970).

[41] Cf. Lanthier, Pierre 'Les constructions électriques en France: Financement et stratégies de six groupes industriels internationaux, 1880-1940' 40 et seq. (Thèse de Doctorat d'État, University of Paris-Nanterre 1988).

[42] Cf. *The Westinghouse Companies in the Railway and Industrial Fields* 43 (Chicago and New York 1905); Lanthier, Pierre 'Westinghouse en France: Histoire d' un échec (1898-1920)' *L' Information historique* 47 (1985) 212-9; Wilkins, supra n. 40, 96.

These multinational structures went together with strategies that were based on quite substantial "competitive advantages." Michael E. Porter's concept of a "global industry" seems to fit precisely the case of these full-line electrotechnical manufacturers, since in his view an industry can be considered to be global ". . . if there is some competitive advantage to integrating activities on a worldwide basis."[43] Going into more detail, one can distinguish five different types of "competitive advantages" which could explain the particular ways and means of expansion used by each of the four members of the international electrotechnical oligopoly:[44]

(1) The *technical complexity* of much of the high-voltage equipment as well as its *systemic character* made it difficult, at least during the first two decades of the industry, to change producer.

(2) By *continuously innovating the various production processes,* these large firms that were provided with a sufficiently large amount of capital and—at least a potential—access to the capital market could adopt *methods of standardizing mass production* combined with other economies of scale.

(3) Each of these firms was able to offer not only sophisticated products but also a well-developed *after-sales service* which was of crucial importance for the users of such technically advanced investment goods.

(4) The *quality of management* and the *quality of the organizational structure* achieved in these large enterprises very soon became important competitive advantages for each of them. According to Alfred D. Chandler, ". . . the structure built at General Electric became and still remains today a standard way of organizing a modern integrated industrial enterprise."[45] Concretely speaking, this meant steady control from the top combined with "a surprising degree of independence" of the various branches and subsidiaries.[46] In the case of AEG, there seems to have been a relatively high degree of centralization under the undisputed leadership of Emil Rathenau, founder and director general of the firm during its first three decades of existence.[47] As to Siemens, there were several attempts, not all of them convincing or successful, to overcome the typical structure of a family enterprise by creating a

[43] Porter, Michael E. 'Competition in Global Industries: A Conceptual Framework' in: Porter, Michael E. (ed.) *Competition in Global Industries* 15-60, 19 (Boston, Mass. 1986).

[44] The single "advantages" have been demonstrated in greater detail in: Hertner, Peter 'Espansione multinazionale e finanziamento internazionale dell' industria elettrotecnica tedesca prima del 1914' *Studi Storici* (1987) 819-60, 826 et seq.

[45] Chandler, Alfred D. *The Visible Hand: The Managerial Revolution in American Business* 433 (Cambridge, Mass. and London 1977).

[46] Passer, supra n. 23, 385.

[47] Cf. Pinner, Felix *Emil Rathenau und das elektrische Zeitalter* 350 et seq. (Leipzig 1918).

hierarchy of employed managers without letting the family lose control over its firm.[48]

(5) By *financing not only production but also the expansion of the market for the firms' products* these big enterprises gained another important competitive advantage. This particular topic will be treated in the next chapter.

If we look at the specific aspects of corporate governance we will soon find out that these large electrotechnical producers did not at first sight distinguish themselves from other big firms insofar as they showed the same variety of modes of ownership and control. Siemens was, as we have seen, a family enterprise which gradually developed beyond this original structure since it had to turn to the capital market for further growth. Until the Second World War and during the immediate postwar period, its commanding heights were still in the hands of the Siemens family, and this made it certainly an exception among firms of its size.[49]

Westinghouse was dominated by its founder George Westinghouse, but his role had ended and it had become a "public" company in all respects after it had gone into receivership in 1907 and had been rescued by outside investors, the banks, and its own employees.[50] The other two firms, AEG and General Electric, had seen important manager entrepreneurs at their top—Rathenau father and son in the case of AEG, Charles Coffin in the case of General Electric—but their shares had always been widely spread among the investing public.[51] AEG had always had close ties with the big German investment banks, with Deutsche Bank as leader of its financing syndicate first and since 1897 with Berliner Handelsgesellschaft.[52] Nevertheless, one does not get the impression that the banks' influence would have been decisive at any moment of the company's history until World War II.[53]

Problems of corporate governance emerged, however, in another part of the big electrotechnical producers' sphere—the financial holding companies—which they had created starting from the mid-1890s. These problems will be analyzed shortly in the following chapter.

[48] Cf. Kocka, supra n. 25, 233 et seq., 390 et seq.

[49] Cf. Siemens, Georg *Der Weg der Elektrotechnik: Geschichte des Hauses Siemens* vol. 2 (Freiburg and Munich 1961).

[50] Cf. Leupp, Francis E. *George Westinghouse: His Life and Achievements* 204 et seq. (London 1919).

[51] Cf. Hertner, Peter 'Gli imprenditori elettrici in una prospettiva storica' *Annali di storia dell' impresa* 9 (1993) 7-16.

[52] Cf., among others, v. Sothen, Hans *Die Wirtschaftspolitik der Allgemeinen Elektrizitäts-Gesellschaft* 87 et seq. (Dissertation University of Freiburg im Breisgau) (Freiburg i.B. 1915).

[53] For the U.S. electrotechnical industry in its early phase, Patrick McGuire has emphasized the influence of financiers on "technocratic development" (McGuire, Patrick 'Money and Power: Financiers and the Electric Manufacturing Industry, 1878-1896' *Social Science Quarterly* 71 (1990) 510-30).

II. Financial Holding Companies and Corporate Governance

The rapid growth of the electrotechnical industry, and particularly of its high-voltage branch, as it has been briefly described above, would not have been possible without an active sales policy pursued by the electrical manufacturing companies themselves. Given the chronic lack of capital and initiative prevailing especially in many countries of the European periphery and in Latin America, the large German electrotechnical producers started to establish local and regional power, tramway, and lighting companies by themselves. These newly founded firms were then obliged by contract or statute to buy their electrotechnical supplies from their big industrial founders. Through these initiatives, the electrotechnical producers tried to create, so to speak, their own market. In the longer run, however, this could not be done without shouldering considerable risk because the producers, by creating their own customers, accumulated a growing volume of equity and bond capital in their portfolios which threatened to endanger their liquidity status. A satisfactory solution to what German contemporary observers called *Unternehmergeschäft*, i.e., the electrotechnical producers becoming on their part entrepreneurs in the business of producing and distributing electricity, consisted in the creation of financial holding companies with the help and the financial participation of important banks both in Germany and abroad.[54] The task of these financial holding companies was then to take over the shares and bonds of the newly created public utility companies, to hold them in their portfolios during the period of construction and initial development—a period which could last several years, particularly in the case of large-scale hydroelectric installations—and to sell most of these securities to the general public as soon as they had "matured" and started to yield a profit. In order to ensure their own liquidity during the construction periods of their various public utility daughter companies, the financial holdings issued their own shares in an act of "securities substitution", as Robert Liefmann has called it.[55] When and if possible, the holding companies preferred to place bonds instead of shares in the capital market in order to collect long-term capital at stable interest rates which was especially desirable for investment in hydroelectric facilities. By establishing these financial holding companies, their founders managed to internalize an apparently high and long-term risk through the creation of an intermediate body.[56]

---

[54] Cf. the important contemporary analysis by Liefmann, Robert *Beteiligungs- und Finanzierungsgesellschaften. Eine Studie über den modernen Kapitalismus und das Effektenwesen* 93 et seq. 1st edn. (Jena 1909).

[55] Liefmann , supra n. 54, 89.

[56] Cf. Hennart, Jean-François 'International Financial Capital Transfers: A Transaction Cost Framework' *Business History* 36 (1994) 51-70, 55-6.

Each of the more important German electrotechnical producers, even the middle-sized ones, controlled one or more of these intermediaries: AEG, among others, founded the Bank für elektrische Unternehmungen at Zurich in 1895 together with a number of important German and Swiss and also with some French and Italian banks.[57] The activities of this so-called "Elektrobank" started with the takeover of the public utility companies which AEG had started shortly before in Genoa, Seville, and Barcelona. Siemens followed shortly afterwards with its Basel-based Schweizerische Gesellschaft für elektrische Industrie and with Elektrische Licht- und Kraftanlagen, Berlin, both of them established in 1895. Schuckert and some of the medium-sized electrotechnical producers possessed their own financial holding companies, most of which, in the aftermath of the 1901/02 crisis, ended up falling under the control of the two "big ones", i.e., Siemens and AEG. Part of these financial holdings, especially those earmarked for operations outside of Germany, took their legal seat in Switzerland or in Belgium. This was mainly due to the rather permissive company laws and stock exchange regulations of these two countries as well as to some tax advantages. It may also have owed something to the participation of the most important Swiss and Belgian banks in these holdings and to the fact that, where business with France was involved, after 1871 this could be done much more easily from a neutral country than from Germany itself.[58] There was a parallel development in the United States: probably the oldest financial holding created for the North American electrical industry was the United Electric Securities Company, founded by Edison General Electric in 1890. In 1904 General Electric established the Electric Securities Corporation, and a year later it followed with the Electric Bond and Share Company.[59]

One can hardly underestimate the importance of the holding companies for their electrotechnical founders, for the electrical industry in general, and for the development of corporate capitalism as a whole. As to their specific corporate governance problems, these companies certainly featured a more complicated structure than the firms which had created them. The ultimate aim of their electrotechnical founders, as has already been said, was to be achieved by a long-

---

[57] Cf. also for the other literature on this subject, Hertner, Peter 'Les sociétés financières suisses et le développement de l' industrie électrique jusqu' à la Première Guerre Mondiale' in: Cardot, Fabienne (ed.) *Un siècle d' électricité dans le monde* 341-55 (Paris 1987).

[58] Cf. Jörgens, Max *Finanzielle Trustgesellschaften* 73 et seq. (Dissertation University of Munich) (Stuttgart 1902); Hafner, Kurt *Die schweizerischen Finanzierungsgesellschaften für elektrische Unternehmungen* 30 et seq. (Dissertation University of Fribourg/Switzerland) (Geneva 1912); Dumoulin, Michel *Les relations économiques italo-belges (1861-1914)* 115-6 (Académie Royale de Belgique. Mémoires de la Classe des Lettres, 2e série, t. LXVIII, fasc. 2) (Brussels 1990).

[59] Cf. Liefmann, Robert *Beteiligungs- und Finanzierungsgesellschaften* 389 et seq. 2nd edn. (Jena 1913).

term guarantee that the various utilities created or controlled by the holding companies would be supplied exclusively with the electrotechnical material manufactured by the same founders. This could be attained in two ways: one could write the exclusivity into the statutes or fix it by special contract. Another, or also complementary, way to obtain this result was to let the engineers of the electrotechnical mother company project the future installations and entrust them with the control of the construction works. This is what happened in Genoa, for instance, where AEG had acquired control of the existing tramway companies in 1893/94 and established a new one in 1895, all in order to electrify the existing network and its future extensions. The tramway companies had then nominated AEG, which in the meantime had transferred their shares to its newly founded finance company, the Zurich-based Elektrobank, to act as the general agent for the entire electrification project. Needless to say, all the electrotechnical material was supplied from Berlin and AEG remained the exclusive supplier until the outbreak of World War I, whereas the majority of the shares of the Genoa tramways had been passed in the meantime by Elektrobank to Italian investors. Even if it no longer owned the majority of the tramway shares, Elektrobank—and AEG through it—did control the situation with a consistent block of votes.[60] More or less the same policy was pursued by AEG in Seville and Barcelona and to a lesser extent with other utility companies founded or controlled by the Zurich Elektrobank. When the latter was established, AEG had subscribed only 4.14 million francs of its nominal capital of 30 million. All the rest was taken by great German and Swiss banks like Deutsche Bank, Crédit Suisse, and Berliner Handelsgesellschaft. By subscribing such an important part of Elektrobank's share capital, AEG's banking partners must of course have had other motives than Rathenau's company. For those banks which were part of AEG's syndicate of issue—Deutsche Bank and Berliner Handelsgesellschaft in the first place—the creation of Elektrobank meant a welcome initiative aiming at alleviating AEG's portfolio and achieving a better distribution of risk. For the other banks participating in Elektrobank's foundation, there was simply the prospect of making good business in a technologically promising new sector and with an industrial partner that guaranteed the feasibility and the quality of the investment projects. How important Elektrobank really became for AEG's strategy of international expansion is demonstrated by the fact that in 1898, AEG, through an exchange of Elektrobank shares with its own, managed to obtain 95% of Elektrobank's share capital, though this percentage diminished again during the following years.[61]

---

[60] Cf. for AEG at Genoa: Hertner, Peter 'Banken und Kapitalbildung in der Giolitti-Ära' *Quellen und Forschungen aus italienischen Archiven und Bibliotheken* 58 (1978) 466-565, 511 et seq.

[61] Cf. Strobel, Albrecht 'Die Gründung des Züricher Elektrotrusts. Ein Beitrag zum Unternehmergeschäft der deutschen Elektroindustrie' in: Hassinger, Erich, J. Heinz Müller, and Hugo Ott (eds.) *Geschichte—Wirtschaft—Gesellschaft* (Festschrift Bauer) 303-32 (Berlin 1974);

Things did not happen exactly in the same way with Siemens and its financial holding company, Schweizerische Gesellschaft für elektrische Industrie, normally called by its abbreviated name *Indelec*. To start with, when Siemens participated in Indelec's establishment in 1896, it subscribed only 10% of its initial nominal capital of 10 million Swiss francs. When Indelec's capital doubled later on, Siemens' share dropped to 5%.[62] So far the exact reason for this relatively small participation has not been discovered, but one might suppose that it had something to do with Siemens' financial weakness during most of the 1890s, a weakness which might be attributed to its specific character as a family firm. The transformation of Siemens into a joint-stock company, accomplished in 1897 thanks to Deutsche Bank, contributed to the solution of at least part of this problem.[63] Besides Siemens, a group of banks from Basel subscribed half of Indelec's capital, followed by some German banks. None of these credit institutions was even remotely as important as the founding banks of Indelec's great rival, Elektrobank of Zurich. As far as Indelec's position in the framework of the well-known *Unternehmergeschäft* was concerned, no formal contract or statutory rule was concluded. There was just a letter of intent which designated Siemens as the firm which would propose concrete projects and offer technical assistance to utilities created and financed by Indelec. Indelec was allowed to obtain electro-technical material also from other suppliers, but Siemens would have a priority status. Again, compared to its rival Elektrobank, Indelec's financial structure was less solid and, as already mentioned, its banking partners were considerably weaker. Thus it was hit much harder by the 1901/02 crisis. On that occasion its relationship with Siemens ran into trouble, in part because the two partners could not agree on how to assess the power plants built by Siemens for Società Elettricità Alta Italia of Torino, a company which had been financed by Indelec. Now the fact that exclusivity of supply had not been fixed by contractual arrangement acted as a boomerang for Siemens since Indelec threatened to pass future orders to some of Siemens' competitors.[64] In the history of the *Unternehmergeschäft* this was certainly an exceptional event. In this particular case, it reflected the weakness of the industrial partner, but one would also have to say that this incident remained unique. On the contrary, Siemens' position as a supplier of advanced technology was duly esteemed right from the beginning.

Grossmann, Heinrich *Die Finanzierungen der Bank für elektrische Unternehmungen in Zürich* (Dissertation University of Zurich) (Zurich 1918).—Cf. also the minutes of AEG's supervisory board of November 23, 1897, where the intended exchange of shares is justified with "the important international operations which have been started and which will not remain exceptional ones" (AEG business archives).

[62] Cf. for this and the following Hertner, supra n. 44, 834 et seq.

[63] Cf. Kocka, supra n. 25, 321.

[64] Cf. Hertner, supra n. 60, 520-1; Hertner, supra n. 44, 849.

Otherwise it would not be understandable why the first leading manager of Indelec was an engineer delegated from Siemens itself.[65]

More than the other cases of financial holding companies for the electricity sector, Indelec's history is apt to demonstrate that this type of intermediary incarnated two different lines of interest: on the one hand, there existed the interests of the electrotechnical manufacturers who used the financial holdings in order to distribute their risks as investors and to minimize their risks as suppliers of investment goods; on the other hand, there were of course the interests of the capital suppliers. Normally these naturally divergent interests came together, but if no clear contractual arrangements had been made, conflicts could not always be avoided. For their time, financial holdings were certainly an innovative instrument for the specific needs of a technologically far advanced branch. Their high degree of sophistication made them, of course, also rather vulnerable.

E. Conclusion

Problems of corporate governance did not necessarily carry more weight in the case of multinational business than in the purely national sphere. The slowness and the other difficulties of information transfer, however, together with high transactions costs rendered monitoring and control more difficult in the early days of international business expansion and of the beginnings of MNE. Principal-agent relations could therefore suffer from additional problems when business structures went beyond the relatively narrow boundaries of nation states. At least some of these problems either no longer exist or have completely changed in a world of high-speed communication and its immensely reduced costs. Historical research can show us that even under 19th-century conditions, new forms of corporate control were developed in order to meet problems of unequal development between metropolitan markets of capital and technology: a possible answer was the creation of free-standing companies. The establishment of financial holding companies in the case of the electrical industry was another response to growing capital needs and to the connected risks on the part of the electrotechnical producers. These same holding companies also responded to the necessity of bridging the gap between a temporarily insufficient demand for investments in infrastructure and the ever-growing production capacities for the goods supplied. The solutions found in this context created new problems of corporate governance. How they were solved has been briefly described above. That they were solved shows that 19th-century capitalism was by no means less inventive and flexible than the business world of today.

---

[65] Cf. Hertner, *supra* n. 44, 842. In 1907 and 1908, two managers of Swiss and Alsatian origin replaced their German colleague (Indelec, annual reports for 1907 and 1908).

Discussion Report

BRIGITTE HAAR

The article contributed by *Dunlavy* stood at the center of this discussion, which can be grouped under four headings.

Legal Factors Contributing to Consolidation in the United States and to Cooperation in Germany

Dunlavy's paper raised the question of which mechanism barred mergers in Germany as opposed to the United States, and what efforts were made to overcome the obstacles in statutory law. From an American perspective, the incentive to merge in the United States changed around 1890 with the Sherman Act prohibiting cartels, forcing things to be done exclusively by merger. *Dunlavy* did not dispute the importance of the antitrust environment in 1890, but wondered why mergers were so easy in the United States. Overall, the issue of her paper was the question of what happened when certain options—i.e., the option to cooperate in a cartel—were foreclosed, not discounting the influence of antitrust on the incentives to merge. For illustrative purposes, *Dunlavy* hinted at the history of the German steel industry and the case of Thyssen. In this industry there were indeed sentiments for consolidation in the American style, as became evident in the cooperation in the Stahlwerkeverbund. In contrast, in the United States this tendency would have brought about consolidation; in an American context, such an environment with sentiments in favor of consolidation rather than cooperation would have resulted in someone buying out the companies. Under these circumstances, American lawyers, and in particular individual states, would always have found a way around the law inhibiting such a development and would have ensured a corresponding set of rules on the state level.

Internal Factors Contributing to Consolidation or to Cooperation

As for the actual decision to merge in any individual company, it was pointed out that mergers would not have happened in the United States except for a corresponding shareholder vote. One might even go so far as to say that shareholders' interests may have diverged in a specific way, and that mergers lay in large shareholders' interest because they wanted the right people in the boardroom to pursue their business policies, thus catching the gains from compliance with fiduciary duties, and seeking additional rent. For this latter point it was held to make no difference for the outcome whether there was a plutocratic or a democratic structure.

The divergence of interests between large and small shareholders was confirmed by *Dunlavy* and illustrated by the example of the railroad industry where shares were sold to foreign investors and to small local stockholders. The latter would vote against mergers, but one cannot be so sure about any actual economic consequences of this divergence of interests.

Underlying Economic Assumptions

The question was raised as to why shareholders in Germany did not vote to have mergers, and whether there were investor utility considerations in the 19th century or the graduated voting structures simply appeared out of nowhere. In *Dunlavy's* paper, shareholders were not assumed to vote only in economic terms. This turned out to be the key to revealing the basic difference in the underlying assumptions of the participants of the discussion. It became clear that those who viewed the shareholder as representing an economic interest and his share as an investment, arrived at an interpretation very different from *Dunlavy's*. Along these lines, the economic argument for the voting structure was pointed out. There was widespread concern that power be limited, but at the same time from an efficiency perspective, capital was to be attracted. From this viewpoint, passive investment was considered to have efficiency advantages, making it socially desirable to have one share, one vote.

Political Perspective and Empirical Data

It was suggested that the graduated voting structure might have disappeared earlier in the United States because of the American distrust towards power. In this ideological dimension, there was a shift from legislative chartering towards bureaucracy. This move towards bureaucracy can be viewed as less democratic, or as more open to anyone and therefore more democratic. In addition, another possible dimension was pointed out: there might be a parallel between the use of corporations and changes in manufacturing in the United States, both of which resulted in a loss of democracy. From a European perspective, it was noted that Europe also changed as the costs and benefits of mergers became better known due to industrial developments and to a greater availability of information in the market.

Empirically speaking, the three forms of the development under discussion were held to not hold true from a historical perspective in the European context. The concentration on voting rights was therefore criticized as bringing about a purely political perspective. One would expect democratic rules to favor small enterprises, but the first large enterprise was the East India Company, which was Dutch. *Dunlavy* pointed out, however, that in the Dutch East India Company one vote per share prevailed. One explanation for the absence of mergers in Germany was held to be that the driving force of the development were the banks, which did not agree to mergers.

According to *Dunlavy*, an overly narrow look at voting rights was admittedly a problem, but the perspective was still assumed to be basically political. There was no normative argument intended behind it, but simply the interest in the impact of the choice of a corporate strategy. The principal distinction between Europe and the United States was pointed out to be the political process in the United States of competition among the states.

In the discussion of his paper, *Hertner* made clear that in 1880-90 the first financial holdings appeared (Swiss Eisenbahnbank, electric industry) because of their better distribution of risk and their concentration on pure finance. In comparison with other European countries, Belgium and Switzerland turned out to be more investor-friendly. At a rather early stage in history a minimum of legal protection was important for investors in Europe.

Chapter 2: Emerging Markets

Inventing a Corporate Monitor for Transitional Economies: The Uncertain Lessons from the Czech and Polish Experiences

JOHN C. COFFEE, JR., New York[*]

In comparison with other Eastern and Central European countries, the Czech Republic (Czechoslovakia in the beginning) jump-started into the process of turning its Communist economy into a market economy with a radical strategy. This article describes and assesses the Czech experience in mass privatization from its early success until its current problems, and contrasts it with the slower Polish approach which grants the government a stronger role. The analysis focuses on the incentive structure attached to the two types of the main vehicle of voucher privatization, the—independent and bank-affiliated—"Investment Privatization Funds" (IPFs). The lessons which can be learned from the investigation of the relationships between privatized companies and independent IPFs, and privatized companies, bank-affiliated IPFs, and banks, and their interaction with the institutional environment (especially legislation, securities markets, and state ownership which remains surprisingly high) are not only relevant in the Czech or transitional economies context. They also represent the results of a natural experiment in corporate governance which may yield some insights for the (comparative) analysis of established corporate governance systems.

Contents

[*] The author would like to acknowledge the valuable assistance received from a variety of persons whose knowledge and experience with the Czech context vastly exceed his own. A partial list would include: Dusan Triska, Jana Matesova, Jan Mladek, Joel Turkewitz, and Stijn Claessens, and various commentators at The World Bank. The author also gratefully acknowledges financial assistance from the Milton Handler Research Fund at Columbia University Law School.

Tables

A. Introduction

Throughout the 1980s, the Czech experience with voucher privatization has been the focal point of a continuing debate.[1] On one side, proponents of a rapid-transition strategy have applauded the Czech model, because it clearly moved ownership into the private sector much more rapidly than have its sister states in Central Europe (in particular, Poland and Hungary). On the other side of this debate, advocates of a more evolutionary transition have warned that uncertain

---

[1] For an overview of this continuing debate, see Slay, Ben 'The Search for Solutions in Enterprise Restructuring' *Transition* 3/1 32-5 (1997).

property rights, an undeveloped legal and regulatory infrastructure, and the dangers of opportunistic behavior made it inadvisable to rush forward with transition to private ownership, at least before a stable regulatory system could be devised.

As we near the end of the 1990s, this debate still continues. Each side has evidence for its view: proponents of the rapid transition can view the Czech experience as fundamentally successful (despite some acknowledged missteps); in contrast, proponents of a more gradual transition point to the slower Polish experience and argue that it has avoided the Czech problems, which clearly have produced a political crisis, possibly caused recently some economic downturn, and have driven Western portfolio investors largely out of its financial markets.

While both sides in this debate can score points, the critics of the Czech approach make a particularly telling one when they claim that the Czech privatization program has failed in its own terms and according to its own criteria. As designed, the Czech voucher privatization program was intended to transfer ownership of state-owned enterprises to "true owners" in order that they could undertake the restructurings necessary to make Czech industry competitive. Today, the consensus among all commentators is that this necessary process of restructuring has either not happened or proceeded very hesitantly, with little visible encouragement from the privatization investment funds on which the architects of Czech privatization relied.[2]

Why has there been such delay? This question can be better rephrased as: Why have the incentives to restructure not adequately motivated the new owners? This question plus an assessment of the strengths and weaknesses of the Czech approach constitute the roadmaps for this article. For those interested in corporate governance, Czech voucher privatization represents a natural experiment in ownership structure—one in which special monitors and a uniquely concentrated shareholder ownership structure were intentionally created to ensure the accountability of managers at the newly privatized companies. This structure had an undeniable logic: large financial intermediaries were created specifically to monitor operating managements. But something went wrong. For some reason, the strategy of relying upon institutional investors to produce necessary restructuring failed.

At this point, any post-mortem inquiry into the reasons for this failure transcends the Eastern European context. For example, in the United States, the capacity and incentive of institutional investors to monitor managements has

---

[2] For representative evaluations, all stressing this theme, see Stanley, Robert 'The Czech with a Kamikaze Mission' *The European* July 3, 1997, 23 ("Widespread privatization has not been followed by restructuring"); 'Czech Companies Looking for Real Owners' *CTK National News Wire* July 3, 1997 (quoting Ulrich Hewer of The World Bank that investment funds have not attempted restructurings); 'Survey—Czech Industry' *Financial Times* May 14, 1997, 1 ("weak voucher privatization . . . failed to encourage industrial restructuring").

been the subject of a continuing academic debate. On one side of this debate, one group of critics argues that institutional investors, if deregulated and liberated from existing restrictive federal regulations, would become active monitors and thus end (or at least reduce) the separation of ownership and control.[3] On the other side, another group is skeptical that institutional investors have adequate incentives to monitor, both because of principal/agent problems and a general preference for liquidity that leads them to limit their ownership stakes.[4] Thus, although they agree that much federal regulation is burdensome, they believe deregulation may produce only marginal differences.

Against the backdrop of this debate, the Czech experience is particularly interesting because the tradeoff between liquidity and control present in economies with developed securities markets simply does not exist within the Czech system. Because the Czech equity markets are extremely "thin", lacking both liquidity and transparency, large shareholders are therefore locked in and may not choose between "exit" and "voice." In addition, the Czech market may be among the most concentrated in the world, and thus the separation of ownership and control normal in many developed economies is minimized. As a result, the Czech market presents a unique natural experiment: To what degree will newly created institutional investors engage in costly monitoring?

Although the Czech experience with privatization is still too brief to permit dispositive assessment, preliminary data and qualitative evidence does lead to one conclusion. Institutional and legal detail is critical. Concentrated ownership without more may not lead to active monitoring because the economic incentives to monitor may be weak or overshadowed by more powerful incentives. In this light, the Czech experience suggests that the incentives of outwardly similar institutions to engage in monitoring can vary greatly, depending in large part on their own institutional affiliations and sponsorships.

At first glance, the Czech institutional context seems roughly to resemble that of Germany, where a small number of "universal" banks have long played a significant role in corporate governance.[5] But there is an important difference:

---

[3] See Roe, Mark J. 'A Political Theory of American Corporate Finance' 91 *Colum. L. Rev.* 10 (1991); Black, Bernard S. 'Shareholder Passivity Reexamined' 89 *Mich. L. Rev.* 520 (1990); Grundfest, Joseph 'Subordination of American Capital' *Journal of Financial Economics* 27 (1990) 89.

[4] See Coffee, John C. 'Liquidity Versus Control: The Institutional Investor As Corporate Monitor' 91 *Colum. L. Rev.* 1277 (1991); Rock, Edward B. 'The Logic and (Uncertain) Significance of Shareholder Activism' 79 *Geo. L.J.* 445 (1991).

[5] For the traditional view of German banks as active monitors, see Cable, John R. 'Capital Market Information and Industrial Performance: The Role of West German Banks' *Economic Journal* 95 (1985) 118; see also, Gorton, Gary and Frank A. Schmid 'Universal Banking and the Performance of German Firms' (NBER Working Paper no. 5453, February 1996). But for a revisionist view that doubts the extent of such monitoring, see Edwards, Jeremy S.S. and Klaus Fischer *Banks, Finance and Investment in Germany* (New York 1994). Cf. also the articles of

the major Czech financial institutions which founded the majority of the investment privatization funds (or IPFs) on which this paper will focus do not themselves hold—at least initially—significant equity stakes in the newly privatized companies. Although they may have possessed de facto control over the IPFs that they have sponsored, their relationship with their IPFs was that of an agent, rather than an owner; they received a management fee, but do not share in equity appreciation. In turn, this means that they may have control over, but not ownership of, the portfolios that their IPFs in turn hold in the newly privatized Czech companies. Control without ownership can create perverse incentives, particularly when Czech financial institutions have a direct creditor relationship with the newly privatized companies. Either because of such a creditor relationship or the desire for it, there is at least a potential conflict of interests. Both these factors—control without ownership and a potentially overshadowing creditor relationship—can undercut the incentive to be an active monitor, even when the structure of share ownership is uniquely concentrated.

Any description of the Czech privatization experience that focuses only on its lack of success is one-sided and unfairly slights the real achievements of the Czech experience. The Czech Republic was unique among the several Central European nations that began refashioning their economies at the same starting point in 1989 with the collapse of the Communist bloc. Alone among these countries, the Czech Republic created functioning capital markets and a truly privatized corporate structure. In this respect, voucher privatization was a substantial success. With the completion of the second privatization wave at the end of 1994, the post-privatization landscape of the Czech economy looked, in at least its broader outlines, as follows:

(1) Over 80% of adult Czech citizens had become shareholders in the 1,849 companies that were privatized (in whole or in part).[6]

(2) Although estimates varied, between 65% and 90% of all assets in the Czech economy was privately owned (up from a mere 4.5% in 1990).[7]

(3) The Czech economy had the lowest rate of inflation in Central Europe (generally around 10%) coupled with an unbelievably low rate of unemployment (between 2.7% and 3.5%).[8]

Breuer, Mülbert, and Wenger and Kaserer in Ch. 6, and Prigge (Sec. B.I., B.II., and C.II.) in Ch. 12 of this volume.

[6] For detailed recent reviews, see 'Czechs Turn Out to Buy Into Industry Privatization' *Los Angeles Times* November 26, 1994 at D-1; see also, 'Czech Sell-off Round Ends' *The Wall Street Journal* November 28, 1994 at A-14; Rocks, David 'Milestone for Privatization: Czechs Finish Share Selection on Bumpy Road to Capitalism' *Chicago Tribune* November 24, 1994, 3.

[7] For the estimate that 65% of "economic activity" has now been transferred to the private sector, see 'Czechs Complete Privatization Plan' *San Francisco Chronicle* November 26, 1994 (available on NEXIS). For the 90% estimate, see Jaros, V. and M. Sanders 'Investment Privatization Funds' 4 (Wood Company Securities, Equity Research Report, June 1994).

(4) The market capitalization of the Czech stock markets is estimated at around $12 billion, and a small debt market has also begun (hesitantly) to develop.[9] Although the Czech stock market suffered a severe 35% decline between April and October 1994, it continues to attract Western institutional interest.[10]

(5) The Czech Republic's sovereign rating of BBB+ in international credit markets was the highest in Central Europe.[11]

(6) Politically, the Czech Republic has a stable, free-market-oriented government which has been able to survive the process of privatization without seriously trimming its sails.

By any standard, these criteria seemed to define success.

Meanwhile, the progress toward privatization in other Eastern and Central European countries has been hesitant and halting, one foot forward followed by one foot backward. Although Poland began at the same starting point, it only adopted privatization legislation in 1994;[12] and the Ukrainian, Bulgarian, and Hungarian efforts were even farther behind the Czech pace. Only Russia had moved with comparable speed, but Russian privatization (although relying on basically similar methods of voucher privatization) produced insider-dominated firms in which management controlled on average 65% of the shares in the privatized firm.[13] As of the end of 1993, outsiders held on average only 21.5% (and a median of 20%) in privatized firms in Russia.[14]

In sharp contrast, Czech privatization granted few concessions to insiders, and at the end of the first wave of privatization, the average employee stake across all

---

[8] For these estimates, see Rehak, Judith 'Are "Emerging Europe" Debt Markets Just for Adventurous Investors?' *International Herald Tribune* November 26, 1994; Cox, Jim 'Czech Leader Sees Higher Unemployment' *USA Today* November 25, 1994 at B-4 (interview with Vaclav Klaus).

[9] Crawford, Phillip 'As Privatization Phase Ends, Prague Market is Maturing' *International Herald Tribune* November 26, 1994.

[10] See, e.g., 'A Surge of Funds to Eastern Europe' *The Financial Post* November 29, 1994, 26. But see Fleming, Charles 'Managed Investing: Retail Fund Investors Avoid Central Europe' *Wall Street Journal Europe* November 22, 1994, 13 (noting retail mutual funds' reluctance to invest in uncertain markets).

[11] See Rehak, supra n. 8.

[12] Polish Prime Minister Pawlak signed legislation clearing the Polish privatization process to begin after several years of delay in late October, 1994. See *Christian Science Monitor* October 24, 1994.

[13] See Blasi, Joseph and Andrei Shleifer 'Corporate Governance in Russia. An Initial Look' in: Frydman, Roman, Cheryl W. Gray, and Andrej Rapaczynski (eds.) *Corporate Governance in Central Europe and Russia* vol. 2 *Insiders and the State* 78, 79-80 (Budapest et al. 1996); see also Frydman, Roman, Katharina Pistor, and Andrzej Rapaczynski 'Investing in Insider-Dominated Firms: A Study of Russian Voucher Privatization Funds' in: Frydman, Gray, and Rapaczynski (eds.), supra, vol. 1 *Banks, Funds, and Foreign Investors* 187.

[14] Frydman, Pistor, and Rapaczynski, supra n. 13.

privatized firms in the program was only 4.4%.[15] In short, the Czech experiment seems to have succeeded without the compromises that (in Russia and elsewhere) undercut the original goal of a rapid transition to a market economy. As of their privatization, Czech corporations seemed fully subject to capital market discipline, whereas elsewhere privatization remains stalled or (as in Russia) has ushered in a long transitional period of managerial domination.

This early success of the Czech approach to privatization tends to be forgotten today in the light of later problems. During 1996 and 1997, scandal followed scandal; assets were stripped from many firms by their controlling shareholders, and some financial institutions collapsed, amidst allegations of embezzlement.[16] Western portfolio investors, dissatisfied with the lack of transparency and the tendency for price manipulation on the Prague Stock Exchange, exited for other emerging markets (including Poland and Hungary). Meanwhile the rate of growth in the Czech gross domestic product declined in relation to other Central European countries (most notably Poland). Nonetheless, the techniques and decisions most identified with Czech privatization—namely (1) the use of vouchers to effect a rapid disposition of state-owned property, (2) the free entry permitted to privately formed Investment Privatization Funds ("IPFs"), and (3) the use of such IPFs as a corporate governance solution to the problem of dispersed share ownership—worked well to end state control of the economy and to facilitate the rapid creation of secondary markets. But, at the same time, even from the outset, this success was qualified by the facts that (1) Czech securities markets lacked both transparency and liquidity, (2) a curious and potentially collusive system of cross-ownership arose among the major banks, and (3) the state continued to hold a potentially decisive "swing" block of stock in the largest corporations and blocks. Most importantly, the efficacy of the IPFs themselves remains unproven.

In truth, the IPFs were in part the product of planning and in part a spontaneous development during the course of Czech privatization. Although bank-affiliated IPFs had been contemplated, the appearance of "private" IPFs surprised Czech regulators and shocked the Czech Parliament into enacting hastily drafted restrictions on their activity. Basically, Czech IPFs can be loosely classified as either "bank-affiliated" or "independent" (that is, neither founded nor managed by a substantial Czech commercial or savings bank). Most assumed that the larger bank-affiliated IPFs would dominate the post-privatization economy, both

[15] See Earle, John S. and Saul Estrin 'Worker Ownership in Transition' in: Frydman, Gray, and Rapaczynski (eds.), supra n. 13, vol. 2 1, 38. They also report that in only seven companies (out of 988 projects approved for privatization) did the employee ownership stake exceed 30%.

[16] The most recent incident was the indictment of three top executives of A-invest, a prominent investment fund sponsor owed by Agrobanka, for the alleged embezzlement of Kc250 million from their shareholders. See 'Three Top A-Invest Execs Charged With Causing Losses of KC250M' *CTK Business News Wire* June 18, 1997.

because their bank relationship gave them a marketing advantage (as Czech citizens were more likely to trust their local bank than strangers) and because banks could realize economies of scope and scale from their joint roles as creditors and equity shareholders in the privatized companies. Yet, as will be seen, Czech privatization was more influenced by the independent IPFs—new entrants who, without ties to the existing Czech financial establishment, successfully competed in the manner of classic entrepreneurs against larger entities with greater resources. Without the best known of these rugged individualists ("Harvard Capital and Consulting ("HC&C")),[17] it is even doubtful that voucher privatization would have won public acceptance. Not only did HC&C perfect the marketing techniques that caused an initially apathetic Czech public to accept IPFs and to identify its own interests with voucher privatization, but HC&C and similar "independent" IPFs outperformed the "bank" funds in designing and bidding for portfolios. More importantly, there are reasons to believe that "bank" and "independent" funds behaved in characteristically different ways. This hypothesis flows from the fundamental fact that these two classes of IPFs face very different incentive structures: the "independent" IPFs have no other relationship with their portfolio companies and can succeed only as fund managers, while the bank funds often may have a greater (or, at least, offsetting) interest in maximizing bank-lending opportunities for their parent.

Both these developments—the aggressive behavior of the independent funds and the cross-ownership phenomenon—force us to focus on a new level of corporate governance at which the interests of principal and agent can diverge: IPF governance. For several reasons, market forces in the Czech Republic appear to have been inadequate to control agency costs at the IPF level. One indication is the fact that most IPFs trade at substantial discounts from the apparent net asset value of their portfolios (sometimes up to 80%). Such a closed-end fund discount (at a lesser level, to be sure) is a well-known phenomenon in mutual funds, but in theory it should attract bidders to acquire these funds and oust at least the worst performing fund managers. For various reasons, this simple scenario for market discipline was blocked in the Czech Republic by a variety of legal obstacles. As a result, the unique institution that the Czech privatization invented to solve the problem of dispersed ownership was from the outset afflicted with very high agency costs.

---

[17] For a review of the controversies surrounding HC&C and its founder, Victor Kozeny, see King, Jr., Neil 'Czech Financier Scores Rich Success Even As Detractors Hope for His Fall' *The Wall Street Journal* August 18, 1993 at A-7. It should be emphasized that HC&C has no connection with Harvard University (other than for the fact that Mr. Kozeny is an alumnus). Although Mr. Kozeny was forced to flee the Czech Republic in 1994 under the threat of an indictment, HC&C remains an active and seemingly successful manager of both IPFs and other (so-called "cash") funds.

This does not mean that the IPF cannot be improved and even perfected. For example, the Polish approach to privatization will use a diametrically different form of investment fund: fifteen government-created and -staffed "National Investment Funds," among which controlling stakes in privatized companies will be assigned by governmental fiat.[18] This article will argue that such an approach suffers from equally severe deficiencies: although it is unlikely to be as scandal-plagued as the Czech system, government-administered funds may be inadequate to focus capital market discipline on inefficient firms.

How then does one design an efficient intermediary that can perform its corporate governance objectives? This problem is compounded by the central fact that concentrated ownership and liquid capital markets are inherently in tension.[19] Whether compromise can be achieved, or is even worth attempting, is the basic question addressed by this article.

B. An Overview of Voucher Privatization

Voucher privatization was the concluding stage in the overall program of Czech privatization. First, it was preceded by a restitution program, which was adopted in 1990 and vigorously pursued during 1990 and 1991. The principal impact of restitution was on housing, retail trade, and agriculture. Then, a second stage —known as "small-scale privatization"—was inaugurated in 1991 and was primarily implemented through public auctions that lasted into late 1993. Neither technique attempted to privatize large companies, but rather typically separated discrete assets from a state enterprise.

Large-scale privatization was the final stage, and focused on the state-owned assets in industry, agriculture, and trade. When the "Velvet Revolution" in 1989 brought the collapse of the Communist government, productive enterprises in Czechoslovakia were almost entirely state owned. 86% of Gross National Product was produced in the state sector, 10% in the cooperative sector, and only 4% in the private sector.[20] Given the relatively small domestic savings of the Czech citizenry, standard privatization techniques—sales, stock flotations, or auctions—would have predictably resulted in transferring most state property to foreign owners (possibly at bargain prices as well). In addition, such a process would have been slow and extended, both because foreign purchasers would want to conduct a "due diligence" investigation of the assets to be purchased and

---

[18] For a brief review of the Polish approach, see 'International Briefing: Poland—Mass Privatization Programme' 16/3 *International Financial Law Review* 60 (1997).

[19] See Coffee, supra n. 4

[20] Mladek, Jan 'Mass Privatization: A First Assessment of the Results' 3 (OECD advisory group on privatization, 5th plenary session, March 2-4, 1994, Paris).

because political controversies would inevitably result over to whom and at what prices the country's national assets were to be sold.

I. The Rationale of Voucher Privatization

Given these realities, voucher privatization had three obvious advantages: (1) it could be effected very quickly, because there was no need to negotiate the terms of a gratuitous transfer; (2) it distributed assets broadly and democratically to the entire citizenry (rather than to the small percentage of the population with financial resources); and (3) it averted the political controversies inherent in selling a majority interest to foreign interests in prized national industries (which the Czechs generically refer to as "the national silver"). In contrast, if the citizens later re-sold these same assets to foreign interests, that was another matter, without the same political overtones. Realistically, a fourth reason may also explain why voucher privatization was politically popular: for those managing the to-be-privatized enterprises, voucher privatization was not perceived as a threat to their position or control because it was expected to result in a very dispersed (and thus weak) class of stockholders. In contrast, private sales would bring in "true" owners, who could control the incumbent managers.

In retrospect, the conclusion now seems inescapable that the Czech privatization program succeeded (albeit imperfectly) in realizing the first three goals, but sorely disappointed those who supported it for the fourth reason. Although there was considerable delay, some favoritism, and occasional controversy, other techniques would probably have exacerbated these problems to a considerably greater degree. But incumbent managers who expected to exploit voucher privatization were generally surprised and frustrated by the success of the IPFs in asserting control.

Initially, voucher privatization was intended to be the exclusive mechanism for privatization. The architects of large-scale privatization rejected arguments that vouchers should be used as only one of several interchangeable techniques for restructuring enterprises. Their view was that privatization should precede restructuring in order that the "true" owners could decide on the form that restructuring should take (e.g., sales to foreign investors, managerial buyouts, strategic partners, employee stock purchases, etc.).[21] Other techniques would preempt that choice, they believed, before the new private owners of the firm appeared on the scene. Alone, voucher privatization was neutral and left all other options open. Given this philosophy, it was originally contemplated that 97% of the shares of all privatized companies would be distributed under the voucher program and 3% would be conveyed to the Restitution Investment Fund.

---

[21] See Kotrba, Joseph 'Czech Privatization: Players and Winners' 5 (CERGE-E1 Working Paper no. 58, April 1994).

In reality, this goal of exclusivity for voucher privatization was quickly compromised. The one major limitation of voucher privatization is that it does not bring new capital into the business. For some enterprises, the need for new capital required that they either be sold to another (usually foreign) firm or that a strategic partner (usually Western) be attracted that could be a source of future capital investments. From the outset of Czech privatization, such buyers and investors have been in short supply. Partly for this reason, the National Property Fund ("NPF") was assigned the custodial role of acting as interim caretaker for firms (and blocks of stock) that were ultimately to be marketed to such buyers.

The degree to which departures were made from the original concept of 97% reliance on voucher privatization appears to have depended on the size of the firm, with larger firms being more successful in arranging to park a controlling block of their stock in the NPF. Looking at the average percentage of stock included in the first "wave" of voucher privatization, one finds that voucher privatization was the method used to distribute 81% of the shares. However, if one looks more closely at the relative value of the stock included in the first wave, this percentage of stock value privatized through vouchers falls to 63.5%.[22] The difference points up the political compromise: larger firms were more successful in limiting voucher privatization to a minority of their shares in the first wave (with most of the balance of their shares remaining in the NPF).[23]

In turn, this disparity highlights the significance of the NPF. Founded in August 1991, it was intended to play a passive role as the midwife of the privatization process. Once a privatization project was approved by the Ministry of Privatization, the project was to be handed over to the NPF for implementation. The NPF would form the joint stock company, register the shares in its name, and act as the new company's sole owner pending the sale or distribution of its shares. However, delay increased the period it acted as the de facto sole owner.

Potentially, the NPF could have functioned as the Treuhand did in Germany, playing the role of a policy-maker, auctioneer, and amateur investment banker. Clearly, it has not attempted such a role. Rather, it largely persisted in playing a self-consciously passive role in order to leave discretion to the true owners. When the NPF became controversial (as it did in 1994), it was for its tendency to delay and avoid decisions, not for bureaucratic empire-building. Tomas Jezek, the Chairman of the NPF until June 1994 and one of the most philosophically

---

[22] Mladek, supra n. 20, 4. This is in effect a weighted average figure. In the second wave, the corresponding figure was 69.6% for companies that were not included in the first wave. Letter to the author from Jan Mladek dated July 7, 1994.

[23] The argument of these firms was that they needed a large foreign corporation or investor that could make substantial investments in them in order to finance restructuring, or, in other cases, to make the firm technologically competitive. This need was clear enough, but such investors were in limited supply and in most cases never materialized during the course of privatization.

committed architects of Czech privatization (and a former Minister of Privatization), strongly resisted the bureaucratic temptation to expand the power and authority of the NPF. Still, for those seeking to emulate the Czech experience, the NPF was a problematic institution, one which could potentially subvert or at least sidetrack Czech privatization if its leaders had been more bureaucratically inclined. Even today, after the completion of privatization, the NPF continues to hold a potentially pivotal role in many major Czech corporations.

II. Timing and Procedure

Serious planning for voucher privatization began in 1991. Under the Large-Scale Privatization Law adopted on February 1, 1991, managements of approximately 70% of (then) Czechoslovakia's 4,800 state-owned enterprises were required to prepare specific plans for converting their enterprises to private ownership.[24] These plans, known as privatization projects, were submitted to the enterprise's supervising governmental ministry (usually the Ministry of Industry and Trade) for initial approval, and then to the Ministry of Privatization for final approval. The process was slow, cumbersome, and created the principal bottleneck in the privatization process.

Management's basic plan for the enterprise had to be submitted by November 30, 1991. However, others could submit competing proposals (including proposals to buy some specific unit or division), and competing proposals were given an extended deadline to January 20, 1992. Final decisions by the Ministry of Privatization were to be made by April 30, 1992, for those units to be included in the first wave. Some 23,478 projects (relating to 4,450 state-owned companies) were submitted. Nearly half were received from prospective buyers, but 21% were submitted by managements.[25] One survey has found that the proposals submitted by management succeeded in over 62% of the cases, while other competitors succeeded in only 17.3% of the cases.[26] Nonetheless, from the outset of privatization, the attempt to ensure active competition seems to have been a primary focus of those overseeing the privatization process. On average, each firm in the first wave was the subject of four privatization proposals.[27] Against

---

[24] This paper will refer to The Act on the Consolidation of Transfer of State Owned Property to Other Persons, Act no. 92/1991 Coll. of 26 February 1991 as the "Large-Scale Privatization Law." See also Mann, Bruce 'Privatization in the Czech Republic' 48 *Bus. Law.* 963, 964 (1993).

[25] Kotrba, supra n. 21, 8.

[26] Kotrba, supra n. 21, 15. However, this study finds that in cases of head-to-head competition (where management and buyers sought the same assets), buyers were more successful than the incumbent management (Kotrba, supra n. 21, 15). Most management proposals did not contemplate significant equity participation by management.

[27] Mladek, supra n. 20, 10.

this backdrop, it may become more understandable why many managements preferred the voucher privatization option to direct sales to third-party buyers who could have immediately removed them from office.

Much of the delay at this stage stemmed from two related factors. Managements tended to propose splitting enterprises into two or more units, each to be separately privatized.[28] Possibly, this tendency was the product of internal tensions within the firm over who should run the privatized enterprise (conflicts which a decision to split the enterprise effectively compromised), or possibly it stemmed from a desire (in a Czech phrase) to "pick the raisins"—that is, to separate quality from junk. In response, the Ministry of Privatization seems to have been strongly committed to inducing competition at the privatization plan stage—but at the cost of slowing down the process. Thus, the first goal of voucher privatization—speed in implementation—was significantly compromised. Voucher privatization was scheduled to occur in "two waves", in theory based on the relative readiness of firms for privatization. Many of the more complex projects—such as those in energy, health services, and agriculture—and some of the largest enterprises (including public utilities and at least one major bank) were postponed until the second wave. For the first wave in 1992, some 2,285 large firms were originally selected for large-scale privatization (in both the Czech and Slovak republics), but the number to be privatized through vouchers was gradually whittled down to 1,491 (with the balance being privatized chiefly through cash sales and auctions). 861 firms were included in the second wave (including minority stakes in firms partially privatized in the first wave).

III. The Voucher System

As adopted in 1991, the voucher system entitled each Czechoslovak adult (i.e., a citizen over the age of 18) to buy a booklet of 1,000 voucher points for a cost of CSK 1,035 (or roughly $34.5), which cost then approximated 25% of the average monthly wage at the end of 1991. At the time of the second wave in 1993, the price for a voucher book of 1,000 points was modestly raised to CZK 1,050 (or $35), but by then this amounted to less that 18% of the average monthly wage. Voucher points could be used exclusively in a given privatization wave and not for other purposes (for example, voucher books could not be used even to purchase other shares in the same privatized company in a public auction by the government). Secondary trading in voucher points was forbidden (although this was not strictly enforced). However, because all voucher books were registered

---

[28] Kotrba, supra n. 21, 17.

on a nationwide computerized system, it was possible to check ownership and minimize this possibility for fraud.

Initially, interest in acquiring voucher books was slow to develop, and the original December deadline for voucher registration had to be extended. As of November 1991, public polls showed that only 25% of the adult population was interested in participating in the voucher scheme. At this point, Harvard Capital and Consulting ("HC&C") began its advertising campaign in November 1991,[29] and public interest quickly increased. By the end of January 1992, the percentage of the adult Czech population that planned to participate had risen to 55%. Ultimately 75% of the adult population participated (77% in the Czech Republic), and over eight million citizens registered to be eligible to buy voucher books.[30] This level of participation nearly doubled the government's predictions, which anticipated the sale of only 4-5 million booklets.

What explained the sudden surge of interest? The answer is twofold: first, massive advertising by the IPFs convinced the citizens that real value could be obtained through purchasing the voucher coupons at low cost. Second and more important, HC&C made its famous (and vague) promise that it would redeem shares in its IPFs beginning in one year at a price equal to ten times the cost of a voucher booklet (CSK 10,350 or $345). As originally announced, Harvard's non-transferable option could be exercised at any time after the first anniversary of the transfer of voucher points by an investor to it.[31] Almost overnight, this tactic monetized the gains and established a short-term profit that motivated citizens to go through the tedious process of registering for vouchers by establishing their citizenship. Other funds followed Harvard's lead and even outdid it. For example, KIS a.s. (a major insurance company's fund) offered CSK 15,000 for a voucher book, and SIS a.s. (the fund established by Ceska Sporitelna, the principal Czech savings bank) offered CSK 11,000.[32] PIAS, the investment company for Investicni Banka, gave investors the option between a CSK 15,000 collateralized loan or a guaranteed buyback at CSK 11,000.[33]

---

[29] Interview with Dusan Triska, December, 1994. Dr. Triska, the former Vice-Minister for Finance, was the Czech official in charge of (and most responsible for the design of) voucher privatization.

[30] See Mladek, supra n. 20, 12.

[31] HC&C later reinterpreted the timing on its pledge, so that it became operative on the first anniversary of the later date on which the NPF transferred the shares in the privatized companies to the IPFs and other private parties.

[32] See Jaros and Sanders, supra n. 7, 6.

[33] See Jaros and Sanders, supra n. 7, 6.

IV. The First Wave: The Rise of the IPFs

The architects of the Czech voucher privatization program—most notably, Dusan Triska—were aware that broad distribution of shares to some substantial percentage of the Czech public would produce an atomized ownership structure. Because this, in turn, implied that collective action among small shareholders would be infeasible, they envisioned from the outset of their planning the formation of intermediary financial institutions modeled loosely after Western mutual funds.[34] Much the same idea was also present in the contemporaneous Polish privatization plan, but the Czech scheme had one critical difference: the state would play no role in creating or staffing these funds, other than in establishing certain minimal ground rules for their creation and operation. Their scheme contemplated a Darwinian competition among funds to attract the voucher points of citizens. Citizens were, however, free to reject the overtures of the funds and invest their voucher points themselves in the stocks of privatized companies (in fact, twenty-eight percent of all voucher points were retained by individuals).

Substantive regulation of the IPFs has in fact been minimal. The rules under which IPFs were to be created were first specified in a Federal Government decree of September 5, 1991.[35] Initially, it specified only three basic requirements:

(1) The IPF must have minimum capital of CSK 100,000 (this was later raised to CSK 1,000,000 or $33,300);
(2) The members of its supervisory board and its offices had to have certain professional qualifications (which were not spelled out with any specificity and never enforced as a practical matter) and a reputation for civic integrity.
(3) The IPF had to contract with a bank to act as its depository.

In addition, the founder/managers of IPFs were required to obtain a license from the Ministry of Finance, but all sources agree that the licensing procedure quickly became perfunctory and, for the remainder of the first wave, applications that satisfied the basic requirements seem not to have been rejected. The actual appearance of IPFs followed swiftly on the heels of the September 5, 1991, decree outlining voucher privatization. Shortly thereafter, on October 1, 1991, the Ministry of Finance issued regulations requiring all IPFs that wished to participate in the first wave to be established by the end of 1991. This three-month deadline effectively discouraged some prospective fund managers, who as a result deferred their participation until the second wave.

---

[34] Dusan Triska reports that the idea of investment privatization funds can be traced back to a special Government Memorandum dated April 6, 1990. See Pauly, Jan and Dusan Triska 'Investment Funds in the Czech Republic' 3 (mimeo, October 1993).

[35] Federal Government Decree No. 383/1991 Coll. This decree was less than three months before the deadline for fund registration on December 31, 1991.

The initial challenge for the Ministry of Finance was to alert and inform the public as to opportunities for profit in voucher privatization. Toward this end, the Ministry began its own advertising campaign in October 1991, to alert the public and inform them as to the procedures necessary to register and obtain voucher booklets. Response was, at best, sluggish, but once HC&C began advertising in November, the Ministry of Finance quickly recognized and accepted that the private IPFs could outperform it at this activity and suspended its own campaign.

HC&C's marketing success prompted, however, a legislative reaction. Its promise to buy back its shares at a tenfold price raised fears of a Ponzi-type financial pyramid, whose failure could discredit voucher privatization. In January 1992, temporary regulations were adopted requiring portfolio diversification.[36] IPFs were required to diversify their assets so that they did not invest more than 10% of their capital in any one security and were restricted from owning more than 20% of the nominal value of securities issued by the same issuer.[37] Unquestionably, these rules reflected a concern on the part of Czech regulators that there might be a "run on the funds." However, the 20% limitation was only crudely related to any diversification goal (because 20% of a single issuer might amount to only 1% of a large IPF's assets) and reflected an independent debate among Czech policy-makers over whether to encourage IPFs to become active owners.

The Czech Parliament was not satisfied with dealing with the problem simply through administrative regulations.[38] Alarmed by the prospect that HC&C would dominate the economy, many legislators demanded a special session of Parliament, which was convened in January 1992. Although the Ministry of Finance opposed additional legislation, the Parliament insisted, but settled largely for codifying the already adopted temporary regulations. Some of the political motivation for this statute appears to have come from concerns about insider trading and the sale of confidential information, and not simply from concerns about fund liquidity or the risk of a "run on the funds."

In any event, the April 28, 1992, Law on Investment Companies and Investment Funds came too late to affect the first wave, but it did make several important changes applicable to the second wave in 1994. First, and most important, it authorized the unit trust format (whereas all IPFs in the first wave were formed as joint stock associations). Second, the statute contained a number of housekeeping rules designed to minimize the risk of fraud and embezzlement. For example, the statute provided that the property of an IPF could be managed only

---

[36] These rules were eventually codified as amendments to Decree No. 383: amendments No. 67/1992 Coll. and 69/1992 Coll.

[37] This provision was finally codified in § 24(3) of The Investment Companies and Investment Funds Act (Act No. 248/1992 Coll. of 28 April, 1992).

[38] In an interview, Dusan Triska described the Czech Parliament as having been in a "panic" during this stage over its fear that HC&C and other entrepreneurs would create a "bubble" and a resulting crash that would discredit Czech privatization.

by itself or by an investment company; personal control of funds by founders was no longer permitted. By November 1992, each IPF was required to appoint a bank as its depository and to deposit all securities and funds with it. By the same date, IPFs were required to appoint managing and supervisory boards. Other rules barred the issuance of bonds by IPFs (thus restricting the degree of leverage they could achieve and hence again reducing the prospect of a "run on the funds"). Finally, limitations were placed on the permissible compensation that IPFs could pay their investment companies under new management contracts (the ceiling was set at 2% of the average value of IPF property or 20% of the profits).[39]

Given the limited regulatory hurdles and a basically permissive attitude on the part of the Ministry of Finance, it is not surprising that a superabundance of IPFs quickly were formed and began to compete for investor's voucher points. Over 420 IPFs participated in the first wave of privatization, of which 260 were based on the Czech side of the Federal Republic and the balance on the Slovak side. Their collective marketing success is evidenced by a simple statistic: IPFs obtained 71.8% of all available voucher points in the first wave.[40] After an initially apathetic reception, public interest in the voucher program picked up markedly in January 1992, and the registration process had to be extended through the end of February. 8.54 million citizens (out of an estimated 11 million eligible citizens) bought and registered voucher books. 5.8 million of these (or 68%) chose to invest their entire voucher booklet with one or more IPFs, while another 4% split their investment, contributing some voucher points to an IPF, but also retaining some points for individual investment.

Despite this ease of entry, success still went to the powerful and well-funded. Those funds with superior marketing and advertising capacities dominated the field and obtained slightly over 60% of all voucher points deposited with IPFs.[41] Bank-affiliated IPFs had three significant advantages in this process. First, banks had a natural and national retail network through their branches by which to reach the public across the country. Second, banks could lend funds to their investment company subsidiaries to cover marketing, advertising, and start-up costs. Third, banks had at least relatively enviable reputations for integrity and competence and were subject to close governmental regulation. If they had not stolen their depositors' funds, voucher holders could logically reason that they would not embezzle the IPF's funds or securities. Lacking these inherent advan-

---

[39] See § 27 of The Investment Companies and Investment Funds Act (Act No. 248/1992 Coll. of 28 April 1992) (discussed infra in text at note 78).

[40] Mladek, supra n. 20, 21.

[41] Roland Egerer estimates that the ten largest bank-sponsored funds held 61% of all points acquired by all IPFs (or about 43% of all voucher points) in the first wave. Egerer, Roland 'Investment Funds and Corporate Governance in Emerging Markets: An Assessment of the Top Ten Voucher Funds in the Czech Republic' (mimeo, The World Bank, 1994).

tages, new entrants (such as HC&C) faced a marketing challenge: how to convince the public that they were safe and better. They responded with promises of a guaranteed return. HC&C was, however, the one "private" IPF to develop an elaborate retail marketing structure. It hired thousands of part-time agents to canvass voucher-holders, even as they waited in line to purchase voucher booklets at the post office or to register their booklets at local centers. Other IPFs used school children to solicit voucher holders. Once Harvard began to succeed with its offer to redeem its shares at ten times their cost (i.e., CSK 1,035), other funds made similar guarantees. Some funds offered cash bonuses of CSK 2,000 to 3,000 for voucher booklet investments.[42]

On the marketing level, HC&C succeeded largely in urban areas (most notably, Prague), while bank-affiliated funds did better in rural areas. The IPF that attracted the largest number of voucher points in the first wave was founded by Ceska Sporitelna, the Czech Savings Bank. Based on its broad retail network, it won over 11% of the voucher points in the first wave; yet it informed us that it received less than 10% of its total from residents of Prague. Essentially, banks won the trust of the rural population, which knew and presumably trusted them as local institutions, while the more sophisticated urban population preferred the financial guarantees of HC&C and others.

Most investment companies created only one fund for the first wave, but some of the more sophisticated companies tried to develop a diversified family of funds that resembled the marketing strategy of a typical U.S. mutual fund sponsor (e.g., Fidelity, Vanguard, or Dreyfus). For example, HC&C created eight funds, one emphasizing growth, another dividends, while a third was a "country" fund focused on Slovak-based companies. Prvni Investicni, a.s. ("PIAS"), the investment company of Investcini Bank, the second largest commercial bank, similarly established eleven funds. This strategy may have also had an ulterior purpose because an investment company was permitted to control up to 40% of the stock in a company through multiple funds (even though an individual IPF faced a 20% ceiling).

From a distance, one might well wonder why Czech regulators permitted HC&C and others to make seemingly dangerous guarantees, which later proved disastrous in the Russian context. Promises of tenfold returns in a single year bring to mind the classic Ponzi schemes, which have historically failed sooner or later. Several reasons probably explain the tolerance of Czech regulators. First, it must be remembered that voucher points were sold for an arbitrarily low price of CSK 1,000 (or about $35). Ultimately, the book value of the 1,849 companies

---

[42] See Brom, Karla and Mitchell Orenstein 'The "Privatized Sector" in the Czech Republic: Government and Bank Control in a Transitional Economy' 21 (Paper, Institute for East-West Studies, New York, 1993)

privatized in the two privatization waves has been estimated at $12.3 billion.[43] Given that roughly six million Czech citizens each purchased 1,000 voucher points for slightly less than $35 each, their aggregate investment was thus in the neighborhood of $210 million. As a result, they collectively acquired $12.3 billion in property at an aggregate price of $210 million, yielding them a profit of roughly $12.1 billion. Viewed differently, the book value of the property that the average Czech citizen acquired was thus $2,000 (i.e., $12.3 billion divided by 6 million). In offering to pay ten times the citizen's voucher purchase price of $35, HC&C was thus offering $350 for $2,000. Rather than an illusory promise that could not be fulfilled, the greater danger may have been that Czech citizens would have accepted this offer and sold too cheap (at least if one accepts the book value estimate).

Second, ideological considerations probably played an equal or larger role in shaping the Czech Government's response to HC&C. Both Vaclav Klaus, then Minister of Finance, and Dusan Triska, then the Vice-Minister and principal architect of voucher privatization, believed strongly in open access, free competition, and limited regulation. In particular, they preferred ex post regulation in response to demonstrated problems to ex ante regulation through potentially overboard prophylactic rules. Thus, the Ministry of Finance had objected to legislative codification of the 20% ceiling on an IPF's stake in a single company.

A third and more political reason for the government's tolerance was simply that the government needed HC&C and the banks at least as much as they needed the government's tacit acquiescence. Alone, the Czech government had not been able to stir up citizen interest in its privatization program. HC&C and its imitators were the major factor in its sudden popularity; without them, it is questionable that a program critical to the government would have succeeded (at least in urban areas). In short, the relationship was symbiotic—each needed the other.

In any event, HC&C and the others making guarantees won their gamble, and it has been estimated that only 7-15% of voucher investors chose to redeem their IPF shares for cash.[44] Although the market price of HC&C's principal IPF has fallen slightly below its guaranteed redemption offer of CSK 10,350, its net asset value per voucher book is estimated to be around CSK 40,000.[45] Thus, HC&C might well benefit handsomely if investors in its IPFs demanded redemption from it, because HC&C would be in effect buying a right to CSK 40,000 per share for CSK 10,350 per share. Having so repurchased much of its IPF shares, HC&C could then liquidate the IPF and sell or distribute its securities to its shareholders (including itself). In such a context, the logical scenario would be

---

[43] See Rocks, supra n. 6, 3.

[44] See Brom and Orenstein, supra n. 42, 26.

[45] See Jaros and Sanders, supra n. 7, 7.

for HC&C to encourage redemptions (at least if it had confidence in its ability to realize the estimated net asset value of its IPFs on the Prague Stock Exchange). In any event, by alone refusing to list its IPFs' shares on the Prague Stock Exchange, HC&C was believed to be protecting itself against any significant market decline in its IPF share price.[46]

In retrospect, the concern that the funds would be unable to honor their financial commitments appears to have rested to some degree on a misconception. The IPFs themselves were not authorized to repurchase their shares, and thus the guarantee came from their parent investment company. Those associated with banks had adequate financial resources to meet their commitments, and the others (such as HC&C) carefully maintained substantial cash reserves. Still, redemptions have occurred, and in consequence, some investment companies have become the largest holders in their own IPFs, thus further complicating the problem of fund accountability.

V. Portfolio Selection

Privately sponsored funds and bank-affiliated funds diverged markedly in their portfolio selection policies. As others have noted, "[t]he largest bank-affiliated funds created broad portfolios, comprised of 200 to 500 companies."[47] In marked contrast, HC&C deliberately and carefully assembled a portfolio of some 51 companies. Creditanstalt and Zivnostenska (two investment companies that were each associated with foreign financial institution) also assembled relatively consolidated portfolios in the first wave.[48] Those IPFs that assembled consolidated portfolios were consciously seeking to approach the 20% ceiling ownership permitted by law in order to assure representation and "clout" on their portfolio companies' boards.

But why did the bank-affiliated funds seek a much larger portfolio of 200 to 500 companies? Several explanations are possible. Ceska Sporitelna, the Czech Savings Bank, explained to us that most persons who deposited voucher points with its IPF were also depositors with the savings bank, and were rural, relatively

---

[46] Investors in the IPFs established by HC&C can trade their shares on the RM-system, but in the auction system, it is easier for HC&C to "stabilize" the price of its funds.

[47] Jaros and Sanders, supra n. 7, 5. SPAS, Ceska Sporitelna's investment company, told us that they held a portfolio of 500 companies at the end of the first wave. Prvni Investicni held a 240-company portfolio and Komercni Bank's investment company held a portfolio of 265 companies. Jaros and Sanders, supra n. 7, 7.

[48] Both Zivnostenska and Creditanstalt seem best classified as "private" IPFs. Although they are banks, they are foreign-controlled banks. A majority stake in the former was sold just prior to the first wave to a German bank and the International Finance Corporation, while Creditanstalt is owned by an Austrian bank. Zivno Fund, owned by the former, held a portfolio of 50 companies, while Creditantstalt assembled a portfolio of 76 firms. Jaros and Sanders, supra n. 7, 7.

unsophisticated persons who could not afford to hold a high-risk, undiversified portfolio of securities. Thus, it claimed, it diversified broadly to reduce risk. Although this portfolio diversification explanation might explain a policy of holding a portfolio of a hundred odd companies, it cannot adequately explain Ceska Sporitelna's decision to hold a five hundred-stock portfolio. Efficient diversification requires far less. Possibly, Ceska Sporitelna, as the sponsor of the IPF that had assembled the greatest number of voucher points at the end of the "zero round" of the first wave, feared that it would not be able to invest all the voucher points it had acquired and so bid for virtually every company reflexively. A number of interviewees expressed the view that Ceska Sporitelna's investment company had behaved reflexively and unthinkingly ("They haven't got a clue" was one characteristic phrase). But the same allegation of incompetence could not be made with respect to Investicni and Komercni, whose investment companies also assembled portfolios with five times the number of companies in HC&C's portfolio, but based on a similar level of voucher points to that held by HC&C.

Close observers in Prague of the bidding policies of the different IPFs saw a different purpose underlying the broad diversification strategy of the bank-affiliated IPFs: namely, a desire to obtain banking business by securing at least a toehold stake in the broadest possible number of companies. As a study by Wood Company Securities observed:

> "The strategy in many of these cases, it seems, was for the bank funds to leverage stakes in companies into seats on their managing boards and later into banking business for the fund's sponsoring bank."[49]

At least at the outset of privatization, an IPF might need a 10% stake to achieve a seat on the board, but not the 20% maximum stake that the privatization law permitted. A 20% stake would be useful if the IPF were intent on pursuing an active restructuring policy, but it was not otherwise essential. If the IPF was used to advance its banking parent's interests, then broad diversification makes sense (at least for the parent). Yet, such a conclusion raises the disquieting possibility that the German corporate governance model of bank participation in corporate governance carries with it more serious conflicts of interest than proponents of the German model have recognized or addressed.

Of course, from the bank's perspective, it might be argued that approaching the legally permissible 20% ceiling was undesirable because it would cost their IPFs liquidity in a thin market. Nonetheless, this same consideration would apply equally to "private" IPFs, and the contrast between the bank-affiliated IPFs and the privately sponsored IPFs seems striking in this regard. Portfolio concentration was pursued to a considerably greater extent by the private IPFs. In turn, this

---

[49] Jaros and Sanders, supra n. 7, 5.

positioned these IPFs to be more aggressive monitors, while observers have generally reported the bank-controlled funds to be somewhat less active.[50]

Although most private funds have not pursued to the same extent HC&C's strategy of holding a highly concentrated portfolio, many of the private funds have tended to focus on particular industries (i.e., glass, engineering, beer, etc.) or regional areas. This deviation from full diversification was in part a matter of marketing necessity, because these funds could stress their special competence and managerial background in these fields (a strategy which may have partially compensated for their lack of instant name recognition or reputation for integrity in comparison to the better-known bank funds). As a result, these private funds may have acquired some monitoring advantages through economies of scope (at the cost of some diversification). For example, having board representation on several firms in the same industry, a non-diversified fund might be better positioned to compare performance among managements, to see industry trends, and to understand technological developments than a bank fund overseeing a portfolio of several hundred companies. At the same time, however, such cross-ownership raises anti-trust issues that will be later discussed.

VI. The Second Wave

The second wave of privatization, which was completed in late 1994, was significantly smaller in scale than the first wave. Some 861 companies were included in the second wave (as opposed to 1,491 in the first wave, of which 988 were Czech companies), but 185 of these 861 were companies that had been partially privatized in the first wave. Both waves followed the same procedures and elicited roughly the same responses from investors as the first wave. Approximately 6.15 million Czech citizens (74% of the eligible Czech population) purchased voucher booklets in the second wave (down slightly from 77% in the first wave).[51] Some 353 IPFs competed to attract voucher points in the second wave, and again they convinced the bulk of the population to invest with them (64% of all voucher points were invested with IPFs in the second wave as opposed to 72% in the first wave).[52] The largest funds again dominated, but the level of concentration declined. The fifteen largest funds obtained approximately 2.5 billion points out of a total 6.15 billion points in the second wave[53] (or

---

[50] See sources cited at notes 17, 20, and 21 supra.

[51] Jaros and Sanders, supra n. 7, 4.

[52] Jaros and Sanders, supra n. 7, 4. The figure 353 comes from Table 1, which was supplied to me by Dusan Triska.

[53] Jaros and Sanders, supra n. 7, 4.

40.65%—slightly below the 42.8% level that the largest 13 investment companies obtained in the first wave).[54]

The decline in the percentage of individuals electing to invest through IPFs may be attributable to several factors. Local observers in Prague emphasized that local newspapers had given considerable publicity to individual shareholders in the first wave who had not invested with IPFs but who had rather invested in individual companies whose stock price had skyrocketed (such as CEZ, the energy public utility whose stock price increased by four to five times).[55] The press attention given to these "instant millionaires" may have dissuaded some from investing with IPFs in the second wave. Another related possibility stems from the fact that stock exchange trading had begun in IPFs prior to the "zero round" of the second wave, and the amount of the closed-end discount on the IPFs had become painfully clear (up to 80% from net asset value in the case of some funds). The desire to avoid incurring such a discount could have influenced sophisticated Czech investors as well. Nonetheless, the consensus view at the beginning of the second wave was that at least some of the IPFs were professionally managed and had shrewdly invested in the first wave.

The marketing of IPFs changed significantly with the second wave, and correspondingly some IPFs that had dominated the first wave performed very poorly in the second. In particular, Ceska Sporitelna's IPF, which had finished in first place with 950 million voucher points (or 11.1%) in the first wave, collected only 124 million points in the second wave and fell to ninth place. The new leader was the IPF established by Agrobanka, a mid-sized Czech bank (but with a national retail network), which had only marginal success in attracting voucher points in the first wave.[56] Nonetheless, under new and aggressive management in the second wave, it collected an estimated 320 million voucher points (or 5.2%). Agrobanka's marketing success rested on two distinct factors: (1) Agrobanka marketed an open-end unit trust, and (2) it offered immediate cash payments for voucher books invested with its IPF. Agrobanka structured its cash payment as a CSK 2,000 "loan" from itself to any investor who invested his voucher booklet with Agrobanka's IPF. The loan was collateralized by a portion of the shares acquired with the voucher booklet. In the typical case, if the voucher points were ultimately converted into 20 IPF shares, Agrobanka would receive two shares (or 10%) in return for its "loan". By using this loan format, Agrobanka deliberately stole a march on its competitors, because the loan could be (and was) made

---

[54] Mladek, supra n. 20, 22.

[55] To give one illustration: fifty shares of Opatovic Electrical Works could have been purchased for one voucher book in the first wave and later traded for CSK 500,000 at one point in 1994—a 500% increase in little over a year.

[56] As discussed later, the leading executives at Agrobanka's subsidiary (A-invest), which served as sponsor to these funds, were indicted in June 1997 on charges of fraud and embezzlement. Agrobanka itself was earlier placed in receivership. See note 16 supra.

weeks before the "zero round" began. Thus, Agrobanka could advance a portion of the loan proceeds on an effectively unsecured basis, retaining the balance until the borrower had registered for, received, and could invest his voucher booklet with Agrobanka's IPF. One consequence of this approach should be underscored: by "lending" in return for voucher points, Agrobanka became the largest investor in its own IPF. In the typical case, it would acquire 10% of the shares eventually issued on each voucher book in return for its "loan". Other investment companies quickly copied Agrobanka's new technique, but they could not overtake its head start.

Viewed from a distance, the success of Agrobanka may seem largely idiosyncratic, the result of its ability to steal a march on its competitors. A clearer pattern emerges, however, if we look at the performance of the major Czech banks relative to the largest "independent" funds. No other major Czech bank finished in the top five. In this light, the interesting and distinctive fact about Agrobanka is that it was privately owned (unlike the major Czech banks over which the state held control). Thus, the privately owned entities (whether or not bank-related) outperformed the state-controlled funds, as a group, at the marketing stage. Finishing in sixth place was HC&C, which also marketed a broad family of funds and also had other of its IPFs finish in 27th, 36th, 41st, 51st, and 66th positions, respectively. In contrast, the highest-ranking fund sponsored by PIAS, the investment company of Investicni Banka, finished in 32nd position. Ceska Sporitelna marketed only one fund, which finished in 7th position (directly behind HC&C in sixth position), and Komercni Banka sponsored the eighth largest fund (but no others in the top 100). On this basis, out of the 100 largest funds, HC&C attracted over 265 million voucher points, more than double what either the much larger Ceska Sporitelna or Komercni collected by themselves. Moreover, despite that fact that Investicni Banka marketed multiple funds, its five leading funds obtained in the aggregate only one-third of the total voucher points that HC&C received.

Nor was HC&C alone in this respect. YSE's three largest funds finished in 14th, 16th, and 87th positions, respectively, and in the aggregate collected more points than either Ceska Sporitelna or Komercni Banka. PPF, another prominent "independent fund," sponsored IPFs that emerged in 13th and 25th positions and thus in the aggregate almost tied both Ceska Sporitelna and Komercni Banka. Several large insurance companies also did very well (in particular, Expandia and K.I.S., which finished in 2nd and 5th positions, respectively), but they did so without the same built-in networks that retail banks possess.

In short, by the second round, when the Czech citizenry had presumably grown more sophisticated about IPFs and voucher privatization in general, the public turned away from the largest banks (except for the privately owned and more entrepreneurial Agrobanka, which had developed a unique cash-on-the-barrel marketing strategy) and toward independent funds (at least in the aggregate).

Table 1: Privatization Funds in the Second Privatization Wave

	1 Joint Stock Companies	2 Open-End Unit Trusts	3 Closed-End Unit Trusts	Total Unit Trusts	Total All Funds
100 Million Voucher Points or More	3	2	3	5	8
50 to 100 Million Voucher Points	7	4	6	10	17
10 to 50 Million Voucher Points	20	8	18	26	46
5 to 10 Million Voucher Points	22	4	17	21	43
1 to 5 Million Voucher Points	48	10	23	33	81
0.5 to 1 Million Voucher Points	27	4	8	12	39
0.1 to 0.5 Million Voucher Points	39	3	15	18	57
Less than 0.1 Million Voucher Points	29	3	30	33	62
Totals:	195	38	120	158	353

As Table 1 shows, another major development in the second wave was the appearance of open-end and closed-end unit trusts. Of the 353 IPFs participating in the second wave, an estimated 195 were joint stock associations (of which 160 had participated in the first wave). These 195 joint stock IPFs received approximately 1.57 billion voucher points in the second wave; another 120 IPFs were closed-end unit trusts (these received 1.48 billion voucher points in the second wave), and, finally, 38 were open-end unit trusts (these received 867 million voucher points in the second wave).[57] Thus, although Agrobanka succeeded with

[57] Mladek, supra n. 20, 13.

an open-end fund, the majority of investors still opted for closed-end funds, but unit trusts (both open-end and closed-end) received more voucher points than did joint stock associations (2.35 billion points to 1.57 billion).

Table 1 summarizes this data and also provides a breakdown of the relative size of IPFs in the second wave.

To understand the foregoing table, it helps to recall that each investor received 1,000 points, and thus 100,000 investors held 100 million voucher points. Hence, the eight funds with over 100 million points each represent at least 100,000 investors (more if some investors split their points among funds or retained some of their points to hold on an individual basis). Of these eight giant funds, Ceska Sporitelna finished seventh and Komercni finished eighth, with the balance being accounted for by independent funds and insurance companies (and, of course, Agrobanka in first place).

What explains these trends? In both the U.K. and the U.S., open-end funds have dominated closed-end funds by a wide margin. The same has not happened in the Czech Republic. Two reasons may explain why. First, Czech law requires a delay of between one to three years from the date of investment before an IPF can agree to redeem shares for the net asset value of their proportionate interest in the fund. That is, an open-end fund may specify a future date (between one and three years away) on which it will redeem its shares at their net asset value, but as a marketing matter that date may seem in the distant future for most investors. Those investment companies electing to offer open-end funds have generally chosen a date between two and three years away. Given the illiquidity in the Czech stock market, there is considerable reason to doubt that any IPF could liquidate a significant portion of its portfolio at or near its existing net asset value. Second, open-ended funds have primarily been organized as unit trusts without voting rights, and some investors may resist this loss of voting rights.

The popularity of the unit trust format among investment company sponsors is much easier to understand. Fund managers defend its use by claiming that it is a cheaper, more efficient vehicle, largely because the unit trust is not a joint stock company. Thus, no annual meeting of shareholders is required, and neither a managing nor supervisory board need be appointed. These cost savings may be real, but they do not truly explain the popularity of the unit trust. In reality, because the unit trust is essentially a contractual device rather than a legal entity, no new legal entity is created, and hence no voting rights arise. Rather, the unit trust's "shareholders" are really just joint owners of an account with the investment company. The absence of voting rights is important chiefly because of the substantial discounts at which closed-end funds trade. For example, if an IPF with a net asset value of CSK 10,000 trades at CSK 4,000, then the prospect arises that a different management team could buy its shares (possibly by paying a small premium), acquire control, and then liquidate the IPF to realize its net asset value. In short, this scenario is that of a hostile takeover. However, if the buyers lack voting rights (as they would in a unit trust), this whole scenario fails.

In truth, the use of the unit trust is not the only defensive technique that allows an incumbent management to frustrate a hostile takeover. Those IPFs that were formed as joint stock companies have typically signed long-term contracts with their investment company (often for ten years or longer) that prevent any termination of the advisory relationship, except with mutual consent. Finally, as a result of buy-backs, collateralized loans, and other guarantees, investment companies (or their banking parents) have become major shareholders in many of the largest IPFs.

VII. Share Ownership Structure and Share Prices

Although IPFs obtained 71.8% of all voucher points distributed, this figure does not closely correlate with the considerably lower percentage that they hold in the typical privatized company. There were several reasons for this divergence: first, some shares were retained by the state, and other blocks of shares were sold directly to strategic investors. Second, IPFs tended to opt for quality, investing their voucher points in higher-priced companies. As a result, the share distribution of the 1,491 Czech and Slovak firms included in the two privatization waves ultimately broke down as follows among five investor classes:[58]

Table 2: Share Distribution of Czech and Slovac Firms Included in the Two Privatization Waves

Investor Class	Mean	Standard Deviation	Minimum	Maximum
State	8.37%	15.38%	0.00%	84.00%
Individuals	36.53%	21.62%	1.56%	96.82%
IPFs	39.39%	22.22%	0.00%	90.89%
Domestic Investors	3.25%	12.51%	0.00%	84.00%
Foreign Investors	1.34%	8.00%	0.00%	80.00%
Not Sold	11.12%	NA	1.14%	92.83%
	100%			
Investment Funds As a Class				
Top 1	13.42%	6.26%	6.00%	32.44%
Top 1 and 2	22.20%	10.86%	0.00%	49.97%
Top Ten	38.36%	21.32%	0.00%	86.52%

[58] See Claessens, Stijn 'Corporate Governance and Equity Prices: Evidence from the Czech and Slovak Republics' 3 and Table 1 (mimeo, The World Bank, 1995).

This data may understate the level of ownership concentration among the larger public firms in which IPFs tended to concentrate their investments. While Table 2 shows that, as of the end of the second wave, all IPFs as a group owned on average 39.39% of the typical privatized company, the largest ten IPF shareholders own an almost equivalent level (38.36%). Apparently then, IPFs do not typically hold small positions. As a result of the bidding process, the percentage of stock held by individuals rose to 36.53% (as opposed to 28% of voucher points), but this seems a statistical artifact, reflecting the preference of individuals to invest in smaller companies at cheaper prices. In some cases, families or residents of one town concentrated their investments in a smaller company to gain leverage.

Although a mean ownership level of 39.4% for all IPFs and 38.4% for the largest ten IPF stockholders suggests that IPFs could exercise de facto control over the typical Czech company (if they acted cooperatively to elect their own directors), it is far from clear that IPFs do cooperate in this fashion or that board composition correlates closely with share ownership. Surveying 1,491 privatized Czech and Slovak firms, Claessens investigated the premise (suggested by others) that effective control can be defined as the ownership of stock equal to, or greater than, 50% of that held by all other strategic investors.[59] On this basis, 10% ownership might carry effective control if, for example, all other strategic investors owned no more than an additional 10%. Applying this standard to his sample of 1,491 Czech and Slovak firms, he concluded that, under this definition of control, some 273 firms would be effectively controlled by a single IPF, whereas two IPFs would be able to control 793 firms, and the stock held by three IPFs could control 1,013 firms.[60] As he recognizes, this finding seems to show the problematic character of its premise. The problem is that a large shareholder can be resisted by a coalition of smaller ones; thus, a 20% shareholder can be effectively resisted by four other shareholders, each holding 5%. Alternatively, each of these five significant shareholders might demand and obtain at least one seat on the board, with the result that the largest shareholder's voting power is diluted at the board level.

Claessens also investigated the relationship between shareholder concentration and stock prices. Examining equity price data for a sample of Czech and Slovak firms, Claessens initially finds that "higher [share] concentration tends to have a positive effect on prices . . . ."[61] But, on closer examination, he found that "high strategic ownership . . . is more important than ownership concentration . . . in terms of its effect on prices."[62] Indeed, "high absolute strategic ownership

[59] Claessens, supra n. 58, 4.
[60] Claessens, supra n. 58, 4.
[61] Claessens, supra n. 58, 11.
[62] Claessens, supra n. 58, 11.

has a positive effect on prices, but effective control, particularly by investment funds, does not have a positive influence on prices—actually a negative influence."[63] In short, the presence of a near majority shareholder seems to raise stock prices, but concentrated ownership among IPFs does not (and may have some negative impact).

What can explain this disparity? In the case of the near majority shareholder, the market may expect that it will seek to buy the remaining shares or has the capital and incentive to make the firm profitable. In contrast, no such presumption apparently attaches to a consortium of IPFs, who, sharing control, may have seen no need to buy additional shares.

VIII. The Market Environment

A 1994 survey by Wood Company Securities found that "first wave" IPFs then traded within three distinct price ranges. Smaller IPFs and others viewed as risky traded at apparent discounts to net asset value of between 70% to 80%. IPFs with a weak portfolio but with the backing of a large financial institution traded at apparent discounts of between 55% and 70%. Strong IPFs with quality portfolios and competent managements traded at discounts of between 25% and 45%.[64] The severity of these discounts may be to some extent illusory, because they depend on the reported prices on the Prague Stock Exchange ("PSE") for the underlying securities in the IPFs' portfolios. Many of these stocks trade infrequently, and the prices on the PSE reflect only a small fraction (probably under 10%) of all trading, because the vast majority occurs off the exchange. Although some 1,000 stocks are traded on the PSE, only about thirty stocks appear to be actively traded.[65]

Because the amount of discount differs among IPFs, this variation suggests that the market does discriminate among them. Still, as a measure of relative IPF performance, these discounts may again be misleading. Investors may believe, it has been suggested, that some of the bank-affiliated IPFs are "too big to fail". That is, they expect the government would step in to protect the largest IPFs from insolvency. Smaller funds may be subject in contrast to an excessive discount if they hold investments that infrequently trade.

As a generalization, Czech IPFs do not seem to engage in the active portfolio management that one observes in the case of U.S. or British mutual funds. The leading reason for their inactivity as traders is the lack of liquidity. Even if they could sell stocks they wished to dump, the IPFs report that they doubt that they

---

[63] Claessens, supra n. 58, 11.

[64] Jaros and Sanders, supra n. 7, 9.

[65] See Crawford, supra n. 9.

could find and purchase replacement equity investments in any substantial quantities. The market, they fear, is frozen. Trading that does occur chiefly takes place in an off-market environment that is totally devoid of transparency. The prices at which transactions occur off the Prague Stock Exchange (and off a smaller computerized over-the-counter system, known as the RM/S system) are simply not reported. Most observers that we interviewed estimated that over 90% of share trading in Czech stocks occurs off-the-exchange in this fashion. Although the IPFs are not permitted in principle, even in off-exchange transactions, to buy or sell stocks at prices better than the last transaction price on the Prague Stock Exchange,[66] compliance with this rule cannot be monitored.

In general, most trading among IPFs seems to be directed at consolidating the portfolios of each IPF-"swap" transaction, as they were described to us. Since the end of the first wave, many IPFs appear to have conceded the basic wisdom of HC&C's strategy of seeking concentrated holdings sufficient to entitle the IPF to board representation and are seeking to develop larger stakes through off-exchange swaps. Small stakes in other stocks are likely to be swapped for positions in companies where the IPF is already a substantial holder.

The absence of liquidity may deter some fund managers from selling even stocks they consider to be overpriced. Their fear is that they could not reinvest the proceeds of a sale (in particular because no bond or money market has yet developed that provides an alternative to equity investments). This does not mean, however, that there are no active traders in the Czech market. The CEO of A-invest, the investment company for Agrobanka, told us that 90% of his firm's profits came from trading activities, while 90% of its costs came from corporate governance activities. His point was that "trading in the dark," at least on a small scale by professionals, can be highly profitable for investment companies, even if it is infeasible (as he also conceded) to implement a broad portfolio re-allocation strategy. In short, lacking exit, the IPFs have the option of exercising voice—but it is a costly option that different IPFs pursue with different levels of enthusiasm.

C. Impacts and Consequences

This section will focus on the impact of IPFs on both the structure of shareholdings and corporate governance generally within the newly privatized Czech economy. Three general areas need to be reviewed in more detail in this section before policy options can be sensibly considered: (1) the extent and significance of cross-ownership among Czech financial institutions; (2) the corporate govern-

---

[66] See § 17(3) of The Investment Companies and Investment Funds Act (Act No. 248/1992 Coll. of 28 April 1992).

ance activities of IPFs; and (3) IPF accountability and the problem of small "voiceless" funds that lack board representation.

I. Corporate Incest: Cross-Ownership in the Czech Financial Sector

At the outset, it must be remembered that two processes were occurring simultaneously in Czech privatization: first, IPFs were seeking to establish themselves as powerful financial intermediaries by acquiring and investing voucher books in privatized firms; and, second, the indirect founders of the leading IPFs (namely, the major Czech financial institutions) were themselves being privatized. Predictably, these two processes did not occur independently of each other. Yet, when the dust ultimately settled, the extent of cross-ownership among the leading financial institutions came as a surprise to most observers.

To understand the level of cross-ownership that resulted, it is useful to start with the largest Czech financial institution, Ceska Sporitelna, the Czech savings bank, which is estimated to hold approximately 80% of the country's demand deposits. Ceska Sporitelna was also the founder of the largest IPF in the first wave. In the first wave, some 37% of its own shares were privatized (with another 40% being retained by the FNP and another 23% held by others). At the end of the first wave, the following firms owned the following equity percentages of Ceska Sporitelna's equity through their controlled IPFs:

Table 3: Ownership of Ceska Sporitelna (After First Wave)

1. FNP	40.0%
2. HC&C	12.9%
3. Investicni banka	8.8%
4. Komercni banka	3.9%
5. Vseobecna uverova	1.6%
6. Slovenska IB	0.8%
7. Agrobanka	0.6%
8. Slovenska poistovna	0.3%
9. Ceska pojistovna	0.2%
Total	69.1%

Even if one excludes the FNP's 40%, the fact remains that of the 37% of Ceska Sporitelna's stock privatized through vouchers in the first wave, roughly 80% (or 29.1% of its total outstanding stock) was acquired by a limited group of eight major financial institutions.

Nor is this example exceptional. In the case of Komercni banka, the largest commercial bank in the Czech Republic, the level of concentration was even greater. 53% of Komercni's stock was privatized through vouchers (while the NPF retained another 44%). At the end of the first wave, Komercni's six largest shareholders proved to be:

Table 4: Ownership of Komercni banka (After First Wave)

1.	FNP	44.0%
2.	HC&C	17.6%
3.	Investicni banka	10.8%
4.	Ceska Sporitelna	4.9%
5.	Vseobecna uverova	4.3%
6.	Komercni banka	3.4%
	Total	85.0%

In the case of Investicni's bank (the third largest Czech bank after the two banks discussed above), a stranger pattern emerged: cross-ownership became coupled with self-ownership. The FNP retained 45% of Investicni's stock, but IPFs founded by Investicni's investment company acquired 17% of Investicni, their own indirect parent. Another 6.9% of Investicni's stock was controlled by the Slovak Investicni bank, which is the parallel institution within Slovakia. Interestingly, IPFs founded by the Slovak Investicni bank acquired a total of 18.8% of their own indirect parent, Slovenska Investicni Banka. Although some IPFs controlled by some other banks also acquired shares in their parent banks (Komercni's IPFs, for example, acquired 3.4% of Komercni), IPFs founded by the Czech and Slovak Investicni banks invested in the stock of their grandparent banks to an unparalleled degree—perhaps to the extent that it is debatable whether these banks have truly been "privatized."

This pattern of cross-ownership has a further dimension: not only do Investicni's funds own a large percentage of Investicni, but Investicni in turn holds more than 10% in each of the IPFs founded by its investment company (Prvni Investicni, a.s., or "PIAS"). This latter form of cross-ownership by which the grandparent owns blocks in the IPF founded by its subsidiary was the result of guarantees made by Investicni during the marketing stage of voucher privatization. Specifically, Investicni promised a CSK 15,000 loan to those who invested their entire voucher book with PIAS-founded IPF. As an alternative, PIAS also offered to buy back a voucher book investment in its sponsored funds at CSK 11,000. Ultimately, some 15% of PIAS's investors accepted one offer or the other.

A strong argument can be made that the high level of cross-ownership between Investicni and its funds has impacted adversely on its fund's shareholders. For example, a principal Investicni-controlled IPF is Rentiersky Investment Fund (Rent IF). As of March 31, 1994, Wood Company Securities reported that over 50% of Rent IF's portfolio was invested in the banking sector (presumably with a substantial portion being invested in Investicni itself), but Rent IF was trading at a deep discount to a net asset value of over 75%. The market price of a voucher book invested with Rent IF stood (as of mid-June 1994) at CSK 9,000— less than half that of a voucher book invested at the same time with Zivno 1. Fund (then trading at CSK 18,300) or the YSE Fund (then trading at CSK 21,600). Possibly, this apparent discount could have been a response to other factors and not necessarily to poor portfolio selection. Second only to HC&C, PIAS has been the subject of repeated criticism and innuendo in the press, suggesting that it was involved in unfair self-dealing and insider trading transactions.

That cross-ownership developed to the degree that Investicni and its sponsored IPFs illustrate must have surprised the original draftsmen of the Czech privatization law. The Czech Investment Companies and Investment Funds Act provides simply:

> "An investment company or investment fund established by a bank or insurance bank may not purchase the shares of its founder, its depository, or other banks and insurance banks."[67]

Yet, notwithstanding this provision, Investicni's IPFs own 17% of it and substantial blocks in Ceska Sporitelna and Komercni banka as well. How could this happen? The answer involves, on one level, a legal technicality and, on another level, an issue of political motivation. Technically, Investicni (as with most other banks) founded an investment company (PIAS) as a wholly owned subsidiary, which in turn founded its various IPFs. From a hyper-technical perspective, because Investicni did not itself "establish" its grandchildren IPFs, they can purchase shares in it and in other banks.[68]

Such a narrow reading seemingly frustrates the statute's apparent intent to prevent bank cross-ownership. One wonders then whether this narrow reading was unavoidable or was the product of political compromise and accommodation. To be sure, civil law has never been read or interpreted in the pragmatic, purposive way that U.S. courts traditionally have sought the legislature's intent in reading U.S. statutes. But, the political accommodation story also sounds promising. Czech privatization did seemingly depend (at least at its outset) on the active cooperation of the major banks in marketing and distributing voucher books. Once HC&C emerged as activist outsider with possible plans for acquiring control of a major bank, it would not be surprising if the major banks sought to protect themselves through collusion. The state may have tacitly cooperated

---

[67] See § 24(11) of The Investment Companies and Investment Funds Act (Act No. 248/1992 Coll. of 28 April 1992).

[68] Presumably, PIAS cannot directly purchase shares in Investicni because it is a first-generation descendant.

(and quietly waived the statute's application by accepting a patent formalism), both as a political quid pro quo and because it, too, feared HC&C and the prospect that it might "loot" any bank that it controlled. This possibility cannot be presented as historical fact, but neither is it fanciful speculation.

In any event, the cross-ownership structure within the banking industry has not remained static. Rather, both Investicni and Komercni have begun by various means to dilute the ownership of the NPF. In 1994, Investicni announced a merger with the Czech postal bank. The strategic objective of the merger was to provide Komercni with a national retail network rivaling that of Ceska Sporitelna, but it also diluted NPF's ownership to under 40%. In contrast, Komercni engineered an equity subscription offering (in which the NPF by pre-arrangement did not subscribe), thus also diluting NPF's equity percentage. However, the NPF has announced that it will retain a minimum one-third interest in each of the major Czech banks to protect against hostile takeovers and mergers (a two-thirds shareholder vote being necessary under Czech law for a merger). In consequence, the managements of both banks seem secure from any threat of a hostile raid. Finally, the Czech national bank has adopted and enforced regulations precluding any person or entity from acquiring more than a 10% interest in a bank without its approval. As a result of these regulations, HC&C is under an obligation to reduce its holdings in Ceska Sporitelna.

This fact that special rules were adopted to limit HC&C in its pursuit of major banks, while Investicni's IPFs have been allowed to invest both in it and other banks, suggests a political interpretation of the cross-ownership phenomenon. Much of the impetus for cross-ownership within the Czech banking sector may well have come as a response to HC&C, which was widely rumored to have intended a takeover of Ceska Sporitelna. Multiple interviewees treated it as common knowledge that HC&C had such a scheme, but was stopped by the Czech National Bank and the Ministry of Finance. Arguably, the fear of HC&C acquiring a major Czech bank caused all Czech banks to make substantial cross-investments in each other through their IPFs as an anticipatory defensive reaction. In interviews with us, representatives of HC&C stressed that the major banks were a "club" or an "old boys' network" and would always protect each other.

Cross-ownership is not, however, a universal phenomenon (as, for example, it tends to be among trading partners in Japan[69]). Only the two Investicni banks (Czech and Slovak) appear to have concentrated their portfolios in the financial sector of the economy (and with seemingly dismal economic results in consequence). Komercni, in contrast, appears not to hold any significant ownership in

---

[69] On cross-ownership in Japan, see also Hoshi (Ch. 11), Kanda (Ch. 12), and Miwa (Ch. 11) in this volume; for the German case, compare Wenger and Kaserer (Ch. 6: Sec. B) and Prigge (Ch. 12: Sec. C.II.).

Investicni (while Investicni's IPFs hold 10.8% of Komercni). Thus, cross-owner-ship is not fully reciprocal, and seldom do others match Investicni's significant holdings in them.

Even a significant block of stock in a bank may not confer much influence. Surprisingly, the Deputy General Manager of PIAS (the investment company for Investicni) told us that he doubted that IPFs could be active investors in the banks, both because, in his judgment, no more than a 5 to 15% stake could be acquired in the market in most of them, and because the NPF tended to favor the status quo and back the incumbent management. As evidence of this contention, he pointed to the fact that IPFs had been unable to secure representation on the managing boards of the banks (although they had secured representation on the managing boards of most other privatized companies). PIAS, he said, focused on bank investments largely because (1) restructuring would not be necessary (at least as compared to the industrial sector), (2) bank investments were safe, and (3) some liquidity was likely to be available in bank stocks.

II. Initial Corporate Governance Activities

At the outset of privatization, considerable evidence suggests that IPFs attempted to cooperate. This early period of cooperation involved several dimensions.

1. Board Representation and Recruitment

At the outset, the major IPFs successfully sought board representation on their portfolio companies, typically on the managing boards (with the exception of the banking sector where they have been forced to settle for seats on the supervisory board). By some accounts, there were informal rules recognized by the larger IPFs as to their relative rights to board representation. According to one commentator,

> "The largest three to six fund-owners nominate up to three non-executive directors each to a company's management board—and usually hold the majority."[70]

Another commentator observed that:

> "[T]he 2-7 largest shareholders, depending on the size of the board, were able to nominate and elect representatives to the Board of directors, while the next largest shareholders got seats on the Supervisory Board."[71]

[70] See Meth-Cohn, Delia 'Good Governance: Czech Investment Funds Are Learning About Corporate Governance Very Quickly' *Business Central Europe* (1994/February) 30.

[71] See Matesova, Jana 'Post-Privatization Restructuring: The Case of the Czech Republic' (Case Study Working Paper, ACE-Phare Project, 1997).

Others told us (not necessarily inconsistently) that any fund owning 10% or more would be entitled to at least one board seat. PIAS, which generally seeks to reach the 20% ceiling on its shareholdings in a company, indicated that it had "strong representation" in about 50-70 companies where it held such a stake, and that in such cases it would have approximately five to seven representatives on such boards (only one to two of which would be individuals from the executive management at PIAS with the others being "outside experts").

An initial concern in our interviews was how IPFs recruited directors. It quickly became apparent that this responsibility was basically handled by the investment company. PIAS, for example, told us that it had between 150 to 170 seats to fill on the managing boards of portfolio companies (its portfolio then consisted of about 300 companies). All of its representatives would have a contract with PIAS, but would be obligated under it to represent the interests of the portfolio company (and not any special interests of PIAS). Usually one representative will serve on two to three boards, and, to avoid conflicts of interest, the representative will be placed on boards of companies that are not in active competition or within the same industry.

How can an investment company recruit the necessary directors to fill the board seats that its IPFs are entitled to fill? We encountered quite different responses. PIAS illustrates the polar case of an investment company assembling a substantial cadre of director nominees. Although conceding that finding sufficient persons with business experience and expertise was a serious problem, PIAS's Deputy General Manager estimated that PIAS had assembled a cadre of 65 persons to serve as its directors, from the following sources:

(1) 20 persons from the top management of PIAS;
(2) 25 persons from the top management of Investicni Banka; and
(3) 20 persons from the regional branches of Investicni Banka (usually to serve on the boards of local companies).

Alone among our interviewees, PIAS thus acknowledged that it used bank employees to staff board positions. Others acknowledged that firewalls between the bank and the investment company were often breached, but they went well out of their way to disclaim the use of bank personnel as directors.

In contrast, HC&C, which assembled the smallest portfolio after the first wave (only 51 companies), estimated that it had a strong supervisory role in some 35 companies. To staff these seats, it employs five to seven outside persons as its board representatives, with each such person sitting on approximately five boards. In addition, HC&C uses its own local employees to serve on boards of regional companies.

At the opposite end of the numerical spectrum from HC&C is SIS, the investment company to Ceska Sporitelna. Having assembled a portfolio of 500 companies, SIS holds a total of 280 board seats (primarily at the managing board level). For the most part, it relies on its own employees to staff these positions, but also uses some 10 to 12 "external collaborators." More importantly, it permits no individual to serve on more than two boards. In total, SIS has about 120 staff employees, and we were told that "almost everyone is engaged" in serving as a director. However, unlike PIAS, no employee of its parent, Ceska Sporitelna, is permitted to serve as a director. Obviously, the use to this extent of lower-echelon staff employees as directors raises questions about their competence and ability to perform. In defense of this approach, SIS personnel argued that the practical role of the director could simply be to vote with a coalition of IPF funds on the board; this coalition would independently decide on the policy to be pursued and would use the actual director merely as a nominee by which to implement that policy. Other interviewees have suggested that SIS's policy of conferring directorships on lower-echelon employees was more a compensation device by which to supplement their modest salaries with director's fees and was regarded by SIS employees as an important fringe benefit of their employment.

Some investment companies recapture all or a portion of the directors' and consulting fees paid to their representatives on the boards of portfolio companies. Although no IPF that we interviewed disclosed or acknowledged this practice, knowledgeable observers at the Czech Management Center (which runs a training program in Prague for new directors) told us that this practice was becoming common (although it was far from standard). Obviously, to the extent this occurs, directors may be under-motivated to perform any true monitoring function and may understandably view such a practice as a signal that their intended role is less that of a monitoring director than an informational agent who is expected to bring valuable information learned at the board meetings to the investment company for trading purposes.

2. Board Governance

Common agreement existed regarding the frequency of meetings and the preference of the IPFs for seats on the managing board—but on little else. Boards of privatized companies are meeting continually, at least once a month and often twice a month, according to most interviewees. Unlike a U.S. or British board, there is generally little delegation of authority to a CEO or management team. Rather, as a representative of Creditanstalt Investment Bank recently told the press: "All the decisions that count have to be approved by the board."[72] But the logistical constraint this imposes on part-time directors serving on multiple boards was thought by a number of interviewees to result in informational overload on these directors and, in turn, a tendency to defer to the firm's managers.[73]

[72] Meth-Cohn, supra n. 70, 30 (quoting Wolfgang Lafite).

[73] Some also attribute this to the typical director's lack of "industry experience." See comments of Wolfgang Lafite in Meth-Cohn, supra n. 70, 30.

Most interviewees were highly skeptical of the supervisory board. It was characterized as a "declining institution", or "useless", or as a cosmetic institution where real issues could not be discussed because of the presence of employee-elected representatives. Others described it as the equivalent of an American audit committee, but without decision-making authority. A few interviewees were equally critical of the managing board. Jan Suchanek, the chief executive of YSE, the investment company which is widely believed to have assembled (on a per share basis) the highest valued portfolio after the first wave, noted that his funds had representatives on 80 boards (out of a portfolio of some 126 companies) and used some 65 persons as directors. Nonetheless, he was highly critical of the performance of most directors (and particularly those appointed by the bank-affiliated funds), whose behavior he viewed as "trying simply to avoid risk." In particular, he saw the large bank funds as staffing boards with "old Communists" whose chief aim was to "avoid embarrassment." Even when the funds owned a majority of the stock, their representatives on the boards had little incentive to become involved in management affairs and saw their primary role as that of conduits for information (much of it presumably non-public) about the company back to the fund manager. Corporate managers in his view were finding the typical IPF board representatives on their boards easy to manipulate.

No one else took this extreme or polar a position. But others, particularly managers, expressed the view that fund representatives lacked any strategy or business plans. Indeed, some felt that the board resisted giving strategic directions to avoid involvement in any failure. As the General Director of Prago, a.s., who was newly appointed to that post on March 30, 1994, phrased it to us:

> "I was given the task of within three months moving the company from the red to the black. I explained that's nonsense in that short term, and, in the end, they said . . . that the last quarter this year must be a profitable quarter."

As he explained, because his company had lost 80% of its market with the insolvency of its major Eastern block customers in Russia and the Ukraine and the dissolution of Comecon, he did not expect to be able to overcome these reversals in the nine months that he had been given.

Some managerial interviewees maintained that IPF directors simply lacked the business acumen and experience to offer specific advice or alternatives. Others stressed that directors did not want to take responsibility, and still others (including the above-quoted individual) felt that time constraints were the most important factor as IPF directors (and their investment companies) were simply attempting in most cases to supervise too large a portfolio of companies. A senior executive at PPF, a respected "private" investment company, remarked to us that he had seen some individuals (apparently connected with bank-affiliated IPFs) occupy as many as 10 to 13 board seats. An official at CKD, one of the largest Czech engineering firms, went this story one better, citing a case of one director (who was incompetent in his judgment) who was then serving on some 40 boards.

Most interviewees agreed that on those boards on which IPFs held a majority, the board was prepared to fire senior management—and had frequently done so. In fact, some noted that there was a general expectation that the incumbent managers in office at the time of privatization would be replaced because they were widely assumed to be "old Communists" whose status in the corporate hierarchy was presumed to result from political affiliations. But the tendency to replace successor managers has continued, and some view it more as an indication of the board's inability to take any alternative step in response to continued unprofitability.

3. From Cooperation to Conflict

The first reports during early 1994 suggested that the major IPFs were cooperating easily on the boards where they shared representation. After all, they had obvious common interests in establishing internal controls, preventing managerial or employee diversions of assets, and securing competent management. As of June 1994, we had not heard reports of conflict among IPFs with regard to portfolio companies. This picture changed, however, later in 1994. Apparently in several instances, dissension had arisen among bank-affiliated IPFs as to which bank a portfolio company should use as its primary lender. In one instance, a board was reportedly split between a faction led by directors aligned with Komercni banka and another faction associated with Investicni banka, and the dispute essentially boiled down to which bank would serve as the lead lender.[74]

Such a conflict suggests that bank-affiliated IPFs at least sometimes may be serving more as agents of their bank sponsors than as agents of their own shareholders. In principle, if a bank controls a corporate board through its agents, it can extract rents from the company in the form of above-market interest rates. Corporate interest rates appear to be high in the Czech Republic (generally around 14%), and if such levels are artificially high, capturing the board would mean that the bank could secure above-market rates. This fear has long been a concern raised about the German banking system, and now appears to have arisen in the Czech context also.

4. Restructuring

Are IPF directors inducing privatized companies to undertake necessary restructuring? This is clearly a critical question, but answering it runs up against the

---

[74] Interview with Jana Matesova, Czech Management Center, December 1994.

enduring problem that chronology does not imply causation. That restructuring occurs does not imply that IPF members of the board induced it. Any visitor to the Czech Republic notices immediately that most enterprises (private or public) are characterized by overemployment. Even most public spaces (from museums to restrooms) are serviced by an inefficient surplus of attendants. During 1996, the monthly unemployment rate in the Czech Republic fluctuated between 2.7% and 3.5%. Given relatively modest economic growth over this period, this suggests that firms have not been systematically downsizing their labor forces.[75] Still, many Czech industries—particularly those in engineering, electronics, and agriculture—have, with the collapse of Comecon, lost their foreign markets in Russia and Eastern Europe that sustained such levels of employment. In consequence, restructuring has been forced on these companies. In these cases, who initiated any necessary restructurings? A series of 17 focus group interviews with Czech managers, conducted in 1995 and 1996, elicited a general reaction from the managers: "the most important pressure came from the process of privatization itself,"[76] not from the board or IPFs. Managers reported that the loss of Eastern bloc markets and the need to prepare a privatization proposal in 1994 during the outset of the privatization process forced them to recognize that some operations could not be continued. Little "outside" involvement (by which the managers meant shareholders) was reported.

Some have suggested to us that a principal reason why IPFs have had only limited impact on the restructuring process is that they lack the ability to provide financing (or, equally important, to withhold financing, unless specific targets were met), technology, or the other forms of assistance that a strategic partner would provide. By definition, voucher funds lack capital, and, although several investment companies have recently established cash funds, their resources are limited. In our interviews, no one phrased it this bluntly, but several management interviewees indicated an inability to make strategic plans until the firm's "true owner" was determined. Many Czech companies have had some 30 to 40% of their shares reserved for sale to a prospective single shareholder (presumably, a foreign corporation). With some consistency, the managers interviewed in this study acknowledged reluctance about making strategic plans, opening plants, or selling possibly peripheral assets without the consent of such a "true owner" (who they also viewed as the source of critical financing). In comparison to these possibly hypothetical future owners, IPF directors tended to be discounted as amateurs. At least implicitly, the NPF has shown a similar attitude, resisting efforts by companies to convert surplus or peripheral assets into cash through sales or dispositions on the ground that the future owner should decide these

---

[75] See Matesova, supra n. 71, 8.

[76] Matesova, supra n. 71, 8.

questions (even in cases where the board has a majority of IPF directors). The result is to leave these companies in a limbo-like transitional stage.

5. IPF Incentives

Participation in corporate governance is not costless. Thus, in evaluating the extent of IPF involvement in the governance of their portfolio companies, it is useful to compare the costs and benefits of "active ownership." Investment companies (and in some cases their banking parents) derive benefits from three sources: (1) from management and start-up fees charged to their IPFs, (2) from share appreciation to the extent that they own or acquire IPF shares, and (3) from independent trading activities (possibly informed—or "tipped"—by information gained from an IPF director). Investment companies are permitted to charge an annual management fee of an IPF of up to either (a) 2% of the average net asset value of the fund, or (b) 20% of the IPF's annual profits.[77] Most investment companies have opted for the former option as the more profitable, and (possibly as a marketing matter) most seem to charge slightly less than 2% (i.e., 1.75% or 1.50% were common annual fees).[78] Given such a fee structure, investment companies have considerable reason to economize on their corporate governance activities. Few, if any, appear to have hired outside consultants, and most rely more on staff employees (whose primary responsibility has been marketing) for board positions than salaried outsiders. Milan Jurceka, the Executive Director of A-Invest (the investment company to Agrobanka), phrased the trade-off to us succinctly:

> "As to the profit of our company, our profit last year of our Investment Company was like this: 4% came from dividends and profits from share companies, and 96% from the [trading] business on the Prague Stock Exchange and RM-S system. As to our expenditures, it was the opposite: 90% of our expenditures were to go to the share companies and 10% from the wages of the specialist on the PSE and RM-S. This is a great difference. It is better to concentrate on the specialist in the PSE/RM-S because I expect a profit from them."

A-Invest was a highly successful trading firm in 1993, earning a 20% return on its capital. Given this disparity between costly participation in corporate governance activities and cheap but lucrative trading profits, investment companies may become increasingly (and rationally) passive as shareholders.

---

[77] See § 27 of The Investment Companies and Investment Funds Act (Act No. 248/1992 Coll. of 28 April, 1992).

[78] None seem to charge the greater of the two options. In addition to the annual fee, investment companies may also charge a one-time start-up or establishment fee, whose size is not regulated. Presumably, this one-time fee will not affect marginal decision making about monitoring. HC&C appears uniquely to charge its IPFs for expenses incurred on their behalf. The amount of this fee (and what it covers) is not known.

Still, one important qualification to any such prediction emerges from the fact that many of the largest investment companies now tend to own between 10% to over 50% of the equity in their IPFs (partly as a result of repurchase guarantees made at the marketing stage). Thus, in these cases, their incentives may be much better aligned with those of the other IPF shareholders, and principal/agent conflicts should be mitigated.

But large equity stakes do not alone logically ensure activism. Investment companies must believe that the marginal benefits of shareholders activism exceed the marginal costs. At present, many seem dubious about costly monitoring. Another possible explanation for apparent IPF passivity involves the set of investment opportunities that they confront. Some fund managers candidly told us that the most interesting investment opportunities in the Czech Republic today involved the shares of other IPFs. Given discounts of possibly up to 80% in IPF shares and (relatively) liquid financial assets if a small IPF could be acquired and liquidated, the expected return from this form of restructuring (in effect to eliminate the closed-end discount) at the IPF level is perceived by some within the Czech financial markets to exceed that from more traditional corporate restructuring. To be sure, Czech law precludes one IPF from acquiring shares in another,[79] and a merger between two IPFs would require Ministry of Finance approval. Still, investment companies can form investor groups to acquire controlling blocks in smaller IPFs and seek their liquidation. A Ministry of Finance official estimated for us that as little as a 10% block could control a smaller IPF (assuming it was formed as a joint stock company) and acknowledged that such control acquisitions had occurred and were in progress.

III. Bank/IPF Contacts: Does the German Banking Analogy Apply?

A common prediction about Czech privatization was that it would evolve in the direction of the German "universal" banking system rather than towards an Anglo-American market-oriented system of corporate governance. The conventional wisdom about the German system was that its major banks acted as careful monitors of managerial performance at client corporations because of their joint position as creditors in their own right and also agents for the shareholders for whom they typically serve as depositary for most shares.[80] According to tradi-

---

[79] See § 24(7) of The Investment Companies and Investment Funds Act (Act No. 248/1992 Coll. of 28 April, 1992).

[80] For the conventional assessment that German banks do monitor corporate managements closely, see Carrington, John T. and George T. Edwards *Financing Industrial Investment* (London 1979); Charkham, Jonathan P. 'Corporate Governance and the Market for Companies' (Bank of England Panel Paper no. 25, 1989). See also Cable, supra n. 5. These reviews have recently been elaborately criticized in a full-scale review of the German banking system, which

tional argument, this dual relationship gives rise to economies of both scope and scale.

Although the evidence about the efficiency advantages of the German banking system is itself much in dispute, the Czech pattern must be recognized as different from the German in several important respects. First, German banks own substantial stock in their own right in their "client" corporations. Although they also typically hold substantially greater voting power through proxies granted them by individual shareholders, the significance of the large equity stakes that they do hold is that it tends to align their interests with that of the other shareholders. In contrast, Czech banks hold virtually no equity in the port-folio companies held by their sponsored IPFs. Where the bank does not own a substantial stake in its own IPF, this contrast with the German system means that the only benefit that a Czech bank receives from equity appreciation of a stock in an IPF's portfolio is an increase in the annual management fee that it receives (typically at or under 2% of the net asset value of the fund).

This distinction has particular importance because the latest research on the German banking system finds that "German banks improved the performance of German firms to the extent that they held the firms' equity."[81] That is, proxy voting power and other variables suggesting the bank's level of influence (i.e., supervisory board seats held) did not correlate closely with improved economic performance. Only when the bank was a substantial blockholder in its own right did a correlation between the bank's presence and the firm's economic perform-ance become clear. Yet, at the outset of Czech privatization, banks were not substantial blockholders. Since 1995, this has begun to change indirectly, as bank ownership in their own IPFs has increased.

Another factor that bears on the extent of bank influence in the Czech systems versus the German is the existence of other large blockholders. Such blockhold-ers are common in Germany. 85% of the largest quoted German companies have a shareholder owning 25% or more.[82] This suggests the likelihood of countervailing power, which could prevent a bank from extracting private bene-fits. Although Czech share ownership is highly concentrated, IPFs appear to reinforce bank control, rather than place a brake on it, because the largest IPF in a firm's ownership is likely to be controlled by the firm's principal bank.

Most IPFs also have only a weak incentive to maximize the value of their portfolio shares, because they do not expect (after the second wave) to have further opportunities to sell their shares. This is in sharp contrast to the typical

finds that it devotes no more attention to monitoring than do banks in economies organized around stock markets. See Edwards and Fischer, supra n. 5.

[81] See Gorton and Schmid, supra n. 5, 30. This statement holds for their 1974 sample but they are unable to detect a significant effect for their 1985 sample (p. 31).

[82] Gorton and Schmid, supra n. 5, 15.

open-end American mutual fund, which regularly offers its shares to the public. To be sure, the investment company sponsoring an IPF can expect a larger annual management fee if portfolio share value increases (basically 2% of the increase annually), but it cannot expect to double its asset value by selling additional shares. It knows that the privatization process is over and that there will be no third wave. Hence, its incentives to monitor to raise share value should logically be weaker.

Even among bank-affiliated IPFs, the pattern of interaction between the bank and its sponsor seems to be highly divergent. Some investment companies that are controlled by Czech banks (for example, S.I.S., the subsidiary of Ceska Sporitelna) protested that they could not (and did not) contact their banking parent for information about privatized companies in their portfolio, but rather maintained a strict firewall between themselves and the bank.[83] In sharp contrast, another prominent investment company (A-Invest) indicated that it participated in regular, formalized discussions through quarterly meetings at which bank-appointed directors, regional managers of the investment company, and regional bank officials would meet to pool information about companies in the investment company's portfolio. A-Invest in particular stressed that what it desired most from these meetings was the financial data that any borrower would be required to provide and update periodically to its banking parent (Agrobanka). A-Invest did insist, however, that these collective conferences would use the information assembled to predict trends, discuss possible mergers and acquisitions, or evaluate management—but not to acquire information for use in securities trading. Still, A-Invest acknowledged that it had profited handsomely from its securities trading activities (it estimated a 20% return on capital last year, primarily from trading activities). No other investment company was as candid about its disregard for firewalls between the bank and an investment company subsidiary, but PIAS did acknowledge relying heavily on employees of its banking parent (Investicni bank) to serve as directors of its portfolio companies.

Most interviewees were familiar with the term "firewall" and some under-stood it to be the Ministry of Finance's policy that there should be a "firewall" between the investment company and its banking parent, at least with regard to IPF activities. No Czech statute seems to mandate such a firewall, however, and others (most notably A-Invest) disputed the need for any such prophylactic rule, pointing out that the most valuable information was already in the hands of the

---

[83] Interviewees may, of course, have been inhibited by their knowledge of § 28 of The Investment Companies and Investment Funds Act (Act No. 248/1992 Coll. of 28 April 1992), which provides that both employees of an investment company and an investment fund (among others) "are bound to treat as confidential all facts concerning the business interests of an invest-ment company, investment fund or depository."

bank in the form of credit date and that efforts to obtain such data could only benefit the IPFs.[84]

D. Post-Privatization Developments: Theory Meets Reality

To this point, this paper has described Czech privatization through the second wave of privatization in 1995. It has described a process in which the bank-affiliated funds performed less aggressively at both the marketing and portfolio selection stages than the more entrepreneurially oriented independent IPFs. In particular, independent IPFs sought larger stakes, while bank-affiliated IPFs chose to hold broader portfolios (with correspondingly smaller percentage stakes in their portfolio companies). In general, the independent IPFs were also the more active monitors. Arguably, the standard conflict-of-interest story about banks as shareholders and lenders can explain (and might well have predicted) this outcome: that is, because bank-controlled IPFs could be used by their banking sponsors to obtain clients through toehold acquisitions, bank-controlled IPFs pursued broad diversification strategies which in turn made them less effective (and less motivated) monitors.

But the story does not end here. In particular, once we move into the post-privatization stage that began essentially in 1995, the private IPFs do not remain the champions of efficiency or the role models that policy planners in other transitional economies would wish to recreate in their own countries. Beginning more or less in 1995 (although the prospect was evident even earlier), the pace of change accelerated, and controversy became commonplace. Both at the IPF level and at the portfolio company level, control contests began to break out in earnest.[85] It is simplest to examine these developments separately, first at the company level and then at the fund level.

I. The Struggle for Majority Control

In the 1994-1995 period at the outset of privatization, IPFs seemed willing to share control among themselves. As of the end of 1995, the top five IPFs owned

---

[84] This argument may have been an effort to distinguish away § 28 of The Investment Companies and Investment Funds Act, which imposes a duty of confidentiality on investment company employees but says nothing about their efforts to gather data from others.

[85] For a recent example of an IPF takeover, see Green, Peter 'Coup Outs Czech Fund Managers' *The European* November 7, 1996, 20 (describing takeover by Regent-Kingpin Czech Value Fund of Trend-VIF Investment Fund an IPF, in which Regent-Kingpin, 2 Western Mutual Fund, bought a 38% stake in Trend-VIF and removed KHB, its Czech management company).

on average 48.8% of a first wave firm and 40.7% of a second wave firm.[86] Over the five-year period from 1991 through 1995, ownership concentration for the average firm, as represented by the percentage held by the top five investors (excluding the state), rose from 47.2% in 1992 to 59.4% in 1995.[87] Since then, however, ownership concentration has significantly increased. Today, it is estimated that "a vast majority of Czech privatized firms of up to ECU 30 mil. of equity have acquired a majority owner," and larger firms usually have at least a controlling block holder.[88] Control acquisition has usually occurred through the sale of strategic blocks among the principal holders, and not by a tender offer to the smaller shareholders.[89] With each sale, the seller's representatives on the board typically resign in favor of nominees of the buyers. Thus, a Czech business school academic has written:

> "It is not unique among Czech companies that their boards have changed their composition five and more times between February 1995 and the end of 1996."[90]

While managerial changes did not necessarily follow these changes in ownership, the ability of the existing management team to follow a consistent stable policy (or make long-term plans in general) was compromised. Insecurity and decreased commitment is a likely corollary of such board reshuffling.

The impact on minority shareholders is even clearer once a majority control block was assembled. The same source reports:

> "In the Czech legal and institutional framework, to protect (the) value of one's ownership in most cases requires (one) to hold a majority. Fifty-one percent stakes in companies are sold at a hundred-percent price of the company. With a few exceptions, stakes in companies dominated by a majority owner have little or no value as they provide little enforceable rights to control the assets . . . and . . . there is no market to sell the remaining shares at any price close to the per share net asset value . . . or any positive price at all."[91]

Even if this assessment overstates to some degree, it captures the popular disillusionment within the community of Czech public shareholders, who generally believed that the value of their shares has been misappropriated from them by the majority holders. It can scarcely be overemphasized that a unique feature of Czech voucher privatization was that it converted most citizens into shareholders (and, as a practical matter, minority shareholders); thus, it created an extraordinarily broad political consistency concerned about the abuse of minority share-

---

[86] See Claessens, Stijn, Simeon Djankov, and Gerhard Pohl 'Ownership and Corporate Governance: Evidence from the Czech Republic' 8 (World Bank Policy Research Working Paper no. 1737, March 1997).

[87] Claessens, Djankov, and Pohl, supra n. 86, 8.

[88] See Matesova, supra n. 70.

[89] Matesova, supra n. 71.

[90] Claessens, Djankov, and Pohl, supra n. 86, 8.

[91] Claessens, Djankov, and Pohl, supra n. 86, 8.

holders. Unfortunately, Czech privatization did not create meaningful minority shareholder protections at the same time, and it thereby sowed the seeds of future political dissatisfaction. In short, while shareholder rights are seldom a political issue in the United States, they have become a major issue in the Czech Republic, both because of the relative absence of protections and because of the sudden impact of such incidents upon a majority of the Czech population. In June 1997, the Czech prime minister, Vaclav Klaus, survived a parliamentary no-confidence vote by a single vote, and his defeat in forthcoming elections in 1998 is widely predicted.[92] Dissatisfaction with the excesses of privatization appears to be a principal cause of the popular dissatisfaction.

II. Asset Stripping

Although the conflict between the interests of a bank-affiliated IPF and those of other shareholders in its portfolio company over the choice of lender for the firm is obvious, this by no means implies that non-bank-related IPFs are exposed to fewer conflicts. In fact, as discussed below, they can probably engage as a practical matter in even more egregious behavior that effectively loots the firm. A variety of techniques became popular in 1995 and 1996:

(1) *Subcontracting.* The majority owner could subcontract to buy the firm's production (or most of it) at cost (or below) and then resell to the firm's former customers at a profit. Alternatively, the parent could sell the firm its raw materials at an inflated price. In either case, the denominator is manipulated transfer pricing.

(2) *Repayment of Bank Loans.* The majority shareholder could require its firm to repay the bank loan by which the majority shareholder acquired its majority interest. For example, the entity that borrowed the money could be merged into the firm, thereby making the firm liable for these debts.

(3) *Sales and Leases of Firm Assets.* The simplest scenario is to sell valuable firm assets at below fair market value prices to the majority shareholder (or to its affiliates, not all of whom will be readily recognizable). In the absence of developed judicial remedies, minority shareholders have little recourse.

Although in principle bank-run IPFs could also strip assets from portfolio companies, most observers report that asset-stripping was primarily engaged in by non-bank IPFs.[93] Several reasons make this lesser involvement of bank-

---

[92] See Longworth, R.C. 'Czechs' Economic 'Miracle' Looking More Like a Nightmare' *Chicago Tribune* August 4, 1997, 1.

[93] See Matesova, supra n. 71 (arguing that "firms dominated by investment funds unrelated to banks are in most cases heavily involved in asset stripping" and attributing this phenomenon to the tendency for non-bank IPFs to be dominated by a single individual or small group with only short-run interests in the portfolio company).

related IPFs in asset stripping logical: first, at least at the outset, the bank may have had only a very small equity stake in its own IPF and hence would not directly profit from exploitation. Second, the portfolio company was probably also a debtor to the bank, and thus stripping its assets to benefit the IPF injured the bank as an unsecured creditor. Similarly, the bank may view the portfolio company as a long-term client whose management it did not wish to antagonize. Third, banks are more closely regulated than most other economic actors, and even in the Czech Republic, banks were subject to the oversight of the Finance Ministry. Finally, banks have reputational capital, which involvement in scandals can injure; the same cannot be said (at least as easily) for start-up independent IPFs (particularly when they are closed-end funds that do not expect to make future equity offerings).

III. IPF Mergers and Conversions

As of late 1995, some funds traded in the Czech market at prices that reflected as much as a 75% to 80% discount from the apparent net asset value of the securities in their portfolio. By acquiring the IPF's shares, one could in theory liquidate the IPF and acquire its assets, thereby realizing this discount. But there are also risks in this strategy. Most importantly, the lack of transparency in the Czech market made it uncertain what assets the particular fund held and also suggested that the market value of these portfolio stocks might have been inflated; if so, the inflated value of market prices may have overstated the amount of the discount. In addition, legislation passed in 1996 that slowed the takeovers of IPFs by restricting partial bids.[94]

The collective result of these restraints has been to reduce the incentive to conduct a hostile takeover of an IPF, but to leave unchilled management's own incentive to acquire control of its own fund—in effect, the Central European equivalent of "going private." Management after all knows better than others the "real" value of its own portfolio and thus also knows the degree to which the apparent discount is real or illusory.[95] Fund managers can exploit these discounts in one of two basic ways: (1) converting the fund from a closed-end fund into an unregulated holding company, or (2) converting the fund into an open-end fund, after first buying the fund's shares at a substantial discount. On announcement of the plan, the prospect of conversion will typically eliminate much of the discount, creating an immediate profit for the fund manager who has acquired shares from his own shareholders prior to the disclosure of this plan.

---

[94] See 'Ministry Casts Cold Eye on Fund Managers' *East European Banker* February 1997.

[95] *East European Banker*, supra n. 94.

The paradigmatic example of opportunistic exploitation of these possibilities is again supplied by Harvard Capital and Consulting. In 1995, Viktor Kozeny entered into an informal alliance with an equally (if not more) controversial American capitalist, Michael Dingman, to restructure target companies. To this end, Kozeny secretly converted his already small portfolio of 50-odd companies into major blocs in some eight Czech industrial companies.[96] Fortune Magazine has reported that Kozeny deliberately sold the holdings of his funds at a loss—to himself (that is, to affiliated companies that he controlled).[97] Predictably, the share value of Harvard Capital's funds began to shrink dramatically. Kozeny then accelerated this process by announcing his intention to convert the Harvard mutual fund family into an industrial holding company. Fortune compared this to the equivalent of Fidelity suddenly announcing that it was selling its diversified holdings and turning itself into a parallel of General Electric. With this announcement, the price of some Harvard Capital funds declined 22% in one week. Over a one-year period, "Harvard's main fund, now a holding company, has lost 83% of its value."[98]

Predictably, Mr. Kozeny bought his funds' shares as this price decline accelerated and became the 51% holder of his principal fund's shares. Having deliberately deflated his own balloon, he then merged all his funds into a new holding company, called Harvard Industrial Holding, which he then merged with an entity that Dingman and Kozeny collectively controlled, to eventually produce (after still other mergers) an entity called Daventree Ltd., which is now based in Cyprus and beyond the effective control of Czech authorities. The fund's former shareholders now hold debt obligations of Daventree, and a forthcoming public offering by Daventree has been widely rumored.

As before, Harvard Capital has been followed by a number of imitators. A number of closed-end funds have converted to unregulated holding companies—simply by surrendering their licenses as broker-dealers.[99] Other closed-end funds have converted to open-end status—often after insiders made substantial purchases of the fund's shares. As a generalization, independent IPFs were probably significantly more implicated in these scandals than were bank-affiliated IPFs. But all generalizations have their exceptions, and probably the most notorious episode of fraud over the 1996-1997 period has involved

---

[96] See Wallace, Charles P. 'The Pirates of Prague' *Fortune* December 23, 1996, 78.

[97] Wallace, supra n. 96. The Czech Finance Ministry eventually ordered Kozeny to pay restitution to his fund shareholders in the amount of $6.8 million and has also fined him for certain of these transactions.

[98] Wallace, supra n. 96. The Czech stock market rose over the same period in 1996.

[99] As examples, two investment funds run by Agrobanka—AGB If 1 and AGB If 2—converted into holding companies (Appollan Holding and AGB Holding, a.s.) on May 31, 1996. See 'Charges Brought Against 11 In connection with Agrobanka' *CTR National News Wire* April 23, 1997.

Agrobanka, the Czech commercial that is the parent of A-Invest, possibly the most successful fund manager in the second wave of Czech privatization. In late April 1997, eleven officers and employees of Agrobanka were arrested as a result of the alleged embezzlement of shareholder funds from Agrobanka-affiliated IPFs.[100] At the center of this scandal was a December 1995 battle for control of Agrobanka between Motoinvest and Investicni. Investicni eventually retreated and sold its 17.5% stake to Motoinvest on the condition that the latter buy a large share (15%) in a troubled bank controlled by Investicni. After an audit of Agrobanka by Price Waterhouse in 1996, an administrator for the bank was appointed, and in 1997, A-invest was replaced as manager of Agrobanka's IPFs by Expandia, another well-known fund manager.

A-Invest and Harvard shared one characteristic in common: both were the most aggressive marketers of IPFs, the two that made the financial promises that seemed the closest to a pyramid scheme. Both profited, but both ultimately ran afoul of regulators in a nation almost notorious for its lack of financial regulation. Although A-Invest was bank-affiliated, a controlling interest in its bank, Agrobanka, had been effectively acquired midway during the privatization process by a small investment firm, Motoinvest, several of whose founders were eventually indicted.[101] If anything, the Motoinvest example shows that a truly privatized bank can be corrupted.

IV. Survival of the Inefficient: What Explains the Dominance of the Bank-Affiliated IPFs?

Investor disenchantment with the status of minority shareholders has had a variety of consequences. First and most obviously, smaller investors have sold their interests in IPFs. Three of the largest Czech banks—Ceska Sporitelna (the largest savings bank), Komercni banka (the largest commercial bank), and Privni Investicni (the fourth largest commercial bank)—exemplify this pattern. Ceska Sporitelna, which was not involved in scandals but which acquired a reputation for bumbling incompetence, saw the number of shareholders in its funds fall from over one million to one-third that level by mid-1997.[102] Privni Investicni, which has been involved in repeated scandals, lost over 50% of the original

---

[100] See 'Czech Bank Fraud Arrests' *Financial Times* April 24, 1997, 2 *CTF National News Wire*, supra n. 99.

[101] Motoinvest, which is itself now in liquidation, seems to have specialized in buying the portfolio assets of Agrobanka, whose sales seem to have led to the bank's eventual insolvency. See 'Motoinvest to End by September 1' *CTK National News Wire* July 27, 1997.

[102] See 'Investment Funds' Number of Shareholders Fall' *CTK Business News Wire* July 9, 1997.

800,000 shareholders in its funds.[103] Komercni, which has been relatively scandal free, saw its number of fund shareholders fall by a somewhat smaller margin from 500,000 to 280,000.[104] Overall, the number of shareholders in investment funds as of mid-1997 had fallen from the original level of approximately "five million to less than a half." With this pattern of disinvestment by small shareholders in IPFs, there has been a necessary increase in the concentration of IPF ownership (paralleling a similar increase at the portfolio company level). In particular, the percentage of bank ownership and cross-ownership of their own funds has increased (while the major banks themselves remain relatively "unprivatized"). This transition has been described by some Czech commentators as the "renationalization of the Czech economy."[105]

In overview, a partially state-owned bank seems an unlikely candidate to push necessary restructuring through against the resistance of portfolio companies' management, for at least two reasons: (1) the prospect of layoffs may produce labor and management appeals to the state to use its influence as a shareholder to call off or mitigate scheduled restructuring; and (2) the bank's status as the principal lender (at high interest rates) might be jeopardized if the bank, as shareholder, sought to tightly to constrain management (at least where the bank did not control an absolute majority of the corporation's stock).

The Czech public seems also to have sensed that bank-run IPFs were less aggressive than their independent rivals, and in the second wave of privatization, public investors opted for independent IPFs. This is shown by a World Bank statistic that bank-sponsored funds at the end of 1995 owned 21.2% of firms in the first privatization wave, but only 9.8% of firms in the second wave. Conversely, private IPFs owned 27.6% of firms in the first wave but 30.9% of firms in the second wave.[106] In short, a trend in favor of the private IPF was evident, as investors learned to contribute their vouchers to non-bank IPFs over the two privatization waves.

Given this early trend and the general observations that bank-run IPFs have not pushed restructuring but have been for the most part complacement monitors, one would expect the shares of listed companies whose principal shareholder was a bank-run IPF to trade at a discount to the market average. Yet the reverse appears to be the case. A World Bank study of 706 publicly traded Czech companies over the 1992 to 1995 period found that companies with a more

---

[103] *CTK Business News Wire*, supra n. 102.

[104] *CTK Business News Wire*, supra n. 102.

[105] At the end of July 1997, Nomura, the Japanese bank, purchased the state share (roughly 36%) of Investicni. This may presage a general sell-off of the state's interest in the major banks. See 'Japanese Nomura Bank Gains Stake in Fourth Largest Czech Bank' *BBC Summary of World Broadcasts* July 31, 1997.

[106] *BBC Summary of World Broadcasts*, supra n. 105.

concentrated ownership had a higher stock market valuation.[107] More importantly, it also examined the relationship between company stock price and
ownership by the most important IPFs (both bank-related and non-bank-related).
Some major banks revealed "significantly positive" coefficients (e.g., Komercni
Banka, Ceska Sporitelna, and Zivnostenska Banka),[108] and only one bank, the
scandal-plagued Agrabanka, revealed a negative relationship. Yet, uniquely
among the major Czech banks, Agrobanka was privately owned and thus outside
the network of cross-ownership that characterized the other banks. A few non-
bank-related IPFs also had a positive relationship, showing that the market could
distinguish individual firms.[109]

Based on this evidence, the authors of this study conclude that it demonstrates
the invalidity of the conflict of interest hypothesis that bank-related funds might
seek to maximize the position of their bank sponsor as creditor. This conclusion
seems, however, well beyond the logical import of their evidence. What such
evidence shows is not the efficiency of bank-sponsored funds, which all observers report to be passive and, in some cases (i.e., Ceska Sporitelna), virtually
incompetent, but the market's greater fear of predatory non-bank IPFs. Put
simply, the market fears the prospect of looting by some independent IPFs (such
as Harvard Capital) far more than it fears the risk of above-market interest rates
charged by a bank-related IPF.

Indeed, when one integrates the quantitative evidence in the World Bank
study with the qualitative evidence supplied almost uniformly by on-the-scene
observers that bank-related IPFs have not pushed for restructurings, the
combined evidence suggests the need for a redefinition of the role of the bank as
monitor. Proponents of the German model have long argued for the efficiency of
the universal bank as a combined shareholder and creditor. Although some close
students of the German system hotly dispute such claims,[110] the Czech context is
in any event different. At least within this context, the market's positive reaction
to the bank as a sponsor of an IPF is not attributable to an expectation that it will
be an active monitor, but that it will be a protective shield. This role takes neither
active oversight nor benevolent intentions; indifference in this context is more a
virtue than a vice. The indifferent supervision of a bank-related IPF may not be
efficient, but its mere presence protects minority shareholders from more predatory owners who would strip assets and loot the firm. Both because a bank has
reputational capital (which it wishes to protect across a variety of markets and
constituencies) and because it views the firm as a debtor whose solvency it

---

[107] Claessens, Djankov, and Pohl, supra n. 86, 8.

[108] Claessens, Djankov, and Pohl, supra n. 86, 13.

[109] Claessens, Djankov, and Pohl, supra n. 86, 13. (In particular, YSE had a positive coefficient).

[110] See Edwards and Fischer, supra n. 5.

instinctively wishes to protect, the bank-related IPF is a natural guardian. If it did not restructure, it also did not loot. In a legal system without meaningful protections for minority shareholders, such a guardian shareholder logically commands a market premium.

Similarly, a high concentration of IPF ownership also may convey useful information. If other IPFs remain as minority shareholders even after majority control is obtained by one of them, this may signal their informed judgment that looting is unlikely. Even if a group of IPFs holds collective control, looting by a group is more difficult and less likely than looting by an absolute majority shareholder (if only because agreement over the allocation of the plunder may be difficult within an informal group of pirates). Again, this could explain the World Bank finding that the market placed a positive value on a high concentration of IPF ownership.[111]

This hypothesis that the role of the bank as a shareholder is less that of an active catalyst than a defensive shield applies beyond the Czech Republic. The assumption which some researchers have made that a positive market response to bank equity ownership implies the bank is an efficient monitor is too glib.[112] In legal systems without significant protection for minority shareholders, the initial hypothesis should be that the bank's ownership or control of a strategic block constitutes a protective shield. For the small price of an above-market interest rate, the bank protects the minority shareholders from a far darker fate at the hands of other possible owners. More ambitious claims that the bank is an optimal monitor should require evidence of actual monitoring, which in the Czech context remains lacking.

E. Policy Options: How Should the Regulatory System Be Changed?

Although the Czech experience is instructive and revealing in its own right, the preceding discussion ultimately sets the stage for a focus on the policy issues in voucher fund regulation—both within the Czech Republic and in other transitional economies. While the early Czech experience with voucher privatization seemingly confirmed the wisdom of a rapid transition to a market economy, the later phases of Czech privatization are now cited by those who favor the slower, more gradual transition, which both Poland and Hungary have pursued. Some critics might go even further and question whether voucher privatization in any

---

[111] An alternative thesis is that there are many small firms which IPFs wisely never invested in because they were worthless and likely to become insolvent, but which uniformed individual investors did buy with their voucher coupons because they were cheap. In this light, firms with low IPF ownership were low quality firms to begin with.

[112] Such an assumption has been made, but not defended, in one well-known study. See Cable, supra n. 5.

form makes sense, on the grounds that minority interests cannot be protected in transitional legal systems. Hence, they would argue that privatized companies should simply be sold to strategic owners (whether foreign or domestic) in order to avoid the wasteful but inevitable process of shareholder concentration.

In addition to these questions about the pace and objectives of voucher privatization, the Czech experience also suggests that some recurring problems will need to be faced in any economy that is to be privatized through the use of voucher funds. One such problem involves the high level of cross-ownership and the consequent consolidation of control within the Czech banking system. Although this last issue of high cross-ownership may prove unique to the circumstances of Czech privatization, privatization achieves little if it only substitutes oligopoly for government ownership. Thus, this paper will group the major regulatory issues under three headings: (1) Motivating the Monitor—What Incentives Are Necessary to Induce Restructuring? (2) Rapid versus Evolutionary Privatization; and (3) Strategic Owners and the Problem of Bank Ownership.

I. Motivating the Monitor

Let us assume that the standard story about the Czech experience is accurate: IPFs did not monitor and did not push for necessary restructurings or layoffs. Viewed in the abstract, this translates into a problem of incentives. How do you give IPFs appropriate incentives to monitor? Why didn't the market automatically provide such incentives?

At least two hypotheses can be offered for why the incentives were inadequate. First, it was simply more profitable to loot firms through self-dealing transactions than to run them for the benefit of others. So long as Czech law provided little restriction on self-dealing, the sponsors of IPFs can profit more in transferring the assets of portfolio firms to themselves than in running the firms for long-term appreciation. Second, even if unfair self-dealing and embezzlement can be controlled, closed-end mutual funds do not necessarily have the in-house expertise or economic incentives to undertake expensive investment in the corporate governance of their portfolio companies. Compounding this problem is the existence of ownership ceilings (20% on an individual IPF, 40% for a family group) on the percentage of stock that an IPF or an IPF group could own in any individual company. Still a further difficulty is the closed-end nature of IPFs. Because an IPF will not sell stock in the future, it loses much of its incentive to develop reputational capital as a successful monitor.

1. The Problem of Self-Dealing

If voucher privatization (which inherently creates a very dispersed ownership structure) is to be used as the primary vehicle for privatization in other transitional economies, the Czech experience strongly suggests that severe limits must be placed on transactions between a portfolio firm and the IPF, its sponsor, and their affiliates. Even if self-dealing transactions can sometimes promote efficiency, transitional legal systems lack the ability to discriminate between fair and unfair self-dealing (or between "efficiency promoting" self-dealing and simple theft). Thus, prophylactic rules appear necessary (if voucher privatization is to be retained). Such rules might broadly forbid asset sales or purchases between large shareholders and the portfolio company, subcontracting, or use of corporate funds to pay the indebtedness of stockholders. It is beyond the scope of this article to offer draft rules, but the key point is that they have to be simple and violations must be transparently observable. Whether private enforcement mechanisms (such as the class action or the derivative suit) should be authorized presents another highly debatable question, but clearly governmental enforcement (possibly through cease and desist orders and civil penalties) needs to be strengthened.

Would such a system work? The Czech experience cannot tell us, because it was never attempted.

2. Ownership Ceilings

The most obvious barrier in Czech law to IPFs behaving as "true" owners was the 20% ceiling on ownership by an IPF or related group of IPFs of a single firm's stock.[113] Clearly, such a rule had only a tenuous relationship to any diversification objective (a goal which is in any event more sensibly addressed by a

---

[113] The actual legal rule has three distinct provisions: Section 24(3) of The Investment Companies And Investment Funds Act (Act No. 248/1992 Coll. of 28 April 1992, as amended by Act No. 591/1992 Coll.) provides:

"(3) Not more than 20 (twenty) percent of the total nominal value of securities issued by the same issuer may be owned by a unit trust or an investment fund."

To prevent evasion through the use of multiple funds controlled by the same investment company, § 24(5)(a) of the same Act further provides:

"(5) An investment company must ensure that:

(a) the assets of all unit trust established and administered by that investment company do not represent more that 20 (twenty) percent of the shares of the same issuer;"

Finally, § 24(6) provides:

"The restrictions under subsection 5 also apply to investment funds established by the same founder."

Thus, the combined effect is that the investment sponsor may not hold more than 40% of a single firm between its investment funds and its unit trust funds.

narrower rule restricting IPFs to investing no more than 10% of their assets in securities of any one issuer).[114] The economic impact of this rule was to aggravate the usual "free rider" problem in corporate governance because a 20% owner will have less incentive to monitor and expend funds on corporate governance activities than will, for example, a 50% owner.

The case for eliminating the ceiling on IPF ownership of individual companies is clear and straightforward: its abolition would facilitate corporate control transactions and permit an activist IPF shareholder to acquire control (or simply threaten to do so) in order to influence or oust a management that is resistant to shareholder pressure. Other shareholders (including even foreign owners) are not restricted by any similar ceiling and can today assemble a majority interest. Why then are IPFs specially singled out? Even when acquisition of control is not feasible (because, for example, of the above-noted 10% diversification restraint), an IPF that acquires 30% will have a greater incentive to monitor managements. For the most part, the economic evidence tends to support the position that large shareholders create value for all shareholders, because they are a partial solution to the "free rider" problem.[115]

Conversely, the case for retaining the ceiling rests instead on political considerations and the fear that minority shareholders (and also other constituencies) will be exploited by a dominant IPF shareholder. Those favoring retention of the ceiling fear that if a controlling block is assembled, the value of the minority shares will decline—either in anticipation of future exploitative conduct or because the "public" minority shares will be shorn of their "control premium." The realism of this scenario is difficult to assess, but it can be addressed in other less drastic ways, such as, for example, by adoption of the British tender offer rules which require anyone seeking to exceed a specified ownership level to make a public tender offer for all remaining shares.[116]

II. Rapid Versus Slow Privatization

The evident problems with Czech voucher privatization and the recent economic revival in Poland (which has experienced relatively greater economic growth over the last few years) has rekindled the debate between proponents of fast and

---

[114] See § 24(1) of The Investment Companies and Investment Funds Act.

[115] See, e.g., Shleifer, Andrei and Robert W. Vishny 'Large Shareholders and Corporate Control' *Journal of Political Economy* 94 (1988) 461 (presenting data from U.S. context that large, but noncontrolling, shareholders increase firm value).

[116] In 1996, the Czech Republic adopted legislation requiring that once a person crosses any of the 50%, 66 2/3%, or 75% thresholds, such person is required to make a public tender offer for the remaining shares within 60 days thereafter at a price equal to the weighted price on the market over the prior six months.

slow privatization. The latter point to the seeming success of Poland and Hungary and argue that the legal and regulatory infrastructure should be developed before firms are placed directly into the hands of private owners. The Polish approach to privatization has been deliberately slow and heavily regulated. Instead of permitting private entrepreneurs to launch independent IPFs, Poland has established some 15 National Investment Funds ("NIFs") which hold controlling stakes in some 512 privatized companies. Each of the NIFs, which remain indirectly under governmental control, will receive controlling stakes (33 1/3%) in some 30 mid-sized companies. In addition, another 27% in each company will be distributed to the other 14 NIFs (or slightly less than 2% each).[117] Thus, each privatized company will have a designated "lead" NIF. The Polish government issued vouchers to citizens in 1996, which can be converted by them into shares in the NIFs this year. Citizens do not, however, receive the opportunity to directly invest their vouchers in individual firms, and each of the NIFs is required to hire a Western investment banking firm to help it plan necessary restructurings and portfolio modifications. The NIFs are permitted to swap their portfolios or sell their stakes in individual companies to strategic owners; some have also begun to sell their stake through IPOs conducted on the Warsaw Stock Exchange. On June 12, 1997, the 15 NIFs were listed on the Warsaw Stock Exchange, and trading began.[118] At least at the outset, the discount from the net asset value per share of these NIFs has been modest (11%) and well below the typical discounts on Czech IPFs.[119]

While it would be premature to appraise the success of Polish privatization at this early stage, the Polish approach is clearly highly paternalistic in comparison to the Czech approach: citizens do not invest in individual firms; investment funds are assigned their initial portfolios; portfolio size was kept small, and the controlling shareholder was in effect appointed by the state (i.e., the NIF given a controlling 33 1/3% stake). In effect, the usual chaos of the free market was strictly prohibited. In addition, the 500-odd firms being privatized represent only between 10% to 12% of the Polish economy.

Will it work? Time will tell, but if one is concerned (as many are) that Czech privatization was only skin deep (because of the pervasive role of bank-related IPFs where the state still maintained control over the principal banks), the Polish approach shows far more pervasive continuing state influence. To be sure, over time, the price of individual NIFs may come to reflect their relative success in managing their portfolios, but it is also possible that many NIFs will resemble

---

[117] For a recent overview of the progress of Polish privatization, see Pechman, Russell 'Country Profile: Poland' *Emerging Markets Weekly* July 21, 1997, 8.

[118] See 'Poland Floats National Investment Funds' *Privatization International* July 1, 1997.

[119] *Privatization International*, supra n. 118.

small index funds and thus will rise or fall with the overall strength of the Polish economy.[120]

Although the idea of restricted small portfolios may well have merit if one wishes to induce close monitoring and restructuring, the downside of the Polish approach is that each NIF may amount to a governmentally imposed economic czar for its thirty firms. If a proposed restructuring is politically sensitive or cuts deeply into local employment, one must suspect that labor interests and others with political clout will know how to protest effectively. Because the initial board of each NIF is governmentally appointed, there is little reason to believe that individual NIFs will feel insulated from such protests.

Poland's refusal to permit private entrepreneurs to form IPFs means that Poland will be spared the occasional embarrassment for the country that Harvard Capital caused for the Czechs, but at the same time Poland may be spared the chaotic but desirable creative destruction that new market forces can unleash. In effect, Poland is relying upon NIFs that resemble bureaucracies more than they do mutual funds to convert state-owned enterprises into competitive businesses.

Although the structure of the Polish privatization program is certainly debatable, the deeper question is its judgment to build up the regulatory infrastructure first before undertaking voucher privatization. Here, the Polish approach has had at least one marked success: the Warsaw Stock Exchange, which is closely regulated and relatively transparent, is much preferred by Western portfolio investors to the Prague Stock Exchange, which, despite recent reforms, is still viewed by many as a pirates' den of manipulators. Yet, although Warsaw stock prices are widely considered more reliable and stable than those in Prague, it is questionable whether this advantage necessitated the several year delay by which Polish privatization lagged behind Czech privatization. The real source of the disparity between the two countries seems to be more the ideological distaste of the Czech government for regulation in any form versus the equally ideological skepticism on the part of Polish officials for market forces. As next suggested, the case for a substantial delay to develop a legal and regulatory infrastructure seems weak, because the true shortcomings of the existing system are not likely to become evident until they are exposed to market forces. Sensible regulation will necessarily have to be largely reactive, even if some problems can be anticipated in advance.

---

[120] While each NIF will receive a controlling 33 1/3% stake in some 30 firms, it will receive a small stake (just under 2%) in the remaining firms. Given that 512 firms are in this first privatization wave, each NIF will therefore receive a nearly 2% stake in 482 firms and a 33 1/3% stake in 30 firms. This resembles a highly diversified index fund.

III. Strategic Owners Versus Public Ownership

One can easily view the Czech experience and conclude pessimistically that dispersed ownership will not work, absent the special legal and institutional framework that exists in the United States, the United Kingdom, and few, if any, other countries. Thus, it can be argued that privatization should be implemented through the sale of controlling blocks to strategic owners. From this perspective, concentrated ownership is the most practical answer to the inadequate legal protections that most existing (and virtually all transitional) legal systems provide minority investors.[121] Of course, at least in theory, voucher privatization through investment privatization funds is precisely an attempt to concentrate ownership, but arguably it has just pushed the agency cost problems back to a different level of dispersed ownership at the IPF level. If so, critics can contend that the state should focus instead on sales to serious owners who can buy controlling or near controlling blocks (and at most distribute the minority interests to the public for free through voucher privatization).

While this question is far from frivolous, it is necessary to assess the costs of concentrated ownership, particularly in transitional economies. Among these costs are the following:

1. The Loss of Liquid Capital Markets

If equity ownership is deliberately concentrated, the remaining minority ownership may be insufficient to maintain a liquid equity market. In addition, the risk that the majority owner will expropriate over time the remaining value of the minority owners will further deter active trading or the development of liquid markets. For transitional economies, this means in turn the loss of Western portfolio investors (e.g., mutual and pension funds that can basically invest only in such markets). Here, the contrast between the Czech and Polish securities markets illustrates this cost: Western portfolio investors appear to have fled from Prague Stock Exchange to the Warsaw Stock Exchange. In Poland, while it is very debatable whether government-run NIFs will be efficient monitors, it is highly unlikely that they will loot portfolio firms (as Harvard Capital appears to have). Thus, Western portfolio investors are safer in Poland (even if the upside proves to be lower on economic growth).

Why should we care about the fate of Western portfolio investors? No one could reasonably suggest that transitional economies should design their ownership structure with the interests of portfolio investors chiefly in mind. But the presence of such portfolio investors (foreign and domestic) increases the possi-

---

[121] For a fuller statement of this perspective, see Shleifer, Andrei and Robert W. Vishny 'A Survey of Corporate Governance' *Journal of Finance* 52 (1997) 737.

bility that privatized firms could finance themselves in the future through lower-cost equity offerings (instead of through reliance on higher-cost and riskier debt financings). In effect, this lowers the cost of corporate capital. More generally, there is some evidence that success in creating a domestic equity market will result in greater economic growth.[122] In this light, the hidden cost in abandoning minority investors to the untender mercies of an unregulated market is lower economic growth. The recent slowdown in Czech economic growth may well be attributable to other causes, but the possibility of a causal relationship also exists.

2. Political Legitimacy: The Stake in the Market Argument

Few forces or trends are irreversible. In a number of formerly socialist countries, the old socialists have made at least a partial political comeback. The extent to which they can undo (or even wish to undo) economic reforms installed in the early 1990s may depend heavily on the degree to which the citizenry perceives itself to have an interest in a market economy. In this light, voucher privatization can be viewed as a political compromise that aligned the self-interests of a majority of Czech citizens with a market economy in general (and the Prague Stock Exchange specifically). Of course, such an alignment also means that citizens will be dissatisfied if their stock ownership is essentially expropriated by majority owners.

In addition, the alternative of selling formerly state-owned enterprises to strategic buyers for cash risks serious political dangers for any regime conducting such sales. If the strategic owners are foreign, a chauvinistic reaction is predictable (such proposed sales were viewed in the Czech Republic as the equivalent of "selling the national silver" and consequently rejected). Sales to domestic buyers raise equivalent dangers of political scandals with charges of favoritism and payoffs. To be sure, an open auction approach may reduce these dangers, but not all large enterprises can be feasibly sold at auction. In any event, giving citizens a "stake in the commonwealth" as voucher privatization does may yield political benefits that can offset its inefficiencies.

All these comments do not mean that concentrated ownership will not still result. But how it results may be the critical issue. The arrival of concentrated ownership through systematic self-dealing carries far greater costs than its attainment through tender offers, mergers, and a corporate control market. In this light, possibly the wisest regulatory reform that the Czech Republic has recently

---

[122] Joseph Stiglitz, chief economist for the World Bank, has argued in this context that "the total economic cost [of an unregulated capital market] is enormous," and some analysts estimate that Czech GDP growth would be up to 2 percentage points higher per year if it had "a properly regulated capital market." See 'Survey-Czech Industry and Finance' *The Financial Times* May 14, 1997, 1.

installed may have been its decision in 1996 to require that purchases over specified thresholds (50%, 66 2/3%, and 75%) in any public company be made by means of a universal tender offer at the average price over the prior six months.[123] This step seemed to follow the British rules on takeovers, which have long required a shareholder seeking to acquire more than 30% to do so by a tender offer for all the remaining shares.[124] In Britain, partial acquisitions above 30% are impossible—unless the minority chooses not to tender its shares. Spain and Australia have also followed the British approach, and a proposed EEC directive on company law has recently advocated generalizing this approach.[125]

A European consensus appears then to be developing on the desirability of a mandatory bid (presumably at the highest price at which shares in the company have been recently purchased) once a specified threshold has been crossed. Although this approach is vulnerable to the objection that if the bidder must pay all shareholders the same price, it may sometimes be unable to pay a control premium to the incumbent group holding control (who may prefer as a result not to sell in order to continue to enjoy the private benefits of control). Thus, some efficient transfer of control may be blocked by this equal sharing rule. Still, this objection has less practical matter in the Czech context, where the threshold has been set at 50% (thus clearly permitting a control premium to be paid).

IV. Establishing Effective IPF Corporate Governance

If minority rights are to be protected, the greater challenge is today at the IPF level. Whatever the corporate governance problems at the level of the newly privatized Czech corporations, they are dwarfed by those at the IPF level for three distinct reasons: first, with the appearance of unit trusts in the second wave of privatization, many funds are simply beyond shareholder control because their shareholders lack any voting rights. Second, even in the case of IPFs organized as joint stock companies (rather than as unit trusts), investment companies have caused their controlled IPFs to enter into non-cancelable multi-year management contracts with them for periods typically equaling or exceeding six years. Third, many of the IPFs organized in the first wave of privatization have become inactive shells, with limited assets and an investment company interested and able to do little more than collect its 2% annual fee until it effectively exhausts the IPF's assets. Still, other entities founded as IPFs have simply surrendered

---

[123] See Wallace, supra n. 96.

[124] See DeMott, Deborah A. 'Comparative Dimensions of Takeover Regulation' 65 *Wash. U. L.Q.* 69, 93-9 (1987).

[125] See Elhauge, Einer 'Toward a European Sale of Control Doctrine' 41 *Am. J. Comp. L.* 627 (1993); see also Lüttmann, Ruth 'Changes of Corporate Control and Mandatory Bids' *International Review of Law and Economics* 12 (1992) 497.

their licenses as investment funds and converted into holding companies (after insiders, as in Harvard Capital's case, first purchased a controlling interest). Many of the remaining IPFs are trading at apparent discounts of up to 80% from their assumed net asset value. In an efficient capital market, such companies would likely be the target of hostile takeovers. But hostile takeover of IPFs are substantially chilled under Czech law by the legal rule that provides that neither IPFs nor investment companies may "purchase participation certificates of other unit trusts or shares of other investment companies and investment funds, or shares of persons whose interest in such investment companies or funds exceeds 25 (twenty-five) percent."[126]

1. Voting Rights in Unit Trusts

Should unit trusts be permitted? Or should their shareholders somehow be legislatively accorded voting rights? Clearly, the sudden popularity of the unit trust form seems more attributable to their character as tame investment vehicles immune from takeovers and control contests.[127] Yet, on a worldwide basis, unit trusts are a well-known investment vehicle, and thus it may seem difficult to justify a prophylactic rule prohibiting an investment form widely used throughout the U.K. and Europe. Why then should they be restricted in the Czech Republic?

One response might be that there is a basic distinction between the unit trust, as known in most securities markets, and its counterpart in the Czech market. Typically, unit trusts are open-ended, meaning that there is an immediate right of redemption. Thus, unit trust holders may lack voting rights, but they have an equally (and possibly more effective) means of disciplining a substandard management: unit trust holders can withdraw their investment (usually on a daily basis) at a price determined by their proportionate interest in the unit trust's net asset value. In such a world, unit trust holders have effectively traded "voice" for "exit."

Such an exchange may make sense elsewhere, but exit is lacking in the Czech market. Not only is there currently no right to immediate redemption (even in the case of funds that will eventually become open-ended), but the thinness of the Czech market makes secondary trading at best a sporadic phenomenon. Reliable financial data about the net asset value of an IPF also remains generally unavailable (with some exceptions). Given their limited ability to trade IPF shares (in

---

[126] See § 24(7) of The Investment Companies and Investment Funds Act (Act No. 248/1992 Coll. of 28 April 1992).

[127] Proponents of the unit trust cited to us two cost savings from its use: it eliminates the need for a costly annual shareholders' meeting and for boards of directors. True as this may be, the costs involved seem modest.

the case of a closed-end fund) or to obtain redemption (in the case of an open-end fund), Czech shareholders in IPFs today lack both voice and exit.

Hence, legislative correction may be appropriate. In any event, the Czech experience might lead planners in other privatization programs to delay the use of the unit trust format until their equity market had matured. At least over the short run, there are strong arguments that the joint stock company form should be preferred.

2. Long-Term Management Contracts

Even when there are voting rights (that is, when the joint stock company form is used), voting rights can still be trivialized by the use of long-term management contracts. As noted above, six-year and longer management contracts between an IPF and its investment company have become common, and these can effectively divest the shareholders of an IPF of any meaningful right to vote.

The U.S. contrast here is instructive. Under U.S. securities law, the investment adviser to an "investment company" (a term which includes all publicly offered mutual funds) must enter into a written contract that "precisely describes all compensation to be paid thereunder"[128] and which "shall continue in effect for a period more than two years from the date of its execution, *only* so long as such continuance is specifically approved at least annually by the board of directors or by vote of a majority of the outstanding voting securities of such company."[129] Moreover, the contract must be terminable at any time (without penalty) by a vote of the mutual fund board of directors,[130] and it must terminate automatically "in the event of its assignment" of the management contract.[131]

In short, annual approval of the management contract (after the second year) is the norm. Intended to promote accountability, this requirement in theory allows an IPF to escape a weak investment company which founded it. Should Czech law adopt this requirement? Because the institution of independent outside directors is not well developed to this point in the Czech environment, it might be more logical to require that both the board and the shareholders must annually approve the contract.

Still, this response leads to two further problems: first, some investment companies now own substantial percentages of their own IPFs as a result of share repurchases pursuant to guarantees made at the marketing stage. Thus, for shareholder approval to be meaningful, it would have to be defined in this context to

---

[128] See Investment Company Act of 1940, § 15(a)(1), 15 U.S.C. § 80a-1 et seq.

[129] Investment Company Act of 1940, § 15(a)(2) (emphasis added).

[130] Investment Company Act of 1940, § 15(a)(3).

[131] Investment Company Act of 1940, § 15(a)(4).

mean independent shareholder approval (excluding the shares held by the interested party). Second, if shareholder approval is withheld, how is a replacement investment company to be chosen? Here, the problem is that even independent shareholders might be threatened or coerced into approving the existing management contract if they feared that the consequence of a rejection of the contract would be that their IPF would be abandoned and left without any investment advisers (even for an interim period). Of course, willing replacements would be at hand in any competitive market. But how are they to be chosen? Many mechanisms could work (a proxy contest, an auction, an obligation on the part of the board to find a replacement, judicial intervention, etc.), but some mechanism needs to be specified legislatively.

Similarly, the problem of sponsor ownership of the fund also invites legislative attention. It seems inconsistent to place a ceiling on the percentage of IPF ownership permitted in a portfolio company, but then allow the sponsor to hold a controlling stake in its own IPF. On the other hand, some sponsor ownership could serve to align interests between the sponsor and the other shareholders and to induce greater investment in corporate monitoring.

Nonetheless, any practical assessment of the likelihood that shareholder democracy can be made to work at the IPF level must be pessimistic. Candidly, even with the additional regulatory controls provided under U.S. law, mutual fund shareholders have remained passive, and the large mutual fund families (Vanguard, Fidelity, Putnam, etc.) have generally dominated the boards of their funds. In this light, two alternative modes of control need to be considered: (a) corporate control contests, and (b) increased state oversight.

a. Corporate Control Contests

The Czech IPF market structure seems plainly in need of efficient consolidation. Several hundred IPFs still remain, and many are powerless, ineffectual, and small; some are mere inactive shells. Many will become insolvent in due course, as administration expenses and the annual management fee gradually consume their remaining assets. How then can their efficient consolidation be encouraged?

The simplest answer is that, if legal obstacles are removed, consolidation is a natural process. Many firms today are interested in acquiring control of inactive IPFs. One incentive is the significant discount at which many IPFs trade in relation to the actual market value of their investment portfolios. Secondly, other investment companies may want to control an IPF founded by a now inactive investment company in order to outflank the 20% ownership ceiling (which applies to all IPFs "established and administered by that investment company").[132] If an investment company can form an alliance with other IPFs not "established" or "administered" by it, it can thus partially evade the 20% limitation.

During the early 1990s, some groups sought to obtain control of less active IPFs for both these reasons. A Ministry of Finance official estimated for us that the purchase of as little as 10% of the stock of an IPF (at least one organized as a joint stock company) could confer control.[133] But investment companies and IPFs are effectively excluded from this process by § 24(7) of The Investment Companies and Investment Funds Act, which precludes both IPFs and investment companies from purchasing shares in other IPFs.[134]

The rationale for such a sweeping prohibition is obscure. It might well be advisable to preclude an investment company from buying shares of its own IPFs, because of the asymmetric information it likely possesses. But precluding only IPFs and investment companies from investing in other IPFs makes little sense, particularly when individuals and other financial institutions are not similarly precluded. If the fear is that existing IPF shareholders will be over-reached or coerced, this problem might be addressed by requiring any person who acquires some threshold level of an IPF (say 10%) to make disclosure to the market and to buy further shares only in a prescribed manner (possibly pursuant to a tender offer or possibly after simply stating the number of shares it intends to acquire within a specified period). Indeed, to the extent that individuals and others are currently purchasing control of smaller, inactive IPFs, permitting other IPFs to do so simply increases the demand for their shares and possibly creates a desirable auction market, thereby improving the price to the original IPF shareholder.

More generally, sensible policy planning should seek additional ways to encourage the consolidation of small IPFs. As a practical matter, only IPFs with sizeable holdings obtain representation on the boards of their portfolio companies, and thus smaller IPFs are essentially "voiceless." Although smaller IPFs can consolidate their portfolios, the 10% diversification requirement implies that a very small IPF will not be able to hold sufficient shares in any company to obtain board representation. Particularly when an IPF cannot obtain board representation, there is little for its investment company to do—except collect their 2% (or so) annual management fee. To be sure, a smaller IPF could contract out for expert management assistance, and a single investment company could efficiently manage a dozen or more small IPFs, thereby achieving economies of

---

[132] See § 24(5) of The Investment Company and Investment Funds Act (Act No. 248/1992 Coll. of 28 April 1992).

[133] This assumes, of course, that there is not a long-term management contract between the IPF and its founding investment company that cannot be canceled.

[134] The text of this statute is set forth in the text at note 126 supra.

scale and aggregating sufficient stock to achieve board representation. But this is a largely illusory hope, because the original investment company has no incentive to surrender any of its annual management fee. Conceivably, management contracts could be assigned (in return for some premium paid to the original management company), but no such market appears to have developed. If it did, special safeguards might be needed.[135]

A market remedy to encourage consolidation could be created. For example, legislation could permit any IPF to make a merger proposal for a "small" IPF (as defined) under which the small IPF would be merged into the larger, "proposing" IPF in return for shares of the latter if some level—say two-thirds—of the smaller IPF's shareholders approved the merger. To be sure, such a process would risk conflict of interests. Sometimes, the larger IPF might make such a proposal believing that the smaller IPF's assets were undervalued. Conversely, the investment company controlling the larger IPF might have an incentive to overpay for the smaller IPF, because its annual management fee would be based on gross assets in the new, merged IPF. Thus, an investment company could rationally pursue an inefficient policy of growth and size maximization that injured its own shareholders. As a result, both funds should be required to approve any such merger by an equivalent supermajority of disinterested shareholders.

Finally, a desirable congruence might be achieved between the legal rules applicable to corporations and those applicable to IPFs if any IPF were permitted to buy up to 30% of another—and then could proceed further only by making an "any-and-all" bid for 100% of the remaining shares at the highest price recently paid by it. Again, this would generalize the British takeover code, which seems on the whole to have worked smoothly.

b. Increased Oversight

When one compares the Czech and Polish approaches toward investment funds, one seeks two extreme, indeed polar positions: the Czechs permitted open access and thus wound up at one point with over 500 IPFs, a number well beyond their effective ability to oversee; in contrast, the Poles have permitted only 15 NIFs to be formed, each staffed by governmental appointees. Whether the latter is sufficient to truly unleash market forces is as questionable as the wisdom of permitting more funds than can be supervised.

---

[135] Serious legal and policy questions exist as to whether a fiduciary should be able to sell its position to another at a profit. See *Rosenfeld v. Black* 445 F.2d 1337 (2d Cir. 1971) (mutual funds may recapture profit made by investment advisor on sale of its advisory contract to new investment advisers). Such transactions are today allowed under U.S. securities law, but are subject to special judicial scrutiny and procedural safeguards.

Obviously, a mean can be struck between these two positions. While no number is inherently optimal, the real issue is the number that can be effectively overseen. Different degrees of oversight can also be imagined between complete control and no control. For example, the government could appoint two directors to a ten-director board. This approach was sometimes used in 19th-century America (then a transitional economy) for corporations that carried on business activities believed to be partly "public" in character. (e.g., banks, bridges, insurance, etc.).

V. Ensuring a Competitive Market: The Problem of Cross-Ownership

From a distance, the most surprising and striking fact about Czech privatization is the level of cross-ownership that resulted. Today, a limited group of financial institutions, which are still subject to state control through partial ownership, control through their wholly owned investment company subsidiaries the largest IPFs, which in turn hold (in the aggregate) controlling positions in much of Czech industry (including positions in these same financial institutions). Critics argue that Czech privatization is thus only "skin deep".

It was not supposed to work this way. The Investment Companies and Investment Funds Act seemed intent on preventing cross-ownership of this character when it provided:

> "An investment company or investment fund established by a bank or insurance bank may not purchase the shares of its founder, its depository, or other banks and insurance banks."[136]

Unfortunately, although the intent of this language seems clear, it was easily sidestepped by the simple evasion of banks forming wholly owned subsidiaries, which in turn established IPFs. Thus, at least arguably, the bank was not the founder of the IPF, and the IPF could purchase the bank's shares. Moreover, such an IPF (because it was not in theory "founded" by a bank) could also buy the shares of other banks.

Whatever the intent of this statutory language, the first lesson from this experience is the need for literalistic precision in civil law legal regimes where neither the bar nor the judiciary is guided by any sense of legislative intent. Perhaps the result would have been different if the same provision had read:

> "An investment company or investment fund organized, established, or controlled, directly or indirectly, by a bank or insurance bank may not purchase the shares of its founder or of any company holding direct or indirect control over it, or of other companies directly or indirectly controlled by, or under the common control with, such a company, or other banks and insurance banks."

---

[136] See Section 24 (11) of The Investment Companies and Investment Funds Act (Act No. 248/1992 Coll. of 28 April (1992).

Such a definition would predictably work in a common law legal regime, but in a civil law country, an elaborate, detailed definition of "indirect control" still seems necessary (and would presumably look to whether any parent or grand-parent possessed the power through stock ownership, contract or otherwise, "to direct or cause the direction of the management or policies" of the other company).[137]

Whatever the level of specificity needed, an adequate definition *could* presumably be drafted to prevent a repetition of the Czech experience. More debatable is whether the level of cross-ownership that actually emerged in Czech privatization was accidental and unplanned or rather the product of an implicit conspiracy or tacit acquiescence by governmental authorities who feared one or more of the following: radical change, loss of governmental influence, or the emergence of new charismatic economic actors whose future conduct could not be easily predicted or controlled. Some have suggested that the government originally believed its privatization program was dependent on the cooperation of the banks in marketing vouchers to the Czech population. Arguably, only the major banks could reach the citizenry in rural areas and hold their confidence. Although this premise seems overstated in hindsight, it could explain the willingness of Czech governmental officials to blink at the obvious evasion of banks using an intermediate tier subsidiary to escape the impact of § 24(11) of The Investment Companies and Investment Funds Act. The government's fear might have been that unless major financial institutions sponsored IPFs, privati-zation would result in a vastly dispersed stock distribution without sufficient concentration for shareholders to pressure for necessary restructuring. Alterna-tively, the appearance of Harvard Capital may have scared and threatened both the government and the financial establishment. Together, they agreed to blink at the law to protect banking institutions from a potential raider whose inclinations were unclear and integrity unproven.

All such scenarios are speculative. The issue for the future is what, if any-thing, should be done about the level of cross-ownership that emerged. Two distinct policy concerns should be acknowledged. First, the existing level of cross-ownership coupled with the government's residual ownership in the banks arguably leaves too much decision-making power in the government's hands. As some see it, privatization has not yet fully occurred because the government has not truly cut the strings by which it can make its puppets dance. Second, cross-ownership raises the prospect of collusion among firms. If the same IPFs and investment companies control the major banks and also major firms in other sectors of the economy, it is possible that such control could be used to share information, restrain competition, and engineer a polite oligopoly. Indeed, to the

---

[137] See SEC Rule 405, 17 C.F.R. 230. 405. A rebuttable presumption might also be estab-lished that 25% direct or indirect stock ownership was sufficient to confer control.

extent that the major banks are also lenders to the major industrial firms, their self-interest is not for fierce, cost-cutting competitive battles to break out, but for stable, sustained growth and shared markets. In particular, because the banks (and their controlled investment companies) do not own much equity in the industrial sector, but rather simply advise IPFs for a fee, their economic center-of-gravity is that of a risk-adverse creditor with a distaste for uncertainty and volatility.

In principle, what steps could be taken? Given the very limited liquidity in the Czech stock market, it seems infeasible to order bank-controlled IPFs to sell all (or most) of their investments in bank and insurance stocks. Indeed, the only persons who could purchase the investments (at a punitively large discount) are the private IPFs (such as Harvard Capital) who would thereby also be placed in a position of controlling competing economic rivals. Moreover, the economic cost of such a radical divestiture policy might be borne by Czech shareholders generally—particularly if it produced a general decline in market price levels.

A simpler, but no less radical, reform might be to spin off the management companies from the banks. Banks and insurance companies could be required to dividend their shareholdings in their controlled investment companies to their own shareholders (possibly excluding the NPF). The result would leave the investment companies in control of many banks, but the banks would no longer be in control of investment companies. To soften this provision, banks could be exempted from this spin-off requirement if (within some period) their investment companies divested their bank holdings so as to fall below some minimal level.

Even these steps are incomplete. Investment companies, even once separated from their banking parents, are in a problematic position when they can hold seats on the boards of competitors. In the U.S., such interlocking boards are severely restricted by the Clayton Antitrust Act, which (subject to some exceptions) prohibits any person from serving as a director of "any two or more corporations . . . if such corporations are or shall have been . . . competitors . . ."[138] Some Czech IPFs seem to be complying with such a policy by not assigning directors to competing firms. What remains uncertain, however, is whether the investment company can still use its board positions to restrict competition between natural rivals.

Adoption of the U.S. pro-competitive approach (either by requiring a divestiture by banks of their investment companies or by restricting an IPF from holding seats on the boards of competitors) would seemingly entail a fundamental rejection of the German model of corporate governance. Unlike the United States, German banks do have representatives on the boards of competitors, and German banks do have interlocking stock ownership. Any Czech divestiture

---

[138] See 15 U.S.C. § 19. See, e.g., *Protectoseal Co. v. Baranick* 484 F.2d 585, 589 (7h Cir. 1973).

proposal by which banks would be separated from their investment companies would seemingly sacrifice the informal synergies and arguably superior monitoring capacity that the German system of corporate governance in theory creates. Indeed, even the firewall policy that the Ministry of Finance seemingly favors seems inconsistent with the conventional understanding of the German system under which a "universal bank" pools the information it acquires as a creditor and as an equity holder and employs this information to reward or discipline management from its position on the Supervisory Board.

Thus, a fundamental policy choice is posed here: Should Czech IPFs be structured along the German model (in which case, the only reform needed might be to restrict one bank from controlling through its IPFs a substantial block in a competitor) or should firewalls and other informational barriers be placed between IPFs and their indirect banking parents? In short, is the close relationship between banks and IPFs a vice or a virtue?

The more skeptical view of the German banking system's impact on German corporate governance holds that it supplies critical industries with a politely collusive "system of coordination by banker".[139] To be sure, others see it differently, and the debate over the relative attractions of the German versus alternative models of corporate governance will undoubtedly continue. However, even those who remain proponents of the German universal banking system have recently stressed that it works precisely to the extent that German banks hold large equity positions in their debtor clients.[140] But this is the critical difference between the German and Czech system. Only by acquiring the shares of their own IPFs do Czech banks typically acquire an indirect equity interest in their portfolio companies.

In fairness, if the Czech system does not truly approximate the German universal banking system, it is even more removed from the U.S./U.K. system of stock market monitoring. Market transparency has long been absent in the Czech market environment, where most trading occurs off market and without any obligation for contemporaneous trade reporting. Nor are accounting or disclosure systems well developed. In addition, because closed-end fund investors cannot flee unsuccessful funds and unit trusts make shareholder voting irrelevant, there is little discipline over the market intermediaries. Given inefficient markets, weak techniques such as incentives fees and stock compensation, which may work adequately in the United States, may only produce a stronger incentive for

---

[139] See Edwards and Fischer, supra n. 5, 239 (citing Shonfield, Andrew *Modern Capitalism* 261 (Oxford 1965)).

[140] See Gorton and Schmid, supra n. 5, 30 ("Our evidence shows that in 1974 German banks improved the performance of German firms to the extent that they held the firms' equity"). However, they were unable to detect a significant relation for their 1985 sample (p. 31).

stock manipulation in the Czech market. The debate then between the German and U.S. models may have to be framed in terms of which is more obtainable.

F. Conclusion

A long article deserves a short summary. The Czech experience is problematic. Its initial success was more than counterbalanced by its later regulatory failures. Some will undoubtedly view this as evidence that privatization funds (and voucher privatization generally) are unworkable and should be abandoned. This, however, overreads the evidence from the Czech experience. Unsurprisingly, the Czech experience primarily shows that if people with control over other people's money are not watched, they will embezzle. Phrased more generally, the market does not automatically cure agency cost problems, and intelligent regulation must fill this gap.

The danger in light of the Czech experience is that overcompensation may occur, with the state permitting only weak or "tame" privatization funds that are so overregulated as to be unable to bring market discipline to bear on firms that desperately need it. It is too soon to evaluate the Polish experience, but its form of privatization fund clearly risks this danger.

The most important practical step in light of the Czech experience is to tighten regulation of IPFs by generally prohibiting self-dealing transactions between the IPF (and its affiliates) and the portfolio company. The only exception (born of necessity) might be bank loans from a banking parent to the portfolio company, and in other countries, the better solution might be to preclude banks from sponsoring IPFs.

The other unexpected finding from the Czech experience that policy planners elsewhere must consider is the surprising persistence of a residual state owner- ship, which cross-ownership and the centrality of the banking system magnify. The state clearly does not wither away of its own volition and can maintain its influence in low visibility ways.

Today, the future evolution of the Czech corporate governance system seems to be headed in two directions at once: (1) toward a more Germanic system of corporate governance with greater concentration of ownership, which is largely impelled by the inadequacy of the legal protections for minority shareholders; and (2) toward a more American-style system of securities regulation with the creation of an American-style SEC in the hopes of luring back Western portfolio investors, who have largely disinvested in the Czech market.

If it is still premature to predict how far the evolution in either direction will go, the tension cannot be ignored. Ideally, IPFs can bridge this divide by creating an investment vehicle that can function effectively in a world of concentrated ownership. Abandonment of this possibility implies a concomitant abandonment of liquid capital markets, which may be an important catalyst for economic growth. Nonetheless, if the failure of the IPF need not yet be conceded, its promise has clearly not yet been realized. The one policy option that has not yet been attempted is close regulation of this new financial intermediary. Given the alternatives, it seems the lowest cost option.

Discussion Report

With respect to the Czech privatization experience, one commentator raised the question of whether the banks' informal role as a "shield" for investors from market manipulation could be supplemented by explicit regulation of the banking sector, drawing attention to the fact that the Czech banking industry is facing serious credibility problems in the international arena. Recently, the Czech Republic has been downgraded by international rating agencies. On this issue, Professor *Coffee* reported that Czech banking regulation was greatly insufficient. While there are still no rules concerning minority ownership, banks—whose monitoring activity has been very limited to date—seem to at least protect the investors from the worst market manipulation and abuses. In his view, active restructuring would be required in a format such as is provided to MBO/LBO participants in the U.S. But reliance on banks and their acquired knowledge of firms proves to be a still more successful tool for privatization than the concept adopted in Poland, where 15 government-sponsored privatization funds were founded in order to keep the private banks out of the process. The firms were chosen by the Polish authorities not according to market forces, but on a discretionary basis. A German commentator observed that bank involvement in the privatization had a significant reputational effect and may generally evoke a positive share price reaction. Another commentator concluded that the Polish example demonstrated the general need for a certain amount of bank involvement in the privatization process of transitional economies.

Chapter 3: Securities Regulation

Empowering Investors: A Market Approach to Securities Regulation

ROBERTA ROMANO, New Haven[*]

This article contends that the current U.S. approach to securities regulation is mistaken. It advocates a market-oriented approach of competitive federalism that would expand the role of the states in securities regulation and would fundamentally reconceptualize the regulatory scheme. Under a system of competitive federalism for securities regulation, only one sovereign will have jurisdiction over all transactions in the securities of a corporation that involve the issuer or its agents and investors: the sovereign chosen by the issuer from among the federal government, the fifty states, or foreign nations. The aim is to replicate for the securities setting the benefits produced by state competition for corporate charters—a responsive legal regime that has tended to maximize share value. A competitive legal market supplants a monopolist federal agency in the fashioning of regulation, it will produce rules more aligned with the preferences of investors, whose decisions drive the capital market. Competitive federalism for U.S. securities regulation also has important implications for international securities regulation. The jurisdictional principle applicable to domestic securities transactions is equally applicable: foreign issuers selling shares in the United States would be able to opt out of the federal securities laws and choose the law of another nation, such as their country of incorporation, or of a U.S. state, to govern those U.S. transactions.

Contents

[*] I have benefited from comments by Barry Adler, Anne Alstott, Yakov Amihud, Ian Ayres, Boris Bittker, John Coates, Ehud Ekamar, Boris Feldman, Merritt Fox, Henry Hansmann, Howell Jackson, Marcel Kahan, Alvin Klevorick, Paul Mahoney, Geoffrey Miller, Peter Schuck, Alan Schwartz, Joel Seligman, Linda Silberman, Michael Solimine, and participants at the Harvard Law School Seminar in Law and Economics, Yale Law School Faculty workshop, the University of California at San Diego Political Science Department Law and Behavioral Studies Seminar, a seminar at the Commissione Nazionale per le Società e la Borsa (CONSOB), Rome, and the Symposium on Comparative Corporate Governance held at the Max-Planck-Institut, Hamburg. A version of this article appears in 107 *Yale L.J.* No. 8 (1998).

A. Introduction

The U.S. securities laws have repeatedly been assailed as burdensome or ineffective. Reform efforts have conversely been attacked for undermining an effective mechanism for shareholder discipline of management. Moreover, even reformers have been dissatisfied with the effectiveness of their product. For example, after enacting the Private Securities Litigation Reform Act in 1995,[1] members of Congress became concerned that their effort to rein in frivolous private lawsuits under the federal securities laws was being circumvented by state court filings and introduced legislation to preempt such action.[2] There is some validity to their concern: in a report to President Clinton on the impact of

---

[1] Pub. L. No. 104-67, 109 Stat. 737 (1995) (codified at 15 U.S.C. §§ 77a et seq.).

[2] See H.R. 1653, 105th Cong., 1st Sess. (1997) (sponsored by Rep. Thomas Campbell and six co-sponsors); H.R. 1689, 105th Cong., 1st Sess. (1997) (sponsored by Rep. Richard White and 134 co-sponsors).

that Act, the Securities and Exchange Commission (SEC) cited preliminary studies indicating a decrease in federal and increase in state court filings.[3]

This article contends that the current legislative approach to securities regulation is mistaken, and that preemption is not the solution to frivolous lawsuits. It advocates instead a market-oriented approach of competitive federalism that would expand, not reduce, the role of the states in securities regulation.[4] It thereby would fundamentally reconceptualize our regulatory approach and is at odds with both sides of the debate over the 1995 Act, which have sought to use national laws as a weapon to beat down their opponents' position by monopolizing the regulatory field.

The market approach to securities regulation advocated in this article takes as its paradigm the successful experience of the U.S. states in corporate law, in which the fifty states and the District of Columbia compete for the business of corporate charters. There is a substantial body of literature on this particular manifestation of U.S. federalism that indicates that shareholders have benefited from the federal system of corporate law, by its production of corporate codes that, for the most part, maximize share value.[5] This article proposes extending the competition among states for corporate charters to two of the three principal components of federal securities regulation: the registration of securities and the related continuous disclosure regime for issuers; and the antifraud provisions which police that system (in short, the components involving securities transactions' claims by investors against issuers of securities). The regulatory regime for market professionals is not included in the proposed reform. This reform can be implemented by modifying the federal securities laws in favor of a menu-approach to securities regulation under which firms elect whether to be covered by federal law or the securities law of a specified state, such as their state of incorporation.

Under a system of competitive federalism for securities regulation, only one sovereign will have jurisdiction over all transactions in the securities of a corporation that involve the issuer or its agents and investors. The aim is to

---

[3] See U.S. Sec. & Exch. Comm'n 'Report to the President and the Congress on the First Year of Practice Under the Private Securities Litigation Reform Act of 1995' pt IV at 22 & pt VII at 72 (Apr. 1997) (summarizing study by National Economic Research Associates of securities litigation filings after the Act). Joseph Grundfest and Michael Perino also document a shift to state court filings. See Grundfest, Joseph A. and Michael A. Perino 'Securities Litigation Reform: The First Year's Experience' (Stanford Law School, John M. Olin Program in Law and Economics Working Paper no. 140, 1997). More recent data, however, suggest a reversal of this trend, with state filings declining and federal filings increasing in the first half of 1997. See '1995 Private Securities Litigation Reform Act of 1995: Federal Securities Class Action Filings Rise as State Filings Fall, NERA Finds' 29 *Sec. Reg. & L. Rep.* (BNA) 1001 (July 18, 1997).

[4] See also Gerum/Wagner (this volume Ch. 5: Sec. E) who deal with the related question of harmonization versus competition with respect to EU law.

[5] See Romano, Roberta *The Genius of American Corporate Law* (Washington, D.C. 1993).

replicate for the securities setting the benefits produced by state competition for corporate charters—a responsive legal regime that has tended to maximize share value—and thereby eliminate the frustration experienced at efforts to reform the national regime. As a competitive legal market supplants a monopolist federal agency in the fashioning of regulation, it will produce rules more aligned with the preferences of investors, whose decisions drive the capital market.

Competitive federalism for U.S. securities regulation also has important implications for international securities regulation. The jurisdictional principle applicable to domestic securities transactions is equally applicable to international securities transactions: foreign issuers selling shares in the United States can opt out of the federal securities laws and choose the law of another nation, such as their country of incorporation, or of a U.S. state, to govern transactions in their securities in the United States. The federal securities laws would also, of course, not apply to transactions by U.S. investors abroad in the shares of firms that opt for a non-U.S. securities domicile. This approach limits the reach of U.S. laws to corporations affirmatively opting to be covered by U.S. law, whether they be U.S.- or non-U.S.-based firms, notwithstanding rulings and efforts to the contrary by the SEC and U.S. courts.[6] It therefore will put an end to the ever-expanding extraterritorial reach of U.S. securities regulation to include transactions abroad involving foreign firms, as long as there are any U.S. shareholders or U.S. effects.

Stemming the trend of extraterritorial application of U.S. law will not harm U.S. investors because they have, in fact, often been disadvantaged by the expansion of U.S. securities jurisdiction. For example, to avoid the application of U.S. law, foreign firms have frequently explicitly excluded U.S. investors from takeover offers, and hence they miss out on bid premiums.[7] In addition, adoption of the market approach will facilitate foreign firms' access to capital, as they will be able to issue securities in the United States without complying with U.S. disclosure and accounting rules that differ substantially from their home rules, a requirement that has been a significant deterrent to listings.[8] This consequence of the proposed modification of U.S. law will also benefit U.S. investors, who will no longer have to incur the higher transaction costs of purchasing shares abroad in order to make direct investments in foreign firms.

The market approach to securities regulation is a natural extension of the literature on state competition for corporate charters, and commentators, recog-

---

[6] For a discussion of these efforts in the context of securities regulation of takeover bids, see Pinto, Arthur R. 'The Internationalization of the Hostile Takeover Market: Its Implications for Choice of Law in Corporate and Securities Law' 16 *Brook. J. Int'l L.* 55 (1990).

[7] See Pinto, supra n. 6, 67-76.

[8] Edwards, Franklin R. 'Listing of Foreign Securities on U.S. Exchanges' in: Lehn, Kenneth and Robert Kamphius (eds) *Modernizing US Securities Regulation: Economic and Legal Perspectives* 53, 53 (Burr Ridge, Ill. 1992).

nizing the possibility of this extension, have occasionally mentioned it as an alternative to the current system of securities regulation.[9] This article advances those earlier suggestions by making a systematic case for competitive federalism by articulating the rationales for the proposal and crafting the mechanics of its implementation. The position advocated in the article—elimination of the exclusive mandatory character of most of the federal securities laws—may seem on first impression to many readers surprising, if not unrealistic or worse. In my judgment a compelling case can be made on the substantive merits of the proposal. There may be an understandable desire to discount the need for the proposal because of the vibrancy of U.S. capital markets and the calls for piecemeal reform rather than comprehensive revamping of the current regime by issuers and investors. This would be a mistake. While U.S. capital markets are among the largest and most liquid in the world, it is incorrect to attribute this fact to the federal regime. U.S. capital markets were the largest and most liquid global markets at the turn of the century before the federal regime was established, and their share of global capitalization has declined markedly over the past two decades,[10] facts at odds with the contention that the current federal regime is the reason for the depth of U.S. capital markets. The absence of calls for comprehensive reform is a function of a lack of imagination rather than evidence that the current regulatory apparatus does not produce deadweight losses.[11] Blind adherence to the securities regulation status quo imposes real costs on investors and firms, and there is a better solution.

Some may, in fact, conclude that the proposal does not go far enough, and that all government interference in capital markets, whether federal or state, should be abolished. I believe that the intermediate position advocated in this article is the more sensible public policy than eliminating all government involvement. This is because state competition does not foreclose the possibility of deregula-

---

[9] See, e.g., MacIntosh, Jeffrey G. 'International Securities Regulation: Of Competition, Cooperation, Convergence and Cartelization' 31-2 (University of Toronto Faculty of Law, Law and Economics Working Paper WPS-48, 1996); Romano, supra n. 5, 99-100, 107-8; Macey, Jonathan R. 'Administrative Agency Obsolescence and Interest Group Formation: A Case Study of the SEC at Sixty' 15 *Cardozo L. Rev.* 909, 935-6 (1994).

[10] See Solnik, Bruno *International Investments* 168, exhibit 6.1, 3rd edn. (Reading, Mass. 1996) (U.S. share dropped from 57% to 36% from 1974 to 1994). With the rising market, the U.S. share rose to 41% in 1996. See Ibbotson Associates 'AI/RI Global Portfolio Intensive Classroom Program 1997' at Day 1—page 16 (data source: Developed Markets, Morgan Stanley Capital International EAFE and World Perspective January 1996, 5, and Emerging Markets— IFC Emerging Market Data Base, Monthly Review of Emerging Stock Markets, 8.)

[11] Issuers have focused their efforts on removing regulatory authority from the states to the federal level because they have not recognized the possibility of removing the source of the state-level problems of plaintiff forum shopping and burdensome registration requirements. This can be achieved by altering the state jurisdictional rule of investor domicile to that proposed in this article, under which only one state, chosen by the issuer, its securities domicile, will have jurisdiction over all transactions in the firm's securities.

tion should that be desired by investors: a state could adopt a securities regime that delegates regulatory authority over issuers to stock exchanges, just as the current federal regime delegates regulatory authority for market professionals to the stock exchanges and National Association of Securities Dealers (NASD). State competition permits experimentation with purely private regulatory arrangements, while retaining a mechanism to reverse course easily—migration to states that do not adopt such an approach—that is not present if the federal regime is replaced with a purely private one. On a more pragmatic level, there is a more immediate point to the article, to caution against the current impetus to extend the federal government's monopoly over securities regulation and suggest that it would be more fruitful for Congress to rationalize state securities regulation by legislatively altering the multijurisdictional transactional basis of state regulatory authority to an issuer-domicile basis, rather than to supplant it.

The article proceeds as follows. In Part B, a market-based approach to U.S. securities regulation is outlined and the mandatory federal system is critiqued. The rationale for excluding the third component of the federal securities regime, the regulation of market professionals, from the proposal, and comparisons with alternative market-oriented reforms, such as regulation by exchanges, are also provided. Part C discusses details for implementing the proposal, including changing the current choice-of-law rule for securities transactions from one that focuses on the site of the transaction to an issuer-based approach analogous to the internal affairs rule applied in corporate law, and conditioning opting out of the federal regime upon compliance with two procedural requirements that insure the integrity of the investor decisions that drive the regulatory competition: disclosure of the issuer's securities domicile at the time of a security purchase, and a shareholder vote to effectuate a change in securities domicile. The final part extends the proposal to international securities regulation.

B. Competitive Federalism: A Market Approach to Securities Regulation

Although both the states and federal government regulate securities transactions, the current regulatory arrangements are a far cry from competitive federalism. The federal securities regime (the Securities Act of 1933 and the Securities Exchange Act of 1934)[12] applies to all publicly traded firms and is a mandatory system of disclosure regulation bolstered by antifraud provisions. While the federal laws do not preempt all state regulation,[13] states cannot lower the regula-

---

[12] 15 U.S.C. §§ 77a-77bbbb (1994 & Supp.), and 15 U.S.C. §§ 78a-78mm (1994 & Supp.).

[13] Although both statutes originally expressly reserved the rights of states to regulate securities, the 1933 Act was amended in 1996 to preempt state regulation of the registration of publicly traded securities. See National Securities Markets Improvement Act of 1996, § 102, Pub. L. No. 104-290, 110 Stat. 3416, 3417 (1996) (codified at 15 U.S.C. § 77r).

tory standards applicable to firms covered by the federal regime (because its laws are mandatory) and have been prevented from raising the standards on some occasions.[14] As a consequence, the states have essentially abandoned the regulation of public firms to the SEC. In the proposed system of competitive federalism, state and federal regulators will stand on an equal regulatory footing, and firms will be able to choose the applicable regulatory regime.

I. The Essence of Competitive Federalism

A market approach to U.S. securities regulation consists of two prongs that differ from current law. First, a public corporation's coverage under the national securities laws is optional rather than mandatory. Second, the securities transactions of a corporation that elects not to be covered by the national securities laws are regulated by the corporation's selected domicile for securities regulation. This approach is premised on the idea that competition among sovereigns—here the fifty states, District of Columbia, and the federal government (represented primarily by the SEC)—in the production of securities laws will benefit investors in public corporations by facilitating the adoption of regulation aligned with investors' preferences, as has been true of the competitive production of corporation codes. The motivation for the proposal is that no government entity can know better than market participants what regulations are in their interest, particularly as their requirements are continually changing as financial market conditions change, but that competing regulators will make fewer policy mistakes than a monopolistic regulator as competition harnesses the incentives of the market to regulatory institutions.

Regulatory competition is desirable because when the choice of investments includes variation in legal regimes, promoters of firms will find that they can obtain a lower cost of capital by choosing the regime that investors prefer. For example, as long as investors are informed of the governing legal regime, if promoters choose a regime that exculpates them from fraud, investors will either not invest in the firm at all or will require a higher return on the investment (that is, pay less for the security), just as bondholders charge higher interest rates to firms bearing greater risk of principal nonrepayment.[15] Investors set the price

---

[14] See, e.g., *Edgar v. MITE* 457 U.S. 624, 640-6 (1982) (invalidating a state takeover regulation that was more extensive than the federal regulation as a burden on interstate commerce). Only a plurality of the Court in *MITE* held the takeover statute to be preempted by the federal act. See id. at 634-40.

[15] See generally Easterbrook, Frank H. and Daniel R. Fischel *The Economic Structure of Corporate Law* 17-21 (Harvard 1991) (entrepreneurs choose terms that enhance investors' expected returns in order to increase securities prices); Winter, Ralph K. 'State Law, Shareholder Protection, and the Theory of the Corporation' 6 *J. Leg. Stud.* 251, 275-6 (1977) (securities of

because financial capital is highly mobile and financial markets are highly competitive (the set of investment opportunities is extensive and with the use of derivatives virtually limitless). It is plausible to assume that investors are informed about liability rules given the sophistication of the institutional investors who comprise the vast majority of stock market investors and whose actions determine market prices on which uninformed investors can rely.[16] Promoters thus bear the cost of operating under a legal regime inimical to investor interests, and they will therefore select the regime that maximizes the joint welfare of promoters and investors.

The analytical point concerning the ability of capital markets to assess legal regimes and consequently the beneficial effect of competition is confirmed by empirical research in the bond indenture and corporate law contexts: creditor

firms incorporated in states with codes unfavorable to shareholders will be unattractive investments).

[16] In 1995, for example, institutional investors—pension funds, insurance companies, mutual funds, and bank-managed investment funds—held 50% of total equity in the United States, see Brancato, Carolyn K. *Institutional Investors and Corporate Governance* 19-20 (Chicago 1997), compared to less than 10% in 1950, see New York Stock Exchange 'Fact Book 1995 Data' 57 (New York 1996). Although there are formal models of informationally inefficient capital markets (markets with, for instance, speculative bubbles) that depend on the existence of irrational, uninformed traders termed "noise traders," these models provide no theory that can predict when irrational pricing will occur and are simply unrealistic with regard to market behavior. Namely, informed investors and arbitrageurs will trade against the irrational individuals, preserving market efficiency, as the noise traders experience significant losses and stop trading. For the development of this critique, see Friedman, Milton 'The Case for Flexible Exchange Rates' in: Friedman, Milton (ed.) *Essays in Positive Economics* 157 (Chicago 1953); Fama, Eugene F. 'The Behavior of Stock Prices' *Journal of Business* 38 (1965) 34, 37-9; and Samuelson, Paul 'The "Fallacy" of Maximizing the Geometric Mean in Long Sequences of Investing or Gambling' *Proc. Nat'l Acad. Sci.* 68 (1971) 2493. Modelers of inefficient markets have been unable to amend the models to respond to these criticisms. For example, in models where noise traders affect price, they cannot be shown to survive over time (and thus to affect prices in the long run), see De Long, J. Bradford, Andrei Shleifer, Lawrence H. Summers, and Robert J. Waldmann 'Noise Trader Risk in Financial Markets' *Journal of Political Economy* 98 (1990) 703, 713, 717, but in the models in which noise traders can "survive" over time (i.e., do not go bankrupt from their irrational trading), their misperceptions do not affect prices (the model is unsolvable if they are allowed to affect prices), see De Long, J. Bradford, Andrei Shleifer, Lawrence H. Summers, and Robert J. Waldmann 'The Survival of Noise Traders in Financial Markets' *Journal of Business* 64 (1991) 1, 2. In addition, more generalized versions of models in which noise traders can affect prices have multiple equilibria which include the classical (efficient pricing) equilibrium, and the noisy (inefficient pricing) equilibria require very strong assumptions concerning noise traders, such as their ability to hold infinite positions, which are unrealistic. See Bhushan, Ravi, David P. Brown, and Antonio S. Mello 'Do Noise Traders "Create Their Own Space?"' *Journal of Financial and Quantitative Analysis* 32 (1997) 25, 28. There is, however, one context in which unsophisticated investors are not protected by the actions of institutional investors (that is, they cannot rely on prices set by informed investors), their relations with brokers, and this is another reason for excluding the regulation of brokers from the proposal, see infra notes 26-8 and accompanying text

protection provisions in bond indentures are positively priced,[17] and firms experience statistically significant positive changes in stock prices upon changing their incorporation state.[18] The entrepreneurial motivation to reduce capital costs that operates in a competitive legal system mitigates the otherwise core problem for a government regulator of identifying what regulation will benefit investors in capital markets.

Federal intervention in capital markets in the 1930s was justified by a contention that securities markets operate poorly on two dimensions: first, that they fail to protect investors from stock price manipulation and fraud; and second, that they produce an inadequate level of corporate disclosure because the benefits of information concerning a firm cannot be appropriated solely by the firm which bears the cost of the information's production (corporate information is a public good).[19] Analytically, a demonstration that there are information externalities that necessitate government intervention depends on the mix of informed and uninformed investors.[20] But a theoretical need for government regulation to prevent a market failure is not equivalent to a need for a monopolist-regulator.

[17] See, e.g., Chatfield, Robert E. and R. Charles Moyer 'Putting Away Bond Risk: An Empirical Examination of the Value of the Put Option on Bonds' *Financial Management* 15/2 (1986) 26, 31-2; Crabbe, Leland 'Event Risk: An Analysis of Losses to Bondholders and "Super Poison Put" Bond Covenants' *Journal of Finance* 46 (1991) 689, 690; Kish, Richard J. and Miles Livingston 'Estimating the Value of Call Options on Corporate Bonds' *Journal of Applied Corporate Finance* 6/3 (1993) 95, 97.

[18] See Romano, Roberta 'Law as Product: Some Pieces of the Incorporation Puzzle' *Journal of Law, Economics, and Organization* 1 (1985) 225, 271; Wang, Jianghong 'Performance of Reincorporated Firms' 14-8 (Unpublished Manuscript, 1995; on file with author).

[19] See Easterbrook and Fischel, supra n. 15, 277 (antifraud rationale); and Seligman, Joel 'The Historical Need for a Mandatory Corporate Disclosure System' 9 *J. Corp. L.* 1, 9 (1983) (optimal disclosure level rationale). It must be noted, however, that the economic theory underlying the argument concerning information production is actually ambiguous: capital markets can overproduce information as well as underproduce it. The informational efficiency of capital markets implies that only the first investor to obtain private information about a firm is likely to realize the value of the information through trading, and this creates an incentive for investors to engage in costly duplicative efforts at information-production (that is, overproduction) in a race to be first. See Hirshleifer, Jack 'The Private and Social Value of Information and the Reward to Inventive Activity' *American Economic Review* 61 (1971) 561, 565-6. From this perspective, mandatory disclosure could be beneficial by reducing the amount of privately produced information.

[20] The formal models indicate that information will not be underproduced if the proportion of investors who are informed (that is, capable of understanding the significance of no disclosure) is not too low. See Fishman, Michael and Kathleen Hagerty 'Mandatory vs. Voluntary Disclosure in Markets with Informed and Uninformed Customers' (Department of Finance, Kellogg Graduate School of Management, Northwestern Univ. Paper no. 233, July 1997); Dye, Ronald A. 'Investor Sophistication and Voluntary Disclosures' (Unpublished Manuscript, 1997; on file with author). As these papers show, if all investors are informed, no information externality exists—investors draw negative inferences from nondisclosure, which forces firms to reveal both good and bad information.

The premise of competitive federalism is that if, for example, corporate information would be under-produced to investors' detriment in an unregulated market, then there would be a demand for, matched by a supply of, mandated disclosure regulation in a regime of state competition for securities regulation as well as in the monopolist SEC system.

A third rationale more recently offered for federal intervention that is a refinement of the public good rationale identifies the information problem as involving information that would benefit an issuer's competitors as well as investors (that is, a problem of third-party externalities).[21] According to this theory, because competitors can use such information to compete more effectively with the issuer and thereby diminish the issuer's profitability, investors as well as firms would not wish to reveal such information, even though investors would be better able to evaluate the firm with this information, and thus mandatory disclosure rules are necessary. It can be shown analytically that even in the case of such third-party externalities, mandatory disclosure is not always optimal compared to voluntary disclosure and it would, in all likelihood, be extremely difficult for a regulator to determine when mandatory disclosure was optimal.[22] But putting aside the theoretical uncertainty of the need for a mandatory regime, even this third-party externality argument does not require an exclusive federal regime. The majority of investors hold portfolios, not single shares of stock, and therefore, unlike the issuer, they will internalize the externality if they make the disclosure decision. Namely, they will desire a regime requiring the information's disclosure because, by definition of a positive externality, the expected gain on their shares in competitors will offset the loss on their shares in the issuer.

Because the antifraud rationale does not depend on the presence of an externality for government action, there is even less of an issue concerning whether competition is desirable under this rationale than the rationales surrounding the mandatory disclosure regime: it is silly to contend that investors will choose regimes that encourage fraud. Joel Seligman states that a federal law was needed in the 1930s because state securities laws did not reach out-of-state sellers.[23] Whatever the merit of the argument then, it is not applicable to modern jurisdictional doctrines and is therefore not relevant to today's policy discussions.[24] If

---

[21] See Easterbrook and Fischel, supra n. 15, 290-1.

[22] See Dye, Ronald A. 'Mandatory Versus Voluntary Disclosures: The Cases of Financial and Real Externalities' *Accounting Review* 65 (1990) 1, 15-6, 18-9 (formal model indicating divergence between voluntary and mandatory disclosure depends on information regulators unlikely to obtain, a detailed *a priori* knowledge of the covariances of firms' returns).

[23] See Seligman, supra n. 19, 21.

[24] Frank Easterbrook and Daniel Fischel suggest an analogous reason for a federal law: the efficiency of enforcing all claims involving a particular transaction in one case, see Easterbrook and Fischel, supra n. 15, 285. The choice-of-law reform discussed in Part C that adopts the issuer-based jurisdictional approach of corporate law for state securities regulation, can resolve

there was concern in the 1930s over the states' capacity to handle securities fraud cases, this is no longer a serious issue. Given the overlapping feature of the current antifraud regime, the states have developed active securities law enforcement divisions as well as coordinating capacities to deal with interstate frauds.[25]

The coverage of the federal securities regime regarding the regulation of securities markets and market professionals who broker transactions between investors and issuers is excluded from the proposed market approach.[26] Brokers are excluded because the domicile choices of their employing organizations are not subject to the same capital market forces that prod regulatory competition to adopt rules preferred by investors as are issuers: the owners of broker-dealers, whose preferences will dictate the choice of securities regime, are not the customers whose interests the securities regime seeks to protect.[27] Unless the interests of broker owners and customers are identical on this dimension (that is, share value is maximized under the securities regime customers prefer), the owners may not choose the regime that is most desired by customers.

this concern; as is true of shareholder class action claims for fiduciary breach, all securities claims can be consolidated into one court action, and one law will apply, that of the issuer's securities domicile. This reform also resolves Easterbrook and Fischel's other explanation for why state competition will not work in the securities context, the potential to exploit out-of-state shareholders with rules favoring in-state shareholders given the multistate jurisdictional rules based on shareholder residence, see Easterbrook and Fischel, supra n. 15, 300-1, because the reform will result in only one state's law governing all shareholders' transactions that is independent of the shareholder's residence.

[25] See, e.g., Sargent, Mark A. 'A Future for Blue Sky Law' 62 *U. Cin. L. Rev.* 471, 504-5 (1993). A recent example illustrates the vigor of state enforcement activity. The New York state prosecutor's criminal enforcement action against a perpetrator of securities fraud (insider trading) was undercut by the federal government: the U.S. attorney seized the case and struck a plea bargain with the defendant after the state prosecutor had developed the case and obtained an indictment. See *Morgenthau v. White*, *N.Y. Times* Dec. 6, 1997 at A18. The states have also agreed to coordinate regulation of electronic offerings on the Internet. See Coffee, Jr., John C. 'Brave New World?: The Impact(s) of the Internet on Modern Securities Regulation' 52 *Bus. Law.* 1195, 1231-2 (1997). Indeed, the Internet is likely to facilitate state enforcement efforts, as it has for the SEC, as state securities regulator websites will offer a ready means of communication of complaints by non-resident investors. See Special Report 'SEC Enforcement, Microcap Fraud, Staffing Issues Top Enforcement Agenda' 29 *Sec. Reg. & L. Rep.* (BNA) 1769, 1773 (Dec. 19, 1997) (SEC Enforcement Division Director states that Internet has made it easier for people to get in touch with the SEC concerning complaints, as well as for the agency to "run down" people engaged in misconduct as their electronic interactions with investors leave identifying trails).

[26] Trading by such professionals that would fall under current antifraud provisions and is not related to their relationship with a customer, such as trading on inside information in violation of section 10(b) of the Securities Exchange Act, 15 U.S.C. § 78j (1994), see *United States v. O'Hagan* 117 S. Ct. 2199 (1997), *is* included in the proposal (as is any such activity conducted by any non-issuer-affiliated third party).

[27] This is also true for investment advisers, who are regulated under the Investment Advisers Act of 1940, 15 U.S.C. §§ 80b-1 to 80b-18a (1994).

Reputational concerns in the competition for customers surely affect brokerage firms' incentives regarding the choice of regime. But they provide lower-powered incentives than in the case of issuers because there are many potential conflicts of interest between broker owners and customers over the desirable rules.[28] This scenario is different from the choice of securities regime by the owners of issuers, as the issuer-related provisions of the securities laws concern precisely the relation between issuers and owners. A further consequence of this distinction between the regulation of issuers and brokers is that brokerage customers who are not informed of the relevant securities regime may not be protected by the presence of informed investors in the market, in contrast to uninformed stockholders who benefit from informed investors' evaluation of issuers, as it is revealed in the stock prices.

There is one change that must be made in the regulation of market professionals, however, to maintain the integrity of the market approach to securities regulation for issuers. In order to prevent the SEC from being able to regulate surreptitiously issuers not subject to its jurisdiction, the small subset of SEC regulations of market professionals that relate their conduct to its substantive regulation of issuers, such as the requirement that brokers and dealers obtain issuers' periodic SEC filings before providing quotations,[29] will have to be modified to refer to the substantive law of the issuer's domicile. Such a reform will not undermine the SEC's responsibility to oversee market professionals because, keeping in mind that none of the SEC's substantive issuer disclosure requirements are drafted with its market professional oversight responsibilities in view, where states require a different or reduced set of issuer disclosures than the SEC, such information will also be adequate for the SEC's oversight purposes, as competition will produce the level of issuer disclosure deemed cost-effective by investors.

Whether exchanges should be included in the proposed regulatory reform is more complicated. Exchanges are also not investor-owned corporations; they are not-for-profit organizations controlled by member trading firms. They are, however, exposed to incentive-aligning market forces as competition for trading

---

[28] Brokers that are also dealers have multiple revenue sources which can create conflict of interest in trading policies, see, e.g., 'E.F. Hutton & Co.' Exchange Act Release No. 34-25887, 41 S.E.C. 413 (1988) (finding conflict between market-making activities and brokerage activities regarding customer limit orders, although SEC commissioners divided on the appropriate practice). After the *E.F. Hutton* decision, the National Association of Securities Dealers (NASD) revised its rules to eliminate the conflict by according priority to customer limit orders, see Exchange Act Release No. 34279, 59 *Fed. Reg.* 34,883 (1994) (approving rule). In addition, although competition should restrain the conflict between brokerage firms and customers over trading costs, the securities industry recently reached a substantial settlement in litigation charging dealer collusion over bid-ask spreads in the over-the-counter market, see McGeehan, Patrick 'Settlement of Nasdaq Suit to Hit Some Firms Harder' *Wall St. J.* Dec. 24, 1997 at C1.

[29] See Rule 15c2-11, 17 C.F.R. § 240.15c2-11.

across exchanges will tend to align exchange members' regulatory choices with investors' preferences, to the extent that trading volume is maximized under trading rules preferred by investors. If there is a conflict between rules maximizing trading volume and investor welfare, the market will not provide exchanges with high-powered incentives.

There is disagreement in the literature over whether there is a conflict between increased trading volume and the trading rules preferred by investors,[30] but the severity of any such conflict is likely to be small, and controllable. Yakov Amihud and Haim Mendelson, who believe there is a conflict, for example, contend that if issuers, rather than exchanges, controlled the listing decision, the incentive problem regarding exchanges' choice of trading rules would be eliminated.[31] There is, moreover, a further, pragmatic reason to exclude exchanges from the proposal that is independent of the debate over exchanges' incentives: to target the proposal where it will do the most good. In contrast to corporate issuers, exchanges are self-regulating under the federal securities scheme (that is, rather than specify regulatory requirements for exchanges and their members, the federal law delegates regulatory authority to the exchanges themselves, subject to oversight by the SEC) and the benefits from regulatory competition would thus be far more attenuated for them than for issuers.[32] However, even more important than in the regulation of market professionals, there is a critical change that must be made to the existing regulatory regime for exchanges in order to integrate successfully the exchange's continued oversight by the SEC with the new competitive regime for issuers. The SEC's authority over exchanges must be statutorily limited to non-issuer-related matters, such as trading rules. Otherwise the agency will be able to undermine the market approach by introducing mandatory rules for issuers in the form of exchange requirements that preempt competing state regimes.

---

[30] Compare Amihud, Yakov and Haim Mendelson 'A New Approach to the Regulation of Trading Across Securities Markets' 71 *N.Y.U. L. Rev.* 1411, 1434-42 (1996) (emphasizing conflicting preferences) with Fischel, Daniel R. 'Organized Exchanges and the Regulation of Dual Class Common Stock' 54 U. *Chicano L. Rev.* 119, 123-5 (1987) (emphasizing compatible preferences).

[31] See Amihud and Mendelson, supra n. 30, 1442-6.

[32] This is not to say that the SEC's oversight of exchange rules has unambiguously benefited investors. It has not. For example, the SEC supported the New York Stock Exchange's (NYSE) anti-competitive fixed commission rule for many years, see Phillips, Susan M. and J. Richard Zecher *The SEC and the Public Interest* 88 (Cambridge, Mass. et al. 1981), and the benefit to investors from the SEC's commitment to developing multiple markets in NYSE stocks has been questioned, see Amihud and Mendelson, supra n. 30, 1454. Rather, it is simply to acknowledge the need for priorities, that the SEC's exclusive jurisdiction over issuers is a source of greater harm to investors than its oversight of exchange rules, for, in contrast to its policies toward issuers, it has not successfully imposed uniformity on exchange rules and practices, see, e.g., Macey, supra n. 9, 937-8 (discussing SEC's failed effort in rule 19c-4 to impose a one-share one-vote requirement for all exchanges).

Finally, mutual funds, which are regulated by the SEC under the Investment Company Act of 1940, a regime that entails far more than disclosure requirements,[33] present a more complicated regulatory context. Some funds could easily come under the proposal, the mutual funds that are subject to the same investor-driven market forces as corporate issuers because their owners are their customers, the objects of securities regulation. There is, however, a potentially important difference between these funds and issuers: the most informed investors in the stock market, large institutions, typically do not invest in mutual funds that are held by individual investors (they hold securities directly). Thus, for competitive federalism to work for mutual fund registration, there must be a sufficient number of individual investors in mutual shares who are informed about legal regimes such that their regulatory preferences will govern fund domicile outcomes. Under such circumstances—a set of informed fund investors—the overall mechanics of competitive federalism for investment companies would follow that for issuers.

Many funds are not, however, customer-owned. For these funds, potential incentive-alignment concerns regarding owner and customer interests would be present as in the broker and exchange contexts. The competitiveness of the mutual fund industry suggests that funds will have incentives to see to it that investors are informed about the benefits of their domiciles compared to those of competitors, just as funds advertise their rates today. Moreover, given the fast-developing access to information concerning securities regulation on the internet, the likelihood that competition will work in this context is quite promising.[34] But the alignment of regime choice across owners and customers is not guaranteed. Accordingly, this article does not provide a detailed proposal to implement the market approach to mutual fund regulation.

II. Is Abandoning a Mandatory Federal Securities Law Justified?

This part first reviews the empirical literature that has sought to measure the impact of the federal securities regime on investors. The analysis rests on contemporary empirical studies because the historical "evidence" of market abuses that was dramatically orchestrated by congressional investigators during the hearings preceding the creation of the federal regime as part of the New Deal

---

[33] 15 U.S.C. §§ 80a-1 to 80a-64 (1994).

[34] See, e.g., 'Technology Issues Priorities for SEC in '98, Barbash States' 29 *Sec. Reg. & L. Rep.* (BNA) 1720 (Dec. 12, 1997) (Director of SEC's Division of Investment Management predicting Web sites containing major securities laws from regulators around the world will be available to investors by the end of 1998).

agenda has been shown to be inaccurate.[35] The hearings were held for the purpose of furthering a political end (federal regulation of the stock market), and the statistical techniques used by modern researchers were not available to researchers in the 1930s to develop the case for or against regulation. There is, in fact, a paucity of empirical evidence that the federal regime has affirmatively benefited investors. For an educated prediction of what the counterfactual would produce, this section then reviews the empirical evidence on investor welfare of the next best thing—state competition for corporate charters; it compares favorably.

The difficulty of discerning an affirmative impact on investors from the federal regime detailed in this section supports abandoning its exclusivity. While it does not prove the counterfactual—that state competition will be better—the near total absence of measurable benefits from the federal regulatory apparatus surely undermines blind adherence to the status quo. Under regulatory competition, lawmakers have incentives to replace regimes that do not measurably support their objectives with those that do. In a competitive regulatory system, undesirable mandatory policies cannot be maintained over time because they are not enforceable—firms will migrate to the regulatory regime that does not impose such mandates. The competitively produced state corporation codes, for instance, in contrast to the federal securities laws, consist primarily of enabling provisions, providing firms and investors with a standardized contractual form to govern their relationships that reduces the cost of doing business. Thus, to the extent the empirical literature suggests that the federal securities laws have been fashioned from a set of misguided premises, adoption of the market approach to securities regulation will weed out inefficiencies in the federal regime by permitting capital market participants to establish a new regulatory equilibrium with a mix of enabling and mandatory provisions, if that is what investors prefer.

1. Empirical Evidence on the Rationales for Federal Securities Regulation

a. Mandated Disclosure[36]

There is little tangible proof of the claim that corporate information is "under-produced" in the absence of mandated disclosure, or that items mandated by the government that would not otherwise be produced in fact benefit investors above their cost of production. For instance, before the enactment of the federal securities laws in the 1930s, public corporations voluntarily disclosed financial state-

---

[35] See Bierman, Jr., Harold *The Great Myths of 1929 and the Lessons to be Learned* 133-46 (New York 1991); and the discussion infra notes 72-4 and accompanying text.

[36] For a general treatment of disclosure, cf. Fox (this volume Ch. 9).

ments, typically under a stock exchange listing requirement, that contained substantially all of the information subsequently required under the federal laws. In an important and still underappreciated study, George Benston found that the only major mandated item that was not reported by a significant set of firms prior to the 1934 legislation was sales; comparing pre- and post-legislation stock returns of the firms for which the legislation was relevant (firms that had not previously reported sales, which were 38% of New York Stock Exchange (NYSE)-listed corporations) to those for which it was not (firms that had always disclosed sales information, the remaining 62% of NYSE corporations), he found no significant price effect from the new mandated disclosure.[37]

Benston's finding, upon reflection, should not be surprising: because firms need capital and investors need information, firms have powerful incentives to disclose information if they are to compete successfully for funds against alternative investment opportunities. Consistent with this explanation, studies have found that the quantity and quality of publicly traded firms' voluntary disclosures (such as earnings forecasts) are positively correlated with the issuance of securities,[38] and with information asymmetry in the market for the firm's stock (that is,

[37] See Benston, George 'Required Disclosure and the Stock Market: An Evaluation of the Securities Exchange Act of 1934' *American Economic Review* 63 (1973) 132, 144-5 [hereinafter Benston 'Evaluation']; Benston, George 'An Appraisal of the Costs and Benefits of Government-Required Disclosure: SEC and FTC Requirements' 41/3 *Law & Contemp. Probs.* 30, 51-2 (1977) [hereinafter Benston 'Appraisal']. Joel Seligman criticizes the significance of this finding, see Seligman, supra n. 19, 16-7, but his objections, which follow those of Irwin Friend and Randolph Westerfield, see Friend, Irwin and Randolph Westerfield 'Required Disclosure and the Stock Market: Comment' *American Economic Review* 65 (1975) 467, actually reinforce Benston's conclusions. For example, Seligman cites in criticism of Benston's finding of no stock price effect of the SEC's disclosure requirements that more recent studies show data in SEC filings affect stock prices and therefore prove the SEC's mandated disclosure program is of value to investors. See Seligman, supra n. 19, 16. But it is not the SEC's disclosure requirements that are affecting stock value in these studies because they have not added any new items into the information mix already disclosed: the information examined in the studies he cites, earnings, was disclosed, as Benston demonstrates, even prior to the creation of the SEC, and would continue to be disclosed if there were no SEC. Seligman realizes this point by adding that the issue is whether the SEC compels information otherwise not voluntarily disclosed, rather than the location where the item is disclosed (SEC report or otherwise). See Seligman, supra n. 19, 16. But the studies he cites do not bear upon this issue. Seligman also objects to Benston's test because it did not adequately distinguish between disclosure and non-disclosure firms as all the firms in his sample disclosed earnings. But this is precisely Benston's point: the SEC's mandated disclosure added only one item—sales—that had not been disclosed by NYSE firms, and release of the new information under its requirement had no effect on stock prices of those firms not previously disclosing sales.

[38] E.g., Frankel, Richard, Maureen McNichols, and G. Peter Wilson 'Discretionary Disclosure and External Financing' *Accounting Review* 70 (1995) 135, 141 (firms significantly more likely to forecast earnings if they access capital markets over sample period); Lang, Mark and Russell Lundholm 'Cross-Sectional Determinants of Analyst Ratings of Corporate Disclosures' *Journal of Accounting Research* 31 (1993) 246, 265, 269 (financial analyst federation disclosure quality rating increases with security issuance); Ruland, William, Samuel

managers release information voluntarily when there is greater information asymmetry, as measured by the stock price's bid-ask spread)[39], and negatively related to the cost of capital (that is, increased voluntary disclosure reduces firms' cost of capital).[40] In addition, European firms listing in London typically comply with the higher United Kingdom disclosure requirements rather than the lower ones of their home countries, which they could do under the European Community disclosure directives.[41] A further datum relevant to the issue of information production is the fact that European stock markets are not any less efficient than U.S. stock markets even though the European accounting and disclosure regimes require the revelation of considerably less information than the SEC.[42]

There is, accordingly, ample evidence that firms voluntarily disclose significant amounts of information beyond that mandated by securities regulators. It is difficult to prove what, if any item, among required disclosures is of less value to investors than items voluntarily disclosed, but the great variety in content across disclosure regimes—a recent study identified 100 SEC disclosure items deemed excessive compared to international standards—[43] is suggestive that a number of

Tung, and Nashwa E. George 'Factors Associated with the Disclosure of Managers' Forecasts' *Accounting Review* 65 (1990) 710, 720 (firms reporting forecasts more likely to issue new capital); Choi, Frederick D.S. 'Financial Disclosure and Entry to the European Capital Market' *Journal of Accounting Research* 11 (1973) 159, 168-70 (firms entering Eurobond market increase disclosure).

[39] See Marquardt, Carol A. and Christine I. Wiedman 'Voluntary Disclosure, Information Asymmetry, and Insider Selling Through Secondary Equity Offerings' 16, 19-20, 22 (John M. Olin School of Business Washington University in St. Louis Working Paper no. 97-05, Apr. 1997) (in secondary offerings, managers act as if reduced information asymmetry is correlated with reduced cost of capital, such that their participation in an offering explains the frequency of voluntary disclosure); Coller, Maribeth and Teri Lombardi Yohn 'Management Forecasts and Information Asymmetry: An Examination of Bid-Ask Spreads' *Journal of Accounting Research* 35 (1997) 1, 6-8, 10 (firms with increasing bid-ask spreads release earnings forecasts to reduce spread).

[40] See Botosan, Christine 'Disclosure Level and the Cost of Equity Capital' *Accounting Review* 72 (1997) 323, 344, 346 (voluntary disclosure in annual report significantly explains cost of capital of firms with small analyst following).

[41] See Meek, Gary K. and Sidney J. Gray 'Globalization of Stock Markets and Foreign Listing Requirements: Voluntary Disclosures by Continental European Companies Listed on the London Stock Exchange' *Journal of International Business Studies* 20 (1989) 315 (sample of European companies trading in London); Scott, Hal S. and Philip A. Wellons *International Finance: Transactions, Policy, and Regulation* 314 3rd edn. (Westbury, N.Y. 1995) (references concerning Danish and French firms' compliance with U.K. standards).

[42] See Hawawini, Gabriel A. *European Equity Markets: Price, Behavior and Efficiency* (New York 1984); Edwards, supra n. 8, 60-2; Baumol, William J. and Burton G. Malkiel 'Redundant Regulation of Foreign Security Trading and U.S. Competitiveness' in: Lehn and Kamphuis (eds.), supra n. 8, 35, 42-6.

[43] See Choi, Frederick D.S. 'Financial Reporting Requirements for Non-US Registrants: International Market Perspectives' *Financial Markets, Institutions & Instruments* 6 (1997) 23, 29. There are also significant differences in the securities disclosure regimes of emerging markets,

mandates are not cost-effective. Although the estimates are extremely crude and conservative, Susan Phillips and J. Richard Zecher calculated in 1975 that the termination of the SEC's mandatory periodic disclosure programs would reduce corporate disclosure costs by at least $213 million.[44] These data make plain the point of this section, that regulators do not have superior knowledge concerning what information investors need (otherwise firms would not on occasion disclose more than required), which bolsters the desirability of regulatory competition, as it will reduce regulatory mistakes.

In a detailed defense of federal legislation, Seligman challenges Benston's findings with data compiled by the SEC during the 1940s and 1950s in order to expand its jurisdiction, data that indicate that small firms not subject to the federal securities laws disclosed less information than the SEC required of its larger-sized registrants.[45] In particular, he notes that the SEC reported that most of the exempt firms did not disclose management compensation or insider trans-actions in proxy statements, and that some firms did not furnish income state-ments or provided inadequate accounting information, compared to SEC requirements, in their balance sheets.[46] But these data do not provide proof of the efficacy of the federal securities regime. The failure to provide voluntarily information that the SEC mandates does not demonstrate that such disclosure enhances investor welfare. It does so only with an additional assumption, that the SEC, and not the firms, has made the correct cost-benefit calculation.

To address the issue of the adequacy of the differential level of disclosure by non-registrants we need to know the answer to several questions: whether finan-cial analysts and shareholders were unable to accurately value firms under the more limited voluntary disclosures; and if so, did they underpay or overpay for the shares (that is, did promoters and insiders bear the cost of the allegedly inadequate disclosure, or did the outside investors)? It would be difficult to make such a judgment directly, although a finding of significant changes in stock prices upon firms' increased disclosures under SEC requirements would be probative on the issue.

There is no study of which I am aware that examines the effect of the 1965 extension of the continuing disclosure requirements to small firms. But there was no significant increase in stock prices after enactment of the 1933 Act for new

where we might expect a need for substantial disclosure to encourage foreign investment. See Saudagaran, Shahrokh M. and Joselito G. Diga 'Financial Reporting in Emerging Capital Markets: Characteristics and Policy Issues' *Accounting Horizons* 11 (1997) 41.

[44] See Phillips and Zecher, supra n. 32, 49-51. Their estimate for extra costs imposed in the 1975 new issue market was $193 million.

[45] See Seligman, supra n. 19, 36-9.

[46] See Seligman, supra n. 19, 36.

issue registration,[47] a finding that strongly suggests that the new federal regime had, at best, no effect on investor welfare. If the 1933 Act did not increase stock prices of covered firms it is unlikely that the 1965 extension of the Act did so, for the absence of a price increase post-1933 suggests that the market elicits the right level of disclosure. A similar conclusion can be drawn from studies of a more specific instance of SEC-mandated disclosure, a requirement that large corporations disclose the current replacement cost of inventories, plant, and equipment: researchers find no stock price effect when firms disclosed the newly mandated replacement cost information, suggesting that investors did not find the SEC's mandated disclosure useful for valuing firms.[48]

---

[47] See Stigler, George 'Public Regulation of Securities Markets' *Journal of Business* 37 (1964) 117, 120-1 (no effect on returns); Jarrell, Gregg 'The Economic Effects of Federal Regulation of the Market for New Securities Issues' *Journal of Law and Economics* 24 (1981) 613, 645, 666 (same, examining returns over five years from issuance); Simon, Carol J. 'The Effect of the 1933 Securities Act on Investor Information and the Performance of New Issues' *American Economic Review* 79 (1989) 295, 305 (no effect on returns of NYSE and seasoned regional exchange issues). Carol Simon did find that one subsample of firms, unseasoned issues traded on regional exchanges, had greater returns after the enactment of the Act (they were overpriced before the Act), but this subsample performed significantly worse in all periods than the other new issues in the study. See Simon, supra, 308. Irwin Friend and Edward Herman, in a study on which Seligman heavily relies, criticized Goerge Stigler's interpretation of his data because although not statistically significant, post-Act issues had higher returns than pre-Act issues, and because there was a significant positive return after four years, Friend, Irwin and Edward S. Herman 'The SEC through A Glass Darkly' *Journal of Business* 37 (1964) 382, 391. These criticisms do not, however, impeach Stigler's findings. The length of the interval over which they find a stock price effect—four years—is so long that it is impossible to attribute the price change to the legislation. Friend and Herman also do not provide a theory explaining why the 1933 Act should improve a new issue's returns only four years after its issuance. Not only is such a result inconsistent with a relatively efficient stock market, but also, we would expect mandated disclosure to have the greatest impact over the shorter interval of Stigler's study as short-term performance would be more predictable from financial disclosures than long-term performance. Nor do Friend and Herman explain why statistically insignificant findings should be given any evidentiary weight, counter to conventional social scientific practice. Further damaging to Friend and Herman's critique is the confirmation of Stigler's basic results by the more recent studies of Jarrell and Simon, supra. One study of existing stocks, rather than new issues, finds that the 1933 Act had a negative price impact, which the author attributes to the Act's restrictions on accounting procedures, that may have adversely affected the firms' ability to comply with debt covenants that were based on accounting numbers. See Chow, Chee W. 'The Impacts of Accounting Regulation on Bondholder and Shareholder Wealth: The Case of the Securities Acts' *Accounting Review* 57 (1983) 485, 489, 502, 507. Chee Chow expected to find a wealth transfer from shareholders to bondholders given the accounting covenants hypothesis, but he was unable to identify such an effect. Because the sample stocks were not new issues (to which the 1933 Act applied), it is difficult to interpret the study's results without knowing whether these firms planned to issue new securities in the future. A further difference, which is a serious shortcoming, between this study and the others is that, in contrast to the other studies, it did not adjust stock returns for market movements, which may account for the results, see Chow, supra, 503.

[48] See Watts, Ross L. and Jerold L. Zimmerman *Positive Accounting Theory* 174 (Englewood Cliffs, N.J. 1986) (citing studies).

The variance of stock returns, however, decreased after the enactment of the 1933 Act.[49] A plausible interpretation is that the legislation simply forced riskier investments off the market.[50] Consistent with this explanation, the proportion of common stock, compared to debt, of outstanding new issues decreased after the 1933 Act and there was also a dramatic increase in private placements of debt concentrated among bonds of higher risk after the Act.[51] Such a result—reduction in the investment opportunity set—does not obviously benefit investors as they simply require higher compensation for riskier securities, while in all likelihood it reduces social welfare by restricting the availability of financing for the riskiest ventures. The finding of a decrease in return variance has also been interpreted as indicating that the disclosure mandated by the Act enabled investors to form more accurate price predictions.[52] Even this alternative explanation does not, however, demonstrate that the Act benefited investors. A core tenet of modern finance theory is that investors are compensated for bearing market risk and it was firm-specific risk and not market risk that was measured to have decreased with the 1933 Act. In this regard, it is not surprising that there is no stock price effect: a reduction in own-return variance (viz, more accurate stock prices) is of no value to diversified investors. Consequently, commentators who point to the return variance reduction as evidence affirming the efficacy of the 1933 Act are mistaken; investors benefit from reductions in risk that is priced.

Seligman provides a further datum in support of the contention that the SEC's mandatory disclosure program benefits investors: from 1955 to 1971, "approximately two percent of the registration statements filed with the SEC were withdrawn after receipt of an SEC letter of comment [seeking additional disclosures] or . . . [an SEC] stop order."[53] This datum does not, however, indicate that the SEC's program aided investors. The key datum, which is not knowable, is whether, had those withdrawn issues been marketed as planned, investors would have overpaid for the issue or otherwise been defrauded concerning the firms' value. Emphasis on registration withdrawal data presupposes gross investor stupidity, that an investor reading a prospectus that SEC staff thought deficient would not similarly recognize the deficiency and discount the share price. Why assume that the analytical ability of the SEC staff is superior to that of financial

---

[49] See Jarrell, supra n. 47, 646; Simon, supra n. 47, 309; Stigler, supra n. 47, 122.

[50] See Jarrell, supra n. 47, 648-9, 668; Stigler, supra n. 47, 122. Seha Tinic offers a further gloss on this explanation, that the kind of securities underwriters were willing to offer changed to larger issues that were less risky after enactment of the 1933 Act, because the underwriters were fearful of their legal liability under the Act. See Tinic, Seha M. 'Anatomy of Initial Public Offerings of Common Stock' *Journal of Finance* 43 (1988) 789, 813.

[51] See Jarrell, supra n. 47, 661, 664, 667, 669.

[52] See Seligman, supra n. 19, 10; Simon, supra n. 47, 313.

[53] Seligman, supra n. 19, 43.

analysts and investors? Such an assumption simply does not square with what we know.

One reason for the surreal character of the arguments raised in support of the federal regime that are based on historical data is that capital markets have changed dramatically since the securities laws were adopted. The institutional investors who dominate today's markets have far greater ability, as well as financial incentives, to process information and price securities than the SEC staff.[54] Institutional investors' pricing determinations better protect unsophisticated investors than any of the SEC's mandated disclosure requirements because securities sell for one price and institutional investors cannot use their superior information-processing ability to extract wealth systematically from uninformed investors, particularly those long-term investors who follow a buy-and-hold strategy, given the efficiency of U.S. capital markets in information aggregation.[55] The federal regime has not adapted well to this changed context. The interests of sophisticated and unsophisticated investors in the choice of securities regime will not diverge for the issuer-investor relations that come under the regime of competitive federalism proposed by this article, and will, in fact, be better served by the new regulatory arrangement.

One particularly egregious example of the SEC's problematic disclosure policies will serve to underscore the point that it would be a profound mistake to presume that the SEC gets things right. The SEC prohibited for decades disclosure of projected earnings, although such information is far more valuable to investors than the accounting information the SEC required because stock value is a function of future cash flows, not historical data.[56] It modified its position in 1979 to permit the disclosure of projections within a "safe harbor" rule,[57] but

---

[54] This discrepancy in expertise is evident in recent rule-making activity by the SEC. In its new rule requiring disclosure of the market risk of derivative securities, the SEC essentially acknowledged that it is, and will always be, woefully behind market participants in understanding and developing the most accurate valuation techniques for these complex instruments, by abandoning its normal approach of standardized disclosure requirements. See 'Disclosure of Accounting Policies for Derivative Financial Instruments and Derivative Commodity Instruments and Disclosure of Qualitative and Quantitative Information about Market Risk Inherent in Derivative Financial Instruments, Other Financial Instruments, and Derivative Commodity Instruments' Release No. 33-7386, 62 *Fed. Reg.* 6044, 6048 n. 45, 6057 (1997) (to be codified at 17 C.F.R. pts 210, 228, 229, 239, 240, and 249) (explaining why rule permits choice of quantitative disclosure methods, including model parameters) [hereinafter SEC 'Derivatives Disclosure'].

[55] For a recent review of the research on market efficiency, see Fama, Eugene F. 'Efficient Capital Markets II' Journal of Finance 46 (1991) 1575, 1600-2.

[56] See, e.g., Kripke, Homer 'Can the SEC Make Disclosure Policy Meaningful?' *Journal of Portfolio Management* 2/4 (1976) 32, 35-7.

[57] See Rule 175, 17 C.F.R. 230.175 (1997) and Rule 3b-6, 17 C.F.R. § 240.3b-6 (1997), originally promulgated in 'Safe Harbor Rule for Projections' Securities Act Release No. 33-6084 (June 25, 1979), available at 1979 WL 16388 (S.E.C.).

even today the agency's approach is still quite guarded when it comes to such disclosures. For instance, when Congress recently legislated a safe harbor from civil liability for forecasts, the SEC was responsible for the extended list of transactions excluded from the safe harbor provision.[58]

The SEC's historic concern was that projections were more susceptible to abuse than accounting data. This concern was premised on a bizarre view of investor decision making, that investors believe all figures are "written on stone," and do not discount managers' optimism and therefore have to be protected from all but "verifiable" information (historical cost).[59] This approach has made SEC disclosure documents of limited value for investment decision making and was the subject of sustained criticisms throughout the 1970s. The SEC's approach, ironically, particularly disadvantaged public investors by closing off their ability to obtain information on projected earnings, as firms would not make public earnings forecasts for fear of liability, although they would provide them to analysts and other professionals.[60]

The 1979 modification did not substantially increase public forecasts, given firms' liability concerns,[61] and was clearly outmoded for modern markets populated by institutional investors. Congress therefore sought to increase the disclosure of forecasts in the 1995 securities reform legislation by explicitly creating a safe harbor from civil liability for the release of forecasts.[62] Whether the legislation will have the intended effect is not yet ascertainable, but early indications suggest that the new law is having minimal impact on the disclosure of projections.[63] The restrictions on the applicability of the safe harbor so vigorously advanced by the SEC surely enhance the likelihood that the statute's impact will be limited, and they serve as a useful reminder of how difficult it is for a monopolist government agency to alter course and implement significant policy changes.

This illustration of utterly misguided SEC disclosure mandates makes plain that an SEC disclosure initiative does not evidence that the market is inade-

---

[58] See, e.g., Matteson, Noelle 'Comment, Private Securities Litigation Reform Act of 1995: Do Issuers Still Get Soaked in the Safe Harbor' 27 *Golden Gate U. L. Rev.* 527, 547 n. 139 (1997) (citing sources indicating SEC supported provision only after Congress agreed to its transaction exclusions).

[59] See Kripke, supra n. 56, 40.

[60] See Kripke, Homer 'The SEC, The Accountants, Some Myths and Some Realities' 45 *N.Y.U. L. Rev.* 1151, 1199 (1970).

[61] See 'Safe Harbor for Forward-Looking Statements' Exchange Act Release No. 7101, 59 *Fed. Reg.* 52723, 52728-29 (1994), available at 1994 WL 562021 (S.E.C.), at *7-8.

[62] See Pub. L. No. 104-67, § 102, 109 Stat. 737 (1995) (codified at 15 U.S.C. §§ 77z-2 & 78u-5).

[63] See, e.g., 'Panelists Dispute Reform Law's Impact on Private Class Securities Fraud Litigation' 29 *Sec. Reg. & L. Rep.* (BNA) 1134 (Aug. 15, 1997); Matteson, supra n. 58, 550-1.

quately producing relevant information and, consequently, should not be privileged by assuming that the agency is always (or more often than not) right. It indicates quite the opposite, that the SEC may not even possess a rudimentary understanding of, much less a superior capacity over anyone else to identify, what information investors require for decision making. Such regulatory mistakes would be far less likely with competition: investors would be able to reveal their preference for particular information by bidding up the price of firms located in a regime in which they could make forecasts, compared to firms in one prohibiting such disclosures.

b. Mandatory Disclosure Involving Third-Party Externalities

Proponents of the third-party externality rationale have not specified what such items would be, let alone whether that information is the focus of SEC disclosure requirements. In fact, such information is at times explicitly excluded from the SEC's mandated disclosure.[64] It is thus difficult to use empirical studies of SEC mandates as tools for investigating this rationale compared to the more general information underproduction rationale. One potential candidate as an instance of mandated disclosure in order to assist third parties is the segment or line-of-business reporting requirements promulgated by the SEC in 1969.[65] These requirements mandated separate disclosure of profits as well as revenues of firms' different business product lines. Such disclosure could enable rival firms to discern more precisely firms' costs, facilitating competitive strategies. The results of studies investigating whether the additional information disclosed under the segment reporting requirements benefited investors essentially duplicate the results of the studies of the 1933 Act. They report no significant change in stock price and an increased consensus among financial statement users concerning predicted earnings, but are in disagreement over whether there was a significant change in firms' market risk from the increased disclosure.[66]

---

[64] See, e.g., Regulation S-K, Item 101, 17 C.F.R. § 229.101(c)(ii) (1997) (issuer not required to disclose information concerning business lines and products "the disclosure of which would affect adversely the registrant's competitive position.")

[65] See 'Adoption of Amendments to Forms S-1, S-7 and 10' Securities Act Release No. 4988 (July 14, 1969), available at 1969 SEC LEXIS 709.

[66] See, e.g., Ajinkya, Bipin B. 'An Empirical Evaluation of Line-of-Business Reporting' *Journal of Accounting Research* 18 (1980) 343, 357-9 (no effect on returns, increased consensus in probability assessments); Collins, Daniel W. and Richard R. Simonds 'SEC Line-of-Business Disclosure and Market Risk Adjustments' *Journal of Accounting Research* 17 (1979) 352, 372-3, 378-80 (change in market risk); Horwitz, Bertrand and Richard Kolodny 'Line of Business Reporting and Security Prices: An Analysis of an SEC Disclosure Rule' *Bell Journal of Economics* 8 (1977) 234, 239, 241-2, 246 (no effect on market risk or on returns); see generally Mohr, Rosanne M. 'The Segmental Reporting Issue: A Review of Empirical Research' *Journal of Accounting Literature* 2 (1983) 39, 45-52, 56-62 (literature review summarizing general results

The absence of any consistent discernible effect on firm value of the line-of-business disclosures is consistent with Edmund Kitch's contention that the SEC's segment reporting requirements do not disclose information of competitive value because of the necessary discretion afforded management, under the disclosure rules, in the allocation of costs and grouping of activities.[67] But if Kitch's analysis is correct and proprietary information is not effectively disclosed by line-of-business reporting, then it is not an example of a disclosure mandate that mitigates third-party externalities. Kitch further contends that it is virtually impossible to implement a disclosure regime which includes proprietary information in practice—either firms will not meaningfully disclose information that can benefit their competitors or they will delist to avoid such disclosure.[68] This contention, supported by the empirical research on segment reporting, highlights an essential weakness of the third-party externality rationale to support the federal regime of mandatory disclosure: a theory that cannot be implemented effectively cannot serve as the basis for public policy.

c. Antifraud Provisions

The federal antifraud laws have not been a focus of as much empirical research as the federal disclosure regime.[69] But even here there is little evidence indicating that federal, as opposed to state, securities laws are necessary to protect investors from fraud and manipulation. In truth, the data that would be probative of the efficacy of the federal antifraud regime have not been compiled. Because all states had antifraud statutes prior to the adoption of the federal securities laws and only Nevada did not have an administrative entity to investigate securities fraud at that time,[70] investigating whether reported instances of investor fraud

---

of no effect on returns, some improvements in analyst forecasts, increased consensus, evidence mixed concerning whether market risk shifted).

[67] See Kitch, Edmund W. 'The Theory and Practice of Securities Disclosure' 61 *Brook. L. Rev.* 763, 858 (1995).

[68] See Kitch, supra n. 67, 874.

[69] If disclosure reduces the frequency of fraud and fraudulent issues are generally of high risk, then one explanation of the finding that the 1933 Act reduced the variance of stock returns could be that the 1933 Act eliminated fraudulent issues. See Jarrell, supra n. 47, 649. Gregg Jarrell sought to test this hypothesis by examining the performance of pre-SEC new issues but excluding from the pre-1934 sample the firms that would have been screened out by the SEC's regulation (the riskiest issues) had the Act been in effect in the earlier years. See Jarrell, supra n. 47, 650. He found that the screened sample performed no better than the entire pre-SEC sample. See Jarrell, supra n. 47, 650. Jarrell concludes that the reduction in variance after the Act is not due to effective deterrence of fraud, because high variance is not connected to poor performance in the unregulated period. Jarrell, supra n. 47, 650.

[70] See Easterbrook and Fischel, supra n. 15, 277.

decreased after enactment of the federal securities laws would be a useful step in determining the efficacy of the federal regime. However, the difficulty of establishing a baseline rate pre-enactment (given, for example, differences in enforcement regimes across states), in all likelihood, makes the task infeasible. Other probative research would examine whether securities issued outside of the SEC's jurisdiction (intra-state issues of small firms, state and local government securities, or foreign issues) have higher frequencies of fraud and price manipulation than SEC-registered securities, although, again, developing good estimates of comparative base-rate frequencies would be quite difficult.

Seligman cites SEC testimony to Congress in the 1940s and a 1963 SEC study, as part of the agency's twenty-year effort to expand its jurisdiction over small firms, indicating that the SEC initiated more fraud investigations against issues exempt from federal registration requirements than those that were registered.[71] These data are of little import. First, we do not know whether the SEC allocated more resources to investigating exempt issues than to investigating registered issues, an altogether plausible possibility given the SEC's agenda at the time, extension of its disclosure requirements to exempt firms. Such an enforcement policy would make it impossible to draw any conclusion concerning relative rates of fraud from the data. And, of course, the initiation of an investigation does not mean that fraud actually occurred. Second, it is important to ascertain the level of state antifraud activity against such issuers, to determine whether federal intervention was necessary. Third, even if one accepted Seligman's contention that massive securities frauds went undeterred by the states and necessitated the enactment of the federal laws, it is important to determine whether fraud occurred more frequently in small rather than large firms, because such a finding would indicate that the lower rate of fraud investigations for firms covered by the 1933 Act would not be a function of the mandatory disclosure regime, but of the population's lower underlying occurrence rate.

But the evidence supporting the contention that rampant fraud necessitated the federal laws is itself quite thin. After reviewing the legislative record and other sources, Benston concludes, in contrast to Seligman, that there is scant evidence of fraudulent financial statements prior to the 1934 Act.[72] Harold Bierman also reviews the evidence concerning stock market fraud and manipulation prior to the 1929 crash, and in particular, the sensational charges raised against several

---

[71] See Seligman, supra n. 19, 34-5. As Seligman discusses, the SEC's concern was directed at small issues (under $100,000) which were exempt from the 1933 Act, see Seligman, supra n. 19, 34, and small firms, which were exempt from the 1934 Act because they were not exchange-traded, with assets of $3,000,000 and 300 shareholders (the minimum size requirements the SEC proposed in 1946 as the basis for applicability of the reporting requirements of the 1934 Act), see Seligman, supra n. 19, 36.

[72] See Benston 'Evaluation', supra n. 37, 135.

prominent financiers in the Pecora hearings that led to the federal securities legislation, and concludes that the hearings and attempted prosecutions in their aftermath did not uncover fraudulent or dishonest behavior on Wall Street and that the amount of manipulation in the 1920s was "surprisingly small".[73] More important, a recent empirical study of the operation of stock pools that were a principal focus of the congressional investigation leading to the enactment of the federal securities laws found no evidence that the pools manipulated stock prices.[74]

In short, a fair reading of the empirical literature on the effects of the federal securities laws points to an expansive regulatory apparatus with an absence of empirical validation for its most fundamental objectives. One cannot but suspect that it is a regulatory edifice without foundation. A competitive regulatory system would put such a characterization to the test, as firms would be able to seek out the securities regime investors prefer.

2. Empirical Evidence on Corporate Charter Competition

The most prudent approach to the considerable data reviewed in the previous part, which cast doubt on the efficacy of the federal securities regime, is to replace the monopolist federal regulator with regulatory competition. This is, of course, the gist of the market approach embedded in a system of competitive federalism. To find fault with a market approach one must maintain that a competitive regulatory setting will do an even worse job than the federal monopolist in achieving the investor-protection goals of securities regulation. For such a contention to be correct, a further assumption is required, that the states will engage in a "race for the bottom" and enact rules that favor promoter/issuers over investors.[75] This assumption cannot be directly tested because there is at present no competitive regime for securities laws (besides the national mandates, the governing regime is fixed by the investor's residence or place of sale). But there is a competitive regime for corporate charters. The most important data bearing on the question whether the federal securities regime should be eliminated is, consequently, the research on the impact on shareholder welfare of state competition for charters. This research indicates convincingly, in my judgment, that investors are at a minimum not harmed from the competition and, in all likelihood, benefit from changes in corporate domicile to states such as Delaware, the leading incorporation state.

[73] See Bierman, supra n. 35, 133-45.

[74] See Mahoney, Paul 'The Stock Pools and the Securities Exchange Act 38' (Unpublished Manuscript, Dec. 2, 1997; on file with author).

[75] Seligman, for example, asserts that there is a need for mandatory national securities laws "because of the history of state corporate law 'chartermongering.'" Seligman, supra n. 19, 53-4.

There have been six studies of the wealth effects of state competition on shareholders, which is accomplished by investigating stock price reactions to domicile changes. Measured over a variety of time periods and sample firms, these studies find either a significant positive stock price effect or no significant price effect upon reincorporation.[76] No study observes a negative stock price effect. The empirical research on state competition undermines the "race for the bottom" argument against eliminating the federal securities monopoly by demonstrating that choice of jurisdiction does not leave investors defenseless against unscrupulous promoters.[77]

---

[76] Bradley, Michael and Cindy Schipani 'The Relevance of the Duty of Care Standard in Corporate Governance' 75 *Iowa L. Rev.* 1, 66-7 (1989) (significant positive returns on event date and approximately one month before); Dodd, Peter and Richard Leftwich 'The Market for Corporate Charters: "Unhealthy Competition" vs. Federal Regulation' *Journal of Business* 53 (1980) 259, 272-5 (significant positive returns two years before event); Hyman, Allen 'The Delaware Controversy—The Legal Debate' 4 *J. Corp. L.* 368, 385 (1979) (positive returns four days before event); Netter, Jeffry and Annette Poulsen 'State Corporation Laws and Shareholders: The Recent Experience' *Financial Management* 18/3 (1989) 29, 35-7 (positive returns one month around event that were significant at 10% level only); Romano, supra n. 18, 270-1 (significant positive returns at three-day, one-week, and one-month intervals before event); Wang, supra n. 18, 14-8, 21 (significant positive returns for full sample over three-day event interval; significant positive returns for Delaware firms over forty days before event, positive returns over three-day event interval significant only at 10% but significant at 5% if shareholder meeting date used as event for three-day interval; returns to Delaware firms consistently higher than those to non-Delaware firms, which are negative throughout most of event interval). To examine whether the positive price effect was a function of investors' responses to other changes in business plan accompanying the reincorporation and not their evaluation of the new legal regime, I compared the returns of the firms in my sample grouped by the type of such activity— engaging in a mergers and acquisitions programs, defending against takeover, and miscellaneous other reasons for reincorporating including tax savings. I found that there were no significant differences across the groups' returns, see Romano, supra n. 18, 272 (analysis of variance test of cumulative residuals). This finding strongly suggests that the significant positive returns upon reincorporation are due to investors' positive assessment of the change in legal regime, and not a confounding of the impact of reincorporating firms' other future projects.

[77] In an attempt to explain away the non-negative stock price effects of reincorporation, Lucian Bebchuk asserts that stock price studies are not probative on whether state competition benefits shareholders because state competition may produce some provisions that are harmful to shareholders even if the overall package of provisions is not, see Bebchuk, Lucian A. 'Federalism and the Corporation: The Desirable Limits on State Competition in Corporate Law' 105 *Harv. L. Rev.* 1435, 1449-50 (1992). This is not a particularly damaging contention against competition and in favor of a federal monopolist for several reasons. First, it is the net wealth effect of a code on investors that is important, and that effect is positive for state corporate law. Second, because state corporation codes are enabling statutes, firms can avoid any such harmful provisions by customizing their charters or by-laws. See infra n. 82 and accompanying text (discussing numerous firms' opting out of Pennsylvania takeover statute). Indeed, Bebchuk does not identify specific mandatory (hence unavoidable) provisions in state codes that he believes benefit managers over shareholders. Third, Bebchuk offers no support for the prediction that a federal corporation code would contain fewer harmful provisions than state codes. An examination of the lobbying process in the corporate context indicates that the differences between federal and state politics are, in fact, minimal. See infra notes 83-6 and accompanying text. Bebchuk offers

The "race for the bottom" view of state competition is no longer the consensus view of scholars in the debate over the efficacy of state competition for corporate charters precisely because its advocates cannot provide tangible proof that competition is, in general, harmful to investors. There is no reason to expect state competition to operate differently for securities law than it does for corporate law. The informational efficiency of capital markets and the dominant presence of institutional investors in such markets ensure that the content of legal regimes will be impounded in the cost of capital, whether they concern only corporate governance or include securities transactions. Accordingly, if mandatory securities rules benefit shareholders, notwithstanding the absence of empirical support in their favor, then competitive federalism will produce mandatory rules as well.

This is not to say that state competition is perfect. In the 1980s, when hostile takeovers emerged as a mechanism for changing control and, correlatively, for replacing incumbent management, the vast majority of states enacted laws that attempted to lower the probability of a hostile takeover. Because shareholders receive substantial premiums in hostile takeovers, most commentators hypothesized that the objective of these statutes was not to enhance shareholder welfare but to entrench management.[78] Indeed, some anti-takeover statutes made explicit a non-shareholder wealth maximization objective. Referred to as other constituency statutes, such statutes permit management to consider interests other than

---

two other speculations to refute the validity of the empirical research, but they are incorrect. His contention (offered to explain insignificant price effects of reincorporation) that both the original and destination state's laws are equally harmful to shareholders, see Bebchuk, supra, 1449-50, is not borne out by the evidence. Not only do some studies find significant positive results, see supra n. 76 (collecting studies), but more important, the legal regimes of the destination states differ significantly from those of the states of origin: the destination states are more responsive to reincorporating firms' demands than the originating states in enacting code innovations; and reincorporating firms perceive significant differences between the legal regimes of the two states and offer them as a reason for moving, see Romano, supra n. 18, 246-7, 258-60. Bebchuk's other contention (offered to explain positive stock price effects) that any price effects of reincorporation are due to changes in the firm's business accompanying or anticipated by the move rather than a reflection of investors' assessment of the new regime, see Bebchuk, supra, 1449, while plausible, is not supported by the data. I tested for significant differences across reincorporating firms grouped according to such potentially confounding transactions, where some categories would be hypothesized to be negative and others positive, for shareholder wealth, and found none. See Romano, supra n. 18, 272. This finding is strong evidence that the positive price effects for the full sample in my study were due to investors' assessments of the domicile change and not accompanying or anticipated transactions.

[78] See, e.g., Easterbrook and Fischel, supra n. 15, 220-2. Some commentators contended, however, that takeover defenses benefited shareholders by solving a coordination problem created by dispersed stock ownership and thereby enabling managers to negotiate higher bid prices. See, e.g., Bebchuk, Lucian A. 'The Sole Owner Standard for Takeover Policy' 17 *J. Leg. Stud.* 197 (1988); Carney, William J. 'Shareholder Coordination Costs, Shark Repellents, and Takeout Mergers: The Case Against Fiduciary Duties' 1983 *Am. B. Found. Res. J.* 341.

shareholders (that is, factors besides the offered price) in deciding whether to oppose a bid.[79]

Consistent with the view that restricting hostile takeovers is not beneficial to shareholders, the enactment of anti-takeover laws produced negative or statistically insignificant stock price reactions.[80] Delaware, with the largest stake in the chartering business, stands out, however, as an anomaly in the takeover statute legislative process. In contrast to its position as an innovator in corporation code provisions, in the takeover statute context, Delaware was a laggard behind other states, and its regulation is considerably less restrictive of bids.[81] More important, charter competition limits the extent to which states can restrict takeovers: when Pennsylvania enacted what was considered to be a draconian statute, a majority of firms opted out of its coverage because of demands made by their investors, who raised the prospect of selling their shares and reinvesting in firms incorporated in states with no or less restrictive statutes, such as California and Delaware.[82] Consequently, other states did not adopt the Pennsylvania statute.

[79] For an analysis of these statutes, see Romano, Roberta 'What Is the Value of Other Constituency Statutes to Shareholders?' 43 *U. Toronto L.J.* 533 (1993). Although I found these statutes had no significant stock price effect on the specific legislative event dates and two-day event intervals, John Alexander, Michael Spivey, and Wayne Marr, infra, found a significant negative price effect (for firms without poison pills or anti-takeover charter amendments) for two of the statutes that I examined for event intervals of two and three days, and for a third statute, Indiana's 1989 statute, that was improperly included in their sample because Indiana had an other-constituency statute in effect since 1986. See Alexander, John C., Michael F. Spivey, and M. Wayne Marr 'Nonshareholder Constituency Statutes and Shareholder Wealth: A Note' *Journal of Banking and Finance* 21 (1997) 417, 427. I, in fact, found a negative effect for the earlier Indiana statute, see Romano, supra, 539, but it is not a "clean" statute (it was passed with another anti-takeover provision). I did not find any difference for firms with or without defensive tactics in place, but the sample was not subdivided by firm characteristics for each state statute separately, and therefore the results cannot be compared. In addition, my sample consisted of larger firms, as it was constructed solely from NYSE listings while Alexander, Spivey, and Marr included American Stock Exchange and NASDAQ-traded firms; because at least one study has found that it is small firms that experience negative price effects from takeover statutes, see Fields, M. Andrew and Janet M. Todd 'Firm Size, Antitakeover Charter Amendments, and the Effect of State Antitakeover Legislation' *Managerial Finance* 21 (1995) 52, the difference in the studies' samples may explain the difference in the results.

[80] The most comprehensive study, which finds a small but significant negative stock price effect is Karpoff, Jonathan and Paul Malatesta 'The Wealth Effects of Second-Generation State Takeover Legislation' *Journal of Financial Economics* 25 (1989) 291 (study of 40 statutes). Romano, supra n. 5, 60-9, reviews the empirical research on takeover statutes.

[81] Correspondingly, in contrast to the anti-takeover statutes of other states, the Delaware statute did not have a negative stock price effect. See Jahera, John S. and William N. Pugh 'State Takeover Legislation: The Case of Delaware' *Journal of Law, Economics, and Organization* 7 (1991) 410, 416-9 (insignificant or positive over eight two-day event intervals); Karpoff and Malatesta, supra n. 80, 315 (insignificant over two-day event interval).

[82] See Romano, supra n. 5, 68-9.

There is also no evidence that a monopolist-regulator enforcing one national corporation law would produce better takeover regulation than the states. Quite to the contrary, in all likelihood, a monopolist-regulator would make the situation worse. The political dynamics over takeover regulation would be unchanged. The groups that are influential in state politics outside of Delaware—local firm managers—are as influential in Washington. They provide, for instance, the bulk of the witnesses testifying for takeover regulation.[83] In addition, members of Congress whose districts included hostile takeover targets were the principal advocates for legislation,[84] just as states with hostile targets were the enactors of protective legislation.[85] Moreover, the congressional legislation on takeovers enacted under the securities laws, the Williams Act, paralleling the state statutes, favors incumbent managers over bidders by delaying bids and the overwhelming majority of bills introduced concerning federal takeover regulation since the Williams Act have sought to make hostile bids more difficult.[86]

With only a national law, there would be no safety valve offered by a competing jurisdiction (such as California and Delaware in the current federal system of corporate law) to constrain takeover legislation, and a legislative or judicial mistake would be more difficult to reverse, as Congress moves considerably more slowly than state legislatures.[87] As the experience with state takeover laws indicates, although in the short run there will be deviations from the optimum in a federal system, in the longer run competitive pressure is exerted when states make mistakes, as in the example of firms opting out of Pennsylvania's takeover statute. Such pressure is absent in an exclusive one-regulator system.

The empirical literature concerning the efficacy of state competition for corporate charters has been my focus of analysis not only because an assessment of the efficacy of charter competition underlies the arguments for and against the market approach to securities regulation, but also because economic theory

---

[83] See Romano, Roberta 'The Future of Hostile Takeovers: Legislation and Public Opinion' 57 *U. Cin. L. Rev.* 457, 485 (1988). Only witnesses employed by the government participated in a greater number of takeover legislation hearings than corporate managers. See Romano, supra.

[84] See Romano, supra, n. 83, 482-4; Lehn, Kenneth and James Jones 'The Legislative Politics of Hostile Corporate Takeovers' (Unpublished Manuscript, 1987; on file with author).

[85] See Butler, Henry N. 'Corporate-Specific Anti-Takeover Statutes and the Market for Corporate Charters' 1988 *Wis. L. Rev.* 365; Romano, supra n. 83, 461.

[86] See Romano, supra n. 83, 470-4.

[87] See Romano, supra n. 5, 48-9. This explains why Congress did not amend the Williams Act to restrict takeovers further in the 1980s. Over the course of its lengthy deliberative process on takeover legislation, the Supreme Court upheld state takeover regulation, and firms redirected their lobbying efforts from Congress to the states, which could provide a target with relief more quickly than Congress.

provides limited guidance concerning whether a monopolist will provide the optimal degree of product quality, variety, or innovation, issues of importance in the regulatory context. Whether a monopolist's choice of quality is socially optimal depends on the difference between the marginal and average consumers' willingness to pay for quality, as is true of price-taking competitors; whether the monopolist will undersupply quality compared to the competitive market depends on the elasticity of demand.[88] There is a similar ambiguity concerning whether a monopolist will produce too few or too many products; the answer again depends on the elasticities of demand and whether the goods in question are substitutes.[89]

Extending the theory of monopolistic firms to regulators, William Albrecht et al. present a model in which multiple regulators provide efficient regulation when the goods regulated are substitutes, in contrast to a monopolist (or collusive regulators).[90] Although it is most plausible to conceptualize the products in the securities regulation context as substitutes, as all states' securities codes are available to all firms, if different states' laws are appropriate for specific types of firms and diversified investors desire to hold such firms in fixed proportions, the products could be conceptualized as complements. Lacking information on demand elasticities for securities laws, Albrecht et al.'s model is only suggestive of the benefits of the policy advocated in this article, and we must rely instead on the best available empirical evidence, the evidence from state competition for corporate charters. Charter competition has not resulted in product differentiation across states (that is, corporate law regimes are substi-

---

[88] In other words, while a social planner would set quality by the average consumer's valuation because she looks at all consumers' welfare, the monopolist, concerned with profits and not social surplus, sets quality by the marginal consumer's valuation because the price increase for higher quality can be passed on to all inframarginal consumers. As the marginal consumer is not likely to be representative of the population, the monopolist's product quality choice will differ from that of the social planner (i.e., it will undersupply quality if the average valuation exceeds the marginal valuation). The bias in quality introduced by the monopolist can be identified only if output will be the same in both cases; this is generally not the case because a monopolist tends to produce less output for a given quality. See Tirole, Jean *The Theory of Industrial Organization* 100-2 (Cambridge, Mass. 1988).

[89] When the monopolist can produce only one product, because the monopolist cannot appropriate the net consumer surplus from introducing a new product design, there may be too few products under monopoly compared to the social optimum; when the monopolist can offer multiple products that are substitutes, it may introduce "too many" products compared to the social optimum because if it charges an above-marginal price for one good it can create demand for a second good, which would not exist if the first good was competitively priced. See Tirole, supra n. 88, 104-5. The analysis concerning the monopolist's choice for product diversity is substantially the same as that for product innovation.

[90] Albrecht, William P., Corinne Bronfman, and Harold C. Messenheimer 'Regulatory Regimes: The Interdependence of Rules and Regulatory Structure' in: Lo, Andrew (ed.) *The Industrial Organization and Regulation of the Securities Industry* 9, 27 (Chicago 1996).

tutes),[91] and investors have benefited from the competition. These data suggest that there will be substantial benefits for investors from opening securities regulation up to competition as well.

III. How Would State Competition for Securities Regulation Work?

For states to compete in the production of specific laws, a state must receive some benefit from the activity. In the corporate law setting, the benefit is financial: states collect franchise tax revenues from locally incorporated firms. Over the past thirty years the franchise tax revenue collected by Delaware, which is the leading incorporation state despite having few local corporations, averaged 16.7% of its total tax revenue (see Table 1). This revenue greatly exceeds what Delaware spends on its corporate law system.[92] If the regulation of securities transactions depended on incorporation state as well, the incentive to obtain franchise tax revenues would increase, as there would be more dimensions on which a state could serve its corporate clientele. That is, a state could increase the number of incorporations, and hence its franchise tax revenues, by offering a desirable securities law as well as a desirable corporate law.

An additional potential revenue source for states competing over securities regulation is filing fees, which accompany the registration of a public offering of securities. These fees can be substantial, as indicated in Table 2, which reproduces the fees collected by the SEC over the past thirty years for the registration of securities and various other filings.[93] Since 1983 the SEC's fee collections

---

[91] See Romano, supra n. 5, 45-8.

[92] The figures in Table 1 provide a conservative estimate of the profitability of Delaware's chartering business because they overstate its expenditures by including—in addition to the appropiations for the Division of Corporations in the Office of the Secretary of State, which administers the corporate registration process—the total appropriations for the Chancery Court and Supreme Court, which hear corporate law cases, at trial and on appeal, respectively, but such cases are only a fraction of their caseload. For example, only thirty percent of Chancery court cases are corporate law cases. See 'Chancery Court High Stakes in Delaware' *Nat'l L. J.* (Feb. 13, 1984) 32. In addition, the outlays for the Division of Corporations were only separately itemized after 1972; for the years before 1972 the table includes the entire appropriation for the Secretary's Office, although in the subsequent years the ratio of the budget for the Division to the budget for the Office is slightly under eighty percent. The appropriations figures come from the 'Laws of Delaware' (volumes 52-70) (1965-95); and the tax revenues from U.S. Bureau of the Census 'State Government Tax Collections' (1966-1996).

[93] The bulk of the SEC's fee revenue comes from securities' registration. For example, in 1996, securities registered under the 1933 Act accounted for 75% of the agency's fee revenue, and transactions of covered exchange-listed securities comprised a further 7%. See SEC '1996 Annual Report' (visited Jan. 5, 1998) <http://www.sec.gov/asec/annrep96/polas.htm>. The figures for fees collected in the 1960-70s include the fees from the registration of exchanges and

Table 1: Delaware's Revenue from Corporate Charters

Year	Franchise Taxes ($000)	% Total Tax Collected	Appropriations ($000)
1966	14,091	10.9	492
1967	17,615	12.6	517
1968	21,414	14.8	606
1969	20,572	13.1	645
1970	43,924	22.5	722
1971	55,212	24.9	836
1972	49,129	19.1	697
1973	50,777	17.7	699
1974	57,073	18.5	984
1975	55,030	16.4	1,051
1976	67,887	18.9	1,208
1977	57,949	14.8	1,255
1978	60,509	13.5	1,385
1979	63,046	12.8	1,482
1980	66,738	12.9	1,899
1981	70,942	12.9	2,230
1982	76,591	12.9	2,448
1983	80,031	12.5	2,847
1984	92,270	12.9	2,721
1985	121,057	14.8	3,242
1986	132,816	15.0	3,809
1987	152,152	15.4	4,746
1988	180,583	17.7	4,719
1989	195,862	17.3	4,873
1990	200,201	17.7	6,398
1991	203,868	17.5	6,953
1992	297,004	22.1	6,591
1993	284,839	21.3	6,831
1994	307,008	21.3	7,980
1995	336,348	21.2	7,104
1996	350,035	20.7	9,462

Note: Appropriations for Delaware's chartering business consist of state outlays, for the fiscal year ending June 30, on the Division of Corporations in the Office of the Secretary of State and on the Supreme Court and Chancery Court.

Sources: U.S. Bureau of the Census 'State Government Tax Collections' (1966-1996); 'Laws of Delaware' (1965-1995).

brokers as well as securities. See, e.g., SEC '36th Annual Report' 210 (1970) (figures for 1968-70); SEC '33rd Annual Report' 149 (1967) (figures for 1965-67).

Table 2: SEC's Financing

Year	Appropriation ($000)	Fees Collected ($000)	% Fees to Appropriation
1966	16,442	6,608	40
1967	17,550	9,706	55
1968	17,730	14,623	82
1969	18,624	21,996	118
1970	21,905	15,526	71
1971	23,615	16,374	69
1972	26,817	19,000	71
1973	30,293	22,000	73
1974	36,227	22,000	60
1975	44,427	24,000	54
1976	49,000[+]	26,000	53
1977	56,270	29,000	52
1978	62,475	26,100	42
1979	67,100	33,000	47
1980	72,739	48,000	66
1981	80,200	65,300	81
1982	83,306	78,200	94
1983	86,690	98,600	110
1984	94,000	121,000	129
1985	106,382	144,000	135
1986	106,323	215,000	202
1987	114,500	263,700	230
1988	135,221	250,000	185
1989	142,640	214,000	150
1990[*]	166,633	232,000	139
1991	189,083	259,000	137
1992	225,792	406,000	180
1993	253,235	517,000	204
1994	259,000	593,000	229
1995	267,000	559,000	209
1996	297,400	774,000	260

Notes: [+] Excludes supplemental appropriations of over $13 million for transitional quarter, accommodating change in fiscal year.
[*] Since 1990, SEC appropriations acts increased registration fees by .01% of offering's dollar value, with increase offsetting SEC costs rather than going into general revenues.
Source: Securities and Exchange Commission 'Annual Reports' (1967-1996); fees collected for 1972-77 were obtained from Henry I. Hoffman, Assistant Comptroller of the SEC.

have been more than 100%, often more than 200%, of its gross outlays.[94] As a monopolist the SEC has been able to charge a higher fee for registration than could competitive states, but competition need not drive such fees to zero. Delaware, for instance, charges higher incorporation fees than other states and is still the leading incorporation state, a phenomenon indicating that firms are willing to pay a premium for a superior legal product.[95] Securities transaction taxes could be a further source of revenue, as they could accrue to the securities-regulating state, but the competitiveness of capital markets has constrained states from imposing substantial taxes on share transfers. The trend in European countries, for example, has been to reduce or eliminate securities transaction taxes because of competition for stock exchange business.[96]

The financial incentives generating state charter competition have resulted in a race that has tended to the top in corporate law. This result suggests that it would be beneficial for investors to create similar financial incentives for states in the securities law context. States presently, however, have little of value to offer firms in return for the payment of securities "franchise" taxes. State securities case law is not as extensive as that for corporate law because the national securities laws until recently have occupied the field, given expansive interpretations of the federal antifraud provisions by the SEC and courts and the desirability of using federal courts. State securities law is not a complete void, however, because some litigants began turning to state actions in the aftermath of the Supreme Court's restrictive interpretations of the federal antifraud provisions, which began in the 1970s, and this trend is expected to increase given Congress's recent tightening of procedural requirements for federal securities actions.[97]

---

[94] See Congressional Budget Office, 104th Cong., 1st Sess., No. 95-J932-26, Memorandum: Growth of Federal User Charges: An Update (Comm. Print 1995). The SEC's revenue is so great that for many years it sought to be self-financing. Congress initially refused its request, preferring to retain a system in which the fees from SEC filings entered into general revenues and the SEC was allocated a budget far lower than the revenues it produced. In 1996, however, Congress enacted legislation reducing SEC fees over time so that eventually the SEC will collect no more in fees than it costs to run the agency. See National Securities Markets Improvement Act of 1996, §§ 402, 404-405, Pub. L. No. 104-290, 110 Stat. 3416, 3441-4 (1996) (to be codified at 15 U.S.C. §§ 78a, 77f(b), 78ee). States do charge filing fees for the in-state registration of new securities under the current regime, and in preempting the states' ability to regulate public corporations' offering registrations, Congress preserved their right to continue to collect such fees.

[95] See Romano, supra n. 18, 257.

[96] See Jamieson, Colin 'Stamp Duties in the European Community: Harmonization by Abolition?' *British Tax Review* 9 (1991) 318, 318-9.

[97] For an overview of the advantages to investors of bringing securities claims in state rather than federal courts, see Steinberg, Marc I. 'The Emergence of State Securities Laws: Partly Sunny Skies for Investors' 62 *U. Cin. L. Rev.* 395, 418-27 (1993). Grundfest and Perino note the incentives created by the 1995 reform act for plaintiffs to use state courts. See Grundfest and Perino, supra n. 3, 39.

The relative dearth of a developed body of securities case law places states at a distinct disadvantage in competing for corporations with the federal government in terms of substantive securities regulation. In choosing their statutory domicile, corporations place a premium on the presence of a comprehensive case law because a stock of precedents facilitates business planning: firms can structure transactions to minimize the possibility of liability.[98] States can, however, compensate for the problem of meager judicial precedents by formally incorporating federal court decisions interpreting the national laws through either legislation or judicial action, to the extent that the state's statutory language tracks the national laws. This approach is not novel and has, in fact, been adopted in the corporate law context. It facilitated the replacement of New Jersey as the leading incorporation state by Delaware when corporations sought an alternative statutory domicile after a lame-duck Governor Woodrow Wilson and the Progressive party majority in the New Jersey legislature drastically revised the corporation code: Delaware's judiciary had incorporated New Jersey precedents in interpreting its code, which was modeled on the former New Jersey statute.[99] Moreover, a state such as Delaware, with a specialized corporate law court, can compensate for the dearth in precedents by offering litigants the prospect of far greater judicial expertise than the federal courts.

The limited experience of states with securities regulation is one important reason for maintaining a federal government option, at a minimum as a transitional mechanism, in the context of creating competitive federalism for securities law in contrast to corporate law where there is no analogous federal government corporation code in the United States. It is, however, probable that opening securities regulation up to state competition will enhance Delaware's dominant position as an incorporation state. For to the extent that the national securities laws have been accurately taken to task for requiring costly and excessive disclosure and fostering frivolous antifraud litigation, Delaware, in all likelihood, will offer a securities regime that mitigates these problems.

Delaware's fiscal prosperity depends to a significant extent upon providing rules that reduce firms' costs of doing business. As a small state it does not have indigenous income sources to replace the substantial revenue it derives from the franchise tax were it to lose incorporations to a state more responsive to business needs. This motivation is a key to Delaware's chartering market success: Delaware's reliance on franchise tax revenues serves as a commitment device to ensure firms that it will continue to enact legislation that firms desire (statutes

---

[98] See Romano, supra n. 5, 32-4 and Romano, supra n. 18, 249-51.

[99] See *Wilmington City Ry. Co. v. People's Ry. Co.*, 47 A.2d 245, 251 (Del. Ch. 1900). For a more recent example of this approach, see *Santa Fe Hills Golf & Country Club v. Safehi Realty Co.*, 349 S.W.2d 27, 34-35 (Mo. 1961).

that maintain share values as new business conditions warrant code revision).[100] Such a commitment device is critical to the production of corporate charters because a corporate charter is a relational contract, extending over many years during which unforeseen contingencies are likely to arise that make it difficult to specify in advance the parties' obligations and, as performance is not simultaneous in a given period, that increase the possibility of opportunistic breach. In particular, firms select their domicile and pay franchise taxes based on the extant legal regime and run the risk that as business conditions change thereafter the state will not adapt its code (or will repeal key provisions to firms' disadvantage). The opportunism problem of relational contracting is exacerbated when one of the contracting parties is the state, given its role as the enforcer of contracts through the court system.

Delaware has surmounted the commitment problem by investing in assets that have no value outside of the chartering market, thus guaranteeing to firms that it will continue to be responsive in its code after they incorporate. These assets include its specialized corporate court system and a reputation for responsiveness dependent on its high ratio of franchise taxes to total revenues. To the extent that Delaware can gain further franchise revenues from crafting a responsive securities regime, the same factors will operate in the securities, as in the chartering, context, and Delaware will have stronger incentives than the SEC to find the desirable regulatory balance.

IV. Regulatory Innovation and Competition: Variety and Uniformity in State Securities Laws

A more traditionally articulated benefit of federalism that is integrally related to the incentive effects of competition is that it permits experimentation in legal rules, as states implement different solutions to specific problems. This, in fact, occurs in the corporate chartering context. Successful corporate law innovations diffuse rapidly across the states.[101] For instance, to address a perceived crisis in directors' and officers' liability insurance in the mid-1980s, states enacted a variety of statutory approaches, including permitting firms to cap or eliminate monetary liability of outside directors for negligence and changing the fiduciary

---

[100] For the details of the argument, see Romano, supra n. 5, 38; and Romano, supra n. 18, 240-2.

[101] See Carney, William 'Federalism and Corporate Law: A Non-Delaware View of the Results of Competition' in: McCahery, Joseph, William W. Bratton, Sol Picciotto, and Colin Scott (eds.) *International Regulatory Competition and Coordination: Perspectives on Economic Regulation in Europe and the United States* 153, 172-4 (Oxford 1996); Romano, supra n. 18, 233-5.

duty standard of care to wilful misconduct or recklessness from negligence.[102] Within a few years, the vast majority of states copied Delaware's approach permitting charter amendments to eliminate liability.[103]

There is, however, far greater variation in state approaches to securities regulation than in corporate law, which has tended to uniformity in key provisions through the diffusion of statutory innovations.[104] Some states, for instance, condition securities' registration on their meeting a standard of investment worthiness or merit (securities regimes referred to as merit regulation), while the majority employ a disclosure approach, similar to the federal securities laws.[105] The distinction across state securities regimes is not, however, entirely clear-cut because merit review for compliance with the investment standard can take the form of requiring greater disclosure of aspects of an issue viewed with disfavor by the regulator, rather than denial of registration.[106] In addition, the import of the difference is limited because only a subset of securities are subject to state regulation: nationally traded shares, as earlier noted, are excluded from state regulation, and individual exemptions are often granted.[107] Investors can also avoid a home state's merit review regime: if a security is not registered in their state, they can acquire it in an unsolicited secondary market transaction rather than in the initial public offering.

The absence of competition in the securities field most probably accounts for the greater variation in regulatory approach across the states than in corporate law, although the limited applicability of the states' registration regimes is undoubtedly also a factor, for where the vast majority of investors prefer a

[102] See Romano, Roberta 'Corporate Governance in the Aftermath of the Insurance Crisis' 39 *Emory L.J.* 1155, 1160-1 (1990).

[103] See Romano, supra n. 102, 1160; see also Carney, supra n. 101, 167. Firms reincorporating in Delaware to take advantage of the limited liability statute experienced positive returns, while event studies of the enactment of Delaware's limited liability statute, and of firms' charter amendments to opt into the statute, do not pick up a significant positive price effect. See Romano, supra n. 5, 19-24.

[104] See Carney, supra n. 101, 165, 174-5; Romano, supra n. 18, 235.

[105] See Ad Hoc Subcommittee on Merit Regulation of the State Regulation of Securities Committee of the American Bar Ass'n 'Report on State Merit Regulation of Securities Offerings' 41 *Bus. Law.* 785, 790 (1986) [hereinafter 'ABA Report']. Variation in states' approaches to securities regulation dates from the initiation of state securities laws at the turn of the century, when only a subset of the states adopted merit regulation modeled after Kansas' pioneering blue sky law (another name for state securities regulation) which predated the federal legislation. See Macey, Jonathan R. and Geoffrey P. Miller 'Origin of the Blue Sky Laws' 70 *Tex. L. Rev.* 347, 377-80 (1991).

[106] See 'ABA Report', supra n. 105, 823.

[107] See 'ABA Report', supra n. 105, 796 (describing exemptions for issues traded on national exchanges or registered with the SEC); Salwen, Kevin G. 'State Laws Are Often Overkill, Some Say' *Wall St. J.* July 20, 1987 at 35 (describing individual exemptions). Of course, these issues are not exempt from the states' antifraud statutes.

particular regime, competition will produce incentives for regulators to choose that regime.[108] Accordingly, if the variation in securities regulation is due, for instance, to regulators' preference for merit review differing from that of investors, in a competitive system merit regulation will not survive. In fact, even in the absence of regulatory competition, merit regulation has been on the decline, for, in addition to the expanding number of exemptions from coverage under merit regimes, several important states, such as Illinois, eliminated their merit review provisions in the 1980s.[109]

The empirical research on state securities laws does not provide much support for merit regulation. Studies find that securities sold in nonmerit review states have higher returns and greater risk than those sold in merit review states;[110] while this result is what merit regulators set out to accomplish, there is no evidence that the reduction in risk is desirable. Namely, there is no evidence that securities risk is positively correlated with fraud, that investments in nonmerit review states are subject to more instances of fraud than those registered in merit review states, or that investors residing in merit review states are more risk-averse, uninformed, or financially unsophisticated than those in nonmerit states to justify the disparate regulatory policies. The absence of a showing of significant benefits to investors from merit regulation suggests that opening state securities regulation up to competition will hasten its demise.

The probability that competition will hasten the demise of merit regulation is important because it sheds light on a potential concern over abandoning the mandatory federal system—will investors be harmed by a subsequent loss of standardized disclosure across firms governed by fifty regimes? Competitive federalism will not necessarily increase variation in the legal regime. State charter competition has, in fact, produced substantial uniformity across corporate

[108] Saul Levmore offers two explanations of variety in legal rules that suggest that differences would remain across securities regimes even in the presence of competition: variety exists because the rules "do not much matter or . . . raise issues about which reasonable people (even in the same culture) could disagree." Levmore, Saul 'Variety and Uniformity in the Treatment of the Good-Faith Purchaser' 16 *J. Leg. Stud.* 43, 44 (1987). If reasonable people can disagree over which securities regime best safeguards investors against fraud and low-quality investments, competition would not eliminate merit regulation but rather would preserve it, as investors (and hence firms) self-selected across states, choosing the regime that they considered preferable for protecting their financial interest. In addition, if the adoption of either merit review or disclosure regulation does not differentially affect the level of investor fraud, then the choice of regime would not matter and variety could be preserved, although, as Levmore notes, the commercial needs of a national market would press toward uniformity despite the inconsequential effect of variety. See Levmore, supra, 60.

[109] See 'ABA Report', supra n. 105, 86 (legislation eliminating merit authority enacted in 1983 in Illinois and in 1985 in Louisiana).

[110] See Brophy, David J. and Joseph A. Verga 'The Influence of Merit Regulation on the Return Performance of Initial Public Offerings' (University of Michigan School of Business Administration Working Paper 91-19, 1991) (reviewing other studies and presenting new data).

codes, preserving variety in its enabling approach to rules, an approach that permits firms to customize their charters if the default provisions of the statutes are not suitable. This situation is likely to be true for competitive disclosure regimes, as the most desirable disclosure standards will diffuse across the states.

More important, the most significant area of standardization, firms' financial reporting, will still be controlled by the private sector under the Financial Accounting Standards Board (FASB) and thus be consistent across firms complying with its rules. States could require compliance with FASB standards to assist firms' needs for uniformity,[111] or stock exchanges could perform a standardizing function, as they did prior to the enactment of the federal regime, by requiring for listing, compliance with FASB or their own disclosure requirements. Even without such requirements, most firms will comply with most FASB standards voluntarily to reduce their cost of capital, just as firms at times disclose information beyond that required by regulators today.[112] It is important to note that although the SEC does not exercise any statutory control over the FASB, it has authority to promulgate accounting rules,[113] and it has therefore exerted significant influence over FASB by the threat that it would adopt its own standards if FASB would not act.[114] Because the market approach eliminates the SEC's prescription of accounting rules for any firms other than those voluntarily submitting to its jurisdiction, its power to affect FASB standards will be greatly reduced under the proposal.

When competition is introduced into securities regulation, specific rules will undoubtedly develop that differ from those imposed by the SEC, even under state disclosure regimes, as states experiment to find the regime most attractive to registering firms. This may be accomplished by two routes: enactment of substantively different rules from SEC rules; or application to securities laws of the enabling approach taken to corporate law, in which state securities laws (which may or may not be the same as SEC rules) operate as default rules from which firms can opt out if they so choose. Where a majority of firms opt out of a default, the state obtains information concerning the appropriateness of that rule, and eventually the rule will be revised by that state or another state which can

---

[111] In fact, most states currently recognize FASB as the accounting standards setter through their regulation of public accountants. State accounting boards, which license public accountants, control accountants' activities by identifying sources of generally accepted accounting principles (GAAP) and enforcing compliance with such principles through ethics regulations, which typically recognize the FASB as the authority on GAAP. See Miller, Paul B.W., Rodney J. Redding, and Paul R. Bahnson *The FASB: The People, the Process, and the Politics* 22 3rd edn. (Boston, Mass. 1994).

[112] See supra notes 38-41 and accompanying text.

[113] See 15 U.S.C. § 78m (1994).

[114] See Gore, Pelham *The FASB Conceptual Framework Project 1973-1985* 18, 22 (Manchester 1992).

obtain new registrations (and hence increased revenue) by choosing the more desirable default.[115] States could further offer firms a menu of regimes from which to choose (such as the choice of an extensive disclosure regime, a more limited disclosure regime, and a merit review regime), analogous to the states' offering of special statutes for small firms, referred to as close corporation statutes, in the chartering context.

If the SEC's rules are optimal, as its supporters contend, then either firms will not opt out of SEC coverage or they will opt into state securities regimes that are identical to the SEC's regime. But if all states simply mimicked the SEC's rules, there would be little purpose in enacting the market approach, as there will be increased transaction costs (firms will have to inform investors, or they will otherwise have to learn, of the firms' securities domicile choice). The weakness of the empirical support for the rationales underlying federal regulation, important instances of misguided SEC disclosure policy, and persistent concerns voiced over frivolous litigation, suggest that the particulars of securities regulation under competition will differ significantly from the present federal regime.

V. Alternative Market-Oriented Proposals

There are two alternatives to the competitive federalism approach to securities regulation advocated in this article that are also market-oriented: eliminating the mandatory features of the federal regime by converting the federal securities laws into default provisions from which firms can opt out, analogous to the enabling form of corporation codes; and replacing the government regulatory apparatus with a private, exchange-based regulatory regime.[116] Both of these alternatives harness market-based incentives to the regulatory system. Neither is precluded by this article's multiple regulator approach.

1. A Federal Default Regime

In a federal default regime, firms that do not wish to be governed by particular SEC rules or statutory provisions specify alternative provisions in their corporate charters or bylaws (or the indenture contracts for debt securities). Congress would either specify itself, or delegate to the SEC to determine, which securities regulations, if any, a firm must opt out of by a charter, as opposed to bylaw,

---

[115] Examples of default rule changes in state corporation codes are the change in the defaults for preemptive rights and cumulative voting. In the earliest corporation codes, shareholders had these rights unless a firm expressly opted out of them in its charter, whereas in modern codes these rights exist only if the firm expressly includes them in its charter.

[116] See, e.g., Romano, supra n. 5, 107.

amendment.[117] A default system would clearly be more desirable than the present "one-size-fits-all" regime, which is difficult to change because consensus must be developed among all participants regarding the new rule, even if their needs are quite different. For example, the SEC has been surveying registrants with a view to updating its rules regulating shareholder proxy proposals, and on the question of whether to retain the current voting thresholds for a proposal's resubmission, ten corporate respondents produced eight different threshold proposals.[118] A lack of consensus among firms on such a matter is of far lesser import under a default system because firms can obtain the threshold level most appropriate for their shareholder configuration by provision in their charter or bylaws.

Under an enabling approach, if a default rule is suboptimal (that is, the rule's compliance costs outweigh benefits to investors), the majority of firms will elect not to be subject to the rule. Assuming the SEC is informed of firms' choices, perhaps by a requirement that firms file securities "charters" with the agency so that it can track deviations from the defaults, this market response will feed back into the SEC's decision-making process, leading it to readjust its beliefs concerning what regulation is most appropriate and, ultimately, to alter the default rule to one more compatible with investors' needs, just as would occur with state competition. There would also be a potential benefit compared to state competition for securities regulation: there would be a reduction in transaction costs because investors would not have to determine which regime governs their transactions. But if the SEC is not attentive in updating its defaults, there will be little savings in transaction costs because investors will have to identify whether a firm is operating under particular outdated SEC defaults or its own alternatives.

An enabling national regime would be preferable to the current mandatory one but, in my judgment, a competitive system of securities regulation is even more preferable. State competition does not preclude a national enabling regime, as Congress (or the SEC) can adopt an enabling regime in competition with the states, as may any or all states. But state competition provides an additional benefit over a federal enabling regime: there is a straightforward mechanism by which regulators learn of firms' adoption of statutory defaults. Under regulatory competition, there will be some variety in defaults across states, even if key innovations diffuse over time across the states, as has occurred in the corporate law context. This phenomenon will accelerate regulators' identification of the rules most desired by investors, as more firms will register in the states with the

---

[117] The difference between charter and bylaw amendment is that state corporation codes require shareholder approval of changes to the charter, but not to the bylaws.

118 See 'Some of Surveyed Firms Show Consensus on "Cracker Barrel," Other Issues' 29 *Sec. Reg. & L. Rep.* (BNA) 567, 569 (Apr. 25, 1997).

more desirable default rules. This will also reduce investors' transaction costs of learning whether a firm has customized an outdated default.

A further benefit of state competition compared to a federal enabling regime is a more rapid updating of undesirable defaults because of financial incentives. A state such as Delaware will be considerably more attentive to the need to reduce the transaction costs generated by obsolete defaults than the SEC because of the state's financial dependence on franchise taxes (or securities taxes if incorporation and security domicile differ). Because firms have no alternative regulator in the monopolist enabling regime, the SEC will not be exposed to the code-updating incentives experienced by states—the declining revenues due to declining registrations.[119] The pressure experienced by the SEC from global competition—whether under an enabling statute or the mandatory regime currently in effect—is quite weak because resort solely to foreign capital markets for financing is not a viable option for publicly traded U.S. firms. The best evidence that global competition is not as effective a motivator for the SEC as direct domestic regulatory competition comes from the regulation of derivative securities. In the derivatives regulatory context, where the SEC has exclusive jurisdiction—the derivatives disclosures of publicly traded domestic companies—it has been minimally responsive to issuers' concerns about regulatory costs and competitiveness,[120] but where it competes with the Commodity Futures Trading Commission (CFTC) for jurisdiction—the regulation of new equity derivatives products—it moved from an initial position of opposing such products to one encouraging and promoting innovation by its regulatees, stock exchanges, in competition against the futures exchanges regulated by the CFTC.[121]

---

[119] A regulatory monopoly also affords the SEC the opportunity to implement policies favoring the interests of financial market professionals rather than investors, see Phillips and Zecher, supra n. 32, 22-3; Haddock, David and Jonathan R. Macey 'Regulation on Demand: A Private Interest Model with an Application to Insider Trading Regulation' *Journal of Law and Economics* 30 (1987) 311, 318-30. Market professionals benefit from receiving information for free from firms under the SEC's mandatory disclosure policies, and from the absence in the market of more informed traders under the insider trading prohibition. Regulatory capture by market professionals is more difficult under the market approach to securities regulation because corporations will opt for the regime more congenial to investors (the providers of capital will direct their funds to firms in those regimes); correspondingly, regulators sensitive to the number of corporations subject to their jurisdiction will adapt their rules to the preferences of investors rather than those of market professionals.

[120] See SEC 'Derivatives Disclosure', supra n. 54, 6054-62 (describing minor changes made in response to comment letters on proposal and presenting superficial cost-benefit analysis of proposal).

[121] See Romano, Roberta 'The Political Dynamics of Derivative Securities Regulation' 14 *Yale J. on Reg.* 279, 354-9 (1997) (discussing shift in SEC's approach to product innovation). Some might attempt to characterize the SEC's loosening of its holding period for the resale of restricted (unregistered) securities under Rule 144, see 'Revision of Holding Period Requirements in Rules 144 and 145' 62 *Fed. Reg.* 9242 (1997) (17 C.F.R. Part 230), as evidence

A further benefit of state competition compared to an enabling national regime turns on whether any mandatory rules are desirable in the securities context, for instance, to facilitate firms' making credible a commitment to investors that they will not engage in opportunistic behavior and alter a securities default to one offering less protection after the investments are made.[122] Mandatory rules cannot be effectuated satisfactorily under a national enabling approach. For if the national enabling regime consisted of a mix of defaults and mandatory provisions, then we would be left with the problem endemic in the current monopolist-regulator setup: there would be no mechanism checking whether the mandatory provisions were, in fact, the ones that firms would voluntarily choose.[123] Multiple regulators permit mandatory provisions without the conse-

of the SEC's responsiveness to competitive pressures, since the reform is a recognition by the agency that compliance costs were too high for small businesses. See id. at 9243-4. In my opinion, this action does not provide evidence that the SEC is particularly responsive to competitive pressure. The holding period revision took almost two years to be adopted. Delaware, by contrast, responds to corporate complaints much more quickly. See Romano, supra n. 102, 1160 (enactment of limited liability statute within one year of insurance crisis and controversial judicial opinion). Moreover, the change has had no effect on the disclosure obligations of the public companies that are the focus of this article's proposal, as it is directed at easing 1933 Act offering requirements for small firms and not at easing the continuing reporting obligations of the 1934 Act. The 1934 Act disclosure obligations have, in contrast to the SEC's moves to limit 1933 Act coverage, significantly increased over time, as the SEC has come to view that Act as the centerpiece of its regulatory authority rather than the 1933 Act, in a policy referred to as "integrated disclosure." See, e.g., Ratner, David L. and Thomas L. Hazen *Securities Regulation* 129-34 5th edn. (St. Paul, Minn. 1996). Finally, and most important, the SEC has sought to eliminate competition and establish its regime internationally, by identifying harmonization of regulatory standards as a central goal of its policy toward international securities regulation. See 'Policy Statement of the Securities and Exchange Commission on Regulation of International Securities Markets' Exchange Act Release No. 6807, 53 *Fed. Reg.* 46,963 (1988) (regulators should "seek to minimize differences between systems"). Although the SEC's policy statement also asserted that regulators should be "sensitive to cultural differences and national sovereignty concerns," see id., this is belied by the SEC's implementation of the policy at home, where it requires foreign firms to reconcile their financial statements with GAAP in order to list in the United States. See infra notes 176-8 and accompanying text.

[122] Jeffrey Gordon has advanced such an argument in the corporate law context. See Gordon, Jeffrey 'The Mandatory Structure of Corporate Law' 89 *Colum. L. Rev.* 1549, 1573-5 (1989). I am, however, skeptical of a justification for mandatory rules involving promoters' need for a commitment device concerning the stability of the initial domicile choice. See Romano, Roberta 'Answering the Wrong Question: The Tenuous Case for Mandatory Corporate Laws' 89 *Colum. L. Rev.* 1599 (1989). A shareholder vote will be required for a change in securities domicile, as it is for a change in incorporation state, see infra Subsection C.II.2., and, accordingly, the need for mandatory rules as a commitment device will be minimal because the successful occurrence of an opportunistic relocation will be extremely remote.

[123] This problem would also arise under an intermediate reform proposal that followed the approach of federal environmental and safety regimes, such as the meat and poultry inspection programs administered by the Department of Agriculture, in which state regulation supplants federal regulation if the federal regulator deems the state regime to be equally or more effective at protecting consumers than the federal schema.

quent costs, as such provisions can vary across jurisdictions and information will therefore be provided concerning which provisions are desirable through the registration decisions of firms.

2. Regulation by Exchanges

A more decidedly deregulatory approach would be to leave securities regulation to the stock exchanges on which firms list.[124] In such a regime, exchange listing conditions would include the substantive content of securities laws, such as periodic disclosure requirements. Exchanges can solve free-rider problems encountered by individual firms concerning information production, as well as coordination problems presented by investor need for standardized disclosure, thus replacing the government as the solution to a securities market failure. Indeed, much of the voluntary disclosure predating the 1934 Act discussed by Benston was an NYSE listing requirement.[125] Moreover, multiple exchanges will compete for listings, to the extent that maximizing trading volume is a function of listings, and they will thus be subject to the same incentives as states competing for charters, leading to listing requirements preferred by investors (or to shares discounted accordingly).[126]

As with a national default regime, an exchange-based regime is likely to save transaction costs compared to state competition, for by trading in the shares investors are directly informed of which regime is applicable.[127] There could still be a role for the states in an exchange-regulated system, however. Although the over-the-counter market for the largest stocks, NASD's Automated Quotation System (NASDAQ), is a sufficiently developed regulatory organization that can offer its own securities regime, if this regime is poorly suited for the smallest

[124] For a recent article advocating this approach, see Mahoney, Paul G. 'The Exchange as Regulator' 83 *Va. L. Rev.* 1453 (1997).

[125] See Benston 'Evaluation', supra n. 37, 133. Paul Mahoney provides a description of the NYSE's pre-SEC disclosure requirements. See Mahoney, supra n. 124, 1466.

[126] See Fischel, supra n. 30, 125; Mahoney, supra n. 124, 1459. Amihud and Mendelson argue that exchanges will provide trading rules that benefit investors only if firms, and not exchanges, choose where a security is listed (in the context of multiple listing of shares or the trading of derivative securities). See Amihud and Mendelson, supra n. 30, 1442-6. The issues of interest here involve issuer-shareholder transactions, which are governed by the firm's principal exchange, an exchange chosen by the firm, and not trading rules. Thus, the concerns of Amihud and Mendelson and other critics of exchange self-regulation (which focus on exchanges' mismatched incentives regarding trading rules that can exploit investors, see Mahoney, supra n. 124, 1462-3) are not relevant to the discussion.

[127] The transaction cost savings will obviously be reduced if a firm's shares are traded on more than one exchange. Even if the secondary exchange adopts a regime that recognizes the primary exchange's rules as governing all issuer shares regardless of transaction location, investors will have to know which exchange is the primary one.

firms traded over-the-counter ("bulletin board" and "pink sheet" issues), it may be more cost-effective for states, than for those firms' market makers, to organize and operate a separate securities regime.

State regulation does offer one decided benefit over stock exchange regulation, a more effective mechanism of private dispute resolution for securities suits against issuers and a public enforcement system, should the deterrent effect of criminal prosecution for securities law violations be a necessary complement to civil liability. Class action litigation is not well suited for private arbitration,[128] and it is not surprising that arbitration programs currently administered by exchanges resolve individual complaints against brokers, not class complaints against issuers. As a consequence, even when courts have permitted classwide arbitration, they have retained substantial judicial involvement, including the initial determination of the certifiability of the class and review of the settlement.[129] Thus, state or federal courts will be required to enforce the exchanges' regulatory regime. This creates two difficulties. First, the use of tribunals not operated by exchanges externalizes the cost of their legal system, which is a disadvantage from a social welfare, as opposed to investor, perspective. With state securities regulation, the fees the states earn in the registration process will defray the costs of administering securities cases.

Second, regulatory competition is most effective when the sovereign's jurisdiction includes both court and legislature. Canada, for instance, has not developed a viable charter competition across the provinces in large part because the provincial governments do not control the adjudication of corporate law disputes; securities administrators (of any province) and the national Supreme Court share that authority with the incorporation province.[130] This renders it impossible for a province to guarantee to prospective incorporators a responsive legal regime,

---

[128] The hybrid use of courts and arbitrators in class arbitration suggest some of the difficulties. See, e.g., *Keating v. Superior Court* 31 Cal. 3d 584, 621-3 (Cal. 1982) (Richardson, J., dissenting) (describing problems with class arbitration). For a discussion of these and other difficulties by proponents of arbitration, see Shell, Richard 'Arbitration and Corporate Governance' 67 *N.C. L. Rev.* 517, 551, 553-4, 561 (1989); Note 'Classwide Arbitration: Efficient Adjudication or Procedural Quagmire?' 67 *Va. L. Rev.* 787, 799, 805-6 (1981).

[129] See *Keating v. Superior Court*, supra n. 128, 613-4 (Cal. 1982) (judicial involvement in class arbitration includes determination of certification and notice to class, supervision of adequacy of counsel, and dismissal or settlement; case remanded to trial court to determine feasibility of class); *Izzi v. Mesquite Country Club* 186 Cal. App. 3d 1309, 1322 & n. 6 (Cal. Ct. App. 1986) (remanding to trial court to determine certifiability of arbitration class and noting preferability of court determination of any class action problems involving notice and discovery); *Lewis v. Prudential Bache Securities* 179 Cal. App. 935, 946 (Cal. Ct. App. 1986) (appeals court found class arbitration feasible, leaving to trial court the determination of all issues necessary to certify class and provide proper notice). None of the cases permitting classwide arbitration have involved securities law claims.

[130] See Daniels, Ronald J. 'Should Provinces Compete? The Case for a Competitive Corporate Law Market' 36 *McGill L.J.* 130, 182-4 (1991).

because a securities administrator could impose obligations on firms counter-manding provincial laws. A similar difficulty will be experienced by exchanges that are unable to adjudicate all of the disputes arising under their securities regimes. This problem is, in fact, raised in a weaker form even under the competitive federalism advocated in this article, for unless firms adopt forum clauses specifying that all securities claims are to be adjudicated in courts of their securities domicile, investors can file in non-domicile courts and, although these courts will apply the law of the domicile, they may lack the expertise to adjudicate disputes as effectively as the domicile.[131] Thus, regulation by exchanges will at best be a dual regulatory system, with much of the enforcement of exchange rules performed by the government.[132]

It is important to note that state competition for securities regulation does not preclude exchange-based regulation. A state could, for instance, adopt a securities regime only for non-exchange-traded corporations, or enact no mandatory disclosure requirements at all, thereby leaving the determination of such requirements to exchanges. Because such an outcome is within the realm of possible outcomes under competitive federalism, the prudent approach to regulatory policy reform is to implement incremental experimentation, replacing the current monopolist-regulator with state competition and permitting that competitive process to reach the judgment that an exchange-based securities regime would provide as or more optimal a set of rules than the states.

C. Implementing the Market Approach to Securities Regulation

Operationalizing a market approach to securities regulation for issuers requires two legislative reforms. The first and more straightforward to accomplish is to make the federal securities laws optional. This can be achieved by an act of Congress. Alternatively, the SEC could cede its exclusive authority over public corporations under its newly granted exemptive power.[133] This solution is, however, akin to asking the agency to put itself out of business, behavior that would be decidedly out of character for an agency which has historically sought to increase, not decrease, its jurisdictional scope.[134] In addition, an act of Congress expressly eliminating the SEC's exclusive regulatory authority over publicly traded firms is the preferable course of action because the statute creating the SEC's exemptive authority also preempted the states from applying

---

[131] See infra Section C.I. and Subsection D.I.2.

[132] Cf. Mahoney, supra n. 124, 1498-9.

[133] See National Securities Markets Improvement Act of 1996, § 105, Pub. L. No. 104-290, 110 Stat. 3416, 3423 (1996) (to be codified at 15 U.S.C. §§ 77z-3, 78mm).

[134] For an analysis of the SEC's failed effort to expand its jurisdiction to include derivative securities, see Romano, supra n. 121, 355-80.

registration requirements to nationally traded securities.[135] The facial inconsistency between using the exemption to increase state authority when Congress was otherwise reducing state authority would provide opponents of the market approach to securities regulation reform the opportunity to delay, if not defeat, its implementation through litigation.

The second major policy reform, adapting the choice-of-law rule governing securities transactions (site of sale) to one compatible with competition (issuer domicile), could be more complicated to accomplish because it entails coordination by the states to adopt a new rule. It would therefore be more expedient for the congressional legislation making the federal regime optional also to institute the requisite change in choice of law, and this article advocates such an approach. But because Congress has not typically legislated choice-of-law rules, this part of the article not only explains the requisite change but also justifies its adoption and critiques the reigning conflicts approach.

Two additional requirements for the successful implementation of the proposal are also detailed in this part: disclosure of the securities domicile to the purchaser of a security at the time of the purchase; and a shareholder vote to accomplish a change in securities domicile. These refinements, which would be included in the authorizing legislation as conditions for opting out of federal regulation, are necessary to ensure that the new market-oriented regime meets the stated goal of the federal securities laws, investor protection.

I. An Internal Affairs Approach to the Choice-of-Law Rule for Securities Transactions

To establish a market approach to securities regulation, only one sovereign's law can apply to an issuer's securities transactions. This means that only one state's securities law can govern securities transactions when the SEC option is not invoked. Similarly, when the SEC regulatory option is selected, it would preempt all state securities regulation, including antifraud provisions. The state with legislative jurisdiction[136] must be connected to the issuer to ensure the proper operation of state competition—that one state's law governs, and it is the state

---

[135] See National Securities Markets Improvement Act of 1996, § 102, 110 Stat. at 3417 (to be codified at 15 U.S.C. § 77r).

[136] I adopt here terminology more commonly used in the international, as opposed to domestic, law setting: legislative or prescriptive jurisdiction is "the authority of a state to make its laws applicable to particular conduct, relationships or status" (whether or not that state is the forum state), see Born, Gary B. *International Civil Litigation in United States Courts* 491 3rd edn. (The Hague 1996), as distinct from judicial jurisdiction, the power of a court to adjudicate a dispute, which, for U.S. courts, requires both personal jurisdiction and subject matter jurisdiction, see Born, supra, 1-2. The federal securities laws confer both prescriptive and subject matter jurisdiction on federal courts.

chosen by the issuer. This necessitates recrafting the reigning choice-of-law approach, which follows the site of the securities transaction and not the issuer's domicile.

1. Applicability of the Internal Affairs Approach to Securities Transactions

The prevailing choice-of-law approach to securities transactions is codified in provisions of the Uniform Securities Act: the law of the site of the transaction, which is either the state in which the offer or the acceptance to buy the security took place, applies.[137] More than one state can claim legislative jurisdiction over a transaction under this approach, and the state whose law governs is not connected to the issuer.

The present choice-of-law rule, under which the securities law varies across a firm's stockholders by where they purchased their shares, has a number of undesirable consequences for a legal system. These include lack of uniform treatment across similarly situated individuals and unpredictable standards of conduct for issuers, given the possible application of fifty-one (state and D.C.) statutes. These difficulties are, in fact, on occasion presented as the reason for the federal securities laws, most typically in cases involving the states' overlapping jurisdiction with the federal regime, such as the regulation of broker-dealers.[138] In the corporation code setting, the operational problems created by an absence of uniformity and predictability due to multistate shareholders are eliminated because the choice-of-law rule recognized by all of the states fixes one state's law as governing all shareholders' claims, the incorporation state's law. This choice-of-law rule is referred to as the "internal affairs" doctrine because the subject matter of corporate law is characterized as the internal affairs of the corporation.

The rationale for application of the internal affairs rule to corporate law disputes is equally applicable to the choice of law for securities transactions. In particular, choice-of-law commentators justify the internal affairs doctrine by the need for uniform treatment of shareholders. For example:

> "[I]t would be intolerable for different holders of the same issue of stock to have different sets of rights and duties by reason of their stockholdings, perhaps according to the laws of

---

[137] See Unif. Securities Act § 414, 7B U.L.A. 672 (1985); see also, e.g., Cal. Corp. Code § 25008 (West 1997) (codifying section 414).

[138] See, e.g., *Orman v. Charles Schwab & Co.* 676 N.E. 2d 241, 246 (Ill. App. Ct. 1996) (refusing to apply state law to claims against broker because such application would frustrate, if not destroy federal uniformity goal, stating that "if uniformity is not to prevail, neither rule 10b-10 nor the SEC would serve any function or purpose in regulating disclosure").

the various places at which they acquired their stock. Unity of treatment is desirable, and the only single law by which it can be achieved is that of the corporation's domicile."[139]

The *Restatement (Second) of Conflicts of Law* similarly stresses as the rationale for preserving the internal affairs rule, the need for "uniform treatment of directors, officers and shareholders. . . which can only be attained by having (their) rights and liabilities . . . governed by a single law."[140] This approach has also been followed by the Supreme Court in its consideration of whether state takeover laws violate the Commerce Clause. The Court's validation of such statutes depends critically on a state's exclusive legislative jurisdiction as the incorporation state (that is, on the internal affairs rule), which avoids the impermissible risk of a corporation's encountering "inconsistent regulation by different States."[141]

Application of the internal affairs rule to securities transactions should go further than cover litigation arising from initial public offerings under state registration requirements and include secondary market trading. Fraud claims against an issuer should be uniformly adjudicated across investors. It is even more troubling to differentiate fraud claims and corporate internal affairs than to differentiate securities registration requirements and corporate law. Namely, there is no plausible rationale for distinguishing a fiduciary standard of conduct to govern an officer's or director's judgment concerning a corporate transaction such as payment of a dividend or undertaking a merger, from that officer's or director's judgment concerning disclosure about the firm's performance in a public document, nor to permit such standard's differentiation across shareholders. Yet choice-of-law rules establish the application of one state's (the incorporation state's) standard to fiduciary duties at corporate law but leave the latter decision on disclosure to vary with the investor's domicile, even though a duty of full and fair disclosure is at the heart of the fiduciary duties of state corporate law. Such intellectual incoherence concerning fiduciary conduct is the fallout of current choice-of-law doctrine.

The bizarre possibility of fiduciary standards differing across shareholders according to their residence (or other location of their stock purchase or sale) has not yet been the focus of legislators' or commentators' attention because there

---

[139] Leflar, Robert A., Luther L. McDougal III, and Robert L. Felix *American Conflicts Law* 700 4th edn. (Charlottesville, Va. 1986). For a similar analysis by a choice-of-law scholar who specializes in corporate law issues, see Kozyris, P. John 'Some Observations on State Regulation of Multistate Takeovers—Controlling Choice of Law through the Commerce Clause' 14 *Del. J. Corp. L.* 499, 509-11 (1989).

[140] Restatement (Second) of Conflicts of Law § 302 cmt. e (1971) [hereinafter 'Restatement'].

[141] *CTS Corp. v. Dynamics Corp. of America* 481 U.S. 69, 89 (1987). For an analysis of the relation of the CTS decision to the corporate choice-of-law rule, see Kozyris, supra n. 139, passim.

have not been many cases involving conflicting fiduciary standards. The vast majority of securities claims are brought in federal court and settled.[142] In particular, the problem of certifying a class when the standard of liability depends on the shareholder's domicile or investment contract situs has not been raised with any frequency in the securities context, in contrast to the mass tort product liability context.[143] If securities cases are filed increasingly in state, rather than federal, courts, whether in response to the 1995 securities litigation reform or for other reasons, such as a more amenable settlement process,[144] then the class certification issue will take on a pressing importance. Extending the internal affairs rule to state securities fraud claims would have the salutary effect, beyond accomplishing this article's immediate aim of empowering investors by creating a competitive regulatory regime, of disposing of a thorny substantive law problem of varying liability standards and thereby ensuring that a class can be certified.

An additional salutary effect of following an internal affairs approach to securities regulation would be eliminating the potential problem of under-enforcement with multiple potential regulators whereby ambiguity in regulatory responsibility can lead to regulatory free-riding, as each regulator expects

---

[142] See O'Brien, Vincent E. *A Study of Class Action Securities Fraud Cases 1988-1996* 4 (visited Dec. 28, 1997) <http://www.lecg.com/study2.htm#att>; Grundfest and Perino, supra n. 3, 9, 31.

[143] Cf. *Amchem Prods., Inc. v. Windsor* 117 S.Ct. 2231, 2249-50 (1997) (affirming appellate court's rejection of an asbestos class action settlement for failing to meet statutory class requirements and suggesting that the predominance of common issues that is a problem in mass torts may not be a problem in securities fraud). In a small number of securities cases when certifying a federal class, the courts have referred to the class certification issue in passing and largely ignored it, adding, on occasion, the proviso that the class could be decertified or divided up at a later date if individual state law issues presented a problem. See, e.g., *Lubin v. Sybedon Corp.* 688 F. Supp. 1425, 1460-1 (S.D. Cal. 1988) (holding that for purposes of the state securities claim, the federal class if certified, would need to be divided into subclasses of California and non-California investors); *Weinberger v. Jackson* 102 F.R.D. 839, 847 (N.D. Ca. 1984) (certifying class despite assertion that the need for individual determinations of state law applicable to members' claims would overwhelm the commonality of the class, by finding the assertion of a conflicts problem premature as the defendants did not show that there was a true conflict among states' interests). Moreover, when the federal suit thereafter settled, there was either no mention of the individual state law determination issue, see *Weinberger v. Jackson* 1991 U.S. Dist. LEXIS 3938 (N.D. Cal. 1991), or the federal class was certified without any mention of the need to subdivide it for the state claims, see In re U.S. Grant Hotel Assoc. Sec. Litig., 740 F. Supp. 1460 (S.D. Ca. 1990) (*Lubin v. Sybedon* litigation). The *Matsushita* case, in which a state court settlement disposed of federal securities claims, did not raise the multijurisdictional issue because the state class action was a corporate law claim for breach of fiduciary duty and thus only one state's law applied to the class members. *Matsushita Elec. Indus. Co. v. Epstein* 116 S. Ct. 873, 882 (1996).

[144] See supra notes 2-3 and accompanying text (discussing impact of 1995 Act on filings) and supra n. 143 (discussing Supreme Court's recognition of a state court settlement extinguishing federal claims in the *Matsushita* case).

another regulator to be responsible. This is an increasing possibility with the expansion of Internet trading.[145] The internal affairs rule specifies precisely one regulator, the issuer's securities domicile, thereby removing the free-riding problem.

2. Flaws in the Reigning Choice-of-Law Approach to Securities Transactions

Conflict-of-law scholars typically rationalize the disparate choice-of-law approach to securities law that insulates state regulation of transactions in foreign corporations' shares from application of the internal affairs rule by contending that individual securities transactions do not implicate concerns over uniformity.[146] The explanation advanced for the distinction has two prongs: (1) in stock transactions, the individual purchasers are not yet shareholders (i.e., not members of the "corporate community") and therefore the transaction can be characterized as of purely local effect, which is said to give the buyer's domicile state an interest in regulation more significant than the issuer's state; and (2) a corporation can avoid a state's regulation by not selling its shares in that state, and thus need not be subject to inconsistent regulations.[147] The choice-of-law distinction between corporate and securities law is a legerdemain but it has a certain practicality: it is more feasible for a corporation to issue fifty different disclosure statements to accompany the registration of securities than it is to operate with fifty different policies on dividend payouts and voting rights.

The flaw in the choice-of-law analysis that distinguishes corporate and securities laws is, however, easy enough to identify. The common shares of a corporation are the same in whatever state they are sold, and it is arbitrary to apply different criteria to transactions in the same securities simply because of differences in purchasers' residences. Indeed, securities litigation between investors and issuers is not individualized litigation: management's defective disclosures are not differentially or personally directed at particular investors in the anonymity of modern capital markets and the composition of the class of affected shareholders (namely, those who entered into transactions in the relevant interval) is therefore fortuitous. In short, neither the prospective feature of the shareholder relation for a buyer of new securities nor the voluntary choice of selling securities in particular states can be characterized as individualizing the multiparty context of the corporate contract to overcome the desirability of regulatory uniformity across security transactions for the issuer, as well as for

[145] Cf. Harris, Clay 'European Regulators Probe Defunct "Virtual' Brokerage'" *Fin. Times* Dec. 22, 1997 at 16 (Internet broker that sold U.S. over-the-counter shares globally being investigated by four nations' regulators after operations ceased).

[146] See 'Restatement', supra n. 140, § 302 cmt. e (1971); Kozyris, supra n. 139, 520-1.

[147] See Kozyris, supra n. 139, 521.

investors, as they bear the increased cost of compliance with a panoply of regimes.

The demand for uniform and consistent treatment across investors is, in fact, recognized by the states' voluntary refusal to exercise regulatory authority over the securities of interstate (exchange-traded) corporations. The shift in legal regime from mandatory to optional federal coverage does not alter the desirability of this approach. Just as the federal law has trumped securities choice-of-law analysis under the exemptive policy of the state statutes, where a public corporation has chosen a specific state over the SEC as its securities regulator, registration requirements should be governed by that state's law.

Moreover, the limitation of a court's exercise of local legislative jurisdiction by a contract's choice-of-law clause selecting a foreign state is well established.[148] Although there are specific circumstances when courts refuse to enforce such provisions—when there are defects in contract clause formation, such as when the contracts are unconscionable adhesion contracts, or when the contracts contravene the public policy of the state that would otherwise exert legislative jurisdiction[149]—they are not relevant for securities law transactions. First, given the multiplicity of investment choices, securities transactions are not adhesion contracts. In addition, the proposed notice requirement concerning which state's law applies[150] will render highly improbable the likelihood that an investor's agreement to a choice-of-law clause is fraudulently obtained. Second, securities transactions specifying the governing law of a state other than the buyer's state are also not contracts in contravention of public policy, the enforcement of which would deprive the plaintiff of an adequate remedy. Even in the remote possibility that the chosen securities domicile had no securities regulation at all, the absence of an appropriate remedy would not be an issue because a defrauded purchaser could still pursue a complaint under that state's common law fraud and fiduciary doctrines.[151]

---

[148] See, e.g., Born, supra n. 136, 654-5 (contemporary approach in U.S. law regards choice-of-law provisions as presumptively enforceable); Leflar, McDougal, and Felix, supra n. 139, 415-9 (right of parties to determine themselves what law governs contracts is generally approved by authorities and is preferred basis for contract choice-of-law in the 'Restatement', supra n. 140).

[149] See, e.g., Born, supra n. 136, 655, 661; Leflar, McDougal, and Felix, supra n. 139, 416-7; cf. *The Bremen v. Zapata Off-Shore Co.* 407 U.S. 1, 12-3, 15-6 (1972) (expressing similar concerns in enforcement of choice-of-forum clause).

[150] See infra Subsection C.II.1.

[151] See *Roby v. Corporation of Lloyd's* 996 F.2d 1353, 1365-6 (2d Cir. 1993) (upholding a United Kingdom choice-of-law contract provision over federal securities law claims, while noting the adequacy of remedies in English common law). The adequacy-of-the-remedy prong of the Supreme Court's exemptions from upholding contractual choice-of-law clauses has been raised in securities law cases because the federal securities laws prohibit waiver of compliance. See 15 U.S.C. §§ 77n, 78cc(a) (1994). Were the federal statutes optional, the anti-waiver

The conventional conflicts-of-law objection to application of an internal affairs-type doctrine to securities transactions, which is captured by the public policy exception to choice-of-law clause enforcement and requirements that the chosen state have a reasonable connection to the transaction or the parties,[152] is that the investor's domiciliary state has a more important "interest" in a securities dispute than the issuer's domicile. The policy concern that is confusedly asserted as a state's "interest" in this instance is that the issuer's state will not provide an adequately protective regulatory regime against fraudulent sales practices because the buyers (or a majority of them) are not its citizens. This concern is, however, founded on a mistaken premise. The research on state competition for charters indicates that states that compete successfully for corporate charters do not enact regimes that diminish investors' wealth. Investors will benefit from an internal affairs rule for securities regulation as well because, as occurs in the chartering market, investors' preferences will drive the regulatory competition. In addition, the proposed requirement that disclosure of securities domicile must be provided upon stock purchases[153] eliminates the concern of the buyer's state that its citizens will be inadequately protected: domicile notice ensures that buyers are informed of which state's regime is applicable. If the regime of the issuer's state is less favorable to investors than that of the buyer's state, the investor will pay less for the shares or not purchase them in the first place. Consequently, a requirement of physical connection to the state for contracting parties' choice of law to be effective, like interest analysis, makes absolutely no sense in the securities context.[154]

3. Which State Should Be the Securities Domicile?

There are three plausible candidates for the single state whose rules will govern a firm's securities transactions in place of the SEC: (1) a state chosen specifically for securities regulation by the issuer; (2) the issuer's incorporation state; and (3) the issuer's principal place of business. The first approach would be implemented

---

provisions would not apply to firms opting out of the federal regime, and the argument against enforcing a choice-of-law clause would be even more attenuated than it is at present.

[152] See Leflar, McDougal, and Felix, supra n. 139, 417 n. 18 (discussing the relationship between the "reasonable relation" requirement and the public policy limitation on choice-of-law clauses under the Uniform Commercial Code).

[153] See infra Subsection C.II.1.

[154] The 'Restatement', supra n. 140, § 187, cmt. f (1971), the Uniform Commercial Code, and many states, see, e.g., N.Y. Gen. Oblig. Law § 5-1401 (Consol. 1997 Supp.) (choice-of-law clause selecting New York is enforceable whether or not the contract bears a reasonable relation to New York for contracts worth at least $250,000), recognize that geographic contacts may be unnecessary for parties' effective choice. See also Leflar, McDougal, and Felix, supra n. 139, 417-8.

as a choice-of-law clause in the corporation's charter (and noticed on the security). It creates, in effect, a statutory domicile for securities law. Under a choice-of-law clause approach, the choice of securities domicile could vary across a firm's financial instruments, as well as differ from the firm's statutory domicile (its incorporation state). The other two approaches operate automatically and hence do not require independent action by the corporation to effect a securities domicile choice (it does so by its choice of incorporation state or corporate headquarters), unless that choice is the federal government.

The least desirable securities domicile approach is to choose the state of principal place of business. This is because a physical presence requirement introduces friction into state competition. When physical and human capital must be relocated in order to effect a change in legal regime, a firm's decision to move to a more preferable securities domicile is considerably, if not prohibitively, more expensive than when such a relocation can be accomplished by means of a paper filing. Few firms will change domicile to take advantage of incremental legal improvements under such a domicile approach compared to the other two approaches and, correspondingly, the incentives of states to provide securities codes responsive to investor preferences would be sharply diminished. The difference between the domicile choice of incorporation state (statutory domicile) and state of physical presence (referred to as the "siège réel," the corporation's real or effective seat, in some European nations) in corporate law is, in fact, a principal reason for the absence of charter competition across the nations of the European Union compared to U.S. states.[155]

Whether the most desirable approach for fostering competition over securities regulation is the choice-of-law clause or incorporation state approach depends, in large part, on whether there are synergies in having one state administer both the corporate and securities law regimes. This is because the incorporation state approach harnesses the in-place apparatus of charter competition to the securities context. In general, such synergies will be substantial because corporate law expertise is readily transferable to securities law. For instance, with one state's law adjudicating both corporate and securities issues, the standard for directors' and officers' fiduciary duties, including disclosure obligations, across corporate and securities transactions would be harmonized.[156] More specifically, all

---

[155] See Romano, supra n. 5, 132-3.

[156] Indeed, two Supreme Court cases interpreting the federal securities law illustrate the difficulties created by the two regimes being different. In *Basic v. Levinson* 485 U.S. 224, 232-4 (1988), while imposing disclosure duties on managers regarding merger negotiations, the Court rejected as a valid concern the acquirer's desire for secrecy when nondisclosure for such reasons would not obviously be a breach of fiduciary duty at state law, while in *Virginia Bankshares v. Sandberg* 501 U.S. 1083, 1102-6 (1991), the Court found the requisite causation for a private right of action under section 14(a) of the 1934 Act, 15 U.S.C. § 78n(a) (1994), lacking, in a case involving proxy statement misstatements where the complaining shareholders' votes were not required by state law to authorize the action subject to the proxy solicitation. The Court left open

litigation relating to conduct during hostile takeovers would be governed by one state's law. In addition, all legal issues concerning shareholder meetings would be subject to the same legal regime, eliminating the considerable confusion surrounding the SEC's rules regulating shareholder proxy proposals, which both look to the allocation of authority across shareholders and managers of state corporate law and ignore it.[157] Where the synergies of an incorporation state securities domicile include the expertise of the judiciary, a firm can adopt a forum clause to ensure that securities claims are filed in the incorporation state.[158]

But even if the substantive law synergies were limited in number, there is a further benefit associated with the incorporation state approach. Litigation costs will be reduced because the need for line-drawing over whether a dispute implicates securities or corporate law is eliminated, as the same sovereign's rules apply in either scenario.

Although the arguments supporting the choice of incorporation state as the securities domicile appear to be compelling, there are countervailing considerations that militate against mandating such an approach rather than leaving the choice of domicile up to the issuer (the choice-of-law clause approach). First and most important, the choice-of-law clause approach obviates the need to guess whether the potential synergies of one regime for corporate and securities law are substantial—market participants' domicile choices will provide the information. It is therefore most consistent with the market approach to securities regulation. Second, given the variety of securities issued by firms, it is possible that states will specialize in different securities, and consequently, that firms would benefit from being able to select a different domicile for different issues. This is particularly relevant for debt securities, where there are no regulatory synergies with the incorporation state because corporate law deals solely with manager-shareholder relations.[159] Third, permitting a self-standing securities domicile

the question whether there would be sufficient causation if the shareholders lost a state remedy otherwise available because of the misstatement. Id. at 1107.

[157] Compare SEC Rules 14a-8(c)(1) & (7), 17 C.F.R. §§ 240.14a-8(c)(1) & (7) (firms can exclude proposals that are "not a proper subject for action by security holders" and involving "ordinary business operations") with 'Adoption of Amendments Relating to Proposals by Security Holders' Exchange Act Release No. 12999, 41 *Fed. Reg.* 52,994 (1976) (qualifying rules by permitting, where the subject is not proper for shareholder action, proposals couched in precatory language because recommendations to the board are not improper actions at state law, and by permitting proposals involving ordinary business operations, such as employment practices, where they implicate social policy).

[158] Such clauses are presumptively enforced at federal common law and by most states. See *Carnival Cruise Lines, Inc. v. Shute* 499 U.S. 585, 593-5 (1991); Solimine, Michael E. 'Forum-Selection Clauses and the Privatization of Procedure' 25 *Cornell Int'l L.J.* 51, 63, 69 (1992).

[159] See, e.g., *Revlon, Inc. v. MacAndrews & Forbes Holdings, Inc.* 506 A.2d 173, 182 (Del. 1985) (finding board breached its fiduciary duty to shareholders in engaging in takeover

might enhance state competition, as a state could decide to compete more vigorously for securities issues than for corporate charters and thus prevent Delaware from being able to slouch on the securities regime it offers because of its success in obtaining incorporations.

4. Adapting the Securities Law Choice-of-Law Regime to the Market Approach

Choice-of-law rules are generally creatures of judicial, rather than legislative, determination. But statutes may codify choice-of-law rules. For instance, some states have enacted the Uniform Securities Act's choice-of-law provisions, which select the most common judge-made choice, the state where the securities are offered for sale.[160] In addition, some states have adopted choice-of-law clause statutes, which guarantee enforcement of contractual choice-of-law provisions regardless of standard conflicts rules, such as whether the contracting parties have any relationship to the state.[161] Coordinated statutory action by the states altering the site-of-sale rule to an issuer securities domicile rule, such as by amendment to the Uniform Securities Act, would be a more expeditious route for implementing the new domicile choice-of-law approach than reliance on judicial action.

An even more efficacious alternative than coordinated state statutory action is for Congress to legislate the mandatory application of the issuer domicile approach as the securities transactions choice-of-law rule in the statute rendering the federal securities regime optional. Although Congress has not mandated choice-of-law rules, it could do so under its Commerce Clause and Article IV powers.[162] Congressional action is the preferred mechanism for implementing the

---

defensive tactic that protected noteholders, whose rights are a matter of contract); *Harff v. Kekorian* 324 A.2d 215, 219-20 (Del. Ch. 1974), aff'd, 347 A.2d 133 (Del. 1975) (bondholders cannot bring derivative suit). A corporate code would be relevant for a bond contract only when a corporation is close to insolvency, for at that point some states might hold that the board's fiduciary duty encompasses creditors. See *Credit Lyonnais Bank Nederland, N.V. v. Pathe Communications Corp.* C.A. No. 12150, 1991 Del. Ch. Lexis 215, at *108 (Del. Ch. Dec. 30, 1991) (suggesting that board's duty shifts away from shareholders when company enters the "vicinity of insolvency").

[160] See, e.g., Cal. Corp. Code § 25008 (West 1997) (codifying section 414 of the Uniform Securities Act).

[161] See, e.g., Del. Code Ann. tit. 6, § 2708(c)(ii) (1993) ($100,000 minimum contractual amount); N.Y. Gen. Oblig. Law § 5-1404 (Consol. 1996) ($250,000 minimum contractual amount).

[162] See Leflar, McDougal, and Felix, supra n. 139, 6 ("[A]ssuming that the local law of a particular American state permits one of its courts to act in a given instance, the only authority which can effectively say that the court may not apply the law that it chooses is that of the federal government, under the powers delegated to it by the Federal Constitution.") Although there is a well-established judicial tradition upholding forum clauses in commercial contexts, including securities transactions, see, e.g., *Scherk v. Alberto-Culver Co.* 417 U.S. 506 (1974);

securities domicile choice-of-law rule, whether the incorporation state or choice-of-law clause approach is chosen, because it is the most expeditious method for achieving that end as it does not require coordination by fifty state courts or legislatures.

Coordination can occur—the universal recognition of the internal affairs approach to corporate law is a prime example—but it takes time. For instance, most states enforce forum selection clauses; this sea change from an earlier era when such clauses were considered presumptively invalid has occurred by a mix of state legislative and judicial action, exemplifying a policy of reciprocity (that is, the states recognize residents' contracts to litigate in another state) rather than conscious coordination through adoption of a uniform act.[163] But, while the gradual shift to acceptance has been led by Supreme Court decisions upholding such clauses in federal cases over the past two decades, there are still some states that do not enforce such clauses.[164] If there is a similar pattern in the securities context as occurred for the recognition of forum selection clauses (increasing acceptance of the concept of securities domicile with an outstanding small number of holdouts after many years), making the federal securities regime optional will not engender successful competition, at a minimum in the short run, in securities regulation because the incentives of issuers, investors, and regulators are not in alignment when the law of the issuer's selected domicile does not govern all securities transactions.[165]

Congressional enactment of a securities domicile conflicts rule shortcuts such an evolutionary process by implementing immediately all states' adherence to the securities domicile choice-of-law approach, and thereby preserves the advantages of the market approach. It is, perhaps, ironic that the byproduct of federal intervention in the states' securities choice-of-law rulemaking will be a greatly invigorated competitive federalism.[166]

The Bremen v. Zapata Off-Shore Co., supra n. 149, to the extent there might be a question whether firms opting out of the federal regime can also opt out of the federal court system, the congressional legislation establishing the market approach should specify that such choices—forum clauses selecting a state court—are to be enforced by the federal courts.

[163] See Solimine, supra n. 158, 75-6.

[164] See Solimine, supra n. 158, 55, 63.

[165] See supra n. 130 and accompanying text.

[166] Bruce Hay has criticized adopting a non-buyer state approach to products liability litigation, contending that state competition in choice-of-law rules is an alternative, substantively more promising, approach to substantive law competition regarding such torts. See Hay, Bruce L. 'Conflicts of Law and State Competition in the Product Liability System' 80 *Geo. L.J.* 617 (1992). He asserts that states' policies of choice-of-law rules and substantive laws are inversely correlated. Thus, when states can follow a choice-of-law rule favorable to their citizen-plaintiffs under what is referred to in choice-of-law as the "governmental interests" approach, they can adopt pro-manufacturer substantive laws to protect in-state firms without harming in-state consumers. He concludes that this scenario indicates that competition over choice-of-law rules

II. Refinements to the Implementation of the Market Approach

In order to ensure that the investor protection goal of the federal securities laws functions smoothly under the market approach, two additional statutory mandates are necessary in the proposed congressional legislation that renders the federal regime optional and fixes an issuer domicile approach to the states' securities choice-of-law rule. These statutory requirements establish investor safeguards at two critical transactional junctures, one occurring at the individual investor level and the other at the aggregate firm level. The first requirement is disclosure of the applicable legal regime (the firm's securities domicile) at the time an investor acquires a security; the second is a vote of the affected security holders in order to accomplish a change in securities domicile.

1. Disclosure of the Applicable Securities Regime

For state competition to function properly, investors must know what regime will apply to a particular security.[167] The domicile disclosure requirement ensures that

---

will produce the optimal level of substantive products liability law, because it enables states to favor consumers in the choice-of-law rule and manufacturers in the substantive law.

Hay's analysis is, however, mistaken. The governmental interest approach looks to the state's substantive policy to determine a state's "interest" in a lawsuit. If a state's law favors defendant-manufacturers, then a court applying the governmental interest standard will not be able to find that the state has expressed an interest in protecting its citizen-plaintiffs. It will therefore not be able to choose a pro-plaintiff state's law to govern the dispute, as Hay expects. As a consequence, Hay's crucial assumption, that the policy underlying a state's choice-of-law rule will be the inverse of the state's substantive law, is incorrect; the two policies must be positively correlated. Hence, competition in choice-of-law rules cannot substitute for substantive law competition in the products liability setting of concern to Hay, nor in any other substantive law setting. The operation of conflicts-of-law interest analysis will prevent opportunistic choices of inconsistent substantive policies and choice-of-law rules. States can, of course, compete on both choice-of-law and substantive dimensions, but the choice-of-law rule that benefits investors in the securities context is straightforward, an issuer securities domicile rule, because that fosters substantive competition, which advantages investors since their preferences will dictate the competitive outcome. States will thus have an incentive to choose the issuer domicile conflicts rule. But to achieve the full benefits from competition, one state's use of the internal affairs rule must be recognized by all the other states to assure that one state's law will govern all of a firm's transactions with investors. This means that the same choice-of-law rule must be uniformly applied as the choice-of-law rule across the states. Over time, states will probably do so. See supra notes 162-3 and accompanying text.

[167] Of course, not every investor need know a stock's domicile; the informed investors will set the price. This is, of course, the meaning of an efficient market. The best available evidence indicates that the U.S. stock market is efficient regarding publicly available information, the type of information that an issuer's securities domicile is. See Fama, supra n. 55, 1607 (event studies [which test the "adjustment of prices to public announcements", id. at 1577] provide "cleanest evidence on market efficiency"). For general models of information aggregation through prices with heterogeneously informed investors, see supra n. 20; and Schwartz, Alan and Louis Wilde

this condition will hold. To accomplish this notice function, security domicile should be indicated on the instrument (stock certificate or note), analogous to the corporate law requirement that restrictions on share transferability, to be effective, must be noticed on the stock certificate.[168] But because investors rarely receive a financial instrument even after purchase (most stock investments transfer electronically and remain physically held by the clearinghouse depositary), a further mode of notice is essential. The most plausible additional means of domicile disclosure entails a two-pronged approach, directed at both brokers and firms. First, brokers should be required to inform prospective buyers of securities domicile at the time of purchase (or short sale). As federal broker regulation is not being transferred from the SEC under the proposed approach, such a requirement could easily be implemented by agency regulation.

Second and more important, issuers should be required to disclose their securities domicile at the time of initial public offerings as a condition of opting out of the federal regime. The required disclosure should be permitted to take a variety of forms. Where the issuer's domicile requires use of a prospectus to sell securities, the federal requirement should be satisfied by indicating the domicile in that offering document. Where there is no prospectus or other offering document requirement, the issuer should have to inform the prospective buyer of the securities domicile in a writing, an obligation that could be satisfied by the issuer's contracting with the underwriting syndicate to provide the information in writing to prospective purchasers. In addition, for public offerings of a firm whose securities are already traded, where a securities domicile imposes periodic reporting requirements, disclosing securities domicile in the required documents should satisfy the issuer's federal notice requirement as long as such reports are matters of public record (i.e., filed with a state office) and thus available to prospective purchasers. Where a domicile imposes no periodic reporting requirements, then voluntary disclosure of securities domicile in a public document available on a continuing periodic basis (such as in an annual financial report or proxy statement sent to shareholders for the annual meeting to elect directors, in the corporate charter on file with the Secretary of State, or in a publicly available record kept by the stock exchange on which the shares trade) should also satisfy the federal disclosure requirement. These latter forms of disclosure will also suffice for any issuer responsibility regarding domicile notice to investors who acquire securities in secondary trading markets.

Domicile disclosure is not a costly requirement for issuers under any of the possible mechanisms that have been outlined. It would also not be costly for brokers to identify an issuer's securities domicile to prospective purchasers. But

---

'Competitive Equilibria in Markets for Heterogeneous Search Goods Under Imperfect Information: A Theoretical Analysis with Policy Implications' *Bell Journal of Economics* 13 (1982) 181.

[168] See, e.g., Del. Code Ann. tit. 8, § 202(a) (1996).

mandating disclosure of securities domicile at the time of a securities purchase is not clearly necessary to protect investors: markets will price significant differences in securities regimes as sophisticated investors will obtain domicile information prior to their purchases even if domicile disclosure is not mandated. However, given the historical application of the federal regime to all securities, mandated domicile disclosure will go a considerable distance toward mitigating the relatively remote possibility of less sophisticated investors' not knowing that the federal regime may no longer apply. Because such confusion is most likely to occur in the initial years following the adoption of the market approach, the domicile disclosure requirement could be enacted as a sunset provision, expiring, for example, three years after the statute's effective date. For securities trading in markets where institutional investors' presence is limited, such as penny stocks, the domicile disclosure requirement could be retained beyond such a transition period, as the absence of a significant number of informed investors trading in such shares may result in security pricing that does not fully incorporate regime information.

The domicile disclosure requirement would not mandate disclosure of the substantive contents of the relevant regime. Firms can, of course, provide such information to investors in their domicile disclosure, but the statutory requirement would leave acquisition of such details to investors. To the extent there might be concern that unsophisticated investors might mistakenly assume all state regimes contain similar protections and could thereby be duped into buying penny stocks registered under a regime that institutional investors shun, a written disclaimer could be required at the time of such securities' acquisition, in addition to the domicile disclosure, that informs investors, in large print, that "their rights under the securities laws may differ significantly across the states." Alternatively, a disclosure requirement could be fashioned for a regime's significant differences. I am reluctant to advocate such an approach given the costly line-drawing questions it is likely to entail. It would, at minimum, require careful drafting to specify the norm against which differences are to be measured, such as a majority of the states, the old federal regime, and so forth. The prospect of litigation over the fulfillment of the domicile disclosure requirement under such an alternative leads me to opt for the more generic disclaimer approach, if any disclosure beyond the domicile is to be required.

2. Security Holder Approval of Securities Domicile Changes

A different set of concerns regarding the securities domicile choice is implicated when an issuer determines to change its securities domicile midstream than when a shareholder purchases a security with a given domicile. Namely, the price the investor paid for their shares will not reflect the value of the new domicile (unless the change was anticipated at the time of purchase). This is of concern if corporate insiders can behave opportunistically and move to a securities domicile that requires less disclosure or has a lower securities fraud standard than the original regime. Such a move could shift value away from the public to insiders' shares, assuming, of course, that outside investors did not anticipate such opportunistic behavior and pay less for the more protective domicile in the first place.

Insider opportunism regarding domicile choice can be mitigated by requiring the voting approval of the affected security holders before a domicile change can be effected.[169] As in the corporate law context, the federal statute would create a minimum default for the required vote of a simple majority. Firms wishing to operate under a higher, supermajority voting requirement would therefore be able to do so. The most practical means of implementing a supermajority voting requirement would be for the corporation to include such a rule in its corporate charter (and, if commitment to such a voting rule was of concern, to subject its repeal to an analogous supermajority vote). States could also establish higher voting minimum defaults in their securities codes. A supermajority voting default to accomplish changes in securities domicile would not, however, be desirable from the perspective of competitive federalism because when exit from a regime is difficult, the signals from migration patterns concerning firms' preferred provisions are weakened and the beneficial effects of competition stymied.

A majority voting requirement for securities domicile changes could actually aid insiders because in the absence of a voting requirement, it is possible that investors would expect value-diminishing moves to occur and pay less for their shares initially. The presence of a voting requirement commits insiders to proposing a domicile change only when the new regime will increase firm value, rather than when it would disproportionately benefit their own shares, and, as a consequence, investors need not discount shares for opportunistic mid-stream domicile changes. To the extent that promoters value such a precommitment device, a federal voting requirement may well be unnecessary because competitive state codes will include such a requirement. But placing the requirement in the federal statute is a more robust commitment device because as an integral part of the regulatory regime, it would be difficult to rescind (for example, as noted earlier, it is more difficult to change congressional than state legislation).

Some commentators contend that shareholder voting is not an effective safeguard against insider opportunism, because it is irrational for shareholders to vote—that is, an individual shareholder's cost of becoming informed in order to vote his or her interest outweighs the pro rata benefit he or she will receive from

---

[169] A change in incorporation state (the firm's statutory domicile) requires a shareholder vote because it is effected by a merger of the corporation into a subsidiary incorporated in the new domicile state and under all state corporation codes a merger requires shareholder approval.

a correct outcome.[170] This contention, in my judgment, is vastly overblown.[171] In a capital market dominated by institutional investors holding portfolios of stock, issues are repeatedly raised across portfolio firms, reducing information costs significantly on any one vote. More important, even if some subjects of shareholder votes are subject to rationally uninformed voting, a vote on securities domicile is similar to a vote in the merger context, where the stakes concerning impact on share value are high enough to change the cost-benefit calculus for even small shareholders to engage in informed voting.

Voting rights in corporate law are often accompanied by appraisal (dissenters') rights—the right of dissenters to be cashed out of the firm at a price set by a court under statutory guidance.[172] Appraisal rights mitigate adverse outcomes due to uninformed voting: informed shareholders can dissent and, under the statutory standard, obtain the cash value of their shares equal to the value "exclusive" of the transaction that was the subject of the vote.[173] Thus, for a value-diminishing transaction such as an unfavorable domicile shift, the share's appraisal value would be the stock price before any adverse effect from the market's assessment of the value in the new domicile (the outcome of the vote). Such rights could be mandated for dissenters to a domicile change. Appraisal rights, however, come with costs, such as the potential for an unwanted cash drain if many shareholders exercise their rights, the hold-up power that comes from shareholders exercising such rights against a non-value-decreasing proposal, and imprecise valuation of the dissenters' shares that may over- or under-compensate them.

There has not been empirical research examining cross-sectionally the functioning of appraisal rights for charter amendments, which could provide information concerning how frequently such rights are used, what the stock price

---

[170] See, e.g., Gordon, supra n. 122, 1575.

[171] In particular, it can be shown that, under plausible assumptions concerning the breakdown of stock ownership among insiders, outside blockholders, and dispersed investors, a rational strategy for an uninformed shareholder concerned about the possibility of opportunism would not be always to support management and vote "yes," which is the strategy emphasized by commentators critical of shareholder voting, but rather, a mixed strategy of voting randomly against management's proposals or a strategy of not voting at all, leaving the decision to the informed voters. Both of these latter strategies are better than always voting "no," as well as always voting "yes." See Romano, supra n. 122, 1607-10.

[172] See, e.g., Del. Code Ann. tit. 8, § 262 (1996) (providing appraisal rights in conjunction with mergers, which require shareholder approval); Model Bus. Corp. Act § 13.02 (1992) (providing appraisal rights in conjunction with mergers, asset sales, amendments of articles of incorporation that materially and adversely affect shares by specified impact, and any actions taken pursuant to a shareholder vote where charter, bylaws, or board resolution provide for such rights).

[173] See, e.g., Del. Code. Ann. tit. 8, § 262(h) (1996) (for merger dissenters entitled to appraisal, court to determine "fair value exclusive of any element of value arising from" the merger).

reaction was to the amendment when they are used, or whether charter amendment proposals and vote outcomes differ systematically across firms when such rights are present. In states where appraisal rights are not statutorily provided for dissenters to charter amendments, firms do not appear to include such rights in their charters.[174] A plausible inference from such behavior is that appraisal costs outweigh the benefits; either they are an inadequate remedy for opportunistic amendments or insiders rarely propose opportunistic charter amendments. Indeed, if midstream opportunism was rampant, institutional investors would become aware of the practice and promoters would have incentives—higher share prices—to bind themselves against engaging in opportunistic charter amendment by providing the appraisal remedy for such votes. Accordingly, rather than have Congress mandate dissenters' rights in the securities domicile context, their presence should be left to the decisions of securities domiciles, which can legislate such rights, and issuers, which can place such rights in the corporate charter or bylaws if the domicile does not mandate them.

D. The Regulation of Foreign (Non-U.S.) Issuers

The desirability of regulatory competition does not stop at national borders, for the same incentives are at work in a global setting: financial capital is as mobile across nations as it is across U.S. states, and capital providers will require higher returns from investments governed by regimes less protective of their interests, prodding firms to seek out the securities regime preferred by investors in order to reduce their cost of capital.[175] The market approach to securities regulation advocated in this article should, accordingly, apply equally to U.S. and non-U.S. issuers of securities.

---

[174] In the course of over a decade of research which required examining hundreds of corporate charters, I have not come across such a provision.

[175] Although investors favor their home countries in their portfolio allocations, see French, Kenneth and James Poterba 'Investor Diversification and International Equity Markets' *American Economic Review* 81 (1991) 222, 222, cross-border flows of capital have dramatically increased over time, and are expected to continue to do so, see Shapiro, Alan C. *Multinational Financial Management* 403-4 4th edn. (Boston 1991), as financial markets have been deregulated globally, international market capitalizations have increased, and the benefits of international diversification are becoming widely recognized, see Solnik, supra n. 10, v-vi. For concise reviews of such investment trends in the legal literature, see MacIntosh, supra n. 9, 6-10; Fox, Merritt 'Securities Disclosure in a Globalizing Market: Who Should Regulate Whom' 95 *Mich. L. Rev.* 2498, 2523-5 (1997).

I. Applying the Market Approach to Non-U.S. Issuers

1. The Market Approach

Under the market approach to securities regulation, the issuer's securities domicile controls, whether that domicile is a U.S. state or a foreign nation, for all securities sold in the United States. This would be a dramatic turnabout from the SEC's current practice, which assumes jurisdiction over all transactions occurring in the United States, and until recently, asserted jurisdiction over foreign transactions involving U.S. citizens,[176] analogous to the states' choice-of-law rule for securities transactions that looks to the sale location or purchaser domicile.

The SEC's territorial approach to jurisdiction prevents foreign issuers who are in compliance with their home states' disclosure requirements (which are less extensive than the SEC's) from listing on U.S. stock exchanges. The principal reason why the vast majority of non-U.S. firms who could qualify for exchange trading do not list in the United States is that their disclosure costs would increase significantly, particularly with respect to accounting data, as they would have to comply with the SEC's regime.[177] Although the precise cost of reconciliation with U.S. generally accepted accounting principles (GAAP) is not publicly available, James Fanto and Roberta Karmel report that given compliance costs, companies find a U.S. listing worthwhile only if large amounts of equity capital (over $300 million) are required.[178] Other data suggestive of the costliness of reconciliation are that the London Stock Exchange lists five times the number of foreign firms than does the NYSE, and that after the SEC extended its reporting requirements to foreign firms trading on the NASDAQ, the number of such listings declined by almost thirty percent over the next seven years, after having tripled over the seven years prior to the change.[179]

---

[176] See Choi, Stephen J. and Andrew T. Guzman 'The Dangerous Extraterritoriality of American Securities Laws' 17 *Nw. J. Int'l L. & Bus.* 207, 221 (1997) (discussing SEC's adoption of Regulation S, governing overseas transactions, which changed regulatory emphasis from "the protection of U.S. investors, wherever . . . located, to the protection of American capital markets").

[177] See, e.g., Fanto, James A. and Roberta S. Karmel 'A Report on the Attitudes of Foreign Companies Regarding a U.S. Listing' 3 *Stan. J.L. Bus. & Fin.* 51, 70 (1997); Cochrane, James L. 'Are U.S. Regulatory Requirements for Foreign Firms Appropriate?' 17 *Fordham Int'l L.J.* S58, S61 (1994).

[178] See Fanto and Karmel, supra n. 177, 71. William Baumol and Burton Malkiel point out that beyond the time and expense entailed in the translation process for GAAP reconciliation, there are difficulties arising from the fact that GAAP requirements are not adapted to the "circumstances of the foreign firm," such as GAAP rules being tailored to U.S. corporate tax rules that vary significantly from other nations' taxation. See Baumol and Malkiel, supra n. 42, 37.

[179] See Baumol and Malkiel, supra n. 42, 37; Edwards, supra n. 8, 58-9.

The market approach would open up U.S. markets to non-U.S. issuers. This is a policy shift that will not only make U.S. securities regulation more respectful of other nations' policy decisions by reaffirming a norm of international comity, but will also benefit U.S. investors. For they will no longer have to incur the substantial costs of purchasing shares on foreign exchanges, as they have been doing in increasing numbers to invest directly in non-U.S. corporations.[180]

Under the market approach, foreign firms (firms not incorporated in the United States) will be able to choose their securities domicile for U.S. trading purposes, and therefore will not need to comply with SEC disclosure requirements to trade in the United States. This result has some precedent: the multijurisdictional disclosure system (MDS) adopted by the SEC and the Ontario and Quebec Securities Commissions in 1991 enables Canadian firms to trade in the United States by complying with Canadian disclosure requirements, although they must reconcile their financial data with GAAP.[181] Canada is the only nation with which the SEC has entered into such an agreement, however, because its disclosure requirements are similar to U.S. requirements.[182] In addition, the SEC has itself relaxed its disclosure requirements for non-U.S. firms for certain nonfinancial items, such as ownership data. The market approach expands the SEC's multijurisdictional disclosure system without requiring disclosure regimes harmonized with the SEC or GAAP reconciliation. But it goes still further than these precedents: it renders inapplicable to such issuers the antifraud provisions of the federal securities laws (unless they opt for SEC regulation), in contrast to the MDS, which retains U.S. antifraud liability for Canadian firms. If all nations adopt the market approach, all of a firm's shareholders would be subject to the same securities regime, wherever they purchased their shares, and there would be uniformity of treatment of investors as occurs in the corporate law context. Rather than harmonization of national securities regime, the universal application of the market approach should be the goal of international securities regulation.

The SEC was unwilling to extend the multijurisdictional accord globally to nations with lower levels of disclosure than it requires because, in its view, investors in U.S. markets would not be adequately protected if firms traded without releasing all of the information that the SEC and U.S. accounting standards mandate. There is, however, an absence of evidence that the lower levels of disclosure in other nations adversely affect investors. Studies of price reactions to foreign issuers' release of information reconciling their financial

---

[180] See Edwards, supra n. 8, 54, 59.

[181] See 'Multijurisdictional Disclosure and Modifications to the Current Registration and Reporting System for Canadian Issuers' Securities Act Release No. 6902, 56 *Fed. Reg.* 30,036 (1991).

[182] See, e.g., Jennings, Richard W., Harold Marsh, Jr., and John C. Coffee, Jr. *Securities Regulation Cases and Materials* 1581 7th edn. (Westbury, N.Y. 1992).

reports with GAAP do not consistently find any effects, leading several economists to conclude that the SEC's requirement that foreign firms' disclosures conform to GAAP is of no benefit to investors.[183] In addition, despite the lower level of disclosure required, foreign markets are not less efficient than U.S. markets.[184] Finally, different accounting systems do not appear to provide less information about firms' financial situations of importance to investors; for instance, although German accounting is considerably less rigorous than GAAP, the information provides as good a probability estimate of a German firm's bankruptcy as GAAP information does for U.S. firms.[185]

If the lower level of disclosure of other nations was, in fact, of concern to U.S. investors or adversely affected investments, they would discount the shares of foreign firms or not invest in them in the first place. Because of such a reaction, many firms would voluntarily reveal more information than required by their home state, albeit less than the SEC would have required, under the market approach.[186] An increase in U.S. listings of non-U.S. issuers that are covered by less extensive disclosure regimes than the SEC requires would not, therefore, be harmful to investors and would instead lower the transaction costs entailed in direct foreign investment.

The securities domicile choice of foreign firms available under the market approach may be limited in practice to their home country (assuming they do not choose the SEC), compared to the choice of U.S. firms because their home countries' choice-of-law rules may not recognize the legislative jurisdiction of a nation that is not the site of the securities transaction. Indeed, for corporate law domicile, many nations do not recognize a statutory domicile and follow instead a physical presence or "seat" rule.[187] If those nations followed this principle for securities domicile as well, then non-U.S. firms would have no securities domicile choice but their home country (or the United States as the site of the transaction). But even if the domicile choice is circumscribed because of home country practices, the number of foreign firms listed on U.S. exchanges would markedly increase under the market approach because it eliminates the need for such firms to undertake costly expenditures to comply with the SEC's disclosure regime, such as the GAAP reconciliation.

---

[183] See, e.g., Baumol and Malkiel, supra n. 42, 43-4; Edwards, supra n. 8, 61-2.

[184] See supra n. 42 and accompanying text.

[185] Baetge/Thiele (this volume Ch. 9).

[186] Firms currently respond to such incentives. See supra notes 38-41 and accompanying text.

[187] See Romano, supra n. 5, 132 (European nations, except the Netherlands and United Kingdom, follow real seat rule).

2. Securities Litigation Involving Non-U.S. Issuers

There is a potential problem for U.S. investors who invest in firms subject to a non-U.S. securities regime should they need to seek redress for a securities law violation. Namely, the collective action problem inherent in any type of shareholder litigation—that the cost of pursuing a lawsuit exceeds a shareholder's pro rata share of any recovery but not the aggregate award[188]—would be exacerbated by requiring prosecution of a claim in a foreign forum, both because of the expense and because of the absence of mechanisms for aggregating claims in many countries.

U.S. investors will, of course, discount the shares of foreign firms against which they can never exercise their rights under foreign securities laws or avoid such securities entirely. Foreign firms may therefore find it in their self-interest to ensure that U.S. investors can prosecute securities claims in U.S. courts. The institutional mechanism for obtaining a foreign corporation's consent to a U.S. court's jurisdiction is not difficult to construct: the issuer could provide such a written consent in the documentation accompanying the sale of stock to a U.S. investor. In addition, U.S. stock exchanges competing for business could require issuers' consent to jurisdiction in the United States as a listing requirement, if they thought that such a rule would enhance the value of listed shares and thereby increase trading interest.

There is, however, a question as to whether U.S. courts will accept jurisdiction as a forum state over a securities dispute between investors and an issuer that is subject to foreign (non-U.S.) securities law. Traditionally, in international litigation, securities law is treated as a species of public law, over which local courts either declined to exercise jurisdiction or accepted jurisdiction but applied their own substantive law. The distinction between public and private law is arcane, and has largely been undone by the Supreme Court in the securities context through its validation of arbitration clauses to resolve securities law disputes, reversing prior convention that arbitration was inappropriate for public, as opposed to private, law subjects.[189] Accordingly, in keeping with the contemporary trend merging the jurisdictional approach in public and private law areas, it would be appropriate for U.S. courts to apply private law jurisdictional

---

[188] See generally Coffee, Jr., John C. 'The Unfaithful Champion: The Plaintiff as Monitor in Shareholder Litigation' 48/3 *Law & Contemp. Probs.* 5 (1985) (discussing collective action problem in shareholder litigation).

[189] See *Rodriguez v. Shearson/American Express, Inc.* 490 U.S. 477 (1989), *Shearson/American Express, Inc. v. McMahon* 482 U.S. 220 (1987); and *Scherk v. Alberto-Culver Co.*, supra n. 162; overruling *Wilko v. Swan* 346 U.S. 427 (1953).

principles to international securities transactions.[190] In the private law setting, forum selection clauses are presumptively enforceable,[191] and the exceptions to this presumption—defects in contract formation, unreasonableness, and public policy,[192] as well as the *forum non conveniens* doctrine—have no relevance for our context: the foreign defendant will have consented to a U.S. forum; federal policy will have expressly authorized foreign legislative jurisdiction; and the plaintiff-investor's local domicile and purchase can provide sufficient "contact" with a U.S. forum to render the local forum's retention of jurisdiction both feasible and desirable.

While U.S. jurisdiction should be readily attainable, a more important question is whether a U.S. court should exercise jurisdiction or, to put it another way, is it desirable from the perspective of regulatory competition for foreign firms to choose a U.S. forum for securities suits? The adjudication of securities disputes by non-domicile courts can undermine the effectiveness of competition, as the legislating state does not control the interpretation of its laws. The problem is not as severe as it is for Canadian provinces competing for corporate charters because the U.S. courts will be attempting in good faith to apply the domicile's law, whereas Canadian securities administrators intentionally apply their own governance standards rather than the law of the domicile province. But the difficulty here is not solely a matter of substantive law interpretation.[193] The U.S. approach that adopts the procedural rules of the forum can have a significant impact on substantive outcomes because, in addition to class action mechanisms to aggregate individual claims not prevalent in other countries, U.S. procedures—including rules on discovery, pleading requirements, contingent fees, and the absence of a "loser pays" cost rule—are far more favorable to plaintiffs than those of foreign courts.[194]

[190] The Supreme Court's forum selection clause jurisprudence has especially emphasized the needs of parties engaged in international commercial transactions when sustaining the parties' contractual choices. See, e.g., *The Bremen v. Zapata Off-Shore Co.*, supra n. 149, 8-18 (1972).

[191] See *The Bremen v. Zapata Off-Shore Co.*, supra n. 149, 17-9; and supra n. 158 and accompanying text.

[192] See, e.g., Born, supra n. 136, 395.

[193] Under current law, U.S. courts have imposed U.S. standards on foreign issuers rather than applied non-U.S. law in their role as a forum, in a misguided attempt to protect U.S. investors. See, e.g., *Consolidated Gold Fields PLC v. Minorco, S.A.* 871 F.2d 252, modified, 890 F.2d 569 (2d Cir. 1989) (applying U.S. law to takeover contest between foreign firms that permitted U.S. residents to tender only if they did so from outside United States); *Leasco Data Processing Equip. Corp. v. Maxwell* 468 F.2d 1326 (2d Cir. 1972) (applying U.S. law to purchase of stock in British corporation on London Stock Exchange by U.S. corporation). The danger of such conduct continuing under the proposed regime is probably low, given that Congress will have expressly authorized the applicability of non-U.S. law to the transactions.

[194] See Born, supra n. 136, 4. The critical differences in litigation procedures may lead some foreign issuers to consider an alternative approach to the selection of a convenient forum for disputes, use of an international arbitration clause. But it is problematic whether investors will

There is a powerful competing consideration in favor of a U.S. forum against the substantive concerns raised by a non-domicile adjudicator: the significant inconvenience for a U.S. investor to prosecute a securities claim abroad. The balancing of the various factors regarding the appropriateness of a U.S. forum is a calculation that is best undertaken by the foreign issuer, rather than by Congress or regulators. As long as investors are informed of the issuer's choice-of-law and choice-of-forum selections, they will be able to price their ability to obtain relief for securities violations, and issuers will respond accordingly, trading off U.S. forum protections that facilitate securities litigation and the cost of capital with the substantive advantages of a foreign forum.

II. Comparison with Other Reform Proposals

The outcome of applying the market approach to non-U.S. issuers—that their shares will be able to trade in U.S. markets under a non-U.S. securities regime— is certainly not a novel idea. Several commentators have advocated reform of the SEC's approach to foreign issuers to enable such issuers' shares to trade in U.S. markets without coming under the SEC's regulatory regime (or its most onerous components, such as GAAP reconciliation).[195] For instance, in a comprehensive effort to rationalize this aspect of securities regulation, Merritt Fox contends that an issuer nationality rule (physical presence domicile) is the rule that maximizes social welfare.[196]

Although the substantive policy outcome between Fox's proposal and this article's may not be significantly different—that is, non-U.S. issuers trading on a U.S. exchange are likely to choose their home country's securities regime under the market approach—the rationales are fundamentally at odds. This is because

place sufficient value on such an approach to make it worthwhile for the issuer to offer arbitration unless some features of U.S. litigation practices are retained in the arbitration agreement, such as the use of representative actions. Although arbitration is less costly than litigation to pursue an individual claim, the profitability of most securities cases comes from the ability of an attorney to aggregate claims. Despite potential difficulties in claim aggregation, in the international securities context there is a significant advantage to arbitration over litigation that may make it highly attractive to U.S. investors: it is easier to enforce arbitration awards worldwide because virtually all nations (including the United States) are signatories to the United Nations Convention recognizing arbitration awards, while there is no global treaty concerning the enforcement of judgments. See Lowenfeld, Andreas F. *International Litigation and Arbitration* 332 (St. Paul, Minn. 1993).

[195] See, e.g., Cochrane, supra n. 177, S61, S63-5; Fox, supra n. 175, 2582; Fox, Merritt 'The Political Economy of Statutory Reach: U.S. Disclosure Rules in a Globalizing Market for Securities' 14-5 (Unpublished Manuscript, 1997; on file with author). Other commentators have simply called for an end to the extraterritorial application of U.S. securities laws. See, e.g., Choi and Guzman, supra n. 176, 240-1; Pinto, supra n. 6, 73.

[196] See Fox, supra n. 175, 2580-3; Fox, supra n. 195, 14-5.

Fox's key assumption is that international regulatory competition will lead to a "race for the bottom" regarding disclosure requirements. Fox provides two reasons for this projected outcome: firms will not voluntarily produce the desirable level of financial information because of third-party externality concerns; and U.S. stock exchanges' interest in increasing listings will dominate the regulatory process, resulting in a lowering of disclosure requirements to enable them to compete for listings against foreign markets.[197] Fox therefore advocates a physical presence rule to stymie such regulatory competition. Not only will firms have to change their nationality in order to change regulators, which is a costly undertaking, but also, more important to Fox's thesis, exchanges will no longer have an incentive to lobby for lower local securities standards in order to increase foreign listings because firms' listing decisions will be independent of the regulatory regime of the stock exchange's location.

This article's proposal for shifting to an issuer-domicile-based rule is premised on an assessment of competition that is the precise opposite of Fox's. As discussed earlier, neither of Fox's rationales depicting destructive competition holds up to scrutiny. The need to internalize third-party externalities is a tenuous rationale for securities regulation, and such externalities are not, in any event, likely to account for the items of mandatory disclosure pursued by the SEC or the differences across national regimes. More important, there is no reason to assume that firms will list on the exchange with the lowest level of disclosure requirements. Rather, they will choose the one whose requirements will lower their cost of capital, which will not be the exchange operating under the least amount of disclosure because investors place affirmative value on information. The supporting evidence against the "race for the bottom" thesis, as already noted, is that firms the world over voluntarily release more information than their securities regulators require in order to raise capital, with the best example being the European firms listing in London that voluntarily choose to meet higher local disclosure requirements.[198] Finally, it should also be noted that Fox's concern

---

[197] See, e.g., Fox, supra n. 195, 34-5.

[198] See supra notes 38-41 and accompanying text. One study of foreign stock exchange listings found an inverse relation between listings and disclosure requirements, but the exchanges with the lowest level of disclosure did not have the most foreign listings (although the United States, with the highest disclosure level, did have the fewest foreign listings), and more important, the inverse relation was not significant when domestic and foreign exchange disclosure levels were compared, that is, the data did not support the hypothesis that the probability of a firm listing on a given foreign exchange is inversely related to the exchange's disclosure level when its disclosure level is higher than the disclosure level of the firm's domestic exchange, the hypothesis concerning listing choice refined to evince a "race-for-the-bottom" phenomenon. See Saudagaran, Shahrokh M. and Gary C. Biddle 'Financial Disclosure Levels and Foreign Stock Exchange Listing Decisions' in: Choi, Frederick and Richard M. Levich (eds.) *International Capital Markets in a World of Accounting Differences* 159, 181, 184 (Burr Ridge, Ill. 1994).

regarding the political process in a competitive regulatory setting—the incentives of stock exchanges to lobby for lowered disclosure—is eliminated under the market reform proposal whether the domicile approach is either statutory or contractual or Fox's preferred domicile of physical presence, because the location of the stock exchange does not determine the issuer's securities regime, the issuer's securities domicile does. Accordingly, while Fox's proposed regulatory reform is compatible with the approach in this article, the rationales could not be much farther apart.

An alternative proposal with a narrower reform agenda in view, that of limiting extraterritorial application of securities laws, by Stephen Choi and Andrew Guzman, adheres to a strict location-of-sale jurisdictional rule as the means of increasing global welfare.[199] In contrast to Fox, Choi and Guzman seek to encourage regulatory competition across nations because they believe that different rules are appropriate for different issuers and investors. A site-of-sale rule is a cheaper mechanism through which firms can exercise choice over regulatory regime to meet their particularized requirements than Fox's home-country rule requiring the firm's physical presence for a regime to apply, and thus facilitates regulatory competition. In this sense, Choi and Guzman's approach is closer to the spirit of this article's competitive federalism than is Fox's proposal, as it provides firms with greater flexibility in their choice of securities regime.

But although the objectives are similar—facilitating regulatory competition—the recommendations differ because Choi and Guzman are not willing to follow through with the implications of regulatory competition. For example, they finesse the question of whether regulatory competition is for the "top" or "bottom" with respect to investor protection by asserting that the question is complicated and need not be resolved because different rules are appropriate for different clienteles. This is a muddled position because, if the competitive race to diversity produces laws disadvantageous to investors (that is, it is a race for the "bottom"), there will be no demand for such differentiated regimes. Despite their disclaimer, it only makes sense to advocate a policy of regulatory diversity if the competition results in regimes desirable to investors (that is, it is a race for the top).

The confusion created by Choi and Guzman's position becomes more apparent when they sidestep the implications of a policy of regulatory competition for domestic regulation. Relying on the existing practice of a monopolist SEC, they contend that investors and issuers within a single nation have homogeneous preferences regarding securities regulation and, therefore, that fostering domestic

---

[199] See Choi, Stephen J. and Andrew T. Guzman 'National Laws, International Money: Regulation in a Global Capital Market' 65 *Fordham L. Rev.* 1855, 1893-4 (1997); see also Choi and Guzman, supra n. 176, 240-1.

regulatory competition is unjustified.[200] This justification of local regulatory monopolies is due to a mistaken understanding of the dynamics of competitive federalism: competition can lead to uniformity as well as diversity in substantive law. Moreover, uniformity produced by regulatory competition is more likely to be of benefit to investors than uniformity derived from a noncompetitive regime.[201]

There is, however, no evidence that diverse securities regimes are appropriate for U.S. and non-U.S. multinationals, or for U.S. investors holding such firms, notwithstanding Choi and Guzman's conjecture. Similar product diversity arguments were hypothesized to explain the benefits of state charter competition, but the empirical evidence does not support such claims.[202] There is also no reason to suppose that the disclosure differences between U.S. and non-U.S. securities regimes is a function of different needs for public information by U.S. firms and investors than other firms and investors; indeed, the lack of empirical research evincing the efficacy of the federal securities regime suggests precisely otherwise. But were international differences due to varying issuer and investor needs, then Choi and Guzman's jurisdictional approach is not likely to lead to the optimal set of regulations: as Fox maintains, a home state (physical presence), as opposed to site-of-sale, jurisdictional approach is more likely to be the key to optimal regulatory diversity because domestic regulators are better situated than foreign ones to identify the regime best suited for local firms.[203]

In part, Choi and Guzman's conclusion that domestic regulation should be noncompetitive is essential for sustaining their policy proposal for eliminating extraterritorial regulation: if there was domestic regulatory competition, then a site-of-sale rule would no longer be applicable to U.S. transactions, as it would make domestic competition ineffective. Nor would the optimal choice for fostering global competition be such a rule, compared to the options proposed in this article, a firm's contractual or statutory domicile. Having identified the international securities problem as extraterritorial application of U.S. law to non-U.S. transactions, they set out to choose a jurisdictional rule that would readily eliminate the problem. Site of sale does this. But when international issues are considered within the broader question of competitive securities regulation examined in this article, it is apparent that another approach, that advanced in

---

[200] See Choi and Guzman, supra n. 199, 1882-3.

[201] See Carney, supra n. 101, 169-72 (comparing uniform corporate law produced competitively in U.S. with that produced by noncompetitive European harmonization process).

[202] See Romano, supra n. 5, 45-8.

[203] See, e.g., Fox, supra n. 175, 2582. Fox's argument relies on the difference in European and U.S. firms' ownership structures (that is, he maintains that greater disclosure is needed for the dispersed ownership structure of U.S. firms, in contrast to the concentrated ownership structures of European firms, since large blockholders can be expected to obtain information directly from firms). See, e.g., Fox, supra n. 195, 26-7.

this article, that permits firms to choose their securities domicile, will both spur competition and resolve the extraterritorial problem more effectively. Moreover, if applied by all nations, the issuer-selected domicile approach will also provide a further benefit of uniformity of investor treatment, for it will result in all of the purchasers of a firm's securities being subject to the same securities regime, in contrast to a site-of-sale rule. Choi and Guzman have recently recognized this critical weakness in their proposal for the promotion of regulatory competition; in a recent paper, they abandon their former position and now advocate a system of "portable reciprocity" for international securities regulation, in which firms choose their securities regime, analogous to this article's proposal.[204]

E. Conclusion

This article has advocated fundamental reform of the current approach to securities regulation by implementing a regulatory approach of competitive federalism, under which firms select their securities regulator from among the fifty states and the District of Columbia, the SEC, or other nations. Competitive federalism harnesses the high-powered incentives of markets to the regulatory state in order to produce regulatory arrangements compatible with investors' preferences. This is because firms will locate in the domicile whose regime investors prefer in order to reduce their cost of capital, and states will have financial incentives (such as, incorporation and registration fees) to adapt their securities regimes to firms' locational decisions. This prediction of securities market participants' and regulators' responses to competition is well grounded: there is a substantial body of literature examining the workings of competitive federalism in the corporate charter setting that indicates that such regulatory competition benefits investors.

To establish competitive federalism in the securities law context, the current choice-of-law rule for securities transactions must be altered to follow the issuer's securities domicile rather than the securities' site of sale. In addition, two procedural safeguards would be required of firms opting out of federal regulation: domicile disclosure upon securities purchases and a security-holder vote to effectuate a domicile change. These requirements assure that informed investor preferences will drive the regulatory competition. When competition is introduced, SEC rules and regulations that are not cost-effective or are otherwise detrimental to investors will be replaced by competing regulators with rules investors prefer, as the domicile choices of capital market participants establish a new regulatory equilibrium.

---

[204] See Choi, Stephen J. and Andrew T. Guzman 'Portable Reciprocity: Rethinking the International Reach of Securities Regulation' *So. Cal. L. Rev.* (forthcoming 1998).

The mandatory federal securities regime has been in place for over sixty years, but the theoretical support for it is thin and there is an absence of empirical evidence indicating that it is effective in achieving its stated objectives. In fact, there is a developing body of literature pointing in the opposite direction. At minimum, this literature suggests that the securities status quo should no longer be privileged, and that it should instead be opened up to market forces by means of competitive federalism; corporation codes have benefited from precisely such competition. Although the current legislative trend in Congress, supported by both the proponents and opponents of the existing regulatory regime, is to seek to monopolize even further securities regulation at the federal level, this article maintains that it would be far better public policy to expand, not restrain, state regulatory involvement. As long as only one state's law, chosen by the issuer, controls the regulation of a firm's securities transactions, regulatory competition will arise, and there are compelling reasons to prefer such a regulatory arrangement to the mandatory federal regime.

Discussion Report

DIRK H. BLIESENER

Before the discussion of her unorthodox proposal, Professor *Romano* had already emphasized that the chances for implementing her new competitive approach to securities regulation in the U.S. were as good as winning in the state lottery without even purchasing a ticket. The very lively debate centered on theoretical challenges as well as practical concerns and explored the possibilities of implementing her ideas in a European framework of financial regulation.

From an economic perspective, U.S. commentators drew attention to the evolution in American corporate law characterized by a competitive concept of regulation of the several states. They criticized the fact that the competitive "genius" of American corporate law had neither reduced the social cost nor brought about the optimal regime of corporate regulation. Also, the social cost of the SEC's disclosure rules is probably significantly lower than the cost of private disclosure would be. Many were worried about the "race to the bottom" that Professor *Romano's* proposal could provoke with respect to securities regulation. Incumbent managers would most probably opt for a low disclosure system. If the SEC were to allow the NYSE to have foreign firms listed without conforming with U.S. GAAP, domestic firms could also ask for non-compliance with those standards. Along these lines, a German speaker explained that actual regulatory differences among U.S. and foreign jurisdictions were smaller than is commonly perceived by the interested public. For example, with respect to U.S. and German financial statements, it could be shown that many of the alleged differences are more a matter of interpretation than a substantial deviation from information quality. Accordingly, the SEC's refusal to accept European-style financial statements appears to be a question of power for the institution.

On a more theoretical note, a European commentator pointed out that there is ample evidence in economic literature that financial regulation cannot reasonably supplement mandatory rules by "enabling" rules. Others sympathized with the idea of competition in securities law in general, while asking Professor *Romano* to clarify the scope of her proposal with respect to the exchange level of regulation as well as her definition of securities law as opposed to corporate law. One commentator made an argument for establishing a minimum set of antifraud regulations since investors are faced with all kinds of fraudulent practices that they realistically cannot anticipate. A German commentator raised the question of how broker-dealer regulation would fit into the new system.

Yet another U.S. commentator claimed that there was no need for regulatory competition since even more efficient competition would soon take place without regulatory interference in the electronic media, in particular in the Internet, where investors, with the SEC's consent, will be able to choose from securities issued by domestic or off-shore firms under the most diverse securities law regimes. A German commentator added that current NYSE regulation already allows a listed issuer chartered under German law to select a U.K. takeover code or Japanese securities regulation for the issuance of new shares.

A German commentator was worried that Professor *Romano's* approach could bring back to U.S. securities regulation the patent inefficiencies created by early blue sky laws in the 1920s. Speakers differed on the question of whether her model was in accordance with current choice-of-law theories in the U.S. Another objection concerned the cost of the proposed transition as such. Apart from an alleged reduction of rules in number, a Japanese commentator doubted that there would be any significant reduction in enforcement cost. In addition, as one German commentator noted, implementing uniform laws in the U.S. is already reported to be a very costly process.

American and non-U.S. speakers had controversial views on the merits of the SEC as the institutional body that would lose most of its functions under Professor *Romano*'s new approach. On the one hand, it was difficult for a number of commentators to imagine that other institutions could accomplish the same tasks, especially in the field of disclosure regulation, with the same enforcement success and the same economies of scale. Speakers who were more skeptical about the SEC's institutional efficiency, on the other hand, expected that new state agencies would be in a better position to modernize SEC standards than the current Commission is.

Finally, European commentators discussed a possible application of Professor *Romano's* model for purposes of harmonizing EU financial regulation. It was observed that European firms are already in a position to shop around Europe for the optimal securities law environment. With respect to actual experience with competing regulations within Europe, the 30-year-old Eurobond market has a very low standard of regulation. Another element of Europe-wide competition was introduced with EASDAQ.

In her brief response, Professor *Romano* took up a number of the issues raised by the several speakers. She emphasized that, based on her approach, many rules would have to be changed, including the relevant choice-of-law concepts. As already explained more fully in her paper, Professor *Romano* suggested that there were significant differences between the pre-1929 blue sky era and the current situation. With respect to antifraud rules, she agreed that investors would expect some antifraud scheme from any jurisdiction. Therefore, no securities regime would eliminate this type of regulation. On the issue of broker-dealer regulation, Professor *Romano* emphasized that she wished to exclude this issue from her approach, as she had pointed out in her paper. Further, she explained that—apart from reputational incentives for broker-dealers to treat their customers fairly—

unsophisticated investors are being afforded substantial protection by sophisticated investors through the pricing of securities.

Professor *Romano* agreed with the commentator who had emphasized the mandatory character of securities regulation. Far from suggesting a non-mandatory regime, she envisioned a system where a number of different mandatory state rules instead of one federal rule compete for issuers and investors. In her view, the SEC should not be eliminated. Given the poor standards of service to the public she has experienced with the SEC, Professor *Romano* was positive that the states could also develop similarly competent or more competent organizations.

With respect to the new media, Professor *Romano* did not expect a significant impact on large U.S. firms since they would continue to have their plants and main operations in the U.S. In her view, the SEC would not let these firms deviate from its regime.

Part II:

Building Blocks of Corporate Governance Systems

Chapter 4: The Board

The German Two-Tier Board: Experience, Theories, Reforms

KLAUS J. HOPT, Hamburg

The role of the two-tier board of the German type in corporate governance cannot be assessed without an analysis of its roots and systemic embedding in the 19th century. This explains also its different types in practice. The main function of the supervisory board (*Aufsichtsrat*) was to organize networks which included banks and later also labor (co-determination). The impact on cartelization is problematic. Economic research on the *Aufsichtsrat* is emerging, though the legal environment is not favorable to it. The findings concern the structure, composition, and functions of the board. Bank and labor representation on the board are characteristic for Germany. The latter is the cause for not reforming the outdated size requirements. Open questions concern the incidence and possible role of independent outside directors as distinguished from affiliated directors. The boards in corporate groups are still a black box. The role of the board may change swiftly together with the economic and legal environment in Germany. A relatively modest board reform has taken place in 1998. Broader market reforms are very necessary. On the whole, one should be very prudent in assessing and reforming the supervisory board and related corporate governance schemes.

Contents

A. Roots and Systemic Embedding of the Two-Tier Board

I. The Legal Framework

In comparative law, the fact that some countries like the United States or the United Kingdom rely on one-tier boards while others like Germany stick to the two-tier board system is common knowledge. Indeed, this division runs through continental Europe. To be sure the landscape is rather tripartite. Besides the U.K., Ireland and the southern European countries such as Italy, Spain, Portugal, and Greece belong to the *one-tier group.* Germany, Switzerland, Austria, the Netherlands, and the Scandinavian countries have the *two-tier system.* In France and Belgium we have a *mixed system,* with both board forms available. In this report the German situation will be presented from a comparative law perspective and with a look into EU harmonization plans.

The legal framework of the German two-tier board has been described elsewhere in English.[1] For legal details in German, the best sources are three commentaries on the German Stock Corporation Act of 1965, two multi-volume commentaries and a small one.[2] For the present purposes it suffices to stress two

---

[1] Cf. Vagts, Detlev F. 'Reforming the "Modern" Corporation: Perspectives from the German' 80 *Harv. L. Rev.* 23-89 (1966); Roth, Guenter H. 'Supervision of Corporate Management: The "Outside" Director and the German Experience' 51 *N.C. L. Rev.* 1369-83 (1973); Meier-Schatz, Christian 'Corporate Governance and Legal Rules: A Transnational Look at Concepts and Problems of Internal Management Control' *Journal of Corporations* 13 (1988) 431-80; André, Thomas J. 'Some Reflections on German Corporate Governance: A Glimpse at German Supervisory Boards' 70 *Tul. L. Rev.* 1819-79 (1996); du Plessis, J.J. 'Corporate Governance: Reflections on the German Two-Tier Board System' *Journal of South African Law (TSAR)* (1996/1) 20-46; Hopt, Klaus J. 'The German Two-Tier Board (Aufsichtsrat), A German View on Corporate Governance' in: Hopt, Klaus J. and Eddy Wymeersch (eds.) *Comparative Corporate Governance: Essays and Materials* 3-20 (Berlin and New York 1997).

[2] Zöllner, Wolfgang *Kölner Kommentar zum AktG* 2ⁿᵈ edn. (Cologne 1986 et seq.); Hopt, Klaus J. and Herbert Wiedemann (eds.) *Großkommentar zum Aktiengesetz* 4ᵗʰ edn. (Berlin and New York 1992 et seq.). The one-volume commentary is Hüffer, Uwe *Aktiengesetz* 3ʳᵈ edn. (Munich 1997).

points. First, the supervisory board (*Aufsichtsrat*) is strictly separated from the management board (*Vorstand*), a separation which the law enforces by an incompatibility rule. Second, the supervisory board is chosen by the shareholders and, in large companies, up to one half of its seats are chosen by labor. It nominates, controls, and dismisses the management board. In addition, the supervisory board has a certain co-responsibility for basic decisions in the company, in particular as far as the annual report is concerned. Under the bylaws of the company or by decision of the supervisory board, certain categories of transactions may be subjected to its prior approval. But the day-to-day management is strictly reserved for the management board.

II. History

1. The So-Called Supervisory Board Debates at the Turn of the Century

A functional discussion of the German two-tier board system should not go right into factual details and economic theories on the supervisory board. The system is better understood if the two boards are set into a historical perspective.[3] The history of and the discussion on the supervisory board have been in turmoil ever since its mandatory introduction in 1870. The *Aufsichtsratsfrage* (supervisory law debate) was already a notorious field of debate for lawyers and social scientists at the turn of the century. Today we not only have a renaissance of this debate with many of the old policy arguments rediscovered and presented as new insights, but we are also in the midst of a full-fledged board reform which is due for 1998.[4] While analysis of this development is essential to business historians and of acute interest to German company lawyers and company law reformers, in the present context a short glimpse at the development of the two boards in business practice must do.

---

[3] See Hopt, Klaus J. 'Zur Funktion des Aufsichtsrats im Verhältnis von Industrie und Bankensystem' in: Horn, Norbert and Jürgen Kocka (eds.) *Law and the Formation of the Big Enterprises in the 19th and Early 20th Centuries* 227-42 (Göttingen 1979); Horn, Norbert 'Aktienrechtliche Unternehmensorganisation in der Hochindustrialisierung (1860-1920)' in: Horn and Kocka, supra, 123-89, 144 et seq.; Hopt, Klaus J. 'Ideelle und wirtschaftliche Grundlagen der Aktien-, Bank- und Börsenrechtsentwicklung im 19. Jahrhundert' in: Coing, Helmut and Walter Wilhelm (eds.) *Wissenschaft und Kodifikation des Privatrechts im 19. Jahrhundert* vol. V *Geld und Banken* 128-68 (Frankfurt am Main 1980). Securities regulation did not exist, but the beginnings of stock exchange law were in place; see Merkt, Hanno 'Zur Entwicklung des deutschen Börsenrechts von den Anfängen bis zum Zweiten Finanzmarktförderungsgesetz' in: Hopt, Klaus J., Bernd Rudolph, and Harald Baum (eds.) *Börsenreform—Eine ökonomische, rechtsvergleichende und rechtspolitische Untersuchung* 17-141 (Stuttgart 1997).

[4] See infra Sec. C.I.

2. The Roots of the Supervisory Board in the 19th Century and Their Impact
    Until Today

At the beginning of the modern stock corporation in Germany—as well as in
other countries—the management board was but the (economic and legal) agent
of the shareholders.[5] The supervisory board was first a mere shareholder
committee which later developed into a unitary governing board (*Verwaltungsrat*) consisting of the shareholders, some bankers, and other related entrepreneurs. Within the latter, government and control were not separated.

The mandatory supervisory board of 1870 and mandatory disclosure were the
prices set by lawmakers for permanently giving up their charter requirement and
former state control. Therefore, the German supervisory board is historically the
incarnation of the idea of a strictly separate outside board to control the
management board for the sake of the shareholders, but also to protect the public
interest. Public interest was considered both before and after 1870 to *extend
beyond the mere shareholders.*

The congenital defect of the supervisory board, if it is one, is that the supervisory board simply continued the tradition of the *Verwaltungsrat*, i.e., the
linkage of the enterprise with its financial and business partners. Before the turn
of the century it was already clear that the controlling function of the supervisory
board was no doubt legally mandated and had to be fulfilled, but that the former
advising and linking function of the supervisory board would continue and was
both legitimate[6] and economically welcome. The "modern" observation that the
supervisory board does not live up to its control function and, indeed, that it does
not act only and may be not even primarily in the interest of dispersed shareholders is, historically speaking, a truism.

Even the wisdom of the modern public choice theory—that the legislators are
also rent-seeking and that this is also relevant for takeover regulation and stock
corporation law—was expressed in nuce as early as 1856 by Robert von Mohl.

---

[5] For the U.S., cf. Buxbaum, Richard M. 'Die Leitung von Gesellschaften—Strukturelle
Reformen im amerikanischen und deutschen Gesellschaftsrecht' in: Feddersen, Dieter, Peter
Hommelhoff, and Uwe H. Schneider (eds.) *Corporate Governance. Optimierung der Unternehmensführung und der Unternehmenskontrolle im deutschen und amerikanischen Aktienrecht*
65-93, 71 et seq. (Cologne 1996). For the U.K., cf. Gower, Laurence C.B. and Paul L. Davies
Principles of Modern Company Law 183 (London 1997). For Germany, cf. Baums, Theodor *Der
Geschäftsleitervertrag* 9 et seq. (Cologne 1987). The agency problem is an old insight: "The
directors of such companies, however, being the managers rather of other people's money than of
their own, it cannot well be expected, that they should watch over it with the same anxious
vigilance with which the partners in a private copartnery frequently watch over their own. . .
Negligence and profusion, therefore, must always prevail, more or less, in the management of the
affairs of such a company." Smith, Adam *An Inquiry into the Nature and Causes of the Wealth of
Nations* Book 5 Ch. 1.3.1.2. 5th edn. (London 1789).

[6] Cf. Kropff, Bruno *Aktiengesetz, Textausgabe* 136 (Ausschußbericht ad § 100 in the context
of the size of the supervisory board) (Düsseldorf 1965).

He feared that stock corporations with large capital could corrupt state legislators in their own interest, and at the expense of other stakeholders such as labor and of the public interest.[7]

It is also revealing to see that by the middle of the last century the search had already begun for other means of control beyond the supervisory board, in particular for control by disclosure and by the market.[8] Of course, real antitrust law sprang up only towards the turn of the century, first in the U.S. and much later in some European countries.[9] In the light of these early insights, it would be more than appropriate for certain critics, while fulfilling a potentially useful role in the annual meetings as well as in German academia, to not only formulate their wisdom in a more nuanced way but to become more modest when looking at corporate and capital market law history.[10]

3. The Different Types of Supervisory Boards in Corporate Practice in the Past and Today

a) Under the practice of corporate statutes in the middle of the 19th century, the supervisory board as an institution already covered very different realities.[11] In corporations with major shareholdings, the real say was always with the shareholders who sat personally or were represented in the *Verwaltungsrat* (or later on the supervisory board). In these cases, the management board was just a recipient of orders. Just the opposite turned out to be true in what was called later the Berle Means corporations: the supervisory board neither governed nor controlled. Though formally elected by the shareholders' general assembly, the supervisory

---

[7] von Mohl, Robert 'Die Aktiengesellschaften, volkswirthschaftlich und politisch betrachtet' *Deutsche Vierteljahrs-Schrift* 4 (1856) 1, 38, 53, 61 et seq., 64.

[8] Hopt 'Ideelle', supra n. 3, 154 et seq.; Großfeld, Bernhard 'Die rechtspolitische Beurteilung der Aktiengesellschaft im 19. Jahrhundert' in: Coing and Wilhelm, supra n. 3, vol. IV *Eigentum und industrielle Entwicklung, Wettbewerbsordnung und Wettbewerbsrecht* 236-54, 239 et seq. (Frankfurt am Main 1979).

[9] Cornish, William R. 'Legal Control over Cartels and Monopolization 1880-1914. A Comparison' in: Horn and Kocka, supra n. 3, 280-305. In Germany one of the first books to deal with cartels was by Kleinwächter, Friedrich *Die Kartelle* (Innsbruck 1883); see Großfeld, Bernhard 'Zur Kartellrechtsdiskussion vor dem Ersten Weltkrieg' in: Coing and Wilhelm, supra n. 8, 255-96. Also the group phenomenon and its problems were first seen in the U.S. In Germany the first full discussion took place in the Deutscher Juristentag 1902; see Großfeld, supra, 252 et seq. Cf. also Baums, Theodor *Kartellrecht in Preußen: von der Reformära zur Gründerkrise* (Tübingen 1990). See also infra Sec. A.III.3.

[10] Cf. the polemics by Wenger, Ekkehard 'Kapitalmarktrecht als Resultat deformierter Anreizstrukturen' in: Sadowski, Dieter, Hans Czap, and Hartmut Wächter (eds.) *Regulierung und Unternehmenspolitik. Methoden und Ergebnisse der betriebswirtschaftlichen Rechtsanalyse* 419-58 (Wiesbaden 1996).

[11] Hopt 'Funktion', supra n. 3, 229 et seq.

board members were chosen by the management. This well-known dichotomy was already in existence in the very beginning of the first half of the 19th century. And it has continued until today.

b) This dichotomy is particularly important when one tries to compare the German two-tier board with boards in other countries:[12] in Germany, many more enterprises are under the influence of major shareholders than, for example, in the U.S. or in the U.K.[13] In 1996, the domestic shares (nominal value) were held overwhelmingly by non-financial companies (37.3%), while private households and institutional investors had a much smaller part of the shares (private households including organizations: 15.7%; banks and investment funds: 9.5 and 5.8%; insurance companies: 5.6%; public sector: 10.9%).[14] 85.4% of the largest quoted companies had a single (major) shareholder owning more than 25% of the voting share, and 57.3% had a majority shareholder.[15] The comparison of ownership of common stock (1990) in Germany and in the U.S. and the U.K. shows an even more striking difference (figures in percentages for 1990): non-financial companies 42/14.1/10.1; banks: 10/0/4.3; other financial institutions including pension funds and insurance companies: 12/30.4/48.5.[16]

It is hardly surprising that this German peculiarity shows in the pattern of appointment of the supervisory board chairman. Where the major shareholder is another company, the proportion of chairmen appointed by the large shareholder was found to be 77.8%. In one-fourth of the cases, the whole board (i.e., shareholder members) was appointed by the major shareholder.[17] Large shareholders

---

[12] See Wymeersch (this volume Ch. 12: Sec. B).

[13] Windolf, Paul and Jürgen Beyer 'Kooperativer Kapitalismus. Unternehmensverflechtungen im internationalen Vergleich' *Kölner Zeitschrift für Soziologie und Sozialpsychologie* 47 (1995) 1-36; Franks, Julian and Colin Mayer 'Ownership and Control' in: Siebert, Horst (ed.) *Trends in Business Organizations: Do Participation and Cooperation Increase Competitiveness?* 171-95 (Tübingen 1995); see generally Edwards, Jeremy S.S. and Klaus Fischer *Banks, Finance and Investment in Germany* (Cambridge 1994).

[14] Deutsche Bundesbank 'Wertpapierdepots' (Statistische Sonderveröffentlichung no. 9, August 1997); see Table 5 in Prigge (this volume Ch. 12), with more data and further research. The *Deutsches Aktieninstitut*, Frankfurt am Main, publishes the DAI-Factbook each year with detailed figures on the shareholders' structure in Germany and in some other countries, 'DAI-Factbook 1997. Statistiken, Analysen und Grafiken zu Aktionären, Aktiengesellschaften und Börsen' Ch. 8 (Frankfurt am Main 1997).

[15] Franks, Julian and Colin Mayer 'Ownership, Control and the Performance of German Corporations' Table 1 (Working Paper, London Business School and University of Oxford, 14.10.1996, revised 25.1.1997).

[16] Prowse, Stephen 'Corporate Governance in an International Perspective: A Survey of Corporate Control Mechanisms Among Large Firms in the U.S., U.K., Japan and Germany' *Financial Markets, Institutions & Instruments* 4/1 (1995) Table 2.

[17] Franks and Mayer, supra n. 15, 10.

are nearly always present on the board in Germany, while this is very rare in the U.S. and in the United Kingdom.[18]

This is bound to lead to differences in the corporate governance problem as well as in the corporate governance discussion in these countries. In the U.S. and the United Kingdom, much attention is given to the typical public company with shares quoted at a stock exchange and without a major shareholder. In Germany this is a relatively infrequent species, not only in absolute numbers (in 1996, 681 domestic corporations were quoted at the German stock exchanges, 2,339 in the United Kingdom, 2,602 at the New York Stock Exchange, and 5,138 at NASDAQ) but also as far as the percentage of shareholders in the population is concerned (in the early 1990s, this was 5.5% in Germany, 21% in the U.S., and 15.8% in the United Kingdom).[19] The problems of the latter company type are, however, exacerbated by the fact that institutional investors play a much smaller role in Germany as compared to the U.S. and the U.K.[20]

III. Formation of Networks and the Board

1. Networks and Advice

The use of other professional experience by the presence of professional business advisers—in particular banks, but also lawyers and others—in the supervisory board seems to be a characteristic element of the German board system as compared to others. The idea of using expertise and advice is also present in many corporations' tradition of having retiring members of the managing board, in particular the president or *CEO, move into the supervisory board*, often even as the president of the latter.[21] Exceptions only confirm the rule, such as Edzard Reuter of Daimler Benz. Reuter claims to have had a succession promise from the president of the supervisory board (Kopper, Deutsche Bank), but he was prevented from following this practice in view of the enormous losses which had

---

[18] Prowse, supra n. 16, 35.

[19] See the figures in German Monopolies Commission 'Ordnungspolitische Leitlinien für ein funktionsfähiges Finanzsystem' 6 et seq. (Special Expert Opinion of the Monopolkommission, Cologne 1998); Hopt, Klaus J. and Harald Baum 'Börsenrechtsreform in Deutschland' in: Hopt, Rudolph, and Baum, supra n. 3, 287-467, 289 et seq.

[20] Cf. Baums, Theodor, Richard M. Buxbaum, and Klaus J. Hopt (eds.) *Institutional Investors and Corporate Governance* (Berlin and New York 1994); for Germany, see in particular Kübler, Friedrich 'Institutional Investors and Corporate Governance' in: Baums, Buxbaum, and Hopt, supra, 565-79. While in Germany institutional investors hold around 20% of the outstanding shares, the figures for the U.S. and the U.K. are around 45 and 51% respectively.

[21] See infra Sec. B.II.2.

arisen from his excessive and mistaken policy of expansion of the automobile producing group into the military aviation business.[22]

These and other characteristics—such as the size of the two boards, the balance between inside and outside directors, the composition of the boards, the origin of its members, the board appointment, etc.—constitute an important factual and typological distinction between the German two-tier board system and those of other European countries.[23]

2. Networks, Relational Banking, and Labor

a) The particular role of the *banks* within the supervisory board and the actual and potential conflicts of interest created thereby[24] were already a cause of concern for entrepreneurs like Camphausen, Hansemann, and Mevissen far back in the 19th century.[25] Yet the close relationship between banks and newly industrialized enterprises in the industrialization process of the last two-thirds of the 19th century was crucial for the economic development in Germany.[26] It has remained so through the different wars and afterwards as the network with and beyond the banks has grown. The supervisory board thus was and has remained a relationship board.

However, it is important to realize that the banks were only part of the network and that the supervisory boards were not much more than a convenient tool of institutionalizing this network. The board is only the form; the key is the network. Therefore, the idea of reducing the role of the banks within supervisory boards is somewhat naive. Apart from the fact that very often bank representation on the board follows major bank shareholdings (and the latter has followed and still quite often follows difficult situations which call for rescue both of the enterprise and of the bank's credits),[27] the network could easily be continued by other means, for example by voluntary advisory boards (*Beirat*).

---

[22] Cf. the chronology given by Küting, Karlheinz 'Die Talfahrt der Daimler-Benz AG' *Blick durch die Wirtschaft* no. 72, 12.4.1996, 9.

[23] Korn/Ferry International 'Board Meeting in Session, European Boards of Directors Study' 9 (London 1996), there corporate leadership structure is mentioned as a further characteristic factor; cf. idem at 42.

[24] See also infra Sec. C.I.

[25] References can be found in Hopt 'Ideelle', supra n. 3, 141, 154.

[26] Riesser, Jakob Die deutschen Großbanken und ihre Konzentration im Zusammenhang mit der Entwicklung der *Gesamtwirtschaft in Deutschland* 4th edn. (Jena 1912, reprint 1971).

[27] The banks' role in rescue situations is seen differently by traditional opinion in Germany and by Edwards and Fischer, supra n. 13, 164; see Hopt, Klaus J. 'Corporate Goverance und deutsche Universalbanken' in: Feddersen, Hommelhoff, and Schneider, supra n. 5, 243-63, 255 et seq.

Such voluntary bodies are frequent in enterprises other than corporations in which supervisory boards are not mandatory, in groups of companies beyond the supervisory boards of the member companies,[28] and in particular in international groups and trusts.

b) It is unclear whether labor—or, more specifically, the trade unions to which the *co-determination* law grants special seats on the labor bench in the supervisory board—form part of this network. The fact that for certain issues the representatives of the banks and of labor occasionally form a coalition—for example, against too high dividend claims on the shareholder side—is of course not yet a sign for a common network. The interviews show overwhelmingly critical remarks concerning the role of trade union representatives on the board. They are considered to be outsiders in the enterprise and to behave as such, making consensus more difficult. There are even reports of occasional clashes between the representatives of the workforce (who usually are trade union members) and those of the trade unions.[29] On the other side, the heads of the influential trade unions such as IG Metall seem to be part of the crowd. This was certainly true for Steinkühler (before his well-deserved fall after an awkward, probably even reckless and prepotentious insider transaction). It may also be true for some "modern" trade union leaders who have not lost sight of economic reality and the ultimate needs of the enterprise and its workforce when sitting on its supervisory board.[30]

3. Networks and Cartelization

In a historical and comparative perspective, the hypothesis could be made that this formation of networks is particularly marked in countries with a strong cartelization. This is of course not to say that these networks are necessarily used for or leading to cartelization. Germany and even more so France are the two European countries with the greatest amount of this networking. Switzerland possibly also belongs to this category. On the other hand, the U.S. seem to be a country without such networks, or with much less of them. While France and

[28] Even the actual supervisory board of the subsidiary corporations in groups of companies have lost much of their influence and control momentum. Vice versa, the role of the supervisory board of the parent has grown almost unnoticed by corporate law. Only most recently has the discussion on the duties of the supervisory board of the parent to the subsidiaries begun. See Götz, Heinrich 'Leitungssorgfalt und Leitungskontrolle der Aktiengesellschaft hinsichtlich abhängiger Unternehmen' *Zeitschrift für Unternehmens- und Gesellschaftsrecht* 27/4 (forthcoming 1998).

[29] Bremeier, Eberhard, Jürgen B. Mülder, and Florian Schilling 'Praxis der Aufsichtsrats-tätigkeit in Deutschland—Chancen zur Professionalisierung' 64 et seq. (AMROP International, Düsseldorf 1994).

[30] For further aspects of labor codetermination, see infra Sec. B.III. 2.

Switzerland have relatively weak antitrust laws and policies even today, Germany's antitrust law is comparatively stern. Yet this is contradictory only at first sight. Until the late 1950s, cartelization was omnipresent in Germany, not only during the special situation of wartime but also in the Weimar Republic and before. The German *Reichsgericht* upheld such cartels in line with the common opinion of their usefulness.[31] Even now the formation and operation of networks via the supervisory boards is not caught by the relatively strict German antitrust laws. Only most recently has there been concern and some reform discussion on this point.[32]

It is another question whether those countries such as the U.S. without such or much networking were instead going the way of concentration. There is evidence of this having been the case.[33] It might be that the concentration movement helped to create the common type of public company which covered its capital needs from a large shareholding public. In any case, early concentration led to the much earlier development of merger control in the U.S. than on the European continent.[34]

IV. Shareholder Versus Stakeholder Philosophy

Another characteristic of German boards can be circumscribed by shareholder versus stakeholder philosophy. In Germany this dichotomy is as old as the institution of the board itself. As mentioned above, the mandatory supervisory board was the direct successor of state oversight over the stock corporation. It was only natural that the public interest, i.e., the interest of the shareholders, but also the interests of the enterprise, its workforce, and its creditors, were part of the supervisory board's concern. Due to historical reasons labor achieved a particular role in this. By the second half of the last century the so-called social question had already arisen, with entrepreneurs feeling responsible to their workforce in addition to and possibly to a greater extent than to their shareholders. The idea of labor co-determination had already been conceived by Robert von Mohl in 1835.[35] Formal boardroom co-determination beyond mere works council

---

[31] See Nörr, Knut Wolfgang 'Die Generalklausel und die Kartelle: ein Rückblick auf die Rechtsprechung des Reichsgerichts' in: Lange, Hermann, Knut Wolfgang Nörr, and Harm Peter Westermann (eds.) *Festschrift für Gernhuber* 919-37 (Tübingen 1993); Möschel, Wernhard *70 Jahre deutsche Kartellpolitik* (Tübingen 1972).

[32] See infra Sec. C.I.

[33] See Dunlavy (this volume Ch. 1: Sec. A).

[34] See Hopt, Klaus J. (ed.) *European Merger Control—Legal and Economic Analyses on Multinational Enterprises* vol. I (Berlin and New York 1982).

[35] von Mohl, Robert 'Ueber die Nachtheile, welche sowohl den Arbeitern selbst als dem Wohlstande und der Sicherheit der gesammten bürgerlichen Gesellschaft von dem fabrikmäßigen

representation was introduced first in 1920 and again in 1952, i.e., both times after the wars when solidarity was badly needed. A further factor may have been the massive loss of private savings by superinflation and two currency reforms. This not only hindered the development of broad capital markets, but it equalized German society more than in other Western countries. Cooperation and *consensus* were the forces needed to deal with collective crises.

In the legal doctrine this was reflected in the discussion that focused on "enterprise law" (*Unternehmensverfassungsrecht/Unternehmensrecht*) rather than on mere corporation law. The Stock Corporation Act of 1937 contained a provision which held the management board responsible not only for the shareholders' interest, but also for those of the workforce and for the public good. This provision was not retained verbatim in the Stock Corporation Act of 1965, but the reason given for this in the legislative debate was that the obligation of the management board to look out for the interest of the workforce is self-evident under the law.[36] The fact that most recent interviews show that German management boards still consider themselves to have a particular duty towards the workforce[37] is fully in line with this tradition. On the other side, according to these interviews the supervisory boards feel obliged primarily to the shareholders. To be sure these are statements of the shareholder members of these supervisory boards. The labor representatives have the interest of their own constituency in mind, even though by law both sides are bound to strive only for the corporation, whatever this means.

Of course, the legal permission for the board to also take into consideration interests other than shareholder interests may work in practice less (or at least not only) for the other stakeholders than for widening the discretion of the board in making business decisions which favor itself. Legally, widening the scope of responsibility of the board beyond shareholders not only acerbates the agency problem for the latter, but it adds the agency problem of labor and gives an excuse for respecting neither of these responsibilities. The same observation has been made in the United States concerning the states' constituency statutes. While these observations are usually meant to be a critique on these statutes, other American commentators have also seen benefits flowing from it insofar as

Betriebe der Industrie zugehen, und ueber die Nothwendigkeit gründlicher Vorbeugungsmittel' *Archiv der politischen Ökonomie und Polizeiwissenschaft* 2 (1835) 141.

[36] Kropff, supra n. 6, 97 et seq. Cf. Großmann, Adolf *Unternehmensziele im Aktienrecht* (Cologne 1980); Teubner, Gunther 'Unternehmensinteresse—das gesellschaftliche Interesse des Unternehmens "an sich"?' *Zeitschrift für das gesamte Handelsrecht und Wirtschaftsrecht* 149 (1985) 470-88.

[37] For example, Korn/Ferry International, supra n. 23, 8, 25: Responsibilities to employees as objective which ranged by a fraction before financial and operational performance and responsibility to shareholders. Cf. also, as one source of many, Schmitz, Ronaldo H. (from Deutsche Bank) 'Praktische Ausgestaltung der Überwachungstätgkeit des Aufsichtsrats in Deutschland' in: Feddersen, Hommelhoff, and Schneider, supra n. 5, 234-42, 235, 238.

this discretion helps the firm to make a decentralized and flexible response to general market pressures, thereby reducing the danger of direct political interference.[38] However, this argument seems too far-fetched for Germany. The view that the board should be bound to act in accordance with a (moderate) shareholder value orientation has the advantage of giving clearer guidelines for action and performance and of reducing conflicts of interest, while at the same time maintaining the expectation that the (implicit) contracts with other stakeholders are fulfilled.[39]

B. Research, Practice, Open Questions

I. Economic Research on the German Supervisory Board

1. Studies

Contrary to what is known by most German academics in business and company law, but also to what is believed by foreign observers, there is a considerable body of economic research on the supervisory board in Germany as well.

Apart from an older study by Vogel in 1980,[40] the Bleicher study of 1987 is probably the most well known.[41] It was based on representative interviews with 779 supervisory board members in 1985 and 1986. Since then other studies have been presented, for example by Gerum, Steinmann, and Fees in 1988,[42] Pfannschmidt in 1993,[43] Bremeier, Mülder, and Schilling in 1994,[44] The German

---

[38] Gordon, Jeffrey N. 'Corporate Governance and the Transition Costs of Capitalism' 17 (Law and Economics Workshop paper, University of Toronto, 16 March 1994).

[39] Schmidt, Reinhard H. and Gerald Spindler 'Shareholder-Value zwischen Ökonomie und Recht' in: Assmann, Heinz-Dieter, Tomas Brinkmann, Georgios Gounalakis, Helmut Kohl, and Rainer Walz (eds.) *Wirtschafts- und Medienrecht in der offenen Demokratie* (Freundesgabe Kübler) 515-55 (Heidelberg 1997); cf. also Mülbert, Peter O. 'Shareholder Value aus rechtlicher Sicht' *Zeitschrift für Unternehmens- und Gesellschaftsrecht* 26 (1997) 129-72; von Werder, Axel 'Shareholder Value-Ansatz als (einzige) Richtschnur des Vorstandshandelns?' *Zeitschrift für Unternehmens- und Gesellschaftsrecht* 27 (1998) 69-91.

[40] Vogel, C. Wolfgang *Aktienrecht und Aktienwirklichkeit. Organisationsrecht und Aufgabenteilung von Vorstand und Aufsichtsrat. Eine empirische Untersuchung deutscher Aktiengesellschaften* (Dissertation University of Giessen 1978/79) (Baden-Baden 1980).

[41] Bleicher, Knut *Der Aufsichtsrat im Wandel* (Gütersloh 1987).

[42] Gerum, Elmar, Horst Steinmann, and Werner Fees *Der mitbestimmte Aufsichtsrat. Eine empirische Untersuchung* (Stuttgart 1988).

[43] Pfannschmidt, Arno *Personelle Verflechtungen über Aufsichtsräte. Mehrfachmandate in deutschen Unternehmen* (Dissertation University of Bonn) (Wiesbaden 1993).

[44] Bremeier, Mülder, and Schilling, supra n. 29.

Private Banks Association in 1995,[45] and Leimkühler in 1996.[46] The most recent data on the composition of the supervisory board were collected by Hansen in 1997 and cover the 30 DAX corporations.[47] The latest comparative contribution was by Korn/Ferry International in 1996.[48] The biannual general reports of the German Monopolies Commission must also be mentioned; they look at corporate governance from the angle of competitive market structures and economic concentration. The latest of these reports dates from 1996. A special report on the financial system, including the underdeveloped share market, the need for more competition and takeover, and the position of financial intermediaries, has just been presented.[49] A number of more specialized studies concern the interrelationships between German enterprises.[50] These are evidenced by participations as well as by interlockings in the supervisory boards. Other studies are also of bearing for the assessment of the German board, for example, various contributions by Theisen on the supervisory board's tasks and information,[51] and by Baums concerning more specifically the influence of German banks via various factors and research on German co-determination.[52]

There is also some economic research on the management board.[53] It concerns inter alia its size, its remuneration including stock options plans[54] which are not yet very common in Germany, its aims and outlook, and the turnover of management. The most comprehensive economic report on German corporate

[45] Bundesverband deutscher Banken 'Erhebungen zu Anteilsbesitz und Aufsichtsratsmandaten. Methodik und Ergebnisse' (Cologne 1995).

[46] Leimkühler, Claudia 'Ist die öffentliche Kritik am deutschen Aufsichtsratssystem gerechtfertigt? Empirische Untersuchung über die personellen Verflechtungen zwischen den Vorständen und Aufsichtsräten der in Deutschland börsennotierten Aktiengesellschaften' *Die Wirtschaftsprüfung* 49 (1996) 305-13.

[47] Hansen, Herbert 'Die Zusammensetzung der Aufsichtsräte bei den DAX-Gesellschaften' *Die Aktiengesellschaft* 42 (1997) R123-R124.

[48] Korn/Ferry International, supra n. 23.

[49] German Monopolies Commission, supra n. 19.

[50] Ziegler in 1984, Biehler and Ortmann in 1985, Pappi, Kappelhoff and Melbeck in 1987, Biehler and Liepmann in 1988, Schreyögg and Papenheim-Tockhorn in 1995, Windolf and Beyer in 1995, and Beyer in 1996. For exact references, see Prigge (this volume Ch. 12: List of References).

[51] See Theisen (this volume Ch. 4); cf. also Theisen, Manuel René and Wolfgang Salzberger 'Die Berichterstattung des Aufsichtsrats. Eine empirische Analyse der Überwachungsberichte von 1984-1994' *Der Betrieb* 50 (1997) 105-15, with an empirical study of the supervisory board reports 1984-1994.

[52] Apart from the early contributions of the Mitbestimmungskommission in 1970 and Ulmer in 1977, in particular the studies by Gerum, Richter, and Steinmann 1981, Bleicher 1987, Gerum, Steinmann, and Fees 1988, and most recently Baums and Frick 1997. For exact references, see Prigge (this volume Ch. 12: List of References).

[53] See the report by Prigge (this volume Ch. 12: Sec. B.I.5.).

[54] On stock option plans, cf. also Wenger/Kaserer (this volume Ch. 6: Sec. C).

governance in general is by H. Schmidt, Drukarczyk, Prigge, and others from 1997.[55] Turning to co-determination, the final report of a large research project on labor co-determination has just been published.[56] The project was financed by the Bertelsmann foundation and directed by Streeck, director at the Cologne Max Planck Institute for the Study of Societies. However, it was not intended to collect such a broad original interview database like the path-breaking Bieden-kopf Commission Study many years ago. The most recent data on Europe are by Wymeersch.[57]

The following contribution is not to present the results of the aforementioned studies. This has been done most in the most recent and comprehensive report on German corporate governance by my economist collaborator, Dr. Prigge.[58] Rather, a few selected findings shall be presented together with some observations on German experience and practice with the hope of formulating some open factual and theoretical questions. But first some comparative remarks are appropriate on the German legal academic environment concerning corporate governance.

2. Academic Environment

As one can see from the list above, much of this research is very recent. Taken as a whole, the quantity and the state of the art of this research on supervisory boards and more generally on corporate governance questions lags far behind what is done in the United States.[59] In addition, quite a number of valuable studies on the German scene stem from abroad, for example, the work by Franks and Mayer[60] and by Edwards and Fischer.[61] Performance studies trying to link board characteristics with the performance of the enterprise are very rare. The very few which exist concern the presence of banks on the supervisory boards

---

[55] Schmidt, Hartmut, Jochen Drukarczyk, Dirk Honold, Stefan Prigge, Andreas Schüler, and Gönke Tetens *Corporate Governance in Germany* (Baden-Baden 1997).

[56] Bertelsmann Stiftung and Hans-Böckler-Stiftung (eds.) 'Mitbestimmung und neue Unter-nehmenskulturen—Bilanz und Perspektiven' (Series "Mitbestimmung und neue Unternehmens-kulturen", Bertelsmann Stiftung, Gütersloh 1998). For a discussion of open questions in co-determination research, cf. Streeck, Wolfgang 'Mitbestimmung: Offene Fragen' (Series "Mitbestimmung und neue Unternehmenskulturen", Bertelsmann Stiftung, Gütersloh 1996).

[57] Wymeersch (this volume Ch. 12).

[58] Prigge (this volume Ch. 12).

[59] Kraakman, Reinier 'Die Professionalisierung des Board' in: Feddersen, Hommelhoff, and Schneider, supra n. 5, 129-42, 136, mentions 27 empirical studies on the correlation between the composition of the board and aspects of behavior or performance of the corporation.

[60] Franks and Mayer, supra n. 13; Franks and Mayer, supra n. 15.

[61] Edwards and Fischer, supra n. 13.

and yield different results.[62] Some have attracted harsh methodological criticism.[63]

It may be more surprising to a foreign observer that in Germany, with very few exceptions, this kind of economic or functional research is done by economists (mostly from microeconomics, i.e., *Betriebswirtschaftslehre*) and a bit by other social scientists. Most law professors, even in business and company law, are either not interested or not qualified to do this kind of work. Nor is historical research on these questions very common. The same is true for most continental European countries. The reaction of a foreign observer to this could be to consider legal academic work in these countries as too dogmatic or conceptual, yet this would be short-sighted. The phenomenon is rather due to a historical division of labor that still makes sense in legal systems in which as a matter of fact courts, lawyers, and legal academia work together on the lex lata in view of elaborating it in a legally consistent way. Legal policy decisions, at least as far as they are prepared and made openly, are left to the legislators. Of course, in continental European company and banking law the functional approach also comes into play, but more subtly. This could be illustrated, for example, by modern case law as shaped by the company and the banking law senates of the German *Bundesgerichtshof,* which embed policy arguments in their law-finding process, at least indirectly. It is shown more openly by the still small law and economics faction, by the long-established and strong comparative law movement, and also in the work of the Max Planck Institutes and others as they help to prepare legal reform such as the Hamburg Institute with its 1996 study on stock exchange reform.[64]

II. The Supervisory Board Under Economic Scrutiny

1. Structure

As to structure, the most striking fact is the size of the German *Aufsichtsrat.* Stock corporation law sets a maximum of 21 members for corporations in general and fixes the number of members in co-determined corporations at 12, 16, or 20 members (depending on the size of the workforce), with slightly different rules for coal and steel co-determination. With this legal background, an

---

[62] The most recent is by Wenger and Kaserer (this volume Ch. 6: Sec. D). See also Nibler, Marcus 'Bank Control and Corporate Performance in Germany: The Evidence' (Working Paper no. 48, St. John's College Cambridge, June 1995).

[63] Perlitz, Manfred and Frank Seger 'The Role of Universal Banks in German Corporate Governance' *Business & the Contemporary World* 6/4 (1994) 49-67.

[64] See Hopt, Rudolph, and Baum, supra n. 3. This interdisciplinary and comparative study originated in a report which was commissioned by the German Ministry of Finance.

average size of 13.25 members was recently counted.[65] It is interesting to see that in 1975, i.e., before the 1976 introduction of quasi-parity labor co-determination for enterprises with more than 2,000 workers, the average size of the supervisory board was reported to be only 7.[66]

Committee work is still underdeveloped in Germany. By 1986, around 25% of the corporations covered still did without a single supervisory board commit-tee.[67] If committees were formed, they were personnel committees (58%). Audit committees made up for only 7%. Interviews with supervisory board members show that today committees are considered to be much more important. An international outlook, including the British example (Cadbury Report[68] and London Stock Exchange) and the German reform discussion,[69] point in the same direction. While more recent figures are not available, it can be taken for granted that, both due to economic insight as well as to the international standard, committees will be more frequent and will gain momentum.[70]

2. Composition

The maximum number of supervisory board memberships is fixed by law at ten, five of which are not counted if they concern the CEO of parent companies with regard to subsidiaries. This reduction by law was in reaction to business practice before 1965 and even more so before 1937 when occasionally much higher numbers of supervisory board seats were held by single persons. Economic studies show that most supervisory board members are members of only one supervisory board. The percentages vary with samples and time from 51.39% to

---

[65] Korn/Ferry International, supra n. 23, 10.

[66] Schiffels, Edmund W. *Der Aufsichtsrat als Instrument der Unternehmenskooperation* 129 (Frankfurt am Main 1981); this source and figure were still used by Bleicher, Knut and Herbert Paul 'Das amerikanische Board-Modell im Vergleich zur deutschen Vorstands-/Aufsichtsratsverfassung—Stand und Entwicklungstendenzen' *Die Betriebswirtschaft* 46 (1986) 263-88, 267.

[67] Bleicher, supra n. 41, 25 et seq.

[68] 'Report of the Committee on the Financial Aspects of Corporate Governance' (Cadbury Report) (London 1992); The Code of Best Practice No. 4.3 recommended an audit committee of at least three non-executive directors with written terms of reference; see also note 11 (the notes give further recommendations, but do not form part of the Code; reprinted in Hopt and Wymeersch, supra n. 1, M-5 et seq.).

[69] Experience on building up an effective internal audit is presented by Mundheim, Robert H. and Simon M. Lorne 'An Essay on Corporate Governance' in: Assmann et al., supra n. 39, 457-64.

[70] Cf. Coenenberg, Adolf Gerhard, Alexander Reinhart, and Jochen Schmitz 'Audit Committees—Ein Instrument der Unternehmensüberwachung? Reformdiskussion im Spiegel einer Befragung der Vorstände deutscher Unternehmen' *Der Betrieb* 50 (1997) 989-97.

66.7%.[71] The given percentages of supervisory board members with seats on more than five boards vary between 7.1% and 3.93% (this includes supervisory board seats held in subsidiary companies). Of course, these figures say nothing about whether this concentration of seats serves particular netting purposes or to what degree it is due to the quality and experience of the individual concerned. Take Röller (ex Dresdner Bank) and Schulte-Noelle (Allianz) who hold eight seats each in the DAX-30 corporations, or Kopper (Deutsche Bank) and Liesen who held seven seats each.[72]

As mentioned above, institutional interlockings and netting have a long tradition in Germany and can even be considered characteristic for the German two-tier system. There are many findings as to personal links among enterprises in Germany, for which reference can be made to the German country report.[73] In sum, it appears that the interlockings are due to relatively few supervisory board members, around 13% in the respective inquiries. In the sample of one study, only 12.8% of the corporations were not linked with another corporation by a common board member. Most prominent and frequent in this linking are the large private banks (Deutsche Bank, Dresdner Bank, Commerzbank) and the largest insurance company, Allianz. Linkage is one of the problems of the German board system and German corporate governance which is discussed most frequently and controversially, and rightly so. Nevertheless, the problem is not treated here in more detail since personal linkage via the supervisory board cannot be separated from the linkage by participations and, in the case of banks and other financial intermediaries, from the role which the latter play within German corporations by means of other factors such as the depository vote and their financial and business relationship to the corporation.[74]

The intertemporal links between the management board and the supervisory board have also been mentioned in the historical survey. It is still common practice today for the retiring management board members, in particular the chairmen, to move to the supervisory board. According to one study, this was the case in 43% of the corporations.[75] This is a frequent practice, even though it is viewed with great reserve by a majority of the interviewed supervisory board members.[76] Sometimes public fights over such a succession of the chairman, as

---

[71] Pfannschmidt, supra n. 43, 86 for 1989; Leimkühler, supra n. 46, 309 for 1992.

[72] Hansen, supra n. 47, R124.

[73] Prigge (this volume Ch. 12: Sec. B.I.2.).

[74] See Chapter 6 in this volume on financial intermediaries and the contributions by Mülbert, Wenger/Kaserer, Breuer, and Baums.

[75] Korn/Ferry International, supra n. 23, 12. See also idem at 17: in two-tier system countries there is a non-executive chairman on over 80% of the supervisory boards.

[76] Bremeier, Mülder, and Schilling, supra n. 29, 37 et seq. Cf. also André, supra n. 1, 1846.

in the cases of Hilger (Hoechst) in 1993 or of Reuter (Daimler Benz),[77] highlight the problem. I shall come back to the recruitment of supervisory board members later.[78]

Still one word about remuneration is appropriate. In Germany, board remuneration is not comparable to the practice in the United States.[79] This is even more striking for management board members because of the traditional infrequency of stock options plans in Germany (most recently there has been a clear change as to stock options, but this has been accompanied by controversial discussions and a number of lawsuits[80]). According to one source, the average remuneration of the management board members was DM 420,000 per year in 1992. The average remuneration of supervisory board members was DM 16,900 per year, while the chairman of the supervisory board gets 50% to 100% more than ordinary members.[81] Even if the figures for the supervisory board were doubled, this would still not be a great incentive. Accordingly, it is common opinion that remuneration should be changed. Yet this will be difficult because the labor representatives must pay over most of what they receive to a labor foundation, and the shareholder side is hardly interested in financing the trade unions in this way.

3. Functions

It is common knowledge that the information flow both from the management board to the supervisory board and within the supervisory board from its

---

[77] See supra Sec. A.III.1.

[78] See infra Sec. B.IV.1.

[79] But cf. also Kraakman, supra n. 59, 140 n. 30 for independent outside directors.

[80] Cf. Hüffer, Uwe 'Aktienbezugsrechte als Bestandteil der Vergütung von Vorstandsmitgliedern und Mitarbeitern—gesellschaftsrechtliche Analyse' *Zeitschrift für das gesamte Handelsrecht und Wirtschaftsrecht* 161 (1997) 214-45; Kohler, Klaus 'Stock Options für Führungskräfte aus Sicht der Praxis' *Zeitschrift für das gesamte Handelsrecht und Wirtschaftsrecht* 161 (1997) 246-68; Lutter, Marcus 'Aktienoptionen für Führungskräfte—de lege lata und de lege ferenda' *Zeitschrift für Wirtschaftsrecht (ZIP)* 18 (1997) 1-9; Knoll, Leonhard 'Der Wert von Bezugsrechten und die materielle Rechtfertigung des Bezugsrechtsausschlusses bei Wandelschuldverschreibungen' *Zeitschrift für Wirtschaftsrecht (ZIP)* 19 (1998) 413-5; LG Frankfurt *Wertpapier-Mitteilungen* 51 (1997) 473-7; LG Stuttgart *Zeitschrift für Wirtschaftsrecht (ZIP)* 19 (1998) 422-8 (Wenger/Daimler Benz).

[81] Hoffmann-Becking, Michael 'Rechtliche Möglichkeiten und Grenzen der Verbesserung der Arbeit des Aufsichtsrats' in: Lanfermann, Josef (ed.) *Internationale Wirtschaftsprüfung* (Festschrift Havermann) 229-46, 245 (Düsseldorf 1995). Cf. also Bremeier, Mülder, and Schilling, supra n. 29, 113. The most recent survey is by Schmid, Frank A. 'Vorstandsbezüge, Aufsichtsratsvergütung und Aktionärsstruktur' *Zeitschrift für Betriebswirtschaft* 67 (1997) 67-83; he finds an average of DM 34,400 per year. For more details, see Prigge (this volume Ch. 12: Sec. B.I.4.).

chairman to the normal members[82] is deficient. It is particularly striking that in many corporations the auditor's report is not handed out to the supervisory board members ahead of the session, a practice which purportedly is to prevent the details of the report leaking out via the labor side. This is in clear violation of the spirit of the law and will be changed in the forthcoming board reform. This reform will grapple more fundamentally with the information problem by increasingly bringing the corporation's auditors into play.[83]

These and other findings support the view that the chairman of the supervisory board (who in co-determined firms is elected by a two-thirds majority or by the shareholder side) is the key figure in practice. This goes much beyond his legal right of casting the decisive second vote in case of a deadlock between capital and labor. Sometimes the chairman is considered to be more influential than the board as a whole.[84] In any case, the appointment and dismissal of members of the management board is in general prepared by the chairman of the supervisory board.

The interview studies tell also about the priorities the supervisory board sets itself in its work. One interesting point is that German supervisory boards, if they have a say (not just legally, but in practice), take the selection of the management board very seriously. In particular, they are aware of the need for succession planning. This seems to be true for most countries with a two-tier system.[85] On the other side, there are inside reports that the supervisory boards pay too little attention to the monitoring of management personnel development.[86]

III. Bank and Labor Representation as Characteristics of German Supervisory Boards

From the data reviewed above, two striking features of the German two-tier system appear that may even be considered characteristic of the German corporate governance system: bank influence and labor co-determination. Each is so important that special sessions of this symposium were devoted to these issues.[87] Therefore, a few words must do.

---

[82] As to the relationship between the chairman of the supervisory board and the normal members, see Bremeier, Mülder, and Schilling, supra n. 29, 43, 57 et seq., 102 et seq.

[83] See infra Sec. C.I.

[84] Bremeier, Mülder, and Schilling, supra n. 29, 57 et seq.; Semler (this volume Ch. 4: Sec. B.I.); Prigge (this volume Ch. 12: Sec. B.I.3.).

[85] Korn/Ferry International, supra n. 23, 8.

[86] Semler (this volume Ch. 4: Sec. B.III.).

[87] See Chapter 5 and 6 in this volume.

1. Bank Representatives on the Board

The most discussed feature is the presence of the *banks* on many supervisory boards. This is clearly distinct from the American system. It marks also a difference between the German two-tier system and other European two-tier systems. In absolute numbers, bank representation on corporate boards is not striking and certainly does not yield a decisive influence. The picture changes, however, if one looks at the concentration of bank representation in the top tier of the German corporations, say the DAX 30, or in particular branches. Besides the discussion on the economic power of the banks, which is more populist and sociopolitical—there is much less bank concentration than in other countries and bank competition is fierce—the real problems which are treated elsewhere[88] are the following:

What does bank representation mean for the information flow from the boards to the banks and vice versa? Effects of bank representation on the credit extended to the corporation concerned seem not to exist, at least not in the sense that there is a causal relationship from the former to the latter.

How do such board representations relate to the prevention of failing company situations and the role of the banks in these situations? It is controversial whether or not having bank representatives on the board increases the chance of early recognition of possible difficulties, and in particular the chance of being rescued.[89]

And maybe the most important and unclear question: What importance do these bank representations have for linking together competing enterprises? The latter would be a most serious problem beyond corporation law and would need to be solved by competition law and policy.[90]

2. Co-Determination of the Board

The second main feature is *co-determination*. In Germany there are 740 companies with quasi-parity co-determination, and around 1,980 firms have labor

[88] See Chapter 6 in this volume on the financial intermediaries with contributions by Mülbert, Wenger/Kaserer, Breuer, and Baums. See also 61. Deutscher Juristentag (ed.) *Empfehlen sich gesetzliche Regelungen zur Einschränkung des Einflusses der Kreditinstitute auf Aktiengesellschaften? Gutachten* Mülbert, *Referat* Kübler, and *Verhandlungen* (Munich 1996 et seq.); Edwards and Fischer, supra n. 13; Hopt, supra n. 27.

[89] Cf. Edwards and Fischer, supra n. 13, 164, 174 et seq., 232 et seq.; Franks and Mayer, supra n. 15, 3 et seq.; Mülbert (this volume Ch. 6: Sec. B.II. and D.I.2.). For Switzerland see Hertig (this volume Ch. 10: Sec. C.I.4.). For the U.S. see Bhagat and Black (this volume Ch. 4: Sec. B). For Scandinavia see Berglöf/Sjögren (this volume Ch. 10: Sec. E).

[90] See Monopolies Commission, supra n. 19, para 183 et seq.

representatives on their board.[91] It is very probable that labor co-determination weakens the control function of the supervisory board. This is because co-determination has led to fractionalization, which is evidenced by the firm practice of separate meetings of the shareholder and the labor sides before the board meeting[92] and by a marked reluctance of the shareholder side to openly criticize the management board. Furthermore, it happens that much of the time spent in the supervisory board meetings is devoted to issues of particular interest to the labor side rather than to the actual supervision of business decisions and entrepreneurial planning in the company.[93]

Yet the voices from inside the supervisory boards are mixed. Some make clear that the input of labor in the board is important and useful. A long-time bank representative made a point of stating that, in practice, co-determination has proved to be efficient and that he had never experienced labor representatives voting against measures which were important and decisive for the future of the enterprise.[94] As Gerum and Wagner suggest,[95] even in merely microeconomic terms, labor co-determination has not only negative, but also positive effects. While there are clear efficiency problems of co-determined supervisory boards, most of these are practically identical with the problems of German supervisory boards in general.[96] The overall assessment becomes even more nuanced if one tries not to exclude a priori systemic, macroeconomic, and sociopolitical consequences, which of course are not easy to ascertain. Some of this is explained elsewhere.[97] In my view, the evaluation may depend inter alia on two key issues:

---

[91] For the former and more figures, see Tegtmeier, Werner 'Sachgerechte Dynamik' *Mitbestimmung* 42 (1996) 28-31; Theisen (this volume Ch. 4: Sec. A).

[92] But quite often there are also intergroup meetings of the shareholder and labor side before the actual supervisory board meeting in which the final solutions and compromises are already worked out. See Schmitz, supra n. 37, 238.

[93] Cf. Semler (this volume Ch. 4: Sec. C.II. para 5).

[94] Schmitz, supra n. 37, 238.

[95] Gerum and Wagner (this volume Ch. 5: Sec. B.I.2., B.I.3., and C).

[96] Gerum and Wagner (this volume Ch. 5: Sec. C). Cf. also Raiser, Thomas 'Bewährung des Mitbestimmungsgesetzes nach zwanzig Jahren?' in: Assmann et al., supra n. 39, 479-92; Theisen, Manuel René 'Die Rechtsprechung zum Mitbestimmungsgesetz 1976—eine vierte Zwischenbilanz' *Die Aktiengesellschaft* 43 (1998) 153-70, reports on recent case law as to labor co-determination.

[97] Hopt, Klaus J. 'Labor Board Representation on Corporate Boards: Impacts and Problems for Corporate Governance and Economic Integration in Europe' *International Review of Law and Economics* 14 (1994) 203-14; Pistor, Katharina 'Co-Determination in Germany: A Socio-Political Model with Governance Externalities' (Paper for a conference on "Employees and Corporate Governance" held at Columbia Law School on November 22, 1996); Sadowski, Dieter, Joachim Junkes, and Cornelia Lent 'Mitbestimmung—Gewinne und Investitionen' (Expertise für das Projekt 'Mitbestimmung und neue Unternehmenskulturen' der Bertelsmann Stiftung und der Hans-Böckler-Stiftung) (Gütersloh 1997) give a good survey on economic research on labor co-

first, whether co-determination fulfills the consensus-building function between capital and labor, not only in the enterprise itself but also beyond; and second, whether the efficiency losses co-determination undoubtedly has are still outbalanced by this consensus building today when the need for quick reaction to global competition is more urgent than at any time before. It is clear that these key issues are even more virulent if supervisory board reform does not succeed in solving the general problems of this board.[98]

3. Size of the Board and Entrepreneurial Representation

There are two major side effects of having labor, banks, and other interest groups represented to such a degree in the supervisory boards of major companies.

The obvious one is the size of the supervisory board. Its average size of 13.25 members makes it the largest both in comparison with supervisory and with one-tier boards in Europe.[99] It is true that for co-determined corporations a relatively large board size is mandated by law. Yet even before parity co-determination came into being, very large boards were common during the Weimar Republic— some had up to 30 members[100]—and also today size provisions probably do not account for the overall high average. It is quite another question whether other particularities of German board behavior, such as infrequency of meetings, rarity of committee work, and in general a somewhat loose control intensity in many supervisory boards, are due to co-determination. There is some truth in this, but very little. It may be true, for example, with respect to the frequent practice of not handing out the auditor's report to each supervisory board member before the session, a practice which will now be changed by law. Yet even without co-determination the management board is not interested in developing the supervisory board as a competing player for the management board, be it only for control purposes. This may even be so in companies with major shareholders if the latter have direct influence on the management board and do not use the supervisory board as their main control instrument. The historical development of the *Verwaltungsrat* in public companies confirms this observation. The same can be shown for committee work since until recently committees were not fully co-determined by law (a decision of the *Bundesgerichtshof* has changed this). The above-mentioned hypothesis that co-determination is the important factor

---

determination both in the supervisory board and by the works council. Cf. also Prigge (this volume Ch. 12: Sec. C.I.).

[98] See infra Sec. C.I. and also C.II.

[99] Korn/Ferry International, supra n. 23, 36.

[100] Hommelhoff, Peter 'Störungen im Recht der Aufsichtsrats-Überwachung: Regelungsvorschläge an den Gesetzgeber' in: Picot, Arnold (ed.) *Corporate Governance* 1-28, 24 n. 29 with references (Stuttgart 1995).

which shapes the function and behavior of the supervisory board is therefore flawed. Co-determination is apt to reduce the influence of the supervisory board, but it is not the source of all this.

Another important side effect is that in Germany, relatively few executives from other enterprises can be found. This is true both for active and retired executives. It is in striking difference to some other European countries and may deprive German boards of valuable business experience. Of course, it is hard to say what is better, more entrepreneurial spirit or finance experience possibly coupled with a more conservative outlook. The supervisory board members themselves, regardless of whether they are bankers, lawyers, or businessmen themselves, seem overwhelmingly to be of the view that it would be useful to have more executives from other enterprises on the supervisory board.[101] One wonders why this is not done more often, given the observation that in practice either the chairman of the management board or the chairman of the supervisory board are most influential in new recruitments.

IV. Experience, Practice, Open Questions

1. Affiliated and Independent Outside Directors

a) German economic studies which look at the composition of the supervisory board usually fail to make a clear-cut division between affiliated outside directors and (really) independent outside directors.[102] It is probable that most of the members of the supervisory board belong to the first category, i.e., retired members of the company's management board, banks, lawyers, and most of the businessmen from other companies. The latter usually come from the enterprises that have business relationships with the company. As the history of the *Verwaltungsrat* and later on the supervisory board shows, this is traditionally the very idea, namely, giving a supplier or another enterprise with which the company cooperates a seat and say in the supervisory board.

Collecting data along this division would enable us to make a more meaningful comparison with the American situation as to outside directors. This would

---

[101] Bremeier, Mülder, and Schilling, supra n. 29, 36.

[102] Affiliated outside directors are, for example, former members of the management board and persons who have or are likely to have business relationships with the company, such as bankers, cf. Bhagat and Black (this volume Ch. 4: Sec. A). Cf. also Cadbury Report, supra n. 68, No. 2.2: "The majority should be independent of management and free from any business or other relationships which could materially interfere with the exercise of their independent judgement, apart from their fees and shareholding." According to note 5 this includes that non-executive directors neither participate in share option schemes nor benefit from pensions. The Hampel Report 3.9 (Committee on Corporate Governance, Final Report, London, January 1998) supports Cadbury fully.

also contribute toward rendering the German discussion on banks' influence more sophisticated and hopefully less polemic. Many bank representatives in the supervisory boards come from banks that have no own relevant participations in the company. It can also be expected that a number of these banks do not even have relevant[103] bank business with the company.

b) It has been observed that in Germany (in contrast to the legal regime), supervisory board members are de facto often selected by the management board,[104] which means that the controlled person selects his controller. This is, of course, more likely in corporations without major shareholders than in others where the management board has less discretion of its own.

On the other hand, a recent study reports that in Germany the most relevant sources of influence on the nomination of outside directors are institutional investors (58%),[105] the "full board" (50%),[106] CEO/Chairman (42%), and a nominating committee (38%). In a comparative view it is interesting to see that in other two-tier system countries, the relevant figures were 57%, 73%, 60%, and 37%, and for the one-tier U.K. they were 4%, 65%, 73%, and 52%. This means that the influence of institutional investors in this selection is more important in Germany than elsewhere, while the influence of the CEO on the selection is overwhelming in some other countries.

Furthermore, in Germany the CEO himself is much more likely to be an out-side appointee (46% identified by advertisement on the labor market and only 40% internally) than in other countries with a two-tier system where 48% of the CEOs were internal appointees. In the U.S., the CEO and the chief officers seem to be dominant if there are no controlling shareholders.[107]

This could lead the comparative observer to the conjecture of whether the contraposition of the one-tier board and the two-tier board is as meaningful as is

---

[103] It seems that most retail banking business—as for example check accounts, normal credits, etc.—do not make the bank's representative an affiliated outside director. This is differ-ent for much of the investment banking business and for major credit relationship. On the other side, in order to be affiliated in the above-mentioned sense, the bank must not be a house bank, a concept which in reality is quickly losing its traditional importance anyhow due to fierce bank competition. For a nuanced view, see Krahnen, Jan P. and Ralf Elsas 'Relationship Banking. Wandel im Kreditgeschäft' *Frankfurter Allgemeine Zeitung* no. 52, 3.3.1998, B7 (newspaper article describing their ongoing research).

[104] Similarly Bremeier, Mülder, and Schilling, supra n. 29, 17; Semler (this volume Ch. 4: Sec. B.I. and B.III.).

[105] Korn/Ferry International, supra n. 23, does not define this term. It means probably not only banks, insurance companies, and other institutional shareholder in the technical sense, but all major shareholders.

[106] Korn/Ferry International, supra n. 23, 18 n. 3: The "full board" constitutes selected members of the supervisory and management boards, forming a full board quorum to vote on fundamental strategic policies for the company.

[107] Kraakman, supra n. 59, 131 et seq.

generally maintained. In a functional sense a more meaningful comparative analysis would focus on the CEO and the *Vorstand* (management board) on the one side, and the board, be it unitary or supervisory, on the other.

Of course, differences remain. For example, under the German two-tier system it is impossible for the chairman of the management board to be a member of the supervisory board, while the practice of the CEO being at the same time the chairman of the board is not only legal but rather frequent in the U.S. Furthermore, management cannot be the domain of the supervisory board in Germany. Still, in many cases and as far as control deficits are concerned, the important dividing line may fall instead between CEO/management board on the one side and unitary/supervisory board on the other.

c) Groups of companies (affiliated enterprises, *Konzerne*[108]) are today's reality, with most corporations belonging to a group. Recent data show that 73.61% of the stock corporations and 96.96% of the listed stock corporations belong to a group.[109] Board members within a group very often come from another group member and serve on the board in view of netting the group. The law takes this into consideration when allowing board members to cumulate more seats if they are in affiliated enterprise. Economic research on German boards has not paid enough attention to distinguishing groups of companies,[110] which is surprising in view of the importance rightly attributed to interlockings and netting in general.[111] In future research the difference between normal boards and board members—be it with business ties to other companies on the one side, and boards of enterprises belonging to the same groups of companies with board members linking them together on the other—could be distinguished for more meaningful results.[112]

Furthermore, the historical survey has shown that groups are not only linked by legally mandated boards, but also by voluntary boards and by other voluntary advisory bodies. I am not aware of a study looking into the corporate governance dimension of these transenterprise and transnational linking bodies.[113] This could be an interesting field of research even though data are not easily available.

---

[108] In the broader sense of the word, not in the technical legal sense of § 18 AktG.

[109] The figures are even higher, if not the numbers, but the statutory capital of the stock corporations is taken as a basis. See Prigge (this volume Ch. 12: Sec. A.II.1. and B.II.2.).

[110] As to legal policy towards groups in Europe, see Forum Europaeum Groups of Companies (Doralt, Druey, Hommelhoff, Hopt, Lutter, and Wymeersch) *Zeitschrift für Unternehmens- und Gesellschaftsrecht* 27/4 (forthcoming 1998).

[111] See supra Sec. B.II.2.

[112] See also Prigge (this volume Ch. 12: Sec. B.I.2.).

[113] As to the role of advisory bodies, see for example Gaugler, Eduard and Wolfgang Heimburger *Firmenbeiräte mittelständischer Unternehmen* (Mannheim 1984); Klaus, Hans *Die Rolle des Beirates bei der Führung von Mittelbetrieben* (Dissertation University of Erlangen-Nuremberg 1987) (Frankfurt am Main et al. 1988).

d) Another remark relates to the close relationship between the members of
the unitary board or the two boards. For the United States this has been referred
to as a club.[114] For Germany the same observation has been made. Indeed, this
seems quite plausible in view of the particular linkage function of the supervisory board. On the other side, German insiders have contested the idea that
there is an "old boys' network" between the (shareholder) members of the supervisory board by pointing to the fact that the (supervisory) board members and,
indeed, more generally the elite in Germany are much less homogeneous than,
for example, in France and in Great Britain.[115] It follows that research would be
fruitful which would look more into the origin, profile, and orientation of the
board members in the different countries.

2. The Supervisory Board in a Swiftly Changing Environment

a) While institutional patterns such as corporate governance patterns do not
change quickly, specific factors may be subject to rather quick evolution.
Recently there have been several cases in which bank representatives have left
the board, not because they were urged to do so, but rather because they themselves or their bank did not consider it necessarily in the best interest of the bank
to keep the seat on the supervisory board.[116] It is too early to state that this is a
trend. But such a trend would not be surprising. As to the reasons, one need not
speculate. The acute public discussion and legislative concern about the role of
the banks in recent failures and scandals, and more generally about bank power,
is certainly one reason.

A more relevant force is competition of Anglo-American investment banks
with German universal banks, both abroad and increasingly also in Germany. A
full network of bank supervisory seats is too much of a drain on their own scarce
board member resources. It simply does not pay. Even worse, it is bound to
create problems of conflict of interest, as shown most vividly in the recent
abortive takeover battle between Krupp and Thyssen. There the large German
banks were severely criticized for having their representatives sitting on the
boards of both companies, the bidder and the target. While this is not illegal in
Germany, it is open to criticism and certainly uncommon in other countries such
as the U.K., not to mention the U.S.

It is not clear what consequences such a retreat of major banks from the
boards will have. If one thinks that the influence of the bank representatives on

---

[114] Kraakman, supra n. 59, 139.

[115] Schmitz, supra n. 37, 237. Cf. also Charkham, Jonathan P. *Keeping Good Company. A
Study of Corporate Governance in Five Countries* 122 et seq. (Oxford 1994) for France.

[116] Schmitz, supra n. 37, 236; André, supra n. 1, 1844.

the board is useful because of their financial expertise and their back office,[117] it is a loss for the company. On the other hand, expectations that the influence of the banks on the company would thereby be considerably reduced are ill-founded. Even without revitalizing the house bank relationship, major banks that have important credit or investment banking business with a company have other and better means to check the company and its management.

b) It has been said that personal links and participations often go together, also for banks. Yet contrary to what is said, the overall number of bank participations in non-bank enterprises has sometimes slightly increased during the last years. It is true that the participations of 25-50% went down. On the contrary, however, participations between 10-25% moved up. The latter are by far more important, both as to absolute numbers as well as to stated capital.[118] It is unclear to what degree the diminution of board seats held by banks also concerns those banks which hold such participations or only others without participations, and whether the banks with such participations choose to exert influence by means other than supervisory board memberships. In any case, most recently several major German banks have reviewed their participation policy and have announced their decision to reduce their participations in non-financial enterprises considerably.[119]

c) From a comparative law perspective, a clear tendency of assimilation is discernible. In the one-tier system one can see forms and methods of breaking up the homogeneity of the board (principal senior executives, inside directors, independent outside directors, and their role in the different board committees).[120] In the United Kingdom, the Cadbury Report has recommended against having the same person as CEO and as chairman of the board.[121] These developments are due in part to law, partly to stock exchange requirements, but in many cases this

---

[117] Back offices also have drawbacks; see Prigge (this volume Ch. 12: Sec. B.I.3.).

[118] Bundesverband Deutscher Banken, supra n. 45.

[119] Deutsche Bank, Hypo-Bank, BHF-Bank and others. See also Mülbert (this volume Ch. 6: Sec. G.II.).

[120] Windbichler, Christine 'Zur Trennung von Geschäftsführung und Kontrolle bei amerikanischen Großgesellschaften. Eine "neue" Entwicklung und europäische Regelungen im Vergleich' *Zeitschrift für Unternehmens- und Gesellschaftsrecht* 14 (1985) 50-73; Buxbaum, supra n. 5, 68 et seq.; Baums, Theodor 'Der Aufsichtsrat—Aufgaben und Reformfragen' *Zeitschrift für Wirtschaftsrecht (ZIP)* 16 (1995) 11-8, 15.

[121] Cadbury Report, supra n. 68, 4.9 and The Code of Best Practice, supra n. 68, No. 1.2, at least in the following way, "that no one individual has unfettered powers of decision. Where the chairman is also the chief executive, it is essential that there should be a strong and independent element on the hoard, with a recognised senior member." This is supported by the Hampel Report, supra n. 102, 3.17, 3.18.

differentiation is just perceived as beneficial by the corporations and their boards themselves. Similar differentiations are discernible in Swiss one-tier boards.[122]

Conversely, in the two-tier board systems the practical interplay between the two boards is becoming closer and closer. Even though the legally imposed incompatibility rules are respected, there are many cases in which either the management board or the supervisory board clearly has the lead, meaning that either the supervisory board is not fulfilling its supervisory task as it should, or that in practice it is interfering in basic management decisions.

d) Finally, there is a rather common feeling that the supervisory boards are not living up to expectations. This shows in the interviews conducted[123] as well as in the discussion and reform plans.

This goes together with retarded capital markets and corporate control markets. Yet which way causation runs is difficult to tell. One of the major reasons for these market deficiencies may be the lack of demand of small and medium-sized firms.[124]

C. Reforms and Conclusion

I. Board Reform

The German discussion on board reform is legion and cannot be summarized here.[125] Some very brief remarks must suffice. One thing is for sure. In the fore-seeable future, the two-tier system will not be changed nor even placed at the disposal of the corporations. While during the last decades there have been some voices recommending such a change,[126] the overwhelming majority of German commentators cannot see an advantage in this or is even convinced of the superi-

---

[122] Böckli, Peter 'Verwaltungsrat oder Aufsichtsrat?' *Festschrift für Walter Reist* 3, 20 (Zurich 1992).

[123] Cf. Korn/Ferry International, supra n. 23, 28 et seq.; Bremeier, Mülder, and Schilling, supra n. 29, 9.

[124] Similarly, OECD 'Eigentumsverhältnisse, Kontrolle und Entscheidungsprozesse in deutschen Unternehmen' in: 'OECD Wirtschaftsberichte: Deutschland 1995' 94-145, 144 (Paris 1995).

[125] A good sample of arguments is given by the contributions to the Parliamentary Hearing on the Draft Act in Bonn, see *Die Aktienrechtsreform 1997 nach den Vorschlägen des Referentenentwurfs eines Gesetzes zur Kontrolle und Transparenz im Unternehmensbereich (KonTraG)* (with contributions by Adams, Assmann, Baums, Claussen, Gelhausen, Götz, Hopt, Kübler, Lutter, Martens, Mertens, Peltzer, Seibert, Wenger) *Die Aktiengesellschaft* (Special Edition, August 1997). As to legislative and self-regulatory board reform in other countries, see the reports, recommendations, and other materials in Hopt and Wymeersch, supra n. 1, Part II.

[126] See the references in Meier-Schatz, supra n. 1, 444.

ority of the two-tier system[127], just as the British and others are convinced of their own system.[128] As mentioned above, this goes together with frequent criticism of the present law and practice of the German supervisory board. This is in line with the parallel discussion in the United States which does not plead for giving up the one-tier system, but concentrates on the structure and the function of the board, its committees—in particular the audit committee—and the profile of the various groups of directors.[129] The experience in France, where a choice between the two board models is open, has not led to dramatic changes in practice.[130]

The German board reform has just become law in April 1998.[131] It has been very fiercely discussed. At the end, the more prudent majority in politics, business, and academia[132] has had its way against the opposition parties, the press, and some outspoken academic critics. The reform deals with several clear deficiencies of the supervisory board. Some of them and the corresponding reforms are minor and rather technical. For example, the requirement of meeting more frequently (at least four times a year) has been taken up, even though it is doubtful whether this should be prescribed by law. The proposals for mandatory legal provisions concerning a professional full-time chairman, minimum resources and back office for the chairman, the number and kind of committees, etc., have rightly been dumped. These improvements can be left to competitive pressures. In general, corporation law (as well as stock exchange law) does not need more technical regulation, but deregulation.[133]

Unfortunately, it was not possible to change the mandatory size provision in the law. In the light of American and international studies, deregulation or at

---

[127] Cf., for example, Kropff, Bruno 'Das amerikanische Board-Modell im Vergleich zur deutschen Vorstands-/Aufsichtsratsverfassung. Stellungnahme' *Die Betriebswirtschaft* 46 (1986) 523-5; Theisen (this volume Ch. 4: Sec. A). See also the OECD Report of Experts on Corporate Governance 'Corporate Governance: Verbesserung der Wettbewerbsfähigkeit und der Kapitalbeschaffung auf globalen Märkten' (Paris 1998), no preference for a one-tier or a two-tier board, but for a professional, independent board.

[128] See Gower and Davies, supra n. 5, 196: "To some extent, therefore, the practice of English public companies resembles that of continental companies with two-tier boards—despite the hostility [of. . .] the English business world." Cf. also Hampel Report, supra n. 102, Summary no. 10: "There is overwhelming support in the UK for the unitary board, and virtually none for the two tier board (3.12)."

[129] Buxbaum, supra n. 5, 69 et seq.

[130] See the figures given in Hopt, supra n. 1, 12 et seq.

[131] *BGBl I* 24/1998, 786-94.

[132] See the references in Hopt, Klaus J. 'Kontrolle und Transparenz im Unternehmensbereich' in: Assmann et al. supra n. 39, 435-56.

[133] Cf. Spindler, Gerald 'Deregulierung des Aktienrechts?' *Die Aktiengesellschaft* 43 (1998) 53-74. For stock exchange law, see Hopt, Rudolph, and Baum supra n. 3, and Monopolies Commission, supra n. 19, para 70 et seq.

least reduction of the mandatory size would have been clearly beneficial.[134] But as to this there was stiff resistance by the trade unions, which feared an intrusion into the "vested rights" of labor co-determination, and by the Federal Ministry of Labor, which had the same fears (or was already looking forward to the elections). This shows once more the immobility of German labor and the widespread, alarming unwillingness of the German politicians and public to reduce anything which concerns social rights.

The core reforms cover three fundamental points:

The first concerns the information of the board and the role of the auditors. The reform aims at adding another layer of monitoring by the latter. The chances of achieving a major improvement of control by this measure are good, according to many observers. Much will depend, of course, on whether professionalism of the auditing firms will prevail over the temptation to foster business ties. This is exactly the reason why other have certain doubts. Some have pleaded for a mandatory change of the auditing firm after a number of years. The Reform Act restricts itself to a mandatory change of auditing team. Indeed, mandatory change rules, while helping to reduce conflicts of interest, tend to diminish the control over the management since the auditing firm needs much time and investment in order to familiarize itself anew with the company to be audited.[135]

The second reform improves the enforcement mechanisms for board member liability, both for the management board and the supervisory board. Individual shareholders with shareholdings of 5% or shares with a nominal value of 2 million marks can sue board members for damages to be paid to the corporation; however, this can only be done upon suspicion of grossly negligent behavior. The Monopolies Commission would have gone further, down to 5% per cent, 1 million marks, and simple negligence, while keeping the normal cost risk of the minority shareholders who lose the case.[136] In my view the better arguments are for the Reform Act.[137]

In general, the Reform Act requires more transparency in order to reduce conflicts of interests. This is certainly beneficial. The Monopolies Commission again goes further and recommends a prohibition of interlocking directorates for the representatives of enterprises and banks to be monitored by the Cartel

---

[134] Cf. also Bhagat and Black (this volume Ch. 4: Sec. C).

[135] Arruñada, Benito and Cándido Paz-Ares 'Mandatory Rotation of Company Auditors: A Critical Examination' *International Review of Law and Economics* 17 (1997) 31-61.

[136] Monopolies Commission, supra n. 19, para 198.

[137] Hopt, supra n. 132, 439 et seq.; Hopt, Klaus J. 'Die Haftung von Vorstand und Aufsichtsrat. Zugleich ein Beitrag zur corporate governance-Debatte' in: Immenga, Ulrich, Wernhard Möschel, and Dieter Reuter (eds.) *Festschrift für Ernst-Joachim Mestmäcker zum siebzigsten Geburtstag* 909-31, 919 et seq. (Baden-Baden 1996). The latest comparative contribution is by Abeltshauser, Thomas E. *Leitungshaftung im Kapitalgesellschaftsrecht* (Cologne et al. 1998).

Commission.[138] It believes that interlocking directorates by trade unions need not to be touched except for a prohibition of the same representative sitting in two competing companies. This distinction is doubtful. In general, the conflict of interest problems are too difficult to be adequately addressed by broad structural measures such as the one proposed by the Monopolies Commission, and dealing with them on a case-by-case basis by the courts may bring better and more flexible results. Also, the American experience with independent directors illustrates these difficulties.[139] It might be that mixed boards with affiliate members who bring in particular knowledge and experience and independent members are more beneficial than legally mandated prohibitions.

II. Market Reforms

The Stock Corporation Reform of 1998 is by no means sufficient. What is needed now is a far-reaching legislative reform which would deregulate and open the markets for competition. This means that the emphasis of practical and legislative reform should be on reforming the German stock exchanges, which are under a dated legal regime, and on developing the German capital markets, the market for corporate control, and the labor markets, which are incredibly rigid compared to other countries.[140]

III. Outlook: A Plea for Prudence

Historical and practical experience as well as theoretical insights and the reform discussion all warrant some rather cautious final remarks.

Practically, all of the economic research mentioned and most of the public attention and reform discussion is on the stock corporation. Yet foreign observers and EU Commission officials should beware: in Germany, there are only 4,088 stock corporations (as of February 1997).[141] This is to be compared with over 600,000 *GmbHs* and far more than 200,000 commercial partnerships.[142] Even though much of large business is done by stock corporations, the other company

---

[138] See Monopolies Commission, supra n. 19, para 183 et seq.

[139] Cf. the neutral evidence on the value of independent directors on large firm boards and its various hypothetical interpretations by Bhagat and Black (this volume Ch. 4: Sec. D).

[140] Cf. Hopt, Rudolph, and Baum, supra n. 3; Monopolies Commission, supra n. 19, para 267 et seq.

[141] 4,043 at the end of 1996, Hansen, supra n. 47, R123.

[142] Former figures were 3,219 stock corporations, 549,659 *GmbHs* (as of 1994), 210,335 commercial partnerships, and 1,305,445 individual enterprises (as of 1980), Hopt, Klaus J., Günther Hehl, and Hans-Joachim Vollrath *Gesellschaftsrecht* 4th edn. 317, Table 15 (Munich 1996). See also Prigge (this volume Ch. 12: Sec. A.I.).

forms are used for large enterprises as well. Some of the largest are *GmbHs*, which need not have a supervisory board and which are not allowed to go public at the stock exchange. It becomes rather obvious that economic reality is not captured by the above-mentioned research. Cross-country comparisons, whether purely academic or legislative in the context of European harmonization work, risk being fallacious if they do not give credit to these differences between Germany and other countries. This is true in particular if one tries to find correlations between corporate governance and economic systems and their performances.

Even without reaching beyond the stock corporation, the hypothesis has been brought forward that different board structures may be related with and suit different firm sizes, industries, and markets.[143] Again, just sticking to the stock corporation or at least to large enterprises, it would be worthwhile to take into consideration not only the supervisory board as a legally mandated organ in the stock corporation, but also other supervisory boards, for example in the *GmbH*, and similar voluntary advisory boards. The observation made in the beginning that these kinds of boards are frequent in multinational companies warrants research on whether the multinational character of the enterprise has specific consequences for boards, supervision, and corporate governance. This kind of research would be particularly relevant in an emerging internal market like the European Union.

In sum, the aforementioned historical, economic, and comparative findings cannot but lead to a prudent assessment of the German two-tier board and more generally of German corporate governance.[144] Both straightforward praise and condemnation are either short-sighted or ideological. Things are much more complicated and interwoven. This lesson must be remembered, particularly if one enacts or recommends legislative reforms as to the board model and corporate governance. Many of the more fundamental reform proposals concerning bank influence in the supervisory boards by participations in non-banks and also via the depository vote would simply be great-scale experiments whose overall results cannot be predicted. In other words, those who support the economic competition theory would consider it to be a "presumption of knowledge" (*Anmassung von Wissen*). This plea for prudence goes together with room and respect for different historical, social, and cultural contingencies and preferences—as long as it is allowed by the forces of globalization and their impact on corporate governance.[145]

---

[143] As to this hypothesis, see Bhagat and Black (this volume Ch. 4: Sec. D). Cf. also the board typology presented by Gerum, Elmar 'Aufsichtsratstypen: Ein Beitrag zur Theorie der Unternehmensführung' *Die Betriebswirtschaft* 51 (1991) 719-31.

[144] Cf. Romano, Roberta 'A Cautionary Note on Drawing Lessons from Comparative Corporate Law' 102 *Yale L.J.* 2021-37 (1993).

[145] Cf., for example, OECD, supra n. 124, 136 et seq., 143 et seq.

Empirical Evidence and Economic Comments on Board Structure in Germany

MANUEL R. THEISEN, Munich

Both the legal board structure and the empirical situation on this subject make this essay's overview of the real situation and its problems necessary. Most of the German supervisory board's legal work is done by committees or in direct contact between the chief executive officer and the chief officer of the supervisory board. Another speciality is co-determination and the influence of the employee representatives, who meet separately before the general meetings take place. To improve the practice of supervision in Germany, this essay calls for generally accepted orderly monitoring principles, developed by specialists for business administration and organization and accepted by the jurisprudence. First steps toward arriving at a consensus on some kind of "best method" in this field are also advocated.

Contents

A. The Legal Model of the German Supervisory Board

The supervisory board (*Aufsichtsrat*) is the main monitoring body in large German stock corporations (*Aktiengesellschaften*). It represents the most important counterpart to the management of a single company or a group of companies; its task is to monitor the management and, as a part of these duties, to advise as well. From an economic point of view, management and supervision of companies and groups of companies must be strictly separated.[1] By statute law, the German supervisory board model guarantees this important characteristic by separating both functions, which are transferred to two different bodies (the two-tier system).[2] From this institutional point of view, the board model cannot

---

[1] See Semler, Johannes *Leitung und Überwachung der Aktiengesellschaft* 2nd rev. edn. (Cologne et al. 1996) with further hints and literature.

[2] For the German *Aufsichtsratssystem* and the specific problems of supervision in groups of companies see Theisen, Manuel R. *Die Überwachung der Unternehmungsführung* (Stuttgart 1987); Theisen, Manuel R. *Der Konzern* 447-9 (Stuttgart 1991), and Scheffler, Eberhard 'Konzernleitung und Konzernüberwachung' in: Scheffler, Eberhard (ed.) *Corporate Governance*

formally provide such a dual system of management and monitoring;[3] it is, therefore, rejected by the majority of German business leaders as well as German academics.[4]

Co-determination of the employees and union representatives is an integral part of business culture in Germany. With regard to management, it is practiced at the level of each plant, each legal entity, and the group of companies as a whole. Concerning monitoring, co-determination of internal and external representatives is justified by the organizational separation of management and supervision. Also in this respect, the separation of day-to-day management on the one side and monitoring on the other documents their different functions. From both a practical and a theoretical point of view, the co-determination of the employees at the supervisory level need not be discussed or questioned because it has proven its worth in Germany for more than four decades.[5]

Formally, supervisory boards in Germany reach the legal conception with nearly no divergence. Since the last fundamental reform of the legal framework of the supervisory board model by the Co-Determination Act of 1976 (MitbestG 1976), more than 20 years ago, the number of legal proceedings and court decisions about the establishment and organization of co-determined supervisory boards has continuously decreased.[6] Currently, about 740 supervisory boards of

147-70 (Wiesbaden 1995); for a comprehensive review of the differences between the German system and the board system, see the articles and theses in Feddersen, Dieter, Peter Hommelhoff, and Uwe H. Schneider (eds.) *Corporate Governance* (Cologne 1996) and Theisen, Manuel, R. 'Das Board-Modell: Lösungsansatz zur Überwindung der "Überwachungslücke" in deutschen Aktiengesellschaften?' *Die Aktiengesellschaft* 34 (1989) 161-8; for a comprehensive analysis of the European approaches, see Wymeersch (this volume Ch. 12: Sec. C).

[3] See Lutter, Marcus 'Das dualistische System der Unternehmensverwaltung' in: Scheffler (ed.), supra n. 2, 5-26; Potthoff, Erich 'Board-System versus duales System der Unternehmensverwaltung—Vor- und Nachteile' *Betriebswirtschaftliche Forschung und Praxis* 48 (1996) 253-68; finally, in contrast, see Dreher, Meinrad 'Die Organisation des Aufsichtsrats' in: Feddersen, Hommelhoff, and Schneider (eds.), supra n. 2, 33-60, 59: "keines der Organisationsmodelle ... eindeutig überlegen." For the newest perspective, see Holzer, Peter and Andreas Makowski 'Corporate Governance' *Der Betrieb* 50 (1997) 688-92.

[4] For an American perspective, see Lorsch, Jay W. 'German Corporate Governance and Management' in: von Werder, Axel (ed.) *Grundsätze ordnungsmäßiger Unternehmungsführung (GoF)* 199-225 (Wiesbaden 1996); Buxbaum, Richard M. 'Die Leitung von Gesellschaften— Strukturelle Reformen im amerikanischen und deutschen Gesellschaftsrecht' in: Feddersen, Hommelhoff, and Schneider (eds.), supra n. 2, 65-93.

[5] For empirical evidence, see Baums, Theodor and Bernd Frick 'Co-determination in Germany: The Impact on the Market Value of the Firm' 29 (Working Paper of the Institut für Handels- und Wirtschaftsrecht, University of Osnabrück, no. 1/1997): "Co-determination is thought to influence the performance of the firms concerned neither negatively nor positively." For further information about the legal environment, see Baums and Frick, supra, 3-5. For a survey of empirical evidence, cf. Gerum/Wagner (this volume Ch. 5: Sec. C).

[6] See Theisen, Manuel R. 'Die Rechtsprechung zum MitbestG 1976—eine vierte Zwischenbilanz' *Die Aktiengesellschaft* 43 (1998) 153-70; Jäger, Axel 'Die Entwicklung der Recht-

the full parity model exist,[7] while strategies to evade or avoid co-determination are no longer a subject for discussion. Quite the reverse, the continuous discussion about function and quality of supervisory boards in Germany —especially during company crises, scandals, and financial difficulties—has seemed to increase the solidarity between their different members more than at anytime before.

B. Practice of the German Supervisory Board

In reality, however, the German supervisory boards work in a way that is quite different from the legally defined model. The supervisory board as a monitoring organ, the members of which are responsible in common, is mostly reduced to a mere formal meeting: according to empirical surveys, this monitoring committee meets about two to five times a year and the meetings last between two and four hours.[8] The legal size of supervisory boards depends on the number of employees and is between 12 and 20 members. In consideration of an average of five to seven members of management boards, one clerk (secretary), and one or two additional experts or specialists, the average attendance of the meetings amounts to 18 to 30 participants. Provided that each of them wants to make at least one verbal contribution, his remarks could last approximately 4 to 13 minutes. On the basis of these organizational conditions, an orderly discussion is neither theoretically nor practically possible.

In company practice, two organizational activities that act in opposition to the actual malfunction of German supervisory boards as a collective organ can be observed: an increasing number of committees within the supervisory board on the one hand, and so-called preliminary meetings on the other.

Committees—as sub-units of the supervisory board—are created to take on special tasks of the monitoring body as a whole, either permanently or on a case-by-case basis. Up to now, the German legislature has not made the setting-up of committees obligatory, but for many years they have been provided for by the

---

sprechung zur Aktiengesellschaft in den Jahren 1994-1996' *Wirtschaftsrechtliche Beratung* 3 (1996) 460-6.

[7] For further details, see Tegtmeier, Werner 'Sachgerechte Dynamik' *Die Mitbestimmung* 42/10 (1996) 28-31, 28: More than 8 million employees are represented in these 740 companies, 406 as stock corporations (*AG*) and 329 as limited liability companies (*GmbH*).

[8] See the empirical results of Bremeier, Eberhard, Jürgen B. Mülder, and Florian Schilling 'Praxis der Aufsichtsratstätigkeit in Deutschland' (AMROP International, Düsseldorf 1994); Deutsche Schutzvereinigung für Wertpapierbesitz (ed.) 'Aufsichtsräte in Deutschland' (Düsseldorf 1995); Ward Howell (ed.) 'Macht und Ohnmacht der Aufsichtsräte in Österreich' (Vienna 1995); Korn/Ferry International (eds.) 'European Boards of Directors Study' (London 1996). The available evidence is surveyed in an internationally comparative context in the respective sections of the articles by Kanda, Prigge, and Wymeersch in Ch. 12 of this volume.

by-laws (charter) of most companies. Committees typically deal with personnel matters, the review of the annual report and the balance sheet, the corporate planning, or special tasks such as the promise of credit. The different committees work together with the members of the executive boards in charge of their specific tasks and/or the external auditor, as well as additional internal and external experts. The assignment of a precise task to a committee is usually—but falsely—interpreted by the other members of the supervisory board as a definite delegation of responsibility.

The work of the supervisory board can be considerably reduced by preliminary meetings, but these are neither laid down by statute law nor welcome in principle. Nevertheless, they undoubtedly are the most important setting praeter legem, especially for the full-parity supervisory boards. Before each meeting of the supervisory board and—in important matters—also before the relevant meeting of the single committees, both the representatives of the shareholders and the representatives of the employees meet separately with the CEO and additional experts, if necessary. At these meetings, important matters of the monitoring work of the supervisory board are discussed, and the participants generally seek for joint positions on all important questions by means of bilateral exchange and bargaining. Only these results of the preliminary meetings will then be reported to the meetings of the complete supervisory board. This is the historical and proven way to deal with the temporal and organizational restrictions the plenary sessions of the supervisory board have to cope with.

In fact, the bulk of the supervisory board's monitoring of management—at least in larger German stock companies—has shifted to other bodies or settings, which is legally possible but not intended by the German legislature. Therefore, the functioning and efficiency of the legal and obligatory work of the supervisory board is more or less beyond the control of third persons or groups of persons. Furthermore, this development permits or forces a further and stronger cooperation of the members of the supervisory board on the one hand and the members of the management board on the other, a probable attribute of the two-tier system. Therefore, it is not impossible that there will be an increased conversion of the German supervisory board model toward a structure quite similar to the board model; however, the functioning of this process can be neither tested nor scrutinized.[9]

---

[9] See also Schneider-Lenné, Ellen R. 'Das anglo-amerikanische Board-System' in: Scheffler (ed.), supra n. 2, 27-55, 50; Kraakman, Reinier 'Die Professionalisierung des Board' in: Feddersen, Hommelhoff, and Schneider (eds.), supra n. 2, 129-48, and others.

C. The Need for Generally Accepted Orderly Monitoring Principles and Other Means of Improving the Activities of German Supervisory Boards

However, the mentioned shift and reduction of the activities of the supervisory board determined by statutory law are not just caused by organizational matters. From an economic point of view, the German supervisory board model's legal pretense cannot operate with success if the following conditions are not solved in an efficient way:

a. The compensation of the members of the supervisory board should be adequate, i.e., in relation to their commitment;

b. a minimum qualification of the members of the supervisory board should be determined; and

c. the liability of the members of the supervisory board should be put in concrete form juridicially.

The compensation of an ordinary member of a supervisory board—excluding its president and vice-president—averages around DM 16,000 (approx. US$ 9,500) per year. In other words, the actual work of the members of a supervisory board is not at all adequately compensated. From an economic point of view (given rational behavior), an additional commitment by the members cannot be expected—even in order to fulfill the legal duties—if the conditions are not changed.[10]

The legislature provides no special requirements that should be met in particular in order to become a member of a supervisory board; special qualifications and skills are not asked for. It is only the legal duty of monitoring which sets the standard that members have to comply with; however, the extent to which they accept and perform that standard is up to potential members themselves.[11] Up to now, proven decisions by a higher court in order to examine that behavior do not exist.

By German statutory law, the liability of each member of a supervisory board is very extensive; however, only few persons are entitled to bring an action. Only

---

[10] For some empirical results of the varying compensations in Germany, see Schmid, Frank A. 'Vorstandsbezüge, Aufsichtsratsvergütung und Aktionärsstruktur' *Zeitschrift für Betriebswirtschaft* 67 (1997) 67-83. For an international comparison see Kaplan, Steven N. 'Corporate Governance und Unternehmenserfolg—Ein Vergleich zwischen Deutschland, Japan und den USA' in: Feddersen, Hommelhoff, and Schneider (eds.), supra n. 2, 301-15.

[11] For the intense discussion about higher quality in the German supervisory board, see Dreher, Meinrad 'Die Qualifikation der Aufsichtsratsmitglieder' in: Ebenroth, Carsten T., Dieter Hesselberger, and Manfred E. Rinne (eds.) *Verantwortung und Gestaltung* (Festschrift Boujong) 71-97 (Munich 1996); Wardenbach, Frank *Interessenkonflikte und mangelnde Sachkunde als Bestellungshindernisse zum Aufsichtsrat der AG* (Cologne 1996); Mülbert, Peter O. 'Die Stellung der Aufsichtsratsmitglieder' in: Feddersen, Hommelhoff, and Schneider (eds.), supra n. 2, 99-123.

the board (which is subject to monitoring), as well as a minority of—still—[12] 10% of the shareholders are able to sue the supervisory board itself as well as certain members.[13] In reality, only liquidators have sued supervisory boards; as a matter of fact, since the last war there has not been any conviction of a supervisory board or its members as long as the company has continued to operate.[14]

Discussions have gone on for decades concerning to what extent a supervisory board has to fulfill its duties, with nearly no further results.[15] For quite some time it has been known to economists that an ordinary member of a German supervisory board, as well as most of the supervisory boards as a monitoring level, are not able to fulfill their duties of supervision in a sufficient manner. The reason for this is that the organizational and personnel preconditions as well as the necessary skills are missing.[16] Nevertheless, supervisory boards can (and do) often report positively about their activities,[17] because neither the legislature nor the courts have exactly determined the duty of monitoring and the extent of monitoring and liability.[18] Consequently, German business leaders as well as German academics should give priority to setting up generally accepted orderly

---

[12] For a related special legislative reform, see Seibert, Ulrich 'Kontrolle und Transparenz im Unternehmensbereich (KonTraG)' *Wertpapier Mitteilungen* 51 (1997) 6-8.

[13] Most recently, see Poseck, Roman 'Die Klage des Aufsichtsrats gegen die Geschäftsführung des Vorstands' *Der Betrieb* 49 (1996) 2165-9; Fischer, Michael 'Der Entscheidungsspielraum des Aufsichtsrats bei der Geltendmachung von Regreßansprüchen gegen Vorstandsmitglieder' *Betriebs-Berater* 51 (1996) 225-30.

[14] See Theisen, Manuel R. 'Haftung und Haftungsrisiko des Aufsichtsrats' *Die Betriebswirtschaft* 53 (1993) 295-318; for the last legislative reforms, see Thümmel, Roderich C. 'Manager- und Aufsichtsratshaftung nach dem Referentenentwurf zur Änderung des AktG und des HGB' *Der Betrieb* 50 (1997) 261-4. For the American situation, see von Werder, Axel and Christa Feld 'Sorgfaltsanforderungen der US-amerikanischen Rechtsprechung an das Top Management' *Recht der Internationalen Wirtschaft* 42 (1996) 481-93; Coffee, John C. 'Organhaftung im amerikanischen Recht' in: Feddersen, Hommelhoff, and Schneider (eds.), supra n. 2, 165-208.

[15] Last contributions in Picot, Arnold (ed.) *Corporate Governance* (Stuttgart 1995); Scheffler (ed.), supra n. 2; Feddersen, Hommelhoff, and Schneider (eds.), supra n. 2.

[16] See Theisen, Manuel R. 'Grundsätze ordnungsgemäßer Kontrolle und Beratung der Geschäftsführung durch den Aufsichtsrat' *Die Aktiengesellschaft* 40 (1995) 193-203.

[17] For a last example, see Semler, Johannes 'Unternehmensüberwachung durch den Kapitalmarkt' in: Picot (ed.), supra n. 15, 29-87, 41: "Die Aufsichtsräte der deutschen Wirtschaft sind besser als ihr Ruf."

[18] Surprisingly, nearly the same intention is found in Mertens, Hans-Joachim 'Unternehmensleitung und Organhaftung' in: Feddersen, Hommelhoff, and Schneider (eds.), supra n. 2, 155-64, 161: "(Es) müßte hier zunächst einmal ein eindeutiges Anforderungsprofil für Aufsichtsratsmitglieder geschaffen werden, wovon das geltende Recht bekanntlich weit entfernt ist. Gäbe es ein solches Profil—und eine entsprechende Bezahlung—, so würden sich Aufsichtsratsmitglieder seinen (ihren?, M. R. T.) Anforderungen wohl durchweg auch unabhängig von Haftungsdrohungen fügen."

monitoring principles (*Grundsätze ordnungsmäßiger Überwachung*); these principles should be tested by German companies for a certain time.[19]

Empirical surveys of German supervisory boards cannot be made in a reliable manner on the basis of legal general provisions. In this regard, exact standards (rules) of monitoring are necessary, developed by specialists for business administration and management and accepted by the jurisprudence. It must be feared—and insofar it is to be discussed—that the relative self-satisfaction of members of supervisory boards, as well as the common satisfaction with the activities of supervisory boards, are principally due to the fact that neither the members of supervisory boards nor those who evaluate their activities are (and can be) aware of the duties asked for by the legislature: expectation and reality do not match.

Another interpretation may come to the conclusion that the legislature as well as the supervisory boards are quite aware of the important economic function of a monitoring organ, but both know—and do not say—that they cannot fulfill that function at all. In the second case, reality and expectation would fit but the monitoring function would not be fulfilled.

The activities of the supervisory board can and have to be considerably improved on the basis of the provisions concerning company law. It is difficult to say whether and to what extent a higher level of efficient and successful monitoring can be reached in the future. Regarding this, there must first be an answer to the question of whether large German companies and groups of companies can still be managed by the bodies required by law in a responsible way.[20] If this cannot be assured—or only in a more or less restricted manner—it is also not possible to efficiently monitor those bodies by the German supervisory board.

[19] For detailed information, see the contributions in von Werder (ed.), supra n. 4; Theisen, Manuel R. *Grundsätze einer ordnungsmäßigen Information des Aufsichtsrats* 2nd rev. edn. (Stuttgart 1996).

[20] The author first mentioned this consideration at the Corporate Governance Discussion of the Schmalenbach-Gesellschaft, Düsseldorf, April 1995, see Theisen, Manuel R. in: Picot (ed.), supra n. 15, 128-9.

The Practice of the German Aufsichtsrat

JOHANNES SEMLER, Frankfurt/M.

There are various types of supervisory boards in Germany with different responsibilities. The essential task of the supervisory board is the appointment of an efficient management board. The management board must report to the supervisory board regularly and on different topics. The supervision by the supervisory board is multifaceted because of different reporting practices. The supervisory board is required to report annually to the shareholders on its activities. Every board member is liable for violation of his duty to exercise due care, even though—in practice—suits against board members are seldom.

Contents

A. Preliminary Remarks

Because of time constraints, my report on the topic "The Practice of the German *Aufsichtsrat*" can highlight only a few aspects of the treatment of corporate governance in German stock corporations.[1] There are several reasons for this.

1. There is not just one type of German supervisory board (*Aufsichtsrat*). The legal basis for the activity of this supervisory body varies according to the legal form of the company involved.

The composition of supervisory boards also varies.

---

[1] For additional information on German supervisory board practice in this volume, cf. Hopt (Ch. 4), Theisen (Ch. 4), and Prigge (Ch. 12: Sec. B.I. and C.I.1.); for a treatment in an international context, see Kanda (Ch. 12: Sec. B.I.) and Wymeersch (Ch. 12: Sec. C.).

In the case of the coal and steel model, there is a so-called "neutral" member in addition to an equal number of representatives of the shareholders and the employees. There are supervisory boards which, in accordance with the Co-Determination Act, consist of an equal number of shareholder and employee representatives. Also, there are supervisory boards in which a third of the members are appointed by the employees. There are no employee representatives on the supervisory boards of so-called *Tendenzunternehmen,* which are enterprises not fully subject to the Employees' Representation Act (*Betriebsver-fassungsgesetz*), nor are there any employee representatives on the supervisory boards of stock corporations with fewer than 500 employees which have been established after August 1994 or family enterprises.

2. The *responsibilities of supervisory boards* also differ according to legal form. The supervisory board of a stock corporation has wide-ranging duties. The supervisory board of a partnership limited by shares is less powerful than that of a stock corporation, and less powerful still is the supervisory board of a liability company with fewer than 2,000 employees.

I myself have not had any experience with supervisory boards in companies subject to coal and steel co-determination. I have had experience with supervisory boards of co-determined stock corporations, partnerships limited by shares, and limited liability companies; with supervisory boards constituted in accordance with the Employees' Representation Act in stock corporations, partnerships limited by shares, and limited liability companies; as well as with supervisory boards without employee representatives in stock corporations and limited liability companies.

3. Not only the size and legal form of the company make a difference in the actual activity of the supervisory board, but the work is also very heavily influenced by the members themselves. The absolute balance of power sought by the law between the board of managing directors and the supervisory board is found rather seldom.

Boards of managing directors whose members have very strong personalities often diminish the influence of the supervisory board. On the other hand, the role of the supervisory board takes on added importance if strong personalities belong to this board, above all if they simultaneously represent shareholder interests. The chairmen often play a more important role than the boards they head. A strong chairman of the board of managing directors can give management dominating influence; a strong supervisory board chairman can transform the supervisory function into important participation in decision-making.

B. Structure of the Supervisory Board

I. Members

There is also no standard answer to the question of how one becomes a member of a supervisory board in Germany.

In the presentation that follows, I will limit myself to the election of shareholder representatives because the election of employee representatives has its own rules and practices.

1. In *corporations with a clearly defined shareholder structure*, the nominations come mostly from the shareholders. It is certainly not to the advantage of the company that the shareholders often nominate individuals representing their interests rather than experts for the supervisory tasks of the supervisory board.

The shareholders' solid support of supervisory board members, however, serves to strengthen the possibilities of the shareholders exercising influence. This often serves to ensure continuity and supervisory influence and applies especially if there is a major shareholder, even if he does not have a controlling position.

2. In purely *publicly-held corporations*, new members are most often nominated by the chairman of the supervisory board. In this regard, the chairman frequently consults with the board of managing directors.

Occasionally, the board of managing directors even completely takes the initiative in nominating new members. Inclusion of the board of managing directors in this process is not without justification. Among other things, the supervisory board is supposed to advise the board of managing directors. For that reason, it is indeed significant whether the board of managing directors views the candidate for membership on the supervisory board as capable of rendering such advising services. However, it is important that the chairman of the supervisory board and the supervisory board as a whole do not permit the board of managing directors to take away their nominating rights.

3. If shareholder groups do not wish to be represented themselves on the supervisory board, an attempt is usually made to staff the supervisory board with experts in all principal *fields of activity of the company*.

Almost always we find one representative of a bank on supervisory boards, occasionally even several bank representatives. These representatives embody special finance expertise. Engineers are selected in order to oversee development and production; marketing experts often are chosen to cover their field of expertise. Internationally active corporations often look for supervisory board members who have acquired business experience in foreign countries or, better still, work abroad. This is very difficult, however, because there are hardly any French citizens, only very few citizens of Spanish-speaking countries, and also not many businesspeople from Anglo-Saxon countries who have a command of the German language. Supervisory board members without such language capabilities are of little value. Because of the employee representatives, it is generally not possible to make English the working language of the supervisory board.

4. *Large corporations* often tend to make representatives of other large corporations members of the supervisory board. It is a correct assessment that representatives of medium-sized corporations usually do not have an adequate enough grasp of the complicated structures of a major corporation to enable them to perform their supervisory duties effectively.

5. For a long time is was customary to elect *representatives of small shareholders* to the supervisory board. This was done essentially so that the existence of these representatives could be pointed out in the shareholders' meeting rather than to benefit from their personal expertise.

However, because these representatives of small shareholders often did not bring additional expertise to the supervisory board, shareholders have recently increasingly gotten away from electing small shareholder representatives to the supervisory board.

6. *On the whole*, a trend can be seen toward electing more professionals to the supervisory board than in the past.

II. Self-Organization

In most companies, the supervisory board organizes its own work.

1. Above all, *rules of procedure* govern formal questions such as the preparation and conduct of meetings and the passing of resolutions.

2. In corporations subject to co-determination, the law requires that a *committee* be set up to prepare appointments to the board of managing directors. These committees as such have absolutely no importance.

I have never experienced that such a committee has met, even though I have belonged and, in some cases, still belong to such committees. However, such committees are very often identical with the executive committee, which is also responsible for personnel matters of the board of managing directors.

3. In *major corporations* there is an increasing tendency to form committees. This is based on the recognition of the fact that large supervisory boards are practically unable to function in plenary session.

In such corporations there is most often an *executive committee,* which supports the work of the chairman of the supervisory board and, in addition, deals with the personnel matters of the managing directors.

The term "executive committee" is often avoided as being too high-sounding, and the term "working committee" or "principal committee" is used instead.

For some time there have been *finance committees,* which, especially if an engineer or natural scientist is chairman of the supervisory board, provide advice regarding finances and prepare the financial supervision. More and more, we are seeing *audit committees* which prepare a thorough analysis for the entire supervisory board of not only the annual statement of accounts but also other financial documents such as intermediate reports. The external auditors (*Wirtschaftsprüfer*) often take part in the sessions of the audit committee.

Investment committees are also important, above all in companies which have an especially active investment program.

III. Appointment and Employment of the Board of Managing Directors, Organization of the Work of the Board of Managing Directors

1. The essential task of the supervisory board is the *appointment* of a good board of managing directors.

Where the supervisory board has authority in personnel matters, every member of the supervisory board knows that he can effectively supervise the company only if he makes sure that the company has a board of managing directors capable of doing the job. However, in the case of smaller partnerships limited by shares or smaller limited liability companies, both of which are not subject to co-determination, other principles apply; most often, the supervisory board is not responsible for the appointment of the board of managing directors.

2. In large companies, the *recommendations of the board of managing directors* carry great weight in the selection of new members of the board of managing directors. For the most part, the members of the supervisory board accept this procedure. However, well-led supervisory boards point out again and again that the board of managing directors cannot base on this a claim to permanent participation in the nomination of the board of managing directors, and that the nominations will only be accepted if they are made with the appropriate expertise and the necessary objectivity.

3. Supervisory boards often, but not often enough, feel it necessary to inform themselves regarding the *young talent potential* in the corporation and to monitor the development of management personnel.

Unfortunately, this task is often neglected. For that reason, it is often necessary to hire personnel consultants (headhunters) to search for suitable personnel. We all know that the probability is low that a good executive who fits perfectly into the corporation can be found by this procedure.

4. In most companies there are rules of procedure for the board of managing directors as well as *plans for the allocation of responsibilities*. In large companies, these rules are always approved by the board of managing directors itself. The rules must be approved unanimously. In medium-sized and small companies, the supervisory board maintains a say in the decision.

5. *The employment contracts* are usually prepared according to widely used standard contracts. They govern remuneration and retirement benefits, supplementary benefits, and often prohibitions against competition as well. The total

remuneration of a member of the board of managing directors is regularly made up of a fixed salary and a performance-oriented bonus, which usually depends on profits. In many cases, it is expressly provided for that the supervisory board may grant additional remuneration if the requirement of appropriate payment of managing directors cannot otherwise be achieved. Up to now, only a few companies have introduced stock options as an element of remuneration.

Increasingly, the principal company is using the group annual surplus as the basis for calculating profit-oriented remuneration. Apart from forms of remuneration that are linked only to the annual surplus, remuneration payments are also sometimes made conditional on the achievement of special objectives agreed upon with the supervisory board, such as the fulfillment of plan, return on investment, or return on equity.

C. Functions of the Supervisory Board

I. Reporting by the Board of Managing Directors to the Supervisory Board

1. Basis for the supervision by the supervisory board are the *reports* of the board of managing directors.

Normally, the supervisory board is not obligated to conduct inquiries itself. The legal possibilities of the supervisory board to make inquiries of its own are hardly ever used. Where reporting is found to be insufficient, it calls on the board of managing directors to make additions and corrections.

2. Reporting by the board of managing directors to the supervisory board has improved in the last few years.

The focus of information based on sound figures has for some time now been on the *documents supporting the annual statement of accounts*. Many companies view the analysis of the annual statement of accounts as the main task of the supervisory board.

The supervisory board is often inundated with figures. In principle, it has the possibility, and thus also the duty, to refer to the reports of the external auditors on the audit of the annual statement of accounts.

I know of many companies in which the audit reports are readily handed out, even to employee representatives. However, there are also companies which continue to treat the audit report, and unjustifiably so, as one of the most important secrets of the company.

3. Only slowly, and not yet in all companies, is *planning* being given special attention in the discussions of the supervisory board.

In many large—but also in several smaller—companies of my practice, it has been taken for granted for several years that we receive well-prepared planning documents with detailed figures. All members of the supervisory board study these documents intensively and look for weak points.

4. Special *investment, product, or sales plans* are, for the most part, supported by thorough pertinent documentation and explained orally.

However, in only a few cases have I received varying model calculations for best case and worst case scenarios. The boards of managing directors concentrate mostly on what they consider to be the probable course and, at the most, make deductions for risk or note further opportunities.

5. Thinking in *alternative scenarios* is not widespread. Reporting on the *profitability of share capital* is gaining increasing importance.

The profitability of share capital is being made more and more the focus of reporting under the expression in vogue, "shareholder value". However, entrepreneurs and business economists certainly know as well as I that the profitability of share capital is by no means a sufficient basis for the judgment of capital profitability.

6. Companies structure their *regular reporting* differently. Very often we see that the supervisory board is overwhelmed with figures. Dozens, even hundreds, of pages of statistical graveyards are presented to all members of the supervisory board without any prioritization or selection being made beforehand.

7. *Special reports* or presentations on specific topics are often requested.

I have never experienced that the board of managing directors of a company has not met such wishes. In my experience, hardly any use has ever been made of the formal rights of enforcing claims to reports and information. Naturally, these rules are always of importance as "fleet in being".

II. Supervision of the Board of Managing Directors

The different reporting practices cause the supervision based on the reporting to be multifaceted.

1. The members of the supervisory board regularly receive *between-meeting* reports on the status and development of the company. These reports are studied just as carefully as any special reports. Each member of the supervisory board thereby compares the contents of the report with his general impressions of the branch of industry and the public impression of the company.

Where proposals for decisions are concerned, each member of the supervisory board attempts to make his own judgment on the completeness of the facts provided as the basis for the decision, to analyze the plausibility of the proposals, to make sure whether alternative scenarios in the sense of best case/worst case scenarios are explained, and to reach his own judgment on how failure of the plans would affect the company.

In Germany, aside from cases of the acquisition of a participation in another enterprise, it is not customary for the proposals of the board of managing directors to be accompanied by legal opinions or any sort of approving presentation by investment bankers. It is at least doubtful whether such presentations are suitable under German law to prove that the necessary care has been exercised. Each individual member of the board is obligated to analyze the plan. This responsibility cannot be met with third-party evaluations. However, if every board member meets his obligation to exercise due care, such expert opinions are mostly unnecessary and the expenditure for such opinions superfluous. This does not affect the carrying out of due diligence analyses.

2. In companies subject to co-determination, the supervisory board members, in practice, take the view that they have a special responsibility vis-à-vis those who elect them, i.e., the shareholders or the employees. The supervisory board members exhibit pronounced *group behavior*. This leads to regular meetings of the employee representatives, often of the shareholder representatives as well, before each meeting of the supervisory board.

In the case of the employee representatives' preparatory meetings, roles or tasks are assigned for the upcoming board meeting; the preparatory meetings of the shareholder representatives, on the other hand, serve for the most part as a forum for open criticism of recommendations of the board of managing directors, which are then suppressed at the full board session.

3. The discussions of the supervisory board occur in *meetings*. The managing directors usually take part in these meetings. The entire supervisory board meets three to four times a year. The meetings last three to four hours. If normal meetings last longer, they are generally either poorly prepared or poorly conducted.

Committee meetings take place between meetings of the entire board.

In large corporations, a *guide* is usually drawn up for the meeting chairman. This guide contains the formal requirements to be observed and the agenda. Where a decision is to be reached regarding an item on the agenda, a recommendation for this decision is formulated.

4. The *object of the discussions* in certainly every meeting is the state of business. Either the last quarterly report serves as a basis for the explanations of the board of managing directors, or more up-to-date information is explained by the board of managing directors with the help of diagrams and documents prepared for the meetings.

Once a year, the supervisory board deals with the annual financial statement prepared by the board of managing directors. It is becoming the usual practice to invite the company's external auditors to attend this meeting.

In many companies, the audit report is provided to all members of the supervisory board in advance. Often it is requested that the report be returned after the meeting. In other companies, the members of the supervisory board have only the possibility of examining the report of the external auditors of the annual statement, but are not issued a copy of the report.

Company planning of the enterprise is likewise discussed once a year. Almost regularly, the budget for the following year is presented to the supervisory board.

In many companies the medium-term planning for the following two to four years is outlined. A long-term concept (strategic planning) is frequently explained, but seldom formulated in detailed figures.

Special plans are dealt with as necessary. They may concern major investments in assets, acquisitions of interests, outstanding plans for development, plant closings or important reductions in the number of employees, or similar matters. Personnel matters can also be the subject of supervisory board discussions, for example, the granting of remuneration above fixed limits, the transfer of functions, or the awarding of titles.

The appointment or dismissal of members of the board of managing directors is usually prepared by the chairman of the supervisory board. He also has the duty to determine the principal contractual questions, which are for the most part discussed in a committee.

5. The *taking up of the individual items of the agenda* by the supervisory board always begins, after call up by the chairman, with an oral report by the board of managing directors; reference is made to documents distributed in advance. Thereafter, the members of the supervisory board ask questions, which are answered by the managing directors.

In companies with poor reporting, meetings of the supervisory board are often spent analyzing figures and calculating differences between target and performance or changes compared to the previous year. In companies with good reporting the emphasis is put on the analysis of the differences between target and performance.

If the board of managing directors thoroughly discusses differences between target and performance and prospects for the future on the basis of carefully prepared, sound reporting, there is often little to discuss. Well-structured presentations with concentrated information for the most part do not give rise to additional questions. More extensive entrepreneurial experience and well-developed critical thinking are indeed necessary to be able to determine weak points in such presentations.

I have never actually experienced a situation where managing directors have not attempted to give complete and sound answers to reasonable and justified *questions*. I can remember cases in which such discussions have caused the board of managing directors to reconsider and occasionally even to withdraw presentations.

The work of the supervisory board is often seriously disrupted by the types of questions asked by employee representatives on the supervisory board. They often ask questions which correspond to their own experiences and consciousness. These are the same questions which are asked and belong in the bodies concerned with industrial democracy, namely, the works council or the economic committee.

Members of the board of managing directors tend to take such questions seriously and to answer them thoroughly because they are naturally interested in having a good relationship with the employee representatives. The chairman of the supervisory board often will not intervene because he wants to avoid the impression of suppressing the employee representatives. I have experienced meetings of the supervisory board in which about 80% of the time was taken up with the discussion of such questions of the employee representatives.

The varying *quality of the presentations* also determines the way in which they are treated. In the case of not completely sound presentations, supervisory board members with entrepreneurial experience attempt to fill gaps in the necessary factual basis by asking additional questions.

In this regard, one of the points of emphasis of the discussion is for the most part a comparison of the existing risks and possible additional chances. The mostly rather positive projections for the future found in the presentations are subjected to critical questioning; attempts are made to analyze the effects if actual events differ from the assumptions of the board of managing directors.

6. The *aim of the discussions* is the acquiring of a sufficient base of information to allow the supervisory board members to make an objective assessment and—if the pending decision is within their scope of authority—to enable them to participate in decision-making.

After all questions have been discussed, the members of the supervisory board first form their *own judgment* concerning the matter dealt with.

Different attitudes exist regarding the *conclusion of the discussion*. In small and medium-sized companies, there is a tendency to use positive resolutions to cause the supervisory board to identify itself with the plans of the board of managing directors. In larger companies and where members of the supervisory board have entrepreneurial experience, the supervisory board is more likely to avoid such identification with the board of managing directors.

Even without knowledge of legal literature on the monitoring function of the supervisory board, experienced entrepreneurs on the supervisory board avoid making determinations beyond the question of the proper nature of presentations and the legality of transactions. Individual positions are not taken if the assessment of the decision of the board of managing directors is within the scope of reasonable discretion with regard to profitability and expedience.

7. German law recognizes differing degrees of *authority to participate in decision-making*.

On certain matters the supervisory board decides alone, for example, always in matters dealing with the board of managing directors. In other questions, the supervisory board has the right to participate in decision-making. These rights are always exercised where the annual statement of accounts is voted on. The law provides for the possibility that charters, rules of procedure, or resolutions can make certain types of transactions dependent on the consent of the supervisory board. In practice, these *reservations of consent* are viewed differently and accordingly are provided for differently. In this regard, ownership structure often plays a role as well.

In the past, the general accounting office of the federal government and the *Länder* (*Rechnungshöfe*) always pointed out that supervisory boards should make comprehensive use of the possibility to lay down reservations of consent, and recommended in this regard a wide-ranging list of transactions that should be made subject to such reservations of consent. For that reason, we frequently find this even today in companies in which the federal government or the *Länder* formerly held an interest: lists of transactions subject to reservations of consent exist which hinder rather than promote efficient monitoring. In the supervisory board meetings, certain matters must be extensively dealt with which other companies feel very comfortable about leaving to the board of managing directors. In the latter case, the supervisory board concentrates on extensive discussion of those questions which cannot so easily be included in reservations of consent, knowing that they are more important for the future of the company.

8. At the end of the meeting of the supervisory board, a *statement* is often released to the press. This press release announces to the public the important resolutions of the supervisory board, above all also to avoid problems with insider dealings.

The *minutes* of the meeting, prepared by an individual who is not a company officer, are signed by the chairman of the meeting and distributed as soon as possible after the meeting.

In many companies, a compilation of the resolutions passed in the meeting and a summary of the matters not brought to a conclusion (also from earlier meetings) are attached to the minutes of the meeting. A list of meeting dates already agreed on is usually included in most minutes.

9. The supervisory board of a German stock corporation has not only the duty to monitor the management, but also the equally important duty to *advise* the *management*. This is often understood to mean the discussion of future plans. This part of monitoring is also called "farsighted monitoring".

In these cases, the job of the supervisory board does not consist of determining in retrospect whether something was right or wrong. It must instead analyze the future plans for their plausibility and put them in their proper place in the company strategy. Experienced members of the supervisory board know that this farsighted monitoring is the most important task of a functioning supervisory board.

III. Monitoring in the Group

The majority of German stock corporations own one or—as is most often the case—several subsidiaries, and are thus the parent company of a group. These stock corporations are controlling enterprises of a group.

1. In such groups the parent company and its subsidiaries are, in practice, almost always viewed as an *economic unit*. At the same time, the numerous legal issues affecting the group receive little treatment. The supervisory board of the parent company is well aware that it properly fulfills its duty only if it monitors the entire group.

2. There are no legal problems with viewing the task of management of the parent company as the *management of the group*. The board of managing directors of the parent company considers itself to be just that and not a separate group board of managing directors. As a consequence, the group supervisory board is the supervisory board of the parent company in the group, and there is no special group supervisory board.

3. The *reports of the board of managing directors* also cover the entire group. The status and development of the parent company and the other companies belonging to the group, considered individually, take a back seat. Frequently, reference is made only to the status and development of the group as a whole.

Only in special cases are specific group companies dealt with on an individual basis. Lines of business, segments, or product areas are generally reported and viewed on a worldwide scale.

The supervisory board monitors the enlarged business units and does not limit its monitoring to the lines of business of the principal company.

The annual statement of accounts and planning are viewed in the context of the group as a whole. In considering the appropriate documents, the figures and plans of the parent company diminish in importance.

4. Even though there is no statutory basis for this, the *authority of the group supervisory board of the parent company to participate in decision-making* is generally viewed as covering the entire group.

The discussion of the annual financial statement of the parent company is, in fact, limited to a discussion of the annual statement's function as a statement of distributed profit. Economic importance is attributed only to the consolidated annual financial statement of the group. Many companies prepare it by applying internationally recommended standards (IAS or U.S. GAAP).

In the same manner, the parent company prepares the company planning in the group on a consolidated, group-wide basis.

Reservations of consent for specific transactions are viewed and observed as affecting the entire group, to the extent that this makes sense. Boards of managing directors and supervisory boards are in agreement that reservations of consent in the parent company may not be avoided by shifting those matters which require consent to a subsidiary.

D. Responsibility of the Supervisory Board

I. Accountability

In all stock corporations, the supervisory board reports in the company's business report on its activity in the past year.

While the reports formerly had almost no substantive content, today they are often very informative. They explain changes in the board of managing directors and supervisory board, describe the formal process of its activity, and state the supervisory board's position on important matters. The account of the supervisory board's examination of the annual financial statement is usually of a schematic nature only.

Only a few companies discuss the report in the shareholders' meeting, as is required by law. Frequently, there is only a reference to the written report.

Shareholders' questions regarding matters involving the members of the board of managing directors and the supervisory board are generally answered thoroughly by the chairman of the supervisory board. The Data Protection Act (*Datenschutzgesetz*) prohibits the answering of questions with regard to remuneration of individual members of the board of managing directors.

II. Responsibility and Liability

Only very seldom do supervisory board members pay damages. Even less frequent are lawsuits against members of the supervisory board for violation of the duty to exercise due care. However, it may not be concluded from this that supervisory board members are not well aware of their duties of care and their responsibility.

Legal provisions with regard to damages are not decisive for the success of entrepreneurs. Much more important and, above all, much more effective is the change in the reputation of an entrepreneur who belongs to the supervisory board of a company which has run into difficulties.

In the business world, the principle "Nothing succeeds better than success" is controlling. Questions concerning cause and fault are not asked. In cases of serious negative developments, every shareholder representative on the supervisory board must expect that, in the future, he will not be considered for board membership. Likewise, every well-respected entrepreneur fears a large number of votes against the motion that he be granted formal approval of his acts (*Entlastung*) by the shareholders' meeting.

This is well known to the shareholder members of the supervisory board. Most often, farsighted entrepreneurs do not wait until the public becomes aware of a problem. If they are not in agreement with the direction of company policies, they give up their seat on the board prematurely, unless they have not taken their seat on the basis of some sort of contractual relationship. Board members who do not recognize early on that problems are approaching and immediately take action run the risk of no longer being able to give up their seat without damage to their reputation. Aside from legal consequences, the general principle applies that a board member, after a reasonable period of time for familiarization, does not leave an enterprise which has run into difficulties.

The Relationship Between Board Composition and Firm Performance

SANJAI BHAGAT, Boulder, and BERNARD BLACK, Stanford

We survey the evidence on the relationship between board composition and firm performance. Boards of directors of American public companies that have a majority of independent directors behave differently, in a number of ways, than boards without a majority of independent directors. Some of these differences appear to increase firm value; others may decrease firm value. Overall, there is no convincing evidence that firms with majority-independent boards perform better than firms without such boards. There is also no empirical support for the current push for firms to establish "supermajority-independent boards" that have only one or two inside directors. On the contrary, there is some evidence to support a correlation between having a moderate number of inside directors and greater profitability. (The literature survey for the article was conducted in early 1997).

Contents

Tables

A. Introduction[1]

Over the last 25 years, the boards of directors of large American public companies have come increasingly to contain a majority of independent directors. Many companies now have "supermajority" independent boards, with only one or two inside directors. For example, a 1996 survey of 100 of the largest Ameri-

---

[1] Cf. also the sections dealing with the board in the comparative contributions of Kanda, Prigge, and Wymeersch in Ch. 12 of this volume.

can public corporations, summarized below, reports that half of the surveyed firms had only one or two inside directors.

Table 1: Inside Directors at SpencerStuart 100 Corporations

Number of Inside Directors	Number of Firms
1	17
2	33
3	20
4	15
5	8
6 or more	7

Source: SpencerStuart (1996).

Many commentators applaud this trend. For example, the National Association of Corporate Directors (1996: 9) notes with apparent approval the increasing number of firms whose only inside director is the CEO, and recommends that boards have a "substantial majority" of independent directors. The Business Roundtable (1997) also recommends that a "substantial majority" of directors be independent. Greater board independence remains high on the agenda of activist institutional investors. For example, CalPERS recently adopted guidelines under which the CEO is the only inside director on an "ideal" board of directors (Bryant 1997).

We survey here the evidence on whether the trend toward greater board independence rests on a sound empirical footing. Many studies document differences in the *behavior* of majority-independent and non-majority-independent boards. But studies of overall firm performance have found no convincing evidence that firms with majority-independent boards achieve better performance than other firms. There is an even greater lack of empirical support for the recent trend toward supermajority-independent boards. The differences between merely majority-independent boards and supermajority-independent boards have not been carefully studied. But the limited evidence that we have suggests caution: there is some evidence that having a moderate number of inside directors correlates with greater profitability.

The weak empirical support for majority- or supermajority-independent boards is mirrored by mixed anecdotal evidence. Independent directors often turn out to be lapdogs rather than watchdogs. The majority-independent board of General Motors did nothing for a decade, while GM floundered. The majority-independent board of American Express fired former CEO James Robinson only when faced with open shareholder revolt, despite a decade of business problems, with a few scandals along the way. Many other companies—including IBM, Kodak, Chrysler, Sears, Westinghouse, and Borden—performed abysmally for years despite majority-independent boards. And chief executive compensation has exploded over the same period during which independent directors became dominant on large firm boards (Crystal 1991).

In this article, we follow the common practice of dividing directors into *inside directors* (persons who are currently officers of the company), *affiliated outside* directors (former company officers, relatives of company officers, and persons who have or are likely to have business relationships with the company, such as investment bankers and lawyers) (sometimes called *grey* directors), and *independent directors* (outside directors without such affiliations). We call a board with at least 50% independent directors a *majority-independent board* and a board with only one or two inside directors a *supermajority-independent board*. We indicate the proportions of inside and independent directors as f_{inside} and f_{indep}, respectively.

Part B of this article reviews evidence on how board composition affects the board's actions on discrete tasks, such as firing the CEO or approving a takeover bid. Part C surveys the evidence on whether board composition affects overall firm performance. Part D explores some implications from these research findings.

B. Research on Board Composition and Discrete Board Tasks

There are two basic approaches to studying the effect of board composition on firm performance. The first involves studying discrete board tasks, such as replacing the CEO, making a takeover bid, or defending against a takeover bid. This approach can provide insight into how different boards behave on particular tasks. It also tends to involve relatively tractable data, which makes it easier for researchers to find statistically significant results. The principal weakness of this approach is that it doesn't tell us how board composition affects overall firm performance. Firms with majority-independent boards could perform better on particular tasks such as replacing the CEO, yet worse on other, unstudied tasks, leading to no net advantage in overall performance.

The second approach involves examining directly how board composition affects overall firm performance. This approach directly examines the "bottom line" of firm performance, thus avoiding the principal weakness of the first approach. But the direct approach raises a different problem. Firm performance must be measured over a long period of time, which leads to noisy data. This could make it difficult to find statistically significant results, even if a relationship between board composition and firm performance in fact exists.

Researchers have used both approaches in studying the effects of board composition on firm behavior and performance. In this part, we review research on how board composition affects how boards perform particular tasks. Part C reviews the evidence on how board composition affects overall firm performance.

CEO Replacement. A central board task is replacing the CEO when necessary. Weisbach (1988) reports that boards with at least 60% independent directors are more likely than other boards to fire a poorly performing CEO. These additional firings are likely to be value increasing, because boards are generally slow to fire CEOs. Only very poor performance, for an extended period of time, leads to measurably shorter tenure in office (Weisbach 1988; Warner/Watts/Wruck 1988). The stock price reaction to a CEO firing is hard to interpret because the firing announcement conveys information to the market both about the event (the firing) and about how the firm performed under the fired CEO, but there is some evidence that investors believe that these firings increase firm value (Scott/Kleidon 1994). There is also evidence that firm performance improves modestly, on average, after a CEO is replaced (Denis/Denis 1995).

The economic significance of the additional firings by 60%-independent boards is small, however. Weisbach finds that the CEO termination rate for firms that ranked in the bottom decile for stock price (earnings) performance is only 1.3% (6.8%) higher for firms with 60%-independent boards than for firms with 40% or fewer independent directors. Mikkelson/Partch (1997) find no significant correlation between firm performance or board composition and CEO tenure during the low takeover period of 1989-1993, despite the dominance of independent directors on large firm boards during this period. Moreover, Weisbach finds that for firms with *above average* stock price (earnings) performance, CEO turnover is *lower* if the firm has a 60%-independent board. Also, Scott/Kleidon (1994) find that firms with majority-outside boards who replace CEOs have worse pre-replacement stock price performance than firms without such boards. These results are consistent with independent directors, who know less about a firm than inside directors, being a bit quicker to replace a CEO if observable performance measures such as stock price and earnings performance are poor, but acting more slowly to replace a bad CEO as long as these indicators remain respectable.[2]

Weisbach's study suggests that independent directors behave *differently* than inside directors with respect to the task of firing the old CEO. But it isn't clear whether independent directors make better or worse decisions, on average. Moreover, a study like Weisbach's, which focuses on only *one* directorial task,

---

[2] Weisbach notes this possible interpretation of his results (Weisbach 1988: 454-5). He attempts to address this possibility by studying stock price reaction to firing announcements by companies with and without 60%-independent boards. But his stock price results are generally statistically insignificant, and his analysis of stock price returns ignores signalling effects (compare Scott/Kleidon 1994).

tells us relatively little about how board composition affects overall firm performance. Even if independent directors perform better *with regard to the task of firing the old CEO*, that need not produce superior economic performance on average.

For every CEO who leaves, another must be hired, not only when the old CEO is fired, but in the more common case when the former CEO retires or leaves voluntarily. Suppose that majority-independent boards (1) are better at firing underperforming CEOs, but (2) know less about the company's business and are therefore worse at choosing new CEOs. Negative effect (2) would occur at *all* companies and could easily swamp positive effect (1), which would occur only at poorly performing companies. Borokhovich/Parrino/Trapani (1996) report that firms with a high proportion of outside directors are more likely to choose an outsider as a new CEO, but we know little about whether these choices are better or worse than the insiders chosen by other boards (the authors' study of stock price returns does not control for signalling effects).

More generally, even if majority-independent boards are better at *monitoring* tasks, such as firing the new CEO or approving a takeover bid, they may be worse at *advising* CEOs because independent directors usually know less about the firm and its industry than inside or affiliated directors. This relative ignorance is strengthened by the Clayton Act, which bars director interlocks between competing firms. Whatever its antitrust justification, this ban tends to reduce the quality of independent directors.

Takeovers. Byrd/Hickman (1992) report that tender offer *bidders* with majority-independent boards earn roughly zero stock price returns on average, while bidders without such boards suffer statistically significant losses of 1.8% on average. Bidders with majority-independent boards also offer lower takeover premia. You et al. (1986) also report a significant negative correlation between proportion of inside directors and bidder stock price returns. This suggests that independent directors may help to restrain the CEO's tendency to build a larger empire, even if this means overpaying to buy another company. However, the economic significance of the lower takeover premia offered by bidders with majority-independent boards is small. Only a minority of firms are active acquirers, and the improvement in returns to these firms is modest. Moreover, the general concern expressed above remains: even if firms with majority-independent boards are less likely to overpay when acquiring other firms, these firms may perform less well at other tasks.

Cotter/Shivdasani/Zenner (1997) report that tender offer *targets* with majority-independent boards realized roughly 20% higher stock price returns between 1989 and 1992 than targets without majority-independent boards. Their study, however, suffers from possible selection bias. The higher returns to targets with majority-independent boards come at the expense of lower bidder returns. In a rational expectations equilibrium, acquirers will realize this and will make fewer takeover bids for firms with majority-independent boards. Shareholders of *potential* target firms may not benefit from majority-independent boards, even if shareholders of *actual* targets realize higher returns if they have majority-independent boards.

There is some evidence in the Cotter/Shivdasani/Zenner (1997) study to support our conjecture about selection bias. The target firms in their sample had, on average, only 36% independent directors—far lower than the 60% or so independent directors found in other contemporaneous studies (Bhagat/Black 1997; Klein 1998; Yermack 1996). This could reflect the smaller size of takeover targets, compared to the large firms that other researchers on boards of directors have studied. But it could also reflect bidders avoiding targets with a high proportion of independent directors.

Lee et al. (1992) study management buyouts—a transaction form where monitoring by independent directors is especially likely to have value because inside directors have a conflict of interest. They find that shareholders receive higher premia in management buyouts of firms with a majority of independent directors. This effect is not observed for divisional buyouts, where inside directors don't participate in buying the division, and thus have an incentive to sell the division at an arm's-length price. But here too, higher prices could lead to fewer management buyouts, and thus lower total premia for a portfolio of firms.

Shivdasani (1993) uses the number of other directorships held by a company's outside directors as a proxy for director quality.[3] Companies with high-quality directors are less likely to become takeover targets. For Shivdasani, this suggests that they are better run, which could be because they have better directors. This is possible, but it seems at least as likely that people whose services as directors are in high demand choose to serve on the boards of already well-run companies.

Kini/Kracaw/Mian (1995) report that after a takeover of a company with a board dominated by inside (independent) directors, the proportion of independent directors increases (decreases); this effect is stronger for targets whose CEO is also replaced. This suggests that board composition can be suboptimal if there are too few *or too many* independent directors.

Poison Pills and Antitakeover Amendments. Brickley/Coles/Terry (1994) report that when firms adopt poison pill defenses, the stock market reaction is significantly positive if the firm has a majority-independent board, and significantly negative if it does not. This suggests that investors believe that majority-independent boards are more likely to use this weapon to receive a higher takeover price than to block a control transaction altogether. But Sundaramurthy/

---

[3] The reasonableness of this choice is uncertain. Kaplan/Reishus (1990) report that CEOs of well-performing companies receive more directorships than CEOs of poor performers. But Davis (1993) reports that social connections are also important, and in an unpublished extension of this work, fails to confirm the Kaplan/Reishus finding.

Mahoney/Mahoney (1996) find the opposite result: a higher proportion of outside directors predicts a more negative stock market reaction to adoption of poison pills and other takeover defenses.

With regard to adoption of takeover defenses, Mallette/Fowler (1992) find no significant correlation between proportion of independent directors and the likelihood that a firm will adopt a poison pill. Similarly, Wahal/Wiles/Zenner (1995) find no significant difference in board composition between firms that did and did not opt out of Pennsylvania's strict antitakeover laws.

Golden Parachutes. The proportion of independent directors correlates with the likelihood that a firm will adopt a golden parachute plan to protect its senior executives if the company is acquired (Cotter/Shivdasani/Zenner 1997; Singh/ Harianto 1989; Cochran/Wood/Jones 1985). These plans reduce the likelihood that a firm will resist a takeover bid (Machlin/Choe/Miles 1993), so they may be value-enhancing if the payout is a small fraction of company value. This is usually but not always the case (Lambert/Larcker 1985).

Greenmail. Kosnik (1990) reports that firms with a high proportion of outside directors are more likely to pay greenmail, after controlling for management stock ownership.[4]

CEO Compensation. Core/Holthausen/Larcker (1997) report that CEO compensation correlates with the proportion of independent directors on a company's board, and that the component of CEO compensation that is predicted by board composition is *negatively* correlated with future performance. Apparently, independent directors aren't very good at compensating the CEO (including developing appropriate incentive compensation). This could perhaps be because many are themselves current or former CEOs. The independent directors' generosity to the CEO filters down—pay for other executives is also higher at firms with a high percentage of outside directors (Lambert/Larcker/Weigelt 1993).

Firm Failure. Chaganti/Mahajan/Sharma (1985) compare 21 matched pairs of firms that failed between 1970 and 1976 and matched nonfailed firms. They find no significant difference in board composition between failed and nonfailed firms and no significant tendency for failed firms to increase their proportion of outside directors in the five years before failure. In contrast, Daily/Dalton (1994) find a correlation between the number of affiliated directors and the likelihood of future bankruptcy.

Financial Reporting and Fraud. Dechow/Sloan/Sweeney (1996) report that firms with a majority of inside directors and without an audit committee are more likely to commit financial fraud, compared to a control sample matched by

---

[4] This study is a reexamination of earlier work (Kosnik 1987), in which the author reported the opposite result—an inverse correlation between proportion of outside directors and propensity to pay greenmail—but only for firms with low CEO ownership.

industry and size. But Wright (1996) finds no evidence that board composition affects the overall quality of financial reporting.

Stock Option Awards. Yermack (1997) finds evidence that greater independence of the compensation committee reduces the tendency for companies to award stock options (with exercise price equal to current market value) shortly before company's stock price increases.

Factors Affecting Changes in Board Composition. Hermalin/Weisbach (1988) and Weisbach (1988: 454) report that the proportion of independent directors on large firm boards increases slightly when a company has performed poorly: firms in the bottom performance decile in year X increased their proportion of independent directors by around 1% in year $X+1$, relative to other firms, during the 1972-1983 period. Consistent with this, Klein (1997) and Bhagat/Black (1998) report that firms with low past profitability have more independent directors. In contrast, Klein (1998) finds no tendency for firms in the bottom quintile for 1991 stock price returns to add more independent directors in 1992 and 1993 than firms in the top quintile, and Denis/Sarin (1997) report that firms that substantially increased the proportion of independent directors had *above-average* stock price returns in the previous year. Denis/Sarin (1997) also report that among a group of firms, average board composition changes slowly over time and tends to regress to the mean, with firms with a high (low) proportion of independent directors reducing (increasing) this percentage over time. Individual firms not infrequently undergo large changes in board composition in a single year, often as a result of a change in block ownership, but these changes usually don't affect whether a board has a majority of independent directors. Taking these studies together, if firms add independent directors in response to poor performance, this tendency is rather weak, if it exists at all.

An early study by Pfeffer (1972) finds evidence that board composition responds to the firm's regulatory environment: highly regulated firms have fewer inside directors and more lawyers on their boards. Mayers/Shivdasani/Smith (1997) report that mutual insurance companies, which have weaker control mechanisms other than the board of directors, have a higher proportion of independent directors than stock insurance companies, and that insurance companies that change their organizational form make corresponding changes to their boards. This suggests that firms adapt their board structures to the principal challenges that they face. However, Kole/Lehn (1996) report various changes in corporate governance mechanisms in the airline industry after deregulation, but no change in the proportion of independent directors on airline boards.

Lack of Evidence on Supermajority-Independent Boards. A number of the studies cited above find differences in behavior between firms with majority-independent boards (60%-independent boards) in Weisbach's (1988) study, and firms without such boards. Noe/Rebello (1996) develop a theoretical argument for why majority control of the board by independent directors can be important;

Hermalin/Weisbach (1998) develop a model in which CEO independence is a continuous decreasing function of the proportion of independent directors. However, no study investigates whether a supermajority-independent board, with only one or two inside directors, behaves differently than a merely majority-independent board.

The Role of Share Ownership. Numerous studies examine the correlation between share ownership and company performance. For Surveys, see Black (1992a: 917-27); Servaes/Zenner (1994); Council of Institutional Investors (1994); see also Lichtenberg/Palia (1996); Loderer/Martin (1995). Some studies find evidence that inside stock ownership correlates with improved performance up to a modest level of ownership (perhaps as low as 5%), but others do not. There is mixed evidence about the correlation between inside ownership and performance at ownership levels above 5%, and some evidence that CEO stock ownership serves more as a reward for past performance than as an incentive for future performance (Kole 1996; Himmelberg/Hubbard/Palia 1996).

The possible correlation between inside ownership and firm performance means that studies of whether board composition affects performance must control for inside stock ownership. Firms with high inside ownership tend to have fewer independent directors (e.g., Hermalin/Weisbach 1991; Rediker/Seth 1995; Denis/Sarin 1997), partly because large inside shareholders want their own representatives on the board, which leaves fewer seats for others. Large outside shareholders also sometimes insist on representation on a company's board of directors. If companies with large outside shareholders perform better, then a study that doesn't control for their presence might mistakenly ascribe this correlation to the presence of independent directors. Yet many studies of the role of directors don't control for stock ownership.

C. The Relationship Between Board Composition and Firm Performance

The studies discussed in Part B evaluate whether majority-independent boards behave differently than other boards on particular tasks, such as replacing the CEO or approving a takeover bid. They do not address the underlying question of whether firms with majority-independent boards achieve better (worse) overall performance than firms without such boards.

Appointment of New Directors. Rosenstein and Wyatt use event study methodology to study investor reaction to the appointment of additional directors. In Rosenstein/Wyatt (1990), they find that stock prices increase by about 0.2%, on average, when companies appoint additional outside directors. This increase is statistically significant, but economically small. Also, appointing an additional independent director could signal that a company plans to address its business problems, even if board composition doesn't affect the company's ability to address these problems. In Rosenstein/Wyatt (1997), they find that stock prices neither increase or decrease on average when an *insider* is added to the board. They find nonrobust evidence that stock price *decreases* when an insider is added to the board of a company where inside directors own less than 5% of the shares and independent directors constitute at least 60% of the board, and more robust evidence that stock price *increases* when an insider is added to the board of a company where inside directors own 5-25% of the shares.

The event study approach, though, suffers from a central problem with no easy solution: the announcement of a change in board composition could easily provide a signal to the market about some other facet of the company's performance. Investors could be responding to the signal, rather than to the substantive announcement.

Board Size. Yermack (1996) reports a strong negative correlation between board size and Tobin's q, and a similar negative correlation between board size and several accounting measures of profitability. He hypothesizes that many corporate boards are simply too large. Eisenberg/Sundgren/Wells (1997) find a negative correlation between board size and return on assets and operating margin for a sample of 900 small and mid-sized Finnish firms. However, Bhagat/Black (1997) report that Yermack's results are not robust to the choice of performance measure.

Composition of Board Committees. Klein (1998) studies whether the existence and staffing of board committees affects firm performance. She finds little evidence that "monitoring" committees that are usually dominated by independent directors—the audit, compensation, and nominating committees—affect performance, regardless of how they are staffed. In contrast, inside director representation on a board's investment committee correlates with improved firm performance. This suggests that companies with supermajority-independent boards may perform worse, because they have too few inside directors to perform this role.

Correlation Between Performance and Board Composition. The most direct approach to assessing whether board composition affects firm performance is simply to measure performance, and see whether it correlates with board composition. This approach has been adopted in a number of papers, with mixed results.

An early study by Vance (1964) reports a correlation between proportion of inside directors and a number of performance measures. Baysinger/Butler (1985), Hermalin/Weisbach (1991), and MacAvoy et al. (1983) all report no significant same-year correlation between board composition and various measures of corporate performance. Baysinger and Butler report that the proportion of independent directors in 1970 correlates with *1980* return on equity, relative to industry norms. Causation seemed to run from more independent directors to higher performance rather than the other way around. However, Baysinger and Butler use only a single performance measure, and their ten-year lag period seems surprisingly long for the hypothesized effects of board composition on performance to develop.

Conversely, several studies suggest that firms with more independent directors may perform *worse*. Yermack (1996) reports a significant *negative* correlation between proportion of independent directors and contemporaneous Tobin's *q*; Agrawal/Knoeber (1996) report a similar negative correlation between proportion of *outside* directors and Tobin's *q*; Baysinger/Kosnik/Turk (1991) report a positive correlation between percentage of *inside* directors and R&D spending per employee. These studies also use only a single performance measure.

Most studies of the effect of board composition on firm performance focus on independent directors or inside directors; affiliated outside directors are excluded from the analysis. The exception is Klein (1997), who finds no evidence of a consistent relationship between different types of affiliated outside directors and firm performance. She also reports that affiliated directors are more likely to be found on the boards of firms that need the affiliated director's expertise, which suggests that these directors have a useful role to play.

International Evidence. Lawrence/Stapledon (1997) seek to replicate for Australian boards of directors the Bhagat/Black (1997) study of American boards of directors discussed below. They report generally similar results—they find only scattered, nonrobust correlations between various performance measures and proportion of independent directors.

Evidence from Bhagat/Black (1997). In light of the scant evidence on the relationship between firm performance and board composition, we recently undertook a careful reexamination of the direct relationship between board composition and firm performance. We attempted to correct the weaknesses in prior work by using a large sample to improve signal-to-noise ratio; measuring performance over a long period of time, rather than just at a single date; using a wide variety of performance measures, including both stock price and accounting-based variables; and employing a large set of control variables, including CEO stock ownership, outside blockholder ownership, independent director ownership, board size, and firm size. Selected results from this study are reported below.

On the whole, our reexamination confirms that the direct relationship between board composition and firm performance, if it exists at all, is weak, and perhaps variable over time. We find no consistent evidence that the proportion of independent directors affects future firm performance. A high proportion of independent directors correlates with slower growth and, less strongly, with lower stock price returns, in the recent past (the several years *before* the date when we measure board composition). However, this correlation disappears for future performance (during the several years *after* the date when we measure board composition). This suggests either that the correlation is not robust to choice of measurement period, or that causation runs *from* low stock price returns and slower growth to a higher proportion of independent directors, rather than the other way around.

We found evidence that the proportion of *inside* directors correlates with higher past (but not future) stock price returns, and with greater profitability for some accounting measures of performance (both retrospectively and prospectively), but not for other accounting measures of performance. Results that appear significant for a single performance variable, such as Tobin's q, often lost significance or changed sign for other plausible performance variables.

Our study was based on the Institutional Shareholder Services database from mid-1991. This database contains information on 957 large U.S. public corporations, principally from early 1991. We supplemented this data on directors with data on the financial performance of these firms between 1983 and 1995, obtained from Compustat; data on the stock price performance of these firms between 1983 and 1995, obtained from CRSP; and data on share ownership by management, the board of directors, and 5% shareholders, obtained by reading 1991 proxy statements.

We studied separately firm performance during the "prospective" period from 1991 through 1995, which mostly follows the date (early 1991) when we collected board composition and stock ownership data, and during the "retrospective" period from 1983 through 1990, which precedes the date at which we collected board composition and stock ownership data. If board composition changes in response to firm performance, then comparing "lead" regressions of performance during the prospective period against 1991 board composition with "lag" regressions of performance during 1983-1990 against 1991 board composition can shed light on whether it is more likely that board composition causes, or responds to, changes in firm performance. Alternatively, if board composition changes only slowly in response to firm performance, similar (different) results for the retrospective and prospective periods will indicate robustness (lack of robustness) for our results.

The median firm in our study had an eleven-member board, including seven independent directors, one affiliated outsider, and three insiders (typically including the chief executive officer and chief financial officer). About 70% of the firms had majority-independent boards. The median of three inside directors in 1991 might be as low as two today, due to changes since 1991 in the composition of a typical board (see Table 1).

To measure stock price performance, we used primarily the simple "market-adjusted returns" (MAR) measure, in which firm-specific returns are adjusted for market-wide returns but *not* for firm-specific risk. We made this choice because there is evidence that MAR is a better-specified measure of stock price performance for long time horizons than measures that adjust for firm-specific risk (e.g., Barber/Lyon 1997).

If investors could perfectly anticipate the effect on firm value of board composition, stock price tests would be of limited value. An event study measures only the departure of actual results from the *expected* results that are already impounded in stock prices. However, other studies of long-term stock price performance—including long-term performance of acquirers of other firms (Agrawal/Jaffe/Mandelker 1992; Loughran/Vijh 1997), and initial public offerings (Ritter 1991)—provide grounds for skepticism about whether investors have perfect foresight. To the extent that investors have imperfect foresight, stock price tests can provide information about the value of different board structures.

Table 2 reports our stock price results. The independent variables are a constant term (not shown), the natural logarithm of the proportion of inside directors $\log(f_{inside})$, the natural logarithm of the proportion of independent directors $\log(f_{indep})$, board size, firm size measured by $\log(1990$ sales), and several measures of stock ownership by insiders and outside blockholders: percentage ownership by the CEO, percentage ownership by all directors and officers, number of outside 5% blockholders, and percentage ownership by all outside 5% blockholders.

The coefficient on $\log(f_{indep})$ is insignificant except for the three-year period preceding the date when we measure board composition, when it correlates *negatively* with stock price performance (we use $p < 0.05$ as the minimum level at which we report statistical significance). The coefficient on $\log(f_{inside})$ is significant and positive for the full retrospective 1983-1990 period and for the 1983-1987 subperiod, but loses significance in the prospective period.[5]

If the significant positive correlation between *retrospective* stock price returns and proportion of inside directors is real, and this correlation either disappears or reverses sign in the prospective period, we have no ready causal explanation for this pattern. Alternatively, the different patterns in the retrospective and prospective periods could reflect lack of robustness in the results or a tendency for poorly performing firms to add more independent directors. This tendency could be strengthened by the conventional wisdom that large firm boards should be dominated by independent directors. We cannot test the hypothesis that board composition changes in response to firm performance because we measure board composition at only one date.

---

[5] We also tested the hypothesis that there are critical breakpoints in board composition (such as majority-independence or 60% independence) that affect how boards behave. We found no evidence of breakpoints.

Table 2: Regression: Stock Price Performance and Log (Board Composition)

MAR measure of mean stock price performance for firms in sample of 934 large U.S. public companies for various periods during 1983-1995. A dependent variable in the form MAR 83-87 means the sample market-adjusted return over the period from 1983 through 1987, and similarly for other periods. Board composition and board size variables are based on early 1991 data. *t*-statistics are shown in parentheses.

	Independent Variables										
Depen-dent Variable	Log (Prop. of Inside Direc tors)	Log (Prop. of Indep. Direc tors)	Board Size	Log (1990 Sales)	CEO Owner-ship	D&O Owner-ship	No. of Outside 5% Holders	Owner-ship by Outside 5% Holders	Adj. R²	F	Sample Size
MAR 83-87	**.807** (3.01)**	.300 (1.42)	**.017** (2.08)*	.022 (1.04)	**-.009** (-2.06)*	.004 (1.41)	**-.099** (-3.11)**	.002 (.79)	.060	5.87	608
MAR 88-90	.164 (.77)	**-.347** (-2.13)*	-.001 (-.20)	.010 (.54)	.003 (.94)	-.001 (-.37)	-.045 (-1.75)	-.003 (-1.47)	.057	6.12	677
MAR 83-90	**1.144** (3.47)**	.080 (.31)	**.021** (2.12)*	.035 (1.32)	-.006 (-1.10)	.005 (1.33)	**-.144** (-3.67)***	-.002 (-.61)	.128	12.1	608
MAR 91-93	.012 (.06)	.223 (1.42)	**.016** (2.34)*	.012 (.68)	.003 (.77)	.003 (1.36)	**.067** (2.79)**	-.002 (-1.19)	.028	3.44	689
MAR 94-95	-.103 (-.68)	.219 (1.85)	.002 (.50)	.028 (2.19)	.001 (.56)	-.001 (-.20)	**-.036** (-1.98)*	.003 (1.92)	.024	3.05	664
MAR 91-95	-0.25 (-1.04)	.287 (1.53)	**.017** (2.16)*	.044 (2.12)	.002 (.43)	.004 (1.43)	.038 (1.32)	-.001 (-.31)	.036	4.11	666

Note: Significant results in **boldface** (not shown for log (1990 sales)): *** (**) (*) = significant at 0.001 (0.01) (0.05) level.

CEO ownership and D&O ownership are insignificant, except for a negative coefficient on CEO ownership in the retrospective 1983-1987 subperiod. We obtain similar results in separate regressions (not shown) in which we replace D&O ownership with ownership by independent directors. Thus, the intuition that independent directors who own a significant stake in the company will be more vigorous monitors is not confirmed.

There is some evidence that outside blockholders play a monitoring role. In the prospective 1991-1993 period, the coefficient on ownership by number of outside 5% blockholders is significantly positive. The number of outside 5% holders correlates with worse stock price performance in the retrospective period, which could reflect outside blockholders buying positions in poorly performing firms. Both findings are consistent with Bethel/Liebeskind/Opler (1996).

We also studied the correlation between board composition and a variety of accounting measures of performance and mixed stock price and accounting measures. Table 3 reports regression results for growth variables, which we used to assess whether firm growth rate correlates with board composition. The growth variables that we use are:

fractional growth in assets (GrAST)

fractional growth in sales (GrSAL)

fractional growth in net income (GrINC)

fractional growth in operating income (INC + interest expense + income taxes) (GrOPI)

fractional growth in number of employees (GrEMP)

fractional growth in spending on new property, plant and equipment (GrPPE)

fractional growth in gross cash flow (OPI + depreciation + amortization) (GrGCF)

Table 3: Regression: Growth Accounting Variables on Board Composition

Growth accounting variables for 928 large U.S. public companies for various periods during 1983-1995. GrAST 83-87 means growth in assets during the period from 1983 through 1987, and similarly for other growth variables. Board composition and board size variables are based on early 1991 data. t-statistics are shown in parentheses. Growth figures are percentages.

Dependent Variable	Log (Proportion of Inside Directors)	Log (Proportion of Independent Directors)	Board Size	Log (1990 Sales)[a]	Adj. R^2	F	Sample Size
GrAST 83-87	34.8 (1.85)	-26.8 (-.97)	-2.01 (-.82)	-13.5 (-2.08)	.023	5.74	795
GrAST 88-90	6.76 (1.94)	-14.7 (-3.04)**	-.38 (-.79)	-3.90 (-3.15)	.056	14.4	914
GrAST 83-90	65.2 (1.49)	-162 (-2.50)*	-6.13 (-1.05)	-29.2 (-1.92)	.040	8.9	761
GrAST 91-93	.86 (.23)	-5.61 (-1.04)	-.38 (-.70)	-6.53 (-4.75)	.042	10.3	857
GrAST 94-95	4.12 (2.67)**	.50 (.23)	.29 (1.29)	-2.67 (-4.79)	.038	8.7	783
GrAST 91-95	11.1 (1.58)	8.05 (.81)	-1.30 (-1.28)	-13.3 (-5.25)	.056	12.9	783
GrSAL 83-87	27.6 (1.18)	-32.7 (-.96)	-4.94 (-1.62)	-18.0 (-2.25)	.025	6.08	794
GrSAL 88-90	-.812 (-.22)	-20.6 (-3.97)***	-.78 (-1.52)	-4.86 (-3.65)	.060	15.3	914
GrSAL 83-90	-73.9 (-.88)	-324.2 (-2.64)**	-17.8 (-1.59)	-75.9 (-2.62)	.031	7.1	761
GrSAL 91-93	4.69 (1.91)	3.95 (1.15)	-.79 (-2.26)*	-5.94 (-6.74)	.097	23.9	857
GrSAL 94-95	-1.11 (-.69)	-2.72 (-1.21)	.33 (1.41)	-2.45 (-4.24)	.021	5.21	782
GrSAL 91-95	8.03 (1.04)	5.29 (.49)	-1.64 (-1.47)	-17.3 (-6.19)	.076	17.0	782
GrINC 83-87	-155 (-1.18)	-46.4 (-.24)	-21.2 (-1.23)	-37.8 (-.82)	.010	1.12	682
GrINC 88-90	-12.2 (-.50)	-91.1 (-2.66)**	-3.26 (-1.00)	-5.20 (-.59)	.012	3.37	778
GrINC 83-90	-3290 (-1.50)	-546 (-.17)	-172 (-.60)	311 (.40)	-.001	.81	717
GrINC 91-93	1547.0 (1.09)	1037.0 (.52)	204.3 (1.02)	-1266.5 (-2.42)	.004	1.77	808
GrINC 94-95	-343.4 (-2.23)*	-759.8 (-3.51)**	-25.2 (-1.14)	110.0 (1.95)	.016	3.97	745
GrINC 91-95	-26.1 (-.43)	-153.9 (-1.80)	-4.61 (-.53)	-28.2 (-1.27)	.006	2.04	742

	Independent Variables						
Dependent Variable	Log (Proportion of Inside Directors)	Log (Proportion of Independent Directors)	Board Size	Log (1990 Sales)[a]	Adj. R^2	F	Sample Size
GrOPI 83-87	-17.8 (-.63)	**-175 (-4.19)*****	**-13.0 (-2.87)****	2.11 (.20)	.057	9.20	547
GrOPI 88-90	9.82 (1.34)	-18.6 (-1.81)	**-2.44 (-2.04)***	-7.42 (-2.60)	.057	10.67	643
GrOPI 83-90	16.9 (.28)	**-207 (-2.53)***	**-32.8 (-3.48)****	19.0 (.87)	.042	6.80	534
GrOPI 91-93	7.90 (1.39)	10.32 (1.32)	-.41 (-.42)	-7.63 (-3.35)	.030	5.41	589
GrOPI 94-95	-2.93 (-.97)	-3.86 (-.93)	-.80 (-1.50)	-1.39 (-1.13)	.010	2.40	575
GrOPI 91-95	19.5 (1.35)	19.2 (.97)	-4.62 (-1.84)	-16.0 (-2.67)	.039	6.49	541
GrEMP 83-87	138 (.04)	4.76 (.02)	-17.6 (-.79)	-9.63 (-.16)	-.002	.65	743
GrEMP 88-90	4.53 (1.59)	**-8.51 (-2.15)***	-.49 (-1.24)	-4.49 (-4.42)	.064	15.7	856
GrEMP 83-90	12.7 (.07)	**-585 (-2.05)***	-28.8 (-1.10)	-14.4 (-.21)	.009	2.68	737
GrEMP 91-93	-3.86 (-1.05)	**-22.3 (-4.37)*****	.48 (.92)	-8.50 (-6.44)	.084	20.3	841
GrEMP 94-95	1.14 (.76)	-2.08 (-.99)	-.18 (-.81)	-1.96 (-3.63)	.031	7.08	763
GrEMP 91-95	5.86 (.77)	-15.2 (-1.44)	-.83 (-.77)	-14.6 (-5.32)	.062	13.5	760
GrPPE 83-87	-.951 (-.24)	**-241 (-4.18)*****	-6.60 (-1.00)	-28.1 (-1.91)	.052	10.5	695
GrPPE 88-90	-18.7 (-1.27)	**-47.0 (-2.33)***	2.75 (1.09)	-17.2 (-3.07)	.017	4.38	782
GrPPE 83-90	-263 (-1.00)	**-1632 (-4.32)*****	-34.5 (-.77)	6.91 (.07)	.030	6.16	669
GrPPE 91-93	-28.9 (-1.39)	-24.7 (-.86)	-4.06 (-1.13)	-22.8 (-2.88)	.023	5.50	761
GrPPE 94-95	6.69 (1.25)	-.63 (-.09)	.07 (.07)	-3.27 (-1.59)	.004	1.63	690
GrPPE 91-95	2.20 (.10)	16.9 (.56)	-5.33 (-1.41)	-24.9 (-2.96)	.027	5.74	692
GrGCF 83-87	-1.42 (-.07)	**-106 (-3.45)*****	**-11.1 (-3.29)****	2.52 (.32)	.054	8.71	537
GrGCF 88-90	7.22 (1.20)	**-23.8 (-2.84)****	**-2.55 (-2.56)****	-4.50 (-1.90)	.071	12.83	618
GrGCF 83-90	17.7 (.31)	**-197.7 (-2.42)***	**-31.9 (-3.40)****	19.8 (.92)	.040	6.50	526
GrGCF 91-93	7.37 (1.55)	7.67 (1.19)	-.34 (-.42)	-7.25 (-3.82)	.040	6.93	568
GrGCF 94-95	-1.89 (-.76)	-2.84 (-.83)	-.62 (-1.40)	-1.28 (-1.26)	.009	2.35	573
GrGCF 91-95	18.5 (1.73)	16.1 (1.10)	-3.69 (-1.95)	-14.5 (-3.23)	.057	8.88	523

Notes: [a]   For the SAL 90 and SAL 91 regressions, we use log(1990 assets) instead of log(1990 sales) as an independent variable.

Significant results in **boldface** (not shown for log(1990 sales)): *** (**) (*) = significant at 0.001 (0.01) (0.05) level.

There is no significant correlation between the proportion of inside directors and any growth variable for the full prospective 1991-1995 period or the full retrospective 1983-1990 period and only two significant correlations, with opposite sign, for subperiods (a positive coefficient on GrAST94-95 and a negative coefficient on GrINC 94-95). Thus, the growth variables do not confirm the hints from retrospective stock price returns that having more inside directors correlates with better performance.

The most striking feature of Table 3 is the negative correlation during the retrospective period between proportion of independent directors and various growth variables. For the full 1983-1990 retrospective period, all growth variables except income are significantly negatively correlated with log(f_{indep}), and for the near-term 1988-1990 subperiod, all variables except operating income take significant negative coefficients. However, none of the growth variables takes a significant negative coefficient during the full prospective 1991-1995 period. Employment growth takes a significant negative coefficient in the 1991-1993 subperiod, perhaps as a delayed reaction to slow growth in the previous period, and income growth turns significantly negative in the 1994-1995 subperiod.

This evidence can be interpreted in two ways. If board composition does not change in response to slow growth, then the difference between the retrospective and prospective periods suggests that our results aren't robust. Alternatively, the retrospective/prospective difference could reflect firms employing different types of boards at different stages in their life cycle. Fast-growing firms could use a higher proportion of inside and affiliated outside directors, to provide advice on managing growth, while mature firms could employ more independent directors to restrain managers' tendency to indulge in unprofitable growth. In effect, board composition could be endogenous—it could be determined by growth or other firm characteristics (compare the evidence in Demsetz/Lehn (1985) on endogeneity of ownership concentration).

The endogeneity story is in tension with the evidence discussed above, from Hermalin/Weisbach (1988) and Klein (1998), that board composition changes slowly, if at all, in response to poor performance. However, these studies measure only board composition changes in the year or two immediately after a poor year, and leave open the possibility of slower change or change in response to several bad years. Moreover, they focus on change in response to poor stock price or earnings performance, which is potentially different from a general growth slowdown.

We also studied a set of ratio variables that provide different measures of whether profitability (as opposed to growth rate) depends on board composition:

Tobin's q

the ratio of earnings to stock price (E/P)

ratio of sales to assets (SAL/AST)

operating margin (ratio of operating income to sales) (OPI/SAL)

return on assets (ratio of operating income to assets) (OPI/AST)

ratio of sales to employees (SAL/EMP)

ratio of gross cash flow to sales (GCF/SAL)

ratio of gross cash flow to assets (GCF/AST)

Table 4 reports the correlation of our ratio variables with the same board composition variables as in Table 3.

Table 4: Regression: Ratio Accounting Variables on Board Composition

Ratio accounting variables for 928 large U.S. public companies for various years during 1983-1995. SAL/AST 90 means the ratio of sales to assets for 1990, and similarly for other ratio variables. *t*-statistics are shown in parentheses. Board composition and board size variables are based on early 1991 data. Dollar figures are in $ millions and number of employees in thousands.

Dependent Variable	Independent Variables				Adj. R^2	F	Sample Size
	Log (Proportion of Inside Directors)	Log (Proportion of Independent Directors)	Board Size	Log (1990 Sales)			
Q 83	.196 (2.54)*	-.292 (-2.57)**	-.074 (-7.25)***	-.133 (-4.94)	.212	51.1	746
Q 87	.404 (4.85)***	-.100 (-.85)	-.050 (-4.49)***	-.126 (-4.32)	.150	38.1	842
Q 90	.240 (3.25)***	-.253 (-2.45)*	-.043 (-4.32)***	-.160 (-6.17)	.172	47.1	886
Q 91	.264 (2.26)*	-.247 (-1.52)	-.061 (-3.69)***	-.245 (-5.91)	.127	33.0	880
Q 93	.173 (2.12)*	-.100 (-.04)	-.048 (-4.23)***	-.141 (-4.93)	.116	28.5	838
Q 95	.047 (.56)	-.101 (-.85)	-.049 (-4.11)***	-.102 (-3.36)	.072	10.1	780
E/P 84	.002 (.20)	.018 (1.05)	.005 (3.63)***	.004 (.92)	.028	6.37	747
E/P 87	-.012 (-.58)	-.002 (-.06)	-.001 (-.41)	.019 (2.52)	.005	1.96	815
E/P 90	.019 (2.66)**	.016 (1.59)	.001 (1.01)	.002 (.63)	.006	2.26	878
E/P 91	.009 (.57)	.003 (.14)	.003 (1.39)	-.001 (-.21)	-.002	.58	877
E/P 93	.056 (.83)	.108 (1.15)	.008 (.79)	-.001 (-.05)	-.002	.58	856
E/P 95	.003 (.30)	.012 (.94)	.003 (2.43)*	.012 (3.53)	.043	9.76	781
SAL/AST 87	.193 (3.47)***	-.244 (-3.09)***	-.062 (-8.22)***	.194 (9.92)	.166	45.5	893
SAL/AST 90	.154 (2.97)**	-.180 (-2.47)*	-.069 (-9.69)***	.183 (9.95)	.161	45.5	928
SAL/AST 91	.119 (2.31)*	-.149 (-2.09)*	-.067 (-9.18)***	.170 (9.28)	.144	38.0	882
SAL/AST 93	.150 (3.04)**	-.048 (-.69)	-.069 (-9.92)***	.158 (8.99)	.148	39.1	877
SAL/AST 95	.103 (2.03)*	-.105 (-1.47)	-.068 (-9.31)***	.149 (8.10)	.142	33.4	782
OPI/SAL 87	.009 (.41)	-.018 (-.58)	.003 (.73)	-.037 (-4.44)	.033	6.85	696
OPI/SAL 90	.006 (.55)	.006 (.43)	.006 (3.27)***	-.028 (-7.16)	.064	13.2	715
OPI/SAL 91	-.009 (-.58)	.007 (.35)	.011 (4.22)***	-.036 (-5.86)	.047	9.16	668
OPI/SAL 93	-.008 (-.51)	.020 (.92)	.010 (3.65)***	-.033 (-5.32)	.041	7.85	638
OPI/SAL 95	-.019 (-1.15)	.017 (.78)	.013 (4.44)***	-.029 (-4.53)	.043	7.80	607
OPI/AST 87	.025 (2.67)**	-.033 (-2.48)*	-.002 (-1.30)	-.007 (-1.87)	.062	12.33	681
OPI/AST 90	.013 (1.53)	-.036 (-3.03)**	-.004 (-2.70)**	-.004 (-1.15)	.060	12.44	717
OPI/AST 91	.012 (1.40)	-.019 (-1.67)	-.003 (-1.81)	-.003 (-.91)	.028	5.75	668
OPI/AST 93	.014 (1.70)	.002 (.18)	-.002 (-1.78)	-.003 (-1.20)	.019	4.04	638
OPI/AST 95	-.001 (-.17)	-.015 (-1.30)	-.003 (-2.09)*	.001 (.15)	.008	2.22	607
SAL/EMP 87	-17.3 (-.81)	-105 (-3.49)***	-.57 (-.20)	12.2 (1.64)	.014	4.06	836
SAL/EMP 90	6.12 (.23)	-100 (-2.74)**	-.019 (-.005)	19.3 (2.08)	.013	3.94	876
SAL/EMP 91	-10.37 (-.31)	-79.37 (-1.73)	-.84 (-.18)	.38 (.03)	-.000	.99	866
SAL/EMP 93	2.96 (.15)	-14.09 (-.50)	-3.82 (-1.33)	22.43 (3.10)	.007	2.48	847
SAL/EMP 95	-16.83 (-.59)	-28.40 (-.71)	-3.15 (-.77)	19.91 (1.93)	.000	1.03	766

GCF/SAL 87	.003 (.11)	-.013 (-.39)	.005 (1.25)	-.046 (-5.13)	.0400	7.94	671
GCF/SAL 90	-.001 (-.11)	.010 (.59)	**.008 (4.15)*****	-.037 (-8.23)	.086	17.1	685
GCF/SAL 91	-.016 (-.90)	.001 (.06)	**.014 (4.85)*****	-.049 (-7.10)	.071	13.3	643
GCF/SAL 93	-.012 (-.70)	.011 (.48)	**.012 (4.08)*****	-.042 (-6.24)	.057	10.3	618
GCF/SAL 95	-.023 (-1.34)	.022 (.93)	**.014 (4.53)*****	-.037 (-5.40)	.055	9.83	605
GCF/AST 87	**.023 (2.36)***	**-.032 (-2.31)***	-.001 (-.23)	-.006 (-1.67)	.043	8.31	659
GCF/AST 90	.015 (1.60)	**-.034 (-2.71)****	-.003 (-1.70)	-.004 (-1.08)	.044	8.83	691
GCF/AST 91	.012 (1.32)	-.021 (-1.74)	-.001 (-.88)	-.003 (-.93)	.019	4.16	643
GCF/AST 93	**.018 (2.08)***	-.001 (-.03)	-.001 (-.63)	-.004 (-1.40)	.015	3.28	618
GCF/AST 95	-.003 (-.31)	-.016 (-1.20)	-.003 (-1.92)	.002 (.54)	.004	1.57	605

Note: Significant results in **boldface** (not shown for log (1990 sales)): *** (**) (*) = significant at 0.001 (0.01) (0.05) level.

Looking first at the results for inside directors, we find evidence of superior use of assets by firms with a high proportion of inside directors. The coefficients on $\log(f_{inside})$ are uniformly positive, often significantly so, in all years except 1995 for ratio variables with assets in the denominator (Q, SAL/AST, OPI/AST, GCF/AST). These results are present for both the retrospective period and the prospective period (through 1993). Proportion of inside directors is insignificant for ratio variables which use sales as the denominator (OPI/SAL, GCF/SAL).

For independent directors, ratio variables with assets in the denominator often take significant negative coefficients in the retrospective period. But the significance weakens in 1991 (SAL/AST is significant, OPI/AST and GCF/AST are marginally significant, Q loses significance), and essentially disappears by 1993. The negative coefficients in the retrospective period are consistent with the correlation reported above between proportion of independent directors and weak retrospective stock price performance (Table 2) and slower growth (Table 3). However, because the ratio variable evidence weakens in the prospective period, we cannot conclude that a high proportion of independent directors causes weak performance; the reverse causal inference is also plausible.

Adjusted R^2 values are tiny, with the exception of the Q and SAL/AST variables. Indeed, some adjusted R^2 values are negative. Our regressions simply don't explain very much of the variation in firm performance.

D. Policy Implications

There remains no convincing evidence that the composition of the board of directors affects overall firm performance. Bhagat/Black (1997) find evidence that the proportion of inside directors on the board correlates with improved performance, but this evidence is stronger for recent *past* than for near-term *future* performance. They find that the proportion of independent directors correlates with slower recent past growth, but not with future performance.

A null result, of course, can never be proved. But, pending the results of additional tests (some of which we plan in future work), the burden of proof should perhaps shift to those who support the conventional wisdom that ever-greater board independence is an important element of improved corporate governance.

The neutral evidence on the value of independent directors on large firm boards can be interpreted in a number of ways. First, it could reflect the limited power of the tests. Stock price and accounting data are noisy, especially over long time horizons.

Second, perhaps today's "independent" directors aren't independent enough. Perhaps, as Gilson/Kraakman (1991: 865) argue, "corporate boards need directors who are not merely independent [of management], but who are *accountable* [to shareholders] as well." But if so, institutional investors may need to put their own representatives on boards of directors, a step that few are interested in and which is hard for them to take under current U.S. legal rules (Black 1990; Roe 1994).

Perhaps, too, some directors who are classified as independent are not truly independent of management, because they are beholden to the company or its current CEO in ways too subtle to be captured in customary definitions of "independence." For example, some nominally independent directors may serve as paid advisors or consultants to a company, may be employed by a university or foundation that receives financial support from the company, or may have a personal relationship with the CEO that compromises their independence. This possibility is consistent with evidence that directors who were appointed during the current CEO's tenure are more generous in determining the CEO's compensation (Core/Holthausen/Larcker 1997; Yermack 1997). It's also possible that directors who have been on the board for a long time, though nominally independent, may be less willing to oppose management. This possibility is consistent with evidence that director tenure correlates with the likelihood that a firm will pay greenmail to get rid of a dissident shareholder (Kosnik 1990).

A third possibility, implicit in Klein's (1998) research on board committee structures, is that independent directors can add value, but only if they are embedded in an appropriate committee structure. This would let independent directors perform the monitoring function that, commentators argue, they are best suited for while letting inside and affiliated outside directors perform the advising function to which they may bring more firm-specific expertise. However, most large firms, like those in our sample, already have such committee structures, and Klein finds little evidence that the principal outsider-dominated "monitoring" committees—audit, compensation, and nominating committees—affect performance, regardless of how they are staffed.

A fourth possibility is that different firms benefit from different board structures. This "endogeneity" story is similar in spirit to Demsetz/Lehn's (1985) argument that stock ownership concentration is endogenous. For example, slowly growing firms may need a high proportion of independent directors to control managers' incentives to reinvest the firm's cash flow rather than pay dividends, even when the firm lacks profitable reinvestment opportunities. Optimal board composition could also vary with a firm's principal industry.

This endogeneity/cash flow conflict story is consistent with the correlation that Agrawal/Knoeber (1996) and Yermack (1996) find between a high proportion of independent directors and lower Tobin's q (which is a measure of growth prospects). It is also consistent with evidence in Bhagat/Black (1997) that a high proportion of independent directors correlates with slower *past* growth across a number of accounting variables, although not slower future growth, and evidence in Bhagat/Black (1997) and Klein (1997) that a high proportion of independent directors correlates with lower past profitability. This could reflect companies who face slow growth increasing the proportion of independent directors on their boards. This endogeneity story, however, suggests that the push by commentators and institutional investors for greater board independence at *all* firms may be misguided.

Another plausible endogeneity hypothesis is that alternate mechanisms for controlling agency costs in large firms (including independent directors, leverage, CEO stock ownership, large outside blockholders, and takeovers) act either as substitutes or complements (e.g., Hermalin/Weisbach 1991; Kini/ Kracaw/Mian 1995; Mehran 1995; Rediker/Seth 1995). These interaction effects are a potentially fruitful avenue for further research.

A fifth explanation for the lack of strong evidence of a correlation between board composition and firm performance is that an optimal board contains a mix of inside, independent, and perhaps also affiliated outside directors, who bring different skills and knowledge to the board (Baysinger/Butler 1985; Fisch 1997; Klein 1997). For example, including insiders on the board may also make it easier for other directors to evaluate them as potential future CEOs (Vancil 1987; Weisbach 1988). This "mixed board" explanation is consistent with the hints in the available data about the value of having at least some inside directors on the board, and with Klein's (1998) finding that inside director representation on investment committees of the board correlates with improved firm performance. But if a mixed board is optimal, then many large companies may have too few inside directors to perform this role.

Sixth, perhaps some types of independent directors are valuable, while others are not. Maybe CEOs of companies in other industries (who are, by number, the majority of independent directors) are too busy with their own business, know too little about a different business, and are overly generous in compensating another CEO. Maybe "visibility" directors—well-known persons with limited business experience, often holding multiple directorships and adding gender or racial diversity to a board—are not effective on average. These possibilities are consistent with Vance's (1978) finding that directors' technical expertise in the company's industry correlates with firm performance. But this explanation, too, suggests that the current push for greater board independence may be fruitless or even counterproductive, unless independent directors have particular attributes, such as close knowledge of the company's industry.

Then, too, board independence may simply not be very important, on average and over time, compared to other factors that influence corporate performance. That hypothesis is consistent with the mixed results from a number of recent studies of the effects of corporate governance activism by institutional investors targeted at specific companies,[6] and with evidence that social connections are important in determining who is chosen to fill board seats, while home-firm performance is not.[7]

---

[6] Daily et al. (1996); Del Guercio/Hawkins (1997); Gillan/Starks (1995); Opler/Sokobin (1997); Smith (1996); Strickland/Wiles/Zenner (1996); Wagster/Prevost (1996); Wahal (1996).

[7] Davis (1993); Davis/Robbins (1996).

References

Agrawal, Anup, Jeffrey F. Jaffe, and Gershon N. Mandelker 'The Post-Merger Performance of Acquiring Firms: A Reexamination of An Anomaly' Journal of Finance 47 (1992) 1605-21.

Agrawal, Anup and Charles R. Knoeber 'Firm Performance and Mechanisms to Control Agency Problems Between Managers and Shareholders' *Journal of Financial and Quantitative Analysis* 31 (1996) 377-97.

Barber, Brad and John Lyon 'Detecting Long-Run Abnormal Stock Returns: The Empirical Power and Specification of Test-Statistics' *Journal of Financial Economics* 43 (1997) 341-72.

Baysinger, Barry D. and Henry N. Butler 'Corporate Governance and the Board of Directors: Performance Effects of Changes in Board Composition' *Journal of Law, Economics & Organization* 1 (1985) 101-24.

Baysinger, Barry D., Rita D. Kosnik, and Thomas A. Turk 'Effects of Board and Ownership Structure on Corporate R&D Strategy' *Academy of Management Journal* 34 (1991) 205-14.

Bethel, Jennifer E., Julia Porter Liebeskind, and Tim Opler 'Block Share Purchases and Corporate Performance' (Working Paper, 1996).

Bhagat, Sanjai and Bernard Black 'Do Independent Directors Matter?' (Working Paper, 1997).

Black, Bernard 'Shareholder Passivity Reexamined' 89 *Mich. L. Rev.* 520-608 (1990).

Black, Bernard 'The Value of Institutional Investor Monitoring: The Empirical Evidence' 39 *UCLA L. Rev.* 895-939 (1992).

Borokhovich, Kenneth A., Robert Parrino, and Teresa Trapani 'Outside Directors and CEO Selection' *Journal of Financial and Quantitative Analysis* 31 (1996) 337-55.

Brickley, James A., Jeffrey L. Coles, and Rory L. Terry 'Outside Directors and the Adoption of Poison Pills' *Journal of Financial Economics* 35 (1994) 371-90.

Bryant, Adam 'Calpers Draws a Blueprint for its Concept of an Ideal Board' *New York Times* June 17, 1997, D1.

Business Roundtable 'Statement on Corporate Governance' (1997).

Byrd, John W. and Kent A. Hickman 'Do Outside Directors Monitor Managers? Evidence from Tender Offer Bids' *Journal of Financial Economics* 32 (1992) 195-222.

Chaganti, Rajeswararao S., Vijay Mahajan, and Subhashi Sharma 'Corporate Board Size, Composition and Corporate Failures in Retailing Industry' *Journal of Management Studies* 22 (1985) 400-17.

Chung, Kee H. and Stephen W. Pruitt 'A Simple Approximation of Tobin's q' *Financial Management* 23/3 (1994) 70-4.

Cochran, Philip L., Robert A. Wood, and Thomas B. Jones 'The Composition of Boards of Directors and Incidence of Golden Parachutes' *Academy of Management Journal* 28 (1985) 664-71.

Core, John E., Robert W. Holthausen, and David F. Larcker 'Corporate Governance, CEO Compensation and Firm Performance' (Working Paper, 1997).

Council of Institutional Investors 'Does Ownership Add Value? A Collection of 100 Empirical Studies' (1994).

Cotter, James F., Anil Shivdasani, and Marc Zenner 'Do Independent Directors Enhance Target Shareholder Wealth During Tender Offers?' *Journal of Financial Economics* 43 (1997) 195-218.

Crystal, Graef *In Search of Excess: The Over-compensation of American Executives* (New York 1991).

Daily, Catherine M. and Dan R. Dalton 'Bankruptcy and Corporate Governance: The Impact of Board Composition and Structure' *Academy of Management Journal* 37 (1994) 1603-17.

Daily, Catherine M., Jonathan L. Johnson, Alan E. Ellstrand, and Dan R. Dalton 'Institutional Investor Activism: Follow the Leaders?' (Working Paper, 1996).

Davis, Gerald F. 'Who Gets Ahead in the Market for Corporate Directors: The Political Economy of Multiple Board Memberships' *Academy of Management Best Papers Proceedings* (1993) 202-6.

Davis, Gerald F. and Gregory E. Robbins 'Changes in the Market for Outside Directors, 1986-1994' (Working Paper, 1996).

Dechow, Patricia M. 'Accounting Earnings and Cash Flows as Measures of Firm Performance: The Role of Accounting Accruals' *Journal of Accounting and Economics* 18 (1994) 3-42.

Dechow, Patricia M., Richard G. Sloan, and Amy P. Sweeney 'Causes and Consequences of Earnings Manipulation: An Analysis of Firms Subject to Enforcement Actions by the SEC' *Contemporary Accounting Research* 13 (1996) 1-36.

Del Guercio, Diane and Jennifer Hawkins 'The Motivation and Impact of Pension Fund Activism' (Working Paper, 1997).

Demsetz, Harold and Kenneth Lehn 'The Structure of Corporate Ownership: Causes and Consequences' *Journal of Political Economy* 93 (1985) 1155-77.

Denis, David J. and Diane K. Denis 'Performance Changes Following Top Management Dismissals' *Journal of Finance* 50 (1995) 1029-57.

Denis, David J. and Atulya Sarin 'Ownership and Board Structures in Publicly Traded Corporations' (Working Paper, 1997).

Eisenberg, Theodore, Stefan Sundgren, and Martin T. Wells 'Larger Board Size and Decreasing Firm Value in Small Firms' (Working Paper, 1997).

Fisch, Jill 'Taking Boards Seriously' (Working Paper, 1997).

Gillan, Stuart L. and Laura T. Starks 'Relationship Investing and Shareholder Activism by Institutional Investors' (Univ. of Texas at Austin, Working Paper, 1995).

Gilson, Ronald J. and Reinier Kraakman 'Reinventing the Outside Director: An Agenda for Institutional Investors' 43 *Stan. L. Rev.* 863-906 (1991).

Hermalin, Benjamin E. and Michael S. Weisbach 'The Determinants of Board Composition' *Rand Journal of Economics* 19 (1988) 589-606.

Hermalin, Benjamin E. and Michael S. Weisbach 'The Effect of Board Composition and Direct Incentives on Firm Performance' *Financial Management* 21/4 (1991) 101-12.

Hermalin, Benjamin E. and Michael S. Weisbach 'Endogenously Chosen Boards of Directors and their Monitoring of the CEO' *American Economic Review* 88 (1998) 96-118.

Himmelberg, Charles P., R. Glenn Hubbard, and Darius Palia 'Understanding Determinants of Managerial Ownership and the Link Between Ownership and Performance' (Working Paper, 1996).

Kaplan, Steven N. and David Reishus 'Outside Directorships and Corporate Performance' *Journal of Financial Economics* 27 (1990) 389-410.

Kini, Omesh, William Kracaw, and Shehzad Mian 'Corporate Takeovers, Firm Performance, and Board Composition' *Journal of Corporate Finance* 1 (1995) 383-412.

Klein, April 'Transaction Costs and Board Structure: Causes and Consequences' (Working Paper, 1997).

Klein, April 'Firm Performance and Board Committee Structure' *Journal of Law and Economics* 41 (1998) 137-65.

Kole, Stacey R. 'Managerial Ownership and Firm Performance: Incentives or Rewards?' (Working Paper, 1996).

Kole, Stacey R. and Kenneth Lehn 'Deregulation and the Adaptation of Governance Structure: The Case of the U.S. Airline Industry' (Working Paper, 1996).

Kosnik, Rita D. 'Greenmail: A Study of Board Performance in Corporate Governance' *Administrative Science Quarterly* 32 (1987) 163-85.

Kosnik, Rita D. 'Effects of Board Demography and Directors' Incentives on Corporate Greenmail Decisions' *Academy of Management Journal* 33 (1990) 129-50.

Lambert, Richard and David Larcker 'Golden Parachutes, Executive Decision-Making, and Shareholder Wealth' *Journal of Accounting and Economics* 7 (1985) 179-203.

Lambert, Richard, David Larcker, and Keith Weigelt 'The Structure of Organizational Incentives' *Administrative Science Quarterly* 38 (1993) 438-61.

Lawrence, Jeffrey and Geof P. Stapledon 'Independent Directors in Australia: Empirical Evidence and Policy Prescriptions' (University of Melbourne Center for Corporate Law and Securities Regulation, Working Paper, 1997).

Lee, Chun I., Stuart Rosenstein, Nanda Rangan, and Wallace N. Davidson, III 'Board Composition and Shareholder Wealth: The Case of Management Buyouts' *Financial Management* 21/1 (1992) 58-72.

Lichtenberg, Frank and Darius Palia 'Managerial Ownership and Firm Performance: A Re-examination Using Productivity Measurement' (Working Paper, 1996).

Loderer, Claudio and Kenneth Martin 'Executive Stock Ownership and Performance: Tracking Faint Traces' (Working Paper, 1995).

Loughran, Tim and Anand M. Vijh 'Do Long-Term Shareholders Benefit from Corporate Acquisitions?' (Working Paper, 1997).

MacAvoy, Paul W., S. Cantor, J. Dana, and S. Peck 'ALI Proposals for Increased Control of the Corporation by the Board of Directors: An Economic Analysis' in: 'Statement of the Business Roundtable on the American Law Institute's Proposed "Principles of Corporate Governance and Structure: Restatement and Recommendations"' (1983).

Machlin, Judith, Hyuk Choe, and James Miles 'The Effects of Golden Parachutes on Takeover Activity' *Journal of Law and Economics* 36 (1993) 861-76.

Mallette, Paul and Karen L. Fowler 'Effects of Board Composition and Stock Ownership on the Adoption of "Poison Pills"' *Academy of Management Journal* 35 (1992) 1010-35.

Mayers, David, Anil Shivdasani, and Clifford W. Smith, Jr. 'Board Composition and Corporate Control: Evidence from the Insurance Industry' *Journal of Business* 70 (1997) 33-62.

Mehran, Hamid 'Executive Compensation Structure, Ownership, and Firm Performance' *Journal of Financial Economics* 38 (1995) 163-84.

Mikkelson, Wayne H. and M. Megan Partch 'The Decline of Takeovers and Disciplinary Management Turnover' *Journal of Financial Economics* 44 (1997) 205-28.

National Association of Corporate Directors 'Report of the NACD Blue Ribbon Commission on Director Professionalism' (1996).

Noe, Thomas H. and Michael J. Rebello 'The Design of Corporate Boards: Composition, Compensation, Factions and Turnover' (Georgia State Univ. College of Business Administration, Working Paper 96-01, 1996).

Opler, Tim C. and Jonathan Sokobin 'Does Coordinated Institutional Activism Work? An Analysis of the Activities of the Council of Institutional Investors' (Working Paper, 1997).

Pfeffer, Jeffrey 'Size and Composition of Corporate Boards of Directors: The Organization and its Environment' *Administrative Science Quarterly* 17 (1972) 218-28.

Rediker, Kenneth J. and Anju Seth 'Boards of Directors and Substitution Effects of Alternative Governance Mechanisms' *Strategic Management Journal* 16 (1995) 85-99.

Ritter, Jay R. 'The Long-Run Performance of Initial Public Offerings' *Journal of Finance* 46 (1991) 3-27.

Roe, Mark J. *Strong Managers, Weak Owners: The Political Roots of American Corporate Finance* (Princeton 1994).

Rosenstein, Stuart and Jeffrey G. Wyatt 'Outside Directors, Board Independence, and Shareholder Wealth' *Journal of Financial Economics* 26 (1990) 175-91.

Rosenstein, Stuart and Jeffrey G. Wyatt 'Inside Directors, Board Effectiveness, and Shareholder Wealth' *Journal of Financial Economics* 44 (1997) 229-50.

Scott, Kenneth E. and Allan W. Kleidon 'CEO Performance, Board Types and Board Performance: A First Cut' in: Baums, Theodor, Richard Buxbaum, and Klaus J. Hopt (eds.) *Institutional Investors and Corporate Governance* 181-99 (Berlin and New York 1994).

Servaes, Henri and Marc Zenner 'Ownership Structure' *Finanzmarkt und Portfolio Management* 8 (1994) 184-96.

Shivdasani, Anil 'Board Composition, Ownership Structure and Hostile Takeovers' *Journal of Accounting and Economics* 16 (1993) 167-98.

Singh, Harbir and Farid Harianto 'Management-Board Relationships, Takeover Risk and the Adoption of Golden Parachutes' *Academy of Management Journal* 32 (1989) 7-24.

Smith, Michael P. 'Shareholder Activism by Institutional Investors: Evidence from CalPERS' *Journal of Finance* 51 (1996) 227-52.

SpencerStuart '1996 Board Index: Board Trends and Practices at Major American Corporations' (1996).

Strickland, Deon, Kenneth W. Wiles, and Marc Zenner 'A Requiem for the USA: Is Small Shareholder Monitoring Effective?' *Journal of Financial Economics* 40 (1996) 319-38.

Sundaramurthy, Chamu, James M. Mahoney, and Joseph T. Mahoney 'Board Structure, Antitakeover Provisions, and Stockholder Wealth' *Strategic Management Journal* 18 (1996) 231-45.

Vance, Stanley C. *Boards of Directors: Structure and Performance* (Eugene 1964).

Vance, Stanley C. 'Corporate Governance: Assessing Corporate Performance by Boardroom Attributes' *Journal of Business Research* 6 (1978) 203-20.

Vancil, Richard F. *Passing the Baton: Managing the Process of CEO Selection* (Boston 1987).

Wagster, John D. and Andrew K. Prevost 'Wealth Effects of the CalPERS' "Hit List" to SEC Changes in the Proxy Rules' (Working Paper, 1996).

Wahal, Sunil 'Pension Fund Activism and Firm Performance' *Journal of Financial and Quantitative Analysis* 31 (1996) 1-23.

Wahal, Sunil, Kenneth W. Wiles, and Marc Zenner 'Who Opts Out of State Antitakeover Protection? The Case of Pennsylvania's SB 1310' *Financial Management* 24/3 (1995) 22-39.

Warner, Jerold B., Ross L. Watts, and Karen H. Wruck 'Stock Prices and Top Management Changes' *Journal of Financial Economics* 20 (1988) 461-92.

Weisbach, Michael S. 'Outside Directors and CEO Turnover' *Journal of Financial Economics* 20 (1988) 431-60.

Wright, David W. 'Evidence on the Relation Between Corporate Governance Characteristics and the Quality of Financial Reporting' (Working Paper, 1996).

Yermack, David 'Higher Market Valuation of Companies with a Small Board of Directors' *Journal of Financial Economics* 40 (1996) 185-212.

Yermack, David 'Good Timing: CEO Stock Option Awards and Company News Announcements' *Journal of Finance* 52 (1997) 449-76.

You, Victor, Richard Caves, Michael Smith, and James Henry 'Mergers and Bidders' Wealth: Managerial and Strategic Factors' in: Thomas, III, Lacy Glenn (ed.) *The Economics of Strategic Planning: Essays in Honor of Joel Dean* 201-21 (Lexington 1986).

The Corporate Director's Fiduciary Duty of Care and the Business Judgment Rule Under U.S. Corporate Law

WILLIAM T. ALLEN, New York

This essay addresses the enforcement of corporate directors' fiduciary duty of care under U.S. law. After describing that duty, it explains the cross-cutting efficiency effects that strict enforcement of this duty of care would have. It then explains the *business judgment rule* as a modified liability rule for claimed violations of the duty of care. It sees the business judgment rule as a method to ameliorate the inefficient effects that strict enforcement of the duty of care would produce. It asserts that the business judgment rule does this by focusing on the subjective good faith of directors rather than on deviation from an "objective" standard of behavior. Lastly, the essay posits that the resulting legal structure implies the view that persons subject to it are not simply rational calculators of self-interest but are moral actors.

Contents

Prologue: The Corporate Governance Context

Over the last fifty years or so the conventional view in the United States of the role of the board of directors in the actual governance of large, publicly financed corporations might be summarized as follows: modern technology gives rise to economies of scale that dictate that efficient production occurs within large-scale economic organizations. The attractions of diversification of risk make financing these enterprises through public distribution of its securities relatively efficient.[1] A consequence of this relative efficiency is that owners[2] effectively disappear. Diversified investors, who suffer from a number of collective action disabilities, take their place. Highly diversified investors who own a relatively small stake in each of their portfolio companies will tend to underinvest the time and money necessary to investigate management performance, to organize monitoring activities, or to change management policies or personnel.[3] Thus, free of effective oversight from investors, the conventional view sees corporate governance and its central instrument—the board of directors—as being essentially captured by management.[4] Management controls the corporation and its treasury, it nominates directors for shareholder endorsement, and spends corporate funds to promote that election. Management thus in effect controls the designation of directors. In the U.S., boards of directors of the large public companies have for decades been seen as passive, largely symbolic groups, whose only residual role of substance was to organize matters in the event of an unforeseen disaster.

The world has not stood still, however. The self-confident interpretation of the world that saw boards of publicly financed enterprises as inevitably passive no longer appears compelling to all.[5] In recent decades, there have been serious efforts in the U.S. to structure U.S. corporate governance so as to promote enhanced monitoring by corporate boards of corporate management performance and to push corporate directors to be more engaged, active "monitors." These

---

[1] Implicitly, of course, this implies a belief that the gains from diversification are greater than the losses from excess agency costs that the form permits. The prevalence of the corporate form in the U.S. economy would appear consistent with that inference. But the prevalence of large-scale integrated economic organizations in Germany or other economies without large public equity markets may cloud that inference. Julian Franks' and Colin Mayer's research tends to suggest, however, that German investors tend to get diversification in other ways; cf. Franks, Julian and Colin Mayer 'Ownership, Control and the Performance of German Corporations' (Paper, London Business School and University of Oxford, 1997).

[2] I simply refer to equity investors whose investment is sufficient large and sufficiently non-diversified that they want and get effective access to information and to the corporate governance machinery that designates senior management.

[3] A basic explanation of the shareholders' collective action problem is set forth in Clark, Robert C. *Corporate Law* 389-94 (Boston et al. 1986).

[4] Berle, Adolf A. and Gardiner C. Means *The Modern Corporation and Private Property* (New York 1933).

[5] Professor Mark Roe has challenged what he sees as the view that passive boards are the *inevitable* consequence of technology and the means the U.S. economy has pursued to finance large-scale economic organizations. Roe reminds us that positive law has in numerous specific ways channeled the way in which finance and governance interrelate in the U.S., as elsewhere. See Roe, Mark J. 'A Political Theory of American Corporate Finance' 91 *Colum. L. Rev.* 10 (1991); see also, Black, Bernard S. 'Shareholder Passivity Reexamined' 89 *Mich. L. Rev.* 520 (1990).

efforts, which appear to have had some effect,[6] may broadly be placed under three headings.

Sources of Pressure for Change in Board Performance: Federal Administrative Law. First, there has been substantial federal regulatory pressure, possibly backed up with a criminal law sanction, for corporate directors to be appropriately attentive.[7] Significantly, that pressure derives in part from the Federal Organization Sentencing Guidelines.[8] The Guidelines issued under the Sentencing Reform Act of 1984 set forth a uniform sentencing structure for organizations to be sentenced for violation of federal criminal statutes and provide for penalties that equal or often massively exceed those previously imposed on corporations. The Guidelines offer powerful incentives for corporations today to have compliance programs in place to detect violations of law, promptly to report violations to appropriate public officials when discovered, and to take prompt, voluntary remedial efforts. Thus those guidelines create substantial incentives for directors to actively assure that the corporation has appropriate structures to reasonably assure compliance with law.

Institutional Investors. Secondly, there is a well-documented and important "good governance" movement, largely built around a loose confederation of large pension funds, other institutional investors, and trade groups for the investment advisory and mutual fund industries. This movement has brought substantial pressure on public companies to reform board of director practices. Their power resides in their stock holdings, which collectively are vast, and in their ability to communicate with corporate management and, under limited circumstances, among themselves. Even though most institutional investors are quite diversified, albeit sometimes within defined sectors of the economy, for a variety of reasons some of them find it attractive either to support trade associations that press governance issues or, in some instances, to devote a small proportion of their budget to their own governance activities. It is widely understood in the U.S. that institutional investor pressure was an important reason why CEOs of huge, household-name firms have been removed by the companies' boards over the last ten years—a previously unimaginable result.

---

[6] For example, corporate boards are getting smaller in the U.S. They are becoming dominated by "outside" directors. Directors are serving on fewer boards, meeting more often, and getting paid more. And perhaps most importantly, the corporations' mechanisms of governance are increasingly being treated as a formal matter for regular outside director attention and consideration. Whether these changes affect performance is uncertain.

[7] The Securities Exchange Commission deserves substantial credit for encouraging the securities exchanges to require listed companies to have key board committees—audit and nominations particularly—dominated by "outsiders".

[8] See United States Sentencing Commission 'Guidelines Manual' Chapter 8 (U.S. Government Printing Office, November 1994).

Corporation Law as a Source of Change in Board Practice. Thirdly, as a source of change in corporate governance, I list corporation law itself, although it is surely the least important source of this change of the three I mention. From 1985 (*Smith v. Van Gorkom*[9]) through 1993 (*QVC Network, Inc. v. Paramount Communications, Inc*[10]), the corporation law of the State of Delaware (and thus, as a practical matter, the corporation law generally in the U.S.[11]) was in a difficult state. During this period, in default of a clear national policy with respect to the powerful social phenomenon of hostile corporate "takeovers", state law of organization form was required, in effect, to fashion such a policy. Courts were required to do so by specifying what the corporate directors' fiduciary duties of care and loyalty required or permitted in various contexts involving prospective hostile or voluntary changes in corporate control. Fiduciary duty is arguably a poor means to fashion such policy. Prospective statements of the content of fiduciary duties are so general as to offer only very limited guidance to transaction planners; as applied in specific cases, the fiduciary obligation is typically so highly particularized that generalizing *ex ante* rules from judicial holdings is a difficult, artistic process which rarely will give the complete confidence that the planner of transactions seeks.

As a result, the institutional legal rules that defined director and officer duty in the face of these merger and acquisition transactions were often problematic.[12] One of the most basic observations that an attentive reader of important corporate law opinions authored by the Delaware Supreme Court during this difficult period inevitably made, however, involved the duty of directors to be actively engaged. The Delaware court repeatedly and firmly stated its view that director passivity was unacceptable. In the face of what it saw as director passivity, the Delaware Supreme Court demonstrated its willingness to enjoin major transactions and even to subject to personal liability disinterested directors who actively participated in board processes. In a series of cases beginning with the 1985 decision in *Smith v. Van Gorkom*, all of which dealt with transactions that involved no conventional conflict of interest, the Delaware Supreme Court

[9] 488 A.2d 858 (Del. 1985). Kahan (this volume Ch. 8) also refers to some of the cases mentioned in this section.

[10] 635 A.2d 1245 (Del. 1993).

[11] Two aspects of U.S. law establish Delaware law as the de facto natural corporation law of the U.S., even though every state in the U.S. has a more or less highly developed law of corporations and much economic activity occurs in corporations chartered in these other states. First, a majority of the largest firms (Fortune 500 firms) are incorporated in Delaware, and secondly, many state judges recognize the experience that the Delaware judiciary has had with respect to corporate law problems. Thus, in many U.S. states, the judicial solution to what is a novel corporation law problem for that jurisdiction will often include consideration of the pertinent Delaware authorities.

[12] With the decision in the *QVC* case, supra n. 10, a substantial improvement in clarity was achieved.

criticized the level of performance of outside directors, enjoined closings of major transactions, and most surprisingly, exposed disinterested directors to possible personal liability. In *Van Gorkom,* over a vigorous dissent, the Delaware Supreme Court held that disinterested outside directors who had approved an arms-length merger had violated their duty to act with due care and were exposed to personal liability.

Later, the Delaware Supreme Court decided the famous *Revlon* case.[13] That case, too, involved a proposed merger as in *Smith,* but this time the merger had been negotiated in reaction to another "hostile" effort to acquire control of Revlon. The Revlon directors had authorized a series of devices that favored the company-chosen buyer, even though the hostile party had consistently evidenced a willingness to top the friendly bidder's price. In that case, too, the board had no conventional conflicting interest in either transaction,[14] and had certainly satisfied traditional standards of involvement with corporate affairs. Yet once again the Delaware Supreme Court closely examined the substance of the directors' conduct, and declared that the directors had failed.

In a series of later cases, all arising out of the negotiation of corporate mergers, the Delaware Supreme Court criticized and enjoined outside directors,[15] and, more notably, once more, in the context of a negotiated sale of the firm, again held that disinterested directors had been "negligent" and were therefore exposed to the possibility of personal liability.[16]

Understanding the Fiduciary Duty of Care and its Enforcement. This essay addresses only the corporation law of directors' duty of care and the liability rule used to exact damages for its breach (the so-called business judgment rule). It does not address institutional investors or federal law as sources of pressure on corporate boards to be more active. In my opinion, those factors do constitute the principal forces pushing for change in the behavior of corporate boards of U.S. companies. Consideration of the director's fiduciary duty of care is nevertheless deserving of our consideration, since that duty and its related doctrine, the "business judgment rule," do play an important part in the legal advice that

---

[13] *Revlon v. MacAndrews & Forbes Holdings, Inc.* 506 A.2d 173 (Del. 1986).

[14] The court's opinion, following the inventive advocacy of counsel, referred to a sort of conflict from the fact that the board had earlier distributed new bonds to the companies' shareholders pro rata . This conflict was plainly a covenant construction, not a substantial fact.

[15] E.g., *Mills Acquisition Corp. v. Macmillan* 559 A.2d 1261 (Del. 1989), *QVC Network, Inc. v. Paramount Communications, Inc.*, supra n. 10.

[16] *Cinerama, Inc. v. Technicolor, Inc.* 663 A.2d 1134 (Del. Ch. 1994), *aff'd,* 663 A.2d 1156 (Del. 1995).

boards are given by their lawyers, and those related doctrines are analytically difficult and, I contend, often misunderstood.[17]

In treating the corporate directors' duty of care we delve into an area of legal doctrine that is deceptive in its apparent simplicity. If one pays attention both to what courts say and what they do, however, a picture of greater complexity emerges. In this short essay I attempt to do several things for a comparative law audience.

First, after an orienting description of fiduciary obligations under U.S. corporate law generally, I want to give a brief, modern statement of the director's duty of care and attention under U.S. law. This duty is stated in "objective" terms, that is, in terms of what a hypothetical third party would do in the same or similar circumstances as those faced by the corporate director defendant.

Second, I want to describe the source of ambiguity and complexity in this doctrine: the competing efficiency effects that enforcement of this objective standard of attention can be expected to have.

Third, I show, albeit not exhaustively, that the Anglo-American corporation law up through the middle part of the 20th century *announced* an "objective reasonable person" standard of care for corporate directors, but when personal liability was at stake, it *enforced* a different rule. Closer to a description of the "rule" that courts enforce, in the absence of a director conflict of interest, would be as follows: in the absence of a conflicting financial interest, a director will be liable for corporate losses caused by board action he authorizes, only if he has authorized such action without at that time having a good faith belief that, in the circumstances present, he has satisfied his obligation to be reasonably informed.

I assert that this practice, observable in the 19th century and earlier 20th-century cases, of announcing an objective standard of attentiveness but enforcing a subjective standard, while subject to certain evident criticisms, arguably has a potential to mediate the cross-efficiency effects that enforcement of the objective standard of care would raise, in a way that may assist in the optimal production of wealth.

Fourth, I note that this approach evidenced in cases throughout the 19th and 20th centuries appears inconsistent with the thread running through recent (post-1984) Delaware corporation law opinions and is inconsistent with the formulation of the "business judgment rule" contained in the American Law Institute's *Principles of Corporate Governance*. I suggest, however, that the Delaware law respecting director diligence and liability has not changed fundamentally, but the courts have modified their conception of independence in the merger context; that the recent cases are reflective of special concerns with change in corporate

---

[17] This essay cannot attempt a complete assay of this very large subject. The leading text on it is Block, Dennis J., Nancey E. Barton, and Stephen A. Radin *The Business Judgment Rule: Fiduciary Duties of Corporate Directors* (Englewood Cliffs, NJ 1994).

control transaction only; and that in other contexts, the traditional approach will be found. I also criticize the ALI definition of business judgment rule because it is not limited as to type of transaction and it does invite second-guessing of decisions by disinterested directors. It therefore will create a disincentive to rational assumption of risk by the corporation.

Fifth, in the last section of the essay I offer an explanation why a system that includes a disjunction between a director's standard of duty and his standard of liability may induce different—and in this instance possibly more efficient— action than a system that itself collapsed the standard of care and the liability standard into a single consistent statement of duty and liability. This explanation is premised on the understanding that human beings seek systematically to advance their interests, but that they are moral beings whose interests include a range of social, moral, and solidaristic concerns.

A. The Corporate Director's Fiduciary Duty of Care and Attention Under U.S. Law

U.S. corporate law statutes—those positive state law enactments that authorize persons to establish corporate entities and describe their character—play an important, albeit rarely controversial, role in the economy. They contribute to the public good in countless transaction in which the availability of the form facilitates the (relatively) inexpensive coordination of interests of various persons desiring to coordinate their efforts or resources in an economic activity. To the extent that corporation law plays a higher profile and perhaps more difficult role, it does so because courts are required to fill in the huge interstitial gaps in defined duty necessarily left open at the creation of the firm. In doing so, courts deploy an ancient body of law dealing with "fiduciaries."

U.S. corporation law affords to stockholders three principal sources of protection of their interests: the stockholder's right to vote his or her stock, to sell stock, and the fiduciary duty of corporate officers and directors, all of which are principally enforced judicially through shareholder-initiated lawsuits. The fiduciary duty may be thought important because it (1) affords a basis for shareholders to recover for the corporation's amounts diverted from the corporation through various types of managerial misconduct; (2) it protects the right to vote against manipulation that may disarm it,[18] and (3) it may protect the mechanism that permits hostile corporate takeovers from manipulation by incumbent managers seeking to protect the *status quo*.[19] Beyond the fiduciary duty, extensive regula-

---

[18] See, e.g., *Blasius Indus. v. Atlas Corp.* 564 A.2d 651 (Del. Ch. 1988).

[19] See, e.g., *Revlon v. MacAndrews & Forbes Holdings, Inc.*, supra n. 13; *Paramount Communications, Inc. v. QVC Network, Inc.* 637 A.2d 34 (Del. 1993); *QVC Network, Inc. v. Paramount Communications, Inc.*, supra n. 10.

tion of disclosure, principally by the federal Securities Exchange Commission, also offers protection to the effectiveness of the right to vote and the takeover mechanism.

I. A General Description of Fiduciary Duties

To understand the nature of fiduciary duties under U.S. law, it is helpful to understand a little English legal history and a distinction that grew up as a result of that history between a realm of *legal rights and duties* and a concurrent realm of *equitable rights and duties*. That history is somewhat beyond the scope of this essay. For present purposes it may be sufficient simply to note that in jurisdictions built upon English law, a fiduciary owes duties (to certain persons) in addition to the legal duties that the law imposes on all residents. It is of the essence of those duties that they can constrain the exercise of otherwise lawful legal right and that a court of equity will specifically enforce such constraint.

Fiduciary duties may be thought of as *judicially defined duties* imposed upon one who agrees to accept broad legal power over property, pursuant to an undertaking to exercise that power for the benefit of another; or upon one who agrees to use information disclosed as part of a relationship of trust and dependency only for the benefit of the party disclosing the information.[20] The classic fiduciary role under Anglo-American law is the trustee (and the trustee's institutional predecessor, a legal owner subject to a use). The trustee owns legally unrestricted title to property, but holds and employs it subject to an equitable duty to advance the purposes of the original grant. The corporation may be seen as in some respects analogous to the trust. In both institutions, property is transferred to another pursuant to an unspecified or general purpose. In both, legal power resides in the holder of legal title, but a general fiduciary obligation of loyalty to the original purpose will be enforced in equity.[21] Other examples of fiduciary relationships in Anglo-American law include the relationship between a guardian and her ward; or between an executor and the estate of a decedent. These relationships may be regarded as classical or pure fiduciary relationships because they involve both the exercise of legal power by one over property which he or she does not equitably own and they involve relationships of dependence by the beneficial owner on the fiduciary. Another class of relationships that traditionally U.S. law has treated as fiduciary in character may not have the same degree of dependency but still presents the same condition of trust: these relationships

---

[20] See generally, Flannagan, Robert 'The Fiduciary Obligation' *Oxford Journal of Legal Studies* 9 (1989) 285.

[21] There are, of course, highly significant legal and economic differences between a trust and a corporation. I described some of these differences in *Cinerama, Inc. v. Technicolor, Inc.*, supra n. 16.

include the agent's relationship with his principal; the relationship between partners; and the relationship between corporate officers or directors and the corporation.

One of the characteristics that make fiduciary duties interesting is their unspecified character. Viewed from an *ex ante* perspective, fiduciary duties are extremely broad in character, typically entailing not much more (or less) than an obligation of scrupulous loyalty and good faith by the fiduciary (the person upon whom the duty rests) to the beneficiary of the duty.

The duties of a fiduciary, whether a trustee, a partner, or a corporate director, are essentially three: first, (it often goes without being said since it is so basic) a fiduciary must act consistently with the legal document or documents that create her authority.[22] Thus, for example, if a Declaration of Trust restricts the trustee's power to deal with an asset, the trustee will be exposed to liability for breach of trust if she does not conform her conduct to that standard. It will not matter that the trustee acted in good faith pursuit of the interests of the trust beneficiary. Similarly, corporate directors are charged by the constitutional documents of the firm to do certain things—to cause the corporation to hold an annual meeting of shareholders, for example, or to recognize the special rights of the holders of any outstanding preferred stock. These obligations that are explicitly imposed by the foundational documents of the office are like any legal obligation.[23] Customarily they are specific and failure to meet the standard they establish may in an appropriate case be enforced by injunction without regard to the fact, if true, that the directors in refusing to comply with the legal obligation did so in the good faith belief that they would thereby advance the corporation's best interest.[24]

The other two foundational duties of fiduciaries generally or corporate directors specifically do not involve the relative clarity or specificity of the first. They are the judicially created *duty of loyalty and duty of care.* The fiduciary's duty of loyalty, speaking very broadly, requires that a corporate director exercise his or

---

[22] An agent, for example, is said to have a duty of obedience to the agent's principal. Unlike an agent, corporate directors are not generally said to have such a duty, since they are to exercise their own honest business judgment, c.f. *Paramount Communications, Inc. v. Time, Inc.* 1989 Del. Ch. LEXIS 77 ("corporate governance is not a town meeting"), but they do have a duty, which may be enforced by injunction, of obedience to the constitutional documents of the corporation. See also Restatement (Second) of Agency § 385 Duty to Obey.

[23] It is, however, highly unlikely that a corporate director would be held liable in damages for losses following from a decision to fail to conform to an express charter provision, unless the facts show a breach of one of the other two sources of fiduciary duty: the duty of care or, more likely, the duty of loyalty.

[24] Under Anglo-American law the grant or denial of the equitable remedy of injunction is always subject to the informed discretion of the court. Thus, it is quite possible that a court would fail to enforce by injunction a duty specified in the constitutional documents of the firm upon a finding that, in the circumstances, the directors were acting for the best interest of the corporation.

her authority over corporate processes or property (including information) only in a good faith attempt to advance the corporation's interests and not for other purposes. Thus, for example, a corporate officer or director is precluded from secretly competing with the corporation, from using its property (including information learned in a confidential capacity) for his advantage or its detriment, from appropriating opportunities that fall within its business, and especially from transacting business with it on terms that are not entirely fair.[25] Much of U.S. corporate law is concerned with the corporate officer's and corporate director's duty of loyalty. The duty of loyalty includes a duty of truthful disclosure to shareholders of relevant information, although the precise boundaries of this duty under general fiduciary law are not fully worked out.[26]

The fiduciary duty of care is in some respects more straightforward. It is the duty of a director or officer to exercise the care of an ordinarily prudent person in the same or similar circumstances. In fact, this formulation, while highly conventional, does lead to special considerations in corporate law, where the law must be especially careful not to over-deter risk taking.

The corporate officer's and director's fiduciary duty of care and attention and its judicial enforcement is the topic of this essay.

II. The Duty of Care

From the earliest stirring of a distinct body of corporation law, courts have expressed the view that corporate directors have a duty to be appropriately attentive to the interests that by accepting the office they have implicitly agreed to protect and advance. The earliest reported judicial opinion in Anglo-American jurisprudence that states that a corporate director owes a duty to act "with reasonable diligence" is the report of the English Chancellor's 1742 decision in *The Charitable Company v. Sutton.*[27] In the U.S., early cases include *Godbold v.*

---

[25] It is sometimes said that the fiduciary duties of a corporate director include three components: good faith, due care, and loyalty, e.g., *Cede v. Technicolor, Inc.* 636 A.2d 956 (Del. Supr. 1994), but despite the frequency with which such statements occur, they are analytically misleading. The duty of loyalty subsumes the obligation to act with respect to the corporation in good faith. Only if one narrowly and mistakenly understood the requirement of loyalty to preclude only financial conflicts of interests would good faith constitute an additional requirement of corporate directors.

[26] The development of the state fiduciary law of director disclosure appeared to be preterminted by the development of federal disclosure law under the Securities Exchange Act of 1934 and the evolution of the rules under that act. Since *Santa Fe Indus., Inc. v. Green* 430 U.S. 462, 97 S.Ct. 1292 (1977), state courts have attempted to develop this area of corporation law consistently with the Supremacy Clause of the U.S. Constitution. See *Lynch v. Vickers Energy Corp.* 383 A.2d 278 (Del. 1977) and *Zirn v. VLI Corp.* 621 A.2d 773 (Del. 1993).

[27] 2 Atk. 400, 26 Eng. Rpts. 642.

Branch Bank, 11 Ala. 191 (1847); *Hodges v. New England Screw Co.*, 1 R.I. 312 (1850); and *Bates v. Dresser*, 251 U.S. 524 (1920) (Holmes, J.).

The fiduciary duty to be appropriately attentive is inevitably captured *ex ante* only in a statement of very great breadth. About the best that can be done with respect to an *ex ante* articulation of a director's obligation to pay attention is to establish an obligation in broad, almost empty terms: reasonable care in the circumstances then present.[28] A director must exercise that degree of care that an ordinarily prudent person would reasonably be expected to exercise under similar circumstances. This, of course, is a very general formulation.[29] But a formula of this duty could not be otherwise than vague and general. At the time the corporation is formed, directors initially recruited, and stock sold, the duration of the capital investment in the corporation is indefinite. There is little dependable information available concerning the sorts of decisons that directors will be called upon to make in future years. The investors and the directors will know, however, that markets and technological environment within which the corporation will function will be dynamic, and that an important part of the utility of the corporate form derives from the information efficiencies that centralized decision-makers allow. There is therefore a fundamental, joint interest in conferring on corporate directors and corporate management wide discretion to react *in a timely way* to changing circumstances. Given the possibility of almost infinite variation in the possible context calling for decision, the time frames that may be presented within which action must be taken or foregone, and the blend of skills and information relevant to a decision, it is impossible to do more than to describe a duty to act as a reasonably prudent person would do in similar circumstances. [30]

---

[28] See generally Mod. Bus. Corp. Act Annot., Section 8.30 et seq. (1994). Relatively recently the statutory laws of various U.S. states have incorporated a standard statutory statement of a duty of care for corporate directors which is generally intended to reflect the common law formulations, such as is stated in text. See 'Report on Committee on Corporate Laws: Changes in the Model Business Corporation Act' 30 *Bus. Law.* 501 (1975). E.g., *Briggs v. Spaulding* 141 U.S. 132, 152 (1891); *Norlin Corp. v. Rooney, Pace, Inc.* 744 F.2d 255, 264 (2d Cir. 1984); Rev. Mod. Bus. Corp. Act. § 8.30.

[29] See *Briggs v. Spaulding* 141 U.S. 132, 11 S.Ct. 924, 35 L.Ed. 662 (1891).

[30] Unlike the designer of a jet engine or a brain surgeon—as to whom one could in principle determine what the relevant profession establishes as the appropriate standard of care in each imagined circumstances in which professional judgment is to be exercised—a corporate director is not necessarily an expert in any specialty and certainly he will not be an expert in all involved specialties. Yet the director must decide questions affecting the corporate welfare (i.e., he or she cannot decline to act).

B. Cross-Cutting Efficiency Effects of an Objective Duty of Care

I. Positive Efficiency Effects of an Objective Duty of Care Standard

It seems intuitive that, in a world without agent opportunism at least, a legal command that an agent exercise care or attention proportional to the magnitude of the decision's impact upon the principal would tend systematically to produce efficiency enhancements, when compared to alternative rules. Such a rule would create incentives for a decision maker to spend time and money becoming informed just to the extent that those expenditures were justified by the estimated improvement in the decision-making process. The command to exercise the care of a reasonable person in the same or similar circumstances is operationally similar to this proportionality rule. Under the objective "reasonable man" standard, we can assume, I believe, that such an imagined person would engage in the same cost-benefit calculation to determine whether he knew enough about the corporation or the particular decision that the board faced, in order to act or to decide not to act. Surely, a legal system that somehow assured that corporate directors would be "reasonably" informed in this sense, would be more efficient than a system that assured that directors would be "too informed" (i.e., invested more than an optimal amount in information) or were under-informed.

But it is evident that determining an appropriate quantum of information needed optimally to authorize or reject a proposed corporate act is never a scientific question, to which there is in principle a correct answer. Determining when an optimum amount of information is available for a decision with a time-fuse on it logically involves estimating the various *unknown costs* associated with getting more information and estimating the *possible value that unknown information may bring*. Moreover, these estimates of unknown future costs and values will be affected by the *attitude towards risk* that the agents (directors)[31] ascribe to the corporate enterprise and to themselves as individuals as well. The result is that, with respect to a director's duty to be attentive and informed, the law may specify some minimums, but can do little more than hold that a director's duty is to act with respect to the corporation as a reasonable man would do in similar circumstances.

Thus, the objective standard of reasonable care may be interpreted as simply a generalized if opaque command to be efficient with respect to the acquisition and use of information.

---

[31] I don't call the directors agents in a legal sense, for it has been long and well decided that individually they are not agents of the corporation (far less of the shareholders) by reason of their status as directors. I use the term in the way that economists might do, to refer to one with delegated power over the legal ownership claim of another.

II. Negative Efficiency Effects of an Objective Duty of Care Standard

The *enforcement* of a legal duty to acquire and use relevant information efficiently is not without its own negative efficiency effects. All other things being equal, uncertainty with respect to the risks of liability associated with service on a board or of authorizing corporate action, can be expected to have an impact on the conduct of directors. The threat of possible liability arising from a later judicial specification of what a reasonable fellow would have done, rather than what this board in fact did, may present a substantial impediment to the optimum functioning of a board. Of course, as a practical matter, the law reduces this liability risk in a number of respects. I note some of these in the margin, but pass over them because, while they have an impact on the practical scope of the effects of legal doctrine that I discuss, they do not affect the doctrine itself, or completely overcome its effects.[32]

I described this unattended efficiency impediment that an objective standard of care may have on corporate directors in a recent judicial opinion, which for economy I will quote:

> [Where there is a large well-developed stock market] shareholders can [cheaply] diversify the risks of their corporate investments. Thus, it is in their economic interest for the corporation to accept, in rank order, all positive net present value investment projects available to the corporation, starting with the *highest risk-adjusted rate of return first.* Shareholders don't want (or shouldn't rationally want) directors to be risk averse. Share-holders' investment interests, across the full range of their diversifiable equity invest-ments, will be maximized if corporate directors and managers honestly assess risk and reward and accept for the corporation the highest risk-adjusted returns available that are above the firm's cost of capital.
>
> But directors will tend to deviate from this rational acceptance of corporate risk *if* in authorizing the corporation to undertake a risky investment, the directors must assume some degree of personal risk relating to *ex post facto* claims of derivative liability for any resulting corporate loss.
>
> Corporate directors of public companies typically have a very small proportionate ownership interest in their corporations and little or no incentive compensation. Thus, they enjoy (as residual owners) only a very small proportion of any "upside" gains earned by the corporation on risky investment projects. If, however, corporate directors were to be found liable for a corporate loss from a risky project on the ground that the investment

---

[32] The corporation laws of the U.S. provide three levels of protection for breach of care liability, in addition to the doctrinal protection discussed in the text. First, corporations are authorized to, and inevitably do, broadly indemnify officers and directors from all expense incurred as a result of their services to the corporation. There are limits however. Notably a judgment recovered in a suit charging a director with breach of duty is not indemnifiable. (But, under Delaware law, at all events, settlement of such a suit is an indemnifiable expense. See 8 Del. Code § 145(e).) Secondly, a corporation may secure directors' and officers' insurance, which may in fact be somewhat broader—and perhaps more secure—than indemnification rights. Thirdly, in reaction to *Smith v. Van Gorkom*, in Delaware and subsequently a great many other jurisdictions, shareholders can approve a charter amendment waiving on the part of the corpora-tion any recovery for alleged breach of duty of care uncomplicated by a breach of loyalty. See 8 Del. Code § 102(b)(7).

was too risky (foolishly risky! stupidly risky! egregiously risky!—you supply the adverb), their liability would be joint and several for the whole loss (with I suppose a right of contribution). Given the scale of operation of modern public corporations, this stupefying disjunction between risk and reward for corporate directors threatens undesirable effects. Given this disjunction, only a very small probability of director liability based on "negligence", "inattention", "waste", etc., could induce a board to avoid authorizing risky investment projects to any extent! Obviously, it is in the shareholders' economic interest to offer sufficient protection to directors from liability for negligence, etc., to allow directors to conclude that, as a practical matter, there is no risk that, if they act in good faith and meet minimal proceduralist standards of attention, they can face liability as a result of a business loss.[33]

Thus, the threat of enforcement of an "objective", "reasonable man" standard of liability tends to create an impediment to the director action authorizing the acceptance of optimum risk on the part of the corporation. The corporate director's objective duty of care therefore constitutes a rose with its thorns.

C. Mediating Cross-Efficiency Effects of "Objective" Duty of Care

Focusing upon the cross-efficiency effects that announcing and enforcing an "objective reasonable person" standard of care would tend to have on corporate directors offers a way to interpret the fact—reflected in more than a century of judicial opinion—that the law has announced a standard for reasonable care, but it has enforced a different standard, one that in substance looks to the good faith of the director in light of the existence of the "objective" duty. It is a mistake to interpret as poor public policy judicial unwillingness to impose standards of "reasonableness" on corporate directors. It is more likely that to enforce through damages claims of compensation for corporate losses arising from "unreasonable" board action would impede rational risk assumption and therefore impede wealth creation.

I. Traditional Law of Director Liability Absent Conflicting Interest

An unwillingness to second-guess the substance of a business decision when made by disinterested corporate directors in good faith is one of the most evident features of reported 19th- and 20th-century corporate law opinions. An influential early English case, *Turquand v. Marshall,*[34] held that no matter how "foolish" or "ridiculous" a decision may seem in retrospect, so long as it is within the legal power of the board, the court will not second-guess it for the purpose of finding liability. *Turquand* was widely followed both in England[35] and in the U.S.[36] A

---

[33] *Gagliardi v. TriFoods Int'l, Inc.* 683 A.2d 1049, 1052 (Del. Ch. 1996).

[34] 4 Ch.App. 376 (1869).

[35] E.g., *Re Forest of Dean Coal Mining Company* (1888); 10 Ch.D. 450 (Jessel, M.R.).

leading U.S. case of the late 19th century, *Spering's Estate*[37], cited *Turquand* approvingly. Indeed, one reading a fair sprinkling of the early English cases on director liability absent conflict of interest cannot escape the inference that during the late 19th century, even the idea of abandonment of office was not a plausible basis for a plaintiff to hope for a monetary recovery from a corporate director. The case that most makes the point is a dying gasp from the feudal past: the *Marquis of Bute's Case (Re Cardiff Savings Bank)*.[38] There the director-defendant had, at six years of age, succeeded to his father's place on the board of the Cardiff Savings Bank. He had attended only one meeting in thirty-eight years, but was nevertheless held not liable for failing to uncover a fraud by a bank officer. See also, e.g., *Re Denham & Co.*, 25 Ch. D. 752 (1884) (failure to attend any meetings in four years held no ground for liability for loss from undiscovered fraud). Such cases give rise to the inference that, at that point, nothing was expected of corporate directors in fact, other than they refrain from deliberately injuring company interests. It was for a very long period conventionally accepted by experts in U.S. corporation law that so long as a director of a non-banking corporation attended meetings when called and attended to other fundamental formalities, there existed virtually no risk of liability as result of a claim that he or she violated a duty of care.[39] That is, for a very long time, Anglo-American courts have announced that directors have a duty to pay appropriate attention to the corporation's welfare, but for equally long they have in effect failed to impose liability on this ground unless there is either (1) conflicting financial interests or (2) conduct that evidences fraud, or lack of good faith. While what conduct short of active participation in a fraud or clear condonation of it might constitute lack of good faith is, under the earlier cases and today, a difficult question, where a director essentially abandons the office by not attending meetings, not making a reasonable effort to be informed about it, etc., he will be deemed to have violated his duty of care.[40] Traditionally such a lack of good faith might be shown by such complete disregard of the duties of the office as to constitute a virtual abandonment.

Delaware judicial opinions until 1985 are representative. First, it is notable that during the whole of the 20th century prior to 1963, the concept of director "negligence" or indeed of director "duty of care," appear to have not generally

---

[36] E.g., *Spering's Estate* 71 Pa. 11, 10 Am.Rep. 684 (1872).

[37] 71 Pa. 11; 10 Am.Rep. 684 (1872).

[38] 2 Ch. 100 (1892).

[39] See Fletcher, William Meade *Fletcher Cyclopedia of the Law of Private Corporations* Vol. 3a § 1039 (Deerfield, IL et al. 1975); Bishop, Jr., Joseph W. 'Sitting Ducks and Decoy Ducks: New Trends in the Indemnification of Corporate Directors and Officers' 77 *Yale L.J.* 1078 (1968).

[40] E.g., *Briggs v. Spaulding*, supra n. 28 (opinion of Harlan, J.).

been a part of the vocabulary of reported Delaware judicial opinions respecting directors' duties.[41] When Delaware courts were required to address the conditions under which directors might be found liable for a corporate loss in a non-self-dealing transaction, they did not refer to "negligence" or "due care" but rather used phrases redolent of fraud, or bad faith: "fraud" or "constructive fraud,"[42] "bad faith and reckless indifference,"[43] or "bad faith or. . . gross abuse of discretion"[44]. As one follows the line of Delaware cases from the 1920s through the 1940s and 1950s, this judicial reliance on *financial independence and good faith* judgment as inconsistent with any determination of director liability continues.[45]

The law of director liability in circumstances where the director suffers from no conflict of interest is not a seamless web. The cases are many and difficult to fit together at a verbal level. Generally, however, it is my assertion that absent conflicting interest or disloyal conduct, American corporation law has consistently based director liability for corporate losses on a standard that looked to the *good faith effort* of directors to be reasonably informed. Where directors are thought to have exercised an honest judgment in the good faith pursuit of corporate interests, there has been no willingness to second-guess this conduct by asking what a hypothetical reasonable person might have done in these circumstances. Thus while many cases state that corporate directors must act in a way consistent with the action that a reasonable attentive person would take, cases that predicate liability on such a statement are very rare.[46] Those few cases that

[41] Retired Justice Henry Horsey of the Delaware Supreme Court, the author of the 1985 *Smith v. Van Gorkom* opinion, noted his surprise in researching a 1994 lecture to realize this fact. Justice Horsey reports that not before *dicta* in a 1963 opinion did a Delaware court expressly acknowledge a duty of care, and at that time the acknowledgment was, according to Justice Horsey, "tentative and almost begrudging". See Horsey, Henry R. 'The Duty of Care Component of the Delaware Business Judgment Rule' 19 *Del. J. Corp. L.* 971, 988 (1994).

[42] *Allied Chemical & Dye Corp. v. Steel & Tube Co.* 120 A.2d. 486 (Del. Ch. 1923); *Robinson v. Pittsburgh Oil Refining Corp.* 126 A.2d 46 (Del. Ch. 1924); *Bodell v. General Gas & Elec. Corp.* 140 A.264, 268 (Del. 1927).

[43] *Cole v. National Cash Credit Ass'n* 156 A.183 (Del. Ch. 1931).

[44] *Warshaw v. Calhoun* 221 A.2d 487, 492 (Del. Ch. 1966).

[45] E.g., *Porges v. Vadsco Sales Corp* 32 A.2d 148 (Del. Ch. 1943); *Cottrell v. Pawcatuck Co.* 128 A.2d 225 (Del. Supr. 1957); *Meyerson v. El Paso Natural Gas Co.* 246 A.2d 789 (Del. Ch. 1967).

[46] In his famous study, Professor Joseph Bishop reported on an exhaustive study of American judicial opinions on this subject. His conclusion was that few cases could be cited as possibly representing liability of disinterested directors arising only out of a violation of due care obligation. See Bishop, Jr., supra n. 39. More recently, Mssrs. Block, Barton, and Radin count nine additional cases, many of which involve failed financial institutions. E.g., *FDIC v. Bierman* 2 F.3d. 1424 (7h Cir. 1993) ("unreasonable loan"). To the extent non-depository companies are involved in these cases, the directors are classified as totally passive or uninformed. E.g., *Stern v. Lucy Webb Hays National Training School* 381 F. Supp. 1003 (D.D.C. 1974). See generally, Block, Barton, and Radin, supra n. 17, 72-5.

do so involve action or inaction that is inconsistent with a good faith belief by the director that he had satisfied the objectively stated duty of care. Most of those few cases are abandonment of office cases, where the degree of inactivity was completely inconsistent with a credible claim by the director that he had concluded in good faith that he had satisfied the objective standard of care. A few others involve directors who exercised judgments that resulted in losses and were found liable for those losses. But the facts of these cases inevitably give rise to suspicions concerning the *bono fides* of director-defendants. Consider *Shelheimer v. Maganese Corporation,*[47] a case that is one of the few American cases widely cited as involving an actual finding of liability for corporate losses arising from decisions that were found to be beyond the range of those that a reasonable person would have made. While certainly language in the Supreme Court of Pennsylvania's opinion can be well cited in support of that conclusion, the facts of the case as found by the trial court and affirmed by the Supreme Court convincingly establish that the case did not involve innocent, albeit uninformed, decisions that might be the basis for a simple negligence finding. The director-defendants were the five directors of Manganese Corporation of America, a start-up company. Before any operations were running, they sold non-controlling stock to the public in an offering exempt from registration under an intra-state exemption from the 1933 Securities Act that required the company to do business in Pennsylvania. In fact the company did not qualify for that exemption. In addition, one of the five directors acted as distributor or under-writer of the stock and received 15% of the proceeds in that way. The directors as a class received compensation that had never been authorized.

Following the initial distribution of stock, the defendants proceeded to invest most of the corporation's funds in an effort to bring a plant at Paterson, New Jersey, into commercial production. The effort was futile in fact and the business fairly promptly failed, with a loss of substantially all of the capital that had just been raised in the public underwriting. The Pennsylvania Supreme Court held that the controlling group—but not the fifth director who owned none of the controlling stock—was liable for the loss.

In justifying this result, the court's opinion employs the phrases "misman-agement", "waste," "negligence," and other terms. It contains language stating that the directors engaged in conduct that was to the court inexplicable. Yet a reading of the entirety of the court's opinion discloses that the court could not have believed that the defendants had exercised a good faith judgment concerning management of the company. The court notes that unauthorized payments had been made to the defendants and never repaid and that "a pattern of self-enrichment by the managing defendants" appeared to have existed.[48] Moreover,

---

[47] 224 A.2d 634 (Pa. 1966).

[48] *Shelheimer v. Maganese Corporation*, supra n. 47, 645.

since the court implies that the exemption to the Securities Act of 1933 was not validly taken, there may have been available a right to rescission under that Act. Indeed, the whole pattern of facts as recounted by the court has the flavor of a misrepresentation. Thus the Supreme Court, in confirming the directors' liability for the loss of the corporation's capital, recounted that

> "Defendants" actions in respect of the Colwyn plant were not the result of errors in judgment or a calculated business risk, nor can such actions be classified as mere negligence. . . . [T]he pouring of Manganese's funds into [the unsuitable Paterson plant] defies explanation; . . . The chancellor found . . . and the record, in our view, fully supports such findings, that [defendants' conduct of the business] *creates a reasonable inference of wilful misconduct and a pattern of self-enrichment by the managing defendants to the prejudice [of the corporation] and militates against their good faith and fair dealing.*[49] (Emphasis added).

Shelheimer is an important precedent for those who wish to support the idea that liability for a corporate loss can properly be imposed upon a disinterested corporate director if, in the judgment of some later judicial body, a hypothetical reasonable person would have decided differently and would have thus avoided the loss. It is weak support for any such claim, however, since it involved facts plainly sufficient to nullify any claim that the defendants might have made that they were disinterested and acting in good faith pursuit of duty.

II. Evolution in Delaware Law and Statutory Response

The long history that was inconsistent with courts directly imposing liability on corporate directors for violation of the objective standard of care was interrupted by the decision of the Delaware Supreme Court in *Smith v. Van Gorkom*. The legal profession had not read the portents of change that started occasionally appearing in Delaware corporate law opinions in the early 1980s.[50] The world was thoroughly shocked *by Smith v. Van Gorkom*,[51] a case in which the defendants were disinterested corporate directors. They had attended meetings and were experienced businessmen. They had approved a merger (subject to shareholder approval) which did not appear even in retrospect to be a particularly poor deal. Nevertheless they were found to have been negligent in the performance of their duties and subject to possible liability. Of course, reasonable attention had always been thought to be a part of the good faith performance of the director's role; what was new in *Smith* was the apparent willingness of the court, in the

---

[49] 423 Pa. 563, 584; *Shelheimer v. Maganese Corporation*, supra n. 47, 646.

[50] See *Aronson v. Lewis* 473 A.2d 805 (Del. Supr. 1984).

[51] *Smith v. Van Gorkom*, supra n. 9.

context of a damage claim, to second-guess the "reasonableness" of the steps directors took to be informed.[52]

In retrospect, *Smith* can be best rationalized not as a standard duty of care case, but as the first case in which the Delaware Supreme Court began to work out its new takeover jurisprudence.[53] The interpretive key is the later *Unocal* case.[54] There the Delaware Supreme Court noted that corporate directors are not entirely disinterested when the transaction under consideration involves a change in corporate control, that indeed in such circumstances directors, who are assumed naturally enough to personally prefer to retain their office, suffer from an inevitable, if generalized, conflict of interest. Thus in such situations it became clear that special rules of judicial review, not the business judgment rule that applied to "run of the mill" business questions and problems, would be utilized.

Smith represented the high-water mark for the "objective" duty of care as an enforceable obligation, but it lasted, in its full effect, hardly longer than the phases of the moon. Almost immediately the Delaware legislature enacted a statute permitting Delaware corporations to place into their corporate charters provisions waiving corporate damage claims against directors except those that involved a breach of loyalty.[55] Similar statutes are now widely adopted and most public corporations have so amended their charters. Thus the notable novelty introduced in U.S. corporate governance by *Smith v. Van Gorkom* has been largely contained within the evolving takeover field,[56] where the prevalence of injunctions rather than damage actions may, in all events, make the efficiency-impeding effects of enforcement of an "objective" standard of care less significant.

---

[52] *Smith v. Van Gorkom*, supra n. 9.

[53] Macey, Jonathan R. and Geoffrey P. Miller *'Trans Union* Reconsidered' 98 *Yale L.J.* 127 (1988).

[54] *Unocal Corp. v. Mesa Petroleum Co.* 493 A.2d 946 (1985).

[55] See 8 Del. Code § 102(b)(7); *Resolution Trust Corp. v. City Fed Fin. Corp.* 57 F.3d 1231, 1239 (3d Cir. 1995).

[56] *QVC Network, Inc. v. Paramount Communications, Inc.*, supra n. 10. In those cases, too, I would offer—but not explore here—the hypothesis that the gist of the motivation for the decision is a judicial interpretation of the motivation of the directors. That is, where the court interprets the facts as indicating that the board is trying to favor one deal over the other for reasons that are inexplicable except on the ground of personal interest or favor (e.g., *QVC*), it will be inclined to intervene, but where discrimination appears to be a good faith business judgment the court will respect it.

III. ALI Principles of Corporate Governance Approach:
Developments in Director Liability

The legal doctrine employed by courts when they are required to evaluate the potential liability of a corporate director to the corporation for damages allegedly sustained as a result of the director's lack of due care or attention is referred to in U.S. law as the business judgment rule. Over the last several decades this "rule" has become an increasingly prominent feature of U.S. corporation law, at least measured by the frequency with which it is discussed in the reported cases.[57] Formulation of a statement of this rule is, however, quite problematic, as the various formulations employed are neither consistent with each other nor clear. What is problematic is both the precise relationship between the director's duty of care and the business judgment rule and the nature of the business judgment rule itself.

The American Law Institute addressed this subject in Section 4.01(c) of its *Principles of Corporate Governance*. The ALI recognized the functional role of the business judgment rule: to establish a modified test for liability for alleged violations of the duty of care, which modified test would, where applicable, establish non-liability. The central condition for application of this modified test—and this is completely non-controversial—is that the director is financially disinterested in the transaction the authorization of which led to the corporate loss.[58] In addition, the ALI project included two other conditions: one a "rationality" requirement, and the second a version of the "good faith" requirement I find in the reported cases. The terms of the ALI proposal is in relevant part as follows:

(c) A director or officer who makes a business judgment in good faith fulfills the duty under this Section if the director or officer:

(1) is not interested [§ 1.23] in the subject of the business judgment;

(2) is informed with respect to the subject of the business judgment to the extent the director or officer reasonably believes to be appropriate under the circumstances; and

(3) rationally believes that the business judgment is in the best interests of the corporation.

---

[57] The place of this concept in the analysis of corporate law is growing at an impressive rate. If one searches for "business judgment rule" in all American databases for each year over the last fifty years one finds a remarkable pattern. Without reproducing the results, the point is made by saying that for each decade starting with 1943, the results are as follows: 16 reported opinions (1943-52); 25 reported opinions (1953-62); 28 opinions (1963-72); 156 opinions (1973-82); 620 opinions (1983-92). The growth continues. In the 18 months following the close of 1992, 149 opinions were published that invoked this term.

[58] What constitutes financial disinterest, however—that is, the test that determines whether it is present—is the subject of some disagreement in the cases. Some cases hold that any financial interest will disqualify a director from application of the business judgment rule, while others hold that only a material financial interest adverse to the corporation will do so.

Thus, under Subsection (c)(2), a court may determine *ex post* if a corporate director "who makes a business judgment in good faith" was reasonable in believing he was appropriately informed. In this way the ALI re-inserts the objective third-party standard into the liability rule for duty of care violations. More pointedly, the quoted section would authorize a court, after the fact, to make a judgment of whether a good faith belief that the transaction was in the best interest of the corporation was, in its view, "rational." The introduction of a "rationality" standard—assuming as I believe is correct that "rationality" is a meaningful different standard than "reasonableness"—certainly reduces the effectiveness of the business judgment rule to protect corporate directors from second-guessing by judges or juries. It will thus have a tendency to increase the risk of *ex post* determinations of personal liability that disinterested directors face.

While the ALI formulation impedes the optimal acceptance of risk, it is not obvious that such loss in efficiency is not offset by efficiency gains that this rule arguably makes possible from the greater incentive to invest in information that it provides. Here, as often, law is formulated in part on intuitions or "practical reason."

IV. Superiority of the Traditional, Subjective Approach from a Moral Point of View

The formulation of the business judgment rule which I advance is more consistent with the holdings of the body of Anglo-American corporation law over the last century or more, than is an approach that directly enforces the standards of care reflected in an objective, "reasonable person" standard. It is possibly more efficient as well since it will, at the margin, render directors more willing to rationally accept business risk on behalf of the corporation. Finally, I suggest that it is a morally more attractive rule. Indeed, one wonders on what moral basis shareholders might attack a *good faith* business decision of a director as "unreasonable" or "irrational". Where a director *in fact exercises a good faith effort to be informed and to exercise appropriate judgment,* he or she should be deemed to satisfy fully the duty of attention. If the shareholders thought themselves entitled to some other quality of judgment than such a director produces in the good faith exercise of the powers of office, then, as more than one case holds, the shareholders should have elected other directors. Directors are not professionals like doctors or engineers who implicitly warrant the quality of their judgment in some special area of human endeavor. Judge Learned Hand made the point rather better than can I. In speaking of the passive director-defendant Mr. Andrews in *Barnes v. Andrews,* Judge Hand said:

> True, he was not very suited by experience for the job he had undertaken, but I cannot hold him on that account. After all it is the same corporation that chose him that now

seeks to charge him.... Directors are not specialists like lawyers or doctors.... They are the general advisors of the business and if they faithfully give such ability as they have to their charge, it would not be lawful to hold them liable. Must a director guarantee that his judgment is good? Can a shareholder call him to account for deficiencies that their votes assured him did not disqualify him for his office? While he may not have been the Cromwell for that Civil War, Andrews did not engage to play any such role.[59]

Given the development of Anglo-American director's liability for corporate losses, it can be said with some confidence that while a director may be thought implicitly to warrant his good faith attempt to advance corporate interests, he does not warrant the results or, of course, the contents of any decision. Thus, from results or from the contents of any decision—including the decision to decide at any given point in time—one may not fairly create a liability.

D. U.S. Corporation Law as a Regulator of Rational, Moral Persons

Whether one accepts the formulation of the business judgment rule that I contend is the correct one, or one accepts the ALI formulation, or another, the central mystery of this body of doctrine remains the same: Why does the law announce a standard of care for corporate directors and then impose a different rule in order to determine whether liability can be created? Why so much indirection? If there is utility in holding independent directors liable for corporate losses on some standard other than an objective "reasonable person" standard, why does the U.S. law not simply modify the *articulated standard of conduct* for corporate officers and directors so that that standard is substantively the same as that reflected in the business judgment rule? In that way the law would at least announce and apply consistent standards! There is no standard answer to why this disjunction exists.

I suggest two possible answers to the question of why this disjunction exists. First, there is today considerable unclarity about the relationship between the duty of care and the standard of judicial review for violations of it. This unclarity offers the possibility that the legal system may extract some of the benefits of encouraging director attentiveness, while avoiding the worst elements of the efficiency costs that actually imposing liability on directors would entail. That is, the *ex post* nature of fiduciary duties generally, including the duty of care, should constrain opportunistic behavior to some extent. The special ambiguity of the duty of care/business judgment dichotomy may have a special efficiency effect: it may confuse the rationally calculating opportunist ("Can I be sure I'll be safe if I am passive and unengaged?").

A second and more interesting account of the efficiency of this dichotomy between the standard of conduct for corporate directors and the standard of

[59] 208 Fed. 614, 618 (S.D.N.Y. 1924).

judicial review would focus on a posited difference between *the law as a utilitarian system of sanctions* designed to deter unwanted conduct and *the law as an expression of community ideals* designed to inspire solidarity around certain values. It would see the duty of care as essentially aspirational: informing well-intentioned persons of what they should be doing in a most general way ("Try to be efficient in acquiring information").

The great American jurist Oliver Wendell Holmes said that he was not much concerned about abstract conceptions of "law"; he thought of the law as a "bad man" would: what sanction may be applied to contemplated conduct and what is the probability of its being applied.[60] For one with this stark utilitarian perspective, the standard of conduct for corporate directors would conflate into the liability standard or the standard of judicial review, for it is only with the standard of review that the person who is solely concerned to avoid a hurtful legal sanction or achieve a helpful legal judgment should be concerned. But if there are persons *who obey law for reasons not fully accounted for by the utilitarian calculus that Holmes projected*, persons who seek to achieve reinforcement of their own sense of moral worth through willing acceptance of authoritative rules of behavior (including but not limited to legal rules), then the presence of a rule of conduct that is not fully enforced may have some effect upon behavior. There almost certainly are such people. Indeed, to a greater or lesser extent we all are such people.[61] Such persons are, of course, not immune to the rational calculation of costs and benefits. But often the view that such persons take of themselves and that they hope their neighbors take of them, as moral beings, will count, perhaps heavily if non-quantifiably, in such intuitive calculations as they may perform.

Thus, one answer to the question of why the standard of care matters at all if, in practice, the "business judgment rule" "punishes" only bad faith (or under the ALI formulation "irrational") director action, is the observation that humans are moral beings. Human actors *are* opportunistic, of course. They can be counted upon over time to tend to exploit opportunities for personal gain presented by

[60] Holmes, Oliver Wendell 'The Path of the Law' in: Holmes, Oliver Wendell (ed.) *Collected Legal Papers* 167, 169-79 (New York 1920).

[61] See Yezer, Anthony M., Robert S. Goldfarb, and Paul J. Poppen 'Does Studying Economics Discourage Cooperation?' *Journal of Economic Perspectives* 10/1 (1996) 177 (data suggest to authors that studying economics affects degree of cooperative behavior that students pursue). In fact, during my term of judicial office, once or twice a year I accepted an invitation to speak at a meeting of corporate directors or senior officers about the responsibilities of a corporate director. I rarely mentioned the business judgment rule, but thoroughly announced the duty of corporate directors to exercise reasonable care. In such talks I typically refer not only to legal duties, but to the moral responsibility that their office confers on directors for the welfare of the community. Directors are exhorted to "do the right thing." I am not completely naive as to the utility of such talks, but I do suppose that there is some margin within which the conduct of real persons may be affected by them or other admonitions from legitimated sources.

social structures within which they find themselves. Risks of losses that such actions may occasion (for example, the legal system's extraction of damages from a "wrongdoer") do probably on average affect exploitation of such opportunities. But human actors are not only opportunistic, they are also members of *moral communities* with allegiances to *moral codes.* Conforming our conduct to such codes, and being perceived as doing so, may be important to us. While these tendencies to consider social solidarities in making decisions may be modeled in a utilitarian calculus, in real life its constituent values are deeply psychological. Therefore, it is logically possible for the exploitation of *ex ante* opportunities that transfer wealth to corporate directors on average to be reduced because an authoritative standard of "right action" is announced, even if there is no enforcement mechanism that will sanction violation of the standard with a monetary penalty.

Thus, the standard of reasonable care for corporate directors would not (does not) collapse in practice into the the liability standard (the business judgment rule). Rational moral beings may and probably do pay some attention to a duty to be reasonably informed and attentive because it is announced as "the right thing to do," despite the practical fact that a damage remedy is unavailable unless there is evidence of "bad faith."[62]

But if one were to find this explanation of the disjunction between the duty of care and the standard of its judicial review plausible, it would still not explain why the disjunction between a standard of conduct and a standard of review sustains itself in corporation law.[63] There are, no doubt, persons in every area of human activity who would be inclined to some greater or lesser extent than others to cleave to an authoritative standard of conduct even in the face of a less demanding standard of review. But I suggest that corporation law provides an especially hospitable environment for the survival of such a disjunction. First I note that we do find this distinction between conduct rules and decisions rules in other areas of law. Consider, for example, the defense of duress in a criminal prosecution. It involves a similar disjunction.[64] A second reason we find this disjunction in corporation law may be that corporate law deals with a subject matter that can more easily sustain this technicality than might an area of more intense concern to the polity. Any such disjunction—to the extent it is recognized—exists as a small embarrassment to the system of law, because it implicitly acknowledges the existence of non-enforced legal duties. The social cost of this disjunction could mean that it would subsist only in areas of law that are not

---

[62] And not even then under most modern corporate charters. See supra n. 59.

[63] E.g., Eisenberg, Melvin A. 'The Divergence of Standards of Conduct and Standards of Review in Corporate Law' 62 *Fordham L. Rev.* 437 (1993).

[64] See Dan-Cohen, Meir 'Decision Rules and Conduct Rules: On Acoustic Separation in Criminal Law' 97 *Harv. L. Rev.* 625 (1984).

open to frequent citizen entanglement, that do not treat interests that are regarded as nearly sacred (e.g., speech, intimate human relations), and that are bathed regularly in the protective lotion of arcane doctrine. All of these conditions seem true with respect to rules concerning liability of corporate officers and directors for breaches of care. Finally, and most importantly for this paper, the pursuit of reasonable efficiency dictates that some means be evolved that offer the possibility of optimizing the two cross-cutting efficiency effects of the duty of care. The equivocal duty of care/business judgment rule dichotomy is a mechanism that makes possible an *ex post* superintendence of director attention and thus permits some trade-off between these effects to occur.

Discussion Report

ANDREA PEDDINGHAUS*

The results of *Black's* studies were discussed intensively. As one participant expressed, there is a strong intuition in favor of *independent directors*. Thus, there was a consensus that the question might not be whether there should be independent directors at all, but whether there should be a majority of independent directors. It was pointed out again that there is some evidence that inside directors serve certain functions better than independent directors. Therefore, the tendency toward super-majority boards seems alarming. The suggestion was made to differentiate between the voting rights of independent directors and inside directors in correlation with specific tasks that the board must fulfill. Thus, for example, independent directors would have the right to fire the CEO, whereas inside directors would be in charge of electing a new one. Although this idea was appreciated, as a matter of fact almost all American boards tend towards the same type.

The results of *Black's* paper concerning the differing negative performance in the period of 1983 to 1990 on the one hand and the period from 1991 to 1995 on the other hand were questioned. An American participant remarked that the results for independent directors in the retrospective period (1983-1990) could also be interpreted the other way around: weakly performing companies could have increased the number of independent directors on their boards. The need for a follow-up study to clarify these points was accepted.

As to the *size of the German supervisory boards*, the generally accepted critique of their being too big to work efficiently was questioned by an American participant. There was agreement that empirical research on the relation between board size and performance is lacking; however, a German professional confirmed the thesis by his own experiences as a member of supervisory boards of various sizes.

Another central topic of debate was the role of *committees*, which are important in Germany even though less so than in some other countries. One explanation relied on the thesis that the number of supervisory board members is too high. Consequently, the delegation of tasks to committees is appropriate. However, it was stressed that in many cases this practice is against the law. If there is a mandatory supervisory board, the law may prohibit the delegation of responsibility to other organs. Given the practical importance of committee work, the

---

* The last paragraph was written by Brigitte Haar.

fact that some members of the supervisory board often do not participate in any of the committees might lead to problems.

American participants questioned the *role of co-determination in committees.* According to the German panel members, the role of co-determination in committees is traditionally low. One reason can be found in the unwillingness of the shareholders' representatives to convey information to the employee members. However, this might change in the future. A recent High Court decision held that in corporations with mandatory co-determination on the enterprise level, the employees must also be represented adequately in the committees, at least in the most important ones. This decision was criticized by American participants as undermining the market mechanisms of corporate governance. If the market leads to a corporate governance model with committees working with reduced or with an absence of employee participation, this legal decision seems to be an inappropriate answer.

A German contributor drew a parallel to those CEO decisions which must be approved by the supervisory board. Although neither the supervisory board nor the committees are allowed to intervene in day-to-day management, German corporate law empowers the supervisory board (or the bylaws) to subject certain management decisions to the condition of approval by the supervisory board (§ 111 AktG). Therefore, a proposal was made to investigate whether the number of such decisions declined after the introduction of co-determination, and whether this number differs in corporations with employee representation on the supervisory board.

According to a German professional, the performance of employee representatives in committees differs. While they tend to perform well in executive committees where they can contribute knowledge from an operational business perspective, in auditing committees they are in most cases less useful due to their lack of knowledge concerning this subject.

The correlation between the professional *qualification* and the performance of board members became a separate topic of the discussion. Various German participants called into question whether the professional qualification of board members is the crucial point for the lack of board performance. Especially with respect to employee representatives, as mentioned before, one should be careful with generalizations. Many employee representatives are trained by the unions. Also, some of the less educated ones perform very well as board members. Taking this into account, the need for a proof of the qualification of board members was questioned. In addition, it was doubted whether a proof of qualification is a realistic option. The problem of how such a proof should be implemented and who should control it would first have to be solved. The idea of establishing a new institution to assure the professional qualification of the board member (e.g., "Amt für die Prüfung von Aufsichtsratsmitgliedern") was generally rejected.

A main part of the discussion was devoted to the question of whether *generally accepted principles of monitoring* would improve the monitoring of the supervisory board. There was consensus that a precondition is the improvement of measuring the performance of the management. Further discussion developed around the use of a comparison with the performance of other companies from the same branch as a firm performance measure. As an objective measure, the stock price performance was mentioned. While this is a common approach in the U.S., it was doubted whether the share prices in Germany reflect the real situation of the company. As an alternative, a German economist suggested the coverage of capital costs as a decisive factor. As an illustration, he mentioned that from 1978 through 1985, 40 to 50% of the firms did not earn their costs of capital. Arguing against the need for a measure of objective performance, one participant drew attention to the network which assures that supervisory boards work professionally. Because supervisory board members are represented in supervisory boards and sometimes also in management boards of different firms, they have adequate information and insights into standards of management board performance. Moreover, in general they are able to measure their firm's performance by comparison with competitors. In addition, the danger was mentioned that generally accepted rules might lead to negligence as board members begin to rely on the principles and feel no more responsibility after basic compliance with the rules. Some German participants favored the idea of leaving the development of monitoring standards to the courts. The existing lack of guidelines from the courts is due to a lack of cases, and cases do not come up because it is difficult for shareholders under German law to sue the supervisory board. Hence, the role of shareholders in this respect should be strengthened.

An American participant questioned the *normative goal of the supervisory board*. In its present form the board cannot be expected to constantly monitor the management; hence, a focus on the task of crisis intervention was suggested. A controversial discussion followed this statement. While recognizing the importance of crisis intervention, German participants reiterated the role of monitoring and stressed the advisory function, the latter being of paramount importance for smaller and medium-sized companies.

The main problem of reducing the function of the supervisory board to *crisis management* was held to be that this would be too late as a time for intervention. An alternative suggestion for the supervisory board to take on the duty of intervention during the initial development of a crisis, before it actually occurs, was questioned by a German professional. In his opinion, experience has shown that the supervisory board is often not in a position to prevent a crisis if the causes of the problem date back 10 to 15 years before the actual crisis. As an example, he cited strategic flaws in the steel or shipyard industry. However, in times of crisis the tasks of the board do increase.

It became clear that there are many different definitions of "crisis". As reported in the U.S., a sudden fall in stock price would fit into the definition; insolvency, on the other hand, would be a less common measure in the U.S. German participants stressed that insolvency would not be a proper element of the definition anyway, because at that time it is already too late for the supervisory board to react. Share prices, on the other hand, often fail to give the right signal because of the common practice of creative accounting.

A German participant stressed the factual importance of the crisis intervention function of the supervisory board in Germany. On the one hand, it is not unusual for management boards to be fired because of an imminent crisis. This is also indicated by the development of CEO insurance. Supervisory boards, on the other hand, are very defensive and thus generally remain in place. This situation was repeatedly labelled as unsatisfactory. The behavior of bank representatives in supervisory boards in crisis situations was mentioned as a point of further investigation.

The business judgment rule was mentioned as an important point in the debate about the *liability* of the boards. However, a differentiation must be made between stock corporations (*AG*) and limited liability companies (*GmbH*). For the latter there is much more case law.

Compensation and its relevance for improving board performance was another point of discussion. One thesis mentioned was that it does not seem rational to assume that board members would perform better without some financial incentive. In Germany, however, compensation tied to performance of the corporation is rather uncommon. This statement is subject to some exemptions, as was illustrated by German participants. There are in fact different compensation models, some of which are performance oriented. For example, there is basic compensation combined with a bonus system linked either to personal performance or frequency of board meeting attendance. Under another scheme, compensation is tied to dividends. A German economist criticized the lack of a significant relationship between development of stock return and remuneration of the supervisory board members. A German professional who himself sits in many supervisory boards gave an example from one of the most important German stock companies, where in years of losses the remuneration of supervisory board members increased. For dividend-oriented compensation this lack of relationship also holds true as the correlation between dividends and stock price development in Germany is rather low. An American participant questioned whether or not available data show that compensation in the form of stock ownership leads to better board performance.

In the discussion of his contribution, *Allen* was skeptical about the efficiency idea that the United States is enamored with. In the discussion, the view was expressed that norms were observed not out of considerations of revelation of information and value, but in order to achieve norm compliance. According to the bad man theory of law, the "bad man . . . cares nothing for an ethical rule which is believed and practised by his neighbors" but only wishes ". . . to avoid an encounter with the public force . . ."[1] *Allen* did not accept Justice Holmes's generalized idea of a bad man's behavior. Overdeterring directors by overly strict rules of behavior might be counterproductive. According to *Allen*, people are assumed to be affected in their behavior by norms not simply because they are opportunistic, but also because they want to be looked at as good neighbors and they want to live in solidarity with others.

---

[1] Holmes, Oliver W. 'The Path of the Law' 10 *Harv. L. Rev.* 457, 459 (1897).

Chapter 5: Labor Co-Determination and Labor Markets

Economics of Labor Co-Determination in View of Corporate Governance

ELMAR GERUM, Marburg, and HELMUT WAGNER, Hagen

The article examines the economic effects of co-determination (by supervisory boards) with regard to theoretical and empirical aspects. We show theoretically that co-determination can be an efficiency-increasing institution in a market-based economy. An empirical check of the economic effects of German co-determination fails because of the non-existence of large companies without co-determination. Co-determination can also be found in corporate governance systems in other European countries. In the EC a harmonization of co-determination on the corporate level has not yet been achieved. The reason is the specific historical development of industrial relations in Europe. Instead of an integration through harmonization, the European Commission has good reason to favor system competition.

Contents

A. Introduction[1]

The question of co-determination for employees can be regarded under purely economic efficiency aspects as an element of corporate governance. However, co-determination can also be examined under socio-political-economic aspects. The opinion may be held that in its essentials, co-determination is concerned with ethical questions such as social justice and human dignity at work, or, put

---

[1] Cf. also the sections dealing with employees and co-determination respectively in the comparative contributions of Kanda, Prigge, and Wymeersch in Ch. 12 of this volume.

more generally, with industrial civil rights or industrial democracy. This latter point of view has dominated previous research into co-determination, particularly in Europe and especially in Germany. This is reflected in the relevant empirical studies. These focus in the main on the distribution of power and influence in a company or its committees and not so much on economic efficiency. Only in the last twenty years have analyses of the economic efficiency of co-determination come more to the foreground, and most of them have been purely theoretical. We will focus on these analyses, which stem mainly from the English-speaking world, in Part B of this article. In Part C we will be examining the empirical studies of the economic effects of co-determination (by supervisory boards). In Part D, co-determination and its future in a European context will be examined and discussed, because national leeway will be reduced in the course of the further Europeanizing of the law. Finally, in Part E, an attempt will be made to explain the heterogeneity of attitudes to co-determination, and also the reversal of the originally planned convergence of co-determination concepts within the European Community.

B. Economic Theory and Co-Determination

In the more recent economic discussions on co-determination, work from neo-institutional economics dominates. In addition, studies from the labor market theory and from the organization theory and business strategy can also be used fruitfully in the discussion on co-determination.

I. Co-Determination in the Light of Neo-Institutional Economics

1. Property Rights and Co-Determination

Alchian/Demsetz (1972) reconstructed the company and its corporate governance as a system of constantly dissolvable individual contracts (contractual model of the firm).

The reason for these contracts lies in the advantages of team production—in other words specialization—and the resulting synergy effects. The problem here is determining the marginal product and thus the rewards for individual team members, which support the tendency to shirk in the team. Insofar it is necessary to have working behavior monitored by a specialist. To make sure that this person does not shirk as well, he is rewarded with the residual income. Along with the right to appropriate this income, the holder of the controlling position must also have the unqualified right to terminate employment and to amend and conclude contracts in order for him to be able to carry out his coordination function in the team efficiently. This central agent is referred to as the "firm's owner and the employer". Specifying and concentrating property rights in the hands of the owner is also deemed to be allocation-efficient. The classical capitalist firm is therefore always the reference case for the analysis of corporate governance.

Compared with this ideal case, co-determination leads to the attenuation of property rights, because the right of co-ordination is divided between the shareholders and representatives of the workforce. This type of redistribution of property rights must not necessarily lead to inefficiency of allocation. However, the introduction of statutory co-determination speaks for this inefficiency. The argument runs that if it was in the mutual interests of the owners of capital and the workers, it would take place voluntarily, or would have long since taken place. In other words, according to the property rights theory, voluntarily granted rights of co-determination lead to the presumption of efficiency; in the case of statutory rules (compulsion), the opposite may be assumed (for a criticism of this, cf. Section B.II. below).

However, this position has experienced a differentiation through the contrast between firm-specific and non-specific resources and services (Alchian 1984). The owners of specific resources do not tend to shirk because their input depends on use in a defined firm and the success of this firm. For this reason there is not only no cause for these team members to shirk, but they must especially also have an original interest in the firm's success. The management is therefore made up of those who own the firm-specific means of production.

The consequence of this construction is co-determination for employees in the corporate board, unless the attitude is taken that the knowledge, skills, and capabilities of employees are generally non-firm-specific. Here, Alchian is strangely contradictory, because on the one hand he lists some examples of firm-specific employee investments, but on the other hand describes co-determination as a "wealth confiscation scheme" (Gerum 1988: 26).

The firm-specific character of human resources also leads Furubotn/Wiggins (1984) under specific conditions to plead in favor of co-determination for employees. Their argument states that where human resources take on a firm-specific character during a contract of employment, this opens up to the employer—given the familiar lesser degree of specification with long-term contracts of employment—the opportunity of post-contractual opportunism, in that he appropriates wholly or partly the quasi rents of specialized human capital investments. The probability of the employer's loss of reputation is assessed as being slight, because of the familiar asymmetry of information. This growth in risk on the employee side requires protection and therefore justifies co-determination. However, the specific human capital investments have to be financed wholly or partly by the employees themselves. In spite of this, co-determination is still appropriate even where, with employer financing, these investments would lead to an increase in risks on the employee side.

However, this reason for co-determination is questioned (Michaelis/Picot 1987: 112). The argument runs that risk for firm-specific capital assets and human resources is not really equal. In fact, there would often be analogous employment opportunities for employee skills with the competition. In addition, the problem of the specific nature of human capital is less significant the simpler and less problematic the processes of imitation in an economy are. It is exactly with administrators and managers that general skills are of considerable significance, and on the whole this is why competition policy is of central importance for this set of problems. However, in relation to capital assets, the question must be asked whether and to what extent "specialized assets" would be formed in companies in the same sector given the appropriate imitation processes (Gerum 1989: 51). In other words, the risk position of capital assets and human capital does not seem to be so dissimilar that it can be used to reject co-determination (in general). Independently of this, a statutory protection of employee investments continues not to appear logical to the property rights theory, because this means that insufficient differentiation between firm-specific and non-firm-specific human resources can be made on an individual company basis.

2.   Co-Determination as a Reduction in Transaction Costs?

According to Coase (1937) and Williamson (1975), the organization of economic activities depends primarily on the transaction costs involved. Under competitive conditions, the institutional arrangement with the lowest transaction costs will prevail, or rather has to be the objective for shaping the organization. Whether and to what extent transaction costs are generated depends basically on the opportunistic behavior of individuals, the intensity of the competition, the complexity and uncertainty of the decision situation, and the limited information-processing capacity of the individuals involved.

Prima facie, statutory co-determination is inefficient for the transaction costs theory as well, because it restricts freedom of contract and therefore obstructs the search for the most favorable organization form regarding costs in each respective case. In addition, distribution of disposal rights to employees is dysfunctional because there is a wide gap between the planning horizon and the willingness of shareholders and employees to take risk in investment and financing decisions (von Weizsäcker 1984: 146 et seq.). There is a danger that for opportunistic considerations, employees will aim for a short-term utility maximization. This leads to sub-optimum results, because the required long-term-oriented allocation decisions by the risk capital owners are obstructed or even prevented. In addition, the costs of coordination would increase, not only in the decision-making phase, but also in the implementation phase under co-determination conditions.

Cost advantages of statutory internalization of employee interests in operating and entrepreneurial decision-making processes, however, are put forward as arguments against the inefficiency of co-determination based on the economics of transaction costs (Brinkmann/Kübler 1981: 685 et seq.). These advantages are in the range of current transaction costs and, in particular, in the establishment of the co-determination institutions themselves. Compared with solutions based on collective agreement or even with the arrangement of individual regulations, statutory co-determination saves negotiations running and repeating at very different levels. These negotiations are very cost-intensive because they are not just a matter of the recognition of co-determination rights, but are at the same time concerned with their use in individual cases. It is also said that in these negotiations, the participants tend to produce conflicts in other negotiation fields for "strategic reasons". These behavioral patterns in fact endanger the productivity of economic systems with a high division of labor, which are very susceptible to sectional disturbances. The usefulness of statutorily controlled co-determination can therefore be explained with the logic of the transaction costs approach.

These divergent assessments of co-determination are based as well on the deficient operationalizing of and lack of a closer definition for the transaction costs. Insofar, a broad scope of discretion opens up for the arguments both ex ante and ex post where there is a comparison of the efficiency of capitalist corporate governance and with co-determination.[2]

3. Co-Determination as a Principal-Agent Problem

The agency theory links up with the principal-agent relationships created in the contractual model for the firm. It analyzes the problems of incentives and controls based on the asymmetrical distribution of information in the principal-agent relationship. The most efficient institutional arrangement is the one with the lowest agency costs. Jensen/Meckling (1976) differentiate here between (1) monitoring costs for the principal, (2) the bonding costs which accrue to the agent through controls and self-engagement, and (3) the residual loss arising in contrast to the case of ideal cooperation.

In the language of the agency theory, a contract of employment is a principal-agent relationship. As the principal, the employer has to pay control costs, because he has to reckon with all forms of withholding of performance and

---

[2] A further, more fundamental problem is included in the paradigm of the transaction cost approach: "Corporate governance follows costs." The opposite is correct: the paradigm has to be turned around. What are supposed to be costs and benefits of economic action are the result of a decision about corporate governance. Corporate governance determines the objective function of the firm and therewith the relevant cost and benefit categories. It prevails: "Costs follow corporate governance."; Gerum/Steinmann (1984: 97).

information by employees. On the other hand, as agents, the employees must reckon with post-contractual opportunism on the part of the employer arising from the specific structure of long-term contracts of employment. The search is therefore for the institutional arrangement with the lowest welfare losses.

Co-determination can make a positive contribution here in many ways. An improvement in the supply of information to workers' representatives in decision-making committees can restrict the opportunities for the employer side to post-contractual opportunism. At the same time, it increases the readiness of employees to participate in firm-specific investments. The improved supply of information for employees is accompanied by the risk for the principal of being caught in opportunist behavior and therefore losing face. The tendency towards this type of behavior will therefore be reduced. In addition, co-determination is suitable for increasing coordination efficiency by reducing the creation of expectation errors (Furubotn/Wiggins 1984: 176 et seq.).

However, according to neo-institutional economics, these positive effects of co-determination do not provide grounds for accepting co-determination as the right to take part in making decisions. Labor market immobility with the corresponding misallocation of resources, or slowing down of technical progress, are deemed to be possible dangers of co-determination. For this reason, only a "strict minority representation on corporate boards" is regarded as being reasonable to restrict a possible loss of steering and control efficiency (Furubotn/Wiggins 1984: 186). A counter-argument might be that the tendency of the agents to shirk and withhold information would disappear if they were able to influence their working conditions. This would then mean that the necessity for and intensity of monitoring would be reduced, and monitoring costs would fall.

II. Key Aspect: Statutory Versus Voluntary Co-Determination

It is interesting that co-determination, insofar as it is institutionalized, has very rarely been privately organized; instead it has usually come into effect as a result of statutes. The conclusion often drawn from this is that co-determination, in contrast to the claims made by its advocates, is not really efficient at all. Jensen/Meckling (1979: 474) express this as follows: "If co-determination is beneficial to both stockholders and labor, why do we need laws which force firms to engage in it? Surely, they would do so voluntarily. The fact that stockholders must be forced by law to accept co-determination is the best evidence we have that they are adversely affected by it".

This argument has been attacked by Levine/Tyson (1990) and Freeman/Lazear (1995), among others. They argue, as do Keynesians with new-classical economists in the field of macroeconomics, that because of the existence of externalities and coordination problems (prisoner's dilemmas), the state may be forced or called upon to prescribe institutional extensions to the private market economy in order to maximize social welfare. It may well be that the total revenue of a firm would be increased by the introduction of co-determination, and all participants may be aware of this. However, uncertainty over the distribution of the larger overall earnings may be so great for both sides because of the changing conditions that there is no incentive for the private introduction of this efficient institution. (To prevent the introduction, it is enough that the uncertainty referred to is too high for one side.) As Levine/Tyson (1990) stress, for a firm which introduces co-determination voluntarily, there is the danger that pressure will grow for erosion of pay differentials and greater protection against dismissals. This is why these firms must be afraid that the introduction of co-determination will mean that they will suffer disadvantages compared to firms without co-determination, namely in the form of "adverse selection" (they will attract the less motivated labor suppliers) and negative externality (their best workers will be poached by firms without co-determination and with less equalized pay structures). This means that no single firm will have an incentive to start the introduction of co-determination. Only if all firms were to introduce co-determination simultaneously would individual firms have an incentive to realize the perceived opportunities for increasing earnings through this institutional innovation. However, because there is no reliable coordination mechanism with regard to the introduction of this type of institution—which does basically increase efficiency—we cannot expect the introduction on a private level. Therefore, if the state is assumed to be oriented towards maximizing social welfare, it is now called upon.[3]

Freeman/Lazear (1995) take the same line. They are convinced that firms' total earnings would increase through the introduction of general co-determination, above all because of a reduction of economic inefficiencies (demands by workers would moderate during tough times), support for new solutions to problems (the exchange of information between management and workers would increase), and an extension of the planning horizon and greater concessions in the workplace on the part of the workers (job security would increase subjectively). Nonetheless, neither employers nor employees have any incentive to introduce co-determination themselves. The main reason given is once again that co-determination not only (as expected) increases total earnings, but it also changes the previous distribution of earnings. There is a danger for both sides that distribution may change to their disadvantage. Employers or the providers of capital fear that the shift of power that accompanies co-determination will reduce

---

[3] The same argument is used by advocates of a "share economy" (profit or revenue sharing), which is also supposed to be socially desirable or superior but privately not introduceable; Wagner (1989, 1998). The most prominent objection to a share economy is, interestingly, that it would only be accepted by the workers or unions if it were combined with co-determination (ibid.). The latter, however, is objected to by the employers and by their associations on the basis of the above arguments.

their share of earnings. For this reason they are not prepared to agree to the optimum level of co-determination for society, above all because of their fear that once co-determination has been introduced privately, it will lead to endogenous expansionary trends and increasingly weaken their distribution position. Therefore, a co-determination platform fixed by law is required to counteract these incentive effects and the accompanying fears.

It may also be argued that the above conclusion drawn by Jensen/Meckling, if it were accurate in the first place, is only valid under the respective institutional framework, in particular political regulations. In other words, other regulatory framework settings also influence the advantageousness and desirability (of certain types) of co-determination.

III. The Coalition Theory and the Resource-Based View of Strategy

The coalition theory provides an alternative approach for co-determination. This theory interprets the firm as a coalition of individuals and interest groups, i.e., of owners of capital, managers, workers, suppliers, customers, tax authorities, and external consultants (Cyert/March 1963). The stakeholder approach also arrives at this type of pluralistic view when it asks about the influence groups relevant for the strategic planning and management process (Ansoff 1965; Freeman 1983). The coalition does not have a joint objective function a priori. This is the result of negotiation processes which serve to compensate conflicting individual and sub-group specific objectives. The objective function is then the expression of the distribution of power between the members of the coalition.

A further explanation and foundation for co-determination for employees in the central decisions of the coalition can be derived from the resource-based view of strategy, which differentiates between tangible/intangible and transferable/non-transferable assets (Barney 1991; Grant 1991; Hall 1993). According to the concept, intangible and non-transferable assets are particularly relevant for achieving competitive advantage and therefore the success of the firm. These resources are, above all, know-how, training specific to the firm, and the implicit knowledge of the employees. The firm experiences sustained competitive advantages if it is successful in binding resources which are difficult to imitate and substitute. This itself demands appropriate chances of influencing things for human resources, such as those provided by a formal system of co-determination.

C. Co-Determination and Efficiency: Some Empirical Findings

The attempt to check empirically the economic effects of co-determination for supervisory boards has to struggle against a whole series of difficulties. In Germany, nearly all large companies are subject to co-determination for their supervisory boards, so that there is almost no way of comparing large companies with co-determination with those without it. On the other hand, a comparison with small companies is a problem because of the significant influence of company size on efficiency. International comparisons are not very helpful either. The objection that other factors of the economic and institutional context may have been more relevant—such as the high average qualifications of the workforce, the economic rationality of the unions, the longer planning horizon used by German managers, or perhaps even the exchange rate—can be raised against all findings on the alleged efficiency or inefficiency of co-determination. Furthermore, the assessment of a national institution such as co-determination also depends on the observer's own value system and his subjective perceptions. Finally, all the relevant studies are of necessity related to the past, and may be doubted to an extent with regard to the present with a reference to possible changes to fundamental competitive relationships. These are probably the reasons why there are few empirical studies on co-determination for supervisory boards. They were carried out in the context of the Co-Determination Act of 1976 and are system-immanent in their focus.

The available studies are related to firm efficiency and are based partly on organization science, such as Witte (1980, 1982), Kirsch/Scholl/Paul (1984), Gerum/Steinmann/Fees (1988), and Bamberg et al. (1987). Other studies, however, orient themselves towards allocation efficiency (in the sense of neo-institutional economics) as a criterion, such as Svejnar (1982), Benelli/Loderer/Lys (1987), Gurdon/Rai (1990), and FitzRoy/Kraft (1993).

Witte's study (1980, 1982) refers to independent industrial corporations covered by the Works Councils Act of 1952 and later to the Co-Determination Act of 1976 for the purposes of comparison. An attempt was made to measure the effects of co-determination using the financial statement and net cash flow as indicators of company success and on the enforcement of workers' interests. The subjective assessments of the works council, board, union officials, and managers of large banks were used to record the realized influence. The findings do not show any dominant influence for co-determination that was actually realized. Logically, therefore, a correlation cannot be verified between the development of a company's success and the degree of the workers' influencing potential. On the other hand, the extension of co-determination in 1976 had a positive effect on the satisfaction of workers' needs. It is also remarkable that Witte, in contrast to his research hypothesis, confirms the enormous significance of formal regulations for co-determination.

The study carried out by Kirsch/Scholl/Paul (1984) is also based on behavioral science. This study concerned companies with various legal forms, sector sizes, and legal dependencies (group members) that fell under the jurisdiction of the Co-Determination Act for the coal, iron, and steel industries, the Co-Determination Act of 1976, and the Works Councils Act of 1952. Here an attempt was made to measure the actual influence of co-determination through a comparison of subjective perceptions of boards and works councils. The efficiency criterion was the company's capacity to act, i.e., on the one hand its decision-making capacity—in other words, the capacity to identify problems, expedite the process of problem solving, and finally come to a decision—and on the other hand the capacity to implement, the target of which is the faithful implementation of the resolutions taken and the acceptance of the measures by those affected. The empirical findings show that a company's capacity to act is guaranteed more in companies with greater co-determination than in those with a weak system, and this holds true in each of the above-mentioned aspects of the capacity to act. This finding is explained by the stable cooperative patterns that have grown up in practical co-determination, and which are based on mutual recognition and regular information. In addition, the significant influence of the statutory foundations of factual distributions of power was once again seen. The influence of the owners of capital, workers, and union representatives in the supervisory board on the whole, and also in individual decisions concerning investment and personnel planning, corresponds to the differences between the Co-Determination Act of 1951 for the coal, iron, and steel industries, the Co-Determination Act of 1976, and the Works Councils Act of 1952.

The study carried out by Gerum/Steinmann/Fees (1988) on the efficiency of supervisory boards with co-determination selected an institutional perspective. To construct a *Realtyp*, exclusively institutional-structural data was collected and evaluated for all stock corporations and limited liability companies subject to the Co-Determination Act of 1976 and stock corporations subject to the Co-Determination Act for the coal, iron, and steel industries, such as articles of associations, ownership relationships, group membership, size characteristics, the relevant trade union, and the degree of union organization. The empirical findings showed clear deficiencies with regard to the functional efficiency of supervisory boards with co-determination. Actual organizational and decision structures offer no guarantee for productive clearing of interests. The main reason for this are the inadequate responsibilities of supervisory boards, but also the counterproductive rules for regulating decision processes created by the owners of capital. It is remarkable that the problems of co-determination in supervisory boards are practically identical with those of supervisory boards in general in the German corporate governance system.

Finally, the examination by Bamberg et al. (1987) is aimed at the mode of operation and efficiency of the Co-Determination Act of 1976 for employee interests. In a combination of institutional-structural data and qualitative case studies, they arrive at the conclusion that although the information of employee representatives in supervisory boards has improved, this has not meant that they have an effective influence on company policy decisions.

The studies discussed here suggest that co-determination has at least not had any negative effects on companies' efficiency.

Similar results were obtained in studies which oriented themselves towards allocation efficiency as a criterion. An early study recording the interplay between co-determination and profitability was made by Svejnar (1982). Svejnar compared the consequences of the Co-Determination Act of 1951 for the coal, iron, and steel industries, the Works Councils Act of 1952, and the Works Councils (*Reform*) Act of 1972 in a cohort study (1950-1976) in 14 different industrial sectors. He found no significant influence of the introduction of or amendment to the co-determination acts on productivity as a determinant of profitability or efficiency. A central criticism of this analysis is that it is based on sectoral data. However, in all the sectors examined there were also companies that were not affected by any of the co-determination acts referred to, and this reduces the probability of valid findings.

Subsequent studies by Benelli/Loderer/Lys (1987) and Gurdon/Rai (1990) on the effects on profitability of co-determination in Germany, which were based on the Co-Determination Act of 1976, used company-related data. However, both studies are also based on simple comparisons of mean values before and after the Co-Determination Act of 1976 without controlling for any other relevant economic and organizational variables. While Benelli/Loderer/Lys were unable to find any relevant effects, contradictory results are found in the Gurdon/Rai study. On the one hand, productivity fell in companies subject to the Co-Determination Act of 1976; on the other hand, their profitability rose. Gurdon/Rai obtained their data (N=63) from a mailing action, which resulted in nearly three-quarters of respondents refusing to reply, so that we cannot speak of a representative sample of German companies. In addition, the sample groups differ greatly in the size of the companies, and this probably leads to a distorting effect on the company comparison. In fact, large companies (N_1=37) subject to the Co-Determination Act of 1976 were compared with smaller companies (N_2=26) subject to the Works Councils Act of 1952 or not subject to any of these co-determination acts.

FitzRoy/Kraft (1993) carried out another study of the effects of co-determination on productivity, costs, and profitability. The database was a sample of 68 large companies subject to the Co-Determination Act of 1976 and 44 smaller stock corporations not subject to the act. Balance-sheet data from the years 1975 and 1983 weres compared with the help of multiple regression analyses. Significant negative productivity and profitability effects were noted in both years in the companies subject to the 1976 act. However, significant (labor) cost effects were not discovered. The main weakness of the analysis by FitzRoy/Kraft, as with Gurdon/Rai (1990), is that in the end small and large stock corporations are compared with one another and significant effects on productivity and profitability of company size differences are neglected. Insofar, our argument above is confirmed, namely that an empirical study of the economic efficiency of German co-determination for supervisory boards encounters great difficulties in practice.

D. Co-Determination and Corporate Governance in Europe

For a complete description of the situation, it is necessary to sum up the status of company co-determination in Europe in the context of corporate governance (Gerum 1998). Since the 1970s, co-determination has become a guiding principle for European corporate governance, and is therefore no longer a purely German specialty. Statutes governing co-determination for employees in supervisory and management boards have been passed in several European countries, for example, the Netherlands in 1971, Denmark in 1973 and 1980, Luxembourg in 1974, or Sweden and Norway in 1976. Even in Great Britain, the 1976 Bullock Committee (1977) recommended co-determination in companies, as did the Rapport Sudreau (1975) in France with its suggestions for a special "co-surveillance". In accordance with the trend towards statutory co-determination in Europe, the EC Commission oriented its proposals towards the German pattern of supervisory board co-determination. The 5th EC Directive of 1972 provided for at least one-third of the seats for employees, and the 1975 proposal for a European stock corporation in the framework of the "three-bench model" provided for exactly one-third of the places for employees. Along with the German representation model, the 5th EC Directive also contained the Netherlands "co-option model" as an option.

As with management structure, this extensive harmonization did not find the expected positive resonance. Once again, the whole range of European social techniques for the participation of employees in company decisions is found today in the drafts from the EC Commission of 1989 and 1991: representation, co-option, independent workers' representatives, and collective agreements. As these variations are supposed to be used not only for supervisory boards but also alternatively for administrative boards, this means that in the end there are no less than eight options. These can be outlined as follows, without going into the legal details:

(1) Supervisory board with co-determination: this German solution was originally favored by the EC Commission and provides for employee representation of between 33% and 50%, whereby if both sides are equally represented the casting vote is to go to the owners' side.

(2) Board with co-determination: on the basis of the difference between executive and non-executive board members, employees are to be entitled to designate between 33% and 50% of the non-executive members. Because of the disposability of the organizational structure in boards it is very difficult to assess the consequences of this rule.

(3) Co-option: co-option on the "Dutch model" means that the supervisory or administrative board voted on by the shareholders' meeting selects its own members. The shareholders' meeting and the employee representatives may only object to the designation of a proposed candidate if there are reasons for doing so. A state arbitration agency then has to decide on the objection. In the Netherlands, this procedure has led in practice to supervisory boards, approximately one-third of whose members are employee representatives.

(4) Independent employee representatives: in this variation, the employee bench is separated completely and placed alongside the supervisory board, which is occupied solely by shareholders, or the administrative board, which consists of shareholders or executive members. This workers' representative board has the same rights to information as the supervisory or administrative boards, but has no decision-making capability. In practice, this rule calls to mind the *Wirtschaftsausschuß* (economic council) of Germany's works constitution. In the discussions on this subject, however, the independent workers' representative body is seen as the so-called "French model" and is also thought of as a possibility for Great Britain.

(5) Collective agreement: under the "Swedish model", a co-determination model for the board or supervisory boards is to be contractually agreed upon in a collective agreement for the company or sector, or at least achieved by means of strikes. The parties to the collective agreement have the choice between the options shown above, but may also create other organizational models for co-determination, at least for the European stock corporation.

(6) The idea from the Commission is that member states may choose between these alternative structures. Under a collective agreement there is even a possibility for each single company to choose one of the options. In sum, harmonization does not exist.

In this muddled situation, the EC Commission attempted at the end of 1995 to provide the discussion with new impulses through a "notification for information and consultation of employees" (EC Commission 1995). This had been preceded in 1994 by the successful publication after 20 years of negotiations of a Directive on European Works Councils (Richtlinie 94/45/EG 1994), which grants employees in transnational companies the right to be informed and consulted in the relevant cross-border situations. Put very briefly and pointedly, the Commission is now aiming for this level of participation to be the common denominator for the whole set of co-determination problems in Europe. The reactions from industry and politicians were predictable. While industrial associations see the right approach here, German trade unions in particular, but also the EC's Economics and Social Committee, reject this concept strictly as a substitute for co-determination on the supervisory board. Consensus cannot be expected in the near future.[4]

E. Convergence or Variety in Europe?

I. Cultural Variety Versus Convergence Induced by Competition

If we want to understand the heterogeneity of attitudes to co-determination and its organization, we have to fall back on the theory of industrial relations. According to this, the attitude to German *Mitbestimmung* (integration, conflict partnership) is characterized predominantly by the specific historical development of industrial relations within a country (Nagels/Sorge 1977). These are oriented alternatively towards two basic strategies: co-determination or countervailing power strategy.

On the one hand, the repression against the labor movement exercised by the state in the 19th century is decisive. The more repressive the actions of the state were, and therefore the more it influenced or was involved in solving industrial conflicts, the earlier there was an institutionalizing of conflict regulation in the form of organs for the representation of interests and therefore a predisposition to co-determination. Further developments depended on the intensity with which co-determination was secured by means of statutory regulations. If this happened relatively early on, and peacefully, as in Germany or the Netherlands, co-determination became the dominant form of the representation of interests. If, however, statutory regulations remained weak, forms of representation of interests developed that were not guaranteed by law, or a re-orientation towards a countervailing power strategy developed. This was the case in France, Belgium, or Italy. In cases in which the state was in general less repressive in the 19th century, the countervailing power strategy developed in the main, and this characterizes industrial relations and the rejection of co-determination right through to the present day in these countries. This applies above all to Great Britain and Switzerland.

The impact of these cultural concepts is not only reflected in the proposal made by the EC Commission. This is shown by empirical surveys of the co-determination potential in German subsidiaries of foreign companies, which are subject to the Co-Determination Act of 1976. According to these, the potential for influence of employees in German companies dominated from the Netherlands is significantly higher than in companies whose parent company is in Great Britain or Switzerland (Gerum/Steinmann/Fees 1988: 137).

We will have to wait and see whether the globalization of markets, which leads to increasing uncertainty with respect to change of environment, will start

---

[4] See, however, the recent expert report 'European Systems of Worker Involvement' (1997).

up learning processes among employers, unions, and politicians in the direction of forms of industrial democracy that are adequate for the problems involved, i.e., which are able to adapt to the respective situations. Convergence through the flexible linking of internal opposition through statutory co-determination and of countervailing power strategy through collective bargaining, such as in Sweden (Gerum/Steinmann 1984), seems at least not implausible.

II. Harmonization Versus System Competition[5]

The deviation from the convergence or harmonization strategy in the co-determination question in the 1980s described in Section D was only one aspect of many parallel developments in Europe. While the EC's integration concept originally aimed at widespread harmonization of regulations in member states, there was a clear reversal of direction in the Community's integration strategy in the 1980s (cf. the European Commission's (1985) White Book). The main reason for this was that integration through harmonization had proved to be infinitely laborious. Harmonization of regulations by the EC was unable to keep pace with the speed with which the number of regulations by member states increased, nor was it possible to bring the different provisions to a common denominator. This is the reason why EC legislation has since then emphasized *competition of systems* as a coordinating mechanism, which is most clearly expressed in the "subsidiarity principle" established in the Maastricht Treaty.[6]

This strategy reversal was accompanied by a fundamental rethinking in the theory of economic policy. In recent years, convergence or harmonization of legal or organizational structures has increasingly been regarded as undesirable. It certainly cannot be denied that harmonization has the effect of reducing certain transaction costs, and therefore also increases efficiency not only in a controlled process of integration, but also in an uncontrolled globalization process. The following reasons are usually put forward in favor of harmonization in order to establish a single market (Ehlermann 1995): the removal of distortions of competition which cause serious costs differences; the protection of "essential interests" which are endangered by the elimination of restrictions on competition; and finally, the elimination of restrictions in the way of the basic freedoms of the single market.

These can, however, be countered by the following arguments (Streit/Mussler 1995): the above reasons for harmonization are considered to be inconclusive.

---

[5] Competition of legislators is subject of Romano's article in Ch. 3 of this volume.

[6] The "subsidiarity principle" states that the European Community may only intervene if the aims of the treaty and the aims of individual measures "cannot be adequately achieved at the level of member states and can therefore be better achieved at Community level because of their range or their effects" (Art. 3b ECT).

Those in favor of competition of systems regard harmonization as a restraint of competition analogous to a cartel, in which third countries are seen as the outsiders. In addition, harmonization as practiced is subject to legal application problems that cause transaction costs. And finally—and this is the main argument—harmonization waives the advantages of system competition.

From the point of view of the classical-evolutionary theory of competition, the advantages of system competition are based on the following "conjectures" (Streit/Mussler 1995):

- System competition is a process that enables institutional innovations to be discovered and checked.
- System competition has a controlling function on the political providers.

The starting point of these assumptions is the constitutional lack of knowledge of all societal agents. Institutions are interpreted as fallible "hypotheses" on the system of human coexistence that have to pass permanent trials (Albert 1986; Mussler/Wohlgemuth 1995). Competing institutional supplies are evaluated by institutional consumers, i.e., by the owners of mobile factors. They provide information on different societal solutions for problems. This is advantageous in that it is to be assumed that the institutional consumers and suppliers are unaware of the most suitable respective solution. Variety of systems or regulations also means system or regulation competition, and is therefore a process for discovering the institutions or regulations that fulfill the desired purpose at the lowest costs (Hayek 1968; Sinn 1992). Exaggerated harmonization would forbid this competition and prevent transaction costs from being lowered. Market integration would be inhibited.

If the possibility of a faulty or unsuitable statutory provision is considered in addition, competition between systems of rules permits a relatively low-risk and low-conflict method of correcting errors, compared with harmonized policies. The controlling effect of competition arises from private agents being able to compare different institutional attempts at solving problems and to sort out inferior ones. There does not necessarily have to be an exchange of the legal system itself, but there may also be, corresponding to the cultural peculiarities, efficient institutional innovations within the prevailing legal system.

System or regulation competition also has a second control function. It consists of system competition imposing restrictions on the room for maneuver of political competitors as institutional suppliers. National governments exposed to system competition are subject to constant control by the owners of mobile factors in that the latter are able to evade the sphere of influence of a government by moving to that of another government. This is also linked to the hope that system or regulation competition can reduce the influence of lobbies to eliminate welfare state incrustations or "institutional sclerosis" (Olson 1982). However, it must be taken into account that international legal uncertainty limits system competition (Wagner 1997).

From these arguments one cannot conclude that harmonization or convergence are never preferable. It would seem that it is to be preferred in cases of cross-border externalities. But the non-existence of privately organized convergence does not imply that it might not be desirable. We have already pointed this out in Section B.II. However, it must be taken into account that variety of regulations such as different co-determination rules reflects a variety of preference and culture on the one hand, and on the other differences in development. As we have shown, different countries have opted for specific institutions and solutions in accordance with their special preferences and cultural peculiarities and on the basis of respective development levels. A forced adaptation to general levels, or the compulsory adoption of outside institutional arrangements, probably has a tendency to cause welfare losses. This is also shown by analyses from development economics (Wagner 1997a).

References

Albert, Hans *Freiheit und Ordnung* (Tübingen 1986).

Alchian, Armen A. and Harold Demsetz 'Production, Information Costs and Economic Organization' *American Economic Review* 62 (1972) 777-95.

Alchian, Armen A. 'Specificity, Specialization, and Coalitions' *Journal of Institutional and Theoretical Economics/Zeitschrift für die gesamte Staatswissenschaft* 140 (1984) 34-49.

Ansoff, H. Igor *Corporate Strategy* (New York 1965).

Bamberg, Ulrich, Michael Bürger, Birgit Mahnkopf, Helmut Martens, and Jörg Tiemann *Aber ob die Karten voll ausgereizt sind... - 10 Jahre Mitbestimmungsgesetz 1976 in der Bilanz* (Cologne 1987).

Barney, Jay 'Firm Resources and Sustained Competitive Advantage' *Journal of Management* 17/1 (1991) 99-120.

Benelli, Giuseppe, Claudio Loderer, and Thomas Lys 'Labor Participation in Corporate Policy-making Decisions: West Germany's Experience with Co-determination' *Journal of Business* 60 (1987) 553-75.

Brinkmann, Thomas and Friedrich Kübler 'Überlegungen zur ökonomischen Analyse von Unternehmensrecht' *Journal of Institutional and Theoretical Economics/Zeitschrift für die gesamte Staatswissenschaft* 137 (1981) 681-8.

Bullock Committee 'Report of the Committee of Inquiry and Industrial Democracy' (HMSO, Cmnd. 6706, London 1987).

Coase, Ronald H. 'The Nature of the Firm' *Economica* 4 (1937) 386-405.

Cyert, Richard M. and James G. March *A Behavioral Theory of the Firm* (Englewood Cliffs, N.J. 1963).

EC Commission 'Weißbuch der Kommission an den Europäischen Rat: Vollendung des Binnenmarkts' (Luxemburg 1985).

EC Commission 'Mitteilung der Kommission der Europäischen Gemeinschaften zur Information und Konsultation der Arbeitnehmer' (KOM (95) 547 endg.; Ratsdok. 11954/95, 1995).

Ehlermann, Claus-Dieter 'Ökonomische Aspekte des Subsidiaritätsprinzips: Harmonisierung versus Wettbewerb der Systeme' *Integration* 18 (1995) 11-21.

FitzRoy, Felix and Kornelius Kraft 'Economic Effects of Co-determination' *Scandinavian Journal of Economics* 95 (1993) 365-75.

Freeman, R. Edward *Strategic Management: A Stakeholder Approach* (Marshfield, Mass. 1983).

Freeman, Richard B. and Edward P. Lazear 'An Economic Analysis of Works Councils' in: Rogers, Joel and Wolfgang Streeck (eds.) *Works Councils: Consultation, Representation and Cooperation in Industrial Relations* 27-52 (Chicago 1995).

Furubotn, Eirik G. and Steven N. Wiggins 'Plant Closing, Worker Reallocation Costs and Efficiency Gains to Labor Representation on Boards of Directors' *Journal of Institutional and Theoretical Economics/Zeitschrift für die gesamte Staatswissenschaft* 140 (1984) 176-92.

Gerum, Elmar 'Unternehmensverfassung und Theorie der Verfügungsrechte' in: Budäus, Dietrich, Elmar Gerum, and Gebhard Zimmermann (eds.) *Betriebswirtschaftslehre und Theorie der Verfügungsrechte* 21-43 (Wiesbaden 1988).

Gerum, Elmar 'Mitbestimmung und Effizienz' in: Eichhorn, Peter (ed.) *Unternehmensverfassung in der privaten und öffentlichen Wirtschaft* 46-60 (Baden-Baden 1989).

Gerum, Elmar 'Corporate Governance in Europa: Konvergenz trotz Varianz' in: Berger, Roland and Ulrich Steger (eds.) *Auf dem Weg zur Europäischen Unternehmensführung* 33-48 (Munich 1998).

Gerum, Elmar and Horst Steinmann *Unternehmensordnung und tarifvertragliche Mitbestimmung* (Berlin 1984).

Gerum, Elmar, Horst Steinmann, and Werner Fees *Der mitbestimmte Aufsichtsrat—Eine empirische Untersuchung* (Stuttgart 1988).

Grant, Robert M. 'The Resource-Based Theory of Competitive Advantage: Implications for Strategy Formulation' *California Management Review* 33 (1991) 114-35.

Group of Experts "European Systems of Worker Envolvement" *'Abschlußbericht'* (EUKOM 1997).

Gurdon, Michael A. and Anoop Rai 'Co-determination and Enterprise Performance: Empirical Evidence from West Germany' *Journal of Economics and Business* 42 (1990) 289-302.

Hall, Richard 'A Framework Linking Intangible Resources and Capabilities to Sustainable Competitive Advantage' *Strategic Management Journal* 14 (1993) 607-18.

von Hayek, Friedrich A. *Der Wettbewerb als Entdeckungsverfahren* (Kieler Vorträge, N.F. 56, 1968).

Jensen, Michael C. and William H. Meckling 'Theory of the Firm: Managerial Behavior, Agency Costs and Ownership Structure' *Journal of Financial Economics* 3 (1976) 305-60.

Jensen, Michael C. and William H. Meckling 'Rights and Production Functions: An Application to Labor-Managed Firms and Co-Determination' *Journal of Business* 52 (1979) 469-506.

Kirsch, Werner, Wolfgang Scholl, and Günter Paul *Mitbestimmung in der Unternehmenspraxis* (Munich 1984).

Levine, David I. and Laura D'Andrea Tyson 'Participation, Productivity and the Firm's Environment' in: Blinder, Alan S. (ed.) *Paying for Productivity: A Look at the Evidence* 183-237 (Washington, D.C. 1990).

Michaelis, Elke and Arnold Picot 'Zur ökonomischen Analyse von Mitarbeiterrechten' in: FitzRoy, Felix R. and Kornelius Kraft (eds.) *Mitarbeiterbeteiligung und Mitbestimmung in Unternehmen* 83-127 (Berlin 1987).

Mussler, Werner and Michael Wohlgemuth 'Institutionen im Wettbewerb—Ordnungstheoretische Anmerkungen zum Systemwettbewerb in Europa' in: Oberender, Peter and Manfred E. Streit (eds.) *Europas Arbeitsmärkte im Integrationsprozeß* 9-45 (Baden-Baden 1995).

Nagels, Karlheinz and Arndt Sorge *Industrielle Demokratie in Europa* (Frankfurt am Main and New York 1977).

Olson, Mancur *The Rise and Decline of Nations: Economic Growth, Stagflation and Social Rigidities* (New Haven and London 1982).

'Richtlinie 94/45/EG des Rates vom 22.11.1994 über die Einsetzung eines Europäischen Betriebsrates oder die Schaffung eines Verfahrens zur Unterrichtung und Anhörung der Arbeitnehmer in gemeinschaftsweit operierenden Unternehmen und Unternehmensgruppen (Richtlinie Europäische Betriebsräte)' (ABl. EG Nr. L 254 v. 30.09.1994: 64-72).

Sinn, Stefan 'The Taming of Leviathan: Competition among Governments' *Constitutional Political Economy* 3 (1992) 177-96.

Streit, Manfred E. and Werner Mussler 'Wettbewerb der Systeme und das Binnenmarktprogramm der Europäischen Union' in: Gerken, Lüder (ed.) *Europa zwischen Ordnungswettbewerb und Harmonisierung. Europäische Ordnungspolitik im Zeichen der Subsidiarität* 75-107 (Berlin 1995).

Sudreau, Pierre *La réforme de l'Enterprise* (Paris 1975).

Svejnar, Jan 'Co-determination and Productivity: Empirical Evidence from the Federal Republic of Germany' in: Jones, Derek C. and Jan Svejnar (eds.) *Participatory and Self-Managed Firms* 199-212 (Lexington 1982).

Wagner, Helmut 'Durch Gewinnbeteiligung zur Vollbeschäftigung? *Konjunkturpolitik* 34 (1989) 329-45.

Wagner, Helmut 'Rechtsunsicherheit und Wirtschaftswachstum' in: Behrends, Sylke (ed.) *Ordnungskonforme Wirtschaftspolitik in der Marktwirtschaft 227-53* (Berlin 1997).

Wagner, Helmut *Wachstum und Entwicklung - Theorie der Entwicklungspolitik* 2nd edn. (Munich 1997a).

Wagner, Helmut *Stabilitätspolitik* 5th edn. (Munich 1998).

von Weizsäcker, Carl Christian 'Was leistet die Property Rights Theorie für aktuelle wirtschaftspolitische Fragen?' in: Neumann, Manfred (ed.) *Ansprüche, Eigentums- und Verfügungsrechte* 123-52 (Berlin 1984).

Williamson, Oliver E. *Markets and Hierarchies: Analysis and Antitrust Implications* (New York and London 1975).

Witte, Eberhard 'Das Einflußpotential der Arbeitnehmer als Grundlage der Mitbestimmung' *Die Betriebswirtschaft* 40 (1980) 3-26.

Witte, Eberhard 'Das Einflußsystem der Unternehmung in den Jahren 1976 und 1981' *Zeitschrift für betriebswirtschaftliche Forschung* 34 (1982) 416-34.

German Co-Determination and German Securities Markets

MARK J. ROE, New York[*]

Germany lacks good securities markets. Initial public offers are infrequent, securities trading is shallow, and even large public firms typically have big blockholders that make the big firms resemble "semi-private" companies. These firm characteristics are often attributed to poor legal protection of minority stockholders, to the lack of an equity-owning and entrepreneurial culture, and to permissive rules that allow big banks and bank blockholding in ways barred in the U.S.

I sketch an additional explanation. German co-determination undermines diffuse ownership. First, stockholders may want the firm's governing institutions to have a blockholding "balance of power," a balance that, because half the supervisory board represents employees, diffusely owned firms may be unable to create.

Second, managers and stockholders kept the supervisory board weaker than it had to have been. Board meetings are infrequent, information flow to the board is poor, and the board is often too big and unwieldy to be effective. Instead, out-of-the-boardroom shareholder caucuses and meetings between managers and large shareholders substitute for effective boardroom action. But, because diffuse stockholders will at key points in a firm's future need a plausible board (due to a succession crisis, a production downfall, or a technological challenge), diffuse ownership for the German firm would deny the firm both boardroom and blockholder governance. Stockholders would face a choice of charging up the board (and hence further empowering its employee-half) or of living with sub-standard (by current world criteria) boardroom governance. In the face of such choices, German firms (i.e., their managers and blockholders) retain their "semi-private," blockholding structure, and German securities markets do not develop.

Contents

A. Introduction

Germany lacks good securities markets. Initial public offers are infrequent, securities trading is shallow, and even large public firms typically have big block-

[*] Paper prepared for the Symposium on Comparative Corporate Governance, held at the Max-Planck-Institut für Ausländisches und Internationales Privatrecht, Hamburg, 15-17 May 1997. The article also appears in 1998 *Colum. Bus. L. Rev.* No. 1.

holders that make the big firms resemble "semi-private" companies. These "private" firm characteristics of German ownership are often attributed to poor legal protection of minority stockholders,[1] the lack of an equity-owning culture,[2] the lack of an entrepreneurial culture (one that would create many new businesses and IPOs), and permissive rules that allow big banks and bank blockholding in ways barred in the U.S.[3]

German institutions, though, provide another, potentially alternative, and plausibly additional explanation for the weakness of German securities markets. German co-determination (by which employees control half of the seats on the German supervisory board) undermines diffuse ownership for two related reasons. One, stockholders may wish that the firm's governing institutions have a blockholding "balance of power," a balance that, given German law's mandate that half the supervisory board represent employees, diffusely owned firms may be unable to create.

Two, managers and stockholders sapped the supervisory board of power (or, more accurately, prevented it from evolving into a serious governance institution in the face of the 1980s' and 1990s' global competition and technological change) to reduce employee influence in the firm. For many firms, board meetings are infrequent, information flow to the board is poor, and the board is often too big and unwieldy to be effective. Instead of boardroom governance, out-of-the-boardroom shareholder caucuses and meetings between managers and large shareholders substitute for effective boardroom action. But, because diffuse stockholders will at key points in a firm's future need a plausible board (due to a succession crisis, a production downfall, or a technological challenge), diffuse ownership for the German firm would deny the firm both boardroom and blockholder governance. Blockholder governance would be gone (if the block dissipated into a diffuse securities market) and board-level governance would be unavailable because the shareholders and managers had sapped the board of authority beforehand. Stockholders would face a choice of charging up the board (and hence further empowering the employee-half of the governance structure) or living with sub-standard (by current world criteria) boardroom governance. In the face of such choices, German firms (i.e., their managers and blockholders) retain their "semi-private," blockholding structure, and German securities markets do not develop.

---

[1] La Porta, Rafael, Florencio Lopez-de-Silanes, Andrei Shleifer, and Robert W. Vishny 'Legal Determinants of External Finance' *Journal of Finance* 52 (1997) 1131-50.

[2] 'Launching Deutsche Telekom' *The Economist* Oct. 26, 1996, 73.

[3] Roe, Mark J. *Strong Managers, Weak Owners: The Political Roots of American Corporate Finance* 94-101, 169-97 (Princeton 1994).

B. The German Boardroom

One might begin to analyze the German boardroom with a handful of observations from the U.S. about what makes for a good board:

1. small size, with specialized subcommittees;
2. frequent meetings;
3. intense information flow; and
4. low conflicts of interest.

To an American, the German boardroom seems poor on all four characteristics.[4] That observation might be taken as advice for German boardroom players—a start on a conversation that could conclude: here's how to improve the German boardroom. Or the observations might begin an analysis of German boardroom origins. Or it might reflect back on the U.S.: because German companies have until now been internationally competitive, maybe these features are not crucial to good operations, and other features, not yet well identified in the corporate governance literature, are.

I shall begin with the second point of entry: I assume that these boardroom features are desirable, that many German boards lack every one, and that one might want to speculate on the origins and persistence of that deficit. For the U.S., I've argued that some prevalent forms plausibly have political origins, and one might speculate similarly for the German boardroom. Mundane features might link to German social politics. In reaction to German co-determination, players inside the firm, namely managers and shareholders, seem to have reacted by weakening the large firm's supervisory board (or, more properly, keeping it weak, despite global business changes that led to its strengthening elsewhere).

Moreover, German businesspeople, the German business press, and business academics point at times to Germany's lack of a vibrant securities markets that would take innovative firms public and help charge-up the Germany economy. To explain the lack of a vibrant German stock market, standard accounts point to the lack of an equity-holding culture (a demand-side perspective), the lack of an entrepreneurial culture of businesspeople who create new firms (a supply-side perspective), inappropriate securities laws, opaque accounting, and the influence of the banks (in business and politics). While I do not deny these explanations, I suggest that even if these problems (which are common in several continental European countries) were overcome, Germany would face an additional, and perhaps even more intractable, difficulty in developing vibrant securities markets with many IPOs, namely that the co-determined structure fits poorly with diffuse ownership. This poor fit makes founders less willing to sell off their block into

---

[4] On German board practice, cf. Hopt, Semler, and Theisen in Ch. 4 of this volume and Prigge (Ch. 12: Sec. B.I.).

IPOs and makes distant buyers potentially more wary of owning stock in the German firm than they'd otherwise be.

C. Co-Determination and Boardroom Reaction

Begin with what seem to be details of the board structure and function: Could information flow, board size, and meeting frequency link to co-determination?[5] Take size of the board. American studies find that smaller boards are more effective than big ones; here linkage is quite explicit because the co-determination statute mandates, depending on company size, that the board's size vary between twelve and twenty members.[6]

The nonmandated features, like the infrequency of board meetings, the formalized information flow, and the frequently conflicted composition of the shareholder side, can also be seen as buttressed by co-determination. Begin with meeting frequency: American boards tend to meet about eight times per year. German boards typically meet two to four times per year and, although the minimum frequency is specified in the German statute, the board is free to meet more frequently, but many do not and those that do typically only meet four times a year.[7] Obviously, a board that meets infrequently will, all else being equal, be less informed and less able to monitor management than one that meets frequently. Moreover, information flow to the infrequent German board meetings is further constricted, with key documents often only placed in front of the board members at the meeting,[8] a practice that disables directors from intensely preparing to examine (if they were so inclined) the firm's current operations. That preparation might lead to closely questioning managers, to see if that information was slanted, and to prepare the directors for closely questioning managers when performance is poor. But even motivated, capable directors will have a hard time being strong monitors if the company's basic information is placed in front of

[5] For the particular influence of co-determination on board practice, see also in this volume the contributions of Hopt (Ch. 4: Sec. B.III.2. and passim), Semler (Ch. 4: Sec: C.II. para 2 and passim), and Prigge (Ch. 12: Sec. B.I.3. and C.I.1).

[6] Pistor, Katharina 'Co-Determination in Germany: A Socio-Political Model with Governance Externalities' 18 n. 40 (Columbia Law School Conference on Employees and Corporate Governance, Nov. 22, 1996) (citing *Mitbestimmung der Arbeitnehmer*, § 7 MitbestG). Companies with more than 20,000 employees must have a 20-person board; those with less than 10,000 must have a 12-person board; and those between 10,000 and 20,000 get a 16-person board.

[7] Edwards, Jeremy S.S. and Klaus Fischer *Banks, Finance and Investment in Germany* 213 (New York 1994). Recent pressures seem to have pushed the supervisory boards up to meeting three or four time a year. Liener, Gerhard 'The Future of German Governance' *Corp. Board* (May 1995) at 1, as cited in André, Thomas J. 'Some Reflections on German Corporate Governance: A Glimpse at German Supervisory Boards' 70 *Tulane L. Rev.* 1819, 1825 n. 21 (1996).

[8] Pistor, supra n. 6.

them only moments before a formalized meeting begins and then is whisked away shortly thereafter.

A question for serious research is whether these features strongly link up to German co-determination. For board size, which is mandated, the linkage is clear. But the deeper question is whether variable matters, like meeting frequency and information flow, also link up to co-determination. Let's assume, as we have been, that intense information flow and more frequent meetings are functional. If so, German boards could have evolved consciously to get better information and to meet more frequently. After errors and missteps, boards could have decided they needed to meet more often to be effective. Or German managers and board members, aware that meeting frequency and information flow could improve the boards' functions, could have led boards to meet more often even before the firm made any errors. Or boards might have stumbled onto more frequent meetings as effective and then continued the practice.[9]

If, in fact, these processes could have occurred but did not, what could explain the roadblock? Once again, dysfunctionality or irrelevance cannot be rejected, but the American experience suggests the contrary. A simple economic analysis suggests a hypothesis: if there are gains to be made by strengthening governance, but it is not strengthened, then perhaps increasing its strength also brings on costs, either to the firm or to players inside the firm. And here co-determination might play a role in the internal calculus of the firm's players, and perhaps in the firm's performance as well.

That the German supervisory board was never formally intended to have a hands-on role is not critical to this discussion. The question put here is *why* the German boardroom didn't *evolve* to be more hands-on. True, one cannot dismiss the possibility that to evolve the German supervisory boards the players needed a formal legal mandate and, absent that mandate, the board could not evolve even if, net, business pressures pushed to increase activity.[10] But this, too, begs our question: even if the lack of formal authority to go beyond nomination of management board personnel blocked evolution (presumably because formalities are more important in German boardrooms than in the American), we would still have to wonder *why* the German corporate system did not turn to the parliamentary granters of formal authority to request that their authority be upgraded. The hypotheses I offer in this paper could help to explain the lack of demand for formal change as precursor to substantive change.

---

[9] Thus one would hypothesize that recent boardroom failures in Germany would have increased the pressure on supervisory boards to meet more often. Liener, supra n. 7.

[10] The supervisory board cannot formally take on management functions. André, supra n. 7, 1824 n. 19 (citing AktG Section 111, para. 4; Stock Company Act (Aktiengesetz) *BGBl. I* 1965, 1089).

Abstract the German firm into three parts: management, labor, and capital.[11] Managers who face the possibility that an independent board might scrutinize them might perform better than those who do not face an independent board. But for boards to scrutinize, they need both to meet frequently and to get good information about the firm. Capital might insist on this scrutiny, or managers might from time to time ask for it, or firms with this scrutiny might tend to prosper and those without it to contract. Normally the board would be the vehicle for this scrutiny.

Now assume that capital does not want labor to be well informed. Their desire here could be functional, dysfunctional, or neutral, but is easy to understand. Their desire here could be functional in that labor could damage the firm sometimes, especially when labor's representatives voice the goals of employees with only a few years left to work at the firm, and greater voice and information in corporate affairs could increase that damage. Conflict, even conflict not arising from capital-labor disputes, is a critical cause of failure in closely held firms when owners side-track the firm while fighting to divide value and thereby harm the firm;[12] increased information could increase conflict, and increased conflict could fritter away firm value. Capital's desire here could be neutral in that internal rent-seeking between capital and labor could be in play; capital might want to keep labor in the dark so that labor is less effective in internal rent-seeking. Or the desire here could be dysfunctional in that some labor-management decisions require trust and well-informed labor—getting good information through the board—could enhance that trust in shop-floor activities. But if this enhanced firm performance is offset by capital's perception that it would lose value because labor would be able to rent-seek more effectively, (or management's fear that their consulting labor would constrict their own autonomy), then capital's (and management's) desire to keep labor in the dark is, net, dysfunctional.[13]

It is easy to see that capital (and management) could prefer that labor be ill informed. But if the supervisory board is theoretically the best (or a good) conduit for information to capital as well, then capital, by cutting down on (or by failing to increase) the information flow to the board, would be cutting information that flowed to itself as well. This cut in information flow could be rational if

[11] Cf. Gerum/Wagner (this volume Ch. 5: Sec. B) for a treatment of economic theories of co-determination.

[12] For the proposition that shareholder disputes are a major cause of business failures for the close corporation, see sources cited in Miller, Sandra K. 'Minority Shareholder Oppression in the Private Company in the European Community: A Comparative Analysis of the German, United Kingdom, and French "Close Corporation Problem"' 30 *Cornell Int'l L.J.* 381, 384 n. 16 (1997).

[13] One study suggests co-determination brought overall *social* gains, but decreased firm-level productivity and profitability (without affecting wage rates). FitzRoy, Felix R. and Kornelius Kraft 'Economic Effects of Codetermination' *Scandinavian Journal of Economics* 95 (1993) 365, 373. These results suggest internal rent-seeking by labor and shareholder governance counters are plausible.

the costs to capital from labor being better informed were greater than the gains to capital by better firm performance: i.e., capital might prefer to take its chance with unmonitored managers than with well-informed labor.

Or capital might decide it can get enough information elsewhere—through informal discussions, through control of the "speaker's" seat of the supervisory board (the chair of the supervisory is from the shareholder side), through separate meetings between management and the shareholder "bench" of the board, or through bank loan channels. Capital might know that these channels could be enhanced with better boardroom information, but if the better boardroom channel comes with the price of better-informed labor, they may prefer the co-determined board to be less well informed than it could be. Bankers believe they get no more information from their seats on the supervisory board than they get as a creditor of the firm.[14]

Shareholders and managers might calculate similarly about meeting frequency. They may know that more monitoring should somewhat improve operations, at least at critical junctures, and they may believe that more meetings should improve monitoring. But more meetings would enhance labor's voice in the co-determined boardroom, making management and capital shy away from more meetings.

The board's large size might contribute to its weakness, by making it harder for the players to coordinate meeting times than if the board were smaller. This is the reason often given by German players on why meetings are infrequent, but I wonder whether those who use it do so to avoid confronting the deeper structural questions that co-determination raises.

Large size also increases the inside-the-boardroom free-rider problem (why prepare, if I'm a small player inside the boardroom?). If free-riding board members will not prepare well, then there's little reason to get the reports out to the supervisory board for early study (because they will not be studied by the free-riders) and small benefits (like maintaining general confidentiality) from last-minute distribution could determine the low information result.

* * *

The evidence available[15] is consistent with this view of a deliberately weakened supervisory board in the face of the 1976 expansion of German co-determination, although the evidence is indirect. Early studies suggest that managers and shareholders sought to weaken the labor side of the co-determined board via, say, equity-dominated subcommittees. More than half of the German boards used one

---

[14] Mülbert, Peter O. *Empfehlen sich gesetzliche Regelungen zur Einschränkung des Einflusses der Kreditinstitute auf Aktiengesellschaften?* 49 (Expert Opinion for the 61ˢᵗ Deutscher Juristentag 1996) (Munich 1996).

[15] For a survey of empirical evidence with respect to co-determination, see Gerum/Wagner (this volume Ch. 5: Sec. C).

or more of these "equity-enhancing" characteristics: 1) added stockholder vice-chairs of the board (the German corporate law's default rule is that the vice-chair come from the labor side, the chair from the equity side), 2) formed equity-controlled subcommittees, 3) enhanced the power of chair (who is from the shareholder side) to control the agenda, 4) instituted quorum rules that favored equity, 5) added authority of the chair to postpone a substantive action if he or she could not be present, 6) required that the chair cast the tie-breaking vote if a board vote was tied, or 7) restrained board members from statements outside of the boardroom.[16] But it's puzzling to this observer that when corporate governance becomes a hot topic in Germany (as it has), the number of seats that the bankers take is an issue (as it should be) and custodial voting becomes an issue (as it should be), but the reports we see in the U.S. do not indicate co-determination's effects as also an issue (but it should be).[17] This is partly because the topic of co-determination is academically passé in Germany, partly because it's a sacred cow that's above direct criticism, and partly because this kind of functional analysis (as opposed to formalist and doctrinal analysis) isn't central to German legal scholarship

Tests are plausible here. The most obvious one is sociological surveying: ask supervisory board members whether meeting frequency and information flow were issues and whether co-determination affected decisions on whether to change.[18] More sophisticated tests are plausible: take a sample of firms and divide them into two, one where internal rent-seeking should be low, the other where it could be high. If the hypotheses I advanced earlier are correct, then the low rent-seeking firms should have more frequent meetings, better information flow, and more diffuse ownership. Smaller matters are tested for U.S. boards and securities markets with delicious detail in the Journal of Financial Economics and Journal of Finance in the U.S., yet with a few exceptions even major matters aren't yet so tested for German boards.[19]

[16] Gerum, Elmar, Horst Steinmann and Werner Fees *Der mitbestimmte Aufsichtsrat—Eine empirische Untersuchung* 98-115 (Stuttgart 1988). The study, however, dealt with data that are now stale.

[17] The Ministry of Justice is focusing on reducing board size from 20, limiting the number of chairmanship that a single person can hold, and moving the authority to appoint auditors from the management board to the supervisory board. The leading shareholder associations are focusing on these matters, and also proposing to limit to 10 the boards a single person can sit on, to upgrade board committees, and to increase required board meetings to four per year. See Arnold, Corinna 'Recent Scandals Place German Boards Under Attack' *IRRC Corporate Governance Bulletin* (July-Sept. 1996) 16, 17.

[18] One quotation, said to be seen as radical: "[C]ritical questions are not asked because you have to take account of the employees." Attributed to the head of the Federation of German Industry [BDI]. Arnold, supra n. 17, 17.

[19] Some exceptions: Baums, Theodor and Bernd Frick 'Co-Determination and Stock Price' (Paper presented at Conference on Employees and Corporate Governance, Sloan Project, Columbia Law School, Nov. 22, 1996); Kaplan, Steven N. and Bernadette Alcamo Minton

D. Securities Markets and Public Choice

Germany lacks a good securities market. One finds sometimes in the United States that incumbent players block passage enforcement of laws that might undermine their position,[20] and it would not be surprising if German incumbent industrial giants did not want competition from upstart, IPO-financed new firms. Nor would it be surprising if incumbent German bankers did not want competition from upstart investment bankers (or if incumbent bank executives did not want to be forced to learn a new set of investment banking skills). These hypotheses seem plausible, but I am unaware of any development or refutation in the literature about the German firm and German securities markets.

A related public choice hypothesis arises from the analysis in this paper. Could German structures have decreased the *demand* for good securities laws? Governance and securities markets are linked. The usual perspective is that securities markets induce special governance features, such as the Berle-Means corporation, takeovers, and enhanced agency costs. That is, a standard refrain in the American literature is that firms went public because of financing needs (either to finance the firm itself or to finance the owners' diversification out from the firm they founded) and, as the new buying owners diversified into small lots, power shifted in the corporation from free-riding shareholders with poor information to concentrated inside managers with good information about the corporation. Governance structures can also affect the "demand" for securities markets. The co-determined German supervisory board might keep corporate issuers' *demand* for securities markets and their supporting apparatus, like good securities laws and transparent accounting, low. This low demand from issuers for good securities rules may be as important as other explanations, such as a correctly suspicious view that banks may prefer a purportedly profitable credit business to the supposedly less profitable underwriting business.[21] Again, although family founders may wish to cash out, diversify, and retire like their Anglo-Saxon counterparts, if the securities buyers will be unwilling to pay "full"

'Appointments of Outsiders to Japanese Boards: Its Determinants and Implications for Managers' *Journal of Financial Economics* 36 (1994) 225; Kaplan, Steven N. 'Top Executives, Turnover and Firm Performance in Germany' *Journal of Law, Economics and Organization* 10 (1994) 142. The available empirical evidence with respect to German boards is surveyed by Prigge (this volume Ch. 12: Sec. B.I. and C.I.1.).

[20] Macey, Jonathan R. and Geoffrey P. Miller 'Origin of the Blue Sky Laws' 70 *Tex. L. Rev.* 347 (1991) (bankers call for laws that regulate stock and bond issuances). Cf. Langevoort, Donald 'Statutory Obsolescence and the Judicial Process: The Revisionist Role of the Courts in Federal Banking Regulation' 85 *Mich. L. Rev.* 672 (1987) (ideology, policy, and small-town bankers and farmers versus city bankers); Macey, Jonathan R. 'Special Interest Group Legislation and the Judicial Function: The Dilemma of Glass-Steagall' 33 *Emory L.J.* 1 (1983) (commercial versus investment bankers).

[21] Mülbert, supra n. 14, 26.

price for the stock because the buyers will have to deal either with a weak board or strong labor inside a strong board, then the founders may find it comparatively worthwhile to retain the block and induce the next generation in the family to enter and run the firm. When they sell, they might sell a block to new blockholders who can monitor the firm and its managers, and the evidence suggests this is so, with many sales of control, but those sales always going as blocks.[22]

This may feed back on the scarcity of entrepreneurs willing to build new firms. If sales have to be made to other blockholders, successful entrepreneurs may be unable to find many bidders for their firm. In the U.S., in contrast, the blockholder bidders face competition from underwriters who can sell into the securities markets. This competition from securities markets in *pricing* an entrepreneur's sell-out may be critical. In Germany, the seller may often be unable to get "full" price because the number of blockholder buyers is small and the few potential buyers do not face competition from public securities market underwriters. Purported cultural attitudes, like the lack of entrepreneurs and a weak equity-holding culture, may accordingly be economically motivated. The weak securities market may partly depend on the mandated co-determined structure of the boardroom.

Consider this abstraction: a founder builds a successful business. The heirs ordinarily do not want to run the business; they would prefer to sell out in public markets and bring in professional managers. (This tracks a common American occurrence). The firm is, say, worth $50 million to the heirs. But a public offering will decrease the power of equity to counterbalance labor in the boardroom and, if the boardroom were to become important, this lack of balance could be costly to stockholders. And if the boardroom does not become important, then agency costs from poorly monitored managers would decrease the value of the firm. Either way, stockholders would lose. If the firm would then be worth, say, not $50 million but only $25 million to public stockholders, who anticipate this lower amount as the value to them of low-voice in a co-determined firm, then it "costs" $25 million to the heirs to sell out their stock instead of managing the firm. They thus have a low "demand" for good securities markets, and that low demand could manifest itself both in fewer IPOs and in a lower demand for good, well-enforced securities and corporate laws that would make such stock sales more effective. Family ownership through several generations may be a German culture feature, as it is said to be. But, again, culture may have an economic base, and family-oriented ownership may also result from an institutional structure that disfavors the fully public, diffusely owned firm. Families thus have economic (and not just cultural) reasons to find and induce the next

[22] See Franks, Julian and Colin Mayer 'Ownership, Control and the Performance of German Corporations' (London Business School and University of Oxford, paper presented at a Columbia Law School Sloan Project Conference, April 1997).

generation to take over the family firm.[23] But because maintaining a firm in a family generation after generation is not a stable result, judging from the American experience, then pressure on the system should eventually increase: demand for secondary sales should rise, and if concentrated equity makes the firms run acceptably in light of Germany's other corporate institutions, then new governance problems could arise and alternative efforts to focus equity could be tried.

Thus, until now, one key source of demand for better securities markets —selling founders—might have been missing from the German system.[24] German businesses may thus stay in a family's hands for more generations than American businesses do.

E. Substitutes

The point here is not that boardroom monitoring is the sine qua non of securities markets. Nor is it that American boardroom monitoring is infinitely superior to Germany's. The point is that securities markets require monitoring of managers from time to time. The principal monitoring mechanisms are market competition (in capital and product markets), takeovers, a good board, and a concentrated shareholder. The U.S. is strong in the first control mechanism (competition) and passable in the next two. Germany has historically been weak on competition, lacks takeovers, and is weaker in boardroom governance. All that's left for large German firms at this time is the fourth, blockholding. Were German firms to dismantle blockholding, via a diffusion in ownership of their largest firms, they would leave themselves with no significant control device, either internal or external. The fact that over 85% of Germany's largest firms persist in having a stockholder owning over 25% of the firm's stock[25] is suggestive. Large blockholders' representatives meet informally with managers, outside of the formal meetings, and this seems to be Germany's significant monitoring mechanism, one for which the U.S. has substitutes (or improvements) and one for which German firms, lacking substitutes, would pay a price if the blocks dissipated.[26] If the

---

[23] A continuing strength of family ownership is based here on a poor securities market and poor monitoring structures. If we observe continuing family ownership, however, we don't know whether the poor securities market is due to poor legal protections or shareholders' fear of diffuse ownership in a co-determined firm.

[24] More generally, German analysts bemoan the lack of presence of good securities markets in Germany. But the connection between securities markets and labor presence does not seem to be well analyzed. Co-determination may have arisen to "balance" power with the German banks and other equity holders, but once it's in place, dispersal of equity interests could debilitate the firm.

[25] Franks and Mayer, supra n. 22; see also Prigge (this volume Ch. 12: Sec. B.II.).

[26] Cf. Kaplan and Minton, supra n. 19; Kaplan, supra n. 19 (articles that show roughly similar corporate governance executive and director turnover results in Germany, Japan, and the U.S., in recent times).

other substitutes improved enough, because of, say, enhanced European product market competition after implementation of Maastricht or a European Monetary Union, then perhaps the German governance trade-off would also change.

F. Conclusion

Much remains to be understood about the German supervisory board, co-determination, and the historical weakness of German securities markets. But by linking the salient institutions, we can pose fundamental questions. The weakness of the supervisory board might be structurally linked to co-determination. If so, prevailing reform proposals (e.g., limiting the number of boards an individual can serve on) may fail to improve the board much, because they fail to address a fundamental structural dilemma for Germany. Moreover, the weakness of German securities markets may in important ways be due to the weakness of the German supervisory board. Diffuse stockholders would face either a labor-dominated board or a weak board. Neither choice may be appealing, so potential buyers may not pay up to buy from blockholders, and blockholders may be unwilling to take the loss. Stock persists in big blocks (85% of the large, purportedly "public" firms have at least one blockholder owning more than a quarter of the stock) and fluidity comes not from IPOs but from blocks changing hands. The demand for good securities market institutions may not be strong, and hence these institutions may not arise.

Institutions can be linked in other ways. If Germany has deficient securities and corporate laws (and enforcement) then one must ask how this came about, because the task of writing a passable law and getting a plausible enforcement agency in place just is not insurmountable and Germany is not incapable of good government administration. Public choice forces could help explain the perceived deficiency. First, the ordinary public choice forces of incumbent firms that did not wish to compete with securities-financed entrants needs to be examined, as does the possibility that incumbent bank leaders preferred to avoid a new competitive arena. Second, I'd suggest linking the weak securities markets to the possibility of a "weak" demand for sell-out by founders in secondary sales: if the firm would be worth *much* less to scattered outside owners because a "balance of power" inside the firm would tilt away from equity, then the firm's founders and heir would seek to preserve concentrated ownership, and good tests could, and should, be made on whether the concentrated ownership that persists is due to the inability to sell out (because securities markets are weak) or because the players' demand to sell is low.

A Note on Labour and Corporate Governance in the U.K.

PAUL L. DAVIES, London

This note explores the historical reasons for the minimalist development of a legal structure for enterprise governance in the U.K. in which representatives of the employees were significantly involved. It analyses the strains which have been placed upon this traditional structure of 'collective laissez-faire' in the U.K. over the past fifty years; and assesses the strength of the incentives currently operating British industrial relations towards the elaboration of statutory structure of employee involvement.

Contents

A. Introduction

A note on this subject from a U.K. perspective might seem supererogatory. This is because U.K. does not have a system of employee representation on corporate boards along the German model, or even along the lines of the less demanding Swedish, Danish, or Austrian models. However, there is something more to be stated than just this negative fact. First, as Streeck reminds us, the significance of labour representation on the supervisory board in Germany 'is part of a broader system of industrial governance'[1] and it thus has to be assessed in the context of its relationship with the functioning of works councils and collective bargaining in Germany. If one adopts this widening of the focus, there emerges a second negative to be explained about the U.K. system, i.e., the absence in that country of a statutorily mandated system of works councils. In fact, the latter negative fact is, in a European context, a more surprising one than the former. Whereas a (small) majority of member states of the European Community does not have a mandatory system of employee representation at board level in the private sector

---

[1] Streeck, Wolfgang 'Co-Determination in Context: Outlines of an Institutionalist Perspective' (Draft paper presented for discussion at the Symposium on 'Comparative Corporate Governance: The State of the Art and Emerging Research' Hamburg, Max-Planck-Institut für ausländisches und internationales Privatrecht, May 1997).

of the economy, only a small number do not have any form of statutory, employee-based works councils.[2]

However, the situation in the U.K. is not one where the third pillar of the German system (i.e., collective bargaining) fails to appear. On the contrary, the distinctive feature of the British system hitherto has been the weight it has placed on collective bargaining as the 'single channel' of representation of the interests of the employees vis-à-vis the employing enterprise. Overall, the contrast with Germany is even greater when attention is given to the industrial governance system as a whole than when it is confined to board representation.

As another paper reminds us, the crucial starting point for many later developments in modern industrial relations systems has to be found in the reaction of the state to the collectivisation of employees' interests in the early stages of industrialisation. The purpose of this note is consequence to do three things. The first is to attempt to explain how the U.K. came to place exclusive reliance on collective bargaining for the representation of employee interests; why that model has increasingly come under pressure over the past 50 years; and how it might react to those pressures in the near future.

B. History

In the U.K., after an initial phase of repression during the first half of the nineteenth century, from the 1870s onwards the policy of the British state towards trade unions became one of toleration, i.e., of permitting them to win a place in the newly industrialised society for their members. This process is associated at governmental level in particular with the statutes of 1871,[3] 1875,[4] and 1906.[5] That represented an early flowering within Europe of the policy of incorporating, rather than suppressing, the trade union movement. Corresponding developments in France and Germany came at a later date. However, it was a curiously passive approach on the part of the state to incorporation. It did not involve active state support for trade union growth and collective bargaining (except during periods of national crisis, such as the First World War) but rather simply removing the legal obstacles which blocked the unions' path.

As a renowned German observer—who became the leading analyst of British labour law—put it, this was a policy on the part of the state of 'collective laissez-

---

[2] European Commission 'Final Report of the Group of Experts on European Systems of Worker Involvement' (Davignon Report) Annex II, Tables 1 and 2 (Luxembourg 1997).

[3] Trade Union Act 1871.

[4] Conspiracy and Protection of Property Act 1875 (something of a misnomer).

[5] Trade Disputes Act 1906.

faire'.[6] This was a policy stance which had profoundly limiting consequences for the role of labour law in the U.K., including the role of law in promoting the representation of employees collectively vis-à-vis their employer. First, leaving the unions to their own devices necessarily meant placing collective bargaining at the centre of the picture. By the end of the nineteenth century collective bargaining had become the method of operation upon which the majority of unions concentrated, replacing attempts at unilateral regulation which worked with craft workers but which was an ineffective tool for the representation of semi-skilled and unskilled workers with no natural job control. As in the United States, collective bargaining, not board representation or employee-based works councils, became the way of bringing democracy to the workplace.[7] However, the laissez-faire aspect of the policy meant that the state did no more than remove the legal obstacles which might make it difficult for unions to expand the scope of collective bargaining arrangements. The state did not act to secure bargaining rights for trade unions, whether by way of the enactment of a duty to bargain along the lines of the Wagner Act in the United States or by more complex methods of giving the union some sort of priority within an ostensibly employee-based system of works councils, as, say, in France.

In fact, the focus of state activity in relation to labour law was on strike law. For many decades, and still today for some, the acid test of state labour policy was whether it granted complete legal freedom to trade unions and workers to deploy peaceful economic sanctions in pursuit of industrial disputes. Once unions had that freedom of action, they were left to sink or swim as far as the recruitment of members and the securing of recognition was concerned.[8] So distant did the state wish to remain from legal regulation of the process of bargaining that the resulting collective agreements were not (and are not even today usually) treated as legally enforceable contracts;[9] and the closed shop was not the subject of regulation. In short, it was a system in which strong unions flourished, and the weak went to the wall.

---

[6] Kahn-Freund, Otto 'Labour Law' in: Ginsberg, Morris (ed.) *Law and Opinion in England in the 20th Century* 215 (London 1959).

[7] It is significant that the Webbs' early and seminal analysis of collective bargaining in the U.K. was entitled *Industrial Democracy* (Webb, Sidney J. and Beatrice Webb *Industrial Democracy* new edn. (1913)).

[8] The absence of legal regulation was not thought to be inconsistent with the provision of conciliation, mediation, and arbitration on a *voluntary* basis. See Industrial Courts Act 1919.

[9] Somewhat inaptly, they are considered 'gentlemen's agreements binding in honour only.' They are neither binding as legally enforceable contracts as between employer and union nor are they automatically and compulsorily incorporated into individual contracts of employment as codes of terms and conditions of employment. See Lord Wedderburn 'Inderogability, Collective Agreements and Community Law' *Industrial Law Journal* 21 (1992) 245.

Second, if the state showed little interest in regulating the institutions of collective representation, it nevertheless relied upon those institutions for the regulation of individual employment relationships. The state delegated that task to collective bargaining, whilst giving the bargaining parties the broadest freedom of manoeuvre. The result was a stunted development of individual employment law in the U.K. To take but a few examples: no general minimum wage law (only in 1998 is one being introduced); no regulation of the working hours of adult male workers (hence the controversy caused in the U.K. by the EC Directive on Working Time,[10] which requires the introduction of such rules); controls over dismissals (other than those of classical contract law) introduced only at the relatively late date of 1971.

It was, thus, the *combination* of delegation by the state of the regulatory task to collective bargaining and the abstention of the state from the regulation of the collective bargaining system which gave the British arrangements their unique character. It is easy to find states which have delegated the task of regulation of employment relationships to collective bargaining, but commonly they have also regulated the collective bargaining process at the same time (for example, the United States and the Wagner, Taft-Hartly, and Landrum-Griffin Acts). Equally, it is possible to find states (say, France until recently) which have not regulated the process of collective bargaining heavily but which equally have kept a much bigger role for the law in the regulation of individual employment relationships. The abstention from state regulation along *both* dimensions is what made the British model of collective *laissez-faire* unique.

It is not surprising that in this context statist institutions for the representation of employees within the enterprise did not develop. Except for a brief period in the incipiently revolutionary times at the end of the First World War, the state steered clear of proposals for statutory works councils.[11] Generally, it had no cause to alter its view that the trade unions needed little help to perform their role. Trade unions successfully occupied the representational space, not just at industry level in multi-employer bargaining but also at workplace level, especially in the period of full employment after the Second World War. During this period, collective bargaining, following the path of social power, became highly decentralised. Multi-employer bargaining went into secular decline and bargain-

[10] Council Directive 93/104/EC of 23 November 1993.

[11] The proposals of the Whitley Committee, produced at the end of the First World War and which might have led to a statutory structure of employee-based workplace representation, were in fact directed towards further state encouragement for voluntary collective bargaining and for statutory fall-back collective bargaining analogues ('wages councils') only in those (few) industries where trade union organisation proved impossible. See Davies, Paul L. and Mark R. Freedland *Labour Legislation and Public Policy* 37-43 (Oxford 1993).

ing arrangements became focused on the plant or enterprise.[12] The neat division of works councils within the plant and multi-employer collective bargaining outside it, on the German model, had no chance to take hold.

It is even less surprising that the U.K. developed no legal structures for the representation of employees within company law. Within a general culture of collective laissez-faire and without the sub-structural support of works councils, the absence of board-level representation is easily explained. In this context, what is surprising is not that the Bullock Committee's proposals[13] for board-level representation in the middle 1970s did not succeed but that they were ever made. The key to understanding this episode (including the level of employer opposition to the proposals) is that they were based upon the model of collective bargaining. The aim was to bring within joint regulation by employers and trade unions a range of employer decisions, especially at the level of strategic planning, which it was thought were not capable of being captured by traditional collective bargaining mechanisms.[14] But the model of collective bargaining was to be found in the form of board representation proposed: parity representation on a unitary board with reserved powers, the representatives to be closely linked to the unions recognised by the company for the purposes of collective bargaining (in the absence of such unions there was to be no board representation). With the failure of the Bullock proposals, U.K. corporate law continued largely unaffected by any employee concerns. That law had always regarded the duties of directors as being owed to the ultimate recipients of the company's income: the shareholders or, in cases of impending insolvency, the creditors. Although in 1980 the company law was amended so as to require directors to take into account the interests of the employees, in the absence of any mechanism for the enforcement of that duty by the employees or their representatives, its effect has probably been marginally to increase the freedom of action of corporate management vis-à-vis shareholders rather than to constrain it vis-à-vis the employees.[15]

---

[12] This development is chronicled in the 'Report of Royal Commission on Trade Unions and Employers' Associations' (Cmnd 3623, London 1968).

[13] 'Report of the Committee of Inquiry on Industrial Democracy' (Cmnd 6706, London 1977).

[14] For this argument in greater detail, see Davies, Paul L. 'The Bullock Report and Employee Participation in Corporate Planning in the UK' *Journal of Comparative Corporate Law and Securities Regulation* 1 (1978) 245.

[15] See Gower, Laurence C.B. and Paul L. Davies *Gower's Principles of Modern Company Law* 601-5 6th edn. (London 1997).

C. The Crisis

In retrospect, the system of collective laissez-faire can be seen to have been a product of particular economic and political circumstances which no longer obtain. Its adoption in the nineteenth century depended upon the conjunction of politically tolerant bourgeois parties, which controlled Parliament, and an industrially strong but politically weak working class.[16] Skilled workers were organised in effective trade unions by the middle of the nineteenth century and semi-skilled and unskilled workers by the end of it. By contrast, the universal male suffrage was not achieved until 1918 and the female suffrage not until 1928. The Trades Union Congress was founded in 1868 but the Labour Party not until 1900. Reversing the process in many other European countries, the Party was created by the unions, not vice versa. Consequently, when the government began to formulate its new policy in the 1870s, it was faced by a workers' movement which made predominantly industrial demands on the government, not political ones. The industrial demand was the freedom to get on with the process of organisation and collective bargaining without restraint from the law, and that was the demand to which the legislation of the time responded. The legal form of what developed was immunities for bargainers from the rigours of the common law, not rights, whether for trade unions or workers. The absence of a written constitution in the U.K. merely reinforced this tendency not to view labour law issues in terms of rights.

However, the continuance of the system of collective laissez-faire depended upon a rough equivalence of power in fact between employers and trade unions and a relative indifference on the part of the state as to the outcomes of collective bargaining. As the post-Second World War period has progressed, these factors have ceased to obtain, notably for our purposes the relative indifference of the state towards the operations and outcome of collective bargaining.[17]

The postwar full employment led to higher levels of industrial conflict than had obtained over the previous thirty years, and to the generation of inflationary pressures within the economy. For most of the thirty years from 1950, governments (both left and right) tried, at first timidly, later with greater boldness and even desperation, to cope with these trends by the deployment of corporatist policies, of which the Bullock proposals were perhaps the acme. Greater political or industrial power was offered to the trade unions in exchange for more 'responsible' use of that power and, in particular, for the trade unions taking up a role in controlling their members at grass roots level in support of policies jointly agreed with the government. These policies involved the abandonment of collective laissez-faire (because government was now far from indifferent to the processes

---

[16] Lord Wedderburn *The Worker and the Law* 21-5 3rd edn. (Harmondsworth 1986).

[17] For an extended account of these matters, see Davies and Freedland, supra n. 11, passim.

and outcomes of collective bargaining), but they still placed collective bargaining at the centre of the picture as the preferred mechanism for determining terms and conditions of employment. However, a union movement built on membership support as the source of its social power proved unsurprisingly inept at implementing the top-down policies which corporatist programmes were based on. In consequence, the attempted shift to a new form of industrial relations, with collective bargaining as a central element in a tripartite social plan concluded at national level among government, employers, and trade unions, proved unsuccessful.[18]

The essence of the 'Thatcher revolution' of the 1980s can perhaps be said to reside in the decision to abandon the policy of seeking to work through the trade unions and collective bargaining and of seeking to replace collective laissez-faire with straightforward individual laissez-faire or individual bargaining.[19] It was thus to be expected that the main focus of this legislation, especially in the early years, was upon strike law, i.e., upon the replacement of the policy that peaceful infliction of economic harm in pursuance of a trade dispute is lawful with a framework of strike law which rivals Germany's in its restrictiveness. Unionism declined from 55% of the workforce to 36% between 1979 and 1995.[20] In later years there was also a concentration upon restructuring of labour markets, especially in the public sector, where unionism was strong and the government could bring to bear its influence as both legislator and employer.[21]

However, this *bouleversement* was the result not just of a change of policy on the part of the government, for it resulted also from a change in the economic environment which was unfavourable to trade unions, especially in the decline of manufacturing and growth of services in their respective contributions to the overall economy. This was in part the result of intensified competition in an increasingly open global economy, which all comparable economies have experienced. Thus, there was a dramatic drop in the number of days lost per thousand employees in industrial disputes between 1975-1979 (when the figure was 509) and 1990-1994 (when the figure was 37). This led to a relative improvement in the U.K.'s international position: it was in the middle of the list of comparable countries in 1980, whereas by 1994 it was among the less strike-prone (it moved from 15th to 5th on the list). Yet, even if the U.K. has remained at 15th on the list, the number of days lost would have fallen to 55.[22] This suggests

---

[18] Davies and Freedland, supra n. 11, Ch. 7 and 8.

[19] The most general statement of the then government's policies is to be found in 'Employment for the 1990s' (Cm 540, London 1988).

[20] Some sources put the current figure even lower, at about 33%. See International Labour Office 'World Labour Report 1997-98' Table 1.2 (Geneva 1997).

[21] Davies and Freedland, supra n. 11, Ch. 9 and 10.

[22] Brown, William, Simon Deakin, and Paul Ryan 'The Effects of British Industrial Relations Legislation 1979-97' *National Institute Economic Review* no. 161 (1997) 78.

that the change in the area was probably more due to the decline in union power brought about by factors which the U.K. shared with other countries and was only to a lesser extent due to changes in governmental policy. This is not to deny that some employers did make very explicit use of the new legal framework either to de-recognise trade unions or to challenge and defeat trade unions in set-piece industrial action; the question that is debated relates to the relative significance of the changes in public policy on the one hand and in economic circumstances on the other.

On the other hand, these general economic developments impacted upon the U.K. in at least two particular ways because of its particular industrial governance structures. First, the impact of the decline in membership on the coverage of collective bargaining was severe. Coverage fell from 83% in 1980 to 48% in 1994 (i.e., coverage fell by over 42% whilst membership fell by 35%). By contrast, in France membership declined by one half whilst the coverage of collective bargaining actually increased by 10%.[23] The explanation for these figures seems to lie in the levels of collective bargaining in the two countries. In particular, in the context of single-employer bargaining, a decline in trade union membership tended to translate itself more directly into lower coverage of employees by collective bargaining than was the case in France in a still-flourishing system of multi-employer, sectoral bargaining, with agreements reached with employers' associations laying down a basic floor for the whole industry. The fall between 1980 and 1994 in the proportion of the workforce covered by collective bargaining in the U.K. was a much bigger proportionate fall than in any other country except, interestingly, the United States, where collective bargaining is also largely single-employer based.

The second particular impact of these general developments on the U.K. can be found in the area of task and numerical flexibility. All European labour relations systems have had to adjust to international competition by seeking greater flexibility, but the form of that flexibility in the U.K. has been heavily influenced by the nature of the employment laws and institutions left in place after this period of turmoil. Given that individual employment law has never provided a high level of employment security in the U.K. and that collective bargaining, which used to do that job in many industries, may no longer be in a position to do so, it is relatively easy for employers to achieve numerical flexibility, for example, by dismissing employees for economic reasons or substituting part-time workers for full-time ones or by sub-contracting tasks to lower paid workers. On the other hand, it is much less easy for employers to generate high-trust relations between employees and employers for lack of institutions which will protect employees who have invested in human-capital development from subsequent opportunistic behaviour on the part of the

---

[23] Brown, Deakin, and Ryan, supra n. 22, Tables 2 and 3.

employer. The relatively open system of takeover regulation, including the mounting of hostile bids, also tends to be destructive of established working relationship. Thus, organisational flexibility has appeared, relatively, the harder road to follow. As Locke and Kochan have put it: "The low-cost approach to market pressures and changes appears to be most frequent in countries with weak institutions, low levels of unionisation, decentralised bargaining systems, and a limited role for government in labour market affairs".[24] The point should not be over-played. Some low-skill employment is a desirable part of any economy; and some firms, domestic and foreign, have made a successful transposition to high-skill, high-wage flexible production methods. But there is enough evidence that the general trend is in the other direction for the point to worry policy-makers in the U.K.

D. The Future

British labour policy (with a new government in power) faces a strategic choice among three ways forward. One is to remain with the newly found emphasis on individual employment relations and a weak trade union movement, on the grounds that this gives the economy the greatest flexibility of response to changing economic conditions and is likely to generate the greatest total number of jobs. The second is to revert to the primacy of collective bargaining, probably not in the sense of collective laissez-faire, but in the sense of collective bargaining, constrained within some appropriate legal and institutional framework, being the preferred method of settling terms and conditions of employment. The third is to move towards what is sometimes referred to as the 'European model' of industrial relations (though in reality no such single model can be found). The essential features of this seem to be the involvement of employers' associations and trade unions at the national level in finding solutions to social and economic problems; a broad state-led system of social protection, including social security and publicly provided services; and significant levels of intervention by the government in the economic life of the country.

To date, one can identify policy decisions which are consistent with each of these three strategies, and the ultimate balance between them waits to be determined. The first strategy involves doing very little beyond keeping the inherited structure of law and policy in place. It seems clear that the new government accepts much of the previous government's analysis of the job creation potential of flexible labour markets. In particular, combating social exclusion is seen very much in terms of getting the young and the long-term unemployed into jobs, and

---

[24] Locke, Richard M., Thomas A. Kochan, and Michael Joseph Piore *Employment Relations in a Changing World Economy* 374 (Cambridge, Mass. 1995).

legislation regulating the individual employment relationship is therefore viewed with suspicion if it is thought likely to make that task harder. On the collective side, in its 'Business Manifesto' the Labour Party specifically stated during the election campaign that "the existing laws on industrial action, picketing and ballots will remain unchanged"; and Mr. Blair said that, even after the government's proposed reforms, "the U.K. would still have the toughest labour laws in the Western world."[25] So the previous government's arguments on the need to reform strike law seem to have won the day, subject to a rather important proposal to improve the position of individual workers engaged in lawful industrial action.

To the extent that the existing structure of industrial conflict law remains in place, so the second policy of placing collective bargaining at the centre of the picture is impeded. However, some steps to support that institution seem likely to be adopted. In particular, there is a commitment to re-introduce a statutory union recognition procedure, containing an obligation to bargain in good faith and based upon majority voting in defined bargaining units. What is unclear at the time of writing is whether this machinery will be designed with the aim of reversing the decline in collective bargaining or only to deal with the most egregious cases of employers' ignoring the expressed desires of a majority of the work-force.

It is difficult to believe that the third model will be implemented at the macro level. The constraints of government financing are likely to cause a contraction rather than an expansion of welfare state expenditures, and the mechanisms for effective social plans in the U.K. seem still not to exist.[26] However, at the micro, or firm level, one can see the possibilities of a strategy of greater involvement by employee representatives in aspects of the firm's decision making, the possibilities of which bring us at least some way back towards the subject of corporate governance with which we started.

The basis of the argument would be as follows. The dense system of enterprise-based, adversarial collective bargaining which grew up in the U.K. in the postwar period led to a high degree of joint regulation of terms and conditions of employment. On some criteria, this system scored highly. For example, it introduced a high degree of democracy into the workplace and it helped the dispersal of power within society, as confident local communities developed around large workplaces. On the other hand, the adversarial nature of the system made

[25] For an analysis of the Labour Party's policy statements during the election campaign and shortly after elections, see Warwick Business School 'The Industrial Relations Consequences of New Labour' (available over the Internet; http://www.wbs.warwick.ac.uk/HotTopics/).

[26] The introduction of a national minimum wage may be seen as a step in the direction of social solidarity, though it will also have the desirable effect (from the government's point of view) of reducing state expenditure on in-work benefits and the wage rate is unlikely to be set at a level which will threaten job creation.

management reluctant to share information about matters outside the bargaining arena (for example, production and investment plans), for fear that such sharing would be a prelude to demands for the extension of joint regulation into the arena of 'business management' and therefore of 'management prerogative'. The strength of employer opposition to the proposals of the Bullock Committee[27] demonstrates the firmness of employer opposition to such a strategy.

However, a strategy which emphasises above all the importance of managerial prerogative, the individualisation of labour relations, and the need to expose the participants in industrial relations to the rigours of the markets strongly discourages investment by both employers and employees in the development of job-related skills, except where those skills are of a generic and transferable type. With the growth of flexible specialisation of production, however, it seems likely that the whole or the majority of the investments of employers and employees in high-level training is lost once the employment relationship within which the training occurred is terminated. As the jargon has it, the investment is 'match specific', i.e., "is one which has value when used by the parties to the match, but has no value otherwise."[28] Once the investment has been made, either side is vulnerable to termination of the employment relationship by the other party, and ex ante perception of this risk is likely to lead to a less than optimum investment in training. A legal and economic structure which makes termination of employment the de facto preferred response to changes in the levels and composition of product demand is likely to discourage both employers and employees from match-specific investment in training, unless that investment has a very short pay-back period. Certainly, training investments which pay back only over the full career of the worker begin to look highly unattractive.

This take on employment relationships has some quite general implications for the structure of employment law, for example, in relation to the termination of employment for economic reasons. Of more immediate relevance to the concerns of this paper, however, is that it suggests a rationale for mechanisms designed to give employees (or their representatives) information about and consultation rights in relation to managerial decision making, though it stops well short of providing an argument for the extension of joint regulation into these areas. The argument concerns not so much the sunk costs thrown away upon the termination of the employment relationship but rather the fact that, even with the employment relationship on foot, each side has difficulty, arising out of asymmetric information, in determining whether the other side is engaging in rent seeking. For the employer the asymmetry arises typically in relation to work

[27] Supra n. 13.

[28] Rock, Edward B. and Michael L. Wachter 'Enforceability of Norms and the Employment Relationship' 144 *U. Pa. L. Rev.* 1913, 1917 n. 12 (1996). Cf. also the survey of economic theories of co-determination in Gerum/Wagner (this volume Ch. 5: Sec. B).

effort; for the employees in relation to business success of the enterprise. The employer's temptation not to recognise and reward the full value of the human capital investments made by the employees by exaggerating the business difficulties the enterprise faces could be counteracted, it is argued, by statutory information and consultation mechanisms.[29]

Within European Community law[30] the use of compulsory information and consultation mechanisms at the point of termination of the employment relationship was recognised in the 1970s, with the directives on collective redundancies[31] and transfers of undertakings.[32] More significantly the European Works Councils Directive,[33] applying to enterprises over a certain size threshold which have operations in two or more member states, ushers in at Community level the notion of a mechanism for the continuing disclosure of information and consultation relating to the employment implications of strategic decisions taken at the level of the multi-national enterprise as a whole.[34] The Commission is currently seeking to extend the principle of mandatory information and consultation to national-level decision making (whether by subsidiaries of multi-national companies or by purely domestic companies) by encouraging the social partners to negotiate an agreement with the social policy provisions[35] which would extend the principles of the European Works Council Directive to this lower level.[36]

It is far from clear that we should limit the institutional mechanisms for dealing with the informational asymmetries of the employees to works councils. There is evidence that the main consequence of board-level representation of

---

[29] The employers' information asymmetry problems in relation to work performance are addressed, positively, by payment and promotion systems and, negatively, by disciplinary and dismissal procedures.

[30] On the development in the EU, see also Gerum/Wagner (this volume Ch. 5: Sec. D and E).

[31] Council Directive 75/129/EEC of 17 February 1975.

[32] Council Directive 77/187/EEC of 14 February 1977.

[33] Council Directive 94/45/EC of 22 September 1994. This directive has been extended to the U.K. in the light of the U.K. government's commitment, reflected in the treaty changes agreed in Amsterdam in 1997, to accept the extended law-making competence of the Community in the social policy area, originally agreed for the other member states at Maastricht and embodied in the Social Policy Agreement which was attached to the Treaty on European Union.

[34] What this will amount to in practice remains to be seen since one strong feature of the directive is the freedom it gives the management and employee representatives in particular enterprises to design their own information and consultation structures, albeit in the light of the fall-back provisions in Annex 1 of the directive, which come into play if agreement is not reached on an alternative set of arrangements.

[35] See Commission of the European Communities 'Communication from the Commission on Worker Information and Consultation' (COM(95) 547 final, Brussels, November 1995).

[36] It may seem paradoxical that the Community should begin by legislating for the more remote level of multi-national decision making, but the subsidiarity objection to Community legislation is more easily met at multi-national level where, by definition, national systems of law find it difficult to establish trans-border machinery, so that the efficacy of Community legislation is clearer.

employees, at least at a minority level, is that it improves the information flow between central management and the institutions of worker representation within and without the enterprise. However, even at the level of works councils, these Community developments provide both a challenge to the existing British law relating to a 'single channel' of employee representation through a trade union, and pressure towards adoption by the U.K. of the third strategic model identified above. Already, in relation to the directives adopted in the 1970s, the European Court of Justice has held that exclusive reliance on the recognised trade unions as the consultation partners of employers in collective redundancies and transfers is inadequate, because there will not necessarily exist a recognised union in all workplaces covered by the directive.[37] Although the then government's response, of giving the employer a free choice to consult a recognised union or employee representatives elected by the workforce as a whole,[38] is likely to be replaced by a rule giving priority to the recognised trade union, if such exists,[39] the union monopoly over representation in respect of statutorily required information and consultation will remain broken. The application of the European Works Councils Directive to the U.K. will reinforce this trend, since its fall-back provisions require that the representatives on the EWC either be chosen from among the employee representatives existing in the national-level firms or "in the absence thereof, by the entire body of employees."[40] Thus, British trade unions, too, are faced with a strategic choice. Should they continue with their traditional policy of opposition to any form of non-union-based representation within the enterprise or, as German experience shows is not impossible, should they see an ostensibly employee-based body as a potential vehicle for the promotion of the benefits of union representation? With the decline in union membership and in the coverage of collective bargaining, the issue presents itself with a force not previously seen this century.[41]

So there is considerable scope for future conflict between the British tradition of representation only via the trade unions and the evolving Community norm which at a minimum requires supplementation of the single channel where no union has been recognised by the employer. In particular, it is unclear how far British unions, which have traditionally depended upon job control at the workplace for their power positions, will be able to embrace a less adversarial and

---

[37] Cases C-382 and 383/92, *Commission v UK* [1994] ECR I-2435, noted by Davies, Paul L. *Industrial Law Journal* 23 (1994) 272.

[38] Collective Redundancies and Transfer of Undertakings (Protection of Employment) (Amendment) Regulations, SI 1995 No 2587.

[39] Department of Trade and Industry 'Employees' Information and Consultation Rights on Transfers of Undertakings and Collective Redundancies' (Consultation Document, February 1998).

[40] Directive 94/45/EC, Annex, para 1(b). See also art. 5(2)(a) on the Special Negotiating Body.

[41] For a cautious initial stab at this issue, see Trades Union Congress 'Your Voice at Work' (London 1995).

more trusting workplace culture and a more 'investment-based' approach to employment relationships. Under EC pressures there may be some convergence on the part of the U.K. towards a 'works council' model of plant-level representation, but whether this will be a significant step and whether it will be part of a more general move away from a low-skill, low-cost strategy for labour relations remains to be seen.

Employee Stock Ownership in Economic Transitions: The Case of United Airlines

JEFFREY N. GORDON, New York[*]

This chapter argues that employee stock ownership transactions (ESOTs) may have decisive advantages in addressing the transition problems associated with significant economic change. Equity ownership by employees can increase value not only because of the better incentive alignment, but also because equity has special value in addressing bargaining problems that interfere with renegotiation of employee contracts in volatile economic environments. One important question is whether ESOTs create only a transitional organizational form, a one-time adjustment of economic claims that will soon revert back to public shareownership, or a durable form for managing economic change.

These issues are explored in the recent employee acquisition of a majority ownership of United Airlines. The transaction provided for long-term employee ownership, not simply a transitional form, and so locked up the employee stock in an employee pension plan and provided employees with long-term governance rights. One objective of the UAL transaction was to catalyze a cultural change to make the airline a better competitor, not just through wage reductions but through operational efficiencies requiring a higher level of employee cooperation. The evidence to date suggests that the ESOT has enhanced UAL's competitive position, but that governance pressure from employees when their interests are directly at stake is a potentially destabilizing force.

Contents

[*] For helpful discussion and comments on earlier drafts, I am grateful to Mark Barenberg, Margaret Blair, Bernie Black, David Charny, Sam Estreicher, Ron Gilson, Henry Hansmann, Eric Orts, Andrzej Rapaczynski, Mark Roe, and Chuck Sabel. For research help I am grateful to Ian Haft. For financial support, I am grateful to the Sloan Foundation and the Columbia/Sloan Corporate Governance Project.

Figures

Tables

A. Introduction

Employee ownership starts with two sorts of normative appeal. First, in the current economic order, equity participation may be a more reliable mechanism for employees to share in the firm's prosperity than wage increases. Real wages for all but the top quintile of wage earners have been essentially stagnant for nearly two decades while real stock prices have increased nearly threefold. Protecting and promoting employees' welfare arguably means giving them a firm-specific ownership stake in the means of production.[1] Second, ownership carries with it governance rights, which means the opportunity to participate in the organization and management of the workplace. As in any large-scale political regime, direct participation may be constrained, but even so, employee ownership brings the dignity of self-control and accountability to one's fellow employees.

Despite these attractive features, employee ownership of controlling stakes is uncommon in large corporations and such ownership as exists typically uses a tax-favored retirement trust, an ESOP ("Employee Stock Ownership Plan"), that ordinarily severely limits employee exercise of ownership prerogatives. There is of course an extensive debate, usually of a polar sort, on why employee owner-

[1] See generally, Gordon, Jeffrey N. 'Employees, Pensions, and the New Economic Order' 97 *Colum. L. Rev.* 1519 (1997).

ship of large firms is so rare. One position is that employee ownership is never efficient because of an array of problems, including monitoring failures, inefficient risk bearing, inadequate incentives for internal capital accumulation, and internal governance failures. The other position is that employee ownership is always efficient (because of incentive alignment that reduces shirking and enhances effort) but that market failures or regulatory barriers have blocked its use.[2]

My approach is somewhat different. I want to suggest that "employee ownership" should be thought of not as a self-defining organizational form but rather a reference to a universe of potential organizational forms that variously combine elements of employee governance participation and profit participation.[3] Imagine governance participation and profit participation as variables on separate axes of a two-dimensional organizational space. No single point in the space constitutes "employee ownership." Different levels of economic participation may be matched with different levels of governance participation. "Employee ownership" refers to a set of points in which the resulting organization is sufficiently different from the traditional firm that the new designation seems apt. Central to my approach are the propositions that employee ownership can take many different forms and that the particular institutions of economic participation and governance participation fashioned for a particular firm may matter crucially to the firm's success. This is not so very different from our evolving concept of the "public corporation" as an organizational form that can house quite different relationships between shareholders and managers. The manager-dominated firm of the 1950s, for example, is quite different from the institutionally influenced firm of the 1990s; the public corporation owned by a dispersed group of shareholders is different from a firm with a controlling shareholder.

Like many other organizational forms, particular employee ownership structures may be especially well-suited to particular economic environments. In particular, certain forms of employee ownership may have decisive advantages in

---

[2] Very useful discussions of employee ownership (and references to further discussion) are found in Blasi, Joseph and Douglas Kruse *The New Owners: The Mass Emergence of Employee Ownership in Public Companies and What It Means for American Business* (New York 1991); Dow, Greg and Louis Putterman 'Why Capital Hires Labor: A Review and Assessment of Some Proposed Explanations' (Working Paper, 1996); Earle, John S. and Saul Estrin 'Employee Ownership in Transition' in: Frydman, Roman, Cheryl Gray, and Andrzej Rapaczynski (eds.) *Corporate Governance in Central Europe and Russia* vol. 2 *Insiders and the State* 1 (Budapest et al. 1996); Hansmann, Henry 'When Does Worker Ownership Work? ESOPS, Law Firms, Codetermination, and Economic Democracy' 99 *Yale L.J.* 1749 (1990); Hansmann, Henry *The Ownership of Enterprise* (Cambridge, Mass. 1996); Hyde, Alan 'In Defense of Employee Ownership' 67 *Chi.-Kent L. Rev.* 159 (1991).

[3] By "profit participation" or "economic participation" I mean to refer to participation in the residual claim usually associated with ownership of common stock but also available through contingent compensation formulas such as profit-sharing.

addressing the transition problems associated with significant economic change. This is not only because the value of some of the commonly identified advantages of employee ownership is likely to be greatest in such circumstances (for example, the better incentive alignment achieved by making employees major stockholders may be crucial for firms in financial distress), but also because equity has special value in solving some of the bargaining problems that can stymie renegotiation of the employees' contract with the firm. Similarly, some of the disadvantages of employee ownership are at their lowest (for example, accepting equity in place of fixed wage claims in a distressed firm may actually reduce employee risks by enhancing the firm's viability). Indeed, many recent examples of employee ownership in the large corporation may be found in two industries facing sharply changed economic circumstances: the airline industries following deregulation in 1978, and the steel industry following the rise of low-cost foreign competition employing new technology. In restructurings of firms in both industries, employees received substantial equity claims in exchange for wage and labor amenity concessions.

One important question is whether these employee stock ownership transactions produce a transitional organizational form or a relatively permanent form for managing transitions. Does the employee transaction amount to simply a one-time adjustment of economic claims, so that we should expect in ordinary course a reversion back to public shareholder ownership? Or do these employee transactions produce a durable organizational form that addresses a series of transition problems in a superior way? Thus there are two possible ways to understand the present examples of employee ownership. First, it may be that they simply restructure fixed wage claims that are no longer sustainable by the distressed firm's cash flows—much like a bondholder's acceptance in similar circumstances of lower yielding, longer maturity bonds with an equity interest. If the crisis passes, the employee, like the bondholder, will be only too happy to give up the role of stockholder, and the firm reverts to the standard form. On the other hand, perhaps the business environment calls for continual readjustments of wage levels and other labor amenities, or perhaps an employee stock ownership transaction can catalyze a change in firm culture and structure that makes the firm a better competitor. In this case employee ownership may turn out to be a superior organizational form for firms in industries undergoing transitions.

An obvious analogy is leveraged buyouts, which had special value in the 1980s in addressing managerial incentive or "agency" problems in firms with free cash flow (that is, firms that were generating more cash flow than they could profitably reinvest in their core businesses).[4] In many cases those firms have

---

[4] See Jensen, Michael 'The Takeover Controversy: Analysis and Evidence' in: Coffee, John, Louis Lowenstein, and Susan-Rose Ackerman (eds.) *Knights, Raiders, & Targets: The Impact of the Hostile Takeover* 314 (New York 1988); Jensen, Michael 'Eclipse of the Public Corporation' *Harvard Business Review* 61/5 (1989) 61.

become public companies once again ("reverse LBOs"), having solved the agency problems (at least for a time) and finding that the risk-bearing advantages of public ownership outweigh the better incentive alignments of private ownership.[5] For such firms the LBO served as a transitional organizational form. Nevertheless, many LBO firms have remained private companies, presumably because of the advantages of close monitoring by the LBO organization. Even if the public corporation has not been eclipsed, the LBO form has established itself as a viable alternative for particular business situations. And just as LBOs can address a number of different organizational problems, not just the stylized free cash flow case, it may be that employee stock ownership transactions ("ESOTs") usefully can address many adjustment problems that arise in cases of economic change.

This paper analyzes the potential advantages of ESOTs in cases of economic transition and then examines one particularly important example, the recent employee acquisition of majority equity in United Airlines ("UAL"). The United transaction can be traced to the transition shock of airline deregulation in 1978 and the competitive aftershocks that followed. The parties in UAL contemplated employee ownership as more than a transitional device, since the deal is structured to lock up employee stock in an ESOP and to provide strong employee governance rights for the next 20 years. One of the objectives of the ESOT was to catalyze a cultural change in UAL's operations so that at least part of the airline could become a low-cost carrier that could compete in the economically important West Coast market, not just through wage reductions but through operational efficiencies that would require a higher level of employee cooperation. The evidence, sketchy thus far, is that UAL is capable of highly profitable performance but that governance pressure from the employees where their economic interests are directly at stake is potentially destabilizing. The UAL case also shows that adjustment to prosperity can raise problems almost as difficult as adjustment to economic adversity.[6]

---

[5] Kaplan, Steven 'The Staying Power of Leveraged Buyouts' *Journal of Applied Corporate Finance* 6/1 (1993) 15.

[6] Although the focus of this paper is the value of ESOTs in solving transition problems in the U.S. setting, it generally supports the use of employee equity ownership in the transitional economies of Eastern Europe and Russia. Insofar as employees start with significant bargaining endowments and unsustainable wage and labor amenity claims, equity can play a useful role in restructuring the economic claims on the firm. This is subject to the important caveat that appropriately contextualized institutional structures of governance participation and gain-sharing are critical to a successful restructuring. Similarly, the general analysis supports the use of significant employee ownership in firms that might be regarded in a continual state of transition because of the intensity of the competitive pressures, for example, in the high-tech area. Thus one way to understand the wide dispersal of stock options among Microsoft employees is not only as an incentive for strenuous activity to increase the value of the firm but also to encourage employees to leave after their period of maximum productivity.

B. Transition Problems

There are four sorts of transition problems that employee stock ownership transactions can address: the just allocation of transition costs as between shareholders and employees; efficient bargaining over the allocation of one-time transition costs; efficient bargaining over ongoing transition costs; and the creation of superior structures for transitional environments. The form of employee ownership and the associated governance arrangements will be a function of the problem addressed.

"Just allocation" problems arise because of changed economic circumstances that reduce the profitability of the firm. In theory, the reduction in cash flow could be allocated against shareholder returns, in the form of reduced dividends (which would presumably lower the stock price) or against employee returns, in the form of reduced wages or layoffs. The normative question is how *should* these transition costs be allocated. If cost-sharing is the answer, then employee stock ownership transactions, in which employees exchange wage claims and other labor cost-reducing measures for equity in the firm, may serve this purpose, depending on the terms of trade.

"Efficient bargaining" problems arise from information asymmetries and from hold-up and other bargaining problems that are likely to interfere with efforts to renegotiate fixed claims in a firm facing reduced cash flows. The starting point is a stakeholder group that has made a firm-specific investment which is protected contractually against expropriation but which loses substantial value in bankruptcy. One example is unsecured bondholders; another is employees covered by a collective bargaining agreement that provides for wages and amenities above the employees' opportunity wage. A successful renegotiation that leads to lower labor costs may well preserve economic value for both the workers and the shareholders, but bargaining failure is a real possibility. Like a restructuring of financial claims that gives bondholders an equity interest, an ESOT reallocates claims on the firm's cash flow in a way that credibly certifies the need for employee concessions and that in other important respects may reduce the risk of bargaining failure. Thus the argument for an ESOT is not a "justice" claim in the reallocation, but that the transactional form promotes the conservation of economic value, given the preexisting bargaining endowments.

"Efficient bargaining over ongoing transition costs" refers to cases in which the firm faces the likelihood of future occasions for renegotiation and will face continuing problems of bargaining breakdown. This is different from a typical restructuring, which is commonly imagined as a one-time event. But if the firm is operating in a dynamic economic environment, it is easy to imagine that the firm may repeatedly be unable to meet fixed wage claims and labor amenities. An ESOT can put in place economic incentives and a governance structure that reduces the likelihood of bargaining failure in the course of successive renegotiations.

"Superior structures" refers to ways of restructuring workplace relations and culture that, in a dynamic economic environment, enables the firm to adapt more quickly than competitors and so minimize the transition costs that must be allocated. There are at least two points of interest here: first, the possibility that the particular governance structure and profit-sharing structure of an ESOT can help promote a more productive, competitively superior environment within the firm; and second, that in such an environment employees are less likely to experience the sudden wipeout of human capital investments that gives rise to the most severe transition costs issues.

Each of these transition problems has been the subject of debate, but I think the analysis can be advanced by considering each through the lens of employee stock ownership transactions in the airline industry, in particular, the UAL transaction. My general view is that although ESOTs could usefully serve as a vehicle for "just allocation" of transition costs, the case for such allocations is not convincing. Nevertheless, in many transition cases ESOTs can play a role in conserving (or enhancing) the value of the firm. Employee stock ownership can serve as a transitional form for solving particular problems that arise in a transition, such as the need to reprice the value of the labor in an uncertain environment. But it also has a place as a form for transitions for environments in which a high degree of employee cooperation may produce competitive advantage.

I. Just Allocation

There are two significant problems in conceiving of ESOTs as addressing the just allocation of transition losses between shareholders and employees. The first is a basic practical issue: absent a legally enforceable wage and labor amenity claim, employees ordinarily have no basis to negotiate for an equity-for-concessions swap. This becomes apparent in contrasting the case of UAL (and other airlines that have undertaken an ESOT) with the case of Delta, which, unlike the other major carriers, is not unionized (except for the pilots). In 1994 Delta announced a program to reduce operating expenditures by 20%, $2 billion. Delta's plan seeks to eliminate 12,000-15,000 jobs (of a workforce of approximately 71,000) and calls for other concessions. The laid-off employees have received no equity and similarly the move for further concessions has not led to an ESOT. The one Delta employee group that has benefited from an ESOT is the pilots, which received approximately 2% of the company's equity in exchange for concessions. The contrast is stark: explicit contractual rights, but not otherwise, trigger an ESOT.[7]

This threshold issue does not necessarily resolve the matter, however, since it would be possible to construct a legal regime that mandatorily gave employees special bargaining endowments in appropriately defined cases of economic transition. It is difficult to identify the normative basis for such an inalienable endowment (necessarily inalienable because the willingness of some employee groups not to exercise the present legal right to bargain collectively shows that employees ex ante might waive or trade such an endowment). Even if as a matter of social justice or policy we decided that it was wrong that specific employee groups should bear economic transition costs, it is not obvious why the solution should be located at the level of the individual firm, fixed there through a bargaining endowment that could lead to stock ownership. Particular firms will differ in their capacity to provide for transition measures; the bargaining position of different employee groups within firms will also differ, and thus the actual benefits will be somewhat randomly distributed. Moreover, receiving stock in an economically threatened enterprise hardly addresses core issues such as the portability of benefits and enhancement of future employability. "Justice" is a feature of a society overall that does not depend on locally just decisions by every economic institution.[8]

---

[7] Actually the UAL case provides a partial counterexample. Among the employee groups that participated in the buyout were the salaried and management employees, who in exchange for a proportionate share of concessions, received approximately 9% of the stock—despite the absence of a collective bargaining agreement covering them. There are two theories as to why they were permitted to participate in the ESOT on equivalent terms. The first is an agency cost explanation: that senior management self-identified with this employee group and under the cover of the general transaction, gave an unnecessary benefit at shareholder expense. The second is an efficiency explanation that sheds light on the underlying purpose of the transaction: that the point of the transaction was to add value going forward, an objective served by expanded participation, or in a somewhat milder form, that white collar concessions were necessary to obtain union membership approval and that to have excluded the salaried and management employees from the ESOT would have demoralized them.

[8] I feel some conflict about this point in the following way. Assume that society decides to provide protection against transition losses, whether as a matter of justice or as a prudential judgment about the necessary sharing of gains and losses from economic change for social and political harmony. Then mechanisms that force firms and employees to internalize (at least partially) such transition costs may reduce the costs ex ante and ex post. Compare, for example, the problem of workplace safety. We have come to a consensus that accidents and hazards are inevitable in an industrialized society, but that medical costs and lost work time should be compensated. Nevertheless if such costs were fully socialized, the costs to be borne by general taxation, firms would have little incentive to reduce the level of workplace harm or to monitor medical and income maintenance costs ex post. The success of worker's compensation system in reducing the level of workplace harm depends upon experience-related insurance premiums. In the same way mechanisms that force individual firms to address transition costs problems may be the lowest-cost way to achieve a social objective, and conceivably the assignment of bargaining endowments is a critical part of the problem. This is the subject of an ongoing project.

A related problem is specifying the employee claim at the firm level. A collective bargaining agreement or other explicit contractual protection is a straightforward specification. Where there is no such contract, many have argued that the basis for the employee claim is an "implicit" contract with the firm, which is entitled to protection, either through courts or through governance mechanisms.[9]

Such implicit contracts protect two sorts of interests: deferred compensation claims, and rents and quasi-rents deriving from firm-specific human capital investment. There are apparently two distinct concerns: first, that the firm will opportunistically expropriate these employee claims; second, that these employee claims should be prior to shareholder claims over a significant range of economic circumstances. I think that expropriation is a much overstated concern and that in any event, the very nature of an implicit contract undermines its use as a basis for renegotiating a sharing of transition costs.

"Deferred compensation" refers to circumstances in which an employee is or will be paid more than marginal product on account of a prior period of employment compensated at less than marginal product. Such circumstances include compensation for initially suppressed wages that represent the employee "match" to the firm's investment in training; compensation for lower wages because of the difficulty in identifying superior performance early in an employee's career; and explicit efforts to structure the compensation ladder to bind employees to the firm during periods of maximum mobility.[10]

"Rents and quasi-rents" refers to circumstances in which an employee is paid marginal product that reflects return on firm-specific human capital investment. For example, assume that a worker learns how to operate a customized machine that makes products that earn economic rents for the owner. Some of these rents may be shared with employees. The quasi-rent reflects the difference between marginal product (taking into account a return on the employee's investment in learning to operate the customized machine) and the employee's opportunity wage (the wage at the next best job).

---

[9] See, e.g., Shleifer, Andrei and Lawrence Summers 'Breach of Trust in Corporate Take-overs' in: Auerbach, Alan (ed.) *Corporate Takeovers: Causes and Consequences* 33 (Chicago et al. 1988); Blair, Margaret *Ownership and Control: Rethinking Corporate Governance for the Twenty-first Century* (Washington 1995); O'Connor, Marleen 'The Human Capital Era: Reconceptualizing Corporate Law to Facilitate Labor-Management Cooperation' 78 *Cornell L. Rev.* 899 (1993); Mitchell, Lawrence 'A Theoretical and Practical Framework for Enforcing Corporate Constituency Statutes' 70 *Tex. L. Rev.* 579 (1992); Singer, Joseph 'The Reliance Interest in Property' 40 *Stan. L. Rev.* 611 (1988).

[10] "Deferred compensation" as used here does not refer to measures commonly thought of within the category, such as pensions (which may vest and increase in the out years), stock options (which may be granted and exercised over a time period), or other forms of explicitly contractible benefits. Indeed, such rights granted by contract stand in contrast to "deferred compensation" arising from implicit understandings.

One important question is the extent to which these employee interests are subject to expropriation. In fact, the "rent and quasi-rent" interest are not systematically expropriable. As long as the firm is earning rents, the owner has every incentive to continue to pay such wages to keep production flowing. There may be jockeying over the division of rents, but the owner's agreement to pay more than the employee's opportunity wage is self-enforcing.[11] This is the sense in which the agreement to pay such wages is "implicit".[12] But assume market conditions change, either because of cheaper versions of the product or a superior substitute; rents disappear. In such circumstances, for the owner to cut the worker's salary or to lay off the worker is not an expropriation. It merely reflects the fact that the owner's investment and the worker's investment have both depreciated in value and that the conditions under which high wages were paid have disappeared. In other words, an implied term of the implicit contract relates to continuation of the economic circumstances on which the payout was predicated.

What about "deferred compensation"; can these interests be expropriated? By hypothesis the employee is receiving greater than marginal product, so the individual contract for the continuation of such compensation cannot be self-enforcing—unless the individual is part of a workforce that the company wants to continue to hire and employ on the same basis as the particular employee. That is, so long as the firm wants employees to make firm-specific human capital investments, then the firm will protect accrued deferred compensation claims; otherwise the firm's claim to protect future deferred compensation would not be credible. In such circumstances the firm's desire to preserve its reputation would sustain its past implicit promise.[13]

---

[11] To be sure, there may be some temptation to reduce wages below marginal product—to appropriate some of the quasi-rent—on the view that any payment above the employee's opportunity wage is sufficient to retain the employee. The employer faces considerable risk in such a calculation, as is demonstrated by the experimental literature on the rejection of "rational" economic bargains that are perceived as unfair. Moreover, insofar as the employee's skills require continual updating—i.e., continued firm-specific human capital investment—the failure to pay on prior investments would be self-defeating. Similarly, if the firms hires new employees expecting firm-specific human capital investments, welshing on implicit contracts to incumbent employees would be self-defeating.

[12] It is important to distinguish between an "implied' contract as a lawyer would understand the term and an "implicit" contract as used in the economics literature but sometimes loosely elsewhere. An implied contract, which represents a binding contract between the parties that may not have been reduced to definitive form, is enforceable if proved; an implicit contract in the economists' customary sense depends on marketplace forces for its enforcement.

[13] One of the complexities is that the reputation effects which in some circumstances sustain implicit contracts are supported by social norms that may be unstable over time. A major economic dislocation, or a rapid change in the behavior of firms in a concentrated time period, can produce a general shift in expectations that could reduce significantly the penalty for deviating from prior expectations.

On the other hand, if background economic conditions have reduced the level of optimal firm-specific human capital, the firm may well want to change its employment policy. Consider the example of the shift from custom configured mainframe computers with highly specialized software to personal computers using off-the-rack software: general capital, physical and human, has replaced specific capital. The value of prior specific capital investments is substantially diminished and the firm does not anticipate such investments in the near future. In such cases the firm's reputational interests may not sustain payment of the deferred compensation. But this is because of a change in real economic variables that provided the basis for the self-enforcing nature of the implied contract, not because of opportunistic behavior by the firm.[14] In other words, implicit deferred compensation claims will be honored only in circumstances where the parties could have reasonably expected them to be honored: where it serves the present interest of the firm. If the claims were contractible (like pensions or stock options), they would have been.[15]

The second question is whether such claims should come ahead of shareholder claims over some range of economic circumstances. This is probably what most defenders of the implicit contract claim actually have in mind—that shareholders

[14] One of the major concerns of 1980s-style leverage buyouts was that the gains were financed out of opportunistic conversion of the employees' deferred compensation claims. The argument was that new owners could treat current employees opportunistically without damaging their continuing reputation. See Knoeber, Charles 'Golden Parachutes, Shark Repellants, and Hostile Tender Offers' *American Economic Review* 76 (1986) 155. This seems implausible: having previously decided to disregard prior claims of deferred compensation, how could new owners credibly commit to protect deferred compensation subsequently? Even if they were unwilling to wield the axe, they could sell to others who would. More generally, the debate in the 1980s was over whether takeover entrepreneurs were acting opportunistically or in response to real economic change; the question about expropriation of implicit deferred compensation claims was part of that debate. The subsequent restructuring, downsizing, and reengineering by large firms that were not under the raiders' gun is strong evidence that a change in real economic variables rather than speculative opportunism played the more important role. See Gordon, Jeffrey N. 'Corporation, Markets, and Courts' 91 *Colum. L. Rev.* 1931, 1953-5, 1975-88 (1991).

[15] This analysis explains why Williamson's account of corporate governance is incomplete. He distinguishes the case of the shareholder (who gets board representation) from the employee (who does not) on the ground that the employee's claim is contractible, whereas the shareholder's residual claim is not; or in the alternative, that shareholders have made an asset-specific investment that is expropriable ex post because it cannot be described by a complete contingent claims contract. Blair, supra n. 9, and others point out that employees have residual claims in Williamson's sense—non-contractible interests that are expropriable ex post. Focusing on the comparative degree of self-enforceability may provide a more convincing explanation of why shareholders control the board. As noted in the text, employees are making continuous firm-specific investments in the firm, either as individuals or as a group; thus the firm's reputational interests protect the employee investment. By contrast, after an initial period of capital raising, shareholder investments in the firm are made infrequently. Most of the firm's capital needs are supplied through retained earnings. This means an implicit contract with shareholders is not self-enforcing, thus calling for a governance structure to provide credible protection against expropriation.

are better situated to bear the losses of economic transition than workers and therefore should honor these implicit contract claims. Shareholders can easily diversify their claims in financial markets (though not all do and recent governance theory suggests that concentrated holdings help constrain agency costs in some settings). By contrast, workers' capacity to diversify is much more limited because the present value of their job-related rents and quasi-rents is much greater than their financial assets, and because it is much harder to acquire a diversified labor skill portfolio (i.e., learn many jobs) than a diversified financial portfolio.[16]

Of course, in such circumstances shareholders have already borne part of the loss, since the economic changes that threaten deferred compensation claims have presumably also reduced firm cash flows and thus the stock price.[17]

The airline industry presents an especially challenging case for the employee-preference argument. Many of the employee rents are the legacy of a regulated market structure, not the result of firm-specific human capital investment. Although airlines do engage in some training, many of the skills—learning to fly an airplane—are acquired elsewhere (the U.S. military, for example). In comparison, because of capital market competition most shareholders at the time of transition are earning only a competitive rate of return. In such circumstances the case for protecting employee rents in preference to shareholder returns is not the strongest.

One deeply troubling aspect of the effort to claim a certain level of employee priority is to determine how much. Without some clear notion, or some procedure that will lead to a determinate result, the priority claim will be deprived of desirable ex ante properties (notably, a sense of security) and also an ex post measure of whether the claim has been satisfied. The nature of implicit contract claims is to resist quantification, which is essential to the task. By contrast, a collective bargaining agreement or other explicit contractual undertaking establishes a very clear basis (and limit) for employee priority.

Another way to ask the question is to consider the differences between the treatment of UAL employees, who received stock in exchange for reduced wages and labor amenities, and Delta employees, where 15%-20% of the workforce was laid off but wages were not cut. Arguably the laid-off Delta employees were deprived of implicit deferred compensation and rents and quasi-rents. On the

---

[16] This is similar to explanations as to why explicit contracts generally give workers fixed claims rather than contingent claims, despite the possible incentive effects of profit-sharing, as discussed below. For an illuminating discussion of these issues, see generally Charny, David 'Nonlegal Sanctions in Commercial Relationships' 104 *Harv. L. Rev.* 373 (1990).

[17] But not always. The changes in the airline industry threaten shareholders as well as employees. On the other hand, the invention of labor-saving technology rarely spreads transition losses evenly between shareholders and employees, for example, the sophisticated switching equipment that has replaced banks of telephone operators.

other hand, the layoffs came following four consecutive money-losing years for Delta in which it lost $2.5 billion and faced a strong competitive attack from low-cost start-ups. Insofar as United's employees received a better deal (not a straightforward conclusion), it was because of their investment in collective organization, in dues and the willingness to bargain collectively.

II. Efficient Allocation

Employee stock ownership transactions may conserve value in firms facing economic transitions by providing a mechanism that promotes agreement rather than deadlock in the renegotiation of the employee share of firm cash flows. The stylized facts of firms in the airline industry (which could generalize to other firms facing drastically changed competitive circumstances) are these. Employee compensation at given firm is a function primarily of compensation levels in the industry, expected revenues of the firm, and employee bargaining power at the firm. This leads to a particular cost (or value) of the labor input. Prior to deregulation (an example of a powerful shock to the industry structure), these factors were relatively stable so that changes in the cost (value) of employee services, as inputs, were incremental and were accommodated in the traditional collective bargaining relationship. But deregulation and the successive forms of newly arising competition in the industry dramatically affected airline revenues. Revenues are a function principally of load factors and ticket prices; new entrants competed on price, which forced incumbents to lower ticket prices or face lower loads. Such competition, in turn, changed the assumptions on which prior compensation levels had been negotiated and forced revaluation of labor inputs. Survival required firms to compete successfully against carriers that charged much lower prices in part because they hired employees at much lower wages and, unconstrained by costly work rules, could make more efficient utilization of their workforce. Competitive price-cutting meant that incumbents could no longer afford to pay the old price for labor, as reflected in explicit or implicit contracts.

In short, the prevailing compensation arrangements, based on the old revenue assumptions, now made the firm unprofitable (or much less profitable) and threatened the firm with liquidation, either through a transaction in which the shareholders sold physical assets and routes to another carrier (to salvage shareholder value) or through eventual bankruptcy. Nevertheless the new marketplace realities could not immediately be reflected in the operation of the firm, because of preexisting contracts, and even more importantly, the collective bargaining relationship, which would prevent shareholders from simply shifting all the transition costs onto employees. In other words, industry-wide changes in competitive conditions reduced the value of both the shareholder's financial capital and the employees' human capital.[18] From the financial perspective, employee compensation is simply a cost, and such cost reduction increases the value of the shareholders' financial capital. Both shareholders and employees have a common interest in the survival of the firm, but antagonistic interests in the allocation of transition costs; the relative bargaining positions mean that neither can impose all of these costs on the other party.

Airline economics make strikes costly and dangerous for firms facing economic distress. Operating leverage is high, meaning most costs are fixed and changes in revenues go right to the bottom line. So relatively small reductions in the firm's ability to fly a full schedule at customary efficiency quickly affect earnings. For this reason, shareholders and employees have a bilateral monopoly over the cash flows of an airline, and organized employees have substantial bargaining endowments. Thus quite apart from any particular conception of justice, the bargaining structure calls for some sharing of the transition costs. In other words, although revenues and revenue expectations changed, the employees' bargaining position remained strong.

The traditional instrument of collective bargaining in the industry—changes in fixed wage levels—often works when small changes are necessary, but is much less likely to produce an efficient settlement when large transition costs must be allocated. This is because the variables that determine compensation (in particular, industry compensation levels, firm revenues, and employee bargaining power) become more volatile, which in turns leads to two sorts of problem: first, an increase in the information gap between employees and managers at precisely the moment that managers claim unprecedented negative financial outcomes; and second, a shift in the compensation function that increases the importance of the high-variance expected firm revenues variable and decreases the importance of the relatively low-variance industry compensation variable. The uncertainty associated with the new environment makes it difficult to set a fixed wage level that respects both the firm's survival and the employees' expectations.[19]

[18] To be sure, both financial capital and human capital impounded the rents associated with the industry structure under regulation, but as those rents have been competed away, shareholders and employees have suffered losses against prior expectations and have suffered losses in light of investments that, but for the rent, might not have been made, for example, the newest model planes (in the shareholder case), or particular careers in the airline industry (in the employee case).

[19] This can be illustrated with a simple example. Assume that employees receive 75% of revenues. In the regulatory era, assume expected revenues of 100 with a 25% chance of a downside realization of 75. Setting wages at 75% of expected revenues yields $0 profit in the worst case scenario and the firm survives. In the deregulatory era, revenue volatility increases, meaning the downside realizations become lower and more likely. So if revenues in a given year are $50, the firm with a fixed wage bill of $75 suffers a loss. The one-year problem becomes a crisis if the pattern repeats itself, draining the firm's accumulated reserves.

An ESOT can help resolve these problems by providing a form of consideration—common stock, or common stock equivalent—with a contingent payout
that is credibly linked to performance of the firm. In fact, there are several ways
in which common stock overcomes bargaining problems in a transition negotiation.[20]

Information Problems. First, the offer of common stock credibly signals to
employees that the firm is facing financial distress. A firm may seek wage
reductions in two instances: (1) to enhance profitability in circumstances where
the firm could afford to pay full wage claims out of cash flow, but is seeking
wage reductions for competitive or perhaps opportunistic reasons; or (2) in
circumstances where cash flows are insufficient to cover full wage claims,
"genuine" distress. Common stock is a signal of genuine distress because, among
other reasons, the relative risk-bearing capacities of public shareholders over
employees will ordinarily make it more expensive to shareholders to deliver a
given expected wage payout through a contingent payout than through a fixed
payout.[21] The firm would propose this arrangement only if the risks of insolvency from a fixed payout are very high. In other words, an ESOT makes sense
for shareholders only where the market discount on the issuance of equity
exceeds the employee discount, a circumstance that is credibly associated with
financial distress.[22] Similarly, shareholders are likely to regard an ESOT as

---

[20] Employee stock ownership transactions in the airline industry are diverse in ways not fully
captured by the stylized facts and thus the bargaining advantages of stock ownership described
below will vary somewhat. There are really three separate cases: first, the base case of a transaction that arises out of an urgent need to transform the firm's cost structure because of changing
competitive conditions, such as the transactions at Eastern and Pan Am; second, the case that
arises because of a perturbation in the market that may correct itself (temporary overcapacity or
an unexpected falloff in demand), especially if the firm is especially vulnerable because of a
high-leveraged financial structure, such as the transactions at Northwest and TWA; third, the
case that is employee-initiated and seeks far-reaching goals of structural and cultural change,
such as the United employee buyout. See generally, Gordon, Jeffrey N. 'Employee Stock Ownership as a Transitional Device: The Case of the Airline Industry' in: Jenkins, Darryl (ed.) *The
Handbook of Airline Economics* 575 (1995). Although these cases start with the same set of
stylized facts about the airline industry in the post-deregulatory era, the differences among firms,
their competitive situations and prior strategic decisions, mean that the employee stock
ownership transactions arise somewhat differently and that different elements associated with the
stock component may be particularly important.

[21] This is because public shareholders can diversify away all but the systematic risk of
holding a particular security; whereas employees will not be able to eliminate the firm-specific
risk of holding stock in their firm and will insist on compensation for this risk bearing. The
problem is even greater if the employees receive the stock subject to liquidity constraints, as with
an ESOP.

[22] Ordinarily the firm's managers resist dilution of the public shareholder, believing that the
market often undervalues the firm's stock, and accordingly will issue new stock to raise funds
only where retained earnings are insufficient. In an employee stock ownership transaction, no
external funds are coming into the enterprise. The "concession capital" is in effect funding oper-

reducing the stock price, from apprehension that employee governance participation will reduce profitability. This means that common stock will be an expensive substitute for fixed wages that the firm would propose only in the case of financial distress.

Second, common stock helps overcomes the information gap by eliciting a credible valuation of the firm from management. There are now two elements in the bargain, wage levels and the amount of stock, traded off against each other. The more negative the management view of the firm's prospects, the more stock workers will insist on receiving in exchange for a given level of wage concessions. Conversely, if management claims a high value for the stock, then workers will accept correspondingly smaller wage cuts. Because managers wish neither to dilute unnecessarily the interest of public shareholders or pay out higher wages than necessary, the use of common stock will produce more credibly candid revelation of management's assessment of the firm's prospect.

Third, a common stock transaction may also provide a special justification for employee board representation, which enhances the credibility of management's valuation by providing a mechanism for ex post review of management's candor. As board members, employee representatives would obtain access to detailed financial information, including the information that formed the basis for management's negotiating position. The discovery of management's lack of candor in prior negotiations would presumably damage ongoing relations with the new employee board members and possibly with employees generally, in a way that could jeopardize management's incumbency and hurt the firm's prospects. So a governance participation add-on that provides future access to information may help overcome a current information problem.[23]

Misvaluation Hedge. The very uncertainty about the range of possible revenue realizations can be an impediment to fixed wage bargaining. If revenues are high, employees will feel cheated if they made wage concessions. If revenues are low, shareholders may feel they gave away too much. The dynamic economic situation may make it very difficult to agree on a likely range of revenue expectations. Moreover, the sense of uncertainty is exacerbated because the whole industry—not just a single firm—is going through a transition shock and thus it is more difficult to benchmark revenue (or wage) expectations against other firms in the industry. The use of common stock reduces the redistributive gains from trade

---

ating expenses, not new investment. A firm's willingness to issue stock on this basis should be a credible signal of financial hardship.

[23] Board membership for employee representatives doesn't require common stock ownership, but may not, without such ownership, sufficiently address all of the information concerns. The new employee directors will not necessarily have been involved in the concessionary negotiations (for example, they may be employee designees rather than current employees), and may feel limited by the fiduciary duties of directorship from sharing non-public information with those who were.

and thus reduces the incentives to hold out because of this uncertainty. If the firm does unexpectedly well, the stock will increase in value—the favorable outcome will be shared between public shareholders and employees. Conversely, if the firm does unexpectedly poorly, the economic consequences of a lower stock price will also be shared. In a transition, the uncertainties increase the costs of contracting. Using common stock, because of its mitigating effects on distributional outcomes, reduces the cost of contracting.[24]

Misvaluation Hedge; Employee Ownership as Adding Value. Another potential source of valuation uncertainty and information asymmetry is the impact of the ESOT itself on the firm's revenues. The cash flow impact of foregone wages and changed work rules will be relatively easy to calculate, but the employees may well contend that the change in culture associated with a successful employee transaction will also affect cash flows, for example, through greater productivity from higher morale. Insofar as employees are right, the stock price will increase, thus raising the value the public stake and the employee stake. But an ESOT also offers possibilities of contingent valuation that does not entail sharing with public stockholders these undervalued elements of employee contribution. In the United Airlines transaction, for example, a dispute over the value of employee ownership was resolved by an agreement that if the average stock market price of the common stock over a yearlong period exceeded a certain threshold, the employees would receive additional stock, up to an additional 8% of the company (thus increasing their ownership stake from 55% to 63%).[25] One year was conceived of as a period long enough for the market to correct an initial suspicion about the value of employee ownership and long enough as well to make manipulation of the stock price impossible.

---

[24] There is also a way in which common stock partially "ensure" against mistakes in bargaining. The stock price will be significantly influenced by the wage agreement. Assume that the agreement results in a wage structure that is unexpectedly low against the stock market's priors—then the stock price should go up, which will compensate employees for wages that may have been unnecessarily foregone. (Part of the complexity here is that the market's assessment of the likely wage outcome will undoubtedly diverge from the cash-flow maximizing outcome, and an increase in stock price as the bargain is achieved will not necessarily reflect a judgment that the workers got too little measured against the most likely revenue expectations; only that the wage settlement was below expectations.) Similarly, if the wage structure is too high, then stock prices will decline and the loss will be shared with employees. (Conceivably the market may have expected even worse and stock prices will increase).

Moreover, since the value of the stock is partly a function of the labor agreement itself, stock price changes will reduce the "winner's" spoils; this too will help the parties converge to agreement.

[25] Similar contingent valuation adjustment mechanisms are often found in stock-for-stock mergers (albeit in the period before consummation of the merger rather than as an ex post settling-up mechanism) as a way of protecting shareholders against valuation losses in the stock to be received as merger consideration.

Credible Payouts. In theory, these various features can be replicated through contractually described contingent compensation that does not involve equity. For example, consider the possible role of profit-sharing in an employee restructuring. As a credible signal of financial distress, profit-sharing could also work, since all other things being equal, workers' risk preferences would result in a higher valuation of fixed wages over profit-sharing of equal expected value. Moreover, the trade-off between the level of profit-sharing and fixed wages should similarly produce sincere revelation of managers' assessment of the firm's prospects, since (as we saw before) both excessively optimistic and pessimistic forecasts would have negative consequences for shareholders. What makes common stock uniquely valuable is that it offers employees a more credible assurance of a payout linked to the performance of the firm than alternative contingent compensation schemes. This is because share price is a publicly available measure of the firm's profitability that is hard to manipulate.

Consider, for example, profit-sharing, the leading alternative. Ordinarily profit-sharing schemes have certain advantages over stock-based systems: profit-sharing can be tailored to performance at a profit center rather than the firm as a whole, which more closely ties compensation to performance. Moreover, the greater influence of market-wide factors on share price than on operating income and other profit-sharing measures drives a wedge between employee compensation and the firm's profitability. But where normal bargaining relationships are unsettled by transition events, the effort to negotiate new profit-sharing arrangements may be very difficult. Uncertainty makes agreement difficult—even assuming forthrightness on both sides—and opens up new possibilities for strategic behavior as well. There are both many possible definitions of profits and many chances for manipulation in the reporting of operating results that feed into a profit calculation. Economic exigency may legitimately require unusual financial maneuvers that may siphon off cash flows for restructurings or refinancing. Too firm a guarantee of profit-sharing creates risks of hold-up or insufficient financial flexibility. Yet the risk of opportunistic manipulation will be great—and the fear of it greater—in an environment in which ordinary reputational constraints are undermined by the changing competitive environment that has led to the transition negotiation in the first place. Common stock has the reassuring attribute that it is the same claim held by the public shareholders, to whom the board owes its chief loyalty, and comes with its own set of monitors on whom employees can partially free ride. Employees need not worry about the validity and reliability of particular profit measures; they share in the stockholder residual.[26]

---

[26] A contingent payout in the form of stock has the additional value that it is self-financing. Even if a struggling firm has now achieved a "profit" on some accounting or cashflow measure, it still might be difficult and more costly to make a cash payout. In theory there is no difference between funding a level of contingent compensation with cash or with stock; the stock could be

Heuristics. Finally, equity may also help overcome some of the heuristic barriers to a transition cost-sharing. One reason wages are sticky going down is the well-known heuristic problem of loss-aversion, the tendency for individuals to overvalue a loss.[27] The problem seems especially important in directly representative bargaining situations, in which a relatively uninformed, unsophisticated electorate must ratify the agent's bargaining outcome. Equity can be fashioned to address this problem. In the 1994 Northwest Airlines transaction, for example, the employees received convertible preferred stock puttable to the company ten years after issuance for the face amount of the concessions. The discounted present value of the exercise price of the put was no more than a third of the concession amount; moreover, the economic circumstances under which the put price would be greater than the conversion value of the preferred would probably be those in which the airline could not perform on its put obligation (approximately $800 million in cash!). The point was to create an appearance that, after all, the employees were protected against losses on their transaction. In effect, one heuristic bias was deployed to combat another. Similarly in the 1983 Eastern transaction, the employees made concessions greater than the market capitalization of the company. The gap between the deemed value of the common stock they received and the concession amount—the extent of possible employee loss—was nominally covered by a class of preferred stock with a liquidation preference conveniently equal to the difference. In an actual liquidation, the value of the preferred shareholders' claim would have been closer to 0 than 100 cents on the dollar.

In sum, an ESOT may add value in ways that are quite different from the familiar story about incentive effects. It may well be that employee stock ownership helps promote desirable behavior—less shirking, more cross-monitoring, higher morale, etc.—but its particular value in a transition (and perhaps more generally) is to address disparities of information and uncertainty. A transition shock upsets conventional valuations of the labor input and of the value of the

---

sold on the market with the proceeds going to employees as easily as giving the employees stock directly, and the level of public shareholder dilution is the same. In practice the outcomes are quite different. The market is likely to take the sale of stock as a negative signal, leading the firm to think of ways to finance the contingent payment out of cash flow or additional borrowings, which may divert the firm from its otherwise optimal business plan and add to bankruptcy risk. Moreover, if the employee stock goes into a retirement plan like an ESOP, there is no subsequent employee sale of stock into the market.

[27] See, e.g., Kahneman, Daniel, Jack Knetsch, and Richard Thaler 'Anomalies: The Endowment Effect, Loss Aversion, and Status Quo Bias' *Journal of Economic Perspectives* 5/1 (1991) 193. "Loss aversion" is different from "risk aversion." A party is "risk averse" if he considers risk and expected return in making an investment and requires compensation for taking on downside risk. A party exhibits "loss aversion" when he will pay more to avoid a loss than to obtain an equal risk-adjusted gain.

firm generally. In such cases employee stock ownership can help structure the sharing of losses and possible gains in the new and uncertain state of the world.

III. Efficient Allocation of Ongoing Transition Costs

The transition problems that lead to an ESOT may not be fully resolvable by a single negotiation. Transition adjustments rarely consist of a one-time restructuring, in which the labor input is simply repriced and the firm moves forward with a new cost structure. This is for two reasons. First, in many cases the labor repricing has not been permanent. Rather, concessions have accrued over the term of a particular collective bargaining agreement, after which the baseline for measuring further (or even continuing) concessions "snaps back" to the preexisting wage level, or even to the industry average at the time of the new negotiation. Second, as the airline industry shows, implications of a major transition become apparent over time. The transition shock of airline deregulation has reverberated for nearly two decades with no clear evidence of the emergence of a stable equilibrium.[28] Thus it is reasonable to anticipate a continuing need to renegotiate wage levels, the size of the workforce, and the organization of work, including work rules that affect productivity. Employee stock ownership may promote the efficient allocation of these continuing transition costs.[29]

At this point it is important to observe that stock ownership entails two distinct features: economic participation and governance participation. Both features have the potential to reduce three barriers to a successful bargaining: asymmetric information, strategic miscalculation about the possible settlement range, and concern about opportunistic behavior ex post. Thus both features can

---

[28] The airline industry really is a remarkable case. The technology is essentially unchanged over the period; the regulatory structure has been stable since the early 1980s; input prices have also been relatively stable (except for a fuel price spike associated with the Gulf War in 1990-91); and, except for the Gulf War period, there have been no sudden shifts in demand for air travel. Nevertheless the intensity of competitive pressures has made the period a turbulent one for almost all of the carriers. A number of well-known incumbents have been forced out of the business (Braniff; Pan Am; Eastern) and others have made trips through Chapter 11 (Continental; TWA). The very recent prosperity across all the airlines is unusual, and, according to many industry observers, not destined to last.

[29] An example that bears elaboration is TWA, in which employees initially received a 35% equity interest in exchange for concessions that were part of TWA's emergence from bankruptcy in 1994. The financial restructuring proved inadequate and as part of another transition negotiation, the employees accepted dilution to a 25% equity stake. The airline barely survived the decline in passenger loads following the 1996 crash of Flight 800 and the ensuing boardroom disagreements among groups representing bondholders, managers, and employees. TWA is currently riding the airline industry's boom but has still not become profitable. See Feder, Barnaby J. 'The St. Louis Phoenix: From Its Heartland Hub, T.W.A. Is Rising, but Wall St. Has Some Doubts' *New York Times* February 10, 1998, D1.

be deployed to work through subsequent transition adjustments and may interact in useful concert.[30]

Governance Participation—Information. The most important form of governance participation comes through representation on the board of directors, although this is not necessarily entailed by even substantial share ownership. For the typical public firm, for which the directors are elected by majority vote of shares, a minority stake will not assure even minimal board representation. Indeed, the trend against cumulative voting as a mandatory term in state corporate law statutes and as an optional feature in the governance of the large public corporation reflects at least some doubt of the value of minority board representation. Nevertheless it is easy to recapitalize the firm to establish special classes of stock with the right to elect directors. This has been the pattern for employee stock ownership transactions that address transition problems. (By contrast, the ordinary establishment of an ESOP—often in anticipation of a control threat—that will occasionally hold as much stock as found in an ESOT, has not led to employee board representation.)

From the perspective of the allocation of ongoing transition costs, the major advantage of board representation is access to credible information about the firm's business and financial condition. This contrasts with information received in the course of collective bargaining, where the risks of strategic misrepresentation are high. Credible information as a basis for negotiation over further transition adjustments reduces the risk of bargaining breakdown because it reduces the risk that parties will be negotiating from radically different premises about the firm's financial condition and reduces the potential for the fact or appearance of bad faith bargaining.

What makes information received at the board level credible is that employee directors can free ride on both the legal rules and informational demands of other directors, especially the public directors. Employee board representatives receive the same information as other directors.[31] As a legal matter, corporate law requires the board, at a minimum, to oversee the business and affairs of the corporation. Directors obtain the protection of the business judgment rule only for decisions taken after reasonable investigation. Most statutes provide for broad exculpation of monetary liability for breach of the duty of care, but no director wants to risk the chance of losing statutory protection because of failure to investigate that may seem ex post to have been in bad faith. Moreover, public

---

[30] The protection against ex post opportunism not only is an aid to negotiation of a further transition adjustment, but also to reaching the initial ESOT.

[31] Conceivably some of the work of the board could be delegated to committees which exclude employee directors. Committee involvement is an element of governance participation and may be necessary to address credibility problems. On the supposed effects of co-determination on the information flow on German supervisory boards, cf. Prigge (this volume Ch. 12: Sec. B.I.3. and C.I.1.).

directors have independent reputations to protect that depend, at minimum, upon knowing the true facts of a firm's condition. Thus directors as a group will insist on a certain level of information disclosure and on the reliability of such information. This would be particularly the case for a firm that is visibly experiencing economic distress, where public directors are likely to want more information than usual. Such information revelation means that employees and management will bargain on the basis of the same facts, reducing the risk of bargaining failure because of factual disagreements or bad faith misrepresentations that are discovered.[32]

Governance Participation—Miscalculation. Board representation can also facilitate subsequent transition adjustments by narrowing the estimate of the settlement range and thus reducing the risks of miscalculation. Employee directors will come to a better understanding of the business environment in which the firm operates, including the competitive pressures. In working through the firm's operational and strategic decisions at the board level, the employee directors should develop a clearer sense of the set of economically feasible contracts between the firm and its employees. This means that bargaining should not be derailed by clearly mistaken beliefs about contracting possibilities.[33] This is particularly important where an industrial sector is in transition and the customary economic relationships no longer obtain.

Governance Participation—Opportunism Ex Post. Stock ownership brings another governance right—the right to vote shares in a matter that is submitted to shareholder vote. Although this right is ordinarily not regarded as the most important feature of corporate governance, it can offer significant protection to a shareholder group against transactions that they regard as expropriative. In the employee ownership case, employees might well worry that wage and productivity concessions that enhance the firm's economic viability merely set the stage for a sale of the firm (in whole or in part) or a merger. The acquirer might try to extract additional concessions from the employees (easy to imagine if the transaction is leveraged), and the new corporate structure which overtakes the original

---

[32] One question that arises is if employee board representation helps solve these information problems, why aren't employee directors more commonly found on the board? There are two obvious answers: first, that in normal times, the information asymmetries may not be so critical, because of a relatively narrow range of revenue realizations and because of reliable benchmarking against other firms; and second, that board membership would give employee directors governance power as well as information. One consequence of an employee ownership transaction is that employee stock ownership partially bonds the employee director promise to act as a fiduciary on behalf of shareholders' interests generally, in direct proportion to the size of the employee stake.

[33] Neither of these propositions about board representation is invariably true. In the case of Eastern Airlines, participants believe that the board membership of a strong-willed, if not willful, union director contributed to the bargaining failure that led to the sale of the firm to the unions' least favorite airline operator, Frank Lorenzo, at a bargain price.

enterprise conceivably may eliminate or truncate the employees' governance rights. Also, the employees would be faced with a difficult choice whether to sell their stock together with the public shareholders (at a premium price, that may be based in part on the assumption of a frozen-in employee minority) or to maintain their possibly diluted investment to protect their governance interests in a relationship not of their choosing.

All this is foreseeable ex ante and can contribute to bargaining failure in the initial ESOT and subsequent transition adjustments. Voting rights, as amplified through charter amendment, can mitigate these risks. Moreover, although typical corporate law provisions appear to require shareholder approval of mergers, acquisitions can often be structured in a way that avoids the requirement of shareholder vote (and even when required, a simple majority vote usually suffices).[34] But charters can be drafted to expand the set of transactions that require shareholder approval and to impose supermajority requirements that give employees a veto and thus overcome the risk of an opportunistic transaction.

Economic Participation—Information. Although stock ownership is typically linked to the solution of information problems through the governance mechanism of board representation, economic participation offers a distinct way in which stock ownership addresses information problems. This is because transforming employees into shareholders makes the stock price a credible and common referent for the business prospects of the firm. A negative stock price movement provides a credible signal of the need for a transition adjustment that is relatively protected from the possibility of managerial misrepresentation or manipulation of information disclosure. For academics, the information value of stock prices of publicly traded firms is obvious and beyond dispute: not only do stock prices impound all publicly available information about the firm (informational efficiency) but the stock price is also the most reliable estimate of the present value of the firm's future cash flows (allocative efficiency). Nevertheless since managers sometimes discredit the reliability of stock prices (it seems that markets always undervalue a company's stock), it is easy to imagine that employees ordinarily disregard the stock price altogether. An ESOT dramatically changes the employees' relation to the stock price. Some substantial fraction of employee wealth will be tied up in the stock. Because of the singularity of the transaction, the stock price will have great saliency. It will be a focal point of discussion at work and owning the stock may be the occasion for discussion of the financial reports received in the mail. Publicly reported financial information is often hard to interpret, and notwithstanding the antifraud protec-

---

[34] Through a triangular merger, for example. See, e.g., *Hariton v. Arco Electronics, Inc.* 188 A.2d 123 (Del. Sup. Ct. 1963). See also *Paramount Communications, Inc. v. Time, Inc.* 571 A.2d 1140 (Del. Sup. Ct. 1990) (Time's stock-for-stock merger with Warner requiring Time shareholder vote converted into cash acquisition requiring no Time shareholder vote).

tion of the federal securities laws, not always credible—in part, because as even a casual reader of financial statements can see, the adjustments, assumptions, and footnotes are a barrier to straightforward interpretation. The stock price distills this information, shakes it loose of management's efforts to spin the facts, and communicates whether the firm is doing relatively well or poorly. Thus apart from governance participation, the economic element of employee stock ownership may also reduce information barriers to successful adjustment negotiations.[35]

Economic Participation—Narrowing the Settlement Range. After an ESOT employees will have two economic interests to protect, the cash flow from their jobs and the value of their stock. The presence of this additional economic interest will facilitate agreement on subsequent transition matters. This is because common stock reduces the redistributive element of contracting, as discussed above, and thus narrows the settlement range. This can be illustrated with a simple example of a two-period negotiation problem. Assume that in period one, survival of the firm depends upon wage concessions. In case A, wage concessions are coupled with an ESOT. In case B, wage concessions are made, but no stock is taken in return (perhaps the wage concessions are somewhat less than case A). In period two, survival of the firm once again depends upon wage concessions (or some modification of the work rules to enhance productivity). In case B, the employees need consider only the value of their firm-specific human capital investment, which had decreased because of the prior wage concessions, and which is ambiguously affected by continued employment at this financially shaky firm (because of the sacrifice of the opportunity to start employment at another firm). In case A, by contrast, the employee has two investments, in stock as well as firm-specific human capital. Further concessions preserve the human capital investment and will also enhance the value of the employee's stock.[36] For a given level of concession, the employee receives a greater gain; or, to bring loss avoidance into play, has a smaller loss. This narrows the differences of

[35] The stock price as a commonly accepted signal of the firm's condition and prospects also may be valuable in addressing a problem that has not yet entered the analysis—the fact that ESOTs are typically negotiated with multiple employee groups that will be competing among themselves to minimize concessions and maximize claims on the firm's cash flows. A common point of valuation can limit certain kinds of strategic bargaining among the employee groups.

[36] Stock ownership can also help overcome some of the conflicts that emerge in bargaining on behalf of an employee group with different job tenure and thus different levels of firm specific human capital investment and opportunity cost. Put somewhat crudely, junior and senior employees may value their jobs differently, but they will value each share of stock the same. An optimal bargain might allocate a disproportionate amount of stock to lower-tenured employees (relative to the amount of apparent concession) to enhance their combined human capital and stock stake in the enterprise.

interest between the employee and the firm, and thus should reduce the possibility of bargaining failure in the second-period negotiation.[37]

Economic Participation—Opportunism Ex Post. Economic participation can also reduce the risk to employees of a subsequent opportunistic transaction. As noted above, a concessionary labor agreement can add substantial economic value to the firm, since going-concern value rapidly dwindles at an enterprise that consistently operates at a deficit. Employees might well be reluctant to enter into such an agreement if they believed it opened the way to a sale of the firm that permitted shareholders to capture the economic value. Employee stock ownership in its economic dimension assures that employees can also capture some of the gain from a subsequent transaction. This assurance may facilitate a transition adjustment, both in the initial transaction and afterwards.

IV. Superior Structures

The greatest potential upside of employee stock ownership, however, is its ability to promote organizational innovations in workplace relations and culture that will make the firm a superior competitor. On this conception, an employee stock ownership transaction can serve not simply as a transitional mechanism, designed to overcome bargaining problems in the allocation of transition costs, but rather as a way of creating a firm that can better manage the stresses and opportunities of a dynamic economic environment. One of the consequences of such an environment is that if the firm is in trouble, no one really knows how to fix things, because once-successful models do not necessarily point the way to a future success. This places a premium on a pragmatic style of learning by monitoring, in which collaboration among and between employees and managers may give the firm a comparative advantage in a competitive market and thus increase its chances for survival and prosperity.[38] If a firm can better govern the shifts of economic transitions, employees are less likely to experience the sudden wipeout of human capital investments that give rise to the most severe transition costs problems.

---

[37] The potential importance of this dynamic is increasing in the level of employee stock ownership. But even at significant levels, ceteris paribus, an employee would prefer a wage increase rather than stock price appreciation enjoyed ratably. The problem is more acute because of problems tracing changes in wages directly to changes in stock price, potential conflict among employee groups in the competition for wage increases that leads to a degenerate equilibrium (or, alternatively, cooperation that leads to logrolling), and the fact that the stock might be locked up in retirement plans, meaning that the consumption value of a stock price increase is much less than the comparable wage increase.

[38] See Sabel, Charles 'Learning By Monitoring: The Institutions of Economic Development' in: Smelser, Neil J. and Richard Swedberg (eds.) *The Handbook of Economic Sociology* 137 (Princeton 1994).

The goal is not simply to persuade employees that competitive conditions require a new cost structure, meaning they must accept lower wages and different work rules to protect the existence of the firm and their jobs—a repricing of the labor input. Rather, the goal is to induce employees to generate cost-savings and other productivity enhancements for a more competitive firm. In most firms this requires a change in what might loosely be called "corporate culture." In its more ambitious versions, the firm may be seeking new ways of collaboration with employees that will promote a commitment to continuous improvements and greater efficiency. The firm may wish to establish discursive practices in which employees participate in goal-setting and in discussions on how to attain those goals, and then how to exceed them, in a way that also shares the gains from such collaboration. An ESOT may serve such objectives through both the governance participation and the economic participation features of equity.[39]

Governance—Board Membership. Board membership can obviously entail more than the absorption of credible information for the next transition negotiation. The board can be structured in a way to make use of information about the firm from employees,[40] to provide a credible signal that such information is regarded as valuable, and to signal that employee interests will be given significant, sometimes decisive weight in matters of apparent conflict with shareholder interests. In these ways board structure can help sustain the creation of a more collaborative corporate culture.

One of the often-asserted advantages of employee ownership is that employees can monitor managers. Employees are often in a good position—much better than outside shareholders—to evaluate the exercise of managerial authority within the firm: whether resources of labor and machinery are efficiently used, whether production moves smoothly, whether managers appear to be capable and well-motivated. Although employees may not be able to monitor directly the decisions of senior managers, they may observe the performance of line managers and, depending on the employee group, staff managers, both groups whose supervision is a major responsibility of senior managers. Employees also have a valuable perspective on the business that is perhaps more operational than big picture but which can still provide a useful addition to the mix of information

---

[39] It is important to note that ESOTs will differ quite significantly depending on the goals. If the purpose merely is to allocate transition costs, then the level of ownership may be rather modest and the governance rights non-existent. If the purpose is a cultural shift, then one would expect a high level of ownership and extensive governance rights. Nor are transactions necessarily in pure form. The ostensible goal of every employee stock transaction is probably to minimize transition costs, even though in looking at the arrangements it becomes apparent that the actual objective was more modest. On the opposite side, even if an ESOT is structured principally to reallocate costs, the incentive effects of employee stock ownership may matter in employee performance.

[40] With respect to this point, cf. Prigge (this volume Ch. 12: Sec. C.I.) on the connection between supervisory board co-determination and works council co-determination.

ordinarily coming into the boardroom. Employee directors can present this information in the course of boardroom discussion, but often agenda constraints and the formality of a full board meeting limit a director's interventions. A more thoroughgoing way to make use of this information—and to signal its use and its value—is to assign employee directors to board committees where much of the actual work (and much of the informal discussion) takes place.[41] Perhaps most important for such purposes are the compensation committee, where senior management is evaluated, and the executive committee, where important policies may be formulated.

The tough governance question is how much power to give to employee directors, as reflected in number of board seats. Even if most board actions are officially by consensus rather than vote, "consensus" outcomes will often reflect the majority opinion on a matter. A substantial minority may be given informal veto power out of the desire to avoid a board split. Because of the concerns of capital suppliers, employees will rarely elect a majority of board members, even where they hold a majority of the shares. In the UAL transaction, for example, only 3 of the 12 board members were union designees. But it is possible through bylaw or charter provisions to give certain groups of directors blocking power over all or some decisions. A provision found in some bylaws lets a group of employee directors plus some number of outside directors (but less than a majority of the whole board) block certain large-scale business decisions, such as the capital budget.

At first glance these provisions may seem to elevate employee interests over shareholder interests in crucial decisions, a strategy that probably is unwise, and perhaps fatal, for the firm in the long run. It may force the firm to do an inefficient thing to satisfy a rent-seeking constituency. On the other hand, such provisions are a credible signal about the importance that the firm now places on employee interests. In reality there may be few occasions in which important decisions will come out differently because of pressure from employee directors (and the employees' economic interests may partially constrain rent seeking), so the efficiency loss may well be small. Thus if the goal is to change culture, the signal may add more value than suboptimal decisions may subtract.[42]

Governance—Voting. As noted above, shareholder voting is an additional element of corporate governance, especially where shareholder approval is

---

[41] This discussion course assumes that employee directors will be good agents—skillful at collecting and reflecting back employee information, loyal to employee interests. This will not always be the case, since agency problems do not disappear when the designations change.

[42] A less strong version of the story is that both shareholders and employees want to maximize the value of the firm (assuming a common definition) but that the employee director veto provisions merely signal in cases of disagreement how seriously employee opinions are weighed. In both cases the goal is to create a culture in which employees are continuously looking for operational improvements.

required not just for the limited set of transactions that require shareholder vote as a mandatory corporate law matter, but for a broader set that would change the business in some substantial way, such as divestitures, assets sales, or other forms of disinvestment. Depending on the voting percentages required, employees can be given influence or a veto. Where the employees are divided into specific subgroups (typically the case), different employee coalitions may have different degrees of influence or veto. It is easy to imagine how this power could protect the status quo despite the efficiency losses. Disinvestment, for example, is likely to be resisted because of its association with layoffs, which runs against the equality norms that employee ownership fosters. Nevertheless including such provisions also credibly signals that employees will not be opportunistically treated in the event of subsequent business restructuring. The employee voting rights should not be seen as making appropriate disinvestments impossible, rather to opening the way to bargaining over the sharing of gains and losses. If the goal is to persuade employees to work to improve the operation of the firm or, more ambitiously, to create a collaborative culture of continuous improvement, it may be valuable to pre-commit to negotiation over gain (or loss) sharing in the event of a significant reshaping of the business.

Economic Participation. Perhaps the most salient feature of employee stock ownership is employee participation in the firm's economic residual. If the firm is more profitable, employees will benefit either from receiving increased dividends or stock appreciation, or both. This should advance the effort to instill a corporate culture of continuous improvement. Economic participation provides incentives for employees to worker harder (and smarter), to cross-monitor one another and to monitor managers, and to undertake discretionary efforts to improve the operations of the firm.[43]

Employee stock ownership may offer advantages over other vehicles for economic participation, such as profit-sharing, if the goal is a culture change. As noted previously, stock ownership more credibly commits the firm to gain-sharing with employees than profit-sharing.[44] Stock ownership also more powerfully transmits the consequences of improvement (or failure), in that it amplifies

---

[43] One fair question is why employees of firms in transitions need such an incentive beyond the desire to hold onto their job at the same level of pay. That is, if the survival (or at least prosperity) of the firm depends upon beating the competition, why isn't ordinary pay enough? There are at least two answers: first, employee stock ownership is a way of sharing the gains of competitive success that doesn't depend on subsequent renegotiation of wages; and second, because of this non-negotiability, an ESOT may credibly signal a desire to change corporate culture.

[44] The risks of opportunism in the definition and accrual of "profits" go both ways in a firm with substantial employee governance participation. Gain-sharing based on stock ownership insulates management from pressure to pursue short-term profits, to fatten current employee payouts, at the expense of long-term value, as might be the case with profit-sharing. This, of course, is a reversal of the usual concern that a focus on stock prices will lead to "short termism."

changes in profitability through a multiplier effect. For example, assume a $1 per share increase in profits for a firm trading at price-earnings multiple of 10. All else being equal, this will lead to a $10 per share stock price increase, a much more vivid addition to employee wealth than an aliquot share of the cash. Stock ownership also automatically locks in prior gains in a way that increases the employees' investment in the firm, which in turn enhances the incentive effects for subsequent periods. In the preceding example, paying out a profit-sharing bonus from year 1 keeps constant the employees' residual claim for year 2. But in case of stock ownership, unless the employee sells off stock, the value of the residual claim will increase for year 2.[45] This gives the employee an economically more valuable ownership stake and the incentive to protect and enhance its value.

Stock ownership serves symbolic purposes as well. All employees have a common mode of economic participation. Unlike a profit figure, which is announced only quarterly, the stock price is a constant reminder of the common endeavor and the potential gains of success.[46]

C. The UAL Transaction

The potential value of employee stock ownership led to a number of transactions in the airline industry following deregulation, including those at Eastern, Northwest, Republic, TWA, UAL, and, as an initial ownership form, at Southwest and Kiwi.[47] The UAL transaction, in which the employees acquired majority equity ownership, is especially important because of its aim to create a new organizational form, a public corporation with large employee blockholders. Unlike many ESOTs, it did not arise under the pressure of imminent financial distress. It's clear that the parties perceived the UAL buyout as not simply a one-time rationalization of transition costs but as a vehicle for making UAL a superior competitor in the industry. The parties also thought that the governance and

---

[45] Most ESOTs place significant limitations on employee stock sales. Some, e.g., UAL, tie up employee stock in ESOPs, meaning that employees cannot dispose of stock until they end their employment relationship (or retire). Others, e.g., Northwest Airlines, provide greater liquidity. Although most employees would surely consume, rather than save, a profit-sharing payment, the Northwest example suggests that employees will not sell stock even when they have the opportunity (i.e., will reinvest rather than consume). This may be because employees, like managers, tend to think that the market undervalues the stock.

[46] Of course this particular symbol can also lead to discouragement, as employees may also experience the frustration associated with a stagnant or declining stock price, despite what they know to be their personal diligence and innovative work and a similar performance by the workforce generally.

[47] I have explored some of the transactions in related work, bearing out the theme that transaction-specific structures matter critically to outcomes. See Gordon, supra n. 20.

economic participation arrangements were crucial. The institutions they devised were somewhat novel, probably as much the result of compromise as a disinterested search for the "best" system, but the success of this particular example of employee stock ownership may turn on their handiwork.

The UAL employee transaction was a July 1994 acquisition of 55% of the company's equity in exchange for wage reductions and work rule changes valued at approximately $4.9 billion. The transaction had its impetus, on the employee side, from the pilots, who decided that employee ownership offered the greatest degree of economic security in the buffeting course of transition in the airline industry. On the management/public shareholder side, the decisive factor seemed to be the necessity for employee cooperation in cost reduction and in the establishment of a low-cost short-haul carrier, later known as "Shuttle by United," to compete with Southwest Airlines in West Coast markets that fed UAL's longer flights. The bargaining endowments of the employees, particularly the pilots, meant that management could not unilaterally impose a labor cost reduction (this alone might have led to an ESOT to allocate transition costs efficiently). Equally important, however, was that competitive success for the Shuttle required a new culture of cooperation. This conclusion led towards an ESOT.

What is extraordinary about the United case is that the play of bargaining endowments and competitive necessity led to a transaction in which employees obtained a majority equity interest in the firm, an unprecedented outcome in a large public corporation not at insolvency's door. The success (or failure) of the transaction will help answer not only the question of whether employee ownership is desirable in a transition environment, but also whether a mixed ownership structure in which employees own a majority of the equity but share control with public shareholders can survive. The implications are significant. The UAL acquisition was financed with a de minimis amount of employee capital, and yet UAL has maintained its customary relationships with capital suppliers to finance the transaction, to finance airline purchases, working capital, and long-term capital needs. Conceivably it is a template for a new organizational form, a public corporation where the large blockholders are employee groups.

I. Transactional Background

The United pilots seemed to understand that they received substantial rents and quasi-rents that were at risk in the increasingly competitive air travel market following deregulation in 1978.[48] Deregulation ended an era of "regulated competition" in which the control of entry, route allocation, mergers, and fares

---

[48] In parallel work, I am trying to quantify the rents and quasi-rents of the various airline worker groups, by airline, over the period 1978-94. At the time of the UAL buyout, the present value of average pilot rents and quasi-rents were in the vicinity of $900,000.

all but guaranteed airline profitability. In adapting to the new regime, shareholders, acting through their managerial agents, had strong incentives to shift the transition costs to employees. In part, the competition from new entrants was so fierce as to make prior labor cost structures unsustainable. In other respects, the question was the allocation of the remaining rents between shareholders and employees.

The risk to the employees was on several fronts. First, the company might use straightforward economic pressure in contract negotiation to force lower labor costs. Indeed, the United pilots took a 29-day strike in 1985 in resisting such pressures. Second, the company might use airline cash flows for alternative business investment, in effect disinvesting from the airline business. Fewer routes and fewer flights would translate into layoffs and lower wages. United did in fact diversify into the non-airline travel business in the mid-1980s, through acquisitions of the Hertz rental car company and two hotel chains. Third, the company might be taken over in a leveraged buyout that, given the cyclical nature of airline profits, would serve as a mechanism for forcing down employee wages. As cash flow fell below debt service, employees would be faced with the Hobson's choice of risking their jobs as the airline went through bankruptcy or reducing their wages. In fact, in 1989 takeover entrepreneur Marvin Davis proposed to put together a leveraged takeover of the airline at $240 a share that led to a management/pilots' union leveraged buyout offer at $300 a share. That transaction (fortunately) collapsed under the weight of its flawed projections.

What precipitated the 1994 employee buyout was a company restructuring proposal that was a peculiar combination of all three of these rent-draining strategies. Over the 1990-93 period, UAL lost over $1 billion, partially because of the industry-wide fall-off in air traffic associated with the Gulf War, but more seriously because of the competitive encroachment of short-haul low-cost carriers like Southwest. The company's restructuring proposal would have led to widespread layoffs, subcontracting of certain services, and spinning off part of the airline's operations into its own low-cost short-haul carrier.

II. Financial Terms

The final terms emerged after a year of bargaining over financial terms and governance arrangements for a restructured, recapitalized UAL. The "old" United shareholders received a total of $2.1 billion in cash and 45% of the common equity equivalents in the recapitalized airline, for total consideration valued at $3.2 billion. The participating employee groups (all participated except the flight attendants) received 55% of common equity equivalent, implicitly valued at $1.9

billion.[49] In exchange, the employee groups agreed to wage cuts of approximately 15% for at least three years, valued at $3.3 billion, and to work rule changes, locked in for 12 years, that would permit the higher pilot utilization, quick-turnarounds, and streamlined service necessary for low-cost operation of a United short-haul carrier. The work rule changes were assigned a value of $1.6 billion, making for a total employee contribution valued at $4.9 billion.

In addition to the 55% equity stake, the union employees also successfully bargained for additional job security provisions. For example, the new collective bargaining agreements provide layoff protection for all present employees, limit domestic and international code-sharing, require labor protective provisions in the case of significant asset sales, and perhaps most importantly, restrict the scope of the United Shuttle operation both as a percentage of the entire system and as to city pairs. The benefits of these provisions are apparently not netted out in the measure of labor savings.

The UAL buyout illustrates the capacity of organized employees to use an employee stock transaction to share transition losses and gains with stockholders on favorable terms. Immediately prior to board approval of the transaction, United's financial advisors estimated that if the airline could implement its initially planned cost-savings, the reference value of the stock would range between $135 and $175; a few months earlier the top of the reference range had been $200. The old shareholders received less than $130, below the bottom of the reference range. Moreover, the adviser's estimate did not take into account the anticipated gains from the United Shuttle ($64 per old share), the implementation of which was mainly a function of work rule changes.

Thus it appears that the employees were well compensated for their concessions. In return for cash labor savings on the order of $3.3 billion they received stock with an implied value of $1.9 billion, as well as highly prized job security provisions (that are difficult to assign a dollar value to). In this particular case the transition costs of economic change in the airline industry were shared in significant measure by the shareholders, not borne by the employees only.

III. Governance Arrangements

Both the employee shareholders and the public shareholders have an interest in governance arrangements that enhance the value of the firm. The key to the

---

[49] This value for the employees' 55% of the equity is more than proportionately greater than the value for the public's 45% share. This is because the employees received ESOP convertible preferred, which carried an 8% dividend and a liquidation preference and was deemed to be worth 138% the value of a common share. Until the share was allocated to an employee account, the dividend was available to pay down the ESOP debt (a leveraged ESOP was used to obtain tax advantages) and higher value associated with the preferred stock increased the tax advantage.

protection and appreciation in value of the employee stock is a governance regime that successfully addresses the many conflicts of employee ownership generally and in this particular transaction. In a sense the critical party in the devising of governance arrangements is not the public shareholders, whose investment in the firm is in effect sunk at the time that negotiations begin, but rather the third parties who have strong exit (or no-show) options, such as lenders, lessors, suppliers, and ultimately, customers. These parties need to be shown that the employees cannot readily expropriate cash flow in a way that will threaten the firm's solvency. This problem was especially salient in the UAL transaction, since the $2 billion cash payout to shareholders was to be financed through the sale of UAL senior securities. Thus the UAL governance arrangements struggle to include all of the following: employee involvement, professional management, and some insulation of employees from labor matters. These matters are played out both in board structure and in shareholder voting.

The Board. The parties fashioned a unique structure for the board to maintain a balance between representatives of public shareholders and employees. The key innovation is a balance wheel group of "independent directors" who are insulated from direct pressures of both employees and public shareholders because they are self-perpetuating. Three aspects of the board structure are particularly notable: the board's composition, the committee structure, and the voting rules.

Board Composition. The board (see Figure 1) consists of 12 members: five "public directors," four "independent directors," two "union directors," and one "salaried and management" director (the latter three directors known collectively as "employee directors"). Three of the public directors must be outsiders with no prior affiliation with the company ("outside public directors"). The other public directors are insiders, the chief executive officer and the chief operating officer. At least two of the independent directors must be either a senior executive of a major company (revenues greater than $1 billion) or a board member of a major public company (market capitalization greater than $1 billion).

The directors will be selected by nominating procedures and class voting that in the end mean that only the three public outside directors are accountable solely to the public shareholder. The employee groups will directly select three directors and have influence in the selection of the remaining six. In the case of the CEO and COO, who will be the management public directors, it seems highly likely that these managers will want to remain on best possible terms with the employee majority shareholders, even if the three employee directors could not act alone to force their dismissal. The current CEO, for example, was selected by the employee coalition at an early stage in the negotiations. The four independent directors are in one sense a self-perpetuating group, in that they will be elected by vote of a special class of preferred stock that they will hold. On the other hand, a shareholders' agreement obligates them to vote that stock for the nomi-

Figure 1: UAL Board and Committee Structure

a) UAL Board of Directors

Employee Directors (3)
Independent Directors* (4)
Public Directors (Inside)* (2)
Public Directors (Outside) (3)

b) Compensation Committee

Outside (1)
CEO* (1)
Independent* (2)
Employee (3)

c) Competitive Action Committee

Union (2)
Independent* (2)
CEO* (1)
Outside (3)

d) Compensation Admin. Committee

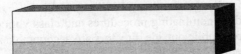

Independent* (2)

Outside (1)

e) Labor Committee

Other Than Employee (1)
Independent (1)
Outside (1)

Note: * Selection influenced by employees.

nees presented by a nominating committee that adds two employee directors to the independent directors and requires the consent of at least one union director to any particular independent director nominee. By contrast, the outside public directors are nominated by a committee that consists of the incumbent outside public directors.

The scope of employee influence over the selection of directors is a potential weakness in the board structure. At crunch time the employee groups could substantially change board composition, an act that would undoubtedly be taken as bad faith by outside capital suppliers as well as public shareholders. The possibility nonetheless exists.

The employee directors, one for each ownership group, will be selected in a manner that illustrates another potential fault line in the governance structure. The employee directors will not be elected by the relevant employees voting as shareholders. Rather, each employee director will be elected by a special class of preferred stock that in the case of the pilots and the machinists is held by the union and presumably voted by the union leadership. In the case of the salaried and management employees, a representative body makes a binding nomination. Thus employee board representation will come through the union leadership rather than direct election.

This will lead to two significant problems. The first is a standard principal/agent problem now applied to the employee ownership setting. The union leaders who control the nomination of directors with "supercharged" voting rights (a phrase from a pilots' union document) may be tempted to pursue personal agendas, including retaining office, rather than pursuing solely the interests of the employee shareholders. The second, more subtle, problem arises from the discontinuity between employment and stock ownership that will grow over time. The buyout is structured so that employees will receive stock to replace foregone wages and benefits during a six-year investment period. New hires toward the end of the period will receive proportionately less stock; those hired after the period will receive no stock. As employee shareholders retire, their preferred stock converts into common, which they can sell. Over time the employee groups will be divided on the basis of shareholder status. The employee leaders will face an inevitable conflict of interests. Internal politics will force the leaders—and the directors whose election they control—to shift their views of optimal company decisions in response to the shifting make-up of the group membership. (Of course, the anticipation of this conflict may lead to negotiation of a further employee stock ownership transaction that would include new employees.)

Board Committee Structure. Many corporate functions will be under the charge of specially designated committees of the board. For example, a "Competitive Action Plan Committee" is responsible for overseeing the United Shuttle rollout and operation. This committee consists of eight directors: the

CEO, three outside public directors, two independent directors, and the two union directors. It has "exclusive authority" to modify the very elaborate arrangements relating to the Shuttle, although the union directors cannot vote on labor issues and any amendment to the collective bargaining agreements must be referred to another committee, the "Labor Committee."

The Labor Committee will consist of three or more directors, including at least one outside public director, one independent director, and at least one other director (but no union director), and will have "exclusive authority" with regard to the company's collective bargaining agreements. The collective bargaining agreements with the pilots and the mechanics specified a three-year salary freeze; wages could be renegotiated after that, subject to arbitration with defined limits and a no-strike clause (including a sympathy strike). Six years out the entire agreement can be renegotiated. All subsequent labor negotiations will be conducted against the background of job security agreements, seniority protection, and similar protective provisions in the initial collective bargaining agreement. The company will also have to bargain with the flight attendants, who did not participate in the buyout and who therefore have made no wage or work rule concessions.

The compensation of senior management, especially the CEO, is obviously a sensitive matter and a complicated committee structure addresses it. In general, managerial compensation will be established by a seven-member "Compensation Committee," consisting of the CEO, one public outside director, two independent directors, and all three employee directors. This obviously gives the employee directors an important voice in setting managerial salaries. On the other hand, the Compensation Committee may delegate to the "Compensation Administration Committee" "specific responsibilities" with respect to compensation of the CEO. That committee consists of two independent directors and one outside public directors, i.e., no employee directors.[50]

The committee structure embodies some interesting innovations. For example, the establishment of a special committee to oversee a particular aspect of the firm's operations may help resist the management effort to aggregate information before it reaches the board. In other words, the committee structure pushes the board's involvement to lower echelons of the hierarchy. This could be particularly important for the UAL case because these particular operations, the United Shuttle, are also the focus of the effort to change culture. It is here where United needs to learn to become a successful low-cost, high-efficiency carrier. In fact

---

[50] This governance structure has led to significant changes in managerial compensation. Apparently it had previously been the practice to give all managers above a certain level a fixed number of stock options, regardless of the share price, i.e., regardless of the value of the options. The employee directors challenged this, hired well-known compensation consultants; the result is a revamped compensation system with a lower level of options overall and explicit performance targets for the grant of options.

the Shuttle's operations have been of such critical importance to the company that matters concerning it are routinely taken up by the entire board; the Competitive Action Plan Committee has rarely, if ever, met.

The Labor Committee is an effort to solve the conflict that generally arises whenever a controlling shareholder does business with the firm, but it is particularly important in the case of employee ownership. The common nightmare scenario is that the anger from difficult contract negotiations will spill out into the boardroom, poisoning relationships and skewing decision making. The objective of a separate committee that has been delegated all board power in these matters is to contain these conflicts outside the boardroom. There are potential weaknesses, however. At present the committee consists of the CEO, one independent director, and one outside public director. As discussed above, this gives the employees influence over two of the members. This fact, plus the concerns that the committee might have about its legitimate exercise of such important responsibility, may well nudge it toward the arbitration option in the collective bargaining agreements. This probably mean a less favorable outcome for public shareholders.

Board Voting Rules. As noted above, the Competitive Action Plan Committee and the Labor Committee will act for the entire board over certain matters. For most other business, board action is by majority vote of a quorum, although "quorum" is defined in a way to limit strategic non-attendance decisions by independent directors. Certain "extraordinary matters" require approval by a 75% board vote (including one union director) or approval of 75% of the vote at a shareholders meeting. These matters include mergers or acquisitions as target or acquirer, entry into new lines of business, asset sales, and the sale of equity equivalent securities that would dilute the employees' ownership interest. The practical consequence is to give the three employee directors veto power over such a transaction, since it seems extremely unlikely that their concerted opposition wouldn't carry at least half the employee voters, which would block shareholder approval.[51] Indeed, the two union directors have an effective veto over such a transaction, since their members hold a total of 45% of the votes. (Once again there is an elaborately crafted exception that would permit an equity issuance even without the employees' concurrence if necessary to avoid insolvency.)

Shareholder Voting. A subsidiary governance mechanism is shareholder voting. As previously discussed, employee shareholders do not elect, in their capacity as shareholders, the employee directors. Those directors are elected by a special class of stock held by the union or other employee group leadership. In the case of "extraordinary matters" the shareholders have the rights provided

---

[51] Fifty percent of 55% is greater than 25%, which is a blocking coalition in cases of a 75% supermajority requirement.

under Delaware law (simple majority voting for charter amendments and limited class of transactions) and, as noted above, voting rights in cases where the board splits. The employee voting stock is held by ESOPs, subject to directions to the trustee to "pass through" votes for allocated shares and to vote unallocated shares in the same proportions, "mirrored voting."[52]

These limited shareholder voting rights can serve useful purposes. For example, they can restrain the enthusiasm of employee directors who might become co-opted by management's vision of corporate expansion. Or they can take the heat off of employee directors who, for the sake of boardroom comity, may not want to oppose management's expansion plans directly and can now lay the matter off on employees. Both factors may have been at work in UAL's unsuccessful investigation of a possible merger with US Air in the fall of 1995.

Economic Participation and Governance Participation. There are two potential mismatches between the employees' economic interests and their governance rights. The first has been noted previously: stock accrues over a six-year concessions period, meaning that newer employees will not necessarily own stock (or very much) yet will vote for union leaders who select directors. Especially as the existing UAL workforce retires, this could lead to a disconnection between the employees' economic stake and their governance power. This is troublesome because the employees' economic interest as shareholders constrains the tendency to use governance power for distributive purposes.

The second arises from the perpetuation of employee governance power long after the employee beneficial ownership interest falls below 50%. The voting structure provides that the employees as a group will continue to have a majority

---

[52] The parties have established these voting rules through an elaborate classification of stock. One class of stock that votes for directors is held by the representatives of the employee groups. The employee stock held by the ESOP is in two classes, one class is a convertible preferred stock that has dividend rights but no voting rights; another class has voting rights but no dividend rights. As concessions accrue, the ESOP allocates stock (of both classes) into employee accounts, but holds onto the stock until the employee retires or leaves the company, at which point the employee receives the common share equivalents of the convertible preferred and the separate voting share is extinguished.

Why the division of employee stock into two classes? First, this gives the employees an immediate 55% voting interest even though the economic interest, the convertible preferred stock will be acquired by the ESOP over the six-year concession accrual period, not immediately. The ESOP stock acquisition was stretched out over the period to maximize expected tax advantages (the company deducts the value of the stock at the time acquired and the parties believed the stock price would increase over time; convertible preferred stock was the favored instrument because its dividend right and conversion privilege are a basis for asserting a valuation higher than the publicly traded common). Second, the ESOP trustee is supposed to vote non-allocated shares via "mirrored voting," but recent Department of Labor rulings may require the trustee to exercise independent judgment as to non-allocated shares. This could have significant consequences in the event of a hostile takeover bid. So the parties have provided that if the trustees ignore the employee instructions, the ESOP voting stock loses its vote, another shareholder vote is required, and the employee voting interest shifts to the director voting stock.

vote (55%) and will retain an influence over the election of 9 of 12 directors until the level of beneficial employee ownership falls below 20%. This falloff will occur principally through retirement of present employees. The "sunset" date is not expected until 2016 and could easily extend beyond.[53] A change in these arrangements would require concurrence by the employee voters and their representatives.

These two problems reinforce one another. In the out years, as the employees' collective economic interest from stock ownership diminishes, full governance power will be exercised by union leaders accountable to a membership that, in the main, owns no stock at all. On its face, this looks like a prescription for disaster. On the other hand, it is a problem that will not materialize for some time. The very point may be to force the parties to ensure a succession of employee owners. That is, one of the limits to employee ownership as a stable form has been the desire of some employee stockholders to cash out sooner rather than later, and the eventual sale by retirees. UAL stock is held by ESOPs on behalf of individual employees, closing off one avenue of employee exit (since employees can sell the stock only if they leave the firm or upon retirement).[54] But retirements and turnover will inevitably come. What is needed is a new program of employee stock ownership, perhaps financed with new concessions or as part of a company-sponsored retirement plan. The potential mismatch may spur the necessary action.

IV. How's It Doing?

The key question is whether the UAL ESOT has produced a structure that has conserved or, better, enhanced value. There are several possible ways of evaluating this: the financial performance of the airline as a whole, both in absolute terms and compared to the industry; the stock price performance in absolute and industry comparative terms; operating performance of the airline as a whole (in particular, cost data, in absolute and industry terms); and the operating performance (and profitability) of the United Shuttle.

Another way to evaluate the UAL ESOT is for its direct impact on measures of employee morale and performance, on the theory that even if not immediately reflected in the bottom line, these measures correlate with the creation of a new

---

[53] The level of share ownership for purposes of the "sunset" includes not only the ESOP stock that is part of the transaction but also stock owned by any United employee benefit plan, including self-directed plans like 401(k) plans and company-directed plans like a defined benefit pension plan.

[54] My view is that this is a mistake because 1) it artificially locks in employee ownership when it may be optimal to convert back to a more conventional form—like a reverse LBO; and 2) it unreasonably lengthens incentive horizons until retirement.

culture that ultimately will be the source of significant added value. A weaker claim could also be made: that unless measures of employee morale and performance improve, the ESOT should not be expected to do more than allocate transition losses, rather than help create a collaborative culture.

Perhaps the most straightforward performance measure is stock price data. As Figures 2 and 3 demonstrate, UAL was an industry laggard in the pre-buyout period and a star after the buyout. UAL's stock price performance in the pre-buyout period from July 1990 through July 1994 was a negative 5.4%, somewhere in the middle of industry performance, between industry standout Southwest (48.5%) and industry laggard US Air (-27.7%), and, in a narrower range, between Delta (-9.3%) and American (-0.2%). (See Table 1.) UAL's post-buyout performance has been splendid, 46.5% annualized returns over the three-year period beginning in July of 1994. But the entire industry has enjoyed sparkling returns, especially Northwest (36.4%) (an LBO saved from bankruptcy by an ESOT), Continental (66.1%) (coming out of bankruptcy), and US Air (77.1%) (aided by the grounding of Valuejet). Putting aside those turnaround situations, UAL's returns significantly dominated all others, including rivals American (14.4%) and Delta (20.5%). Even when the 1994 et seq. industry index is broadened in Figure 4 to include Continental and Northwest (which were not publicly traded throughout the earlier period), UAL's post-buyout stock performance is still above the industry average.

Figure 2: UAL Versus a Composite of American, Delta, Southwest, and USAir, 1/1/1990-7/14/1994

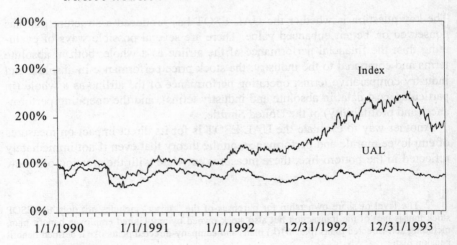

Source: Own calculations.

Figure 3:   UAL Versus a Composite of American, Delta, Southwest, and USAir, 7/13/1994-8/5/1997

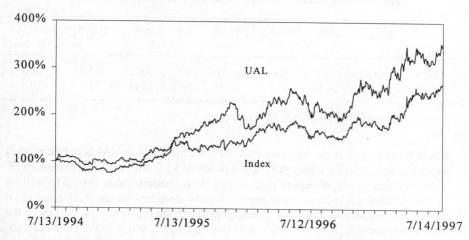

Source: Own calculations.

Figure 4:   UAL Versus a Composite of American, Continental (B), Delta, Northwest, Southwest, and USAir, 7/13/1994-8/5/1997

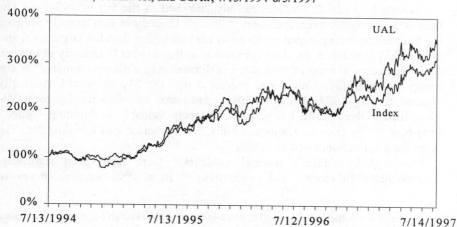

Source: Own calculations.

Table 1: Annualized Stock Returns (Including Reinvested Dividends) of UAL and
          Other Publicly Traded Major Airlines, 1990-1997

	UAL	AMR	CONT.B	DELTA	NW	SW	USAIR	Non-UAL Avg.
90-94	(5.4)	(0.2)	n.a.	(9.3)	n.a.	48.5	(27.7)	(2.9)
94-97	46.5	14.4	66.1	20.5	36.4	(1.0)	77.1	39.6

Note: Figures in %; July 14-July 13 of each year.

Another reflection of the buyout's success is the increase in UAL's public market capitalization from $1.1 billion to approximately $5.5 billion as of yearend 1997. Similarly, the employee equity appreciated in its shadow value from $1.9 billion to $10 billion, an increase that approximately doubles the deemed amount of employee investment. This data strongly supports the efficiency properties of the United transaction: for sure, value was not destroyed, and it looks as if substantial value has been created.

Ironically, the performance of the Shuttle—whose establishment was probably the critical variable in persuading the 1993 United board to approve the buyout—has been quite mixed.

"Shuttle by United" was successfully launched in the fall of 1994, but has been at best a break-even operation. Although United has substantially reduced the Shuttle's operating expenses, its costs are still higher than the target level and higher than Southwest, its chief competitor in that market.[55] Industry observers, moreover, seem to regard the Shuttle's performance as a disappointment.[56] In the runup to the ESOT, United had predicted that the Shuttle would eventually account for 20% of United's domestic operations; currently the figure is 3%. Nevertheless the Shuttle has proved extremely valuable in building United's long-haul traffic from its California hubs, San Francisco and Los Angeles. The main loser is not Southwest but Delta.[57]

Measured by United's internal yardsticks, there have been significant improvements in morale and productivity.[58] In a 1995 internal survey of

[55] The cost reduction was substantial, down to 8c per ASM (available seat mile), but against a target of 7.4c per ASM and Southwest's 7.1c.

[56] See McCartney, Scott and Michael McCarthy 'Airlines: Southwest Flies Circles Around United's Shuttle' *Wall Street Journal* February 20, 1996, B1. The Shuttle's chief operating officer was replaced in the fall of 1995.

[57] See Carey, Susan 'Aided by Its Shuttle, United Air is Taking Los Angeles by Storm' *Wall Street Journal* January 16, 1998, 1.

[58] This data is based on a first-quarter 1996 presentation to security analysts by John Edwardson, United's chief operating officer.

employee attitudes, 62% of the employees say they had seen positive changes in the company's culture over the past year, 62% claimed to believe in the effectiveness of "task teams" (employee-led work groups), 93% professed to be committed to improving the way they do their work, and 87% said they were looking for opportunities to keep quality high and costs low. This self-generated evidence of employee attitude changes—soft data at best—positively correlates with some concrete measures of employee morale and performance. On the morale side, sick time was down 17% over the prior year, worker's compensation claims were down 17%, disability claims were down by 15%, and 75% fewer grievances were filed. On the performance side: United asserted that "task teams" had produced fuel conservation savings of $30 million annually and aircraft scheduling savings of $25 million annually, and noted significant improvements in on-time performance and baggage handling.

One very interesting performance comparison is between UAL and Delta, which, as noted above, addressed transition problems by making substantial layoffs beginning in 1994, the same year as the UAL employee buyout. As Table 2 indicates, using 1993 as a benchmark, both UAL and Delta achieved substantial labor savings in subsequent years, as measured in labor costs per available seat mile. Nevertheless, UAL's average annualized stock return of 46.5% during the 1994-1997 period was substantially higher than Delta's 20.5%. Although direct comparisons are difficult because of differences in route structure and competitive pressures, the comparative stock price performance of UAL and Delta offers suggestive support for the efficiency of an ESOT in managing a transition. Moreover, despite Delta's positive stock price performance, the Delta board perceived that the job cuts had precipitated a crisis in the Delta "family" culture that both degraded service to passengers and led to increased union organizing activity. The CEO who initiated the downsizing was forced out.[59] This suggests that Delta's layoffs may not have been the optimal transition strategy.

Table 2: Percentage Reduction in Labor Cost per Available Seat Mile, 1993 as Baseline

	1994	1995	1996
Delta	+0.08	-11.20	-6.22
UAL	+0.04	-5.96	-4.30

Source: Computed from Form 41 Data, airline submissions to Department of Transportation.

[59] See Brannigan, Martha and Joseph White "'So Be It": Why Delta Decided It Was Time For CEO To Take Off' *Wall Street Journal* May 30, 1997.

At best, only very tentative conclusions about United's performance are possible at this point. This is partially because of the relatively short time that has elapsed since the transaction and because of the unusually favorable conditions that have prevailed in the air travel market in the period. Air travel demand has increased, fuel prices have decreased, secular inflation is low, safety concerns have slowed the entry of new carriers, and the airlines have avoided rapid capacity expansions and all-out price wars that have undermined profitability in the past. Virtually every airline has made money and stock prices have moved upwards. The real test of the United ESOT, in particular the resiliency of its governance structure, will come when general economic conditions worsen or the inevitable fare wars break out.[60]

V. Mid-Term Wage Negotiations

The recent wage negotiations between United and the pilots and the machinists, which extended from the fall of 1996 into the spring of 1997, revealed both the fragility and the strength of United's employee ownership structure. The negotiation was occasioned by the terms of the 1994 buyout, which permitted a mid-stream reopening of the wage settlement against the possibility that industry wage levels changed relative to prior expectations. The buyout agreement precommitted the parties to arbitration in the event of deadlock, capped the amount of the arbitration award to a 10% wage increase in the last two years of the ESOP accumulation period (1998 and 1999),[61] and barred a strike until the collective bargaining agreement became amendable in 2000. The company proposed a deal significantly better than the arbitration baseline, including a significant element of profit-sharing.

Nevertheless, in January 1997, the pilots and the mechanics, the most important subgroup of the machinists, rejected the company proposal. The pilots were particularly indignant, rejecting the company's "business-as-usual attitude that has no place in an employee-owned company."[62] Although the pilots could not threaten to strike, they did threaten to end the culture of employee ownership: "They can expect no cooperation. . . . They will find every interaction with us

---

[60] For another account and assessment of the UAL transaction, see Oakeshott, Robert 'Majority Employee Ownership at United Airlines: Evidence of Big Wins for Both Jobs *and* Investors' (Job Ownership Ltd. Working Paper, July 1997).

[61] Ziemba, Stanley 'More United Labor Woes: Mechanics, Technicians, Reject Pact; Ramp Workers and Other Approve It; But New Turbulence Adds to Questions About Employee Ownership' *Chicago Tribune* January 10, 1997, 1.

[62] Podmolik, Mary Ellen 'United Pilots Reject Contract; Arbitration Will Follow Lopsided Vote' *Chicago Sun-Times* January 17, 1997, 45.

equally as difficult as they have made this negotiation."[63] Although the company made moves to submit the matter to binding arbitration, eventually the parties came to an agreement much closer to the pilots' position: a 10% wage increase apportioned over two years, a recovery of certain pension benefits, and a guaranteed "snapback" by 2000 to wage levels prevailing prior to the employee buyout.

The implications of this outcome for the United employee buyout are complex. First, it shows the way that significant employee ownership can transform contracts with strict terms into "relational" contracts that can be renegotiated in midstream. There is nothing inherently unreasonable about the employees' desire for an extra-contractual wage increase. The performance of UAL and the industry generally since the 1994 transaction significantly exceeded the parties' expectations. For example, "Status Quo" projections prepared in connection with the evaluation of the 1994 transaction anticipated operating income for 1995 and 1996 of $377 million and $502 million respectively, and net income of $118 million and $244 million. The labor savings associated with the transaction were estimated to add $250 million to net income in 1995, increasing net income to $370 million the first year, and presumably equivalent amounts in subsequent years.[64] The actual results were significantly better: operating income/net income of $829 and net income of $662 million for 1995, and $1.12 billion and net income of $960 million for 1996. These results were nearly double the estimates!

Moreover, the 10% wage increase on a lower base is not out of line with the 9% wage increase (over 1997-2001), plus stock options, that the American Airline pilots received at the conclusion of their difficult wage negotiations in April 1997. Pilot wages at United will still be approximately 15% less than comparable wages at American.[65]

Nevertheless, the mid-term negotiation does represent a retrading of the deal. In the classic contract story, parties calibrate their demands in the light of a probability distribution over outcomes; part of the return of the public shareholders was the upside of unusually good results. Indeed, the parties specifically contracted over this possibility by imposing a ceiling on the wage increase available in arbitration, and had explicitly ruled out the strike option. There are three possible reasons why management did not assert its contract right and, by some notions, may be deemed to have capitulated. First is the possible loss of the immediate economic benefits of the employee ownership culture. Although likely to be of some value, these have proven difficult to quantify. As mentioned

[63] Driscoll, Paul A. 'Employee Ownership Threatened By Pilots United Airlines Dispute Over Wages Termed "Serious"' *Arizona Republic* January 10, 1997, E8 (Associated Press story).

[64] UAL Proxy Statement, 6/10/94, 21-3.

[65] McCartney, Scott 'American Airlines Pilots Are Expected By Union Leaders to Ratify New Pact' *Wall Street Journal* April 7, 1997, B2.

above, a 1995 internal survey identified reduced annual operating costs of approximately $50 million from fuel conservation measures and better aircraft scheduling because of employee "task teams."[66] These savings are not trivial, but the factors most significantly accounting for United's superior results have been industry conditions: a growing economy that has led to an increased demand for air travel, which translates into higher passenger "yields" (i.e., fare increases) and higher load factors.[67]

The second possibility is the threat against incumbent management specifically and the company generally via the employees' governance rights. On the specific threat: Gerald Greenwald, the CEO, was brought into the transaction by the employees, the pilots in particular. To lose the goodwill of the pilots would be a major blow to his leadership. Moreover, although his performance is reviewed and compensation set by a committee composed of non-employee directors (the "Compensation Administration Committee"), two of the three directors are independent directors, nominated through a mechanism that, as discussed above, gives a union director a veto. Additionally, two union directors sit on the Compensation Committee, which determines the compensation for the rest of the management team.

Concerns about general boardroom conflict seem very real, in part because of the particular governance regime at United. The company's negotiations were orchestrated through its Labor Committee, which means that directors were involved in an unusually immediate way in the formulation of the company's strategy (common practice is simply for management to present its proposed strategy to the board at the outset and make routine reports along the way unless there is a major problem). The negotiations were brought into the boardroom through reports of the Labor Committee to the board. Even though the UAL charter devolves the board's authority in labor negotiations to the Labor Committee, apparently the directors on that committee felt it was inappropriate not to share information (and perhaps responsibility). The employee directors were present during at least some of the reports, possibly affecting candor both positively and negatively, and articulated the employee position. There are reports that the negotiations changed the "temperature" of the boardroom over a several-month period, including in deliberations on matters that did not directly bear on the labor negotiations. Failure to resolve the conflict—the first of many to come—obviously carried the risk of a downward spiral in boardroom cooperation that could undermine the company.

---

[66] This data is based on a first-quarter 1996 presentation to security analysts by John Edwardson, United's chief operating officer.

[67] See UAL Proxy Statement, 3/31/97, A.6 (Management Discussion and Analysis).

The Eastern Airlines case is a vivid demonstration of the potential havoc of boardroom conflict.[68] There employee representatives with far less influence over the board's agenda and procedures than in the United case became vocally disenchanted with the management team. This proved to be regrettable. The fact of substantial employee stock ownership, 25% in the Eastern case, proved to be an insufficient bulwark against spiraling antagonism. United's management could not but be aware of the risks.

The third possibility is the bright side—namely, that cooperation and flexibility in the good times will be reciprocated in the tough times. Historically the airline business has been highly cyclical, the result of high operating leverage as discussed above. After all, the profits of 1995-96 barely offset the losses of 1990-93. If employee stock ownership is to induce a willingness to share economic adjustment costs in the face of new competitive scenarios, then presumably the converse must follow: that public shareholders must share some of the unanticipated rents. Sometimes the challenges of prosperity equal the challenges of adversity. Certainly if United management had insisted on enforcement of its contract, concession bargaining with employees in an economic downturn would have been much harder. If this was the strategy, it seems that management may have resisted the employees' effort to renegotiate too vigorously.

Another major implication of the United mid-negotiation is the demonstration of the weakness of employee stock ownership as an economic incentive, at least in the ESOP structure. Regardless of the employees' sense of unfairness in the turn of economic events, they had in fact profited hugely on their stock ownership and had more than recouped their investment of foregone wages. The price of United common stock trebled over the July 1994-January 1997 period (when the pilots and machinists rejected the contract proposal based on the arbitration ceiling). By my calculation, the average pilot contributed approximately $50,000 over the period and received stock worth approximately $150,000 (plus accrued dividends). In the month after the settlement was announced, removing a cloud over the airline, the stock rallied by another 25%, adding another $37,000 to the value of a pilot's stock.. (Presumably the stock price increase also reflected the market's general belief that the employees' midstream renegotiation did not signal a major shift away from the shareholder-oriented focus of United's management and that the governance arrangements were not going to unravel in a pathological way.) Of course a more favorable (to the public shareholders) wage settlement would have led to a further stock price increase, at a time when the market multiple of United's earnings has been approximately 11.

The problem here is that the stock appreciation is locked up in the ESOP, not available for consumption purposes until the employee retires or quits. In theory there is a substitution effect among various forms of savings, so that an increase

---

[68] See Gordon, supra n. 20.

in an ESOP account will be offset by reduced savings in other respects, making greater consumption possible. The general empirical evidence on saving and consumption patterns conflicts with this idea, however, and at least some of those very close to the UAL negotiation realized the employee frustration at being unable to realize on the fruits of their investment and sought, unsuccessfully, to devise an instrument that could deliver economic value to employee shareholders that would not significantly dilute earnings per share.

Moreover, expecting ESOP stock to deliver significant economic incentives for line employees seems to contradict the pattern of "incenting" high-level managerial employees: stock options that upon vesting typically have an exercise period of two to ten years and various other sorts of stock-based rights (stock appreciation rights, phantom stock, etc.) that deliver near-term economic return. Because of their average greater wealth (and the declining marginal utility of money), high-ranking managerial employees would be more favorably disposed to longer term incentives than line employees, yet line employees are given an appreciating asset that can't be cashed out until retirement! ESOP stock is not an "incentive-compatible" contract.

There are three hypotheses that explain the common use of ESOP's in employee stock ownership transactions. First is that the tax benefits of a leveraged ESOP may blind the parties to the incentive failures of ESOP stock ownership. Often the goal is to achieve as much value as possible for the public stockholder seller; the appeal of the immediate tax savings may be overwhelming. Second is that the ESOP is a convenient way to lock-in employee ownership, where "lock-in" serves the economic interests of other parties. For example, ESOPs were commonly instituted in the 1980s as a way of putting a substantial block of employer stock in the hands of parties likely to reject a hostile takeover bid. In United, the role of employee representatives on the board is tied to the maintenance of a certain level of employee stock ownership that might quickly evaporate if employees could freely dispose of the stock. Third is that the ESOP locks in employee ownership where lock-in serves the economic interests of the employees. The midstream renegotiation in United illustrates one such case: a high level of employee stock ownership gives weight to the insistence of board-level employee representatives. Another case would be a firm where a high level of employee stock ownership was necessary to cement a value-increasing corporate culture; this may be United as well.

In any event, the economic benefits to employees of the ESOP form are clearly in tension with its economic limitations. The field is open for the design of transactional alternatives that might maintain long-term employee ownership while connecting present employee compensation to equity-type returns.

D. Conclusion

The UAL transaction illustrates a central point: that standard conceptions of ownership and governance may be far more malleable than previously thought. In particular, "employee ownership" is not a unitary thing, but rather a transactional framework that needs to be filled in with key institutional design parameters. Transactions that produce significant employee ownership and governance participation may solve particular problems in economic transitions—and not just through one-time adjustments, but in environments where continued flexibility is important, trust is hard to sustain, and high employee morale can contribute significantly to competitive success. It also appears that the success of the venture, especially over the long term, may be sensitive to particular institutional design choices that structure employee ownership and governance participation. The UAL structure is a first cut at accomplishing these objectives: to let employees face the incidence of stock price changes while preserving employee ownership and to bring employee concerns into the boardroom while insulating board decision making from redistributive bargaining over interests. It would be a mistake to take the UAL precedent as a standard form, both because its experiment in ownership and governance design is still underway and because the problems of information, credibility, commitment, and incentives may vary significantly across firms.

In economic terms, both UAL's public shareholders and employees have prospered in the buyout years, in part because of the favorable conditions for airlines generally. The mid-term labor negotiations at UAL were a crucial moment because failure at an early stage would have been irreversible. Their resolution, if not total success, opens up two or so years to build both institutional trust and perhaps subinstitutions of incentive alignment and governance participation. It's ironic that a structure designed for adversity should face its first challenge of economic adjustment from prosperity. And whether United will establish a successful precedent for a new organizational form—the large corporation of mixed public and employee ownership, uniquely suited for industries of sharp transition—is still an open question.

Discussion Report

HANS-CHRISTOPH VOIGT

The following discussion focused mainly on the contributions of *Roe* and *Gordon,* whose hypotheses were discussed intensively and, in part, controversially.

Regarding *Roe's* thesis of German corporate issuers' 'low demand for good securities markets,' participants discussed possible correlations between German supervisory boards, co-determination, and the historical weakness of German securities markets. One central topic of debate was whether governance structures can affect the demand for good securities markets, and whether this kind of 'reverse' view might apply to Germany.

To begin with, an American academic reported that there presumably had been good securities markets in Germany at the beginning of this century. He wanted to know whether board-level co-determination was already established at this time (it was not prior to 1922). In addition, a cross-country comparison covering the development of capital markets in proportion to co-determination could be revealing.

Relating to *Streeck's* paper, an American colleague asked for empirical data on whether the number of transactions requiring board approval (§ 111 IV 2 AktG) has changed since the introduction of board-level co-determination. Furthermore, it would be interesting to know how many of the not officially traded corporations are in fact family-owned.

Given the low demand for good securities markets, a German academic questioned *Roe's* thesis that it might be conditioned by board-level co-determination. According to *Roe*, co-determination following an IPO could possibly cause some lack of balance between power of equity and labor in the co-determined boardroom. He pointed out that the heirs of a family-owned company with concentrated ownership normally face two possible ways of running the business: either they want to manage the firm by themselves or they want to sell out in public markets in order to bring in professional managers. In the former case, they tend to shy away from an IPO because they do not want to be controlled in any way. Board-level co-determination does not threaten them in the first place because they are accustomed to it from plant-level co-determination. In the latter case, they do not care about board-level co-determination at all.

Roe objected to this argument by pointing out that the stock market will anticipate any lack of balance through lower stock prices. Selling out their stock instead of managing the firm could thus become costly for the heirs.

In reference to this, an American academic suggested selling out in blocks of shares as a possible way out of this dilemma. This would simultaneously meet the heirs' demand for selling out in public markets and preserve the power of equity to counterbalance labor in the co-determined boardroom. She noted that the sample presented by *Franks* and *Mayer*[1] could verify German corporate issuers' affection for this additional possibility, although it covered only those corporations quoted on the stock exchange. Still, some significant block sales were registered in Germany during the period from 1988 to 1991. *Roe* subscribed to this view and emphasized that it strongly supported his thesis.

According to a German participant, there has been a growing number of IPOs initiated by German family-owned companies since the law relating to small stock corporations (less than 500 employees) became effective in 1994. As they are not subject to board-level co-determination, provided registration took place after August 9, 1994 (§ 76 VI 1 BetrVG), *Roe* noted that this development also confirmed his hypothesis.

Some German academics questioned whether the generally criticized weakness of the German supervisory board is in fact caused by board-level co-determination. As one German participant expressed, the long-lasting debate on German supervisory boards has indeed led to several amendments of the German Stock Corporation Code (AktG). Nevertheless, these corrections were not motivated by board-level co-determination but by systemic failures between managing board and supervisory board. For example, the provisions regulating the information flow from the managing board to the supervisory board (§ 90 AktG) have been amended no fewer than three times since 1965.

Another German participant pointed out that empirical facts might induce one to draw a parallel between strong capital markets and strong boards in the U.S. and weak capital markets and weak supervisory boards in Germany. Nevertheless, according to this participant, no interdependence between capital markets and board monitoring efficiency can be observed. He expressed the opinion that Germany's capital market for IPOs might be small but was not compellingly weak, as was shown recently by the German Telekom case. By considering possible effects of board-level co-determination on monitoring efficiency, a distinction must be made between formal and informal boards, the latter of which are working very well. Furthermore, he doubted that board-level co-determination was the driving force in concentrating ownership to counterbalance labor in the boardroom. Concentrated ownership is not a characteristic of the German capital market. On the contrary, it can be found in many other European countries that are not familiar with co-determination. Therefore, research must look for other driving forces for concentration. For this, a reference to Germany's most frequent company form, the German 'limited liability company' (*GmbH*),

---

[1] At the symposium, Franks and Mayer presented their paper 'Ownership, Control, and the Performance of German Corporations' (Working Paper, London Business School and University of Oxford, 1997).

could be revealing. As it is the shareholders' meeting itself which exercises strong control over the management, maybe conclusions for co-determination can be drawn from this.

In response to this, *Roe* pointed out that strong informal boards could not disprove his arguments. They were the typical result of concentrated ownership being in the position to organize itself.

With regard to the cited German Telekom case, an American participant questioned its relevance to prove or disprove the German capital market's strength. He noted that equity risk was limited beyond the normal range by promising fixed dividends from the beginning and not to sell out a second block of shares held by the German government prior to 1999.

One German contributor confirmed his predecessor's doubts about co-determination as the driving force for concentrated ownership. If *Roe* was right, different ownership structures had to be expected depending on whether labor representation in the supervisory board runs up to one half or one third of its legal members. But such differing structures could not be observed. Those few stock corporations that are widely held were those subjected to one half board-level co-determination. Even though other facts might influence ownership structures as well, e.g., the size of a corporation, this calls *Roe's* thesis into question because, according to him, especially the co-determined corporations were expected to be closely held in order to counterbalance labor.

A German participant showed another possible impact of board-level co-determination. It could aggravate the free cash flow problem, thereby enlarging the management's latitude to invest the firm's free cash flow in the acquisition of other firms, which in the end led to today's tight interlinking of business enterprises. *Roe* admitted that this could be a possible explanation, too.

Finally, a European participant agreed with his German colleague's doubts about board-level co-determination as the driving force for concentrated ownership. As in other European countries, the main problem while selling out in public markets was to preserve any control in the corporation.

Turning back again to German supervisory boards' monitoring efficiency, one American academic noted that identical problems could be observed in the U.S. He reported on irregular board meetings and insufficient information flow.

In responding to this, *Roe* pointed out that even if American boards turned out to be worse than their German counterparts, it would not disprove his assumptions presented in the paper because other governance structures existed to settle possible defects, i.e., strong capital markets, incentive management compensation, proxy fights, etc. These features do not exist in Germany.

Regarding *Gordon's* paper, there was consensus that 'employee ownership is not a self-defining organizational form'. Nevertheless, employee ownership structures could be especially well-suited in times of economic transition. As one American participant expressed, the UAL construction could probably decrease bargaining problems that emerge in a situation of low trust between management and employees. That could pay off in times of economic distress. Furthermore, employee stock ownership was a good way to give people equity. Employees recognized that if they don't control the board, they don't own the firm. With respect to the panelist's criticism about locking in employee ownership in an ESOP (employee stock ownership plan), the participant wondered why the parties concerned did not choose convertible claims instead. He presumed two reasons, the most convincing of which was that it was chosen for fiscal reasons. Besides, an ESOP could provide solutions to decrease collective action problems that emerge from direct stock ownership on behalf of individual employees. The major problem would be to measure the economic success of this solution.

A German participant was amazed by the panelist's reservations referring to ESOPs. Contrary to the appraisal given in the paper, employees could take advantages of the ESOP structure even before retiring or quitting.

With regard to bargaining problems in situations of low trust, an American participant questioned whether employee stock ownership actually offered any advantages. According to him, this applied only to dual-monopoly situations. But employees could not be considered as a homogenous group that forms a counterpart to management, e.g., while bargaining over the just allocation of transition costs. The participant referred to stakeholders that may not primarily be interested in the corporation's rise in value. To take their interests into account would tremendously increase the complexity of any bargaining situation despite employee stock ownership structures.

Stimulated by a European participant, *Gordon* turned to the great influence achieved by labor while negotiating the UAL transaction. He admitted that the unique governance arrangements in favor of the employees could be attributed to labor appreciation as well as employee ownership structures. Nevertheless, the most interesting question was whether the UAL transaction could lead the way in reducing transition costs. He noted that it was difficult to measure its economic success, but in the very case of UAL, employees had more than recouped their investment of foregone wages over the period of two and a half years. Unfortunately, the stock appreciation was locked up in an ESOP and therefore not available for consumption purposes until the employees retired or quit. The panelist stated that it was the responsibility of the lawyers to design transactional alternatives that deliver near-term economic returns.

Another American participant argued that the situation at UAL could differ from other American airlines. However, the entire airline industry might be a special branch because wages were usually bound to the years of service. She wanted to know how board-level co-determination influenced wages and other micro data of the enterprise, e.g., costs of purchase, service, etc.

As a German participant noted, the UAL construction considerably aggravated the risk diversification of the employees. In addition, German employees were fundamentally risk-averse, i.e., they preferred fixed wage claims to stock ownership. Having no guarantee that stock prices will increase in the future, they fear being expropriated of fixed wage claims without any equivalent. He asked whether such considerations occurred in the U.S. and whether any 'insurance' existed to prevent such losses.

A German participant pointed out that employee stock ownership was no innovation with respect to Germany. At Siemens and Bertelsmann, for example, employees held respectively 6% and 25% of the common stock.

Chapter 6: Financial Intermediaries

Bank Equity Holdings in Non-Financial Firms and Corporate Governance: The Case of German Universal Banks

PETER O. MÜLBERT, Trier[*]/[**]

According to American observers, "it is not exaggeration to say that the universal bank sits at the epicenter of German corporate governance." In this context German banks' long-term shareholdings are widely perceived as a key instrument for wielding influence in non-financial firms. Regarding the effect of bank shareholdings on corporate governance, though, observers disagree. While some credit the banks' involvement as being beneficial to a corporation, its shareholders, and even to societal welfare, others take the opposite stance. In discussing these contradictory assertions the article starts by analyzing the number and size of German banks' equity stakes of at least 5% of voting stock in 424 non-financial corporations. It goes on to examine the banks' motives for holding long-term equity positions and provides a novel explanation based on the banks' interests in the deposit-taking business as a major source of refinancing. These considerations strongly imply that the bank's interests as a partial owner will substantially differ from those shareholders who hold sufficiently diversified portfolios. Finally the article reviews the existing empirical evidence on the banks' impact on German corporate governance.

Contents

[*] The author acknowledges the helpful comments of Hellmuth Milde on a previous version of this paper.

[**] Final version August 1997. The paper therefore does not reflect the acquisition of Bayerische Hypotheken- und Wechselbank AG by Bayerische Vereinsbank AG in September 1997.

A. Introduction

Bank equity holdings in non-financial corporations[1] cause substantial misgivings and even anxiety among lawyers, economists, and politicians. Criticism based on legal and economic considerations stresses the threat to depositors, to competition in the banking and non-banking sectors, and to the development of the capital market. In addition, the potential financial and political power of such corporate interlocking is regarded with distrust. On an international scale, there have been very different responses to this problem. Since 1933 the Glass-Steagall Act has forbidden U.S. banks to acquire holdings in non-financial institutions, while bank holding companies may not hold more than 5% as passive shareholders. In 1987 Japan lowered the ceiling for bank equity holdings from 10% to 5% of a company's capital stock. So far EU law does not contain any such percentual limits based on a company's capital stock, but only restrictions relating to a bank's liable equity. Nevertheless, the most recent German discussion on the "power of banks"[2] appears to be ending with a regulation which will act as an indirect restriction.[3] This is once more an expression of the traditional age-old mistrust of banks owning large equity positions in non-financial corporations.

At the end of the eighties, a different view of bank shareholdings emerged for the first time in the course of the U.S. discussion on corporate governance. Essentially, there were two aspects which drew attention to the Japanese and German systems of corporate governance, (i) the potential role of financial intermediaries as active institutional investors and (ii) the effects of different systems of corporate governance on corporate performance. From this point of view,

---

[1] As used in this paper, the term excludes firms that furnish bank services in the sense of the universal banking system, as well as insurance companies.

[2] From the current discussion, see Hopt, Klaus J. 'Corporate Governance und deutsche Universalbanken' in: Feddersen, Dieter, Peter Hommelhoff, and Uwe H. Schneider (eds.) *Corporate Governance* 243-63 (Cologne 1996); Mülbert, Peter O. *Empfehlen sich gesetzliche Regelungen zur Einschränkung des Einflusses der Kreditinstitute auf Aktiengesellschaften?* (Expert Opinion E for the 61st Deutscher Juristentag 1996) (Munich 1996); the lectures at the 61st convention of German jurists by Kübler, Semler, and Köhler in: Deutscher Juristentag (ed.) *Verhandlungen des 61. Deutschen Juristentages* vol. II/1 at N11-N27, N29-N45, N47-N58 (Munich 1996); Raiser, Thomas 'Empfehlen sich gesetzliche Regelungen zur Einschränkung des Einflusses der Kreditinstitute auf Aktiengesellschaften?' *Neue Juristische Wochenschrift* 49 (1996) 2257-62; Peltzer, Martin 'Empfehlen sich gesetzliche Regeln zur Einschränkung des Einflusses der Kreditinstitute auf Aktiengesellschaften?' *Juristenzeitung* 51 (1996) 842-51; Hammen, Horst 'Beschränkung von Beteiligungen der Kreditinstitute an Nichtbanken' *Zeitschrift für das gesamte Handelsrecht und Wirtschaftsrecht* 160 (1996) 133-62.

[3] Formally, the planned regulation will amend the rules on "depository voting rights", i.e., on giving proxies to banks. It stipulates that banks cannot vote the brokerage stock they hold as custodians if they own more than 5% of company's outstanding voting stock as well as vote all or part of their own stock.

German universal banks with their extensive shareholdings are a true alternative to the Anglo-Saxon mechanisms of market-based corporate control, or, more precisely, they appear to offer an alternative solution to the problems of corporate control afflicting companies of the Berle-Means type.

Against this background, this paper concentrates on the role of universal bank shareholdings in corporate governance, using German universal bank holdings in stock corporations as an example.[4] Already at this point it should be pointed out, though, that the effects of universal bank shareholdings are not fully grasped if universal banks are treated as "pure" investors like any other financial intermediary, e.g., pension funds, mutual funds, etc. Universal banks pursue a different set of interests via equity holdings than other financial intermediaries. Their role in corporate governance can be evaluated properly only by analyzing their corporate monitoring activities in the context of their banking operations in their entirety, this being a central issue of this paper. This perspective also gives us some idea of how the German system of corporate governance will develop in the future.[5] In contrast to Mark Roe's[6] suggestions, there are several arguments

---

[4] Banks also hold equity positions in companies of other legal forms. These, however, are not admitted to the Stock Exchange and therefore, almost without exception, have a highly concentrated shareholder structure. Thus, the following reflections deal only with bank holdings in stock corporations.

[5] Equity holdings—and depository voting rights—of universal banks are not the only distinct features of the German system of corporate governance. In addition, the overwhelming number of stock corporations have a highly concentrated ownership structure. Most stock corporations are not even listed on the stock exchange and even the majority of listed companies is a far cry from being widely held. The following figures are revealing:

(i) At the end of 1995, only 678 companies out of approx. 4300 corporations were listed on the German stock exchanges. 437 companies were officially quoted in the top tier (*Amtlicher Handel*), 147 traded in the regulated market as the second tier (*Geregelter Markt*), and 94 were traded in the lowest tier (*Freiverkehr*).

(ii) 429 among the 435 officially listed companies on September 30, 1996, had a well-known ownership structure. 270 firms were owned by a single majority shareholder, holding a qualified majority (75%) in 171 firms and a simple majority (50% + 1 share) in 99 firms. An additional 71 firms exhibited a blocking minority (25% + 1 share). Adding up the ownership stakes of the five largest shareholders yields the following figures: 351 (261/90) majority-owned firms/51 firms with a blocking minority (see Appendix B, Tables 1/2).

Taking into account that officially listed companies on average still show the broadest dispersion of shareholdings, these numbers indicate that direct shareholder monitoring by non-financial firms and private persons is of prime importance in the German system of corporate governance (this aspect is rightly emphasized, for example, by Prowse, Stephen 'Corporate Governance in an International Perspective' 35 et seq. (BIS Economic Papers no. 41, 1994); OECD 'Wirtschaftsberichte: Deutschland 1995' 97 et seq. (Paris 1995); Franks, Julian and Colin P. Mayer 'The Ownership and Control of German Corporations' 8 et seq. (London Business School and University of Oxford Working Paper, 1996); Mayer, Colin P. 'Corporate Governance, Competition, and Performance' 7-34, 22 et seq. *OECD Economic Studies* no. 27 (1996/II)). Of course, banks' shareholdings and depository voting rights are particularly important with the largest German non-financial firms. See Appendix B, Table 8 for a list of banks' shareholdings in the 53 largest German non-financial stock corporations, Appendix B, Table 9 for a list of banks' holdings in the

indicating that the bank-centered German system does not constitute a path-dependent alternative to the U.S. system, but rather will move in the direction of U.S. corporate governance, which is dominated by financial markets.

The remainder of this paper is organized as follows. The next section outlines the actual and legal conditions pertaining to corporate control by banks. Section C raises the question as to why banks as shareholders engage in monitoring activities at all. Section D analyzes possible motives which could induce banks to own a permanent interest in non-financial companies. The results hereof serve as a basis for Section E, which studies the objectives pursued by universal banks when monitoring and controlling a corporation in their capacity as owners. Based on the theoretical considerations in this section, various hypotheses are derived which are evaluated in Section F by referring to empirical studies of the German system. Section G is a résumé of the significance of bank shareholdings for corporate governance. It also gives some intuition on the future role of German universal banks in corporate governance.

B. Foundations

German universal banks are entitled to acquire holdings in companies regardless of the firms' legal form. Most holdings are acquired in companies structured as stock corporations. Limitations on holdings are, for the most part, contained in banking supervisory regulations (Sections 10, 12 I, V, 13 IV, German Banking Act),[7] implementing EU directives.[8] In practice, these restrictions are of no real significance.

---

23 non-financial corporations included in the DAX 30 Index, and Baums, Theodor and Christian Fraune 'Institutionelle Anleger und Publikumsgesellschaft: Eine empirische Untersuchung' *Die Aktiengesellschaft* 40 (1995) 97-112 for proxy voting by banks in the 24 largest firms which show a majority of widely held stock.

Cf. also the comparative reports of Kanda, Prigge, and Wymeersch in Ch. 12 of this volume who also investigate the role of banks in corporate governance.

[6] Roe, Mark J. *Strong Managers, Weak Owners* (Princeton 1994); Roe, Mark J. 'Some Differences in Corporate Structure in Germany, Japan, and the United States' 102 *Yale L.J.* 1927-2003 (1993); Roe, Mark J. 'Einige Unterschiede bei der Leitung von Unternehmen in Deutschland und Amerika' in: Ott, Claus and Hans-Bernd Schäfer (eds.) *Ökonomische Analyse des Unternehmensrechts* 333-68 (Heidelberg 1993); Roe, Mark J. 'German "Populism" and the Large Public Corporation' in: Buxbaum, Richard M., Gérard Hertig, Alain Hirsch, and Klaus J. Hopt (eds.) *European Economic and Business Law* 241-60 (Berlin and New York 1996).

[7] For a detailed description of these provisions, see Baums, Theodor and Michael Gruson 'The German Banking System: System of the Future?' 19 *Brook. J. Int'l L.* 101-29, 108 et seq. (1993), with further references.

[8] Council Directive 89/646 of December 15, 1989, on the Coordination of Laws, Regulations and Administrative Provisions Relating to the Taking Up and Pursuit of the Business of Credit Institutions and Amending Directive *OJEC* L 386/1, 1989; Council Directive 91/121 of

I. Data on Shareholdings

Larger blocks of shares of non-financial firms are held mainly by large private banks, i.e., the three big banks—Deutsche Bank, Dresdner Bank, Commerzbank—plus Bayerische Vereinsbank and Bayerische Hypotheken- und Wechselbank.[9] Other banks with blockholdings include DG Bank (which is the head of the agricultural credit cooperatives and cooperative banks sector) and the *Landesbanken* (the leading regional institutions in the savings bank sector), particularly Westdeutsche Landesbank and Bayerische Landesbank. In the past two decades, several empirical studies of the extent and development of bank shareholdings have been published. Unfortunately, they do not fully reflect the actual volume.[10] However, it is clear that holdings are concentrated in listed stock corporations, notably in those which are officially traded. Moreover, the figures available allow us to conclude that banks, altogether, own no more than some 5% of outstanding common stock of all non-financial stock corporations.

For officially traded corporations, the Securities Trading Act which came into effect on January 1, 1995, has clarified the ownership pattern to a much higher degree. Sections 21 et seq., 25, of the Act require all companies and private individuals to report all voting shares they hold directly or indirectly in officially traded companies, and where such holdings amount to at least 5%. On September 30, 1996, a total of 435 corporations were officially quoted on the stock exchange.[11] Stakes of at least 5% were reported for as many as 404 companies, and at least 24 of the remaining 31 companies[12] were not publicly held.[13] 377 of

December 21, 1992 on Monitoring and Controlling Large Exposures of Credit Institutions *OJEC* L 29/1, 1993.

[9] Baums and Gruson, supra n. 7, 103 et seq., and Edwards, Jeremy S.S. and Klaus Fischer *Banks, Finance and Investment in Germany* 97-107 (Cambridge et. al. 1994) describe the structure of the German banking industry in some detail.

[10] Mülbert, supra n. 2, E16 et seq. summarizes the findings of some of the most recent surveys. See also Prigge (this volume Ch. 12: Sec. B.II.). All studies carried out so far have suffered from a lack of publicly available information on shareholdings by individual banks. Some surveys tried to circumvent this problem by using highly aggregated data. For a number of reasons the results obtained were rather misleading (for details see Mülbert, supra n. 2, E16 et seq.). The Federal Association of German Banks (*Bundesverband deutscher Banken e.V.*) in particular published several surveys based on individual shareholdings by the ten largest private banks. However, comparing these figures with the compilation of direct and indirect bank holdings presented in this paper (see Appendix A) reveals that the figures reported by the Federal Association of German Banks were far too low.

[11] At the end of 1995, 437 companies were officially listed. 11 of these companies were listed only with preferred non-voting stock.

[12] These 31 companies include: Allerthal-Werke AG; Allweiler AG; Amira Verwaltungs AG; Berentzen-Gruppe AG; Bremer Vulkan Verbund AG; Commerzbank AG von 1870; Energieversorgung Ostbayern AG; Ford-Werke AG; Fröhlich Bau AG; GARANT SCHUH AG; Heinrich Lehmann AG; Hypothekenbank in Hamburg AG; Keramag Keramische Werke AG; Krauss-Maffei AG; Leica Camera AG; MACROTON Aktiengesellschaft für Datenerfassungs-

the 435 companies belonged to the non-financial sector. In 67 of the 377 non-financial corporations, German banks owned a total of 87 holdings of at least 5% of the voting stock directly or indirectly (Appendix A lists all holdings in detail), mostly within the range of 5% to 25% (Appendix B, Table 3 gives details on the size distribution). In 14 (3) of these 67 companies there were 2 (3) banks each of them holding at least 5% of the voting stock. The corresponding numbers for bank holdings of at least 10% read as follows: a total of 55 companies, including 11 (1) companies in which 2 (3) banks held at least 10% of the voting stock (see Appendix B, Tables 6, 7). Finally, the banking sector as a whole held less than a blocking minority in 46 companies, a blocking minority in 16 companies, a simple majority in 7 companies, and a qualified majority in 3 companies (see Appendix B, Table 4).[14]

II. Monitoring Instruments

As shareholders, universal banks have three channels through which they obtain information and exert influence: (i) bank shareholdings, (ii) banks' membership on supervisory boards, and (iii) banking operations.

ad (i) Little influence and even less information is obtained through shareholdings. Under the German Stock Corporation Act, the annual shareholder meeting is restricted to voting on a narrow catalog of vital measures (Section 119 (I), Stock Corporation Act). In the German two-tier board system, election of members to the supervisory board by a simple majority is especially important since it is the supervisory board that appoints, controls, and—if need be—dismisses members of the management board. The shareholder meeting also decides on the increase of capital, structural changes such as mergers, and other amendments to the by-laws, all of which require a qualified majority (75%). Shareholders are only entitled to ask for information at the annual shareholder

systeme; Maschinenfabrik Esterer AG; Merck KGaA; MLF Holding für Umwelttechnologien AG; Nino AG; Norddeutsches Steingut AG; Plettac AG; Porzellan Waldsassen AG; Quante AG; Rathgeber AG; Reichelbräu AG; JIL SANDER AG; TERREX Handels-AG; Traub AG; Westag & Getalit AG; Würzburger Hofbräu AG.

[13] GARANT SCHUH AG serves as a de facto cooperative for 2800 shoeshop owners. In case of 6 corporations—Bremer Vulkan Verbund AG; Commerzbank AG von 1870; Heinrich Lehmann AG; Nino AG; Norddeutsches Steingut AG; Porzellan Waldsassen AG—detailed information on ownership structures was not available. As to the degree of ownership concentration, see in more detail supra n. 5.

[14] German critics, however, argue that the magnitude of the banks' influence on non-financial corporations has to be assessed by adding shareholdings of insurance companies as well. But a comparison of the figures contained in Appendix B, Tables 4 and 5 respectively reveals that the summing up of all stakes held by the German financial sector (funds excluded) leaves the overall picture fairly unchanged.

meeting if the information is required to enable shareholders to reach an informed opinion concerning any subject on the meeting's agenda (Section 131 (I-III), Stock Corporation Act). Outside the shareholder meeting, the company is at liberty to supply information to those shareholders requesting such information. However, to ensure that shareholders are treated equally, the information given must be supplied again if requested by other shareholders at the shareholder meeting (Section 131 (IV), Stock Corporation Act).

ad (ii) Shareholders do not elect members of the supervisory board by a cumulative voting system. Nevertheless, if a bank has a holding of at least 10%, a member of the bank's management board is frequently elected to the supervisory board.[15] According to the letter of the law, though, such a bank has little potential for obtaining information and excercising control. The supervisory board member must only safeguard the interests of the company supervised. He must maintain secrecy vis-a-vis his employer with regard to information obtained in exercising this function (Section 93 (I 2), Stock Corporation Act). However, it is questionable whether these rules are strictly observed in practice. At any rate, proceedings for damages against supervisory board members belonging to a bank are unknown. On the other hand, the current debate about reforming supervisory boards shows that it is mostly the chairman of the supervisory board and not a simple board member who has superior information and opportunities to exercise influence. Whether a bank, by managing to have a simple member on the supervisory board, permanently enhances its opportunities in exercising influence and in obtaining in particular more information with regard to the lending transaction is therefore very doubtful.[16] And even the advantages connected with the position of supervisory board chairman no longer seem indispensable for banks.[17]

---

[15] Gorton, Gary and Frank A. Schmid 'Universal Banking and the Performance of German Firms' (NBER Working Paper no. 5453, 1996) found a statistically significant positive relationship between shareholdings and membership in supervisory boards (Schmid, Frank A. 'Banken, Aktionärsstruktur und Unternehmenssteuerung' (Part II) *Kredit und Kapital* 29 (1996) 545-64 presents the same study).

[16] Baums, Theodor 'The German Banking System and its Impact on Corporate Finance and Governance' in: Aoki, Masahiko and Hugh Patrick (eds.) *The Japanese Main Bank System* 409-49, 417, 421 et seq., 433 et seq. (Oxford 1994); Hopt, supra n. 2, 253; Edwards and Fischer, supra n. 9, 151 (summary); Mülbert, supra n. 2, E48 et seq. See also the most revealing statements of *Hilmar Kopper* as former Chairman of the Management Board of Deutsche Bank. When asked in an interview how he could serve as full-time director of Deutsche Bank and at the same time control ten of the largest German companies by sitting on their supervisory boards, he replied: "I don't control these firms. There can be no control. It can't be done." (*Der Spiegel* 31/1996, 60, 63).

[17] In the last couple of months, *Rolf-E. Breuer* as present Chairman of the Management Board of Deutsche Bank repeatedly announced that representatives of Deutsche Bank will relinquish their positions as supervisory board chairman. See, e.g., *Süddeutsche Zeitung* 14/15.6. 1997, no. 134, 29. In the past, though, bank representatives have held the position of chairman of the supervisory board in disproportionately high numbers. See figures in Mülbert, supra n. 2, E21. Hansen, Herbert 'Die Zusammensetzung der Aufsichtsräte bei den DAX-Gesellschaften'

ad (iii) The "natural" source for any bank's special position as information insider and influential monitor of a corporation is the relationship established by banking operations, notably extending loans and providing payment and settlement services. Recently, two developments have lowered the importance of the banking relationship for corporate governance: decreasing informational insider advantages and decreasing traditional loan contracting.

Until just a few years ago the special edge of universal banks in terms of information could be explained by modelling banks as a black box: all information from the entire banking relationship was available (virtually) free of charge at all times to every bank department for monitoring purposes. However, the legal environment changed radically when the Securities Trading Act went into effect on January 1, 1995. Implementing an EC directive, it proscribes various forms of insider trading (Sections 12-14, 38, Securities Trading Act), e.g., the passing on of insider facts (Section 14 (I) No. 2, Securities Trading Act). In addition, Section 33 (Nos. 2, 3) of the Act requires, among others, universal banks to create internal organizational structures that minimize the potential for conflicts of interests between the bank and its customers and to establish adequate internal control systems that prevent bank employees from violating the prohibition on insider trading. Admittedly, it is not yet clear whether the aforementioned proscription of the passing on of inside information as stipulated in Section 14 (1) No. 2 of the Act in fact forbids all internal passing on of insider facts not absolutely essential for the carrying on of banking operations in the ordinary course of business.[18] To meet the requirements of Section 33 (Nos. 2, 3) of the Act, banks have created new internal compliance organization structures. Securities departments are protected from insider facts by Chinese walls, and compliance-relevant information must be passed on to central clearing offices that decide on other possibilities of using this information internally. Such compliance management procedures are a considerable obstacle to the bank-internal flow of information.[19] This automatically reduces the informational advantages of universal banks with regard to corporate control, even if the entire impact of these changes cannot be foreseen today.

Die Aktiengesellschaft 42 (1997) R123-R124, provides most recent data for the corporations included in the DAX 30 Index; André, Thomas J. 'Some Reflections on German Corporate Governance: A Glimpse at German Supervisory Boards' 70 *Tulane L. Rev.* 1819-79 (1996) provides most comprehensive but slightly older data for the same set of corporations. On the board, see also Prigge (this volume Ch. 12: Sec. B.I.).

[18] As to this problem, see Assmann, Heinz-Dieter 'Insiderrecht und Kreditwirtschaft' *Wertpapiermitteilungen* 50 (1996), 1337-56, 1349 et seq., with further references.

[19] As to the practical relevance of this effect, see, for example, Bülow, Stephan 'Chinese Walls: Vertraulichkeit und Effizienz' *Die Bank* (1997) 290-3 (working as a compliance officer).

Today lending operations have practically no significance as a disciplinary instrument, the exception being corporations in financial distress.[20] The following figures for big corporations with sales of more than DM 100 million and at least 250 employees speak for themselves: for all companies, including those not structured as stock corporations, the ratio of long-term bank loans to total assets in 1989 was 3.9%, and the percentage of all bank loans was 7.6%.[21] The position is even clearer when one considers only the big stock corporations: from 1981 to 1991, the ratio of long-term bank loans declined from 3% to 1%; if short-term bank loans were included, total bank loans accounted for 5.5% of total assets.[22] In line with these figures, both the German Bundesbank and the OECD conclude that (long-term) bank financing no longer plays an important role, at least not for large companies.[23]

III. Additional Control-Related Features

A number of other factors determine to a large extent the actual potential for control inherent in a bank holding: (i) bearer shares, (ii) concentrated ownership structure, (iii) proxy voting rights, (iv) co-determination, and (v) agency problems on the level of the bank.

[20] For example Roe 'Unterschiede', supra n. 6, 354; Coffee, John C. 'Liquidity versus Control: The Institutional Investor as Corporate Monitor' 91 *Colum. L. Rev.* 1277-1368, 1304-5 (1991). Prowse, supra n. 5, 31 et seq., Neuberger, Doris and Manfred Neumann 'Banking and Antitrust: Limiting Industrial Ownership by Banks?' *Journal of Institutional and Theoretical Economics* 147 (1991) 188-99, 189 disagree. However, they base their arguments on highly aggregated data. This is misleading because small and very small firms show a dramatically higher percentage of loan financing by banks than large companies.

See also Ch. 10 of this volume with contributions dealing with lenders as a force in corporate governance.

[21] Deutsche Bundesbank 'Längerfristige Entwicklung der Finanzierungsstrukturen west-deutscher Unternehmen' *Monatsberichte der Deutschen Bundesbank* 44/10 (1992) 25-39; the OECD, supra n. 5, 106 gives somewhat higher figures.

[22] Figures are taken from Huth, Andreas H.-J. *Industriefinanzierung in Deutschland und Frankreich* 59 et seq. (Wiesbaden 1996). On the development between 1970 and 1985, see Fischer, Klaus 'Hausbankbeziehungen als Instrument der Bindung zwischen Banken und Unternehmen' 60 (Dissertation, University of Bonn 1990): The percentage of long-term bank loans declined from 4.9% to 2.2%, the combined percentage of short- and long-term bank loan financing decreased from 14.8% to 6.4%.

[23] Deutsche Bundesbank, supra n. 21, 25 et seq.; OECD, supra n. 5, 107.

These figures also refute the widely held belief that German banks extend more long-term than short-term credits—according to a widely cited rule of thumb the ratio is 2 to 1 (e.g., Mayer, Colin P. 'The City and Corporate Performance: Condemned or Exonerated?' *Cambridge Journal of Economics* 21 (1997) 291-302, 293)—towards its corporate customers in general.

Cf. also the analysis of lending of German companies in Prigge (this volume Ch. 12: Sec. C.II.).

ad (i) In Germany, bearer shares are the most common type. Registered shares are issued almost exclusively by insurance companies. As a result, attendance at shareholder meetings, especially at those of widely-held companies, is rather low these days. In some cases, less than 50% of the voting stock is represented. Drawing inferences based on these figures one has to bear in mind, that attendance at shareholder meetings has declined in recent years mostly because ownership structures have become more international, i.e., mainly because British and American institutional investors have bought stock in German companies.[24]

ad (ii) The degree of influence a bank may wield by holding 10% - 15% of the voting stock critically depends on the ownership structure of a corporation. Generally speaking, German corporations show a high degree of ownership concentration, much higher than their counterparts in the U.K., U.S., or even Japan. However, of special interest in the present context is the existence of non-financial large shareholders in partly bank-owned corporations. In both respects a rather clear picture of officially listed companies has emerged, thanks to the new reporting requirements mandated by the Securities Trading Act.[25] With regard to non-financial blockowners whose holdings are larger than the highest stake of a bank, the numbers are as follows:[26] of the 67 corporations referred to above as being partly ($\geq$5%) bank-owned, one blockholder was registered in 31 companies, two in 7 companies, and as many as three in 4 companies. Considering only those corporations in which at least one bank owns an interest of at least 10%, the figures read as follows: 27/3/1. In 6 out of these 31 companies the largest non-bank blockholder held a blocking minority (25% + 1 share), and in another 11 companies even a simple or a qualified majority. In all, these figures allow us to conclude that the concentrated shareholder structure of German companies does indeed dilute German banks' equity-based potential for control.

ad (iii) Bank proxies are of great significance for widely held stock corporations. A shareholder who deposits its shares with a bank frequently authorizes this bank to vote the shares by a revocable proxy ("depository voting right") that may last up to 15 months (Section 135 (1), Stock Corporation Act). In practice, proxies are concentrated with the big banks and in particular the three largest private banks. It is widely accepted that in order to properly assess a bank's

---

[24] See the data in Bundesverband deutscher Banken 'Macht der Banken' 16 (Cologne 1995); cf. also Prigge (this volume Ch. 12: Sec. B.II.4.). Schneider, Uwe H. and Ulrich Burgard 'Maßnahmen zur Verbesserung der Präsenz auf der Hauptversammlung einer Aktiengesellschaft' in: Beisse, Heinrich, Marcus Lutter, and Heribald Närger (eds.) *Festschrift für Karl Beusch* 783-803, 787 et seq. (Berlin and New York 1993) discuss the reasons for decreasing attendance of shareholder meetings in some detail.

[25] See supra n. 5.

[26] For more details, see Appendix B, Tables 5/6. A general analysis of German ownership structure is provided by Prigge (this volume Ch. 12: Sec. B.II.).

potential for monitoring and controlling a corporation, one has to add up the voting rights from the bank's own shareholdings as well as the voting rights that may be exercised by proxies. According to such calculation, banks owning stakes of 10% - 20%, i.e., mostly the three biggest private banks, sometimes even reach a blocking minority.

However, this simple addition neglects two important factors. (i) Under Sections 128, 135, Stock Corporation Act, banks are not entirely free in how to exercise their clients' proxies but face statutory restrictions: if a bank intends voting by proxy at a shareholder meeting, it has to inform the depositors of management's own suggestions concerning how to vote the items on the meeting's agenda. In addition, the bank has to draw up its own voting proposals based solely on the interest of the shareholders and then to submit these proposals to its depositors as well. Finally, even if the bank receives no instructions from its depositors, it is still not free to exercise the proxy at will but has to vote in accordance with its own voting proposals. Because of this mechanism, already the formulation of the voting proposal decides how the bank will vote by proxy in the future. (ii) For several reasons, banks almost always recommend that their clients vote in accordance with the management's suggestions.[27] But if the bank owns a larger stake in the company, the management will consult the bank as a shareholder prior to the shareholder meeting in order to hear its views on the various points on the agenda, e.g., on a raise of nominal capital and on the election of members to the supervisory board. Therefore, managements' own suggestions concerning how to vote the items on the meeting's agenda will often already reflect the interests of shareholding banks (and other blockowners). Taken together, these two factors explain to a large extent, why banks, almost without exception, vote their own shares and the shares held as custodians in parallel. Furthermore, the specific significance of German-style proxies becomes much clearer: proxies to a lesser extent serve as an independent source of a bank's influence rather than making it more difficult (and expensive) for third parties to acquire a controlling position in the corporation.

ad (iv) Co-determination on the level of the supervisory board also plays a role in enhancing a bank's influence. To a high degree, management's interests coincide with those of a bank as business partner of the company.[28] Checking, for example, the preference of management (and workers) for an overly risk-adverse business strategy by supervisory board monitoring becomes far more

---

[27] For details, see Mülbert, supra n. 2, E43 et seq.

[28] This alignment of interests is explained, inter alia, by management's limited ability to diversify its firm-specific risk and at least according to the assertions of managerialists by its interest in pursuing alternative corporate goals such as sales growth, etc. See in more detail, for example, Böhm, Jürgen *Der Einfluß der Banken auf Großunternehmen* 147-56 (Hamburg 1992).

For further treatments of co-determination in this volume, refer to the articles in Ch. 5 and the respective sections in the comparative articles by Kanda, Prigge, and Wymeersch in Ch. 12.

difficult when workers' interests are explicitly introduced by setting up a co-determined supervisory board. Moreover, bank representatives on supervisory boards are offered the opportunity to form implicit coalitions with worker representatives at the expense of outside shareholders.[29] This effect is of special importance for large corporations with at least 2,000 employees falling under the Co-Determination Act of 1976, as their supervisory boards must comprise equal numbers of shareholder and worker representatives. Smaller corporations are subject to the Works Council Act of 1952, according to which only one-third of supervisory board members must be elected by workers. Corporations with less than 500 employees that are family owned or that are incorporated since August 10, 1994, are even totally exempt from co-determination.

ad (v) The big German private banks are corporations with fairly dispersed ownership patterns, the exceptions being Dresdner Bank and Bayerische Hypotheken- und Wechsel-Bank. But as the two Munich-based "twin" insurance companies—Allianz AG and Münchener Rückversicherungs-Gesellschaft AG—[30] together own a stake of around 25% in Dresdner Bank as well as in Bayerische Hypotheken- und Wechsel-Bank, even these two banks can be classified as management-controlled. The actual consequences of this observation, however, are unclear. According to the assertions of managerialists, management will use its freedom to pursue its own goals that are different from those of shareholders. But since 1996, Deutsche Bank has published its consolidated financial statements according to the International Accounting Standards (IAS) in order to give shareholders full insight into the development of the value of their shares,[31] thus voluntarily strengthening the monitoring function of the stock market. Whether this behavior indicates that the problems associated with the separation of ownership and control are less severe for (some) German banks than implied by managerialists is still an open question.

---

[29] From this perspective it is no longer obvious that banks' blockholdings—and depository voting rights—are a necessary counterweight to non-shareholder interests advanced in Germany's Stock Corporation Act. For an assertion to the contrary see Romano, Roberta 'A Cautionary Note on Drawing Lessons from Comparative Corporate Law' 102 *Yale L.J.* 2021-37, 2030-1 (1993).

[30] Allianz AG and Münchener Rückversicherungs-Gesellschaft AG are linked by cross-shareholdings of 25% each. As a result, both companies show outstanding management entrenchment.

[31] See *Frankfurter Allgemeine Zeitung* 21.12.1995, no. 296, 16. The other large banks adopted this reorientation of accounting policy only to varying degrees (see *Frankfurter Allgemeine Zeitung* 2.3.1996, no. 79, 20). These differing reactions may partly reflect differences in the banks' competitiveness.

C. Incentives for Corporate Monitoring

I. Universal Banks

"Pure" investors, e.g., funds, can increase the value of their shares only by carrying out costly monitoring activities. The higher a shareholder's stake, the more likely he is to engage in these activities. Therefore, large blockholdings of "pure" investors can create sufficient incentives for spending funds. In the case of universal banks the incentives are less obvious. The position of lender provides a strong incentive to produce extensive information about the borrower and to monitor and control his activities in order to minimize the credit risk. One may therefore question, whether banks have any incentive at all to invest additional resources, e.g., the working time of their managing directors, in exercising monitoring and controlling activities as shareholders.

One might argue that the continual monitoring activities going on within the scope of the banking relationship pursue other goals than monitoring from the owner's point of view. A bank must therefore endeavor to control and monitor the company not only as lender but also as shareholder. To give but two examples: for a lender, agency costs resulting from management's shirking and self-dealing are only of significance if these costs threaten the existence of the company. This is particularly true if a bank has sufficient collateral. However, from the shareholders' point of view, these agency costs are not trivial. The same applies when managers shirk by pursuing projects with a negative net present value instead of maximizing the company's market value. The second argument presupposes that the bank wants management to act in the interests of a "pure" investor. However, as explained in greater detail in Section E, this is by no means obvious. There is therefore no simple answer to the question of whether banks in their capacity as owners have any incentives at all to act as corporate monitors.

Essentially there are three arguments in favor of an affirmative answer. First of all, lenders can exercise control and impose penalties only in some states of the world. The ratio of bank loans to total external financing, competition from other lenders, and the availability of other forms of financing all determine whether the lending bank can effectively threaten to terminate the loans extended and thereby discipline the borrower. Moreover, many forms of shirking and self-dealing cannot sufficiently be reduced by the monitoring and disciplining mechanisms inherent in the banking relationship. Lending permits effective "negative" control by restricting management's scope for action, but "positive" entrepreneurial control aimed at making the company more competitive and profitable in the future cannot be achieved solely by appropriately designed lending transactions.

Finally, a blockholder whose company does not perform as expected may have to rely on "voice", because the alternative, i.e., "exit", is prohibitively costly. Anyone trying to sell a large block of shares in the market because of a company's poor performance runs the risk of triggering a plunge in share prices. Alternatively, if the shares are sold over the counter—provided that a potent buyer can be found at all—he runs the risk of having to accept a hefty block markdown. For universal banks holding blocks, the trade-off between liquidity and control tends to be even more biased at the expense of liquidity. For several reasons, they must fear that the sale of a block could bring a drastic reduction, if not the end of the business relationship with the company: the buyer may have close business ties with other banks or break up the company in the course of a bust-up takeover. It is even conceivable that company management is opposed to the sale[32] and will try to "punish" the bank by terminating the existing banking relationship. The likelihood of this reaction would be especially high if the bank sold its block to a bidder attempting a hostile takeover. The banks' fears in this respect might partly explain why the big German banks have opposed hostile takeovers until very recently, and why this mechanism so far has failed to gain ground in Germany as a means of acquiring control.[33]

II. Additional Incentives of German Banks

The trade-off between liquidity and control still has a stronger bias at the expense of liquidity when it comes to shareholdings of German banks. They mainly own stock listed on the first and second tier of the German stock market;[34] on the other hand, some of the stakes reach 20% or even more of all outstanding voting stock. Furthermore, even many of the officially listed companies lack liquidity

---

[32] The recently failed attempt of BHF-Bank in selling a 49.9% stake in AGIV to Metallgesellschaft is an example of even stronger management resistance. The management of AGIV, fearing a sort of bust-up sale of control, restricted Metallgesellschaft's access to company data within the due diligence process. As a result, Metallgesellschaft withdrew from the sale and the Chairman of the Management Board of BHF-Bank withdrew from his position. See *Süddeutsche Zeitung* 14.1.1997, no. 10, 19; 15./16.2.1997, no. 38, 25; 27./28.3.1997, no. 72, 23; *Frankfurter Allgemeine Zeitung* 14.2.1997, no. 38, 21; 15.2.1997, no. 39, 15.

[33] Mülbert, supra n. 2, E63 et seq. describes in more detail the interests of banks with regard to hostile takeovers. A comment by *Martin Kohlhaussen* (Chairman of the Management Board) dealing with Commerzbank's position in Krupp-Hoesch's failed attempt to take over Thyssen provides confirming evidence: "Commerzbank (which owns a stake in Thyssen) will certainly profit from the fact that it supported Thyssen by being lead manager if Thyssen decides to raise its nominal capital." See *Frankfurter Allgemeine Zeitung* 9.4.1997, no. 82, 19.

[34] See the data in Bundesverband deutscher Banken, supra n. 24, 24: In 1994 the nominal capital of all shareholdings in non-financial firms held by the ten biggest private banks reached DM 2,004 million. 79.2% (= DM 1,537 million) accounted for stakes held in corporations that are listed on the first and second tier of the German stock markets.

and market depth. The following figures are telling: only 166 companies consecutively quoted on the Frankfurt stock exchange have a fixed ownership ratio of less than 85%. The 10 most heavily traded companies account for 63.4% of total turnover of all German stocks traded on the Frankfurt Stock Exchange in 1996, and the 25 most heavily traded companies account for as much as 94.1%.[35] Even banks would have difficulties selling a large block rapidly without upsetting the market unless an over-the-counter buyer was found. In addition, for tax and other reasons, banks often hold their equity positions via subsidiaries in which insurance companies and/or industrial corporations own a stake as well.[36] These frequent pool solutions also tend to reduce liquidity. The most important impediment probably results from the interaction between balance sheet and tax regulations. Shareholdings must normally be shown at historical cost in the balance sheet. Special regulations designed for banks allow them more freedom in drawing up their balance sheets.[37] For example, shares allocated to the so-called liquidity reserve (*Liquiditätsreserve*) can be shown at less than historical cost if certain rather lenient criteria are fulfilled (Section 340f, German Commercial Code).[38] These regulations permit banks to set up large hidden reserves, particularly with older equity holdings. When such holdings are sold, these hidden reserves are dissolved and tax must be paid on the realized capital gains. Statements made by banks in the current discussion of curbing the "power of banks" strongly testify to the liquidity-reducing effect of these regulations. Banks will only agree to the introduction of statutory ceilings on shareholdings in non-financial corporations if they can reduce their holdings in a tax-neutral manner.[39]

---

[35] Source: Hansen, Herbert 'Die Kopflastigkeit des deutschen Kurszettels' *Die Aktiengesellschaft* 42 (1997) R78-R82. The 25 stocks with the highest volume of turnover are contained in the DAX 30 Index, with one exception.

[36] The annotations in Appendix A give a first impression of the extent of this practice.

[37] See, for example, Hölscher, Reinhold 'Stille Reserven in den Jahresabschlüssen deutscher und schweizerischer Banken' *Die Betriebswirtschaft* 55 (1995) 45-60, 49 et seq.; Bieg, Hartmut 'Erfordert die Vertrauensempfindlichkeit des Kreditgewerbes bankenspezifische Bilanzierungsvorschriften?' (Part II) *Die Wirtschaftsprüfung* 39 (1986) 299-307; Wenger, Ekkehard 'Kapitalmarktrecht als Resultat deformierter Anreizstrukturen' in: Sadowski, Dieter, Hans Czap, and Hartmut Wächter (eds.) *Regulierung und Unternehmenspolitik* 419-58, 436-42 (Wiesbaden 1996) deal very critically with the argument that banks need more flexibility in accounting because of the special nature of the deposit-taking business.

[38] In the judgment of a reasonable banker, the lower valuation must be a necessary precaution against special risks pertaining to banking.

[39] For the Deutsche Bank, see *Rolf-E. Breuer Frankfurter Allgemeine Zeitung* 10.5.1996, no. 109, 27; *Hilmar Kopper Süddeutsche Zeitung* 27./28.3.1997, no. 72, 23.

D. Motives for Permanent Equity Holdings

Permanent large holdings in the hands of universal banks pose a sort of puzzle. As discussed, these holdings tend to be of a rather illiquid type of capital investment. Furthermore, theoretical work suggests that bank loans are the most efficient method of supplying capital in the presence of informational or monitoring problems.[40] Why, then, do banks not confine themselves to their role as lender instead of acquiring permanent holdings in some of their borrowers? Financial theorists and practitioners from the banking industry have come up with two very different sets of answers to this question. In what follows, theory will be discussed first.

I. Split Financing as a Superior Financing Technique

1. Creating an Advantageous Control Structure

To overcome conflicts of interests, a combination of loan financing and long-term shareholding (split financing) seems to be a more useful instrument than pure loan financing. There are two arguments supporting this idea: (i) controlling moral hazard in the bank-lender relationship, and (ii) mitigating conflicts of interests between the company's shareholders and lenders.[41]

ad (i) The critical point in the relationship between *lender* and *borrower* is moral hazard: controlling opportunistic behavior on the part of the borrower. Given certain conditions, it is advantageous for the borrower to switch to riskier projects after the loan agreement has been agreed upon. High cash flows are claimed by the borrower alone while the risk of low cash flows or even losses is shifted mainly to lenders. Split financing reduces this problem in two ways. First, the control rights of banks as shareholders make it easier to counteract this type of opportunistic behavior on the part of the company. Second, the bank's shareholding reduces the portion of profit available for management and outside shareholders and thus the incentive for opportunism at the lender's expense.

---

[40] The seminal work is Diamond, Douglas 'Financial Intermediation and Delegated Monitoring' *Review of Economic Studies* 51 (1984) 393-414. Bhattacharya, Sudipto and Anjan Thakor 'Contemporary Banking Theory' *Journal of Financial Intermediation* 3 (1993) 2-50 and Scholtens, Lambertus J.R. 'On the Foundation of Financial Intermediation: A Review of the Literature' *Kredit und Kapital* 26 (1993) 112-41 provide a review. Mayer, Colin P. 'The Assessment: Money and Banking: Theory and Evidence' *Oxford Review of Economic Policy* 10 (1994) 1-13, 7 et seq. provides a critique and stresses the need for alternative explanations. See also Thakor, Anjan 'The Design of Financial Systems: An Overview' *Journal of Banking & Finance* 20 (1996) 917-48.

[41] The following discussion is partly based on Baums, supra n. 16, 413 et seq.

However, the assumed positive effects presuppose that the bank has a substantial holding in the company. Even if one cannot specify a minimum, a stake of at least 20% - 25% seems to be necessary. A smaller portion in the hands of the lender will not substantially reduce the incentive for the borrower to engage in more profitable but also highly risky projects, nor does a small block of shares enable its owner to influence the behavior of the governing bodies of the company.[42] In addition, this idea fails to explain why banks do not protect themselves against opportunism by requiring collateral, but instead acquire shareholder claims which have lower priority to the firm's cash flow compared to debtholder claims, and which even increase the total risk exposure of the bank towards a single customer.

ad (ii) The relationship between *shareholders* and *lenders* is characterized by a conflict of interests pertaining to the riskiness of the company's business strategy. Fixed claimants (such as banks) prefer less risky business operations than residual owners, i.e., shareholders, even if the less risky operations show a lower expected return than the more risky projects preferred by shareholders.[43] When the company is faced with a financial crisis, the conflict becomes even more acute. While shareholders will advocate still riskier operations, external lenders support exactly the opposite policy of further minimizing the riskiness of cash flow. Despite assertions to the contrary,[44] split financing cannot mitigate this conflict of interests. However, because the bank in its dual role as shareholder and debtholder internalizes this conflict of interests, it will prevent the firm from taking actions which might destroy the existing equilibrium between shareholders and fixed claimants by arbitrarily benefitting one type of claimant at the expense of another. Split financing by a bank, therefore, protects each of the two groups of financial claimants against opportunistic behavior on the part of the other group. This reduced risk of exploitation, especially in financial distress situations, reduces the firm's cost of capital on equity and debt.

Again, this explanation is only plausible under very limited conditions. First, it presupposes relatively high equity holdings. Otherwise the bank would not be in a position to induce the management—if necessary by replacing the current managers—to change its corporate strategy. Second, this neutral stance on the part of the bank is only plausible if marginal changes in corporate strategy do not increase the bank's total cash flow—if, in other words, its cash flow from the

---

[42] Baums, supra n. 16, 414 et seq.

[43] As to this conflict of interest, see more generally, for example, Macey, Jonathan R. and Geoffrey P. Miller 'Corporate Governance and Commercial Banking: A Comparative Examination of Germany, Japan, and the United States' 48 *Stan. L. Rev.* 73-112, 77 et seq. (1995), with further references.

[44] See, for example, Neuberger, Doris 'Anteilsbesitz von Banken: Wohlfahrtsverlust oder Wohlfahrtsgewinn?' *ifo Studien—Zeitschrift für empirische Wirtschaftsforschung* 43 (1997) 15-34, 17.

banking relationship on the one hand and the shareholding on the other hand balance each other out. Even in an initial commitment, it should be quite difficult determining the appropriate size of the share stake. Moreover, as the original equilibrium would not remain stable over time, the bank's interest in the company would have to be continuously readjusted. Above all, this idea only explains the overall gains from split financing, whereas the bank's incentives to use split financing are not addressed.

2. Creating an Advantageous Industrial Organization Pattern

Both explanations of bank shareholdings discussed so far concentrate on advantages regarding corporate control. If this interlocking is seen as a kind of vertical integration in the market for banking services, additional effects come into view. These effects pertain to informational asymmetries between (i) the bank and the borrowing firm, (ii) the firm and its outside shareholders/debtholders, and (iii) the firm and third business partners.[45]

ad (i) Firstly, shareholdings by banks serve to align the conflicting interests of the bank and the borrowing firm by lessening the bank's incentives to behave opportunistically with regard to the banking relationship. This effect, in turn, helps to mitigate problems of informational asymmetries between the two parties. Take the example of confidentiality: as a blockowner, a bank is less likely to misuse confidential information to the detriment of its customer, e.g., by prematurely terminating the banking relationship, by charging excessive fees when the firm is in financial distress, or by promoting the interests of one of the company's competitors, be it a bank's client or a partially bank-owned company. The bank's holding in the firm acts as a bonding device that helps to overcome the informational asymmetry between the two parties by allowing the firm to submit better information to the bank. This superior flow of information, in turn, makes it possible for the bank to reduce the price of and/or to expand banking services, especially lending. Secondly, temporary liquidity constraints impede the company's investment activities to a lesser extent since the bank's better knowledge of its client increases the chances of it extending additional loans to the company. Finally, bankruptcy costs are likely to be lower. Possessing superior information allows a bank to detect crises early on and thereby enables it to reorganize the company before bankruptcy proceedings are initiated. Moreover, linking debt to equity leads to a concentration of shareholders and debtholders and thereby reduces the cost of financial distress by simplifying renegotiations.

---

[45] For the following discussion, refer also to Baums, supra n. 16, 414; Neuberger and Neumann, supra n. 20, 193.

ad (ii) A bank's equity position can also mitigate the problem of informational asymmetry between the firm and its outside shareholders and/or outside debtholders. A bank's equity interest credibly signals lower agency costs and a lower risk of insolvency. Third parties will therefore demand lower risk premiums, thus reducing the cost of capital on equity and debt.

ad (iii) Finally, the signalling effect associated with a bank's equity position reinforces a company's competitive position in output and input markets and thus enhances its profitablity.

For the bank,[46] these positive effects of vertical integration boil down to two motives for permanent shareholdings: (i) improving its competitive position insofar as a shareholding bank can offer its services, notably loans, at more favorable conditions or in greater volumes, and (ii) seeking additional compensation for information costs and control costs incurred as lender. As outside shareholders profit at least in part from these expenses, the stock market interprets the granting of a loan as a positive signal and responds with a positive share price reaction.[47] Via shareholding, the bank not only eliminates free-riding of outside shareholders to some extent, but also receives compensation for its monitoring costs by capturing part of the additional stock return generated by its monitoring activities as a lender.[48]

3. The Structure of Equity Portfolios of German Banks

Despite all theoretical advantages of split financing, there is no empirical evidence that they affect the behavior of German banks apart from financial distress situations.[49] First, in recent years banks have reduced the number of their holdings of more than 25%. Today most holdings in publicly traded companies are below 15% and thus too small for the specific advantages of split financing to

---

[46] Neuberger and Neumann, supra n. 20, 193 try to explain bank shareholdings as a result of inter-bank competition for customers in the lending business. However, their explanation relies crucially on a special feature of the German system of corporate control, the depository voting right. Therefore, holdings by, for example, French banks cannot be explained by inter-bank competition.

[47] James, Christopher 'Some Evidence on the Uniqueness of Bank Loans' *Journal of Financial Economics* 19 (1987) 217-35. Lummer, Scott and John McConnell 'Further Evidence on the Bank Lending Process and the Capital Market Response to Bank Loan Agreements' Journal of Financial Economics 25 (1989) 99-122 and Slovin, Myron B., Marie E. Sushka, and John A. Polonchek 'The Value of Bank Durability: Borrowers as Stakeholders' *Journal of Finance* 48 (1993) 247-66 provide further evidence of the special role of bank loans in the stock market.

[48] Frankel, Allen B. and John D. Montgomery 'Financial Structure: An International Perspective' *Brooking Papers on Economic Activity* vol. 1 (1991) 257-97, 286 argue along these lines.

[49] In the same sense, see Baums, supra n. 16, 420 et seq.

carry any weight. Second, even with the big private banks, the number of holdings varies widely, while lending operations do not reflect any comparable differences. Third, most banks only own an interest in a small percentage of all borrowers. The rate of shareholdings by banks is highest in the companies included in the DAX 30 Index, although the ratio of bank loans to total assets is at its lowest for large corporations.

Explanations of split financing to the effect that an ownership stake lessens the problems of informational asymmetries and gives the bank informational advantages are subject to even further objections: if the bank had greater access to inside information on the basis of its shareholding, it should be in a position to identify crises in the company early on and, as an influential shareholder, induce the management to introduce reorganization measures. As a result, compared to companies with non-bank blockholders, these companies should have a lower rate of bankruptcy. While empirical studies are lacking,[50] anecdotal evidence belies such an effect. The big private banks began setting up specialized departments dealing with reorganizations only a few years ago.

In addition: if a shareholding considerably reduced problems of informational asymmetries, this should be reflecting in financing. In particular, companies in which a bank owns an interest should suffer significantly less from financing constraints than companies in which there are no bank holdings. A number of studies have tried discriminating between more and less constrained firms by using the sensitivity of firm investment to fluctuations in cash flow as proxy. Adopting this methodology,[51] the studies by Hoshi, Kashyap and Scharfstein[52] of Japanese companies of the *keiretsu* type produced strong evidence on the sensitivity-reducing effects of banks' shareholdings, whereas the study by Elston and

---

[50] A potential problem of such studies is noted: perhaps banks are afraid that their reputation would suffer if a partially bank-owned company goes bankrupt. Then a comparatively higher percentage of successful reorganizations outside bankruptcy proceedings might simply reflect the fact that banks are more willing to support an informal workout if they own a stake in the company. However, on account of the way the reorganization of Metallgesellschaft was handled, even bankers doubt such a willingness on the part of banks. See *Franz Neubauer Frankfurter Allgemeine Zeitung* 28.1.1994, no. 23, 18 (Chairman of the Management Board of Bayerische Landesbank).

[51] Note, however, the objections by Kaplan, Steven N. and Luigi Zingales 'Do Investment-Cash Flow Sensitivities Provide Useful Measures of Financing Constraints?' *Quarterly Journal of Economics* 112 (1997) 169-215 based on theoretical arguments and econometric problems.

[52] Hoshi, Takeo, Anil Kashyap, and David Scharfstein 'Bank Monitoring and Investment: Evidence from the Changing Structure of Japanese Corporate Banking Relationships' in: Hubbard, Glenn (ed.) *Asymmetric Information, Corporate Finance and Investment* 105-26 (Chicago 1990); Hoshi, Takeo, Anil Kashyap, and David Scharfstein 'Corporate Structure, Liquidity, and Investment: Evidence from Industrial Groups' *Quarterly Journal of Economics* 106 (1991) 33-60.

Albach[53] found only a weak confirmation of this effect. Their sample of 29 "bank-controlled" firms consisted of at least 20 companies in which a bank held an interest of more than 20%. As expected for this group, the investment volume in the three periods studied (1967-72, 1973-82, and 1983-92) stood up well against liquidity constraints. But the investment behavior of the companies in which no banks had blockholdings only just suffered from liquidity constraints in the period from 1983-1992. This is all the more surprising since bank loan financing lost in importance across the board in this period.

II. Equity Holdings as Capital Investment

1. Practical Explanations

Practitioners in the banking business list numerous reasons as to why German banks acquire shareholdings. These include:

- supporting companies with a thin equity layer, growth financing and settlement of succession problems, acting as underwriters, capital investment, acquisition as a result of reorganization, collateralizing loans, privatization in the new German states;[54]
- protection against (hostile) takeovers and promotion of the banking relationship with the company;[55]
- entering into a banking relationship as a result of an acquisition.[56]

Most of these motives cannot explain why banks carry long-term shareholdings. For the purpose of reorganizing companies or taking them public, a temporary ownership position suffices. As far as the establishment of a banking relationship is concerned, representatives of banks attested in the 1970s that the acquisition of a 5% stake is enough to win a company as a customer for banking services.[57] However, not even a permanent holding of this small size is necessary in order to maintain the business relationship once it is established. Accordingly, West-

---

[53] Elston, Julie Ann and Horst Albach 'Bank Affiliation and Firm Capital Investment' *ifo Studien—Zeitschrift für empirische Wirtschaftsforschung* 41 (1995) 3-16. Note, though, their rather thin data basis.

[54] Bundesverband deutscher Banken, supra n. 24, 20; Bundesverband deutscher Banken 'Banken zum Sechsten Hauptgutachten der Monopolkommission' *Die Bank* (1986) 584-9, 586.

[55] Schneider-Lenné, Ellen R. 'Corporate Control in Germany' *Oxford Review of Economic Policy* 8 (1993) 11-23, 19.

[56] *Friedel Neuber Süddeutsche Zeitung* 27.12.1990, no. 296, 30 (Chairman of the Management Board of Westdeutsche Landesbank).

[57] Monopolkommission *Mehr Wettbewerb ist möglich* Tz. 563 (Hauptgutachten 1973/1975, Baden-Baden 1976).

deutsche Landesbank acquired some 25-30 equity positions over a three-year period (1988-1990) and then sold them after only one to two years.[58]

Eliminating all acquisitions motives that require no permanent equity holdings leaves basically a single motive: shareholdings as a capital investment. Numerous statements of German banks that strongly emphasize the character of their shareholdings as a means of achieving better internal risk diversification in the operation of the banking business are quite in line with this reasoning.[59] Still more to the point, banks offer essentially two reasons for holding long-term equity positions. Firstly, they point out that the fluctuations in cash flows from banking operations as such can, at least in part, be evened out by dividend payments of the portfolio companies.[60] Secondly, shareholdings make it possible to form hidden reserves as a buffer in times of financial crisis.[61]

From a theoretical point of view, this explanation given by practitioners from the banking industry begs two questions: (i) Why do banks at all strive for internal risk diversification instead of concentrating on the banking business, leaving risk diversification to their stockholders? And (ii), what is the optimal structure of a universal bank's portfolio of shareholdings in non-financial firms? Both these questions will be taken up seriatim.

2. Maximizing the Banks' Market Value Via Equity Holdings

Assume a universal bank structured as a stock corporation and pursuing the goal of maximizing its net present value. Diversification by way of acquiring large-scale shareholdings in non-financial corporations creates a conglomerate comprising a number of totally unrelated lines of business and whose market value depends on the total market value of its shareholdings plus the bank's own market value as part of the conglomerate.[62] In recent years, though, numerous studies of mostly non-financial firms have found that the shares of conglomerates ceteris paribus tend to suffer from a "conglomerate discount", i.e., the shares tend

---

[58] *Friedel Neuber,* supra n. 56.

[59] See Schneider-Lenné, supra n. 55, 19; Mertin, Klaus 'Substanzwert Industrieschachteln' *Zeitschrift für das gesamte Kreditwesen* 35 (1982) 226-30, 228.

[60] See, for example, Schneider-Lenné, supra n. 55, 19; Bundesverband deutscher Banken, supra n. 54, 586; Bundesverband deutscher Banken 'Zur Diskussion um die Macht der Banken' *Die Bank* (1989) 556-62, 560.

[61] For example Mertin, supra n. 59, 228; Bundesverband deutscher Banken, supra n. 54, 586; Bundesverband deutscher Banken, supra n. 60, 560.

[62] As to this approach, see Walter, Ingo 'Universal Banking: A Shareholder Value Perspective' *Finanzmarkt und Portfolio Management* 11 (1997) 14-34, 29 et seq.

to trade at prices lower than shares of more narrowly-focused firms.[63] In order to explain why firms nevertheless continue to maintain value-reducing diversification strategies, a number of agency cost-based explanations have been advanced: Managers may derive private benefits from diversification because of the power and prestige associated with managing a larger firm, because their compensation is related to firm size, because diversification helps to make them indispensable to the firm, or because the risk of their undiversified personal portfolio is lowered.

The general agency cost-based explanation for diversification stands in stark contrast to statements of German banks, claiming a value-increasing effect of diversification via shareholdings in non-financial firms. The question arises of whether diversification of this type by universal banks is really an exception to the rule, i.e., whether, for banks, it basically is a value-increasing strategy, and, if so, how to explain this effect. The answer flows from the economics of banking, or, more precisely, from the character of (commercial and) universal banks as institutions, which simultaneously operate as lenders (i.e., extend loans) and as borrowers (i.e., take deposits).

Unlike "pure" investors, universal banks as shareholders are not interested in maximizing the (net present) stand-alone value of their holdings. Rather, they are interested in maximizing the net present value of total returns from all their business activities. Furthermore, banks as highly leveraged institutions regularly operate with only a thin equity layer. Their profitability, therefore, depends crucially on the spread between their cost of debt funds and their return on assets, such as loans. Now, the deposit-taking business, especially with small savers, offers one of the cheapest refinancing sources. A high volume of deposits serves to considerably enhance the profitability of banks. But deposits come with strings attached: one factor which is supposed to influence the deposit-taking business, particularly with small savers, is the confidence of the depositors that the bank will repay the savings deposits in (virtually) any contingent future state of the world. For this reason, banks do their best to avoid incidents which could undermine the confidence of depositors in their ability to make repayments.

For banks structured as stock corporations, one event which may have a negative effect on their deposit-taking business is a sharp reduction in the dividend payment or—worse yet—a total failure to pay a dividend. Such an incident and the attendant speculation in trade journals and the daily press about the bank's position could lead many savers with a limited knowledge of finance to assume that their deposits were threatened and to withdraw their funds. To avoid this risk, a bank will pay out a constant annual dividend which does not depend on

---

[63] For example Denis, David J., Diane K. Denis, and Atulya Sarin 'Agency Problems, Equity Ownership, and Corporate Diversification' *Journal of Finance* 52 (1997) 135-60 with further references.

actual annual earnings.[64] Thus, the incentive for smoothing dividend payments becomes even stronger as the deposit-taking business acquires more significance as a refinancing source.

In this context, the special role of bank shareholdings in non-financial firms finally comes into play. First of all, equity holdings serve as a diversified source of cash flow. If a bank's earnings from its banking operations shrink and dividend payments from the portfolio companies are high enough, the bank can show a profit and use the cash flow generated by its shareholdings to make dividend payments.[65] Moreover, if these cash flows are not sufficient to finance a constant dividend payment, the hidden reserves associated with equity holdings come into play.[66] By dissolving part of these hidden reserves, the bank can show a balance sheet profit which allows it to pay a dividend in the amount customary in past years.[67] To be really effective, though, banks must be able to keep such acts of "creative accounting" hidden from the general public. In this respect, German accounting rules are very obliging. Under Section 340f of the German Commercial Code banks may set off gains from dissolving hidden reserves against, among other items, depreciations on outstanding loans and newly set-up reserves for credit risks, without having to report the dissolution of hidden reserves at all.

Just taken together, a case could be made out for diversification of (commercial and) universal banks via holdings in non-financial corporations for it to be the exception to the rule, namely a value-increasing business strategy. Still, critics might argue that debt claims are less risky than equity claims and there-

---

[64] Frankel and Montgomery, supra n. 48, 268 offer some support for this line of reasoning. They find that profits of German banks appear to vary less from year to year than those of British, Japanese, and American banks.

[65] Steinherr, Alfred and Christian Huveneers 'Universal Banks: The Prototype of Successful Banks in the Integrated European Market?—A View Inspired by German Experience' (Centre for European Policy Studies Research Report, Brussels 1990) 26 are very critical of this reasoning by pointing out that a bank's shareholders can achieve the desired risk reduction by individually holding diversified portfolios. However, they fail to take into account the effect of diversification on the level of the bank for its deposit-taking business.

[66] Thus despite suggestions to the contrary (see Allen, Franklin and Douglas Gale 'A Welfare Comparison of Intermediaries and Financial Markets in Germany and the US' *European Economic Review* 39 (1995) 179-209, 197) there is no inherent contradiction between creating hidden reserves and maximizing net market value. Admittedly, however, the hidden reserves of the large German banks are not fully reflected in share prices on the stock exchange: at the annual press conference in connection with publication of Deutsche Bank's financial statements for 1996, the former Chairman of the Management Board of Deutsche Bank, *Hilmar Kopper*, pointed out that the current stock market valuation of Deutsche Bank did not take hidden reserves into account. See *Süddeutsche Zeitung* 27./28.3.1997, no. 72, 23.

[67] BHF-Bank presents an actual example: despite lower earnings in 1996, the bank paid the same dividend for the 1996 fiscal year as for the year before by using around 15% of its hidden reserves. See *Frankfurter Allgemeine Zeitung* 27.3.1997, no. 73, 23.

fore universal banks as value-maximizers would be better off using their funds to further diversify their credit portfolio instead of taking on permanent equity positions in non-financial firms. This argument is flawed, however. Firstly, the present Chairman of the Management Board of Deutsche Bank, Rolf-E. Breuer (in the course of the discussion at the Hamburg conference) assessed the credit business as the more risky one by pointing out that in the past, Deutsche Bank incurred much higher losses (to the extent of several billion DM) on its portfolio of credit claims than on its portfolio of equity holdings.[68] Moreover, a portfolio of equity holdings offers far greater opportunities for amassing hidden reserves and, as a consequence, for window-dressing the balance sheet. Therefore, even assuming that debt claims are less risky in the long run, universal banks will find it more profitable holding a portfolio of equity positions in non-financial firms if their benefits from the lower cost of refinancing outweigh those losses due to a less diversified credit portfolio.

Quite apart from these considerations, a definite assessment of the relative costs and benefits of (commercial and/or) universal bank shareholdings in non-financial corporations is problematic. A number of preconditions have to be fulfilled before the beneficial diversification-associated effects to really take place: the tax and balance sheet regulations must be structured accordingly, deposits and especially savings deposits must be an important source of refinancing, depositors must be unsophisticated, and deposit insurance must not exist or depositors are either ignorant of its existence or mistrust its effectiveness.[69] There is therefore no generally applicable answer as to the value-maximizing effects of diversification by universal banks.

3. Structuring a Value-Maximizing Portfolio of Equity Holdings

As to the optimal structure of a universal bank's portfolio of equity positions in non-financial firms, financial theorists seem to assume that banks should hold a well-diversified portfolio when striving for value-maximization. Quite obviously, this idea is not matched by the structure of shareholdings of German banks. Instead of numerous blocks of up to 5%, they hold a small number of large blocks of at least 10%, and different sectors of industry are unevenly repre-

---

[68] Taking risk and volume into account may lead to a different conclusion. But regardless of objective data, the actual behavior of Deutsche Bank—and that of other banks as well—will be determined by the subjective risk perception of top management.

[69] Whether these conditions would ever fully be attained in Germany seems doubtful. At any rate, the often-stated and recently demonstrated willingness of German banks to part with their holdings in non-financial corporations (see infra n. 105 et seq. and accompanying text) indicates that at least these conditions no longer prevail.

sented in banks' portfolios. On top of this, holdings are illiquid, many holdings dating back to the inflation-induced economic crisis of 1923/24.[70]

German critics of universal banks holding equity positions in non-financial corporations have taken issue with both features. In their opinion, the lack of adequate diversification and the far too low portfolio turnover implies that bank equity holdings are not to be understood in terms of portfolio investment but as a means of exerting influence on the companies in question.[71] For additional support for such reasoning, one could point to the fact that banks voluntarily create illiquid ownership structures by sometimes pooling their shareholdings with insurance or industrial companies even if not required by tax considerations, and that banks rarely invest in preferred non-voting stock[72] even though such an investment would also strengthen portfolio diversification.

Tax reasons provide at least a partial explanation for both features. To begin with, until 1977, extensive preferential tax treatment of profits and losses for affiliated companies was granted for holdings of at least 25%. After two amendments in 1977 and 1984, this privilege had far less effect on taxes and, on the other hand, already applied to holdings of at least 10%. In line with these changes, banks from 1977 onwards substantially reduced their holdings of 25% or more but held on to existing or even acquired further smaller blocks.[73] Second, for the reasons already discussed above (Section C.II.), namely the interaction of tax and balance sheet regulations and the prevalence of concentrated ownership structures respectively the low liquidity of most stocks traded on German stock exchanges, particularly those equity holdings in existence for some time are not very liquid.

Given the German economic and regulatory environment up to now, the banks may even have pursued a value-maximizing business strategy by holding a number of large equity positions in a smaller number of companies instead of holding a well-diversified portfolio. Maximizing returns from shareholdings becomes less important if banks use their shareholdings to secure their own consistent dividend payments, and if furthermore they use their holdings as a

---

[70] An example is the holding of the Deutsche Bank in Daimler-Benz AG.

[71] See, for example, Münchow, Malte-Maria *Bankenmacht oder Kontrolle durch Banken* 165-6 (Sinzheim 1995). Similarily Mülhaupt, Ludwig 'Das Problem der Bankenmacht aus wettbewerbspolitischer Sicht' *Die Betriebswirtschaft* 40 (1980) 513-26, 521 because of inadequate portfolio diversification; Böhm, supra n. 28, 50 because of low bank portfolio turnover.

[72] A known exception is Dresdner Bank's 4.9% stake of preferred non-voting stock in Dyckerhoff AG.

[73] With figures, Mülbert, supra n. 2, E36. Roggenbuck Harald E. *Begrenzung des Anteils-besitzes von Kreditinstituten und Nichtbanken—Gesetzliche Regelungen, empirischer Befund sowie anlage- und geschäftspolitische Bedeutung* 164 et seq. (Frankfurt am Main et. al. 1992) describes this development for the years 1976-1991 in detail; Böhm, supra n. 28, 38 et seq. offers confirming data for the period 1972-1990.

means to create hidden reserves. Rather, banks must give priority to holding stock on a long-term basis, because they would otherwise not be able to build up substantial hidden reserves. Put differently, the function of shareholdings as a source of hidden reserves makes illiquidity a necessary precondition. In the light of these considerations, then, the large size of numerous bank shareholdings can be easily understood. As long as their shareholdings are to serve as an important source of hidden reserves, banks which are dissatisfied with the performance of portfolio companies cannot follow the Wall Street-rule and sell their stock. Lacking the exit option, they need instead a voice in the affairs of the company. Therefore, in order to perform an effective monitoring and controlling function, bank shareholdings must be high enough to give some leverage over corporations.

E. Control Objectives

The previous section discussed universal banks' shareholdings in non-financial firms in terms of the economics of banking. This section takes up the corporate governance perspective and examines how the incentives derived above reflect in the behavior of universal banks when exercising their ownership-based monitoring and controlling function. In this respect, possible intra-bank conflicts of interests are of prime importance. Does the bank perform its ownership function as a "pure" investor, thus acting in the interest of the other investors holding well-diversified portfolios, or does the bank's interest differ from that of a "pure" investor?[74] Any answer to this question depends on the bank's objectives when acting as corporate monitor. To simplify our discussion of these objectives, let us first consider the "pure" financial holding and then the "complex" holding, which goes hand in hand with an extensive banking relationship.

I. "Pure" Shareholdings

One mechanism for controlling stock corporations is monitoring by active shareholders, i.e., inside shareholders, outside blockholders, or institutional inves-

---

[74] Theoretically, universal banks structured as stock corporations with widely held ownership should strive to maximize net present market value. According to many observers, however, the behavior of German banks casts doubts on the assumption that universal banks pursue the maximization goal in their banking business and, more specifically, in their activities as corporate monitors. This raises the most interesting question of "Who monitors the monitor?" For the purpose of this paper, there is no need to take up this problem. The basic result emerging from the following discussion, namely that universal banks do not qualify as "ideal" corporate monitors, remains true when the agency problems within the monitoring bank itself are also taken into account.

tors.[75] In a German-type universal bank, these three types of shareholders are melted into one: by holding equity positions as a financial intermediary, universal banks qualify as institutional investors; through the supervisory board mandates, which are de facto linked to larger shareholdings, they have a voice in major internal decisions such as the selection of members of the management board and thus qualifing as inside shareholders; by owning stakes of at least 10% in many companies, they qualify as blockholder.[76]

Admittedly, objectives pursued by universal banks regarding corporate control cannot be deduced from this categorization alone. A short digression on the control objectives of blockholders in general helps to further clarify the problem.

1. "Pure" Blockholders in General

Blockholders may hold their interest as a capital investment, but also for (other) entrepreneurial or private reasons. This distinction is critical. Take the case of groups of companies: minority shareholders in subsidiaries cannot—and this is an important motive underlying the German body of law on groups of companies—expect the blockholder or majority shareholder to safeguard their capital interests through the monitoring activities exercised in its own interest.[77] In the case of a large shareholder who owns his equity position as a "pure" investment, however, there seems to be no conflict of interest between small shareholders and this large shareholder, be it a financial institution in the broadest sense of the word or a wealthy private individual. Both types of shareholders would want the company to maximize its net present value. Alas, the situation is more complicated than it appears at first glance.

Most blockholders' portfolios show little diversification for many reasons, one being lack of necessary funds. Among the German banks, only the three big

---

[75] A comprehensive list of control mechanisms would include: inside/managerial shareholding, outside blockholdings, institutional holdings, outside board representation, lender monitoring, the labor market for managers, takeovers/the market for corporate control. These mechanisms can reinforce as well as hinder each other. See, for example, Agrawal, Anup and Charles R. Knoeber 'Firm Performance and Mechanisms to Control Agency Problems between Managers and Shareholders' *Journal of Financial and Quantitative Analysis* 31 (1996) 377-97, 380 et seq.

[76] While the special role of blockholders as corporate monitors is generally acknowledged, opinions vary as to the size of the stake required for qualifying as a blockholder. Values from 5% to 15% to 50% have been named (references in Short, Helen 'Ownership, Control, Financial Structure and the Performance of Firms' *Journal of Economic Surveys* 8 (1994) 203-49, 223). This problem, however, pertains only to empirical studies of blockholding-associated effects, not to the following theoretical discussion of possible goals pursued by blockholders.

[77] For the U.S., see Rosenstein, Stuart and David Rush 'The Stock Performance of Corporations That are Partially Owned by Other Corporations' *Journal of Financial Research* 13 (1990) 39-57.

banks—Deutsche Bank, Dresdner Bank, Commerzbank—and Westdeutsche Landesbank hold somewhat diversified portfolios in non-financial companies. But even Deutsche Bank's portfolio lacks adequate diversification since the stake in Daimler-Benz gears the portfolio towards the automobile sector.

Blockholders with insufficiently[78] diversified portfolios, as Stiglitz[79] already pointed out, will pursue other goals than adequately diversified shareholders. In particular, since these blockholders bear firm-specific risks that could be diversified away, they do *not* aim at maximizing the market value of the company.[80] Their position would be different only if they were compensated for taking on diversifiable risks, i.e., if they could realize additional private benefits by diverting parts of corporate resources for private purposes. However, this alternative also works to the detriment of other shareholders. Consequently, there is no solution to the conflict of interests between inadequately diversified owners of large blocks and those shareholders who own a small stake as part of a well-diversified portfolio.

Thus, discussing the benefits and costs of corporate monitoring by large shareholders, distinguishing between well-diversified and inadequately diversified blockholders is critical.[81] Only large shareholders falling within the second

---

[78] As to the minimum number of stocks needed, see, for example, Stratman, Meir 'How Many Stocks Do Make a Diversified Portfolio?' *Journal of Financial and Quantitative Analysis* 22 (1987) 353-63, with further references; with special emphasis on the German stock market, see Hellevik, Jan Sverre and Ralf Herrmann 'Diversifikation am deutschen Aktienmarkt—eine empirische Betrachtung' *Zeitschrift für Bankrecht und Bankwirtschaft* 8 (1996) 131-9.

[79] Stiglitz, Joseph 'Credit Markets and the Control of Capital' *Journal of Money, Credit, and Banking* 17 (1985) 133-52, 140.

[80] See, for example, Mülbert, Peter O. 'Shareholder Value aus rechtlicher Sicht' *Zeitschrift für Unternehmens- und Gesellschaftsrecht* 26 (1997), 129-72, 159-61. The case of *Bluhdorn* as blockholder of Gulf and Western provides an illustrative example. He used the company to hold a large portfolio of stocks in other companies. By doing so he reduced his firm-specific risk as a blockholder of Gulf and Western. However, investors holding an adequately diversified portfolio would not benefit from this strategy and might even have been hurt. Within a week after *Bluhdorn's* death, the share price of Gulf and Western rose by 42%. See Demsetz, Harold and Kenneth Lehn 'The Structure of Corporate Ownership' *Journal of Political Economy* 66 (1985) 1155-77, 1162 n. 1.

In this context, see also Hansen, Robert G. and John R. Lott 'Externalities and Corporate Objectives in a World with Diversified Shareholder-Consumers' *Journal of Financial and Quantitative Analysis* 31 (1996) 43-68, 57. They try to explain the 5% limitation placed on shareholdings by Japanese banks as "one method of preventing each bank from acquiring too much of a company—too much in the same sense that the bank would then want to maximize the value of that one company alone".

[81] Most empirical studies on the value of monitoring by large-scale shareholders agree in their finding that beyond a certain point, the presence of a large shareholder reduces the performance of the firm (as to this and to the costs of large investors in general, see, for example, Shleifer, Andrei and Robert W. Vishny 'A Survey of Corporate Governance' *Journal of Finance* 52 (1997) 737-83, 758 et seq., with further references). If blockholders are inadequately diversified, this is to be expected. Well-diversified blockholders will, however, only extract private

category would want the company's management to pursue a value-maximizing corporate strategy and, as corporate monitors, would act accordingly. On the other hand, even assuming diverging interests, well-diversified shareholders holding only a small stake in the company can in the end still profit from the corporate oversight exercised by a non-diversified large shareholder. All things being equal, this depends on whether the resulting reduction of agency costs exceeds the assets claimed by the large shareholder as compensation for his inadequate degree of diversification.

2. Banks as "Pure" Blockholders

At first glance, the aforegoing discussion of "pure" blockholders' objectives with regard to corporate monitoring and control seems also to apply to banks as "pure" blockholders, i.e., if a bank at most entertains a marginal business relationship with the company whose shares it owns. However, Macey and Miller have recently argued that as a consequence of commercial banks' highly leveraged capital structure, their incentives as fixed claimants will dwarf their interests as residual claimants, i.e., as shareholders. This bias not only leads to incompatible risk preferences of bank and non-bank equity holders, but severely compromises the ownership-based role of banks that act as corporate monitors in the interest of other shareholders.[82]

The suggested link between a value-maximizing bank's preference for a risk-adverse business strategy of its portfolio company and the bank's highly leveraged capital structure is problematic, though. Compared to firms operating in other lines of business, banks on average show a much thinner equity layer. Therefore, a bank's likelihood for going bankrupt ceteris paribus is higher than that of a less highly leveraged institution. Given such a situation, standard economic theory tells us that shareholders would want the firm to take on more risky projects instead of less risky ones. As residual owners, shareholders reap all the benefits from more profitable but also more risky operations, whereas fixed claimants only share in the higher risk. Deposit-taking business acts as a check on the tendency of value-maximizing banks in taking excessive risk, though. If a bank switches to more risky projects, depositors will either withdraw their funds or demand an additional risk premium, i.e., higher interest rates on deposits. Both effects lead to an increase in the bank's cost of refinancing. A value-maximizing bank would therefore choose such risky projects so that the additional benefits from a marginal increase in risk equal the additional cost.

---

benefits if the value of these gains exceeds the opportunity costs in the form of a lower market-valuation of the company. Unfortunately, the studies do not control for the degree of diversification of different blockholders.

[82] Macey and Miller, supra n. 43, 94 et seq., 108.

Admittedly, while this line of reasoning establishes a relationship between the riskiness of the bank's shareholdings (and other operations such as lending) and the deposit-taking business in terms of value maximization, the implications for a bank's behavior as a monitoring shareholder still await further clarification. In this respect, the above discussion (Section D.II.2.) of universal banks' motives for holding equity positions on a long-term basis could serve as a starting point. To recall but the most important results: given a value-maximizing business strategy, such holdings could be explained by a (assumed) positive correlation between the consistency of the bank's dividend payments over time and the volume of its deposit-taking business as a significant source of refinancing. Shareholdings in turn are of twofold importance for smoothing the time path of the bank's own dividend payments: first, the bank could use the dividend payments by the portfolio company to fund its own dividend payments; second, by dissolving part of the hidden reserves associated with the shareholding, the bank can show a balance sheet profit even in times when its core banking business is unprofitable.

These observations have straightforward implications with regard to the banks' role in corporate governance. The twofold function of bank shareholdings in non-financial companies will reflect in the dividend and business policy which a bank prefers for its portfolio companies.[83] These companies' dividend payouts over time must be as smooth as possible in order to ensure that the bank itself can pay out a constant dividend from the cash flow generated by its shareholdings. In the long run, however, such consistent dividends can only be paid out if a firm's corporate strategy is designed accordingly. A portfolio company's corporate strategy must therefore be aimed at reducing the variance of its returns as much as possible for any given (satisficing) level of earnings, and not at maximizing net present market value by accepting more volatile returns.

Universal banks prefer a risk-adverse corporate strategy of listed non-financial companies for yet another reason. In order to conduct their securities operations, brokerage services, block trading, etc., universal banks frequently own larger blocks of shares (trading stock). A corporate strategy of non-financial firms which lowers fluctuations in returns also smooths the companies' stock price variations. From a universal bank's point of view, the reduced volatility of stock prices in turn reduces any need to write down trading stock and thus helps to keep the bank's own earnings stable.

Finally, the particular functions of banks' shareholdings affect the portfolio firm's decision whether to pay out dividends or to retain earnings. At minimum, a

---

[83] Note, however, that dividend-smoothing practices have also been observed for market-based financial systems, i.e., the U.S. and the U.K. See, for example, Browne, Francis X. 'Corporate Finance: Stylized Facts and Tentative Explanantions' *Applied Economics* 26 (1994) 485-508, 491, with further references.

bank will support a payment ratio that reflects its requirements with regard to its own dividend payments. Less clear, however, is a bank's position with regard to the alternative between paying out an even higher dividend or retaining these earnings. While retentions do strengthen a bank's hidden reserves associated with the shareholding, two contradictory effects are associated with this increase. On the one hand, this may act as a signal for the deposit-taking business which strengthens customers' confidence in the safety of their deposits and in turn improves the bank's refinancing conditions. On the other hand, retentions augment the free cash flow of the company and thus its scope for self-financing. Less need for debt capital and fresh equity reduces the effectiveness of corporate control as exercised by the capital market and the bank as lender. In the sense of Jensen's[84] free cash flow theory, this widens management's discretionary powers for investment in negative net present value projects. From a value maximizing bank's point of view, the point at issue when choosing between retentions and payouts is the trade-off between lowering the bank's refinancing cost and earning higher returns from its shareholdings by reducing agency costs in portfolio companies. This trade-off delimits the bank's incentives to advocate retention of all profits above the minimum threshold just outlined.

To summarize our discussion, the following interim result emerges: even assuming that a universal bank strives for maximizing net market value and does not maintain an extensive banking relationship with its portfolio company, the bank's interests differ from those of "pure" investors holding a diversified portfolio. From the latter's point of view, universal banks are not ideal corporate monitors.[85]

II. Concomitance of Holdings and Ties Derived from Banking Relationships

The aforegoing discussion used equilibrium analysis to determine the bank's objectives when acting as a monitoring shareholder. This approach can also be applied to situations in which the bank is both a shareholder and a business partner maintaining an extensive banking relationship with the portfolio com-

---

[84] Jensen, Michael C. 'Agency Costs of Free-Cash Flow, Corporate Finance, and Takeovers' *American Economic Review Papers and Proceedings* 76 (1986) 323-9.

[85] That banks support a low risk corporate strategy with low stock price volatility may have positive welfare effects. Because of the reduction in price volatility, investors who have liquidity needs may be better off. For more details, see Allen and Gale, supra n. 66, 195 with further references. By pointing to the German example, they argue that the dampening effect of the universal banking system results from the fact that even for listed companies only very little information is available. The arguments here given provide a more direct explanation for the link between the universal banking system and lower stock market volatility.

pany.[86] In this case, the bank will attempt to maximize the net present value of total returns from its entire business operations, i.e., from its core banking activities and from its portfolio of shareholdings. Therefore, if there is a trade-off between earnings from the banking relationship on the one hand and the share-holding on the other, it will not suffice to maximize the stand-alone returns from the two lines of business independently. Rather, the bank must also consider possible spill-over effects of its corporate control activities on its banking relationship with the portfolio company as client.

The literature has frequently dealt with this trade-off[87] and has established at least four effects with regard to the portfolio company: (i) a preference for growth of sales, (ii) a preference for a risk-adverse corporate strategy, (iii) a preference for excessive bank loans, and (iv) a preference for the non-listing of companies.

ad (i) As business partners, banks want their portfolio companies to maximize the growth of sales rather than profit. The reason is straightforward: increased turnover also expands the volume of the banking services these companies require. This preference particularly affects the companies' dividend policy since banks may approve of profit retention even if the companies lack investment opportunities, the minimum return of which equals the company's cost of equity capital. However, a higher self-financing ratio makes management less subject to control by either the lender or the capital market. This consideration acts as a check on the bank's willingness to support profit retention.

ad (ii) As a lender, the bank's prime interest is the loan being paid back in all possible future states of the world. Therefore, banks prefer a risk-adverse corpo-rate strategy with less volatile earnings and approve of profit retention even though these funds could be reinvested only at below-market rates, i.e., when the return on all feasible investment projects is less than the cost of equity capital.

ad (iii) For the sake of returns from its lending business, the bank is interested in having the company take out loans that exceed the level which maximizes the firm's value.[88]

ad (iv) Because of the loan business, the bank is anxious detering companies from tapping the capital market and in keeping unlisted companies from going public. Investment banking, e.g., underwriting, generates a once-off return while lending generates an on-going income stream.

---

[86] Aoki, Masahiko 'Shareholders' Non-Unanimity on Investment Financing: Banks vs. Individual Investors' in: Aoki, Masahiko (ed.) *The Economic Analysis of the Japanese Firm* 193-224 (New York 1984) develops a formal model based on this approach. Neuberger, supra n. 44, 17 et seq. adopts this approach as well.

[87] See, for example, Hoshi, Kashyap, and Scharfstein, supra n. 52, 122. See also Böhm, supra n. 28, 146-56.

[88] This aspect is stressed by Aoki, supra n. 86, 205 et seq.; c.f. Baums, supra n. 16, 439.

Summarizing these considerations leads to the following conclusion: the combination of equity ownership in the company and extensive banking business with the company causes the bank, as shareholder, to have substantially divergent control objectives compared to those of diversified "pure" investors.[89] In part, the bank's control objectives within such a "complex" bank-firm relationship coincide with those of universal banks acting as "pure" blockholders. This is particularly true with regard to the preference for a risk-adverse business strategy of the portfolio company. For the rest, however, a "complex" bank-firm relationship provides a value-maximizing bank with even less incentives to support a value-maximizing strategy of its portfolio company than is true for banks as "pure" blockholders. The extent to which a bank will try to realize (private) benefits from the banking relationship instead of profiting from maximizing the portfolio company's market value depends on, inter alia, the size of the bank's shareholding and the ratio of total bank services required by the company to the services provided by the bank. The higher the shareholding stake[90] and the lower the banking-business stake, the less incentive there will be to exploit the company and its shareholders via the banking relationship.

F. Corporate Control by German Banks

The theoretical analysis in Section E showed that universal banks as blockholders pursue different control objectives from those of sufficiently diversified "pure" investors. Of course, it is another question whether banks are in fact in a position to push their specific interests through, under given circumstances. This depends both on the legal environment, e.g., the regulations pertaining to shareholder control of the company, and on factual conditions such as the company's shareholder structure. Moreover, even if the banks pursue their own interests with regard to corporate control and monitoring, their controlling activities can, in the end, still be advantageous for "pure" investors as well. This presupposes, however, that the management-induced agency costs would be substantially reduced if it is the bank exercising control. Bank-specific advantages would, inter alia, include better access to inside information regarding management conduct and the position of the company.

---

[89] Therefore, contrary to the assertion of Jensen, Michael C. 'The Modern Industrial Revolution, Exit, and the Failure of Internal Control Systems' *Journal of Finance* 48 (1993) 831-80, 867, not all financial institutions are equally well-suited to act as "natural active investors" who monitor firm management and policies in an unbiased way. Obviously, commercial banks and other financial intermediaries entertaining extensive business ties with non-financial firms qualify even less as "natural active investors".

[90] Neuberger, supra n. 44, 18 et seq., 28 offers a more formal presentation of the argument.

To sum up: purely theoretical reasoning yields no clear-cut result as to the effects of universal banks on corporate governance. The banks' monitoring and controlling activities are subject to a varying set of restrictions depending on the concrete legal and economic system in question. Therefore, the role of universal banks has to be assessed individually for each corporate governance system. In what follows, an attempt will be made with regard to the German system by considering the available empirical data.

I. Control Based on Superior Information

If banks, as partial owners, had better inside information than other blockholders, they should sooner and/or more often succeed in identifying incapable or self-serving management and dismiss the managers. Management board turnover, therefore, is an indication of the quality of corporate control exercised by banks (and other blockholders). Two studies of management board turnover published so far arrive at quite different conclusions. However, both agree about the point in issue here: companies with banks as blockholders and companies with other large shareholders do not differ significantly in terms of management board turnover.[91] The hypothesis that banks as blockholders have greater incentives and/or ability to control companies is therefore not confirmed. This result is in line with the above doubts (Section D.I.3.) that banks have significantly better inside information.

II. Control Based on Self-Interest

If universal banks use their position as blockholders to exercise influence in their own interest, these companies should show a significantly higher ratio of bank loans to external financing than companies in which banks do not hold an equity position. Schwiete and Weigand tested this hypothesis for a sample of 230 stock corporations from 24 lines of business within the industrial sector. However, when comparing the debt structure of 34 companies in which banks owned an interest of at least 5% with the debt structure of the other sample companies, they found no differences with regard to banks' holdings.[92] Furthermore, even if empirical tests produced evidence for a higher ratio, any attempt at explaining this fact would have to consider that banks, as partial owners, might provide long-term loans on more favorable conditions thanks to their position as an

---

[91] Kaplan, Steven N. 'Top Executives, Turnover, and Firm Performance in Germany' *Journal of Law, Economics & Organization* 10 (1994) 142-59, 155; Franks and Mayer, supra n. 5, 25.

[92] Schwiete, Mark and Jürgen Weigand 'Bankbeteiligungen und das Verschuldungsverhalten deutscher Unternehmen' *Kredit und Kapital* 30 (1997) 1-34, 27 (summary).

informational insider. If this second explanation were correct, companies with a bank, as partial owner, should not tend over time to turn to the stock market for financing as an alternative to long-term bank loans. Huth established such a trend for a sample of 340 stock corporations in manufacturing with sales of at least DM 100 million and 250 employees.[93] Unfortunately, he failed to distinguish between companies which were partially bank-owned and others, so ultimately his survey does not allow one to draw any conclusions.

Not only credit operations but the deposit-taking business as well can justify the bank's interest in excessive retained earnings. As late as 1995, Schneider-Lenné, former member of the management board of Deutsche Bank, confirmed that in the past banks had expressed this interest to companies.[94] However, any study of this hypothesis must bear in mind that differences in the payout pattern of partially bank-owned companies and other corporations could also be explained by signalling effects. If a bank's equity position signals that the port-folio company is especially profitable, companies without a bank as shareholder could attempt to signal the prospect of high earnings by paying comparatively higher dividends. However, the second alternative would not explain smooth dividend payments of partially bank-owned companies, i.e., payout patterns which do reflect the volatility of annual earnings. This consideration leads to the final hypothesis.

Because of the deposit-taking business with the general public and also because of the credit business, banks may urge their portfolio companies to pursue less risky operations, thus ensuring smoother returns and consistent dividend payouts by these companies. Anecdotal evidence suggests that the dividend policy of German stock corporations up to the eighties was primarily aimed at keeping annual dividends as constant as possible.[95] However, no studies have been published so far which explicitly consider the effect of bank holdings, nor are there studies on whether partly bank-owned firms have pursued a signifi-cantly more risk-adverse corporate strategy in the past.

---

[93] Huth, supra n. 22, 59 et seq. During the period 1981-1991, equity financing as a percent-age of the balance sheet total rose from 16% to approx. 18.5%, while financing by long-term bank loans fell from 3% to 1%.

[94] *Ellen R. Schneider-Lenné Frankfurter Allgemeine Zeitung* 16.2.1995, no. 40, 19.

[95] A study by Fischer, Otfried, Helge Jansen, and Werner Mayer (*Langfristige Finanzpla-nung deutscher Unternehmen—Ergebnisse einer empirischen Untersuchung anhand ausge-wählter Aktiengesellschaften* 79 (Hamburg 1975)) on the dividend policy of 30 large German corporations established that for all these firms, constant dividend payments enjoy top priority. However, a later study revealed that the *Lintner* model on dividend payouts by American corpo-rations almost succeeds in explaining the dividend policy of German stock corporations as well. See, for details, Hort, Helmut *Zur Dividendenpolitik der Aktiengesellschaften des Verarbeitenden Gewerbes der Bundesrepublik Deutschland* (Dissertation, University of Saarbrücken 1984). Cf. also Prigge (this volume Ch. 12: Sec. B.III.) on the dividend policy of German comapnies.

III. Profitability of the Controlled Company and Corporate Governance

1. Testable Hypotheses

In recent years, several econometric studies attempted to determine the significance of banks' shareholdings for corporate governance by using the performance of portfolio companies as proxy. However, interpreting these studies with regard to corporate governance poses difficulties. Both the result that partly-owned companies perform comparatively better as well as the opposite result could be explained by different and sometimes even contradictory mechanisms.

Partly bank-owned firms may be more profitable because banks as monitors succeed more effectively in reducing management-induced agency costs than other blockholders or other control mechanisms. On the other hand, bank blockholdings may serve as a superior mechanism for overcoming informational asymmetries; in other words, corporate interlockings via bank equity holdings in non-financial firms may form an effective industrial organization pattern.

If, on the contrary, partly bank-owned companies perform significantly below average, this may be because universal banks as blockholders are in a position to assert their special interests with regard to corporate control. An alternative explanation particularly favored by Wenger and Kaserer suggests that the poorer performance of these companies may have to do with the big German private banks themselves being management-controlled stock corporations of the Berle-Means type. Thus, corporate control exercised by these blockholders serves the interests of the bank's management, but not the interest of the company's shareholders.[96]

The performance studies to date have not specified independently testable hypotheses with regard to these various interactions. This must not be overlooked when interpreting their results.

2. The Studies[97]

An initial study of the effect of bank shareholdings was undertaken by Gorton and Schmid.[98] They examined the performance of companies in the years 1974

---

[96] Wenger, Ekkehard and Christoph Kaserer 'The German System of Corporate Governance: A Model Which Should Not Be Imitated' in: Black, Stanley and Matthias Moersch (eds.) *Competition and Convergence: The German and Anglo-American Models* 40-81 (Washington, D.C. 1998).

[97] Cf. also the study conducted by Wenger/Kaserer (this volume Ch. 6: Sec. D); for a comprehensive survey of these studies, see also Prigge (this volume Ch. 12: Sec. B.II.5. and C.II.).

[98] Gorton and Schmid, supra n. 15; (Schmid, supra n. 15, is based on the same study).

and 1985 on the basis of two differently constructed samples. While the 1974 sample showed a uniquely significant positive influence of bank holdings on equity capital ratios and overall return on capital, the effect of bank holdings in the 1985 sample was in line with the significantly positive influence of non-bank blockholders.

Nibler's[99] later study essentially confirms the result for the 1985 sample. On the basis of a sample of 158 of the 200 largest German non-financial companies, he examined corporate performance for the years 1988-1992, testing for several criteria. The result was a significantly positive influence for banks as blockholders. However, firms with a concentrated shareholder structure showed a significantly positive influence even in the absence of banks as blockholders. Nibler therefore summarizes his own findings as follows: "Banks certainly do not appear to perform this (monitoring) task any better than significantly large non-bank shareholders."

Schmid's[100] study for the year 1991 is based on the sum of the shareholdings of all banks in one company. He obtained highly differentiated results. If the shareholding ratio is relatively low, return on equity first declines and then rises as the shareholding ratio grows. This U-shaped curve is determined by the number of banks involved and ownership concentration. At the same time, Schmid finds a significantly positive relationship between the amount of interest paid for debt capital and the extent and concentration of bank shareholdings. According to his interpretation of these two results, it is relatively more attractive for banks with a bigger share stake to be compensated for exercising a corporate control function by increasing the value of their holding than by receiving additional interest payments.

Wenger and Kaserer[101] studied the long-term performance of large companies in which banks or insurance companies owned an interest of at least 10% on the basis of the share-price performance of these companies in the years 1974-1993. According to their findings, the share price return for the companies in which the financial sector had a blockholding was significantly lower than for companies without such a holding.

Finally, the above-described study by Schwiete and Weigand also tested for the long-term (1965-1988) performance of the sample corporations. According to their results, neither the existence of a bank holding of at least 5% nor the degree of ownership concentration had a significant effect on the return on equity.[102]

---

[99] Nibler, Marcus 'Bank Control and Corporate Performance in Germany: The Evidence' 14 et seq. (University of Cambridge, Faculty of Economics and Politics, Research Paper Series no. 48, 1995).

[100] Schmid, Frank A. 'Beteiligungen deutscher Geschäftsbanken und Corporate Performance' *Zeitschrift für Wirtschafts- und Sozialforschung* 116 (1996) 273-310, 300 et seq.

[101] Wenger and Kaserer, supra n. 96.

[102] Schwiete and Weigand, supra n. 92, 27 (summary).

In sum, the findings of the different performance studies not only vary but are to some extent even contradictory. The evidence produced so far is at best inconclusive. Judging by the findings so far, the hypothesis cannot be rejected that bank blockholdings do not affect the profitability of the company at all or that banks, at any rate, do not exercise more effective corporation control than non-financial blockholders.[103] Least of all do these studies show which of the conceivable effects of banks' shareholdings caused the performance effects observed in each case.

G. Conclusion

I. Banks' Equity Holdings and Corporate Governance

The interlocking of universal banks and non-financial firms based on bank shareholdings forms a distinctive industrial organization pattern. Theoretically, this combination increases efficiency by reducing problems of informational asymmetries on the one hand and by allowing efficient corporate monitoring on the other hand. The second aspect touches on the role of banks' shareholdings in corporate governance. Bank equity holdings acting as a distinct control mechanism clearly produce benefits for other shareholders as well as additional agency costs allocated to them. Even as blockholders, banks are not in the position of "pure" investors and will therefore associate corporate control with other objectives than well-diversified shareholders. As a consequence, blockholding banks, acting as corporate monitors, lack effective incentives to enforce management's exclusive concentration on increasing shareholder value. In addition, universal banks do not want an active market for hostile takeovers to set off the control deficit attributable to their particular monitoring objectives. Not only for this reason, but also to protect their banking relationship with the company, they will shield their portfolio companies against hostile takeovers.

These considerations suggest that blockholdings of universal banks tend to impair the formation and functioning of some corporate governance mechanisms. Admittedly, though, this partial analysis offers no conclusive judgment on the overall economic efficiency of banks' shareholdings. To fully assess their welfare implications, any benefits resulting from this industrial organization pattern

---

[103] This conclusion finds a parallel in the ambiguous findings of studies that measured the performance of corporations with large shareholders in general. Even overviews covering a nearly identical set of studies offer vastly different evaluations. Contrast, for example, Short, supra n. 76, 222 ("inconclusive evidence") and Servaes, Henri and Marc Zenner 'Ownership Structure' *Finanzmarkt und Portfolio Management* 8 (1994) 184-96, 192 ("mere presence of a large shareholder does not seem to be sufficient to affect corporate value") with the "very optimistic survey" (Rock, Edward B. 'America's Fascination with German Corporate Governance' *Die Aktiengesellschaft* 40 (1995) 291-9, 298, n. 52) by Black, Bernard S. 'The Value of Institutional Investor Monitoring: The Empirical Evidence' 39 *UCLA L. Rev.* 895-939 (1992).

would also have to be taken into account. In this respect, the most important question is whether interlockings via bank shareholdings in fact act as a particularly efficient mechanism for overcoming informational asymmetries between the bank and its customers. There are doubts whether purely theoretical reasoning succeeds in adequately performing such a cost-benefits analysis.

Turning to the example of the German universal banks, the findings so far are inconclusive. On the one hand, there is no evidence to support the hypothesis that the integration of banks and non-financial firms via bank shareholdings is a superior industrial organization pattern with regard to overcoming informational asymmetries. On the other hand, there is no definitive proof that this control structure generates substantial additional agency costs for investors. Evidence on the banks' leeway in using their blockholdings for exercising corporate control, primarily in their own interest, could be found, e.g., if the decline of bank loans as a source of financing was less pronounced for partially bank-owned companies than for other firms.

II. Equity Holdings of German Banks in Perspective

The fact that lending to large corporate customers has become less important reflects a change in banking in general. The big German banks have responded to the challenge by expanding their investment banking operations. The most striking example in this regard is the acquisition of London-based investment banks by Deutsche Bank (Morgan Grenfell) and Dresdner Bank (Kleinwort Benson). In addition, the changes in banking also affect the relative importance of the banks' various refinancing sources. While deposit-taking business has become less significant, the stock market has become more attractive for the big private banks structured as stock corporations. This change is reflected in the already-mentioned decision of Deutsche Bank in 1995 to publish its consolidated financial statements according to the International Accounting Standards (IAS) in order to allow shareholders to fully appreciate the development of the value of their shares.[104]

These developments may affect the monitoring behavior of banks and thus the significance of bank equity holdings for corporate governance. The two business lines of universal banks which are currently decreasing in importance, namely lending and deposit-taking, are the ones which most strongly taint the banks' role as corporate monitors. The on-going changes, therefore, reduce the banks' incentives to control companies with a view to their interests in deposit-taking and lending operations and thus tend to transform the universal banks into large shareholders like any other. If their shareholdings are a "pure" investment,

---

[104] See supra n. 31 and accompanying text.

however, greater emphasis will be placed on portfolio diversification. At best, only the three big private banks—Deutsche Bank, Dresdner Bank, and Commerzbank—can probably afford a sufficiently diversified portfolio with blockholdings of between 10% and 15%. It is therefore probably not pure chance that of all banks, it is Bayerische Hypotheken- und Wechsel-Bank and BHF-Bank which have recently announced their intention to radically scale back their holdings in non-financial firms.[105]

Finally, the growing importance of investment banking activities may affect the position of German banks—and in particular of the three big private banks—towards their blockholdings in non-financial corporations. Expanding the investment banking operations has proven to be a very expensive undertaking. In order to obtain the funds required to finance this expansion, German banks may find it necessary to sell some of their blockholdings in non-financial corporations. It is therefore probably not pure chance that only very recently Dresdner Bank sold its stakes in Degussa AG and Hapag-Lloyd AG,[106] while Deutsche Bank and Commerzbank respectively sold their long-standing positions in Karstadt AG.[107]

[105] See *Frankfurter Allgemeine Zeitung* 7.1.1995, no. 6, 12 (Hypo-Bank); 26.3.1997, no. 72, 24, and 27.3.1997, no. 73, 23 (BHF-Bank).

[106] As to the sale of Degussa AG, see *Frankfurter Allgemeine Zeitung* 24.5.1997, no. 118, 17, and the confirming interview statement by *Jürgen Sarrazin Frankfurter Allgemeine Zeitung* 2.6.1997, no. 124, 16 (Chairman of the Management Board of Dresdner Bank); as to the sale of Hapag-Lloyd AG, see *Frankfurter Allgemeine Zeitung* 3.9.1997, no. 204, 25.

[107] The equity stakes date back to mid-1930. See *Frankfurter Allgemeine Zeitung* 13.8.1997, no. 186, 15.

Appendix A

Directly and Indirectly Held Equity Positions of German Banks in 404 Non-Financial Stock Corporations Listed on the First Tier (*Amtlicher Handel*) of the German Stock Exchanges as of September 30, 1996[*]/[**]

I. Private Banks (*Privatbanken*)

	Percentage of Voting Rights[***] (+ x shares)	Nominal Capital (Mil. DM)
Deutsche Bank AG		
– VOSSLOH AG	49.05[108]	36.000
– Deutsche Beteiligungs AG Unternehmens-beteiligungsgesellschaft	approx. 48.18[109]	45.000
– Klöckner-Humboldt-Deutz AG	approx. 45.91[110]	298.125
– Philipp Holzmann AG	25.83	219.375
– Hutschenreuther AG	25.1[111]	21.330
– Hindrichs-Auffermann AG	24.96	7.612

[*] Source: Bundesaufsichtsamt für den Wertpapierhandel (ed.) 'Bedeutende Stimmrechts-anteile an amtlich notierten Aktiengesellschaften zum 30. September 1996' (Frankfurt am Main 1997), and further also see Bayerische Hypotheken- und Wechselbank 'Wegweiser durch deutsche Unternehmen 1996' (Munich 1997); Commerzbank 'Wer gehört zu wem' 19th edn. (Frankfurt am Main 1997).

[**] Shareholdings by bank-owned investment funds are not included.

[***] Three caveats seem to be appropriate: (i) The data may not fully reflect all indirectly held stakes because the bank can abstain from disclosing its holding if the subsidiary is jointly held by another (non-financial) firm and the bank owns no more than 50% of the subsidiary. (ii) Disclosure is not required for changes in share ownership between the threshold levels of 5%, 10%, 25% 50%, and 75%. Thus, if a bank sold or acquired shares after having disclosed its holding, the change might not be reflected in the data. (iii) The figures pertain to voting rights instead of nominal capital. Thus, if the corporation issued preferred non-voting stock or a (second) class of stock with multiple voting rights attached, or if shareholders pooled their stakes, the percentages in terms of nominal capital will be different.

[108] The high percentage results from a pool agreement. Deutsche Bank indirectly owns 100% of Deutsche Herold Lebensversicherungs AG, which in turn holds a 11.43% stake in VOSSLOH. Deutsche Herold Lebensversicherungs AG and members of the Vossloh family pooled their stakes (11.43% resp. 37.62%) in Schutzgemeinschaft Vossloh GbR.

[109] Approx. 23.6% are indirectly held by owning 45% of DBG Vermögensverwaltungs-gesellschaft mbH, which in turn holds a 52.5% stake in Deutsche Beteiligungs AG.

[110] A 20.23% stake is held indirectly via owning 100% of ALMA Beteiligungsgesellschaft mbH, which holds 100% of KCB-Beteiligungs-AG. KCB in turn owns 72.6% of Klöckner Industriebeteiligungsgesellschaft mbH, which holds a 10.06% stake in KHD.

[111] By owning 100% of ALMA Beteiligungsgesellschaft mbH, which in turn holds a 25.1% stake in Hutschenreuther.

– Daimler-Benz AG	24.4	2,568.437
– WMF Württembergische Metallwarenfabrik AG	17.0[112]	70.000
– Metallgesellschaft AG	13.09	669.602
– Leonische Drahtwerke AG	approx. 12.5[113]	24.000
– Leifheit AG	11.0	25.000
– Salamander AG	10.7	93.606
– Continental AG	10.25	469.940
– Linde AG	10.01	420.270
– KARSTADT AG	10.0 + 20	420.000
– VERSEIDAG AG	10.0 + 20	50.000
– Schmalbach-Lubeca AG	10.0	187.500
– PHOENIX AG	10.0	75.000
– Heidelberger Zement AG	10.0	220.000
– FUCHS Petrolub AG Oel + Chemie	9.37	7.609
– VK Mühlen AG	approx. 7.4[114]	49.900
– VEW AG	approx. 3.875[115]	1,000.000

Dresdner Bank AG

– Bilfinger+Berger Bauaktiengesellschaft	25.1[116]	180.000
– Heidelberger Zement AG	20.5	220.000
– Brau und Brunnen AG	17.3	224.457
– Bremer Woll-Kämmerei AG	approx. 14.7[117]	37.300
– Metallgesellschaft AG	14.2	669.602
– Fresenius AG	11.2[118]	90.000
– Buderus AG	11.1	126.875
– Degussa AG	approx. 10.6[119]	429.930
– Paulaner-Salvator Beteiligungs-Aktiengesellschaft	10.0[120]	18.891

[112] By owning LIBA Beteiligungsgesellschaft mbH as a 100% subsidiary.

[113] By holding 50% of GROGA Beteiligungsgesellschaft mbH, which in turn owns 25% of Leonische Drahtwerke.

[114] By owning 25% of AIH Agrar-Industrie-Holding GmbH, which in turn holds a 29.6% stake in VK Mühlen.

[115] By owning 25% of EVG Energie-Verwaltungs-Gesellschaft mbH, which in turn holds 15.5% of voting rights in VEW.

[116] By owning FGI Frankfurter Gesellschaft für Industriewerte mbH as a 100% subsidiary.

[117] By owning 44.6% of Bremer Wolle Beteiligungsgesellschaft mbH, which in turn holds a 32.95% stake in Bremer Woll-Kämmerei.

[118] By owning 50% of H.O.F. Beteiligungs-GmbH, which in turn holds a 22.4% stake in Fresenius.

[119] By owning 27.13% of GFC Gesellschaft für Chemiewerte mbH, which in turn holds a 39.07% stake in Degussa.

[120] Indirectly held via Dresdner Bank, Switzerland.

– FUCHS Petrolub AG Oel+Chemie	7.2[121]	77.609
– Continental AG	6.5	469.940
– Bayerische Motorenwerke AG	approx. 5.01[122]	986.850
– Deutsche Lufthansa AG	approx. 4.47[123]	1,908.000
– PREUSSAG AG	approx. 3.1[124]	761.576
– Hoechst AG	approx. 2.04[125]	2,939.768

Commerzbank AG

– Kolbenschmidt AG	49.99	134.545
– ALNO AG	27.57	39.000
– Buderus AG	13.7	126.875
– Kaufring AG	approx. 12.5[126]	90.000
– Salamander AG	10.7	93.606
– KARSTADT AG	10.3	420.000
– Linde AG	10.2	420.270
– Philipp Holzmann AG	10.0 + 1	219.375
– MAN AG	approx. 9.02[127]	771.000
– Linotype-Hell AG	6.67[128]	120.000
– Thyssen AG	approx. 5.0[129]	1,565.000
– Hochtief AG	approx. 2.5[130]	350.000

[121] By owning a stake in Beteiligungsgesellschaft für die deutsche Wirtschaft mbH, which in turn holds a stake in BdW Beteiligungsgesellschaft für die deutsche Wirtschaft mbH.

[122] By owning 50% of GFA Gesellschaft für Automobilwerte mbH, which in turn holds a 10.02% stake in BMW.

[123] By owning 44.5% of MGL Münchener Gesellschaft für Luftfahrtwerte, which in turn holds a 10.02% stake in Lufthansa.

[124] By directly owning 70% and (via Oldenburgische Landesbank AG) indirectly owning another 22% of C.F. Beteiligungsgesellschaft mbH, which in turn owns 33.3% of Niedersachsen Holding GmbH. The latter holds a 10.4% stake in PREUSSAG.

[125] By owning 20% of FGC Frankfurter Gesellschaft für Chemiewerte mbH, which in turn holds a 10.2% stake in Hoechst.

[126] By owning 100% of Atlas Vermögensverwaltungsgesellschaft mbH, which in turn holds a 50% stake in Kaufring Beteiligungsgesellschaft GbR.

[127] By owning a 25% stake in Almüco GmbH. Almüco owns 100% of Regina-Verwaltungsgesellschaft mbH, which in turn holds a 36.07% stake in MAN.

[128] By owning 40% of Frega Vermögensverwaltungsgesellschaft mbH, which in turn holds a 16.67% stake in Linotype-Hell.

[129] By owning 50% of Thyssen Beteiligungsverwaltung GmbH, which in turn holds 10.0001% of Thyssen.

[130] By owning a 25% Beteiligung in Almüco GmbH. Almüco holds 40% of Francommerz Vermögensverwaltungsgesellschaft mbH (via Pan-Vermögensverwaltungsgesellschaft mbH?), which in turn owns 25% of Hochtief.

Bayerische Hypotheken– und Wechsel-Bank AG

– AGROB AG	52.72	19.482
– Brau und Brunnen AG	approx. 45.7785[131]	224.557
– Neue Baumwoll-Spinnerei und Weberei Hof AG	26.33	24.75
– Rosenthal AG	15.0	30.000
– Isar-Amperwerke AG	approx. 11.25[132]	376.000
– VIAG AG	approx. 5.03[133]	1,325.723

Bayerische Vereinsbank AG

– HASEN-BRÄU AG	77.3	2.400
– Aktienbrauerei Kaufbeuren AG	75.7	2.500
– Neue Baumwoll-Spinnerei und Weberei Hof AG	42.4	24.75
– VIAG AG	approx. 5.25[134]	1,325.723

BHF-Bank Berliner Handels– und Frankfurter Bank AG

– AGIV Aktiengesellschaft für Industrie und Verkehrswesen	48.7	200.000
– Wayss & Freytag AG	5.1	62.000
– Deutsche Babcock AG	< 5.0	350.000

Bankgesellschaft Berlin AG

– Markt- und Kühlhallen AG	approx. 20.7[135]	29.800
– Isar-Amperwerke AG	approx. 12.85[136]	376.000

---

[131] 12.4135% are indirectly held by owning 50% of PORTA Vermögensverwaltung GmbH, which in turn holds a 24.827% stake in Brau und Brunnen.

[132] By owning 14% of Isarwerke GmbH, which in turn holds a 80.5296% stake in Isar-Amperwerke.

[133] By owning 50% of HI-Vermögensverwaltungsgesellschaft mbH, which in turn holds a 10.06% stake in VIAG.

[134] By owning 50% of VI-Vermögensverwaltungsgesellschaft mbH, which in turn holds a 10.5% stake in VIAG.

[135] By holding a 50% stake in BB-Kapitalbeteiligungsgesellschaft mbH, which in turn owns 41.7% of MUK.

[136] By holding a 14% stake in Isarwerke GmbH, which in turn owns 80.5296% of Isar-Amperwerke.

BW Bank Baden-Württembergische Bank AG		
– DLW AG	12.6[137]	70.500
– ZEAG Zementwerk Lauffen-Elektrizitätswerk		
Heilbronn	6.25	35.075
Delbrück & Co. Privatbankiers		
– Süd-Chemie AG	5.46	40.600
Frankfurter Bankgesellschaft gegr. 1899 AG		
– Binding-Brauerei AG	36.04	54.640
Anton Hafner, Bankgeschäft		
– Eichbaum-Brauereien AG	11.59	12.739
Sal. Oppenheimer jr & Cie. KGaA		
– Rütgers AG	23.91[138]	230.000
Schmidt Bank KG aA		
– Deutsche Beteiligungs AG Unternehmens-		
beteiligungsgesellschaft	6.25	45.000

II. Banks Structured as Public Corporations
   (*Landesbanken/öffentlich-rechtliche Banken*)

Westdeutsche Landesbank Girozentrale		
– PREUSSAG AG	approx. 32.6[139]	761.576
– VEW AG	approx. 12.4[140]	1,000.000
– Deutsche Babcock AG	10.0	350.000
– Horten AG	approx. 10.0[141]	250.000

[137] By owning 100% of ANSELM Verwaltungsunion GmbH, which in turn holds a 12.6% stake in DLW.

[138] By owning 100% (?) of NEPTUNO Verwaltungs- und Treuhand Gesellschaft mbH, which in turn holds a 23.91% stake in Rütgerswerke.

[139] A 29.1% stake is indirectly held via GEV Gesellschaft für Energie- und Versorgungs-werte mbH as 100% subsidiary. Another 3.5% stake is indirectly held by owning 33.3% of Niedersachsen Holding GmbH, which in turn holds a 10.4% stake in PREUSSAG.

[140] By owning 28.3% of Kommunale Energie-Beteiligungsgesellschaft mbH, which in turn holds 43.84% of voting rights in VEW.

[141] By owning 20% of WestBTL Handel-Beteiligungsgesellschaft mbH, which in turn holds a 50.1% stake in Horten.

– Fuchs Petrolub AG Oel+Chemie	9.74	77.609
– Gildemeiser AG	8.53	95.243
– Fried. Krupp AG Hoesch-Krupp	7.21	1,050.144
– Gerresheimer Glas AG	4.68	113.500
– KÖLN-DÜSSELDORFER Deutsche Rheinschiffahrt AG	?[142]	16.200

Bayerische Landesbank Girozentrale

– Bürgerliches Brauhaus Ingolstadt AG	61.4[143]	3.000
– Thüga AG	29.7	290.000
– Walter Bau AG	16.9	75.000
– Isar-Amperwerke AG	approx. 12.88[144]	376.000
– Süd-Chemie AG	10.01[145]	40.600
– SGL Carbon AG	4.962	104.669
– Lufthansa AG	approx. 4.47[146]	1,908.000

Landesbank Schleswig-Holstein Girozentrale

– W. Jacobsen AG	59.03	3.630

Norddeutsche Landesbank Girozentrale

– Continental AG	16.9388	469.940
– PREUSSAG AG	approx. 3.5[147]	761.576

Südwestdeutsche Landesbank

– Bürgerliches Brauhaus Ravensburg-Lindau AG	15.83	1.365

Landwirtschaftliche Rentenbank

– BM Bäckermühlen AG	96.4	13.500

---

[142] Indirectly held via WestKD Gesellschaft für Finanzanlagen mbH, which in turn owns 89.1% of KÖLN-DÜSSELDORFER.

[143] Indirectly held via Bankhaus H. Aufhäuser.

[144] By owning 16% of Isarwerke GmbH, which in turn holds a 80.5296% stake in Isar-Amperwerke.

[145] Indirectly held via Bankhaus H. Aufhäuser.

[146] By owning 44.5% of MGL Münchener Gesellschaft für Luftfahrtwerte mbH, which in turn holds a 10.02% stake in Lufthansa.

[147] By owning 33.3% of Niedersachsen Holding GmbH, which in turn holds a 10.4% stake in PREUSSAG.

– AGAB Aktiengesellschaft für Anlagen und Beteiligungen	25.5[148]	138.557

III. Cooperative Banks (*Genossenschaftsbanken*)

DG Bank

– AGAB Aktiengesellschaft für Anlagen und Beteiligungen	24.65	138.557
– Fröhlich Bau AG	18.92	20.250
– VK Mühlen AG	approx. 14.32[149]	49.900
– Andreae-Norris Zahn AG	7.44	47.940
– SPAR Handels-Aktiengesellschaft	5.4	301.570
– PREUSSAG AG	3.5	761.576

[148] A 22.7% stake is indirectly held via LR Beteiligungsgesellschaft mbH as a 100% subsidiary.

[149] A 6.92% stake is directly held (?). Another 7.4% stake is held indirectly by owning 25% of AIH Agrar-Industrie-Holding GmbH, which in turn holds a 29.6% stake in VK Mühlen.

Appendix B

Ownership Concentration and Direct/Indirect Shareholdings of German Banks in 435 Stock Corporations Listed on the First Tier (*Amtlicher Handel*) of the German Stock Exchanges as of September 30, 1996*

Table 1: Ownership Concentration in 435 Companies: Single Largest Blockholding

Size of Largest Blockholding	$\leq 25\%$	$25\% < x \leq 50\%$	$50\% < x < 75\%$	$\geq 75\%$	unknown
Number of Companies	88	71	99	171	6

Table 2: Ownership Concentration in 435 Companies: Added Holdings of the 5 Largest Shareholders

Size of Added Blockholding	$\leq 25\%$	$25\% < x \leq 50\%$	$50\% < x < 75\%$	$\geq 75\%$	unknown
Number of Companies	27	51	90	261	6

Table 3: Banks' Shareholdings in the 377[1] Non-Financial Companies

Size	< 5%	$5\% \leq x < 10\%$	$10\% \leq x \leq 25\%$	$25\% < x \leq 50\%$	$50\% < x \leq 75\%$	> 75%
Number of Stakes (min.)	9	19	46	16	3	3
Number of Companies (min.)	5	12	35	14	3	3

Note: [1] 58 of the 435 officially quoted companies belonged to the financial sector.

Table 4: Added Banks' Shareholdings in 72 out of 377[1] Non-Financial Companies

Size	< 5%	$5\% \leq x < 10\%$	$10\% \leq x \leq 25\%$	$25\% < x \leq 50\%$	$50\% < x \leq 75\%$	> 75%
Number of Companies (min.)	4	12	30	16	7	3

Note: [1] 58 of the 435 officially quoted companies belonged to the financial sector.

*   As to sources, exclusion of bank-owned investment companies, and caveats, see Appendix A, ns. */**/***.

Table 5: Added Holdings of Banks and Insurance Companies in 72 out of 377[1] Non-Financial Companies

Size	< 5%	5% ≤ x < 10%	10% ≤ x ≤ 25%	25% < x ≤ 50%	50% < x ≤ 75%	> 75%
Number of Companies (min.)	4	7	29	20	9	3

Note: [1] 58 of the 435 officially quoted companies belonged to the financial sector.

Table 6: Number of Companies with Banks' Shareholdings ≥ 5% of the 377[1] Non-Financial Companies

	Number of Banks:			Number of Other Owners:[2]			Size of Other Holdings:[2]	
	1	2	3	1	2	3	25% < x < 50%	> 50%
Number of Companies	50	14	3	31[3]	7[4]	4	10	16

Notes: [1] 58 of the 435 officially quoted companies belonged to the financial sector.
   [2] Holdings by non-banks which exceed the highest stake of any bank.
   [3] In three cases, the largest shareholder was an insurance company.
   [4] In one case, the largest two shareholders were insurance companies.

Table 7: Number of Companies with Banks' Shareholdings ≥ 10% of the 377[1] Non-Financial Companies

	Number of Banks:			Number of Other Owners:[2]			Size of Other Holdings:[2]	
	1	2	3	1	2	3	25% < x < 50%	> 50%
Number of Companies	43	11	1	27	3	1	7	11

Notes: [1] 58 of the 435 officially quoted companies belonged to the financial sector.
   [2] Holdings by non-banks which exceed the highest stake of any bank.

Table 8: Banks' Shareholdings in the 53 Non-Financial Stock Corporations Among the 100[1] Largest German Enterprises as of 1994[2]

No.	Name	Banks' Holdings as a Percentage of Voting Rights	Other Holdings $\geq$ 5% as a Percentage of Voting Rights
2	Daimler-Benz AG	24.4	12.96
11	Thyssen AG	5.0	8.58//5.0[3]
14	Hoechst AG	2.04	24.5
16	Bayerische Motorenwerke AG	5.01	17.9//17//13.2
18	Deutsche Lufthansa AG	4.47//4.47	35.68
19	PREUSSAG AG	32.6//3.5//3.5//3.1	approx. 5
20	Karstadt AG	10.3//10.0	29.4
21	VIAG AG	5.25//5.03	32.63
22	Friedrich Krupp AG	7.21	51.6
29	MAN AG	9.02	9.02//9.02//9.02[4]
37	AGIV Aktiengesellschaft für Industrie und Verkehrswesen	48.7	10.01//10.01
38	Philipp Holzmann AG	25.83//10.0	34.9[5]
40	Deutsche Babcock AG	10.0//approx. 5.0	
44	VEW AG	12.4//3.875	21.1/10.3//9.1//6.8[6]
55	Linde AG	10.2//10.01	13.09[7]
57	Continental AG	16.9388//10.25//6.5	5.03[8]
60	Degussa AG	10.6	17//10.6[9]//3.92
69	SPAR Handels-AG	5.4	approx. 27.25//25.0001//14.7
70	Bilfinger + Berger Bauaktiengesellschaft	25.1	
94	Buderus AG	13.7//11.1	14.76

Notes:
[1] The top 100 list includes 19 financial companies. 15 of which were structured as a stock corporation.
[2] Ranking of companies is according to the *Monopolkommission* (German Monopolies Commission) 'Unterrichtung durch die Bundesregierung: Elftes Hauptgutachten der Monopolkommission' (Bundestags-Drucksache 13/5309, 19.7.1996, 240-4) and is based on *Wertschöpfung* (surplus adjusted for certain items).
[3] Allianz AG.
[4] Allianz AG//Allianz Lebensversicherungs-AG//Münchener Rückversicherungs-Gesellschaft AG.
[5] RWE AG.
[6] Allianz-Lebensversicherungs-AG.
[7] Allianz AG.
[8] Allianz AG.
[9] Münchener Rückversicherungs-Gesellschaft AG.

Table 9: Banks' Shareholdings in Non-Financial Companies Included in the DAX 30 Index as of September 30, 1996[1]

Name	Banks' Holdings as a Percentage of Voting Rights	Other Holdings $\geq$ 5% as a Percentage of Voting Rights
Bayerische Motorenwerke AG	5.01	17.9//17//13.2
Daimler-Benz AG	24. 4	12.96
Degussa AG	10.6	17//10.6[2]//3.92
Deutsche Lufthansa AG	4.47//4.47	35.68
Hoechst AG	2.04	24.5
Karstadt AG	10.3//10.0	29.4
Linde AG	10.2//10.01	13.09[3]
MAN AG	9.02	9.02//9.02//9.02[4]
Metallgesellschaft	14.2//13.09	20.2//7.33//4.014[5]
PREUSSAG AG	32.6//3.5//3.5//3.1	approx. 5
Thyssen AG	5.0	8.58//5.0[6]
VIAG AG	5.25//5.03	32.63

Notes: [1] As of September 30, 1996, the DAX 30 Index included:
23 non-financial companies: BASF, Bayer, BWM, Daimler-Benz, Degussa, Henkel, Hoechst, Karstadt, Linde, Lufthansa, Metallgesellschaft, MAN, Mannesmann, Metro, Preussag, RWE, Schering, Siemens, Thyssen, VEBA, VIAG, VW.
7 financial companies: Allianz, Bayerische HYPO-Bank, Bayerische Vereinsbank, Commerzbank, Deutsche Bank, Dresdner Bank, Münchener Rückversicherung.
[2] Münchener Rückversicherungs-Gesellschaft AG.
[3] Allianz AG.
[4] Allianz AG//Allianz Lebensversicherungs-AG//Münchener Rückversicherungs-Gesellschaft AG.
[5] Allianz AG.
[6] Allianz AG.

German Banks and Corporate Governance: A Critical View*

EKKEHARD WENGER and CHRISTOPH KASERER, Würzburg

It is the aim of this paper to take issue with the widespread—but erroneous—belief that blockholdings—mainly by banks—in large German companies are suited to mitigate the free-rider problem of corporate control. In reality, managers of large German banks are not forced to pursue a value-maximizing investment policy because they are sheltered from capital market pressures by a dense network of cross-holdings and underdeveloped disclosure obligations. Therefore, the first part of the paper shows how far-reaching the German system of mutual shareholdings is. In the second part, newly introduced stock option programs are analyzed. The findings suggest that there is a great danger of collusion among managers tied together by a system of cross-holdings. In the final part of the paper, the impact of bank control on the economic performance of industrial companies is analyzed. By measuring bank control in terms of long-run equity holdings of the financial sector, we show that there is a significant difference between bank-dominated companies and a control group in terms of total shareholder returns.

Contents

* Our special thanks go to Richard Rösener for his valuable assistance regarding the empirical part of the paper.

b.   The Treynor Ratio as a Measure of Risk-Adjusted Performance
E.   Conclusion
References

Figures

Tables

A. Introduction

It is widely known that the separation of ownership and control specific to all publicly traded companies is the source of a variety of agency problems.[1] These problems can be mitigated as far as shareholders are in a position to control and punish corporate management. For this purpose they can rely on internal as well as external control mechanisms. Internal control is exerted mainly through the supervisory board[2], while capital markets are supposed to provide external control. Of course, the effectiveness of these control mechanisms depends crucially on the institutional and legal environment. As far as legal rules governing internal control activities in Germany are concerned, shareholders are virtually unprotected. German board members enjoy far-reaching immunity from damage claims because shareholders are not entitled to sue for damages unless they hold an equity stake of at least 10%. For private shareholders this threshold is usually prohibitive; corporate shareholdings, on the other hand, cannot be

---

[1] The seminal paper of Jensen/Meckling (1976) marks the beginning of a comprehensive academic discussion on these issues.

[2] Foreign readers should note that Germany has a two-tier board system. According to § 111 Aktiengesetz (Stock Corporation Act), supervisory board members are obliged to control the board of executive directors (or "management board").

mobilized against the very board members who control them.[3] If one looks at internal control incentives, the compensation system for supervisory board members should be of special interest. As Knoll/Knoesel/Probst (1997) have shown, the typical German supervisory board member earned about DM 30,000 in 1993 with no significant dependence of his compensation on the share price performance.[4] Therefore, one should not expect internal control mechanisms to work very well in Germany. The chain of shocking losses that became public during the nineties was certainly more than an unfortunate accident. The cases of Metallgesellschaft, Daimler Benz, Klöckner-Humboldt-Deutz, Jürgen Schneider, and so forth, truly justify the following comment of a leading business newspaper: *"The control exercised by bankers, auditors, and Germany's two-tier board system has proven woefully inadequate."*[5]

It should be noted that the failure of internal control systems has been documented for other countries, too. Jensen (1993) reports an opportunity loss on R&D investments and capital expenditures of General Motors during the eighties exceeding $100 billion. He concludes " . . . *that the infrequency with which large corporate organizations restructure or redirect themselves solely on the basis of the internal control mechanisms in the absence of crises in the product, factor, or capital markets or the regulatory sector is strong testimony to the inadequacy of these control mechanisms."*[6] One reason for the weakness of internal control systems might be that they are prone to the same agency conflicts as the relationship between shareholders and management. Therefore, we would expect that their efficiency finally depends on the effectiveness of outside pressures. As already mentioned, these pressures should come primarily from the capital markets.[7]

---

[3] A more detailed description of the difficulties to sue board members in Germany can be found in Wenger/Kaserer (1998: 67 et seq.). Especially interesting in this regard is the case of Metallgesellschaft, where supervisory board members had to bear no consequences although a lack of control became evident; cf. Wenger/Kaserer (1998: 42 et seq.) and Wenger (1996a). After harsh critique of the liability rules in academic and non-academic circles, the ministry of justice has made a proposal to give minorities the right to sue for damages if they hold shares with a par value of at least DM 2 million; the proposal is still pending in the federal parliament.

[4] They studied 125 publicly quoted corporations over a period of five years from 1989 to 1993. It is interesting in this regard that Knoll/Knoesel/Probst (1997) even found a negative— although not significant—correlation between supervisory board compensation in large corporations and share price return.

[5] *Financial Times* May 29, 1996, 14. In all these cases German banks played a major role as stockholders and supervisors. For a more detailed description of the case of Metallgesellschaft and Daimler Benz, cf. Wenger/Kaserer (1998: 42 et seq.) and Wenger (1996a).

[6] Jensen (1993: 854).

[7] Obviously, pressures by product and factor markets should also be taken into account, even though it can take a very long time before incapable management is forced to resign solely because of crises in product and/or factor markets.

Even in countries where capital markets traditionally play an important role —as in the U.S.—their functioning becomes more and more threatened by several legal rules which Jensen (1991) assumes to be the result of *"politics of finance"*. Therefore, some authors are asking whether the U.S. should adopt German-type solutions with a more important role of banks in corporate governance.[8] Indeed, in academic circles in the English-speaking world, it is conventional wisdom that in Germany the agency problems arising from the separation of ownership and control are much less important than in the U.K. or U.S.[9], because in most industrial companies there are large blockholders, especially banks, which are toughly monitoring the management of the companies in their portfolio.[10] This conventional wisdom, however, is the result of a fundamental misunderstanding. As we have already pointed out, internal control mechanisms can only be supposed to work if agency problems are mitigated by outside pressures. Therefore, corporate control by banks can only be expected to be effective if controlling bank managers are themselves controlled by the ultimate residual claimants, i.e., private shareholders. It is hard to believe that the latter is true of Germany, since German banks and insurance and industrial companies are sheltered from capital market pressures through a dense network of equity cross-holdings.[11]

These cross-holdings are not the only pillar upon which the shelter from active capital market oversight is established. The lack of disclosure obligations and the proxy voting system are other important devices for the immunization

---

[8] Cf., e.g., Roe (1990), Grundfest (1990).

[9] *America's Fascination with German Corporate Governance* is the title of a recent article of Rock (1995).

[10] A notable exception in this regard is the paper of La Porta et al. (1996). According to their comprehensive empirical study of 49 countries, concentrated corporate ownership is negatively related to investor protection. We definitely agree.

[11] The former CEO and current chairman of the supervisory board of Deutsche Bank can be quoted as a crown witness for this purpose of cross-holdings. In an interview given to a leading German magazine, Hilmar Kopper was confronted with a question regarding his membership in the supervisory boards of numerous big corporations: *"Don't you feel overburdened from time to time by having to control so many companies?"* He answered: *"I do not control these firms. There can be no control. This claim cannot be satisfied"* (Translated by the authors; for the original quotation, see *Der Spiegel* July 29, 1996, 62 et seq.). Similar statements of Mr. Kopper can be found in other sources. According to him, *"It makes no difference for a company if we hold a large block of shares.... We are a plain and quiet shareholder and that is the reason why we are so welcome."* (Translated by the authors from *Finanz und Wirtschaft* September 25, 1993, 17), Even more instructive is how Kopper explains the reason why German banks hold equity stakes and why they participated in the defense of Continental AG, a leading tiremaker, against a (finally thwarted) hostile takeover attempt by Pirelli, an Italian competitor. In an authorized interview with Euromoney, Kopper is quoted as follows: *"We had 5%... of Conti... We said to Leopoldo Pirelli that we would not dispose of our 5% unless the management of Conti asked us to, and that until then we would keep it in the interest of Conti's management (!!)."* (*Euromoney* January 1994, 44).

against external control systems.[12] However, the second part of this paper is only focused on a documentation of how external control mechanisms in Germany are undermined by a dense network of equity cross-holdings. Furthermore, one would expect this shelter to be used by management to accumulate private benefits. This is all the easier the more complex and obscure the underlying structures and mechanisms are. As is pointed out in the third part of the paper, the new rhetoric of "shareholder value", which nowadays has spilled over even into corporate Germany, has created a new and not yet understood opportunity to plunder private shareholders: stock option programs enacted by several companies during the last year under the banner of "shareholder value" provide convincing evidence that corporate control by banks and other non-private shareholders promotes underhanded exploitation of the ultimate residual claimants in favor of corporate management. Finally, the control efficiency of the German banking system will be subjected to an empirical test. According to our results, the conventional wisdom that corporate control by German banks is a valuable service to the economy does not hold—at least not from the perspective of shareholders who invest in companies allegedly under bank control.

B. Cross-Holdings in Germany

I. The Status Quo

The main feature of the German system of corporate control is a network of mutual shareholdings[13] financed with retained earnings or coordinated capital increases serving the sole purpose of exchanging equity among colluding companies. This state of affairs has been fostered by at least two institutional factors. First, there are only minor legal obstacles regarding the accumulation of influential holdings in public corporations by banks, mutual funds, insurance companies, or any other financial, commercial, or industrial firms in Germany.[14] This is also true for cross-holdings between two or more companies. According to § 328

---

[12] For a detailed description of these immunization mechanisms, cf. Wenger/Kaserer (1998: 63 et seq.), Wenger (1992), Baums (1996), and Baums/Fraune (1995). For a comprehensive overview of the German corporate governance system, see also Schmidt et al. (1997).

[13] On the German ownership structure, see also Prigge (this volume Ch. 12: Sec: B.II.).

[14] In this regard two legal rules have to be mentioned. First, § 8a Gesetz über Kapitalanlagegesellschaften (Investment Company Act) prohibits an investment company from acquiring more than 10% of the voting rights of a stock company. Second, insurance companies have to observe certain investment restrictions enumerated in §§ 54 and 54a Versicherungsaufsichtsgesetz (Insurance Supervision Law). This law forbids an insurance company to hold more than 10% of the equity of a company. But this restriction is only valid for those parts of the assets representing the actuarial obligations of the insurance company (*gebundenes Vermögen*). Therefore the limit of 10% is meaningless.

Aktiengesetz, the only restriction in German company law[15] applies to the case of two corporations holding more than 25% of each other's stock; according to this paragraph, it is forbidden to exercise more than 25% of the votes "in both directions". The intention is to prevent cross-holdings that curtail the rights of shareholders in favor of management.[16] The aforementioned provision, however, evidently fails to achieve its purpose. Apart from the fact that a block of 25% is often sufficient to dominate a shareholder meeting of a widely held public corporation,[17] the provision is completely ineffective if more than two companies establish cross-holdings amongst each other. Even if only three companies collude, 50% of the voting rights of each of the three companies could be controlled by the other two companies without violating the law.

Second, the German co-determination system has undoubtedly supported the emergence of cross-holdings. Employees tend to collude with management in this regard because they have a strong bias against distributing a company's profits and any other kind of downsizing.[18] As far as the payout policy of a company is concerned, cross-holdings are nothing else than a hidden increase of retained earnings. If two companies with equal profits hold 25% of each other's stock, a payout ratio of 60% means that effectively only 45% of the profits are paid out to external shareholders. Furthermore, by preventing the company from being taken over, cross-holdings allow employees to preserve their claims to the company's cash flows. Therefore, the opening of German supervisory boards to employees' representatives as required by various co-determination laws was an important support for management in search of shelters against capital market pressures.

It is very difficult for an insider and impossible for an outsider to get a complete picture of the network of cross-holdings among large German corporations. If a comprehensive measure is needed, one has to compare the market value of all domestic corporations quoted on a German stock exchange before and after correcting for the value of all shares owned by other listed corporations

[15] Another potential obstacle is the German Anti-Trust Act (*Gesetz gegen Wettbewerbsbeschränkungen*). According to § 23 of the Anti-Trust Act, the acquisition of a stake of at least 25% has to be reported to the anti-trust office if aggregate turnover amounts to at least DM 500 million. The anti-trust office can prohibit the acquisition if it may lead to a market-dominating position of the combined companies.

[16] This statement could be found in parliamentary documents on the history of the German Stock Corporation Act; see Kropff (1965: 35).

[17] According to Baums/Fraune (1995: 40), the average participation rate on the shareholder meetings of the 24 largest widely held German stock corporations in 1992 was 58.05%. Furthermore, as soon as a large bank is involved in a cross-holding scheme, a block of 25% can be topped up with proxy votes averaging 60.95% of the voting rights present at the meeting. Thus, the average share of voting rights exercised by banks on the shareholder meetings of widely held corporations amounts to 84.09%; cf. Baums/Fraune (1995: 37).

[18] Cf. Wenger (1986).

themselves. The corrected market capitalization may be taken as a measure of the amount of capital that is effectively invested in the stock market. Prowse (1994) reported that in 1985 the market capitalization of listed German corporations would have been less than half as high if corrected for cross-holdings. Comparing this finding to other important industrialized countries leads to the result that only Japan has comparably sizable cross-holdings, as can be seen from Table 1.

Table 1:   Market Capitalization of Publicly Quoted Domestic Companies
in Percent of GDP, 1985

	U.S.	U.K.	Japan	Germany
Gross	51	90	71	29
Net of Cross-Holdings	48	81	37	14

Source: Prowse (1994: 30).

We cannot assess the reliability of Prowse's estimation; he has relied on data from Borio (1990) and other unmentioned sources. For this reason and also because this estimate is now more than ten years old, we have done our own calculations. For this purpose we examined cross-holdings among listed domestic companies as they existed on December 31, 1994.[19] The main problem of such a research program is that most German companies have issued bearer shares only. Hence, shareholders are unknown unless disclosure rules of the Securities Dealing Act (*Wertpapierhandelsgesetz*) apply. According to § 21 Wertpapierhandelsgesetz, holdings of at least 5% of a listed company have to be reported.[20] However, there are several ways to bypass this legal rule.[21] One of

---

[19] Therefore all cross-holdings between domestic and foreign companies are neglected. Actually this should not cause a significant estimation error, although the amount of such international cross-holdings has become more important in the last years. Furthermore, strong ties between the Swiss and the German insurance industry have existed for a long time.

[20] It should be mentioned that before the Securities Dealing Act became effective in 1995, the threshold had been 25% as stated in § 21 Aktiengesetz. This is a good example of the bias of German company law in favor of the "cross-holding society". A first major inroad was made by court rulings initiated by one of the authors in the early nineties; three of the largest German corporations, Allianz Holding, Siemens, and Münchener Rückversicherung, were forced to disclose all shareholdings with a market value of at least DM 100 million.

[21] § 23 Wertpapierhandelsgesetz contains several important exceptions from the obligation to disclose stakes of 5% and more. Companies belonging to the financial sector can hold up to 5% of another company's shares, which are not counted under the 5% disclosure rule if certain conditions are met. Among the requirements are that no influence on the portfolio company is intended, and that a newly established government agency grants a general permission that stakes of up to 5% need not to be counted. Such permission, which is routinely granted upon

them is pooling the stakes of several companies. For this purpose a holding company has to be set up in which none of the founding corporations has a stake of more than 50%. As a consequence, the asset-holding company is not legally classified as a controlled company; therefore, disclosure rules do not require that its assets be proportionally allocated to the parent companies. As long as this asset-holding company is—as usual—not quoted on a stock exchange, the reporting provisions of the Security Dealing Act are ineffective. Furthermore, if the holding company has issued bearer shares only, it is impossible to find out its owners. Although we evaluated all available sources—i.e., not only the announcements required by § 21 Wertpapierhandelsgesetz, but also the outcome of lawsuits, voluntary disclosure by single companies, participation lists of stockholder meetings, or lists of registered shares—we have to strongly emphasize that our estimation can only be regarded as a lower boundary of the actual size of cross-holdings because of the reporting limit of 5% and the various methods to bypass it.

At the end of 1994, the market capitalization of all domestic listed companies amounted to DM 803 billion.[22] The market value of stock holdings in listed companies belonging to the largest German insurance company alone, Allianz AG Holding, amounted to nearly DM 40 billion or 5% of the total stock exchange capitalization at this time. The leading German bank, Deutsche Bank AG, held stocks of listed companies with a market value of nearly DM 28 billion or 3.4% of stock market capitalization.[23] Because of the extraordinary complexity of the whole system of cross-holdings, it is actually impossible to condense it in one picture. Nevertheless, for the sole purpose of giving an optical idea of the density of existing cross-holding, we have summarized our findings in Figure 1.

Summing up all identified cross-holdings among domestic listed companies leads to the result that the net market value of all domestic companies amounts to 73% of the gross market capitalization.[24] As mentioned above, this number is only an upper limit of the "net" market capitalization. Preliminary evidence that the amount of undetected holdings may be rather high can be concluded from voluntary disclosure of one of the top ten insurance companies during a stockholder meeting in October 1995. After having been questioned by one of the authors, Württembergische AG Versicherungs-Beteiligungsgesellschaft disclosed

application, makes it possible to hold stakes of 10% minus one share without any legal duty to disclose them.

[22] This figure, as well as the following, is based on our own calculations. For a more detailed analysis, see Wenger (1996c: Ch. 3).

[23] For a more detailed documentation of the German system of cross-holdings, cf. Wenger/Kaserer (1998: 53 et seq.).

[24] It should be kept in mind that the gross market capitalization measured as percentage of GDP is already very low in Germany compared to other industrialized countries. Cf. Wenger/Kaserer (1998: 64).

Figure 1: Network of Cross-Holdings Among Large German Stock Corporations

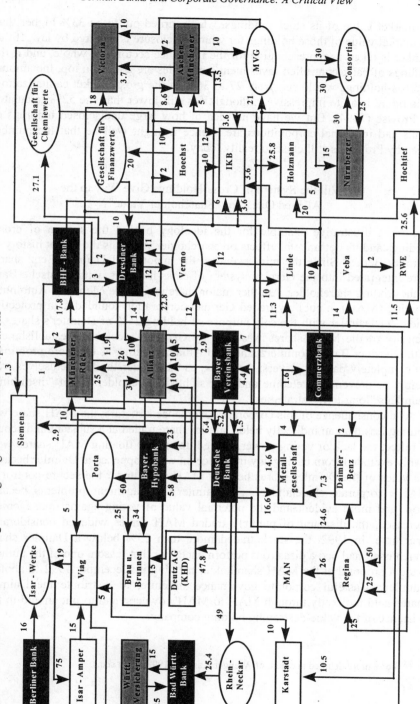

the market value of its stock holdings, which turned out to be 33% higher than the market value of those holdings for which disclosure is required by law. If this number is taken as representative for the insurance sector as a whole, and if the holdings of bank-controlled investment companies are added on top, the amount of cross-holdings would rise from 27 to 36% of the gross market capitalization. This figure is quite impressive, although it is still lower than the 52% calculated by Prowse (1994). But we have no idea of how large undisclosed holdings of banks and industrial corporations are. Hence it might well be that the number given by Prowse is still close to reality today.

II. Will the System of Cross-Holdings Give Way to the Alleged Quest for "Shareholder Value"?

The most illustrative example for the ideology behind the system of cross-holdings and its detrimental effects on shareholder wealth is the recent history of Daimler Benz.[25] Since the mid-seventies, the majority of Daimler Benz shares were integrated into the German system of cross-holdings, with Deutsche Bank as the leading shareholder. Another major shareholder was Mercedes Automobil Holding (MAH), a publicly traded German corporation founded as a protective shield for Daimler with the sole purpose of holding 25% of Daimler's shares. A majority of the MAH shares was held by Germany's corporate establishment, with Dresdner Bank, Commerzbank, and Allianz Holding as the more prominent yet completely passive players; their task, as they understood it themselves, was simply to prevent unwelcome and shortsighted shareholders from "disturbing" Daimler's "long-term" strategies.

As a consequence of this corporate governance structure, the MAH share was nothing less than an indirectly held Daimler share traded at a substantial discount to reflect the lack of voting power. Indeed, the freely floating MAH shares were firmly excluded from having any influence on what happened at Daimler because the votes of the Daimler shares held by MAH were under the secure control of MAH's corporate shareholders. As Daimler's management problems became more and more evident and the potential value of voting against management increased, the discount of publicly traded MAH shares widened considerably over time. In 1992, the stock traded more than 25% below a Daimler share, which itself had had a disastrous performance. For that reason, one of the authors made a proposal at the MAH shareholder meeting in December 1992 to abolish Daimler's wasteful corporate governance structure, to distribute the Daimler shares held indirectly through MAH to MAH's owners, and to put an end to the existence of the value-destroying holding company.

---

[25] For a more detailed account, cf. Wenger/Kaserer (1998: 44 et seq.).

What followed was an unprecedented example of unintended cabaret. MAH's management, which was nothing other than an appendix of Daimler's corporate governance structure, was strongly opposed to the proposals, which in their opinion came from an "academic horror cabinet".[26] MAH's existence was defended on the ground that "every shareholder knew what he had to expect when he bought MAH shares: a company established to serve a well-defined purpose." Accordingly, MAH still had "to protect the independence" of Daimler and should not be managed in order "to create short-term profits for shareholders". The board members emphasized that they were "*committed to a long-term strategy, not to quotations on the stock exchange. . . . A good business policy is a long-term policy. We know that the thinking of the stock market is different. . . . We know that we cannot convince all shareholders; we are satisfied if we can convince those who want to achieve more than the 'fast buck*[27]." After all these compelling arguments, the line of reasoning adopted by MAH's directors ended with a remarkable invention that truly deserves to be labeled as the "inverted shareholder value principle": "*We have to remind you that new shareholders should have the opportunity to participate in Daimler's future by paying an attractively low share price. Moreover, we feel permitted to ask why our long-term shareholders should be deprived of a favorable opportunity to buy more shares.* "

It is indeed true that a long-term shareholder who sticks to his company and buys more and more stocks at continuously declining prices will end up with average acquisition costs which are favorably low. Between December 1992 and March 1993, however, the combined management of Daimler and MAH must somehow have abandoned its commitment to the inverted shareholder value principle. On April 2, 1993, Daimler Benz announced that MAH would soon cease to exist; within minutes, the discount on the MAH shares had almost vanished because their exchange into Daimler shares at a ratio of 1:1 was now only a matter of one year pending the required legal procedures. Within less than four months, the unsound grabbing for the fast buck had turned into a sufficiently slow long-term strategy—so slow that even a member of the supervisory board could exploit the opportunity to buy into MAH shares at favorably low prices.[28]

---

[26] All quotes referring to the MAH case are translations from the management's report to the shareholder meeting on December 18, 1992. The report has been published in Fonk (1993).

[27] In German: "*schnelle Mark*".

[28] Franz Steinkühler, president of the influential labor union IG-Metall and a worker representative sitting on Daimler's supervisory board as required by German codetermination laws, later had to resign when his insider trades accidentally became known to the public. The behavior of MAH's stock price and its trading volume support the conclusion that Steinkühler's activities were only the tip of the iceberg; but as Germany had no legal ban on insider trading at that time, no other insider who had traded in MAH shares has been identified. Internal sources at Daimler, however, have at least admitted that Daimler had to announce the exchange of MAH

Why Daimler suddenly wanted to get rid of MAH in early 1993 is still not fully clear. The intended listing on the New York stock exchange, which was accomplished in autumn of 1993, might have been one reason; having disappointed domestic shareholders for years and suffering from a continuous cash drain, Daimler felt the need to tap the U.S. capital market before long.

Whatever the true reasons might have been, it must have dawned even on Daimler's management that U.S. investors would not scramble for the shares of a company governed by the inverted principle of shareholder value. Indeed, within two years and a new CEO, Daimler's management began to profess a strong and uninverted commitment to "shareholder value"[29] which had suddenly become fashionable among German executives. The pretended quest for shareholder value is hardly compatible with public professions that companies need to be shielded against short-sighted shareholders who fail to understand the benefits of low purchase prices; as a consequence, open support for the system of cross-holdings has become outmoded, and even Deutsche Bank, meanwhile also under a new CEO, has begun to regret "frozen shareholdings" and to complain about tax rules preventing their sale.[30]

What seems to be more important is the fact that in spite of the tax rules, at least some cross-holdings have been considerably reduced or even sold in the recent past.[31] Superficial observers, therefore, may feel induced to bid "farewell to Germany, Inc."[32] Such an assessment, however, would be premature. The reduction or sale of larger stakes may just be a natural reaction to increased capital requirements in the banking sector and stricter disclosure rules for shareholdings in listed companies. The protective effects of a multilateral network of cross-holdings can easily be maintained if larger stakes of 10 or 25% are substituted by correspondingly more and smaller stakes just below the new disclosure limit of 5%. Such tendencies are reinforced by the still increasing involvement of the life insurance industry in the German stock market. A special tax privilege for life insurance policies drives huge amounts of money into the coffers of insurance companies. If only a fraction of this money is invested into the German stock market, it is only a matter of time until all widely held companies can be controlled by means of insurance money. As insurance companies are heavily

---

stocks two months earlier than originally planned because of abnormal activities in the stock market which must have been due to insider trading.

[29] How serious this was may be concluded from the fact that the new CEO publicly announced he would stop the talk on shareholder value after he had a less than successful clash with the work council and the union on sick pay; cf. *Wirtschaftswoche* May 15, 1997, 112.

[30] Even before he was appointed as new CEO of Deutsche Bank, Mr. Breuer complained about "*festgefrorenen Beteiligungsbesitz*", cf. *Frankfurter Allgemeine Zeitung* May 10, 1996, 27.

[31] An important example is Germany's leading chain store, Karstadt, where Deutsche Bank and Commerzbank's former holdings of 25% each have been sold step by step until August 1997.

[32] "Abschied von der Deutschland AG?" (*Wirtschaftsdienst* 77 (1997) 251 et seq.).

intertwined among themselves and with the banking sector, there is no reason to believe that German companies will soon be exposed to the forces of an open capital market. Unless the tax privilege for life insurance policies is abolished, the German stock market will remain firmly under the control of corporate bureaucrats.[33]

C. Stock Option Plans and the Failure of Corporate Control

I. Preliminary Reflections

From a theoretical point of view, it is widely accepted that pecuniary incentives should be set in order to induce management to act in the best interest of shareholders. Since the latter is closely linked to the maximization of the company's market value, management compensation should depend at least partially on the performance of the share price. Management, however, is not responsible for the stock's performance as far as the latter reflects general conditions in the market; consequently, compensation should depend on share returns adjusted for factors beyond management's control. As long as a company's shares are listed on a stock exchange, the relevant share returns can be measured easily by comparing their stock price return with a benchmark capturing "market factors" beyond management's control. It is of secondary importance in this regard whether a portfolio of stocks with comparable market capitalization, a comprehensive market index, or an industry-specific index is used as a benchmark. The main point is that stock options are designed in a manner to ensure that management is only rewarded for stock price increases in excess of market returns.[34]

As Angel/McCabe (1996) report, U.S. firms do not use this kind of market-adjusted stock option; as a possible explanation, they point to biased accounting rules which give management a strong incentive not to adjust the exercise price to market movements since such an adjustment would result in a higher reported expense for management compensation holding the market value of stock options constant.[35] If this is an empirically relevant explanation of the non-existence of market-adjusted stock option plans, two remarks should be made. First, the company could set the exercise price of the stock option at a level which exceeds the stock price at the date of issue by a factor derived from the expected rate of return of the relevant market index until maturity. Therefore, if the company does not use market-adjusted options, it should issue at least deep out of the money options. Second, in Germany there are no special accounting and

---

[33] Cf. Wenger (1997: 258).

[34] Cf. Angel/McCabe (1996). For a summary of the executive compensation debate, cf. Jarrell (1993).

[35] Cf. Angel/McCabe (1996: 11 et seq.).

disclosure rules for stock options.[36] Hence, the objection raised in the U.S. against market-adjusted stock options does not make sense in Germany. Therefore, an executive compensation plan based on stock options should be expected to be market-adjusted as long as incentive effects are its primary goal.

An incentive-driven stock option plan should be subject to another adjustment, too. As revenues from stock options are dependent on stock prices, management has the incentive to retain earnings, thereby increasing the value of the stock. A well-designed stock option plan should therefore be based on stock returns, including dividends and subscription rights, or should require a pre-specified dividend policy.

It is well-known that in the U.S., stock options are widely used as an incentive mechanism for executives. About 80% of the largest 500 U.S. firms have such plans.[37] Nevertheless, the pay-performance relationship for U.S. firms should not be overstated. As Jensen/Murphy (1990) found out in an empirical study of the compensation schemes of more than 2,000 CEOs over the last five decades, there is on average a $3.25 wealth change for CEOs for every $1,000 change in shareholder wealth.[38] Furthermore, this relationship is less strong for large companies than for small and has declined over the last five decades. The authors argue that the lack of a strong pay-performance relationship for CEOs in the U.S. might be due to political forces, which limit large payoffs for exceptional performance. Although this might be one explanation, the dependence of top managers' compensation schemes on internal corporate control systems should be taken into account, too. We have already mentioned Jensen (1993) as a crown witness for the lack of effectiveness of these control systems in the U.S. Therefore, compensation schemes of CEOs in the U.S. should be expected to be biased against incentive compatibility wherever boards are not under tight outside control.[39] From this perspective it is hard to imagine that stock option programs in the U.S. are not used as a device for the enrichment of colluding directors. Although as foreign observers we are not familiar with the details of compensation structures in publicly held U.S. corporations, our view is consistent with the structure of most U.S. stock option programs, which offer generous awards even for managers who fail to beat the market. Hence, in order to emphasize that our critique of the structure of board compensation in Germany is by no means confined to this country, we conclude these few remarks with the following statement of a former

---

[36] Even the exercise of stock options by executives does not need to be disclosed.

[37] Cf. Kohler (1997: 249). In the U.K. this ratio is about 30%.

[38] According to Jensen/Murphy (1990: 233), only $0.15 of CEO's wealth increase for every $1,000 shareholder wealth increase is due to stock options.

[39] It is interesting in this regard that Boyd (1994) found out in a sample of 193 publicly held U.S. firms that management compensation is negatively correlated with the intensity of board control.

member of the U.S. corporate establishment: "*It is a sad commentary on the intellectual vigor and financial discipline of the U.S. business community that so many corporate executives are receiving entrepreneurs' rewards for doing bureaucrats' jobs.*"[40]

II. The Situation in Germany

It is not our goal to discuss whether the compensation schemes for executives implemented in U.S. firms are at a socially desirable level. The aim of this chapter is rather to give an overview of the stock option programs initiated in Germany during the last year from a corporate governance point of view. Apart from a few less important cases which did not attract public attention[41], stock options were almost non-existent in Germany until the year 1996. The first important stock option programs were on the agenda of the stockholder meetings of Daimler Benz AG and Deutsche Bank AG in 1996. They stirred up a public debate among academics, corporate representatives, and the business press.[42] Among other leading German companies included in the main stock index DAX, the car maker Volkswagen AG and the chemical company Henkel KGaA had option programs on the agenda of their stockholder meetings in 1997. In the same year, Daimler Benz's management sought an authorization to increase the volume of the option plan passed in 1996.

Of course, it cannot be seen as an accident that the introduction of stock option plans is occurring simultaneously with a smooth but fundamental change in corporate Germany. As corporations become more and more intertwined with international capital markets, the ongoing disregard of private shareholder interests is becoming increasingly difficult for German companies. Especially Anglo-American investors are strongly asking for more disclosure and shareholder wealth orientation. Therefore, several companies have begun to prepare their annual reports according to the more informative IAS or GAAP standards. At the same time, some of them planned the introduction of executive compensation schemes depending on stock price performance. During all the years before, the

---

[40] Mason (1988: 72).

[41] Shareholders of the software company SAP AG decided to introduce a stock option program as early as 1994. On the basis of this program, convertible bonds were issued in 1996. It should be noted, however, that they cannot be subscribed by members of the board. The program is a compensation instrument for all employees of the company. Moreover, the SAP case is peculiar insofar as members of the board still hold a majority of SAP's voting stock; consequently, one would expect the incentive problems at the top level to be of minor importance. Therefore, the stock option program of SAP is neglected in the following.

[42] Cf. among others Baums (1997), Menichetti (1996), Kohler (1997), and Lutter (1997). For a critical review of these programs, cf. Wenger (1998).

salary of German executives was only related to performance measures such as accounting profits or dividends, if there was any relation to performance at all.

But option programs are still not very well understood; as long as management can make shareholders believe that stock options promote "shareholder value", nearly everything is possible. Especially in those companies where private shareholder interests are staved off through equity holdings of other large corporations or significant proxy voting by banks, stock option programs approved by shareholder meetings have had more to do with an outrageous exploitation of stockholders in favor of management than with the goal of introducing more incentive compatibility into executive compensation. Obviously, with a well-functioning internal control system, such compensation systems could not have been introduced. In regard to what has been said about corporate control in Germany in the preceding chapters, however, one should not be surprised that internal control systems are prone to collusion among management. Therefore, the less a company is controlled by a private shareholder, the more such a complex and intransparent compensation mechanism like a stock option program will be abused for management's own advantage.[43] This temptation is strengthened by the lack of disclosure obligations regarding option-related executive compensation. Therefore, we would expect stock option programs to be incentive-compatible in companies with influential private shareholders. In companies that are sheltered from capital market oversight, however, stock option programs are expected to be ill-designed; if the latter is true, their sole or main purpose is to disguise an increase in management compensation regardless of any incentive effects. Although the number of cases is still too small to draw far-reaching conclusions, deeper analysis of the following examples seems to support our hypothesis.

1. Stock Options as an Instrument to Exploit Private Shareholders

Before portraying the characteristics of German stock option programs, it should be noted that the German Stock Corporation Act gives a company only the right to issue convertible bonds or bundles of bonds and warrants. "Naked options" are not allowed[44] because the spirit of the law is opposed to "excessive speculation", whatever this means. German stock option programs, therefore, always consist of bonds which management has to buy. But this restriction is virtually meaningless as long as companies are allowed to introduce option programs with an arbitrarily low percentage of their value attributable to the bond component. It may well be, however, that the courts will finally declare such programs to bypass the law

---

[43] Cf. on this point Wenger (1997, 1998).

[44] At the time this paper was written, however, a draft of the German company law was discussed that would allow corporations to issue "naked" stock options.

illegal. The most outrageous stock option programs were conceived by Deutsche Bank AG, Daimler Benz AG, and Volkswagen AG. These companies are a part of the German corporate establishment and are sheltered from capital market pressures because of their mere size and the existing shareholder structure.[45] Their stock option plans are so ill-designed that all the companies have been and still are the target of legal action brought forward by one of the authors.

a. The Case of Deutsche Bank

The shareholder meeting of Deutsche Bank in 1996 authorized the board of executive directors to issue stock options within a five-year period. For every single issue, management has to obtain the consent of the supervisory board; but in the case of Deutsche Bank this is only a pro-forma restriction.[46] According to the authorization, about 200 top managers will be entitled to subscribe to a bond with a maturity of ten years and a total volume of DM 40 million. The interest rate on this bond is supposed to be near the market rate. For every DM 5 bond par value, the subscriber has the right to buy one Deutsche Bank stock with a par value of DM 5. The option has a maturity of up to ten years, and its exercise price is allowed to be as low as the stock price at the time when the board of directors decides to grant the pertaining subscription rights. Furthermore, in order to shelter the option value against dilution effects, the exercise price is lowered whenever Deutsche Bank grants its shareholders subscription rights to newly issued shares. There is no payout policy commitment. The option is American-style, i.e., the right can be exercised at any point in time until maturity. However, this right is restricted by the rule that the stock price at the time of exercise has to be at least 10% higher than the exercise price.

---

[45] 24.40% of Daimler's equity is owned by Deutsche Bank. Apart from Kuwait, which owns almost 13%, several other shareholders among large German industrial and financial corporations contribute enough votes to form a stable majority in the shareholder meeting. The same seems to be true of Deutsche Bank, although only Allianz AG and Münchener Rückversicherungs AG are known to hold a combined equity stake of at least 6.5%. But more than 80% of voting rights present at the annual shareholder meeting of Deutsche Bank are exercised by banks as proxy votes. The company's management exercised proxy votes for approximately 32% of all shares present at the shareholder meeting of Deutsche Bank; cf. Baums/Fraune (1995: 102 et seq.). Volkswagen is under the control of the state of Lower Saxony. The prime minister, who is the dominant member of the supervisory board, has always emphasized that he does not feel committed to "shareholder value". Moreover, he enjoys the reputation of celebrating private events together with members of Volkswagen's top management.

[46] For a detailed description of the different programs set up during the last year, cf. Kohler (1997: 251 et seq.) and Knoll (1997). It should be noted that the authorization passed in the shareholder meeting of Deutsche Bank was very vague. The stock option program could not be implemented because of the legal action mentioned above. Therefore, some of the characteristics explained below rest on an interpretation of various hints given by board members on several occasions. Since the lawsuit is pending, management remains conspicuously silent as to what would have been done had the plan not been contested in court.

It is easy to see that this stock option program is ill-designed from the perspective of incentive compatibility. Even if one ignores the incentive for management to retain profits and assumes an unchanged payout policy keeping the dividend return at the current level of 3% of Deutsche Bank's stock price, an option with a strike price that remains unchanged for ten years will end up deep in the money unless the total return for shareholders lies far below the interest on government bonds. This means that the restriction regarding the minimum stock price increase of 10% is virtually meaningless; much more important, however, is the obvious consequence that management would have been rewarded for mediocre or even dismal performance if the board had felt free to take full advantage of the authorization granted by the 1996 stockholder meeting. With 3% dividend return, the stock would have to appreciate 4% per year just to match the average long-term yield of German government bonds of 7%. With a stock price of DM 72 immediately after the 1996 shareholder meeting and an authorization to issue 8 million shares, management would finally have made DM 277 million on top of their cash salaries, while shareholders would have been left with a return which could easily have been earned without Deutsche Bank's expensive directors. The present value of this redistribution in favor of management amounts to DM 141 million.

Evidently, this number has been calculated under the assumption that the volatility of the stock is zero and, therefore, understates the actual value of the rip-off.[47] According to the Black-Scholes option-pricing formula, an annual volatility of 20% leads to a present value of the program of DM 236 million. No reduction in cash salaries was offered in exchange for this impressive pay rise, and no restriction was imposed upon the maximum share of the loot that may be granted to a single person or the board of directors as a whole. Moreover, one should bear in mind that the program allows the top management of the company to pocket several hundred million DM without having to undertake any effort to beat the return on government bonds.

This lack of incentive compatibility can also be illustrated by taking a look at the actual performance of Deutsche Bank's stock in the aftermath of the 1996 shareholder meeting. One day thereafter, on May 29, 1996, the stock traded at DM 72.20. Had the options been granted on this date, management would have profited from an increase of DM 49.90 per share until August 1, 1997, when the stock price of Deutsche Bank stood at DM 122.10. Had the authorization to issue options on 8 million shares been exploited to full advantage, management could have earned DM 400 million in 14 months by exercising the options. Sharehold-

---

[47] In the language of the Financial Accounting Standards Board, the amount of DM 141 million is the "minimum value" of the stock option plan. Feeding a volatility of zero into the Black-Scholes formula is another method of computing the "minimum value". Cf. FASB (1995: 135).

ers, however, would have given up these DM 400 million in exchange for a stock that underperformed the German stock market. The DAX index, which measures the performance of 30 German blue chips, soared 72.8% during the 14-month period in question, whereas the increase of Deutsche Bank's shares from DM 72.20 to DM 122.10 and an adjustment for a dividend of DM 1.80 results in a slightly lower increase of 72.2%. Although the underperformance is negligible, a reasonable shareholder would certainly not want to distribute an additional bonus of DM 400 million within 14 months to a management team that fails to beat the market.

Nevertheless, the stock option program of Deutsche Bank was supported by more than 99% of the votes in the 1996 stockholder meeting. Resistance of private shareholders was easily overcome by proxy votes and cross-holdings under the control of Germany's corporate establishment, whose members can count on Deutsche Bank's support for similar option plans elsewhere. Even among private shareholders, opposition to the plan was limited because most of them did not understand the lack of incentive compatibility nor did they have the slightest idea of the volume of the rip-off scheme proposed by management. Perhaps this is even true of some board members. CEO Hilmar Kopper failed to answer crucial questions regarding the value and the structure of the program, and it was not clear whether this was due to unwillingness or incapability. In any case, shareholders passed a resolution without having been properly informed. This is one of the reasons why the plan may eventually founder in the courts.[48]

b. The Case of Daimler Benz

A very similar stock option program was passed in the shareholder meetings of Daimler Benz in 1996 and 1997. This is certainly not an accident, as Deutsche Bank is the major shareholder of Daimler Benz and Mr. Kopper, former CEO of Deutsche Bank, is the chairman of the supervisory board of Daimler Benz and Deutsche Bank. As opposed to the Deutsche Bank case, the authorization of Daimler's board does not refer to a bundle of bonds and options; instead, top management can be offered the right to subscribe to convertible bonds with a maturity of up to ten years. The aggregate par value of the 1996 and 1997 authorizations is DM 150 million.[49] Every DM 5 par value of the convertible

---

[48] The case is now pending in the provincial court. The local court in Frankfurt dismissed the complaint. But this does not mean anything because in Germany the lower courts with jurisdiction over corporate law have a strong bias in favor of management. Two of the three judges considering a case are local business people subject to economic repercussions if they decide against corparate leaders. Even higher courts, however, are often not so independent as they should be. Cf. Wenger (1996b: 447) and *Der Spiegel* December 6, 1993, 132.

[49] The stock option program passed in 1996 had a volume of DM 40 million and was reserved for a group of approximately 170 top managers. In 1997, the volume was increased by DM 110 million and the program was expanded to a larger group of beneficiaries. The first

bonds bears an exchange right into one share with the same par value. If this right is exercised, the difference between the pre-specified exercise price and the par value has to be paid in cash. The date of issue and the beneficiaries are determined by the board of executive directors in agreement with the supervisory board.[50]

One of the especially delicate characteristics of the program is the rule governing the determination of the exercise price. What matters is the stock price of Daimler Benz on the Frankfurt stock exchange on the day after the share-holder meeting of that year in which the convertible bonds are issued. As the shareholder meeting of Daimler Benz is usually held in May, the board of direc-tors can adopt a wait-and-see strategy a normal investor can only dream of: they can wait for about seven months before having to decide whether the stock price has risen enough. If that is the case, they will take advantage of their authoriza-tion and issue convertibles which are already deep in the money; if not, no issue will take place and the unexhausted volume will be reserved for the next year.[51] Under these circumstances, the additional restriction that exercise is not allowed unless the stock price has risen by at least 15% becomes even more meaningless than the corresponding 10% rule in the Deutsche Bank plan.

From the perspective of incentive compatibility, the Daimler Benz program is as ill-designed as that of Deutsche Bank. The value of Daimler's rip-off scheme, however, is much higher, because the par value of the shares under the program as well as the ratio between market and par value exceeds the corresponding figures for Deutsche Bank. The 1997 authorization alone, with a par value of DM 110 million and a stock price of DM 132 on the day after the stockholder meet-ing, creates a value of DM 1.8 billion upon expiration, assuming zero volatility, a 7% return on government bonds, and a dividend return of 2%. This corresponds to a present value of DM 928 million. With 20% annual volatility, the Black-Scholes value is DM 1.3 billion. But a conventional calculation on the basis of the Black-Scholes formula ignores the considerable effects of the right to follow the wait-and-see strategy mentioned above. Complicated calculations which we

resolution was not contested in court because management should have the opportunity to give one awful example of how an ill-designed program might be implemented; this was sufficient to justify legal action against the expanded authorization passed in 1997. The case is still pending in the lower court.

[50] This is also valid for the interest rate of the convertible bond, which was set 50 basis points lower than the market rate.

[51] In the year 1996 the stock price rose from DM 83.77 on the day after the shareholder meeting to DM 105.50 at the end of the year. Under these circumstances, top management can buy into the share with an 20% discount if those beneficiaries of the program who sit on the board of directors take advantage of their authorization to issue convertibles. To obtain the consent of the supervisory board should not be a problem, as long as the chairman feels committed to a policy of non-interference; see footnote 11.

have not yet undertaken are necessary to find out how much this drives the value of the loot up.

The ex ante value of the 1996 program with a par value of DM 40 million is of the same order of magnitude as the value of the Deutsche Bank plan. Ex post, within one year huge awards for underperformance could have been pocketed as in the Deutsche Bank case. With an actual stock price appreciation of DM 53 per share, Daimler's management could have cashed in more than DM 400 million if they had taken full advantage of the authorization and had exercised their conversion rights after one year. This would have been the reward for the fact that Daimler Benz was the worst performer among four listed German car makers.[52] In reality the loot was much smaller, mainly because Daimler's management exercised the majority of the conversion rights granted within less than six months.[53] Such a value-destroying exercise policy is a clear sign that even the program's beneficiaries themselves had no understanding of its potential value. Even less understood is the purpose which should underlie a well-designed program: to establish sound long-term incentives for corporate management instead of creating opportunities to speculate on market-driven stock price movements with a time horizon of six months.

As a consequence of all these failures, Daimler's management was confronted with harsh criticism by private shareholders in the 1997 annual meeting when the expansion of the program's volume was on the agenda.[54] Of course, this had no influence on the consent of Germany's corporate establishment. Even though Daimler's management persistently refused to reveal an estimate of the value of the extended program, more than 99% of the votes were cast for the truly gigantic redistribution scheme. The only concession management made to their critics was a ridiculous tribute to demands for more long-term orientation: they promised to impose a minimum waiting period of two years before beneficiaries of the new program are allowed to exercise their conversion rights

c. Other Ill-Designed Stock Option Programs

Volkswagen AG decided to introduce a stock option plan in 1997. This plan is as misguided as those of Deutsche Bank and Daimler Benz. For an investment of DM 5 into a convertible, a beneficiary of the Volkswagen plan is granted an exchange right on one Volkswagen share which traded at DM 1,257 on the day after the 1997 stockholder meeting. When the exchange right is exercised, the difference between the investment into the convertible and the pre-specified exchange price has to be paid in cash. The exchange price is set to the stock price

---

[52] Cf. *Börsen-Zeitung* April 16, 1997, 4, and *Manager-Magazin* September 1997, 188.

[53] Cf. *Der Spiegel* 21/1997, 63.

[54] Cf. *Börsen-Zeitung* May 30, 1997.

on the issue date of the bond and remains constant until the conversion right expires after five years. Under the assumptions made in the Daimler Benz case, the Black-Scholes value of the program is slightly below DM 1 billion. This compares to an annual dividend of DM 315 million. Moreover, what was only a conjecture in the Daimler and Deutsche Bank cases became evident during the discussion in the stockholder meeting of Volkswagen: management was not only unwilling to give proper information on the value of the rip-off scheme, but was definitely incapable of doing so. It is not clear whether this was the reason that the consent of stockholders fell short of the notorious 99% level. At any rate, "only" 95% of the shares voted for the expropriation of stockholders as proposed by Volkswagen's management.

The Volkswagen plan has the notable peculiarity that the class of beneficiaries is extended to common workers. This may in part be due to the fact that Volkswagen as a company under government control has always been subject to an exceptionally strong influence of the German Metal Workers' Union (IG Metall). But it may also have played a role that by taking the whole workforce into their boat, management could hope to sell the planned enrichment scheme to the shareholders by appealing to considerations of "social justice". It remains an open question whether such considerations will count in the Braunschweig court, where the case is now pending.

A somewhat smaller case which has gone uncontested is Continental AG. The largest German tire maker introduced a stock option program reserved for management as early as 1995. Without going into the details, one can safely contend that it suffers from the same deficiencies as the three plans mentioned before. Regarding the corporate governance structure of Continental, this does not come as a surprise. The company belongs to the German corporate establishment, with Allianz AG and Deutsche Bank AG as leading shareholders.[55]

2. Examples of Well-Designed Stock Option Programs

Our theoretical approach suggested that the quality of a stock option program will crucially depend on the corporate governance structure of a company. Therefore, we would expect well-designed stock option programs in companies with influential private shareholders. Among companies included in the DAX, there is only one which fits into this category and has already introduced a stock option plan. This was the large chemical company Henkel KGaA, which is under the control of the Henkel family. The stock option plan approved by the shareholder meeting of 1997 had all the main characteristics to be incentive-compatible. According to the plan, all directors of the Henkel group have the right to

---

[55] It was Deutsche Bank that prevented the company from being taken over by the Italian competitor Pirelli; cf. footnote 11 and Baums (1993).

subscribe to a five-year bond with a market-determined interest. The total volume of the plan is limited to a par value of DM 10 million. For every DM 5 par value of the bond, the subscribers have the right to buy one quoted Henkel share with a par value of DM 5. This option cannot be exercised within the first three years after issue.

The most important feature of this option plan is the determination of the exercise price. It is set at the level of the stock price at the time of exercise, diminished by a factor which is determined by the outperformance of the Henkel share compared to the DAX index. This index is corrected for subscription rights and for dividends; consequently, the calculation of the Henkel stock price return is corrected for dividends and subscription rights, too. Therefore, the payout policy of the company is without any influence on executive compensation. As we already mentioned in Chapter C.I., these are the two most important characteristics for an incentive-compatible stock option program. It should also be noted that Henkel is not the only company to introduce a well-designed stock option program. Similar compensation schemes have been adopted by Schwarz Pharma AG and Böwe Systec AG in 1997. It is not surprising that the corporate governance structure of these two companies is characterized by the existence of influential private shareholders.[56] Under a corporate governance point of view, all these findings can be summarized in the following Table 2.

3. A Summary of Recent Stock Option Plans

Table 2: Synopsis of Stock Option Programs Introduced in Listed German Companies Between 01/1995 - 08/1997

Company	Year of Issue	Corporate Governance Structure	Incentive Compatibility
Daimler Benz	1996, 1997	corporate establishment	no
Deutsche Bank	1996	corporate establishment	no
Volkswagen	1997	government/union	no
Continental	1995	corporate establishment	no
Puma	1996	foreign parent company	indecisive
SGL Carbon	1996	widely held (no influential private shareholder known)	indecisive
Henkel	1997	influential private shareholders	yes
Schwarz Pharma	1997	influential private shareholders	yes
Böwe Systec	1997	influential private shareholders	yes

[56] More than 75% of the equity capital of Schwarz Pharma is controlled by the family of the founder. Almost 54% of the equity capital of Böwe Systec is owned by Wanderer Werke AG, the shares of which are owned for nearly 60% by three large shareholders.

Two inconclusive cases should be added to the summary of well- and ill-designed plans in Table 2. The first one is SGL Carbon AG. Its existence as a listed company is due to an equity carve-out arranged in 1995 by Hoechst AG, one of the largest conglomerates in the chemical industry. Although Hoechst has retained a small equity stake of less than 10%, SGL Carbon seems to be a widely held company. Influential private shareholders are not known. The company's so-called stock appreciation rights plan is a mixed bag with a lot of restrictions imposed on the right to buy and sell the shares under the plan. These restrictions mitigate the problems existing in the three cases we classified as ill-designed; there is, however, no systematic link between rewards and outperformance of an alternative investment in the stock or bond market.

The same is true for Puma, the second inconclusive case. Puma is not under the control of Germany's corporate establishment, but has a foreign parent company. Its stock option plan is similar to that of Daimler Benz. It is somewhat superior insofar as the exercise price of the option must be at least 20% higher than the stock price on the issue date of the option. This is, however, a very modest improvement over the Daimler Benz plan, because the option can have maturity of up to ten years. Consequently, management can be awarded to the extent that it beats an alternative investment with a return of approximately 2% p.a.

D. Empirical Investigation

I. Introduction

Our thesis is that the German system of corporate control cannot work very well because of a dense network of mutual shareholdings. These cross-holdings, together with several other politically supported rules—for example, the lack of disclosure obligations or the proxy voting system—are suited to shelter management from capital market pressure. The discussion of the brand new compensation instrument of stock options in the preceding chapter can be seen as an example of Germany's deficient corporate governance system. Of course, one could object that this is not more than a case study without any general validity. However, as our theory regarding the interaction between the corporate governance structure and the characteristics of stock option programs was corroborated by the nine cases discussed, this can hardly be seen as a pure accident. Nevertheless, our view of the German corporate governance system, and especially the alleged monitoring activity of banks, should also be put to test based on conventional methods of empirical research. The results we present in this chapter are concerned with bank control on the share price performance of controlled companies. Because bank influence can only be expected to be stable in the long run if it is supported by equity holdings, it is measured only through such equity holdings in this study.

Sometimes it is argued that the impressive economic performance of Germany after World War II could not have been possible without a well-functioning corporate system.[57] As banks have played a crucial role in corporate control for several decades, they necessarily have to be seen as efficiency-enhancing block-holders. In this view—especially popular among Anglo-American writers—it is implicitly assumed that bank managers are provided with the right incentives to monitor their portfolio companies. We have already suggested that there are serious doubts about the existence of such incentives, as it is difficult to make bank managers liable for control failures. Therefore, we would expect bank-dominated companies to perform worse than privately owned or even widely held companies.

Here is not the right place to give a comprehensive overview of the extensive empirical discussion regarding the monitoring efficiency of banks in Germany as well as in other countries.[58] These studies shed a critical light on the conventional view that bank involvement can mitigate the agency problems arising from the separation of ownership and control.[59] This is especially true of the supposed benefits of proxy votes and supervisory board representation, which in reality seem to be of no influence at best. Nevertheless, some studies find a positive influence of banks on corporate performance in those cases in which banks hold equity stakes for their own accounts; if one takes a closer look, however, these findings merely suggest that banks as blockholders are not necessarily worse than other owners of large stakes. However, what should be pointed out here is that we have some fundamental objections regarding the methodological

---

[57] In this regard it is often pointed out that listed companies play a much less important role in Germany than in countries like the U.S. or the U.K. While it is estimated that listed companies contribute 35% to GDP in the U.K., this figure is probably not higher than 10% in Germany. For these figures, as well as for a detailed discussion of the importance of the incorporated sector, see Edwards/Fischer (1994: Ch. 4). Obviously these figures give no indication of the amount of the welfare loss due to unresolved agency problems in the sector of listed companies because its relatively small size could by itself be a consequence of these agency problems. Should the listed sector indeed be too small, there is a welfare loss due to suboptimal use of the risk-sharing effects of capital markets.

[58] For such an overview, cf. Wenger/Kaserer (1998: 68 et seq.), Gorton/Schmid (1996: 26 et seq.), Seger (1997: 141 et seq.), Edwards/Fischer (1994: 221 et seq.), Perlitz/Seger (1994), and Böhm (1992). For an overview regarding the features of the German corporate governance system, see also Schmidt et al. (1997).

[59] In this regard the studies of Wenger/Kaserer (1998) and Perlitz/Seger (1994) are unequivocal. The results of the studies of Gorton/Schmid (1996), Nibler (1995), and Franks/Mayer (1994) are going in the same direction, although they are partially inconclusive. This is also true for the study of Kaplan (1995), while the only study lending support to the view that banks are superior monitors is presented in the comparatively old paper of Cable (1985). See also the brief synopsis of available evidence in Prigge (this volume Ch. 12: end of Sec. C.II.).

approach of these studies. The reason is that they all use only a cross-sectional approach with practically no longitudinal perspective. Therefore, they analyze the influence of banks on corporate performance at one point in time, assuming in this way that bank influence does not vary over time. This is a fundamental misconception, because the net of relationships governing such a complex organization as a large industrial company will only change smoothly and over a longer period in time.

The decline of Daimler Benz during the eighties and nineties can be seen as an example of this dynamic aspect of bank influence.[60] As Deutsche Bank became the dominant shareholder in the mid-seventies, Daimler's profitability didn't change immediately. The economic decline was a long-lasting process, the consequences of which did not become evident until the early nineties. Therefore, in order to get a complete picture of the monitoring role of banks, one has to control for the intertemporal pattern of bank influence. It is our aim to incorporate this aspect in our empirical investigation. In this way one can also prevent an objection that is frequently raised against studies like those quoted above. The objection has to do with the observation that banks occasionally take over equity stakes in companies that are under reorganization. In several cases this might be rational behavior, because in this way companies can be kept out of a formal bankruptcy procedure. After a successful reorganization, the bank can sell out its equity stake, realizing a revenue which—depending on the specific situation of the case—could be higher than the revenue from liquidating the company's assets under a formal bankruptcy procedure. If one measures bank influence at one point in time, an overrepresentation of distressed firms in the sample of bank-dominated companies might lead to the erroneous conclusion that banks tend to ruin the companies in their portfolio. In our approach, it is very unlikely for rescue attempts to be interpreted as bank-induced failures because bank influence is measured over a longer period of time. Therefore, a company where a bank holds an equity stake only for a short reorganization period would not be counted as bank-dominated.

Finally, compared with a former study, we will try to incorporate risk in our analysis.[61] If the performance of a sample of bank-dominated companies is compared with a control group, one could object that the lower return of the bank-dominated sample could be due to lower risk exposure. Although it seems difficult to find theoretical reasons why banks should focus their equity stakes on low-risk companies, the study will be designed in a manner to incorporate this risk-return aspect.

---

[60] For a detailed description of this case, cf. Wenger/Kaserer (1998: 44 et seq.).

[61] Cf. Wenger/Kaserer (1998: 70 et seq.).

II. The Design of the Study

As already mentioned, our empirical approach tries to take into account the stability of the pattern of bank influence on a company's performance.[62] Therefore, we analyzed the long-term performance of 48 large non-financial German companies.[63] They were selected on the basis of the following criteria: the companies had to have been listed on a stock exchange since the end of 1973, their market value as of June 1990 had to have been greater than DM 750 million, and the percentage of shares belonging to all other companies in the sample was limited to 60%. We excluded companies with a formal control agreement, which forces management to obey the instructions of a parent company even if it is to the disadvantage of the controlled company.[64] Based on the market value of all sample companies, stock prices of June 1990 amounted to nearly DM 300 billion, or 56% of the total market capitalization in this year.

For every company, the share price return between the end of the year 1973 and the end of the year 1995 was calculated. Declared dividends and subscription rights were properly taken into account. R_i is the geometric average of the annual return of company i. The shareholder structure as it existed at the beginning and at the end of the testing period was collected. With this information, every company was characterized by two dummy variables. BANK_95 was set to one, if the financial sector[65] held an equity stake of at least 10% at the end of the year 1995 in the company examined.[66] Accordingly, BANK_73 was set to one if the financial sector held a 10% stake at the end of the year 1973. On the basis of this

---

[62] It should be mentioned here that one solution of the methodological problems resulting from the intertemporal instability of bank influence would be to analyze only firms with a very short (price) history. It is interesting in this regard that Kaserer (1996) found out that the performance of the share value of newly issued non-financial companies in the first year after the IPO is significantly lower for those firms having a banker as chairman of the supervisory board.

[63] "Non-financial" means that the company is neither a bank nor an insurance company. This sample is identical with that analyzed in Wenger/Kaserer (1998). A list of all companies can be found in Table 8 at the end of the paper.

[64] In such cases, minority shareholders are entitled to a guaranteed dividend and the parent company has to make an offer to buy their shares at their "intrinsic value"; cf. Wenger/Hecker (1995).

[65] As financial sector we defined the eight largest German banks and the insurance companies Münchener Rückversicherung and Allianz Holding because—as we already pointed out—these two companies are heavily intertwined with the banking sector. Therefore, one might prefer the term "financial sector-dominated"; nevertheless, we stick to the more familiar term "bank-dominated".

[66] It should be noted that this classification is based on those holdings which are known to the authors. Due to the lack of sufficiently strict disclosure rules, we cannot rule out that the financial sector altogether holds more stakes of 10 or more percent than we have used for dividing our sample. It is very likely, however, that holdings which are hidden by their owners have no or at least comparatively weak effects on the pattern of influence on the pertinent company.

information, two different sample classifications were made. First, all companies where the financial sector held a 10% equity stake in 1995 were defined as bank-dominated. Therefore, the control sample consisted of all companies with BANK_95$_i$=0. Second, as we already pointed out, bank influence should be measured over a longer period. Therefore, a second sample classification was made where only those companies were defined as bank-dominated where both dummy variables assumed the value one: i.e., BANK_73$_i$=BANK_95$_i$=1. This sub-sample was then compared with a control sample of companies which were—presumably—never under bank influence. Hence, only companies with BANK_73$_i$=BANK_95$_i$=0 were included in this second sub-sample. Obviously, one can object that there might be companies in this sub-sample where the financial sector held a 10% stake bought after 1973 and sold before 1995. Admittedly, such cases cannot be ruled out. But as we are interested in bank influence as a long-term phenomenon, we do not care too much about these cases.

III. Empirical Results

1. Bank Influence and Share Price Returns

In a first step, share price returns of the sample of bank-dominated companies are compared with the sample of non-bank-dominated companies. In order to exclude sectoral effects, sectoral specific excess returns were calculated for every company, too. This was done by subtracting the average market portfolio return per year of sector j (CDAX^j) from the average share price return per year of company i belonging to the sector j (R$_i^j$). The sectoral market portfolio return was measured by the relevant sectoral German stock index CDAX. Table 3 summarizes the results.

Table 3:   Two-Sample t-Test of Annual Share Price Returns (Assuming Different Variances) for the First Sample Classification

	R$_i^j$ BANK_95$_i$=0	R$_i^j$ BANK_95$_i$=1	R$_i^j$ - CDAX^j BANK_95$_i$=0	R$_i^j$ - CDAX^j BANK_95$_i$=1
Sample Mean	9.66%	8.52%	0.84%	-0.24%
Sample Variance	0.20%	0.13%	0.21%	0.12%
Observations	31	17	31	17
t-Statistic (mean diff.=0)	0.98		0.93	
Prob. (one-sided)	0.1676		0.1781	

The geometric average of the annual share price return during the testing period was 9.66% for the control group, while the sub-sample of bank-dominated companies achieved a return of 8.52% per year. If the outperformance of the share price return relative to a sectoral stock index is calculated, the annual performance difference decreases from 1.14 to 1.08 percentage points, as one can see from Table 3. These differences are not statistically significant at a usual 5% level.

This picture changes if bank influence is measured over the long run: for this purpose, only those companies were defined as bank-dominated where the financial sector held an equity stake of at least 10% in 1973 and 1995. In this way, the sub-sample of bank-dominated companies is reduced from 31 to 27 and that of the control group from 17 to 11. Therefore, with this second sample classification, ten companies were excluded from the sample because their corporate governance structure definitely changed during the testing period. As one can see from Table 4, the average annual share price return of the group of firms with a long-lasting bank influence is 2.68 percentage points lower per year than that of firms which were allegedly never bank-influenced. This difference is statistically significant at a level of approximately 3%. The performance difference between the two sub-samples decreases to 1.89 percentage points per year, as far as the outperformance of the share price return relative to a sectoral stock index is concerned. This difference is no longer statistically significant. The important result so far is that the performance comparison picture will be significantly changed if a long-term definition of bank influence is applied. As we would expect according to our theoretical considerations, the performance of companies with a long-term bank influence is more negatively affected than the performance of companies where this influence lasted only for a short period.

Table 4: Two-Sample t-Test of Annual Share Price Returns (Assuming Different Variances) for the Second Sample Classification

	R_i^j BANK_73$_i$= BANK_95$_i$=0	R_i^j BANK_73$_i$= BANK_95$_i$=1	R_i^j - CDAX^j BANK_73$_i$= BANK_95$_i$=0	R_i^j - CDAX^j BANK_73$_i$= BANK_95$_i$=1
Sample Mean	9.93%	7.25%	0.84%	-1.05%
Sample Variance	0.20%	0.13%	0.22%	0.14%
Observations	27	11	27	11
t-Statistic (mean diff.=0)	1.95		1.30	
Prob. (one-sided)	0.0316		0.1031	

2. Bank Influence and Risk-Adjusted Performance Measures

Against the results presented above, the objection could be raised that the lower equity performance of the sample of bank-dominated companies might be caused by a lower equity risk. Although we find it too difficult to explain why the financial sector should concentrate its equity holdings in companies with lower equity risk, we have tried to shed some light on the question of potential risk effects. In financial economics, two relevant measures are known. These are the so-called Sharpe ratio or reward-to-variability ratio and the so-called Treynor ratio or reward-to-volatility ratio.[67] The first is the ratio between excess return and volatility, while the second is the ratio between excess return and systematic risk.

a. The Sharpe Ratio as a Measure of Risk-Adjusted Performance

The Sharpe ratio is a return measure which is standardized with respect to the variability of stock returns. For every company i, the Sharpe ratio is defined in the following manner:

$$SR_i = \frac{R_i - R_s}{\sigma_i}$$

R_s is the average annual return on government bonds during the testing period[68], while σ_i is the square root of the variance of the 22 consecutive annual returns the individual stock has earned over the whole testing period. In Table 5, the Sharpe ratios of the two sub-samples are compared.

Table 5:   Two-Sample t-Test of the Sharpe Ratio (Assuming Different Variances)

	SR_i BANK_95$_i$=0	SR_i BANK_95$_i$=1	SR_i BANK_73$_i$= BANK_95$_i$=0	SR_i BANK_73$_i$= BANK_95$_i$=1
Sample Mean	7.69%	4.39%	8.81%	-1.11%
Sample Variance	1.82%	1.50%	1.75%	0.97%
Observations	31	17	27	11
t-Statistic (mean diff.=0)		0.86		2.54
Prob. (one-sided)		0.1976		0.0088

Regardless of the sample classification, the reward-to-variability ratio is higher for the sub-sample of companies which are not bank-controlled. Furthermore, this difference is statistically highly significant if the long-term-oriented subdivision of the sample is used. The negative sign of the Sharpe ratio for the sub-sample of companies under long-term bank control indicates that their share price returns are even lower than the return on the safe asset. These results

---

[67] Cf. Sharpe/Alexander (1990: 749 et seq.). It should be mentioned that the often-used Jensen measure does not contain more information than the Treynor measure. Therefore, it will not be used here.

[68] This return was calculated on the basis of the German bond performance index REXP.

Figure 2:   Reward-to-Variability Ratio

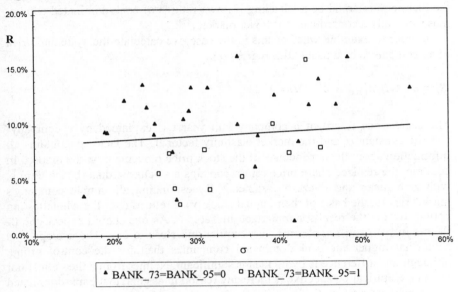

strongly confirm our hypothesis that the effects of bank influence take their time. In the long run, the detrimental effects of the lack of control incentives seem to be disastrous. This is also confirmed by Figure 2, where the risk-return relationship for the long-term-oriented subdivision of the sample is depicted. As one can see, in only 2 of 11 cases is the risk-return ratio of a bank-dominated company above the sample average represented by the straight line. Therefore, we can conclude that as far as the Sharpe ratio is taken as a measure of risk-adjusted performance, bank-dominated companies perform worse than the control group.

b. The Treynor Ratio as a Measure of Risk-Adjusted Performance

Finally, we should consider the objection that the relevant risk measure on capital markets is not the total return variability but only market-correlated variability. This part of return variability is usually called systematic or market risk. All other risks will become very small or even disappear through portfolio diversification. In a perfect capital market, diversifiable risks will not influence market prices of risky assets.[69] In such an environment, conclusions relying on the Sharpe ratio could be misleading if lower returns of bank-dominated companies were only a consequence of lower market risk.

In order to examine whether this is the case, we calculate the systematic risk of all companies by a usual OLS regression:

$$R_i^t = \alpha_i + \beta_i R_{CDAX}^t + \varepsilon_i^t \quad \forall t = 1..22$$

The share price return of a company i in year t is explained by a company-specific constant α_i and the market elasticity factor β_i. The factor β_i contains all information about the dependence of the stock price movement on the market. In addition, the realized share price return contains a stochastic disturbance term ε_{it} with zero mean and nonzero variance.[70] By estimating all sample company's market risk on the basis of their annual stock price returns over the whole testing period, we get the results summarized in Table 6. As one should expect, the β-factors in both sub-samples are very similar and close to one. The average β is somewhat higher for bank-dominated companies than for the control group, although this difference is by no means significant. Neither from a theoretical nor from an empirical perspective is there any reason to assume that bank-dominated companies are systematically different from non-bank-dominated companies in terms of market risk.

Table 6:   Two-Sample t-Test of the β-Risk (Assuming Different Variances)

	β_i BANK_95$_i$=0	β_i BANK_95$_i$=1	β_i BANK_73$_i$= BANK_95$_i$=0	β_i BANK_73$_i$= BANK_95$_i$=1
Sample Mean	1.03	1.08	1.05	1.12
Sample Variance	0.25	0.05	0.25	0.02
Observations	31	17	27	11
t-Statistic (mean diff.=0)		-0.53		-0.62
Prob. (one-sided)		0.2992		0.2693

[69] This can be shown in the Capital Asset Pricing Model (CAPM), the basic model of a perfect market for risky assets. For a detailed description of this equilibrium model, cf. among others Sharpe/Alexander (1990: 194 et seq.).

[70] This is nothing else than the empirically testable version of the security market line developed within the framework of the CAPM; cf. Sharpe/Alexander (1990: 259 et seq.).

In a second step, the Treynor ratio for all sample companies was calculated. It is defined as follows:

$$TR_i = \frac{R_i - R_s}{\beta_i}$$

The Treynor ratio brings the excess stock return of a risky over a safe asset in relation to β-risk. In Table 7 the Treynor ratios of the different sub-samples are compared. Regarding the insignificant findings shown in Table 6, it is not surprising that the results for the Treynor ratio are very similar to those found for the Sharpe ratio in the last section. Regardless of the method of risk adjustment, the share price return of bank-dominated companies is lower per unit market risk than for the control group. As we would expect, this difference increases in significance if bank influence is stable over a longer period.

Table 7:   Two-Sample t-Test of the Treynor Ratio (Assuming Different Variances)

	TR_i BANK_95$_i$=0	TR_i BANK_95$_i$=1	TR_i BANK_73$_i$= BANK_95$_i$=0	TR_i BANK_73$_i$= BANK_95$_i$=1
Sample Mean	6.72%	3.43%	7.85%	-0.02%
Sample Variance	1.82%	1.49%	1.75%	0.99%
Observations	31	17	27	11
t-Statistic (mean diff.=0)	0.86		2.50	
Prob. (one-sided)	0.1977		0.0096	

E. Conclusion

It was the aim of this paper to take issue with the widespread belief that block-holdings—mainly by banks—in large German companies are suited to mitigate the free-rider problem of corporate control. This fundamental misunderstanding, especially popular among Anglo-American academic circles, is the result of the erroneous belief that German banks are located at the top of a hierarchically structured network of shareholdings and are acting in the interest of their own private shareholders. In reality, large German banks are sheltered from outside pressures by a dense network of cross-holdings, proxy votes, and underdeveloped disclosure obligations. Therefore, bank managers are not forced to pursue a value-maximizing investment and monitoring policy. Furthermore, one would expect that such a tight network of capital and personal relationships would enhance collusion among management of all involved companies.

In the first part of the paper it was shown how dense and far-reaching the German system of mutual shareholdings is. In the second part of the paper, we analyzed newly introduced stock option programs. The findings suggest that there is indeed a great danger of collusion among managers tied together by a system of cross-holdings. Stock options are especially prone to collusive agreements because of the lack of relevant disclosure obligations and the almost complete absence of any understanding of these instruments. As we find out in our case-oriented analysis, stock option programs are more likely to be used as an instrument to exploit shareholders if the company is bank-dominated or sheltered from capital market pressures through other arrangements. In companies with influential private shareholders, executive compensation by means of stock options was found to be incentive-compatible.

In order to support our view, in the final part of the paper the impact of bank control on the economic performance of industrial companies was analyzed from an empirical perspective. By measuring bank control in terms of long-run equity holdings of the financial sector, we found out that there is a significant difference between bank-dominated companies and a control group in terms of total shareholder returns. Furthermore, it was shown that the difference in share price return between bank-dominated companies and the control group is not due to risk effects. By using two alternative measures for risk-adjusted returns, we found that the performance differences became even more significant.

Table 8:   The 48 Companies of the Sample

Security Code	Name of Company	Market Capitalization in 1990 (mil. DM)
502820	AGIV	1,584.0
515100	BASF	17,418.7
575200	Bayer	19,776.0
520000	Beiersdorf	2,971.5
590900	Bilfinger & Berger Bau	1,575.0
519000	BMW	8,775.0
527100	Bremer Vulkan	1,000.4
543900	Continental	2,719.3
550000	Daimler Benz	35,391.7
551200	Degussa	3,452.9
550700	Deutsche Babcock	1,215.3
823210	Deutsche Lufthansa	3,811.5
551800	DLW	956.6
609900	Douglas Holding	1,785.0
559100	Dyckerhoff	1,045.5
557550	Dyckerhoff & Widmann	912.0
585800	Gehe	1,117.8
776000	Gelsenwasser	1,137.1
589300	Goldschmidt	816.4
825150	Hapag-Lloyd	1,060.8
603400	Harpener	1,208.3
607000	Hochtief	8,900.0
575800	Hoechst	17,401.2
608200	Holzmann Philipp	3,491.7
608370	Horten	1,352.5
504500	Isar-Amperwerke	3,891.6
627500	Karstadt	4,896.0
781900	Kaufhof Holding	5,059.9
630500	KHD	1,780.8
678000	Klöckner Werke	1,110.0
648300	Linde	5,810.8
593700	MAN	4,742.8
656000	Mannesmann	9,213.2
660200	Metallgesellschaft	4,003.2
503000	Paulaner	894.0
620200	Preussag	3,650.1
688980	PWA	1,602.7
707200	Rütgerswerke	1,725.5
703700	RWE	14,634.0
717200	Schering	5,278.0
723600	Siemens	36,935.4
728300	Strabag Bau	1,514.0
729700	Südzucker	2,141.7
748500	Thyssen	9,045.7
761440	Veba	19,323.6
761221	VEW	4,480.0
766400	VW	14,976.0
780300	WMF	819.0
	Total	298,404.2

References

Angel, James J. and Douglas M. McCabe 'Market-Adjusted Options for Executive Compensation' (Working Paper FINC-1377-32-596, Georgetown University, School of Business Administration, Washington, D.C. 1996).

Baums, Theodor 'Hostile Takeovers in Germany. A Case Study on Pirelli vs. Continental AG' (Working Paper, Institut für Handels- und Wirtschaftsrecht, University of Osnabrück, 1993).

Baums, Theodor 'Universal Banks and Investment Companies in Germany' in: Saunders, Anthony and Ingo Walter (eds.) *Universal Banking: Financial System Design Reconsidered* 124-60 (Chicago et al. 1996).

Baums, Theodor 'Aktienoptionen für Vorstandsmitglieder' in: Martens, Klaus-Peter, Harm Peter Westermann, and Wolfgang Zöllner (eds.) *Festschrift für Carsten Peter Claussen* 3-48 (Cologne et al. 1997).

Baums, Theodor and Christian Fraune 'Institutionelle Anleger und Publikumsgesellschaft: Eine empirische Untersuchung' *Die Aktiengesellschaft* 40 (1995) 97-112.

Böhm, Jürgen *Der Einfluß der Banken auf Großunternehmen* (Hamburg 1992).

Borio, Claudio E.V. 'Leverage and Financing of Non-Financial Companies: An International Perspective' (BIS Economic Papers no. 27, Basle 1990).

Boyd, Brian K. 'Board Control and CEO Compensation' *Strategic Management Journal* 15 (1994) 335-44.

Cable, John 'Capital Market Information and Industrial Performance: The Role of West German Banks' *Economic Journal* 95 (1985) 118-32.

Edwards, Jeremy and Klaus Fischer *Banks, Finance and Investment in Germany* (Cambridge 1994).

FASB 'Statement of Financial Accounting Standards No. 123' (Norwalk, Connecticut 1995).

Fonk, Hans-Joachim 'Bericht des Vorstands auf der Hauptversammlung der Mercedes Automobil Holding AG vom 18. Dezember 1992' *Das Wertpapier* 41 (Supplement to no. 2/93, 22.1.1993 "Männer der Wirtschaft").

Franks, Julian and Colin Mayer 'The Ownership and Control of German Corporations' (Draft, London Business School and University of Oxford, 1994).

Gorton, Gary and Frank Schmid 'Universal Banking and the Performance of German Firms' (NBER Working Paper no. 5453, 1996).

Grundfest, Joseph A. 'Subordination of American Capital' *Journal of Financial Economics* 27 (1990) 89-114.

Jarrell, Gregg A. 'An Overview of the Executive Compensation Debate' *Journal of Applied Corporate Finance* 5/4 (1993) 76-82.

Jensen, Michael C. 'Corporate Control and the Politics of Finance' *Journal of Applied Corporate Finance* 4/2 (1991) 13-33.

Jensen, Michael C. 'The Modern Industrial Revolution, Exit, and the Failure of Internal Control Systems' *Journal of Finance* 48 (1993) 831-80.

Jensen, Michael C. and William H. Meckling 'Theory of the Firm: Managerial Behavior, Agency Costs and Ownership Structure' *Journal of Financial Economics* 3 (1976) 305-60.

Jensen, Michael C. and Kevin J. Murphy 'Performance Pay and Top-Management Incentives' *Journal of Political Economy* 98 (1990) 225-64.

Kaplan, Steven N. 'Corporate Governance and Incentives in German Companies: Evidence from Top Executive Turnover and Firm Performance' *European Financial Management* 1 (1995) 23-36.

Kaserer, Christoph 'Underpricing, Unternehmenskontrolle und die Rolle der Banken' (Working Paper, Department of Economics, University of Wuerzburg, 1996).

Knoll, Leonhard 'Aktien-Optionsprogramme im Vergleich' *Personalwirtschaft* 24/11 (1997) 34-42

Knoll, Leonhard, Jochen Knoesel, and Uwe Probst 'Aufsichtsratsvergütungen in Deutschland: Empirische Befunde' *Zeitschrift für betriebswirtschaftliche Forschung* 49 (1997) 236-53.

Kohler, Klaus 'Stock Options für Führungskräfte aus der Sicht der Praxis' *Zeitschrift für das gesamte Handelsrecht und Wirtschaftsrecht* 161 (1997) 246-68.

Kropff, Bruno *Aktiengesetz* (Düsseldorf 1965).

La Porta, Rafael, Florencio Lopez-de-Silanes, Andrei Shleifer, and Robert W. Vishny 'Law and Finance' (NBER Working Paper no. 5661, 1996).

Lutter, Marcus 'Aktienoptionen für Führungskräfte - de lege lata und de lege ferenda' *Zeitschrift für Wirtschaftsrecht* 18 (1997) 1-9.

Mason, Kenneth 'Four Ways to Overpay Yourself Enough' *Harvard Business Review* 66/4 (1988) 69-74.

Menichetti, Marco J. 'Aktien-Optionsprogramme für das Top-Management' *Der Betrieb* 50 (1997) 1688-92.

Nibler, Marcus 'Bank Control and Corporate Performance in Germany: The Evidence' (Research Paper Series no. 48, Faculty of Economics and Politics, University of Cambridge, 1995).

Perlitz, Manfred and Frank Seger 'The Role of Universal Banks in German Corporate Governance' *Business and the Contemporary World* 6/4 (1994) 49-67.

Prowse, Stephen 'Corporate Governance in an International Perspective' (BIS Economic Papers no. 41, Basle 1994).

Rock, Edward B. 'America's Fascination with German Corporate Governance' *Die Aktiengesellschaft* 40 (1995) 291-9.

Roe, Mark J. 'Political and Legal Restraints on Ownership and Control of Public Companies' *Journal of Financial Economics* 27 (1990) 7-41.

Schmidt, Hartmut, Jochen Drukarczyk, Dirk Honold, Stefan Prigge, Andreas Schüler, and Gönke Tetens *Corporate Governance in Germany* (Baden-Baden 1997).

Seger, Frank *Das Verhältnis von Banken zu Industrieunternehmen* (Wiesbaden 1997).

Sharpe, William F. and Gordon J. Alexander *Investments* 4th edn. (Englewood Cliffs, N.J. 1990).

Wenger, Ekkehard 'Die Berücksichtigung von Arbeitnehmerinteressen im Entscheidungsprozeß der Unternehmung' in: Leipold, Helmut and Alfred Schüller (eds.) *Zur Interdependenz von Unternehmens- und Wirtschaftsordnung* 153-85 (Schriften zum Vergleich von Wirtschaftsordnungen 38, Stuttgart 1986).

Wenger, Ekkehard 'Universalbankensystem und Depotstimmrecht' in: Gröner, Helmut (ed.) *Der Markt für Unternehmenskontrolle* 73-118 (Schriften des Vereins für Socialpolitik 214, Berlin 1992).

Wenger, Ekkehard 'Die Organisation des Aufsichtsrates als Problem der politischen Ökonomie' *Wirtschaftsdienst* 76 (1996a) 175-80.

Wenger, Ekkehard 'Kapitalmarktrecht als Resultat deformierter Anreizstrukturen' in: Sadowski, Dieter, Hans Czap, and Hartmut Wächter (eds.) *Regulierung und Unternehmenspolitik* 419-58 (Wiesbaden 1996b).

Wenger, Ekkehard 'Institutionelle Defizite am deutschen Kapitalmarkt' (Expert Opinion for the Monopolkommission, Unpublished, Wuerzburg 1996c).

Wenger, Ekkehard 'Im Selbstbedienungsladen des Konzernmanagements wird der Privatanleger noch immer verhöhnt' *Wirtschaftsdienst* 77 (1997) 254-8.

Wenger, Ekkehard 'Aktienoptionsprogramme aus der Sicht des Aktionärs' in: Meffert, Heribert and Klaus Backhaus (eds.) 'Stock Options and Shareholder Value' 51-69 (Working Paper no. 116, Wissenschaftliche Gesellschaft für Marketing und Unternehmensführung e.V., Münster 1998)

Wenger, Wenger, Ekkehard and Renate Hecker 'Übernahme- und Abfindungsregeln am deutschen Aktienmarkt' *ifo Studien—Zeitschrift für empirische Wirtschaftsforschung* 41 (1995) 51-87.

Wenger, Ekkehard and Christoph Kaserer 'The German System of Corporate Governance: A Model Which Should Not Be Imitated' in: Black, Stanley and Matthias Moersch (eds.) *Competition and Convergence: The German and Anglo-American Models* 40-81 (Washington, D.C. 1998).

Wenger, Ekkehard, Christoph Kaserer, and Richard Kölling 'Die Bedeutung von Anleger-interessen für das Ausschüttungsverhalten deutscher Publikumsaktiengesellschaften: Das Standortsicherungsgesetz als Testfall' (Draft, University of Wuerzburg, 1996).

The Role of Financial Intermediaries and Capital Markets

ROLF-E. BREUER, Frankfurt/M.

In general, the influence of German universal banks on corporate governance at commercial and industrial companies is greatly overestimated. In fact, the trend is towards a reduction in banks' industrial holdings. Bank representatives are retiring from supervisory board mandates on a growing scale, and there is still no better alternative to the proxy voting right. The German model of corporate governance has generally proved to be efficient. Certain features of the system are gradually being introduced by other Anglo-Saxon countries. At the same time, there is a clear trend in the German system towards fulfilling investors' wishes by various means and strengthening the German capital market as an effective control mechanism. Ultimately, however, corporate governance in the Anglo-Saxon and continental European spheres will continue to show traces of national legal traditions, historical developments, and institutional specialities.

Contents

Table

A. The Role of Financial Intermediaries

I. Overview

The discussion surrounding the German universal banking system[1] contains certain grey areas which can easily lead to misconceptions. Sometimes there is a

---

[1] A description and analysis of the German universal banking system can be found in Hopt, Klaus J. 'Corporate Governance und deutsche Universalbanken' 243-63 in: Feddersen, Dieter, Peter Hommelhoff, and Uwe H. Schneider (eds.) *Corporate Governance. Optimierung der Unternehmensführung und der Unternehmenskontrolle im deutschen und amerikanischen Aktienrecht* (Cologne 1996).

narrower view which has less to do with business and business law than with corporate governance. In this respect, there are three parameters[2] in the German universal banking system:

(1) banks' participating interests in companies,
(2) banks' supervisory board mandates, and
(3) proxy voting rights.

But this does not tally with the real situation. The vast majority of German banks conduct universal banking business without these three parameters. Three big groups of banks—private banks, savings banks, and credit cooperatives—are in competition with each other. The private banks have a market share of only about 35%. In the group of private banks, the questions of industrial holdings, supervisory board mandates, and proxy voting rights have primary importance for the biggest five to ten banks and for certain central institutions of the credit cooperatives and savings banks.

II. Banks' Shareholdings

Banks' shareholdings are greatly overestimated. Private banks, for example, hold 4% of the nominal capital of DAX companies. The ten biggest private banks in Germany hold only 0.4% of corporate equity capital (joint stock corporations, limited liability companies) and have reduced this share substantially in the last 20 years (1976: 1.3%).[3] The main shareholders of German companies are other companies which own 42% of all shares, both listed and unlisted; banks account for 10%.[4]

The roots of the banks' shareholdings are diverse: they stem from restructurings or—in most cases—from traditional relations going back to the early days of industrialization. Moreover, the size of the holdings is determined largely by tax optimization—*Schachtelbeteiligungen* (tax-privileged holding).

The taxation of capital gains on the sale of shareholdings is a major obstacle to the banks' reducing their shareholdings—especially in the case of larger holdings—and restructuring their portfolio. Instead of fewer large holdings almost exclusively in Germany with an unfavorable risk-return structure, they would prefer more broadly dispersed holdings with smaller percentages, in foreign companies, too.

---

[2] For a detailed analysis of these three parameters with facts and figures, see Bundesverband deutscher Banken 'Macht der Banken. Erhebungen zu Anteilsbesitz und Aufsichtsratsmandaten. Methodik und Ergebnisse' (Cologne 1995).

[3] See Bundesverband deutscher Banken, supra n. 2, 9.

[4] See Table 1 below.

III. Supervisory Board

Corrections are also necessary with regard to the supervisory board. The influence of banks through their supervisory board mandates is exaggerated.[5]

6% of mandates at the 100 biggest German companies are held by representatives of private banks. Industry has 27% of all mandates. Trade unions hold 14%, but you don't hear much about the trade unions exercising power over German companies through this channel.

Banks do not bend over backwards to obtain supervisory board mandates; the initiative is taken by companies wanting to use the specialized knowledge and experience of banks in financial questions, economic analysis, and in the evaluation of strategic decisions in lending and investment business.

The banks' representatives do not seek short-term yield maximization at any price in exercising their mandates, but regard that activity as being more in the company's long-term strategic interest. This does not mean that banks are structural conservers or barriers to modernization. Banks must allow flexible adjustment and do so. This applied in the phase of industrialization in Germany, and also applies today to what is in many cases necessary restructuring or conversion projects. Here, the banks are guided by the best interests of the companies and take long-term performance in competition as the benchmark.

The influence of the supervisory board should not be overestimated. It meets, as a rule, only four times a year. It often only discusses fundamental questions of business policy. Business decisions are only tied to the supervisory board's approval in individual cases. A good number of companies, e.g., Siemens, have no points requiring approval at all. The reason for this is that supervisory boards with up to 20 members are too big to discuss individual questions. Furthermore, equal parity co-determination has led to a reduction in the supervisory board's involvement in day-to-day business.

Great expectations are meanwhile attached to the company's auditor. The auditor is required to inspect not only the annual financial statements, but also internal controlling and risk management. More effective supervision is expected from the critical assessment of these areas than from the supervisory board, which very often only has the role of a business consultant.

IV. Proxy Voting Rights

The proxy voting right is often wrongly criticized. For the private shareholder, the direct representation of his interests at general meetings is possible, but in many cases makes little sense economically. He can, however, delegate the

---

[5] See Bundesverband deutscher Banken, supra n. 2, 14.

representation of his interests, and there is a priori no reason why he should not delegate it to banks. The Federal Association of German Industry has stated clearly that it does not agree with the abolition of proxy voting rights.

In this context, banks have made it clear for a long time now that they are open to alternative solutions, provided the extensive representation of private shareholders is ensured. The new communication technologies—for example, Internet, multimedia or videoconferences—could be instrumental for the future.

V. Conclusion

There is no reason for fundamentally abandoning the German model of corporate governance,[6] especially as certain features of this system are being taken over gradually by other countries[7] which so far have concentrated extensively on capital procurement through the stock market.

We should beware, in my opinion, of the temptation of being too quick to make international comparisons between banking systems and their impact on corporate governance. These systems are not only complex, but are embedded above all in very divergent traditions of law, business activity, and conduct. Reform plans can therefore always be only tentative from one country to another. The above-mentioned three parameters of influence of the private banks are in my opinion less important, taken together, than promoting the capital market and the market for corporate governance.

B. The Role of Capital Markets

I. Deficient Equity Culture

The real alternative to influence by banks, industrial companies, and institutional investors is probably to be found solely in the development of the capital markets themselves. In Germany, we suffer from a deficient equity culture,[8] the causes of

---

[6] In this sense, see Henkel, Hans-Olaf 'Neue Beschränkungen für das Kreditgewerbe: Schaden für den Industriestandort Deutschland?' *Zeitschrift für das gesamte Kreditwesen* 48 (1995) 308-12. And: Weber, Manfred 'Phänomen "Bankenmacht"' *Die Bank* (1995) 196-8.

[7] In the U.S. and U.K., a development in the direction of a continental European model can be observed, e.g., the increasingly common German-style separation of the positions of chairman and chief executive in Anglo-Saxon countries, efforts to abolish the Glass-Steagall-Act, and a discussion on "greater social responsibility" and on "stakeholder capitalism". And institutions in the U.K. and the U.S. have increasingly found themselves so large that they can no longer trade without affecting the price, and thus, reluctantly, have taken on more long-term positions in individual firms. "If you can't sell, you must care."

[8] An overview on the equity culture in Germany is given in Deutsche Bundesbank 'Die Aktie als Finanzierungs- und Anlageinstrument' Deutsche Bundesbank *Monatsbericht* 49/1 (1997) 27-

which should be sought not among banks, but among entrepreneurs and investors.

Listed stock corporations in Germany—in terms of number and market capitalization—have much less weight than in the Anglo-Saxon countries. Of 4,000 joint stock corporations, but 450,000 limited liability companies, only about 700 are listed. The new issue volume is well below the average of Western industrialized nations, although the number has increased substantially in the last ten years. Market capitalization is only about 30% of gross national product; the figure is substantially higher in other countries (U.K. 152%, U.S. 122%, Sweden 103%, France 38%).[9]

There are many reasons for this on the entrepreneur side, including the desire for independence, distaste for co-determination, dislike of disclosure, and taxes (property transfer tax, trade tax), but probably also what has been for many decades the high efficiency of the German universal banking system.

Share ownership in Germany is in many cases concentrated in firm hands, and thus much less broadly dispersed than in the U.S. and the U.K. 85% of joint stock corporations in Germany (U.K. 16%, France 79%) have one big shareholder holding more than 25% of shares.[10]

Table 1: Distribution of Outstanding Corporate Equity Among Different Categories of Shareholders

	Germany	U.S.	U.K.	France
Households	15%	37%	30%	20%
Companies	42%	15%	4%	58%
Banks	10%	0%	2%	4%
Mutual Funds	8%	13%	10%	2%
Insurance Companies (+Pension Funds)	12%	31%	40%	2%

Source: Deutsche Bundesbank, supra n. 8, 29.

The main shareholders of German companies are not banks (10%), but other companies, who own 42% of all shares, both listed and unlisted. This ownership structure indicates, too, that large public companies with diversified ownership

41. See also OECD 'Eigentumsverhältnisse, Kontrolle und Entscheidungsprozesse in deutschen Unternehmen' in: 'OECD Wirtschaftsberichte: Deutschland 1995' 94-145 (Paris 1995).

[9] See Deutsche Bundesbank, supra n. 8, 28.

[10] An overview about ownership concentration in listed firms is given by Berglöf, Erik 'Corporate Governance' in: Steil, Benn (ed.) *The European Equity Markets* 147-84, 151 (Copenhagen 1996).

are relatively rare. This is related to the fact that Germany lacks the big institutional investors, such as pension funds, that are found in the Anglo-Saxon countries. Pension funds assets in Germany amounted to just US$ 140 billion in 1995, compared with US$ 879 billion in Britain and as much as US$ 4,258 billion in the United States.[11]

The main reason for that peculiar discrepancy is that the German pension system rests to a large degree on the pay-as-you-go principle. Only 15% of the payments accruing to pensioners are funded. About 10% are accounted for by private life insurance and another 5% by occupational pensions. For the latter, it is standard practice in German companies to retain the provisions for future pension payments within the company, where they serve general financing purposes, instead of putting them into a pension fund. The reason is the favorable tax treatment of pension reserves.[12]

Obviously, this practice constrains the role of the capital market in corporate governance as it reduces, simultaneously, the supply of and the demand for capital via the capital market. In addition, those few and small German pension funds allocate just 11% of their assets to equities compared with a ratio of 80% in the U.K. The upshot of all this is that institutional investors other than banks own no more than about 15% of German equities. This compares with a figure of more than 60% for Britain.[13]

One of the consequences of the ownership structure of German companies in general and of listed companies in particular is that the German capital market plays a negligible role in corporate governance.

Hostile takeovers have been the absolute exception in Germany, although they do occasionally happen. This has to do with the fact that there are not too many companies which are typical takeover targets with shares broadly distributed among individual owners and institutional investors. Many shares are held on a long-term basis. As shareholders, they are regarded by companies as reliable long-term investors who would not readily act against the company's interests.

II. Necessary Reforms

For Germany, it would be advisable to take market-oriented measures to promote the development of the stock market or to increase the supply of listed companies and change the shareholder structure.

[11] See InterSec Research Corp. 'Global Briefing Service' (March 1996).

[12] See Deutsche Bank Research 'From Pension Reserves to Pension Funds' (Paper, Frankfurt am Main 1995).

[13] See De Ryck, Koen 'European Pensions Funds—Their Impact on European Capital Markets and Competitiveness' 35 (Report commissioned by the European Federation for Retirement Provision) (Brussels 1996).

What would be the most important reforms?

• Legal and tax adjustments should be made to offer companies, in addition to the existing efficient debt capital market, an efficient equity market as well, and to facilitate equal tax treatment of all forms of investment for investors.

• More institutional investment capital would be an important precondition for the development of a broader share market in Germany. From a corporate governance point of view, only institutional investors can form a real counterweight in the long term to companies and banks as principal shareholders, because their investment decisions are guided by criteria other than short-term yield maximization.

• A gradual conversion of the funding of retirement pensions from today's "generations contract" to vested capital funding could precipitate a sudden increase in demand for capital investment and help the breakthrough for Germany's equity culture. The spin-off of company pension fund contributions to external pension institutions—under the heading pension funds—would have a similar effect. There are tax obstacles here, too.

• It would be important, as a flanking measure, to improve the level of awareness among the general public and, within the scope of education and training systems—starting in schools—to work towards a change in our equity culture. An increase in information, promotion, and marketing work on behalf of the share would certainly strengthen acceptance of, and confidence in, the equity and help to engineer a change in the mentality of broad sectors of the population.

III. Outlook

The role of the German capital markets is comparatively limited, but it is growing. Attempts to modernize capital market regulation, to attract more companies to the stock exchange, and to change the ownership structure have been to a certain extent successful:

• Passing of a new Takeover Code,[14] which adopts principal provisions from the City Code of London, e.g., the principle of equal treatment, of suffcient and correct information, the mandatory offer at current market price, and the Takeover Panel.

---

[14] German Takeover Code of the Exchange Expert Commission at the Federal Ministry of Finance (Frankfurt am Main 1995). The code allows flexible reactions to continously developing market conditions, and conforming applicable rules to international standards. For further details see also Schuster, Stephan and Christian Zschocke *Übernahmerecht/Takeover Law* (Frankfurt am Main 1996). Cf. also Baumann (this volume Ch. 8) for a report of the experiences with the *Übernahmekodex* and its recent amendment.

- The New Securities Trade Act guarantees more transparency by obliging the listed companies to disclose all relevant information immediately, and protect investors by regulations ensuring that the misuse of insider information is a criminal offense.[15] With the third Act for Promoting Financial Markets enacted in 1998, the initial public offerings is made easier for companies.

There are also trends in corporate governance which have been observed in the U.S. and in Great Britan for some time and are now increasingly being felt in Germany and in continental Europe more or less equally:[16]

- Concerning investor relations, companies are communicating and taking steps to improve business performance to the capital markets in a better way than before. Companies now recognize that they must "know their shareholders" and anticipate their expectations.
- Changes in accounting disclosure reflect the trend towards improved communication as well. Many German and European companies are beginning to see the benefits of adopting an internationally recognized accounting framework, such as International Accounting Standards.
- Increased financial disclosure in annual reports is being matched by expanded narrative reporting. This gives companies an opportunity to communicate their strategy and to explain how they have dealt with operational and financial risks.
- There is a greater attention to shareholder value, as management has become more responsive to the demands of equity investors. Companies are beginning to review their operations and concentrate on those core activities which they do best.

It seems premature, however, to expect the whole German capital market system, including the corporate governance system, to move in the direction of the Anglo-Saxon countries. This will occur, but it will probably be more or less limited to the big global players, while changes in the small- and medium-sized companies will be slow in coming.

---

[15] See Breuer, Rolf.-E. 'Neues Leben für den Finanzplatz Deutschland' *Die Bank* (1994) 444-9.

[16] See the analysis of Price Waterhouse 'Converging Cultures—Trends in European Corporate Governance' (London 1997).

Shareholder Representation and Proxy Voting in the European Union: A Comparative Study

THEODOR BAUMS, Osnabrück

The article deals with shareholder voting in the countries forming the European Union. The focus of the comparative study is on informed voting by both domestic and foreign shareholders in the various legal systems. Voting by proxies and cost-reducing new technologies are included. The study shows some quite similar regulations and patterns. But there are also very distinctive features and institutions, and, not surprisingly, the different stages of development of the various capital markets are revealed. It will be up to further research to refine this preliminary picture and add findings on the practical functioning, criticisms of the various systems, and proposals for further developments.

Contents

A. Introduction

Recent research has shown growing interest in comparative studies on corporate governance, and on shareholders' representation and proxy voting abroad in particular.[1] There are several reasons for this. First, the investors' internationalization of capital investments and the raising of funds globally by companies lead institutional and associations of private investors to ask how their interests are protected abroad. Second, the EU Commission aims at simplifying the operating regulations for public limited companies in the EU and has therefore commissioned a comparative study dealing, inter alia, with shareholders' representation at general meetings in the EU member states.[2] Third, from a microeconomic point of view, the question is whether and what specific features of a given corporate governance system might contribute to better performance of the firms. Fourth, discontent with domestic regulations or the search for improvements of the local voting system leads quite naturally to the question of how this is organized in other legislations.

Of course, not all of these perspectives focus on the same points and follow the same lines. The global institutional investor will, for instance, be interested in learning about all different kinds of corporate governance features, such as voting rights of shareholders and voting by a proxy, disclosure of financial information, takeover and insider regulations, transferability of shares, protection of minority rights, and so on. However, this paper will be confined to one specific aspect only, the exercise of the shareholders' voting rights at the general meeting. The paper is intended as the first part of a larger research project, which, as currently planned, will consist of three parts. As the first part, this article will attempt to describe the regulatory provisions and institutional arrangements concerning proxy voting in the EU member states according to

---

[1] For comparative studies on corporate governance, see most recently Wymeersch, Eddy 'Corporate Governance: Converging Patterns?' (Paper, Melbourne Law School 1997) and the survey in Baums, Theodor 'Corporate Governance Systems in Europe: Differences and Tendencies of Convergence' (Crafoord Lecture Lund, Sweden 1996), n. 1, 2.

For comparative reports and studies on shareholder voting, see Lerman, Rachel O., Stephen M. Davis, and Corinna Arnold *Global Voting. Shareholder Decisions 1991-1992* (IRRC Washington 1993); Hohn Abad, Marion *Das Institut der Stimmrechtsvertretung im Aktienrecht. Ein europäischer Vergleich* (Dissertation, Münster 1995); La Porta, Rafael, Florencio Lopez-de-Silanes, Andrei Shleifer, and Robert W. Vishny 'Law and Finance' (NBER Working Paper 5661, July 1996); Davis, Stephen M. and Karel Lannoo 'Shareholder Voting in Europe' (CEPS Center for European Policy Studies 1997); Davis Global Advisors *Corporate Governance: An International Comparison* (Newton, M.A. 1996); Investor Responsibility Research Center/IRRC (ed.) *Global Shareholder Service Proxy Voting Guide* (Washington, D.C.) (various country reports); International Society of Securities Administrators/ISSA (ed.) *Handbook* 4 vols 6th edn. (Zurich 1996).

[2] European Commission (ed.) 'The Simplification of the Operating Regulations for Public Limited Companies in the European Union. Final Report' (Luxembourg 1995).

information available at this time. In a second step, experts from the various countries will be asked to review the respective reports and add their own remarks on the practical functioning, criticisms of their systems, and possible improvements as seen from their domestic perspective. A symposium as the final part of the project will then bring these experts together and give them a chance to discuss international aspects of shareholder voting and policy recommendations.

B. Shareholder Voting: Reasons, Problems, New Issues

Shareholder voting is an integral part of the governance structure of publicly held corporations. Requiring shareholder consent for any fundamental change in corporate policy is a safeguard for the residual risk-bearers of a corporation against ex post expropriation by the management. The right to vote assures the shareholders that the basic terms of their investment cannot be altered without their approval. In essence, then, voting rights are to stockholders what covenants are to bondholders: by limiting managerial discretion, they serve as a protection against moral hazard.[3] Unlike bondholders, however, shareholders receive most of the marginal costs and benefits of fundamental corporate decisions. Thus, shareholders as residual risk-bearers have the appropriate incentives to decide on those matters.[4] Also, vesting voting rights in shareholders is the only feasible method to implement major improvements of corporate policy that affect the terms of their investment. Because of the dispersion of equity holdings, renegotiations are difficult to organize.[5] Moreover, renegotiations would require unanimity, thus giving veto power to all shareholders, including those who hold only a small fraction of shares. By allowing a majority to implement fundamental changes of corporate policy, however, veto power can only be exerted if a shareholder holds a substantial proportion of the shares; thus, a vetoing shareholder is forced to internalize at least part of the impact of his decision on firm value.

Unfortunately, voting as a decision mechanism suffers from collective action problems. Widely dispersed shareholders are likely to be "rational-apathetic" when it comes to acquiring information on changes of corporate policy proposed by management. The cost of informing oneself in order to cast an intelligent vote on a management proposal will exceed the expected benefits, even if one

---

[3] Easterbrook, Frank H. and Daniel R. Fischel 'The Corporate Contract' in: Bebchuk, Lucian Arye (ed.) *Corporate Law and Economic Analysis* 182, 186 (Cambridge 1990).

[4] Easterbrook, Frank H. and Daniel R. Fischel *The Economic Structure of Corporate Law* 67, 69 (Cambridge 1991).

[5] Bebchuk, Lucian Arye 'Limiting Contractual Freedom in Corporate Law: The Desirable . Constraints on Charter Amendments' 102 *Harv. L. Rev.* 1820 (1989).

assumes that that vote will be decisive. Therefore, voters who hold only a small fraction of shares will remain rationally ignorant. If the management controls the agenda, as it does in most legal systems, shareholders will give their approval, assuming that the management acts on superior knowledge.[6] Moreover, even if some shareholders have determined that a particular proposal will result in a loss in share value, "free-rider" problems will discourage formation of an opposition. Each shareholder may gain from opposition, but each will gain more if other shareholders bear the costs. Shareholders are not rewarded for contributing to decision making. Thus, while it is better for all if everyone contributes, it is better for everyone not to contribute, with the result that the activities (information gathering, casting votes) will not be undertaken. There is no cost-sharing mechanism that forces all the shareholders who gained from the efforts of forming an opposition to pay for these activities.[7]

As a result, changes of corporate policy might be adopted even though they are value-decreasing. Selling shares is not a viable alternative; informed traders would anticipate the approval of a value-decreasing change of corporate policy, and they would lower their willingness to pay accordingly. Thus, investors cannot escape the detrimental effects of their collective action problems by selling shares. True, if a buyer acquires large blocks of shares, he can change the course of action of a particular firm and dismiss the incumbent management. Voting rights, then, help to provide incentives to the management to work hard on behalf of the shareholders because a poorly performing firm may become a target for a takeover. But large equity holdings come at a cost—they reduce liquidity in the market and thereby limit the informational content of share trading.[8] This cost is ultimately borne by the shareholders themselves, because reductions in market liquidity make performance evaluation of the management more difficult.[9]

This short overview of the microeconomic literature on shareholder voting shows that the right and possibility to vote remains the decisive feature of stock ownership in companies, be they privately or widely held. Our comparative study will show how easy or difficult informed voting by shareholders is made in the various legal systems, to what extent cost-reducing new technologies may be used, and whether they allow for informed voting. Another important aspect is how and in what forms voting by proxies is admitted. May proxies be given to the incumbent management? May banks with business links to a company vote

---

[6] Easterbrook and Fischel, supra n. 4, 67.

[7] Gordon, Jeffrey N. 'Ties that Bond: Dual Class Common Stock and the Problem of Shareholder Choice' in: Bebchuk (ed.), supra n. 3, 74.

[8] Holmström, Bengt and Jean Tirole 'Market Liquidity and Performance Monitoring' *Journal of Political Economy* 101 (1993) 678.

[9] Holmström and Tirole, supra n. 8.

their clients' shares in the company at the same time? What incentives do proxies have to act solely in the shareholders' interest, and how and by whom are they compensated?

A third question will address the role of institutional investors in corporate governance: Are fund managers obliged to vote the shares they hold in their portfolios?

A last question in this context concerns the level of ease or difficulty for foreign institutional and private investors to exercise their right to informed voting: How are they informed about time, place, and agenda of the meeting? Are there institutions in place which provide for a voting service? Are there specific obstacles to voting by foreign shareholders?

In what follows, a first attempt will be made to address these questions.

C. Country Reports

I. Austria

1. General Remarks

Austria's Company Law of 1965 (*Aktiengesetz*)[10] is modeled after Germany's postwar Stock Corporation Act (*Aktiengesetz*) of 1965, and many provisions are similar, if not identical. The AGM of an Austrian Aktiengesellschaft is convoked by the management board (*Vorstand*). It sets the agenda for the meeting, but shareholders can add items to the agenda if they surmount a threshold of 5%. The Aktiengesetz requires companies to publish an announcement of the general meeting, including the agenda, at least 14 days before the meeting in the domestic official gazette. As most shares are bearer shares, most companies require that shareholders prove their right to attend the meeting and vote by depositing shares with a custodian (a notary public, a bank) several days before the meeting. This is the common form in practice of proving ownership.

Under the Austrian Stock Corporation Code there is no proxy statement similar to that in the U.S. with detailed information on, e.g., the management's remuneration or grounds for the management's motions of the meeting's resolutions. Shareholders are notified of meetings by the meeting announcement published in the domestic media (official gazette and financial press) and by the information sent to them by the management through the custodian banks. As to foreign investors, it is up to banks, investment managers, or global custodians to pass the information on to the actual shareholders.

---

[10] Bundesgesetz vom 31. März 1965 über Aktiengesellschaften (Aktiengesetz 1965), BGBl. 98/1965.

2. Personal or Proxy Voting

Shareholders of Austrian companies may not vote by mail. If they wish to vote, they must either attend the meeting in person or give a proxy to a representative who will act in their place.

A proxy may be given either to a bank or to another person. As a practical matter, most smaller shareholders are represented by their custodian banks. Most banks, especially the country's three largest banks (Bank Austria, Creditanstalt-Bankverein, and Giro Credit), offer custodian services including voting the depositors' shares.

3. The Role of the Banks

The Stock Corporation Code permits a custodian bank to obtain a standing proxy from the shareholder. The standing proxy is valid for a maximum of 15 months and the shareholder may revoke it at any time. If the bank is not given specific instructions by its clients, it may vote at its discretion.

Banks, especially the three big banks, hold substantial and long-term equity stakes in many Austrian companies, exercise influence by sitting on these companies' supervisory boards, and act as lenders as well as smaller shareholders' proxies. As such, they wield considerable power and play an eminent role in Austrian corporate governance. The system very much resembles the German one, with the exception that the influence of the Austrian state seems to be stronger through its control of the country's two largest banks.

II. Belgium

1. General Remarks

The legal rules concerning general meetings and voting in Belgian public companies (*société anonyme*) are part of the *Lois Coordennées sur les Sociétés*, which themselves form a part of the Belgian Commercial Code. The AGM is convoked by the administrative board (*conseil d'administration*) or by shareholders who hold at least 20% of the company's share capital. The majority of shares in Belgium are bearer shares. To reach these shareholders, the company must publish a meeting notice in the *Moniteur Belge* (the official gazette) at least eight days before the meeting, and two meeting announcements in at least two (national and local) Belgian newspapers eight days apart, with the last notice published no later than eight days before the meeting. Companies with registered shareholders only may send meeting announcements to them instead of following these publishing requirements.

Where shares are held in bearer form, the company will require that its share-holders prove their right to attend the meeting and cast their votes by depositing their shares with the company itself or a designated financial institution at least three days before the meeting. Bearer and registered shares remain blocked until the day after the meeting.

Companies do not send proxy material and annual reports directly to bearer shareholders. Banks also do not usually inform their clients of forthcoming meetings. Bearer shareholders must find out about meetings from a newspaper, the official gazette, or, on request, from the custodian bank.

2. Voting by Mail, in Person, or by Proxy

Belgian law leaves it to the companies and their by-laws to decide whether share-holders can vote by mail or in person. Voting by mail, introduced in 1991, is still very rare, as companies must provide for this voting technique in their articles of incorporation and very few seem to do so.[11] Some companies even forbid mail voting. The reason for this hesitation seems to be the uncertainties connected with the identification of the shareholders when voting by mail. A shareholder may also designate an agent to vote on his behalf, provided the company's by-laws do not forbid it. Proxy voting is relatively frequent.[12] If admitted, a proxy can be given to another shareholder, to a relative, a lawyer, or to the custodian bank. Local custodians often act as voting agents for non-Belgian investors. In any event, shareholders must notify the company at least three days before the meeting that they intend to vote in person or by a proxy.

III. Denmark

1. General Remarks

Danish public limited companies (*aktieselskab*) are regulated under the Public Limited Companies Act (*Lov om aktieselskaber*). The AGM is convoked by the administrative board (*bestyrelse*). It sets the agenda for the meeting, but any shareholder can add items to the agenda. Danish companies must publish the ordinary meeting agenda between four weeks and eight days before the meeting. Most shares of publicly traded companies are bearer shares. To contact these shareholders, companies publish the meeting announcement and the agenda in

---

[11] However, according to a survey done by the IRRC in 1994, the majority of companies in the sample allowed for voting by mail; cf. IRRC (ed.), supra n. 1 (Belgium (1995), at 6).

[12] For a contrasting view, see ISSA (ed.), supra n. 1 (vol. 1, at p. BE 58): Proxy voting is rare in Belgium.

the official gazette and a national newspaper. As to registered shareholders, company law requires firms to send the meeting announcement and the annual accounts to them personally if they so wish. There are no specific requirements for reaching foreign owners of bearer shares.

In order to be admitted to the general meeting, shareholders must have announced their wish to participate a few days (not more than five) before the general meeting.

2. Personal or Proxy Voting

Shareholders of Danish companies may not vote by mail. If they wish to vote, they must either attend the meeting in person or give a proxy to a representative who will act in their place. Shareholders can also appoint as a proxy the meeting's chairman, who essentially casts a pro-management vote.[13] The by-laws of a company may require that the proxy also be a shareholder. Shareholders must sign a written power of attorney with the proxy's name and the duration of the proxy, which cannot exceed one year. The proxy must notify the company at least five days before the meeting that he plans to attend. As to foreign investors, banks and other financial institutions will typically act as their proxies.

IV. Finland

1. General Remarks

The rules and regulations for shareholders' meetings and voting by shareholders in Finnish public limited companies are laid down in the Finnish Companies Act of 1978. A fundamental reform is right now under way. Shareholders' meetings are convened by the board only. In Finland, shares are issued in registered form. It is therefore up to the by-laws of the companies to lay down whether the company will announce a shareholders' meeting by sending a notice to all registered shareholders or by publishing a notice in the official gazette and a national newspaper. The law does not require an announcement in the foreign press. All matters which will be presented for a decision at the meeting must be sufficiently specified in the announcement.

Registration with the company's share register or with the Central Share Register of Finland serves as proof of ownership.

---

[13] Cf. IRRC (ed.), supra n. 1 (Denmark (1995), at 3).

2. Personal or Proxy Voting

Shareholders of Finnish companies may not vote by mail. If they wish to vote, they must either attend the meeting in person or give a proxy to a representative who will act in their place. If a shareholder plans to attend a general meeting or send a representative, he must inform the company if the articles of the association so prescribe. A deadline for notification may be stated in the articles of association or in the meeting notice. A nominee without a written authorization may not act as a proxy for the shareholder.

Nominee-registered shares (nominee registration being available only to foreign investors) entitle neither the nominee nor the shareholder to attend or vote at an AGM.

V. France

1. General Remarks

The rules of French company law on general meetings and shareholder voting in public limited companies (*société anonyme*) are part of the Law No. 66-537 of July 24, 1966, on commercial companies. The AGM is convened by the administrative board (*conseil d'administration*) or, where applicable, by the managing board (*directoire*).[14] It sets the agenda for the meeting. A company must publish its meeting agenda at least 30 days in advance, and send out proxy documents and notice of the date at least 15 days before the meeting dates. Notice is made by mail to registered shareholders and by public announcement in newspapers and the financial press. Meeting agendas and details of the proposals are published in the official gazette (*Bulletin des Annonces Légales Obligatoires—BALO*).

French company law allows companies to require that shareholders own their stock as long as five days before the meeting date. Holders of bearer shares may have to prove ownership by depositing their stock with an institution designated by the company so that it may be blocked from trading until after the meeting.

Many foreign institutions own French stock through a custodian or subcustodian, which might in turn hold the shares under a street, or nominee, name. A stockholder owning bearer shares who wishes to vote by proxy must inform the custodian institution, which in turn asks the company to issue the appropriate forms. These are sent to the custodian 15 days in advance of the meeting, and then forwarded to the beneficial owner for instructions.

---

[14] On the different organizational forms of a *société à conseil d'administration* and a *société à directoire* cf. Guyon, Yves *Droit des Affaires* vol. 1 320 et seq. 9th edn. (Paris 1996).

Interestingly, French pension funds (*fonds d'epargne retraite*) are required by law to vote shares held by them. The relatively new corresponding legislation was recently upheld by France's constitutional court.[15]

2. Voting by Mail (Fax) or in Person

Voting by mail is permitted by the law. Shareholders may also vote by fax, as long as they also mail the official ballot to the company.

Shareholders may, of course, also attend the AGM in person unless the company refuses to admit a shareholder who holds less than ten shares.

Ballots are designed to make it simple for shareowners to give their proxies to the chairman to vote as he sees fit on their behalf. Shareholders wishing to have their votes cast according to instructions on management proposals are assumed to vote for a proposal unless they signify the box corresponding to the proposal number.

3. Voting by Proxy: *Mandats en Blanc*

The shareholders may also be represented by a proxy who must either be their spouse or another shareholder. The scope of the proxy is regulated in detail by a decree[16] and, in principle, is not valid for more than one shareholders' meeting.

The board of directors (or the managing board) generally benefits from this possibility by being empowered *en blanc* (that is, without indicating the name of the proxy holder). However, the proxy form sent by the company to the shareholder must inform the shareholder of this use (Decree art. 134). In addition, all proxy forms sent by the company must be accompanied by certain documents to inform the shareholder (Decree art. 133, amended by Decree of Jan. 2, 1968). These *en blanc* powers must be used by the president of the AGM to cast a vote in favor of the adoption of resolution proposals approved by the board of directors (or the managing board) and against the adoption of all other resolution proposals.

---

[15] Cf. Davis Global Advisors (ed.) 'Global Proxy Watch' vol. 1, no. 17 of May 2, 1997. The law dates from March 25, 1997. The respective implementing decree has, however, not yet been published.

[16] Decree of March 23, 1967.

VI. Germany

1. General Remarks

Germany has a special statute on public limited companies or joint stock corporations (*Aktiengesellschaften*), the *Aktiengesetz* of 1965. The largest part of this statute is mandatory. According to this statute, shareholders' meetings are convened either by the management board (*Vorstand*) or by shareholders owning 5% or more of the company's share capital. The announcement has to be published one month before the meeting in the official gazette and, if the by-laws of the company provide for that, in other newspapers. Only in a case where all shareholders are known by name may the company invite them by letter.

As most shares in public limited companies are held in bearer form, the by-laws of the company may provide that the right to participate and vote at the meeting can only be exercised if the shares have been deposited with a notary public, a depositary bank, or the company itself not more than ten days before the meeting.

Under the German Stock Corporation Code, there is no proxy statement similar to that in the U.S. with detailed information on, e.g., management compensation and the like. However, the agenda and the items on which the meeting is asked to make a resolution are published together with the announcement of the meeting. Shareholders with 5% or more shares may add items to the agenda. The announcement, the agenda with the proposals of management, and counter motions of opposing shareholders are also transmitted to the shareholders through depositary banks and shareholders' associations.

2. Personal or Proxy Voting

Shareholders of German companies may not vote by mail or electronic devices. If they wish to vote, they must either attend the meeting in person or give a proxy to a representative who will act in their place. A proxy may be given to any person (shareholder or not), to a bank, or a shareholders' association. As a practical matter, most smaller shareholders are represented by their custodian banks. Most banks offer custodian services including voting the depositors' shares. German institutional investors such as insurance companies or investment companies are not obliged to vote the shares they hold. Pension funds have not played a practical role so far.

3. The Role of the Banks

The Stock Corporation Code permits custodian banks to ask their clients for a standing proxy. If given, the standing proxy is valid for a maximum of 15 months, and the shareholder may revoke it at any time. If the bank is not given specific instructions by its clients, it may vote at its discretion in the best interest of the shareholder.

Banks, especially the big banks, hold substantial and long-term equity stakes in many large German firms, exercise influence through their subsidiary investment companies and by sitting on the supervisory boards of large firms, and act as lenders and providers of all kinds of financial services to these firms as well as proxies of smaller shareholders. As such, they wield considerable power and play an eminent role in German corporate governance. Plans to curb this power have been discussed and on the political agenda for years. The outcome of the most recent parliamentary motions and plans of the federal government is not yet clear.

VII. Greece

The rules for shareholders' meetings and voting in a Greek public limited company (*anonymi etairia*) are part of the Greek Stock Corporation Code. The general meeting is convened by the administrative board or by shareholders who together hold more than 5% of the share capital. The corporation must notify shareholders 20 days before by publishing a notice in the official gazette, and in at least one financial and one daily newspaper. Shareholders who want to attend the general meeting must deposit their securities with the Consignation and Loan Fund, any bank located in Greece, or at the company at least five days preceding the meeting. Proxy voting is permitted as long as the proxy documents are deposited with a bank or at the company at least five days preceding the meeting.

VIII. Ireland

The law of public limited companies of the Republic of Ireland is laid down in several Companies Acts and in court rulings. Normally the administrative board convenes the shareholders' meeting once a year. The shareholders are notified of this and of the items on the agenda. Proxy voting is allowed; the proxies may be shareholders or not. The by-laws of a company may state that it be notified at least 48 hours in advance if a proxy rather than the shareholder will attend the meeting. Shareholders may also solicit other shareholders for proxies; in such a case, management must hand out the other shareholders' names and addresses from the company's register. The cost of such a proxy solicitation, however, must be borne by the shareholder rather than the company.

IX. Italy

1. General Remarks

In Italy, the rules applicable to companies and public limited companies in particular (*società per azioni*) are those primarily contained in the Civil Code of April 21, 1942, Book V. These rules are complemented by various special laws. According to the Civil Code, shares may be registered or bearer. However, for tax reasons, the royal Decree of October 25, 1941, requires that "shares of companies having their registered office in Italy must be registered." In order to attend a meeting, shareholders must be registered in the company book or deposit their shares at the company's registered office or a designated depositary bank. The deposit date must be at least five days before the meeting.

The meeting is called by the board of directors. It must be called by a notice published in the official gazette at least 15 days prior to the date set for the meeting. The list of issues to be discussed must be published as well. Companies usually announce their AGM also in the national press.

2. Voting in Person or by Proxy

After depositing their shares, shareholders receive an admission ticket for the meeting entitling them to vote either in person or by sending a representative. Italy's recently privatized listed firms are granted the right to introduce voting by mail, but this is not applicable generally.

If the shareholder has decided to vote by proxy, the name of the person voting for him must be on the admission ticket. The proxy is valid for the respective meeting only. Proxies in blank are forbidden. The Civil Code forbids delegating voting power to employees or members of the company's board, its subsidiaries, outside auditors, or to representatives of any bank. This latter regulation is a reaction to the former system in which banks used to cast smaller shareholders' votes, mostly in favor of large blockholders or the companies' managements. Circumventions by giving employees of a bank proxies seem possible. For companies with a share capital of L 50 billion or more, a single proxy agent may represent a maximum of 200 shareholders. Proxy voting in Italy seems to be prohibitively costly if professional proxy voting agents, usually attorneys or consultants, are asked to act because they often charge hundreds of dollars to attend a meeting.[17]

X. Luxembourg

Company law in Luxembourg is codified in the Act on Commercial Companies of August 15, 1915, and the Civil Code. AGMs of public limited companies are convened by the administrative board. The date and the agenda of the meeting must be published in the official gazette (*Mémorial*) and in a local newspaper. Registered shareholders have to be invited by letter eight days in advance. Each shareholder has the right to attend the meeting personally or be represented by a proxy. The former rule that no shareholder may vote more than 20% of all shares and more than two-fifths of the shares present at the meeting has since been repealed.

XI. The Netherlands

1. General Remarks

The rules of Dutch law on stock corporations (*naamloze vennootschap*) form a part of the Dutch Civil Code (2nd book of the *Burgerlijk Wetboek* as of July 26, 1976).

General meetings of shareholders of a Dutch public limited company are normally convened by the management board. The company must notify its shareholders of the meeting at least 15 days in advance. Most shares of large publicly traded companies are in bearer form. To reach them, corporations must publish an announcement in a national newspaper. Holders of registered shares get proxy materials and annual reports directly from the company. The agenda is either published as well or available to the public at the company's head office.

Bearer shareholders must deposit their shares, mostly five days in advance, to prove their ownership.

2. Voting in Person or by Proxy

Dutch corporations do not permit shareholders to vote by mail or fax. Shareholders must either attend the meeting in person or send a proxy to vote there.

The by-laws of a company may limit the power to vote by proxy. However, a shareholder can in any event give a power of attorney with the right to cast his

---

[17] Cf. Lerman, Rachel O. in: IRRC (ed.), supra n. 1 (Italy (1996), at 4).

votes to a notary public, an attorney, or a public auditor. Dutch law also does not prohibit members of the management board or the supervisory board to act as proxies on behalf of other shareholders, but there is not widespread use made of this.

If not forbidden by the by-laws of the company, banks, accountants, attorneys, or brokers can act as a proxy for foreign shareholders as well as Dutch investors. Some seem to have refused to vote against managements' positions, despite instructions, because of their concerns for business relationships with the company. VEB, the Dutch Shareholders' Association, also often acts as a proxy for its members and other shareholders.[18]

XII. Portugal

1. General Remarks

The rules of Portuguese law on general meetings and shareholder voting in public limited companies by shares (*sociedade anónima*) are basically provided for by articles 373° to 389° of the Code of Commercial companies (*Código das Sociedades Comerciais*), enacted by the Decree Law n° 262/86, of September 2, 1986.

The general meeting (*assembleia geral*) is usually convened by the board of administration, but the law also gives this right to the company's supervisory organs and to shareholders owning 5% or more of the company's share capital. The announcement has to be published at least one month before the meeting in the official gazette (*Diário da República*) and in a newspaper of the company's domicile; however, the by-laws of the company may provide for other forms of announcement, and, in cases where there are only registered shares, may substitute private letters for the public announcement.

2. Voting in Person or by Proxy

The concrete form by which voting rights are exercised by shareholders may be determined by the company's by-laws, by a general meeting decision, or by the president of the general meeting himself. Concerning the *voting in person*, there is of course no legal restriction except for the fact that the company's by-laws may require shareholders to hold a minimum number of shares in order to attend

---

[18] According to Myers, Loretta L. in: IRRC (ed.), supra n. 1 (The Netherlands (1994), at 4). For a discussion of reform plans, see Gelauff, George M.M. and Corina den Broeder 'Governance of Stakeholder Relationships' 70-1 (The Hague, Onderzoeksmemorandum, Centraal Planbureau 1996).

and to vote in the general meeting. Concerning voting by mail (or similar electronic devices, e.g., by fax), Portuguese law omits any express regulation, and part of the doctrine considers it as inadmissible. Finally, the law expressly permits shareholders to be represented by a proxy under the following conditions.

The company's by-laws may not forbid a shareholder to vote by a representative who must be a spouse or close relative, another shareholder, or a member of the board of administration; and it may allow the representation in all other cases. Should the same person represent more than five shareholders, the scope of the proxy suffers several legal and mandatory restrictions: namely, it is not valid for more than one general meeting, it may be revoked by the shareholder at any time, and it must indicate precisely the name of the proxy holder.

XIII. Spain

1. General Remarks

The Spanish rules on public limited companies (*sociedad anónima*) have been reformed and are now codified in the Stock Corporations Act (*Ley de Sociedades Anónimas*) of December 22, 1989. Moreover, some provisions contained in the Trade Registry Regulations of 1996 (Royal Decree 1784/1996), and in the Securities Market Act of July 28, 1988, and in its regulations are relevant concerning the shareholders meeting and the proxy system.

General meetings of shareholders are normally convened by the administrative board and must be, together with the agenda, announced at least 15 days in advance in the official gazette and a daily newspaper. The by-laws of a company may require that bearer shareholders prove their right to attend the meeting by depositing their shares five days before the meeting. Registered shareholders prove their right through registration in the company's books. The by-laws may furthermore provide that a shareholder must hold shares at least equal to one one-thousandth of the company's share capital to have the right to attend the meeting.

2. Voting in Person or by Proxy

Shareholders may vote in person or by a proxy. Some companies on some occasions have paid a premium for the participation in general meetings in order to obtain a more substantial attendance of shareholders.[19] The proxy must be in written form and is valid for one single meeting only. It is revocable at any time.

---

[19] ISSA (ed.), supra n. 1 (vol. 4, at p. ES 39).

The by-laws may also require that the proxy be given only to another shareholder of the company.

The Spanish Stock Corporations Act contains detailed rules for voting by publicly solicited proxies, whether they are solicited by the company's directors, a depositary bank, or other persons or institutions. In such a case the proxy must include the agenda and the request for specified instructions on how to vote; and it must indicate in what sense the proxy will have to cast his vote if no specific instructions are given to him. These conditions do not apply to the so-called family representation.

Investment firms (*Sociedades y Agencias de valores*) acting as depositaries cannot receive proxies from the shareholders.

XIV. Sweden

1. General Remarks

Swedish limited liability companies (*aktiebolag*) are regulated under the Swedish Companies Act of 1975. The Act contains provisions concerning four corporate entities: the general meeting of shareholders, the board of directors, the managing director, and the auditors. The general meeting of shareholders is the supreme governing body of the company. The board of directors, which is usually elected in its entirety by the general meeting, is responsible for the organization of the company and the management of its affairs. The managing director, who is appointed by the board of directors, is in charge of the day-to-day management.

The convening of the general meeting is the responsibility of the board of directors. Notice of the general meeting shall never be issued earlier than four weeks before the meeting and, unless a longer period is stated in the articles of association, not later than two weeks before the meeting. The meeting shall be convened pursuant to the articles of association. For public companies this normally means that the notice is advertised in one or more daily newspapers.

In the notice, the items to be dealt with at the meeting shall be clearly stated. This also includes items that the law states must be dealt with at the meeting. Special regulations apply to certain items. For example, where the meeting is to deal with an amendment of the articles of association, the notice shall contain the essential contents of the proposed amendment. Similar regulations apply when the share capital is to be increased through a new issue of shares, when there is a proposal to issue convertibles or warrants, and also when there are proposals concerning the reduction of share capital. Matters not included in the articles may also be presented at the general meeting at the request of a shareholder, provided that he requests this early enough to include the matter in the notice convening the meeting.

2. Personal or Proxy Voting

Shares in a Swedish company must always be issued in the name of a specific person, so-called registered shares. In all companies, the board of directors shall maintain a register of all shares and shareholders. Public companies can facilitate their administration of shares by joining the Securities Register Center System. Briefly, this entails that a separate institution ("VPC") is assigned the task of maintaining the company's share register as well as processing all transactions concerning its shares. Traditional manual processing of share certificates and other legal documents pertaining to shares are thereby replaced by a computerized system.

In a "VPC company", a nominee—a bank or securities institution that is specially authorized to administer shares on behalf of shareholders—may be entered in the share register instead of the shareholder for the shares managed by the nominee.

A person who acquires a share is not compelled to be registered in the share register. However, he may only participate in the general meeting if he is registered.

Shareholders may also exercise their rights at a general meeting through a representative in possession of a written and dated proxy. Such a proxy is not valid for more than one year from its issuance. A proxy may be given to any person, to a bank, or a shareholders' association.

Shareholders may not vote by mail or electronically.

The ownership structure of Swedish public companies is dominated by institutional investors. Today more than 80% of the market value of all shares listed on the Stockholm Exchange is in the hands of institutions. These institutions—insurance companies, pension funds, etc.—are under no legal obligation to vote their shares.

XV. United Kingdom

1. General Remarks

There are several acts on company law in the U.K.: the Company Act of 1985 and the supplementary Company Act of 1989 for England and Scotland, and the Companies Order of 1986 and the supplementary Companies Order of 1989 for Northern Ireland (the latter with roughly the same rules as those contained in the Companies Acts). The Isles (Man, Jersey, Guernsey) have separate laws on companies.

Shareholders' meetings are convened by the board of directors. Notices and proxy documents are sent out no later than 21 days before an annual meeting. Because shares in Britain are almost always registered rather than bearer, companies mail annual reports, meeting notices, the list of agenda, and proxy forms directly to shareholders as they appear on the register. When an investor owns stock through a custodian or subcustodian, which might in turn hold the shares under a street or nominee name, the burden is on the shareholder's local agent to pass the meeting information to the owner. The nominee may, however, be obliged to make available to investors who wish it copies of the annual report and accounts and to arrange for them to attend and vote at shareholders' meetings.[20]

There is no requirement in British company law to "block" or deposit shares with an institution or the company itself before and during the meeting.

2. Voting in Person or by Proxy

Every person who is entitled to attend and vote at a general meeting may appoint another person, whether a member or not, to attend and vote in his place as his proxy. Every notice calling a general meeting must contain a statement of members' rights to appoint proxies. Proxy voting by mail is permitted and widely practiced by institutional investors.

If a group of shareholders wishes to obtain the support of other members for their proposals, they can, of course, solicit proxy appointments from those members and use their votes at the meeting in addition to their own.

3. Institutional Investors and Duty to Vote

The voting behavior of institutional investors in the U.K. is critical because U.K. institutional investors currently account for approximately 60% of stock market capitalization. A further 16% is accounted for by foreign investors who are primarily financial institutions: U.S. investors alone are responsible for an estimated 8% of the market's value. Other investors include private shareholders who account for an estimated 20% of the market. But even a proportion of these private holdings are also under the management of U.K. fund managers through PEPs and other pooled vehicles.[21] Recent research using major companies' own analysis of shareholder proxy votes has shown that voting levels seldom exceed 40% even on contentious issues. This analysis shows also, however, that voting

---

[20] For more details, see Gower, Laurence C.B. *Principles of Modern Company Law* 596 6th edn. (London 1997).

[21] Cf. the study by Mallin, Chris 'Voting: The Role of Institutional Investors in Corporate Governance' 21 et seq. (Research Board of the Institute of Chartered Accountants in England and Wales, London 1995).

levels have increased over recent years.[22] That may have to do with the discussion in the U.K. about the duty of institutional investors and their fund managers to vote. So far, other than under the ERISA legislation in the U.S.,[23] there exists no statutory obligation or regulatory provision for fund managers to vote the shares in funds managed by them. But the fiduciary duty of fund and investment managers to vote has recently been increasingly stressed.[24]

D. Conclusion

This paper deals with shareholder voting in the countries forming the European Union. The focus of the comparative study is on four points:
- How easy or how difficult is informed voting made in the various legal systems for both domestic and foreign shareholders?
- Is voting by proxies permitted, and if so, in what forms and under what restrictions?
- What duties do institutional investors have with respect to voting the shares they hold in their portfolios?

Not surprisingly, the study shows some quite similar regulations and patterns. But there are also very distinctive features and institutions, and, not astonishingly, the different stages of development of the various capital markets is revealed. It will be up to further research to refine this preliminary picture, and add findings on the practical functioning, criticisms of the various systems, and proposals for further developments.

---

[22] Manifest (ed.) 'The Committee on Corporate Governance' at 7 ("The Hampel Committee", 1996).

[23] ERISA: Employee Retirement Income Schemes Act. On the duty to vote under ERISA, cf. e.g., Langbein, John H. and Bruce A. Wolk *Pension and Employee Benefit Law* 765 et seq. 2nd edn. (Westbury, N.Y. 1995); The Conference Board 'Voting Corporate Pension Fund Proxies' (Report no. 971, 1991).

[24] Cf. Mallin, supra n. 21, 4 et seq.; furthermore (critical) Stapledon, Geof P. *Institutional Shareholders and Corporate Governance* 85 et seq. and own recommendations at 285 et seq. (Oxford 1996).

Discussion Report

STEFAN PRIGGE

Voting rights were one focal point of this discussion. From the American side it was asked whether the current voting right structure in Germany with the prominent position of the banks has been a consequence of the dominance of bearer shares, and if proxy voting by banks, usually supporting management, is an equivalent to proxy voting by the management in the U.S. With respect to the first question, it was generally agreed that bearer shares could have been one cause for the current structure. But *Baums*, referring to his current comparative research in this field, remarked that there have been quite different developments in different countries, so that bearer shares should not be seen as the only explaining factor. Regarding the second topic, *Baums* pointed out that banks usually do vote in accordance with management, but they are not obliged to and sometimes actually oppose management's proposals. Looking into the future from both the practical and the academic side, it was hypothesized that progress in communication technology might radically change voting right structures. Once again the issue of how banks are compensated for their service was raised. *Breuer* reported that banks receive their compensation indirectly in a lump sum to cover several securities-related services. Exercising voting rights is not a profitable business. *Baums* expressed his impression that banks obtain revenues from this activity in other fields as well. As to the question of who the customers are that are using the proxy service, no research is available. According to *Breuer*, small shareholders tend to make use of the service, while the voting rights attached to larger holdings are exercised by the owners themselves. *Baums* doubted the latter part of that statement, arguing that banks sometimes also act as proxies for larger shareholders.

Shareholdings of banks and investment banking versus lending was a second focus of discussion, sparked by the remark of an American academic to *Mülbert's* paper that holding shares is riskier than lending. *Mülbert* replied that securitization lowers the quality of the average borrower, thus increasing risk in the intermediated lending business.[1] *Breuer* reported that lending is riskier than investing. The importance of banks as financial intermediaries decreases; consequently, the revenues generated by this line of business also decrease. Thus, banks have to emphasize investment banking, which he predicted will gain

---

[1] With respect to the argument put forward in his paper, Mülbert added that competition often limits the banks' ability to expand lending; moreover, loans are not so convenient a means to build up hidden reserves when compared with equity holdings.

importance in the banking business. The present German tax environment is a strong impediment to an active management of banks' equity portfolios; currently Deutsche Bank is forced to hold an ill-diversified portfolio. Concerning the empirical part of the paper by *Wenger* and *Kaserer* as presented at the symposium, which, among other things, analyzes banks' equity holdings, the lack of an adjustment for risk was criticized. The results presented are also compatible with the interpretation that banks prefer low-risk companies with accordingly low returns because, for instance, they usually take a lender's perspective. *Kaserer* replied that company size can serve as a kind of proxy for risk, but cannot substitute for an adjustment for systematic risk.[2]

With the recent hostile takeover attempt by Krupp in mind, *Breuer* was asked to comment on the connection between banks playing a role in hostile takeovers and their status as an outstanding component of the linkage within the German corporate sector. *Breuer* answered that takeovers by raiders of the Anglo-Saxon type are generally disliked in Germany and are not financed by the Deutsche Bank. In contrast to that, contested takeovers, a notion he prefers to hostile takeovers, can be appropriate and often turn into friendly takeovers. Their significance will increase. Turning to the core of the question, *Breuer* remarked that reputation and credibility rather than the current legal environment are at the root of the problem. In the long run, Chinese walls are not credible. Consequently, banks have to choose whether to have no supervisory board seats or to run their investment banking completely separated, which is not feasible due to the extreme importance of cross selling. Therefore, members of Deutsche Bank are beginning to reduce their supervisory board seats at other companies, especially the particularly exposed and expensive chairmanships. Some board seats of bankers truly do not make any sense, and they will increasingly be replaced by early retirees from industry.

Remarking on the low market capitalization by international standards of the German share market relative to GDP, an American participant asked whether this could reflect higher debt-equity ratios or a higher significance of private equity in Germany. *Breuer* supported the latter point: family-owned companies are one reason for low market capitalization. Families try to avoid IPOs since they dislike disclosure requirements, tax disadvantages for listed companies, and supervisory board co-determination, while having no problems with works council co-determination. Only capital needs that cannot be covered internally cause an IPO. The pension system and universal banking were mentioned as further reasons for the low market capitalization.

---

[2] In their paper in this volume, Wenger and Kaserer also analyze risk-adjusted performance.

Chapter 7: Capital Markets and Venture Capital

Going Public: A Corporate Governance Perspective

WOLFGANG BESSLER, Gießen, FRED R. KAEN, Durham,
and HEIDEMARIE C. SHERMAN, Munich

This paper explores corporate governance issues in the context of owner-manager decisions to "go public" through selling an initial public offering of common stock (IPO) and the subsequent short- and long-term performance of the companies. We find little evidence that the post-IPO performance of firms is related to ownership governance structures in and of themselves and conclude that a more promising approach for understanding the behavior of publicly held firms and, by implication, the going public event, is a research design informed by history and law. What may matter more than ownership structure is the institutional arrangements governing firms and the protection afforded public shareholders from not only managers but also single entity and large (privileged) blockholders.

Contents

Tables

A. Introduction

This paper explores corporate governance issues in the context of owner-manager decisions to "go public" by publicly selling stock for the first time—an event called an initial public offering (IPO). We begin with some definitions of corporate governance and use them to explore reasons why people care about governance structures. Here, our objective is to explain how the corporate governance interests of security holders are part of more fundamental political interests in corporate governance as a means for achieving (American) values of liberty and equity. We then address the questions of why firms go public and what firms, in theory, are likely to go public. We follow this section with a survey of the empirical literature with regard to the post-issue financial and operating performance of IPOs and report some preliminary findings regarding the correlation between IPO initial returns and attributes of a country's legal and accounting systems. We also report our own preliminary analysis of the post-IPO financial and operating performance of German IPOs issued between 1987 and 1992. Our final section contains our conclusions.

The evidence, to date, suggests privately owned firms, on average, perform poorly after going public. This outcome obtains regardless of whether the firm goes public in an Anglo-American capital market-based or a German financial intermediary-based corporate governance environment. Consistent with this finding, we uncover very little evidence supporting a widely held view that concentrated ownership is associated with better than average post-IPO performance and some evidence that just the opposite is likely to be the case.

Our overall assessment is that the option of going public is more important than the act itself with respect to achieving broad societal objectives of economic liberty, social equity, and economic efficiency. For the U.S., at least, the option to go public serves traditional American values of letting individuals escape dependency and capture the fruits of their labor through the market. We also argue that the publicly held firms became an American solution to the problems of concentrated wealth and government ownership of large-scale firms. We believe a set of similar concerns about the power of banks and concentrated ownership of wealth is motivating legislation in Germany to control bank ownership and bank control of German firms.

B. What Is Corporate Governance?

Corporate governance is an intractable term; many definitions exist. For example, Margaret Blair (1995), writing about ownership and control, uses a very broad definition. She defines corporate governance as "the whole set of legal, cultural, and institutional arrangements that determine what publicly traded corporations can do, who controls them, how that control is exercised, and how the risks and returns from the activities they undertake are allocated".[1] Monks/ Minow (1995) also use a broad definition, but one which focuses primarily on the stakeholders of the firm; they define corporate governance as "the relationship among various participants [chief executive officer, management, shareholders, employees, and so forth] in determining the direction and performance of corporations".[2] In contrast, Shleifer/Vishny (1997) prefer a more tightly knit and less open-ended definition. They say corporate governance deals with "the ways in which suppliers of finance assure themselves of getting a return on their investment." They then frame the problem in terms of how suppliers of finance get managers to return some of the profits to them, how the suppliers make sure that managers do not steal the capital they supply or invest it in bad projects, and how suppliers of finance control managers.

These different definitions of corporate governance reflect different perspectives on what corporate governance is supposed to do and the problems it should mitigate if not solve. One perspective approaches the corporate governance debate as part of the larger question of how to organize economic activity to achieve more fundamental societal objectives related to equity, fairness, freedom, and citizen responsibilities. The other perspective is more narrowly concerned with economic efficiency objectives and, at the risk of exaggeration, considers economic efficiency to be an end in itself rather than a means to non-economic societal objectives. For example, Blair (1995) is concerned with the societal role of the firm; Shleifer/Vishny (1997) are concerned with the financial status of security holders and implicitly accept that suppliers of finance should control managers (presumably to optimize some economic efficiency objective such as shareholder wealth maximization).

We believe the broader, societal perspective is necessary for understanding why the public corporation and "going public" is more common in the U.S. than other countries and why Americans historically have been concerned about more than purely economic efficiency questions surrounding the separation of owners and managers.

I. The American Debate[3]

The key feature of the transition from a privately held firm to a publicly held firm is the transfer of cash flow and control rights to individuals and institutions not directly involved in managing the company. The American public policy

---

[1] Blair (1995: 3).

[2] Monks/Minow (1995: 1).

[3] This section draws from Kaen/Kaufman/Zacharias (1988) and from Kaufman/ Zacharias/Karson (1995).

(values) debates about the implications and desirability of this organizational form and the governance structures needed to "control" it have their American origin in the two major 19th-century visions of how to maintain a political economy which sustained both freedom and equality: civic republicanism and liberalism (Appleby 1985).

Civic republicans viewed physical property ownership (possession) as necessary for the development of the citizen's moral character. This character development was an integral part of the citizen's personality, and civic republicans saw the market as a meeting place for independent producers where exchanges would take place based on economic merit in contrast to a dependency culture. The objective was to shape the citizen's personality so as to direct the actions of the citizen toward socially beneficial ends.

The civic republicans forged a strong link between personality (moral development) and responsible individual behavior. Citizens learned to act responsibly through their participation in the market and community politics. In both cases, the citizen's responsible participation was motivated by property ownership. The citizen sought to retain the benefits of his property's productivity and to protect his property from the opportunistic behavior of others through such participation. The ends civic republicans sought to achieve were liberty and equality. Liberty meant not only political freedom but also the freedom of economic self-determination. Equality meant not only equal standing before the law but also economic equality through wide distribution (non-concentration) of productive resources which were equated with property. Freedom and equality were mutually reinforcing and inseparable, for it was the wide distribution of property (equality) which operationalized the attainment of economic self-sufficiency and determination.

Liberalism, the competing view, defined property in purely instrumental terms, not in terms of physical ownership. Physical ownership of property was not deemed necessary to achieve the democratic goals of liberty (social freedom) and equality (fairness). Instead, emphasis was placed on using property to maximize the economic wealth of society.

Liberals believed the civic republican objective of a republic composed of moral, benevolent, and independent producers was naive and blind to human nature. Opportunistic behavior and avarice would dominate the very market economy on which freedom depended and America would become a class-divided society as was the case in Europe. So, the liberals called for a different "technology" to foster democratic virtues. The liberals did not try to change human nature through the market place and widespread ownership of property. Instead, they called for institutional structures, procedures, and governance systems which would fragment power and provide mechanisms for monitoring power and guarding against its abuses so that no single interest group could dominate.

The absence of any moral development function in the liberal scheme of things meant that liberals had a very different view of property and the market than civic republicans. Liberals saw property as a means to achieving an end, not an end in itself. Individuals should use property to become more prosperous and increase the wealth of the community. Property played primarily an economic efficiency role, not a political role, and property rights were needed primarily to insure that property owners would use property for this economic efficiency purpose. As for the market, the market also played primarily an economic efficiency role. It was a utilitarian expediter of economic efficiency, not a developer of personal values ensuring liberty and equality.

The emergence of the corporation in the latter half of the 19th century complicated life for both civic republicans and liberals. For civic republicans, the goal of widespread ownership of property would be eviscerated unless the size of corporations could be controlled and concentrations of wealth (property) broken up. Economic efficiency, per se, was not the criterion by which to judge the corporation. The real question was whether increasing the size of the firm would reduce opportunities for property ownership among the large body of citizens and create a "wealthy" class which would dominate society. Concentrations of wealth (large block holders?) were bad in and of themselves regardless of whether such holdings increased economic efficiency. Furthermore, as civic republicans watched the growth of corporations, they became increasingly concerned with the personality (social responsibility) of the corporation. Did it have one and was it being perverted through concentrations of wealth?

For the liberals, the problem was to show that a concentration of corporate capital would not undermine the economic efficiency function of markets by destroying competition and that concentrations of wealth would not undermine (democratic) politics. Liberals had to find ways to insure the perpetuation of majoritarian electoral politics without eliminating private property rights needed to support economic growth *and* protect the citizen from the state.

Civic republican reformers suggested reforming the governance structure of the corporation by restricting its size and having workers becoming participating owners. Liberals confronted the problems by arguing that the corrupting tendencies of size and concentration should be handled through the political process; not by destroying the corporation which was worth more than the sum of its parts.

In the early twentieth century, the political debate intensified as people looked out the window and saw a rapidly changing industrial world. Veblen (1904), Lippman (1914), and Brandeis (1934) asserted that the owners of corporations had been divested of control. Consequently, managers and insider control groups could serve their own interests in the corporation without benefiting the public shareholders and, hence, society's need for growth in general. Here is where the debate, in America, focused on the question of to whom and how management could be held accountable so as to achieve the goal of economic growth—the debate about corporate governance and whether corporate governance matters. And this debate led to events which probably have as much to do with explaining the level of IPOs and firm formation in the United States as anything else. Note that the purpose of this debate was not how to maximize the wealth of shareholders or any related economic efficiency objective. It was over how to accommodate the corporation to the (American) democratic ideals of liberty and equality!

II. Accommodating the Corporation to American Values

Two dominant strategies for accommodating the (public) corporation to democratic ideals emerged. The civic republican strategy emphasized the role of managers acting as trustees for society at large. The liberal strategy emphasized the role of contractual relationships and the accountability of managers to stockholders as the key for controlling the corporation and directing it towards society's interests. Both strategies can be found in the early writings of Adolph Berle, Jr. (1931, 1932, 1933).

Berle saw that the public corporation drew its capital from an increasingly fragmented investor and creditor base. Berle concluded that this separation of ownership from management severed any connections between property rights of the corporation's owners and the development of these owners' personalities (social responsibility) through the exercise of these property rights. However, Berle also recognized the economic utility in the separation of the management function and the financial risk-bearing function. So, what could be done?

A trustee theory of corporate management could be developed. In this model, managers would be defined as legal trustees for the stockholders' property and be held accountable for performance not by direct shareholder actions but by the courts. This trustee idea was carried further by Dodd (1932), who asked why the managers should be trustees for only the shareholders (making sure the shareholders behaved in the way they would had physical property ownership and responsibility for the management of the property remained in their hands). After all, it was the community's interests which were to be ultimately served by the corporation, so why not have the managers act as trustees for all the stakeholders of the firm—society at large?

Ultimately, Berle questioned the technical competence of the courts to monitor the managers and the complex financial transactions of the firm. More importantly, what reason was there to believe that judicial officials were any less self-seeking than managers? Under the trustee theory, problems of managerial self-seeking behavior are not solved; they are only pushed upward to a higher level—the courts. And, under government ownership, government bureaucracies.

So Berle proposed a second alternative which was essentially a contractual as opposed to a trustee solution. Instead of having managers take on the responsibility of forming the corporation's personality, he had them act as contracting parties between the firm's customers, suppliers, employees, creditors, and shareholders. The self-seeking behavior of all but the residual risk bearers would be held in check by managers responsible for carrying our their contract written with the residual risk bearers—the public shareholders. Managers would be motivated to write the best contracts they could with the workers, suppliers, and other managers because it was in their self-interest to do so. If they didn't, they would be replaced.

But who was going to monitor the monitors and hold the self-interest of the shareholders in place? Berle (1932) wasn't very clear about this. However, he and others were probably relying on a competitive and efficient financial market—not financial institutions and investment bankers—to do this. He wanted a federal agency with special expertise to guard the sanctity of financial markets and insure they weren't subject to managerial and insider manipulation. Unless these markets worked well, his contractual theory would be short-circuited and a trustee theory of management would be viewed as a better solution to social justice and what we now call agency problems from a societal perspective.

From the perspective of today, it is fascinating to look back and see that Berle was calling for ways to discipline managers through financial markets, including a market for corporate control, as a way for achieving American democratic values of liberty and equality. He wanted a governance structure that would assure suppliers of finance of getting a return on their investment, that would make sure that managers do not steal the capital or invest it in bad projects, and that would give suppliers of finance control over managers.

Berle, as well as many others, was struggling with perceived tradeoffs among the following: the economic contributions that corporations could make toward enhancing the well-being of all citizens (economic efficiency, economic growth, and employment); concentrations of wealth in the hands of a few, including financial institutions which were themselves corporations and raised the same concerns about the personality of the corporation; the emergence of an elite managerial class which could extract rents from everyone in the name of the trusteeship theory of corporate governance; and the role of (fragmented) public investors in mitigating or exacerbating the aforementioned problems. Implicit in these debates was the assumption that governance structures mattered. And, in the context of the governance debates, what especially mattered was (1) the size of the firm, (2) the ownership structure of privately and publicly held corporations, and (3) who controls the managers of a publicly held corporation. What was not on Berle's agenda was an optimal ownership structure for maximizing the value of the firm!

Size of firm mattered because size was equated with concentrations of power and control, both of which would lead to political and economic inequalities and the severing of any connections which were left between property ownership and the citizen's personality. The ownership structure of privately held firms mattered because these firms could be controlled by inside owners, including bankers, who would not direct the firm in society's best interests. Who controls the managers of publicly held corporations mattered because economic efficiency of the firm and its ability to raise capital could be damaged by managers who extracted perks for themselves or inappropriately assigned these rights to other corporate stakeholders—employees, creditors, government officials, and so forth.

Approaching the publicly held corporation within this historical context may yield insights into why the United States has "so many" publicly held firms relative to other countries and why the level of IPOs and new firm formation in the United States is so much higher as well. It may also help us understand why firms go or are forced to go public and how the option of going public is far more important than the act itself (because even in the U.S., the vast majority of firms remain private). We also believe it provides a framework for considering privatization of state-owned enterprises and the deregulation of energy, telecommunication, and other industries as part of "going public" governance issues and clarifying some issues about the post-"going public" financial and operating performance of the now publicly owned firms.

We begin with the question of why firms go or become public and relate these decisions to the public policy concerns of modern-day civic republicans and liberals. The analytical structure we use is financial agency theory—a contractual approach—which historically is best understood as the liberal response to managerial capitalism, a trustee approach. Agency theory's heritage extends back to Berle's contractual thesis through the work of Coase (1937).

C. Why Do Firms Go Public?

Why owners of privately held firms choose to take them public or, conversely, not to take them public continues to elude the modeling attempts of financial economists. Instead, a series of independent but not necessarily mutually exclusive reasons for going public have been compiled. Our list follows:

I. The Company Needs Money to Grow

The need for funds to support growth is a popular story because it appeals to common sense. In its simplest version, it is told as follows: the company founders have insufficient capital to finance expansion and, therefore, raise the funds from the public through a sale of common stock. Assumptions about the availability and/or desirability of debt capital are implicit if not explicit in this story. So are assumptions about the availability and/or desirability of obtaining funds from private investors.

Debt capital could be used as an alternative to equity capital for financing the firm. However, either the owners or potential creditors may decide that additional debt financing is undesirable because it is: (a) too expensive, (b) imposes excessive constraints on the investment and operating decisions of the founders, (c) substantially increases the agency costs associated with financial distress, and/or (d) too risky for the creditor. If we take a look at current thinking about why and which firms use financial leverage, we would predict that firms less likely to use debt capital are those which face intangible growth opportunities, are relatively profitable, and want to escape creditor restrictions on new investment activities. We would also find that firms selling products and services whose quality is difficult to measure but whose performance is essential to the survival of the customer would use less debt than the "average" firm.

The firm we just described is often called a new technology-based firm (NTBF). But describing the NTBF as one which can no longer obtain debt financing under acceptable circumstances doesn't explain why the owners choose to raise equity capital through a public offering. At least three other alternatives exist: financing the firm through retention of earnings, slowing down the rate of growth, and/or seeking private equity investors—family, friends, venture capitalists, and so forth.

Retaining earnings instead of distributing them as dividends to the founders assumes the firm has the cash to pay dividends and that the owners are not already reinvesting all of the earnings back in the firm. It also means further concentrating the wealth of the owners in the company rather than permitting them to diversify into other investments. In effect, the decision not to pay cash dividends is a decision to increase the owner's investment in the firm. Reluctance on the part of owners to retain earnings suggests the owners are seeking to diversify their investments, increase the liquidity of their investments, or simply need the cash for consumption purposes.

Not growing or slowing down the rate of growth may not be feasible. The viability of this alternative may well be determined by the presence of product market competitors and the sources of financing available to these competitors. If all competitors face "restricted" equity capital funding sources, the slow growth strategy may be viable. However, if the problem is not the availability of equity capital but the willingness of the owners to share cash flow and control rights, the slow growth strategy becomes questionable.

The remaining alternatives to selling the company to another firm are to finance the growth with private equity capital or go public. Setting aside the sale option, the critical questions become: (1) Why would a private investor pay a premium for buying the equity of a privately as opposed to publicly held corporation? and (2) Why would the existing owners prefer to bring in large block-holders instead of selling shares to the general public and ending up with fragmented public ownership?

The first question is really a question about whether private investors are more than portfolio investors. Private investors always have the alternative of investing in publicly held corporations. So why would they take an equity position in a privately held firm if the expected risk-adjusted returns were no different from those available on existing public corporations?

A common answer to this question is that private investors bring more than capital to the company. They bring technical, managerial, and financial expertise which adds value to the firm. They may also have better knowledge about the quality of the company, its long-run prospects, and the true value of the firm; in other words, the informational asymmetries between the current owners of the company and the private investors may be less than between the current owners and the public investors. Private investors may also be able to exert more control over the investment and financing decisions of the owner/managers through informed and very close monitoring of the company and, most likely, influential positions on the governing board (or equivalent) of the company. All these factors are "value creation" factors. And, from the perspective of the private investor(s), the greater the percentage of the firm owned by the private investor, the greater will be the benefits captured by the investor relative to those shared with passive fragmented public investors.

Of course, other than purely wealth maximization reasons may explain the willingness of private investors to supply the equity. Friendship, family ties, status, and employment for the investors' friends and family may also motivate the private investor.

An answer to the question of why existing owners would prefer the private investor to public ownership can also be framed in terms of a value added and informational asymmetry story—indeed, the other side of the private investor story. Relative to public investors, the private investor(s) adds value to the company through supplying expertise, reputation, and evidence of close monitoring of firm performance. So, the value of the firm is greater under concentrated private ownership than fragmented public ownership. As for informational asymmetries and adverse selection problems, private investors reduce the likelihood of adverse selection and face lower informational asymmetries. So the private investors are willing to pay more for the firm than public investors.

But private investors supplying capital and not interested in becoming permanent owner/managers probably expect to get their money out of the company in the not too distant future. Recall that the "company needs more money" story is a story about a growing, expanding company, not a mature company in a declining industry throwing off cash which can be used to buy back the owners' shares. So, the private investor expects to sell his interest to either another investor, a trade buyer, or to the public through an IPO.

Now, let's work backwards from the trade buyer and IPO stage to the founder stage of the "firm that needs the money to grow" or NTBF. These companies are often founded by engineers and scientists who have limited personal wealth and they need financial assistance. A common financing sequence would be seed capital, start-up capital, venture capital, and then trade sale or IPO. In the absence of a well-developed secondary market for common stock, the attractiveness of taking a private position in these firms is reduced for private investors right back down to the seed capital stage, which means the formation of these companies is truncated at the formative stage. Hence, the number of NTBFs being started is, ultimately, related to the ability of professional "firm-builders" to cash out their investments. And the ability to cash out is related to the existence of capital markets, with the emphasis being on markets. (We will come back to markets later because the existence of markets was deemed critical by those who wanted to facilitate the citizen's economic freedom and secure for the individual the just rewards of his labor. By having a public market, founders are able to protect themselves from oligopolistic and oligarchic interests buying their firms at bargain basement prices.)

Under what circumstances is it likely that the founders of NTBFs and the private investors would agree that going public is a preferred arrangement to remaining private? The circumstances would likely include a substantial reduction in the informational asymmetries between the public investors and the firm—a reduction in adverse selection costs—and in the value-creating benefits brought by the private investors in contrast to public, including large block public, investors. The benefits which would remain associated with large block holders would be benefits associated with monitoring rather than active management. In other words, when the returns on the private investors' position are no different from those which could be earned on portfolio investments in publicly held firms without the benefits of liquidity offered by publicly held firms, the time for the active firm-builder to exit has arrived.

The exit of the "firm-builder" does leave a void with respect to monitoring the remaining managers and owner-managers of the firm and protecting the interests of the new public shareholders. But is this situation any different from a non-NTBF company going public? In other words, if the only value large block holders bring is close monitoring, then why should we expect any difference in the post-IPO performance of NTBFs relative to other kinds of IPO companies? The post-issue performance should be similar. And, as we report later, this is the case.

II. Diversification and Liquidity

Another reason for going public arises out of the owner's desire to diversify risk and obtain liquidity. Going public for this reason is qualitatively different from the "more money to grow the company" reason. In the "pure" case, no new funds are injected into the firm; instead, a change in ownership occurs.

From a purely diversification perspective, going public is not necessary. The owner(s) could sell a portion of the firm to private investors. But why would private investors want to purchase these positions unless they offered returns better than those available from public portfolio investments? Only if the private investors could add value (or gain control) would they be inclined to take a position.

From the owner's perspective, large positions held by non-passive large block holders may be unappealing. These large block holders may be deemed too intrusive by the existing owners because they exert too much influence on the investment, financing, and dividend decisions.

So, firms taken public for primarily personal wealth diversification motives are likely to be firms which would not benefit from active investor management and which pose limited adverse selection risks to public investors. In other words, the value of these firms to a group of private investors is not much different than their value as public firms unless the private investors could control the firm in the event that the founder control group attempted to consume managerial perks.

Bebchuk/Zingales (1996) have tried to formalize this question first addressed by Berle (1926). They have identified an important corporate governance issue in this type of transaction: the percentage of control retained by the private owners relative to their claims on the cash flows of the firm.

Building on the work of Grossman/Hart (1988), Ruback (1988), and Bebchuk (1994), Bebchuk/Zingales (1996) argue that the original owners, by separating ownership and cash flow rights, are able to retain control of the firm, with all of the private benefits that go along with ownership, by selling only the cash flow rights to the public. This outcome could be obtained through selling dual class shares or by selling participating preferred stock with no voting rights, a common type of IPO offering in Germany.

The empirical implications of the Bebchuk/Zingales (1996) argument are that the post-IPO operating performance of companies issuing inferior voting rights IPOs should be worse than full voting rights IPO companies. Furthermore, the value of full voting rights securities should be "greater" than the value of restricted or non-voting rights securities.

III. Escaping the Control of Banks and Increased Financial Flexibility

Not addressed by Bebchuk/Zingales (1996) is what happens to the firm's cost of capital and its financial flexibility as it goes public. Presumably, the increase in liquidity which comes with public trading of securities lowers the firm's cost of equity capital, other things being equal. Whether this results in a reduction of the overall cost of capital to the firm is another question and has to do with cost and availability of debt funds as well as financial flexibility.

A common IPO story told by investment bankers is that established firms go public in order to escape the monitoring and control of banks and to set the stage for selling public debt. The public debt is less expensive than private debt and the firm achieves greater financial flexibility through reductions in debt covenants and being able to issue a wide range of securities to public, including convertible securities. Rajan (1992) has developed a theoretical model along these lines and Pagano/Panetta/Zingales (1995) find supporting evidence in Italian IPOs.

Substituting public debt for bank debt is a major change from a broad governance perspective. It is a move away from a banking-oriented-relationship governance structure toward a capital market governance structure. So, given the supposed virtues of a bank-dominated governance structure with respect to providing a low-cost overall cost of capital (presumably higher interest rates are offset by the ability to use more leverage and reductions in financial distress and agency costs) and lengthening the investment horizon time of managers, what types of privately held firms would be likely to forego these benefits and choose public ownership?

Most likely, these firms have an established track record such that the quality of the firm's cash flows are publicly known or could be deduced from public information, meaning that access to inside information about the firm's financial situation has little value. One would also expect that the need for creditors to control managerial decisions would be limited or, at least, the control exerted through bond covenants would be adequate.

Berlin (1996) provides an excellent description of this transition process. Berlin (1996) maintains that as firms grow and prosper, their owners believe that by diversifying funding sources, including going public, they can get more discretion over investment and financing decisions and improve their bargaining power in negotiations with banks. But, Berlin (1996) also suggests that this transition is more likely if banking markets are concentrated so as to reduce the lending alternatives of their borrowers. This prediction seems counter to the German experience unless German banks are able to control the going public decision and "prevent" firms from going public by making it too costly.

We can think of another interesting (and some would say tongue-in-cheek) prediction of the Berlin model. Suppose the advocates of the German universal-relationship banking system are right. Suppose bank monitoring and control (and, in Anglo-American systems, private investor monitoring and control) does discipline managers and discourage them from undertaking "overly optimistic" projects. But suppose the owner-managers of the companies which have performed exceedingly well suffer from hubris (Roll 1986). The managers ignore the advice and go public to fund the next round of "growth opportunities." Under these assumptions, we would expect to find that German IPOs underperformed the market in the post-IPO period. In reality this underperformance is what has happened, although this outcome is consistent with any number of other hypotheses as well. Further complicating the interpretation is the extent to which market underperformance is sensitive to the selected benchmark portfolio.

IV. Maximizing the Price of Selling Control

Going public is also a way to sell control of the company. We differentiate this motivation from the diversification/liquidation motivation by emphasizing that the existing owners give up managerial control of the firm as well as control over the cash flows. The alternatives to going public are to sell the company to a trade buyer or to another group of private investors. So here the question becomes why the public would be willing to pay more than a trade buyer or private investors.

This question is a variation on the question of why corporations pay a premium to acquire another publicly held firm, why a particular firm is worth more to one bidder than another, and why corporations divest themselves of certain operations through spinoffs and equity carveouts.

One answer is that going public allows a price discovery process to take place and puts the owners in a better bargaining position for sale of their remaining shares either to the public or to a trade buyer who would be willing to pay a control premium over the market price. Such a story is formally developed by Ellingsen/Rydqvist (1996), who describe the going public transaction as a screening device for reducing the risks of adverse selection.

The driving force behind the Ellingsen and Rydqvist model is that the private owner has private information about the value of the firm which, for some reason(s), cannot be ascertained by other buyers. Once the firm goes public, however, this information is released and causes a higher valuation of the firm. Subsequently, the owner can sell his remaining shares at the higher price.

Left unanswered is why the trade buyer or other private investors cannot assess the so-called private information of the existing owner and why the private information eventually becomes public, unless it is simply a matter of time with the existing owner not having the financial resources or tastes for risk that would enable him to delay any public offering until the private information is revealed.

Another way of looking at this sale of control reason is as a vehicle for bringing more participants into an auction and setting a minimum price for the company. By going public, the non-control value of the firm is its floor and trade buyers then make bids for the control value of the company.

But an equally compelling reason for why a trade buyer doesn't acquire the firm is that the firm run as an independent entity can operate more efficiently than as part of a corporate bureaucracy or conglomerate. In other words, the high-powered incentives and freedom from corporate hierarchies outweigh the benefits of belonging to a large corporation. In the jargon of the management literature, by remaining independent, the management of the firm can focus on its core competencies.

Williamson (1985), in answering the question of why firms do not comprehensively integrate, identifies a number of circumstances which may result in the firm being worth more as an independent firm than as part of a bureaucracy. Among them, he lists asset utilization losses, accounting contrivances and incentive schemes, innovation, and bureaucracy costs associated with the internal politics of the corporation.

Williamson is primarily concerned with the question of why hierarchies replace markets and conditions under which markets work better than bureaucracies. A critical factor is asset specificity, including firm-specific human assets. In general, the more specific the asset, the more likely the operation is to become part of a bureaucracy (firm) with transactions taken out of the market.

Now, suppose a privately held corporation exists which produces a product requiring no firm-specific human capital or assets. Previously, the owner-manager of this firm was compensated with a high-powered incentive system (a system which tied pay to performance). If this firm is acquired by another company and made a division of the acquiring firm, the new manager (who may or may not be the old owner) is kept on a high-powered incentive system. Williamson argues that the new manager no longer has the same incentives to utilize equipment with the same care as before and, in the extreme case, may run the division into the ground before leaving the firm to take a similar position elsewhere (remember, the manager has little firm-specific human capital at stake).

The acquiring firm could solve some of these problems by closely monitoring the division manager for compliance. However, this monitoring is costly and was not needed in the independent state. Williamson concludes that "efficient asset utilization and the use of high-powered incentives experience tensions in an integrated firm—tensions that do not arise when the two production stages are independent."[4]

Internal accounting conventions and corporate politics can exacerbate the problems of using high-powered incentives in the firm. The price at which goods are transferred to other divisions in the firm is now determined within the firm and becomes subject to corporate politics and power plays, especially if the manager is not permitted to source outside the firm at lower than internal transfer prices.[5] Determining the cost of the product also becomes more difficult and subject to the same politics.

---

[4] Williamson (1985: 138).

[5] As this paper was being written, an example of these costs appeared at the University of New Hampshire. The telecommunications division of the University "shut off" access to a private Internet server who was charging faculty, including academic departments, lower access fees than the University.

Williamson continues by suggesting that low-powered incentives (salaries) could be used to avoid the high-powered incentive and internal accounting problems. However, in circumstances where no reduction in transaction costs are to be gained by integrating the firm, the governance costs of integration exceed those of an independent firm. Williamson further argues that such a situation is most likely to arise where asset specificity is very low. In these cases, firms should remain independent.

At the opposite extreme of firms which should remain independent are firms where maintaining innovation is critical. Here, the argument is that innovation is stifled by corporate bureaucracies and that the culture of large corporations is ill-suited for creative managers, engineers, and others who are integral to the innovation process. After citing a number of examples supporting his thesis, Williamson summarizes the cases by saying that "large companies are becoming increasingly aware that the bureaucratic apparatus they use to manage mature products is less well-suited to supporting early stage entrepreneurial activity." (p. 159) Williamson suggests that one solution to this "problem" is to have technological development and innovation concentrated in small independent firms with the successful developments either acquired or licensed by the large firms.

We think Williamson's insights into the vertical integration process can be used to enhance our understanding of why some firms go public, provided an equity market exists, rather than being sold to trade buyers. We offer the following explanation:

The independent firm is well-suited organizationally for fostering innovative activities. It is worth more as an independent company than as part of a corporate bureaucracy. So, in the absence of wealthy owner-innovators, a financing problem exists. Financing could be provided by banks; but these are risky firms and for reasons already listed, the owners probably want to avoid the constraints of bank financing. Financing may also be available from other corporations or private investors, but now the liquidity or exit problem re-emerges. So what happens? The firm can go public if a well-functioning equity market exists. If not, perhaps the outcome is a reduction in innovation.

The critical point we are making is that innovation requires an organizational form which is "small" and "independent." Also needed are high-powered incentive systems. Publicly held firms (or the possibility of going public) solve these organizational problems.

Using Williamson's analytical framework, we would predict two types of firms would go public rather than being acquired by trade buyers (or, in Williamson's terms, vertically integrate): firms using non-specific assets and requiring non-specific human capital, and firms dedicated to continuous innovation. We would also predict that, of the firms which do go public, firms with these characteristics would remain independent.

V. Solving Ownership Squabbles

Even in privately held and family-controlled firms, conflicts of interest arise between the owners (family members) who manage the firm and those who supply the capital.[6] Going public is a way of solving these problems without having to sell the company to a trade buyer.

This story, though, is a variation on the partial control argument and/or on the liquidity and diversification arguments. But, like the partial control story, the decision to go public may be part of a buyout of the dissenting owners with public ownership replacing private ownership at the expense of overall economic efficiency. The remaining control block may or may not manage the firm so as to "maximize" economic efficiency.

VI. Breaking Up Concentrated Holdings of Banks and Cross Holdings

A public policy designed to reduce concentrations of wealth and oligopolistic as well as oligarchic control of economic and, by implication, political power, may lead to firms being forced to go public. This story is particularly appropriate for the United States.

As described by Kaufman/Zacharias/Karson (1995), the merger movement of the late 19th century had transformed the American economy into a modern industrial system. Instead of a decentralized economy run by family-controlled firms, the country appeared to have been transformed into an industrial complex dominated by a few banking houses acting as a ruling plutocracy. The apparent control by bankers through their membership on corporate boards and other interlocking relationships led to a national debate over the role of these banks and finance capitalism—a debate which became part of the 1912 three-party Presidential contest among Woodrow Wilson, William Taft, and Teddy Roosevelt and the 1912 Pujo hearings.

Roe (1994) summarizes the American experience in this regard as well as anyone. He concludes that: "Politics never allowed [American] financial institutions to become powerful enough to control operating firms; American politics preferred Berle-Means corporations [ownership separated from management] to the alternative of concentrated institutional ownership, which it precluded." (p. 22)

Whether the American approach of "forcing" fragmented public ownership of (large) firms was and is economically efficient relative to other types of governance structures has become a hotly debated public policy question. We believe

---

[6] A very recent example of such a conflict occurred in New Hampshire and led to the highly unusual situation of the State of New Hampshire guaranteeing a loan to the owner-manager to fend off an attempt by other family members to sell the firm to an out-of-state corporation.

that the outcome was one which led to the development of secondary equity markets and, as an intended or unintended by-product, provided exit routes for what we now call venture capitalists.

VII. Privatization

Publicly held firms are an alternative to government ownership of large-scale enterprises. These enterprises require large capital investments and provide services and products which people consider essential and believe should be priced to provide only a fair return to the owners—zero net present value returns. At the risk of oversimplification, government ownership can be thought of as an example of a trustee concept of governance. The managers of the firm, appointed directly or indirectly by those in control of the government, including government bureaucracies, ostensibly were to run the firm in the best interests of everyone.

These government-owned firms obtained financing in a variety of ways. At one extreme, the firms were simply financed as part of the government budget process. At the other extreme, the firms were set up as quasi-private corporations which borrowed funds in the capital markets. Applying the Shleifer/Vishny (1997) definition of corporate governance raises some interesting questions.

The suppliers of finance to these firms were creditors and taxpayers, with the taxpayers being the residual claimants of the cash flows of the state-owned enterprise (SOE). Who represented the taxpayers? How did the taxpayers assure themselves of getting a return on their investment? How did the taxpayers make sure that the managers did not steal the capital and invest in bad projects? How did the taxpayers control managers?

Apparently, for many countries, the outcome of government ownership of firms was not satisfactory. The electorate, through their elected representatives, decided the government-appointed "trustees" were not adequately representing them as the ultimate financing source of government-owned firms and the result has been the privatizations we have observed in many democratic countries. In other counties, this privatization process accompanied a massive change in all governance structures.

This transition from centrally planned government ownership of firms to private and quasi-private ownership, along with the privatization of SOEs in already market-oriented and capitalistic countries, may offer some of the best insights into whether and how corporate governance matters. For example, Boycko/Shleifer/Vishny (1995) conclude that the weakness of corporate governance mechanisms in Russia have led to misuse of assets by Russian managers and the virtual non-existence of external capital for Russian firms.

D. Going Public and Firm Performance

Do publicly held firms perform differently than privately held firms? Should we expect any differences in performance?

Very little empirical work exists with regard to the question of whether privately held firms perform differently than publicly held firms. The one piece we are familiar with is Pagano/Panetta/Zingales (1995). These authors studied going public decisions in Italy and found that those firms which did go public, compared to those which remained private, were larger, more profitable, had grown more rapidly, and had higher leverage. Fortuitously, the authors had access to a data bank which contained financial information about all Italian firms. A major reason for the absence of comparative analyses in other countries, of course, is the absence of financial data for privately held firms.

What has been examined is the post-IPO stock price (market) and operating performance of IPOs. To the extent pre-IPO data is available for the companies from security prospectuses and other sources, comparisons of pre- and post-IPO performance of the *same* company can be made. Even here, though, most of the work to date is concerned with the stock market performance of the IPOs.

I. Stock Market Performance

Numerous studies of the post-issue performance have been undertaken, with one of the first being by Logue (1973). Until recently, most studies, as would be expected, have focused on the United States. The early studies examined IPO returns at and around the offering date. These studies reported that IPOs in the U.S. were underpriced by 15% or so based on the difference between the offering price and the first trading prices (Ibbotson/Sindelar/Ritter 1994). Subsequently, underpricing of IPOs was identified in many other countries as well (Loughran/ Ritter/Rydqvist 1994), including Germany (Ljungqvist 1996).

These empirical results motivated individuals to explain the results. Rock (1986) has constructed an explanation which proved to be very popular among financial economists. Rock (1986) divides investors into two groups: informed and uninformed. The informed investors buy shares only if they are underpriced, leading to an excess demand for the shares in fixed price offering. Uninformed investors buy IPOs only if they are consistently underpriced. Rock's (1986) explanation is basically an adverse selection under informational asymmetries story. Other so-called rational explanations have been offered, including signalling,[7] underpricing as a quality risk premium to solve an Akerlof lemons problem, and strategies used by underwriters to get investors to reveal informa-

---

[7] Allen/Faulhaber (1989); Welch (1989); Grinblatt/Hwang (1989).

tion about the true value of the firm in the the pre-selling period (Benveniste/ Spindt 1989). Our primary interest in this paper, though, is whether the underpricing is somehow connected to governance structures, including ownership and institutional structures.

Brennan/Franks (1995) have argued that managers and founders may underprice offerings to keep better control of the firm through fragmented ownership. This strategy would be consistent with going public to retain the private benefits of control and could lead to a less than socially optimal outcome. Practitioners have made similar arguments. One empirical implication of these arguments is that the greater the intent of "entrenched managers" to retain the private control benefits, the greater would be the underpricing.

Empirically, the evidence supporting financial agency theory predictions that initial underpricing is correlated with such governance variables as ownership structure and large block holdings is mixed. Lee/Taylor/Walter (1996) find a positive relationship between underpricing and ownership retention for the Australian market. In other words, the larger the percentage of equity retained by the owners, the greater the initial underpricing. Levis (1993) reports similar results for the U.K. But why would "high" ownership be associated with more underpricing?

One story is the signalling story, which says that underpricing is done to signal the company is a "good" company and any "losses" resulting from the underpricing of the IPO will be more than recovered with a subsequent offering. Unfortunately, the empirical evidence[8] doesn't support this story, although these studies did not explicitly control for ownership retention in examining seasoned equity offerings following IPOs. Furthermore, in contrast to Lee/Taylor/Walter (1996) and Levis (1993), Aussenegg's (1996) study of Austrian IPOs finds no relationship between ownership retention and underpricing.

Of particular interest to observers of United States IPOs has been the role of venture capitalists. Venture capitalists closely monitor firm performance and serve on the boards of their portfolio companies. So the expectation was that IPOs backed by venture capitalists would be less underpriced than non-venture-capital-backed IPOs. Barry et al. (1990), however, report that "the average initial-day return of venture-capital-backed IPOs is not significantly different from that of the IPOs without venture capital backing." (p. 458) Apparently, the backing of venture capitalists cannot be used to explain differences in underpricing. But Barry et al. (1990) do find that within their venture capital sample, ownership and governance structure variables matter. Within the venture capital IPO sample, underpricing is negatively correlated with length of time the lead venture capitalist has been on the company's board and the fraction of the issuer's shares held by the venture capitalist prior to the IPO.

---

[8] Garfinkel (1993) and Jegadeesh/Weinstein/Welch (1993).

As well documented as the underpricing of IPOs on the first trading day is the stock market underperformance of IPO companies during the first three to five years of their public life. A classic study is Loughran/Ritter (1995), who report that "an investor would have had to invest 44 percent more money in the issuers (IPOs) than in nonissuers of the same size to have the same wealth five years after the offering date." This feature of post-IPO underperformance of privately owned companies going public has also been documented for Brazil (Leal/Hernandez 1993), Finland (Keloharju 1993), Germany (Ljungqvist 1996), Singapore, and the U.K. (Levis 1993).

Many stories have been told about why the initial underpricing occurs, but no "rigorous" models explain the long-term underperformance. Loughran/Ritter (1995) simply call it a "puzzle." Again, we focus on attempts to explain this long-run underperformance with governance variables.

Lee/Taylor/Walter (1996) found a negative relationship between long-run market performance of Australian IPOs and the percentage of equity retained by the owners. Ausseneg (1996), examining Austrian IPOs, found a negative relationship between long-run IPO performance and family ownership. In sharp contrast, Ausseneg (1996) reported positive abnormal long-run performance for privatized firms. So the evidence in favor of an agency theory story about the long-run market performance of IPOs is not very compelling. If anything, within IPOs themselves, long-run performance is negatively, not positively, associated with owner/family control. This outcome has been confirmed for Germany by Ljungqvist (1996).

One interesting conjecture with regard to family IPOs is the possible connection between going public, cashing out, and management succession. Consider the following situation recently reported in the *Wall Street Journal*.[9]

The family owners of Automotive Moulding decided that to remain competitive in the automotive supply industry they had to expand the company's product line and enlarge the company. The owners decided not to do so and began considering how to sell the business. The arrangement they negotiated was a private trade sale. But, a condition of the sale was that the owners retain 30% of the company for no less than three years and remain on as managers. Apparently, management succession was a real problem in this case and the trade buyer was able to mitigate the management succession problem by having the owners stay on for a few years. Had the company gone public, an entirely new management team would have had to be installed and, if the concerns of the trade buyer were valid, increased the likelihood that the firm under new management would do poorly. In other words, going public was precluded by the absence of adequate replacement management.

---

[9] Lipin, Steven and Gabriella Stern 'Family Firm, Pressed to Get Big or Get Out, Takes the Buyout Cash' *Wall Street Journal* February 28, 1997, 1.

II. Post-IPO Operating Performance

Researchers who have studied the operating performance of IPO firms have also uncovered extensive evidence of underperformance. Jain/Kini (1994) examined the post-issue operating performance of 682 U.S. IPOs between 1976 and 1988. They found the IPO firms exhibited a substantial decline in operating perform- ance during the five years after going public. This decline was reflected in lower profitability and lower asset turnover. These declines occurred despite continued growth in sales and total assets.

Jain/Kini (1994) identified a positive correlation between the percentage of stock retained by the original owners and post-issue operating performance. However, they find no correlation between post-issue operating performance and initial underpricing.

Mikkelson/Partch/Shah (1996) also find that post-issue operating performance of IPOs declines. However—unlike Jain/Kini (1994)—Mikkelson/Partch/Shah (1996) say that going public "is unrelated to the prior change in or the level of post-offer ownership stake of officers and directors . . . [and that] . . . perform- ance in the first and second five-year periods of public trading is unrelated to the change in ownership during the first five years of public trading" (p. 2).

So, what do we have? Essentially, the following: both the market and operat- ing performance of IPOs declines for up to five years after the firm goes public. This decline in operating performance may or may not be related to ownership structure and seems to bear no relationship to the initial underpricing of the IPO.

What does seem to matter with respect to pre-IPO ownership is whether the firm was "owned" by the government and the IPO was a privatization. The post- issue performance of privatized firms does improve considerably.

III. Timing and Windows of Opportunity

A third well-established characteristic of IPOs is that they occur in bunches and these bunches are correlated with rising stock markets. First documented in the U.S. by Ibbotson/Jaffe (1975), this phenomenon has subsequently been identified in many other countries including Austria (Aussenegg 1996) and Germany (Uhlir 1988).

Rigorous rational explanations for this phenomenon are lacking. A widely accepted street view is that owners of these businesses are very smart and are able to time markets. But why would such timing skills be uniquely possessed by the owners of firms going public?

A more sanguine story may be that periods of "high" stock prices are periods when the cost of equity relative to debt is falling. Whether for rational or irrational reasons, investors lower the price for risk leading to an increase in stock prices and a corresponding increase in the quantity of equity supplied to the market.

Evidence of changes in risk premiums over the business cycle does exist. These changes have been documented with respect to the interest rate spreads on bonds rated by Moody's and Standard and Poor's.

Bunching has also been observed in the debt markets, especially the Eurobond markets. Typically, a surge of new debt issues follows a fall in interest rates in these markets.

E. Going Public and Legal Systems

Historians and legal scholars have long argued that laws, politics, and institutions may better explain how a society organizes economic activity than immediate concerns with economic efficiency or shareholder wealth maximization. Recently, these arguments have once again captured the attention of financial economists. For example, Pagano/Panetta/Zingales (1995) suggest the major reason Italian firms rarely go public is the absence of legal protections for shareholders.

Much has been written about the virtues and vices of comparative corporate governance structures in the last few years. A popular story in the U.S. for many years was that U.S. firms performed poorly relative to their German and Japanese competitors because U.S. managers were short-sighted and unwilling to invest in new technologies and product development. Instead, managers focused on the so-called "bottom line" and engaged in paper entrepreneurship. For many, the explanation behind the managers' behavior was the alleged shortsightedness and greed of financial speculators and the myopia of financial market participants, including small public investors. For the critics of Anglo-American corporate governance, the solution was simple: become more like the Japanese or Germans.[10]

The German system of corporate governance, viewed through the lenses of the critics, had the following advantage: banks played a key role in the German system. Not only did they lend money to German firms, they also owned shares in German firms. So, the banks were both creditors (providers of debt capital) and shareholders (providers of equity capital). With their equity holdings came the right to vote the shares so the banks had control rights over the firm as well as cash flow rights. These control rights, but not the cash flow rights, were further enhanced by traditional institutional arrangements whereby banks were able to vote the shares they held in trust for their clients.

---

[10] See Porter (1992).

The typical story about the advantages of the German system revolved around the dual role of banks and the influence of nonbank large blockholders on the investment, financing, and operating decisions of management. The German system was supposedly better than the American system because large block-holders were motivated to monitor corporate managers so as to insure the managers did not transfer wealth from shareholders to themselves. Furthermore, the fact that banks held both debt and equity positions in the same firm (unification of security ownership) meant that agency costs normally associated with conflicts of interest between bondholders and shareholders were minimized if not entirely eliminated. And, with representatives of large blockholders and banks on the various boards of German firms, managers could not escape the scrutiny of informed investors about the performance of the firm. Consequently, proponents of the German universal banking/corporate governance system argued that German managers were more likely to take a long-term perspective and, presumably, make investments in research and development, new technologies, production processes, and products than American managers. Also, because the agency costs of debt were reduced through unification of debt and equity ownership, the cost of capital for German firms was supposedly lower than for American firms, thereby also giving the German firms a competitive advantage over Anglo-American competitors.

La Porta et al. (1996) have "quantified" legal rules and institutional arrangements on a number of dimensions related to corporate governance issues. They report substantial differences among countries with respect to shareholder rights, the provision of accounting information, and related legal attributes. Using their classification and quantification scheme, we sought to explain differences in IPO underpricing across countries. Our IPO underpricing data comes from Loughran/ Ritter/Rydqvist (1994) with additions and updates from other sources. We have IPO returns for 28 countries; they are listed in Table 1 along with the country's legal system type.

We first evaluated whether underpricing was correlated with broad definitions of legal systems. The legal systems are English, French, German, and Scandinavian. These legal systems may be instrumental variables for usually recognized differences in corporate governance systems, especially Anglo-American versus German and Japanese.

We find little evidence that IPO underpricing is correlated with a legal system classification variable. We regressed initial returns against indicator variables for French, German, and Scandinavian legal systems with the results reported in the upper half of Table 2. The intercept captures the "effects" of the English system. The sign on underpricing was positive for the French and German systems and negative for Scandinavia. However, no coefficient was significant and the R-square was only 0.02. So, the fundamental roots of a legal system, by itself, do not explain underpricing.

Table 1: Offering Day IPO Underpricing and Legal System Classification

Country	Underpricing[#]	Legal System[*]
Australia	11.90	English
Austria	6.50	German
Belgium	10.10	French
Brazil	78.50	French
Canada	5.40	English
Chile	16.30	French
Finland	9.60	Scandinavian
France	4.20	French
Germany	10.90	German
Greece	48.50	French
Hong Kong	17.60	English
India	35.30	English
Italy	27.10	French
Japan	32.50	German
Korea	78.10	German
Malaysia	80.30	English
Mexico	33.00	French
Netherlands	7.20	French
New Zealand	28.80	English
Norway	18.00	Scandinavian
Portugal	54.40	French
Singapore	31.40	English
Spain	35.00	French
Sweden	39.00	Scandinavian
Switzerland	35.80	German
Taiwan	45.00	German
Thailand	58.10	English
United Kingdom	12.00	English
United States	15.50	English

[#] Sources: Austria: Aussenegg (1996); Norway: Nurland (1995); all others: Loughran/ Ritter/Rydqvist (1994).

[*] Source: La Porta et al. (1996).

Table 2: Legal System Classification Regression

Initial returns are from Table 1. Legal system variables are indicator variables with the intercept representing the English legal system. Attribute variables are those used by La Porta et al. (1996).

Dependent Variable	Intercept	French	German	Scandinavian	Adj. R²
Initial Return	29.630	1.800	5.170	-7.430	0.02
	(3.978)*	(0.171)	(0.425)	(-0.479)	

Legal System and Accounting Attribute Regressions

Dependent Variable	Intercept	Shareholder Rights	Efficiency of Justice System	Rule of Law	Accounting Standards	Owner Concentration	Adj. R²
Initial Return	31.976	-0.582					0.00
	(3.41)*	(-0.170)					
Initial Return	88.979		-6.980				0.33*
	(5.65)*		(-3.80)*				
Initial Return	99.143			-8.176			0.38*
	(6.01)*			(-4.24)*			
Initial Return	70.747				-0.616		0.04
	(2.47)*				(-1.42)		
Initial Return	20.727					23.165	0.00
	(1.55)					(0.772)	
Initial Return	105.062	1.555		-8.124	-0.139	-2.489	0.31*
	(2.92)*	(0.488)		(-3.65)*	(-0.32)	(-0.085)	

*   Statistically significant at 0.05 level.

We then considered the more specific measures of institutional characteristics and legal systems developed by La Porta et al. (1996). The variables are: (1) an index of shareholder rights based on voting rights; (2) a measure of the efficiency and integrity of the judicial system based on ratings from *Business International Corporation*; (3) a rule of law index based on a country's tradition of law and order from *Business International Corporation*; (4) a measure of accounting standards compiled by La Porta et al. (1996) based on financial disclosure; and (5) a measure of ownership concentration based on ownership concentration of the country's ten largest privately owned corporations.[11]

The regressions are contained in the lower half of Table 2. Initial IPO returns were negatively correlated with measures of shareholder rights, the efficiency of the judicial system, the rule of law, and accounting standards.

One can—and La Porta et al. (1996) do—tell a story about the relationship of these law and accounting attributes to shareholder rights and the protection of public shareholders. Basically, the more efficient the judicial system and the "better" and "fairer" is the enforcement of law, the more is the protection afforded public shareholders. The better the accounting standards, the better and more reliable is the information provided to public shareholders and the lesser are the informational asymmetries between insiders and outsiders.

Our results in Table 2 are consistent with theoretical models of underpricing which explain underpricing in terms of adverse selection risks and the ability of public investors to monitor and control managers. A major theme of financial agency theory is that mechanisms are needed to allow shareholders to monitor and control managers so as to motivate managers to act in the interests of the shareholders. Laws, the enforcement of laws, and accounting standards are ways for public investors to hold managers accountable regardless of the broad nature of the legal system or whether the country has a market-oriented or bank-oriented corporate governance structure.

We also found IPO returns positively correlated with ownership concentration of public firms. (Although not reported in Table 2, ownership concentration is negatively correlated with the shareholder rights, "quality" of legal system, and accounting information variables.) La Porta et al. (1996) argue that concentrated ownership of public corporations is the "solution" to problems associated with the absence of protection for public investors and our regression results are consistent with this hypothesis.

Recently, Ljungqvist (1996) has reported that within Germany ownership retention of shares in an initial public offering is negatively and significantly correlated with the post-issue market performance of German IPOs. The higher the ownership retained by the owners, the worse the subsequent five-year performance of the stock. This finding is intriguing in the context of La Porta's et al. (1996) argument. Germany offers minimal shareholder rights to investors (La Porta et al. (1996) rank it among the lowest of countries listed in Table 1). The negative correlation between insider control and the aftermarket share perform-

---

[11] A complete definition of these variables may be found in La Porta et al. (1996).

ance of IPOs may be confirmation of the inability of public shareholders to control the ability of insiders to consume private benefits.

F. The German Experience

As reported earlier, some evidence has accumulated that German IPOs underperform benchmark indexes from three to five years after the offering. But, according to Ljungqvist, this underperformance is especially apparent among IPOs where the original owners retain strong control. This latter outcome is contrary to what would be expected if owner-managers were more likely to adopt wealth maximization strategies than pure managers and large blockholders acted as delegated monitors for public shareholders.

Our preliminary results with regard to both the market and operating performance of German IPOs also does not support predictions that superior performance is positively associated with the percentage of stock retained by the original owners or by large block delegated monitoring. To date, we have examined the market and operating performance of 47 German IPOs between 1987 and 1992.

I. Stock Price Performance

The average underpricing of these issues was 8.64% with a range of 0% to 57.6%. To determine whether this underpricing was related to ownership structure, we are collecting ownership data for the companies from the time they went public until 1995. Our preliminary results are based on ownership data for 1994/95, which is readily available in computerized form.[12] Following Ljungqvist, we classified the firms into three ownership categories: firms with less than 25% of their shares owned by a single entity; firms with 25% to less than 50% of their shares owned by a single entity; and firms with 50% or more of their shares owned by a single entity. The 25% breaking point was used because 25% or more of shares held by a single entity can be used as a blocking minority. The 50% and over break represents majority control. We also summed up the holdings of the three largest shareholding entities (SUMBLK) and used it as a measure of large block delegated monitoring.

We then regressed IPO underpricing (UNPR) against indicator variables for the 25% to under 50% ownership class (BLKMIN) and the 50% and above ownership class (MAJ). The intercept captures the effects of the under 25% ownership class. Our regression result with t-statistics in parentheses was:

---

[12] For additional empirical evidence on the relation between ownership structure and performance for German companies, see also Wenger/Kaserer (Ch. 6) and Prigge (Ch. 12: Sec. B.II.5.) in this volume.

$$UNPR_j = 0.062 + 0.033(BLKMIN)_j + 0.024(MAJ)_j \qquad R^2 = 0.03$$
$$(1.82) \qquad\quad (0.81) \qquad\qquad (0.44)$$

For our sample, we found no relationship between IPO underpricing and the percentage of the firm subsequently controlled by a single entity. If anything, the greater the percentage of the firm in the hands of a single entity, the greater the underpricing—an outcome similar to Ljungqvist. (The positive sign on the indicator variables means the underpricing was positively related to single entity control.)

We also regressed the underpricing variable (UNPR) against the summation (SUMBLK) of the percentage of shares owned by the three largest block holders. The result was:

$$UNPR_j = 0.076 + 0.000(SUMBLK)_j \qquad\qquad R^2 = 0.02$$

Again, no statistical relationship was uncovered between underpricing and subsequent large block holdings.

We examined the long-run market performance of the IPOs by first calculating their one-, two-, three-, four-, and five-year price relatives. These relatives are calculated as the ratio of the company's common stock price at the end of the respective years to the price of the IPO at the end of its first trading day. The average price relatives for our sample of IPOs are reported in Table 3. On average, the price of an IPO at the end of its second through fifth year of trading hovered around 90% of the closing price on its IPO date. So, the evidence suggests "underperformance" by the IPOs.

To determine whether ownership structure affected this post-market performance, we regressed the three-year (PR REL 3) and five-year (PR REL 5) price relatives against our ownership concentration variables. The results are reported in the lower half of Table 3. The coefficients on the ownership concentration variables are positive and, perhaps worth noting, the coefficient on the blocking minority coefficient is larger than on the majority ownership coefficient. However, none is statistically significant at usually accepted levels. Therefore, we are unable to reject the hypothesis that improved stock price performance is associated with increased concentration of ownership.

We next considered how the stock price of the IPOs performed relative to a broad German stock market index. We chose the MDAX because it is an index of middle capitalization companies traded in Germany. To compare the performance of the IPOs relative to the MDAX, we calculated the ratio of the individual IPO stock price relatives to the respective year MDAX price relative. For example, if the IPO started trading on June 1, 1988, the one-year IPO relative was based on the ratio of the May 31, 1989, IPO price to the closing IPO price on

June 1, 1988, and the MDAX price relative was the ratio of the MDAX price on May 31, 1989, to its price on June 1, 1988.

Table 3: Long-Term IPO Stock Price Performance

Price Relatives

Price Relatives	Year 1	Year 2	Year 3	Year 4	Year 5
IPO Stock Price Relatives (PR REL 1 through 5)	1.001	0.965	0.901	0.920	0.917
Ratio of Average IPO Stock Price Relative to MDAX Price Relative	1.040	0.929	0.909	0.951	0.952

Regression Models

The dependent variables PR REL 3 and PR REL 5 are stock price relatives calculated as the stock price three years and five years from the initial trading day divided by the stock price at the end of the first trading day. PR REL/MDAX 3 and PR REL/MDAX 5 are the ratios of the IPO price relatives for three and five years to the respective price relatives for the MDAX Index. MAJ and BLKMIN are indicator variables with MAJ being 1 if single entity ownership is 50% or greater and BLKMIN being 1 if single entity ownership is 25% to less than 50%. t-statistics are in parentheses.

		Independent Variables		
Dependent Variable	Intercept	MaJ	BLKMIN	Adj. R^2
PR REL 3	0.690 (3.01)	0.328 (1.24)	0.423 (1.18)	0.02
PR REL 5	0.500 (2.42)*	0.319 (1.31)	0.530 (1.31)	0.00
PR REL/MDAX 3	0.835 (14.51)*	0.064 (0.942)	0.170 (1.989)	0.04
PR REL/MDAX 5	0.889 (22.35)*	0.064 (1.375)	0.135 (2.154)*	0.07

Note: Statistically significant at the 0.05 level.

Our average MDAX adjusted price relatives for one-, two-, three-, four-, and five-year post-IPO stock price performance are reported in the top half of Table 3. Except for the first year, the average IPO (an equally weighted IPO portfolio) underperformed the MDAX benchmark portfolio.

We examined whether this MDAX relative performance was related to ownership concentration by repeating our earlier regressions using the MDAX relative performance measure as the dependent variable. The results are reported in Table 3 under the IPO price relative regressions.

Again, the coefficients on the concentration variables are positive and the coefficients on the blocking minority positions are greater than the majority positions. We did pick up a statistically significant coefficient on the blocking minority variable (in contrast to the majority control variable) for the five-year performance regression, but the regression equation as a whole was not significant at the 0.05 level. So it may be that at some point, increased single entity control is associated with worse rather than better performance, an outcome consistent with Ljungqvist's (1996) findings.

II. Operating Performance

To evaluate operating performance we calculated and analyzed the following financial ratios: operating profit to sales, operating profit to total assets, sales to total assets, equity to total assets, and total liabilities to total assets. Operating profit is ordinary earnings before interest income, interest payments, and taxes. Equity is the book value of shareholders equity. Total liabilities is current liabilities, bank debt, and outstanding bonds; provisions are excluded from total liabilities. Table 4 contains the financial ratios for IPOs grouped by year and an average of all companies in event time.

Table 4: Financial Ratios for German IPO Firms

Operating profit to sales is ordinary earnings before interest income and payments and taxes. Equity is book value of shareholders equity. Total liabilities are current liabilities, bank debt, and outstanding bonds. No provisions are included in liabilities.

Year and Ratios	IPO Year	IPO + 1	IPO + 2	IPO + 3	IPO + 4	IPO + 5
1987 (4 firms)						
Operating Profit/Sales	0.103	0.075	0.079	0.067	0.041	0.032
Operating Profit/Total Assets	0.138	0.109	0.124	0.081	0.066	0.053
Sales/Total Assets	1.238	1.365	1.609	1.212	1.451	1.316
Equity/Total Assets	0.369	0.394	0.471	0.414	0.422	0.482
Total Liabilities/Total Assets	0.316	0.285	0.315	0.341	0.330	0.305
1988 (6 firms)						
Operating Profit/Sales	0.111	0.076	0.050	0.030	0.047	0.053
Operating Profit/Total Assets	0.210	0.148	0.100	0.083	0.132	0.101
Sales/Total Assets	2.358	2.417	2.292	2.311	5.815	2.625
Equity/Total Assets	0.486	0.450	0.453	0.392	0.362	0.361
Total Liabilities/Total Assets	0.352	0.393	0.402	0.454	0.501	0.523

1989 (11 firms)

Operating Profit/Sales	0.076	0.051	0.043	0.011	0.038	0.014
Operating Profit/Total Assets	0.118	0.089	0.080	0.055	0.059	0.055
Sales/Total Assets	1.452	1.445	1.502	1.533	1.453	1.330
Equity/Total Assets	0.437	0.455	0.413	0.376	0.383	0.369
Total Liabilities/Total Assets	0.436	0.429	0.449	0.460	0.463	0.470

1990 (11 firms)

Operating Profit/Sales	0.064	0.046	-0.140	0.022	-0.054	0.017
Operating Profit/Total Assets	0.105	0.081	0.026	0.058	0.038	0.037
Sales/Total Assets	1.708	1.666	1.670	1.572	0.609	1.689
Equity/Total Assets	0.458	0.462	0.454	0.471	0.459	0.430
Total Liabilities/Total Assets	0.371	0.381	0.387	0.374	0.376	0.410

1991 (5 firms)

Operating Profit/Sales	0.080	0.069	0.042	0.050	0.038
Operating Profit/Total Assets	0.097	0.082	0.059	0.065	0.041
Sales/Total Assets	1.438	1.315	1.351	1.288	1.298
Equity/Total Assets	0.427	0.403	0.434	0.433	0.365
Total Liabilities/Total Assets	0.382	0.420	0.389	0.405	0.458

1992 (4 firms)

Operating Profit/Sales	0.167	0.091	0.003	0.022
Operating Profit/Total Assets	0.124	0.073	0.014	0.023
Sales/Total Assets	0.975	0.929	0.965	0.981
Equity/Total Assets	0.404	0.403	0.379	0.413
Total Liabilities/Total Assets	0.438	0.447	0.437	0.445

1993 (6 firms)

Operating Profit/Sales	0.187	0.098	-0.079
Operating Profit/Total Assets	0.135	0.077	-0.011
Sales/Total Assets	0.888	0.876	0.851
Equity/Total Assets	0.462	0.454	0.425
Total Liabilities/Total Assets	0.401	0.418	0.429

1994 (5 firms)

Operating Profit/Sales	0.068	0.057
Operating Profit/Total Assets	0.085	0.064
Sales/Total Assets	1.396	1.372
Equity/Total Assets	0.431	0.463
Total Liabilities/Total Assets	0.396	0.405

Event Time Summary (52 firms)

Operating Profit/Sales	0.084	0.061	-0.028	0.027	-0.007	0.018
Operating Profit/Total Assets	0.121	0.092	0.057	0.060	0.055	0.048
Sales/Total Assets	1.576	1.549	1.588	1.540	2.074	1.652
Equity/Total Assets	0.431	0.463	0.429	0.428	0.416	0.431
Total Liabilities/Total Assets	0.396	0.405	0.409	0.408	0.418	0.431

The general deterioration in profitability during the five years after going public is readily apparent. By the fifth year, the operating income to sales ratio has declined by 50% for almost every IPO cohort year. A similar pattern is evident in the operating income to assets ratio. Although not reported, the same deterioration is evident in return on equity ratios. Our results for Germany are typical of those reported for the United States by Mikkelson/Partch/Shah (1996).

Little change is evident in the ratio of sales to total assets, a measure of asset utilization and, possibly, post-going public expenditures on fixed assets. Also, little change occurs in the leverage ratios. In particular, no evidence exists that the IPO was connected with a reduction in outstanding debt leading to a reduction in debt ratios.

To evaluate whether post-IPO operating performance was related to ownership structure, we regressed the changes in three-year operating income (CHG 3YR OP/S) to sales against the ownership structure variables. The resulting regression equation is:

$$\text{CHG 3YR OP/S}_j = -0.086 + 0.032(\text{MAJ})_j + 0.063(\text{BLKMIN})_j \qquad R^2 = 0.003$$
$$\qquad\qquad\; (-2.97) \qquad (0.93) \qquad\qquad\quad (1.34)$$

Although the coefficients are positive, none is statistically significant at less than the 0.15 level. Like Mikkelson/Partch/Shah (1996), we found little evidence that post-IPO operating performance was explained by single entity or block ownership levels. (Although note that once again the coefficient on the blocking minority variable is greater than the majority control variable.)

Our overall results offer little support for hypotheses which link operating performance to retention of control by IPO existing owners and to large blockholders acting as delegated monitors for public shareholders. However, our results are preliminary and we have not divided ownership into categories such as family, other corporations, and foundations. We also have yet to consider changes in ownership. And, given the degree of concentrated ownership typically found in German firms, we may not have enough variability in ownership to matter in terms of producing differences in long-term performance. Still, our preliminary results are consistent with the results obtained by Ljungqvist (1996).

G. Conclusion

The going public decision has attracted the attention of financial economists because of the insights it can provide into corporate governance questions and the role of the public corporation in the contemporary world. Because the policy debates about the merits of alternative corporate governance systems have focused on the implications of separating management from ownership and the role of large blockholders as delegated monitors of public firms, these debates have also informed research into IPOs. Typically, researchers have used some version of financial agency theory to structure their research. Consequently, attempts to explain IPO underpricing and subsequent stock price and operating performance have relied on hypotheses informed by financial agency theory.

The essence of these agency-based theories is that the well-documented "poor" long-run stock price and operating performance of IPO firms could be explained by changes in ownership structure. The predictions were that a positive correlation would exist between the percentage of the firm retained by the original owners and post-IPO financial performance. Also, the expectation was that continued concentrated ownership, acting as delegated monitors for public shareholders, would produce "better" performance. The evidence to date does not support these predictions. And, in the case of Germany, just the opposite may be true.

What appears to be a more promising approach for understanding the behavior of publicly held firms and, by implication, the going public event, is a research design informed by history and law. What may matter more than ownership structure are the institutional arrangements governing firms and the protection afforded public shareholders from not only managers but also single entity and large (privileged) blockholders. Consistent with the work of La Porta et al. (1996), we found that legal system attributes did more to explain IPO underpricing than any operating or ownership concentration attributes.

Admittedly from an American political perspective, we believe going public is an arrangement which lets individuals obtain the full value of their entrepreneurial efforts. The "process" is simply an extension of the important role of markets for permitting Americans to escape the dependency associated with (economic) oligarchies and/or governments. From this perspective, the option of going public is more important than the act itself and needs to be understood in a historical-political context where the economically rational person doing financial calculations is a part of a larger humanistic personality.

Although we cannot document it scientifically, at the moment we suspect a connection exists between the option of going public and the amount of investment finding its way into private sector enterprises, especially investment in new technologies growth options. We also see going public as a solution to the problems of concentrated wealth and government ownership of firms that employ large numbers of people and supply critical goods and services.

References

Allen, Franklin and Gerald R. Faulhaber 'Signalling by Underpricing in the IPO Market' *Journal of Financial Economics* 23 (1989) 303-23.

Appleby, Joice Oldham 'Introduction: Republicanism and Ideology' *American Quarterly* (1985) 461-73.

Aussenegg, Wolfgang 'Short- and Long-Run Performance of Initial Public Offerings in the Austrian Stock Market' (mimeo, Vienna University of Technology, Department of Finance, 1996).

Barry, Christopher, Chris Muscarella, John W. Peavy, and Michael R. Vetsuypens 'The Role of Venture Capital in the Creation of Public Companies' *Journal of Financial Economics* 27 (1990) 447-71.

Bebchuk, Lucian A. 'Efficient and Inefficient Sales of Corporate Control' *Quarterly Journal of Economics* 59 (1994) 957-94.

Bebchuk, Lucian A. and Luigi Zingales 'Corporate Ownership Structures: Private Versus Social Optimality' (NBER Working Paper no. 5584, 1996).

Benveniste, Larry and Paul A. Spindt 'How Investment Bankers Determine the Offer Price and Allocation of New Issues' *Journal of Financial Economics* 24 (1989) 343-61.

Berle, Adolf A. 'Non-Voting Stock and 'Bankers' Control' 39 *Harv. L. Rev.* 673-93 (1926).

Berle, Adolf A. 'Corporate Powers as Powers in Trust' 44 *Harv. L. Rev.* 1049-74 (1931).

Berle, Adolf A. 'For Whom Corporate Managers Are Trustees: A Note' 45 *Harv. L. Rev.* 1365-72 (1932).

Berle, Adolf A. and Gardiner C. Means *The Modern Corporation and Private Property* (New York 1933).

Berlin, Mitchell 'For Better and for Worse: Three Lending Relationships' *Business Review* (Federal Reserve Bank of Philadelphia) (1996/6) 3-12.

Blair, Margaret M. *Ownership and Control* (Washington, D.C. 1995).

Boycko, Maxim, Andrei Shleifer, and Robert W. Vishny *Privatizing Russia* (Cambridge, Mass. 1995).

Brandeis, Louis D. *The Curse of Bigness: Miscellaneous Papers* (O. Fraenkel, ed.) (New York 1934).

Brennan, Michael and Julian Franks 'Underpricing, Ownership and Control in Initial Public Offerings of Equity Securities in the U.K.' (mimeo, London Business School, 1995).

Coase, Ronald H. 'The Nature of the Firm' *Economica N.S.* 4 (1937) 386-405.

Demsetz, Harold and Kenneth Lehn 'The Structure of Corporate Ownership: Causes and Consequences' *Journal of Political Economy* 93 (1985) 1155-77.

Dodd, E. Merrick 'For Whom Corporate Managers are Trustees' 45 *Harv. L. Rev.* 1145-63 (1932).

Ellingsen, Tore and Kristian Rydqvist 'The Stock Market as a Screening Device and the Decision to Go Public' (mimeo, University of Wisconsin-Madison, 1996).

Garfinkel, Jon 'IPO Underpricing, Insider Selling and Subsequent Equity Offerings: Is Underpricing a Signal of Quality?' *Financial Management* 22/1 (1993) 74-83.

Grinblatt, Mark and Chuan Yang Hwang 'Signalling and the Pricing of New Issues' *Journal of Finance* 44 (1989) 393-420.

Grossman, Sanford and Oliver Hart 'One Share-One Vote and the Market for Corporate Control' *Journal of Financial Economics* 20 (1988) 203-35.

Ibbotson, Roger and Jeffrey F. Jaffe 'Hot Issues Markets *Journal of Finance* 30 (1975) 1027-42.

Ibbotson, Roger, Jody Sindelar, and Jay Ritter 'The Market's Problem With the Pricing of Initial Public Offerings' *Journal of Applied Corporate Finance* 7/1 (1994) 66-74.

Jain, Bharat and Omesh Kini 'The Post Issue Operating Performance of IPO Firms' *Journal of Finance* 49 (1994) 1699-726.

Jegadeesh, Narasimhan, Mark Weinstein, and Ivo Welsh 'An Empirical Investigation of IPO Returns and Subsequent Equity Offerings' *Journal of Financial Economics* 34 (1993) 153-75.

Kaen, Fred R., Allen Kaufman, and Larry Zacharias 'American Political Values and Agency Theory: A Perspective' *Journal of Business Ethics* 7 (1988) 805-20.

Kaufman, Allen, Lawrence Zacharias, and Marvin Karson *Managers vs. Owners: The Struggle for Corporate Control in American Democracy* (New York 1995).

Keoharju, Matti 'The Winner's Curse, Legal Liability and the Long-Run Price Performance of Initial Public Offerings in Finland' *Journal of Financial Economics* 34 (1993) 251-77.

Kim, Moonchul and Jay R. Ritter 'Valuing IPOs' in: Volk, Gerrit (ed.) *Going Public: der Gang an die Börse* (Stuttgart 1996).

La Porta, Rafael, Florencio Lopez-de-Silanes, Andrei Shleifer, and Robert W. Vishny 'Law and Finance' (NBER Working Paper no. 5661, 1996).

Lee, Philip, Stephen L. Taylor, and Terry S. Walter 'Australian IPO Pricing in the Short and Long Run' *Journal of Banking and Finance* 20 (1996) 1189-210.

Lerner, Joshua 'Venture Capitalists and the Decision to Go Public' *Journal of Financial Economics* 35 (1994) 293-316.

Levis, Mario 'The Long-Run Performance of Initial Public Offerings: The UK Experience 1980-1988' *Financial Management* 22/1 (1993) 28-41.

Lippman, Walter *Drift and Mastery: An Attempt to Diagnose the Current Unrest* (New York 1914).

Ljungqvist, Alexander P. 'When Do Firms Go Public? Poisson Evidence from Germany' (mimeo, University of Oxford, 1995).

Ljungqvist, Alexander P. 'Can Firms Outwit the Market? Timing Ability and the Long-Run Performance of IPOs' in: *Empirical Issues in Raising Equity Capital* 215-44 (Advances in Finance, Investment, and Banking 2) (Amsterdam 1996).

Logue, Dennis E. 'Premia on Unseasoned Equity Issues' *Journal of Economics and Business* 25 (1973) 133-41.

Loughran, Tim and Jay Ritter 'The New Issues Puzzle' *Journal of Finance* 50 (1995) 23-52.

Loughran, Tim, Jay Ritter, and Kristian Rydqvist 'Initial Public Offerings: International Insights' *Pacific-Basin Finance Journal* 2 (1994) 165-99.

McConnell, John J. and Henri Servaes 'Additional Evidence on Equity Ownership and Corporate Value' *Journal of Financial Economics* 27 (1990) 595-613.

McConnell, John J. and Henri Servaes 'Equity Ownership and the Two Faces of Debt' *Journal of Financial Economics* 39 (1995) 131-57.

Mikkelson, Wayne E., M. Megan Partch, and Ken Shah 'Ownership and Operating Performance of Companies that Go Public' (mimeo, University of Oregon, 1996).

Monks, Robert A.G. and Nell Minow *Corporate Governance* (Cambridge, Mass. 1995).

Nurland, Morten 'Børsintroduksjoner avkastning på kort og lang sikt' *Praktisk økonomi* 2 (1995) 83-8.

Pagano, Marco 'The Flotation of Companies on the Stock Market: A Coordination Failure Model' *European Economic Review* 37 (1993) 1102-25.

Pagano, Marco, Fabio Panetta, and Luigi Zingales 'Why Do Companies Go Public? An Empirical Analysis' (mimeo, University of Chicago, 1995).

Porter, Michael E. 'Capital Choices: Changing the Way America Invests in Industry' *Journal of Applied Corporate Finance* 5/2 (1992) 4-16.

Rajan, Raghuram 'Insiders and Outsiders: The Choice Between Relationship and Arms-Length Debt' *Journal of Finance* 47 (1992) 1367-400.

Rock, Kevin 'Why New Issues Are Underpriced' *Journal of Financial Economics* 15 (1986) 187-212.

Roe, Mark J. *Strong Managers, Weak Owners* (Princeton 1994).

Roll, Richard 'The Hubris Hypothesis of Corporate Takeovers' *Journal of Business* 59 (1986) 197-216.

Ruback, Richard S. 'Coercive Dual Class Exchange Offers' *Journal of Financial Economics* 20 (1988) 153-73.

Rydqvist, Kristian and Kenneth Högholm 'Going Public in the 1980s—Evidence from Sweden' *European Financial Management* 1 (1995) 287-315.

Schultz, Paul 'Unit Initial Public Offerings: A Form of Staged Financing' *Journal of Financial Economics* 34 (1993) 199-229.

Shleifer, Andrei and Robert W. Vishny 'A Survey of Corporate Governance' *Journal of Finance* 52 (1997) 737-83.

Uhlir, Helmut 'Going Public in the F.R.G.' in: Guimaraes, Rui M.C., Brian G. Kingsman, and Stephen J. Taylor (eds.) *A Reappraisal of the Efficiency of Financial Markets* 369-93 (New York 1989).

Veblen, Thorstein *The Theory of the Business Enterprise* (New York 1904).

Welch, Ivo 'Seasoned Offerings, Imitation Costs and the Underpricing of Initial Public Offerings' *Journal of Finance* 44 (1989) 421-49.

Williamson, Oliver E. *The Economic Institutions of Capitalism* (New York 1985).

Wruck, Karen 'Equity Ownership Concentration and Firm Value: Evidence from Private Equity Financings' *Journal of Financial Economics* 23 (1989) 3-28.

Zingales, Luigi 'Insider Ownership and the Decision to Go Public' *Review of Economic Studies* 62 (1995) 425-48.

Market Failure in Venture Capital Markets for New Medium and Small Enterprises

WOLFGANG GERKE, Erlangen-Nuremberg

The paper on market failure in venture capital markets for new medium and small enterprises deals with the private investor's role with regard to financing new and small enterprises, his suitability, his discrimination, and his liquidity preferences. It also looks at the growing influence of institutional investors and at the role banks play when granting credits. Furthermore, it highlights the information asymmetries that lead to a market failure in the equity markets and the fact that there is nothing equivalent to NASDAQ in Europe. A possible measure against market failure could be the setting up of an information exchange that functions as a meeting point and as a rating agency. Finally, the role of the state in providing free entry in the capital markets to new enterprises is taken into account.

Contents

Figures

A. Hypothesis on Disadvantages of New Firms

Nowadays, big companies operate on a global rather than a national scale. More and more, they prepare their balance sheet according to needs of the capital markets. The American structure is the example. In spite of this, significant differences in the financial structures of companies, in the efficiency of banks and venture capital companies, as well as in the different stock exchange segments still prevail. New enterprises in particular seem to have a far better chance of getting capital in the U.S. This could result from differing corporate governance structures. On the one hand, German businessmen have a different approach to taking on new partners and to going public than their American counterparts, and, on the other hand, German banks and venture capital companies prefer to finance companies that have already developed instead of financing newly founded ones. Furthermore, when advising clients, universal bank managers do not as actively promote stock markets as American brokers do.

Despite all efforts to find the best possible corporate governance structure,[1] and despite comparative corporate governance studies, there is no optimum solution that is applicable in the United States, Japan, and Germany at the same time. This is a warning to those who try to prove the superiority of a certain corporate governance structure solely by means of empirical comparison. When examining individual cause-effect relations, we should never forget that they take place under circumstances with very differing backgrounds. Of course, one could also try to harmonize these circumstances. If at all desirable, such a process would take a very long time. For example, American venture capital companies could become more active in Germany without delay, but the disapproving attitude of German companies towards influential additional owners would only change very slowly. Furthermore, in their strategy of buying and selling they would have to take into consideration that for legal reasons there is a different corporate governance structure in Germany, where the position of German trade unions is very strong and worker participation is common practice.

It is one of the basic principles of modern American capitalism that each individual has a fair chance to become an entrepreneur and rise from being an owner of a small business to becoming a millionaire. In the U.S., according to the belief influenced by Calvinism, the individual only has to make the most of his abilities, and his resulting God-pleasing success as a businessman will be his worldly reward. For a corresponding outstanding position in the hereafter, the

---

[1] The term "corporate governance" is used as follows in this paper: "Corporate governance is the totality of the institutional and organizational mechanisms, and the corresponding decision-making, intervention and control rights, which serve to resolve conflicts of interest between the various groups which have a stake in a firm and which, either in isolation or in their interaction, determine how important decisions are taken in a firm, and ultimately also determine which decisions are taken"; Schmidt (1997).

successful businessman invests in some good deeds in this world, just to be on the safe side. The market has thus taken over the function of the Last Judgment. Among the new companies, it is the market that separates the wheat from the chaff, partly through venture capital companies as well. Therefore, it is no surprise that those who have doubts about the fair selection of the market are being labelled and fought against as unbelieving people. With their planned economy concepts they destroy entrepreneurial freedom and the salutary selection force of the market. It amounts to a declaration of war on the present prevailing capitalist ideology to maintain that there is a market failure for the free entry of new companies in Germany.

Free markets often do serve individual human beings. When this is not the case, legislative power must safeguard the interests of the individuals with its regulating hand. This might include the support of new companies. There is hope that the founders of new enterprises will take on some of the workers dismissed by other companies. There is also hope that, by coming up with new inventions in the high-tech industry and by offering new services in the service sector, they will stop society from becoming encrusted. However, the founders of new enterprises will only be able to realize their new ideas if they are provided with sufficient capital to do so. The corporate governance structure in German firms, universal banks, and venture capital companies might be a barrier to financing small companies. In the following, an analysis will be made of whether or not free markets alone will be sufficient to provide young enterprises with capital, and which financial barriers hinder young enterprises. The following working hypotheses form the basis of this study:

(1) In many countries, there is sufficient private investment capital that could be used for direct investment in new enterprises. Yet the importance of the private investor's direct investment in company stock is on the decline in all the big industrial countries. Professional investors oust private investors from direct investment in company stock as the latter are at a disadvantage when analyzing new companies.

(2) Because of this handicap, it is more attractive to private investors—unlike professional ones—to invest in well-diversified funds rather than risk the venture of investing in a single individual enterprise. The strong growth of investment and pension funds can thus be explained as rational behavior of investors, especially if they want to invest in new companies and distrust the unknown entrepreneur's integrity.

(3) Young enterprises are not able to compensate the blocked access to the private investors' capital by means of bank credit. At best, they get a bank loan only at an unattractively high interest rate due to nearly insurmountable asymmetries in information between enterprise and investor. In general, they are completely barred from credit unless they provide special guarantees.

Therefore, when we speak of credit financing of young enterprises, it must be said that, at least in Germany, there is a true market failure.

(4) When it comes to the financing of young enterprises by means of investment, these enterprises also get worse terms than would be appropriate in view of their economic risk. Again, the reason can be found in the entrepreneur-investor information asymmetries.

(5) If it were possible to establish a rating agency and information exchange specializing in new and small companies, this would decrease the expenses incurred when looking for capital and reduce information asymmetries.

B. New Firms' Deficient Access to Capital in Detail

I. The Private Investors' Discrimination on the Capital Markets Results in Discrimination of Small Enterprises

The German venture capital market for stand-up-stage financing largely depends on private investors' willingness to provide capital. The German capital market is indeed dominated by big private banks, numerous savings banks, and cooperative banks. In addition, some venture capital companies are looking for investment in companies, but these financial institutions avoid stand-up-stage financing. Usually, they consider the company founders' risk too high and obscure, the amount of capital asked for too small, and the cost of company rating too high. It is in this very special market segment where the demands on financing are highest that private investors have to take over the start-up-stage financing in Germany. Whether they are prepared and suited for direct investment will be briefly analyzed in this paper.

In the big industrial nations, private investors hold considerable financial assets ready for investment.[2] It can be assumed that there is also sufficient investment capital to finance small and medium-sized new enterprises that run a high risk, yet often offer considerable expansion chances. Of course, the ratio of these financial assets invested in risky new companies will always be rather low since many risk-averted investors prefer life insurance and government bonds. However, a small part of these financial assets can already meet the young enterprises' capital demand.

Taking into account that some investors are prepared to invest in highly risky options, it can be assumed that there is sufficient private capital for young enterprises. Instead, however, investors are on a general drawback from direct investment in company stock. In a single investor, this behavior may be deemed

---

[2] In 1995, private financial assets in Germany amounted to DM 4,657.1 billion. Source: Deutsche Bundesbank (1997).

irrational. If, however, private investors on the whole shrink back from direct investment in company stock, this kind of investment must be considered comparatively unattractive. It seems obvious that the private investor's direct investment meets with severe handicaps in the capital markets.

Along with the globalization of international equity markets, a tendency towards more institutionalized and professionalized market participants can be observed, often resulting in the ousting of small and medium-sized companies and of private investors.[3] In many cases, it is quite favorable for ill-informed and inexperienced private investors to hand over their money to institutional investors and not to invest in new, small and mid caps. However, the well-informed and experienced private investor dislikes the institutional investors' advantage.

The competition for gains deriving from early and better information has become so tough that only professional investors stand a chance to gain a profit in this league of professional players. But who offers the financial reward for a particularly fast reaction to an adverse change in a firm's fundamental data?

The private investors certainly did not intend to write an option on the stocks of a small company when they placed their buy order with a price limit below the company's current market price, but actually they are caught in the trap of a free trading option that cannot be changed at short notice. By the time they get the information, e.g., on unexpected company losses, their orders will have been processed. Therefore, it is the private investor who provides the financial reward in the race for better information.

In the case of big companies such as IBM or Daimler-Benz, the private investors' discrimination generally does not bear much weight. As these companies are in the limelight of public interest, quotations generally reflect the updated situation using the maximum of information obtainable on the enterprises. The situation changes considerably if we look at unlisted new companies. This is where private investors are at the mercy of the better-informed professionals.

In theoretical models or empirical studies it is always difficult to prove that private investors are discriminated against. On the one hand, theoretical models can only partly reflect the often not entirely rational behavior of company managers and of institutional and private investors. On the other hand, in view of the superimposition of many additional factors of influence, it is often very difficult to isolate the effect studied by empirical capital market research and thus to receive clear results. Therefore, we have also used the experimental capital research approach. We created a computerized stock exchange where human beings—with all their strengths and weaknesses—perform transactions in a simulation model controlled by us. To do so, they are given financial data on several enterprises that change each round of period. They can place orders to

---

[3] See also Hopt/Baum (1997: 293).

buy or sell on the basis of these data, or they may invest their money at a fixed rate or take up a credit. This is an epitomized stock exchange in an economic scientist's laboratory, and our participants have to invest a small amount of their own money, which they may lose or multiply depending on their relative success.

The great advantage of our research method is that in the computerized laboratory trade, there is an automatic recording of any action. Thus, at any time, we know which information is asked for by any participant, which assets he holds, and what actions he performs. This controlled ambience allows us to study how the various market participants behave in a market where some participants have an advantage in information, and to analyze how their behavior influences the market prices. It would be beyond the scope of this paper to describe the specific research design of our computerized stock exchange (called CAT), and we therefore refer to the corresponding publications.[4]

In our experiments, the so-called professional insiders skillfully used the market-inherent information asymmetry to their own benefit, using their information advantage so that the quotes did not change in accordance with the insider information. By placing orders in a tactical way, they successfully managed to stabilize the quotes on a level so that insider information was not taken into account, even with an open order book. This strategy is to the disadvantage of the ill-informed private investor. This result underlines the importance of the measures to protect investors from insider trading that have become law (*2. Finanzmarktförderungsgesetz*) in Germany. Furthermore, it shows that, within the framework of legal transactions, it will never be possible to level out the information asymmetries between professional investors and private investors.[5]

In capital markets, the inequality of opportunities between private investors and institutional investors shows itself in the distribution of share ownership. For example, Figure 1 shows the especially significant changes in the distribution of capital in Germany.

The share invested in equities decreased by 50% between 1970 and 1995. There are no further statistics on the capital invested in new companies. In a country where only 5% of private capital is invested in equities, there is no scope for the private financing of company foundations. As the big financial institutions avoid that business, numerous economically desirable company foundations are not realized.

---

[4] See Gerke/Bienert (1998, 1994).
[5] See Gerke/Arneth (1997).

Figure 1: Private Households' Liquid Assets in 1996 in Germany

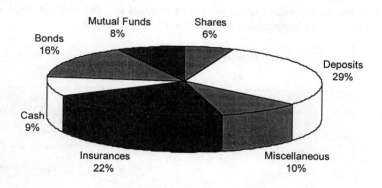

Source: Deutsche Bundesbank (1997: 40).

In Great Britain, this tendency is not quite so dramatic, but there, as well, it can be observed clearly how the percentage of private shareholders fell from 54% to 17.7% of total share ownership between 1963 and 1993.[6] At the same time, the financial institutions' share rose from 30.3% to 62.2%.

Japan is no exception with regard to this development. There, the number of private shareholders declined from 61.3% to 19.9% of total share ownership between 1950 and 1995. The percentage of financial institutions (former investment trusts) rose from 12.6% in 1950 to 44% in 1995. Moreover, it can be noticed that the investment of mutual funds in companies gained significant importance at the same time. In 1950, business corporations owned 11% of all shares, whereas in 1995 they already held 27.7%. The huge blocks of shares, especially the ones of the Japanese banking industry and of corporations, are generally not being traded at the stock exchange, which could endanger the market efficiency in Japan in the long term.[7]

Today, the United States is still a country where direct investment in shares ranks highly among private investors. In spite of this, private investors are being ousted by institutional investors there as well. In 1970, 47% of the private households' liquid financial assets were invested directly in equities, not including pension fund reserves. In 1992 this share dropped to 31.1%. These changing

[6] London Stock Exchange (1982, 1994).

[7] Japan Securities Research Institute (1992) and Japan Securities Dealers Association (1995).

preferences concerning capital investment have caused shifts in the ownership of U.S. equities as well.[8]

American households owned 60.9% of equities in 1980, but by 1994 the rate of households owning equities declined to 47.7%.[9]

Figure 2: Ownership of U.S. Equities

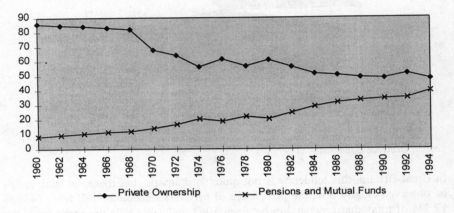

II. Private Investors' Rational Behavior as Underinvesting in New Companies

The comparison of international data shows that the private investor rather withdraws from directly financing enterprises. Figure 3 shows that he does not react irrationally in doing so.

There are huge differences between the market chances of private investors and those of institutional investors. According to the capital asset pricing model, every investor could set up the market portfolio (M) that comprises all risky shares including those of new companies. Depending on his attitude towards taking risks, he would invest more or less of his budget in the stock index (M) or in less risky government bond issues with the interest r_f. In our example, Figure 3, he would split up his budget according to his willingness to run risks in P_M between the stock index and the government bond issues. A portfolio with such a high utility level that cannot be outstripped can only be realized in theory. Getting information on individual companies is rather expensive, for the market for newly set-up companies is hardly transparent. Furthermore, investment in

[8] Securities Industry Association (1993).
[9] New York Stock Exchange (1995).

small companies cannot be distributed in the same way as is possible with listed companies, so that numerous assumptions of neo-classical portfolio theory can only be adopted partially.

Figure 3: The Decision Situation of Private Investors

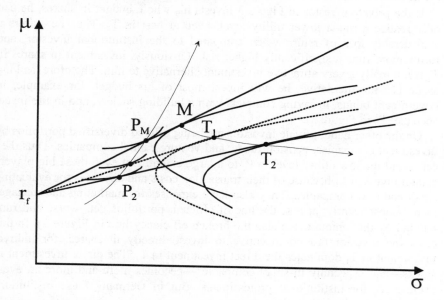

The private investor, and especially the small private investor, cannot realize this utility level in P_M. To him, it is even more difficult to understand the venture capital risks and the complex changes in the capital markets. Derivatives, index contracts, hedging strategies, butterfly and bull spread positions, etc., offer a variety that is very difficult to understand. Therefore, the private investor in general will only invest in a few known shares rather than in small companies, and especially not in new ones. Furthermore, if he divided his budget among many small new companies, the transaction costs would be too high. But that means that the efficient portfolios that can be realized by the private investor are less attractive than the ones realized by institutional investors. Due to transaction costs and information costs, the private investor's obtainable returns from investment in shares decline.[10] When investing in new companies, private investors run higher risks because of information asymmetries and slower

---

[10] See also Levy/Livingston (1995).

reaction possibilities. This is further increased by their low degree of diversification. When compared to the institutional investor, the private investor not only takes the systematic risk for which he at least gets paid, but he also takes the unsystematic risk to a large degree for which the market offers no payment. Especially small and new companies have a very high unsystematic risk that only the institutional investor can eliminate by means of diversification.

If the private investor in Figure 3 invests his whole budget in shares, he can only realize a much lower utility level, even at best in T_2. Thus he suffers a considerable loss of return when compared to the institutional investor, and furthermore runs a significantly higher risk. Obviously, investment in shares in T_2 is not really a very attractive investment alternative to him. Therefore, as long as he has no alternative, he will invest most of his budget, for example, in government bonds, in saving contracts with a building society, and in life insurance (see P_2 in Figure 3).

On the other hand, private investors are being offered diversified portfolios by investment companies, pension funds, and venture capital companies. Thus they can avoid the low utility level in P_2 to a large extent. But even these big players cannot invest in M because of their transaction costs and expenses for evaluating small and new companies. They also have expenses for marketing and management. Consequently, at best the line of efficient portfolios gets worse and runs parallel by that amount (see also the broken efficiency line in Figure 3). In this case, the investor has no incentive to invest directly in shares, for indirect investment in T_1 dominates the direct investment in T_2. The direct investment in stocks—and especially in small companies—becomes more and more an event exclusively for institutional professionals. But in Germany these institutions neglect the stand-up-stage financing.

If private investors invest directly in small companies despite the described disadvantage in comparison to institutional investors, then this can mostly be attributed to their willingness to run a higher risk for part of their budget, or to the fact that they as especially big investors get the same favorable conditions as institutional investors. But as they are not paid for the undiversified risks, it is not in the private investors' interest to invest directly in new companies. It could well be desirable that risky investments, especially in new enterprises, are only possible for professional investors. They are used to assessing and handling risks. But the economy needs the private investor's capital to finance promising future investments if credit institutions or banks do not provide capital to a sufficient degree.

In the long term, financing new companies will be dominantly dealt with by financial intermediaries. This is not automatically a disadvantage to new companies, for professional investors are better at correctly assessing the chances of a company. On the other hand, new problems arise. For financial reasons, investment in small companies is only worthwhile for big funds if they can buy a substantial amount of equities. With that, they are confronted with the problem that they can hardly sell their equities for a narrow market because sell orders can cause severe price losses. In spite of these problems, financial intermediaries are often the 'sole hope' of small companies when they have to get venture capital. At first, in view of a very efficient banking industry in Germany, the question arises of whether new and small companies can at least rely on a functioning credit market.

III. Corporate Governance Structure in Germany a Barrier to Equity Financing

Due to their bargaining power, it is no problem for big corporations with a sufficiently good standing to get credit from banks at favorable conditions. Furthermore, their degree of publicity provides easy access to the equity markets. The low equity capital ratio of successful companies that have already existed for a while can be put down to a very special corporate governance structure in Germany. In Germany, the entrepreneurs of small companies attach great importance to their independence. They would rather do without additional profit and development possibilities than have another partner. In this respect, there is a difference in mentality in the corporate governance structure between the United States and Germany, for the American businessman is more profit-oriented.

It can only be assumed and not proven scientifically to what extent the German entrepreneurs' disapproving attitude towards the new partners' influence can be attributed to legally determined differences in corporate governance structure between Germany and the United States. An unproven assumption is that German owners of companies react especially sensitively to a further decline of their decision-making power because of the employees' extensive rights of co-determination and the German trade unions' relatively strong position.

To many German companies that have already been in the market for some time, their low equity capitalization ratio cannot be explained by a market failure in the equity market, but by special corporate governance structures, the businessmen's distinct patronizing behavior, and by tax reasons. But things have been changing lately. In Germany, young entrepreneurs have a different attitude toward corporate governance and they are more willing to share responsibility with new partners. However, they rely on bank credit due to poorly functioning venture capital markets.

IV. Banks Unsuitable for Credit Lending to New Companies

The financing situation for business founders is quite different from the position of established entrepreneurs. They have to finance the capital from their own resources, relatives, friends, and other private investors because the banks ration their capital. This is shown in Figure 4.

Figure 4: Market Refusal for New Companies Due to Credit Rationing

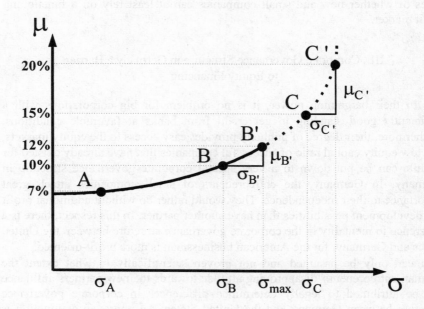

If it were so easy—as assumed in theory—to identify and assess differing risk structures of a company, then every businessman would get his credit at a risk-adjusted price. Figure 4 makes that clear. A well-known big company or an old, established family business (A) with low risk σ_A, high financing power from its own resources, high equity capital quota, and property in land as a collateral, but low additional growth potential, would get a loan at $\mu = 7\%$, for example. The fast-expanding high tech company (B) that can produce considerably higher profit expectations, whose investment plans consistently require additional capital, and whose collaterals are already used to finance growth, would pay an interest rate of $\mu = 10\%$ in view of his risk σ_B. And the often-quoted Schumpeter entrepreneur (C), who as a founder and inventive person achieves high monopoly returns, would get an interest rate of $\mu = 15\%$ because of his high risk σ_C.

Capital market theory, market, and politics would be in harmony. In view of higher chances and higher risks—as far as systematic risks (that is risks that cannot be diversified) are concerned—the financing of innovations would be possible on terms that provide interest rates in accordance with market conditions, thus regulating the means in an economically optimal way.[11]

However, real capital markets are quite different. Banks have to be prepared for receiving glossed-over data for their credit investigation. Only by investing a high amount of additional energy and cost would they be able to reduce the information asymmetries between themselves and the capital-searching company. This is why the business risk that a bank expects to take exceeds the real risk involved, even for companies with a good financial standing that provide accurate information. As the bank can hardly prevent being given manipulated or incomplete information, company B pays an interest rate of 12% instead of an interest rate of 10% that would be risk-adequate. The bank then acts neither maliciously nor irrationally. Its subjectively felt risk is now higher by $\sigma_{B'}$, and that is why it requests an additional interest of $\mu_{B'}$. This risk premium for asymmetric information is especially high for the more risky new company C.[12] Instead of the objectively necessary 15%, the bank would have to demand 20% interest as sufficient risk provision. In Germany, such a credit contract is not possible any more. For the 'good' businessman, this interest rate is too high and the German bank prefers to protect itself from high business risks by credit rationing instead of offering flexible interest rates.

In Figure 4, the bank rations its credit from risk σ_{max} and $\mu = 12\%$ onwards. Thus it not only avoids additional loan losses and the cost involved, but also accusations of charging extortionate interest rates.

Furthermore, especially high interest rates tend to attract companies with a poor reputation. After having been granted the loan, the borrower could be induced to invest in even more risky projects in contradiction to the credit contract, as the bank runs the major risk but does not participate in possible excess returns from this investment.[13]

Most of the credit financing problems of smaller companies and of fast-growing new companies can consequently be put down to credit rationing and low interest flexibility of the banks, that is, a failure of the market due to asymmetric information. Especially old, established companies that can offer securites are granted interest rates in line with overall market conditions. But often enough, these are not the ones with the highest innovative force.

---

[11] In Figure 4, the over-proportionally rising line for the lending rate in accordance with the rising risk σ is a consequence of the lenders' risk-aversion.

[12] See Akerlof (1970).

[13] Stieglitz/Weiss (1981).

V. Credit Rationing for New Companies a Corporate Governance Problem of Banks

Credit rationing due to asymmetric information is further increased by personal clashes of interest in the banking industry that can be explained by the corporate governance structure of banks. The bank clerk handling loan applications is usually not the manager and most of all not the owner. The clerks pursue their own career interests and adjust their credit-granting policy accordingly. But it is asking too much of the person in charge to evaluate new patents and company ideas. Especially in Germany, they are still used to thinking in terms of debt secured by real property, which makes it possible to give only second priority to the company's profit prospects.

Bank clerks handling loan applications are often not as long-term-oriented as the bank owner. In view of the given corporate governance structure of the bank, they act in a rational way. In most cases, they are not directly involved in the results of their credit-granting policy. But this is not the most decisive corporate governance effect, for it is even more important that they are being much more associated with their loss-making credit-granting than with their successful one. Even if they achieve higher interest when giving a loan to a new firm, this is taken for granted. In case of loan losses, however, they have to see their superior and they keep the central law department busy with the bankruptcy proceedings. As they do not want to risk their career with such negative incidents, they rather avoid credit to new firms that would have to be given without being secured by real property.

Finally, it has to be taken into consideration that German banks are not destined for venture capital financing due to their corporate governance structure. Their shareholders might be prepared to accept such a step from a profit-risk point of view. But the majority of the bank clients, the deposit guaranty fund institution, and the banking supervisory authority primarily pursue security interests.[14]

To sum up, even banks need incentives if they are to grant a loan to developing smaller companies with low equity capitalization. We have to admit a market failure on credit lending to new companies, and, as pointed out, we have to give up the hope that private investors might help to finance small and medium-sized companies. We obviously need institutional investors, special stock markets for new companies, and venture capital companies at first to improve the equity capitalization of companies to get bank credits. But there might be a failure of that market, too.

---

[14] See also Hopt (1996: 544).

VI. Organized Equity Markets Not Efficient for New Companies

Analogous to NASDAQ, the *Nouveau Marché*, EASDAQ, and the *Neue Markt* have been set up. But a fundamental improvement in financing the setting-up of new companies has not been achieved so far.[15] However, this is not an argument against the new market segments, for they take over important tasks in financing already successful companies. The number of companies listed on these markets is very small in relation to the capital demand of new companies. Furthermore, the offering terms that are necessary for financing new companies, and that are indispensable for reasons of investor protection, are too strict. Often it can be observed that in countries with a universal banking system, the liquidity of the stock market for small caps is normally quite low. This can be seen in the typical development of an initial public offering in Germany.

While the "wheel" of turnovers in the big international quoted securities and, in particular, in derivatives, is turning faster and faster in Germany, the listed and unlisted primary markets are being neglected. There are several reasons for the low liquidity of smaller companies brought to the German exchange. To give an example, these can be proven by the idealized historical course of a new issue (Figure 5).

Generally, an issuing German bank launches its new offerings with a lot of publicity into the market. In doing this, the bank has given the wheel of stock trading a push in an initial public offering (IPO), which is profitable for itself and promising for the issuer. But even the issuing bank's trading department will not like the new offering as much as the issuing department, because for them dealing in important blue chips and in derivatives is far more profitable than cultivating the market in small IPOs.

Mutual fund managers will only show little interest in small new issues since their performance is rated according to the comparison of yield and risk development of international companies. But also private investors invest only very hesitantly in small IPOs. Quite often, adequate information is not available, for German managers generally pursue a policy of publicity that is limited to the most necessary facts, and investment advisors hardly ever recommend second-line stocks to their clients. Thus, the media interest in publishing information on the economic development of smaller listed companies declines.

Big German banks and insurance companies have set up their own research departments. For them, expertise is only profitable if huge sums of capital are thus controlled. This is the main reason why they neglect second-line stocks as well. Instead, capital intermediaries increasingly turn their attention to international stock markets.

---

[15] See also Hopt/Baum (1997: 357).

Figure 5: Crash Landing of IPOs in Germany

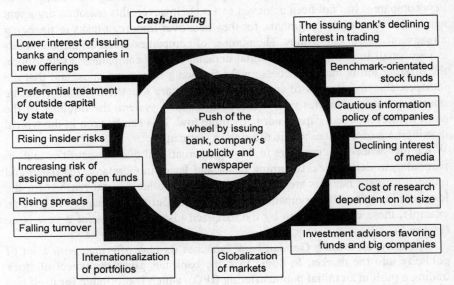

In view of the low turnover in second-line stocks on the stock exchange, not only are the high transaction costs growing, but also the risks of insider trading. In the segment of the organized German stock market dominated by universal banks, most of the IPOs are a failure from a liquidity point of view. The organized stock market fails to meet the liquidity factors listed in Figure 6 to such an extent that most IPOs can be considered a crash landing. But, according to our knowledge now, this is not true for the newly established stock exchange segment *Neuer Markt*. Due to a special supervision system, new issues in this segment have been a success up to now. However, this is no help to new companies on the whole, for only very few companies will meet the requirements of the *Neuer Markt* after having been temporarily financed by venture capital companies. In this respect, the underdeveloped venture capital scene in Germany can largely be put down to the fact that it is still far more difficult to successfully carry out a disinvestment in the German stock market than in the United States. In the past, the special corporate governance structure of German banks could be blamed for the market failure of IPOs. Due to their many-sided interests in credit financing, property, insurance, and bank deposits, they did not pay as much attention to the IPOs as an American broker facing tough competition would have done. That policy was further enhanced by the already-mentioned corporate governance behavior of German businessmen who were not prepared to share their decision-making power with new partners. Up to now, there has been a lack of an investment banking culture for small companies that intensively attends to these primary and secondary markets.[16] Furthermore, the liquidity of traded titles is often diminished by a high ratio of firm ownership of private and institutional investors.[17]

Figure 6: Factors of Stock Exchange Efficiency

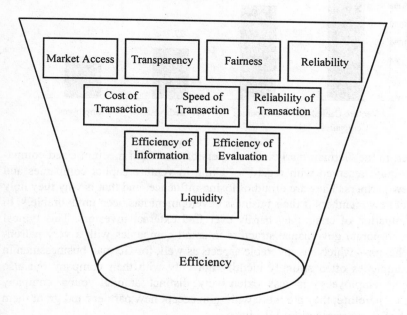

VII. Venture Capital Companies and Their Role in Financing New Companies

Venture capital companies cannot compete with the stock exchange with regard to transparency, liquidity, and transaction cost. But they offer new companies considerably easier access to the market instead. Venture capital companies would be the ideal partner of small and especially new companies insofar as they

---

[16] See Hopt/Baum (1997: 303).
[17] See Baums (1996).

would have more trust in them than, for instance, in the participation of employees or private investors, as was shown in a study conducted among medium-sized companies.[18]

Figure 7: Investors Preferred by Medium-Sized Companies

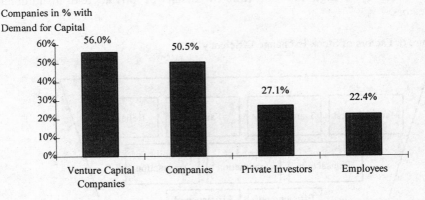

However, in the German market, the owners of small and medium-sized companies are quite reserved with regard to taking in venture capital companies and other new partners. They are afraid of losing influence, and that is why they only try to get new members if their business development has been unfavorable.[19] In such a situation of crisis they hardly ever find external investors. This typical German corporate governance structure in small companies with a very patronizing behavior—which has favorable aspects as well, for German businessmen in small companies often strongly identify not only with their company but also with their employees—is less extensively distinct among young company founders. Therefore, they are more willing to accept new partners and grant them the right of co-determination and advice.

However, not only the German businessmen's striving for independence can be made responsible for the poor performance of the venture capital market in Germany. As a banking subsidiary of the German universal banks, numerous capital investment companies have pursued a policy that is strongly influenced by the banking industry. That is why German venture capital companies have only achieved little publicity among their potential clients, for in the branches of the parent company, out of short-term egoistic interest, the successful businessman's attention was hardly ever drawn to venture capital companies. The German

[18] See Gerke/v. Rüth/Schöner (1992).
[19] See Hopt/Baum (1997: 301).

corporate governance structure in big banks is so unfavorable for venture capital financing that even the employees in the different bank departments have only very little knowledge of their own banks' venture capital companies and of the special quality of the venture capital business at all. Furthermore, the German capital investment companies have not given away real equity capital for a long time. They often negotiated minimum and maximum interest payment and a limited amount of capital with fixed repayment price. Therefore, their portfolios offered no possibility for a high flyer financing several flops, and in the long term they showed a negative portfolio selection.

In Germany, information on the venture capital market is very contradictory. Venture capital companies claim not to find suitable company founders, and business founders claim that there is not sufficient venture capital. According to the BVK (Association of Venture Capital Investment Companies), the companies organized in the association invest DM 9.2 billion in venture capital. This amount would refute the business founders' claims. However, the BVK's statistics give a wrong impression. The largest part of the assigned venture capital is merely a loan with profit participation. Furthermore, companies already established in the market are primarily financed.

When German venture capital companies boast of having to write off just 2% of the money invested, then this clearly demonstrates that they are engaged in another business than they claim to be in and that they do not finance company set-ups. Often former employees of German banks and involved in the governance structure of their own parent bank, they act like banks but in the wrong field.

In the United States, successful venture capital companies could never boast of a 2% deficiency rate. With their high-flyer investments they finance unavoidable flops, and this definitely amounts to more than just 2%. To disinvest from successful business, the American venture capital companies prefer NASDAQ, while the German venture capital companies prefer to resell their shares to the original owner of companies and even often negotiate the terms and conditions when agreeing to an investment.

But even with improved acceptance of venture capital companies, the riskiness of financing new companies continues to make it a difficult process. In the German venture capital companies that are dominated by the universal banks, the entrepreneurial skill of lending money without securities is often missing. They are simply not used to evaluating new ways of process engineering or products. Often, the investing venture capital companies have to assess procedures that have not been tested in the market yet. As specialists in the financial field, they need external expertise to do so. In no case can they only rely on the information provided by the company founders. First, the company founders tend to overestimate their own development chances, for they have very good technical skills but hardly any experience and management skills in judging the market.

Second, it is obvious that the business founders deliberately idealize their expectations for the future in order to get external capital at favorable conditions from the venture capital company. Again, information asymmetry between a little-known company and the external investor prevents successful contracts. There are not only uncertainties about the company's quality, but often poor market transparency on the capital-demanding small and mid caps. At the stock exchange, supply and demand are met every day and the price movements are published, but there is a lack of a similar market transparency for off-board capital markets. Due to that, high expenses for searching for investment capital incur, to which the high cost for reducing information asymmetry between investor and debtor add up. The market efficiency would be increased if it were possible to create a financial situation that—analogous to the traditional stock markets—reduces the information asymmetry between small and mid caps and investors. Consequently, state support of such an institution would not result in a distortion of the market, but stimulate the market instead. Therefore, the setting-up of a European information exchange and rating agency for small and mid caps is being suggested.

C. Proposals to Improve New Firms' Access to Capital

I. The European Information Exchange

Most of all, an information exchange would be a meeting point for those who would like to invest and those who have a demand for capital. Thus, it would especially reduce the searching expenses of potential contracting parties, with the Internet providing a cheap meeting point. An information exchange will not relieve the venture capital companies and other investors of an intensive examination of the capital-demanding company, but it can initiate negotiation processes and point to promising investment possibilities. In order to do this, the companies listed there would have to provide a minimum of information on their field, their capital demand, and their economic situation.

According to Figure 8, it could provide important services with regard to mediation, such as data bases of companies looking for stockholders, of investors offering capital, and of venture capital companies; it could also mediate investment negotiations. Furthermore it could provide services with regard to information, such as differentiated information on investors and capital demand, externally checked data on balances, products and companies, company rating, business sites and negotiations of subsidies, and cooperation with technology and business centers.

Figure 8: Intermediation Against Information Asymmetries

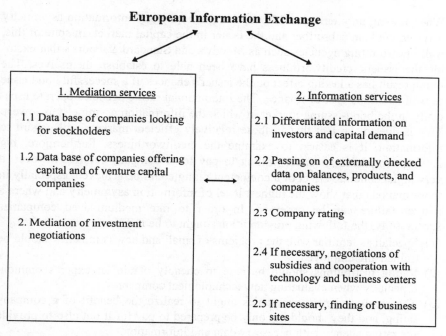

European Information Exchange

1. Mediation services	2. Information services
1.1 Data base of companies looking for stockholders	2.1 Differentiated information on investors and capital demand
1.2 Data base of companies offering capital and of venture capital companies	2.2 Passing on of externally checked data on balances, products, and companies
2. Mediation of investment negotiations	2.3 Company rating
	2.4 If necessary, negotiations of subsidies and cooperation with technology and business centers
	2.5 If necessary, finding of business sites

At the European Information Exchange no equities would be traded and no prices fixed, for the traditional stock exchange is the best place to do this. This means that the terms and conditions of contracts, and especially capital investment, have to be negotiated bilaterally. However, as a neutral authority, the information exchange could make an important contribution by rating the listed companies at their wish. Such a rating is certainly a difficult and sometimes faulty process. In all probability, it would be made easier by the fact that only those companies that expect a favorable rating result would like to be rated. They will be prepared to pay the price for this neutral signalling because it is worthwhile to them. The Internet makes it possible to create the information exchange in such a flexible way that only very few problems with regard to acceptance occur. Thus, new companies that are looking for capital but also fear disclosing research results and company internal affairs could only provide very general information at first. Then, after having received the inquiries, the company could make a decision as to whether further information on the company should be revealed.

II. Rating Arrangements Concerning Medium-Sized Companies

When issuing an international bond, there is hardly any information asymmetry between the loan subscriber and the issuer in the capital market. In spite of this, well-known rating agencies such as Moody's and Standard & Poors's that examine the issuers' creditworthiness have been able to establish themselves. The rating result has a lasting effect on the issuer's chances of a successful bond issue as well as on his cost of finance. The international rating agencies operate especially in the bond-issuing market in which the information asymmetry is lowest. This is due to the fact that in these relatively efficient markets with regard to information, it is easiest to examine the creditworthiness. Furthermore, big issuing companies are more willing to pay for a company rating. However, a very high economic effect of a competent rating could be achieved, especially in those markets that show the highest level of information asymmetry and where a market failure can be observed. In order to rate medium-sized companies successfully, the following pre-conditions ought to be fulfilled:

(1) Specialists familiar with the problems of small and new companies should be trained and employed.

(2) Rating institutions should be able to cheaply obtain an expert's opinion, especially when evaluating new technological companies.

(3) The small and new companies ought to realize the benefit of a company rating, and they should not only be prepared to pay for it but also to provide the rating agency with necessary data and information.

(4) The rating should not be too expensive. Therefore, without considerably reducing accuracy, a standardization of the testing procedure would be necessary.

(5) Finally, high rating accuracy is the pre-condition for being recognized and accepted by institutional and private investors.

Setting up a rating agency for small and new companies proves to be a difficult task. However, this should not be an obstacle to installing such an institution, for a competent rating is very beneficial because of the extremely high information asymmetries in the market for young companies. The main problem will be to establish such a market in the first place, because company rating depends on the confidence gained in the market. This is why the most difficult task is to provide evidence that shows that the small company's rating result on growth and risk prospect is a real quality mark.

To achieve general acceptance, the rating agency for small caps has to be absolutely neutral. Therefore, it should be neither an institution of big banks nor just an initiative of the state. However, in spite of significant information asymmetries, no important rating agency for small and mid caps has been established up till now. Therefore, it can be assumed that it is very difficult to set up such an institution without state support. Such initial financial support by the state should not be handed over directly to the rating agency. It is more efficient if young companies that want to be rated be supported financially till the rating agencies' quality marks are considered an independent and viable service in the market.

Initially, a suggestion was made to integrate the rating of companies unable to issue into an information exchange for investment in young companies.[20] The task of the information exchange was to bring together capital-demanding companies and institutional investors as well as private investors. To do that, a company rating is not absolutely necessary. In particular cases, it is sufficient to provide information on the capital-searching company and its special features. The capital-providing investors will then check the capital-searching company's creditworthiness. However, a rating agency does not have to be integrated into such an information exchange, but could also be set up as an independent institution.

It is true that every day banks have to determine the creditworthiness of small and mid caps in their credit investigation, but there is no neutral rating agency that would offer the lender a kind of pre-selection and inform investors about interesting possibilities. A concept for setting up a rating agency for small and mid caps has already been developed in literature.[21] With regard to content, the mid caps' rating is considerably different from the rating of big companies, and that is why it is not possible to take over the concept of a rating agency for big companies as proposed by Everling.[22] In particular, it is not sufficient to show company creditworthiness in such a condensed form of letters and numbers. These special features are suitable for classifying company risk and profit expectations of big companies. For small companies, it is advisable to state additional similarly standardized judgments on management quality, financial position, industry position and product prospects, and product development. Particularly with new companies, a venture capital company or a new investor will be prepared to meet the requirement to catch up in certain company areas if all other development prospects for the company are attractive.

But even a rating agency for small and mid caps will make a misjudgment every now and again. Even established rating agencies like Moody's occasionally only adapt their company rating to the deteriorated company situation after this news has already been published. Therefore, when rating small and mid caps, their development prospects should be given particular consideration. Before signing a contract of participation, a new investor will always have to make his own judgment about the company independent from the rating agency.

The rating agency's evaluation helps investors choose from interesting investment possibilities and examine their own company rating. Therefore, small

---

[20] See Gerke/v. Rüth/Schöner (1992).

[21] See also Wagner (1991) as well as Gerke (1993, 1995).

[22] See Everling (1991, 1995) as well as Steiner/Heinke (1996), Meyer-Parpant (1996).

and mid cap rating is especially interesting to venture capital companies, to other capital investment companies, and in all probability to pension funds as well as to insurance companies to some extent. Furthermore, the rating will be interesting to wealthy private investors who are prepared to take risks as well as to expanding companies that would like to buy new companies.

But this does not mean that rating addressees ought to finance the rating of small and mid caps. This is only the case when, e.g., a venture capital company wants a rating agency to analyze a company in a particular investment situation. The rating mainly ought to be paid for by the capital-demanding company.

III. Derivation of Rating Utilization

With a favorable rating result, young companies can demonstrate to prospective investors that investment is worthwhile. This means that on the one hand they will try to get attention by means of external company rating, and on the other hand they will hope to reduce their financing cost.[23] But as a prerequisite, it is necessary that a company can show better profit expectations than generally assumed, or, at least, that the general level of uncertainty concerning the future company profits can be lowered considerably. This precondition will have a positive side effect, for only those companies convinced of their company quality will be prepared to face a rating. This positive pre-selection makes the rating agency's work easier, but it still has to conscientiously analyze the company.

To simplify the above-mentioned decision making, we assume that the investor can either invest DM 1 million in a listed company (B) or participate in a medium-sized company (M), with mid cap (M) involving a slightly higher risk $(\sigma_M > \sigma_B)$ and showing a considerably higher profit than (B) $(\mu_M > \mu_B)$. If we further assume that the investor is a wealthy private person with a slightly risk-averse attitude, then he will invest the whole amount, DM 1 million, in a mid cap new on the market, for in doing this he achieves the highest utility level. In Figure 9, his indifference curve (U_M) is tangent to the investment in the medium-sized company (M) in the optimum. Investment in listed companies (B) results in a lower utility $(U_M > U_B)$.[24] Now we can concentrate on why so little is invested

[23] See Paul (1996) concerning the advertising effects of rating.

[24] To complete this scenario, we should also take into account how investment in medium-sized companies is correlated to investment in a listed company in order to quantify possible risk-reducing effects. Furthermore, it should be taken into account to what extent the investor is prepared to invest part of his wealth in fixed-interest, low-risk instruments. The additional recording of these points causes no problems and is sufficiently dealt with in capital market theory.

in young companies, and why the listed companies have the highest refinancing chances.[25]

Figure 9: Derivation of Rating Utility

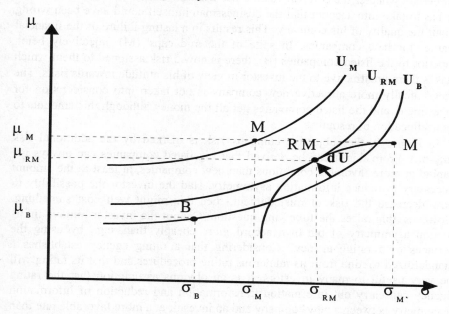

The gap between objective company risk (σ_M) and subjectively perceived investment risk (σ_M) has a detrimental effect on the mid caps' chances of getting capital. A variety of information can be obtained on big listed companies, and the market price of these companies is fixed by opinion forming between different market players. This means that the investor can get information at a considerably lower price, and, furthermore, that he can also rely on a rough degree of certainty that the company rating corresponds to the current economic and information situation. The situation of a newly set-up medium-sized company is completely different. Here, the investor has to rely on himself to a large extent. He has to try to find out the right market price by contacting the company. This

[25] Investment in medium-sized companies causes additional risk for the investor. First of all it is a liquidity risk. Since there is no functioning capital market for medium-sized companies, the investor has to take into account not only his profit expectations, but also that he might find it difficult to realize the company value at short notice. This reduces his freedom of action, for should he want to sell his equities because of better investment possibilities or because of shortage in liquidity, it will either take him quite a long time or he will have to reckon with the possibility that he cannot realize the objective value of the company at short notice.

is not only very expensive, but there is also a high risk of misjudgment. Even if the new company owner is prepared to put every piece of information at the investor's disposal, the investor will remain suspicious, for he will never know for certain whether the company owner has truthfully informed him. In addition, he has to take into account that the businessman himself could have been wrong about the quality of his company. This results in a lasting failure of the financial market for new companies. In spite of the mid caps' (M) objectively being superior to the listed companies (B), there is now a risk assigned to them which makes them unattractive to the investor in view of his attitude towards risks. The economically more attractive new company is not taken into consideration for investment, and the listed companies get all the money although this amounts to a misallocation of resources.

In Figure 9, the subjective company risk is marked by the additional risk $(\sigma_M\text{-}\sigma_M)$. From this it can be derived that big listed companies can always get capital at more favorable conditions than new companies, at least to the amount necessary to reduce information asymmetry. Had the investor the possibility to now decrease the risk of misjudgment, then this might well cost something. However, this raises the following question: Cannot the investor remove information asymmetry of his own accord more cheaply than, e.g., by using the services of a rating agency? Considering that a rating agency establishes a standardized routine from its numerous rating procedures and that its rating will be very useful to many investors, it is an obvious assumption that the rating agency can carry out information transformation and reduction of information asymmetry between a new company and an investor at a more favorable rate than the individual. Therefore, rating agencies ought to be able to diminish the effects of market failure in financing new technological companies and other medium-sized companies. It is then a business management problem to what extent the rating agency should carry out a company analysis. As a rule, it can be assumed that the higher the effort the better the quality of the analytical result, and the lower the risk of a quality misinterpretation and subsequently the subjective investment risk. However, the marginal rate of risk reduction will decrease with increasing effort. From the point of view of a particular investor, Figure 9 shows, e.g., to what extent external company rating would be favorable for him. This is actually exactly the case when the new subjectively felt return-risk structure of the mid cap is tangent to its highest possible risk utility (see RM). It makes a difference whether the rating expenses are being paid for by the investor or by the companies. The investor's profit expectations are diminished in both cases, but if the rating is initiated by the mid cap, the rating result is to the benefit of several potential investors. In Figure 9, dU marks the rating benefit of a particular investor.

D. Conclusion

For Germany, it can be said that in financing small companies and especially in setting up companies, there is an extensive market failure due to inadequate market transparency and information asymmetry. This is true for direct financing of new companies by private investors, for loan financing by banks, for the stock markets in second-line stocks, as well as for venture capital financing. To reduce this failure, those measures are especially recommended that give the new companies a push. Permanent subsidies cannot solve the problems caused by the market failure in the German venture capital market.[26]

The following measures are suggested to reduce the discrimination against young enterprises:

(1) In view of ever-increasing private investment in investment funds, it should be an object to win these funds for investment in small enterprises as well. Therefore, the selling of closed-end funds should be admitted. German open-end investment companies are hardly able to invest in new enterprises of little liquidity as they always have to reckon with the certificate holders' desire to redeem their certificates, which then might force the investment company to an unduly hasty sale of the funds' assets.

(2) Specialized venture capital companies are the most suitable instrument for foundation financing. However, so far, even the achievements of these companies must be considered modest in Germany. Thus, governmental financing schemes and interest subsidies continue to be of great importance to young enterprises. Venture capital companies specializing in financing new companies could be promoted by means of interest-reduced state loans and tax relief on investment earnings if they re-invest in new companies.

(3) Young enterprises growing at a steep rate need organized liquid stock exchange markets in order to raise additional money. Venture capital companies, then, could disinvest via these stock exchange markets; thereupon, the investment funds with big capital behind them could pass the money accumulated from private investors on to young enterprises to finance them for expansion. The organized stock exchange as a stock market segment for small companies should be revitalized in Germany.

(4) Furthermore, creating financial incentives could enhance the financing of new companies. These could include reduced-interest loans granted by the state for setting up a company as well as tax relief offered to people investing directly in new companies or through venture capital companies. A good starting point for the promotion of private investment in companies can be seen in the inheritance tax regulation. In Germany, within a period of five years, about 1.7 million people left approximately DM 2.6 trillion. The heirs'

---

[26] See Hopt (1996: 545).

investment in productive capital, either directly or in funds, could be granted a tax deferral up to a fixed maximum. Furthermore, 10% annually of the original tax could be remitted if the investment in equities remains. If, for social-political reasons, the revenue from inheritance tax should remain unchanged, the same could be achieved by raising the inheritance tax rates at the same time. By means of a gift tax amended analogously to the inheritance tax, the alternation of generations in medium companies could be made easier. Especially in Germany, there is an opportunity to enhance pension schemes with pension funds and their investment in equities. The shareholding limit of insurance companies should be increased to 25% according to § 54a VAG (*Versicherungsaufsichtsgesetz*). Furthermore, banks and insurance companies should not be liable for equity funding of their venture capital companies in addition to their own credit according to § 32a GmbHG.

(5) Creating an information exchange would reduce the information asymmetries between capital-seeking enterprises and potential investors. Such an information exchange would make it easier for venture capital companies and other investors to discover suitable investment opportunities by finding all the major entrepreneurial data ready to be called up.

(6) The setting-up of a rating agency would be another major step in reducing the information asymmetries between capital-seeking enterprises and investors. Such a rating agency might rate the enterprises impartially on the basis of fixed criteria with regard to their standing in order to thus emit signals of their goodwill and risk rating to the investors.

Because of their very special corporate governance idea, numerous German entrepreneurs prefer financiers that give credit without time limit that can be cancelled any time. Furthermore, these financiers should ideally be content with an interest achieved for government bonds and simultaneously bear the entrepreneurial risk. Such altruistic financiers do not exist in a free capital market, and that is why entrepreneurs in Germany request state support for company set-ups.

Due to their corporate governance structure shaped by banks, numerous German venture capital companies prefer so-called investment in companies already established in the market, for which the owner in question can provide securities or for which the state offers deficiency guarantee. This pseudo venture capital is to be paid back by the entrepreneur after a fixed period of time and at a fixed price agreed upon in advance and, of course, with high interest. There is no market for such preferences either.

With growing internationalization of venture capital markets, the corporate governance structures of German companies and venture capital companies will change as well. They will both pursue a business policy that is strongly market-oriented. This process has already started and will accelerate considerably.

References

Akerlof, George A. 'The Market for Lemons' *Quarterly Journal of Economics* 84 (1970) 488-500.

Baums, Theodor 'Mittelständische Unternehmen und Börse. Eine rechtsvergleichende Untersuchung' in: Immenga, Ulrich, Wernhard Möschel, and Dieter Reuter (eds.) *Festschrift für Ernst-Joachim Mestmäcker* 815-29 (Baden-Baden 1996).

Deutsche Bundesbank *Monatsberichte* 49/5 (1997).

Everling, Oliver *Credit Rating durch internationale Agenturen: Eine Untersuchung zu den Komponenten und instrumentalen Funktionen des Rating* (Wiesbaden 1991).

Everling, Oliver 'Rating' in: Gerke, Wolfgang and Manfred Steiner (eds.) *Handwörterbuch des Bank- und Finanzwesens* 1601-9 2nd edn. (Stuttgart 1995).

Gerke, Wolfgang 'Informationsasymmetrien am Markt für Beteiligungen an mittelständischen Unternehmen' in: Gebhardt, Günther, Wolfgang Gerke, and Manfred Steiner (eds.) *Handbuch des Finanzmanagements* 619-40 (Munich 1993).

Gerke, Wolfgang 'Venture Capital' in: Gerke, Wolfgang and Manfred Steiner (eds.) *Handwörterbuch des Bank- und Finanzwesens* 1884-90 2nd edn. (Stuttgart 1995).

Gerke, Wolfgang and Stefan Arneth 'Die Wirkungen von Insiderinformationen an Börsenmärkten' in: Gerke, Wolfgang (ed.) *Die Börse der Zukunft—Märkte, Plätze, Netze* 165-91 (Stuttgart 1997).

Gerke, Wolfgang and Horst Bienert 'Computerisierte Börsenexperimente—Ein Beitrag zu einer Experimentellen Kapitalmarktforschung' *Zeitschrift für Wirtschafts- und Sozialwissenschaften* 114 (1994) 91-105.

Gerke, Wolfgang and Horst Bienert 'Market Design, Trading Behavior: An Experimental Stock Market Model' in: (DFG-Sammelband [Anthology of the Deutsche Forschungsgemeinschaft] 1998, forthcoming).

Gerke, Wolfgang, Volker van Rüth, and Manfred A. Schöner *Informationsbörse für Beteiligungen an mittelständischen Unternehmen* (Stuttgart 1992).

Hopt, Klaus J. 'Verbesserter Zugang zu Risikokapital für Existenzgründer sowie kleine und mittlere Unternehmen' in: Pfeiffer, Gerd, Joachim Kummer, and Silke Scheuch (eds.) *Festschrift für Hans Erich Brandner* 541-54 (Cologne 1996).

Hopt, Klaus J. and Harald Baum 'Börsenrechtsreform in Deutschland' in: Hopt, Klaus J., Bernd Rudolph, and Harald Baum (eds.) *Börsenreform. Eine ökonomische, rechtsvergleichende und rechtspolitische Untersuchung* 287-467 (Stuttgart 1997).

Levy, Azriel and Miles Livingston 'The Gains from Diversification Reconsidered: Transaction Costs and Superior Information' *Financial Markets, Institutions & Instruments* 4/3 (1995).

London Stock Exchange 'Survey of Shareownership' (London 1982 and 1994).

Meyer-Parpant, Wolfgang 'Ratingkriterien für Unternehmen' in: Büschgen, Hans E. and Oliver Everling (eds.) *Handbuch Rating* 111-73 (Wiesbaden 1996).

New York Stock Exchange 'Shareownership' (New York 1995).

Japan Securities Dealers Association 'Fact Book 1995' (Tokyo 1995).

Japan Securities Research Institute 'Securities Market in Japan 1992' (Tokyo 1992).

Paul, Walter 'Rating als Instrument des Finanzmarketing' in: Büschgen, Hans E. and Oliver Everling (eds.) *Handbuch Rating* 373-417 (Wiesbaden 1996).

Schmidt, Reinhard H. 'Corporate Governance: The Role of Other Constituencies' (Working Paper no. 3, July 1997) (to appear in: Pezard, A. and J.-M. Thiveaud (eds) *Workable Corporate Governance: Cross-Border Perspectives* (Montchrestien, Paris forthcoming).

Securities Industry Association 'Factbook' (New York 1993).

Steiner, Manfred and Volker G. Heinke 'Rating aus Sicht der modernen Finanzierungstheorie' in: Büschgen, Hans E. and Oliver Everling (eds.) *Handbuch Rating* 579-625 (Wiesbaden 1996).

Stiglitz, Joseph E. and Andrew Weiss 'Credit Rationing in Markets with Imperfect Information' *American Economic Review* 71 (1981) 393-410.

Wagner, Wolf-Christof *Rating mittelständischer Unternehmungen* (Frankfurt am Main 1991).

Discussion Report

DIRK H. BLIESENER

A German commentator generally agreed with Professor *Gerke's* suggestion of a rating concept for venture capital companies. Concern was expressed with respect to the financial information those firms would make available to the venture capitalist, since in many cases properly audited financial statements are not available. In response, Professor *Gerke* pointed out that in his model, a rating would realistically be offered only to companies with proper data available. Otherwise the rating would be negative, causing the company to not want to publish and pay for it anyway.

Dissemination and exchange of information could, in Professor *Gerke's* perspective, also be brought about by informal discussions between the venture capitalist and the portfolio company. Generally, the German venture capital market is in need of such information or formalized ratings since it suffers from a significant informational asymmetry. U.S. commentators explicitly denied this proposition of a mere asymmetry, but instead suggested that there was substantial uncertainty on both sides as to whether the company would survive at all, not only whether the return on capital would be 15% or 20%. Others added that the task envisioned by Professor *Gerke* for German venture capitalist companies was exactly what U.S. venture capital companies were already doing.

On a factual note, Professor *Gerke* explained that there were only three to four independent venture capital firms operating in Germany. One reason for this small representation is the capital market's lack of liquidity. On the other hand, many commentators agreed that it stems from the underdeveloped equity culture, in which too few German entrepreneurs call for venture capital services although the industry appears to require this type of capital. Another explanation is linked to the fact that staff advisers within banks that have venture capital subsidiaries probably do not sufficiently promote those services. A U.S. commentator suggested that the restrictive use of ratings in general reflects the traditionally strong focus on creditor protection in Germany. Also, at least in the U.S., venture capital financing was usually equity financing instead of debt, because the return on equity capital tends to be larger than on bonds.

As a comment on Professor *Kaen's* contribution on the relationship between ownership structure and underpricing of IPOs, commentators wished to see the expectations of a company's future performance reflected in the model. A German commentator pointed to his own research, according to which disclosure behavior of the issuing company and the composition of its board did have a significant impact on underpricing. Professor *Kaen* responded that, at least in the

U.S., there is evidence that board composition has no effect on underpricing and post-issue performance of the company.

Chapter 8: The Market for Corporate Control

Bank Control, Takeovers, and Corporate Governance in Germany

JULIAN FRANKS, London, and COLIN MAYER, Oxford*

This paper examines the three cases of hostile takeovers in Germany in the post-Second World War period. It describes the important role played by banks in affecting the outcome of the bids: bank representatives were chairmen of the supervisory board in all three cases and banks voted a large number of proxies in important decisions affecting the bids. The paper reports that low returns were earned by shareholders of two of the target firms and offers an explanation in terms of bank control and the regulatory regime operating in Germany.

Contents

Tables

* This paper is part of an ESRC-funded project on "Capital Markets, Corporate Governance and the Market for Corporate Control", no. W102251103 and has been published in the *Journal of Banking and Finance* 22/10 (1998), Special Issue on "Credit risk management and relationship banking".

It has benefited from interviews with numerous individuals in Germany and the U.K. We are particularly grateful to Gerhard Hablizer of Commerzbank, Ellen Schneider-Lenné and Ulrich Weiss of Deutsche Bank, Charles Lowe of Deutsche Bank UK, Dr. Klaus Christian Hubner and Berndt Jonas of Fried. Krupp AG, Dr. Peter Krailic of McKinsey, Peter von Elten and Andreas Buddenbrock of JP Morgan, Greg Morgan of Munger, Tolles & Olson, Malcolm Thwaites of Morgan Grenfell, Dr. Kiran Bhojani and Dr. Wilhelm Heilmann of Veba AG, Michael Treichl of Warburg, Nicholas Weickart of Weickart, Simon, & Westpfahl, Hans Peter Peters, and Andrew Neumann of WestLB.

A. Introduction

The recent attempted hostile acquisition of Thyssen AG by Krupp AG[1] has once again brought to the fore the operation of the German corporate governance system and the role of the banks.[2] The banks have been seen to be instrumental in orchestrating and organising the raid. To some, most notably German steel workers and particular politicians, the banks have abused the social values of the German governance system. To others, they have let shareholders down in failing to push through the bid to the bitter end.

Hostile takeovers in Germany are an important subject of study for two reasons. Firstly, there are not many of them: only three in the whole of the post-Second World War period. Secondly, although they are the earthquakes of German corporate governance and should not therefore be regarded as examples of normal practice, they do allow us to observe the operation of German corporate governance and the behaviour of banks with an unusual measure of clarity. In addition, they provide an interesting laboratory on how a virtually unregulated takeover market affects shareholder returns.

In particular, we want to use the hostile bids to examine two questions: firstly, do banks exercise substantial control during these turbulent periods? and, secondly, if they do, in whose interests do they act? There is continuing discussion amongst both academics and policy makers about the power of German banks. In principle, concentration of control through proxy votes should encourage more active corporate governance by German banks than by U.K. and U.S. financial institutions which hold much smaller stakes and large highly diversified portfolios of shares. Since banks' own shareholdings are in general modest, where conflicts arise between shareholder interests and incumbent management, banks may attach less significance to their custodian functions than to the margin and fee income which they derive from commercial and investment banking. Banks may also feel they have obligations to other stakeholders such as employees and managers.

We find that banks do exert significant influence over the outcomes of bids, their power in large part deriving from their chairmanship of supervisory boards, and the proxy votes which they cast on behalf of individual shareholders. The latter may be especially important where there are restrictions on voting rights: these limit the votes that large blockholders can cast but not those of banks acting as custodians of small shareholders. We find that returns to shareholders who do not sell their shares to acquirors are very low and even negative in two of the bids. These low bid premia may be explained by banks' concern with interests other than

---

[1] On this event, cf. Prigge (this volume Ch. 12: Sec. B.IV.). On the market for corporate control in general, see also the respective sections in the comparative contributions of Kanda, Prigge, and Wymeersch in Ch. 12 of this volume.

[2] On the role of banks in German corporate governance, see in this volume also the articles in Ch. 6 as well as the country report by Prigge in Ch. 12.

those of shareholders; alternatively, they may result from the virtual absence of takeover regulation in Germany.

We begin by describing the methodology and data used in the study in Section B. The three cases of hostile acquisitions are discussed in Section C. Section D analyses the returns to shareholders of the target firms, the role of takeover regulation, and the power of the banks. Finally, we derive some conclusions in Section E.

B. Methodology and Data

This paper reports the results of detailed studies of the three cases of hostile acquisitions which have occurred in Germany in the post-Second World War period. Jenkinson and Ljungqvist (1996) have correctly pointed out that the incidence of hostility may be much more pervasive than the three cases would suggest. There is an active market in share blocks (see Franks/Mayer 1997) and the transfers in control to which these trades give rise are often opposed by the management concerned. However, what distinguishes the three cases of hostile bids is that they involve companies whose shares are widely held and where a change in control could not be secured by agreement between a small number of large blockholders. As a result, banks derive a greater degree of control in these cases from their chairmanship of the board and their custodianship of small shareholdings.

The three cases are the bid for Feldmühle Nobel AG by the Flick Brothers in 1988 and then by Veba AG in 1989; the bid for Continental AG by Pirelli AG in 1990 and 1991; and the bid for Hoesch AG by Krupp AG in 1991 and 1992. Case studies of the three hostile takeovers were compiled from original source data. They included company accounts, press reports in both German and U.K. newspapers, and Textline services. They were supplemented by interviews with representatives of the bidder and target, supervisory board members (for example, Dr. Ulrich Weiss, Deutsche Bank board representative and chairman of Continental's supervisory board and Ellen Schneider-Lenne, Deutsche Bank board representative), investment advisors (for example, Dr. Weickart, advisor to the investment group of Feldmühle Nobel), investment banks (for example, Morgan Grenfell), and management consultants (for example, McKinsey, Frankfurt).

Franks and Mayer (1997) report that 85% of a sample of 171 large companies in 1991 had a single shareholder owning more than 25% of shares. None of the three targets of hostile acquisitions had a single shareholder owning more than 25% of shares prior to the bid. They also record that banks are represented on the supervisory boards of many widely held companies, frequently in the all-important position of chairman. Data on board composition for the firms involved in the acquisitions were collected from Hoppenstedt and Wer ist Wer. In all three target firms, Deutsche Bank occupied the position of chairman of the supervisory board.

Shares in Germany are held in bearer form and banks act as custodians of individual shareholders. In this capacity they offer a free service to shareholders, whereby the bank will offer advice and vote on behalf of shareholders in company resolutions. They are required to obtain permission annually from shareholders to use their proxies and they must inform shareholders of impending resolutions and how they intend to vote. Nibler (1997) reports that for 38 firms, the top three banks controlled 29.5% of the votes at the AGMs in 1991, and the votes for all banks totaled 62.6%. However, for a larger sample of companies totaling 158 firms, the average held by all banks was 24.7%. This lower percentage is explained by greater concentration of ownership in the larger sample.

Consistent with the observation that the targets are widely held, Gottschalk (1988) records that in 1986 the three main banks (Deutsche Bank, Dresdner Bank, and Commerzbank) between them held 48% of Hoesch AG and 39% of Continental AG. In the case of Feldmühle Nobel, Deutsche Bank cast 55% of the votes in a resolution supporting the introduction of a voting right restriction of 5%.

Voting right restrictions limit the maximum number of votes which any one shareholder can cast, irrespective of the number of shares which they hold. They are commonly observed in the minority of German companies which are widely held. Continental AG introduced a voting right restriction of 5% in 1984 and Hoesch AG introduced a restriction of 15% in 1977. As described below, the 5% voting right restriction in Feldmühle Nobel was introduced in 1988 in the middle of the bid by the Flick Brothers.

Voting right restrictions are virtually never observed in the large majority of companies which have dominant shareholders, since they undermine the ability of the dominant shareholder to exercise control. In a list of 19 companies which had voting right restrictions in 1988, we found that 17 had no single shareholder owning more than 25% of shares.[3]

The performance of the acquisitions was measured by abnormal share price returns relative to the DAX index. Share price data on the bidder and target firms were collected from Datastream for the entire period of the bid from the date at which the acquiror started share purchases to the date at which the bid was completed or abandoned.

---

[3] See Prigge (this volume Ch. 12: Sec. B.II.) for a survey of the ownership and voting right structures of German corporations.

C. The Bids for Feldmühle Nobel AG, Hoesch AG, and Continental AG

I. The Bid for Feldmühle Nobel AG

1. Background to the Bid

In 1985, ownership of the Flick Group was transferred from Friedrich Karl Flick to Deutsche Bank. The Group included substantial share stakes in other companies and some industrial subsidiaries (Dynamit Nobel, Buderus, and Feldmühle). The latter were grouped together to form a new company, Feldmühle Nobel. The sale by Flick was made so as to realize a large sum for the payment of taxes; he did not anticipate any family succession. Almost as soon as it took control, Deutsche Bank sold Feldmühle Nobel's share stakes in Daimler-Benz, WR Grace, and Versicherungs-Holding der Deutschen Industrie for about DM 5.9 billion. In April 1986, the shares of Feldmühle Nobel were offered for sale at a price of DM 285 per share. The issue was the largest in German history (DM 2 billion) and it was the first time that 100% of a company's share capital was offered via a new issue. The issue was also unusual in that the shares were in the form of ordinary voting as against non-voting preference shares.

Except for a stake of about 10% held by Deutsche Bank, the shares were widely held. Some believed that the failure of a large stakeholder to emerge reflected a lack of industrial logic in the structure of the new company. The combined value of the earlier sales of share stakes, subsidiaries, and the flotation amounted to DM 7.9 billion.

2. The Bid

In June 1987, Gert-Rudolf Flick and Friedrich Christian Flick, nephews of Friedrich Karl Flick, shareholders in Feldmühle Nobel, proposed a resolution at the company's AGM that an investigation be undertaken into the sale of shares of WR Grace and Co. which took place in 1985. They accused the chairman of Feldmühle Nobel, Dr. Herbert Blaschke, of failing to obtain the highest price possible in the sale.

In June 1988 it was reported that the Flick brothers were attempting to put together a tender offer for the company for a price of DM 350 per share with the clear intention of replacing the management. Following the failure of the bid to materialize, the share price dropped to DM 260. However, it was well known that the Flick brothers and other investors were accumulating a large stake and were being advised by specialists in control contests, a commercial lawyer, Dr. Weickart, and Merrill Lynch.

Subsequently, the management learnt that the Flick Brothers and others associated with them had a block stake of 36.5% and attempted to forestall any hostile action by proposing a resolution at its AGM restricting the voting rights of any one shareholder to 5% of the total shares outstanding. The resolution was supported by Deutsche Bank, which held a share stake of about 8% on its own account and was able to vote a large proportion of the shares through proxies and shares held in investment funds administered by the bank. The resolution was passed with Deutsche Bank voting 55% of the shares cast.

Some of the shares had been purchased directly in the market while others had been acquired through the conversion of options bought from institutions with significant stakes. Sellers of the options were required not to reveal information about the transaction for fear of stimulating a rise in the share price. In the latter part of 1988 there were rumors that a takeover bid was again being made for Feldmühle Nobel. Trading in the shares was unusually high and the share price increased to DM 310. In May 1989, Veba AG declared that it was acquiring a 46% stake, including the stake held by the group of shareholders led by the Flick Brothers.

Veba secured two seats on the supervisory board, one for its chairman, Rudolph von Bennigsen-Foerder, and one other. The former became chairman on July 18, 1989, but died on October 28, 1989. In December 1989, Veba confirmed that it had increased its stake to just over 50% by buying further shares mainly from investment funds, and expressed its intention to raise its stake to 61%.

Unknown to Veba, the Flick brothers had retained a stake in Feldmühle Nobel either in the hope that von Bennigsen-Foerder would successfully restructure the company, or that Veba would eventually buy them out. However, following the unexpected death of von Bennigsen-Foerder, the new management was less inclined to purchase further shares because of the price that the minority shareholders led by the Flick brothers were demanding.

Reluctant to make a full bid at a price required by the minority and unable to take managerial control of the company in the face of opposition from the Flick brothers, Veba put their stake up for auction. In April 1990, Stora Kopparbergs Bergslags, with another Swedish company, Patricia, acquired an 85% stake in Feldmühle Nobel at a price of DM 567 and made an offer of DM 540 to small shareholders for the outstanding 15%. Stora purchased 60.1% of Feldmühle Nobel and Patricia 24.9%. The sellers included Veba (51%), SCA of Sweden (5%), and the Flick brothers (between 10-20%). Whereas Stora and Feldmühle Nobel's paper activities were thought to be good complements, other activities of Feldmühle Nobel were to be sold (Dynamit Nobel and Buderus).

In June 1990, the voting rights restrictions on Feldmühle Nobel's shares were lifted. The head of Veba, Klaus Piltz, vacated his position as head of the supervisory board and was replaced by Dr. Hellmut Kruse, board chairman of Beiersdorf. In August 1990, the takeover was approved by the Cartel Office.

II. The Bid for Hoesch AG

1. Background to the Bid

Prior to the bid by Krupp for Hoesch in 1991, there had been a series of unsuccessful attempts to arrange mergers in the steel industry. In 1981, Krupp approached Hoesch; in 1983 Krupp approached Thyssen; failed negotiations took place with Klöckner Werke, and in 1989 with Salzgitter.

This history of failed friendly mergers convinced Krupp that a merger could only succeed where control could be purchased in the market. Hoesch conformed to these requirements since there was no large industrial stakeholder. The bid by Krupp was motivated by a need to restructure the steel industry which could not be achieved by internal means.

2. The Bid

In October 1991, Krupp announced the purchase of 24.9% of Hoesch's shares and expressed a wish to seek a "close alliance." Unusually, this was announced without prior consultation with Hoesch. The shares were purchased over a five-month period from January to June 1991. The accumulation of shares was facilitated by the Gulf War, which caused substantial selling, and by the presence of foreign shareholdings—15 to 18% of the shares were held in London. The success of this bid was crucially dependent on the ability to acquire control covertly through the accumulation of shares before Hoesch could amass support. Secrecy was maintained with a Swiss bank responsible for the transactions; in September it was rumored that a Japanese firm was about to bid.

None of Krupp's major banks, including Deutsche Bank, were informed of the share accumulation and the intention to bid. The lack of consultation reflected the need for secrecy and the changing relationships of some large companies with their banks. Krupp did not regard any of its banks as the 'house bank.'

Hoesch called the Krupp purchase unfriendly. Neukirchen, who had become CEO of Hoesch three months before at Deutsche Bank's instigation, strongly opposed the bid. Neukirchen addressed workers' meetings and attacked the merger with Krupp, as did the Workers' Council. As a response, the Hoesch supervisory board considered a programme of restructuring called "Hoesch 2000." In addition, talks were initiated with British Steel about taking a blocking minority stake.

In November, Krupp announced that, with its own stake of 24.9% and with 30.4% controlled by banks and institutional investors favourable to the merger, it could exercise effective control. It also purchased shares in Hoesch's convertible, which did not count in any stake that formed the basis of the 25% disclosure rule, prior to conversion. The purchase was necessary to prevent other parties from buying and then converting the shares. Krupp was able to exert effective control with only a slender majority, not the 75% that is frequently cited (see, for example, Franks/Mayer 1990).

Although there were voting restrictions in Hoesch, the limitation was 15% compared with only 5% in Feldmühle Nobel. As a result, a minority shareholder would have required a large stake of 15% to match the size of Krupp's votes.

The attitude of the banks was mixed. When informed, Deutsche Bank did not oppose the bid, possibly recognizing that mergers in the steel industry were necessary and had proved difficult to arrange in the past. WestLB, the one major shareholder in Hoesch, which held about 17% and was also represented on the board of Krupp, did not give public support to the bid and their attitude to the bid was uncertain. This uncertainty may have reflected the fact that the *Land* was a major shareholder in the bank and wished to maintain a low public stance in a merger that potentially involved extensive restructurings and a loss of jobs.

Late in November, Krupp and Hoesch agreed to merger talks. A share for share exchange was proposed, with the terms to be decided after the businesses had been valued. It was also decided that Neukirchen would leave the management board in the event of a successful merger being negotiated. The success of the bid with only a small majority shareholding, therefore, came in the face of strenuous opposition from the management board and workers of the target.

In December, Krupp increased its share stake to 51%. Subsequently, it was increased to 62% so as to provide the Krupp Foundation, which had a 75% stake in Krupp, with a majority of 54% in the merged company. Other shareholders in Krupp were Iran (25%) and WestLB (10%), and dispersed shareholdings amounted to 10-13%. The acquisition of a majority of the shares ensured that Krupp had control even in the event of the merger failing to take place.

In February 1992, trade union officials listed their demands to Krupp. They included the maintenance of production sites and jobs. Krupp announced that additional job losses resulting directly from the merger, over and above those contained in the "Hoesch 2000" plan, would be limited to 1,800 from a total of 110,000. However, while this meant that large plants would not be closed, smaller plants were vulnerable.

In March, Hilmar Kopper, Deutsche Bank's chief executive, announced his support for the bid because it made "good industrial sense." Deutsche Bank's nominee, Herbert Zapp, was chairman of Hoesch's supervisory board and Kopper stated that Zapp had no obligation to defend Hoesch against the bid. It was unusual for a bank to support a merger which had been so vehemently opposed by the head of the management board.

In March 1992, Krupp announced that it was to be transformed into an AG. In June Hoesch accepted Krupp's proposal to merge at its AGM and voted to abolish the voting right restriction. 99.7% of shareholders agreed to the merger. Gerhard Cromme of Krupp and three others were voted onto the supervisory board, and it was agreed that Neukirchen would leave the company with a payment of DM 6 million in November 1992.

In July, Hoesch announced it was to become part of Fried. Krupp AG Hoesch-Krupp. However, by November 1992 the merger had not taken place because of complaints by three small shareholders to the courts. The court action prevented the immediate registration of the merger. One of the complainants, a former employee of Hoesch, objected to the name of the new company. The other shareholders objected to the treatment of minorities. Subsequently, objections to the merger were dropped and the merger became effective on December 8.

III. The Bid for Continental AG

1. Background to the Bid

In 1989, Continental and Pirelli were the fourth and fifth largest tyre producers respectively, each with approximately 8% of world market share; however, together their turnover fell short of that of either Goodyear or Michelin. At the end of the 1980s, serious overcapacity emerged in the tyre industry which necessitated consolidation. Continental purchased General Tyre of the U.S. in 1987 and, in 1988, Pirelli competed unsuccessfully with Bridgestone for ownership of Firestone Tyre of the U.S. In September 1990 Pirelli announced a proposal to merge with Continental.

2. The Bid

Pirelli proposed a 'reversed acquisition.' Continental was to acquire the tyre business of Pirelli through Pirelli Tyre Holding of Amsterdam for between DM 1.8 billion and DM 2.2 billion. Half of this was to be financed by a rights issue amounting to an increase in Continental's capital of between 50% and 60%; the remainder was to be raised through borrowings. Pirelli was to use the payments to increase its share stake in Continental to nearly 28%. Combined with the 23% shareholding held by investors who supported the bid, Pirelli would then have a controlling holding.

Pirelli viewed its approach to Continental as a friendly merging of interests in difficult market conditions. However, Continental rejected the offer, describing it as a "hostile takeover with several serious defects." In particular, it argued that the price proposed by Pirelli for its Tyre Holding's assets was well above Continental's estimate of its value of DM 800 million. Continental also argued that the borrowings would take Pirelli's gearing to unacceptably high levels, and that Pirelli had overestimated the gains to the merger at DM 400 million over four years.

While rejecting the bid, Continental left open the possibility of negotiations occurring at some future date. However, as a precondition it required Pirelli to give an undertaking that no trade in Continental shares occur for two to three years and no confidential or sensitive financial information be disclosed while talks were underway. Pirelli refused to give such an undertaking, thereby confirming Continental's view that the bid was hostile.

In December 1990, a private shareholder, Mr. Alberto Vicari, led a small group of Continental shareholders controlling about 5% of Continental shares in calling for an extraordinary general meeting to resolve uncertainty surrounding the merger and to give shareholders the opportunity to express their views about the merger. Two sets of motions were proposed. The first favoured continued independence: they involved raising the majority required to overturn the 5% voting right restriction from 50% to 75%, raising the majority required to dismiss supervisory board members from 50% to 75%, and requiring a 75% majority to sell important parts of the business. The second set of proposals opened the way for a merger: the voting right restriction would be eliminated and the management required to prepare a merger with Pirelli for the next annual meeting. At the 1989 AGM a proposal to remove the voting restriction had been rejected by a very slender margin of 2%.

The Continental supervisory board supported the management board in opposing the bid. They recommended that shareholders vote against the resolutions with the exception of the one requiring a 75% majority to eliminate the 5% voting right restriction. They recommended that shareholders vote against the resolutions requiring 75% majorities for dismissal of members of the supervisory board and disposal of large assets on the grounds that a minority shareholding would then potentially be able to prevent desirable changes in the board and the company's corporate strategy.

However, the supervisory board, in particular its chairman, Ulrich Weiss from Deutsche Bank, did not oppose the concept of a merger. Weiss had close associations with several Italian firms: he was Deutsche Bank's board member at Fiat, the Italian car maker closely linked to Pirelli, chairman of Banca d'America e d'Italia, and a member of the board of the Fiat automotive group. Through one of these associations he met Leopoldo Pirelli, the chairman of Pirelli, and early in 1990 Leopoldo Pirelli proposed cooperation between the two companies.

There were large share transactions prior to the EGM in March 1991. These created two groups of shareholders: supporters of Pirelli and Continental. As at March 1991, disclosed share stakes were:

Pirelli Supporters		Continental Supporters	
Allianz Group	5%	BMW	5%
Italmobiliare	3%	Daimler-Benz	5%
Mediobanca	5%	Deutsche Bank	5%
Nord. Landesbank	3%	Volkswagen	5%
Pirelli Verwaltungs-Gesellschaft	5%		
Sopaf (Italy)	5%		

Source: *Financial Times* July 29, 1990.

The suspicion arose that Pirelli's supporters were acting in concert and thereby violating the 5% voting right restriction. Just before the meeting, Continental wrote to its principal shareholders asking them to declare the amount held, whether they were acting as beneficiaries for other parties, and whether they had entered into indemnities to reimburse any losses or expenses of third parties. Pirelli strenuously denied any such schemes.

At the shareholders' meeting on March 13, 66% of shareholders voted in favour of rescinding the voting right restriction. The rule requiring Continental to commence negotiations with Pirelli was defeated. However, elimination of the voting right restriction could not be implemented. In April, two lawsuits opposing the elimination of the voting right restriction were lodged—one of these was a class action on behalf of minority shareholders. The concern seemed to arise that elimination of voting right restrictions left minority shareholders exposed to the accumulation of share stakes and of discriminatory pricing.

On May 3, in exchange for Pirelli relinquishing their demand for two places on the supervisory board, to which their shareholding entitled them, the supervisory board of Continental voted unanimously (with one abstention) to request the resignation of the Chief Executive Officer, Horst Urban. The supervisory board wanted negotiations on cooperation with Pirelli to proceed in a constructive way and Urban's presence was viewed as an impediment to this. Wilhelm Winterstein, the longest serving member of the Continental board, was elected as a temporary replacement for Urban and in July he was succeeded by Hubertus von Grünberg. In June 1991, Pirelli responded by replacing the managing director of Pirelli, Gianbattista De Giorgi; he was felt to be taking too aggressive a stance on the merger to promote constructive negotiations.

Thereafter negotiations over cooperation between Pirelli and Continental proceeded steadily. There were discussions about joint purchasing, warehousing, and R&D activities. Talks were organised at two levels: strategy was formulated by top management and detailed implementation discussed by heads of divisions. Impetus was given to the negotiations by the worsening financial conditions of the two companies.

As late as the end of October 1991, reports appeared suggesting that cooperation pacts were about to be signed before the end of the year, but on December 1 the talks collapsed in disarray. Pirelli's shares plunged 25% and it emerged that Pirelli had offered its Italian allies indemnities for losses sustained contingent on no agreement being reached on a merger by November 30. Pirelli's allies had been acting in concert and thereby violating the 5% rule. The indemnities cost Pirelli L 350 billion and considerable loss of face. On February 17, 1992, Leopoldo Pirelli resigned and management control was vested in a seven-member executive committee.

D. Analysis of the Bids

I. Bid Premia and Takeover Regulation

Table 1 records abnormal share price returns measured relative to the DAX of the three targets from nine months before to nine months after the bids. Table 2 reports dividends per share of the three companies. In two out of three of the bids (Feldmühle Nobel and Hoesch) there is no evidence of poor financial perform-ance prior to the bids. There were positive share price movements over nine months prior to the announcement of bids and dividends per share increased or remained unchanged. In the case of Continental, there was little overall move-ment in its share price over the nine months prior to the bid but there was a reduction in dividends per share in the year of the bid (1990).

Table 1:   Cumulative Abnormal Returns Around the Announcement of the
            Three Hostile Takeover Bids

Target	9 Months Before	3 Months Before	1 Month Before	Week of the Announce-ment	1 Month After	3 Months After	9 Months After
Hoesch AG	16.5%	3.7%	-12.8%	-10.8%	0.1%	-12.2%	-2.3%
ContinentalAG	-1.2%	2.1%	-9.5%	-7.7%	4.2%	-13.0%	-39.6%
Feldmühle Nobel AG							
1st Bid	19.9%	12.0%	8.3%	-0.3%	0.4%	-15.7%	-20.4%
2nd Bid	15.0%	12.6%	7.4%	2.6%	-2.5%	-8.2%	9.7%

There were negative share price reactions to the announcement of the bids for Continental and Hoesch both in the week of the announcement and in the month leading up to the announcement of the bids. Neither bid was opposed and, at least in some respects, was supported by Deutsche Bank. In contrast, the one bid which was resolutely opposed by Deutsche Bank, the attempted acquisition of

Feldmühle Nobel by the Flick Brothers, displayed positive share price movements in the month prior to the bid although little movement in the week of the announcement. In no case were bid premia commensurate with those paid in the U.K. or the U.S., between 20 and 30%.

Table 2:   Dividends per Share (DM)

Target	1985	1986	1987	1988	1989	1990	1991	1992
Hoesch AG	5	5	5	8	10	10	n.a.	n.a.
Continental AG	5	6	7	8	8	4	0	0
Feldmühle Nobel AG	10	10	10	10	10	12	30	n.a.

Source: Annual Reports.

The share price movements suggest marked differences between prices paid for blocks of shares by the Flick Brothers and Krupp and those accruing to other minority shareholders. For example, shareholders in Hoesch who sold out prior to the announcement of the takeover received a bid premium of up to 16.5%, whereas those who waited for the announcement received a negative bid premium of up to -12.8%. Such price discrimination would not be possible in the U.K., where the Takeover Code requires bidders to offer a price at least as high as that paid to target shareholders at any time in the previous prior twelve months. There was no equivalent rule in Germany during this period. There are also marked differences between Germany and the U.K. concerning two-tier offers. In the final bid for Feldmühle Nobel by Stora, the bidder offered to purchase an 85% stake at a price of DM 567 and DM 540 to small shareholders for the outstanding 15%. In the U.K., two-tier offers are not permitted.

The low bid premiums offered may have been affected by the ability of the bidder to acquire substantial stakes in the market surreptitiously. In Germany, a company is required to disclose a stake only when it exceeds 25% of the outstanding equity capital. Furthermore, it is unclear whether the purchase of convertibles or options to purchase other parties' stakes are included in the threshold. Krupp acquired 24.9% of Hoesch's equity before announcing their stake. They also purchased shares in the convertible and secured the support of other shareholders before the bid so that when the bid was first announced they had control over a majority of the shares. In contrast, in the U.K., company legislation prescribes a disclosure threshold of 3% of a company's equity and the Takeover Code requires a company to include convertibles and options in calculating this threshold.

Rules regarding voting restrictions and concert parties could also have affected bid premia. The incumbent management of Feldmühle Nobel thwarted a probable tender offer by the Flick Brothers by subjecting their stake of 36.5% to a 5% voting restriction. Pirelli attempted to circumvent Continental's 5% voting right restriction by encouraging allies to purchase blocks of 5% each and guaranteeing them against loss. Such a concert party is not illegal but is subject to the voting restriction determined by the German courts. As a consequence, when the concert party was revealed, it was deemed to have violated the rules under which the extraordinary General Meeting voting was conducted. In the U.K., the former chairman of Guinness was sentenced to imprisonment for giving guarantees against losses on share purchases by individuals who promised to vote in Guinness' favour.

The ability to discriminate between shareholders means that changes in control can be engineered in Germany at lower gains to shareholders than in the U.K.; this makes takeovers in Germany cheaper than in the U.K. and means that restructurings can be organized at lower cost. The failure of the recent bid by Krupp for Thyssen, in which it was stated that Krupp would offer all target shareholders the same price, may reflect the recent growth of shareholder activism and changes to takeover rules in Germany.[4]

II. The Power Exerted by the Banks

Table 3 summarizes the methods, motives, and outcomes of the three bids. Table 4 summarizes the bid tactics and defences which the companies employed. Table 5 records the influence exerted by the banks and their attitude to the bids.

Deutsche Bank exerted considerable influence on all three bids. In Feldmühle Nobel, Deutsche Bank played a key role in introducing a voting right restriction which prevented the Flick brothers from seizing control. The voting right restriction not only prevented the Flick brothers from gaining control, it also prevented control by Veba AG despite the fact that they acquired a majority holding and were favourably inclined to the management of Feldmühle Nobel. Our interpretation of the bank's conduct was that it did not wish to see the break-up of a company which it had so recently brought to the market and it did not believe that there was a need for the bid on industrial restructuring grounds.

The bids for Hoesch and Continental illustrate the limitations on the control conferred by proxy votes. In Hoesch, Deutsche Bank installed the head of the management board three months prior to the bid by Krupp. However, it was unable to prevent the bid from taking place because, by covertly acquiring shares in the market, Krupp was able to diminish the proxy votes which the banks could cast. In Continental, the chairman of the supervisory board engaged in preliminary discussions about the bid and played an important role in replacing the

---

[4] See Baumann (this volume Ch. 8) on the *Übernahmekodex* and its recent amendment.

chairman of the management board to facilitate the acquisition. But here, too, the significance of the banks' proxies in Continental was diminished by the acquisition of share blocks by supporters of both Continental and Pirelli.

Table 3:   Summary of Three Hostile Bids

Target	Date	Bidder	Industry	Method	Motive for Bid	Outcome
Feldmühle Nobel	June 1988	Group of investors headed by Flick brothers	Paper, chemicals and explosives	1 Accumulation of sharestakes (36.5%) 2 Purchase of stake by Veba 3 Sale to Stora	Changing management	Flick brothers sell stake to Veba which is unable to exercise control (Sept 1990)
Hoesch	October 1991	Krupp	Steel and other steel-based activities	1 Accumulated stake of 24.9% by Krupp 2 Merger negotiations	Industrial re-structuring Previous failed attempts at friendly mergers	Krupp gains managerial control. Merger held up by courts (July 1992)
Continental	September 1990	Pirelli	Tyres	1 Merger proposal 2 Bidder stake 3 Concert party 4 Merger negotiation	Industrial restructuring	Bid fails (Dec 1991)

There is an explanation other than self-interest or impotence for the apparent failure of banks to protect the interests of minority shareholders. Support for the bids by Pirelli for Continental and by Krupp for Hoesch was justified by the required rationalizations of the European tyre and the German steel industries respectively.[5] These rationalizations imposed considerable costs on workers in the two companies and these would have been still higher if large bid premia had been paid. Banks may therefore have been balancing the interests of different parties in moderating the gains to shareholders.

---

[5] The recent support of the banks for the attempted acquisition of Thyssen by Krupp was also justified by a continuing need for rationalization of the German steel industry.

Table 4:   Bid Strategies and Bid Defences

Target	Bid Strategy	Bid Defence
Feldmühle Nobel	*Ownership*—Covert purchase of 38.5% stake by Flick brothers et al. Veba purchases Flick stake and acquires 51%	*Ownership*—Use of proxy votes by "housebank" to introduce voting rights restriction
	Voting Restrictions—Limits ability of Veba to take management control	*Voting Restrictions*—5% voting rights restriction introduced after stake purchased by Flick brothers
	Supervisory Board Control—Veba takes two seats on supervisory board including chairman	*Supervisory Board Control*—No action
Hoesch	*Ownership*—Covert purchase of 24.4%	*Ownership*—Large shareholder—West LB does not support bid—Discussions with British Steel on blocking minority
	Control over additional 30.4%	
	Stake increased to 62% to give Krupp majority ownership of merged company	
	Voting Restrictions—No action	*Voting Restrictions*—Restriction of 15%
	Supervisory Board Control—Krupp takes two seats on supervisory board including chairman	*Supervisory Board Control*—Attempt to extend co-determination to Krupp's steel interests
Continental	*Ownership*—Pirelli acquires 5%— Allies acquire 22%—Pirelli indemnifies allies for potential losses—Purchases dilute proxies held by banks	*Ownership*—Allies (BMW, Daimler-Benz, Volkswagen) purchased shares
	Voting Restrictions—Pirelli attempts to remove restriction	*Voting Restrictions*—5% restriction (1990)—Shareholder proposed increasing majority required to overturn voting restriction to 75%— Accused Pirelli and associates of acting as a "concert party"
	Supervisory Board Control—Fails to gain any seats on supervisory board	*Supervisory Board Control*—No action

E. Conclusion

This paper has examined the role of German banks in hostile takeovers in Germany. It has considered the degree of control exercised by banks and whether they acted in shareholders', their own, or some other party's interests. It has also examined the role of regulation in affecting returns to shareholders.

Table 5: Position and Influence of Banks

	Bank's Influence with Company	Attitude to Bid	Action
Feldmühle Nobel	Deutsche Bank chaired supervisory board. Held stake of 8%. Voted large number of proxies.	Opposed Flick brothers.	Supported voting right restriction.
Hoesch	Deutsche Bank chaired supervisory board. Had three months previously installed new head of management board.	Deutsche Bank supported bid even though opposed by head of management board.	None
Continental	Deutsche Bank chaired supervisory board. Voted large number of proxy votes. Closely involved in shaping attitude to the bid.	Opposed bid but supported merger talks.	Opposed removal of voting right restriction. Dismissed head of management board when he opposed merger talks.

The paper has found that banks' influence derives from their chairmanship of supervisory boards and the proxy votes which they can cast on behalf of individual shareholders. As the Feldmühle Nobel case illustrates, proxy votes provide banks with the means to protect minority shareholders. When combined with voting right restrictions, they can require acquirors to purchase nearly all of the shares of a target in the market before gaining control. The fact that the banks did not succeed in securing a bid premium in the bids for Continental and Hoesch suggests that they did not place much weight on shareholder interests. Whether they were in fact frustrated in their attempts to protect minority shareholders by market purchases of proxy votes by the predators or whether their actions reflected self-interest or those of other stakeholders is difficult to determine.

An alternative explanation is that the low bid premia resulted from ineffective regulation. The ability to price discriminate over time and between different shareholder groups and to accumulate substantial share blocks without having to disclose them all reduce the cost of acquisition. However, they also mean that minority shareholders stand to earn low or negative returns from takeovers.

References

Franks, Julian and Colin Mayer 'Capital Markets and Corporate Control: A Study of France, Germany and the U.K.' *Economic Policy* 10 (1990) 191-231.

Franks, Julian and Colin Mayer 'Ownership, Control and the Performance of German Corporations' (mimeo 1997).

Gottschalk, Arno 'Der Stimmrechtseinfluß der Banken in den Aktionärsversammlungen von Großunternehmen' *WSI-Mitteilungen* 41 (1988) 294-304.

Jenkinson, Tim and Alexander Ljungqvist 'Hostile Takeovers and the Role of Banks in German Corporate Governance' (mimeo 1996).

Nibler, Marcus 'Bank Control and Corporate Performance: the Evidence' (mimeo, Cambridge University, 1997).

Takeovers in Germany and EU Regulation
Experience and Practice

KARL-HERMANN BAUMANN, Munich

The essential elements of the German Takeover Code are the intention to achieve transparency in takeover offers, equal treatment of all participants, the same information for all shareholders, and a fairer share of the takeover price for all shareholders. By the end of April 1997, the Code had been accepted by 80% of the DAX 30 companies and 59% of the MDAX companies. The Code is widely recognized by German banks as well as in the corporate community. Its practical experience is encouraging. Although it has no legal force, its rules have been complied with in most takeover offers so far. The Takeover Code can serve as a model set of rules for the transformation of the planned EC directive on takeovers into German law, thereby combining self-regulation with legal enforceability of mandatory rules.

Contents

I have been asked to comment on takeovers with a view to the German experience and practice and EU Regulation. I would like to briefly outline the main elements of the German Code of Conduct for Takeovers and the EC Directive proposal, and say some words on the German experience with self-regulation.[1]

A. Introduction

The German Code entered into effect on October 1, 1995. Its aim was to secure the reputation of Germany as a center of finance, and to set up a reliable framework for takeover offers so that investors from in- and outside Germany would know how public offers are to be conducted.

The Code does not contain any binding legal norms. It serves merely as a recommendation. It has no legislative origin. It follows the thought that market participants should be able to set their own rules of conduct. Potential offerors, target companies, and investments firms are requested to recognize and accept the terms of this Code of Conduct.

After an unsuccessful attempt in 1991, the EC Commission published a new proposal for a takeover directive in early 1996. This directive also aims at setting minimum standards for public offers all over the European Union, thereby ensuring a level playing field for all capital markets within Europe. Although previous attempts have been unsuccessful, the likelihood for this proposal to become law has increased and the European Parliament has already discussed it.

B. Essential Elements

I. Essential Elements of the Code

The essential elements of the Takeover Code are the intention to achieve
- transparency in takeover offers,
- equal treatment of all participants to secure
  - the same information for all shareholders, and
  - a fair share of the takeover price for all shareholders.

The Code contains no provisions concerning the suitability of takeover offers, but aims primarily at setting the conditions that guarantee the shareholders of the target company a free decision with regard to the acceptance of the offer.

All shareholders must receive the same information in order to be able to make a free decision. To ensure proper information, the Code sets minimum disclosure requirements for an offer, including the purpose of the offer, the intentions of the offeror with the target company, and the effect of the takeover on the financial status of the offeror and the target company.

---

[1] Cf. also the sections dealing with the market for corporate control in the comparative contributions of Kanda, Prigge, and Wymeersch in Ch. 12 of this volume.

All shareholders must receive a fair share of the takeover price. That means that all shareholders must be offered the same price, if their shares are acquired. However, offers are permissible when the offeror only intends to acquire part of the shares of the target company.

Art. 16 of the German Takeover Code provides for a mandatory takeover offer once a person has acquired more than 50% of the voting rights in the target company. The mandatory takeover offer must be made within 18 months. This period was chosen to give an offeror the opportunity to take other legal measures offered by German company law, e.g., a contract for control of the corporate entity or the integration of a subsidiary company. In both cases the German Stock Corporation Act and the *Umwandlungsgesetz* (Transformation of Companies Act) contain detailed provisions to ensure the protection of minority shareholders.

The Code contains a flexible pricing formula to limit the price risk for the offeror during the 18-month period. In accordance with Art. 17 of the Code, the price of the mandatory takeover offer must be in a reasonable relation to the current price quoted on a stock exchange, but not more than 25% below the highest price paid by the offeror during the six months before reaching the 50% threshold. In the event that more recent purchases were made after the 50% threshold was exceeded, the price of the mandatory offer is the weighted average of the prices paid for these purchases, provided that it is higher.[2] The mandatory takeover offer has been the subject of long discussion. In the U.S. there is no such obligation. The widely accepted opinion is that there is a functioning market for control of companies. The better management team will gain control of the target company, which will in the end benefit all shareholders. Shareholders who sell receive the consideration for their shares; shareholders who stay earn more by receiving higher dividends and by the increase of the share price. The opposite view is taken by some European countries, namely the U.K., Switzerland, and France. Under the laws of these countries the offeror has to make an offer for all shares of the company once he has acquired a controlling stake. They differ as

---

[2] Effective January 1, 1998 the German Takeover Code has been changed. Now, a takeover offer is mandatory when a person has acquired a controlling stake in a company. A controlling stake is assumed when the threshold of 50% is passed or someone acquires the right to appoint or dismiss directors of the company or enters into a voting right pool with other persons whereby joint control of the company is exercised or the shareholding of a person, although below 50%, is enough to exercise effective control over a company. This effective control is deemed to exist if, having regard to the actual presence of shareholders at the last three annual general meetings, a shareholding of a given person gives him 75% or more of the voting rights represented at the meeting.

The second change concerns the price of the offer. Now the price has to be in a reasonable relation to the highest price noted on a stock exchange in the last three months before the takeover offer. The third change concerns the grace period of 18 months for the making of the takeover offer. Now the person who has acquired control has immediately either to make an offer or to declare his intentions to take other measures available under German company law.

to the size of the controlling stake. In the U.K., 30% are deemed enough, while the German Code sets the threshold at 50%.

To ensure the free decision of all shareholders as to the acceptance of the offer, the target company must refrain from any measures that may impede the takeover offer. The reason is that the takeover offer is an offer made to the owners of a company by someone who wants to acquire the company. The management of the company itself has no right to frustrate the offer and to deprive the owners of the company of a chance to sell it to someone else. The target company may only resort to defense measures once the owners have given permission by means of a shareholders' meeting decision. The management nevertheless has the obligation to point out that the terms of a takeover offer are not sufficient and not in the interest of the shareholders of the target company.

II. Essential Elements of the EC Directive

The EC Directive has the same goals and the same essential elements as the Takeover Code. Most important, it leaves member states the choice between self-regulation and mandatory rules. Member states may allow self-regulation if such is enough to achieve the goals of the Directive, especially the fair and equal treatment of all shareholders. Also, the Directive does not require mandatory offer rules if the same degree of protection for minority shareholders is achieved by other means.

C. Acceptance and Practice of the Code

I. Acceptance of the Code

By the end of April 1997, the Code had been accepted by 363 companies, of which 259 are listed on German stock exchanges. 85 companies in the financial service industry, as well as 19 other companies that are not listed on the stock exchange, have expressed their willingness to comply with the provisions of the Takeover Code. That means that all in all, 80%—in numbers and in terms of market capitalization—of the DAX 30 companies, and 59%—in numbers—of the MDAX companies have accepted the Code. In total, more than 65% of the listed companies—in terms of market capitalization—are now bound by it.

At first sight this might appear to be not enough. But the role of domestic banks or security investment companies must not be underestimated. Their involvement in the successful execution of a takeover offer is, for practical, tactical, and strategic reasons, crucial to takeover offers. The Code has already been recognized by most German banks, and these banks have committed themselves to asking their clients to comply with the Code. This is an additional element for the acceptance of the Code. It is a fact that these banks request their clients to observe the terms of the Code if financing is sought for a takeover.

II. Practical Experience

The number of companies that have accepted the Code is only one aspect. Much more important are the application of the Code in takeover situations and its factual enforcement. From October 1, 1995, through the end of April 1997, 29 takeover offers were published. All of these have been subject to review by the Takeover Commission as to whether they have complied or do comply with the requirements of the Code. This includes well-known companies such as Linotype-Hell, Ex-Cell-O Holding, Frankona, and Hermes. In only three cases did the Commission point out that the takeover offer violated the provisions of the Code and made by companies with a questionable background. All other bids were found to comply with the Code.

In one case, the Takeover Commission granted a waiver from the obligation to make a mandatory takeover offer. In other cases, where the requirements of Art. 16 of the Code had been met, the offeror has started to enter into a contract of control or to integrate the target company, or the period of 18 months for the offer has not yet expired.

Considering this experience, one can say that the Takeover Code is already widely accepted.

D. Opposition to the Code

I do not want to disguise the fact that there is opposition to the Code. It comes from different sides and I want to highlight two aspects, namely, the mandatory takeover offer and the question of enforceability.

I. Mandatory Takeover Offer

In some cases it has been argued that the mandatory takeover offer goes too far and is a restriction of the free conduct of business and that the German Stock Corporation Act already protects the interest of minority shareholders to a sufficient extent.

Others who are in favor of the mandatory takeover offer argue that the threshold of 50% is too high and the time period of 18 months for making the offer after the acquisition of the majority is too long. I believe it is right to set the threshold at 50%, because 30% is normally not enough to gain control given the usual turnout at German annual general meetings of around 50% of the outstanding shares, and the fact that a majority of 75% is needed to dismiss the representatives of the shareholders on the supervisory board.[3]

The time period during which the majority shareholder may decide whether he wants to make a takeover offer for the rest of the shares or wants to start other legal procedures may be too long. It may be useful in the future to ask for a declaration of the intentions soon after the acquisition of the majority of shares.[4]

It should be noted that the EC Directive also does not provide for a mandatory takeover offer if the national laws achieve the same level of protection of minorities by other means. This might lead to discussions of whether the German Stock Corporation Act already secures the same level of protection.

II. Enforceability of the Code

Critics of the Code often refer to the fact that the provisions of the Code are not legally binding and thus are not enforceable. Participants in a takeover cannot turn to the courts if the rules of the Code have not been complied with. Although some writers have tried to derive legal or contractual obligations from the Code, it is by no means certain that its rules can be relied upon in a civil lawsuit.

On the other hand, the disadvantages of detailed legal norms regulating takeovers are often referred to. A takeover may be blocked by litigation because of the likelihood of one of the participants of a takeover not being satisfied with the terms of the offer. In such cases, long delays in court proceedings prevent the outcome of litigation from being known for several years, thereby rendering any takeover practically impossible.

If the EC Directive is passed by the European authorities, it would oblige the member states either to introduce takeover legislation into the national law or to establish other procedures or provisions, provided these procedures or provisions are generally accepted and contain sufficient sanctions to ensure the enforceability of the Directive's rules. Member states may also set up a self-regulatory body to safeguard application of the Takeover Directive. This will depend on the general acceptance of such organizations in their specific states and will require that these organizations have sufficient sanctioning power to ensure enforceability of the Takeover Code.

---

[3] See supra n. 2 and the subsequent changes of the Code.

[4] See supra n. 2 and the subsequent changes of the Code.

E. Conclusion

The decision between self-regulation and mandatory rules is still open. If the Directive is passed, the German Ministry of Justice has already expressed its opinion that at least some legal provisions will be necessary to comply with the Directive. Maybe this will lead to the coexistence of both, thereby combining legal enforceability of mandatory rules with the flexibility of self-regulation.

Appendix 1: Takeover Bids Under the *Übernahmekodex* Since October 1, 1995

I. Voluntary Public Tender Offers

No.	Target Company	Offeror	Offer	Offer Period	Offered Price	Percentage Share of Bidder Prior to Offer	Percentage Share Bought by Public Offer	Percentage Share of Bidder After the Offer	Result
1.	Rösler Draht AG, Schwalmtal	N.V. Bekaert S.A. Zwevegem, Belgium	11-18-95	11-20-95 to 12-19-95	DM 2,000.- per share (face value DM 1,000.-) DM 200.- per share (face value DM 100.-) DM 100.- per share (face value DM 50.-)	>99%	0.3%	>99.3%	12-29-95 purchase of shares for DM 18,950.-
2.	aqua signal AG, Bremen	Glamox, AS, Molde, Norway	9-12-95	12-13-95 to 1-12-96	DM 115.- per share (face value DM 50.-)	ca. 70%	16.97%	ca. 87%	1-25-96 purchase of 58,560 shares
3.	Sachsenmilch AG i.L., Dresden	Sachsenmilch Anlagen Holding AG, Leppersdorf	1-12-96	1-12-96 to 2-12-96	DM 35.- per share (face value DM 50.-)	87.85%	0%	87.85%	2-14-96 no purchase because less than 107,291 shares were offered
4.	AESCULAP AG, Tuttingen	B. Braun Surgical GmbH, Melsungen	1-30-96	2-19-96 to 4-16-96	DM 950.- per share (face value DM 50.-)	78.84%	20.04%	99.13%	4-20-96 purchase of 88,185 shares
5.	F. Reichelt AG, Heilbronn	PH Pharma-Holding AG, Hamburg	4-17-96	4-29-96 to 5-31-96	DM 75.- per common share (face value DM 50.-) DM 75.- per preference share (face value DM 50.-)	50-75%	0.17% (common shares) 0.07% (preference shares)	50-75%	6-7-96 purchase of 1,012 common shares and of 220 preference shares
6.	Brauerei Cluss AG, Heilbronn	Dinkelacker Brauerei AG, Heilbronn	2-24-96	5-2-96 to 6-30-96	DM 320.- per share (face value DM 50.-)	ca. 89.50%	1.46%	ca.90.96%	7-16-96 purchase of 1,473 shares
7.	AESCULAP AG, Tuttingen	B. Braun Surgical GmbH, Melsungen	4-27-96	4-30-96 to 5-28-96	DM 930.- per share (face value DM 50.-)	99.13%	0.309%	99.44%	6-8-96 purchase of 1,360 shares
8.	Revell AG, Bünde	Revell Monogram, Inc. Morton Grove, USA	5-10-96	5-13-96 to 6-20-96	DM 305.- per share (face value DM 50.-)	98.32%	0.93%	99.25%	6-28-96 purchase of 1,499 shares

No.	Target Company	Offeror	Offer	Offer Period	Offered Price	Percentage Share of Bidder Prior to Offer	Percentage Share Bought by Public Offer	Percentage Share of Bidder After the Offer	Result
9.	Chemische Werke Brockhues AG, Walluf im Rheingau	Laporte Pigmente Holding GmbH, Pullach	6-29-96	7-22-96 to 8-30-96	DM 860.- per share (face value DM 50.-)	85.95%	1.87%	87.82%	11-28-96 purchase of 1,866 shares
10.	Linotype Hell AG, Eschborn	Commerzbank AG, Frankfurt (Heidelberger Druck)	7-29-96	8-2-96 to 9-13-96	DM 95.- per share (face value DM 50.-)	0.00%	29.20%	79.20% (including 50% + one share bought from Siemens AG and Frega Vermögensverwaltungs GmbH)	9-20-96 purchase of 700,756 shares
11.	MHM Mode Holding München AG, Munich	Hucke AG, Lübbecke	8-3-96	8-9-96 to 10-7-96	DM 160.- per share (face value DM 50.-)	ca. 83%	10.04%	94.01%	10-11-96 purchase of 44,187 shares
12.	Spobag Holding AG, Düsseldorf	WCM Beteiligungs- und Grundbesitz AG, Mönchengladbach	9-13-96	9-16-96 to 10-14-96	DM 132.- per share (face value DM 50.-)	no statement	89.014%	no statement	10-22-96 purchase of 80,113 shares
13.	Nordhäuser Tabakfabriken AG, Achern	AHAG Aktienhandelsgesellschaft für Spezialwerte AG, Dortmund	10-22-96	11-8-96 to 11-22-96	DM 300.- per share (face value DM 50.-)				no publication of result
14.	EX-CELL-O Holding Aktiengesellschaft, Esslingen	IWKA Aktiengesellschaft, Karlsruhe	11-21-96 / 1-17-97 [prolongation of offer period]	11-25-96 to 1-23-97 [offer period prolonged until 1-31-97]	DM 170.- per share (face value DM 50.-)	49.4%	15.5%	64.86%	2-8-97 purchase of 137,819 shares

No.	Target Company	Offeror	Offer	Offer Period	Offered Price	Percentage Share of Bidder Prior to Offer	Percentage Share Bought by Public Offer	Percentage Share of Bidder After the Offer	Result
15.	AGAB Aktiengesellschaft für Anlagen und Beteiligungen, Frankfurt	Deutsche Genossenschaftsbank, Frankfurt; Landwirtschaftliche Rentenbank, Frankfurt	11-25-96	11-25-96 to 12-23-96	DM 125.- per share (face value DM 50.-) DM 1.- per warrant each granting the right to buy one AGAB share	95.5% (shares) 0.00% (warrants)	2.85% of equity capital and 62.78% of the option rights on shares of the authorized but unissued capital of AGAB.	98.35% of equity capital and 62.78% of outstanding warrants of AGAB.	12-31-96 purchase of 78,976 shares and 200,886 warrants. Listing of AGAB shares and warrants at the official segment of the Frankfurt stock exchange and at the unregulated segment at the stock exchanges of Berlin, Düsseldorf, and Hamburg was suspended on 12-27-96.
16.	Hermes Kreditversicherungs-Aktiengesellschaft, Hamburg/Berlin	Allianz Aktiengesellschaft Holding, Berlin/Munich	1-14-97	1-20-97 to 3-20-97	DM 385.- per share	75.3%	1.3%	89% (including shares bought during the offer period, but not being part of the offer)	3-27-97 purchase of shares with a face value of DM 1,322,950.-

No.	Target Company	Offeror	Offer	Offer Period	Offered Price	Percentage Share of Bidder Prior to Offer	Percentage Share Bought by Public Offer	Percentage Share of Bidder After the Offer	Result
17.	Vereinte Versicherung, Munich	Vereinte Holding AG, Munich	1-14-97	1-20-97 to 3-20-97	DM 2,850 per bearer share with dividend guaranty (face value DM 100.-) DM 1,050.- per registered share not freely transferable with dividend guaranty and extended guaranteed distribution of dividends (face value DM 50.-) DM 1,050.- per registered share not freely transferable with dividend guaranty (face value DM 50.-) DM 2,100 per registered share not freely transferable with dividend guaranty (face value DM 100.-)	no statement	ca. 1%	98.7%	3-27-97 purchase of shares with a face value of DM 1,031,400.-
18.	MagnaMedia Verlag AG, Haar	WEKA Firmengruppe GmbH & Co. KG, Kissing	1-25-97	1-28-97 to 2-26-97	DM 20.- per share (face value DM 5.-)	86%	9.58%	95.63%	3-7-97 purchase of 287,371 shares
19.	Actiengesellschaft Norddeutsche Steingutfabrik	SPARTA Beteiligungen AG, Hamburg	2-8-97	2-8-97 to 3-10-97	DM 25.- per share (face value DM 5.-)	no statement	2.17%	no statement	4-16-97 purchase of 52,044 shares
20.	Rabobank Deutschland AG, Frankfurt am Main	Rabobank International Holding B.V., Utrecht, The Netherlands	2-26-97	2-26-97 to 4-27-97	DM 115.- per bearer share (face value DM 50.-)	ca. 96.5%	ca. 0.9%	ca. 97.4%	5-3-97 purchase of 27,152 shares

No.	Target Company	Offeror	Offer	Offer Period	Offered Price	Percentage Share of Bidder Prior to Offer	Percentage Share Bought by Public Offer	Percentage Share of Bidder After the Offer	Result
21.	Geestemünder Bank Aktiengesellschaft, Bremerhaven	Vereins- und Westbank Aktiengesellschaft, Hamburg	3-13-97	3-14-97 to 4-14-97	DM 200.- per share (face value DM 50.-)	ca. 95%	3.231%	98.553%	4-23-97 purchase of 9,952 shares
22.	Massa AG, Alzey	Metro Aktiengesellschaft, Cologne	4-11-97	4-28-97 to 6-20-97	DM 150.- per share (face value DM 50.-)	>96%	1.643%	98.35%	7-12-97 purchase of 61,628 shares
23.	MTD Products AG, Saarbrücken (formerly Gudbrod AG)	MTD Europa Holding GmbH, Saarbrücken	5-17-97	5-21-97 to 6-19-97	DM 55.- per share (face value DM 20.-)	98.80%	0.67%	99.48%	6-27-97 purchase of 7,580 shares
24.	Bayerische Hypotheken- und Wechselbank AG, Munich	Vereins- und Westbank AG, Hamburg	8-2-97	8-4-97 to 9-10-97	Exchange of six common bearer shares of Hypo-Bank (face value DM 5.-) against one registered share with restricted transferability of Allianz AG (face value DM 5.-)	no statement		no statement	9-17-97 123,441,646 shares offered (representing 47.14% of Hypo-Bank's capital); 95.45% of the shares offered were exchanged against Allianz shares
25.	Rabobank Deutschland AG, Berlin and Frankfurt am Main	Rabobank International Holding B.V., Utrecht, The Netherlands	8-14-97	8-18-97 to 10-13-97	DM 115.- per share (face value DM 50.-)	ca. 97.92%		no statement	11-28-97 purchase of 27,244 shares
26.	Tarkett AG, Frankenthal	Sommer S.A., Luxembourg	10-21-97	10-21-97 to 12-1-97	DM 32.75 per share (face value DM 5.-) and one stock-option for every six Tarkett shares sold, or, alternatively, DM 1.79 premium for every Tarkett share sold	no statement		60%	12-5-97 purchase of one share

No.	Target Company	Offeror	Offer	Offer Period	Offered Price	Percentage Share of Bidder Prior to Offer	Percentage Share Bought by Public Offer	Percentage Share of Bidder After the Offer	Result
28.	Rosenthal AG, Selb	Waterford Wedgwood GmbH, Düsseldorf	12-9-97	12-8-97 to 2-5-98	DM 200.- per share (face value DM 50.-)	32.9%		84.62%	2-16-98 purchase of 312,449 shares
29.	Oppermann Versand AG, Neumünster	Hach AG, Groß-Bieberach	12-18-97	12-18-97 to 2-13-97	DM 196.- per share (face value DM 50.-)	ca. 85%		98.30%	2-21-1998

II. Mandatory Offers

No.	Target Company	Offeror	Offer	Offer Period	Offered Price	Percentage Share of Bidder Prior to Offer	Percentage Share Bought by Public Offer	Percentage Share of Bidder After the Offer	Result
1.	Sektkellerei Schloß Wachenheim AG, Wachenheim	Günther Reh AG, Trier	7-25-96 (request for exemption)						Exemption from a mandatory offer according to Art. 16 *Übernahmekodex* on request; decision of the office of the *Übernahmekommission* published on 8-3-97.
2.	Gelsenwasser AG, Gelsenkirchen	WWB Wasserwerks-Beteiligungs-GmbH, Gelsenkirchen	3-1-97	3-1-97 to 4-1-97	DM 415.- per share (face value DM 50.-) DM 830.- per share (face value DM 100.-) DM 8,300.- per share (face value DM 1,000.-)	50.01%	2.07%	52.08%	4-8-97 purchase of shares with a face value of DM 2,846,550.-
3.	Macrotron AG für Datenerfassungssysteme, Munich	Tech Date Corporation, Florida, USA	7-4-97	7-10-97 to 9-5-97	DM 730.- per common share (face value DM 50.-) DM 600.- per preference share (face value DM 50.-)	42.48%			

III. Other Matters

No.	Target Company	Offeror	Offer	Offer Period	Offered Price	Percentage Share of Bidder Prior to Offer	Percentage Share Bought by Public Offer	Percentage Share of Bidder After the Offer	Result
1.	Glunz AG, Hamm	Future Holding AG, Rheda-Wiedenbrück	7-16-96	to 8-9-96	DM 75.- per common share (face value DM 50.-) DM 75.- per preference share (face value DM 50.-) or, instead of the cash payment, four preference shares (face value DM 5.-) of Future Holding AG				Criticized offer; decision of the office of the *Übernahmekommission* published on 8-3-96.
2.	AGIV AG, Frankfurt	Kapas Börsenmakler AG, Rheda-Wiedenbrück	9-13-96	to 9-26-96	For one share (face value DM 5.-) of AGIV AG Kapas delivers one bearer common share (face value DM 5.-) of Kapas Börsenmakler AG				Criticized offer, decision of the office of the *Übernahmekommission* published on 9-26-96.
3.	Traub AG, Reichenbach	Rheierstieg Holzlager AG, Cologne	2-11-97	to 3-4-97	For three shares (face value DM 5.-) of Traub AG including the current dividend coupons Rheierstieg Holzlager AG delivers one common share (face value DM 5.-) of Kapas Börsenmakler AG entitled to dividend from 1-1-1996 on.				Criticized offer; decision of the office of the *Übernahmekommission* published on 2-21-97.
4.	Macrotron AG für Datenerfassungssysteme, Munich	Sparta Beteiligungen Aktiengesellschaft, Hamburg	4-25-97	4-26-97 to 5-27-97	DM 510.- per share (face value DM 50.-)	no statement	<0.1%	no statement	Criticized offer; decision of the office of the *Übernahmekommission* published on 5-16-97 6-17-97 Publication of the result: purchase of 45 shares.

Sources: Bad Homburger Kreis, Forum für Übernahmerecht and Übernahmekommission, Geschäftsstelle 'Übernahmeangebote. Öffentliche Kauf- und Umtauschangebote nach dem Übernahmekodex der Börsensachverständigenkommission beim Bundesministerium der Finanzen vom 14. Juli 1995' vols. 1 et seq. (1997 et seq.) and additional information provided by the Übernahmekommission.

Appendix 2:   The Bid of SPARTA Beteiligungen AG for Macrotron AG für Datenerfassungssysteme*

T.22
SPARTA Beteiligungen AG/
Macrotron AG für Datenerfassungssysteme

Kaufangebot:	Kauf von Vorzugsaktien
Anlaß für das Angebot:	Übernahme der Mehrheit durch die TechData; soll den Vorzugsaktionären eine Verkaufs-möglichkeit eröffnen
Angebotsfrist:	26. April bis 27. Mai 1997 einschließlich
Beteiligung *vor* dem Angebot:	keine Angabe
Erwerb durch das Angebot:	<0,1%
Beteiligung *nach* dem Angebot:	keine Angabe

I. Kaufangebot[1]

SPARTA Beteiligungen Aktiengesellschaft
Hamburg

Kaufangebot
an die Vorzugsaktionäre der

Macrotron AG für Datenerfassungssysteme
– Wertpapierkenn-Nr. 654 913 –

Wir unterbreiten den Vorzugsaktionären der oben aufgeführten Gesellschaft folgendes
Kaufangebot: Für eine Vorzugsaktie der Macrotron AG im Nennwert von DM 50,- mit
Coupons Nr. 10 ff. zahlt die SPARTA Beteiligungen AG (SPARTA AG) einen Kauf-
preis von

DM 510,- je Aktie.

---

*   Taken from: Bad Homburger Kreis, Forum für Übernahmerecht and Übernahmekommission, Geschäftsstelle 'Übernahmeangebote. Öffentliche Kauf- und Umtauschangebote
nach dem Übernahmekodex der Börsensachverständigenkommission beim Bundesministerium
der Finanzen vom 14. Juli 1995' vol. 2/1 (1997) 46-53 (12.7.1997).

1   Bundesanzeiger vom 26. April 1997.

Folgende Bedingungen gelten:

Befristung

Das Kaufangebot gilt ab 26.4.1997 und ist befristet bis zum 27.5.1997. Nach Zahlung der Dividende 95/96 von DM 13,- je Vorzugsaktie zzgl. Steuergutschrift (Hauptversammlung am 28.4.1997) ermäßigt sich der Kaufpreis auf DM 492,- pro Aktie.

Beschränkung

Das Angebot ist gültig für alle Vorzugsaktien der genannten Gesellschaft bis zum Gesamtnennbetrag von DM 550.000,-, d.h. für bis zu 11.000 Aktien. Übersteigt die Zahl der angebotenen Aktien den Gesamtnennbetrag von DM 550.000,- werden die Wertpapierinhaber pro rata berücksichtigt. Eine jeweils volle Abnahme der angebotenen Aktien behält sich die SPARTA AG vor.

Abwicklung

Diejenigen Aktionäre, welche das oben aufgeführte Angebot annehmen möchten, werden gebeten, ihrer Depotbank oder der SPARTA AG die Annahme des Kaufangebotes formlos mitzuteilen und die Aktien auf das Depot Nr. 55 89 66 der SPARTA AG bei der Westfalenbank AG, Bochum, einzuliefern.

Die Veräußerung der Aktien im Rahmen des Kaufangebotes ist für die Aktionäre der Macrotron AG provisions- und spesenfrei. Durch Einlieferung der Aktien bei der Westfalenbank AG und Begleichung des Gegenwertes auf das vom Veräußerer benannte Konto gilt der Geschäftsabschluß als vollendet.

Stellungnahme des Vorstandes der Macrotron AG

Das Kaufangebot wurde dem Vorstand der Macrotron AG vorgelegt. Eine Stellungnahme des Vorstands steht noch aus.

Nachbesserungsgarantie

Die SPARTA AG verpflichtet sich, allen Aktionären, die dieses Kaufangebot annehmen, eine zusätzliche Zahlung (Nachbesserung) für den Fall zu gewähren, daß die SPARTA AG bis zum 31.05.1998 ein höheres Kaufangebot für Aktien der Macrotron AG abgibt, Die Nachbesserungszahlung wird in diesem Fall pro jetzt eingereichter Aktie der Differenz zu dem vorliegenden Angebot entsprechen.

Bestimmung der Angebotshöhe

Der Preis von DM 510,- liegt höher als der höchste Börsenkurs der letzten 5 Jahre und ca. 70% über dem Ultimo-Kurs 1996.

Begründung des Kaufangebotes

Vorbehaltlich der Kartellamtszustimmung etc. hat der zweitgrößte US-Distributor TechData mehr als 75% der Stammaktien von Macrotron übernommen. Nach Angaben der Macrotron AG ist derzeit kein Abfindungsangebot an die freien Aktionäre geplant. Bei einer Übernahme nach US-Recht oder UK-Recht wäre ein solches Angebot zum Schutz der freien Aktionäre zwingend vorgeschrieben.

Seit 1988 haben die Stammaktionäre nicht mehr zur Finanzierung des Macrotron-Wachstums beigetragen. Bei den Kapitalerhöhungen 1990 und 1994 wurden ausschließlich Vorzugsaktien ausgegeben. Die Vorzugsaktionäre haben 1990 und 1994 insgesamt 38 Mio. DM eingezahlt, dies entspricht über 80% des gesamten in die Macrotron eingezahlten Kapitals. Dieses Angebot soll denjenigen Vorzugsaktionären, die nach dem Einstieg von TechData nicht Aktionäre eines Konzernteils einer US-Gesellschaft bleiben wollen, die Möglichkeit zur Abgabe ihrer Aktien bieten.

Nach Erwerb mindestens von 10% der Vorzugsaktien durch dieses Angebot sollen die gemeinsamen Interessen mit anderen Vorzugsaktionären vertreten werden.

Übernahmekodex

Die SPARTA AG unterwirft sich für dieses Kaufangebot den im Übernahmekodex in der Fassung vom 14. Juli 1995 genannten Bieterpflichten (Art. 12 ff).

Ergebnis des Kaufangebotes

Die Anzahl der im Rahmen des Kaufangebotes erworbenen Aktien der Macrotron AG wird die SPARTA AG voraussichtlich am 4. Juni 1997 im Bundesanzeiger veröffentlichen.

Hamburg, im April 1997

Der Vorstand
SPARTA Beteiligungen AG
Tesdorpfstraße 22
20148 Hamburg
Telefon: 040/450 13 40
Telefax: 040/45 01 34 50

II.a Stellungnahme der Macrotron[2]

MACROTRON
Aktiengesellschaft für Datenerfassungssysteme
München

An die
Vorzugsaktionäre der
MACROTRON AG für Datenerfassungssysteme
– Wertpapier-Kenn-Nr. 654 913 –

Stellungnahme des Vorstands
zu dem limitierten Kaufangebot
von der SPARTA Beteiligungen AG,
Hamburg,
an die Vorzugsaktionäre der MACROTRON AG

Sehr geehrte Vorzugsaktionäre,

der Vorstand der MACROTRON AG hat das vorliegende Angebot der SPARTA Beteiligungen AG, Hamburg, vom 26.04.1997 an die Vorzugsaktionäre zur Kenntnis genommen. Der Vorstand der MACROTRON AG nimmt zu diesem Angebot weder empfehlend noch ablehnend Stellung. Die Bewertung dieses Angebots bleibt den Vorzugsaktionären überlassen. Allerdings weisen wir unsere Vorzugsaktionäre auf Folgendes hin:

1. Die MACROTRON AG hat zur Frage eines "Abfindungsangebotes" bisher keine Angaben gemacht und es kann auch nicht Sache der Gesellschaft sein, dazu Aussagen zu tätigen.

2. Die Hinweise auf das englische und amerikanische Aktienrecht erscheinen uns in Deutschland ohne Bedeutung.

    Die Begründung des Kaufangebotes ist für uns im übrigen nicht nachvollziehbar. Der Hinweis auf eingezahltes Aktienkapital durch verschiedene Aktionärsgattungen ergibt keine Begründung für die Übernahme oder Abgabe von Aktien.

    Der letzte Satz der Begründung deutet eine Polarisierung der Aktionäre an. Eine solche Polarisierung ist nicht im Interesse der Gesellschaft.

---

2   Bundesanzeiger vom 30. April 1997.

II.a Stellungnahme der Macrotron[2]

MACROTRON
Aktiengesellschaft für Datenerfassungssysteme
München

An die
Vorzugsaktionäre der
MACROTRON AG für Datenerfassungssysteme
– Wertpapier-Kenn-Nr. 654 913 –

Stellungnahme des Vorstands
zu dem limitierten Kaufangebot
von der SPARTA Beteiligungen AG,
Hamburg,
an die Vorzugsaktionäre der MACROTRON AG

Sehr geehrte Vorzugsaktionäre,

der Vorstand der MACROTRON AG hat das vorliegende Angebot der SPARTA Beteiligungen AG, Hamburg, vom 26.04.1997 an die Vorzugsaktionäre zur Kenntnis genommen. Der Vorstand der MACROTRON AG nimmt zu diesem Angebot weder empfehlend noch ablehnend Stellung. Die Bewertung dieses Angebots bleibt den Vorzugsaktionären überlassen. Allerdings weisen wir unsere Vorzugsaktionäre auf Folgendes hin:

1. Die MACROTRON AG hat zur Frage eines "Abfindungsangebotes" bisher keine Angaben gemacht und es kann auch nicht Sache der Gesellschaft sein, dazu Aussagen zu tätigen.

2. Die Hinweise auf das englische und amerikanische Aktienrecht erscheinen uns in Deutschland ohne Bedeutung.

    Die Begründung des Kaufangebotes ist für uns im übrigen nicht nachvollziehbar. Der Hinweis auf eingezahltes Aktienkapital durch verschiedene Aktionärs-gattungen ergibt keine Begründung für die Übernahme oder Abgabe von Aktien.

    Der letzte Satz der Begründung deutet eine Polarisierung der Aktionäre an. Eine solche Polarisierung ist nicht im Interesse der Gesellschaft.

---

[2] Bundesanzeiger vom 30. April 1997.

II.b Stellungnahme der Geschäftsstelle der Übernahmekommission[3]

**Stellungnahme der
Geschäftsstelle der Übernahmekommission
zum Übernahmeangebot**

der

**SPARTA Beteiligungen Aktiengesellschaft,
Hamburg,**

an die Vorzugsaktionäre der

**MACROTRON AG
für Datenerfassungssysteme**

Das Übernahmeangebot, das am 26. April 1997 im Bundesanzeiger und am 28. April 1997 in der Frankfurter Allgemeine Zeitung veröffentlicht wurde, entspricht formal und inhaltlich nicht dem im Oktober 1995 in Kraft getretenen freiwilligen Übernahmekodex der Börsensachverständigenkommission beim Bundesministerium der Finanzen:

1. Das Angebot enthält eine Erklärung, wonach sich die SPARTA AG den im Übernahmekodex genannten Bieterpflichten unterwirft. Dies ist grundsätzlich zu begrüßen; die Formulierung läßt jedoch nicht genügend erkennen, daß es sich nur um eine teilweise Anerkennung der Regeln des Übernahmekodex handelt. Der Klammerzusatz "Art. 12 ff " ist nicht ausreichend.

2. Nach Artikel 5 des Übernahmekodex hat der Bieter vor Abgabe eines öffentlichen Angebotes Informationspflichten u.a. gegenüber der Geschäftsstelle der Übernahmekommission. Dieser Pflicht ist der Bieter nicht rechtzeitig nachgekommen.

3. Die Angabe eines Kaufpreises von DM 510,- für nur einen Tag – und das am Tage der Hauptversammlung – ist ein Verstoß gegen Artikel 8.

4. Es fehlt ein Hinweis auf die Rücktrittsmöglichkeit nach Artikel 14 Ziffer 7[4].

5. Das Angebot ist einerseits auf die Annahme von DM 550.000,- beschränkt, andererseits besteht ein Vorbehalt auf volle Abnahme. Hierfür werden keine

---

[3]   Bundesanzeiger vom 16. Mai 1997.
[4]   Gemeint ist Artikel 7 Ziffer 4.

Kriterien genannt, die außerhalb des Einflußbereiches des Bieters liegen. Damit ist ein Verstoß gegen Artikel 9 verbunden.

6. Es fehlen Angaben zur Höhe der gehaltenen Aktien und dazu noch nicht erfüllten Verträgen (Artikel 7 Ziffer 8). Dies gilt ebenso hinsichtlich der Auswirkungen eines erfolgreichen Angebotes, insbesondere hinsichtlich der finanziellen Verhältnisse des Bieters und der Zielgesellschaft (Artikel 7 Ziffer 14).

7. Der angesprochene Zweck, gemeinsame Interessen mit anderen Vorzugsaktionären (in Zukunft) zu vertreten, läßt für den am Angebot Interessierten den (mißverständlichen) Schluß zu, er sei an diesem gemeinsamen Vorgehen beteiligt (nochmaliger Verstoß gegen Artikel 8).

Insgesamt können die nur teilweise Anerkennung des Übernahmekodex und die angesprochenen Mängel darauf schließen lassen, daß bei dem Angebot eine Maßnahme zur Marktbeeinflussung nicht ausgeschlossen werden kann.

Frankfurt am Main, den 12. Mai 1997

Übernahmekommission
Geschäftsstelle

III. Ergebnismitteilung[5]

SPARTA Beteiligungen AG
Hamburg

Mitteilung über das Ergebnis
des limitierten freiwilligen Kaufangebotes
an die Vorzugsaktionäre der
Macrotron AG für Datenerfassungssysteme

– Wertpapier-Kenn-Nr. 654 913 –

Im Rahmen eines limitierten öffentlichen Kaufangebotes haben wir innerhalb der bis zum 27. Mai 1997 laufenden Angebotsfrist insgesamt 45 Aktien der Macrotron AG für Datenerfassungssysteme erworben.

Hamburg, im Juni 1997

SPARTA Beteiligungen AG

---

[5] Bundesanzeiger vom 17. Juni 1997.

Jurisprudential and Transactional Developments in Takeovers

MARCEL KAHAN, New York[*]

I survey jurisprudential and transactional developments in hostile takeovers. Recent Delaware court opinions in *Unitrin*, *Wells Fargo*, and *Kidsco* clarify both that "just say no" is a valid takeover defense subject only to minimal judicial scrutiny, and that courts will subject takeover defenses that go beyond "just say no" to process-based as well as heightened substantive scrutiny. I show how this doctrinal stance stems from the court's view of the proper allocation of power between directors, shareholders, and judges: directors manage the company, shareholders express their view by electing directors, and judges should interfere in this interplay of powers only if it fails to function properly. Several transactional developments—specifically, the coupling of hostile takeover bids with proxy contests and the replacement of cash-financed, financial bids by equity-financed, strategic bids—can be understood, in part, as responses to these jurisprudential developments.

Contents

A. Jurisprudential Developments
B. Transactional Developments

In this paper, I will sketch some of the jurisprudential and transactional developments regarding hostile takeovers in the 1990s. The story I will tell is a simple one. Contrary to many other corporate law commentators, I will suggest that the Delaware Supreme Court's takeover jurisprudence establishes a coherent and consistent set of fairly straightforward standards guiding when a court will interfere in the corporate decision-making process and that some of the transactional developments are responses to this jurisprudence.

A. Jurisprudential Developments

Two cases establish Delaware's broad doctrinal framework for analyzing the duty of a board of directors when faced with a hostile takeover bid: *Unocal*[1] and

---

[*] I would like to thank the participants at the Symposium on Comparative Corporate Governance, organized by the Max-Planck-Institut für Ausländisches und Internationales Privatrecht, for helpful comments and the Filomen D'Agostino and Max E. Greenberg Research Fund for financial support.

[1] *Unocal Corp. v. Mesa Petroleum Co.* 493 A.2d 946 (Del. 1985).

Revlon[2]. In *Unocal*, the Supreme Court announced a two-part test for assessing defensive actions by a board of directors. First, the directors "must show that they had reasonable grounds for believing that a danger to corporate policy and effectiveness existed. . . ."[3] Second, the defensive measure "must be reasonable in relation to the threat posed."[4]

The words of the *Unocal* test, of course, do not have a clear inherent meaning. Whether a defensive action passes the test depends on what counts as a threat, how intensely courts scrutinize the board's grounds for believing that a threat exists, and what measures constitute a reasonable response. Of particular importance is when a board may "just say no" and refuse to redeem a poison pill: modern "flip-in" poison pills, which have been adopted by a large portion of all public corporations,[5] make it in practice impossible to complete a hostile tender offer unless they are redeemed.

As it has developed, the *Unocal* test demands for a rejection of a tender offer little more than the backing by the board's independent directors and an investment banker's opinion stating that the price offered is inadequate. Indeed, no Supreme Court case has ever invalidated a board's defensive action under *Unocal*.

Things look different once a company is in so-called *Revlon*[6]-mode. A board of directors becomes subject to *Revlon* when it is about to sell the company, to break it up, or to sell control in it. Once in *Revlon*-mode, the court generally forces the target to give shareholders the opportunity to accept the hostile tender offer and mandates a high degree of impartiality between the board-favored and the hostile bidder.[7] Thus, under *Revlon*, the locus of power shifts from the directors to the courts—who scrutinize the substantive merits of board actions—and to the shareholders—who ordinarily have the opportunity to accept a hostile bid.

This bifurcated framework established by *Unocal* and *Revlon* raises two important questions. Why does the Court generally validate a board's rejection of

---

[2] *Revlon, Inc. v. MacAndrews & Forbes Holdings, Inc.* 506 A.2d 173 (Del. 1986).

[3] *Unocal Corp. v. Mesa Petroleum Co.*, supra n. 1, 955.

[4] *Unocal Corp. v. Mesa Petroleum Co.*, supra n. 1, 955.

[5] A study by the Investor Responsibility Research Center found that, in 1995, 799 of the 1,500 companies covered by the study had adopted a poison pill and 1,275 of the 1,500 companies have authorized blank check preferred stock and would thus be able to adopt a standard poison pill if a hostile bid were made. See 'Defenses Du Jour' *Corporate Control Alert* (Oct. 1995) 8.

[6] *Revlon, Inc. v. MacAndrews & Forbes Holdings, Inc.*, supra n. 2.

[7] See, e.g., *Revlon, Inc. v. MacAndrews & Forbes Holdings, Inc.*, supra n. 2, 182 (selective dealing to fend off a hostile bidder is no longer proper); *Mills Acquisition Co. v. Macmillan, Inc.* 559 A.2d 1261, 1288 (Del. 1988) (preferential treatment of one bidder only permissible if action reasonable in relation to advantage sought or to threat avoided); *Paramount Communications, Inc. v. QVC Network, Inc.* 637 A.2d 34 (Del. 1994) (under *Revlon*, courts have to scrutinize reasonableness of both process and substance).

a tender offer under *Unocal*? And why does the Court, in some circumstances but not in others, radically depart from the apparently permissive *Unocal* standard and shift to the exacting *Revlon* test?

As I have argued,[8] the answers to both of these questions flow from the Court's view of the proper allocation of power between directors, shareholders, and courts in deciding whether or not to accept a takeover bid. As Delaware courts have repeatedly stated, it is the board of directors that manages the company—a power which includes, with some qualifications, the power to decide whether or not to accept a takeover bid. Shareholders legitimately express their views of how a company should be run by electing directors whose views they share. If shareholders are dissatisfied with a board decision to reject a take-over bid, their proper response is to elect a different board. Courts should be reluctant to interfere in this interplay of powers. But courts may have to do so when it fails to function properly.

The framework established by *Unocal* and *Revlon* establishes when, and in what manner, courts need to interfere. In particular, courts scrutinize board deci-sions under three different standards, one process-based (i.e., courts review the adequacy of the board's decision-making process) and two substantive (i.e., courts review the effects of and reasons for the board's decision). Process scrutiny arises under the first prong of *Unocal* and is applied to any defensive device. The first prong of *Unocal* essentially vests the initial decision to accept or reject a takeover bid with the independent directors and subjects their deci-sion-making process to heightened process requirements. If independent direc-tors, after a process designed to show good faith and reasonable investigation, decide to reject a bid (i.e., not to redeem the poison pill) *and do not otherwise change the company's business strategy*—that is "*JUST* say no"—courts will not review the decision any further. In that case, the normal interplay of powers can run its course: shareholders, if dissatisfied with the decision, can elect different directors at the next occasion.

Substantive scrutiny is applied if directors adopt affirmative defenses that go beyond a mere refusal to redeem a poison pill. These additional defenses may not unduly interfere with the normal interplay of powers. The most stringent substantive scrutiny is applied to actions that *deprive* shareholders of the ability to elect a board disposed towards accepting a takeover bid, to wit: a sale of the company, a change of control, and a break-up. These actions trigger review under *Revlon,* which makes it very difficult for directors to inhibit shareholders' choice between accepting the hostile bid and proceeding with the board-favored trans-action. Lesser scrutiny applies to defensive actions that materially interfere with the ability of shareholders to elect a board disposed towards accepting a takeover

---

[8] See Kahan, Marcel 'Paramount or Paradox: The Delaware Supreme Court's Takeover Jurisprudence' 19 *J. Corp. L.* 583 (1994).

bid, but fall short of depriving them of that ability. Such actions, I have argued, need to be substantively reviewed under the second prong of the *Unocal*-test: whether they are reasonable in relation to the threat posed by the bid.

Recent Delaware case law is consistent with my arguments. The most recent Delaware Supreme Court's opinion expounding on the *Unocal/Revlon* framework is *Unitrin, Inc.* v. *American General Corp.*[9] American General made an unsolicited offer to acquire Unitrin at a 30% premium over its pre-offer market price. The board of Unitrin rejected the bid, adopted a poison pill that precluded American General from acquiring more than 15% of Unitrin's stock, and authorized a program to repurchase up to 10 million (out of 51.8 million) of Unitrin's outstanding shares in open market transactions. Board members announced that they would not sell any of their shares in the repurchase program. Unitrin did, in fact, repurchase 5 million shares at an average price slightly above American General's bid.[10]

One additional fact makes this case unusual. Two members of Unitrin's board, both unaffiliated with Unitrin's management, held substantial blocks of shares. Henry Singleton, the founder of Teledyne (from which Unitrin is a spin-off), owned 7.2 million shares; and Fayez Sarofim, an investment manager, personally owned 1.1 million shares.[11]

American General sued to preliminarily enjoin any further share repurchases. The Chancery Court granted the injunction and Unitrin appealed. The Supreme Court reversed. The main part of the Supreme Court's opinion was addressed to the second prong of the *Unocal* test: whether the repurchase program was a reasonable response to the threat of an inadequate bid.

---

[9] *Unitrin, Inc.* v. *American General Corp.* 651 A.2d 1361 (1995). Another related Delaware Supreme Court case is *Williams v. Geier* 671 A.2d 1368 (Del. 1996). In that case, the Delaware Supreme Court, in a rare split opinion, dealt with the standard of review applicable to the adoption, by Cincinnati Milacron, of a charter amendment establishing "tenure voting"-shares held by the same person for three years that would have ten votes, rather than one. *Williams v. Geier*, supra, 1370. At the time of the adoption, Cincinnati Milacron was controlled by the Geier family and the "tenure voting" scheme presumably enabled the Geier family to sell some of its shares without losing voting control. The Court rejected arguments that the adoption of amendment should be reviewed under *Unocal*, under the "entire fairness" standard, or under *Blasius Industries v. Atlas Corp.* 564 A.2d 651 (Del. Ch. 1988) (which subjects actions intended to impede shareholder franchise to heightened scrutiny), and instead held that the proper standard of review was the business judgment rule. Regarding the inapplicability of *Unocal*, the court stated that "*Unocal* analysis should be used only when a board unilaterally (i.e., without shareholder approval) adopts defensive measures in reaction to a perceived threat." 671 A.2d at 1377. This, of course, is a logical consequence of viewing *Unocal* as protection against board actions that interfere with shareholders' governance rights (to wit, their right to elect a new board disposed towards accepting a takeover bid). The issue of whether the court should apply heightened scrutiny under *Blasius* or under the "entire fairness" standard is, of course, a different one and is not addressed by the analysis above.

[10] *Unitrin, Inc.* v. *American General Corp.*, supra n. 9, 1366–70.

[11] *Unitrin, Inc.* v. *American General Corp.*, supra n. 9, 1368.

How could the share repurchase program inhibit Unitrin's shareholders, if they wanted to accept American General's bid, from electing a board inclined to do so? Allegedly, Unitrin's repurchases changed Unitrin's shareholder profile; specifically, they increased the share ownership of Unitrin's incumbent board members, who had pledged not to participate in the share repurchase program, from 23% to 28%.[12] The Court, however, found that American General's chances of prevailing, if its offer was attractive, remained high. In particular, the Court found that one should not assume that Unitrin's outside directors *who were substantial stockholders* would vote against their economic interests as stockholders just to preserve the "prestige and perquisites"[13] of membership of Unitrin's board. And even assuming that all board members would vote against American General, a proxy contest remained a "viable alternative",[14] since ownership of Unitrin's stock by institutional shareholder was high and relatively concentrated. Finally, the extent to which the repurchase program inhibited a takeover bid had to be weighted against the risk that Unitrin's shareholders might accept American General's bid because of "mistaken or ignorant" belief regarding Unitrin's long-term value and the benefit of offering "liquidity" to some shareholders.[15] The Supreme Court then remanded the case to the Chancery Court for an ultimate assessment of whether the repurchase program fell within a range of reasonable responses.

Two features of the Delaware Supreme Court opinion are noteworthy. On one hand, the Court's analysis of the impact of the repurchase program on General American's ability to wage a proxy contest is highly contextual and substantive—just the type of analysis that I suggested should be undertaken under the second prong of *Unocal*. On the other hand, the analysis of the proper balancing between the risk of American General's offer and the impact of the repurchase program on American General is more cursory. Although I would have preferred a substantive evaluation on this latter front as well, its absence may be due to the particular circumstances of the case. As noted, two directors unaffiliated with management—Singleton and Sarofim—held collectively 8.3 million shares of Unitrin. If Unitrin stock was *not* undervalued prior to American General's offer, Singleton and Sarofim stood to gain close to $100 million from American General's bid.[16] Although *Unocal* recognizes an "omnipresent specter that the board," including its outside directors, "may be acting primarily in its own inter-

---

[12] *Unitrin, Inc. v. American General Corp.*, supra n. 9, 1377-8.

[13] *Unitrin, Inc. v. American General Corp.*, supra n. 9, 1380.

[14] *Unitrin, Inc. v. American General Corp.*, supra n. 9, 1383.

[15] *Unitrin, Inc. v. American General Corp.*, supra n. 9, 1388-90.

[16] American General's bids represented about an $11.50 per share premium. For 8.3 million shares, the aggregate premium is about $95.5 million.

ests, rather than those of the corporation and its shareholders,"[17] this specter is presumably less powerful—and the standard of review is arguably more deferential—when outside directors would have gained $100 million by accepting a takeover bid.

Moreover, the repurchase program could plausibly be viewed as a "put your money where your mouth is" defense, tailored to the threat that Unitrin's shareholders may underestimate its value. The market price of Unitrin at which shares were, and presumably would continue to be, repurchased, was slightly above American General's bid. If Unitrin was not undervalued prior to American General's bid, the program would be a rather expensive defensive device: Singleton and Sarofim, who did not participate in the repurchase program, would stand to lose, respectively, about $20 million and $3 million.[18] Thus, rather than a means to increase the board's proportional share ownership, the repurchase program may be a signal of its credibility—we don't just say that $50-3/8 is inadequate, we show that we mean it by taking an action that is highly detrimental to us if we are wrong. Viewed from this perspective, the repurchase program is a rather appropriate device to counter the threat that shareholders may view the board's protestations of price inadequacy as non-credible cheap talk.

Two recent Chancery Court cases also bear mention. *Wells Fargo & Co. v. First Interstate Bancorp.*,[19] dealt with the takeover battle over First Interstate. After Wells Fargo had made an unsolicited offer to merge with First Interstate, First Interstate entered into a merger agreement with First Bank. The agreement provided for a stock exchange ratio that was, at current market prices, inferior to the offer by Wells Fargo, as well as for breakup fees and reciprocal stock options. Wells Fargo commenced an exchange offer for First Interstate stock, but was precluded from consummating it by First Interstate's poison pill.[20] After dismissing a claim under *Revlon,* the court denied defendant's motion to dismiss the *Unocal* claim. Suggesting that it was concerned over First Interstate's attempt to force a vote on the merger with First Bank without redeeming the poison pill, the court held that "whether there were reasonable grounds for concluding that a threat was posed and whether the response was proportional to that threat are generally questions of fact to be decided at trial, not on the pleadings."[21]

[17] *Unocal Corp. v. Mesa Petroleum Co.*, supra n. 1, 954.

[18] At a pre-offer price of $39 and with 51.8 million shares outstanding, the aggregate value of Unitrin's equity is about $2 billion. Repurchasing 10 million shares for about $50.50 per share reduces Unitrin's aggregate equity value to about $1.5 billion, or about $36.25 per share. The value of Singleton's 7.2 million shares drops from about $280 million to about $260 million; the value of Sarofim's 1.1 million shares drops from about $43 million to about $40 million.

[19] *Wells Fargo & Co. v. First Interstate Bancorp.* 1996 Del. Ch. LEXIS 3.

[20] *Wells Fargo & Co. v. First Interstate Bancorp.*, supra n. 19, at *5-9.

[21] *Wells Fargo & Co. v. First Interstate Bancorp.*, supra n. 19, at *19.

In *Kidsco, Inc. v. Dinsmore,*[22] The Learning Company ("TLC") and Broder-bund had entered into a stock merger agreement (not resulting in a change of control) with the shareholder vote set for November 9, 1995. On October 30, SoftKey announced a two-tier tender offer for TLC's shares and started to solicit proxies to call a special meeting to replace TLC's directors. In response, TLC and Broderbund revised the merger agreement to make it more favorable to TLC, changed the date for the shareholder vote on the revised merger to December 11, and approved a by-law amendment extending from 35 days to 60 days, the minimum time for calling a stockholder-initiated shareholder meeting. As a result, the shareholder meeting on the replacement of TLC's board could not take place until about 25 days after the vote on the revised merger (as opposed to as little as two days after the vote under the original by-law).[23] The asserted reason for the amendment was to enable TLC's board to seek alternatives to SoftKey's offer, or to establish an auction process, should TLC's shareholders not approve the merger with Broderbund.[24] The court, analyzing the by-law amendment under *Unocal,* found that TLC had a valid interest in establishing a process that would yield the highest value for its stock if the Broderbund transaction is turned down and that a 25-day delay in a shareholder meeting called by SoftKey was a reasonable way to achieve this goal.[25] These Chancery Court opinions confirm that review of defenses beyond "just say no" under the second prong of *Unocal* is contextual and substantive.

B. Transactional Developments

On the transactional side, three developments are noteworthy. First, to an increasing extent, hostile takeover bids are coupled with proxy contests to replace the incumbent board of directors. In return, so-called "dead-hand poison pills," the legal validity of which is largely untested, have become an increasingly popular defensive device.[26] Second, to an increasing extent, hostile take-over bids are financed by equity, rather than by cash. Third, to an increasing extent, bids are made by strategic, rather than financial, acquirers.

The first of these developments, of course, follows directly from what I discussed above. If the board has the power to "just say no", the only way for a hostile takeover to succeed is to either "persuade" the board to say "yes" or to

---

[22] *Kidsco, Inc. v. Dinsmore* 674 A.2d 483 (1995).

[23] *Kidsco, Inc. v. Dinsmore,* supra n. 22, 486-9.

[24] *Kidsco, Inc. v. Dinsmore,* supra n. 22, 490.

[25] *Kidsco, Inc. v. Dinsmore,* supra n. 22, 496-7.

[26] Lipton, M. 'Poison Pills' (Wachtell, Lipton, Rosen & Katz Letter to clients, July 18, 1997) (noting that poison pills "continue to be the subject of efforts to strengthen their defensive attributes by the 'dead hand' route").

replace it. An announcement to wage a proxy contest is helpful in either respect. A recalcitrant board, as phone calls by large institutional shareholders start rolling in, may often see the handwriting on the wall and commence negotiations with the hostile bidder or institute an auction process. If it does not, it risks replacement at the next shareholder meeting. This, in fact, is what has happened on many occasions. To wit, in the two Chancery Court cases mentioned earlier —Wells Fargo's bid for First Interstate and SoftKey's bid for TLC—the hostile bidder prevailed even though it lost, or at least did not win, in court.

The countermove to takeovers coupled with proxy contests has been for target boards to adopt so-called dead-hand poison pills.[27] Dead-hand poison pills are designed to prevent the redemption of a poison pill by the new board elected in a proxy contest. Dead-hand poison pills achieve this by making poison pills redeemable only by so-called "continuing directors:" the directors incumbent when the pill was adopted and any new director whose election was approved by, or who was appointed by, other "continuing directors."

No Delaware court has authoritatively ruled on the validity of dead-hand poison pills. Courts in other jurisdictions have split on the validity of dead-hand poison pills, finding them invalid under New York law,[28] but valid under Georgia law.[29] The analysis of the Delaware takeover jurisprudence suggests that Delaware law has no place for dead-hand poison pills. Such pills undermine the very premises of the allocation of powers established by Delaware law: *direc-tors*—that is, present rather than former directors—run the company; and *share-*

[27] Another device that is relatively effective in dealing with takeover bids coupled with proxy contests is a staggered board, where only one-third of the directors come up for election in any single year. See, e.g., 'Moore-Wallace Highlights the Downside of Hostiles' *Mergers & Acquisitions Rep.* Apr. 1, 1996, 1 (reporting that Moore's bid for Wallace failed even though Moore succeeded in replacing one-third of Wallace's directors in a proxy contest). However, the establishment of a staggered board, unlike the adoption of a poison pill, requires shareholder approval. See Delaware General Corporation Law, §141(d). Possibly for that reason, the number of companies with staggered boards does not seem to have significantly increased in the 1990s. See *Corporate Control Alert*, supra n. 5, 8 (reporting that number of companies with staggered boards in sample of 1,500 companies increased from 850 in 1990 to 895 in 1995). A more novel variant of a "staggered board" defense was recently pioneered by ITT in its takeover defense against Hilton. ITT, which did not have a staggered board, decided to spin-off its hotel opera-tions (the major part of its business and the part of interest to Hilton) into a newly-created company, ITT Destinations, which would have a staggered board. See 'ITT Board Opts for Three-Way Split' *Financial Times* July 17, 1997, 33. Under corporate law, a spin-off dividend ordinarily does not require shareholder approval and the charter provisions of the spun-off company are determined by the directors of the spinning-off company. How effective this novel strategy is, and what legal limits are placed on it by the *Unocal/Revlon* framework, remains to be seen.

[28] *Bank of New York Co., Inc. v. Irving Bank Corp.* 528 N.Y.S.2d 482 (Sup. Ct., NY Cty., 1988).

[29] See Lipin, Steven 'Healthdyne Wins Victory Over Invacare As Federal Court Upholds "Poison-Pill"' *Wall Street Journal* July 4, 1997, at B5.

holders properly and legitimately express their views of how the corporation should be run—and whether a takeover bid should be accepted—by electing directors who share these views. These premises do not permit incumbent directors to unilaterally[30] divest different future directors of the power to accept a takeover bid—and thereby shareholders of the power to elect different future directors with a power to accept a bid—according to such future directors' business judgment. Or expressed in more doctrinal terms, the "threat" to which dead-hand poison pills are addressed—that the current target board will be ousted in a proxy contest and that a new board will accept a takeover bid that is not in the interest of target shareholders—is not a cognizable threat in the *Unocal* framework.[31]

Even if dead-hand poison pills are not valid, however, coupling a hostile bid with a proxy contest requires more staying power. To consummate a bid, a bidder may have to wait until it can replace a majority of the board members in a proxy contest. Since most companies do not permit shareholders to remove board members by written consent, this means that the bidder has to wait at least until the next annual meeting. (The date of that meeting, of course, is within some constraints in the discretion of the company's directors.) When a company has a staggered board, it may even require staying power of more than one year, as it may take two annual meetings to elect a majority of directors that is favorably disposed to accepting a takeover bid.[32]

This requirement of more staying power may have marginally contributed to the change in financing method from cash offers to equity offers. Compared with equity offers, it is relatively costly for a hostile bidder to keep the necessary assurances of financing for a cash offer—bank commitment letters and the like—open for extended periods of time. These higher costs are significant in two

[30] An issue not addressed by, and beyond the scope of, this paper is whether dead-hand poison pills are valid if they are approved by the company's shareholders.

[31] A premise of this argument is that a board has no independent business justification to adopt a poison pill (other than the effect of the pill on the raider's ability to consummate a tender offer). A dead-hand poison pill would then have no justification other than to prevent a future board from accepting a takeover bid. In this respect, a continuing director provision in a poison pill differs from such a provision in other contracts, such as in a "golden parachute" agreement or a "poison put" bond covenant. See Kahan, Marcel and Michael Klausner 'Anti-Takeover Provisions in Bonds: Bondholder Protection or Management Entrenchment' 40 *U.C.L.A. L. Rev.* 931 (1993) (discussing use of such provisions in bonds). Such contracts have at least a potential independent business justification: attracting capable executives and providing them with employment security in case of a golden parachute and protecting bondholders against losses in case of poison puts.

[32] See, e.g., *Mergers & Acquisitions Rep.*, supra n. 27, 1 (reporting that Moore's bid for Wallace failed even though Moore succeeded in replacing one-third of Wallace's directors in a proxy contest); see also *Corporate Control Alert*, supra n. 5, 8 (describing study by the Investor Responsibility Research Center that found that, in 1995, 895 of the 1,500 companies covered by the study had a staggered board).

respects. They will directly lead fewer bidders to make hostile cash offers in order to avoid these costs. And they may induce a target to resist a cash offer for longer than it would resist an equity offer in the hope that the bidder will go away, thereby both reducing the likelihood that the bidder will succeed and further raising its costs if it does. Thus, as it takes longer in the 1990s to consummate a hostile bid than in the 1980s, equity bids become relatively more attractive than cash bids.

But even though it is more expensive to keep cash offers open for extended periods than it is to keep equity offers open, and even though the cost difference may not be small as an absolute matter, the cost difference is small in relation to the total premium typically paid in a takeover bid.[33] Thus, it is likely that other factors are primarily responsible for the change in financing method. Such factors may include the fact that stock prices have continued to hit record highs, cheapening (for non-adherents of the efficient markets hypothesis)[34] stocks as a takeover currency or the possibility that junk-bonds were overpriced in the 1980s.

Regardless of the reason why bidders in the 1990s prefer equity bids over cash bids, in practical terms only a bidder whose stock is publicly traded and whose equity base is large compared to the target's can make an offer financed by its own stock. Bidders that are closely held have no publicly traded stock to offer in an equity bid. Bidders whose stock is publicly traded, but whose equity base is small compared to the target's equity base, can offer publicly traded stock, but have difficulty in financing a premium equity-financed bid.

An example will illustrate this difficulty. Assume that Bidder, Inc., with a total equity value of $20 million, wants to acquire Target Corp., with an equity value of $60 million, at a modest 20% premium. Assume further that the market does not believe that such an acquisition will result in efficiency gains. If Bidder, Inc. wanted to offer its stock to Target Corp. shareholders, Target Corp. share-

---

[33] See, e.g., Jarrell, Gregg A., James A. Brickley, and Jeffry M. Netter 'The Market for Corporate Control: The Empirical Evidence Since 1980' *Journal of Economic Perspectives* 2/1 (1988) 49, 51-3 (summarizing various studies that find average gains to target shareholders between 16% and 53%). In comparison, the monthly costs of maintaining a line of credit as estimated by Bebchuk is about 0.1% of the amount of the line of credit. Bebchuk, Lucian A. 'The Case for Facilitating Competing Tender Offers: A Reply and Extension' 35 *Stan. L. Rev.* 23, 32 n. 28 (1982).

[34] According to the efficient markets hypothesis, stocks are accurately valued given the available information. See, e.g., Kahan, Marcel 'Securities Laws and the Social Costs of "Inaccurate" Stock Prices' 1992 *Duke L.J.* 977 (1992) (reviewing hypothesis and discussing implications). I note that, for purposes of explaining the change in financing method, it is significant whether the bidder's decision-makers (its managers and investment bankers) believe in the validity of the efficient market hypothesis, and not whether the hypothesis is valid as an absolute matter. Anecdotal evidence suggests that managers and investment bankers are not among the most avid adherents of the hypothesis.

holders would end up with 90% of the stock of Bidder, Inc. and the (pre-bid) Bidder, Inc. shareholders would retain just 10% of Bidder, Inc.'s stock.[35] Apart from the fact that most companies would need shareholder approval to issue so much stock,[36] which causes delay and complications, Bidder, Inc.'s shareholder may revolt against a transaction that results in such a significant dilution of their share ownership.[37]

The increase in time it takes to consummate a hostile bid may also have contributed to the change in bidder type. More time means more opportunities for a competing bid to be made or a competing transaction to be proposed. This danger is not as stark for a proposed acquisition that offers gains that are hard to replicate, such as unique synergies available from the combination of two specific companies. The danger, however, is stark for a proposed transaction that offers gains that are otherwise available—gains from a change in capital structure, gains from removing inefficient managers. Though many proposed acquisitions will entail both types of gains, my sense is that strategic acquisitions involve relatively more unreplicable gains than financial ones, and are thus less exposed to competition.

I do not claim, of course, that takeover jurisprudence is exclusively, or even primarily, responsible for the increase in equity-financed and strategic acquisitions. Other factors may well be more important: possibly, junk-bonds were

---

[35] The combined equity value of the companies would be $80 million and the value of the shares given to Target Corp. would be $72 million. This amounts to 90% of the total share value.

[36] Shareholder approval would be required as a matter of state corporation law if the company does not have a sufficient number of authorized and unissued shares to finance the takeover. See, e.g., Delaware General Corporation Law, §§ 102(a)(4) and 242. The number of authorized and unissued shares of most companies is substantially below nine times the number of issued shares. Shareholder approval would also be required as a matter of stock exchange rules. U.S. stock exchanges require shareholder approval if an issuance of new shares results in an increase by 20% or more of outstanding shares. See, e.g., NYSE Listed Company Manual §703.08(A).

[37] To be sure, if Bidder Inc. financed such an acquisition with debt, it would end up with a highly leveraged capital structure (90% debt if neither company had any debt prior to the acquisition). However, debt-financed acquisitions with extremely high levels of leverage were not uncommon in the 1980s. See, e.g., *City Capital Associates v. Interco, Inc.* 551 A.2d 787 (Del. Ch. 1988) (describing defensive recapitalization of Interco in which Interco would make payments in cash, debt securities, and preferred stock to shareholders valued at $66 per share and Interco's pre-hostile bid share price was in the low 40s). In contrast, an equity-financed acquisition that results in a 90% dilution is difficult to conceive.

In addition, if an acquisition results in efficiency gains, it may be easier to convince a small number of lenders that such gains exist than to convince the market. (For example, the acquiring company can more easily disclose non-public information related to the presence and size of efficiency gains to lenders.) Finally, the mere fact that an acquisition is financed with debt may lead the market to view the acquisition more favorably. See Kraakman, Reinier 'Taking Discounts Seriously: The Implications of "Discounted" Share Prices as an Acquisition Motive' 88 *Colum. L. Rev.* 891 (1994) (proposing 'discounts' hypothesis according to which acquisition targets are undervalued in the stock market and increases in leverage eliminate these discounts).

overpriced during the 1980s, making junk-bond financing a relatively more attractive financing tool; possibly, stocks are overvalued during the 1990s, making stock-financed acquisitions relatively more attractive in today's environment; possibly, the gains to be had from 1980s-style cash-financed bust-up takeovers—removal of inefficient managers, decrease in free cash flows, deconglomeratization—have been exhausted and only takeovers that offer synergies remain. Without further study it is impossible, and even with further study it will be difficult, to determine the exact causes for these transactional developments. I suggest, however, that the legal developments I discussed above are primarily responsible for the increase in takeovers coupled with proxy contests and the emergence of dead-hand poison pills and may well have at least reinforced the trend to equity-financed and strategic acquisitions.

Discussion Report

HANNO MERKT

The Delaware Courts' Approach to Defensive Strategies

According to a British participant, there is much uncertainty about the values furthered by Delaware case law in this area. In particular, it is unclear why the courts do not simply get rid of the so-called 'just-say-no defense'. Moreover, it is hard to find any justification for mandatory proxy contests. In response to *Kahan*, a German legal scholar pointed to differences in the degree of court involvement in the issue of takeover defense control. Traditionally, in America and England court involvement is perceived more positively than in Germany.

In the case of the Delaware courts, an American academic noted that cases dealing with so-called 'dead hand pills' are not always sufficiently protective to the shareholder franchise; as an example, he cited the complete rejection of fiduciary duties to minority shareholders. On the other hand, the so-called 'just-say-no defense' is impermissible according to Delaware case law. In more general terms, U.S. takeover law is, according to this participant, similar to the City Code and the EC Takeover Directive. The mandatory bid as a practical (not a legal) matter in a hostile deal is a factual requirement. *Kahan* added that current Delaware cases on the permissibility of 'dead hand poison pills' pending before Delaware courts will be test cases with respect to the protection of minority rights. Since Delaware courts are in general very speedy, a result can be expected within months.

Allen reported that there is a great deal of moving around on the doctrinal level of the minority protection debate. Notwithstanding this discussion, the Delaware courts' general aim will be to protect and to further the integrity of the voting process since the board's power is derived from the elections. In general, Delaware courts do a good job of mediating between the conflicting interests. In particular, an attempt will be made to avoid any infringement of takeover activities. The protection of market forces will be paramount. The experience of the past has taught that if the market wants certain types of transactions, it will finally get it, even if the price is higher because of delay.

Germany's Takeover Codex

A British academic asked whether, in the view of the panelists, the Codex is consistent with the 13th EC Directive on takeovers, particularly in the light of the fact that the Codex does not provide for access to state courts and for enforcement of individual minority shareholder's rights.

A German economist fiercely advocated a stronger protection of minority shareholders. In the current Codex, minority shareholders are insufficiently protected: there is no class action provision, and the 10% threshold for shareholder action under the current stock corporation law is much too high. In addition, the provision permitting appraisal of minority shareholders for 25% less than the current stock price amounts to a blatant expropriation of minority shareholders. According to this economist, the Siemens/Düwag case is a good illustration of such expropriation and, moreover, makes a compelling case for improved minority shareholder protection.

Baumann noted that it is too early to judge the Takeover Codex. There is some evidence for a need to amend the Codex; however, amendment is a complicated procedure given the purely contractual nature of the duties under the Codex. Furthermore, *Baumann* strongly objected to the above-mentioned criticism with respect to minority shareholder protection, claiming that the Codex by no means excludes access of minority shareholders to courts as was asserted. On the other hand, review by a panel established under the Codex is preferable to court review, according to *Baumann*, because the panel has more expertise. With regard to the economist's statement about appraisal right price determination, *Baumann* pointed to inherent complications caused by particular provisions of the German Stock Corporation Code (*AktG*) regarding squeeze-outs. Moreover, a 25% discount would be justified given the possibility of falling stock prices. Swiss law on this issue would be identical. *Baumann* added that there will be a regulation on minority shareholder protection that will be tougher than the actual regulation. In general, any regulation of that type must acknowledge the inherent difficulties of enforcing a Codex that is exclusively contractual in nature. An American participant noted that from a U.S. perspective, the purely voluntary acceptance of takeover rules in Germany appears odd. Moreover, research has shown that the cost of time in takeover transactions is less significant than traditionally asserted.

A European participant asked *Baumann* whether he would accept the Swiss solution which provides for an optional statutory 50% threshold that can be modified in the bylaws.

In his response to various contributors to the discussion, *Baumann* underlined that no Codex should or could overrule statutory law. In general, a preference of company over market interests prevails in Germany.

Regarding the above-mentioned criticism of a fraudulously low minority shareholder compensation in the Siemens/Düwag case, an American legal scholar noted that even a share price considerably lower than the market price would be something at least. Hence, there had to be some type of bargaining going on behind the scenes that led to a certain equilibrium point. A closer look into this equilibrium process would be very interesting.

Chapter 9: Disclosure and Auditing

Required Disclosure and Corporate Governance

MERRITT B. FOX, Ann Arbor

Corporate governance, not investor protection, provides the most persuasive justification for imposing on issuers the obligation to provide ongoing disclosure. Such disclosure is not necessary to protect investors against unfair prices or risk. It does, however, assist shareholders in effectively exercising their voting franchise and enforcing management's fiduciary duties. It also positively affects four of the economy's key mechanisms for controlling corporate management—the market for corporate control, share price-based managerial compensation, the cost of capital and monitoring by external sources of finance. It probably improves managerial performance as well simply by forcing managers to become more aware of reality.

This helps identify the relationship between national differences in firm governance structures and in their mandatory disclosure regimes. An examination of these differences suggests that disclosure will be less valuable in Germany and Japan, for example, than in the United States. And in fact, Germany and Japan do require less disclosure of their issuers. More study is needed, however, to determine whether differences in the amount of required disclosure has led to different national firm governance structures, or whether the disclosure differences have been naturally efficient outgrowths of firm governance structures that differ for other reasons.

Contents

A. Introduction[1]

One of the most distinctive features of American business law is the stringent requirements it imposes on the issuers of publicly traded securities to produce ongoing disclosure.[2] This scheme has usually been justified as necessary to protect investors from making damaging trading decisions as a result of being poorly informed. Little scholarly attention has been paid to the corporate governance effects of such required disclosure, the subject of this paper.[3] I conclude that required disclosure can improve corporate governance in important ways. Indeed, it is corporate governance, not investor protection, that provides the most persuasive justification for imposing on issuers the obligation to provide ongoing disclosure.

---

[1] Cf. also the sections dealing with auditing, accounting, and disclosure in the comparative contributions of Kanda and Prigge in Ch. 12 of this volume.

[2] The United Kingdom is a convenient benchmark country for comparison with the United States. The United Kingdom is considered by the SEC to have disclosure requirements that are closer to those of the United States than those of any other country except Canada. SEC Securities Act Release No. 33-6568 (Feb. 28, 1985). Nevertheless, a detailed comparison between the disclosure requirements of the United States and the United Kingdom for companies that issue equity securities reveals that the U.S. requires significantly more information. Differences include the amount of detail that must be provided describing the nature of the issuer's business, data concerning the results of the different lines of business in which the issuer participates, discussion of trends that management identifies that may affect its future liquidity, capital needs or operating results, and information about management compensation and share ownership. Landau, David, Note 'SEC Proposals to Facilitate Multinational Securities Offerings: Disclosure Requirements in the United States and the United Kingdom' 19 *N.Y.U. J. Int'l L. & Pol.* 457, 459-68 (1987). See also Benston, George *Corporate Financial Disclosure in the UK and the USA* 20-1, 37 (Westmead 1976); SEC 'Report of the Staff of the U.S. Securities and Exchange Commission to the Senate Committee on Banking, Housing and Urban Affairs and the House Committee on Energy and Commerce on the Internationalization of the Securities Market' at III-91 (1984) (hereinafter SEC 'Internationalization Report'). European countries in general put much less emphasis on full disclosure. Widmer, Peter 'The U.S. Securiti Laws—Banking Law of the World? (A Reply to Messrs. Loomis and Grant)' 1 *J. Comp. Corp. L. & Sec. Reg.* 39 (1978). Japan has a securities statute that closely parallels the Securities Act and Exchange Act of the United States. However, the staff responsible for promulgating and implementing regulations and enforcement is very small compared to that of the SEC and many provisions of the statute are treated as inoperative. The emphasis is on *de facto* screening of issuers by regulatory authorities rather than full disclosure. Hamada, Kunio and Keiji Matumator 'Securities Transaction Law in General' in: Kitagawa, Zentaro (ed.) *Doing Business in Japan* Secs. 1.02[1] and 1.02[4] (New York 1987); SEC 'Internationalization Report', supra, III-127.

The United States, in addition to having a set of regulations and an administrative apparatus that solicit more information from issuers than those of other countries, has a liability system as well that prods more information out of issuers. The liability system in the United Kingdom, for example, is not as far reaching. SEC 'Internationaliza on Report', supra, III-116.

[3] One notable exception is Lowenstein, Louis 'Financial Transparency and Corporate Governance: You Manage What You Measure' 96 *Colum L. Rev.* 1335 (1996).

Before delving further into this topic, I will define more precisely my use of the terms "required disclosure" and "corporate governance." "Required disclosure" means any kind of legal obligation that requires an issuer's management to provide on a regular basis information that it otherwise might not be inclined to provide.[4] In the United States, the primary source of required disclosure is the periodic disclosure requirements imposed on publicly traded companies under the Securities Exchange Act of 1934 (the "Exchange Act").[5] Other potential sources of required disclosure include obligations imposed by the law of the issuer's state of incorporation, by rules of a stock exchange on which the issuer's shares are listed, and by requirements imposed by the issuer's articles of incorporation.[6] Required disclosure, as I have defined it here, should be distinguished from the one-time disclosure associated with the registered offering of a new issue of securities. By "corporate governance" I mean the myriad mechanisms

---

[4] There are a number of reasons why an issuer's management might not want to produce information if it were under no legal obligation to do so. Both positive and negative information, for example, can be helpful to competitors, major suppliers, or major customers. Both positive and negative information can help a potential acquiror of the issuer better understand the issuer's business and hence decrease the risk the acquiror would incur by engaging in a hostile tender offer for the issuer. See Part C.III.1. infra. Negative information can make management look bad and increase the risk of ouster by hostile takeover or a proxy fight, threats that if postponed through non-disclosure, might by chance go away as a result of subsequent good news. Negative information can also injure the public reputations of managers and with it their sense of self-worth. See Part C.IV. infra. If management thinks that a leveraged management buyout might be in its interests, positive information would, by increasing share price, make the buyout more expensive. A variety of failures in the market for information, including "end game" problems and "market for lemons" problems, limit the usefulness of reputation alone as a method of policing this problem and create the need for a legal obligation.

[5] I am referring here to an issuer's obligations to file Form 10-K's, 10-Q's, 8-K's and its annual proxy statement.

[6] By defining required disclosure in this fashion, I seek to focus specifically on the question of the role that requiring disclosure can have on corporate governance. This is a separate question from the debate about whether the source of the requirements needs to be mandated by a national or multinational authority or whether an issuer should be able to choose the disclosure requirements, if any, under which it operates through its decisions concerning where to incorporate, where to list its stock, and what terms to include in its articles of incorporation. Commentators who believe disclosure mandated by national statute is necessary include Easterbrook, Frank and Daniel Fischel 'Mandatory Disclosure and The Protection of Investors' 70 *Va. L. Rev.* 669, 684-5 (1984); Coffee, Jr., John C. 'Market Failure and the Economic Case for a Mandatory Disclosure System' 70 *Va. L. Rev.* 717 (1984); Fox, Merritt B. 'Securities Disclosure in a Globalizing Market: Who Should Regulate Whom' 95 *Mich. L. Rev.* 2498 (1997); Bebchuk, Lucian A. 'Federalism and the Corporation: The Desirable Limits on State Competition in Corporate Law' 105 *Harv. L. Rev.* 1435, 1490-1 (1992) (placing the regulation of corporate disclosure under the authority of state corporate law rather than federal securities law would, because of regulatory competition, result in a suboptimally low level of disclosure). Commentators who believe that issuer choice, disciplined by market forces, is superior include Macey, Jonathan R. 'Administrative Agency Obsolescence and Interest Group Formation: A Case Study of the SEC at Sixty' 15 *Cardozo L. Rev.* 909, 922 (1994); Romano (this volume Ch. 3).

704   *Merritt B. Fox*   *Chapter 9*

that shape the structure of incentives, disincentives, and prohibitions in which an issuer's management makes decisions.

My inquiry will be further confined in two respects. First, while disclosure can influence corporate governance in ways that impact a variety of interests including labor, environmental quality, and the local community in which the issuer operates, my focus will be exclusively on shareholder welfare. Second, my concern here is with the corporate governance of established issuers that have shares actively trading in a public market and that do not have a control shareholder or shareholder group.

B. Corporate Governance as the Central Justification for Required Disclosure

Required disclosure is usually justified as a means of providing investors buying and selling shares in the secondary market with protection comparable to what investors buying in the primary market receive through new issue registration disclosure. Contrary to popular belief, however, required disclosure's primary social benefit is its influence on corporate governance.[7] Investor protection is a worthy goal of securities legislation in its regulation of many kinds of behavior. It is not, however, a persuasive justification for the affirmative regulation of issuer disclosure.[8] Disclosure is not necessary to protect investors against either unfair prices or risk.

To see why, first consider unfair prices. Under the efficient market hypothesis, securities prices are unbiased regardless of the amount of publicly available information about an issuer.[9] In other words, share prices will on average equal

---

[7] The discussion in this Part B is based on a portion of a recent article: Fox, Merritt B. 'Rethinking Disclosure Liability in the Modern Era' 75 *Wash. U. L.Q.* 903 (1997).

[8] I have discussed this point in considerably more detail elsewhere. Fox, supra n. 6.

[9] Empirical work showing unbiased reactions to announcements of corporate information suggests that the market is unbiased as well to issuer absences of comment about certain matters. This work consists of a large body of financial economics literature that evaluates the market reaction to the affirmative public announcement of various kinds of important events affecting particular issuers. For a classic review, see Garbade, Kenneth *Securities Markets* 249-59 (New York 1982). The typical such "event study" involves a large number of issuers, each of which has experienced at one time or another the announcement of a particular kind of important event, for example, a stock split. The studies show that the shares of the affected firms as a group experience statistically significant abnormal returns at the time of the announcement and, starting almost immediately thereafter, normal returns for the duration of the study, which is sometimes as long as several years. Thus, while some issuers' share prices go up in the periods following the announcement (compared to the market as a whole) and others go down, the average change is near 0. This suggests that as information diffuses out to a larger and larger number of investors, the price on average does not change. Thus the initial price reaction is on average the same "as if" this larger group of investors also knew the information as soon as it was released. The

the actual value of the shares involved whether issuers are required to produce a lot of disclosure or only a little. Thus greater disclosure is not necessary to protect investors from buying their shares at prices that are, on average, unfair, i.e., greater than their actual values.[10]

Now consider risk. It is true that with less information available about an issuer, share price, while still unbiased, is less accurate, i.e., it is more likely to be significantly off one way or the other from the share's actual value. If an investor has a less than fully diversified portfolio, greater share price inaccuracy can make his portfolio more risky. High quality disclosure would, to some extent, protect such an investor by reducing this risk. The investor, however, can protect himself much more effectively and at less social cost by simply diversifying more.[11]

Thus, if required disclosure has a useful function, it is its influence on corporate governance. The discussion below suggests that it has an important role in this regard.

C. Corporate Governance Effects of Required Disclosure

I. Required Disclosure's Role in Assisting the Effective Exercise of the Shareholder Franchise

The most obvious story one can tell concerning required disclosure's influence on corporate governance is that it can assist shareholders in exercising their voting franchise effectively. If shareholders are better informed when they vote to choose an issuer's directors, they are more likely to know whether their interests favor retention or ouster of the incumbents. The same is true of particular propositions subject to shareholder vote such as an amendment to the articles of incorporation, a merger, or a ratification of a transaction in which management is interested. This story, of course, is the idea behind one portion of required disclosure for U.S. issuers—the proxy rules under Section 14 of the Exchange Act—but it is applicable to all other required disclosure as well.

A sophisticated observer might respond that this story ignores the realities both of the typical individual shareholder, who has only a tiny portion of the total

announcements of events tested in this fashion are similar in kind to the types of information contained in Exchange Act filings.

[10] For an analysis of why the noise theory critique of the efficient market hypothesis still does not create a strong fairness justification for mandatory disclosure, see Fox, supra n. 6, 2533-9.

[11] In portfolio theory terms, issuer disclosure reduces firm-specific ("unsystematic") risk. Firm-specific risk can be completely eliminated by sufficient diversification. See Banoff, Barbara 'Regulatory Subsidies, Efficient Markets, and Shelf Registration: An Analysis of Rule 415' 70 *Va. L. Rev.* 135 (1984).

number of shares outstanding, and of the large shareholder, a wealthy individual or institution holding up to perhaps a few percent of the issuer's outstanding shares. The sophisticated observer would argue that in the case of the typical individual shareholder, the story rests on a mistakenly idealized view of shareholders as citizens, imbued with civic virtue, acting within a corporate democracy. In reality, all that is usually at stake in the outcome of a corporate election is money. The behavior of the typical individual shareholder can be analyzed accordingly. To such a shareholder, the information made available by required disclosure is useless. Learning this information is not worth the effort, even if the information is placed for free in her physical possession. There is only a minuscule chance that her vote will affect the outcome of the election. And in the unlikely event that it does, she receives only a tiny fraction of whatever gain her better-informed vote brings about.

As for the large shareholder, the sophisticated observer would argue that required disclosure serves no important social function. Such a shareholder can make its own inquiries of the issuer's management. It can ask a wide range of searching questions and make the appropriate negative inferences if it does not receive full answers. The information sought would be the information the large shareholder believes is most useful at the time, not a set of answers to an infrequently changed, "one-size-fits-all" set of government-mandated questions.

The sophisticated observer would be correct about the typical individual shareholder. He would be wrong about the large shareholder. Some of the very same factors that cause the typical individual shareholder to find the information not worth learning help make required disclosure vital if large shareholders are to play their most socially useful role.

The essential distinction between the typical individual shareholder and the large shareholder is that the large shareholder has a big enough stake that it would find the kind of information made freely available by required disclosure worth learning. The problem is that the large shareholder is insufficiently motivated to acquire the information if it is not made freely available. Ideally, as we will see, the amount of information that should be made available to each large shareholder would be the amount that a single owner of the same enterprise would want from an agent who was managing the enterprise. In a world without required disclosure, however, no large shareholder would be motivated to incur individually the costs of seeking out this amount of information. Huge collective action problems stand in the way.[12] Each large shareholder's expected return

---

[12] These collective action problems are reviewed in Black, Bernard S. 'Shareholder Passivity Re-examined' 89 *Mich. L. Rev.* 520 (1990). Professor Black correctly argues in his article that the problems described in the text could be at least partly overcome by cooperative action among major institutional shareholders if it were not for certain legal rules that chill such cooperation. That point, however, does invalidate the description in the text below of required disclosure as a useful antidote to these collective action problems. First of all, the existing legal regime contin-

from seeking out information is much less than that of the single owner dealing with a managing agent. Again, it is still far from certain that even the large shareholder's vote will affect the outcome of the election. If it does, the large investor would receive at most only a few percent of any gain produced by the change in outcome. There are substantial externalities when a large shareholder does receive information because that generally increases the likelihood that the shareholder will exercise its franchise in a way that will enhance the interests of all shareholders. These externalities are such that, when added up, each shareholder would find it cost-justified for it and every other shareholder to receive the same amount of information from management as the single owner would want.[13] Required disclosure can be seen, therefore, as a way of aggregating the information demands of each large shareholder for information to be provided both to itself and to other large shareholders.

A couple of other considerations favor required disclosure over each large shareholder seeking out information for itself. First, since the same information is useful to all large shareholders, there are substantial economies of scale in the issuer producing it once, for all of them, rather than giving it to each shareholder individually in response to the shareholder's particular requests. Second, in any country that prohibits trading on material non-public information received from an issuer, the large shareholder faces an additional cost in making individual inquiries. If the shareholder receives any such information in response, it is frozen in its trading of the issuer's shares until the information becomes public. Required disclosure solves this problem since the very method by which the shareholder is provided information makes it public.

---

ues to have such a chilling effect despite some recent ameliorating reforms to the proxy rules. Also, even if all rules with such a chilling effect were eliminated, the transaction costs associated with arranging the production and distribution of a public good such as information would still make cooperation expensive and imperfect. Finally, the class of shareholders that Professor Black imagines cooperating in the absence of these chilling rules—institutions each holding perhaps a few percent of the shares of an issuer that can usefully cooperate in a small coalition to affect corporate governance—are a subset of all the shareholders that I label as "large." For me, a shareholder is "large" if it is big enough that when it is presented with the information that required disclosure makes available for free, it finds the information at least worth the trouble of learning. For many issuers in many situations, the votes of shareholders that I consider "large" can in the aggregate have the potential to change the outcome of an election even though individually they are not big enough to be in the subset on which Black focuses.

[13] One qualification is in order. A single owner, who can keep the information it receives from the issuer confidential, might want information that shareholders of a publicly traded issuer might not want because the only way required disclosure can provide the information is publicly. Publicly provided information then becomes available as well to the issuer's competitors, major customers, and major suppliers, thus injuring the issuer. Mandatory disclosure imposed by a national government can be a solution to this problem, however, by putting all firms on an equal footing so that they would gain as much from the disclosure of others as they are hurt by their disclosure to others.

II. Required Disclosure's Role in Assisting Shareholders to Enforce
Management's Fiduciary Duties

A second way that required disclosure can influence corporate governance is the assistance it provides shareholders in enforcing management's fiduciary duties.[14] Absent required disclosure, when a breach of a fiduciary duty occurs, managers are not inclined to provide information suggesting its existence. Without that information, it is often impossible for shareholders to know about the breach.

A couple of examples help illustrate this point. One focus of the Exchange Act's periodic disclosure rules is the existence of transactions entered into by the issuer in which managers have an interest. Once the existence of such a conflict of interest transaction is known, shareholders can force management to meet its burden of establishing the validity of the transaction. To do this, management must show either that the taint of conflict has been removed by appropriate procedures being followed in the transaction's authorization or, alternatively, that the terms of the transaction are clearly fair to the issuer. Without shareholders knowing of the existence of such a transaction, this burden placed on management by corporate law is meaningless. Another focus of these disclosure rules is on segmented reporting: issuer performance in each of its separate lines of business. With segmented reporting, it is much easier for a shareholder to detect a decision so poor as to suggest a violation of management's duty of care. Aggregate figures, which mix such a failure in with the performances of ordinarily successful operations, are far less revealing.

The primary method for enforcement of these fiduciary duties is the shareholder derivative action. The derivative action is controversial, however, because of its "strike suit" potential. A strike suit is a non-meritorious action brought to blackmail management into a settlement so that management can avoid the costly process of continued litigation, particularly discovery. There is a tension in corporate law. It is often difficult to identify before discovery which plaintiffs have non-meritorious suits and which have meritorious ones. Thus, measures that reduce the derivative action's strike suit potential by allowing easier dismissal of derivative suits before discovery tend to be rather blunt instruments that discourage meritorious suits as well as non-meritorious ones. Without the current level of required disclosure in the United States, this tension would be much greater and the instruments much blunter, a point generally missed in the discussion of this controversy. Without required disclosure, most suits, even the ones against managers who in fact did breach their duties, would inevitably start out as "fishing expeditions." The amount of discovery that would have to be allowed for shareholder's actions to perform any deterrent function at all would have much more strike suit potential than derivative suits have today. The United

---

[14] On fiduciary duties, cf. Allen (this volume Ch. 4).

States would be faced with the unenviable choice of foreclosing even more meritorious suits or subjecting issuers to even more strike suits.

It might be argued that required disclosure will not really be that helpful in assisting enforcement of fiduciary duties because management is unlikely to disclose information indicating the breach of such a duty, even if it is supposed to do so. Because of a number of devices designed to promote disclosure, including the required involvement of independent accountants, this concern is exaggerated. To the extent that there is some truth in it, however, the concern suggests a second related function of required disclosure. An undisclosed breach of a required disclosure obligation, if ultimately detected, generates a securities law cause of action available to shareholders that is often easier to pursue than the underlying corporate law claim. Required disclosure thus creates an additional deterrent against managers breaching their fiduciary duties in the first place.

III. Required Disclosure's Indirect Impact on Corporate Governance

Required disclosure's most important, but perhaps least recognized, influences on corporate governance are indirect. These are through its positive effects on the functioning of four of the economy's key mechanisms for controlling corporate management: the market for corporate control, share-price-based managerial compensation, the cost of capital, and monitoring by external sources of finance. Through its effects on these mechanisms, required disclosure improves the selection of proposed new investment projects in the economy and the operation of its existing productive capacity.[15]

---

[15] The discussion in this Part C.III. is based on a portion of another article. See Fox, supra n. 7. See also Fox, Merritt B. 'Shelf Registration, Integrated Disclosure, and Underwriter Due Diligence: An Economic Analysis' 70 *Va. L. Rev.* 1005, 1017-25 (1984); Kahan, Marcel 'Securities Laws and the Social Costs of "Inaccurate" Stock Prices' 41 *Duke L.J.* 977 (1992). For other perspectives on the efficiency-enhancing features of securities disclosure, see Mahoney, Paul G. 'Mandatory Disclosure as a Solution to Agency Problems' 62 *U. Chi. L. Rev.* 1047 (1995) (arguing that the goal of disclosure should be focused on and limited to helping investors uncover breaches of contractual or fiduciary obligations); Kitch, Edmund W. 'The Theory and Practice of Securities Disclosure' 61 *Brook. L. Rev.* 763 (1995) (arguing that while regulators chase the goal of price accuracy enhancement, the laws enacted under this banner actually work to reduce the flow of information relevant to accurate pricing of securities); Stout, Lynn A. 'The Unimportance of Being Efficient: An Economic Analysis of Market Pricing and Securities Regulation' 87 *Mich. L. Rev.* 613 (1988) (disputing the premise that an efficient market is able to monitor or structure the allocation of scarce resources in the economy).

1. The Market for Corporate Control[16]

The market for corporate control is a well-recognized device for limiting the agency costs of management where ownership is separated from control, as in the typical publicly held corporation. More information and the resulting increase in price accuracy improves the control market's effectiveness in performing this role. A potential acquiror, in deciding whether it is worth paying what it would need to pay to acquire a target that the acquiror feels is mismanaged, must make an assessment of what the target would be worth in the acquiror's hands. This assessment is inherently risky and acquiror management is likely to be risk averse. Greater disclosure, however, reduces the riskiness of this assessment. Hence, with greater disclosure, a smaller apparent deviation between incumbent management decision making and what would maximize share value is needed to impel a potential acquiror into action.

Also, when share price is inaccurately high, even a potential acquiror that believes for sure that it can run the target better than can incumbent management may find the target not worth paying for. The increase in share price accuracy that results from greater disclosure reduces the chance that this will happen.

Greater disclosure thus makes the hostile takeover threat more real. Incumbent managers will be less tempted to implement negative net present value projects in order to maintain or enlarge their empires or to operate existing projects in ways that sacrifice profits to satisfy their personal aims. Those that nevertheless do these things are more likely to be replaced.

2. Share-Price-Based Managerial Compensation

Greater disclosure can reduce the agency cost of management in a second way, by increasing the use of share-price-based managerial compensation.[17] The problem with share-price-based compensation is risk.[18] Because of this, managers, being risk averse, will not want all of their compensation in share-price-

---

[16] Cf. also the articles in Ch. 8 of this volume on the market for corporate control.

[17] Share-price-based compensation is an affirmative way to better align the interests of management with those of shareholders. See, e.g., Jensen, Michael C. and Kevin J. Murphy 'CEO Incentives—It's Not How Much You Pay, But How' *Harvard Business Review* 68/3 (1990) 138-53. A critical review of the literature advocating greater share-price-based compensation for management can be found in Fox, Merritt B. 'Insider Trading Deterrence Versus Managerial Incentives: A Unified Theory of Section 16 (b)' 92 *Mich. L. Rev.* 2088, 2096-106 (1994).

[18] Job compensation is a large part of the typical manager's annual income. Therefore, the risk associated from receiving part or all of such compensation in share-price-based form cannot be diversified away.

based form.[19] More accurate share prices make such compensation less risky, however. As a result, managers, offered a total compensation package with a given expected value, will be willing to take a larger portion of it in stock-price-based form.

3. Capital Allocation

Required disclosure, with its resulting increase in share price accuracy, can also improve the selection of proposed new investment projects in the economy through more direct effects on the investment behavior of individual firms. This is obvious when the project under consideration would be financed with a stock sale. The important thing, however, for this inquiry, with its focus on ongoing periodic disclosure, is that share price can have a similar effect even when the firm finances the project some other way. On the supply side, share price can affect the cost of a project by affecting the terms at which intermediaries are willing to extend the firm alternative forms of external financing.[20] On the demand side, share price can affect management's willingness to use funds to implement a new project in a couple of ways. It can affect management's willingness to use debt financing because of the prospect that the firm will subsequently want to counterbalance any new debt with new equity financing in order to maintain its optimal debt/equity ratio.[21] More generally, because of

[19] There is empirical evidence to support the proposition that a reduction in the riskiness of an issuer's stock will increase the proportion of compensation a manager will be willing to take in stock-price-based form. Randall Kroszner compares the percentage of shares owned by officers and directors in a representative sample of exchange-listed U.S. firms in 1935 and one in 1995 and finds that it increased from 13% to 22%. He finds that the relationship between ownership and performance is very similar in the two periods and that the most promising explanation of the change is the reduction in stock price volatility between the first and second period. Kroszner, Randall 'Were the Good Old Days that Good? Evolution of Managerial Stock Ownership and Corporate Governance Since the Great Depression' (unpublished paper presented at the University of Michigan Department of Economics History Seminar, October 8, 1996).

[20] Kripke, Homer *The SEC and Corporate Disclosure: Regulation in Search of a Purpose* 123 (New York et al. 1979).

[21] Some financial theorists, of course, suggest that there is no optimal debt/equity ratio. For the classic statement of this view, see Modilgiani, Franco and Merton Miller 'The Cost of Capital, Corporation Finance and the Theory of Investment' *American Economic Review* 48 (1958) 261. The more orthodox view today is, however, that there are factors weighing against both too little debt and too much. Too little debt deprives a firm of its tax deductible interest payments. Too much debt leads to increased agency costs because of the resulting increased divergence between the interests of debt and equity. It also increases the likelihood of bankruptcy, which would involve real costs. For an overview of these points and the responses of the adherents of financial structure irrelevance, see Brealey, Richard A. and Stewart C. Myers *Principles of Corporate Finance* 447-66 5th edn. (New York 1996).

concern with public perceptions, low share price can constrain use of both external and internal funds.[22]

Putting these supply and demand factors together, if share price is inaccurately low, management may decide not to pursue relatively promising proposed investment projects. If it is inaccurately high, it may implement relatively unpromising proposed projects. Required disclosure, through its enhancement of price accuracy, limits this problem.

4. Reducing the Disincentives for Using External Finance

Required disclosure can reduce a managerial bias that exists toward choosing internal over external finance. Use of external finance has a favorable impact on corporate governance and so a reduction in the bias for internal finance is socially beneficial.

In the United States, as in most countries, the sale of publicly issued securities requires a disclosure-based registration of the offering. Some of the disclosure prompted by this process involves producing information that managers would rather not produce. That is why the disclosure needs to be mandated. By funding new projects with internally generated funds instead, managers can avoid having to comply with these requirements. This is a gain to them, but only if they do not need to disclose the same information, anyway, for some other reason. With required disclosure, they do. The more such information must be disclosed pursuant to required disclosure, the smaller the disclosure-avoidance-based incentive to avoid outside finance.

External finance's favorable impact on corporate governance comes from the fact that it forces managers to subject their real investment choices to the discipline and scrutiny of the market.[23] There is evidence that such scrutiny can have a very beneficial effect. Studies show that the investment projects chosen by firms relying predominantly on internal finance are considerably inferior to those chosen by other firms, an inefficiency which significantly damages the economy's growth in productivity.[24]

---

[22] See Fox, Merritt B. *Finance and Industrial Performance in a Dynamic Economy: Theory, Practice, and Policy* 282-7 (New York et al. 1987).

[23] See Easterbrook, Frank 'Two Agency-Cost Explanations of Dividends' *American Economic Review* 74 (1984) 650, 654; Fox, supra n. 22, 132-40.

[24] See, for example, Donaldson, Gordon *Corporate Debt Capacity* (Homewood, Ill. 1961); Baumol, William J., Peggy Heim, Burton G. Malkiel, and Richard E. Quandt 'Earnings Retention, New Capital and the Growth of the Firm' *Review of Economics and Statistics* 52 (1970) 345. For a critical review of these and several other studies, as well as an estimate of the magnitude of the effects on the economy, see Fox, supra n. 22, 233-7.

The hostile takeover activity of the late 1980s can be seen as a reaction to this problem. It was concentrated in industries where firms had large "free cash flows."[25] In such cases, often the object of the acquiror was to undertake a leveraged financial restructuring of the target in order to increase the payout of cash flow to the market. Alternatively, it was to "bust up" the target by separating, into different corporations, operations producing high cash flows from operations into which these cash flows were previously being inadvisedly poured.[26] The hostile takeover boom may have partially corrected the problem of suboptimal projects funded by internal funds, but it entailed enormous transaction costs. And, with the subsequent spate of state anti-takeover statutes, hostile takeovers may be less effective at playing this role today. Required disclosure, by increasing what firms disclose as a matter of course, reduces the amount of additional disclosure needed when a firm publicly offers new securities. By reducing one of the disincentives for external finance, it can help diminish the problem of poor investment projects in a much less expensive way than hostile takeovers.

IV. Required Disclosure's Role in Raising Managerial Consciousness

Professor Louis Lowenstein has argued that required disclosure can improve managerial performance simply by forcing managers to become more aware of reality. He is thus suggesting that required disclosure will favorably change managerial behavior in ways above and beyond the effects it will have on the various outside forces bearing down on management discussed above: shareholder votes, shareholder enforcement of managerial fiduciary duties, and the various indirect mechanisms of control in our economy. Lowenstein states that a CEO's "capacity for denial is no less than ours."[27]

The idea here is that when managers have the legal obligation to disclose certain information, they may have to gather and analyze a variety of information they would otherwise ignore. The proposition that this consciousness raising will lead to an improvement in shareholder welfare rests on two assumptions. The first assumption is that without required disclosure, management will not gather

---

[25] Jensen, Michael C. 'Agency Costs of Free Cash Flow, Corporate Finance and Takeovers' *American Economic Review Papers and Proceedings* 76 (1986) 323.

[26] Jensen, Michael C. 'The Modern Industrial Revolution, Exit, and the Failure of Internal Control Systems' *Journal of Finance* 48 (1993) 831; Kraakman, Reinier 'Taking Discounts Seriously: The Implications of "Discounted" Share Prices as an Acquisition Motive' 88 *Colum. L. Rev.* 891 (1988).

[27] Lowenstein, supra n. 3, 1342. Lowenstein suggests, as examples of this kind of benefit from required disclosure, the testimony of officials of two European firms that their firms enjoyed managerial improvements as a result of submitting to the U.S. mandatory disclosure regime. Lowenstein, supra n. 3, 1357.

and analyze all of the information that could, in a cost-effective fashion, help it pursue its own objective function. The second assumption is that the managerial objective function is sufficiently congruent with the best interests of shareholders that if management, because of required disclosure, figures out better how to pursue its objective function, the actions it will take will also improve shareholder welfare. Both assumptions, though debatable, are plausible.

Despite the outside forces bearing down on management, few people would insist that management does not have at least some degree of slack. In other words, agency costs can be minimized, but not eliminated. Within this zone of slack, managerial behavior can appropriately be analyzed in accordance with the behavioral theory of the firm. Using this theory, it is easy to imagine that management might not gather and analyze certain kinds of negative information even though knowing the information would help management maximize its own objective function.[28] Required disclosure, because of its "investor protection" emphasis on negative information, might help correct the problem.

There are also reasons to believe that management's objective function and the best interests of shareholders are reasonably congruent in the ways that matter here. A corporate manager, like anyone, can be expected to value compensation, perquisites, respect, power, affection, a sense of rectitude, and job security. The sources of these valued things are the firm's current and future cash flow, firm size and firm growth. To maximize these sources, management must operate each of the firm's existing facilities in a way that maximizes the discounted present value of its cash flow and must identify, in rank order, as many promising new projects as possible for possible implementation. Both kinds of actions are ones that shareholders would want managers to undertake.[29] It is certainly

---

[28] See March, James and Herbert Simon *Organizations* (New York 1958); Cyert, Richard and James March *A Behavioral Theory of the Firm*, (Englewood Cliffs, N.J. 1963). In these models of organizational behavior, of all the information potentially available to a firm, a select subgroup is processed and evokes reaction. The selection and reaction is characterized by stable decision rules which in the past have satisfied management's performance aspirations and which will remain in effect until there is a failure to meet these aspirations.

It is reasonable to think that the blind spots resulting from these rules of information selection can be shaped by, among other things, cognitive dissonance. See Akerlof, George and R. William Pickens 'The Economic Consequences of Cognitive Dissonance' *American Economic Review* 72 (1982) 307. In accordance with the behavioral theory of the firm, the consequence is that certain kinds of bad news will be avoided until, if ever, the practice of avoiding it leads to serious trouble.

[29] The primary divergence between the managerial objective function and the best interests of shareholders develops where management cannot identify a sufficient number of positive net present value projects to exhaust its current cash flow. In such a situation, shareholders would want the remaining cash flow paid out to them, whereas management would want to retain it to fund additional projects. The management of such a firm, as long as it can keep its job, gains from using these internally generated funds to implement any project that has a positive expected return, even if the project's expected return is well below what shareholders could earn on the

plausible that required disclosure could enhance management's ability to perform the first action and there is no reason to believe that it would hinder its ability to perform the second. By revealing problems in existing operations with respect to which a firm's information system would otherwise have a blind spot, required disclosure can help management pursue its objective function (holding constant, for purposes of this part of the analysis, outside forces bearing down on management) and help shareholders at the same time. Reinforcing all of this is the fact that the typical manager's self-esteem depends in part on his public image and required disclosure will therefore make him try harder to avoid taking actions that will generate negative information.

D. National Differences in Mandatory Disclosure

This paper can help identify the relationship between national differences in firm governance structures and in their mandatory disclosure regimes. Disclosure has costs associated with it as well as benefits. Given existing differences in firm governance structures among countries, there are likely to be important differences among issuers worldwide in terms of the level of disclosure that will maximize the returns (net of the costs of this disclosure) that their capital-utilizing productive activities generate.

The decisions of a publicly held firm are the product of both its internal decision-making structure and the external environment that provides the inputs that make this structure function (most importantly for our concerns, shareholder votes and new capital). The internal decision-making structure arises out of a combination of the law of the jurisdiction of incorporation and the issuer country's traditional business customs and practices.[30] The external environment is determined by a number of factors including the degree of concentration of share ownership, the nature of the holders of any such concentrated blocks, the rules and practices under which these holders use their voting power singly and in cooperation with others, the extent to which the legal system and suppliers of finance facilitate or hinder hostile takeovers, and the relative availability of financing in different forms (equity versus debt) and from different sources (private versus public markets.)

Comparative corporate governance has become an important subject for legal and financial scholars in recent years and the resulting studies show significant contrasts among countries in both internal decision structures and external

money, i.e., the project has a negative net present value. I work out these points about the managerial objective function in significantly more detail in Fox, supra n. 22, 116-50.

[30] Custom and practice includes both the typical terms of the firm's articles of incorporation and how people typically behave within a given set of publicly and privately imposed legal constraints.

environments.[31] These contrasts suggest differences in the extent to which required disclosure will be effective in helping to align managerial and shareholder interests and in assuring the best choice of real investment projects. That, in turn, suggests that one country's optimal level of disclosure may be higher than another's (optimal being defined as the level at which the required disclosure's marginal benefits just equal its marginal costs).

By way of illustration, a set of rough contrasts can be made between the U.S. (and Canada and, to a lesser extent, the U.K.) on the one hand and Germany and Japan on the other. These contrasts suggest significant differences in the value of disclosure. Voting power in U.S. issuers is less concentrated and institutional investors in U.S. issuers are less inclined, separately or together, to exercise their voting power to influence corporate decisions.[32] Debt/equity ratios are lower[33] and there is more use of publicly offered equity as a source of finance,[34] particularly by relatively new companies financing major projects. Hostile tender offers are more frequent, as are solicitations of public shareholders in proxy fights. In contrast, in Germany and Japan, institutional investors play a larger role both in monitoring managerial behavior and in supplying finance, mostly debt.[35]

The picture painted here suggests that the optimal level of disclosure for U.S. issuers would be higher than for German and Japanese ones. U.S. institutional investors monitor less the way managers of U.S. issuers make both operating and project choice decisions. They collect, analyze, and act on less information (both public and non-public) concerning these matters. Thus more of the work of aligning managerial and shareholder interests with respect to these decisions falls to the hostile takeover threat and share-price-based managerial compensation, both of which are assisted by greater public disclosure. Greater disclosure and its enhancement of share price accuracy is also of more assistance to good project choice in the U.S. because of the greater reliance by U.S. "start-up" companies

[31] See, e.g., Roe, Mark J. *Strong Managers, Weak Owners: The Political Roots of American Corporate Finance* (Princeton 1994); Black Bernard S. and John C. Coffee, Jr. 'Hail Britannia? Institutional Investor Behavior Under Limited Regulation' 92 *U. Mich. L. Rev.* 1997 (1994).

[32] See, e.g., Roe, supra n. 31, 22, 169-70.

[33] E.g., Browne, Francis X. 'Corporate Finance: Stylized Facts and Tentative Explanations' *Applied Economics* 26 (1994) 485, 488. ("[Non-financial f]irms in securities-based financial systems (the United States, the United Kingdom, and Canada . . .) have quite low debt/equity ratios compared to those in the bank-based systems of Japan, Germany and France.")

[34] E.g., Browne, supra n. 33, 494 (stating that external funding is significantly greater in the United States, the United Kingdom, and Canada than in Japan and continental Europe).

[35] Japanese firms borrow $5.33 from banks for every dollar they raise in the capital markets, German firms $4.20, and American firms $0.85. Macey, Jonathan R. and Geoffrey P. Miller 'Corporate Governance and Commercial Banking: A Comparative Examination of Germany, Japan, and the United States' 48 *Stan. L. Rev.* 73, 85, 89 (1995).

on the public equity markets.[36] The choice of required disclosure levels by these different countries conforms with what this rough illustration calls for. The United States and Canada require the most, Germany and Japan the least, with the U.K. somewhere in between.[37]

E. Conclusion

This paper demonstrates that required disclosure can play an important role in corporate governance. It assists shareholders in effectively exercising their voting franchise and enforcing management's fiduciary duties. It has positive effects on four of the economy's key mechanisms for controlling corporate management— the market for corporate control, share-price-based managerial compensation, the cost of capital, and monitoring by external sources of finance. In so doing, it improves the selection of proposed new investment projects in the economy and the operation of existing facilities. Finally it also probably improves managerial performance simply by forcing managers to become more aware of reality.

All of this can help identify the relationship between national differences in firm governance structures and in their mandatory disclosure regimes. Disclosure has costs associated with it as well as benefits. Existing differences in firm governance structures from one country to another would suggest that the efficient level of required disclosure for firms of one country is not necessarily the same as the efficient level for firms of another country. In fact, we see that countries whose firm governance structures suggest disclosure would be of less value—Germany and Japan—have lower levels of mandatory disclosure than in the United States.

What is less clear is the direction of causation in this observed relationship between disclosure and governance structures. Did differences in the amount of required disclosure lead to different national firm governance structures or are the disclosure differences naturally efficient outgrowths of firm governance structures that differ for other reasons? Would the introduction of U.S.-style mandatory disclosure in Germany and Japan lead to changes in their firm governance structures, and if so would the changes be desirable? If it would not lead to such changes, would it nevertheless improve in a cost-effective way the functioning of their current governance structures? This paper is at most only

---

[36] Ronald Gilson and Bernard Black show that the prospect of a vibrant market for initial public offerings in the United States for issuers that have shown a certain degree of success greatly facilitates the earlier provision of venture capital to get them off the ground in the first place and explains why there is so much more venture capital available in the United States. Black, Bernard S. and Ronald J. Gilson 'Venture Capital and the Structure of Capital Markets: Banks versus Stock Markets' *Journal of Financial Economics* 47 (1998) 243-77.

[37] See supra n. 2.

suggestive in helping to answer these important questions and they are worthy topics of discussion and further research.

Disclosure and Auditing as Affecting Corporate Governance

JÖRG BAETGE and STEFAN THIELE, Münster

The authors discuss the role of disclosure and auditing within the system of corporate governance. As basic functions of disclosure, the direct and the indirect monitoring effect can be distinguished. Accordingly, there are specific basic demands to be met by disclosure. The actual accounting rules do not fulfill the requirements resulting from the task of management monitoring to an "optimum" extent. By means of creative accounting, the managers seem to be able to cover up the financial position shown in the annual report. The problem of the traditional financial statement analysis is that the correct ratios must be selected and interpreted by the analyst in a subjective way. With the help of mathematical-statistical methods, the relevant ratios can be selected and weighted objectively. Another empirical research project shows that the quality of German annual reports has continually improved within recent years.

Within the system of corporate governance, the auditor actually has two functions: first, the auditor guarantees the reliability of the information disclosed by the company; and second, the auditor must evaluate and report on the economic position of the company in the auditor's report.

Contents

Figures

Tables

A. Introduction[1]

In Germany as well as in the U.S., the discussion on the corporate governance of public corporations has a long history. Retrospectively, it becomes obvious that corporate crises have often given rise to scientific inquiries into this issue and, in addition, have resulted in modifications of statutory provisions. In the past, such changes in statutory provisions resulting from corporate crises have most often also affected the regulations concerning disclosure and auditing, as shown by the reaction to the so-called *Gründerkrise* (founders' crisis) in the form of the stock corporation law reform of 1884 in Germany, or by reforms subsequent to the Great Depression, i.e., the introduction of an obligatory annual audit in Germany in 1931 and the creation of the capital market law in the U.S. in 1933/34.

At this point, parallels to the current situation—which is characterized by a discussion on corporate law in almost every industrialized country[2]—become evident. Again, corporate breakdowns in Germany,[3] such as the ones connected with the names *Metallgesellschaft* or *Bremer Vulkan*, have led to a renewed discussion on corporate governance in quoted companies, and once again this discussion includes questions of disclosure and auditing. It must be noted, however, that the discussion about corporate law in quoted companies is not only a topical issue in Germany.

Accordingly, the role of disclosure and auditing within the system of corporate governance shall be assessed in the following. The terms "disclosure" or

---

[1] Cf. also the sections dealing with auditing, accounting, and disclosure in the comparative contributions of Kanda and Prigge in Ch. 12 of this volume.

[2] See the extensive reports including recommendations concerning the shaping of corporate law in the U.S. and the United Kingdom: American Law Institute (1994), Cadbury Committee (1992).

[3] Similarly spectacular breakdowns of renowned companies have also taken place in other industrialized countries, e.g., Maxwell companies, BCCI, and Barings in the U.K.

"financial reporting" usually cover all forms of corporate reporting as to third parties. Besides the financial statements, this also includes the management report, interim financial reporting, and timely disclosure of material events, as well as other special duties of disclosure of capital market law, e.g., in case of security issues. In the following, however, the discussion will be restricted to the financial statements, since they are still of prime importance as compared to the numerous other duties of disclosure.

B. Disclosure and Corporate Governance

I. Monitoring Effects of Disclosure

On account of the separation of ownership and control,[4] in the current discussion on corporate governance all experts agree that it is necessary to provide instruments safeguarding management activities that go together with shareholder interests.[5] And yet, the discussion over which incentive and monitoring instruments might be the right ones for this purpose is quite controversial.[6] With regard to this study, monitoring mechanisms implemented inside the company organization as well as monitoring mechanisms related to the market prove to be relevant.

Monitoring mechanisms inside the company organization are set to work by units of supervision independent of the management and endowed with decision-making and monitoring power. These units put limits on management power (e.g., through duties of approval) and control the exertion of power. In accordance with German corporate law, the supervisory board functions as a monitoring unit independent of the management. In the Anglo-Saxon board model, such a monitoring unit is not explicitly included. In American publications, however, it has been strongly called for,[7] and within large quoted U.S. companies, management supervision by an independent audit committee is customary.[8] Hence, the American board model shows a tendency towards the dual system.[9] In order to become able to work effectively, the supervisory board as well as the audit committee must be provided with enough information to make it possible

---

[4] This problem was already described in detail by Berle/Means (1932).

[5] See Ebke (1994: 9); Hart (1995: 681).

[6] For a survey of this discussion, see Eisenberg (1976: 18-29); Klein/Coffee (1996: 177-206); Merkt (1991: 67-112).

[7] See Eisenberg (1975: 375-439); American Law Institute (1994: 103-4). For the U.K., see also the suggestions of the Cadbury Committee (1992: par. 4.13).

[8] See Windbichler (1985: 50); American Law Institute (1994: 107) with further references.

[9] Buxbaum (1996: 69).

to decide on potential approvals and to unmask management errors.[10] The corporate financial statements supply additional information in this respect. It must be noted, however, that the supervisory board's rights to be given information in accordance with German corporate law [par. 90, 111 (2), 170, 337 AktG (German Stock Corporation Act)] are more far-reaching, so that the financial statements are not the only source of information. Supplying the supervisory board with information is rather a by-product of accounting that is irrelevant for what is going to be further discussed in this study.

The supervisory board and the audit committee are certainly the most important but by no means the only monitoring institutions in a quoted company. The management power is further restricted and controlled by the participatory rights of shareholders in the general meeting, e.g., through the participation of the shareholders in crucial corporate decision making and through the discharge of the managing board.[11] This requires providing information to the shareholders by means of corporate disclosure, thereby creating a *direct monitoring effect*.

By means of the disclosed financial statements, the management informs investors about the activities of the past financial year. Thus, disclosure enables the investors to judge what the management was able to realize with the capital left at its disposal. On the basis of the disclosed information, the shareholders get the chance to assess the achievement of their management, e.g., in comparison to the achievements of other managers. Therefore, disclosure is also an essential instrument with regard to the general meeting because it supplies the shareholders with the information needed to exert their rights there. Thus, the management is forced to justify its activities to the shareholders. The monitoring effect resulting from this has primarily a preventive function.

The organizational monitoring mechanisms that have been discussed so far are juxtaposed with the supervision of the management through the capital market. In this context, the *indirect monitoring effect* of corporate disclosure must be seen, since for shareholders and potential shareholders, disclosure functions as an important basis of their investment decisions. Hence, indirectly, it is required to make the monitoring of the management by the capital market "work". The monitoring function of the capital market is based on the fact that the information on the corporate economic position is mirrored by the share prices. The disclosure of negative financial data will lead to falling share prices and thereby to rising corporate capital costs which, from the point of view of the management, should be avoided. In addition, some experts focus on the monitoring effect resulting from impending unfriendly takeovers.[12] If the bad company earnings are a result of management errors, there will be the danger of

---

[10] See Ordelheide (1995: 94).

[11] See Großfeld/Ebke (1978: 409-10); Hart (1995: 682).

[12] See Beaver (1981: 168); Schildbach (1986: 16).

an unfriendly takeover, since potential buyers will try to make better use of the resources inherent in the company.[13] As a rule, the managers of a company will lose their jobs if their company is taken over. Therefore, managers committed to acting reasonably will be strongly interested in good economic results and high share prices to counter unfriendly takeovers. In aggregate economic terms, the indirect monitoring effect of disclosure also makes the capital invested on the capital market work as effectively as possible (the capital allocation function of accounting). For it is nothing but evident that only a detailed and reliable corporate disclosure enables the shareholders to assess the consequences of their investment decisions well enough to direct the capital to the most profitable ventures.

Accordingly, within the field of corporate monitoring, accounting and disclosure with their direct and indirect monitoring effects are of double importance.

II. Demands to Be Met by Accounting When Functioning as a Monitoring Instrument

Because of the double function of accounting within the system of corporate monitoring described above, two basic demands to be met by disclosure can be distinguished:

- By revealing the management results to the shareholders, disclosure makes a direct monitoring of the management possible.
- By providing the information required by the shareholders to invest or disinvest as efficiently as possible, disclosure makes an indirect monitoring of the management possible.

These two statements will have to be further explained in the following.

The direct monitoring of the management by the shareholders is influenced by the principal-agent relationship between management and shareholders that has often been described before.[14] The core problem of that relationship is that the agent need not necessarily act according to the interests of his principal, whereas the principal has to bear the consequences of the agent's activities in any case. This problem can be solved—or at least reduced—either by means of incentives offered to the agent, which will not be further discussed in this paper, or by a supervision of the agent from the side of the principal. It is, however, characteristic of the principal-agent relationship between shareholders and management that an effective monitoring of the management by the shareholders or by the supervisory board does not work that easily. As a matter of course, the management is better informed than its supervisors, and the management activities can

---

13 See Manne (1965); Meier-Schatz (1985).
14 See, e. g., Jensen/Meckling (1976: 305).

of course not be monitored by means of a target-performance comparison. Managers must make decisions, an activity which necessarily requires a subjective assessment of future events. Thus, for the supervisors, the management activities are only observable to a limited extent, leaving the danger of hidden action.[15]

In contrast, the financial result of all management activities to be measured by accounting and to be brought to their notice can be seen by the shareholders. Still, the problem remains that this financial result does not exclusively correspond to the achievements of the management but is also influenced by other factors, e.g., unforeseen setbacks in economic activity, an economic upspring above average, reunification, strike, or other extraordinary events. Thus, accounting must make sure that the past financial year is shown in such a way that the achievement of the management can be adequately assessed. And yet, in accordance with the basic idea of calling someone to account, it should be the main concern of accounting to provide a basis for the assessment of management achievements.

Far from any claims to completeness, this means in detail:
• The calculation of an operating profit which is not influenced by extraordinary, nonoperating, or aperiodical expenses or income, and thus discloses the profit resulting from the bottom line.
• Accounting principles as clear as possible that make it almost impossible for the management to present the economic position according to their personal desires by making use of options to include assets or liabilities into the balance sheets, by choosing different methods of valuation, or by arranging facts.
• The disclosure of the sales and profits of individual corporate segments (segment reporting) in order to ensure that mismanagement in one segment cannot be concealed by balancing it with profits from another segment.

The indirect monitoring of management by the shareholders comes into effect through the decision of the shareholders concerning the purchase or sale of shares and the corresponding market reactions. Accordingly, shareholders require the kind of information that gives them a basis for their investment decisions. In an ideal case, the shareholders would require the data necessary for the calculation of earning power, i.e., information on the future corporate profits or cash flows and on the future dividends. These demands comprise the starting point for the reflections on the objective of decision-usefulness, which is mentioned as a guiding principle in the framework of U.S. accounting (SFAC No. 1).

For some good reason, however, this guiding principle has not been transformed into precise regulations in the U.S. GAAP in such a manner that the companies are to report only on their future projects. Only data from the past can

---

[15] For the basic idea of hidden action, see Arrow (1985: 43-5).

be checked by the shareholders; moreover, these data form the basis of future corporate development.[16] Information purely related to the future may in principle be very useful to the shareholders; and yet at the same time it is not very reliable because it is influenced to a high degree by subjective estimates. Thus, it comes to a conflict between the usefulness and the reliability of data: the more useful a piece of information is to a shareholder, the less reliable it proves to be and vice versa. Despite the decision-usefulness approach in principle, U.S. accounting is therefore also based on data from the past.

In the end, this means that the indirect monitoring of management can be based on the same accounting as the direct monitoring. And yet, the accounting oriented at the past should be completed by information related to the future. This is also an integral part of the German accounting principles which force the company to report on prospective corporate development in the management report. One argument that is frequently put forward against a reporting practice related to the future is that future development is subject to insecurity and depends on numerous external factors. This is true, but it does not speak against the future-related disclosure, for this level of insecurity can be taken into account by not merely stating the prospective corporate development but also the assumptions concerning the general framework (e.g., concerning the development of the dollar exchange rate) underlying the corporate planning.

III. Do German and American Accounting Principles Meet These Requirements?

As depicted above, accounting principles ought to be as clear as possible and should limit the influence of the management on the annual financial statements as much as possible. This requirement is countered by the fact that companies may have options to include assets or liabilities into the balance sheet and choose between different techniques of valuation in accounting (alternative accounting methods), since the latter are likely to distort the information on the corporate economic position with the passage of time and in comparison to other companies. Thus, the alternative accounting methods provided by the German accounting rules have become subject to severe criticism.[17] The intentional creation of hidden reserves is also contrary to the aim of a clear and unambiguous net income statement since these hidden reserves may secretly be released in less profitable years or in periods of losses. Accordingly, the management might thereby be able to cover up a critical economic situation for some time.

---

[16] See Lowenstein (1996: 1343-4).

[17] See Ordelheide (1995: 92).

However, the basic problem of management monitoring by means of disclosure will continue to exist even if the alternative accounting methods are abolished and the intentional creation of hidden reserves is prohibited: the preparation of the financial statements as a monitoring instrument is still an assignment of the body to be supervised. As there is always room for estimation and creative thinking that approaches manipulation, managers will always feel inclined to shape the financial statements according to their own interests. That this is also true for the U.S. GAAP is shown by the discussion on restructuring costs that has been going on there since the beginning of the nineties.[18] Under the item "restructuring", many large U.S. companies listed high lump-sum spending, especially depreciation costs, so that subsequent financial years showed considerably less spending.[19] Through this high lump-sum depreciation, the total and equity capital was also considerably reduced, thus leading to a positive development of the ratios "return on equity" and "return on investment". Because of their nature as lump-sum and extraordinary expenses, the restructuring costs were not taken into account by the analysts; the same is true for the positive effect on subsequent financial years.[20] Nowadays the SEC checks the cases in which restructuring costs are disclosed on an individual basis.

The examples given above show that there is no accounting which fulfills the requirements resulting from the task of management monitoring to an "optimum" extent. And yet, the empirical studies to be further explained on the following pages have confirmed the high validity of the "suboptimal" accounting instruments currently being used.

IV. Empirical Results as to the Validity of Financial Statements

Financial statements are meant to enable their users to evaluate the corporate economic position. With the traditional financial statement analysis there is, however, the problem that the correct ratios must be selected by the analyst subjectively (on an empirical basis); moreover, this analyst must also sum up the messages of these ratios—that might even be contradictory—in a "correct" but subjective final judgment on the corporate economic position. In order to handle the assignments of ratio selection and the shaping of a final judgment in an objective way, the relevant ratios were, with reference to mathematical-statistical methods, selected and weighted by means of artificial neuronal networks on a broad empirical basis at the Institute of Accounting and Auditing (IRW) at

---

[18] See Monks/Minow (1991: 175-6); Lowenstein (1996: 1350-2).

[19] Lowenstein (1996: 1350), refers to an inquiry that describes that in the years 1991-1993, 80% of the 30 Dow Jones Industrial companies claimed restructuring costs.

[20] See Lowenstein (1996: 1351).

Münster University.[21] Thousands of financial statements of partly "sound" and partly future insolvent companies supplied the empirical basis. With the help of the mathematical-statistical methods, a large number of financial statements of solvent and future insolvent companies could be analyzed objectively in order to find out which ratios—out of a catalog of 209 ratios—best separated solvent companies and companies in danger of insolvency, thereby considering the right combinations and weighting. By means of the discriminatory algorithms derived thereof, most of the companies that will become insolvent in the future can reliably be identified three years prior to the start of the crisis; this was checked on the basis of a large-scale validation sample. Here the optimum artificial neuronal network BP-14[22], developed by means of artificial neuronal network analysis, separated future solvent from future insolvent companies with an α-error of 8.75% and a β-error of 33.55%. Consequently, out of a number of 100 future insolvent companies, only 8.75 companies were wrongly classified as solvent, whereas out of a number of 100 future solvent companies, 33.55 companies were strongly classified as being in danger of insolvency. The following diagram shows the ratios of the artificial neuronal network BP-14 that were selected as optimum ones and the corresponding working hypotheses (Hyp.). The hypothesis $I < S$ with respect to the capital structure ratios (CS 1 and CS 2), for example, signifies that the average values of the ratios from the insolvent companies (I) are smaller than the average values from the solvent companies (S).

Table 1: Ratios of the Artificial Neuronal Network BP-14

Duration of Capital Turnover		
Ratio	Definition	Hyp.
DCT 1	$\dfrac{\text{(acceptance liabilities + trade liabilities)} \times 360}{\text{gross performance}}$	I>S
DCT 2	$\dfrac{\text{(acceptance liabilities + trade liabilities)} \times 360}{\text{sales}}$	I>S

[21] See Niehaus (1987); Baetge/Huß/Niehaus (1988); Baetge (1989); Feidicker (1992); Krause (1993); Baetge (1994); Baetge/Feidicker (1994); Baetge et al. (1994); Stibi (1994); Hüls (1995); Baetge/Kruse/Uthoff (1996); Uthoff (1997). Former studies in this field came from Beaver (1966) and Altman (1968).

[22] BP-14 stands for *back*propagation network with *14* ratios. For further information, see Baetge/Kruse/Uthoff (1996); Wilhelm (1997) and the interview with Baetge in *manager-magazin* (September 1997) 106-11.

Capital Turnover		
Ratio	Definition	Hyp.
CT	short-term bank liabilities + short-term trade liabilities + acceptance liabilities + short-term other liabilities —————————————————— sales	I>S

Indebtment		
Ratio	Definition	Hyp.
IDM 1	short-term outside capital —————————— balance sheet total	I>S
IDM 2	trade liabilities + acceptance liabilities + bank liabilities —————————————————————— outside capital - advance payment from customers	I>S

Capital Structure		
Ratio	Definition	Hyp.
CS 1	equity capital - intangible assets ———————————————————————————— balance sheet total - intangible assets - liquid funds - land and buildings	I<S
CS 2	equity capital + provision ———————————————————— balance sheet total - liquid funds - land and buildings	I<S

Financial Power		
Ratio	Definition	Hyp.
FP 1	cash flow relating to income ———————————————————— outside capital - advance payments from customers	I<S
FP 2	cash flow relating to income ———————————————————— short-term outside capital + medium-term outside capital	I<S

Coverage		
Ratio	Definition	Hyp.
CVR	equity capital	I<S
	tangible fixed assets + land and buildings	

Profitability		
Ratio	Definition	Hyp.
PFT 1	operating result	I<S
	sales	
PFT 2	cash flow relating to income	I<S
	balance sheet total	
PFT 3	cash flow relating to income + pension provision influx	I<S
	balance sheet total	

Personnel Expenses Ratio		
Ratio	Definition	Hyp.
PER	personnel expenses	I>S
	gross performance	

As shown in Table 1, the suitability of financial statements as a monitoring instrument is considerably reduced through alternative accounting methods and chances of estimation. By means of creative accounting, the managers seem to be able to cover up the actual corporate economic position. In the research program of the IRW, the challenge inherent in creative accounting was accepted and countered by means of a system of creative analyzing. In other words, ratios were developed which are not influenced or influenced only to a very small degree by accounting policy. These ratios resistant to accounting policy can be arrived at by eliminating those elements of the financial statements from the computational formula that can be influenced to a large extent by accounting policy. An example of a "creative ratio" is the first equity ratio (CS 1) used in BP-14. Whenever this equity ratio is calculated, the intangible assets, liquid funds, and buildings are left aside. The reason for this is that there are many possibilities of alternative accounting for intangibles. In addition, managers often enough increase liquid funds only for balance sheet day to dress their windows. Some companies sell and lease back their land and buildings to increase their equity ratios. In order to possibly make a better comparison among all the rated companies, the equity ratio CS 1 is contructed in this way.

In addition, the BP-14 ratios have revealed that a change in accounting from HGB (= German Commercial Code) to U.S. GAAP or to the International Accounting Standards (IAS) has only a marginal impact on the amount of the calculated total index (N-value). Table 2 shows the net income and the equity amounts of the Daimler-Benz Group for the years 1995 and 1996, each calculated according to HGB and U.S. GAAP.

Table 2:   Profit/Net Loss, Cash Flow, Equity Amounts, and N-Values of the Daimler-Benz Group for the Years 1995-1996

	Accounting According to HGB				Accounting According to U.S. GAAP			
Year	Profit or Net Loss (million DM)	Cash Flow (million DM)	Equity (million DM)	N-Value	Profit or Net Loss (million DM)	Cash Flow (million DM)	Equity (million DM)	N-Value
1995	−5,734	4,400	13,842	2.38	−5,729	3,800	24,184	2.44
1996	2,689	5,800	16,787	2.65	2,762	6,900	27,329	3.17

Source: Annual Reports 1995 and 1996 of the Daimler-Benz AG.

In 1995, the Daimler-Benz Group reported an equity capital of DM 13.8 billion according to HGB, and of DM 24.1 billion according to U.S. GAAP. In spite of this enormous difference in equity representing DM 10.3 billion, the difference in the N-values only came to 0.06. Although the equity capital was almost doubled by Daimler-Benz, the N-value only changed by 0.3% on the basis of the 20 N-points of the whole N-scale. In 1996 the Daimler-Benz equity capital amounted to DM 16.8 billion according to HGB. In the U.S. GAAP statements of the same group, an equity capital of DM 27.3 billion was shown. The difference in cash flow for 1996 was even DM 1.1 billion. Despite these great differences in equity (DM 10.5 billion) and cash flows, the difference in N-values only came to 0.52 (2.6%). Figure 1 shows the N-value slope of the Daimler-Benz Group for accounting in accordance with either HGB or U.S. GAAP.

The same applies to the VEBA Group, for which the N-values on the basis of the 1993 HGB statements were contrasted with the respective U.S. GAAP statements (Figure 2). The deviation was so small that it could be ignored.

The comparison between HGB and IAS accounting for the Hoechst Group led to a similar result (Figure 3).

Figure 1: N-Value Slope of the Daimler-Benz Group for Accounting According to Either HGB or to U.S. GAAP

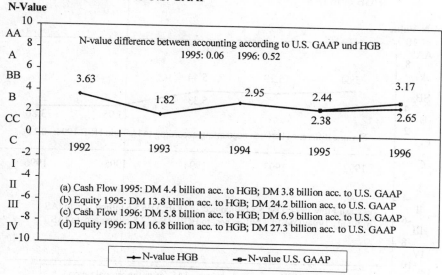

Figure 2: N-Value Slope of the VEBA Group for Accounting According to Either HGB or to U.S. GAAP

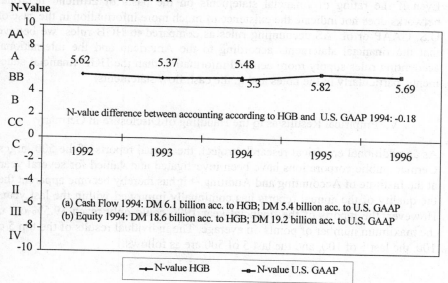

Figure 3:   N-Value Slope of the Hoechst Group for Accounting According to Either
             HGB or to IAS

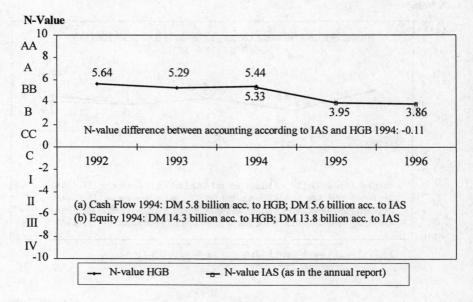

Even if the rating of financial statements on the basis of artificial neuronal networks does not indicate the existence of much more information in the case of U.S. GAAP or of IAS accounting rules as compared to HGB rules, we believe that the financial statements according to the American and the international accounting rules supply more detailed information than the HGB financial statements, particularly in the notes and in the cash flow statements.

V. Empirical Results as to the Handling of Disclosure in Germany

As an additional empirical research project, the annual reports of the 500 largest German public corporations have been investigated and valued for several years at the Institute of Accounting and Auditing.[23] It has thereby become apparent that the quality of the annual reports has continually improved within the last years. However, the reports of the financial year 1996 could only reach 39.5% out of the maximum number of points on average. The individual results of the top 5 of 100, the last 5 of 100, and the last 5 of 500 are as follows:

---

[23] See Baetge/Armeloh/Schulze (1997a, b).

Table 3: Quality of the Annual Reports for the Financial Year 1996 for the 500 Largest German Quoted Companies

Annual Report (total)	Company	Quality max. 100%
Top 5 of 100	VEBA AG	76.3%
	Bayer AG	75.7%
	Thyssen AG	74.4%
	RWE AG	69.9%
	Daimler-Benz AG	69.6%
Last 5 of 100	Herlitz AG	49.1%
	Preussag Stahl AG	49.0%
	WERU AG	49.0%
	PWA AG	48.8%
	KM Europa Metal AG	48.7%
Last 5 of 500	Rathgeber AG	14.2%
	Maschinenfabrik Esslingen AG	14.1%
	MCS AG	13.8%
	Tucher Bräu AG	13.7%
	Hamburger Getreide-Lagerhaus AG	12.4%

Especially striking is the extremely poor reporting on future corporate development. The respective parts of the annual report were valued at not more than 17% out of the maximum number of points on average. Compared to the other sections of the annual report, the reporting on the future corporate development showed the most obvious shortcomings. In contrast, qualified certified public accountants and financial analysts consulted as experts considered forecast reporting to be extremely important.[24] Also, the American Institute of Certified Public Accountants (AICPA) has emphasized the importance of corporate disclosures of forward-looking information.[25]

With regard to the reporting on the future corporate development, the individual results of the top 5 of 100, the last 5 of 100, and the last 5 of 500 were as follows:

[24] See Baetge/Armeloh/Schulze (1997a: 177).
[25] See AICPA, Special Committee on Financial Reporting (1994).

Table 4: Quality of the Reporting on Future Corporate Development for the Financial
Year 1996 for the 500 Largest German Quoted Stock Companies

Report on Future Corporate Development	Company	Quality max. 100%
Top 5 of 100	VEBA AG	58.3%
	Bayer AG	57.3%
	Thyssen AG	52.3%
	Heidelberger Zement AG	50.0%
	Vossloh AG	49.7%
Last 5 of 100	A. Flender AG	11.3%
	Linde AG	11.0%
	Carl Schenk AG	10.0%
	Degussa AG	9.3%
	Th. Goldschmidt AG	7.7%
Last 5 of 500	HADEDA AG	1.1%
	HACH AG	0.7%
	Koepp AG	0.0%
	Gebrüder Bernard AG	0.0%
	BM Bäckermühlen AG	0.0%

It must be noted, however, that in Germany more and more companies are stating precise target values of ratios to be realized in the future and also reporting on the degree of target realization in subsequent years. In the Germany of the 1980s, that was far beyond imagination. An example of the current statement of financial target values is Daimler-Benz, since this group states a total return on investment (operating profit in relation to capital employed) of 12% as a target value in its annual report.[26] The chairman of the managing board of the Mannesmann Group also mentions a corporate objective of 15% return on investment in his annual report.[27]

Due to German disclosure rules, the functional area "research and development" must be commented on as well. From this the shareholders might obtain important information about the future corporate marketing opportunities. Empirical studies have revealed that reporting on research and development differs greatly among German companies. Whereas in the majority of cases the information policy in this functional area is very conservative, it is above all the

[26] See Daimler-Benz AG 'Annual Report 1996' 45.

[27] See Mannesmann AG 'Annual Report 1996' 4.

large companies of the chemicals industry that do an excellent job in this sector of reporting. A positive example of investment-oriented reporting is supplied by the Hoechst Group which, in its 1996 annual report, described in detail each type of pharmaceutical and its stage of development.[28]

Concerning reporting on research and development, the following individual results of the top 5 of 100, the last 5 of 100, and the last 5 of 500 must be taken into account:

Table 5:   Quality of the Reporting on Research and Development for the Financial Year 1996 for the 500 Largest German Quoted Companies

Report on R & D	Company	Quality max. 100%
Top 5 of 100	Schwarz Pharma AG	95.0%
	Merck KGaA	92.5%
	SAP AG	90.0%
	BASF AG	90.0%
	Schering AG	90.0%
Last 5 of 100	Ehlebracht AG	27.5%
	PWA AG	25.0%
	Nordstern AG	25.0%
	Badenwerk AG	15.0%
	TA Triumph-Adler AG	10.0%
Last 5 of 500	ESCADA AG	0.0%
	Diering Holding AG	0.0%
	Jean Pascale AG	0.0%
	Hymer AG	0.0%
	Steffen AG	0.0%

Besides German annual reports, the 1996 annual reports of the 21 European quoted companies with the highest degree of market capitalization were analyzed.[29] All in all, it became apparent that these companies showed a tendency towards worse reporting than the large German companies.

The best of the European reports under investigation was compiled by Unilever. And yet, with 64.17%, Unilever reached about 12% less than the best

---

[28] See Hoechst AG 'Annual Report 1996' 32.

[29] For an international comparison of corporate financial disclosure, see also Frost/Ramin (1997).

German annual report presented by the VEBA AG (76.28%). Above all, the fact that the international annual reports come off worse must be seen as a consequence of their management discussion and analysis, which is comparatively worse in quality. Especially striking was the reporting on future corporate development, which, in comparison with German companies, proved to be even worse. Moreover, none of the international companies under investigation prepared a value added account.

C. The Monitoring Task of the Auditor

I. Preliminary Note

Within the system of corporate governance, the annual audit is often regarded as highly important. At the same time, however, there is the so-called expectation gap—i.e., a discrepancy between what the shareholders and other addressees of the annual audit expect and what the audit is actually able to achieve—to be observed on either side of the Atlantic.[30] In accordance with current law, the auditor already has two functions within the system of corporate governance: on the one hand, the auditor guarantees the reliability of the information disclosed by the company; on the other hand, the auditor also has to evaluate and to report on the economic position of the company in the auditor's report that must not become subject to public disclosure. Both of these aspects will be further discussed in the following.

II. Safeguarding the Reliability of the Disclosed Information

Disclosure can only result in supervision of the management if the disclosed information is reliable. Without an audit performed by an independent third party, however, the reliability of the information will be subject to well-founded doubts on the side of the shareholders. This is because the financial statements meant to serve the monitoring of management are prepared by the supervised themselves. Thus, it is the audit that safeguards the trustworthiness of accounting.[31]

In order to arrive at this trustworthiness, the auditor ought to be as independent as possible. For his position within the system of corporate governance, this means that the legal regulations must make sure that the auditor is far from the board of management (or the inside directors) and close to the supervisory board

---

[30] See Allvey (1995: 66-9); Dörner (1995: 190-203).
[31] See Hopt (1977: 401).

(or the audit committee).[32] The annual audit will not be able to guarantee the reliability of accounting if the auditor (the supervisor) is suspected of being dependent on the board of management (the supervised). Hence, in Germany, the regulations of the audit should be changed in such a way that the auditor is authorized by the supervisory board and not by the board of management; in addition, the auditor ought to report to the supervisory board directly. Pending reform plans [33] go in that direction.

Against these changes, it might be objected that a responsible auditor will also maintain his independence under the current regulations. This is certainly true. And yet, the supervision of the management by accounting is based on the fact that the shareholders put their trust in the independence and, as a result thereof, in the reliability of accounting. Thus, within the system of corporate governance, the legislative body ought to look for a place where the auditor can do his job in accordance with the following basic idea to be found in the U.S. Statements of Auditing Standards (SAS No. 1):

> "Independent auditors should not only be independent in fact, they should avoid situations that may lead outsiders to doubt their independence."

III. Assessment of the Financial Position and Warning Function in Periods of Crisis

Above all, it is the task of the auditor to check the correctness of the financial statements. To what extent the auditor should additionally investigate the economic and financial position of the company—and if he must do so at all—is quite a controversial issue in Germany. However, the legal provisions make the auditor fulfill various auditing and reporting assignments that can only be carried out properly if the auditor judges the financial situation of the company as well:

- The financial statements are based on the going-concern conception [Par. 252 (1) No. 2 HGB (German Commercial Code)]. Accordingly, the auditor must assess whether there is substantial doubt with regard to the going-concern assumption. The same applies to the annual audit in the U.S.
- The auditor is obliged to report on negative changes in the economic position, on relevant losses, and on negative trends in a staggered form [Par. 321 HGB (German Commercial Code)]. SAS 58 of the U. S. Generally Accepted Auditing Standards contains an obligation that is very similar.

---

[32] See Hommelhoff (1995: 15-7).

[33] See the draft statute of a law concerning the improvement of control and transparency in companies (KonTraG) dating from November 22, 1996, printed in: *Zeitschrift für Wirtschaftsrecht* 17 (1996: 2129-35 and 2193-8).

The German auditor's opinion must include the following:

> "With due regard to the [German] accounting principles the annual financial statements give a true and fair view of the company's assets, liabilities, financial position and profit and loss."

Likewise, a U.S. auditor must declare the following:

> "In our opinion, the financial statements ... present fairly, in all material aspects, the financial position of the company as of December 31, 19XX, and the results of its operations and its cash flows for the year then ended in conformity with generally accepted accounting principles."

• Hence, the auditor must confirm the "true and fair view" and a "fair presentation". And yet, the scope of these wordings is subject to interpretation. It is clear, however, that the auditor is not allowed to give an auditor's opinion on doubtful financial statements without explanatory remarks.

• Moreover, in Germany, the auditor's opinion must include that the management report goes along with the financial statements and does not convey a false impression of the corporate position [Par. 317 (1) No. 2 HGB (German Commercial Code)].

The aspects mentioned above show that the role of the auditor within the system of corporate governance cannot be limited to safeguarding the reliability of the financial statements. In addition, the auditor also has to investigate the current economic position as well as the prospective future development of the company being audited. The results must be reported to the supervisory board in the first place so that the supervisory board is informed in time about an impending financial crisis of the company. As long as confidentiality among the members of the supervisory board can be taken for granted, an early warning addressed to the supervisory board will not give rise to the problem of self-fulfilling prophecy. And yet, the latter is frequently employed as an argument against a warning by the auditor in periods of crisis. With regard to an early warning of the supervisory board, this is not very convincing. The problem of self-fulfilling prophecy must, however, be given some importance if the auditor feels obliged to include some well-founded doubt as to the going-concern assumption in his auditor's opinion. In such a case, the auditor must also take the potential consequences into account.

For the purpose of assessing the economic position of the company being audited, the auditor can make use of the traditional financial statement analysis. By doing so, various ratios are usually made up, since a single ratio alone is not enough. Therefore, the auditor must select, weight, and finally judge the ratios supposed to be relevant in each case. These requirements cannot be met by the conventional financial statement analysis. Thus, it is strongly recommendable that the auditor make use of the modern techniques of financial statement analysis depicted above. By making use of these modern methods, the auditor arrives at a statistically founded and thus objective final judgment on the economic position of the company which can also be reported to the supervisory board. On the basis of this assessment resulting from modern techniques of financial statement analysis, the auditor can further decide if additional analyses might become necessary because of a critical situation.

References

Allvey, David Philip 'Corporate Governance in the United Kingdom' in: Scheffler, Eberhard (ed.) *Corporate Governance* 57-77 (Wiesbaden 1995).

Altman, Edward I. 'Financial Ratios, Discriminant Analysis and the Prediction of Corporate Bankruptcy' *Journal of Finance* 33 (1968) 589-609.

American Law Institute 'Principles of Corporate Governance' (Vol. II) (St. Paul, Minn. 1994).

Arrow, Kenneth J. 'The Economics of Agency' in: Pratt John W. and Richard J. Zeckhauser (eds.) *Principals and Agents: The Structure of Business* 37-51 (Boston, Mass. 1985).

Baetge, Jörg 'Möglichkeiten der Früherkennung von Unternehmenskrisen mit Hilfe statistischer Jahresabschlußanalysen' *Zeitschrift für betriebswirtschaftliche Forschung* 41 (1989) 793-811.

Baetge, Jörg 'Rating von Unternehmen anhand von Bilanzen' *Die Wirtschaftsprüfung* 47 (1994) 1-10.

Baetge, Jörg, Karl-Heinz Armeloh, and Dennis Schulze 'Anforderungen an die Geschäftsbericht-erstattung aus betriebswirtschaftlicher und handelsrechtlicher Sicht' *Deutsches Steuerrecht* 35 (1997a) 176-80.

Baetge, Jörg, Karl-Heinz Armeloh, and Dennis Schulze 'Empirische Befunde über die Qualität der Geschäftsberichterstattung börsennotierter deutscher Kapitalgesellschaften' *Deutsches Steuerrecht* 35 (1997b) 212-9.

Baetge, Jörg and Markus Feidicker 'Discriminatory Analysis Procedures for Corporate Assessment' in: Dülfer, Eberhard (ed.) *International Handbook of Cooperative Organizations* 259-65 (Göttingen 1994).

Baetge, Jörg, Michael Huß, and Hans-Jürgen Niehaus 'The Use of Statistical Analysis to Identify the Financial Strength of Corporations in Germany' *Studies in Banking and Finance* 7 (1988) 183-96.

Baetge, Jörg, Ariane Kruse, and Carsten Uthoff 'Bonitätsklassifikationen von Unternehmen mit Neuronalen Netzen' *Wirtschaftsinformatik* 38 (1996) 273-81.

Baetge, Jörg, Ulrich Schmedt, Dagmar Hüls, Clemens Krause, and Carsten Uthoff 'Die Bonitäts-beurteilung von Jahresabschlüssen nach neuem Recht (HGB 1985) mit Künstlichen Neuronalen Netzen auf der Basis von Clusteranalysen' *Der Betrieb* 47 (1994) 337-43.

Beaver, William H. 'Financial Ratios as Predictiors of Failure' *Journal of Accounting Research* 4 (1966) 71-111.

Beaver, William H. *Financial Reporting: An Accounting Revolution* (Englewood Cliffs, N. J. 1981).

Berle, Adolf A. and Gardiner C. Means *The Modern Corporation and Private Property* (New York 1932).

Buxbaum, Richard M. 'Die Leitung von Gesellschaften—Strukturelle Reformen im ameri-kanischen und deutschen Gesellschaftsrecht' in: Feddersen, Dieter, Peter Hommelhoff, and Uwe H. Schneider (eds.) *Corporate Governance* 65-93 (Cologne 1996).

Cadbury Committee 'Financial Aspects of Corporate Governance' (London 1992).

Dörner, Dietrich 'Der Abschlußprüfer als Überwachungsorgan' in: Scheffler, Eberhard (ed.) *Corporate Governance* 171-207 (Wiesbaden 1995).

Ebke, Werner F. 'Unternehmenskontrolle durch Gesellschafter und Markt' in: Sandrock, Otto and Wilhelm Jäger (eds.) *Internationale Unternehmenskontrolle und Unternehmenskultur* 7-35 (Tübingen 1994).

Eisenberg, Melvin A. 'Legal Models of Management Structure in the Modern Corporation: Officers, Directors and Accountants' 63 *Cal. L. Rev.* 375-439 (1975).

Eisenberg, Melvin A. *The Structure of the Corporation—A Legal Analysis* (Boston et al. 1976).

Feidicker, Markus *Kreditwürdigkeitsprüfung* (Düsseldorf 1992).

Frost, Carol A. and Kurt P. Ramin 'Corporate Financial Disclosure: A Global Assessment' in: Choi, Frederick D.S. (eds.) *International Accounting and Finance Handbook* Chapter 18 2nd edn. (New York et. al. 1997).

Großfeld, Bernhard and Werner Ebke 'Controlling the Modern Corporation: A Comparative View of Corporate Power in the United States and Europe' 26 *Am. J. Comp. L.* 397-433 (1978).

Hart, Oliver 'Corporate Governance: Some Theory and Implications' *Economic Journal* 105 (1995) 678-89.

Hommelhoff, Peter 'Störungen im Recht der Aufsichtsrats-Überwachung: Regelungsvorschläge an den Gesetzgeber' in: Picot, Arnold (ed.) *Corporate Governance—Unternehmensüberwachung auf dem Prüfstand* 1-28 (Stuttgart 1995).

Hopt, Klaus J. 'Vom Aktien- und Börsenrecht zum Kapitalmarktrecht? Teil 2: Die deutsche Entwicklung im internationalen Vergleich' *Zeitschrift für das gesamte Handelsrecht und Wirtschaftsrecht* 141 (1977) 389-441.

Hüls, Dagmar *Früherkennung insolvenzgefährdeter Unternehmen* (Düsseldorf 1995).

Jensen, Michael C. and William H. Meckling 'Theory of the Firm: Managerial Behavior, Agency Costs and Ownership Structure' *Journal of Financial Economics* 3 (1976) 305-360.

Klein, William A. and John C. Coffee *Business Organization and Finance* 6th edn. (Westbury, N.Y. 1996).

Krause, Clemens *Kreditwürdigkeitsprüfung mit Neuronalen Netzen* (Düsseldorf 1993).

Lowenstein, Louis 'Financial Transparency and Corporate Governance: You Manage What You Measure' 96 *Colum. L. Rev.* 1335-62 (1996).

Manne, Henry G. 'Mergers and the Market for Corporate Control' *Journal of Political Economy* 73 (1965) 110-20.

Meier-Schatz, Christian J. 'Managermacht und Marktkontrolle' *Zeitschrift für das gesamte Handelsrecht und Wirtschaftsrecht* 149 (1985) 76-108.

Merkt, Hanno *US-amerikanisches Gesellschaftsrecht* (Heidelberg 1991).

Monks, Robert A.G. and Nell Minow *Power and Accountability* (New York 1991).

Niehaus, Hans-Jürgen *Früherkennung von Unternehmenskrisen* (Düsseldorf 1987).

Ordelheide, Dieter 'Brauchen wir für die Unternehmensüberwachung mehr Publizität?' in: Picot, Arnold (ed.) *Corporate Governance—Unternehmensüberwachung auf dem Prüfstand* 89-109 (Stuttgart 1995).

Schildbach, Thomas *Jahresabschluß und Markt* (Heidelberg 1986).

Stibi, Bernd *Statistische Jahresabschlußanalyse als Instrument der steuerlichen Betriebsprüfung* (Düsseldorf 1994).

Uthoff, Carsten *Erfolgsoptimale Kreditwürdigkeitsprüfung auf der Basis von Jahresabschlüssen und Wirtschaftsauskünften mit Künstlichen Neuronalen Netzen* (Stuttgart 1997).

Wilhelm, Winfried 'Wie gut sind die Blue Chips?' *manager-magazin* Sept. 1997, 102-6.

Windbichler, Christine 'Zur Trennung der Geschäftsführung und Kontrolle bei amerikanischen Großgesellschaften' *Zeitschrift für Unternehmens- und Gesellschaftsrecht* 14 (1985) 50-73.

Disclosure and Auditing
A German Auditor's Perspective

PETER-J. SCHMIDT, Hanover

Accounting and disclosure in Germany is not primarily aimed at the decision useful-ness for investors, but is predominantly governed by the scope of protection of credi-tors as well as the company as an ongoing enterprise. Therefore, the precise regulations in the relevant laws are based on the prudence concept as the fundamental accounting assumption. Income tax regulations emphasize the prudence concept even more because the computation of the company's tax base is closely linked to the statutory accounts. The German government has proposed a new law (*Kapitalaufnahmeerleich-terungsgesetz*) which will allow German corporations to prepare consolidated state-ments in accordance with internationally applied accounting principles. This will bring group accounts to German listed companies in line with the accounting methods that are more or less accepted by the worldwide corporate community. In a further law, the government is proposing amendments to the stock corporation law (*Aktiengesetz*) and the *Handelsgesetzbuch* (Commercial Code) that will widen the disclosure obligations for German listed companies with respect to reporting that will be more oriented to the future development and the potential risks of the company. Consequently, the statutory audit will be extended to the evaluation of the company's future prospects and the prevailing risk potential.

Contents

A. Introduction

When discussing disclosure, we refer to the requirements German law imposes on issuers of publicly traded securities, as well as the disclosure which a statutory auditor makes under German law in his long form report (*Prüfungsbericht*) addressed to the supervisory board (*Aufsichtsrat*) and in his auditor's opinion directed to the public. Disclosure is not only a means to protect investors and other shareholders; it has corporate governance effects, too.

Disclosure and auditing are precisely regulated in the *Handelsgesetzbuch*, HGB, (Commercial Code) and *Aktiengesetz*, AktG, (Stock Corporation Law). Germany has no accounting standard-setting body like FASB. Generally accepted accounting principles beyond those which are laid down in the law are derived from the good practice of companies as well as the jurisdiction of the Supreme Civil Court (*Bundesgerichtshof*) and the Supreme Tax Court (*Bundesfinanzhof*), and are widely influenced by the accounting guidelines pronounced by the German Auditors' Institute (*Institut der Wirtschaftsprüfer*).

As shall be discussed later, accounting and disclosure in Germany is not primarily governed by the scope of decision usefulness for an average prudent investor, but is aimed instead at the protection of creditors and the company as an ongoing enterprise. Consequently the prudence concept is the fundamental accounting assumption. This perception has led to a growing criticism by international investors, in particular from the Anglo-Saxon business community.[1]

The German government is realizing the danger of the prevailing accounting, disclosure, and corporate governance leading to disadvantages for German corporations in the global competition for investors' capital. Therefore, the Ministry of Justice (*Bundesjustizministerium*) has published two drafts for the amendment of several sections of the HGB (Commercial Code) and the AktG (Stock Corporation Law) with the aim of opening German accounting for consolidated financial statements to the application of internationally applied accounting standards as well as widening disclosure requirements and improving the means for corporate governance.[2,3]

[1] See 'Stille Rücklagen bleiben für Breeden (SEC-chairman) ein "rotes Tuch"' *Handelsblatt* 9./10.10.92, 45; 'Ausländische Banker kritisieren deutsche Finanzmärke' *Frankfurter Allgemeine Zeitung* 12.9.96, 33.

[2] See 'Entwurf eines Gesetzes zur Verbesserung der Wettbewerbsfähigkeit deutscher Konzerne an internationalen Kapitalmärkten und zur erleichterten Aufnahme von Gesellschafterdarlehen (Kapitalaufnahmeerleichterungsgesetz)' (7.6.1996).

[3] See 'Entwurf eines Gesetzes zur Kontrolle und Transparenz im Unternehmensbereich (KonTraG)' (22.11.1996).

B. Disclosure Required by German Law

I. Corporate Reporting by Management

A corporation must publish annual financial statements (balance sheet, profit and loss statement, notes to the financial statements) as well as a directors' report.

At least once a year, after the first six months of a fiscal year, a corporation has to publish an interim report. Ad hoc information must be given with respect to issues which might have a significant impact on the listing of the company's shares. These two means of disclosure shall not be discussed in this article.

1. Financial Statements and Their Underlying Basic Accounting Assumptions

Accounting under the HGB (Commercial Code) is governed by the prudence concept. Section 252 (general valuation principles) states in para (1), No. 4:

> Values must be determined prudently, namely all foreseeable risks and losses which have arisen up to the balance sheet date must be taken into account even if these become known only between the balance sheet date and the date on which the financial statements are prepared; profits may only be taken up if they are realized at the balance sheet date.

This fundamental accounting assumption is to protect lenders as well as the corporation as a going concern.[4] This is in contrast to the conceptual framework of the FASB pronouncements, for example. The statement of financial accounting concepts (SFAC) No. 1 states:

> "Financial reporting should provide information that is useful to present and potential investors and creditors and other users in making rational investment, credit and similar decisions."[5]

Within the framework of International Accounting Standards as pronounced by IAS, prudence is encompassed by the requirement of reliability, and is therefore far from being a fundamental assumption.[6]

The application of the prudence concept is enhanced by the Income Tax Law (*Einkommensteuergesetz*), which in section 5 para 1 provides that the accounting

---

[4] See Grund, Matthias 'Internationale Entwicklung und Bilanzrecht: Reform oder Resignation?' *Der Betrieb* 49 (1996) 1293; Schneider, Dieter *Betriebswirtschaftslehre. Vol. 2: Rechnungswesen* 110-1 (Munich and Vienna 1997); Adler, Hans, Walther Düring, and Kurt Schmaltz *Rechnungslegung und Prüfung der Unternehmen* §§ 252-6 Tz. 15 6th edn. (Stuttgart 1995). On auditing, accounting, and disclosure in Germany, cf. also Prigge (this volume Ch. 12: Sec. B.V.).

[5] See FASB 'SFAC, No. 1: Objectives of Financial Reporting by Business Enterprises, 1978' in: FASB *Original Pronouncements, Accounting Standards as of June 1, 1995* Vol. 2 1005-20 para 34 (1995).

[6] See Niehus, Rudolf F. '"Vorsichtsprinzip" und "Accrual Basis"—Disparitäten bei den Determinanten der "Fair Presentation" in der sog. internationalen Rechnungslegung' *Der Betrieb* 50 (1997) 1421, 1422.

for certain items needs to be based on the same principles as the accounting for such items for financial accounting purposes.[7],[8] It seems obvious that this legally required link (conformity principle = *Maßgeblichkeitsprinzip*) between statutory accounting and tax accounting is a steady temptation for management to use the prudence concept as far as possible as a means to reduce income taxes.

The link between statutory accounting and tax accounting under the conformity principle is accompanied by the so-called reversed conformity principle (*umgekehrtes Maßgeblichkeitsprinzip*) as codified in section 5 para 1 sentence 2 of the Income Tax Law (*Einkommensteuergesetz*). Under this principle, a taxpayer who wants to make use of specific tax incentives has to account for those not only in his tax accounting but also in his statutory accounting. This means, e.g., that a tax incentive in the form of a special depreciation on machinery or equipment of 50% in the year of acquisition must be applied on the statutory accounts to make it effective for tax purposes. Insofar the tax accounting becomes relevant to the statutory accounting.[9],[10] To avoid the distortion caused by this tax-related accounting, relevant information is to be given in the notes in accordance with sections 280 para 2, 281 para 2 and 285 No. 5 HGB (Commercial Code). Whether the information given in the notes is always adequate to lead to a true and fair view—in particular as far as the impact of such a tax accounting on future years' income is concerned—shall not be discussed here. From an international point of view it should, however, be mentioned that in accordance with U.S. GAAP as well as IAS, the notes accompanying financial statements do have the scope to give additional information and should not be deemed sufficient to enable an average prudent investor to make a reconciliation from accounting figures which are not true and fair to figures which might be true and fair under the prevailing accounting concept.[11]

Tax-related accounting, which gives management room for an earnings management, has long been criticized in Germany.[12] As early as 1988,

[7] See Schmidt, Peter-J. 'Wird die Handelsbilanz zur Steuerbilanz?' *Die Wirtschaftsprüfung* 44 (1991) 605.

[8] See Schmidt, Peter-J. 'Wie maßgeblich bleibt die Maßgeblichkeit?' in: Baetge, Jörg, Dietrich Börner, Karl-Heinz Forster, and Lothar Schruff (eds.) *Rechnungslegung, Prüfung und Beratung: Herausforderungen für den Wirtschaftsprüfer* (Festschrift Ludewig) 903 (Düsseldorf 1996).

[9] See Lischer, Jr., Henry J. and Peter N. Märkl 'Conformity Between Financial Accounting and Tax Accounting in the United States and Germany' *Wirtschaftsprüferkammer-Mitteilungen* 36 (1997) 91, 111.

[10] See Schmidt, supra n. 7.

[11] See Niehus, Rudolf J. 'Der Wirtschaftsprüfer des vereinten Deutschlands: ein freier Beruf in dem einen Markt' in: *Das vereinigte Deutschland im europäischen Markt* (Bericht über die Fachtagung 1991 des IDW) 67-98 (Düsseldorf 1992).

[12] See Küting, Karlheinz 'Theorie und Praxis des neuen Bilanzrechts' *Neue Wirtschaftsbriefe* (Supplement 1, Issue 28/1989).

Havermann, then President of the *Institut der Wirtschaftsprüfer*, pointed out that the conformity principle was an obstacle to the international acceptance of German accounting.[13]

But the corporate community wanted to maintain the options for a most flexible accounting policy.

2. Directors' Report (*Lagebericht*)

The management report should contain a description of the development of the business and the situation of the company in such a manner as to provide a true and fair view. In particular the report should comment on the anticipated development of the company.

In management reports, it has to be stated that, in general, directors report in detail about the development during the relevant fiscal year, give an overall but not too detailed view of the present situation, and make only purely general comments on the anticipated development of the company, although after the implementation of the EC Fourth Directive in 1985 the importance of the report on the anticipated development of the company was widely emphasized,[14] empirical results show a fairly pure reporting on the future corporate development.[15]

3. Expected Legislation

The proposed *Kapitalaufnahmeerleichterungsgesetz*[16] will allow German corporations with foreign subsidiaries to prepare consolidated statements in accordance with accounting principles which are internationally applied, provided that the information given therein is at least equal to the information required by German law. If this amendment to the HGB (Commercial Code) goes through, German groups operating internationally could prepare their consolidated statements in accordance with internationally applied standards without having to prepare separate group accounts in accordance with German law. This would mean that the prudence concept as the fundamental accounting assumption as well as tax considerations would no longer influence the information disclosed

[13] See Havermann, Hans 'Der Aussagewert des Jahresabschlusses' *Die Wirtschaftsprüfung* 41 (1988) 612, 614.

[14] See Emmerich, Gerhard and Martin Künnemann 'Zum Lagebericht der Kapitalgesellschaft' *Die Wirtschaftsprüfung* 39 (1986) 145.

[15] See Dörner, Dietrich 'Der Prognosebericht nach § 289 Abs. 2 Nr. 2 HGB: Überlegungen zur Verminderung der Diskrepanz zwischen Publizitätsanforderungen und Publizitätspraxis' in: Baetge et al., supra n. 8, 219.

[16] See supra n. 2 and Prigge (this volume Ch. 12: Sec. D).

by the consolidated financial statements. On the other hand, this would mean that the consolidated statements would in most cases not coincide with the financial statements of the corporation as a single entity. The result of this would be that the profit that would be available for dividend distribution would be accounted for by applying accounting standards which could differ significantly from the accounting standards being applied for the consolidated statements. It is difficult to imagine that such a disparity will be accepted by investors over a longer period of time. It seems more likely that after having made the first step, the German legislator has either to adopt the main principles of U.S. GAAP or IAS in general or to allow companies to apply the accounting principles which they use for their consolidated statements for their single entity statements, too. Because of these foreseeable impacts on German accounting in general, the proposed amendments are currently subject to a very controversial discussion. Two main arguments against these amendments have been voiced:

- German accounting will no longer be based on German law, but will be dependent on accounting standards developed by private foreign organizations, e.g., FASB or IASC.
- The amendment will eventuallly lead to a cut of the link between statutory accounting and tax accounting with adverse tax implications.

The outcome of this discussion will show whether the German legislature as well as the business community will accept a future with accounting standards not primarily regulated by national law but increasingly developed internationally and oriented to the requirements of the market.[17]

Among other things, *KonTraG*[18] will inter alia improve corporate disclosure and corporate governance.

As far as disclosure is concerned, the proposed amendments are related to the directors' report. The main amendments in section 289 HGB (Commercial Code) would be the following ones:

- The report should give all relevant information, which in addition to the financial statements could have a decision usefulness for interested parties.
- The information shall in particular indicate the future development of the company.
- The report has to deal specifically with the risks management sees related to the company's future development.

In addition to these proposed amendments, it can be stated that both the business community and auditors do accept that the reporting in the directors' report has to be improved. Therefore, the *Institut der Wirtschaftsprüfer* has released a draft for

---

[17] See Ebke, Werner F. 'Rechnungslegung und Abschlußprüfung im Umbruch' *Wirtschafts-prüferkammer-Mitteilungen* (Special Issue 'Rechnungslegung und Abschlußprüfung in globalen Kapitalmärkten') (1997) 12, 17.

[18] See supra n. 3, and Hopt (Ch. 4: Sec. C.I.) and Prigge (Ch. 12: Sec. D) in this volume.

the preparation of the directors' report.[19] This draft is currently under discussion within the profession and between the *Institut der Wirtschaftsprüfer* and the corporate public.

II. Reporting by the Statutory Auditor

1. Scope of the Audit and Nature of the Audit Examination

The scope of the audit is to determine:

- Whether the legal regulations and additional provisions of the articles of association have been observed and whether the financial statements, in compliance with generally accepted (German) accounting principles, represent a true and fair view of the net worth, financial position, and results of the company.
- Whether the management report agrees with the financial statements and whether the other information included in the management report does not give a false impression of the position of the company. This audit requirement does not fully co-incide with the required content of the report (see Section B.I.2.). The auditor does not have to determine whether the description of the development of the business and the situation of the company provides a true and fair view. Although the gap between not providing a true and fair view and giving a false impression may be fairly narrow, this lack of coincidence between reporting requirements and auditing requirements illustrates a specific audit approach under German law.

The audit examination is basically a comparison of stated facts with the prevailing legal requirements. German law requires an evaluation or appraisal by the auditor only insofar as he has to determine:

- Whether the financial statements in compliance with generally accepted (German) accounting principles present a true and fair view of the net worth, financial position, and results of the company.
- Whether the going concern assumption is adequately applied.
- Whether the information included in the management report gives a false impression of the position of the company.

2. Assignment of the Auditor

The statutory auditor must be elected annually by the shareholders' meeting and is assigned by the board of directors (*Vorstand*). There is no time limitation for

---

[19] 'Entwurf einer Verlautbarung: Zur Aufstellung des Lageberichts' *IDW-Fachnachrichten* (1997) 213.

re-election. The supervisory board (*Aufsichtsrat*) is not formally involved in that assignment. The auditor must present his long form report to the board of directors, who in turn must deliver that report to the supervisory board. It is a widespread custom that not all of the board members get this long form report. This applies in particular to the labor representatives on the board. There is no legal requirement that the auditor be present at the board meeting where the annual financial statements are discussed. In the recent past, however, it has become a practice to invite the auditor to participate in that meeting.

Notwithstanding this procedure, the main addressee of the long form report is the supervisory board. "The main scope of the long form report is to inform the supervisory board independently from the board of directors."[20]

3. Auditor's Opinion

The auditor has to render an opinion, the wording of which is laid down in section 322 para 1 HGB (Commercial Code). This opinion is closely related to the scope of the audit as described above. The auditor is not required or even allowed to make explanatory additions to the prescribed wording. However, he must add such information as is necessary in his opinion to avoid a wrong impression concerning the nature of the audit and scope of his opinion.

In case of material objections, the auditor has to qualify his opinion and explain the reasons for the qualification. In case of significant findings which would concern the reliability of the financial statements in total, the auditor must disclaim his opinion. The reasons for the disclaimer have to be explained.

The statutory auditor reports to the interested public through his auditor's opinion (*Bestätigungsvermerk*), and he reports to the supervisory board through his long form report (*Prüfungsbericht*).

4. Auditor's Long Form Report

In the auditor's long form report, the items included in the financial statements must be analyzed and adequately commented upon. The auditor must state expressively and explain adverse changes of the financial position and the earnings situation as compared with the prior year, and he must comment on losses which considerably affected the previous year's results. In accordance with section 321 para 2 HGB (Commercial Code), the auditor must report in particular

---

[20] See Hense, Burkhard 'Der Prüfungsbericht hat zu viele Empfänger: Auch ein Beitrag zur besseren Zusammenarbeit von Aufsichtsrat und Abschlußprüfer' in: Fröschle, Gerhart, Klaus Kaiser, and Adolf Moxter *Rechenschaftslegung im Wandel* (Festschrift Budde) 287, 293 (Munich 1995). For German practice, cf. Hopt (Ch. 4: Sec. B.II.3. and B.III.3.) and Prigge (Ch. 12: Sec. B.I.3.) in this volume.

on facts which could endanger the existence of the enterprise or which could materially hinder its development, and he also must report on facts which indicate serious violations by the legal representatives against the law or the articles of association.

5. Expected Legislation, Proposed Additional Reporting Requirements by *KonTraG*[21]

Corporations shall be required by law to establish an adequate risk management system and to provide for appropriate internal audit procedures to guard the performance of that risk management system.

The auditor shall determine whether the board of directors did establish a risk management system and appropriate internal audit functions. The auditor will be required to evaluate the system and to state whether it is adequate to fulfill the above requirements under the circumstances given in the corporation. In his long form report, the auditor shall comment on this part of his audit examinations in a separate segment.

The auditor will be specifically required to evaluate the adequacy of the information which the board of directors gives with respect to anticipated risks related to the future development of the company.

In his auditor's opinion, the auditor will have to report on risk areas which he believes could adversely affect the future development of the company.

As far as the audit of the directors' report is concerned, the auditor shall not only determine whether the report agrees with the financial statements but shall determine whether the information given in the report provides a true and fair view of the state of the company's affairs. Although the extension of the scope of the audit should be welcomed, it has to be stated that this extended requirement will lead to evaluation problems as long as the prevailing accounting concept is not changed.[22]

There is a tendency in the proposed *KonTraG* to require the auditor to evaluate the situation and the prospects of the company independently from the statements and evaluations given by the management. This would extend the scope of the statutory audit to an appraisal of the enterprise and could lead to a new expectation gap. The auditor's duty and responsibility should be confined to a judgment of the reliability and plausibility of the financial statements and additional information provided by the management.[23]

---

[21] See supra n. 3, and Hopt (Ch. 4: Sec. C.I.) and Prigge (Ch. 12: Sec. D) in this volume.

[22] See Moxter, Adolf 'Die Vorschriften zur Rechnungslegung und Abschlußprüfung im Referentenentwurf eines Gesetzes zur Kontrolle und Transparenz im Unternehmensbereich' *Betriebs-Berater* 52 (1997) 722.

[23] See Schmidt, Peter-J. 'Überlegungen zur Erweiterung der gesetzlichen Regelungen über die Abschlußprüfung' *Betriebswirtschaftliche Forschung und Praxis* 48 (1996) 52.

A further amendment to the AktG (Stock Corporation Law) proposed by *KonTraG* is designed to improve the disclosure of the result of the statutory audit to the supervisory board. The auditor's long form report would be sent to all members and the auditor would be required to be present at that meeting of the supervisory board which deals with the annual financial statements. On this occasion the auditor would inform the supervisory board about the significant findings of his audit examinations. The supervisory board, however, may decide to establish an audit committee and to deliver the long form report to the members of that committee only. It would further be at the supervisory board's discretion to decide whether the auditor shall report on his audit examinations at the relevant supervisory board meeting or at a meeting of an audit committee.

C. Conclusion

There is a growing expectation that the auditor should not only confirm the reliability of the information disclosed by the company. It is expected that the auditor should give a comprehensive judgment on the state of the company's affairs and in particular on its future prospects. This expectation contrasts widely to the legal framework governing disclosure and auditing in Germany.

The corporate community as well as the government are realizing that international investors and institutional investors in particular require disclosure which is in line with internationally accepted standards like U.S. GAAP and IAS. As a consequence, several German groups are already preparing consolidated accounts in accordance with U.S. GAAP or IAS.

The German government is endeavoring by two proposed laws to enable the application of international standards for the consolidated accounts of German groups and to increase disclosure and audit requirements for listed companies. Both proposals, however, leave the basic German accounting approach untouched.

As far as the statutory audit is concerned, it should be noted that the scope of the audit not be extended beyond the examination of the reliability and plausibility of the disclosure given by the management. Otherwise a new expectation gap could develop.

It must still be discussed within the business community whether the globalization and the worldwide competition for investors' capital will further allow German companies to follow an accounting and disclosure concept which is not governed predominantly by the scope of decision usefulness for the present and potential investor.

Discussion Report

HANNO MERKT

Functions of Mandatory Disclosure

Relating to *Fox's* functional analysis of disclosure in the corporate context, an American participant questioned the relevance of disclosure for management compensation and for the allocation of capital. As he pointed out, his own research had produced opposite results.

The necessity of mandatory disclosure was doubted by a Japanese academic. According to him, positive data would be disclosed voluntarily and negative data would be reflected in the share price according to the Efficient Capital Market Hypothesis regardless of disclosure. *Fox* explained that the most commonly accepted rationale for mandatory disclosure is the unwillingness of managers to disclose negative information that would be useful for potential investors.

Another Japanese participant questioned the wisdom of mandating prospective information given the limited scope of reliability of such information. In addition, he had doubts about the overall relevance of accounting figures. *Baetge* replied that, according to his understanding, the market would discount for a lack of reliability of prospective information. A German academic pointed to the situation in Germany where disclosure has long been an integral part of the concept of investor protection. However, it is unclear whether disclosure would function efficiently and in a timely manner as an instrument for preventing losses caused by insolvency in small and medium enterprises. According to *Baetge*, even smaller enterprises and family businesses are becoming more conscious of the advantages of accounting and disclosure, especially in the reduction of agency costs.

A German participant objected to the notion of insolvency prevention as the main or unique function of the so-called 'n-value' analysis as suggested by *Baetge*. There are many forms of management failure and misbehavior apart from running the corporation bankrupt that could and should be detected by means of accounting. *Baetge* agreed that insolvency prediction and prevention would be only one function among others. However, this function has previously been neglected.

An American legal scholar wondered whether mandatory disclosure requirements could be squared regulatorily with the need for keeping sensitive business information away from competitors. *Fox* agreed that any regulatory scheme will have to take into account the private cost of disclosure as well as the social cost of disclosing involuntarily to competitors. However, if all corporations have to disclose their sensitive information equally, any disadvantage would be washed out.

Empirical Analysis of Accounting

Various participants presented methodological questions related to *Baetge's* empirical research. An American participant asked whether *Baetge's* application of neuronal net-supported analysis shows significant similarities to research methods applied by Americans since the seventies. Moreover, he asked for information about the reliability and the advantages of such research methods. According to *Baetge*, his research methods were originally adapted from Edward Altman. Over time, however, these methods have had to be geared to the specific needs of the German system, e.g., the smaller size of the capital market. In the process, the reliability of these methods with respect to insolvency prediction had been significantly improved. Moreover, neuronal net-supported analysis has made insolvency predictable three years in advance in 90% of all insolvency cases. In addition, empirical research has produced valuable insight into the mechanics of so-called 'creative equity ratios'. These ratios were developed in order to respond to specific accounting regulations varying from country to country.

Concerning flaws in accounting statements observed by *Baetge's* research group, a participant from the U.S. suggested systematic bias as a possible explanation. In addition, he pointed to the traditional role of "reputational bonding" in the process of choosing a particular accountant. He asked whether the reputation has diminished as a factor in choosing the accountant. According to *Fox*, no evidence has been found in favor of the suggested systematic bias theory.

Comparison and Unification of Accounting Standards

With respect to *Baetge's* report, an American academic questioned *Baetge's* conclusion that accounting under U.S. GAAP and under German accounting standards would not produce tremendously different results. *Baetge* clarified his position in that the only hypothesis derived from the results would be that such differences are less revealing than originally expected. According to a German legal scholar, a comparison between U.S. GAAP and European accounting standards today could differ considerably from such a comparison five years from now. In the years to come it will become clear what standards are important.

Regarding harmonization, a Japanese participant asked whether in the area of accounting more harmonization or more market competition would be needed in the view of the panelists. According to a German academic, the 4th EC Directive on harmonization of accounting standards had no true harmonizing effect. In particular, the concept of true and fair view imported from the U.S. could not be satisfactorily integrated into the national legal systems of the member states. In German law this concept can be found only in a rather dismantled way. In replying to these comments, *Baetge* indicated his skepticism about the usefulness of harmonization in the field of accounting. However, harmonization would be necessary unless the market is able to look through different regulatory systems. Concerning the quality of the harmonization implemented by the 4th EC Directive, *Baetge's* research did not produce any clear evidence. Obviously the 4th Directive did not cause significant changes in accounting practice. However, insolvency prediction has slightly improved under the harmonized principles.

Another German participant objected to the assessment of the 4th EC Directive put forward by the German academic above. It should be kept in mind that the 4th Directive did not aim at the unification of accounting standards, but merely at making different national accounting standards understandable by setting certain common minimum standards.

From the American side, empirical data were requested on whether the composition of the shareholder population has any impact on the choice of accounting principles. In response to that question, *Franks* reported that according to his investigations, a widely dispersed ownership as in the typical U.S. or U.K. corporation has a higher incentive to disclose than the typical dominating majority shareholder in a Continental corporation, since disclosure might affect private benefit taking of large dominating shareholders. Therefore, mandatory disclosure regulation of the U.S. type would be necessary in Continental countries, particularly in order to prevent insider trading.

Auditing and the Board

With regard to the imminent German supervisory board reform, a German legal scholar favored a more active role of auditors in the board deliberations. Under German law, auditors traditionally have an important role. Moreover, there is a current German law proposal introducing a rotation requirement in order to ensure a certain fluctuation of the auditors in charge. Additionally, he favored whistleblowing as a means of controlling management. A German professional agreed as to board meetings and meetings of board committees, but held whistleblowing within the shareholders' meeting to be problematic.

Chapter 10: Lenders as a Force in Corporate Governance

Chapter 10: Lenders as a Force in Corporate Governance

Lenders as a Force in Corporate Governance Enabling Covenants and the Impact of Bankruptcy Law

JOCHEN DRUKARCZYK, Regensburg, and HARTMUT SCHMIDT, Hamburg

We see corporate governance as the network of arrangements and rules, contractual or legal, which are designed to facilitate and to foster value-maximizing behavior of firms. Our focus is on risky debt. Lenders in a world without lender-specific regulations have to protect themselves contractually. If, contrary to the prevailing static view, a dynamic view is taken, effective lender protection is not feasible at the time when the debt is issued. Much of the debt value-increasing effect of contractual lender protection rests on the lender's monitoring. This view requires and legitimizes an active lender role in corporate governance. In a world with lender-specific regulations the legitimate lender control may be impeded by lender liability and bankruptcy law. A comparison of bankruptcy law in the U.S., in France, and in Germany reveals substantial country-to-country differences. It is hypothesized that such differences affect the relative size of credit and equity markets in these countries and that risk premia on loans to more risky firms are partly an artifact of the legal environment.

Contents

Tables

A. Introduction[1]

This paper focuses on the rich and complex world of risky debt. The problem of lenders to companies is the unpredictable post-contractual behavior of owners and their managers, who, under certain circumstances, act to reduce the total value of the firm at the expense of the lenders. Alternatively, owner-managers may extract value from the lenders' position and, at the same time, increase the value of the shareholders' stake without reducing the total value of the firm. In either instance, lenders suffer from strategic action of owners. The most common transfer-of-wealth mechanisms, widely discussed in the economic literature, are claim dilution,[2] asset substitution,[3] overinvestment,[4] underinvestment,[5] and reduction of assets liable to lenders by paying unexpectedly high dividends.[6] In addition, the value of the lenders' stake may be affected by managerial slack.

Under a corporate governance perspective, post-contractual behavior of the firm that reduces the value of debt is a challenge to lenders. It has to be met by monitoring and restraining countermeasures. It requires lenders to take an active role, to become a force in corporate governance. If, as we see it, corporate governance is the network of arrangements and rules aimed at maximizing total market value of the firm, lenders contribute to this network and act in line with the spirit of its rules. This paper focuses on this role. First, we ask how lenders should structure their control approach if they aim at effective protection. In an agency theory sense, we attempt to provide a rough sketch of a second-best solution.[7] For this theoretical exercise, we assume a fairly unregulated world, a world void of lender-specific regulation. Lender protection has to be achieved by contractual means. Therefore, this part borrows much from the covenants litera-

---

[1] Cf. also the sections dealing with lenders' role in corporate governance in the comparative contributions of Kanda and Prigge in Ch. 12 of this volume.

[2] Lenders buy bonds under the premise that no additonal debt will be issued, but later they see the value of these bonds decline as the firm incurs additional debt of same or higher priority and distributes the newly raised funds to shareholders.

[3] Bonds are sold for the stated purpose of financing low-risk projects and the bonds are priced accordingly, but these projects are later replaced by high-risk investments. The value of bonds is reduced while the value of equity rises.

[4] In addition to existing assets, stockholders approve and fund high-risk projects with negative net present value if these projects decrease the amount and probability of debt payments sufficiently to make up the present value shortfall and augment stockholder wealth.

[5] In contrast, certain projects may increase the probability and amount of debt payments and thus the value of outstanding debt. Given a net present project value, stockholders may still decline to fund these projects if the investment required exceeds the part of the net present value accruing to equity.

[6] These dividends may or may not be distributed as formally declared and paid dividends. Repurchase of stock and other forms of distribution should also be viewed as dividends.

[7] A substantial part of the agency costs is the opportunity cost of owners that results from restrictions on value-maximizing policies imposed by the lending agreements.

ture. We do not deal with collateral and its well-known advantages for the individual lender.[8]

Then, in a second step, we analyze whether lender-specific law comes anywhere near to a second-best solution. A full-scale analysis would require an in-depth study of areas such as secured transactions, lender liability, and bankruptcy in various jurisdictions. This is beyond the scope of this paper, yet we believe it is possible to derive the key message of a full-scale analysis by a rather limited approach. Therefore, we compare the monitioring roles of lenders under the bankruptcy regimes which French, U.S., and German laws provide. We find substantial differences in the lenders' ability to protect themselves. These differences, without doubt, affect the value of debt. This raises the question as to the impact of lender-specific regulation. There are a direct and an indirect implication for corporate governance: if severe restrictions on protective lender monitoring constrain the value of debt, the lenders' role in governance is diminished; but so is the use of debt. This further downgrades lenders as a force in corporate governance and tends to scale down the relative size of the credit or banking sector in the relevant jurisdiction. We suggest that lender-specific regulation is a neglected, but powerful determinant of financial system structure.

B. Lenders' Control Needs and Contractual Arrangements: A Covenants Perspective

I. Static View

What should lenders do to protect themselves against strategic post-contractual action? For the subsequent discussion we assume
- limited liability of firms,
- firms are managed by owners or by an owner-appointed management,
- issues related to groups of companies are excluded,
- intra-shareholder conflicts and
- conflicts between different lenders9 of a firm do not exist,
- lenders do not hold equity stakes in the firm they lend to, and
- the value of the debt instrument of the lender is large enough to warrant considerable monitoring and control efforts.

---

[8] If collateral turns risky debt into safe debt, it is outside the scope of this paper. If it does not, collateral is a tool for the control of implementation of lending agreements, which is beyond the conceptional issues to be addressed here. In bankruptcy, the consequences of collateral are a complicated issue and the related payments to the secured lender differ from jurisdiction to jurisdiction.

[9] Cf. Drukarczyk (1995a) for an analysis of intra-lender conflicts under § 32a GmbHG.

Omniscient lenders fully and correctly anticipate any imminent strategic action, managerial slack,[10] and bad luck[11]. They accept bonds only at prices which already reflect wealth redistribution opportunities, inefficiencies, and other losses. If full default on interest and principal is certain, any attempt at debt financing fails. Omniscience removes the incentive of management or stockholders for slack or strategic action.

Real lenders and owners, in contrast, are likely to make mistakes in anticipating wealth transfers and losses. Consequently, lenders may pay too much or too little for bonds, which hurts either themselves or stockholders who, for tax or other legitimate reasons, prefer a levered firm. Thus, both lenders and stockholders have an interest in contractual and institutional arrangements which effectively restrict slack and strategic action. In this section, we focus on contractual arrangements.

Lenders are prepared to pay the highest price for debt issued by a firm if the debt contract effectively constrains the borrower in all future states of the world to act against the lender's interest. Such contracts would require an excessively detailed menu of permissible investment choices given the expected future states of the borrowing firm. Obviously, it is impossible to write contracts which are complete in this sense. The alternative to such highly intrusive and unfeasible contracts is not necessarily contracts which do not at all constrain the borrower. Debt instruments issued on this basis would fetch the lowest price, if any. It appears sensible to target certain key measurable borrower activities that are not too difficult to monitor and that are unambiguous to a comparatively uninformed third-party enforcer like the courts (Berlin/Mester 1992).

Partial control through restrictive covenants may be viewed in different ways. According to a static view, covenants effectively constrain the borrower in certain areas until the debt matures. In a dynamic view, the breach of covenants triggers some action by both lender and borrower. The value-of-debt increasing effect of covenants is caused, under the static view, directly by the constraint. Under the dynamic view, in contrast, it rests on the action triggered by a breach of covenant. In this section we continue to adhere to the static view.[12]

---

[10] Incompetence, perquisite consumption, excessive compensation, empire building, and other inefficiencies.

[11] States of the world which reduce the borrower's ability to make debt payment as scheduled.

[12] Under both views, covenants are more likely to be included in credit agreements with firms having high default risk or high debt-equity ratios. Cf. Citron (1992: 14). The reader may be inclined to associate the static view with covenants of publicly issued bonds, and the dynamic view with bank loan covenants. Obviously, active monitoring as required by the dynamic view is facilitated if the firm faces a single lender. Bank loans, however, are not necessarily single lender loans. Multiple lenders are involved in syndicated bank loans.

Smith/Warner (1979) focus on the constraints imposed by covenants and on how these constraints benefit lenders. Their reading of the American Bar Foundation's *Commentaries on Indentures* produces three main groups of covenants aimed at constraining strategic borrower action: covenants targeting high risk investments, additional debt, and dividend hikes.[13]

Covenants which reflect concern with high-risk investments restrict mergers and acquisition of third-party common stock or other financial instruments. Mergers are either contractually prohibited or subject to lender approval or certain conditions. In the case of secured debt or a sinking fund, the company cannot dispose of the pledged assets without permission of the lenders. This makes it difficult to replace existing assets by more risky investments. For the same reason, the disposal of any substantial part of the borrower's assets is frequently restricted in debt contracts. Since lack of maintenance of productive assets may result in a higher probability of work disruption by malfunction, defect, or lack of sufficient resources, covenants also require a certain level of assets and servicing schedules. Maintenance may be viewed as investment in a loss control project. Insurance serves the same purpose and its purchase may be required in debt contracts. In addition to all these measures, the incentive of stockholders to increase the riskiness of assets at the expense of lenders may be reduced by convertibility provisions; lenders are given the right to exchange their claims for shares of common stocks.

Additional debt which may dilute the lenders' claims is checked by various restrictions on new debt. The issuance of higher priority debt may be prohibited by covenant. Additional debt of the same priority may be subject to dollar amount or, preferably, financial-ratio ceilings. Financial-ratio ceilings encourage additional positive present value investments. To impede circumvention, debt is defined on a consolidated basis and encompasses guarantees, leases, rents, and other debt-like obligations; moreover, accounting principles specification is required if financial-ratio covenants are employed.[14]

Dividend covenants generally establish that dividends must be paid out of net earnings, not out of borrowed funds (Drukarczyk 1993). These covenants also require specification of accounting principles. If not all net earnings are eligible for distribution to shareholders, they may be used to retire debt or for investment, which may make it difficult for stockholders to reject positive net present value projects benefiting lenders but not stockholders.

---

[13] Covenants are also divided into positive (affirmative) and negative covenants, or in financial-ratio and other covenants. For a survey of covenants, cf. McDaniel (1986), Thießen (1996), and Wittig (1997).

[14] Citron (1992) interprets existing evidence to show that higher debt ratios are associated with the adoption of earnings-increasing accounting methods.

All these covenants which are seen by Smith/Warner (1979) to defease borrower opportunism can also be used as remedies against management incompetence or other managerial slack. Basically, these covenants shore up company assets. This also serves lenders well if states of the world materialize which are adverse to the company. For the additional protection of lenders in case of slack and bad luck, these covenants may be complemented by the requirement of a certain amount of net worth, by a maximum debt ratio or maximum debt-equity clauses, by minimum interest or fixed charges coverages, and by minimum current ratios.[15]

II. Dynamic View

Under the static view, the covenants, agreed upon at the time the debt instruments are placed, assure substantial lender protection until the debt matures. In contrast, under the dynamic view, covenants facilitate actions which contribute to lender protection during the time to maturity. Effective lender protection, according to the dynamic view, is not feasible when the debt is issued. However, as time goes on and new states of the world unfold, previously unknown action in the lender's interest can be taken. This requires a more active lender role in corporate governance.

Risky debt of a company is frequently interpreted as the purchase of a risk-free claim by the lender who, at the same time, sells a put option to the borrower; the put entitles the borrower to sell the company assets to the lender at the face value of the risk-free claim.[16] The bundle "risky debt" promises to yield a higher rate to maturity than the risk-free rate because the price of the put is netted against the price paid for the riskless claim. The lender acquires the risky claim at a discount. If the company does well, it pays interest and principal. Otherwise, the company goes bankrupt: it exercises the put, debt repayment and exercise price cancel, and the lender is left with the company assets. Obviously, it depends on the quality of the company assets whether the put is exercised. The lender prefers assets which, in future states of the world, are worth more than the debt; then the borrower will not exercise the put.

Covenants, under the dynamic view, implant an "option" to renegotiate (Berlin/Mester 1992) into the borrower's put option. This option to renegotiate can be exercised after any breach of covenants or, more realistically, when the borrower reports that a breach is imminent (Citron 1992: 24). An imminent breach of a debt ceiling covenant, for example, may reflect favorable or unfavor-

---

[15] Wittig (1997). These financial ratios may or may not, in the same contract, be used as debt ceilings or maintenance requirements as mentioned above.

[16] Cox/Rubinstein (1985: 376-84); Jurgeit (1989).

able developments. It may be caused by debt funding of fixed charges due to declining sales or, if the imminent breach is good news, by booming demand for the borrowers' products which suggests expansion financing. Obviously, the lender's response to the imminent breach is state-dependent. He will approve activities of the firm only if clearly targeted to the then prevailing market conditions and, at least equally important, if these activities tilt the quality of the firm in a way that makes the exercise of the borrower's put less likely.[17] Expansion activities may appear as a win-win strategy. Thus, a waiver for the breach of covenant is granted. The same may apply to certain safety activities. Therefore, the option to renegotiate implied by covenants can be interpreted as an option of the lender to replace or to restructure from time to time the underlying of the borrower's put.[18] Obviously, whether this arrangement works and increases the price which the lender will pay for debt instruments depends on the nature of the debtor's business. Giving the lender a conditional voice as to the risk profile of the debtor's assets is effective only if default risk-reducing investment choices exist when a breach of covenants occurs.[19]

Consequently, the use of covenants may vary from firm to firm[20] and from industry to industry. Goswani/Noe/Rebello (1995) show that the use of covenants is not necessarily based on the existence of informational asymmetries, but on their temporal distribution. If there is little doubt in the market that a company—for example, a tunnel or bridge operator—will ultimately be able to run a profitable business in spite of disturbing near-term asymmetric information, the company will use uncovenanted long-term debt. Of course, it could also try short-term credit to be rolled over. However, because at the respective dates the long-term cash flows would hopefully dominate the lenders' decisions, the roll-over would imply transaction costs, but serve no useful purpose. In contrast, covenanted long-term debt is the financing instrument of choice when informational asymmetries are concentrated around long-term cash flows and previous

---

[17] In this sense, breaches of covenants have been viewed as checkpoints that permit the lender to review proposed actions by the borrower (Zinbarg 1975).

[18] The value of the put determines the default premium on the risk-free interest rate. The option to renegotiate, if effective, reduces the put value and thus the interest rate at which the loan is originally granted.

[19] Gorton/Kahn (1993) point to situations where there is no alternative to an increase of the riskiness of the debtor's business. Renegotiation will then lead to an upward adjustment of the originally agreed interest rate. In this view, renegotiation allows the lender to make adjustments required due to endogeneous volatility of the underlying of the put.

[20] Malitz (1986) provides evidence that firms with a high debt-equity ratio and a high potential of informational asymmetry have the most to gain from dividend constraints and debt ceilings. They use these covenants more frequently than other bond-issuing companies.

cash flows are expected to be stable.[21] If there is no rollover risk or if there is uniformly distributed asymmetric information on cash flows, short-term debt financing is preferred.[22]

Professional lenders tend to assure a sufficient flow of information on the debtor company by various means. If this flow of information is forthcoming, relevant financial ratios and early-warning conclusions to be drawn therefrom can be obtained from the incoming reports. In addition, borrowers may undertake, in a bonding effort, to provide lenders with special reports certifying that all covenants have been complied with. If there is a breach, an ad hoc report is required. Frequently, this report is preceded by an informal notification that a specific breach is imminent. In most instances, there is an incentive to obtain and to use this information: the loan's effective priority is contingent on the lenders' monitoring effort if covenants[23] provide for requests of additional collateral and for early exit (Rajan/Winton 1995). Viewed in the framework where the value of the default risk is reflected by the borrower's put, the lender obviously gains if, by monitoring, he obtains a less risky underlying or shortens the life of the put.

Any action taken by the lender may support monitoring activities by other stakeholders. Triantis/Daniels (1995) view the various stakeholders as engaged in a process of uncoordinated information collection and interpretation. In interactive governance, exits of active or even passive stakeholders serve as information fragments which sophisticated active stakeholders need for the monitoring puzzle. Of course, sophisticated lenders or other mosaicking stakeholders can only act on a third-party control measure if they learn about it. Affirmative covenants may be used by lenders to assure the ready availability of this information.

So far, the lender-protective effects of covenants have been discussed for a solvent company where the primary control rests with owners or their management. As pointed out, covenants are and should be designed and used in a way that corresponds to the lender-protection needs and opportunities, which vary from firm to firm and, moreover, are state-dependent. The dynamic view suggests that lenders, in their own legitimate interest, should participate in corporate decision making. Obviously, an even more active lender involvement is

---

[21] Goswani/Noe/Rebello (1995) hypothesize that covenanted long-term bonds should have a negative announcement effect, and uncovenanted long-term bonds should have a positive announcement effect.

[22] Hoven Stohs/Mauer (1996) view earnings volatility as a good proxy for asymmetric information and find that firms with high earnings volatility tend to use shorter-term debt. If other variables such as interest rate expectations of management are introduced, this may affect instrument choice. Barclay/Smith (1995) provide evidence that short-term debt is used to limit wealth transfers from shareholders to lenders, whereas Hoven Stohs and Mauer, based on different data, suggest that many firms employ low leverage to avoid this conflict of interests.

[23] Or equivalent contractual provisions such as the German banks' General Business Conditions.

required once the incumbent owner-management has demonstrated its inability to run the company successfully and to meet its obligations under the lending agreements. For this case, the agreements ought to provide that the control rights of the owners are transferred to the lenders. Thießen (1996) suggests replacement of incompetent management, triggered by early warning covenants, by the lender who is capable of value-maximizing decisions. If various covenanted stakeholders obtain control rights, these rights should be transferred to this best decision maker, who could afford to pay most for the control rights available. Admittedly, it may be quite difficult to achieve this transfer. But the principle of contractual bankruptcy is clear enough: control should pass over to the lender who attains a higher total firm value than any other stakeholder.[24] In this case, lenders stand the best chance of having their repayment and interest claims met. Lenders' chances are improved by an early dismissal of incompetent management. It is paramount to the protection of lenders that a value-destroying management be stopped long before the company's resources are depleted.

To sum up, the incentive of interactive lenders to monitor and their capacity to act upon a breach of covenants holds the promise of timely and effective control. Consequently, covenanted lending agreements can be expected to minimize the impact of post-contractual strategic action and of managerial slack on the value of debt. So far, we have assumed a world without any lender-specific regulation. This assumption is now relaxed. At first glance, one might expect that lender-specific regulation draws on the experience with contractual lender protection arrangements and merely reflects covenants that have stood the test of time. This view would imply that this regulation aims at a value of debt unimpaired by potential slack and strategic action. In the following section, we challenge this notion by a brief survey of bankruptcy law. Lender liability law would have been an equally promising field. Lender liability, like bankruptcy law, can be used to reduce much of the legitimate control pressure on owners and management which is to be expected under a purely contractual arrangement. Since, in our view, there is sufficient evidence that lender liability threatens the active governance role of lenders which a contractual-arrangement approach requires,[25] we focus on bankruptcy law.

The reluctance of lenders to employ covenants in some jurisdictions reflects this threat. However, provided their loans are substantial enough to warrant the monitoring effort, the keen interest of sophisticated lenders remains to participate

---

[24] Along similar lines, Triantis/Daniels (1995) propose to screen stakeholders. The actor with the best incentive and expertise to correct managerial slack should exercise voice and instigate change, not lenders entangled in conflicts of interest.

[25] Köndgen (1995), Häuser (1995), Obermüller (1991), Thießen (1996), Triantis/Daniels (1995). McDaniel (1986: 439-41) argues that in the U.S., the reluctance to issue contingent voting bonds or to have bondholder representatives on the board of directors is motivated by lender liability.

in the processes which lead up to decisions on dividends, repurchases, acquisitions, changes in product lines, and other major uses of funds. If lender monitoring is constrained by the notion of improper interference in company matters and subsequent liability, the need to participate in the decision making may be met on a formal or informal basis which, on the surface, appears unrelated to lending and, ideally, provides a safe harbor. Supervisory boards in Germany mandated by company or co-determination law seem to be a case in point.[26] We suggest that the prominent role of bankers on these boards reflects a unique constellation of lender needs, lender liability, and bankruptcy law.

C. Bankruptcy Law and Lenders' Monitoring

I. Objectives of Bankruptcy Law

Bankruptcy proceedings can be triggered by lenders or the borrower himself if there is a high probability that the firm cannot meet its contractual payments to lenders. It is important how the law defines the criterion allowing lenders and/or borrowers to trigger proceedings, since the opinion that proceedings are triggered too late and that this is a wealth-decreasing feature of bankruptcy proceedings is widespread.[27] We will come back to this point later. When a proceeding is triggered, at least two problems have to be solved. The first is the "common pool problem":[28] how can lenders be restrained from using their rights to seize the firm's assets? The grab rules destroy the possible excess value that the pool of assets is supposed to have irrespective of insolvency. The most common answer of bankruptcy law to this problem is an automatic stay[29] for at least the first months of the proceedings. This permits the claimholders to obtain sufficient information about the options available.

The second point is a problem of collective action: how should the proceeding, that is information gathering, valuation of different options to dispose of the assets of the firm, and the decision making, be organized to produce a result for the usually great number of claimholders? This result should not deviate from the outcome which the decisions of a single owner would have. While the automatic stay is considered to be an acceptable answer to the common pool problem, there are no similarly convincing answers to the second problem. Different jurisdictions have found quite different answers to the problem of collective action of

[26] Schmidt et al. (1997: 159-61). It is a long-held notion that supervisory board representation of German banks serves to control credit risk. Cf. Fischer (1956: 46).

[27] For the U.S., see Jackson (1986); for Germany, see Kilger (1975); for France, see Paillusseau/Petiteau (1985) and Campana (1986: 183).

[28] Jackson (1982).

[29] *Suspension provisoire des poursuites*; *Herausgabesperre*.

claimholders and virtually none of these is near to the theoretical ideal, that the decisions of claimholders inside bankruptcy proceedings should be very close to actions a single owner would take.

II. Costs of Bankruptcy

Costs of bankruptcy are usually separated into direct and indirect costs. Direct costs are defined as the costs caused by the formal proceedings: costs of court, administrator and expert fees, and the costs of creditors' committees.

Indirect costs are harder to define and to measure. It is useful to distinguish different aspects of indirect costs of bankruptcy.

(1) Bankruptcy proceedings are a filtering device:[30] insolvent firms which are economically efficient should survive; other insolvent firms should be shut down. Given uncertainty, conflicts of interest and the problems of organizing collective decisions produce filtering failure. Type I error means that economically not viable firms are continued, thus increasing wealth reductions of creditors. Type II error means that viable firms, earning their cost of capital, are liquidated, thus producing losses to equity holders and creditors, and temporary disruptions when employees are laid off and relationships to suppliers and customers are cut. The probabilities of both errors should be minimized.

(2) Managers or owners can be treated differently in the proceedings. If they are replaced automatically by an administrator and if the code is biased toward liquidation, they will try hard to avoid insolvency via optimal investment decisions. If they expect to keep their positions in the insolvent firm and to profit from lenient rules of a code, the managerial input and the value of the firm will be reduced: the "punishment effect"[31], determined by lost market value, is high.

(3) Managers of a firm facing insolvency may choose to "gamble".[32] They increase business risk to avoid formal proceedings.[33] This "gambling effect" depends on how managers and owners are treated in the proceedings. A lenient treatment could reduce the gambling effect.

(4) Another observable reaction of managers (owners) in firms with declining performance is the delay strategy. They continue operations even if the firm

---

[30] White (1992).

[31] White (1993: 13-5).

[32] White (1993: 16-9).

[33] Gambling occurs at the expense of creditors, when the decisions are NPV-negative or when they do not profit from the payoffs.

is insolvent. This delay effect can be expected to be the more pronounced the less lenient the code treats managers and owners in the proceedings.

(5) The fifth aspect is the problem of lost investment opportunities (under-investment) or overinvestment induced by features of the insolvency proceedings. Investment projects might lapse because of conflicts between lenders and equity holders or because new financing is not available. In contrast, overinvestment may take place if lenders cannot stop value-decreasing decisions of the debtor in possession.

(6) Finally, the costs depend on the extent to which terms of pre-petition debt contracts are observed. Observation of the absolute priority rule (APR) could reduce negotiation problems and direct costs, since it contributes to streamlined, speedy proceedings. Non-observation of APR may affect the pricing of debt and the willingness of lenders to lend.

III. Bankruptcy Regimes and Lenders' Control

In principle, bankruptcy proceedings could support the monitoring strategies of creditors, since triggering proceedings enhances the strategic possibilities of creditors in defending their claims. In Germany, e.g., a creditor-based initiation of bankruptcy proceedings is allowed only if claims are not fully secured. This emphasizes the supplementary character of bankruptcy proceedings. But bankruptcy proceedings do not only enlarge the strategic possibilities of *individual* creditors. Bankruptcy rules are the basis for *collective* actions of creditors, where the claims of uninformed creditors with weak contractual rights should and could be defended by putting them under the umbrella held up by informed creditors with stronger contractual rights.

The question of whether bankruptcy proceedings support the monitoring activities of creditors at all and to what degree cannot be answered without a detailed analysis of the bankruptcy rules. We will look at the core rules of insolvency codes in France, the United States, and Germany in order to show that the interrelation between creditors' monitoring and bankruptcy proceedings varies greatly indeed.

1. France

The French insolvency code is characterized by an early warning system (*procédure d'alerte*), composition proceedings (*règlement amiable*), and bankruptcy proceedings (*redressement et liquidation judicaires*).

The *règlement amiable* (*RA*) can[34] be triggered only by incumbent managers or owners if the firm is not insolvent but unable to meet payments which will become due soon.[35] The proceedings are opened by the president of the tribunal de commerce and organized by a conciliateur, who orchestrates the (re)negotiations with all or the main creditors of the firm. The proceedings must come to an end within four months. An automatic stay eliminates exit options of creditors and preserves the excess value of the common pool of assets. Suboptimal investment decisions are unlikely to be continued or taken during the *RA* given the control of the conciliateur and the limited time of the proceedings. Direct costs are presumably low. Empirical data, which are scarce,[36] seem to show that the *RA* is not often used. We will come back to this point later.

The proceedings called *redressement et liquidation judiciaire* (*RLJ*) were introduced in 1985[37] and slightly improved in 1994. The main functions of the proceedings are (1) the continuation of the firm's activities, (2) maintenance of its employment, and (3) the satisfaction of creditors' claims. There is no doubt among legal scholars nor after an economic analysis of the rules that creditors' interests are clearly subordinated to the goals of preserving the firm's activities. Any creditor may initiate insolvency proceedings, whereas managers and owners must initiate insolvency proceedings if the firm is insolvent. The court nominates an administrator and a representative of the creditors (*représentant des créanciers*). It is the court which decides whether the incumbent managers must relinquish control. Alternatively, the administrator, by order of the court, merely controls the decisions of the debtor in possession (surveillance). The administrator has to design a reorganization plan[38] or a liquidation plan during an observation period of given length. The court, not the lenders, decides on continuation or liquidation.[39] At no point in the proceedings are creditors invited to decide on the use of the assets. Their grab rights are stayed, and post-petition interest does not accrue during the period of observation for many of them. They receive individual invitations from the administrator to extend loan maturities and/or to agree to reductions of claims. Lenders who do not accept the modifications proposed by the administrator or at least respond within 30 days run the risk of the court

---

[34] We will not discuss the interesting structure of the early warning system, even if the *procédure d'alerte* might produce the appropriate signals necessary for entering into a *RA*.

[35] "... entreprise, qui, sans être en cessation des paiements, éprouve une difficulté ... financière ou des besoins ne pouvant être couverts par un financement adapté aux possibilités de l'entreprise".

[36] Rey (1993); Bauch (1996: 88-90).

[37] Loi No 85-98 du 25 janvier 1985 relative au redressement et à la liquidation judiciaires des entreprises.

[38] *Plan de redressement* (Art. 18 L).

[39] Art. 8, Art. 61 L.

determining new maturities and repayment schedules.[40] Courts, in extending maturity, should adjust interest payments in a way that preserves the present value of the lender's claim; but this is not the case, as an analysis of court decisions reveals. Non-compensated extensions are equivalent to claim reductions. Since the law does not discriminate between secured and unsecured claims, continuation also threatens secured claims.[41]

The claims of pre-petition creditors may be reduced further by new financing during the observation period. Since the French code favors the maintenance of firms' activities, the superpriority of new creditors seems straightforward.[42] Superpriority reduces the value of old claims if no corresponding investment with positive net present values takes place. As shown above, lenders do not have much say on these issues.

If the firm is sold to a third party (cession)—and it is the court which decides on a sale—the rights of secured creditors concerning the collateral perish. In order to compensate this, the court allocates a part of the proceeds from the sale to the previous holders of collateral. Allocation rules are not fixed by law.[43]

Consequently, we do not suggest classifying the French code as a creditor-oriented regime. Grab rights are stayed, post-petition interest is denied, creditors lose all meaningful decision rights, courts decide on continuation, sale, or liquidation, and on compensation payments for lost collateral. It is an interesting question why the *RA* procedure, where most of the above restrictions on creditors' action do not prevail, is not used more often. Empirical data are not available. Of course, the restrictions on creditors imposed by law enlarge the scope of managers and owners if they seek protection under the *RLJ* instead. Therefore, managers and owners do not prefer *RA* proceedings where creditors are considerably less constrained. On the other hand, creditors are obviously not successful in "sending" firms into *RA* proceedings. One reason could be that the window for entering an *RA* is narrow: the firm must not be insolvent but unable to meet payments which will become due soon. Given a narrow window, informational lags of creditors may be responsible for their apparent inability to force firms into an *RA*.

---

[40] Art. 74 L.

[41] Automatic stay is an element of the reorganization plan.

[42] Art. 40 L.

[43] Art. 93L. It is not clear whether the market value of the security is relevant or an APR analogy is followed by courts. Exceptions from the above rule become relevant when the finance contract secured by the collateral served to finance the collateral.

2. United States

The Bankruptcy Code in Chapter 11 allows a firm to remain in operation while a plan of reorganization is worked out with its creditors. Chapter 7 is available for the purpose of liquidation. The initiation of bankruptcy proceedings is mostly triggered by incumbent managers or owners who, under the pressure of creditors' actions, decide to find a solution under the protection of Chapter 11. To facilitate reorganization and renegotiations, the rights of creditors are stayed. Incumbent managers are permitted to remain in charge and are equipped with substantial rights. Once under Chapter 11, the debtor in possession continues to operate his firm and has the exclusive right, for the first 120 days after filing (exclusivity period), to propose a reorganization plan, and another 60 days to obtain creditor approval. The court can and often does extend the exclusivity period. Lenders are represented by creditors' committees. Post-petition interest continues to accrue on fully secured debt only.

A plan of reorganization has to be voted on by classes of creditors of substantially similar claims. Equity is always a separate class. Approval of a plan of reorganization requires a majority of each class by number and two thirds by face value of claims. Under certain circumstances, the proposer of a plan can use the "cram down" rules to prevent a particular class from holding out. The proposer must show that the plan follows the absolute priority rule, thus observing the pre-bankruptcy rights.

The rules try to offer protection to creditors even though the core of the code is debtor-oriented: creditors may petition for immediate liquidation or for a trustee (for cause); minorities of classes are protected by minimum standards defined by liquidation values; dissenting classes are protected by the absolute priority rule.

Empirical data on Chapter 11 proceedings are plentiful. The main results are:

(1) The renegotiation process of Chapter 11 is time-consuming. The average time between petition date and reorganization plan confirmation date is approximately two years (Table 1).

(2) The direct costs of the proceedings are considerable. Below, the costs are given in percent of the value of the involved claims or in percent of relevant liquidation value (Table 2).

(3) Absolute Priority Rule (APR) is generally not observed (Table 3).

(4) Decisions of courts on the valuation of collateral, risk-adjusted discount rates and the feasibility of reorganization plans—feasibility is a necessary requirement for the confirmation of plans—appear in empirical studies to be of low quality. Gilson (1992, 1997) shows that 80% of the firms of his sample (111) leave Chapter 11 with a leverage ratio above industry average.

Table 1: Number of Months Required for Reorganization Plan Preparation and
          Approval

Authors of Studies	Year	Number of Firms	Proceedings Taking Place in	Number in Months
Flynn, E.	1989	2,395	1979-1986	22[c]
Jensen-Conklin, S.	1991	45	1980-1989	22
White, M.J.	1990	26	n.b.	17
Weiss, L.A.	1990	37[a]	1979-1986	30
Franks/Torous	1989	14	1979-1986	32
Lopucki/Whitford	1990	43[b]	1979-1988	30
Lopucki, L.M.	1983	57	1979-1982	10

Notes: [a] Corporations with shares quoted on NYSE or AMEX.
         [b] Firms with total assets of more than $100 Mill.
         [c] With a range between 461 and 941 days.

Table 2: Direct Costs of Bankruptcy Proceedings

Authors of Studies	Year	Number of Firms	Time Span Covered	Costs in Percent
White, M.J.[a]	1989	26	1979-1986	3.4[c]
Weiss, L.A.[a]	1990	37	1979-1986	3.1[d]
Ang/Chua/McConnell[b]	1982	55	1963-1979	7.5[e]
Gessner et al.[b]	1978	ca. 400	1970-1977	4.5[f]

Notes: [a] Direct costs of Chapter 11 proceedings.
         [b] Direct costs of liquidation (Chapter 7).
         [c] Of present value of all payments to creditors fixed by the plan.
         [d] Of value of equity plus face value of debt at the end of the last year before entrance
              into the proceedings.
         [e] Of liquidation value.
         [f] Of liquidation value minus claims of fully secured creditors.

Table 3: Non-Observation of APR in Percent of Chapter 11 Firms

Authors of Studies	Year	Number of Firms	Time Span Covered	Non-Observation of APR in Percent
Lopucki/Whitford	1990	43	1979-1988	95%
Weiss, L.A.	1990	37	1979-1986	78%
Franks/Torous	1989	27	1979-1986	78%
Eberhart/Moore/Roenfeldt	1990	30	1979-1986	77%

Lopucki/Whitford[44] report a refiling rate of 32%. Jensen-Conklin (1991) shows that only 60% of firms whose plan of reorganization is confirmed by court complete all required distributions and provisions of the plan. Out of these, 25% of the firms are liquidated.

(5) The intended balance of power between debtor in possession and controlling creditors' committees seems to be biased in favor of the debtor. The case study of Eastern Airlines (Weiss 1992) shows that even informed creditors' committees do not succeed in stopping value-decreasing strategies of incumbent managers and owners. The study of Hotchkiss (1994) analyzing the post-confirmation performance of firms (197) supports this bias. Based on accounting data, 70% of the firms show a below-average performance in their industry. Approximately 40% of firms show negative operating cash flows up to five years after confirmation. The consummation of plans of reorganization is not the rule. 15% of the firms refiled after Chapter 11 or Chapter 7 proceedings.

3. Germany

We will address only the new code, which will come into force in 1999 (*Insolvenzordnung*). The objective of the code is to maximize the financial result to all parties. The code contains rules on liquidation, total sale, and reorganization. There is an automatic stay for some creditors and a stay to be triggered by the administrator for others. Preferred creditors no longer exist. As a rule, the proceedings are orchestrated by an administrator. A debtor in possession is only permitted in minor cases. Both the administrator and the debtor are allowed to design reorganization plans. These plans are prepared in cooperation with creditors' committees. Creditors vote on plans in separate groups. Simple majority by number and by claims is required. Minorities of groups are protected by minimum standards. Hold-out strategies of dissenting groups can be attacked by rules called *Obstruktionsverbot*, an analogy to the "cram down" rules of Chapter 11 BC. They provide a guarantee that groups of creditors cannot gain at the expense of another group given the pre-bankruptcy distribution of rights. It is this voting procedure on reorganization plans that reduces the powers of the administrator. Since empirical data will not be available for some time, we provide some preliminary conjectures:

(1) Since the monopoly rights of a debtor in possession do not exist, the new German code is, like the *Konkursordnung*, creditor-oriented. Strong deviations from the APR are not to be expected.

(2) Automatic stay bars the exit option to creditors for the reason explained

---

[44] Lopucki and Whitford (1993); 12 out of 38 firms.

above. The new code provides for compensation of any lender losses which might result from the stay.

(3) Direct costs of bankruptcy are to a considerable degree costs of the administrator and a function of the size of the firm, duration of proceedings, and number of expert opinions used. Although the administrator seems to avoid the conflicts of interest created by a debtor in possession, some direct costs are unavoidable. We expect that the direct costs under the new code will be rather modest.

(4) For creditor-oriented codes, the delay problem is a tough issue: proceedings are initiated too late. The German code(s) rely heavily on the obligation of managers and owners to initiate a proceeding as the company hits the trigger point defined by law: inability to pay its debt and/or overindebtedness. It is doubtful whether these trigger points are well defined and are observed in practice.

Table 4 summarizes the main characteristics of the three codes.

IV. Bankruptcy Law, Costs, and Contractual Arrangements

Given the structure of bankruptcy codes and the various indirect costs defined above, a summary like Table 5 would be desirable. Even if the costs cannot be quantified exactly, comparative suggestions are possible: the French code produces higher errors of type I than the German code; the observation of APR under the French code is less strict than under the U.S. code. We will leave more specified answers to further research and turn to the question of the role of contractual arrangements in a regime of bankruptcy law.

(1) Whether contractual arrangements of lenders (collateral-based contract, me-first rules) extend into the period of insolvency depends on the code.

(2) The more a code is creditor-oriented, the higher the probability that APR and pre-bankruptcy rights are observed.

(3) Creditor-orientation is no guarantee that the optimal decisions are made. This is due to the principle that the residual claimants should decide. Therefore, the problem of who holds the decision rights has to be solved first. This can be done by giving all equity rights to creditors and giving options to equity holders whose exercise price corresponds to the face value of debt.[45] After the exercise of the options, it is clear who holds the residual claims and who makes the final decisions. No code of insolvency implements this idea.

(4) In the shadow of bankruptcy law, contractual arrangements and lenders' monitoring do contribute to the initiation of insolvency proceedings. If the monitoring lenders detect declining performance, informal workouts follow.

---

[45] Bebchuk (1988); Aghion/Hart/Moore (1995).

Table 4: Main Characteristics of the Insolvency Proceedings in France, Germany, and the United States

	France	
	Règlement amiable	*Redressement et liquidation judiciaires*
Managerial control	Incumbent managers (owners) keep control; *conciliateur* organizes negotiations.	Incumbent managers may keep control but are controlled by an *administrateur*. Court decides upon distribution of competences.
Insolvency triggers	Firm must not be insolvent in the sense of cessation des paiements, but must have serious financial problems.	Firm is insolvent; *cessation des paiements*.
Automatic stay	All creditor claims are stayed for a maximum of three months.	All creditor claims are stayed.
Going concern versus liquidation	Liquidation is not a relevant issue.	Primary goals of the law is the preservation of the firm and of the jobs of the employees. Court decides whether liquidation takes place or not.
Rearrangement of capital structure	Renegotiation is initiated with all or the main creditors.	Creditors are invited to offer claim reductions or longer repayment schedules; court can impose longer repayment schedules.
Quality of decisions inside the process	Due to time restrictions (four months) and restrictions on managerial control, inefficient decisions are unlikely.	Due to long periods of observation and reduced monitoring activities of creditors, quality of decisions may deteriorate.
Post-bankruptcy financing		New financing is facilitated by priority positions given to new creditors.
Deviations from absolute priority rule	Deviations in favor of equity seem plausible.	Deviations in favor of equity holders are highly probable; empirical studies are not available.
Direct costs	Low due to time restrictions.	High due to liberal time horizons and diluted monitoring rights of creditors.

Table 4 continued

	Germany *Insolvenzordnung* (new code, effective in 1999)	U.S. *Chapter 11 Bankruptcy Code*
Managerial control	Incumbent managers must as a rule relinquish control.	Debtor in possession as a rule; creditors' committees in proceedings of large companies.
Insolvency triggers	a) Inability to pay fixed obligations when they come due. b) Overindebtedness.	Voluntary petition as a rule.
Automatic stay	All claims are stayed automatically or can be stayed by the administrator.	All claims are stayed; minor exceptions (e.g., lease payments).
Going concern versus liquidation	Creditors, separated into classes, decide on liquidation, sale, or reorganization (going concern).	Substantial influence of debtor in possession if operating cash flows are positive; courts often oppose early liquidations.
Rearrangement of capital structure	Renegotiation is initiated with all creditors.	Renegotiation is initiated with all creditors.
Quality of decisions inside the process	Better results than in Chapter 11 BC to be expected due to more intensive monitoring by creditors and less influence of previous managers.	Poor: firms leave proceedings with above average degrees of leverage; reorganization plans are not realized; high refiling rate; long duration of proceedings.
Post-bankruptcy financing	New financing can be raised; creditors decide whether new claims should have superpriority or not in case of refiling.	New financing is available.
Deviations from absolute priority rule	No data available.	Deviations from APR are a common feature of Chapter 11 proceedings.
Direct costs	No data available.	High because (1) high fees for lawyers, (2) long duration of proceedings, (3) extensive influence of courts.

Table 5: Determinants and Scope of Indirect Costs of Bankruptcy

Scope	Determinants of Indirect Costs of Bankruptcy						
	Punishment Effect	Gambling Effect	Delay Effect	Error Type I	Error Type II	Underinvestment, Overinvestment	Observation of APR
Time during which costs occur	Before insolvency	Between insolvency and initiation of proceedings		During the proceedings		During the proceedings	During the proceedings
Firms affected	All firms	Insolvent firms	Insolvent firms	Insolvent, not viable	Insolvent but viable	Insolvent	Insolvent
Relevance of costs when no lenient treatment of managers and owners can be expected.	Low	High	High	Low	High	Costs depend on who holds the decision rights and on the ease and structure of new financing.	Costs depend on primary goals of the code and the permitted intensity of lender control.

If they are not successful, insolvency proceedings are unavoidable. Monitoring lenders "send" unsuccesful firms into proceedings. This is an important aspect of the control hypothesis of debt (Jensen 1986).

(5) Contractual arrangements may speed up insolvency proceedings. This happens when "prepackaged bankruptcy" occurs. The incentive to design "prepackaged bankruptcy" is higher the less bankruptcy proceedings themselves are streamlined. Prepackaging then assumes a function that proceedings aimed at minimizing costs should or could accomplish.

D. Implications and Conclusion

We see corporate governance as the network of arrangements and rules, contractual or legal, which are designed to facilitate and to foster value-maximizing behavior of firms. Our focus is on risky debt. Lenders who put their money at risk in a world without lender-specific regulation have to protect themselves contractually by covenants. Alternative contractual safeguards are early maturity, seniority, and collateral. Compared to covenants, they are less encompassing and not dealt with here. Under the static view, covenants are seen to effectively constrain the borrower, from the issue to the maturity of the debt instrument, and to assure substantial lender protection. The value-of-debt increasing effect is caused directly by the covenant. The lender's contribution to corporate governance is rather limited. The key activity is designing the contract.

Under the dynamic view, in contrast, effective lender protection is not feasible at the time when the debt is issued. As time goes on, new states of the world unfold, and the lenders obtain a reasonably complete picture of the necessities and opportunities to protect their position. Overinvestment and underinvestment become real and concrete issues as the financial situation of a previously strong debtor deteriorates. Previously unknown action in the lender's interest can be taken. Therefore, much of the value-increasing effect rests on the lender's monitoring and on the action triggered by a breach of covenant. This realistic view requires and legitimizes an active lender role in corporate governance. Any sophisticated lender, provided that his loan is substantial enough to warrant the monitoring effort, has a keen interest in taking a role in the process which leads up to decisions on dividends, repurchases, acquisitions, changes in product lines, and other major uses of funds. Seen in this light, the Jensen argument on the control effect of debt gains strength if it relates to high business risk and high-leverage companies. At companies with low business risk and low debt ratios, however, we encounter low-risk or safe debt, and the attendant constraints on management and owners are rather weak and limited to the capture of some potentially free cash flow.

A breach of covenants opens up a window of opportunity to renegotiate. Risky debt implies a put option of the borrower with an exercise price equal to the face value of debt. The key issue for the lender is to contribute to the value of the underlying, i.e., to a sufficiently high value of the firm's assets in all states of the world. This objective is maintained even if contractual bankruptcy results in a transfer of control to lenders. Obviously, very little lender action is required while the value of the firm's assets is way above the face value of all debt and a high margin of safety is being maintained. Much more lender monitoring and action is needed, however, as the value of the firm's assets drops and gets close to the debt's face value. As the financial situation of a firm deteriorates, the intensity of the lenders' corporate governance activities gradually increases. Their interest in maximizing the total value of the firm becomes keen as the value of equity diminishes. A black and white approach to lenders' role in corporate governance—i.e., no active involvement before bankruptcy, but an active role thereafter—is clearly misconceived.[46]

In the second part of our paper we turn to a world with lender-specific regulation, such as lender liability and bankruptcy law. For lender liability, it is well-documented that it impedes lender monitoring and control. The legitimate need to participate in corporate governance is not met on a formal level directly relating to lending. This may or may not decrease the value of debt, depending on alternative platforms and substitutes, formal or informal, for direct lender monitoring.[47] Members of a German supervisory board are legally in a uniquely protected position to exert lender control. We hypothesize that this contributes much to the prominent role of bankers on these boards.

Bankruptcy law provides a legal framework for lenders and owners to renegotiate. Lenders may seek this opportunity. Whether they can and do initiate bankruptcy proceedings depends on the features of the bankruptcy code. The bankruptcy law of the relevant jurisdiction determines (1) the intensity of lender monitoring during bankruptcy proceedings, and (2) the value of pre-bankruptcy contractual arrangements. There are substantial country-to-country differences, as our analysis of the French, the U.S., and the new German codes shows. Compared with German law, the French and U.S. codes are manager- or owner-oriented and impede lenders in protecting themselves.

These differences have important consequences even before bankruptcy, although tax and other institutional factors may reinforce or dull their impact. Under an owner-oriented regime, lenders are reluctant to make loans to risky firms. If they lend at all, they accept otherwise equal risky debt instruments only at interest rates which are higher than the rates at which lenders in countries with

---

[46] If there is junior and senior debt, subordinated lenders are affected first by deteriorating performance and, therefore, should be in a position to exercise voice at an early state. Of course, their incentive and their ability to monitor effectively is reduced unless they can call their loans.

[47] A well-known formal substitute or complement is monitoring by third parties such as rating agencies. Much informal monitoring is face-to-face and difficult to observe.

a creditor-oriented code would provide funds. For further research, we hypothesize that risk premia on loans to more risky firms are to a large extent an artifact
of the legal environment. In jurisdictions which impede lender monitoring, we
expect to find, due to the higher relative attractiveness of equity, lower debt-
equity ratios.[48] Consequently, financial structure is affected. In countries with
owner-oriented codes we expect well-developed equity and venture capital
markets, whereas a creditor-oriented law fosters credit markets and non-
standardized bank lending even to small and risky firms. Our analysis supports
the path dependency proposition: the task of corporate governance is the same in
all market economies, but country-specific institutions determine how it is taken
care of.

---

[48] Tax-shield differences between the jurisdictions may or may not have reverse influence
(as may have other factors). Substantial tax benefits may be used to compensate lenders for poor
bankruptcy protection.

References

Aghion, Philippe, Oliver Hart, and John Moore 'Insolvency Reform in the UK: A Revised Proposal' 11 *Insolvency Law and Practice* 65-74 (1995).

Ang, James S., J.H. Chua, and John McConnell 'The Administrative Costs of Corporate Bankruptcy: A Note' *Journal of Finance* 37 (1982) 219-26.

Baird, Douglas G. 'The Uneasy Case for Corporate Reorganization' 15 *J. Leg. Stud.* 127-47 (1986).

Baird, Douglas G. 'Revisiting Auctions in Chapter 11' *Journal of Law and Economics* 36 (1993) 633-69.

Barclay, Michael J. and Clifford W. Smith 'The Maturity Structure of Corporate Debt' *Journal of Finance* 50 (1995) 609-31.

Barclay, Michael J. and Clifford W. Smith 'The Priority Structure of Corporate Liabilities' *Journal of Finance* 50 (1995a) 899-917.

Bauch, Matthias *Unternehmensinsolvenzen: Prophylaxe und Bewältigung in Frankreich* (Dissertation University of Regensburg 1996).

Bebchuk, Lucian A. 'A New Model for Corporate Reorganizations' 110 *Harv. L. Rev.* 775-884 (1988).

Beranek, William, Robert Boehmer, and Brooke Smith 'Much Ado about Nothing: Absolute Priority Deviations in Chapter 11' *Financial Management* 25/3 (1996) 102-9.

Berle, Adolf A. and Gardiner C. Means *The Modern Corporation and Private Property* (New York 1932).

Berlin, Mitchell and Loretta J. Mester 'Debt Covenants and Renegotiation' *Journal of Financial Intermediation* 2/2 (1992) 95-133.

Campana, Marie-Jeanne 'La Situation des Créanciers' *Les Innovations de la Loi sur le Redressement Judiciaire des Entreprises* (Revue Trimestrielle de Droit Commercial et de Droit Economiqu, Numéro Special, vol. 1 (1986)) 171-86.

Chatterjee, Sris, Upinder S. Dhillon, and, Gabriel G. Raimirez 'Resolution of Financial Distress: Debt Restructuring via Chapter 11, Prepackaged Bankruptcies, and Workouts' *Financial Management* 25/1 (1996) 5-18.

Citron, David B. 'The Use of Financial Ratio Covenants in UK Bank Loan Contracts and the Implications for Accounting Method Choice' (Working Paper, City University Business School, London 1992).

Cox, John C. and Mark Rubinstein *Options Markets* (Englewood Cliffs, N.J. 1985).

Derrida, Fernand 'Le Financement de l'Entreprise' *Les Innovations de la Loi sur le Redressement Judiciaire des Entreprises* (Revue Trimestrielle de Droit Commercial et de Droit Economiqu, Numéro Special, vol. 1 (1986)) 61-73.

Drukarczyk, Jochen 'Insolvenzrechtsreform: Reformkonzeptionen und aktueller Stand' *Die Betriebswirtschaft* 52 (1992) 161-82.

Drukarczyk, Jochen *Theorie und Politik der Finanzierung* 2nd edn. (Munich 1993).

Drukarczyk, Jochen 'Soll das Insolvenzrecht eine Reorganisation zulassen?' in: Gerke, Wolfgang (ed.) *Planwirtschaft am Ende—Marktwirtschaft in der Krise?* (Festschrift W. Engels) 109-37 (Stuttgart 1994).

Drukarczyk, Jochen 'Verwertungsformen und Kosten der Insolvenz' *Betriebswirtschaftliche Forschung und Praxis* 47 (1995) 40-57.

Drukarczyk, Jochen 'Gesellschafterdarlehen, Rechtsprechungsgrundsätze des BGH und § 32a GmbHG—Einige kritische Anmerkungen' in: Elschen, Rainer, Theodor Siegel, and Franz W. Wagner (eds.) *Unternehmenstheorie und Besteuerung* (Festschrift D. Schneider) 171-202 (Wiesbaden 1995a).

Easterbrook, Frank H. 'Is Corporate Bankruptcy Efficient?' *Journal of Financial Economics* 27 (1990) 411-7.

Eberhart, Allan C., William T. Moore, and Rodney L. Roenfeldt 'Security Pricing and Deviations from the Absolute Priority Rule in Bankruptcy Proceedings' *Journal of Finance* 45 (1990) 1457-69.

'Entwurf einer Insolvenzordnung (InsO), Gesetzentwurf der Bundesregierung' *BT-Drucksache* 12/R 443 (15.4.1992).

Fischer, Otfrid *Bankbilanz-Analyse* (Meisenheim 1956).

Flynn, E. 'Statistical Analysis of Chapter 11' (ed. by Administrative Office of the United States Courts) (Washington, D.C. 1989).

Franke, Günter 'Zur rechtzeitigen Auslösung von Sanierungsverfahren' *Zeitschrift für Betriebswirtschaft* 54 (1984) 160-79.

Franks, Julian R., Kjelle Nyborg, and Walter N. Torous 'A Comparison of US, UK and German Insolvency Codes' (IFA Working Paper 206, London 1995).

Franks, Julian R. and Walter N. Torous 'An Empirical Investigation of US Firms in Reorganization' *Journal of Finance* 64 (1989) 747-69.

Galai, Dan and Ronald W. Masulis 'The Option Pricing Model and the Risk Factor of Stock' *Journal of Financial Economics* 3 (1976) 53-81.

Gelauff, George M.M. and Corina den Broeder 'Governance of Stakeholder Relationships. The German and Dutch Experience' (SUERF [Société Universitaire Européene de Recherches Financières] Studies no. 1, Amsterdam 1997).

Gessner, Volkmar, Barbara Rhode, Gerhard Strate, and Klaus A. *Zieger Die Praxis der Konkursabwicklung in der Bundesrepublik Deutschland* (Cologne 1978).

Gilson, Stuart C. 'Capital Structure Rearrangements in Firms that Default: An Empirical Study' (Working Paper, Harvard Business School 1992).

Gilson, Stuart C. 'Transactions Cost and Capital Structure Choice: Evidence from Financially Distressed Firms' *Journal of Finance* 52 (1997) 161-96.

Gilson, Stuart C., Kose John, and Larry H.P. Lang 'Troubled Debt Restructurings' *Journal of Financial Economics* 27 (1990) 315-53.

Gilson, Stuart C. and Michael R. Vetsuypen 'CEO Compensation in Financially Distressed Firms: An Empirical Analysis' (Working Paper, Harvard Law School 1992).

Gorton, Gary and Jones A. Kahn 'The Design of Bank Loan Contracts, Collateral, and Renegotiation' (NBER Working Paper no. 4273, 1993).

Goswami, Gautam, Thomas Noe, and Michael Rebello 'Debt Financing under Asymmetric Information' *Journal of Finance* 50 (1993) 633-59.

Häuser, Franz (1995) 'Rechte und Pflichten der Kreditinstitute bei der Sanierung von Unternehmen' in: Hadding, Walther, Klaus J. Hopt, and Herbert Schimansky (eds.) *Sicherheitenfreigabe und Unternehmenssanierung—Aktuelle Rechtsfragen* 75-125 (Berlin 1995).

Hax, Herbert 'Economic Aspects of Bankruptcy Law' *Zeitschrift für die gesamte Staatswissenschaft* 141 (1985) 80-98.

Hotchkiss, Edith 'The Post-Bankruptcy Performance of Firms Emerging from Chapter 11' (Working Paper, Harvard Law School 1994).

Hoven Stohs, Mark and David C. Mauer 'The Determinants of Corporate Maturity Structure' *Journal of Business* 69 (1996) 279-312.

Jackson, Thomas H. 'Bankruptcy, Non Bankruptcy Entitlements and the Creditor's Bargain' 91 *Yale L.J.* 857-907 (1982).

Jackson, Thomas H. *The Logic and Limits of Bankruptcy Law* (Cambridge 1986).

Jackson, Thomas H. 'Comment on Baird: "Revisiting Auctions in Chapter 11"' *Journal of Law and Economics* 36 (1993) 655-9.

Jensen, Michael C. 'Agency Costs of Free Cash Flow, Corporate Finance, and Takeovers' *American Economic Review Papers and Proceedings* 76 (1986) 323-9.

Jensen-Conklin, Susan 'Do Confirmed Chapter 11 Plans Consummate? The Results of a Study and Analysis of the Law' 40 *Comm. L.J.* 297-331 (1991).

Jurgeit, Ludwig (1989), *Bewertung von Optionen und bonitätsrisikobehafteten Finanztiteln.* (Wiesbaden 1989).

Kaiser, Kevin M.J. 'European Bankruptcy Laws: Implications for Corporations Facing Financial Distress' *Financial Management* 25/ 3 (1996) 67-85.

Kemper, Markus *Die U.S.-amerikanischen Erfahrungen mit "Chapter 11"* (Frankfurt am Main 1996).

Kilger, Joachim 'Der Konkurs des Konkurses' *Konkurs, Treuhand, Sanierung—Zeitschrift für Insolvenzrecht* 28 (1975) 142-66.

Klee, Kenneth N. 'All You Ever Wanted to Know About the Cram Down Under the New Bankruptcy Code' 53 *Am. Bankr. L.J.* 133-171 (1979).

Köndgen, Johannes 'Risiken der Kreditinstitute bei der Sanierung von Unternehmen: Rechtsvergleichende Erfahrungen aus den USA, England und Frankreich' in: Hadding, Walther, Klaus J. Hopt, and Herbert Schimansky (eds.) *Sicherheitenfreigabe und Unternehmenssanierung—Aktuelle Rechtsfragen* 141-194 (Berlin 1995).

Lopucki, Lynn M. 'The Debtor in Full Control: Systems Failure Under Chapter 11 of the Bankruptcy Code?' 57 *Am. Bankr. L.J.* 99-117 and 247-73 (1983).

Lopucki, Lynn M. and William C. Whitford 'Bargaining over Equity's Share in the Bankruptcy Reorganization of Large, Publicly Held Companies' 139 *U. Pa. L. Rev.* 125-96 (1990).

Lopucki, Lynn M. and William C. Whitford 'Patterns in the Bankruptcy Reorganization of Large, Publicly Held Companies' 139 *Cornell L. Rev.* 580-607 (1993).

Malitz, Ileen 'On Financial Contracting: The Determinants of Bond Covenants' *Financial Management* 15/2 (1986) 18-25.

McDaniel, Morey W. 'Bondholders and Corporate Governance' 41 *Bus. Law.* 413-60 (1986).

Myers, Stewart C. 'Determinants of Corporate Borrowing' *Journal of Financial Economics* 5 (1977) 147-75.

Obermüller, Manfred *Handbuch Insolvenzrecht für die Kreditwirtschaft. Leitfaden für Konkurs, Vergleich und Gesamtvollstreckung* 4th edn. (Wiesbaden 1991).

Paillusseau, Jean and Gérard Petiteau *Les difficultés des entreprises, prévention et règlement amiable* (Paris 1984).

Rajan, Raghuram and Andrew Winton 'Covenants and Collateral as Incentives to Monitor' *Journal of Finance* 50 (1995) 1113-46.

Rey, Perrette *De l'Usage de la Loi du ler mars 1984 relative à la Prévention et au Réglement amiable des difficultés des Entreprises* (Dissertation, Paris 1993).

Roe, Mark J. 'Commentary on "On the Nature of Bankruptcy": Bankruptcy, Priority and Economics' 75 *Va. L. Rev.* 219-40 (1989).

Schmidt, Hartmut, Jochen Drukarczyk, Dirk Honold, Stefan Prigge, Andreas Schüler, and Gönke Tetens *Corporate Governance in Germany* (Baden-Baden 1997).

Shleifer, Andrei and Robert W. Vishny 'Liquidation Values and Debt Capacity: A Market Equilibrium Approach' *Journal of Finance* 47 (1992) 1343-66.

Smith, Clifford W. and Jerold B. Warner 'On Financial Contracting' *Journal of Financial Economics* 7 (1979) 117-61.

Soinne, Bernard 'La Continuation de l'Entreprise' *Les Innovations de la Loi sur le Redressement Judiciaire des Entreprises* (Revue Trimestrielle de Droit Commercial et de Droit Economiqu, Numéro Special, vol. 1 (1986)) 87-117).

Terhart, Peter *Chapter 11 Bankruptcy Code: Eine Alternative für Deutschland?* (Regensburger Beiträge zur betriebswirtschaftlichen Forschung 10) (Frankfurt am Main et al. 1995).

Thießen, Friedrich 'Covenants in Kreditverträgen: Alternative oder Ergänzung zum Insolvenzrecht' *Zeitschrift für Bankrecht und Bankwirtschaft* 8 (1996) 19-37.

Triantis, George G. and Ronald J. Daniels 'The Role of Debt in Interactive Corporate Governance' 83 *Cal. L. Rev.* 1073-113 (1995).

Trost, Ronald J. 'Business Reorganizations Under Chapter 11 of the New Bankruptcy Code' 21 *UCLA L. Rev.* 540-52 (1973).

Weiss, Lawrence A. 'Bankruptcy Resolution: Direct Costs and Violation of Priority of Claims' *Journal of Financial Economics* 27 (1990) 285-314.

Weiss, Lawrence A. 'Restructuring Complications in Bankruptcy: The Eastern Airlines Bankruptcy Case' (Working Paper, Tulane University, New Orleans 1992).

White, Michelle J. 'The Corporate Bankruptcy Decision' *Journal of Economic Perspectives* 3/2 (1989) 129-51.

White, Michelle J. 'Bankruptcy, Liquidation and Reorganization' in: Logue, Dennis E. (ed.) *Handbook of Modern Finance* Chapter 37 2nd edn. (Boston, New York 1990).

White, Michelle J. 'Corporate Bankruptcy as a Filtering Device' (Working Paper, University of Michigan 1992).

White, Michelle J. 'Corporate Bankruptcy: A US-European Comparison' (Working Paper, University of Michigan 1993).

Wittig, Arne 'Sonstige Sicherheiten' in: Hellner, Thorwald and Stefan Steuer (eds.) *Bankrecht und Bankpraxis* Vol. 2 1251-7, 1279-83, 1285-98 (Cologne 1997).

Zinbarg, Edward D. 'The Private Placement Loan Agreement' *Financial Analysts' Journal* 31/4 (1975), 33-5, 52.

Combining Arm's-Length and Control-Oriented Finance
Evidence from Main Bank Relationships in Sweden

ERIK BERGLÖF and HANS SJÖGREN, Stockholm*

The close and stable relationships between the large commercial banks and non-financial corporations in Sweden came under severe strain over the last decade. The financial system experienced wide-ranging financial deregulation and a rapid expansion of bank lending followed by a dramatic banking crisis and a severe contraction of credits. Using detailed, confidential, and internationally unique data on individual credit contracts, this paper documents the main bank relationships and their evolution during this period. The main findings are: (1) firms continue to rely on a single dominant bank lender throughout the period; (2) the turnover of main bank relationships increases dramatically; (3) the level of bank exposure in individual firms jumps as a result of both higher credit volumes and falling collateralization of credits; (4) many firms establish a second, underutilized, credit facility with another bank; (5) main banks have less collateral than these side banks; and (6) main banks have substantial ownership of equity in borrower firms through related institutions. The strong link between lending and such indirect equity ownership is perhaps the most striking aspect of the Swedish main bank arrangement, and equity holdings are important in sustaining these relationships.

Contents

* We wish to thank Gilles Chemla, Caroline Frohlin, Mats Isaksson, Steve Kaplan, Colin Mayer, Rolf Skog, Luigi Zingales, Yishay Yafeh, and, in particular, Denis Gromb for helpful discussions of earlier versions. Jan Wallander contributed valuable institutional insights and Karin Thorburn competent research assistance.

Figures

Tables

A. Introduction

A corporate governance system can be defined as the mechanisms whereby signals from product and factor markets are channeled into investments decisions.[1] Both the academic and policy discussions have often focused on the role of shareholders and equity markets in providing corporate governance, but the above definition implies that a much larger set of actors and institutional arrangements are potentially involved. In particular, creditors and debt markets, and debtor-creditor law, could play important roles in governance. There may also be significant ties between shareholders and creditors, and between equity and debt markets; when there are such links, studying only the equity side of corporate governance may be grossly misleading. Whether creditors do, in fact, play a role in corporate governance or not is ultimately an empirical, and it seems highly contentious, issue.[2]

This paper studies the role of creditors in corporate governance in the context of main, or house, bank relationships in Sweden. Based on confidential, and internationally unique, detailed data on credit contracts and equity ownership, we characterize the basic structure of the house bank and other major creditor relationships the firm may have and how these relationships were affected by the

---

[1] Another more limited, but essentially equivalent, definition would emphasize the mechanisms whereby investors ensure that they receive promised returns.

[2] On the one hand, evidence from the Japanese main bank system and junk bond financing in the United States suggests that the bank relationships and debt structure, respectively, affect investment decisions; Hoshi/Kashyap/Scharfstein (1990a and 1991a); Asquith/Gertner/Scharfstein (1994). On the other hand, the recent debate over the role of commercial banks in German corporate governance has questioned the conventional wisdom that these institutions play an important, and beneficial, role in corporate governance; see Edwards/Fischer (1994) and Gorton/Schmid (1996) for two different views. Cf. also the following articles in this volume: on German banks, the contributions in Ch. 6 and the respective sections in Prigge (Ch. 12), and on Japanese banks, the respective sections in Hoshi (Ch. 11), Miwa (Ch. 11), and Kanda (Ch. 12).

changes in firm performance and the external environment. The study is based on data on large exposures of the four major Swedish commercial banks in large nonfinancial corporations during the period 1985-1993. These data are then supplemented by accounting information on firm performance and general information on developments in the financial system.

Given the selection criteria of large exposures, it should not be surprising that we find a dominant creditor in the overwhelming majority of firms; more than 90% of the firms in the sample had only one large bank or one bank with a utilized credit at least twice as large as that of the second bank, but many firms also maintained a large credit line with a second bank. More interestingly, there were important differences between the contract of the main bank and that of the side bank. In particular, the credit limit of the main bank was much more utilized than that of the side bank. The main bank also had significantly lower collateral, much higher equity ownership through related institutions (basically investment companies), and a disproportionately high share of the firm's deposits.

We interpret the Swedish main bank arrangements as combining two generic forms of corporate finance—the control-oriented house bank relationship supplemented by an arm's-length relationship to its side bank. The house bank offers monitoring services and possibly ex post flexibility in unforeseen circumstances, holding less collateral and more equity through related institutions. The side bank, by providing the firm with the option to easily change its main bank, serves as a check on rent extraction by the house bank once the relationship has been established.

The study also shows, by historical standards, a very high turnover in bank-firm relationships; more than half of the firms in our sample changed main banks at least once during the period.[3] The greater turnover in these relationships is in general agreement with a commonly held view that firms became more independent during the period and diversified their lending. However, the overwhelming majority of firms in our sample continued to rely on one dominant bank. The increased turnover in these relationships suggests that accumulated information and trust play a lesser role in determining choice of credit relationships; we conjecture that the increasing sophistication of financial markets has decreased the informational advantage of the house bank, shifting its function towards the provision of ex post flexibility.

To understand better the determinants of switches in main bank relationship, we divided the period into two subperiods: the first period is characterized by an economic boom with a rapid expansion of lending activity; and the second period by deep recession, a banking crisis, and a strong contraction in lending. We find

---

[3] From previous studies we know that main bank relationships until the early 1980s were remarkably stable, most of them lasting more than twenty years and in several cases more than 50 years; 'Koncentrationsutredningen (1968); Sjögren (1991).

firm liquidity and ownership links (indirect ownership through related institutions) to be positively correlated with the switch of a main bank during the former period. In the latter period, profitability (return on total capital) was negatively correlated with a switch. One possible interpretation is that the switch in the period of economic boom came at the initiative of the firm, whereas the decision to break a relationship was more likely to be that of the bank during the recession. This suggests that the corporate governance role of banks, and more generally creditors, is less important during periods when firms have high liquidity.

These close relationships between banks and firms are not unique to Sweden but can be found in many, if not most, industrialized countries. Main bank relationships are even common in the United States, in particular in local markets with a concentrated banking sector (Peterson/Rajan 1993). While these arrangements have some traits common across countries, there also seem to be considerable international variations in their structure and behavior (Aoki/Patrick/Sheard 1994; Edwards/Fischer 1994). Unfortunately, due to its sensitive nature, only limited information is available on the structure of these relationships, e.g., the relative size of different bank holdings, the degree of utilization of existing credit lines, and the nature of underlying collateral.[4] There is also little publicly available data on the size of firm deposits in banks and the correlation between debt and equity holdings by banks and related institutions in individual firms. The detailed data used for this study contain such information.

The findings should therefore not only help explain the specifics of the Swedish house banks but hopefully also contribute to the general understanding of main bank relationships, and the role of creditors in corporate governance. In particular, we believe the data shed some light on how house bank relationships are sustained over time and how they may be affected by firm performance and changes in the environment, e.g., in the level of competition in the banking sector and fluctuations in aggregate lending. Finally, the study highlights some properties of the larger financial systems, in particular the complementarities between different forms of finance and the need to study both equity and debt when analyzing corporate governance.

The paper begins by providing a brief overview of the theories of main bank relationships. Section C offers a background to the Swedish financial system and the most important developments during the period 1985-1993—an exceptional period by most standards. Section D presents detailed data on individual credit contracts and related equity holdings in our population of large bank exposures. The observations are discussed and interpreted in Section E, and Section F provides some concluding remarks.

---

[4] A noticeable exception is Japan where detailed data on individual credits are published on a regular basis.

B. Theories of Main Bank Relationships

The recent corporate finance literature has suggested that debt and equity is not the only, and perhaps not the most important, distinction in characterizing financial contracts. This literature instead identifies two generic types of relationships between outside investors and firms. One possibility is for investors not to intervene in the company, at least not as long as payment obligations are met. In the case of such *arm's-length finance,* intervention typically is engineered by a third party, via the market for corporate control or through a court in the case of bankruptcy. Under this form of finance, the firm can commit to behave efficiently and repay investors by, for example, providing collateral, i.e., contingent property rights to individual well-specified and verifiable assets (Hart/Moore 1994; Bolton/Scharfstein, 1993; Berglöf/von Thadden 1994). In arm's-length finance, the liquidity of markets for collateralizable assets thus plays an important role.

The other generic form of corporate finance—*control-oriented finance*—allows investors to intervene in investment decisions (Grossman/Hart 1986; Aghion/Bolton 1992; Dewatripont/Tirole 1994). This is done, for example, through a control block of equity or a position as exclusive or dominant creditor. In control-oriented finance, collateral presumably plays a less important role since investors have other ways of ensuring a return on their investment. Banks can provide both control-oriented and arm's-length finance, and firms often raise both types of finance.

The main bank relationship could be thought of as a form of control-oriented finance extended in the form of secured and unsecured debt, and sometimes supplemented by equity holdings. There are basically two main strands in the literature rationalizing the existence of main bank relationships. One strand focuses on the monitoring, or information collection and governance, role of the bank, and the other emphasizes the role of bank finance in the renegotiation of initial contracts. We here briefly review some of these theories and their implications for the main bank contract, in particular for the choice between exclusivity and having additional credit relationships, and of the level of collateral in monitoring arrangements.

In the monitoring literature, the benefits from main bank relationships stem from the fact that they mitigate asymmetric information problems associated with market-based finance (see, e.g., von Thadden 1990). The monitoring exercised by the bank prevents projects with low short-term returns but long-term viability from being prematurely discontinued. An obvious cost in such an arrangement is the cost of information collection. A more subtle cost, however, stems from the possibility of rent extraction by the bank given its monopoly position ex post. Von Thadden (1992) shows that despite the costs of duplicated monitoring, it may therefore be beneficial to have more than one bank. In a similar vein, Rajan (1992) suggests that to mitigate the problem of ex post rent extraction by informed lenders, the borrowing firm will attempt to weaken the bargaining power of these lenders by giving higher priority, or better collateral, to uninformed lenders.

Another interesting question is why main banks have collateral at all given that they can exercise influence over investment decision, i.e., why not all main bank finance is in the form of unsecured debt.[5] Of course, there may be regulatory restrictions requiring banks to keep down risk exposure in individual firms. Another possible explanation is that the contingent liquidation rights associated with secured debt increases the effectiveness of control. Effective control may also reduce the uncertainty about underlying assets, thus increasing the firm's capacity to raise arm's-length finance. Rajan/Winton (1994) see collateral and monitoring as complements; collateral makes effective priority in financial distress contingent on monitoring. However, according to this view the main bank should hold more collateral than other banks.

Yet another explanation as to why main banks take collateral has been provided by Burkart/Gromb/Panunzi (1995): if the amount of information the bank possesses ex post influences its bargaining power, the bank would want to commit to a certain level of information collection. The use of collateral builds in a bias towards emphasis on liquidation value of the collateralized assets rather than on profits, reducing the incentives for the bank to collect information. The more collateral, the more credible is the commitment not to monitor, and intervene; intervention based on poor information is costly. This theory would also imply that main banks take less collateral than banks extending arm's-length finance; the latter banks would basically like to commit not to intervene at all.

The strand of the literature emphasizing the greater ease by which bank debt, as compared to bonds, can be renegotiated views this either as a benefit or as a cost. In Bolton/Freixas (1994), ex post flexibility is a virtue. They compare bank and bond financing, arguing that the main differences between the two are the relative costs and the degree of flexibility they offer firms and investors ex post. Bank finance is more expensive but allows for a valuable renegotiation option ex post. For Dewatripont/Maskin (1995), flexibility represents a cost due to lack of commitment ex ante; the bank may get stuck refinancing unprofitable projects because the initial investment is "sunk" at the time of refinancing (leading to "soft budget constraints"). Such ex post softness can possibly be mitigated by having multiple banks, because they can commit to behaving inefficiently ex post (Bolton/Scharfstein 1996).

---

[5] Main banks seem to care about collateral. For example, Japanese main banks seldom refrain completely from taking collateral, and they typically care about their priority in bankruptcy; in corporate bankruptcies in Japan main banks vigorously pursue their collateralized assets; Packer/Ryzer (1992).

These two views of the main bank arrangement are not always easily distinguished in theory, and even less so in practice.[6] The series of articles by Hoshi/Kashyap/Scharfstein (1990a, 1990b, 1991a) show that Japanese firms closely affiliated with main banks are less vulnerable to fluctuations in cash flows, and have lower costs of financial distress, than independent firms. With weaker data, Elston (1994) and Bond et al. (1994) provide similar evidence for main bank relationships in Germany and other continental European countries.

Some attempts have been made to more directly document the costs and benefits of main bank monitoring. Yafeh/Yosha (1995) document a significant reduction in activities with scope for moral hazard in firms subject to main bank monitoring. Weinstein/Yafeh (1994) find some evidence from Japan that there are considerable costs to close relationships between banks and firms. More specifically, banks, as debtholders, appear to be more risk-averse than other shareholders. These arrangements also allow banks to extract significant rents from enterprises. However, the exact role of the banks and other investors can only be indirectly inferred from these studies.

A final issue in the literature that this study addresses is the role of equity holdings by main banks or institutions related to the main bank. None of the theories have been able to provide a satisfactory rationale for this pattern. Possibly, if equity is viewed as the least collateralized form of claim on the firm, such holdings would be consistent with the earlier monitoring stories. An alternative explanation is provided by Holmström/Tirole (1997). They argue that the investor can make efficient monitoring more credible by contributing equity; an equity stake gives the monitor incentives to veto inefficient investment decisions (the notion of control in Holmström/Tirole). Yet another interpretation is that the bank by holding equity may commit to a type of monitoring which is not only in the interest of debtholders (Gorton/Schmid 1996).

C. The Swedish Financial System—Brief Background

The Swedish financial system went through dramatic developments during the 1980s and early 1990s. A marked increase in activity on the financial markets, fueled in part by far-reaching deregulation, was followed by a severe banking crisis where the entire payment system seemed threatened. This development is well-described elsewhere (Jonung/Stymne 1995; Wallander 1994), and here we focus on the aspects most relevant to the relationship between banks and firms. The period 1985-1993 can be divided into two subperiods—the expansion phase 1985-1989 and the contraction phase 1990-1993.

---

[6] Note that the monitoring and renegotiation explanations are not mutually exclusive. In fact, Burkart/Gromb/Panunzi (1997) argue that they are related; having information implies flexibility.

I. The Expansion Phase

The period 1985-1989 was a protracted but maturing boom period with high liquidity in the corporate sector and very active financial markets. Activity levels were also high in markets for real assets, and prices rose substantially. Bank lending to the public, in particular to the enterprise sector, increased dramatically, both in absolute numbers and when related to GDP (see Figure 1). The savings and loans associations and the cooperative banks, as well as the smaller commercial banks with only limited experience in lending to the enterprise sector, expanded particularly strongly during this period (Wallander, 1994). The composition and extent of underlying collateral also changed markedly during this phase with an increasing share of credits being provided completely without collateral or against weak collateral (claims on financial institutes and name securities).[7]

Figure 1: Total Lending by Credit Institutions to the Public

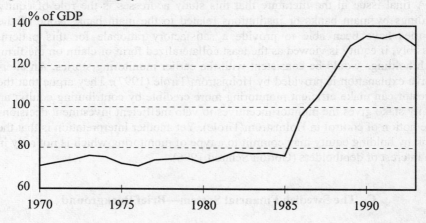

Source: Jonung/Stymne (1995).

---

[7] The decreasing role of collateral is not unique for Sweden, and it was brought about by deregulation under pressure from large firms active on financial markets in the United States and the United Kingdom; see Rajan/Zingales (1994) for international comparisons of collateral levels in large firms. It is also important to remember that the quality of different forms of collateral change over time; the assets considered most safe at the time, real estate, turned out to be the most risky. The previous financial crises in recent Swedish history all rested on different sources of miscalculations of asset values: bonds (in the crisis of 1870), equity (the crisis of the 1920s), and real estate (in the 1990s); Lindgren (1994).

Aggregated statistics show that the financing patterns in the Swedish corporate sector during the second half of the 1980s were exceptional, both by Swedish and international standards. Using the methodology developed in Mayer (1990), Table 1 compares net financing flows during the period 1986-1990 to the previous five-year period 1981-1985, and four other OECD countries (Corbett/ Jenkinson 1994). While it is well known that liquidity in the corporate sector was good during the period, the table shows that the corporate sector, in fact, was a net lender throughout the 1980s.[8] However, the size of the net contribution of internal finance (43% over investments) during 1986-1990 clearly stands out both in a historical perspective and an international comparison.

Table 1: Net Financing in Five OECD Countries

	United States		Japan		Germany		U.K.		Sweden	
	I	II	I	II	I	II	I	II	I	II
Internal Funds	89.6	103.7	74.6	70.7	79.8	89.1	115.4	81.0	110.4	142.0
Bank	12.9	15.0	31.7	23.1	11.1	9.3	12.4	29.9	9.8	66.0
Bonds	10.9	24.8	0.6	8.6	-2.1	0.4	2.0	8.8	-3.0	-38.2
Shares	-4.8	-29.6	3.6	4.4	-0.5	2.4	-7.6	-20.6	-10.9	-51.9
Trade Credits	-1.7	-4.7	-8.4	-5.7	-2.8	-1.8	-3.1	-0.6	-4.6	-0.1
Others	-0.6	1.8	-2.1	-1.1	4.7	-7.9	-12.2	-0.8	-0.8	-6.3
Transfers Within Corporations	..	..	..	..	9.7	8.4	1.6	0.4	-0.9	-11.4
Statistical Adjustment	-6.3	-11.0	..	..	..	..	-8.4	-1.8	..	..
Total	**100**	**100**	**100**	**100**	**100**	**100**	**100**	**100**	**100**	**100**

Notes   Period I: 1980-84; Period II: 1985-1989; in the case of Sweden, 1981-1985 and 1986-1990, respectively.
Figures in %.
Sources: Corbett/Jenkinson (1994); own calculations.

Table 1 further suggests that also the relative net contributions of different sources of external finance during the period 1986-1990 differed from normal

---

[8] Part of the excess liquidity and the high level of bank financing can be explained by the interest rate arbitrage engaged in by large Swedish corporations utilizing the high interest rate differential between Sweden and other countries at the time.

patterns. The net financing patterns in the Swedish corporate sector during the first half of the 1980s were not conspicuously different from those of other countries, and most closely resembled the United Kingdom. However, during the second half of the decade, bank lending expanded dramatically, and other sources of funds made negative contributions. This patterns reflects the increased orientation of firms towards financial rather than real investment during the period. The decrease in the net contribution from equity can also be attributed to the wave of mergers and acquisitions where equity was bought for cash (outright share repurchases are not allowed by Swedish law).

II. The Contraction Phase

The contraction phase was characterized by a severe recession and worsened liquidity in the corporate sector. Prices for real estate, in particular commercial real estate, plummeted, and all commercial banks suffered heavy losses from their exposure in these assets, but also from other lending activity in the corporate sector. The failure of the finance company *Nyckeln* in the fall of 1990 constituted the first sign that the entire financial system was threatened (Jonung/Stymne 1995). The company was largely funded through short-term certificates of deposits, and its failure caused the market for these instruments to completely collapse. One year later, the solvency of *Nordbanken*, a major commercial bank partly owned by the government, came into question, and the government stepped in to support the financial system. Over the next year or so, the government had to provide repeated loan guarantees and loans at subsidized rates to first the large savings bank *Forsta Sparbanken*, and later to another major commercial bank, *Gota Bank*. The government then had to issue an explicit guarantee of banks and "certain other credit institutions" (as it was expressed in the official statement). At one stage, even the important commercial bank, *SE-Banken*, was in jeopardy and had entered into discussions with the government.

The loan losses were concentrated to the commercial banks (82.3 and 64.4% in 1992 and 1993 respectively) and to the customer segment of non-financial corporations (72.8 and 75.2% respectively); as much as 71% of the banks' losses were in this latter category. In addition, a relatively small number of large credits accounted for a disproportionately large share of the losses (Wallander 1994). Lending to the corporate sector decreased by 2% in 1990 and another 9% in 1991 to slowly increase in 1992 and 1993.

III. Control-Oriented Finance with Close Bank-Firm Ties

These dramatic events played themselves out in the context of a system traditionally dominated by control-oriented finance. Ownership concentration has traditionally been high by international standards, and during the 1980s it increased substantially (Isaksson/Skog 1994). At the end of 1991, the largest shareholder held on average 46% of the votes in 63 listed companies with a market value over 1,000 million krona; the five largest owners had a total of 72% of the votes. This is 15 percentage points more than at the end of the 1970s. Crossholdings of shares also became more widespread over the period. The concentration of ownership was further accentuated, at least in small and medium-sized companies, by the banking crisis and the credit crunch that followed. In the illiquid market for corporate assets, many commercial banks chose to take over management of insolvent firms and real estate seized as collateral for unpaid loans.

The banks have played a central role in corporate finance and governance throughout most of this century. The two major corporate groupings are both centered around a commercial bank, but ownership and control patterns differ (see Figure 2). In the traditionally dominant *Wallenberg Sphere,* a family controls, through various formal and informal means, both the commercial bank *SE-Banken* and the two investment companies, *Investor* and *Providentia*. These investment companies incorporated as closed-end mutual funds with bank-controlled institutions as the most important owners, in turn, hold large blocks in a large number of companies. In the *Handelsbanken Sphere* the commercial bank and the investment company *Affärsvärden* have no formal ownership ties. A third much smaller sphere is centered around the state-owned *Nordbanken*.

The term *related ownership* used in the paper refers to holdings within these spheres of influence. The exact classification of individual enterprises in terms of sphere affiliation is a source of some controversy. Here we follow Sundqvist (1994), earlier employed by—among others—the Government Commission on Ownership and Control in Swedish Industry (summarized in Isaksson/Skog 1994). His classifications are primarily based on direct and indirect ownership ties. The most important vehicles for related ownership of the large commercial banks are the investment companies, with the banks and bank-related institutions as the largest shareholders.

Related ownership is a reasonably well-documented aspect of the house bank relationships in Sweden, but the nature of the credit contract between the bank and the enterprise is much less known. We do, however, know that these relationships have been stable over time. A comprehensive study from the mid-60s found that 91% of single bank, or main bank, ties in listed firms had been in existence for more than 15 years, and 35% for more than 35 years ('Koncentrationsutredningen' 1968). In an analysis of the period 1916-1947,

Sjögren (1991) finds that most of the relatively rare breaks in main bank relationships came as a result of mergers between banks. In a few cases changes in ownership triggered a switch in house bank.

There is a widespread perception of weakening and increased turnover in house bank relationships over the last decade. Aggregate statistics of the entire corporate sector in Sweden show that companies increased the number of banks with which they had contacts (Sjögren 1991). This paper sets out to document in detail the house bank contract in large corporations, and the extent to which it changed during the period 1985-1993. In particular, we want to know if these relationships really were weakened, and the extent to which there was increased turnover. If so, what triggered a switch in house bank, and who initiates such changes—the firm or the bank?

Figure 2: Related Ownership—Two Models

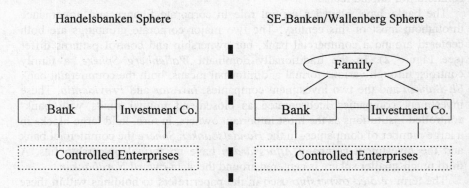

Handelsbanken Sphere   SE-Banken/Wallenberg Sphere

Family

Bank — Investment Co.   Bank — Investment Co.

Controlled Enterprises   Controlled Enterprises

D. Bank-Firm Relationships—The Data

The data on individual credit contracts are based on confidential reports by banks to the supervisory authority, the Banking Inspection Board (later renamed as the Finance Supervisory Authority). Until 1991, the board required banks to report both individual credits above a certain (rather small) size, and large exposures in individual companies or groups of companies (since 1991 only the latter type of information is collected). The thresholds for reporting and the information requirements have changed over time, but the reports contain information on, among other things, approved credit limits, utilized credits, and underlying collateral.[9] The data have been supplemented by information on equity owner-ship (Sundqvist 1994). We report percentage of votes rather than capital.

The study focuses on the four largest commercial banks—*SE-Bank, Handels-banken, Gota Bank,* and *Nordbanken*—which together accounted for 95% of total lending to the corporate sector in 1990. We examine exposures over 15% of the banks' capital base as reported by the banks on June 30, 1990, the last report before the outbreak of the banking crisis.[10] Altogether, the four banks had 50 such large exposures in 34 nonfinancial corporations (here called Population A). In ten of the companies there was more than one large exposure. To study the effects of deregulation and the banking crisis, we reconstruct the bank relation-ships of those of the 34 firms for which we could find data at year-end 1984 and June 30, 1993 (see Table 2). Unfortunately, data for all three occasions are only available for 18 companies (Population B). To avoid losing valuable information we study both populations.

Table 2: The Large Credits of Major Commercial Banks

	1984	1990	1993
Number of Firms	27 (18)	34 (18)	20 (18)
– One-Bank Firm	10 (7)	24 (10)	11 (10)
– Multibank Firms	17 (11)	10 (8)	9 (8)
Number of Large Credits	65 (44)	50 (32)	36 (30)
– In Multibank Firms	55 (30)	26 (16)	25 (18)

Note: Population A; Population B within parentheses.

I. The Large Exposures in 1990

Table 3 provides averages (and medians) of the bank credits for the three years in the study. The total value of the credit limits was 271,000 million Swedish krona in 1990 (Population A), or 5,400 million on average (median: 4,200 million). On average, less than half (45%) of these credit limits were utilized. The largest credit limit exceeded 20,000 million krona and the smallest was 192 million krona. In Population B average credit limits and utilized credits were slightly larger, 6,200 million and 2,700 million krona respectively. Comparable data on

---

[9] The changes in reporting requirements make comparisons over time more difficult. The board also had a policy to destroy information more than three years old. Luckily for the purposes of this study, this policy was only imperfectly implemented.

[10] Loosely speaking, a bank's capital base corresponds to its equity capital.

credit limits were not available for 1984 and 1993, but utilized credits were 493 and 2,539 (medians: 181,000 million and 2,054,000 million) respectively. The average size of utilized credits increased sharply between 1985 and 1990 in both current and fixed prices, and continued increasing but at a slower average rate over the period 1990-1993.

Our data confirm the high level of exposure in individual firms by Swedish commercial banks, and the dramatic increase in this exposure over the period; in two cases individual credits exceeded 40% of the capital base of the bank at mid-year 1990. While international data allowing direct comparisons are not publicly available, existing regulation at the time suggests that none of the exposures in our study would have been allowed in the United States and the United Kingdom, with a maximum of 15% (in most states) and 25% respectively (Borio 1990). Regulatory authorities in Japan, seemingly the only country to regularly publish statistics on bank credits to individual firms, would not permit exposures to reach these levels either (maximum 30%, but now lowered to 20%). Germany and Italy, however, would have allowed even larger bank exposures (maximum 50 and 100% respectively). Current regulation in the European Union prohibits exposures over 25% of the bank's capital base, a limit surpassed by many credits in our study.

The market value of the collateral underlying these loans was estimated at 52,000 million in 1990 (Population A), corresponding to 19% of total credit limits and 41% of utilized credits. There was considerable variation in the collateralization ratio in the data; ten credits from 1990 had been given completely *in blanco*, i.e., without security, whereas the estimated market value of collateral in eight cases exceeded the utilized credit. The lack of collateral could in some cases have been compensated for by deposits from borrowing companies. However, as shown in Table 3, these deposits were small relative to approved credit limits and underlying collateral, on average 45 million krona in 1990. The collateralization ratio (collateral over utilized credits) decreased dramatically over the period; the market value of the underlying collateral decreased from 66% at the end of 1984 to 27% in mid-1993 (Population B).

To study the effect of indirect holdings of equity through related institutions we also compiled data on equity holdings. The information is revealing. In nine of the 34 firms the largest shareholder was closely related to the largest creditor, i.e., the shareholder was classified as a member of the same sphere of influence as the commercial bank. In another 14 firms, one of the five largest shareholders was closely related to the largest creditor. In other words, there were significant related ownership ties in close to 80% of the firms. The average share of related ownership was 9%, and in firms with related ownership the average size of the block was 13% (Table 3). A closer analysis of the data shows that if a related institution was the largest owner, then the bank was the largest creditor. In addition, in one of the banks the reverse was also true, i.e., if the bank was the largest creditor, then related institutions were also the largest owners.

Table 3: The Large Credits and Related Ownership

	Population A		Population B	
Reporting Date	6/30/1990	12/31/1984	06/30/1990	06/30/1993
Credit Limits	5,430 (4,200)	—	6,251 (5,147)	—
Utilized Credits	2,466 (1,355)	493 (255)	1,656 (1,922)	2,539 (2,054)
Collateral[1]	1,021 (637)	317 (181)	1,173 (620)	676 (63)
Deposits	65	—	45	—
Utilization Ratio	45	—	42	—
Collateralization Ratio	41	66	44	27
Related Ownership I[2]	9	6	7	13
Related Ownership II[3]	13	10	10	22

Notes: [1] Market value as estimated by the banks.
[2] Related institutions' average share of votes in all firms.
[3] Related institutions' average share of votes in firms with ownership by institutions related to the bank.
Averages; median within parentheses; current prices. Figures in % and million krona respectively.

There was a clear trend in related ownership: fewer firms had the strong equity ties, but in the firms with such ties still in place the average size of the voting block had increased. Data on related ownership in 1984 were available only in 22 firms. In no less than 50% of these firms the largest creditor and the largest shareholder were closely related; 73% of the firms had a shareholder related to the largest creditor among its five largest shareholders. By mid-1993 we could only identify four firms where the largest shareholder and the largest creditor were closely related. However, more than half of the firms still had a bank-related owner among their five largest owners, and the average share of related ownership increased from 6 to 13% over the period (Population B). If only firms with bank-related shareholdings are included, the average share increased from 10 to 22%. The tendency towards a concentration of ownership is particularly strong in the years during and following the banking crisis.

To further explore the effect of related ownership we designate the 11 firms with the largest related shareholder and creditor in 1984 as *core companies*. These companies had a lower level of collateralization than average, and much higher deposits in the bank than other firms, despite the fact that their credits were smaller.

II. Multibank Relationships

To better understand the role of multibank relationships, this section examines more closely 26 bank credits in 10 companies in 1990. We distinguish between the main bank (the bank with the largest utilized credit in the company), the side bank (the second largest bank), and third-tier banks. The small number of companies in this subsample makes it difficult to draw strong conclusions, but the observations are nevertheless suggestive.

Table 4 summarizes the information on multibank companies. As expected, the average credit limits and utilized credits are larger in these firms than in the entire sample. The share of *in blanco* credits is also significantly larger. The average voting shares were about the same.

Table 4: Large Credits in Multibank Firms, 1990

	Credit Limits	Utilized Credits	Collateral	Deposits	Utilization Ratio[1]	Collaterali- zation Ratio[2]	Share of Votes
Multibank Company	6,889	3,212	1,105	70	47	34	9.0
— Main Bank	8,654	5,904	1,663	140	69	28	22.1
— Side Bank	7,954	2,594	1,278	29	33	49	1.3
Core Companies	6,604	3,483	872	108	52	25	11.8
— Main Bank	10,023	6,595	1,745	187	66	26	33.1
— Side Banks	6,755	2,523	1,057	41	37	42	0.6
Population A	5,430	2,466	1,021	65	45	41	9.0

Notes: [1] Utilized credit / credit limit.
         [2] Collateral / utilized credit.
         Figures in % and million krona respectively.

A first observation is that, despite the increased mobility, in the absolute majority of cases firms chose to have one dominating bank; 31 of the companies in Population A in 1990 had only one large bank or a main bank at least twice as large as the side bank (our operational definition of a house bank). Given the selection criterion of large bank exposures it is only natural that we find many firms with one dominating bank, but it is nevertheless conspicuous that so few firms choose to have two banks of approximately equal size, and play them out against each other.

It is also interesting to note that despite the fact that the main bank always had the largest approved credit limit, the credit limit of the side bank was almost the same order of magnitude but with a much lower utilization ratio, 69% against 33%. The collateralization ratio of main bank credits was, on average, lower than for side bank credits, 28 and 49% respectively. In the seven core companies with more than one large bank credit the corresponding figures were 26 and 42%.

Normally, only the main bank has sufficient related equity interest to exercise influence over borrowing firms. In the firms with more than one large bank, creditor institutions related to the largest bank had on average 22% of the votes in 1990; corresponding holdings by side banks were negligible. In the core companies the average voting share was 33%.

III. Turnover of Main Bank Relationships

It is striking that, in this admittedly biased sample, there is no evidence of large firms attempting to balance their relationship by drawing the same amount of credit from two or more banks; approximately the same proportion of firms have main bank relationships at the end of the period as at the beginning. The number of firms without such relationships decreases during the expansion phase of the late '80s and increases during the first years of the '90s. As noted, though, the role of collateral decreases, while the related ownership becomes stronger but limited to a smaller number of firms.

Perhaps the most interesting observation regards the stability of the relationship between firms and their main banks. The study shows a dramatic increase in the turnover of main banks. At least 17 of the firms in Population A changed their largest bank at least once during the period 1985-1993, and five of these firms changed at least once during each of the two subperiods (the real figures are probably higher since we do not have data on all firms for all years). Turnover was slightly higher during the period leading up to the banking crisis than in the last years of the period—13 as compared to 9 documented cases. Movements were primarily between the two largest banks, *SE-Banken* and *Handelsbanken*, and only in a few cases to and from the "newcomers", *Nordbanken* and *Gota*. There is a clear correlation between the likelihood of turnover and the strength of related ownership at the beginning of the period; only two of the 11 core companies changed main bank during the period.

To further understand the determinants of main bank turnover it would be desirable to examine firm financial data. Unfortunately, the standard database— TRUST—only covers firms listed on the Stockholm Exchange, and in addition is incomplete for some of the firms covered by our study. We are in the process of collecting the missing data and here only report some provisional statistics. Table 5 shows subperiod averages for the ratio of equity to total capital, return on equity, and interest coverage ratios for firms that changed main banks and those that maintained the same main bank respectively.

Table 5: Financial Determinants of Main Bank Turnover

	Subperiod I 1985:1-1990:6		Subperiod II 1990:7-1993:6	
	Main Bank Change	No Main Bank Change	Main Bank Change	No Main Bank Change
Equity/Total Capital	29.8	28.6	22.5	25.0
Return on Equity	19.1	13.3	0.7	3.7
Interest Coverage Ratio	3.2	2.2	0.7	1.2

Notes: Average over the two subperiods; figures in %.
Source: TRUST Database, 1995, Stockholm: Findata.

The figures in Table 5 should be interpreted with the utmost caution. The data refer to averages over each period, and we do not know when in the period the company changed its main bank (it could have done so several times for that matter). The number of companies is also still not large enough to draw any conclusions. However, there is an interesting suggestion that the financial determinants are different in the two periods. In Subperiod I, the firms with higher return on equity and interest coverage ratios were more likely to change their main bank; in Subperiod II, firms that changed bank were, if anything, less profitable, less solvent, and had lower interest coverage ratios.

E. Discussion

The population of large exposures is small and caution is warranted in drawing conclusions, but the study generates some preliminary stylized facts regarding the relationships between commercial banks and large firms in Sweden. Our discussion focuses on the rationale behind the main bank relationship and the possible role of a second creditor in this relationship. In particular, we are interested in explaining the difference in structure between the contract of the main bank and that of the side bank.

This study, and observations from other countries (see, e.g., Aoki/Patrick/ Sheard 1994 and Edwards/Fischer 1994), suggest that a main bank relationship often is not exclusive, the contracts of the main bank differ from that of other banks, and the latter contracts may have bearing on the main bank relationship. The bank-firm relationships in Sweden contain elements of both arm's-length and control-oriented finance. On the one hand, the strong dominance of one bank with large equity holdings through related institutions and relatively low levels of collateral clearly are features of control-oriented finance. The side bank contract, on the other hand, more closely resembles an arm's-length relationship with high levels of collateral and negligible indirect holdings of equity in borrowing firms.

The theory suggested that arm's-length and control-oriented finance are not necessarily substitutes; they may also complement each other in the individual firm. The predictions are largely consistent with observations from the Swedish bank-firm relationships, with the dominance of one bank and main bank credits that are less collateralized than side bank credits. An interesting issue is why firms maintain a secondary bank facility and do not just rely on the credit market as a check on the rent extraction by the main bank. One hypothetical explanation may be that excessive competition ex post is detrimental to incentives to collect information and that a secondary bank represents an intermediate level of competition.

The small size of our population, and the few firms without main bank relationships, have prevented us from comparing the role of liquidity constraints in firms with main bank relationships to those of firms with several creditors of comparable size. However, there is ample casual evidence that main banks are important in providing ex post flexibility. A study of corporate restructurings also suggests that firms with main bank relationships, and firms with bank equity holdings, are less likely to file for bankruptcy when faced with liquidity shortage (Sundgren 1994). However, all these observations of ex post advantages of flexibility give little guidance as to its ex ante costs, and to the possible role of the information collected by main banks in influencing the outcome of financial distress.

The increased turnover in main bank relationships in Sweden suggests that the relative importance of these two aspects of the main bank relationship—mitigating informational asymmetries and providing ex post flexibility—may have shifted towards the latter; such turnover should have been detrimental to any stock of information or trust established over time. The rapid development of the Swedish financial markets in the last decade is also likely to have reduced any informational advantage of the main banks. This interpretation is also broadly consistent with a decreasing role for collateral in lending.

In an international perspective, perhaps the most striking observation in the study is the large blocks of equity controlled by institutions closely related to the main banks. There is considerable support for a control-based explanation of equity holdings. First, and foremost, related ownership typically makes use of the possibility to separate voting power and capital contribution through dual class shares and pyramiding. Most related holdings are in the form of high-voting shares. Second, related ownership clearly seems to have played a role in maintaining the relationship between the bank and the firm in a time of increased turnover of main banks.

Of course, equity holdings by banks and bank-related institutions can also serve as an entrenchment device maintaining inefficient contractual relationships;

the fact that only one of the core companies in our study changed its main bank during the period suggests this as a possible explanation. However, to the extent that entrenchment implies inefficiency, and not just redistribution of surplus, the fact that most firms, also those firms that changed main bank, preferred to rely on one dominant bank indicates that these relationships were beneficial to both parties. It is also hard to reconcile the bank entrenchment story with the very high liquidity of most large Swedish corporations, and the rapid development of financial markets during the second half of the 1980s. The need for external finance decreased substantially, and the corporate sector as a whole became a net lender in the economy. These developments dramatically shifted the bargaining power in favor of firms, allowing them to play out banks against each other and against alternative sources of finance.

F. Conclusion

The study opens up a number of issues regarding the relationship between main and side bank contracts. Unfortunately, the small sample size prevents us from drawing strong conclusions. The data on individual credits are in the process of being complemented with financial data on enterprises. Without such information it is hard to evaluate the riskiness of individual credits, and how differences in risk may affect the relationships between the firms and its banks. It would also have been interesting to have information on differences in maturity and interest rates. We are commencing a comprehensive interview survey to gather more institutional data, in particular regarding the change of main banks.

Ideally, we would also like to obtain information on credit losses, in particular whether they were larger in main banks or side banks. Aggregate statistics show that large exposures were overrepresented in the credit losses in the banking sector, and in commercial banks likely to have been third-tier banks. Preliminary analysis suggests that only a few of the major credit losses are covered by our study. This finding should perhaps not be surprising since the criteria for reporting was based solely on the size of the credit and not its risk content.

References

Aghion, Philippe and Patrick Bolton 'An "Incomplete Contract" Approach to Bankruptcy and the Financial Structure of the Firm' *Review of Economic Studies* 59 (1992) 473-94.

Aoki, Masahiko, Hugh Patrick, and Paul Sheard 'The Role of the Main Bank in the Corporate Governance Structure in Japan' in: Aoki, Masahiko and Hugh Patrick (eds.) *The Japanese Main Bank System: Its Relevance for Developing and Transforming Economies* 1-50 (Oxford 1994).

Asquith, Paul, Robert Gertner, and David Scharfstein 'Anatomy of Financial Distress: An Analysis of Junk Bond Issuers' *Quarterly Journal of Economics* 109 (1994) 625-58.

Berglöf, Erik and Hans Sjögren 'Husbanksrelationen i omvandling' in: 'Bankerna under krisen' (Ministry of Finance, Stockholm 1995).

Berglöf, Erik and Ernst-Ludwig von Thadden 'Long-Term vs. Short-Term Interests: Capital Structure with Multiple Investors' *Quarterly Journal of Economics* 109 (1994) 1055-84.

Bolton, Patrick and Xavier Freixas 'Direct Bond Financing, Financial Intermediation and Investment: An Incomplete Contract Perspective' (mimeo, Université Libre de Bruxelles, 1994).

Bolton, Patrick and David Scharfstein 'Optimal Debt Structure and the Number of Creditors' *Journal of Political Economy* 104 (1996) 1-25.

Bond, Stephen, Julie Ann Elston, Jaques Mairesse, and Benoît Mulkay 'A Comparison of Empirical Investment Equations Using Company Panel Data for France, Germany, Belgium and the UK' (mimeo, Oxford University, 1994).

Borio, Claudio 'Leverage and Financing of Non-Financial Companies: An International Perspective' (Bank of International Settlements, Economic Papers, 1990).

Burkart, Mike, Denis Gromb, and Fausto Panunzi 'Debt Design, Liquidation Value and Monitoring' (mimeo, Université Libre de Bruxelles, 1995).

Burkart, Mike, Denis Gromb, and Fausto Panunzi 'Large Shareholders, Monitoring and the Value of the Firm' *Quarterly Journal of Economics* 112 (1997) 693-728.

Corbett, Jenny and Tim Jenkinson 'The Financing of Industry, 1970-89: An International Comparison' (Working Paper 948, Centre for Economic Policy Research, London, 1994).

Dewatripont, Mathias and Eric Maskin 'Credit and Efficiency in Centralized and Decentralized Economies' *Review of Economic Studies* 62 (1995) 541-55.

Dewatripont, Mathias and Jean Tirole 'A Theory of Debt and Equity—Diversity of Securities and Management-Shareholder Congruence' *Quarterly Journal of Economics* 109 (1994) 1027-54.

Edwards, Jeremy S.S. and Klaus Fischer *Banks, Finance and Investment in Germany* (Cambridge 1994).

Elston, Julie Ann 'Firm Ownership Structure and Investment: Theory and Evidence from German Panel Data' (mimeo, Wissenschaftszentrum, Berlin, 1994).

Franks, Julian and Colin Mayer 'Corporate Control in Germany' (mimeo, London Business School, 1993).

Gilson, Stuart C., Kose John, and Larry H.P. Lang 'Troubled Debt Restructurings' *Journal of Financial Economics* 27 (1990) 315-53.

Gorton, Gary and Frank A. Schmid 'Universal Banking and the Performance of German Firms' (NBER Working Paper no. 5453, February 1996).

Grossman, Sanford and Oliver Hart 'The Costs and Benefits of Ownership: A Theory of Vertical and Lateral Integration' *Journal of Political Economy* 94 (1986) 691-719.

Hart, Oliver and John Moore 'Default and Renegotiation: A Dynamic Model of Debt' (mimeo, London School of Economics, 1989).

Hart, Oliver and John Moore 'A Theory of Debt Based on the Inalienability of Human Capital' *Quarterly Journal of Economics* 109 (1994) 841-79.

Holmström, Bengt and Jean Tirole 'Financial Intermediation, Loanable Funds, and the Real Sector' *Quarterly Journal of Economics* 112 (1997) 665-91.

Hoshi, Takeo, Anil Kashyap, and David Scharfstein 'Bank Monitoring and Investment: Evidence from the Changing Structure of Japanese Corporate Banking Relationships' in: Hubbard, Glenn (ed.) *Asymmetric Information, Corporate Finance, and Investment* 105-26 (Chicago 1990a).

Hoshi, Takeo, Anil Kashyap, and David Scharfstein 'The Role of Banks in Reducing the Costs of Financial Distress in Japan' *Journal of Financial Economics* 27 (1990b) 67-88.

Hoshi, Takeo, Anil Kashyap, and David Scharfstein 'Corporate Structure, Liquidity, and Investment: Evidence from Japanese Industrial Groups' *Quarterly Journal of Economics* 106 (1991a) 33-60.

Hoshi, Takeo, Anil Kashyap, and David Scharfstein 'The Choice Between Public and Private Debt: An Examination of Post-Regulation Corporate Finance in Japan' (mimeo, U.C., San Diego, 1991b)

Isaksson, Mats and Rolf Skog 'Corporate Governance in Swedish Listed Companies' in: Baums, Theodor, Richard M. Buxbaum, and Klaus J. Hopt (eds.) *Institutional Investors and Corporate Governance* 287-310 (Berlin and New York 1994).

Jonung, Lars and Joakim Stymne 'The Great Regime Shift. Asset Markets and Economic Activity in Sweden, 1985-1993' (mimeo, Stockholm School of Economics, 1995).

'Koncentrationsutredningen' (Ministry of Finance, SOU 68: 3, 1968).

Lindgren, Håkan 'Att lära av historien. Några erfarenheter av finanskrisen' 7-32 (Bankkriskommittén, Finansdepartementet, 1994).

Mayer, Colin 'Financial Systems, Corporate Finance, and Economic Development' in: Hubbard, Glenn (ed.) *Asymmetric Information, Corporate Finance, and Investment* 307-32 (Chicago 1990).

Mayer, Colin 'Ownership—An Inaugural Lecture' (mimeo, University of Warwick, 1993).

Packer, Frank and Marc Ryser 'The Governance of Failure: An Anatomy of Corporate Bankruptcy in Japan' (mimeo, Columbia University, New York, 1992).

Peterson, Mitchell and Raghuram Rajan 'The Effect of Credit Market Competition on Firm-Creditor Relationships' (mimeo, University of Chicago, 1993).

Rajan, Raghuram 'Insiders and Outsider: The Choice Between Informed and Arm's-Length Debt' *Journal of Finance* 47 (1992) 1367-400.

Rajan, Raghuram and Andrew Winton 'Covenants and Collateral as Incentives to Monitor' (mimeo, University of Chicago, 1994).

Rajan Raghuram and Luigi Zingales 'What Do We Know About Capital Structure? Some Evidence from International Data' (mimeo, University of Chicago, 1994).

Sjögren, Hans *Bank och Näringsliv* (Stockholm 1991).

Sundgren, Stefan 'Bankruptcy Costs and the Bankruptcy Code—A Case Study of the Finnish Code' (mimeo, Swedish School of Economics, 1994).

Sundqvist, Sven-Ivan *Ägarna och makten i svenska börsföretag* (Stockholm 1985-1993).

von Thadden, Ernst-Ludwig 'Bank Finance and Long-Term Investment' (mimeo, University of Basle, 1990).

von Thadden, Ernst-Ludwig 'The Commitment of Finance, Duplicated Monitoring, and the Investment Horizon' (mimeo, University of Basle, 1992).

Wallander, Jan 'Bankkrisen—Omfattning. Orsaker. Lärdomar' in: 'Bankkrisen' (Banking Crisis Commission, Ministry of Finance, Stockholm, 1994).

Weinstein, David and Yishag Yafeh 'On the Costs of a Bank-Centered Financial System: Evidence from the Changing Main Bank Relationships in Japan' (mimeo, Harvard Institute of Economic Research, 1994).

Yafeh, Yishag and Oved Yosha 'Large Shareholders, Banks, and Managerial Moral Hazard: An Empirical Investigation' (mimeo, Harvard University, 1995).

Lenders as a Force in Corporate Governance Criteria and Practical Examples for Switzerland

GÉRARD HERTIG, Zurich[*]

Most enterprises in Switzerland are very dependent on loans. However, the role of lenders from the standpoint of corporate governance is rarely discussed. The purpose of this paper is to offer criteria for evaluating the influence of banks, which are the typical lenders in Switzerland, and to apply these criteria to various categories of firms.

The analysis will show that banks only play a significant corporate governance role in workouts and MBOs—and that this is a quite recent occurrence. In contrast, in "normal" situations lenders have, up to now, been an almost insignificant force, be it for listed companies or for small to medium-sized firms. As for the future, MBO and workout lending practices could be instrumental in setting new standards, with greater focus on risk-adjusted pricing and on cash flow rather than asset-based lending.

Contents

Figures

[*] I would like to thank the participants in the Symposium on Comparative Corporate Governance—The State of the Art and Emerging Research (Max-Planck-Institut, Hamburg, May 15-17, 1997) for comments. I am also especially grateful to representatives of various financial institutions for having provided me with their assessment of market conditions.

A. Introduction

Most enterprises in Switzerland are very dependent on loans. However, the role of lenders from the standpoint of corporate governance is rarely discussed. The purpose of this paper is to offer criteria for evaluating the influence of banks, which are the typical lenders in Switzerland, and to apply these criteria to various categories of firms.

With the Swiss economy as well as its lending scene being in turmoil, historical data is not sufficient for deciding how to evaluate lenders' influence: we will also have to take into account current structural and behavioral changes (Part B). The results will serve as a basis for specific analyses. For confidentiality reasons, a "representative firm" rather than a case study approach has been adopted. The categories selected are: major listed corporations (Part C.I.); small to medium-sized corporations (C.II.); management buyout processes (C.III.); and workout situations (C.IV.).

The analysis will show that lenders only play a significant corporate governance role in workouts and MBOs—and that even this is a quite recent occurrence. In these situations, lenders' influence is not exercised through board memberships, but rather by imposing tight contractual covenants that ensure frequent high-quality flows of information and which can seriously limit management's discretion. In contrast, in "normal" situations lenders have, up to now, been an almost insignificant force, be it for listed companies or for small to medium-sized firms. Interestingly, what little influence lenders had was exercised through board representation. As for the future, it can be expected that MBO and workout lending practices will set new *general* lending standards. This implies that, except for major companies or very small loans, lenders' corporate governance role in Switzerland should increase across the board.

How significant this role will be is a function of whether state-owned cantonal banks will adopt risk-adjusted pricing and lending policies. This in turn will in great part depend upon the equilibrium reached between political pressure to provide local corporations with new loans, and political unwillingness to support cantonal banks with taxpayers' money. Hence, well-meant efforts to contribute to Switzerland's economic recovery by making "cheap" money available could ironically have damaging long-term effects by permitting inefficient firms to survive or, at least, by preventing overdue management improvements to occur more rapidly through lenders' influence.

B. Evaluating Lenders' Corporate Governance Role

Corporate governance, meaning here shareholders and stakeholders monitoring and/or participation in management, is an issue that had not been specifically addressed by Swiss legal literature until a few years ago.[1]

This does not merely reflect a reluctance to use U.S. terminology. Corporate governance activities have long remained a "black box" in Switzerland.[2] For example, it is only recently that the role of institutional investors in Swiss firms has started to be the object of studies.[3] More importantly, even though the corporate governance debate has finally reached Switzerland, the role of lenders is an issue that is generally[4] ignored, even in "executive forums" totally dedicated to

---

[1] See Böckli, Peter 'Corporate Governance: The "Cadbury Report" and the Swiss Board Concept of 1991' *Swiss Review of Business Law* 68 (1996) 149-63; Nobel, Peter 'Corporate Governance—Möglichkeiten und Schranken gesellschaftsrechtlicher Gestaltung' *Der Schweizer Treuhänder* (1995) 1057-63.

On the subject of lenders' role in corporate governance, cf. also the respective sections in the comparative contributions of Kanda and Prigge in Ch. 12 of this volume.

[2] Obviously, the "black box" problem has not been limited to Switzerland: see Gilson, Ronald J. 'Corporate Governance and Economic Efficiency' in: Isaksson, Mats and Rolf Skog (eds.) *Aspects of Corporate Governance* 131-41, especially 131 (Stockholm 1994).

[3] See Anderson, Martin and Thierry Hertig 'Institutional Investors in Switzerland' in: Baums, Theodor, Richard M. Buxbaum, and Klaus J. Hopt (eds.) *Institutional Investors and Corporate Governance* 489-529 (Berlin 1994); Anderson, Martin and Thierry Hertig (eds.) *Role of Institutional Investors vis-à-vis Financial Intermediaries and Public Companies* (Conference Proceedings) (Zurich 1993).

[4] However, two specific issues that could reflect or result in corporate governance interventions have been the subject of legal analyses.

One is the private law issue of lender's *liability*: see Thalmann, Christian 'Die privatrechtliche Haftung der Bank für fehlende Sorgfalt bei der Abwicklung von Bankgeschäften' in: Wiegand, Wolfgang (ed.) *Konsequenzen aus der Krise* 75-92 (Bern 1995); Chaudet, François 'L'obligation de diligence du banquier en droit privé' *Zeitschrift für Schweizerisches Recht II* 113 (1994) 1-114; Länzlinger, Andreas *Die Haftung des Kreditgebers* (Zurich 1992); Schönle, Herbert 'La responsabilité extra-contractuelle du donneur de crédit en droit suisse' in: Feduci (Fondation pour l'étude du droit et des usages du commerce international) (ed.) *La responsabilité extra-contractuelle du donneur de crédit en droit comparé* 117-32 (Paris 1984).

The other is the regulatory issue of lenders' duty to investigate the economic background of *client transactions*. See Zulauf, Urs 'Gläubigerschutz und Vertrauensschutz—zur Sorgfaltspflicht der Bank im öffentlichen Recht der Schweiz' *Zeitschrift für Schweizerisches Recht II* 113 (1994) 359-535, especially 493-506.

the subject of corporate governance.[5] To evaluate the significance of such a lack of interest, it is useful to first assess the identity and importance of lenders in Switzerland.

I. The Importance of Bank Lending

According to a recent study,[6] Swiss firms' dependence upon lending facilities is considered large by international standards (see Figure 1).

Figure 1: Loans Outstanding as % of Bonds Outstanding

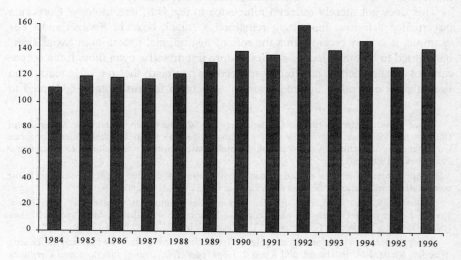

Source: Schmid and Varnholt, supra n. 6, 310.

According to the authors of the study, the above ratios are higher than those in the U.S., the U.K., or even Germany. Taking 1995 as an example, they calculated that the ratio of outstanding credits / outstanding bonds was above 140% in Switzerland, compared to 83% in the U.S., 75% in the U.K. and 94% in Germany.[7]

---

[5] See the proceedings of the '2. St. Galler Executive Forum', published in the special December 1995 issue of *Der Schweizer Treuhänder*.

[6] Schmid, Christian and Burkhard Varnholt 'Kreditgeschäft im Wandel' in: Schmid, Christian and Burkhard Varnholt (eds.) *Finanzplatz Schweiz. Probleme und Zukunftsperspektiven* 309-31 (Zurich 1997).

[7] Schmid and Varnholt, supra n. 6, 310.

This does not necessarily imply that *banks* are in a better position to influence firms in Switzerland than in the U.S., the U.K., or Germany. Their power is a function of factors such as firms' potential access to other sources of financing (e.g., non-bank lending and capital markets) and the firms' own internal funds-generating capacity. However, especially because Swiss firms and Swiss domestic capital markets[8] are generally less sophisticated than, e.g., Anglo-Saxon firms and Anglo-Saxon capital markets,[9] bank loans are the main source of financing for most corporations.[10] This obviously means that bank lending policies are of great significance to Swiss firms and explains why the perception that such policies are becoming more restrictive has caused heated reactions.

Nowadays, big banks (currently Credit Suisse and the soon to be merged SBC and UBS) and state-owned cantonal banks are the main lenders to Swiss firms, with a combined market share of over 75%. The other categories of banks operating in Switzerland either play a much less important role (regional banks and Raffeisenbanks) or are insignificant players (broker-dealers and foreign-dominated banks).

Given the importance of bank credit, the lack of research regarding lending banks' corporate governance role is surprising. In our opinion, there are three possible explanations for this disinterest. The first that comes to mind is that, as in Germany, an important web of cross-shareholdings and the universal banks' ability to vote their and/or their clients' shares are sufficient to ensure banks a corporate governance role, making specific lending-oriented research superfluous. The second is that lenders in Switzerland may not play a monitoring role. The third might be that the issue of lenders as a force in corporate governance is, at least in Switzerland, difficult to document.

II. Banks as Shareholders

The Swiss regulatory framework allows for universal banking, which implies that banks are not limited to lending, but may also engage in investment banking

---

[8] The sophistication of Swiss financial markets was ranked No. 3 worldwide by the World Economic Forum (ed.) *The Global Competitiveness Report 1996* 189 (Geneva 1996). However, this assessment is mainly valid for large firms (see also infra C.I.), and only an extremely small fraction of the total number of Swiss firms can be considered as such.

[9] Note, e.g., that, according to a Daiwa Europe 1997 estimate (cited in *Wall Street Journal Europe* May 12, 1997, 1) 28% of the U.S. and 18% of the U.K. population own stock or stock funds, whereas this percentage drops to 7% for Germany—a percentage which should be comparable to the one valid for Switzerland (see *Journal de Genève* May 29, 1997, 17).

[10] For 1990, 1992, and 1995 data on the (higher) indebtedness of Swiss firms compared to the U.S., U.K., and (to some extent) German firms, see Varnholt, Burkhard *Modernes Kreditrisiko-Management* 17 (Zurich 1997).

and asset management. Banks are thus permitted to own shares in financial as well as non-financial firms.

Among banks, only the big banks are players when it comes to holding equity positions in Swiss firms.[11] However, recent data[12] show that big banks have less than 4% of their assets in permanent holdings that provide at least 10% of voting rights in the targeted firm. More specifically, according to the Swiss National Bank statistics, big banks' investment stake in industrial Swiss firms is of almost negligible importance (see Figure 2).

Figure 2: Big Banks' Permanent Equity Holdings in Industrial Firms (Million SFR)

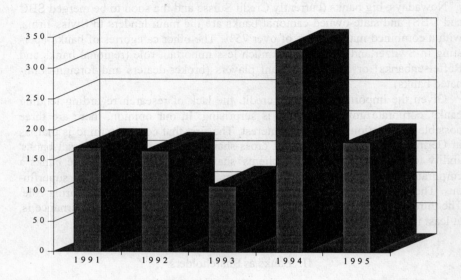

Source: Swiss National Bank, supra n. 12, A52.

Admittedly, Figure 2 could be misleading as its focus is on *investments* providing *more* than 10% of voting rights. Not taken into account are less significant investments, holdings in non-industrial firms, securities held by big banks' foreign subsidiaries, securities held in connection with derivative transactions, securities lent or borrowed, etc. These are significant quantitative omissions. For

[11] See 'Institutional Investors in Switzerland' in: Bank Julius Baer (ed.) 'Market View Switzerland' 28-9 (Zurich, November 1996).

For shareholdings of banks, see also the contributions by Breuer, Mülbert, and Wenger/Kaserer in Ch. 6, and the respective sections in the comparative articles by Kanda (Sec. B.II.), Prigge (Sec. B.II.), and Wymeersch (Sec. D.I.-III.) in Ch. 12.

[12] See Swiss National Bank 'Les banques en Suisse: 1995' at A52-A54 (Zurich 1996).

example,[13] the big banks' annual reports showed their total securities holdings to be SFr. 196 billion at the end of 1995.

However, as far as banks' corporate governance role is concerned, their significant investments in Swiss industrial firms should be the most telling. We believe that other equity positions are of less significance in the analysis of corporate governance, either because they relate to dominated but unconsolidated banking subsidiaries or because they are linked to other financial transactions such as derivatives. Consequently, one can conclude that banks' role as shareholders is generally quite limited in Switzerland.[14]

On the other hand, there has been an extensive and long-lasting debate regarding the banks' ability to vote their clients' shares.[15] This could be because these voting rights are the instrument giving the banks the power to monitor and influence management—and thus makes a direct analysis of their lending role unnecessary. However, this explanation is mainly valid for listed companies, which represent an extremely small fraction of the total number of Swiss firms. For example, at the end of 1995, there were 236 Swiss companies which had their shares listed on the main board of one of the Swiss exchanges;[16] in contrast, taking into account only comparable limited liability companies, there were approximately 170,000 *Aktiengesellschaften* (AG)[17] and 10,000 *Gesellschaften mit beschränkter Haftung* (GmbH).[18] In addition, the 1991 *Aktienrecht* revision limited banks' influence by obliging them to seek their clients' instructions and to vote in favor of management proposals in the absence of such instructions.

As a matter of fact, this procedure has proven so costly for retail clients that banks now normally make the corporation's acceptance to reimburse their expenses a precondition for acting as proxies.[19] For their part, institutional investors increasingly use non-bank proxies.[20] Indeed, even "captive" mutual funds (which, inside Switzerland, are less important institutional investors than are insurers and pension funds)[21] are getting more and more independent from their parent bank. To some extent this reflects new regulation which has

---

[13] 'Institutional Investors in Switzerland', supra n. 11, 28.

[14] See also Bereuter, Rolf *In-House-Banking-Aktivitäten schweizerischer Industriekonzerne und die Abgrenzung zum Tätigkeitsbereich von Banken* 300 (Bern 1995); Schuster, Leo *Bankpolitik im Spiegel aktueller Themen* especially 15 (Bern 1990).

[15] See recently Scherrer, Eric R. *Die Stimmrechtsausübung durch Depotvertreter* (Zurich 1996) and the mentioned literature.

[16] Swiss Exchange 'Jahresbericht 1995' 40.

[17] Nobel, supra n. 1, 1060.

[18] Wohlmann, Herbert *GmbH-Recht* 4 (Basle 1997); von Büren, Roland and Thomas Bähler 'Gründe für die gesteigerte Attraktivität der GmbH' *Recht* (1996) 17-28, 18.

[19] See Scherrer, supra n. 15, 70-1.

[20] See Böckli, Peter *Schweizer Aktienrecht* No. 1334 2nd edn. (Basle 1996).

[21] 'Institutional Investors in Switzerland', supra n. 11, 22.

(formally) improved mutual funds' independence;[22] more importantly, mutual fund managers are under heavy performance pressure and thus resist acting in the parent bank's lending interest, at least when such interest is not aligned with their own interest as investors.

Thus, it is only for listed corporations that the banks' "shareholder influence" may substitute for a lending corporate governance role and may therefore explain the lack of interest in analyzing the latter. Moreover, the extent of the power provided to banks by their ability to act as proxies or to influence voting decisions at the general meeting is debatable.

III. Lenders' Passivity

A second possible explanation for the apparent disinterest in the lenders' role could be that lenders have not acted as monitors or managers. The reason for such passivity could either be that Swiss firms were generally performing so well that such interference would not have been profitable, or that competition among lenders was such that all that counted was to court customers, not to monitor or manage them.

There is quite some evidence that lenders may have been passive. First, there are almost no court cases on lender's liability for involvement in the management of a firm, despite the fact that such a lender would be considered a *de facto* director[23] and that the Federal Tribunal has proven sympathetic to plaintiffs suing lenders that have participated in management decisions.[24] Second, one of the important lessons drawn from the 1990's real estate and commercial credit debacle, which has resulted in huge write-offs,[25] is that insufficient attention was given to companies' activities.

---

[22] In the interest of Euro-compatibility, the revised law regulating mutual funds requires formal as well as management independence from the parent bank see, e.g., Forstmoser, Peter 'Das revidierte schweizerische Anlagefondsrecht. Eine Einführung' in: Zobl, Dieter (ed.) *Aktuelle Fragen des Kapitalmarktrechts* 131-58, 150 (Zurich 1996). However, the parents' representatives can sit on the board of the mutual fund, although there are some qualitative restrictions: see Buttschardt, Alfred 'Article 9 AFG' in: Forstmoser, Peter (ed.) *Kommentar zum schweizerischen Anlagefondsgesetz* No. 13-13a (Zurich 1997).

[23] See, e.g., Gross, Kurt J. *Analyse der haftpflichtrechtlichen Situation des Verwaltungsrates* 90-3 (Zurich 1990). The *Aktienrecht* revision of 1991 has subtly integrated de facto directors in its liability provision (Art. 754 OR), with potentially significant practical consequences: see Böckli, Peter 'Neuerungen im Verantwortlichkeitsrecht für den Verwaltungsrat' *Swiss Review of Business Law* (1993) 261-79, 263.

[24] BGE *Baumgartner v. Schweiz. Krankenkasse für das Bau- und Holzgewerbe* 107 II 349 (1981); see also Homburger, Eric 'Der Verwaltungsrat' in: Forstmoser, Peter (ed.) *Zürcher Kommentar* No. 133-6 ad Art.707 OR (Zurich 1997).

[25] At the Swiss Banking Commission's 1997 press conference, it was indicated that Swiss banks' domestic loan losses (including bad loan provisions, interest lost, and writing down of

However, the lack of court cases and the existence of heavy lending losses do not definitively lead to the conclusion that lenders had no or very little corporate governance influence. First, for at least the past two decades, the specific issue of lender's liability has time and again been addressed in legal literature.[26] Admittedly, until very recently,[27] the focus was on information or signals given by the lender to third parties rather than on its corporate governance role. However, arguing that a lender may be liable because its involvement has had an impact on the debtor's reputation (signaling effect) is very close to arguing that it has general monitoring duties. Although mostly applicable to special situations, this discussion is probably driven by the perception that lenders were indeed monitoring and thus a corporate governance force.

Second, and more importantly, bank consultants as well as bank managers have recently started to underline the need to de-emphasize the importance of relationship banking in favor of financial and credit portfolio analysis,[28] or at least to strongly develop such analytical techniques alongside relationship banking. In our opinion, this confirms that lenders were or, better, thought they were a force in corporate governance, but realized they had not managed to monitor or to play an influential role. This view is also, in our opinion, at the origin of recent proposals made in legal literature, aiming at increasing lenders' liability.[29]

The lack of interest in lenders' influence is thus partly explained by the fact that, up to the 1990s, lenders often had a limited corporate governance impact. Although relationship bankers were supposed to monitor borrowers, they either were content to rely on "seat of the pants" analysis[30] or, to the extent that they realized better monitoring was necessary, refrained from doing so to avoid the risk of losing clients to competitors.

---

property taken over from insolvent customer) amounted to US$ 29.32 billion for the period 1991-1996: see *Neue Zürcher Zeitung* April 23, 1997, No. 93, 21; *Wall Street Journal Europe* April 23, 1997, 12.

[26] See supra n. 4 and Bertheau, Fortunat *Die Haftung der Kreditgeberbank gegenüber dem Kreditnehmer* (Zurich 1998).

[27] See Chaudet, supra n. 4, especially 53-4, 76, 99-108; Länzlinger, supra n. 4, 166-208. In the banking literature, see already Zellweger, Bruno *Überwachung kommerzieller Bankkredite* (Bamberg 1982).

[28] See Schmid and Varnholt, supra n. 6.

[29] See Chaudet, supra n. 4.

[30] E.g., many bankers believed that credit covenants were only necessary for loans to major corporations and there was no need to seriously manage credit risk (and price their loans accordingly) as long as they were the beneficiary of collateral: see Gauch, Urs Peter *Credit Covenants* 14, 42 (Bern 1996).

IV. Lack of Evidence

We believe that there is a third and complementary explanation for the lack of research into lenders' corporate governance role: namely, that it is, if not "taboo", at least difficult to document. Banks and entrepreneurs are both understandably reluctant to address the subject. Even academics can prove surprisingly evasive. Proposals aiming at improving commercial credit policies recognize both past monitoring failures and the need to individually evaluate the creditworthiness of clients on a continuous basis, but provide little indication about practical implementation.[31] In addition, published statistical data in Switzerland has historically been scarce compared to other countries, especially regarding equity holdings and securities trading.

V. Criteria for Detecting and Measuring Lenders' Role

The previous sections have shown that lenders have played some corporate governance role. However, their influence has arguably been weak for listed corporations and their monitoring apparently insufficient for other firms. These rather imprecise conclusions reflect the lack of research and statistical data regarding lenders as a force in corporate governance. The aim of the present section is thus to provide criteria leading to a more precise understanding of lenders' role.

Such criteria cannot be proposed without taking into account some very important changes that have taken place in Switzerland over the past years or even months. Specifically, rapid concentration in the banking industry, as well as modernization of business and lending practices, are likely to fundamentally alter lenders' requirements, and therefore their corporate governance role.

First of all, the number of lenders has dramatically diminished over the past decade. This is partly a result of a reduction in anti-competitive practices following the Cartel Commission's investigation of the banking industry,[32] which implied that weaker players were no longer subsidized through fixed commissions and the like. However, concentration occurred mainly because real estate prices crashed and because of post-1991 economic downturn in Switzerland. Regional banks were the first affected and many had to be quietly (or not so

---

[31] See Mettler, Alfred 'Das inländische Kreditgeschäft im Wandel der Zeit' in: Geiger, Hans, Christine Hirszowicz, Rudolf Volkart, and Peter F. Weibel (eds.) *Schweizerisches Bankwesen im Umbruch* 133-50, 147-8 (Bern 1996); Volkart, Rudolf 'Kommerzielle Kreditpolitik in schwierigen Zeiten. Deutlich zurückhaltenderes Geschäftsverhalten der Banken' *Der Schweizer Treuhänder* (1992) 109-12, 110.

[32] 'Die gesamtschweizerisch wirkenden Vereinbarungen im Bankgewerbe' 1-98 (1989/3 Veröffentlichungen der Schweizerischen Kartellkommission und des Preisüberwachers).

quietly) "bought" by more solid establishments—mainly the three big banks. State-owned cantonal banks also have had their share of trouble, which necessitated various bail-outs. Even one of the larger banks (Volksbank) had to be absorbed by another major bank (Credit Suisse).

Up to now, concentration in the banking industry does not seem to have reduced competition. There are still a significant number of players, mainly the big banks and the cantonal banks. However, growing international exposure, elimination of less competent institutions, and increased accountability vis-a-vis shareholders and taxpayers has made lending a more professional business. Pricing can reflect economic reality and is becoming more elastic. There is an ongoing evolution from asset-based to cash flow-based lending. Borrowers are the subject of greater scrutiny and conditions increasingly vary depending upon internal ratings of the client's creditworthiness.

This obviously cannot remain without corporate governance implications. For example, cash flow-based lending implies that bank employees will pay attention to current and future management practices of their clients. Similarly, firms dealing with lenders with internal rating systems will be quick to realize that a small "downgrading" can result in an exponential rise in the cost of borrowing. Quite naturally, these firms will try to improve their standing and may ask the lender to advise them about changes in their organization and practices.

Admittedly, these changes are only now in the making and do not affect equally all banks and firms. It also does not imply that all previous lending practices will disappear. Thus, it could happen that the state-owned cantonal banks, for social and political reasons, refrain from modernizing pricing and lending requirements as far as small to medium-sized enterprises are concerned. Therefore, it would be wrong to analyze the role of lenders as if all banks had the same behavior; it would also be wrong to only concentrate on current changes and simply disregard historical data.

Nevertheless, for purposes of this analysis it is possible to operate with a limited set of criteria, relating either to a) the flow of information, b) banks' human resources, or c) borrowers' independence and freedom to maneuver. At this stage, it is also possible to get a sufficiently accurate picture by applying those criteria to four representative categories of firms: major listed corporations (the top 25); small to medium-sized firms;[33] enterprises going through management buyouts; and companies in the midst of a "workout".

a) Without any doubt, any lender's monitoring or managing role depends upon *information flow*.

There are various ways to test the quantity and/or quality of information provided to lenders. We will concentrate on *board memberships, applicable*

---

[33] See infra Part C, Section II. regarding the reasons for not having a representative category of firms with less than ten employees.

accounting standards, and *identity of auditors.* Although reliable historical data mainly exist for major listed companies, we will nevertheless be able to use at least one of these three criteria for each of our representative categories of firms.

b) One cannot be a force in corporate governance without devoting the necessary *human resources* to the task. As a matter of fact, this element might be considered as important as insufficient professional competence or laxity when it comes to establishing the causes of past monitoring failures and lending losses.

Again, there are several ways to measure the quantity and/or quality of human resources devoted by lenders to monitoring and influencing debtors' management. Because of a lack of data, we are not yet in a position to suggest criteria concerning human resources normally devoted to monitoring and influencing debtors' management. At this stage, we will concentrate on *the number of people devoted to workouts.* Obviously, this means that this criterion will be used for the workout category only.

c) Finally, the role of lenders might be measured by evaluating *the borrowers' independence and freedom to maneuver.*

Here also, assessing the quantity and/or quality of a borrower's freedom can be done using different methods. At this stage, we will concentrate on *access to capital markets* (securitization), *voting rights,* and *loan covenants.* We will assume that access to capital markets is generally only feasible for listed companies and that they are the only ones for which voting rights play a role. The third criterion, loan covenants, will be used for both the management buyout and the workout categories.

C. Representative Firms

As already pointed out, a "representative firms" rather than a case study approach has been adopted in this paper. The following will be the subject of analysis: major listed corporations (C.I.); small to medium-sized firms (C.II.); management buyout processes (C.III.); and workout situations (C.IV.).

I. Major Listed Corporations

It is first necessary to reexamine the validity of our general conclusion[34] about the importance of lending for this category of firm. Indeed, a major listed company's access to capital markets is significantly different from that of other Swiss firms. This is especially the case for the top 25 Swiss firms, on which we will therefore focus—although, given the scarcity of available data, statistics concerning larger samples of listed companies will also be considered.

---

[34] See supra Part B, Section I.

1. Specific Importance of Lending

Major Swiss listed companies' demand for bank loans has been continuously decreasing over the past years, especially because of securitization and the development of so-called "in-house banking" activities.

This evolution has had an impact not only on bank lending activities. Recently published[35] case studies regarding in-house banking activities by, e.g., ABB Asea Brown Boveri, Sulzer, Ciba-Geigy (now merged into Novartis), and Nestlé provide interesting insights. These studies show that the decrease in lending to major Swiss companies has been accompanied by a change in the structure of the companies' relations with banks. Whereas big Swiss companies used to have a limited number of "*Haus*banken" (house banks), they now try to work with a larger (but still small) number of "*Haupt*banken" (main or core banks). Interestingly, the idea does not seem to be to get better pricing or banking services (competition is fierce even among the former *Hausbanken*), but rather to develop close working relationships with a group of well-known banks, in order to be able to count on solid support in case of hard times.[36]

This implies that lenders' influence should not be totally discounted. First, the framework and functions of "in-house banking" vary according to the firm's culture and its management attitude.[37] Second, bank loans remain interesting to the extent that they are cheaper than other financing methods. Third, and more importantly, major companies' interest in keeping a close relationship with a select number of banks has a price, i.e., there is no such thing as a free lunch.

To evaluate such lenders' corporate governance role, the traditional "board membership" criterion probably remains the most adequate, because it is the only area where hard data is available. However, because they can affect lenders' power within the board, it is interesting to start with two other criteria, accounting standards and voting rights.

2. Accounting Standards[38]

Swiss companies, including listed companies, had the reputation of being anything but transparent, especially as far as their financial statements were

---

[35] See Bereuter, supra n. 14, 165-234.

[36] See Bereuter, supra n. 14, 357. Such strategy seems to have its limits: see, e.g., the recent criminal inquiry regarding drastic reductions in two big banks' equity positions in a listed company during the two years preceding bankruptcy, as reported in *Journal de Genève* April 18, 1997, 11.

[37] Bereuter, supra n. 14, 352.

[38] On accounting and disclosure, cf. also the contributions in Ch. 9 as well as the respective sections in the comparative articles of Kanda and Prigge in Ch. 12 of this volume.

concerned. Analysts, investors, and possibly even bankers or board members were thus unable or seriously hampered in reasonably assessing the financial condition of Swiss firms.

Growth, globalization, and regulatory requirements obliged many major Swiss corporations to increase their capital. Due to the small size of the domestic financial market, there was a need to attract foreign investors, especially institutional investors. It was realized that this meant a change of attitude regarding transparency, especially accounting standards. Quite surprisingly for many observers, fundamental adjustments took place relatively quickly. Whereas the 1980s were still dominated by the old "hiding" approach, significantly more transparent accounting requirements have recently been imposed on listed companies.[39] More to the point is the fact that, by as early as 1995, many listed companies had voluntarily adopted those or the even more stringent European Union or Anglo-Saxon accounting standards (International Accounting Standards or U.S. Generally Accepted Accounting Principles) (Figure 3).

Figure 3:   Accounting Standards Used by the 200 Swiss Listed Companies That Are Not Banks or Insurance Companies, 1995

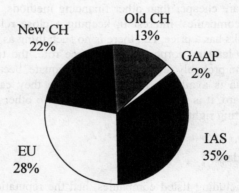

Source: Coopers & Lybrand, cited in 'Den Trends der Rechnungslegung auf der Spur' *Neue Zürcher Zeitung* November 21, 1995, No. 271, 33.

---

[39] See Schweizer Börse 'Kotierungsreglement' (January 24, 1996).

This means that lenders, although possibly not in a position to demand detailed specific information from major listed companies, should now get better general financial information than in the past.

3. Voting Rights

We have suggested[40] that it is only in the case of listed companies that the ability to vote at shareholders meetings potentially provides lenders with additional corporate governance power. To evaluate such lenders' influence, it is useful to start by examining the shareholding structure of listed Swiss companies.

As confirmed[41] by recent data,[42] many large Swiss companies are still dominated by one shareholder or by a group of shareholders (see Figure 4).[43]

Figure 4:   Voting Rights of the Largest Shareholder/Group of Shareholders in 25 Large Swiss Listed Companies, 1994

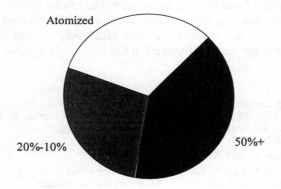

Source: Hertig, supra n. 42, 12.

The voting structure depicted above makes it unlikely that lenders will routinely be able to increase their bargaining power, and thus their influence, due to their

---

[40] Supra Part B, Section II.

[41] See also the empirical studies referred to by Drill, Michael *Investor Relations* 16 (Bern 1995).

[42] Hertig, Thierry 'The Board of Directors: Structure and Role. An Empirical Study Based on the Largest Swiss Listed Companies' 12 (Working Paper, Zurich 1995).

[43] For comparative evidence with respect to ownership structure, see the respective sections in the contributions of Kanda, Prigge, and Wymeersch in Ch. 12 of this volume.

direct and indirect voting rights. This should be true even for the companies that, like 8 of the 25 companies[44] in the Figure 4 sample, have a somewhat atomized shareholder structure. First, their lenders should not be significant minority equity holders, as they have been reducing their minority positions in recent years.[45] Second, banks' proxy role should, generally speaking, not be a credible threat for management because the company pays for banks to represent small shareholders, and because institutional investors tend to use proxies other than banks.[46]

Thus, voting rights do not seem to be a decisive element for lenders' corporate governance role in major listed companies.

4. Board Representation: Lenders' Presence and Impact[47]

Although the "board establishment" that long dominated the scene is being shaken,[48] cross-board memberships are still a frequent occurrence between banks and their major Swiss clients.[49] It therefore comes as no surprise that, at the end of 1995, of the 25 companies referred to in Figure 4,[50] 18 had a bank's representative on their board.[51] In addition, a recent study has emphasized that lenders are also indirectly represented on boards, because of co-optation and networking.[52]

However, Bereuter has pointed out that interviews he had with bankers revealed that their appreciation of lenders' influence within a board ranged from

[44] The following companies were selected: Alusuisse-Lonza, Ares-Sereno, Baer, Bâloise, BBC, CS Holding, Ciba, Elektrowatt, EMS-Chemie, Holderbank, Landis & Gyr, Oerlikon-Bührle, Nestlé, Roche, Rückversicherung, Sandoz, SBC, Schindler, SGS, SMH, Sulzer, Swissair, UBS, Winterthur, and Zurich.

[45] Bereuter, supra n. 14, 298. See also Figure 2.

[46] See supra Part B, Section II. The need for some companies to meet quorum rules could provide some leeway to banks, but this should be of marginal importance.

[47] Board representation of banks, as typical lenders, is also dealt with in this volume by Hopt (Ch. 4: Sec. B.II.1. and passim), Wenger/Kaser (Ch. 6), Prigge (Ch. 12: Sec. B.I.2., B.II.5., and C.II.), and Wymeersch (Ch. 12: Sec. C).

[48] See Flammer, Dominik 'Les Conseils d'administration continuent de maigrir' *Journal de Genève* June 26, 1997, at V; Spogat, Iris 'Verwaltungsräte I' *Bilanz* (April 1997) 93-9; see also Zehnder, Egon P. '"Corporate Governance" darf kein Papiertiger sein. Vielfältige Herausforderung für den Verwaltungsrat' *Neue Zürcher Zeitung* June 7/8, 1997, No. 129, 29; cp. Anderson and Hertig, supra n. 3, 520.

[49] Bereuter, supra n. 14, 299.

[50] For their identity, see supra n. 44.

[51] See Hertig, supra n. 42, 12.

[52] See Nollert, Michael 'Verflechtungen schweizerischer Verwaltungsräte: Eine Analyse des Netzwerkzentrums' (Working Paper, Zurich, April 1997—to be published in *Schweizerische Zeitschrift für Soziologie* Vol. I (1998)).

nil to substantial.[53] Hence, providing a banker with board membership might signal nothing more than the company's willingness to maintain and develop good relations with a group of *Hauptbanken.*

There are three reasons to believe that lenders are indeed not a significant corporate governance force for major listed companies. First, it is usually not one, but several banks that have representatives on the board, which should neutralize their influence. Second, variations in bankers' perceptions of their influence probably mean that it is the bankers' individual qualities which enable them to play a corporate governance role, rather than their status as lenders' representatives.

Third, although prior empirical research concluded that 12.5% of the board members of a sample of 17 major firms had been elected because of their being bankers,[54] a recently published survey[55] among the 100 biggest Swiss firms (with 40% of them answering) does not demonstrate that being a banker is still seen as a determinant in becoming a board member (see Figure 5).

Figure 5: Ideal Qualifications for Swiss Board Members, 1996

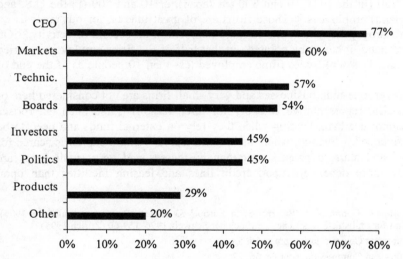

Source: Egon Zehnder International, supra n. 55, 11.

---

[53] Bereuter, supra n. 14, 313.

[54] Glaus, Bruno U. *Unternehmungsüberwachung durch schweizerische Verwaltungsräte* 114 (Zurich 1990).

[55] Egon Zehnder International *Nicht-Schweizer in Schweizer Verwaltungsräten. Zur Funktion und Rolle ausländischer Verwaltungsratmitglieder* 11 (Zurich 1996). See also Hertig, supra n. 42, 14-5, for similar conclusions regarding current board members.

To summarize, lenders may, because of the professional qualities of their representatives, play a monitoring and even a strategic role in major Swiss listed companies. However, it would be excessive to say that they are a corporate governance "force". All banks try to have a strong relationship with such clients, permitting them to act as trusted advisers or even to enter into some sort of "partnership". But they are not in a position of strength. Their influence is a function of the value added they may provide (e.g., with the support of the bank's specialist team for the firm's industry) and is thus quite volatile.

II. Small to Medium-Sized Firms

Obviously, listed companies represent only an extremely small fraction of the total number of Swiss firms. Therefore, the analysis of a second representative category of enterprises, small to medium-sized firms, should provide a better picture of lenders' corporate governance role in Switzerland.

Small to medium-sized firms are generally defined as firms having between 10 and 250 (in the EU), 10 and 300 (in Japan), or 10 and 500 (in the U.S. and Switzerland) employees.[56] Those firms are of great interest for our analysis: at least in Europe, they are found in huge numbers in all sectors of activity.[57] On the other hand, it has to be pointed out that half of EU firms employ no salaried staff,[58] and 87.8% of Swiss firms employed less than 10 people as of the end of 1995.[59]

However, one-man businesses and very small firms are not considered here or in a specific representative category for three reasons. First, such enterprises often cannot use bank lending when they rely on external funds and need to be equity financed.[60] Second, when, as in Switzerland, venture capital is scarce for the seed and start-up phase,[61] one-man businesses and very small firms are normally more dependent upon credit lines and leasing facilities than upon

---

[56] European Commission 'Enterprises in Europe' 53 (Fourth Report, Luxembourg 1996); Bundesamt für Statistik 'Statistisches Jahrbuch der Schweiz 1996' 159-60 (Zurich 1995).

[57] European Commission, supra n. 56, 53

[58] European Commission, supra n. 56, 27.

[59] Bender, André and René Baumi 'Les PME romandes ont des difficultés insurmontables de financement' *Journal de Genève* April 24, 1997, Special Section, at IV.

[60] They often have no specific collateral to offer to lenders and insufficient near-term cash flows to service debt payments. On equity being the most suitable financing tool when debt contracts are difficult to enforce, see recently Shleifer, Andrei and Robert W. Vishny 'A Survey of Corporate Governance' *Journal of Finance* 52 (1997) 737-83, 765.

[61] See 'Parlamentarische Initiative Risikokapital. Bericht der Kommission für Wirtschaft und Abgaben des Nationalrates' *Bundesblatt* 1997 II 1008, 1013. The same assessment is valid at the EU level: see European Commission 'The First Action Plan for Innovation in Europe' Annex 2.3, Table 16 (Brussels 1997).

medium-term loans. Third, to the extent that lenders play a noticeable corporate governance role with this category of firms, it is most likely to be in workout situations (our fourth representative category).

Small to medium-sized firms clearly have fewer alternatives to bank loans than large corporations.[62] In addition, they are often not very sophisticated regarding the financing of their activities. Thus, lenders should be able to play more of a corporate governance role with small to medium-sized firms. But even for this category of firms, lenders have not, up to now, generally played a monitoring or managing role, either because sophistication was lacking or because of competition from other lenders who were less vigilant.[63] The costs of such an approach have been made clear by the real estate debacle and through the economic downturn.

As a result, the major lenders, especially the big banks, are in the process of switching from asset-based to cash flow-based lending. Borrowers will still have to provide financial information, but they increasingly will also be required to produce business plans and management succession planning, and their performance will be benchmarked. The data gathered, combined with the lender's historical data base, will with greater frequency result in the allocation of a rating, which in turn will determine the initial pricing of credit facilities or lead to its adjustment.

Such evolution being in the making, it is not yet possible to evaluate the extent to which it will affect lending practices overall and to measure the likelihood of a resulting increase in lenders' corporate governance role. For example, it is too soon to detect whether the development of internal rating systems by sophisticated lenders will encourage borrowers to implement measures allowing them to get an improvement of their ratings. This will especially depend upon the credibility of the banks' requirements, which among other things will be a function of credit officers as well as relationship bankers having not only financial but also industry specific knowledge. Up to now, the only visible reaction has been small firms' public protests regarding substantial constraints on managerial autonomy resulting from big banks' new lending policies. Moreover, an important part of the lending industry, i.e., state-owned cantonal banks, may refuse to modernize their lending practices for lack of sophistication or for social and political reasons.

Indeed, given that cantonal banks normally are at least implicitly "guaranteed" by their canton, this enables them to undercut other lenders should they wish to do so, either because they get cheaper (subsidized) financing or because they will

---

[62] For an empirical study regarding financing issues for 136 Swiss small and medium-sized firms, see Frei, Regula *Alternative Finanzierungsmöglichkeiten von Klein- und Mittelunternehmen in der Schweiz* especially 154-6 (Bamberg 1994).

[63] See supra Part B, Sections III. and V.

be bailed out if necessary.[64] Thus, an unsophisticated cantonal bank clearly has less than optimal incentives to improve the factoring of risks into pricing or to adjust its lending policies to permit for efficient monitoring of the borrower. But even a sophisticated cantonal bank may not price its loans correctly or ensure for proper monitoring. Especially because of unemployment levels,[65] there are political calls for Swiss lenders to support small to medium-sized corporations through the economic downturn and cantonal banks are in a more difficult position to resist such pressures.[66]

Consequently, there is a not negligible risk that the desirable adjustments of pricing and lending practices will be hampered, possibly leading to a decrease of the big banks' involvement in domestic lending (especially considering the cost of regulatory capital and the need to provide shareholders with satisfying returns). If this happens, well-meant efforts to contribute to Switzerland's economic recovery by making "cheap" money available could ironically result in damaging long-term effects by permitting inefficient firms to survive or, at least, by preventing overdue management improvements to occur more rapidly through lenders' influence.

We nevertheless believe that there is a fair chance that Switzerland's pricing and lending practices will improve, not least because of the realization that lenders' corporate governance influence can be a positive development. First, at the preliminary and anecdotal level, there are indications that small to medium-sized borrowers are prepared to "suffer" more expensive risk-adjusted pricing, to the extent that it permits them to get lender's advice regarding strategy, organization, and management. To some extent, this reflects the U.S. experience in the venture capital area[67]—and means that new lending policies may indirectly contribute to the much needed development of venture capital financing in Switzerland. Second, there is regulatory pressure for banks to adopt risk-adjusted credit policies. Such pressure should have a not negligible impact, given that the

---

[64] On this issue, see the Cartel Commission's investigation of cantonal banks' role: 'Stellung der Kantonalbanken im Bankgewerbe' 23-94 (1995/3 Veröffentlichungen der Schweizerischen Kartellkommission und des Preisüberwachers).

[65] At the end of March 1997, 202,207 persons were officially registered as unemployed in Switzerland, representing an unemployment rate of 5.6% of the workforce (*Neue Zürcher Zeitung* April 9, 1997, No. 81, 14). This is very high by Swiss historical standards, although significantly lower than the EU average unemployment rate, which has exceeded 10% of the workforce for the 1991-1996 period (European Monetary Institute 'Annual Report 1996' 25).

[66] It is not easy to evaluate how difficult it is for small to medium-sized firms to get loans. Recent surveys seem to show that access to lending is better than according to popular belief: see Bender and Baumi, supra n. 59; Chenaux, Jean-Philippe *Les banques ne prêtent-elles qu'aux riches? Le crédit commercial dans tous ses états* 11-3 (Lausanne 1996); Meier, Paul 'Kranken Banken an Kreditschranken' *Neue Zürcher Zeitung* December 27/28, 1997, No. 300, 25.

[67] See Black, Bernard S. and Ronald J. Gilson 'Venture Capital and the Structure of Capital Markets: Banks versus Stock Markets' *Journal of Financial Economics* 47 (1998) 243-77.

industry learned its lesson the hard way during the 1990s[68] and due to the fact that cantonal banks are increasingly subject to the Federal Banking Commission's supervision.[69]

Third, at a more fundamental level, current behavioral changes regarding the role of boards in small to medium-sized corporations should result in a significant increase in the corporate governance role of lenders.

It was fairly common for lenders to have representatives on the boards of small to medium-sized corporations.[70] This was easy to do: such firms are closely held and designating a board member is still a smooth process even for the biggest firms of that category and, beyond, for the smaller listed corporations (see Figure 6).

Figure 6:   Procedure for Choosing a New Board Member in the Top 100 French-Swiss Companies, 1996

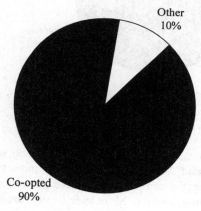

Other
10%

Co-opted
90%

Source: Spencer Stuart, infra n. 71, 19.

Logically, such boards are likely to "rubber stamp" decisions made by the owner of the firm or its management. And for decades this was the case, whether or not lenders sat on the board.

---

[68] See supra n. 25.

[69] The recently revised Art. 3a § 2 Bundesgesetz über die Banken und Sparkassen (SR 952.0), now permits cantons to have their cantonal banks fully submitted to the supervision of the federal regulator—and not mainly to cantonal "supervision". Cantons have been quick to make use of that possibility, which is understandable given the current economic environment and the problems cantonal banks are facing.

[70] Chaudet, supra n. 4, 105; see also the studies and data mentioned by Trindade, Rita Trigo *Le conseil d'administration de la société anonyme* 54-6 (Basle 1996).

However, a recent survey has shown a growing perception that even for small to medium-sized firms (an important part of the sample), a board has to truly function. A new generation of more aggressive outside directors seems to be penetrating the market,[71] and boards are now expected to fulfill significant monitoring and strategic tasks (Figure 7).[72]

Figure 7:   Functions of the Board as Seen by Board Members of 100 French-Swiss
            Corporations, 1996

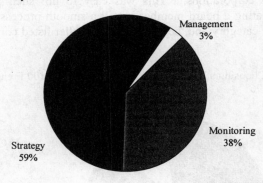

Source: Spencer Stuart, supra n. 71, 19.

It is possible that such surveys reflect wishful thinking or lip service to the corporate governance trend. We believe that there is more to it. Board members have begun to realize that the competitive environment requires them to be more active for the corporation to survive. More specifically, the sophisticated lenders' willingness to implement tougher policies has not gone unnoticed. To preempt a possible shift in corporate governance forces, or simply to contribute to the firm's standing as a borrower, boards of leading companies will have to perform better. This, in turn, should make the new lending strategies of the big banks profitable and render social or political loans an increasingly unattractive strategy for cantonal banks: potential beneficiaries of such loans would mostly be the less fit firms.

To summarize, it is already perceptible that lenders will have a greater influence on firms' corporate governance. How this will materialize is not yet clear. The most likely scenario is the one where discussions regarding the pricing of

---

[71] Spencer Stuart *Enquête sur les conseils d'administration* 11 (Geneva 1996).

[72] See also Böckli, Peter *Die unentziehbaren Kernkompetenzen des Verwaltungsrates* 55-7 (Zurich 1994).

loans will lead firms to adjust their organization and performance. Indeed, as the next two sections will show, this is already the case in "intense" lending situations such as MBOs and workouts and it would make sense for a harmonized approach to develop.

III. A Management Buy-Out

Management buy-outs and leveraged acquisitions have become increasingly common in Switzerland over the past years.[73] There are three main reasons for this development. First, spin-offs due to mergers and firms' focus on core businesses, as well as estate planning for family-owned firms, have supplied the market with MBO/LBO targets.[74] Second, because of the expertise gained in those areas through their international activities, Swiss banks have set up new domestic business units specializing in MBOs and LBOs (providing advisory services, senior debt, and/or equity). Those units are generally run by specialized professionals who have been exposed to cross-border transactions. Therefore they are both more knowledgeable than the average domestic professional and better able to market MBO/LBO transactions. Third, non-Swiss LBO equity funds have started to invest in Switzerland, contributing to the trend.

By definition, a firm that is going through an MBO needs financial support. It has to find new equity providers and (because capitalization nevertheless remains very thin) it has to secure substantial senior and mezzanine debt financing. Until recently, equity was typically provided either by a bank or by a fund, whereas lending was provided by a non-equity-holding bank (to avoid intra-institutional conflicts of interest). This remains generally true, but the strict separation of equity and debt is getting diluted. There is a demand for one-stop solutions, to permit quicker decisions, and, more importantly, because Swiss managers have shown resistance to providing the needed detailed information about their firms to banks that are not ready to hold equity.

In any event, both equity and credit providers know that the success of the MBO depends upon cash flow generation. Therefore, their monitoring and influence on management is incomparably higher than for the average small to medium-sized firm. The difference is not only quantitative, it is also qualitative.

---

[73] According to the Swiss Private Equity & Corporate Finance Association (SECA), the number of MBOs in Switzerland has developed as follows: 5 in 1988, 21 in 1989, 15 in 1990, 18 in 1991, 31 in 1992, 38 in 1993, 45 in 1994, 38 in 1995, 48 in 1996, and 60 in 1997.

[74] A study of 134 Swiss MBOs for the period of 1988-1994 has shown that two thirds were linked to spin-offs and one third to estate planning: see von Hachenburg, Alexander and Maximilian Koch 'Management Buyouts in der Schweiz. Ein Instrument zur Steigerung des Shareholder value' *Neue Zürcher Zeitung* August 9, 1996, No. 183, 23.

We have seen that MBO lenders normally refrain from taking equity positions. This means that they will not have voting rights as an instrument to support their corporate governance role. But providers of senior debt will also usually refuse to be board members, as they fear liability or other legal risks if they are seen as exercising too much management influence.[75] Thus, there is a major difference with the listed company and small to medium-sized firm situations.

Lenders' influence will be secured through three techniques. First, lenders have a lock on the company's balance sheet by virtue of the fact that third-party financing is restricted, and the senior debt providers have pledges on all or virtually all of the company's assets. Second, lenders will increase their requests regarding quantity and quality of the information to be provided. Not only will ex ante due diligence activities be extremely thorough, but lenders will require monthly reporting, quarterly covenants checks, and impose the designation of a recognized accounting firm as auditor. Hence, there is no comparison with "normal" domestic loans regarding the knowledge gained about the company or the ex ante and ex post information obtained from it.

Third, to ensure debt-servicing capabilities, the loan agreement will contain covenants dealing with most issues that affect cash flow. Most importantly from a corporate governance perspective and often the major point of contention during negotiations, management will typically be prevented from deciding alone about acquisitions, capital expenditures exceeding a certain amount, or other important decisions.[76]

On the other hand, it appears that lenders' influence is less pronounced for Swiss MBOs than on the international scene. The pricing and lending practices of other players, especially the cantonal banks, force the big banks to relax their requirements for some transactions, as it is feared that applying "pure" European standards would mean losing many of the smaller but nevertheless interesting deals. Thus, for those situations, information gathering is less intrusive as basic due diligence and data processing are left to more junior (and less costly) staff than at the international level.

Consequently, as for small to medium-sized firms in general, lenders' corporate governance role is partly a function of banks' sophistication and socio-political consideration. Nevertheless, it would be a mistake to underestimate lenders' influence in Swiss MBO situations. Even if European standards are not fully

---

[75] Such fears reflect the perception that the Anglo-Saxon doctrine of "equitable subordination" could be received in Swiss law, either directly or by extension of the de facto director concept. Interestingly, providers of mezzanine financing seem less concerned by the issue and normally want the board to recognize their observer status.

[76] Note that, from a theoretical perspective, the main costs of debt as a source of finance are that the firms may be prevented from undertaking good projects because debt covenants keep them from raising additional funds: see Shleifer and Vishny, supra n. 60, 763.

applicable, the major lenders are not prepared to give up minimum standards concerning on-site visits, industry analyses, business and management succession plans, or loan covenants. This is a significant improvement compared to former Swiss lending practices. In addition, the relaxing of standards mainly concerns relatively small deals, in the range of 10-15 million Swiss francs. Even for those, undercutting pricing and lending requirements is not necessarily a successful strategy. Entrepreneurs start to realize that lenders' involvement has advantages for them as it permits them to improve their management practices, and some are ready to pay higher interest rates for such services.

To summarize, MBOs are on the rise in Switzerland. They are dealt with by specialized units that apply more professional lending standards. As a consequence, lenders are beginning to play a significant corporate governance role.

IV. Workouts

A lender confronts a workout situation when its borrower faces financial problems that cannot simply be reflected into the pricing of the loan and that make it unlikely that a third party can be found to provide substitute financing.

From the bank's perspective, the options are not numerous but are clear: the firm has to receive additional financing, to be restructured, and/or to be liquidated. These are drastic choices that require time-consuming analyses and the commitment of substantial human resources. In the past when bankruptcies were an infrequent occurrence in Switzerland, it often made sense to leave the company to itself and hope for the best.

The increase in lending losses and bad loans has made such a passive approach increasingly unpalatable. As a consequence, most important Swiss banks have both set up specialized workout departments and adopted specific workout policies. Given that firms finding themselves in a workout situation are not in a particularly strong bargaining position, the adoption of a more hands-on approach should have major consequences regarding lenders' corporate governance role.

There are clear indicators that this is the case. First, there has been a massive headcount increase in the workout departments of the major Swiss banks.[77] Second, from a qualitative standpoint, these workout teams consist of specialists whose professional background permits them to adopt a deeper and more comprehensive analysis than the loan managers from whom they take over the critical loan positions.

---

[77] According to the UBS 1996 'Annual Report' (at 35), the credit workout teams consist of some 250 specialists whose task is to minimize losses and optimize the level of recoveries.

As a consequence, the cash flow generation approach that has been used for MBOs is already making inroads in the workout area. Because of the nature of the situation, lenders have to decide quickly about the probability of survival of the firm, given the shape of the industry, the competitive position of the firms' products, and the quality of its management. Obviously, if the decision is taken to have the firm liquidated, lenders' corporate governance role is both massive and final. More interesting is the case where the assessment is that the firm can survive, either through restructuring or acquisitionsby a third party.

It appears that lenders then avoid taking a visible corporate governance role, e.g., through having representatives on the board or by acting as corporate advisor. As for MBOs, the reason is that they do not want to add a liability risk to the existing lending risk. Therefore, they often suggest the hiring of a consultant to devise a restructuring strategy or to help during the transition phase before a merger or an asset sale can take place. In reality, this does not prevent the lenders from playing an essential corporate governance role. They constantly get information, the quantity and quality of which at least equates data flows in an MBO situation. They closely monitor both the consultant and the borrower's management. As a rule, no significant decision is taken without the workout team at least knowing about it.

To summarize, workout situations are significantly more frequent than in the past, both because of the state of the economy and because lenders no longer remain passive during critical situations. The high number of specialists currently dealing with workouts, coupled with experience gained internationally and in MBO situations, results in lenders playing a corporate governance role going beyond what had been the norm up to a few years ago.

D. Conclusion

Previously, lenders were not a significant corporate governance force for Swiss firms. Huge credit losses, the increase in competition, and experience gained at the international level have made it possible and necessary for lenders to be more influential.

This transformation is made easier by quantitative and qualitative improvements in flows of information, resulting from a general evolution in the accounting area. An increase in professional competence, both within banks and firms, also helps. However, the modernization of lending policies will have an impact on borrowers' independence and freedom to maneuver. This is already noticeable for MBOs and workout situations.

In our opinion, practices established for these areas should result in the *general* applicability of new, cash flow-based lending standards. But for the major companies or very small loans, lending officers have learned that the future activities of the borrower will be of paramount importance to the continued creditworthiness of the company, implying that lenders' corporate governance role is due to increase across the board. How significant a force lenders will be will to some extent depend upon the credibility of the big banks' new lending requirements, which among other things will be a function of credit officers as well as relationship bankers having not only financial but also industry specific knowledge. However, the main factor will be the extent to which the cantonal banks will adopt risk-adjusted pricing and lending policies. This in turn will be partly a function of how seriously cantonal banks take political calls for lenders to support local firms. In short, there is a risk that well-meant efforts may paradoxically have damaging long-term effects by permitting inefficient firms to survive or, at least, by preventing overdue management improvements to occur more rapidly through lenders' influence.

Discussion Report

Following the lectures and the general comment by *Macey*, the discussions focused on the role of lending banks as a force in corporate governance. In addition to a vivid discussion on the lectures themselves, the participants also reported on the role of banks in the German corporate governance system. In the general discussion, there was a consensus as to the necessity of distinguishing between the specific situations of lenders in each country.

Lenders and Corporate Governance in Sweden

The Swedish speaker *Berglöf* commented on *Macey's* remark that lenders are at the bottom of the list of forces in corporate governance by arguing that lenders may not be the most important force in corporate governance. But he confirmed his own thesis that the role of lenders as a force in corporate governance depends on arm's-length or control-oriented lending, and he stressed that from an international perspective, banks as main lenders must be accounted for. A European law participant argued that the relationship between banks and companies has become closer and that the equity holding of banks has increased in Sweden. In his view, lending with equity support is less risky. Concerning the relationship between banks and companies, a German lawyer questioned the role of the spheres of influence in Swedish corporate governance. He stated that one sphere of influence with high equity ownership obviously means control. If, on the other hand, the side bank comes from another sphere of influence, it is clear that there can only be arm's-length lending as there are fewer possibilities of control. In his last question, he asked about what happens in Sweden after switching the main bank, and specifically if there is any downgrading of the former main bank. *Berglöf* explained that if the firm and the main bank belong to the same sphere, then it is not likely that there will be a change. In a block, a firm is also protected against hostile takeovers, which plays an important role because 50% of the biggest Swedish firms are linked. Furthermore, *Berglöf* stressed that as in Germany, equity holding in Sweden is more profitable for banks than lending. Putting the importance of lenders as a force in corporate governance in perspective, he finally argued that the fundamental question in Swedish corporate governance depends on the spheres of influence: the question is who monitors at what level of the group and how the influence is used.

State-Guaranteed Banks and Corporate Governance by Lenders

The Swiss lecturer *Hertig* responded to *Macey's* statement that the share market in Switzerland is underdeveloped, that the IPO and the venture capital markets are weak, while the secondary market is not. In answering the question of a German economist as to whether the *Kantonalbanken* in Switzerland will survive, he said that they probably will. These government-guaranteed banks which were intended to do local business only not only help little firms with venture capital, but also go abroad. Because of the current crisis of the *Kantonalbanken*, they are now under the supervision of the Federal Banking Commission. With an ongoing government guarantee they will survive, but if people no longer want to pay for the government guarantee there might be a change. The best option for the future is more competition. There is a connection between the *Kantonalbanken* and the lack of skilled people necessary for a change in credit handling at the three big private banks: private banks cannot afford the monitoring because *Kantonalbanken* sell cheaper loans, which prevents the change from asset-oriented lending to cash-flow-oriented lending. That is a big problem because major losses do not happen because of wrong lending decisions, but because banks do not follow up with information and the development of loans. But if banks do internal ratings which are needed for corporate governance, the lending costs will increase and make a lender unattractive for credit customers. A German lawyer stated that in Germany there is a similar problem. The *Landesbanken* are also state owned or publicly controlled, and venture capital is thus guaranteed by the state. He thinks there is no need for *Landesbanken* to be involved in this kind of business. If the *Landesbanken* make bad choices it is up to the state to pay, and that will lead to problems with the EC.

Theoretical View on the Role of Lenders as a Force in Corporate Governance

The paper by *Drukarczyk* and *H. Schmidt* was presented by the latter, but questions were answered by both. An American participant asked whether covenants are used in the same way in Germany as they are in the U.S.: static covenants for public debt and dynamic covenants for private debt. *Drukarczyk* answered that covenants are rarely seen in Germany. As lenders, banks normally rely on collateral and general terms and conditions (*AGB = Allgemeine Geschäftsbedingungen*). The function of the covenants is particularly taken by the *AGB*: they give the lenders the right to call the loan when the firm performs badly, and also the right to call for additional collateral. Then *H. Schmidt* explained why his definition of corporate governance was not inherent to his analysis: the role of lenders as a major force in corporate governance only occurs in the moment of crisis—not before—and is forced by the problems of the credit customer. If the credit customer is in a crisis, it is the aim of the lender to increase the value of the company. This corresponds to his definition of corporate governance as a network of arrangements and rules aimed at maximizing the total market value of a firm. *Drukarczyk* confirmed this by remarking that banks are contingent monitors, contingent on the ratio of total assets to net lending. While there is no reason for monitoring when there is a wide gap between loans and assets, there is a need for monitoring if there is only a small gap, especially if the bank is the main claim holder.

Macey's thesis of the minor importance of banks in corporate governance was questioned by an American participant: If banks rank at the bottom of the list of corporate governance, who will then have the better incentive structures for corporate governance monitoring? Even if banks have many problems in corporate governance, maybe their role should be improved. For *Macey*, the question is what kind of role a lender shall play in corporate governance. In a global perspective, banks should say yes to projects which increase the value of the company. Therefore, agency costs and transaction costs must be reduced. In that context, it is uncontroversial that banks should get their benefit of the bargain but no excess return. He doubted that banks should play an important role in corporate governance in addition to that.

Comparative Research and the Role of Banks in German Corporate Governance

In the more general part of the discussion, it was common ground that more research on the specific subject of the role of lenders as a force in corporate governance is needed. It was also widely accepted that a comparative study would be difficult; the role of banks as lenders should instead be looked at distinctively from country to country, but also according to size, ownership, and financial wealth of the credit customer.

An American lawyer related the interactive corporate governance idea of Triantis[1] and stated that there is yet another form for banks participating in corporate governance: if a bank fires a firm, this is a signal to shareholders, a signal of impending distress. But it is a question of culture whether the shareholders have much to say. The role of banks is determined by other features, which makes a comparative analysis difficult. To examine the role of banks in corporate governance, one needs to know the shareholder's role, the compensation of the managers, the equity, and the voting. This is why any comparison is hard and troublesome. *Drukarczyk* commented on the beginning of the lawyer's statement by saying that to see the role of banks in corporate governance as nothing but a signal-giver to equity holders is not very helpful for the equity

---

[1] Triantis, George G. and Ronald J. Daniels 'The Role of Debt in Interactive Corporate Governance' 83 *Cal. L. Rev.* 1073-113 (1995).

holders, because this information comes too late. *Macey* agreed to the latter part of the statement. The difficulties for comparative studies were also stressed by German lawyers who stated that what *Berglöf* said about main and side banks is a Swedish phenomenon, and that there are many differences in the corporate governance of Germany and Sweden, such as those of law, tax, and tradition. *Macey* illustrated the problems of a comparative study by focusing on the role of lenders in Germany and in Italy. *Macey* went on to say that banks play an important role in corporate governance in Germany, as opposed to Italy where banks play no role. In northern Italy there is no capital market and no bank interference. From his point of view, the economic system has proven innovative with respect to the corporate governance problem of having very small enterprises in the form of family-run firms. He says that it is difficult to predict what would happen if banks were left out of corporate governance in Germany. To be sure, the structure would change, but the economy would not necessarily have to suffer. As soon as banks are involved as lenders, they tend to avoid risky business, even if equity holders are willing to pay for the risk.

With this remark, the discussion shifted to the German banking system. A German lawyer objected to the description of the role of banks in corporate governance in Germany by saying that the differences between big firms on the one hand and small and medium firms on the other hand should be looked at carefully. Large firms are in a strong bargaining position, which results in a minor importance of the influence of banks. But also family-run small and medium-sized firms fear a tendency of banks to influence their business decisions and tend to avoid borrowing from banks. Nevertheless, it may be said that banks have considerable influence in small and medium-sized firms. Often their influence is even too strong, considering their possible lack of knowledge of the special business of the borrower. But there is no empirical evidence on this subject. A German economist pointed out that there is also a distinction between banks as lenders and banks as investment banks. As lenders, banks play no significant role in corporate governance. Especially big firms are hostile to bank interference. But even small firms do not want to invite lenders to sit in their boards except in cases of crisis. The reason for this is that it would be normal practice for the bank member in the supervisory board to ask for the long version of the audit report. That would be possible even if he were not a member of the audit committee, and most firms want to avoid this information flow. *H. Schmidt* stated that the thesis according to which big firms with less debt are subject to little influence and small and medium-sized firms with much debt are subject to higher bank influence is in line with his theory that indebted firms are subject to corporate governance by lenders. He also remarked that according to their executives, companies often try to avoid lending from big banks with nationwide business because they fear that in case of a crisis of a competitor, their data would be used by the bank to help the competitor survive. For this reason they often choose *Landesbanken*, which have less specific knowledge of the respective business sector.

Part III:

Comparative Corporate Governance

Chapter 11: Understanding Japanese Corporate Governance

Japanese Corporate Governance as a System

TAKEO HOSHI, San Diego[*]

Corporate governance can be defined as the way the management of a firm is influenced by many stakeholders. Depending on which stakeholders are involved, we can identify five aspects of corporate governance. Those aspects address the agency problems between (i) shareholders and managers, (ii) creditors and managers, (iii) workers and managers, (iv) suppliers and customers, and (v) government and firms. The mechanisms used to address each of these aspects differentiate various systems of corporate governance. Other institutional features, such as (a) human resource management, (b) managerial labor market, (c) competitive product markets, and (d) corporate laws also influence the system of corporate governance. This paper characterizes Japanese corporate governance, relying on past empirical studies on those various aspects of corporate governance. Complementarity between various aspects of Japanese corporate governance is examined. Consistency between Japanese corporate governance and the four institutional features is also discussed. The paper also examines the benefits and costs of the Japanese system relative to an alternative system. The Japanese system seems to do better for an economy characterized by (1) substantial noise in the financial markets, (2) high cost of developing markets, (3) an important role of relation-specific capital in production, (4) low monitoring cost, (5) low adversarial incentive effects of possible contract renegotiation, (6) the government's interest aligned with social welfare, and (7) low cost of concentrated political power.

Contents

[*] This paper was completed while the author was Tokio Marine & Fire Visiting Associate Professor at Osaka University. The author thanks Osaka University for its hospitality. The paper was presented at the 11th EDI/FASID Joint Seminar "Regulatory and Institutional Aspects of the East Asian Models," Hakone, November 1995, at the Truman Institute Conference "Lessons from East Asia for the Development of the Middle East in the Era of Peace," Jerusalem, January 1997, at the International Conference on Corporate Governance "Corporate Governance in the Telecom Industry," Seoul, May 1997, at the symposium on "Comparative Corporate Governance - The State of the Art and Emerging Research -," Hamburg, May 1997, at Kobe University, and at Copenhagen Business School. The author thanks the participants at these conferences and seminars for helpful comments. The author is also grateful for comments and suggestions from Noritaka Akamatsu, Dae-Hong Chang, Ronald Dore, Reinosuke Hara, Takenori Inoki, Hiroshi Izawa, Ku-Hyun Jung, Kenji Kojima, Colin McKenzie, Takuya Negami, Kyung-Suh Park, Ulrike Schaede, Juro Teranishi, Chris Woodruff, Yishay Yafeh, Shin'ichi Yufu.

Table

Table 1: Benefits and Costs of the Japanese Corporate Governance

A. Introduction

Corporate governance can be defined as the way the management of a firm is influenced by many stakeholders, including owners/shareholders, creditors, managers, employees, suppliers, customers, local residents, and the government. Different economies have systems of corporate governance that differ in the relative strength of influence exercised by the stakeholders and how they influence the management. The purpose of this paper is to characterize the system of Japanese corporate governance by examining each aspect of the system and its benefits and costs.

The definition of corporate governance in this paper is broader than a probably more popular definition that focuses on how owners/shareholders control a firm.[1] The conflict between owners and managers, albeit important, is only one of many governance problems that a firm faces. Moreover, how the problem between owners and managers is mitigated is related to the remedies for the other problems. This paper argues that interrelation between different aspects of corporate governance is a very important issue that one must examine when one evaluates a system of corporate governance.[2]

The paper primarily summarizes what we currently know from past research about the system of Japanese corporate governance rather than trying to make new findings.[3] The paper is organized as follows. The next section identifies

---

[1] Kester (1992) defines the corporate governance broadly as I do here.

[2] The issue of interrelation between owner-manager relation and other aspects of a firm is also pursued by Aoki (1989) and Garvey/Swan (1994).

[3] Recently there have been numerous surveys on corporate governance in general and Japanese corporate governance in particular. To name a few, Hart (1995a, b) reviews recent development in the theory of incomplete contracts and discusses some implications for corporate governance; Garvey/Swan (1994) also examine corporate governance from the incomplete contract point of view; and Shleifer/Vishny (1997) survey the recent literature on corporate governance, focusing on the agency problem between shareholders and managers. For surveys of Japanese corporate governance in particular, Fukao (1995) compares corporate governance in

several aspects of corporate governance according to the types of stakeholders involved. We show that the shareholder-manager conflict is not the only problem that a firm faces. We also see several alternative mechanisms to address each type of governance problem. Section C characterizes the Japanese system of corporate governance by examining each aspect of corporate governance pointed out in Section B. Section D discusses the complementarity between different aspects of corporate governance and consistency between the system of corporate governance and some other relevant economic institutions. Section E examines relative benefits and costs of the Japanese corporate governance system when it is compared to an alternative system based on a totally different type of complementarity consideration.

Throughout this paper, I refer to "the Japanese system of corporate governance" as if such a system has continued to exist without changing its characteristics. In reality, the Japanese economic system experienced major changes in the past and is currently going through a major change, as many observers suggest. The discussion in this paper should be understood as the one on "the system of corporate governance" that was prominent in most of the post-war period (mid-1950s to mid-1980s). During this period, the system of corporate governance exhibited the characteristics that I point out in this paper. Ideally, we would want to examine why the system has started to change since the mid-1980s, but that is beyond the task of this paper and left for future research.[4]

B. Aspects of Corporate Governance

Corporate governance becomes an issue only when firms face the problem of information. If all the stakeholders shared the same information, shareholders and creditors would not worry about the manager wasting their money on unworthy projects; suppliers would not worry about the buyer firm reneging its promise to buy parts in the future; customers would not worry about a supplier failing to deliver the parts with pre-specified quality by the pre-specified date. In fact, in the (imaginary) world of complete information, we do not even need corporate organizations. As a textbook microeconomic theory would tell us, one can hire workers and rent capital by paying them according to their marginal products.

Japan, U.S., U.K., France, and Germany, and Kojima (1997a) surveys a vast amount of literature on Japanese corporate governance.

[4] The paper also mainly discusses the large corporations in Japan as many other studies have done. The corporate governance of small firms is expected to be different from the corporate governance of large firms, but this is an under-researched area. As an empirical study which examines the difference for large firms and medium firms in Japan, see Izawa/Itoh/Dohmyo (1997).

In the real world, information is incomplete, and each economic agent is tempted to use his informational advantage to pursue his own objective, which may differ from the objectives of those who are influenced by his action. Economics of information has classified the informational problem into two categories. One is the problem of adverse selection or "hidden information", and the other is the problem of moral hazard or "hidden action". For example, consider a debt contract between a lender and firms. The problem arises when the lender does not have crucial information that the firms possess, or when the lender cannot observe the firms' behavior, such as their project choices. Then, the lender can end up with a pool of high-risk firms because they have higher probability of default and are willing to accept high interest rates. Alternatively, if the firms can choose the riskiness of the projects, debt contracts may give them the incentive to choose high-risk projects because they can benefit from upside gain while the lender bears all the downside risk.

The informational problem is not limited to the relation between firm managers and creditors. Similar problems arise between different types of stakeholders of a corporation. The existence of an informational problem alone, however, does not necessarily require corporate governance. As Garvey/Swan (1994) and Hart (1995a, b) point out, if complete contracts are available, corporate governance does not matter. Complete contracts would specify all the relevant actions of the parties contingent on the observed state of the world and leave no room for governance.

Complete contracts are, however, impossible to write in many real-life situations. We cannot foresee all the contingencies. A system of corporate governance can be considered as an institution that mitigates the informational problems between various stakeholders when complete contracts are not available. Depending on which stakeholders are involved, we can identify five aspects of corporate governance. First, problems arise because shareholders do not have all the information that the manager has. Second, similar problems arise because creditors do not have all the information that the manager has. Third, informational asymmetry between the managers and the workers can lead to a problem. Fourth, the informational asymmetry may exist also between a firm and its suppliers and/or customers. Finally, the government can be a stakeholder of a firm. The manager's decision may influence the welfare of local residents, which a local government represents, or the firm's decision may influence some national policy objectives of the government.

These informational problems are often called "principal-agent" problems or simply "agency" problems, because they involve a "principal" and an "agent": the agent's actions influence the welfare of the principal and the principal would like the agent to behave according to the principal's interest. For example, in the relation between shareholders and the manager, shareholders are the principal and the manager is the agent. We can distinguish between different systems of corporate governance by examining the mechanism to alleviate each agency problem.

I. Agency Problem Between Shareholders and Managers

The agency problem between shareholders and managers is the most important aspect of corporate governance.[5] The problem arises because managers have an informational advantage that can be misused against the shareholders' interest. There are several possible mechanisms that can alleviate the problem, but we can classify those into two types. First, the shareholders can closely monitor the manager so that the manager does not harm the shareholders' interest. Alternatively, the shareholders can try to align the manager's incentive with theirs. These two types of approaches correspond to what Berglöf (1995) calls "control-oriented" financing and "arm's-length" financing.[6] Following this terminology, I will refer to "control-oriented" shareholding and "arm's-length" shareholding.

Control-oriented shareholders monitor the behavior of the management and, if necessary, intervene in the management. The monitoring is often delegated to the board of directors elected by shareholders. The board provides monitoring and the shareholders monitor the performance of the board. If the shareholders are dissatisfied with the performance, they can mount a proxy fight to replace the board members. Since it is costly to monitor the board performance and start proxy fights if necessary, control-oriented shareholders are more likely to be large shareholders whose benefits from such active intervention are sufficiently large. In control-oriented shareholding, monitoring and intervention of the shareholders prevent the managers from abusing their informational advantage.[7]

Arm's-length shareholders, on the contrary, do not actively intervene in the management of a corporation. When they are not satisfied with the corporation's performance, however, they take some actions that hurt the management. For

---

[5] Some large firms in Japan, such as many insurance companies, are mutual companies and do not have shareholders. This paper does not address the issue of corporate governance of mutual companies or co-ops, which do not have shareholders.

See also the articles in Ch. 4 of this volume on the board and the respective sections in the comparative contributions of Kanda, Prigge, and Wymeersch in Ch. 12.

[6] Berglöf (1995) uses these to describe two different types of arrangements between a manager and investors, which include both equity holders and debt holders.

[7] This paragraph is a brief description of control-oriented shareholding if it works perfectly. Unless there is a shareholder who holds 100% of the firm, the mechanism may not work perfectly, because small shareholders always want to free ride on the efforts of large shareholders. Some empirical studies using the U.S. data find the monitoring by the board to be not as strong as one might expect. For example, Weisbach (1988) finds that only those boards which are dominated by outsiders tend to replace their CEOs following the companies' poor performance. Main/O'Reilly/Wade (1995) find that many boards for U.S. companies are socially influenced or captured by the CEO to a considerable extent.

example, they can sell their shares, which lowers the share price and makes a firm a target for a hostile takeover. If a takeover imposes sufficient costs on the current manager, the threat will help motivate him to satisfy the shareholders' interests. Another mechanism that can be classified into the arm's-length shareholding category is a high-powered incentive mechanism that aligns the management's interest with that of shareholders. Under such a mechanism, managers' compensation will be tied to the profitability of the company through (profit-sensitive) bonuses or stock options. Thus, arm's-length shareholders can (or at least try to) mitigate the informational problem without actively intervening in the management.

One should note that the effectiveness of two types of solutions to the agency problem depends on other conditions in the economy. In arm's-length shareholding, for example, the threat by a shareholder to dump her shares in the market is credible only when she holds only a small portion of the shares. Otherwise, she would not be able to sell her shares without depressing the share price.

The control-oriented shareholding, on the other hand, requires some concentration of stock ownership. Since monitoring the board (and starting a proxy fight if necessary) is a public good, diffused ownership of stocks will create a serious collective action problem among the shareholders, and no shareholders would have an incentive to monitor the board.

No economy uses only arm's-length shareholding or only control-oriented shareholding to solve the agency problem between managers and shareholders. Arm's-length shareholding and control-oriented shareholding coexist in the same economy. They coexist even at a firm level: some shareholders can provide control-oriented shareholding while others provide arm's-length shareholding.

What one finds, however, is that arm's-length shareholding is more prominent in some economies compared with other economies, and that control-oriented shareholding is more prominent in other economies. For example, the U.S. economy has more liquid stock markets and more frequent hostile takeovers compared with other economies, and takeover threats help discipline the managers. In this sense, the U.S. economy is characterized more by arm's-length shareholding. In contrast, hostile takeovers rarely happen in the Japanese economy, and the main bank, which is also one of the largest shareholders of the firm, takes the responsibility of monitoring and disciplining the management. Thus, by examining the most frequently observed arrangement between shareholders and managers, we can characterize corporate governance of an economy as either dominated by arm's-length shareholding or by control-oriented shareholding.

II. Agency Problem Between Creditors and Managers

Although the relationship between shareholders and managers is the most important aspect of corporate governance, it is not the only component of a system of corporate governance. The system also includes some mechanism to address agency problems between the management and the stakeholders other than shareholders. As Garvey/Swan (1994) argue, recent empirical studies have found that managers are influenced by many types of stakeholders. In other words, it is not sufficient for a manager to maximize the value of shares; he is forced to care about the welfare of other constituencies.

The agency problem between creditors and managers[8] resembles that between shareholders and managers; managers may exploit their informational advantage. To the extent the management's interest is aligned with that of shareholders, the different attitudes toward risk may constitute another aspect of the agency problem. Because shareholders/managers gain from upside risk but creditors do not, the management's decision can be too risky from creditors' point of view.

One way to mitigate the agency problem between creditors and the management is to give creditors some equity stake. In this way, the creditors become shareholders and can benefit from whatever corporate governance mechanism that exists to reduce the agency problem between shareholders and the management. This is an especially easy way to mitigate the problem arising from the differing attitudes toward risk between shareholders and creditors.

Giving ownership to stakeholders always helps in reducing the agency problem to the extent the problem between shareholders and the management is already alleviated. We will see below that this "solution" can be used also to mitigate the problems between the management and workers, suppliers, customers, and the government.

In addition to giving ownership stake to the creditors, there are again two types of approaches to address the agency problem between creditors and the management: "arm's-length" lending and "control-oriented" lending. In the arm's-length lending, the creditors do not intervene in the management of a corporation. But, when they do not get the interest payment that the manager has promised, they can force bankruptcy and take the case to a bankruptcy court. If bankruptcy is sufficiently costly, the threat will help motivate him to satisfy the creditors' interests. This is essentially how arm's-length lending reduces the problem of information and incentive.

In contrast, the control-oriented creditors monitor the behavior of the manager and, if necessary, intervene to limit the choice of the manager. For example, creditors (especially banks) may closely monitor the firm's activities to prevent

---

[8] On lenders as a force in corporate governance, cf. also the articles in Ch. 10 of this volume and the respective sections in Kanda's and Prigge's reports in Ch. 12.

the firm from engaging in too risky projects. By providing transactions and settlement services (besides loans) to the firm, banks can increase their ability to monitor the firm. In control-oriented lending, monitoring and intervention of the creditors prevent the managers from exploiting their informational advantage.

III. Agency Problems Between Managers and Workers[9]

When one discusses the agency problem between a manager and employees, one usually considers a case where the manager is a principal and the employees are agents. The problem arises because the manager cannot know each worker's productivity precisely (adverse selection) and cannot observe their efforts exactly (moral hazard). The manager has to worry about getting low productivity workers only, because they are more likely to find the wage level that the manager proposes attractive than workers with higher productivity (and hence higher opportunity costs). The manager has to worry about workers failing to put in enough effort if he cannot infer the level of effort exactly by observing the level of output. This type of agency problem can also be called the problem of human resource management.

There is, however, a different set of agency problems between managers and workers. Since workers are influenced by the company's decision and performance, they are also stakeholders of the company. In this sense, workers can also be the principal of managers. They face agency problems that are similar to those faced by investors: How can they prevent the manager from spending the company's resource for his own benefits?

What is relevant for corporate governance is the latter type of agency problem. Although the former type of agency problem is important for a firm, corporate governance (the question of who controls the management) does not address this type of agency problem. But, we should also note that a system of corporate governance is indirectly related to the mechanism to address human resource management problems. More specifically, a certain form of corporate governance may be complementary to a certain way of human resource management. I will come back to this point in Section B.VI. below.

We can identify a couple of ways to alleviate the agency problem by letting workers influence the management. First, giving them ownership stakes works again as far as the agency problem between shareholders and the management has already been reduced. This can be achieved, for example, by establishing ESOP (Employee Stock Ownership Program). In the extreme case, a firm can be 100% controlled by workers collectively.

---

[9] On the relation between management and employees with a special focus on co-determination, see also the contributions in Ch. 5 of this volume as well as the respective sections in the comparative articles delivered by Kanda, Prigge, and Wymeersch in Ch. 12.

Second, workers can influence the management through other institutional arrangements without formally owning the firm. A good example is the two-tier board structure for German stock companies (*Aktiengesellschaft*, or *AG*) (See Fukao 1995: 13-5 and Schaede 1995: 99-104). Half of the members of the supervisory board are chosen by shareholders and the other half are elected by workers. Since the supervisory board appoints the management board members, workers can indirectly influence the management.

In most economies, employee-controlled firms occupy only a small share of the total economy. Other institutions that require workers' voice in the management have not gained popularity in many economies. French companies can also choose to have German-style two-tier boards, but most companies choose not to (Fukao 1995: 15). Even in Germany, many companies choose to become limited liability companies (*Gesellschaft mit beschränkter Haftung*, or *GmbH*) rather than *AG*, because being a *GmbH* does not require the company to have a two-tier board.[10] Thus, workers in many firms in many countries do not have a formal way to exercise their influence on the management.

IV. Agency Problems in Customer/Supplier Relations

There are two broad types of agency problems that can arise between a supplier firm and its customer firm. First, the supplier firm may wonder if the customer firm will buy the goods when they are produced. This is a "hold-up" problem. The customer may also suffer from the hold-up problem if he has to make some investment that is productive only if the supplier delivers the goods. Second, if the quality or the cost of goods depends on the supplier's efforts, the customer may wonder whether the supplier will exert a sufficient level of effort.

There are three types of approaches to solving these agency problems. The first is to write a price incentive contract. For example, consider the case where the cost of producing goods depends on the suppliers' efforts (and noise), which cannot be observed by the customer. Then, giving the fixed price (per unit of goods) is best from the incentive point of view; the supplier will put in the optimal level of cost-reducing efforts because he can enjoy all the benefits of cost reduction. One potential problem of the fixed-price contract is that the supplier bears all the risk if the production cost is influenced by some random factors that are beyond the supplier's control. If the supplier firm is risk-averse, the principal (customer here) may want to strike a balance between incentive and risk sharing. The optimal contract would adjust the price according to the observed cost of producing goods. Note that if such a contract is written, it leaves

---

[10] The two-tier board is mandatory for *GmbH*s subject to supervisory board co-determination, i.e., roughly speaking, *GmbH*s with a workforce exceeding 500 employees.

little room for corporate governance, because the contract clearly specifies the price as a function of the (observable and verifiable) production cost.

Second, the information and incentive problems in the customer/supplier relationship may be reduced by letting one own the other, if there already exists a mechanism to mitigate the agency problem between shareholders and the management. This role of ownership in solving the information problem was first elaborated by Grossman/Hart (1986). As they point out, however, if both the supplier and the customer face the hold-up problem, giving ownership to one does not solve the problem completely. The arrangement would improve the incentive for the owner firm to invest in relation-specific assets, but it would hurt the other (owned) firm's incentive to invest. They in fact show that the cost of one-firm ownership can outweigh its benefit.

We can also consider arm's-length share ownership to address the problem caused by many suppliers (customers) dealing with a customer (supplier). The suppliers can threaten the customer with selling the shares if they find misconduct. The possibility of low share price and takeover can discipline the customer.

Finally, the customer and the supplier can enter a long-term relationship that includes mutual monitoring. As we discuss below, a good example is the subcontracting relationship found in the Japanese auto industry. Although the relationship includes a price incentive component as Kawasaki/McMillan (1987) point out, both their empirical study and Asanuma/Kikutani (1992) find that the parameter estimates of their model suggest the contract is more influenced by risk sharing than incentive considerations. Thus, the long-term relationship with monitoring seems to be a more important element of the Japanese subcontracting from the incentive point of view. The Japanese car assemblers maintain long-term relationship with their first-tier suppliers, and those suppliers are closely involved in the designing process of new models, as Asanuma (1989) finds.

V. Government as a Stakeholder

Occasionally, the government cares about a firm's behavior. For example, the firm may be a dominant employer in the local economy and the local government cares about employment in the local community. Or, the firm's operation may create external diseconomy, such as pollution, for local residents, and the government may want to restrict the firm's operation for the welfare of the residents. In these cases, the government is also a stakeholder of the firm, and we can expect agency problems to arise between the government and the firm. The problem is that the government does not have all the information that the manager of the firm has and cannot observe some actions of the manager.

Again there are several ways for the government to tackle the agency problem. First, the government can have ownership stake in the company. The extreme form of the ownership is nationalization, but even without nationalizing the firm, the government can become a control-oriented shareholder and influence the company's management. It is also possible for the local residents to hold shares directly and become either arm's-length or control-oriented shareholders.[11]

The government can intervene in a firm's management without any ownership by imposing regulations. Although any government has at least some regulations on some sectors of the economy, some governments intervene more often than others. Examining government involvement in corporate governance through regulation is one way to distinguish one system from another.

VI. Other Institutions Relevant for Corporate Governance

We have looked at five types of agency problems that a firm may encounter and several mechanisms to reduce each problem. As we will find for the Japanese case, these mechanisms are interrelated with each other. One mechanism to address a certain problem may increase the effectiveness of another mechanism on another problem, making them complements in the sense of Holmstrom/ Milgrom (1994). Two mechanisms can be substitutes, in the sense the existence of one mechanism reduces the need for another mechanism.

The aspects of corporate governance are not only related with each other, but also with some other economic institutions. Here I list four important institutions that influence the nature of corporate governance. Those are (a) system of human resource management, (b) managerial labor market, (c) product market competition, and (d) corporate law. In the next section, we will find that limited empirical results suggest that the Japanese system of corporate governance is consistent with the conditions in these four aspects.

The first one is the system of human resource management. This can be considered as the institution to reduce the first type of agency problem between the management and workers discussed above: the management is the principal and workers are the agents. There are many types of arrangements that can mitigate this type of agency problem, but we can again identify two broad classes of approaches: the arm's-length approach that relies on a well-organized labor market, and the control-oriented approach that relies more on long-term relation in internal labor markets.

---

[11] Examples of companies that are significantly owned by the government or local residents are found in many former socialist economies. Pistor/Turkewitz (1996) find that the state government retained significant share ownership in former state firms even after the privatization in Hungary, Czech Republic, and Russia. Stark (1996) also finds that in Hungary the state government still has direct and indirect (through some firms) share ownership in many former state firms. Qian (1995: 216-7) reports that the Chinese government holds more than 50% of shares in many non-state-owned enterprises. The township-village enterprises in China, which are owned by local communities, present another example (Che/Qian 1994).

In the arm's-length approach, the manager finds workers in a well-organized labor market, where each worker is priced according to the market assessment of his productivity. A well-functioning market will reflect all the observable characteristics of workers related to their productivity, including the levels of education, the experience, and the past wages. Thus, market wages can serve as good signals about workers' quality, and reduce the problem of adverse selection.

A control-oriented approach creates an internal labor market that enhances learning of workers' abilities and gives the right incentive for workers to exert their efforts. A good example for such an institution is what Aoki (1988: Ch. 3) calls "ranking hierarchy." In a ranking hierarchy, workers are classified into ranks, and workers in higher ranks get higher salaries than those in lower ranks. A worker's rank is the only thing that decides his salary and it is not related to his job or output. New workers start from the lowest rank with equal salaries. The management monitors the workers' performance. Workers are promoted to the next rank if their performances meet certain criteria. If a worker is found failing to make efforts to satisfy the performance criteria to move up to the next rank, his promotion is suspended or—worse—he is separated. Aoki (1988: Ch. 3) argues that such ranking hierarchy is found in many Japanese corporations.[12] Since a ranking hierarchy provides the manager with observations of workers' performances over a long period of time, the manager can get good signals about workers' quality and promote high quality workers fast, thus alleviating the problem of adverse selection.

Note that the control-oriented human resource management requires a long-term commitment of both the employers and the employees. An employer needs a long time to find out the quality of her employees and the employees need a long time to climb up the ranking hierarchy to achieve high earnings (that come with high ranks). Thus, a corporate governance mechanism that relies on corporate takeovers to reduce the agency problem between shareholders and management may be too disruptive to a control-oriented human resource management. Control-oriented shareholding, in which management changes are carried out by stable shareholders, may be more conducive to such a labor management.

The second institution that influences the nature of corporate governance is the labor market for the managers. If there is a well-organized market for managers, any misconduct by a manager toward stakeholders may hurt the reputation of the manager in the labor market and reduce the probability of getting a lucrative management position in the future. This pressure from the managerial labor market can prevent managers from abusing their informational advantage against the stakeholders. In this sense, a well-functioning labor market for managers can be a substitute for corporate governance.

---

[12] See Itoh (1994) for more on ranking hierarchy in Japan.

Third, the product market competition also disciplines the managers and may substitute for corporate governance. In a competitive product market, any inefficiency resulting from agency problems in the firm can reduce the probability of its survival. The threat of failure of the company in the competitive market may induce the manager to work hard to reduce the inefficiency from the agency costs as much as he can. Or, a competitive market will eventually weed out inefficient managers, and only efficient managers will survive the selection of the market.

In the sense that a competitive product market provides valuable information about how a company is performing, it may well be complementary to the system of corporate governance that uses such information. Without a reasonably competitive product market, even control-oriented stakeholders may have trouble assessing the performance of the firm.

Finally, corporate laws influence corporate governance. Roe (1990) points out many impediments in the corporate law in the U.S. that discourage or prohibit control-oriented shareholding. Fukao (1995) also finds obstacles for shareholders who want to intervene in the management actively in the U.S. and the U.K., while shareholders in Japan, Germany, and France do not encounter many of the restrictions. He also finds that there are many legal constraints on cash distributions to shareholders in Japan, Germany, France, and the U.K., while few restrictions exist in the U.S. Thus, the stakeholders in Japan, Germany, France, and the U.K. do not have to worry much about the possibility of the manager (colluding with shareholders) making too much distribution to shareholders. This influences the nature of the corporate governance developed in these countries. Finally, as La Porta et al. (1996) examine the relation between corporate law and corporate governance for 49 economies, they find the ownership concentration tends to be very high in the countries with less shareholder protection measure, less enforcement of corporate law, and poor accounting standards. Thus, their result suggests that control-oriented shareholding is more likely to develop when the country has a poor corporate law.

C. Characteristics of Japanese Corporate Governance

We can characterize the corporate governance observed in an economy by identifying the mechanism most often used to address each of the agency problems described in the last section. Further, by examining the characteristics of four institutions listed at the end of the last section, one can examine how corporate governance is related to other parts of the economic system. This section tries to identify the characteristics of Japanese corporate governance, relying on recent empirical studies, and examines its internal consistency as well as consistency with other parts of the economic system.

An alternative approach would be to characterize a system of corporate governance by examining which agency problem is taken most seriously or which stakeholder has the largest influence on the management. For example, Fukao (1995) takes this approach and characterizes the Japanese system as the one where creditors play the most important role in corporate governance. Kojima (1997a) argues that the agency problem between shareholders and management occupies the central position in U.S. corporate governance because other agency problems are handled through contracts. These approaches are not inconsistent with the approach taken in this paper and rather would complement the current discussion. By looking at both the remedial mechanisms and the relative importance of each agency problem, we can gain an even better under-standing of a system of corporate governance.

Shareholding in Japan is closer to control-oriented than arm's-length. The majority of shares of major corporations in Japan are held by stable shareholders, which include other corporations in the same business group, major creditors, and major customers/suppliers. As Ide (1996) points out, these shareholders hold shares primarily to maintain their relationships rather than for financial gains. Often shareholding is reciprocal and forms a dense network of cross-sharehold-ing. As a consequence of stable shareholding, a hostile takeover is very difficult and in fact rarely happens. Thus, arm's-length shareholding, which relies on takeover threats to discipline managers, would not work.

Instead, shareholders in Japan are more control-oriented. Stable shareholders, especially banks, often place their retired employees as board members. The cases of financially distressed firms accepting the executives dispatched by their main banks to senior directors' positions are well-documented. Thus, a main bank, which is one of the largest shareholders, intervenes in the management of the customers in financial trouble by sending their employees to sit on the board. The cases of financial distress are the clearest evidence for the control-oriented nature of Japanese corporate governance, but directors dispatched by stable shareholders are also observed during normal times. Sheard (1996) finds that directors sent by stable corporate shareholders are more likely to be observed for those firms with high leverage, concentrated shareholding, small size, and short history. He also examines bank-dispatched directors and finds that they are more pronounced in those firms with high leverage, high dependence on the main bank, low profitability, small size, and short history.

A relatively more concentrated shareholding structure in Japan compared with the U.S. makes it easier to have control-oriented shareholding because a collec-tive action problem among small shareholders is mitigated. For example, Prowse (1996) calculates the average concentration of the top five shareholders as 33% for large Japanese firms, compared to 25% for the U.S. large firms.

It is important to note that the dominant majority of stable shareholders in Japan are corporations that have business relations with the company. They are shareholders but also other stakeholders at the same time. They are creditors, suppliers, and customers. Thus, even though we observe control-oriented shareholding, it is exercised by the corporations, which also have other types of stake in the company, and the role played by individual shareholders is minimal.

In addition to being major shareholders, creditors (especially banks) in Japan influence the management through another mechanism. Again their approach is control-oriented rather than arm's-length. Rather than relying on the threat of bankruptcy, banks monitor the management of a corporation and intervene when the company gets into financial trouble. The director dispatch discussed above provides a convenient vehicle for such monitoring and intervention.

Not all creditors monitor management carefully. In many cases, one can identify the "main bank" that plays the leading role in monitoring and, if necessary, intervention. The other creditors delegate monitoring to the main bank, which is expected to represent the interest of all creditors. The main bank system economizes on the monitoring costs through mutually delegated monitoring.[13]

Japanese workers do not have formal representation in a supervisory board. Many Japanese companies have ESOP. According to Jones/Kato (1995), more than 80% of Japanese firms listed in the first section of the Tokyo Stock Exchange had ESOP in 1980.[14] But, the workers never seem to actively exercise their control rights. Nevertheless, they are considered to be important stakeholders, and consideration of workers' welfare influences major decisions relating to corporate governance, such as mergers and rescue operations of financially troubled firms led by their main banks.

For example, Kester (1991) finds that Nippon Steel planned to diversify itself into some areas in which the company did not have any experience, in order to continue to employ workers who had become redundant in steel production. He argues:

...... the unambiguous beneficiaries of ongoing investment in new businesses are the employees no longer required in steelmaking activities. Indeed, it is clear that finding uses for their skills as a means of satisfying lifetime employment expectations was central to the planning process that led to the restructuring plan. Whether or not suppliers of capital will benefit from these investments is far less clear at the present time. (Kester 1991: 183)

Sustaining lifetime employment is often an important concern in a main bank-led rescue operation. For example, Pascale/Rohlen (1983) report that in the rescue operation of Mazda led by Sumitomo Bank, the labor union obtained the management's promise to not lay anyone off.

Thus, even though Japanese workers do not have a mechanism to formally represent themselves in the board, they can influence major corporate decisions in critical times. As the quotation from Kester (1991) above suggests, the ability

---

[13] See chapters 1-10 in Aoki/Patrick (1994) for the main bank system in Japan. For the delegated monitoring aspect of the main bank system, see Sheard (1994).

[14] Their study finds substantial effects of ESOP on total factor productivity. They estimate that the introduction of an ESOP leads to 4-5% increase in productivity over three to four years.

of labor to influence corporate decisions seems to be related to the Japanese labor practice characterized by lifetime employment and seniority wages.

Suppliers and customers are often members of stable shareholders. This is especially the case when a series of suppliers are organized under a prime manufacturer to form production *keiretsu,* or when a series of distributors are organized under a manufacturer to form distribution *keiretsu.*[15] Thus, Japanese corporate governance often gives suppliers and customers equity stakes in each other to reduce the agency problem between them.[16]

Customer-suppliers relationship observed in Japanese production *keiretsu* is not limited to cross-shareholding. Many studies on the suppliers network in Japan have focused on the automobile industry, where production *keiretsu* is the best organized. The studies have shown that production *keiretsu* includes an elaborate mechanism to reduce agency problems between customers and suppliers based on long-term relationship.

The Japanese government did not intervene in the economy by owning companies. The government ownership was limited to some industries, such as communication and railroads, and has been declining since the early 1980s. Nonetheless, the Japanese government has been very much actively influencing private business. A device used by the Japanese government to direct private business without owning shares is the industrial policy, which is often implemented through administrative guidance without specifically relying on formal laws.

Another tool is *amakudari*, which is a practice for retired government officials to be invited to be board members of private companies. As other stakeholders, such as banks and firms in the same business group, send their employees to sit on the board, the government, though it is not a shareholder, sends in the retired officials to be board members. This in itself shows the influence of the government over private firms, and it gives the government a communication channel to intervene in the management if necessary.[17]

Much anecdotal evidence suggests the involvement of the Japanese government in corporate governance. For example, MITI (Ministry of International Trade and Industry) encouraged mergers of major industrial firms in the 1960s and played an active role in some major mergers, including the merger between

---

[15] Toyota *keiretsu* organized by Toyota Auto is an example of production *keiretsu*. Many Japanese consumer electronics manufacturers, such as Matsushita and Hitachi, form their own distribution *keiretsu*. See Gerlach (1992) for more on *keiretsu*.

[16] The role of cross-shareholding in reducing the hold-up problem between a supplier and a customer was pointed out by Flath (1996).

[17] This is not the only reason why amakudari exists. Inoki (1996: 207-27) motivates amakudari as a human resource management device for bureaucrats. By sending many senior bureaucrats to private and semi-private companies, the government can maintain a pyramid type bureaucracy with competition between young bureaucrats.

two large automobile companies, Nissan and Prince, in 1965, and the merger of two major steel companies, Fuji and Yawata, in 1970.[18] Another example is the involvement of the Japanese government in some main bank-led rescue operations. Pascale/Rohlen (1983) argue that MITI played a key role in persuading Sumitomo Bank to rescue Mazda. Thus, past research suggests that the Japanese government was much involved in the corporate governance process, even though it was not a major shareholder.

To summarize the arguments in this section, Japanese corporate governance is characterized by (1) control-oriented shareholding, (2) shareholding by creditors and control-oriented lending, (3) involvement of labor without formal representation, (4) shareholding by suppliers/customers and long-term relationship, and (5) interventionist government without shareholding.

D. Japanese Corporate Governance as a System

These five aspects of Japanese corporate governance are interrelated. In other words, the Japanese system of corporate governance forms a *system* in the sense that all the aspects are linked and the mechanism for one aspect may not fully work if complementary incentive mechanisms are not in place for other aspects.[19] This section checks this internal consistency of the system of Japanese corporate governance. Its consistency with four institutions that influence the nature of corporate governance (human resource management, managerial labor market, product market competition, and corporate laws) is also examined.

First, the control-oriented nature of shareholding and lending is complementary to the mechanism to reduce the hold-up problem between suppliers and customers based on repeated transactions. Compared with arm's-length financing that relies on takeovers to discipline the management, the control-oriented approach is better at protecting long-term relationship, which is essential to the Japanese mechanism to minimize customers/suppliers conflicts. At the same time, the long-term nature of customers/suppliers relationship also improves the efficiency of control-oriented shareholding by including those business trading partners in the group of stable shareholders. They can accumulate knowledge about the firm through long-term transactions and use it to monitor the company.

Second, control-oriented shareholding and lending are complementary to government interventions to private business. The practice of director dispatch from stable shareholders gives a convenient vehicle for the government to place retired government officials on the boards of private companies. The government

---

[18] See Kester (1991: Ch. 4) for more on the role of MITI in the merger of Fuji Steel and Yawata Steel.

[19] McMillan (1995) points this out in discussing implementation of the market system for former socialist economies.

establishes a channel of close communication with private firms through the *amakudari* officials. Since this allows the government to potentially get access to sensitive information of private firms, intervention based on administrative guidance, which can reflect the sensitive information without making it public, may be better than intervention based on explicit laws.

One aspect of Japanese corporate governance that fails to show strong complementarity with other aspects is the involvement of workers. Certainly, this aspect is not detrimental to the other parts of the system of corporate governance. But, the complementarity with the other aspects is not obvious. The Japanese human resource management discussed below, which requires workers to have long-term commitment, may make it desirable to give some power to workers. If this is the case, however, it is puzzling to find that there is no formal mechanism (like the two-tier boards in Germany) to represent workers' voice in corporate governance. Many companies have ESOP, but the total shareholding by employees is often very small (no more than a few percent).

I now turn to the question of consistency of the system of Japanese corporate governance with its external environment, which includes human resource management practice, the (lack of a) managerial labor market, the degree of competition in product markets, and corporate laws. Japanese human resource management is characterized by the ranking hierarchy discussed in the last section. A typical Japanese worker joins a firm right after he has finished his education and is expected to stay in the same company until the compulsory retirement age. The company is expected not to lay off the workers before their retirement ages. Even in a recession, the company relies on reduction of overtime, voluntary retirement, and suspension of new hires to adjust the labor force. Thus, both workers and the company commit to a long-term relation in Japan. The workers' performance is monitored by their supervisors and they are promoted to higher ranks as they satisfy certain criteria at each rank. The earnings of workers are tied to their ranks.

Control-oriented shareholding and lending in Japan is very much conducive to the ranking hierarchy, which relies on the long-term relationship between workers and the management. The use of control-oriented financing (instead of arm's-length financing that relies on the threat of takeover and bankruptcy) allows the manager to establish long-term relationships with workers. This makes the ranking hierarchy more effective. Arm's-length financing would be too disruptive for human resource management that is based on the long-term relationship.

The model by Prendergast/Topel (1993) suggests another interesting link between the ranking hierarchy and the control-oriented shareholding. They argue that if the manager is a residual claimant (because of a high-powered incentive scheme, for example), she tends to bias the ratings of workers downward. A high-powered managerial incentive may be an important component of arm's-length shareholding, but it is less important in control-oriented shareholding, where shareholders can influence the manager more directly. Thus, control-oriented shareholding, which does not have to rely on a high-powered incentive scheme, is better at guaranteeing fair assessment of workers by the manager, which is important in ranking hierarchy.

A well-organized labor market for managers does not exist in Japan. The majority of managers of Japanese companies are promoted internally, and the board of directors is just the finishing stage for the winners of internal tournament. Even when directors come from outside, they are most often dispatched by stable shareholders or retired government officials. The lack of a managerial labor market makes sense if it is substituted for by a well-functioning mechanism of corporate governance. If the system of corporate governance is working reasonably well, the managerial labor market is not necessary. There is also an argument for complementarity between the *lack of* a managerial labor market and the Japanese system of corporate governance. The lack of a managerial labor market makes it hard for Japanese managers to move from one company to another, and improves the credibility of their long-term commitment. Since Japanese corporate governance is based on such long-term commitments with stakeholders, the lack of a managerial labor market actually increases the effectiveness of corporate governance.[20]

It is difficult to talk about the degree of product market competition in Japan. We expect to see a substantial variation of competitiveness across different industries. In some industries, such as construction, the competition is often impeded through an elaborate mechanism of collusion.[21] In other industries, such as automobile or electronics, the companies compete fiercely in the international markets.

The relation between product market competition and corporate governance is not theoretically obvious. One may argue that product market competition and tight corporate governance are substitutes. Then, we would expect to see a well-functioning system of corporate governance in an economy with little market competition, because tighter discipline is necessary to overcome the lack of market competition. Alternatively, it seems also reasonable to assume that product market competition and corporate governance are complements. For example, bank control, which is often a central part of control-oriented financing, is often contingent on firm performance. The bank intervenes in the firm only when the firm has trouble meeting the interest payment. In a highly competitive product market, the firm cannot ignore the possibility of poor performance and bank intervention. This makes control-oriented bank financing more effective. Under arm's-length financing, the presence of highly competitive product

---

[20] Whether the long-term commitment between corporations requires personal commitments at the level of managers may be arguable.

[21] See McMillan (1991) for such a mechanism in the construction industry.

markets makes the threat of bankruptcy more realistic. Thus, a competitive product market seems to be complementary to both arm's-length and control-oriented approaches to corporate governance.

The relation between product market competition and corporate governance is an empirical issue, but I am not aware of any empirical study that examines the hypothesis for Japan. We need more empirical studies on this point.[22]

According to La Porta et al. (1996), corporate law in Japan is comparable to that of other developed countries, such as the U.S., in its enforcement and protection of investor rights.[23] They also find Japanese companies' shareholders concentration low compared with less-developed countries.[24] Thus, the Japanese data are consistent with their overall result that concentrated ownership structure is found in a country with little investors' protection and poor enforcement of law. But their results shed little light on the differences between developed countries.

Fukao (1995) carries out a systematic comparison of corporate laws relevant to corporate governance for Japan, U.S., U.K., Germany, and France. He finds some interesting differences between U.S. law and Japanese law (and German law), and argues that the difference in law is consistent with the difference in corporate governance. For example, he finds the U.S. rules on insider trading to be defined vaguely, but the rules are explicit in Japanese law. This is consistent with Japanese corporate governance where control-oriented stakeholders play important roles.[25] They can carry out close communication with the management without worrying about violating the insider trading rules. In the U.S., the ambiguity of the rules makes control-oriented financing more difficult.

---

[22] Hoshi/McMillan/Schaede (1998) test the hypothesis using data on Japanese manufacturing firms. Their preliminary results suggest that the market competition and financial discipline can be either substitutes or complements, depending on the type of financial discipline.

[23] One interesting result of their paper is that the corporate laws in developed countries are similar to each other in their degrees of enforcement and investors' protection, except for the difference in relative importance of shareholders' protection and creditors' protection. The result seems striking if we note the difference in their origins, which La Porta et al. (1996) argue to be an important cause for the difference between the current laws. The laws of less-developed countries, however, seem to show the differences according to the origin of laws, as they point out.

[24] Their shareholding concentration measures cover only the ten largest companies for each country. This is too small a sample, at least for countries like Japan and the U.S., where thousands of listed companies exist.

[25] Here the causality runs from the corporate governance to the corporate laws. The Securites Exchange Act in Japan had an article against "unfair" trades, but it was never applied to insider tradings. When the Act was revised in 1988, what would constitute insider trading was explicitly specified.

E. Benefits and Costs of the Japanese Corporate Governance

The Japanese system of corporate governance is characterized by long-term relationship between stakeholders and management. In the last section, we found that the Japanese system exhibits not only internal consistency but also consistency with some external environments, including the conditions in human resource management and corporate law. The Japanese system, however, is not the only system of corporate governance that is internally and externally consistent. One can think of other systems that are motivated by different sets of complementarity considerations. This section first presents such an alternative system and discusses the benefits and costs of the Japanese system relative to the alternative.

I call the alternative system the "market-oriented" system, because it relies heavily on price signals generated in markets. The system is defined by the following characteristics. Shareholders and lenders have an arm's-length relationship with the manager. The majority of firms have no dedicated mechanism to address the principal-agent problem for workers-managers. Price incentives are used to reduce the agency problems between suppliers and customers, and long-term relationship between them is rarely observed. Government is not a substantial owner of firms, and does not intervene in private business in a discretionary way.

As its human resource management, this system is likely to have the arm's-length approach, which is based on a well-organized labor market. The managerial labor market is also well-developed. The product market competition may or may not be intense. As we noted above, the link between product market competition and corporate governance is not clear. Corporate laws will have strong protection for small shareholders and strong creditors' rights during the bankruptcy procedure.

Complementarity considerations that motivate the market-oriented system are the following. In arm's-length shareholding, corporate control is typically exercised through a change in the management by takeovers. Such a change is easier if the company does not have much long-term commitment. Thus, the absence of long-term trading relationship is conducive to arm's-length shareholding. The lack of involvement of labor in the corporate governance process is also favorable to the development of arm's-length shareholding, because the new management after a takeover has one less problem to worry about. We can make a similar argument for the link between arm's-length lending and other aspects of corporate governance. Bankruptcies, which are another mechanism to discipline management, are handled more smoothly if firms do not engage in long-term relationship. Finally, the lack of government intervention in firms is complementary to arm's-length shareholding. The governments in many countries often rescue a troubled company if it is a big company. The "too big to fail" principle may impair the effectiveness of arm's-length lending in an economy (or an industry) where the government is believed to be ready to intervene in private business.

The external environment of the system (arm's-length labor contracts, well-organized managerial market, protection of small shareholders, and strong creditors' rights) is also consistent with the system of corporate governance. Arm's-length labor contracts are convenient when financing is also arm's-length. To cope with frequent management changes under arm's-length financing, a managerial market is useful. Arm's-length shareholders will benefit from strong protection of their rights, and the threat of bankruptcy under arm's-length lending will be more credible with strong creditors' rights in bankruptcy courts.

What are the benefits and costs of Japanese corporate governance compared to the market-oriented system? First, the market-oriented system uses market signals that reflect the information possessed by many participants in the market. In contrast, the Japanese system uses the information held by those stakeholders who exercise control in a particular aspect. Thus, if the information relevant for an efficient decision is spread across many individuals, the market-oriented system will do a better job of collecting the information widely. However, the extent of decentralization of information may be smaller than one expects if information acquisition is costly. As Grossman/Stiglitz (1980) showed, a fully informationally efficient market cannot exist if information acquisition is costly, and the market price may contain a substantial amount of noise.[26] In a very noisy market, relying on a price signal that reflects worthless noise may be inefficient. If relevant information is concentrated among a few stakeholders, the Japanese system of corporate governance has the benefit of eliminating noise.

Second, concentration of information and control often leads to political power. Thus, political power is more likely to be concentrated under the Japanese system. This can be an important cost of the system. A market-oriented system, in contrast, does not suggest such a tendency toward concentration of power because information is held by many individuals and control is spread among those individuals.

Third, a difference exists in the role of government as a stakeholder under the two systems. In the Japanese system, the government is more likely to intervene as a stakeholder than it would be in a market-oriented system. Whether such interventions are desirable from society's point of view depends on how well the government represents the society's welfare. If the government represents the public's welfare and intervenes as a stakeholder to restrict a firm's behavior, the government interventions will be consistent with the economy-wide welfare. Then, the Japanese system makes the government's job easier and it will be

---

[26] See, for example, Black (1986) and De Long et al. (1990) for implications of such noise in financial markets.

welfare-enhancing. If, however, the government represents the interest of a specific group of people, the interventions are not necessarily welfare-enhancing. Thus, depending on how the government's interest coincides with that of the society, the relative benefits of a market-oriented system and the Japanese system change.

Fourth, in the Japanese system, which is based on many long-term relationships and involves a small number of informed stakeholders, renegotiations of contracts are relatively easy. A good example is a debt renegotiation in financial distress. Consider a firm that cannot meet the interest payment this period, but its net present value—if it survives—is still positive. Under arm's-length lending, which characterizes a market-oriented system, the firm has loans from many small lenders that do not have long-term relationship. It makes sense for creditors as a whole to forgive the debt today, allow the firm to survive, and reap the benefit in the future. A collective action problem, however, may prevent them from coming up with such a rescue plan. Every creditor will try to free ride on other creditors' debt forgiveness and to receive future benefits without paying the cost today. In the Japanese system, the debt is concentrated in the hands of a small number of core banks, and the main bank plays an important role in solving the collective action problem, giving a better chance for the firm to recover from financial distress.[27]

The Japanese system makes welfare-enhancing (cost-reducing) renegotiation more likely. But, this may create a bad ex ante incentive. For example, assume the probability of financial distress partially depends on the efforts of the manager. Knowing that the creditors will renegotiate the terms in financial distress, the manager may fail to make sufficient efforts to avoid financial distress. Close monitoring mitigates this problem, but if monitoring is not perfect, the problem remains. Thus, the Japanese system is better at reducing ex post inefficiency. In contrast, the market-oriented system is better at giving the right ex ante incentive to managers.

Fifth, since monitoring is not free, extensive monitoring in the Japanese system can be quite costly. The market-oriented system, relying mainly on price incentives, can save on the monitoring cost. This can be an important benefit of the market-oriented system.

The market-oriented system, however, requires well-functioning markets. As McMillan (1995) argues, one cannot create markets overnight. The development of markets is a slow process and can be a costly one.[28] The Japanese-type system can be built more quickly, because it does not require well-organized markets.

---

[27] See Hoshi/Kashyap/Scharfstein (1990) for empirical evidence on the role of banks in reducing the cost of financial distress in Japan. For a theoretical model that studies the difficulties in debt renegotiation, see Gertner/Scharfstein (1991).

[28] The use of market signals in corporate governance, however, may encourage the development of well-organized markets. This is a relation similar to that between chickens and

Finally, the Japanese system encourages accumulation of relation-specific capital. For example, the system is conducive to ranking hierarchy, under which workers typically stay in the same company for a long time. Expecting this, the workers are willing to acquire firm-specific skills. The firm also has the incentive to stress firm-specific skills in the training program, because it increases the penalty of being fired and makes the threat of separation more effective: once they quit the current company, their skills are not so useful. Similarly, suppliers can invest in capital that is useful only for the parts it is producing for the current customer, and a bank can accumulate knowledge that is only useful in making loans to a specific borrower.

In contrast to the Japanese system, the market-oriented system rather discourages the development of relation-specific skills, because the system is likely to encourage the development of well-organized labor markets for both managers and workers. Well-organized labor markets increase the mobility of workers and managers. They will try to accumulate skills that are valuable in a wide range of firms to increase their value in the labor market. Thus, if the production system of the economy stresses firm-specific skills and relation-specific capital, the Japanese system is more suitable than the market-oriented system.

Table 1 summarizes the discussion above.[29] Note that whether a certain property of a system brings benefits to an economy often depends on other conditions in the economy. This makes it difficult for policymakers to pick a better system. One has to identify the conditions of the economy very carefully and weigh the relative benefits of the alternative systems. If one believes the conditions will gradually change, one system may be better in the short run but the other may be better in the long run.

---

eggs. Development of markets makes the price signals more informative and useful; use of price signals in turn encourages development of markets.

[29] If we examine the relative importance of each stakeholder and characterize the Japanese system as the one where creditors play the most important role (rather than shareholders), we can point out the possibility of too much creditor influence as a possible cost of such a system. For example, Aoki (1994) discusses the possibility that a firm under bank influence may take in more bank debt than optimal (for profit maximization). Munshi/Reich (1993) argue that the investment choice of a firm under bank influence is biased toward safer projects. Rajan (1992) shows that a bank's informational monopoly over a firm can have detrimental effects on the firm's incentive. Although these are clearly costs to shareholders, those should be compared to the benefits enjoyed by creditors in order to assess the net costs to the whole economy.

Table 1: Benefits and Costs of the Japanese Corporate Governance

Japanese System	Market-Oriented System
Use of Limited Information (Cost if relevant information is diffusely held; benefit if market signals are mostly noise)	Wide Use of Information in Markets (Benefit if relevant information is diffusely held; cost if market signals are mostly noise)
Concentration of Political Power (Cost)	Deconcentration of Political Power (Benefit)
High Government Intervention (Cost if the government's interest does not represent the public welfare; benefit if the government represents the society very well)	Low Government Intervention (Benefit if the government's interest does not represent the public welfare; cost if the government represents the society very well)
Easy Renegotiation (Bad ex ante incentives, but low ex post costs)	Difficult Renegotiation (Good ex ante incentives, but high ex post costs)
Reliance on Monitoring (Cost of monitoring)	Reliance on Price Incentives (Not have to pay monitoring cost)
Does not Require Markets (Not have to pay market development costs)	Requires Markets (Cost of market development)
Encourages Accumulation of Relation-Specific Capital (Benefit for a production system that stresses relation-specific capital; cost for a production system that does not require relation-specific capital)	Encourages Accumulation of General Capital (Cost for a production system that stresses relation-specific capital; benefit for a production system that does not require relation-specific capital)

F. Conclusion

A system of corporate governance can be characterized by examining how it addresses the agency problems between the management and other stakeholders of the firm, including shareholders, creditors, workers, suppliers/customers, and possibly government. Other economic institutions, such as human resource management, managerial labor market, product markets competition, and corporate laws also influence the system of corporate governance. From this viewpoint, this paper has characterized the system of Japanese corporate governance.

The paper has also compared the benefits and costs of the Japanese system to another system based on an alternative complementarity consideration.

One important issue that the paper did not address is the recent change in the Japanese system of corporate governance. Starting sometime in the 1980s, the system of corporate governance in Japan started to change in many aspects. Accumulation of internal funds and financial deregulation have made bank loans less important as a source of funds, and the role of banks in Japanese corporate governance has been declining.[30] The relations between suppliers and customers seem to have started to change as many Japanese companies have expanded their production networks globally. The changes in the system of corporate governance have been accompanied by changes in other institutions, such as human resource management. Many observers argue that the Japanese practice of labor management is finally changing. Simultaneous changes in many aspects of the economic system are consistent with an argument in this paper that elements of a system are linked by complementarities.

Documenting these changes in the Japanese system of corporate governance and examining their causes and implications is beyond the scope of this paper. It will also be important to disentangle the causalities between the transformation of the economic system and the serious decline of economic growth in the 1990s. These tasks are left for future research.

[30] See, for example, Hoshi (1996) and Kojima (1997b) for recent changes in Japanese corporate finance and their implications for the future.

References

Aoki, Masahiko *Information, Incentives, and Bargaining in the Japanese Economy* (Cambridge 1988).

Aoki, Masahiko 'The Nature of the Japanese Firm as a Nexus of Employment and Financial Contracts: An Overview' *Journal of the Japanese and International Economies* 3 (1989) 345-66.

Aoki, Masahiko 'Contingent Governance of Teams: Analysis of Institutional Complementarity' *International Economic Review* 35 (1994) 657-76.

Aoki, Masahiko and Hugh Patrick (eds.) *The Japanese Main Bank System: Its Relevance for Developing and Transforming Economies* (Oxford 1994).

Asanuma, Banri 'Manufacturer-Supplier Relationships in Japan and the Concept of Relation-Specific Skill' *Journal of the Japanese and International Economies* 3 (1989) 1-30.

Asanuma, Banri and Tatsuya Kikutani 'Risk Absorption in Japanese Subcontracting: A Microeconometric Study of the Automobile Industry' *Journal of the Japanese and International Economies* 6 (1992) 1-29.

Berglöf, Erik 'Corporate Governance in Transition Economies: The Theory and Its Policy Implications' in: Aoki, Masahiko and Hyung-Ki Kim (eds.) *Corporate Governance in Transitional Economies: Insider Control and the Role of Banks* 59-95 (The World Bank, Washington, DC 1995).

Black, Fischer 'Noise' *Journal of Finance* 41 (1986) 529-43.

Che, Jiahua and Yingyi Qian 'Understanding China's Township-Village Enterprises' (Manuscript, Stanford University, 1994).

De Long, Bradford, Andrei Shleifer, Lawrence Summers, and Robert Waldmann 'Noise Trader Risk in Financial Markets' *Journal of Political Economy* 98 (1990) 703-38.

Flath, David 'The Keiretsu Puzzle' *Journal of the Japanese and International Economies* 10 (1996) 101-21.

Fukao, Mitsuhiro *Financial Integration, Corporate Governance, and the Performance of Multinational Companies* (The Brookings Institution, Washington, DC 1995).

Garvey, Gerald T. and Peter L. Swan 'The Economics of Corporate Governance: Beyond the Marshallian Firm' *Journal of Corporate Finance* 1 (1994) 139-74.

Gerlach, Michael *Alliance Capitalism: The Social Organization of Japanese Business* (Berkeley, CA 1992).

Gertner, Robert and David Scharfstein 'A Theory of Workouts and the Effects of Reorganization Law' *Journal of Finance* 46 (1991) 1189-222.

Grossman, Sanford and Oliver Hart 'The Costs and Benefits of Ownership: A Theory of Vertical and Lateral Integration' *Journal of Political Economy* 94 (1986) 691-718.

Grossman, Sanford and Joseph Stiglitz 'On the Impossibility of Informationally Efficient Markets' *American Economic Review* 70 (1980) 393-408.

Hart, Oliver *Firms, Contracts, and Financial Structure* (Oxford 1995a).

Hart, Oliver 'Corporate Governance: Some Theory and Implications' *Economic Journal* 105 (1995b) 678-89.

Holmstrom, Bengt and Paul Milgrom 'The Firm as an Incentive System' *American Economic Review* 84 (1994) 972-91.

Hoshi, Takeo 'The Impact of Financial Deregulation on Corporate Financing' in: Sheard, Paul (ed.) *Japanese Firms, Finance and Markets* 222-48 (Melbourne 1996).

Hoshi, Takeo, Anil Kashyap, and David Scharfstein 'The Role of Banks in Reducing the Costs of Financial Distress in Japan' *Journal of Financial Economics* 27 (1990) 67-88.

Hoshi, Takeo, John McMillan, and Ulrike Schaede 'Market Competition and Financial Structure: Evidence from Japan' (In preparation, 1998).

Ide, Masasuke 'The Financial System and Corporate Competitiveness' in: Sheard, Paul (ed.) *Japanese Firms, Finance and Markets* 191-221 (Melbourne 1996).

Inoki, Takenori *Gakko to Kojo: Nihon no Jin-teki Shigen (School and Factory: Japanese Human Resources)* (Tokyo 1996).

Itoh, Hideshi 'Japanese Human Resource Management from the Viewpoint of Incentive Theory' in: Aoki, Masahiko and Ronald Dore (eds.) *The Japanese Firm: Sources of Competitive Strength* 233-64 (Oxford 1994).

Izawa, Hiroshi, Ken'ichi Itoh, and Yoshihiro Dohmyo 'Lending Relationships, Managerial Incentives, and Institutional Complementarity in Japanese Firms: An Empirical Analysis of Panel Data, 1982-1994' (Manuscript, Ritsumeikan University, 1997).

Jones, Derek C. and Takao Kato 'The Productivity Effects of Employee Stock-Ownership Plans and Bonuses: Evidence from Japanese Panel Data' *American Economic Review* 85 (1995) 391-414.

Kawasaki, Seiichi and John McMillan 'The Design of Contracts: Evidence from Japanese Subcontracting' *Journal of the Japanese and International Economies* 1 (1987) 327-49.

Kester, Carl *Japanese Takeovers* (Boston, MA 1991).

Kester, Carl 'Industrial Groups as Systems of Contractual Governance' *Oxford Review of Economic Policy* 8 (1992) 24-44.

Kogut, Bruce 'Direct Investment and Corporate Governance in Transition Economies' (Paper presented at the Conference "Corporate Governance in Central Europe and Russia", December 15-16, 1994, Washington, DC).

Kojima, Kenji *Japanese Corporate Governance: An International Perspective* (Kobe 1997a).

Kojima, Kenji 'Japanese Financial Relationships in Transition' (RIEB Discussion Paper no.74, Kobe University, 1997b).

La Porta, Rafael, Florencio Lopez-de-Silanes, Andrei Shleifer, and Robert W. Vishny 'Law and Finance' (NBER Working Paper no. 5661, July 1996).

Main, Brian G., Charles A. O'Reilly III, and James Wade 'The CEO, the Board of Directors and Executive Compensation: Economic and Psychological Perspectives' *Industrial and Corporate Change* 4 (1995) 293-332.

McMillan, John 'Dango: Japan's Price-Fixing Conspiracies' *Economics and Politics* 3 (1991) 201-18.

McMillan, John 'Markets in Transition' (Symposium Address at the Seventh World Congress of the Econometric Society, Tokyo, August 1995).

Munshi, Kaivan D. and Michael R. Reich 'Investment Behavior and Financial Structure: The Case of the Japanese Pharmaceutical Industry' (Manuscript, Massachusetts Institute of Technology, 1993).

Pascale, Richard and Thomas P. Rohlen 'The Mazda Turnaround' *Journal of Japanese Studies* 9 (1983) 219-63.

Pistor, Katharina and Joel Turkewitz 'Coping with Hydra—State Ownership after Privatization: A Comparative Study of the Czech Republic, Hungary, and Russia' in: Frydman, Roman, Cheryl W. Gray, and Andrzej Rapaczynski (eds.) *Corporate Governance in Central Europe and Russia* Vol. 2: Insiders and the State 192-244 (Budapest et al. 1996).

Prendergast, Canice and Robert Topel 'Discretion and Bias in Performance Evaluation' *European Economic Review* 37 (1993) 355-65.

Prowse, Stephen D. 'Corporate Finance in International Perspective: Legal and Regulatory Influences on Financial System Development' *Economic Review (Federal Reserve Bank of Dallas)* (1996/3) 2-15.

Qian, Yingyi 'Reforming Corporate Governance and Finance in China' in: Aoki, Masahiko and Hyung-Ki Kim (eds.) *Corporate Governance in Transitional Economies: Insider Control and the Role of Banks* 215-52 (The World Bank, Washington, D.C. 1995).

Rajan, Raghuram G. 'Insiders and Outsiders: The Choice between Informed and Arm's-Length Debt' *Journal of Finance* 47 (1992) 1367-1400.

Roe, Mark J. '"Political and Legal Restraints on Ownership and Control of Public Companies"' *Journal of Financial Economics* 27 (1990) 7-41.

Schaede, Ulrike 'Toward a New System of Corporate Governance in the European Union: An Integrative Model of the Anglo-American and Germanic Systems' in: Eichengreen, Barry, Jeffry Frieden, and Jürgen von Hagen (eds.) *Politics and Institutions in an Integrated Europe* 93-119 (New York, NY 1995).

Sheard, Paul 'Reciprocal Delegated Monitoring in the Main Bank System' *Journal of the Japanese and International Economies* 8 (1994) 1-21.

Sheard, Paul 'Banks, Blockholders and Corporate Governance: The Role of External Appointees to the Board' in: Sheard, Paul (ed.) *Japanese Firms, Finance and Markets* 166-87 (Melbourne 1996).

Shleifer, Andrei and Robert W. Vishny 'A Survey of Corporate Governance' *Journal of Finance* 52 (1997) 737-83.

Stark, David 'Networks of Assets, Chains of Debt: Recombinant Property in Hungary' in: Frydman, Roman, Cheryl W. Gray, and Andrzej Rapaczynski (eds.) *Corporate Governance in Central Europe and Russia* Vol. 2: Insiders and the State 109-50 (Budapest et al. 1996).

Weisbach, Michael S. 'Outside Directors and CEO Turnover' *Journal of Financial Economics* 20 (1988) 431-60.

The Economics of Corporate Governance in Japan

YOSHIRO MIWA, Tokyo[*]

Discussions of today's Japanese economy are full of misconceptions, upon which not only political debates but also academic works heavily depend. Discussion of corporate governance in Japanese firms is no exception, influenced by such misconceptions as the dominance of large firms, the dominance of corporate groups, the importance of main bank relationships, the undeveloped capital market, and the important role of cross-shareholdings among firms. Taking the nexus of contract view of a firm, this paper argues that employees are the most important stakeholder in most Japanese firms, which means that the controlling group is the body of employees. In such firms, the directors and managers are selected from among employees, and can almost always expect strong support from the majority of employees, as long as their decision making is consistent with employees' interests. From this we can draw a conclusion contrary to the conventional view of the Japanese economy: the friendly shareholders, the sources of corporate funds (including banks), and the board members are all selected because they are supposed to be friendly to the present directors and managers.

Contents

[*] Revised version of the paper prepared for the Conference on Corporate Governance, held by the Max-Planck-Institut für Ausländisches und Internationales Privatrecht in Hamburg, on 15-17 May 1997. The author would like to thank participants of the conference for helpful comments. The discussion is based on Chapter 11 of my *Firms and Industrial Organization in Japan* (London: Macmillan 1996), entitled 'Corporate Governance in Japanese Firms: The Body of Employees as the Controlling Group and Friendly Shareholders'.

A. Introduction[1]

Talk about today's Japanese economy is full of misconceptions, upon which not only political debates but also academic works heavily depend. Most of these misconceptions prevailed in the 1960s and survive even today, often with only cosmetic changes like that of *keiretsu* loans to main bank relationships. Many people adopt them as stylized facts without close examination of whether these 'facts' ever really existed. They were misconceptions even in the 1960s, when dogmatic Germanic theory or Marxian theories dominated discussions of the Japanese economy. (Frequent use of terms such as 'monopoly capital', 'finance capital,' and 'exploitation' symbolizes this tradition.) Many argue, for instance, that industrial policy was tremendously effective in the 1960s, and that it is still effective although diminishingly so. But if industrial policy was ineffective in the 1960s, as I believe,[2] then it cannot be effective today. Talk about corporate governance in Japanese firms is no exception, particularly influenced by such misconceptions as the dominance of large firms, dominance of corporate groups, importance of main bank relationships, undeveloped capital market, the important role of cross-shareholdings among firms, and the closed nature either of individual corporate groups or of Japan's economy.

The reader may be happy enough not to have any such misconceptions. But the world is full of talks and articles based, often unconsciously, on these misconceptions, and, like little Red Riding Hood, this happy reader has no way to defend herself against them. In Miwa (1996), therefore, as a beginner's guide to studying today's Japanese economy, I point out five misconceptions: the dominance of large firms, the dominance of corporate groups including the role of 'main banks', the effectiveness of industrial policy by the strong government, the argument that all trade relationships are long term and exclusive, and the important role of cross-shareholdings among firms. It is not a purpose of this paper, however, to discuss those misconceptions for themselves, and I ask the reader to refer to Section 1.3 of Miwa (1996), entitled 'Five Misconceptions of the Japanese Economy' (8-16) with endnotes (239-41), whenever she/he stumbles upon something strange in my discussion, presumably due to 'misconceptions'.[3]

As in other countries, in Japan the issue of corporate governance has received an enormous amount of attention in the past several decades. Due to the dominance of Marxian theories until very recently, a number of commentators have argued that the primary focus of the government policy toward business

---

[1] For a treatment of Japanese corporate governance, cf. also Kanda's country report in Ch. 12 of this volume.

[2] For details, see Part III of Miwa (1996).

[3] Also see the last three pages from Chapter 6 on 'Main Bank and its Functions' (120-2) with endnotes, the last two pages from Chapter 7 on 'the Corporate-Group View' (140-1) with endnotes, and 'Conclusion' (236-8).

should be placed upon an attack on the predominance of big business, or a social control of large firms, reflecting their basic view that a free market results in much higher concentration and/or monopoly. Although in recent years commentators have argued that corporations have failed to meet their responsibilities to shareholders and the public, a closer examination of their argument reveals the resemblance to the traditional view. Many, including businesspeople, conclude that something is 'wrong' with the way the corporation is governed, with such characterizations as 'breakdown in accountability,' 'widespread illegality,' and 'lack of legitimacy,' quite often referring to relatively advanced corporate governance models, for instance in the United States and/or Germany. Those arguments, however, tend not to mention that in those countries also commentators propose a wide variety of methods to make corporations more 'socially responsible,' including the requirement of a stated percentage of independent directors, increased shareholder democracy, and stricter enforcement of fiduciary duties.

'Corporate governance' is a catchy but ill-defined term, and so many discuss 'corporate governance' issues without any clear definition of the term, making the discussion heated and futile. In this short paper I do not use this term as a key concept. Instead, I ask who the founders of the corporation are and who takes their position when the firm grows larger—in Simon's (1976) words, who makes up 'the controlling group?'[4]

Note, however, the three points.[5] First, the basic logic underlying the argument below on the formation and maintenance of organization-specific human capital and its importance, resulting in the position of 'the controlling group,' is technological, which means it can be applied everywhere, including Japan, the U.S., and Germany. Therefore, my argument concerning Japanese organization must also be applied to organizations outside Japan. Second, each individual resource owner makes the best use of his or her own resource under given constraints. When a group of human capital investors establishes an organization and takes the controlling group position in many organizations, its prevalence constitutes a constraint binding each individual agent's choice. Under these constraints, individuals, organizations, and industries make decisions and compete. This results in the existing corporate governance within Japanese firms, the industrial structure of the economy, and the international division of labor. Third, the reader may ask whether my argument is different from that of 'a labor-managed firm,' to which my answer is 'yes.' The view of organizations underlying my discussion does not depend on the legal definition of a firm. My focus

---

[4] Of nine sections in Chapter 11 of Miwa (1996), five sections, from 11.3-11.7, are the core parts for this paper's discussion.

[5] For details of the first two points, see pp. 214-5, and for the third point Section 11.8, both from Miwa (1996).

is placed upon how 'the effective boundaries' are relevant and important to the decision making of the controlling group. The controlling group is often a union of several groups, each of which does not necessarily exercise equal bargaining power. Employees are a collection of different groups of workers, and one group of workers or a collection of groups of workers form the controlling group. Thus the discussion does not imply that employees in a firm are strongly united and form the controlling group as a whole. Other groups of workers outside the controlling group may be in a relatively weak position.

B. Actual Figures of Directors and Friendly Shareholders

The view one takes of firms and organizations is apt to depend on one's assumption of how investors, employees, and other players come to be associated in a common venture. In what follows, I take the view of Easterbrook and Fischel (1990: 185):

> The corporation and its securities are products to as great an extent as the sewing machines . . . the firm makes. Just as the founders of a firm have incentives to make the kinds of sewing machines people want to buy, they have incentives to create the kind of firm, governance structure, and securities people value. The founders of the firm will find it profitable to establish the governance structure that is most beneficial to investors, net of the costs of maintaining the structure. People who seek resources to control will have to deliver more returns to investors. Those who promise highest returns—and make the promises binding and hence believable—will obtain the largest investments.

Managers who control such resources do their best to take advantage of investors, but they find that the dynamics of the market drive them to act as if they had investors' interests at heart. It is almost as if there were an invisible hand.

The basic issues are who the founders of the corporation are and who takes their position when the firm grows larger. The fundamental question is, in Simon's (1976) words, who makes up 'the controlling group?' By the term *controlling group* he means 'the group that has the power to set the terms of membership for all the participants,' and the group that selects for the organization '[t]he basic value criteria that will be employed in making decisions and choices among alternatives in an organization' (p. 119). Here I do not intend to develop a general theory. Instead, following Dore (1992), I focus on the controlling group of large Japanese firms and the role of shareholders in corporate management. As mentioned later, the same argument applies to small businesses.

The essence of Dore's argument is found in the following statement.

> In the conception of the firms—or at least of the large corporation— . . . the one stakeholder whose stake is seen to be of paramount importance is the body of employees. The primary definition of the firm is a community of people, rather than a property of the shareholders, and this conception shapes business practice. . . . The economic behavior encouraged by these underlying conceptions is more conducive to business efficiency . . .

than behavior based on the assumptions embodied in American—or for that matter Japanese—corporation law (p. 18).

Employees are the most important stakeholder in most large Japanese firms, which means that the controlling group is the body of employees. In such firms, the directors and managers are selected from among employees, and are almost always able to expect strong support from the majority of employees, as long as their decision making is generally consistent with employees' interests.

Friendly Shareholders (Antei-Kabunushi). The question is how the body of employees, as the controlling group, secures its interests and defends itself from other stakeholders, especially shareholders. The most basic and important reason is that such attacks generally do not benefit other stakeholders. An additional reason is the role played by *antei-kabunushi*, those stable shareholders friendly to the existing management (hereafter, friendly shareholders). This is important for the defense of management's position against hostile shareholders, especially during takeover bids. Dore (1992: 20) states, '[a] large part of a firm's equity is in the hands of friendly, corporate stockholders: the suppliers, banks, insurers, trading companies, dealers it does business with.'

Two observations characterize large firms' shareholdings: first, for most large Japanese firms, a large part of the equity is in the hands of a small number of shareholders; second, the largest shareholders are corporations, mainly financial institutions and trade partners.

The term *antei-kabunushi* is widely used, but ill-defined. *Antei* [literally, stable] here has a dual meaning, one for their stable position as shareholders and the other for their contribution to the stable position of the existing directors. Emphasizing the importance of the latter, I choose 'friendly shareholders' as its English translation. The position of large shareholders has remained stable for a long time. Of the ten largest shareholders in 1990 for the 11 transport equipment manufacturing firms with over 10,000 employees, on average seven to eight were also on the top ten list in 1980. Most large shareholders new to the list in 1990 were financial institutions which in 1980 were listed in the top 11 to 20 shareholders. There were only two non-financial institutions new to the top ten list in these cases: Ford as the largest shareholder of Mazda with 24%, and GM as the third largest of Suzuki with 3.6%.

In most large Japanese firms, the controlling group is the body of employees. In such firms, the directors and managers are selected from among the firm's employees, and are almost always able to expect strong support from the majority of employees, as long as their actions are generally consistent with the interests of these employees. Large shareholders remain as such and faithfully support existing management. They maintain the right as large shareholders under the present corporate law and legal system to deprive the existing management of their leadership in the firm. However, we are in a world of exchange by agreement rather than by coercion, therefore, these shareholders have no incentive to unite for this purpose. Otherwise, nothing prevents them from uniting in order to realize the benefits. If such a situation were to occur, the positions of directors and managers would not be stable. Thus, they are friendly to the existing management, and called 'friendly shareholders [*antei-kabunushi*].'

In a large Japanese firm most members of the board of directors are selected from among employees. For instance, all 55 directors of Toyota in June 1993 were former employees. The same was true for 31 of 33 directors of Honda in March 1993. Of the two remaining seats, one was occupied by a former high official of the Ministry of Foreign Affairs and the other by an interlocking directorate of the chairman of Mitsubishi Bank. In December 1993 at Nihon Denso, with 41,996 employees the largest auto-parts manufacturer in Japan—of which Toyota owned 23.07% of the equity and Toyota Automatic Loom 7.28%—only one of the 35 directors was not a former employee. The only exception was an interlocking directorate of the chairman of Toyota.

On average, an employee/manager is elected to be a director in his or her early fifties, and stays on the board for six to seven years. For instance, in 1993 most directors of Toyota first became members when they were between 50 and 53 years old. Unless they resigned, on average these new directors were promoted to a higher position four years later, such as managing director, executive managing director, vice-president, or president. Of Toyota's 55 directors, 23 held a higher position and ten were newly selected at the general meeting of shareholders in September 1993. Three facts are important. First, every year new directors are selected from among the employees to fill the seats of resigning board members. Second, directors chosen from the body of employees consistently dominate the board. Finally, the large shareholders, individually and as a group, consistently support—with the selection of board members from among company employees—the resulting employee-dominated board itself.

The Japanese Commercial Code requires only that the number of directors should be over three, which is non-binding in most large firms. The basic picture mentioned above of the board members has not much changed, at least over several decades; however, the number of directors has dramatically increased, both in well-established firms such as Hitachi, Tokyo Electric, and Fuji Bank, and in rapidly growing firms such as Toyota, Honda, and Sony. The number grew in Fuji Bank from 19 in 1966 to 30 in 1981, and finally to 36 in 1996. The corresponding numbers in Toyota were 18, 35, and 55, and those in Honda and Sony were (11, 32, 35) and (14, 27, 38).

C. The Body of Employees as the Controlling Group

Why is the body of employees the controlling group and why do large shareholders accept and support this group?[6] To survive and grow, a firm has to accumulate a stock of human capital with which it establishes an organization suitable for its task. This accumulation process takes a long time and the guarantee that in the foreseeable future nothing will drastically devalue the accumulated human capital. This requires friendly shareholders.

This process, when effective, has four characteristics. First, it requires each participant's long-term investment in his or her own human capital. Second, the required investment is more or less specific to the particular organization, that is, the skill is organization-specific. Third, it is used in the team production process described by Alchian/Demsetz (1972: 782-3), in that the product is not a sum of the separable outputs of each cooperating resource, and that not all the resources used in the team production belong to any one person. Fourth, with long-term investment, each participant acquires the right to be a member of the organization, but can recover the investment cost and receive its reward not by selling the right but by staying with the organization. Quitting the organization will devalue the skill gained since it is organization-specific. When the stability of the organizational structure is uncertain—when there remains the possibility of change in the incentive system, such as economic rewards and promotion, and in the basic corporate strategy—participants hesitate to invest in the formation of the required skill. This results in the firm's low performance, discouraging talented young candidates from joining the firm. When only some participants are confident in the organization's stability, the value of confident worker's skills will be lower than otherwise because of the lower skill of less confident workers. Thus, by making the stability of the organization certain, the body of employees can make the best use of its resources.

Besides securing large, stable shareholders supportive of the existing management, the selection of employees as directors and top managers is an indication of the organization's stability. A director who was a former employee, say for 30 years, has already made a long-term organization-specific investment which allows him to understand the firm's core assets and the firm's business nature. This director also understands the importance of the organization's stability to its prosperity. Moreover, once a *de facto* rule of selecting directors from the employees is established, every participant is confident in the organization's stability since directors unfamiliar with or hostile to the existing nature and structure of the firm are generally avoided or can be easily removed.

[6] For a discussion of economic theories of co-determination, see Gerum/Wagner (this volume Ch. 5: Sec. B).

The economic organization through which resource owners cooperate will make better use of its comparative advantages to the extent it facilitates the payment of rewards based on productivity. This applies to every resource owner. Investors, for instance, part with their money willingly, putting it in equities rather than other investment alternatives because they believe the returns of equities are relatively more attractive. The same analysis is true in determining investment alternatives in the case of firms. Once owning the equity of a firm, the investor realizes the importance of the organization's stability and wants to be a friendly, but profitable, shareholder. Investors can recover their investment and receive their reward by selling the equity. They can also decrease the risk of investment by diversifying their portfolio. Neither option is feasible, however, for an employee investing in an organization-specific skill.

D. Why Does a Friendly Shareholder Remain Friendly?

In a world of exchange by agreement, a shareholder agrees to be friendly and stays friendly because the expected rewards of being friendly are higher than the alternative. The controlling group of a firm has to deliver rewards large enough to attract suppliers of other resources. In order to induce a large shareholder to be friendly and remain friendly, the controlling group has to offer additional incentives beyond those available to an ordinary shareholder. Otherwise, those who hold rather pessimistic expectations of the firm's future prospects relative to the market will cease to be friendly.

Three types of incentives are popular. First, cross-holding equity ensures the stability of both organizations, functioning as mutual hostages between friendly shareholders. Second, trade partners often benefit from the other organization's stability and are willing to pay a premium for this benefit. Since stability is the basis of the firm's prosperity, contributions to its stability increase the seller's profits and enable it to provide better products at lower prices to the buyer. It also serves the buyer as a guarantee that the supply of products will not cease, either at the supplier's will or due to an invasion, such as a takeover, by a buyer's rival. In this case, the seller's skill also becomes relation-specific. Third, it can offer additional incentives through allocating profitable business opportunities.

Mutual life insurance companies, some of which are the largest shareholders in Japan, are typical of the third type of beneficiary. Since they are not corporations but mutual companies, cross-holding is not possible. Usually they are neither big purchasers of the manufacturing firms they own nor do they have much interest in the stability of the manufacturing firm's organization. We observe, however, both loan transactions and insurer-customer relationships between life insurance companies and their shareholding firms. Almost the same picture applies to other financial institutions, such as banks and trust banks. However, in the case of these financial institutions, cross-holding does prevail.

For instance, of the ten largest shareholders of Toyota in June 1993, nine were financial institutions, including two mutual life insurance companies. The largest three shareholders, each with 4.9% ownership, were banks. Toyota was a large shareholder in all three banks: the largest shareholder of Tokai Bank and the fifth largest shareholder of both Sakura Bank and Sanwa Bank.

When the body of employees establishes its controlling group position within a firm and is supported by friendly shareholders, it is costly for large shareholders to unite in order to deprive the existing management of their leadership in the firm. Management is strongly supported by the body of employees. New management, whether invited from outside or selected from inside among employees, intent on changing the nature of the organization or corporate policy will face strong resistance from the body of employees since its accumulated human capital is organization-specific. Moreover, as a result of the prevalence of such firms, the external market for managers is not well developed. It is difficult to find a new body of management capable of improving the firm's performance for shareholders. When a bank with a large share of a firm's equity appoints its manager as the president of the firm, there is unlikely to be any significant change in the firm. Unless accepted by the body of employees as its representative, the director cannot change corporate policy. Hence, appointing a leading director from the outside is rarely effective in improving the firm's performance.

E. Related Issues: Role of Other Stakeholders and Agency Costs

I. Role of Shareholders, Banks, and Directors

The basic reason why the body of employees is able to secure its stability and defend itself from attacks from other stakeholders is that such attacks generally do not benefit other stakeholders. An additional reason is the role played by friendly shareholders. With the understanding that the controlling group is the body of employees and that it has the implied power to select the friendly shareholders and to choose the sources of corporate funds, we can draw three logical conclusions, all of which are contrary to the conventional view of the Japanese economy.

(1) The friendly shareholders are selected because they are *supposed* to be friendly to the present directors and managers. When once friendly large shareholders threaten the present management, the directors change their selection of the friendly shareholders. Cross-holdings or group holdings (e.g., among 'corporate group' firms) are the result of such voluntary selection. Accordingly, the shareholding patterns and the names of large shareholders give us limited information: In other words, identifying the friendly shareholders seldom reveals the true distribution of power.

(2) Sources of corporate funds, including banks, are selected based on the lender's support of the present body of directors. Therefore, when once friendly large lenders, such as the main bank(s) or lead bank(s), become hostile to the present management, the directors change their source of funding. The phenomenon that the largest lender often has a large share of the borrower's stock is only one result of such voluntary selection.

(3) Members of the board of directors and top managers are selected based on their support of the present directors and employees. Even directors who are supposed to represent the interests of other stakeholders are friendly to the present body of directors, and they remain in such a position unless they become troublesome. The structure of the board of directors is a result of this voluntary selection. Accordingly, the number of directors who formerly represented other stakeholders within the corporate structure, such as banks and trade partners, gives us little information about the distribution of power.

II. Agency Costs and the Separation of Ownership and Management

Since the time of Adam Smith, the separation of ownership and management, or the separation of management from control, within a large modern corporation has gathered wide attention. Berle/Means (1932) further provoked public interest in the firm's form of social control. In postwar Japan the same argument has prevailed, and many have insisted that the separation was even more clearly realized in Japan than in the U.S.

My argument presents a different view of this ownership-management separation. The classical view states that each shareholder is so small that the cost of uniting is prohibitive, limiting the effective control of management. In Japan, however, a small number of large shareholders own the dominant portion of equity, and for them the cost of uniting is not high. They support the existing management as friendly shareholders, since it is more profitable for them to do so than to manage the firm by themselves or to replace the management. Here, the separation of ownership and management, and that of management from control, is not a serious social problem.

The same is true for the argument about non-zero agency costs. As Jensen/Meckling (1976: 328) pointed out, these costs (monitoring and bonding costs and 'residual loss') are an unavoidable result of the agency relationship. To conclude that the agency relationship is non-optimal is what Demsetz (1969) characterizes as the 'Nirvana' form of analysis. Friendly shareholders choose to accept these costs instead of avoiding them by managing the firm by themselves.

The same logic also applies to large unlisted firms, and even to small unlisted firms. What would happen if an owner of a large unlisted firm where the body of employees is the controlling group makes a decision against the interests of this group, for instance, suggesting to sell the organization to some other firm in ten years? Such a firm can neither attract young talent nor induce employees to invest in organization-specific skill formation, resulting in the firm's poor performance. Thus, an owner-manager chooses to be friendly to the body of employees, and the non-separation, or non-dispersion, of ownership does not affect the firm's basic decisions. The same holds true for small businesses. In order to survive and grow, even an owner-manager of a small business has to follow the same path.

F. The Body of Employees as the Controlling Group Revisited

In a world of exchange by agreement, who 'controls' the firm is a matter of definition. It is difficult to identify the controlling group that holds the power to set the terms of membership for all participants and to select the basic value criteria that will be employed in the organization's decision-making process. However, with two observations concerning the distribution of surplus within firms, I conclude that the body of employees is the controlling group. When other stakeholders, such as shareholders, trade partners, and banks, join the organization, they accept their leader's position and stay friendly unless circumstances change.

First, large firms usually do not increase dividend payments even when there are large profits. Instead, firms expand retained earnings and reinvest this profit into the organization mainly for the employees' benefit. Over long periods of boom and depression, other stakeholders have stayed friendly unless circumstances change.

Second, large firms spend large sums of money on their employees in preparation for periods of hardship, such as a business depression. Many large firms begin to diversify in their heyday when they spend retained profits. Merger & Acquisitions (M&As) are not popular for this objective,[7] since the purpose is not profit itself through efficient use of internal funds but the creation of an expanded workplace for employees. As a result, diversification attempts on average have not been very successful, and thus financial statements tend to show weak profits. Besides investments for diversification, large firms often pay extra money to employees working outside the firm, called *shukko*. In a world of exchange by agreement, at any moment each agent can reevaluate the future prospects. The last case demonstrates that shareholders cannot force the directors to refrain from decreasing dividends to zero instead of continuing these extra payments.

---

[7] M&As, particularly those through takeovers, are not popular in Japan. Note, however, that takeovers, and in particular hostile bids, are not the normal form of corporate control. As Jenkinson/Mayer (1993) point out, outside the U.K. and U.S. hostile takeovers are largely absent in most countries, including Continental Europe and Japan.

G. Conclusion

'It is difficult to escape the conclusion that the corporate governance movement, despite its durability and widely held support, is much ado about nothing.' This final statement of Fischel (1982: 1292) surely applies to Japan.[8]

As is well-recognized, 'corporate governance' is an ill-defined term. In this paper focusing on 'the controlling group,' I investigate who in a Japanese firm makes up the group that has the power to set the terms of membership for all the participants and to select the organization's basic value criteria that will be employed in making decisions and choices among alternatives in an organization.

The basic question and the basic logic underlying the argument to this question on the formation and maintenance of organization-specific human capital and its importance is technological, which means it can be applied everywhere, including Japan, the U.S., and Germany. At least in this respect, the analysis of the paper suggests that there are no such peculiar firms as those labeled with 'Japanese-style management' or those under 'Japanese corporate governance.' For instance, in Japan—as everywhere—shareholders are empowered by law both to select and dismiss board members.

Although opinions may differ greatly, most agree that such Japanese firms as Toyota, Honda, and Sony have been well-run. A simple observation that each of those firms has been managed by a board with such a huge number of members, and moreover with a steadily increasing number, suggests that it is too simplistic to draw an optimal number of board members relevant to any firm under any situation. In the past several decades, Japan has made a series of commercial code revisions in order to improve the 'corporate governance' of firms, and nobody, in my view, argues today that they were quite effective.

I close my paper with my favorite statement from Kay (1996: 18), which applies to everywhere: 'Any governance structure—political or corporate, democratic or authoritarian, American or Japanese—has a natural tendency to embrace those who share the basic values of those who currently operate it, and reject those who do not.'

---

[8] Here, readers who read Japanese should refer to Miwa (1994).

References

Alchian, Armen A. and Harold Demsetz 'Production, Information Costs, and Economic Organization' *American Economic Review* 62 (1972) 777-95.

Berle, Adolf A. and Gardiner C. Means *The Modern Corporation and Private Property* (New York 1932).

Demsetz, Harold 'Information and Efficiency: Another Viewpoint' *Journal of Law and Economics* 12 (1969) 1-12.

Dore, Ronald 'Japan's Version of Managerial Capitalism' in: Kochan, Thomas A. and Michael Useem (eds.) *Transforming Organizations* 17-27 (Oxford 1992).

Easterbrook, Frank H. and Daniel R. Fischel 'The Corporate Contract' in: Bebchuck, Lucian A. (ed.) *Corporate Law and Economic Analysis* 182-215 (Cambridge 1990).

Fischel, Daniel R. 'The Corporate Governance Movement' 35 *Vand. L. Rev.* 1259-92 (1982).

Jenkinson, Tim and Colin Mayer 'The Assessment: Corporate Governance and Corporate Control' *Oxford Review of Economic Policy* 9 (1993) 1-10.

Jensen, Michael C. and William H. Meckling 'Theory of the Firm: Managerial Behavior, Agency Costs and Ownership Structure' *Journal of Financial Economics* 3 (1976) 305-60.

Kay, John *The Business of Economics* (Oxford 1996).

Miwa, Yoshiro 'Shijô ni okeru kyôsô no yakuwari [The Roles of Market Competition]' *Jurisuto* no. 1050 (August 1-15, 1994) (A Special Issue on Corporate Governance) 94-100.

Miwa, Yoshiro *Firms and Industrial Organization in Japan* (London 1996).

Simon, Herbert A. *Administrative Behavior: A Study of Decision-Making Process in Administrative Organizations* 3rd edn. (New York 1976).

References

Adler, Arthur A. and Harold Demsetz, 'Production, Information Costs and Economic Organization', *American Economic Review*, 62 (1972) 777–95.

Alchian, Armen A. and Harold Demsetz, ...

...

Notes on Corporate Governance in Japan

HIDEKI KANDA, Tokyo

It is often said that monitoring tasks are spread out in Japanese corporate governance. Shareholders, employees, and lenders—particularly a main bank—all play some role in Japanese corporate governance. It is, however, difficult to show how exactly each constituency monitors management in Japanese publicly held business corporations. I show that two recent theories—substitutabilities and complementarities—would enrich the analysis in this area. Substitutabilities suggest that as capital markets grow further, the importance of monitoring mechanisms by banks and employees is reduced. Complementarities suggest different stories. Monitoring by shareholders and in capital markets may not function well unless the mechanism of law enforcement is improved. Where lifetime employees are dominant in the firm's decision making, information supplied by banks and other business partners may produce more value; bank monitoring therefore works better where managers are selected from employees who worked for the firm for many years than where they are brought in from outside. The combination of substitutabilities and complementarities is also useful in the analysis of scandals.

Contents

A. Introduction

In this short essay, I will comment on corporate governance in Japan.[1] In my view, Japanese corporate governance has the following characteristics.

First, in Japan, the role of shareholders in corporate governance is not entirely clear. As in other countries, shareholders are highly institutionalized in Japan. In addition to banks and insurance companies, industrial companies often own shares of other companies in Japan. These institutional and corporate sharehold-

---

[1] Here I do not discuss basic legal rules and data on, and recent trends in, corporate governance in Japan. For basic legal rules and data, see the country report by Kanda (this volume Ch. 12). For recent trends, see Kanda, Hideki 'Trends in Japanese Corporate Governance' in: Hopt, Klaus J. and Eddy Wymeersch (eds.) *Comparative Corporate Governance* 185-93 (Berlin 1997).

ers, however, do not play an active role in Japanese corporate governance. But there is no evidence to show that shareholders are victimized in Japan.

Second, employees are important in Japan. Indeed, while Japanese company law provides that shareholders are the owners of the company, it is commonly believed that Japanese companies are in fact owned by employees and are run according to the best interest of employees, not the best interest of shareholders. It is true that executives and directors in Japanese companies are, in almost all cases, former employees of those companies. But it is difficult to develop a meaningful argument from this: again, there is no evidence to show that shareholders are victimized in Japan.

Third, in Japan, it is often said that banks are powerful and important in corporate governance. While this statement is not entirely mistaken, in discussing corporate governance one must distinguish between two notions: giving influence to the company and monitoring management of the company. I think that banks are strong in giving influence, but it is difficult to show that banks are strong monitors in Japanese corporate governance.

Finally, scandals in certain public companies in recent years suggest that the corporate governance debate does not eliminate fraud.

In the discussion that follows for the exposition of these points, I view Japanese corporate governance according to two ideas that have been developed in recent years: substitutabilities and complementarities.

B. Constituencies

Shareholders own Japanese public companies. This is what the law says. In practice, it is difficult to find cases in which shareholders play an active role in corporate governance. Institutional shareholders in Japan in most cases serve as friendly shareholders.

In Japan, in addition to insurance companies and banks, industrial companies often own shares of other companies. First, insurance companies and banks are often top shareholders of a typical public firm. Second, mutual shareholdings—often known as keiretsu—are popular in Japan. But straightforward mutual shareholdings are not often observed. A situation where Company A has, for instance, 40% of Company B's shares and Company B has 30% of Company A's shares is unpopular. Rather, it is common for Company A to have 40% of Company B's shares and for Company B to have 3% of Company A's shares. It is also common in this situation for Company A to have ten to twenty institutional and corporate shareholders, each of which owns 2 to 3% of Company A's shares.

Why do insurance companies, banks, and industrial companies own shares of other companies? They have business relationships with the firm, so they behave as friendly shareholders to keep these business relationships. The puzzle is why they need to own shares to do business. There has not been any satisfactory answer to this question. In theory, shareownership may serve as a hostage. An insurance company, for instance, may keep its business with the customer firm with a threat of the possibility of selling their shares to a non-friendly person. But the fact is that a typical public firm has more than ten of these institutional shareholders, each of which has 2 to 3% of total issued shares of the firm, and thus even if one of them sells its shares it does not cause effective damage to the firm.

In recent years, individual shareholders have begun to sue managers through derivative actions. Under this scheme, when the plaintiff prevails, the money paid by the defendants as damages goes to the company, not the plaintiff. Why then do shareholders use this means? In the United States, the plaintiff's attorney has every incentive to bring this action. In Japan, the structure of attorney's fee is not as drastic as in the United States. Is it then the case that these shareholders sue for "justice"?

Among non-stockholder constituencies of Japanese companies, employees and banks are important. While employees are not the owners of their company under the Japanese legal system, a traditional oft-made statement is that Japanese companies are run for the best interest of employees and not the best interest of shareholders. Thus, a common phenomenon is that when a Japanese company faces financial distress, management cuts dividends before it starts firing employees. Under Japanese practice, most directors and statutory auditors are elected from former employees of the company. Lifetime employment, compensation tied to seniority, and company-by-company labor unions are often pointed out as three distinctive characteristics of Japanese companies and have functioned to keep employee supremacy alive in the past decades.

However, even if Japanese companies are run for the benefit of employees, it does not necessarily mean that shareholders are victimized. The proposition that Japanese companies are not run for the best interest of shareholders lacks empirical support.

Do employees, then, monitor management of their company? If so, it is difficult to show how. At the theoretical level, the role of employees, or the interaction between employees and managers, must await future research.

Banks are often said to be important players in Japan. Japanese companies rely more on banks than on capital markets for debt finance. The relative underdevelopment of the Japanese bond markets might be the result of a political victory by the banking industry. Banks thus are important. But how they operate is far from clear.

As discussed elsewhere,[2] banks obtain a strong legal position under a standard form contract known as the Banking Transactions Agreement, but they sometimes show behavior that looks quite inconsistent with their strong legal position.

---

[2] See Kanda 'Trends', supra n. 1, 190-2.

To take a familiar situation where a firm is in financial trouble, the traditional behavior of a "main bank" (which usually has a first mortgage over the firm's property securing its loans) is to pay off other debts (debts which are legally subordinated to the bank's claim) and pay off publicly outstanding bonds. Despite several interesting theories on bank behavior in Japan, the above-mentioned behavior cannot be explained by these theories.[3]

C. Scandals

While academics tend to debate the most efficient form of decision-making system in public companies or the most efficient form of monitoring in public companies, history shows that the debate on corporate governance and the discussion on the reform of the present governance system arise when fraud or other abuses are uncovered in certain public companies. Japan (like Germany and elsewhere) is not an exception. In 1995, U.S. regulators prohibited Daiwa Bank, a leading Japanese bank, from continuing U.S. operations due to management's failure to uncover (and to report in a timely manner) the fraud conducted by its employee in U.S. bond markets. In 1996, Sumitomo Corporation announced that it had failed to detect its employee's fraud in commodity trading, resulting in the loss of $2.6 billion. In 1997, Nomura Securities, the largest securities firm in Japan, had to report that its senior directors and key employees engaged in illegal trading to benefit a *sokaiya* corporate racketeer. As a result, all representative directors resigned. At about the same time, Dai-Ichi Kangyo Bank, a leading Japanese bank, was convicted of fraud after it was revealed that its top manages and executives made illegal payments to sokaiya of more than 10 billion yen. The mass media and others blamed these scandals on poor corporate governance.

While this is hardly the place to discuss the details of these scandals, it must be noted that the actual discussion today on the reform of company law is more concerned with how to have public companies stop abuses or fraud than about which governance system is better for enhancing economic efficiency of public companies. And as an empirical matter, the corporate governance debate is unlikely to lead to solutions for dealing with these types of fraud.

D. Substitutabilities and Complementarities

Recent theories provide analytical tools in understanding corporate governance more deeply. The idea of substitutabilities—though not uncommon in traditional legal scholarship—suggests that one component of the system serves as a

---

[3] Kanda 'Trends', supra n. 1, 190-2.

substitute for others.[4] Thus, for example, where the market for corporate control is active, there is less need for other monitoring mechanisms. Similarly, a country having less developed capital markets may have stronger bank monitoring. In that country, if bank monitoring does not work, something else must function, such as a strong board of directors.

In this vein, nothing seems strong in Japanese corporate governance. One could still argue that each constituency serves some—though not necessarily strong—monitoring role, so that in total the system functions. There is, however, almost no way of proving this in a scientific fashion.

Another interesting idea is complementarities. This idea is that certain factors of the system are complementary to one another in certain situations.[5] This suggests that the same mechanism—bank monitoring, for instance—has a different effect in corporate governance when it has complementarities with other components of the system. Where employees under the lifetime employment system are dominant in the firm's decision-making, managers (who are former employees) are relatively better at daily business, and thus information provided by banks and other business partners may be more valuable to them. If managers who come from outside are relatively ill-equipped in using valuable information supplied by banks or other business partners, as a relative matter the value of monitoring by banks and other business partners increases when lifetime employees become managers. Similarly, the value of monitoring by shareholders, or in the capital markets in general, will increase when legal rules in the capital markets are enforced in a less costly manner. This suggests that monitoring by the capital markets functions better in the United States than elsewhere, because the United States has the class action system and other less costly law enforcement systems compared to other major countries.

Scandals can be viewed in this vein. They happen within the system having complementary components. Those in the United States tend to come primarily from fraud in the market place. Those in Japan—and perhaps in Germany—tend to come from lack of effective detection within the firm. Needed prescriptions thus may be different, and strengthening the board of directors, while it itself is not necessarily a bad idea, may make complementarities among the system's components obscure and may lead to an inefficient solution.

---

[4] For application in corporate governance, see Roe (this volume Ch. 5); Gilson, Ronald J. 'Corporate Governance and Economic Efficiency: When Do Institutions Matter?' 74 *Wash. U. L.Q.* 327-45 (1996).

[5] See Milgrom, Paul and John Roberts 'Complementarities and Systems: Understanding Japanese Economic Organization' *Estudios Economicos* 9 (1994) 17-42. See also, Aoki, Masahiko 'The Japanese Firm as a System of Attributes' in: Aoki, Masahiko and Ronald Philip Dore (eds.) *The Japanese Firm: The Sources of Competitive Strength* 11-40 (Oxford 1994); Gilson, Ronald J. 'Reflections in a Distant Mirror: Japanese Corporate Governance through American Eyes' (Draft 1997).

E. Conclusion

It is easy to say that monitoring tasks are spread out in Japanese corporate governance. Even if this is correct, it is difficult to show how exactly each constituency monitors management in Japanese publicly held business corporations. Substitutabilities suggest that as capital markets grow further, the importance of monitoring mechanisms by banks and employees is reduced. Complementarities suggest different stories. Monitoring by shareholders and in capital markets may not function well unless the mechanism of law enforcement is improved. Where lifetime employees are dominant in the firm's decision making, information supplied by banks and other business partners may produce more value, so that bank monitoring works better than where managers are not selected from among long-time employees. The combination of substitutabilities and complementarities also aids in the analysis of scandals.

Discussion Report

HARALD BAUM

The discussion of the three presentations focused primarily on two controversial aspects of corporate governance in Japan: (1) the role of shareholders and (2) the role of employees as stakeholders and possible monitors. An additional general subject, (3) historical origins and possible future changes of the present system, also received repeated attention.

The Role of Shareholders

Given the widespread practice of cross-shareholding among large Japanese corporations, a German participant wondered about the importance of shareholdings that amount to just one or two percent of the outstanding shares. Although the individual small holdings do not matter as such, if various members of an enterprise group (*keiretsu*) *each* have between one and two percent, that amounts to a potentially important stake if the group members coordinate their influence as happens in times of distress. Generally, however, even major shareholders are passive and friendly towards management, though not necessarily towards the firm, as *Miwa* pointed out. From the European perspective, the question was raised of how an incumbent management can "elect" its shareholders. Mostly they are chosen from among trade partners who have an economic incentive to invest as they profit from a stable relationship in various ways.

With respect to monitoring functions, the discussions focused on the controversial role of the banks, especially the so-called main bank. Whereas *Hoshi*—in accordance with widespread opinion—assigned to them a prominent role in monitoring, *Miwa* strongly opposed this view, dismissing their importance in comparison with another group of stakeholders: the employees. *Kanda*, though also skeptical about an overly emphasized role of the main bank, thought them to be at least *indirectly* important by exerting influence rather than doing direct monitoring.

Consistent with the setting of friendly and rather passive shareholders in Japan, American participants raised the question of how boards are composed and whether there are no conflicts with the president (CEO) if all board members are from inside the company, with virtually no outside directors on the average Japanese board. *Miwa* confirmed the analysis that, despite the absence of a legal rule, it is common practice even within large Japanese companies to elect only board members from within their own ranks. He mentioned Toyota as an example where all 55 present board members are former employees. As a rule, he saw little conflict with the CEO, whereas *Kanda* cautioned that there are conflicts within the board which are resolved in different ways depending on the given case.

The Role of Employees

Various Anglo-American participants were especially interested in the question of whether Japanese firms are *really* run in the interest of employees and, if so, why and whether that means in the interest of *all* employees. One participant raised the objection that if a company is, for example, partly based on the work of slaves, one could hardly say that it is also run in their interest. *Miwa* pointed out that employees are indeed the controlling group, but the company is not necessarily run solely in their interest. He confirmed that there are of course differences between different groups of employees, and therefore conflicts of interest exist. In *Kanda's* view, shareholders are not victimized for the sake of the employees, although they may not necessarily be the most important constituency and the best candidates with respect to monitoring. The question of how conflicts of interest between the various stakeholders are solved remained open, as no general answer seemed possible; solutions obviously depend on each individual case. *Hoshi* denied that firms behave as if employees are the owners. He saw their interests as *not* dominating; in his view, this can be observed in times of distress when it becomes clear that creditors are more important and layoffs do happen.

An American participant emphasized a basic difference between the U.S. and Japan. In Japan, wages have to be flexible to keep employment fixed (meaning lifetime employment); this is achieved by paying a part of the salary in the form of a bonus. In the U.S., the situation is the opposite: wages are constant, but layoffs are possible and frequent. He wondered whether the varying models of Japanese corporate governance are coherent. His main objection was that they are all static and not dynamic, and therefore do not answer the question of how the present structures developed. *Kanda* agreed that a good theory explaining the dynamics has yet to be formulated.

Historical Development and Future Change

A German participant asked what role the state had played in the historical development of the present structure. The influence of the government in shaping economic institutions was seen as changing over time. The state played a very important role in the late 19th century when Japan was opening up to the West and modernizing the country within a remarkable short period of time. During the 1910s and 1920s, the private sector was perceived as dominant, whereas before and during World War II, government regained control and maintained this control until—in one view—the early 1980s. *Miwa* cautioned against drawing overly general conclusions. In his view, government intervention, e.g., in the manufacturing sector, was only prominent from the 1930s through the end of World War II. However, he drew a different picture with respect to the financial industry, where active state intervention can still be observed today.

The relative importance of the employees as stakeholders was seen as connected to the widespread system of lifetime employment. One questioner asked when that specific form of employment was first introduced. *Miwa* traced the origins back to the turn of the century when large companies needed skilled labor. He saw no strong connection with more recent labor unrest, as one U.S. participant assumed. *Hoshi* emphasized that workers had a great deal of power in the post-World War II corporate governance vacuum of the late '40s and early '50s. In his view, the resulting fight for control between creditors and workers was won by the creditors, thus reducing the role of the employees in corporate governance. It was pointed out that after lost wars, employee participation has always been politically important, Germany being a prominent example for such a development.

Various European participants were especially interested in the possible future course of the present Japanese industrial system and its governance structures. Is there a change in the friendly/stable shareholding context? As many Japanese companies are increasingly active outside Japan, do they adhere to Japanese enterprise and management culture or do they adopt to foreign practices? If the latter is true, does that have an influence back home? The Japanese response was that the future direction is still open, depending on each individual firm, with no general trend yet in sight. *Hoshi* did not believe that Japanese firms are significantly changing their corporate behavior abroad; he saw no change with respect to creditors and shareholders, but confirmed a limited change as far as suppliers are concerned. Potential feedback effects seem to still be unclear. *Miwa* repeated his basic understanding that a number of successful Japanese companies like Toyota or Sony are internationally just as successful as their American competitors, with no significant differences in performance. This would seem to indicate that differences in corporate governance styles between the U.S. and Japan do not matter very much.

The discussion concluded with a query as to the existence of any studies about a possible link between corporate governance structures and performance on the level of individual companies. *Hoshi* answered affirmatively, mentioning ongoing research by himself and colleagues from the United States.

Chapter 12: Comparative Corporate Governance Research

Institutional Investors and Corporate Monitoring: A Demand-Side Perspective in a Comparative View

JONATHAN R. MACEY, Ithaca

Comparative corporate governance is hampered by the absence of generally accepted criteria for the appropriate means to empirically measure alternative schemes of corporate governance. This article proposes three such criteria: first, the success of a system at impeding managers' ability to divert firm resources to their own private uses; second, the willingness of entrepreneurs to make initial public offerings of stock; and third, the functioning of internal and external markets for corporate control.

Without attempting to fully test alternative systems of corporate governance, this article analyzes the systems, in light of these criteria, enough to make tentative observations. Institutional investors have not demonstrated that they are willing to become more involved in the monitoring function. Institutional investors in America have been designed to perform the function of eliminating firm-specific risk, a function that is incompatible with greater monitoring. Thus, applying the comparative empirical criteria, I conclude that the American system of corporate governance would not benefit from greater involvement by institutional investors.

Contents

A. Introduction

Corporate governance refers to the mechanisms and processes by which corporations are governed. Ever since Berle and Means,[1] many have believed that there are significant problems with the American system of corporate governance.[2] In

---

[1] Berle, Jr., Adolf A. and Gardiner C. Means *The Modern Corporation and Private Property* (New York 1932).

[2] Roe, Mark J. *Strong Managers, Weak Owners: The Political Roots of American Corporate Governance* 6-17 (Princeton 1994); Black, Bernard S. 'Agents Watching Agents: The Promise of Institutional Investor Voice' 39 *UCLA L. Rev.* 811 (1992) (arguing that the American system of

particular, the separation of ownership and control identified with the American publicly held corporation is said to produce an organizational structure in which shareholders face collective action problems that make it impossible for them to effectively monitor and discipline the management of the firms in which they have invested.[3] Professional managers are said to be virtually unaccountable to shareholders.

Recently, scholars have suggested that institutional investors are the group most likely to resolve America's corporate governance "problem."[4] Other commentators have questioned the merits of having institutional investors take a more active role in corporate governance in order to solve the "problem" created by the separation of ownership and control. Roberta Romano has shown that public pension funds face political constraints that are likely to prevent them from serving very effectively as corporate managers.[5] As for corporate pension funds and financial institutions, it has long been recognized that these institutions face conflicts of interest that prevent them from serving as effective representatives of the interest of outside shareholders.[6] Jack Coffee has pointed out that the long-term, relational investment required to make institutional investors a voice in corporate governance may be too costly to such investors because it will require them to sacrifice liquidity.[7] Jill Fisch has argued that institutional investors may not find it rational to engage in so-called "relational investing" unless they are given special benefits, which they are unlikely to receive.[8]

The previous scholarship has focused largely on the supply side of the debate. It has focused on the institutional investors who might become more involved in

corporate governance needs to induce institutional investors to take a more active role in monitoring); Rock, Edward B. 'The Logic and (Uncertain) Significance of Institutional Shareholder Activism' 79 *Geo. L.J.* 445, 454 n. 29 (1991) (discussing literature discussing collective action problems facing shareholders).

[3] See, e.g., Gilson, Ronald J. and Reinier Kraakman 'Reinventing the Outside Director: An Agenda for Institutional Investors' 43 *Stan. L. Rev.* 863, 875 (1991) (arguing that directors lack the time, the information, and the economic incentive to actively discipline management); Dent, Jr., George W. 'Toward Unifying Ownership and Control in the Public Corporation' 1989 *Wis. L. Rev.* 881, 898-901 (arguing that directors' deference to management contributes further to the lack of accountability of management).

[4] Black, Bernard S. 'Shareholder Passivity Reexamined' 89 *Mich. L. Rev.* 520, 575-91 (1990); Gilson and Kraakman, supra n. 3.

[5] Romano, Roberta 'Public Pension Fund Activism in Corporate Governance Reconsidered' 93 *Colum. L. Rev.* 795 (1993).

[6] Brooks, John *Conflicts of Interest: Corporate Pension Fund Asset Management: Report to the Twentieth Century Fund Steering Committee on Conflicts of Interest in the Securities Markets* 224 (Twentieth Century Fund 1975).

[7] Coffee, Jr., John C. 'Liquidity versus Control: The Institutional Investor as Corporate Monitor' 91 *Colum. L. Rev.* 1277 (1991).

[8] Fisch, Jill E. 'Relationship Investing: Will It Happen? Will It Work?' 55 *Ohio St. L.J.* 1009 (1994).

corporate governance, and it has analyzed how much, if any, good it would do to have such investors more involved in corporate governance.[9] This article starts with the premise that it is necessary to look at the demand side of the issue of the role of institutional investors in corporate governance. Considering the demand side of this debate requires us to address the issue of how good or bad the existing system is working. It is clear from the existing literature that it will not be costless for the market to provide a greater supply of institutional investor monitoring.[10] To the extent that the existing corporate governance mechanisms are working well, incurring the costs of moving institutional investors into a more active role will probably not be worthwhile. On the other hand, if there are large inefficiencies associated with the corporate governance mechanisms already in place, then providing incentives for institutional investors to expand their role in corporate governance becomes a more attractive policy option.

Unfortunately, as Shleifer and Vishny point out, "even in advanced market economies, there is a great deal of disagreement on how good or bad the existing corporate governance mechanisms are functioning. For example, Easterbrook and Fischel, and Romano make a very optimistic assessment of the United States' corporate governance system, whereas Jensen believes that it is deeply flawed."[11]

The purpose of this article is to make two modest points that, I believe, would improve our current understanding of what our goals should be concerning the ideal role for institutional investors in corporate governance. First, I assert that the quality of the debate would be improved if we had a better empirical sense of how badly (or how well) the American system of corporate governance is operating. More precisely, given the lack of consensus on the issue, it would be helpful to have some systematic understanding of how far away the current system of corporate governance lies from the production possibility frontier defined by corporate governance alternatives. If there is huge room for improvement, i.e, if the American system is a long way from being the best that it could be given current technology, then perhaps radical change is warranted. If, however, the American system of corporate governance already is producing results close to the maximum of what is possible, then it is more doubtful that costly changes will be worth the marginal investment.

---

[9] Black, supra n. 2; Coffee, supra n. 7; Conard, Alfred F. 'Beyond Managerialism: Investor Capitalism?' 22 *U. Mich. J.L. Ref.* 117 (1988); Gilson and Kraakman, supra n. 3; Lipton, Martin 'Corporate Governance in the Age of Finance Corporatism' 136 *U. Pa. L. Rev.* 1 (1987); Roe, Mark J. 'A Political Theory of American Corporate Finance' 91 *Colum. L. Rev.* 10 (1991).

[10] Shleifer, Andrei and Robert W. Vishny 'A Survey of Corporate Governance' *Journal of Finance* 52 (1997) 737.

[11] Shleifer and Vishny, supra n. 10 (citing Easterbrook, Frank H. and Daniel R. Fischel *The Economic Structure of Corporate Law* (Harvard 1991); Romano, Roberta *The Genius of American Corporate Law* (Washington, D.C. 1993); Jensen, Michael C. 'Eclipse of the Public Corporation' *Harvard Business Review* 67/5 (1989) 60; Jensen, Michael C. 'The Modern Industrial Revolution, Exit, and the Failure of Internal Control Systems' Journal of Finance 48 (1993) 831).

The second goal of this article is to point out that there exist marketplace alternatives for achieving all of the goals that commentators hope will induce institutional investors to become more involved in corporate governance. In evaluating the efficacy of greater institutional investor involvement in corporate governance, one must compare the costs and benefits of such institutional investor involvement with the costs and benefits of the available substitute governance mechanisms. Specifically, the market for corporate control and leverage both provide a mechanism for monitoring management that directly substitutes for the monitoring offered by institutional investors. This article offers a direct comparison of the relative merits of these mechanisms.

The first section of this article (Sec. B) sets the stage for the analysis by describing what I believe is a reasonable consensus about the goals of corporate governance. In the second part of the article (Sec. C) I describe the empirically testable, objective criteria by which I believe we might test the operation of systems of corporate governance, and I pose the question of why the use of institutional investors in corporate governance might produce better results than would the market for corporate control in reducing the agency costs associated with investing.

B. Background: The Goals of Corporate Governance

Corporate governance can be described as the processes by which investors attempt to minimize the transactions costs[12] and agency costs[13] associated with doing business within a firm. Andrei Shleifer and Robert Vishny framed the issue very well:

> Corporate governance deals with the ways in which suppliers of finance to corporations assure themselves of getting a stream of return on their investment. How do the suppliers of finance get managers to return some of the profits to them? How do they make sure that managers do not steal the capital they supply or divert it to other uses? How do suppliers of finance control managers?
>
> At first glance, it is not entirely obvious why suppliers of capital get anything back. After all, they part with their money, and have little to contribute to the enterprise afterwards. The professional managers or entrepreneurs who run the firm might as well abscond with the money.[14]

Early academic discussions about corporate governance in the United States focused on such things as the merits of the conglomerate merger and the hostile

---

[12] Coase's classic explanation for the existence of the firm in a modern exchange economy focused on transaction costs, see Coase, Ronald H. 'The Nature of the Firm' *Economica* 4 (1937) 386.

[13] Jensen, Michael C. and William H. Meckling 'Theory of the Firm, Managerial Behavior, Agency Costs and Ownership Structure' *Journal of Financial Economics* 3 (1976) 305.

[14] Shleifer and Vishny, supra n. 10.

takeover as mechanisms for controlling agency costs.[15] More recently, there has been renewed focus on the legal responsibilities of corporate boards of directors, about the efficacy of shareholder litigation as a mechanism for controlling agency costs,[16] and perhaps, above all, about the role of institutional investors as corporate monitors.[17]

Serious comparative corporate governance is an even newer phenomenon for Americans. Of great interest recently has been the efficacy of jurisdictional competition for corporate charters,[18] and, once again, the role played in corporate governance by institutional investors, particularly banks in the U.S. and abroad.[19] While there is a tremendous amount of debate about the specifics, one can identify the general goals of the corporate governance system that has emerged.

I believe that a consensus exists on at least two important issues. There seems to be agreement among scholars and commentators about: (1) the incomplete nature of the corporate contract, and the need for corporate governance principles that fill in the gaps in these incomplete, contingent contracts;[20] and (2) the need to control managerial shirking, i.e., to control agency costs.[21]

It is well known that corporate law provides, *inter alia*, a set of standard, off-the-rack terms that permit participants in a corporation to economize on contracting costs. The formal contracts among entrepreneurs, managers, investors, etc., are necessarily incomplete, and corporate law provides an important mechanism for supplementing the actual bargains that people make by supplying background terms and filling in the gaps in contracts.[22]

Thus, while there is robust debate about whether the missing terms supplied by the legal system should be mandatory or enabling, there is no debate that corporate governance systems should supply the missing terms.

A second goal of a properly functioning system of corporate governance is controlling managerial shirking. While this goal can also be characterized as a subset of the first goal of enforcing contracts, it is important enough to deserve special mention. Any corporation of any size will have outside investors. The

---

[15] Manne, Henry G. 'Mergers and the Market for Corporate Control' *Journal of Political Economy* 73 (1965) 110; Easterbrook, Frank H. and Daniel R. Fischel 'The Proper Role of a Target's Management in Responding to a Tender Offer' 94 *Harv. L. Rev.* 1161, 1169-82 (1981).

[16] Black, supra n. 4, 530-53.

[17] Black, supra n. 2, 820-9.

[18] Romano, supra n. 11.

[19] Roe, supra n. 2; Macey, Jonathan R. and Geoffrey P. Miller 'Corporate Governance and Commercial Banking: A Comparative Examination of Germany, Japan, and the United States' 48 *Stan. L. Rev.* 73 (1995).

[20] See generally American Law Institute *Principles of Corporate Governance: Analysis and Recommendations* (1992).

[21] Easterbrook and Fischel, supra n. 15, 1170.

[22] Easterbrook and Fischel, supra n. 11, 34.

presence of these outside investors requires the separation of management and finance, commonly described as the separation of ownership and control.[23] Takeovers, proxy fights, and public contests for control are among the ways that capital-markets-oriented corporate governance systems (such as the U.S. and the U.K.) deal with the problem of agency costs. In corporate governance regimes with a weak or non-existent market for corporate control, but relatively strong banks, a company's relationships with its main bank, its corporate shareholders, its corporate group, and other institutional investors may substitute, to some extent, for the role played by the market for corporate control in its various incarnations.[24]

C. Measuring the Performance of Alternative Systems of Corporate Governance

While there may be a measure of consensus on certain broad issues in the field of corporate governance, as discussed above, there certainly is no consensus about which corporate governance system is best. Part of this lack of consensus undoubtedly stems from the fact that there are no generally accepted criteria for the appropriate means to *measure* alternative systems of corporate governance. That is to say, there are no formalized, generally accepted criteria for determining whether a particular system of corporate governance is working. Once such criteria are developed, it should be possible to begin serious comparative empirical work in corporate governance.

Drawing on some recent research in corporate finance I identify three ways to measure empirically the performance of corporate governance systems. First, following the suggestion of Shleifer and Vishny[25] and building on the work of Zingales[26], we can categorize the performance of corporate governance systems on the basis of how well they impede managers' ability to divert firm resources to their own private uses.

Second, we can compare corporate governance systems empirically on the basis of the willingness of entrepreneurs to make initial public offerings of stock.

[23] Coase, supra n. 12; Jensen and Meckling, supra n. 13; Fama, Eugene F. and Michael C. Jensen 'Separation of Ownership and Control' *Journal of Law and Economics* 26 (1983) 301; Fama, Eugene F. and Michael C. Jensen 'Agency Problems and Residual Claims' *Journal of Law and Economics* 26 (1983) 327.

[24] Aoki, Misahiko 'Towards an Economic Model of the Japanese Firm' *Journal of Economic Literature* 28 (1990) 1; Aoki, Misahiko, Hugh Patrick, and Paul Sheard 'The Japanese Main Bank System: An Introductory Overview' in: Aoki, Misahiko and Hugh Patrick (eds.) *The Japanese Main Bank System: Its Relevancy for Developing and Transforming Economies* 1 (Oxford 1994).

[25] Shleifer and Vishny, supra n. 10.

[26] Zingales, infra n. 28.

Investors who are confident that a particular system of corporate governance adequately protects them from managerial self-interest will be more inclined to make investments in the first place. Entrepreneurs in firms with dysfunctional governance systems will be unable to make credible commitments to the investing public that they will not act opportunistically ex post, that is, after the shareholders' initial investments have been made. Thus another empirically testable measure of corporate governance systems emerges: the relative proclivity of firms under rival governance schemes to go public. Firms that operate under a properly functioning corporate governance system will be able to sell their shares to the public, while firms that operate under a dysfunctional system will not.

A third measure of the performance of a corporate governance system will be the functioning of internal and external markets for corporate control. Put simply, if a particular system of corporate governance is functioning properly, inefficient management will be replaced, either through a hostile takeover, or through appointments of new management by (presumably independent) directors.[27]

I. Measuring Managements' Ability to Obtain Private Benefits from Control

Comparing the variations among legal systems in the size of premiums paid for voting stock as distinct from non-voting stock provides one empirical measure of the performance of a particular system of corporate governance. As Zingales has observed, the fact that outsiders often are willing to pay sizeable premiums for voting as opposed to non-voting stock suggests that there are high private benefits to control, and that these private benefits are not shared with outside, non-voting shareholders.[28] The right to control a corporation brings with it the right to realize all of the private benefits associated with such control, particularly the right to divert wealth away from shareholders and other groups in favor of the controlling coalition. Large premiums for the shares needed to control a corporation suggest that the private benefits for control—including the ability to transfer wealth from minority shareholders—are great. Such large premiums also indicate that the protections for outside investors in general and minority shareholders in particular, are weak.

As Zingales observes:

> The right to control a corporation is valuable per se because it guarantees the owner of this right some unique benefits. Votes allocate control. Therefore, even if outside share-

---

[27] Kaplan, Steven N. and Bernadette A. Minton 'Appointments of Outsiders to Japanese Boards, Determinants and Implications for Managers' *Journal of Financial Economics* 36 (1994) 224.

[28] See generally Zingales, Luigi 'The Value of the Voting Right: A Study of the Milan Stock Exchange Experience' *Review of Financial Studies* 7 (1994) 125.

holders do not enjoy these private benefits, they may attribute some value to voting rights as long as there is competition among different management teams to acquire those votes. In particular, votes held by small outside shareholders become very valuable when they are pivotal, that is when they are decisive in attributing control to any of the management teams fighting for it. Therefore, the observed size of the voting premium is related to the size of the private benefits and to the degree of competition in the market for corporate control.[29]

From an empirical perspective, therefore, a high premium paid for voting shares in companies that have voting and non-voting stock with similar economic rights is strong evidence of the costs of this lack of protection for non-controlling shareholders. Similarly, the premium for the voting shares can be viewed as a discount for the non-voting savings shares.

While it is not entirely appropriate to compare across studies, there have been studies of differential voting rights in different countries which have taken into account the different economic rights of the shares (i.e., the fact that the non-voting shares may have different dividend and liquidation rights).[30] In summarizing these studies, Zingales found that "voting rights are generally worth 10 percent to 20 percent of the value of the common stock."[31] Particular studies have found the following results:

Country	Premium	Study
U.S.	5.4%	Lease, McConnell, and Mikkelson
Sweden	6.5%	Rydqvist
England	13.3%	Megginson
Switzerland	20.0%	Horner
Canada	23.3%	Robinson & White
Israel	45.5%	Levy
Italy	82.0%	Zingales[32]

---

[29] Zingales, supra n. 28, 126.

[30] See infra, n. 32 and accompanying data.

[31] Zingales, supra n. 28, 125.

[32] Lease, Ronald C., John J. McConnell, and Wayne E. Mikkelson 'The Market Value of Control in Publicly Traded Corporations' *Journal of Financial Economics* 11 (1983) 439; Rydqvist, Kristian 'Takeover Bids and the Relative Prices of Shares that Differ in Their Voting Rights' (Stockholm School of Economics Working Paper, 1992); Megginson, Leon C. 'Restricted Voting Stock, Acquisition Premiums, and the Market Value of Corporate Control' *Financial Review* 25 (1990) 175; Horner, Melchior R. 'The Value of the Corporate Voting Right' *Journal of Banking and Finance* 12 (1988) 69; Robinson, C. and A. White 'The Value of a Vote in the Market for Corporate Control' (York University Working Paper, 1990); Levy, Haim 'Economic Evaluation of Voting Power in Common Stock' *Journal of Finance* 38 (1982) 79; Zingales, supra n. 28.

The above chart indicates that the U.S. corporate governance system is functioning extremely well, at least by this measure of performance.

II. Going Public[33]

If a corporate governance system is functioning well, then *ceteris paribus*, public markets for capital will function well. Firms will be anxious to go public, because doing so provides a low-cost method of funding projects. On the other hand, if the corporate governance system in a particular jurisdiction is not functioning well, entrepreneurs will not be able to make credible commitments to outside investors that they will be treated fairly ex post, i.e., after their initial investments have been made. Thus, the fact that there are large numbers of firms that are eligible to go public but refrain from doing so indicates the existence of a corporate governance system that is not functioning well.

The analytical approach in this section builds on the well-known "lemons" problem identified by Akerlof.[34] Investors will not invest in firms by management without discounting the price they are willing to pay by an amount necessary to compensate themselves for any expected ex-post exploitation by management. This will, in turn, lead to a situation in which entrepreneurs refuse to sell their shares to the public because they cannot receive an adequate price. Thus, where a corporate governance system is not performing well, there will be relatively few public offerings.

In Italy, for example, which was the country that performed the worst in the previous premium-for-voting-shares measure of performance, of the 12,391 companies that satisfied the listing requirements of the Milan Exchange during the period from 1982 to 1992, only 66 chose to do so.[35] The size of the median firm that goes public in Italy is four times that of its U.S. counterpart.[36] And there were approximately the same number of firms listed on the Milan Stock Exchange in October of 1996 (218) as there were in 1910 (210). By contrast, there are 2,907 firms listed on the New York Stock Exchange (NYSE) today, while there were only 426 firms listed on the NYSE in 1910. And, of course, in addition to this, there are 5,451 public companies whose shares trade on the NASDAQ, which did not even exist in 1910. By contrast, in the United States, most firms that are eligible to go public do, in fact, go public. While there are, of

[33] Cf. also the treatment of this subject in Ch. 7 of this volume and in the comparative articles by Wymeersch (Sec. A.III.) and Prigge (Sec. B.III.) in Ch. 12.

[34] Akerlof, George A. 'The Market for 'Lemons': Quality Uncertainty and the Market Mechanism' *Quarterly Journal of Economics* 84 (1970) 488.

[35] Pagano, Marco, Fabio Panetta, and Luigi Zingales 'Why Do Companies Go Public? An Empirical and Legal Analysis' (NBER Working Paper 5367, November 1995).

[36] Pagano, Panetta, and Zingales, supra n. 35.

course, some notable exceptions in the United States, such as Cargill, Koch Industries, and UPS, the New York Stock Exchange views its most significant opportunity for growth as being in the international arena. There are 600-700 domestic firms on what the NYSE characterizes as its "prospect list," while there are 2,300 foreign firms on this so-called "prospect list."[37]

It might be possible to argue that the decision to go public is not a good benchmark of the quality of a particular corporate governance structure because it does not take into account the relative attractiveness of alternative sources of capital. The idea here is that if a certain country has a particularly strong *banking system*, then it might not need to have access to the public equity market because it can meet all of its capital needs through bank borrowing. But this argument runs contrary to much of the learning in modern corporate finance, which posits that capital markets are more efficient sources of capital than banks. In a nutshell, modern corporate finance teaches that those assets that can be securitized will be:

> The heart of financial intermediation is the ability to obtain and use information. The high cost of gathering and using facts in the past meant that banks and other intermediaries could profit from their cumulative store of knowledge about borrowers by making significantly more informed credit decisions than most other market participants. These other market participants were thus obliged to permit depository intermediaries to make credit decisions in financial markets and therefore allow bank credit to substitute for what would otherwise be their own direct acquisition of credit market instruments.[38]

In an open economy with free entry into lending markets and capital markets, it becomes difficult for banks to compete with public capital markets, because "on-line databases, coupled with powerful computers and wide-ranging telecommunication facilities, can now provide potential investors with virtually the same timely credit and market information that was once available only to [banks]."[39]

A variety of new securities projects, including mortgage-backed securities, consumer receivables financing, consumer loan-based securities, and commercial paper, all have been introduced to replace relatively costly bank financing with relatively cheap capital market financing. Thus, the argument that strong banks can replace public equity markets does not seem plausible.[40]

---

[37] I am grateful to conversations with George Sophianis, Chief Economist of the New York Stock Exchange, for this information.

[38] Greenspan, Alan 'Statement Before the Committee on Banking, Housing, and Urban Affairs, U.S. Senate (Dec. 1, 1987)' *Federal Reserve Bulletin* 74 (1988) 91, 99.

[39] Greenspan, supra n. 38, 93.

[40] I am grateful to Luigi Zingales for bringing this point to my attention.

III. The Market for Corporate Control[41]

An important part of any system of corporate governance is some mechanism for controlling managerial shirking. As Jensen and Meckling observed, because investors will discount the price they are willing to pay for a firm's shares by the expected levels of managerial shirking,[42] firms must be able to make a credible commitment to controlling such shirking if the firm is to attract significant outside funds.

As noted above, there is no agreement among corporate governance scholars as to whether the best mechanism for controlling managers is a robust market for corporate control (the U.S. model) or active monitoring by institutional investors (the German model). But it seems indisputable that the existence of *some* form of control is critical.

As Geoffrey Miller and I have pointed out, "the market for corporate control lies at the heart of the American system of corporate governance."[43] As early as 1965, Henry Manne pointed out that takeovers are the mechanism by which the market for corporate control disciplines managers, because, unlike mergers, takeovers do not require the approval of the board of directors of the target firm.[44] Thus, outside bidders can appeal directly to target shareholders for their approval. And, as Roberta Romano has observed, takeovers provide a backstop mechanism for monitoring corporate performance when other corporate governance devices fail.[45] Hostile takeovers target poorly performing firms and replace their inadequate or shirking managers with rival management teams, thereby keeping the capital market competitive and constraining managers to maximize value for shareholders.[46] The basic theory is simple: outside bidders have an incentive to monitor incumbent managers because they can profit by buying the shares of poorly managed firms and installing better management teams.[47] Bidders must share these gains with target-firm shareholders, but as long as bidders can earn a risk-adjusted market rate of return on their investments, they will find it in their interests to monitor target management teams on behalf of incumbent firm shareholders. Roberta Romano has made an extensive review of

---

[41] On the market for corporate control, see also Ch. 8 in this volume and the respective sections in the articles of Kanda, Prigge, and Wymeersch in Ch. 12.

[42] Jensen and Meckling, supra n. 13.

[43] Macey and Miller, supra n. 19, 101.

[44] Manne, supra n. 15.

[45] Romano, Roberta 'A Guide to Takeovers: Theory, Evidence and Regulation' in 9 *Yale J. on Reg.* 119, 129-31 (1992) as well as in Hopt, Klaus J. and Eddy Wymeersch (eds.) *European Takeovers—Law and Practice* 3-48 (London et al. 1992).

[46] Romano, supra n. 45.

[47] Manne, supra n. 15.

the empirical evidence, and finds that it is consistent with this "inefficient management explanation of takeovers."[48]

Professor Romano also says, however, that the inefficient management explanation is incomplete because it does not explain acquisitions in which the acquiror retains incumbent management, and particularly management-led leveraged buy-outs (so-called MBOs), because top management is part of the acquiring group and stays on the job. However, as Romano observes, the inefficient management explanation is convincing even in these contexts.[49] In the MBO context, superior performance after an MBO can be explained by the fact that management had weak incentives before the takeover because they had such a small stake in the firm they were managing. After the MBO, management's far greater equity stake, coupled with the personal guarantees that management often gives to their bankers to secure financing for the MBO transaction, provide very strong incentives for them to do a better job than they were doing prior to the MBO. Similarly, as Professor Romano recognizes, leveraged buyouts in general can reduce agency costs because the increased debt associated with such restructurings constrains them from dissipating their firms' free cash flow.[50]

From a corporate governance perspective, one must wonder why takeovers are not a complete response to the complaint that the market for corporate control solves the monitoring problems associated with the separation of ownership and corporate control that characterizes the classic, American-style Berle-Means corporation. One possible complaint is that takeovers are costly and that, therefore, "companies have to go further off course before attracting a hostile bid than they might if managers were monitored continuously."[51] Because it is costly to search for, identify, and successfully replace target managers, a firm must be substantially undervalued before a takeover bid can be attempted.

However, while takeovers are very costly, it is important to recognize that a robust market for corporate control has important third-party effects. An active takeover market affects managerial performance in a positive way, *even in the absence of a formally announced takeover bid*, because target managers will want to keep their share price high in order to reduce the probability that they will be displaced by a hostile takeover. Thus, even if the probability of a takeover is slight, risk-averse managers can be expected to work harder when there is a positive probability that a hostile bid will be announced:

---

48 Romano, supra n. 45, 131.

49 Romano, supra n. 45, 133.

50 Romano, supra n. 45, 131 (discussing Jensen, Michael C. 'The Takeover Controversy: Analysis and Evidence' in: Coffee, Jr., John C., Louis Lowenstein, and Susan-Rose Ackerman (eds.) *Knights, Raiders and Targets: The Impact of the Hostile Takeover* 314 (New York 1988).

51 'Watching the Boss: A Survey of Corporate Governance' *The Economist* January 29, 1994, 13.

A robust market for corporate control improves managements' performance because incumbents inevitably prefer to reduce the probability that an outside bid will be made. Incumbent management will be unsure how much better a particular rival management team is; consequently, management will be unsure how far the firm's share price must fall before attracting a hostile bid. This uncertainty creates an incentive for managers to improve a firm's performance, even if a hostile offer never actually materializes.[52]

Further, those who argue that takeovers are too expensive and therefore too "lumpy" to be an effective governance device ignore the fact that an investor need not launch a full-blown tender offer to put a target company effectively "in play." Investors may launch a proxy contest for as little as $5,000 (down from $1 million a few years ago).

The point here is that the market for corporate control serves as a mechanism for replacing weak managers with superior managers, and for giving managers greater incentives to do a better job, which is exactly what institutional investors are supposed to do. In fact, studies of Japanese firms show that poor performance leads to an increased probability that institutional investors—i.e., banks—will replace incumbent officers and directors with their own nominees.[53] Kaplan and Minton observed in their important article on the appointment of outside directors to the boards of large non-financial Japanese corporations that their findings are:

> consistent with an important monitoring and disciplining role for banks, corporate shareholders, and corporate groups in Japan. The results are also consistent with the view that the relationship-oriented system of corporate governance in Japan substitutes for the more market-oriented system in the U.S. Banks, corporate shareholders, and corporate groups appear to play a role that is similar to that of takeovers in the U.S.[54]

The point here is not that takeovers are superior to "continued and textured monitoring by institutional investors." Rather, I want to make two different points. First, takeovers provide a form of continued and textured monitoring that substitutes for the monitoring provided by institutional investors. This monitoring may be inferior because it is costly, but it may also be superior because, unlike institutional investor monitoring in a corporate governance system that lacks a market for corporate control, the market for corporate control affects all firms, not just the one in which an institutional investor has a stake.

The second point is that one can generalize from the above discussion in order to develop an empirical measure of corporate governance performance across different systems. In a properly functioning corporate governance system, poorly performing management teams will be replaced.[55] Consequently, comparing the

---

[52] Macey and Miller, supra n. 19, 104.

[53] Kaplan and Minton, supra n. 27; Morck, Randall and Masao Nakamura 'Banks and Corporate Control in Japan' 4-5 (Institute for Financial Research, Faculty of Business, University of Alberta, Working Paper no. 6-92, rev. July 26, 1993).

[54] Kaplan and Minton, supra n. 27, 257.

[55] Manne, supra n. 15.

sensitivity of management changes to share-price performance provides a means of testing the efficacy of alternative corporate governance structures. A corporate governance system that does not replace poorly performing managers is not working very well.

D. Mechanisms of Corporate Governance

A criticism that might be made of the above analysis is that, by focusing exclusively on outcomes, it ignores the mechanisms by which corporate governance can be improved. In particular, the analysis seems to ignore the ways that institutional investors can work together with other mechanisms to achieve superior corporate governance.[56] For example, in the preceding section, the case was made that a properly functioning corporate governance system will replace poorly performing management teams. In certain contexts, concentrated institutional investor ownership can make takeovers less costly by lowering the transactions costs to an outside acquiror of gaining control.

However, facilitating control transactions by selling shares, which is an exit strategy, is much different than engaging in corporate monitoring at the operational level. While there is some evidence that institutional investors have become involved in the former, there is not much evidence that they have become involved in the latter. Specifically, as Jill Fisch has observed, "it is possible to explain the rapid growth in institutional activism as simply a second order institutional response to the takeover era."[57] Fisch points out that institutional activism in the United States first arose in the context of corporate control transactions. The takeover wave of the 1980s was met with a combination of state anti-takeover statutes and court-sanctioned anti-takeover devices. This, in turn, was met by an increase in activism by institutional investors who opposed management efforts to erect powerful barriers to outside acquisitions.[58]

The point here is that institutional investors do not seem to be engaging in the continuous, textured monitoring that demands active involvement in influencing corporate policy. Institutional investors, like other investors, appear to rely on market forces, particularly market forces in the form of the market for corporate control. Institutional investors do not utilize the strategy of giving corporate governance advice and guidance to firms as a means of increasing their investment returns. There are several reasons for this.

First, institutional investors operate in a competitive environment. It is easy to monitor their performance and there are a lot of them. Modern portfolio theory

---

[56] Rock, supra n. 2, 478-501.

[57] Fisch, supra n. 8, 1030-2.

[58] Fisch, supra n. 8, 1030.

teaches that firm-specific risk can be diversified away by investors.[59] The logic behind the Capital Asset Pricing Model supposes that investors will be compensated only for the non-diversifiable risks they bear.[60] Additionally, the Efficient Capital Markets Hypothesis posits that the process of fundamental analysis of a stock's value is not going to produce superior investment results.[61] As such, institutional investors should concentrate on constructing portfolios of stocks that are designed effectively to eliminate firm-specific risk, and on keeping costs down. Neither of these strategies is consistent with the "continuous and textured monitoring" proposed by some. Thus it is not surprising that, as an observational matter, "American institutional investors do not have a . . . skilled pool of employees" capable of offering suggestions and advice that would improve corporate performance.[62]

Put differently, it is not clear that the human capital skills needed to be a successful fund manager are the same as the human capital skills necessary to provide operational advice to the firms in which a fund are invested.[63] And, if the skills are different—and modern financial theory suggests they are—there are no obvious synergies or economies of scale associated with having institutional investors more actively involved in corporate management.

A second reason why institutional investors—particularly mutual funds—are not actively involved with management of the firms in which they have invested is because any gains associated with this sort of activity must be shared with other investors, including rival investment funds. As Jill Fisch has pointed out, many institutional investors are evaluated by how well they do against similarly situated competitors.[64] An institution that invests a large amount in efforts to increase the performance of one firm will not be able to share the costs of this investment. But the returns will have to be shared with other investors, including other institutional investors who own the same stock.

A third explanation for the observed lack of institutional involvement in corporate governance is that institutional investors do not want to sacrifice

---

[59] Brealey, Richard A. and Stewart C. Myers *Principles of Corporate Finance* 165 5ᵗʰ edn. (New York 1996).

[60] Sharpe, William F. 'Capital Asset Prices: A Theory of Market Equilibrium Under Conditions of Risk' *Journal of Finance* 19 (1964) 425; Lintner, John 'The Valuation of Risk Assets and Selection of Risky Investments in Stock Portfolios and Capital Budgets' *Review of Economics and Statistics* 47 (1965) 13.

[61] Jensen, Michael C. and Clifford W. Smith, Jr. 'The Theory of Corporate Finance: A Historical Overview' in: Jensen, Michael C. and Clifford W. Smith, Jr. (eds) *The Modern Theory of Corporate Finance* 10 (New York 1984).

[62] Vanecko, Robert G. 'Regulations 14A and 13D and the Role of Institutional Investors in Corporate Governance' 87 *Nw. U. L. Rev.* 376, 406-8 (1992).

[63] Gilson and Kraakman, supra n. 3, 880.

[64] Fisch, supra n. 8, 1020.

investment liquidity in order to achieve a greater voice in the activities of the firms in which they have invested.[65] In particular, board membership in a company brings responsibilities as well as information. Since it is highly doubtful that an institutional investor could use any information received in that capacity, or in any other role that could be defined as creating a fiduciary relationship, the incentives to assume an active role in corporate governance are greatly diminished.

Greater involvement in corporate governance will involve significant new costs. These costs include: (1) new investments in human capital; (2) significant free-rider problems; (3) loss of liquidity; and (4) potential legal liability for insider trading and for breach of fiduciary duty to other shareholders where the insiders have assumed a role as a director or an active participant in management.

E. Conclusion

This article has explored the need for greater institutional investor involvement in corporate governance. In light of the fact that greater institutional involvement in corporate governance entails substantial costs and risks to institutions, the potential benefits from institutional investor involvement should be considered. One way of measuring these benefits is to measure how well the current system is performing. I suggest three ways for measuring the performance of a corporate governance system. First, I propose measuring the private benefits of control by examining the relative share price performance of voting and non-voting shares in firms with a capital structure that includes both voting and non-voting stock.

Second, I propose looking at the willingness of firms to go public. Investors will not pay full value for firms with weak corporate governance because they will discount the price they pay for such firms by an amount sufficient to compensate them in the future for possible exploitation by management. This will, in turn, lead to a situation in which entrepreneurs refuse to sell their shares to the public because they cannot receive an adequate price. Thus, where a corporate governance system is not performing well, there will be relative few public offerings.

Finally, I argue that a good corporate governance system can be measured by the speed with which management is replaced for sustained poor performance. Systems with weak corporate governance systems will not replace management very often.

The purpose of this article has been to suggest some ways of measuring the performance of a corporate governance system. This seems superior to simply asserting that the U.S. system of corporate governance is dysfunctional. The

---

[65] Coffee, supra n. 7.

article does not purport to fully test the performance of the U.S. system, although it does make some tentative observations. In particular, I find no evidence that the U.S. system is performing badly, and indeed, the U.S. system seems to be used as the benchmark for comparing the performance of rival systems. This is what Kaplan and Minton did, for example, when they examined Japan's system of corporate governance by determining whether that system was as successful in ousting incumbent management as the U.S. system.[66]

It should be clear that none of the tests suggested in this article are meant to be used in isolation to measure the performance of a system of corporate governance. Rather, they should be used together, since shortcomings in one measurement can be compensated for by strengths in another. Finally, it goes without saying, I think, that the U.S.'s market-oriented system of corporate governance has been hurt in recent years by the wave of anti-takeover statutes and court decisions that are hampering the market for corporate control.[67] One of bthe few salutory effects that institutional investors are having on U.S. corporate governance are their actions directed at lowering or removing some of these barriers.

[66] Kaplan and Minton, supra n. 27.
[67] Manne, supra n. 15.

Comparative Corporate Governance Country Report: Japan

HIDEKI KANDA, Tokyo

There are about 9,000 publicly held business corporations in Japan. Among them, about 2,300 are listed on stock exchanges. All these corporations take the legal form of *kabushikigaisha* (stock company). Shareownership of public companies is highly institutionalized. It has two characteristics: (1) financial institutions and industrial corporations are major shareholders; and (2) these shareholders serve as stable shareholders but usually own a small fraction of the total shares of each public company. The board of directors almost always consists of former employees, and there is a unique system of statutory auditors in Japan. Public companies used to raise funds more often by bank borrowing than by issuing debt securities, so that banks were important stakeholders. Monitoring tasks thus are spread out in Japanese corporate governance. Shareholders, employees, and lenders all play some role in Japanese corporate governance. Today, there is a current toward change both in law and practice.

Contents

Figures

Tables

A. Introduction[1]

I. Corporate Sector

In Japan, aside from sole proprietorships, businesses can be organized in one of the six organizational, or legal, forms: *kumiai* (partnership), *tokumeikumiai* (limited partnership), *gomeigaisha* (incorporated partnership), *goshigaisha* (incorporated limited partnership), *yugengaisha* (limited company), and *kabushikigaisha* (stock company).[2]

Among these six forms, only the first two—namely, *kumiai* and *tokumeikumiai*—enjoy single-tiered income taxation, by which income tax is not imposed at the "entity" level and individual investors report their proportional share of the profits earned by the entity in their personal tax return. But *kumiai* does not offer limited liability to investors, and although *tokumeikumiai* does offer limited liability to investors, if the number of investors is ten or more, withholding tax will be imposed, making the *tokumeikumiai* form costly. For these reasons, *kumiai* and *tokumeikumiai* are unpopular for large businesses in Japan. The other four forms are all incorporated types (some of which provide investors with limited liability and others which do not) and are subject to "double taxation." While *gomeigaisha*, *goshigaisha*, and *yugengaisha* are given flexibility under the statutes as to their internal governance structure and related matters, they are unsuitable for raising a large amount of funds in the capital markets. Thus, in Japanese practice, all major businesses take the *kabushikigaisha* (stock company) form, which is similar to a business corporation in the U.S., a public company in

[1] For a treatment of Japanese corporate governance, cf. also Ch. 11 in this volume.

[2] Note also that a trust is sometimes used to do business in Japan. The most well known of these is an arrangement called a "land trust."

the U.K., a German *Aktiengesellschaft*, and a French and Belgian *société par action*.

Table 1:   Number of Corporations in Japan, 1996

Type	Amount of Capital	Number	%
Kabushikigaisha (Stock Company)	Less than 50 million	1,131,000	39.3
	50 million yen or more and less than 100 million yen	48,000	1.7
	100 million yen or more and less than 500 million yen	27,000	1.0
	500 million yen or more	9,000	0.3
	Subtotal	1,215,00	42.3
Gomeigaisha (Incorporated Partnership)		19,000	0.7
Goshigaisha (Incorporated Limited Partnership)		79,000	2.7
Yugengaisha (Limited Liability Company)		1,562,00	54.3
Total		2,875,00	100.0

Note: As of November, 1996; numbers of *kumiai* and *tokumeikumiai* are not available.
Source: Ministry of Justice.

Today, there are about 1.2 million stock companies in Japan, but most of them are closely held companies, and the number of "large" publicly held companies is roughly 9,000.[3] Japan has eight stock exchanges, of which the largest is the Tokyo Stock Exchange. As of March 31, 1997, there were 2,334 publicly held business companies listed on the eight stock exchanges in Japan, and the Tokyo Stock Exchange had 1,766 listed stock companies.

[3] In this report, "large publicly held companies" or "large companies" mean "large stock companies" defined under the statute. A large stock company is a stock company having either capital in the amount of 500 million yen or more, or total debt (on its balance sheet) in the amount of 20 billion yen or more. See the Special Audit Law (Law No. 22 of 1974, as amended).

II. Institutional Settings

1. Legal Structure of the Relevant Company Types

Various organizational rules—commonly known as corporate law or company law—are found in the Japanese Commercial Code (Law No. 48 of 1899, as amended) ("the Code"). The Code was originally modeled on the German Commercial Code of the late 19th century, but after World War II, a number of American rules were incorporated into the German-based rules.

The Code provides corporate law rules for *kabushikigaisha*, *gomeigaisha*, *goshigaisha*, and *tokumeikumiai*. A separate statute, called the Limited Company Act (Law No. 74 of 1928, as amended), governs *yugengaisha*. The Japanese Civil Code (Law No. 89 of 1896, as amended) provides rules for *kumiai*. The essence of the provisions of the Code regarding the governance structure of *kabushikigaisha* (or stock company) can be summarized as follows.[4]

The Code begins with the familiar position that shareholders are the owners of a stock company. A shareholders' meeting elects directors and makes decisions about "fundamental changes" to the company, such as a merger, a sale of substantially all the firm's assets, and an amendment to the firm's charter. There must be at least three directors. Directors are elected at the shareholders' meeting. Criminals and others are disqualified from directorship. Directors constitute the board of directors. The board elects representative directors, the Japanese counterparts of U.S. officers or executives. There must be at least one representative director. Representative directors are managers, and they run the company.

The Code requires that the board of directors make important corporate decisions and supervise the management.[5] Each director, as a member of the board, owes a duty of care and loyalty to the company. There is a unique statutory provision that directors must pay damages to third parties if they act in bad faith or are grossly negligent in running the company or supervising other directors.[6] A director's liability to the company may be enforced by shareholders through a derivative law suit. Shareholders have familiar rights, such as the right to make proposals, the right to ask questions to directors and statutory auditors

---

[4] For a detailed description of corporate law in Japan, see, for example, Kusano, Koichi 'Corporate Law of Japan' in: Oghigian, Haig (ed.) *The Law of Commerce in Japan—A Collection of Introductory Essays* 19-37 (New York 1993).

[5] Commercial Code Art. 260.

[6] Commercial Code Art. 266-3. This provision was often enforced where a closely held company went into bankruptcy and its creditors sued the directors for the amount of the company's debt owed to the creditors. The provision has almost never been triggered for publicly held corporations. The recent popularity of the shareholder's derivative suit in public corporations (which enforces the director's liability against the company), however, may suggest that litigations concerning the director's liability against third parties in large public companies may arise in the future.

(although the Code calls this the director or auditor's "duty to explain"), and the right to examine the company's books and records.

Compensation of directors and statutory auditors must be set either in the charter or at the shareholders' meeting,[7] but an annual shareholders' meeting can set the maximum amount for all directors and for all auditors without specifying the exact amount for each director and auditor.

2. Structure of the Law Governing Groups of Affiliated Companies

There are few statutory rules governing groups of companies in Japan, and general company law rules apply to the group situations. This is similar to the U.S.

One of the statutory rules governing groups of stock companies is the rule on mutual stockholding. If Company A holds more than 25% of Company B's shares, Company B is prohibited from voting on Company A's share(s) which B owns. In practice, this rule seldom applies. In a typical "cross holding" situation, using the above hypothetical example, Company B owns 100% to 1% of Company A's shares, but Company A owns 25% or less of B's shares. Also, a situation where A owns B, B owns C, and C owns A is popular, without triggering the above voting restriction rule. Also, for certain narrow exceptions, subsidiaries are prohibited from acquiring the shares of the parent company, a rule extending the prohibition of the share repurchase. When subsidiaries hold the parent's shares as an exception, they do not have voting rights.

For accounting and disclosure, as noted later, the Securities and Exchange Law requires reporting companies (as defined below) to prepare and disclose financial statements on a consolidated basis twice a year.

3. Securities Regulation

The Securities and Exchange Law in Japan (Law No. 25 of 1948, as amended) ("SEL") was modeled on the U.S. federal securities laws, specifically the Securities Act of 1933 and the Securities Exchange Act of 1934. The SEL provides two basic sets of rules for investor protection: mandatory disclosure and anti-fraud rules. Thus, when a firm attempts to issue "securities", it must file a registration statement with the Ministry of Finance ("MOF"), which must include certain information specified under the rules promulgated by the MOF. A company whose securities are listed on a stock exchange, traded "over the counter," or the number of whose registered shareholders is 500 or more is subject to the reporting requirements of the SEL. Reporting is semi-annual, and the company's

---

[7] Commercial Code Art. 269.

annual report must be audited by a certified public accountant. Also, a company which files a registration statement with the MOF when it issues securities is subject to the same rules.

The anti-fraud rules include prohibitions of somewhat broadly defined fraudulent activities—such as those prohibited under Section 10(b) of the U.S. Securities Exchange Act of 1934—and more specific activities of securities companies, such as fraudulent solicitation of customers. Also, insider trading is prohibited with criminal sanction. One of the important facts in this area in Japan is that there has been little private litigation associated with violations of the disclosure or anti-fraud rules under the SEL.[8]

B. Owners

I. Board Representation[9]

Japanese company law operates on a one-tier board system. Employee participation, or co-determination, is not adopted in Japan. Employees, however, are important constituencies in Japan, as described later.

As noted above, there must be at least three directors. Directors are elected at the shareholders' meeting to form the board of directors. The board elects representative directors, the Japanese counterparts of U.S. officers or executives. There must be at least one representative director. Representative directors are managers who run the company, thus forming the one-tier board system (see supra A.II.).

Boards of directors in Japan are homogeneous. The board of directors in a typical large Japanese company consists of about 25 men, most of whom are at least fifty years old. They are all former employees of the company. There are almost no executives of other firms, no women, no academics, and no outsiders of any kind. These directors elect managers. Managers, with the top position of president, have attained the highest rank in the life of "salary man", the word which describes a typical university graduate under the lifetime employment system in Japan. Japanese company law does not require outside directors. Instead, it requires outside statutory auditors, as noted later.

It is a common practice in most listed companies for the board to meet once a month, and a separate executive committee (usually known as *jomukai*) is established with top executives to meet once a week. The average number of directors

---

[8] Note, however, that there is a vast amount of litigation between brokers and customers. Also, the Securities Trading Surveillance Committee, which was established in 1992 to detect fraud in capital markets, has convicted several cases of insider trading and other fraudulent activities.

[9] See also Ch. 4 in this volume on the board.

and auditors in all listed companies is 19, but there are several companies having more than 40 directors.

Figure 1:   Board Composition, 1979-1994

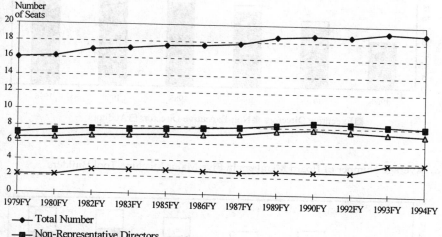

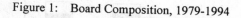

Note: Average number of directors and auditors in all listed companies.
Source: Miwa, Yoshiro 'Directors and the Board' in: Miwa, Yoshiro et al. (eds.) *An Economic Analysis of Corporate Law* (Tokyo 1998) (in Japanese).

Figure 2:   Board Composition in Selected Business Sectors, 1960-1996

a) Average Number of Board Members in Five Major Construction Companies

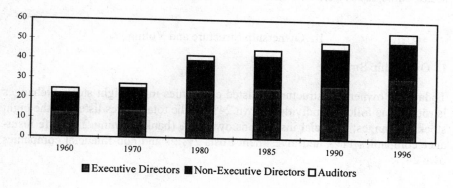

b) Average Number of Board Members in Five Major City Banks

c) Average Number of Board Members in Five Major Machine Tool Builders

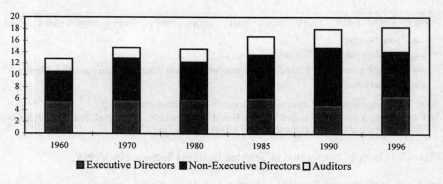

Source: Miwa, supra Figure 1.

II. Ownership Structure and Voting

1. Ownership Structure

Today, the ownership structure of listed companies in the eight stock exchanges is roughly as follows: individuals own 24% of the total shares listed on the eight stock exchanges; financial institutions own 43% (banks owning 22%, life insurance companies 11%, and investment trusts 2%);[10] and non-financial companies own 24%.

---

[10] Note that trust banks and life insurance companies manage pensions in Japan.

Figure 3:   Change in Share Ownership, 1949-1995

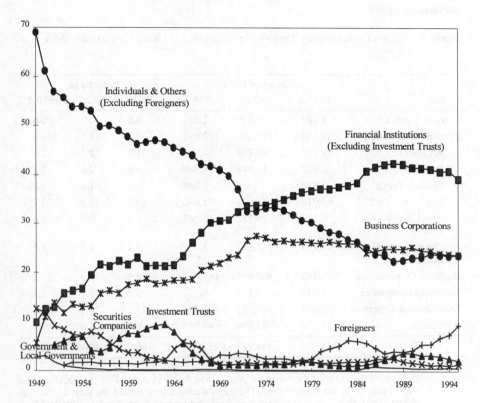

Source: Tokyo Stock Exchange 'Fact Book' (1997).

Unlike in the U.S., banks may hold shares of other companies for investment purposes (under Article 65 of the SEL, the Japanese version of Glass-Steagall), but they cannot own more than 5% of a single company under the Anti-Monopoly Law. For insurance companies, this limitation is 10%. Thus, typically, a manufacturing company, for instance, has ten bank shareholders, each owning 2 to 3%, as well as twenty other major corporate shareholders. Also, mutual stockholding by companies is common, and known as *keiretsu*. But high percentage two-way holdings are unpopular. That is, Company A's holding of Company B's shares may range from 1% to 100%, but Company B typically owns 1 to 2% of A's shares. For banks and insurance companies, the antitrust limitations apply.[11]

Table 2: Share Ownership by Types of Investors of All Listed Companies, 1994-1996

	Thous. of Units			Percentage		
	1994.3	1995.3	1996.3	1994.3	1995.3	1996.3
Gov't. & Local Gov't.	2,589	2,919	2,868	0.6	0.7	0.6
Financial Institutions	186,452	193,488	189,493	43.8	43.5	41.4
All Banks	92,373	98,801	98,908	21.7	22.2	21.6
Investment Trusts	12,607	11,688	9,769	3.0	2.6	2.1
Annuity Trusts	5,920	7,069	8,088	1.4	1.6	1.8
Life Insurance Cos.	54,016	54,474	51,086	12.7	12.2	11.2
Non-Life Insurance Cos.	16,259	16,352	16,262	3.8	3.7	3.6
Other Financial Institutions	5,274	5,102	5,377	1.2	1.1	1.2
Business Corporations	101,792	105,975	108,017	23.9	23.8	23.6
Securities Companies	5,621	5,115	6,252	1.3	1.1	1.4
Individuals & Others	100,821	104,385	107,771	23.7	23.5	23.6
Foreigners	28,374	32,996	43,035	6.7	7.4	9.4
Total	425,650	444,881	457,439	100.0	100.0	100.0

Notes: Data as of the close of the business year ending between April 1 of the previous year and March 31 of the present year. The 1996 statistics thus reflect the total of the individual company's figures at the business year-end ranging from April 1, 1995 to March 31, 1996. The data cover only such shareholders who own one or more "unit of shares". One unit generally consists of 1,000 shares.
"Individuals & Others" includes unincorporated associations.
Source: Tokyo Stock Exchange, supra Figure 3.

Note that the Anti-Monopoly Law prohibited a pure holding company,[12] a company formed solely for owning other companies' shares, but this prohibition was lifted by the amendment in 1997. As a result, the holding company structure may become popular in the future.

---

[11] Who owns banks and insurance companies in Japan? The top ten shareholders of a typical bank are life insurance companies and other banks.

[12] Anti-Monopoly Law Art. 9.

Table 3:   Operating Funds of Life Insurance Companies, 1992-1996

End of Year/ Month	Total		Securities Domestic				Foreign Securities		Total Operating Funds	
			Stocks		Bonds					
1992.3	61,534	44.3	30,692	22.1	12,220	8.8	17,394	12.5	138,903	100.0
1993.3	67,441	44.5	31,338	20.7	18,268	12.0	16,641	11.0	151,651	100.0
1994.3	69,009	41.9	32,897	20.0	21,072	12.8	13,718	8.3	164,617	100.0
1995.3	77,392	44.7	32,974	19.1	30,697	17.7	12,578	7.3	173,072	100.0
1996.3	87,403	47.3	31,860	17.2	40,454	21.9	13,292	7.2	184,976	100.0

Note: ¥ bil., %.
Source: Tokyo Stock Exchange, supra Figure 3.

Table 4:   Trust Accounts of All Domestic Banks, 1992-1996

End of Year/ Month	Total		Securities Domestic				Foreign Securities		Total Trust Accounts	
			Stocks		Bonds					
1992.3	58,094	31.6	19,725	10.7	24,381	13.2	12,952	7.0	184,020	100.0
1993.3	61,690	31.6	20,090	10.3	25,761	13.2	14,527	7.5	194,949	100.0
1994.3	65,615	32.4	21,674	10.7	27,878	13.8	15,084	7.4	202,534	100.0
1995.3	71,728	36.4	24,997	12.7	30,012	15.2	15,643	7.9	196,928	100.0
1996.3	75,682	38.8	25,208	12.9	33,748	17.3	15,900	8.1	195,264	100.0

Note: ¥ bil., %.
Source: Tokyo Stock Exchange, supra Figure 3.

2. Voting

A strict one-share one-vote rule is adopted in company law.[13] Dual voting shares are prohibited. Non-voting shares are only allowed as preference shares in dividend; up to one-third of the total issued shares may be of this type. If the dividend is not paid to the preference shareholders, they receive voting rights instead.[14]

[13] Commercial Code Art. 241(1).
[14] Commercial Code Art. 242.

3. Proxy System[15]

The SEL requires "reporting companies"[16] to conform to its proxy rules when management solicits proxies for shareholders meeting. Management must send the shareholders a proxy statement where certain information required by MOF rules must be disclosed. The company law, however, overrides this rule partially. The Special Audit Law requires all "large" companies (defined above) having 1,000 or more shareholders to send shareholders a form for "mail voting" before every shareholders meeting. A statement with certain information must be sent with this form; reporting companies must send the proxy statement required under the SEL. As a result, in Japanese practice, mail voting rather than proxy voting is common in major public companies today.

III. Stock Market

As noted above, there are eight stock exchanges in Japan. The most important is the Tokyo Stock Exchange, and the second largest is the Osaka Stock Exchange. Stock markets on these exchanges are the major trading markets for the shares of public companies in Japan, and there are over 2,200 companies listed on these exchanges. There are also OTC markets. In practice, the only OTC market (called *Tento toroku shijo*) of importance is administered by the Japan Securities Dealers Association ("JASD"), a Japanese counterpart of the U.S. NASDAQ market. Shares of about 700 companies are traded on this JASD market (as compared with about 5,000 companies in the U.S. NASDAQ market). There is a provision in SEL that prohibits "a place similar to the securities market on an exchange". Also, the charter provision of the Tokyo Stock Exchange (and that of others, too) does not permit its members off-board trades of the shares listed on the exchange. Because of these rules, Japanese OTC stock markets are relatively underdeveloped. JASD recently liberalized its listing standard to invite venture-type companies, and the JASD market may become more popular in the future.

---

[15] For a comparative report on shareholder representation and proxy voting in the EU, cf. Baums (this volume Ch. 6).

[16] Under the SEL, a "reporting company" is (1) a company whose securities are listed on a stock exchange, (2) a company whose shares are traded "over the counter," (3) a company who has 500 or more registered shareholders, and (4) a company which files a registration statement with the MOF when it issues securities. The reporting company is subject to the continuous reporting requirements of the SEL: reporting is semi-annual, and the company's annual report must be audited by a certified public accountant.

Figure 4:   Number of Listed Companies on Tokyo Stock Exchange & Other
Exchanges, 1992-1996

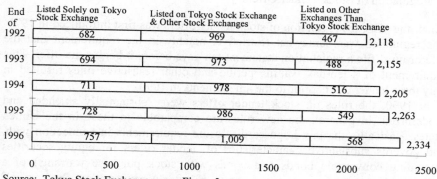

Source: Tokyo Stock Exchange, supra Figure 3.

Table 5:   Listed Companies, 1949-1996

End of Year	Number of Companies Listed		Market Value (¥ bil.)	
	Tokyo	All Japan	Tokyo	All Japan
1949	529	681	122	128
1960	599	785	5,411	5,643
1970	1,280	1,580	16,235	16,824
1980	1,402	1,729	77,074	79,952
1990	1,627	2,071	379,231	393,594
1996	1,766	2,334	347,578	358,538

Source: Tokyo Stock Exchange, supra Figure 3.

Table 6:   Number of Companies Listed on All Stock Exchanges, End of 1996

	Tokyo		Osaka		Nagoya		Kyoto	Hiro-shima	Fuku-oka	Nii-gata	Sap-poro
	1st sec.	2nd sec.	1st sec.	2nd sec.	1st sec.	2nd sec.					
No. of Listed Companies	1,293	473	868	388	438	139	247	206	269	201	194

Source: Tokyo Stock Exchange, supra Figure 3.

IV. Market for Corporate Control[17]

1. Regulation of Stock Tender Offers

Under the SEL, the regulation of stock tender offers was first introduced in 1971. The regulation was somewhat restrictive, notably in the requirement that the offeror must file a registration statement ten days before it begins the offer. This requirement of a ten-day waiting period and other restrictive rules resulted in only three tender offers prior to the amendments in 1990.

In 1990, the rules on stock tender offers were substantially amended and modernized. In general, the new rules are comparable to those in the United States. Basically, the law imposes disclosure requirements in connection with, and governs substantive characteristics of, tender offers for equity securities (including convertible bonds and bonds with stock purchase warrants) of a "reporting" company as explained above, if, after consummation, the person[18] making the offer would be the owner of more than 5% of the securities in question. The person making the offer must file a registration statement with the MOF and make a public announcement, typically in a newspaper. He may commence the offer on the day following the public announcement. The items for disclosure in the registration statement and the public announcement are specified in detail by the MOF regulations. Also, as in the United States, there are detailed rules governing the tender offer process. Among others, rules on the withdrawal of the offer, changes in the condition of the original offer, the mandatory period of the offer, and the fair treatment of those who respond to the offer are important.

There are at least two differences in the regulation of this area between the United States and Japan. First, in Japan, an open market purchase—that is, a purchase of stock in the stock market provided at a stock exchange—is not subject to tender offer regulations. Second and more importantly, while a tender offer typically means an offer to many stockholders, the Japanese regulation is applicable when the offeror acquires stock from a small number of stockholders (ten or less), if, after consummation, the acquiror would be the owner of more than one-third of the securities. The premise underlying the second rule is that even a private purchase must be disclosed when a big stockholder (of more than one-third ownership) would emerge. But the necessity of this rule is controversial, and indeed, an "inadvertent" tender offer may occur where, for instance, a creditor who holds securities as collateral attempts to enforce his security interest.

---

[17] Cf. also Ch. 8 in this volume on the market for corporate control.

[18] The term "person" is broad, to include groups of two or more persons who are "insiders" or act together.

Finally, an ownership disclosure rule, a popular companion of the tender offer regulation, was also introduced in Japan in 1990. Certain disclosure obligations are imposed on persons owning more than 5% of the equity securities of the company, as under Section 13(d) of the U.S. Securities Exchange Act of 1934.

2. Practice

As noted above, there were three tender offers consummated between 1971 and 1990. The first case took place in 1972 when Bendix, a U.S. company, through its wholly owned subsidiary increased the level of its ownership in a Japanese manufacturer of auto parts from 15% to above 20% to be able to include the company in the consolidated accounting. Bendix, rather than its subsidiary, was treated as the offeror for regulatory purposes. The second case occurred in 1975 when Okinawa Denryoku acquired two electricity supply companies in the local market to consolidate the enterprise. The third case appeared in 1990, immediately before the amendment of the regulation, when Orix, a leading leasing company in Japan, increased its ownership interest in Orix Ichioka from 80% to 100% to avoid possible losses that might have been incurred by the "delisting" of Orix Ichioka from the OTC market.

After the new regime was introduced in 1990, nine tender offers took place by the end of 1993, all of which were friendly. First, Gadelius, an affiliate of a Swiss company, acquired Fuso Donetsu Kogyo in 1991. Second, also in 1991, New Home Credit fell into an "inadvertent" tender offer when it acquired the stock of Kokusai Kogyo from the debtor as an in-kind repayment of the debt, resulting in the creditor holding more than one-third of the stock in question. Third, also in 1991, Daiei, a large supermarket operator, acquired the stock of Maruetsu, a similar company, to expand its customer base and obtain scale economies. Fourth, in 1992, again by a similar acquisition, Daiei and Maruetsu acquired the stock of Chujitsuya. Fifth, Avon Beauty Products and its affiliate increased their ownership in Avon Products, a Japanese subsidiary of the Avon group, by a tender offer. Sixth, Mitsubishi Kasei, the largest chemical manufacturer in Japan, made a friendly acquisition of Emoto Industry, a unit bath manufacturer, in 1992. Seventh, in 1993, Nippon Steel Europe BV, a Dutch subsidiary of the largest steel company in Japan, purchased NMB Semiconductor, a subsidiary of the world's top miniature bearing manufacturer, Minebear. Minebear sold this unprofitable operation to the steel company because the latter wanted to expand into semiconductor production. Eighth, the president of a relatively small listed company acquired the company's stock through a tender offer in 1993. Finally, Electronic Data Systems acquired control of Japan Systems, a medium-sized software development firm, in 1993. Electronic Data Systems, as the top stockholder of Japan Systems, decided to take management control.

3. Evaluation

Despite the large number of mergers, consolidations, and asset sales in Japan, the number of stock tender offers has been limited. There have been no (successful) hostile takeovers in Japan. One might ask why this is. In light of the fact that hostile takeovers, at least according to economists, helped to discipline ineffi- cient management in the United States in the 1980s, a related question may be whether Japan lacks effective mechanisms to discipline management in public corporations. A somewhat more difficult question is whether the law, particularly the regulation of tender offers, has something to do with the unpopularity of tender offers, and the nonexistence of hostile takeovers in Japan. While answer- ing these questions is beyond the scope of this paper, it has been proposed that there are a variety of mechanisms other than hostile takeovers by which manag- ers of public companies in Japan are monitored and disciplined.[19]

V. Auditing, Accounting, and Disclosure[20]

1. Auditors

A stock company must have *kansayaku*, often (somewhat misleadingly) trans- lated as statutory auditor. Statutory auditors are elected at the shareholders' meeting, and do not have to be accountants or other professionals. A "large company," which is defined under the statute as a stock company having either capital in the amount of 500 million yen or more, or total (on balance sheet) debt in the amount of 20 billion yen or more, must have at least three statutory audi- tors, and at least one of them must be an "outside" statutory auditor. An auditor is "outside" when he did not serve as a director or employee of the company or its subsidiary for at least five years preceding his appointment as auditor. In a large company, there must be a full-time auditor.

In addition, a "large company" must have an accounting auditor (*kaikei- kansanin*), who must be a certified public accountant (CPA) or certified auditing firm. An accounting auditor is elected at the shareholders meeting, and is respon- sible for auditing the company's financial documents annually before they are submitted to the annual shareholders' meeting, where the audit opinion is also submitted. In contrast, a statutory auditor is responsible for overseeing the activities of management. This is understood to mean confirming the legality of management's activities. The statute requires collaboration between accounting

---

[19] See Ramseyer, J. Mark 'Takeovers in Japan: Opportunism, Ideology and Corporate Control' 35 *UCLA L. Rev.* 1 (1987).

[20] On disclosure and auditing from a corporate governance perspective, see also Ch. 9 in this volume.

auditors and statutory auditors by providing complex rules, but, for instance, if an accounting auditor "notices" an illegal matter in the course of an accounting audit, he must report it to the statutory auditor. Thus, the role of accounting auditors in discovering fraud or the like is limited, as compared to that in the U.S., where a more active role by CPAs is recognized in law.

2. Accounting

Among major industrial countries, Germany and Japan are distinctive as two countries in which company law provides detailed rules on accounting. In Japan, the Code provides accounting rules on recognition, measurement, and reporting of major assets (and some liabilities) of a stock company. For most assets, the Code adopts the principle of historical cost accounting, but for some assets, when the market value declines below the historical cost, the company must adjust booking to the market value (known as the conservative accounting principle). The purpose of the "company law accounting" lies for the most part in the measurement of the company's annual "profits" in connection with the Code's dividend regulation: dividends may only be paid out of the company's (accumulated) profits. Large companies must have their annual financial documents audited by accounting auditors (who must be CPAs) before submission to annual shareholder meeting.

In addition, the SEL requires all "reporting companies" to prepare financial statements, on both unconsolidated and consolidated bases, twice a year. Their annual financial statements must be audited by CPAs. Accounting rules (for recognition, measurement, and reporting of assets and liabilities) are promulgated under the SEL. Accounting rules for recognition and measurement are known as the "Japanese GAAP". This dual accounting system of company law and securities law comes from Japanese history: company law comes from the 19th-century German law, and securities law was imported from the U.S. after World War II. But accounting standards between these two accounting systems have been harmonized over the decades, and today the existence of this dual system does not put much burden on the companies subject to both accounting requirements.

3. Disclosure

Accounting documents prepared in accordance with the rules in company law must be submitted to the company's shareholders before the annual shareholder meeting. The Code requires "large" companies to make public the summaries of their annual balance sheet and profit and loss statement. Under the SEL, all reporting companies must have their financial statement disclosed to the public at the MOF, stock exchanges, and the company's principal office twice a year. In addition, a reporting company must file a disclosure statement when an unusual matter happens, such as a merger. Also, stock exchanges require timely disclosure of certain information.

C. Other Stakeholders

I. Employees[21]

Among non-stockholder constituencies of Japanese companies, employees and banks are important. While employees are not the owners of their company under the Japanese legal system, a traditional oft-made statement is that Japanese companies are run for the best interest of employees and not the best interest of shareholders. Thus, a common phenomenon is that when a Japanese company faces financial distress, management cuts dividends before it starts firing employees. Under Japanese practice, most directors and statutory auditors are elected from former employees of the company (see supra B.I.). Lifetime employment, compensation tied to seniority, and company-by-company labor unions are often pointed out as three distinctive characteristics of Japanese companies that have functioned to keep employee supremacy alive in the past decades.

Thus, employees are important in Japanese companies. However, even if Japanese companies are run for the benefit of employees, it does not necessarily mean that shareholders are victimized. A proposition that Japanese companies are not run for the best interest of shareholders lacks empirical support.[22]

II. Lenders[23]

Public companies in Japan have a variety of sources of capital. Bank borrowing used to be the most important source of capital even for large public companies. In recent years, however, they have been active in issuing debentures and commercial papers, as well as in issuing new shares.

---

[21] On the role of employees in corporate governance, see also Ch. 5 in this volume.

[22] Recent empirical studies suggest that Japanese companies are run for the best interest of shareholders. See Kaplan, Steven N. 'Top Executive Rewards and Firm Performance: A Comparison of Japan and the U.S.' *Journal of Political Economy* 102 (1994) 510; Kaplan, Steven N. and Bernadette Minton 'Appointments of Outsiders to Japanese Boards: Determinants and Implications for Managers' *Journal of Financial Economics* 36 (1994) 225. See also Berglöf, Erik and Enrico Perotti 'The Governance Structure of the Japanese Financial Keiretsu' *Journal of Financial Economics* 36 (1994) 259.

[23] The contributions in Ch. 10 of this volume analyze lenders as a force in corporate governance.

Table 7:   Balance Sheet of All Non-Financial Companies Listed on the Tokyo Stock Exchange, 1993-1995

Fiscal Year	1993		1994		1995	
Number of Companies	1,464		1,472		1,503	
Assets	¥ tril.	%	¥ tril.	%	¥ tril.	%
Current Assets	178.3	55.7	172.6	55.5	176.2	55.6
Cash & Deposits	35.9	11.2	33.1	10.7	30.3	9.6
Notes Receivables & Trade Debtors	63.9	20.0	63.6	20.5	69.2	21.8
Securities	19.1	6.0	18.5	6.0	19.4	6.1
Inventory Assets	43.5	13.6	42.3	13.6	42.3	13.3
Fixed Assets	141.4	44.2	138.2	44.4	140.8	44.4
Tangible Fixed Assets	81.6	25.5	79.8	25.7	80.9	25.5
Intangible Fixed Assets	1.4	0.4	1.4	0.4	1.6	0.5
Investments & Other Assets	58.4	18.3	56.8	18.3	58.2	18.4
Deferred Assets	0.1	0.0	0.1	0.0	0.1	0.1
Total	319.8	100.0	310.9	100.0	317.3	100.0
Liabilities	212.3	66.4	206.2	66.3	209.6	66.1
Current Liabilities	133.4	41.7	130.4	42.0	136.7	43.1
Notes Payable & Trade Creditors	47.7	14.9	47.8	15.4	52.0	16.4
Short-Term Borrowings	41.4	12.9	39.4	12.7	40.3	12.7
Reserves	1.7	0.5	1.7	0.6	1.6	0.5
Fixed Liabilities	78.9	24.7	75.7	24.4	72.8	23.0
Bonds	36.4	11.4	34.4	11.1	17.0	5.4
Long-Term Bonds	27.0	8.4	26.2	8.4	25.5	8.0
Reserves	10.9	3.4	10.6	3.4	10.6	3.4
Shareholders' Equity	107.5	33.6	104.7	33.7	107.6	33.9
Capital Stock	25.8	8.1	25.9	8.3	26.2	8.3
Capital Reserves	28.0	8.8	28.9	9.3	28.9	9.1
Profit Reserves	3.2	1.0	3.2	1.0	3.3	1.0
Other Surpluses	50.5	15.8	46.6	15.0	49.0	15.5

Note: Based on figures of domestic companies whose full 12-month business year ended during each fiscal year (ex. 1995: from April 1995 to March 1996) excluding financial, insurance, railway, electric power, and gas companies.

Source: Tokyo Stock Exchange, supra Figure 3.

Banks are important players in Japan. Japanese companies rely more on banks than on capital markets for debt finance. The relative underdevelopment of the Japanese bond markets might be the result of a political victory by the banking industry. Banks are thus important, but how they operate is far from clear.

The bank-customer relationship in Japan has several distinct characteristics. Some of them are common in other business relationships in Japan, and others are unique to banking transactions. Banking transactions between banks and their customer firms in Japan show three unique characteristics. First, banks and their customer firms engage in a very wide range of transactions, from straightforward lending to a new type of transaction, such as swap transactions, and even to a bank's stockholding in their customer firms. Second, a company usually estab-

Table 8: Business Results and Distribution of Profits of All Non-Financial Listed Companies, 1989-1995

Fiscal Year		1989	1990	1991	1992	1993	1994	1995
Number of Companies		1,797	1,868	1,905	1,920	1,968	1,996	2,081
Total Liabilities & Net Worth	(¥ tril.) A	340.3	373.9	388.7	389.2	394.3	387.6	409.7
Amount of Shareholders' Equity	(¥ tril.) B	100.1	110.4	116.7	119.0	122.8	120.2	131.3
Current Profits	(¥ tril.) C	14.6	15.3	13.3	10.2	8.5	8.9	11.2
Financial Expenses	(¥ tril.) D	7.1	9.3	9.4	7.9	7.1	6.5	5.8
After-Tax Profits	(¥ tril.) E	7.1	7.6	6.7	4.5	3.4	3.2	4.8
Amount of Cash Dividends	(¥ tril.) F	2.2	2.4	2.4	2.4	2.2	2.1	2.3
Shareholders' Equity Ratio	(%) B/A	29.4	29.5	30.0	30.6	31.1	31.0	32.0
Ratio of Before-Interest Current Profits to Total Assets	(%) (C+D)/A	6.8	6.8	5.9	4.7	3.9	4.0	4.2
Ratio of After-Tax Profits to Shareholders' Equity	(%) E/B	7.7	7.2	5.9	3.8	2.8	2.8	3.7
Ratio of Dividends to Shareholders' Equity	(%) F/B	2.4	2.2	2.1	2.0	1.8	1.8	1.8
Dividend Payout Ratio	(%) F/E	31.7	31.3	36.2	53.3	65.9	65.3	48.3

Source: Tokyo Stock Exchange, supra Figure 3.

lishes a long-term contractual relationship with more than one, and typically several, banks. One of these banks typically serves as the "main bank". Third, banks obtain a strong legal position under a standard form contract known as the Banking Transactions Agreement, but they sometimes show behavior that looks quite inconsistent with their strong legal position. To take a familiar situation where a firm is in financial trouble, the traditional behavior of the main bank (which usually has a first mortgage over the firm's property securing its loans) often is to pay off other debts (debts which are legally subordinated to the bank's claim) and pay off publicly outstanding bonds.

All of these characteristics, however, have begun to evaporate in recent years. In particular because of the development of capital markets and their deregulation, large Japanese companies today can obtain cheaper capital from capital markets, and so the presence of banks as lenders is inevitably reduced. And in fact, bank borrowing by large Japanese companies has been decreasing. On the

Table 9: New Issues of Bonds by Public Offering, 1957-1996

Year	Government Bonds Long-Term	Medium-Term	Discount Gov't. Notes & Bills	Munici-pal Bonds	Gov't. Guaran-teed Bonds	Corporate Bonds Elec. Power	NTT JR	Others	Convert-ible Bonds	Yen-Denomi-nated Foreign Bonds
1957	—	—	—	15	33	42	—	47	—	—
1965	—	—	—	58	273	138	—	202	—	—
1975	4,011	—	—	239	448	580	88	885	408	20
1985	16,699	3,752	682	766	2,455	538	235	112	1,904	1,115
1986	16,219	3,322	3,879	903	2,907	490	300	186	2,744	637
1987	17,986	3,027	5,366	846	2,202	530	385	28	5,257	448
1988	17,557	2,506	4,709	1,101	2,513	688	150	72	6,640	635
1989	14,541	1,620	9,016	791	2,033	520	60	4	6,867	1,101
1990	9,716	1,845	20,654	996	1,774	1,678	150	6	2,727	1,203
1991	11,263	1,870	19,231	903	1,952	1,765	200	417	1,092	681
1992	11,292	1,529	22,874	1,027	1,853	1,785	180	1,045	566	1,149
1993	11,850	2,707	24,527	1,396	2,123	1,810	160	1,740	1,690	1,685
1994	16,245	5,673	25,570	1,552	2,747	1,345	290	1,335	2,860	1,213
1995	18,560	5,479	30,623	1,967	2,952	1,625	150	3,271	737	1,616
1996	17,111	5,576	32,136	1,893	3,106	1,515	285	4,346	3,289	3,923

Note: All amounts in ¥ bil.; excluding those issued in foreign countries.
Source: Tokyo Stock Exchange, supra Figure 3.

bank's side, today banks say that they will not "rescue" their customer firm as often as in the past, and they also say that they will not buy defaulted bonds from public bondholders. Thus, banks' power seems now to be decreasing. Japanese economists say that in the past, banks were the most powerful monitor in Japanese corporate governance; today there is no single powerful monitor, so that monitoring is spread out.

D. Conclusion

There is no single powerful monitor in Japanese publicly held business corporations. Shareholders, banks, employees, and others are all important. How they provide influence on the firm is not quite clear. Also, providing influence does not necessarily mean monitoring management. Empirical studies must be awaited.

Table 10: Equity Financing of All Listed Companies, 1955-1996

Year	Rights Offerings		Public Offerings		Private Placements		Exercise of Warrants		**Total**	
	No. of Cases	Amount Raised (¥ bil.)	No. of Cases	Amount Raised (¥ bil.)	No. of Cases	Amount Raised (¥ bil.)	No. of Cases	Amount Raised (¥ bil.)	No. of Cases	Amount Raised (¥ bil.)
1955	126	64	4	0	11	0	—	—	141	64
1960	275	331	100	34	4	0	—	—	379	366
1965	95	114	19	0	8	2	—	—	122	117
1970	316	538	203	138	18	5	—	—	537	681
1975	166	771	103	221	16	8	—	—	285	1,001
1980	34	90	218	880	28	80	—	—	280	1,052
1985	40	182	103	505	18	33	70	137	231	859
1986	27	69	76	399	16	30	116	372	235	872
1987	26	436	99	1,393	22	109	241	1,073	388	3,013
1988	40	787	157	2,582	23	103	316	1,309	536	4,782
1989	32	726	227	5,830	22	102	435	2,189	716	8,848
1990	39	824	121	1,975	21	314	397	677	578	3,792
1991	40	218	27	125	19	103	309	360	395	807
1992	20	110	3	4	22	102	127	203	172	419
1993	9	47	4	7	14	150	184	617	211	822
1994	2	9	18	236	8	238	180	450	208	935
1995	12	95	8	33	19	160	118	299	157	588
1996	9	337	36	305	20	218	187	673	253	1,533

Note: Including those issued in foreign countries.

Source: Tokyo Stock Exchange, supra Figure 3.

In May 1997, the ruling party (the Liberal Democratic Party) began to consider a drastic change in the statutory auditor system with a view to enhancing corporate governance. Its Subcommittee on Commercial Law will make a legislative proposal in the near future. On the practical side, Sony, a leading manufacturer of electronic home appliances, announced in July 1997 that it would completely restructure its board of directors by increasing the number of outside directors and transferring most ex-employee directors to a non-director status. Quite a few companies have announced that they will reduce the number of directors. Japan will therefore experience a drastic change both in law and practice in corporate governance in the coming years.

A Survey of German Corporate Governance

This survey provides a broad investigation of a major part of the German corporate governance structure, though not in its entirety. It is selective in its choice of the U.S. perspective of corporate governance, causing it to concentrate on the core agency relation between management and external owners. But this selected subject is treated encompassingly in the study's analysis of the core relation and the numerous other parties and mechanisms affecting it: supervisory board; management board; ownership structure, voting rights structure, and control structure; significance of share market and market for corporate control; auditing, accounting, and disclosure in view of corporate governance; employees; and lenders, with a summary of German banks. It is less an analytical study than a structured, very extensive guide through available evidence, and, as such, is intended to complement the parallel articles by Kanda and Wymeersch. The key feature of German corporate governance is the almost complete absence of open markets—with the exception of competitive product markets—as forces in corporate governance. This is even true for the small group of quoted companies: control is often stable and large shareholdings are mainly long-term; there is a strong capital (hinting at the special feature of *Konzerne*) and personal linkage among companies; funding is often internal, and in cases of external funding, open markets play a minor role. In general, it is a non-open-market or insider system, and abrupt breaches—at least obvious ones—are the great exception.

Contents

Tables

A. Introduction

Corporate governance is a fairly recent area of research, the exact boundaries of which are not yet settled. The diversity of less abstract definitions reveals this fluidity. See, for example:

> Corporate governance deals with the ways in which suppliers of finance to corporations assure themselves of getting a return on their investments. How do the suppliers of finance get managers to return some of the profits to them? How do they make sure that managers do not steal the capital they supply or invest it in bad projects? How do suppliers of finance control managers?...Our perspective on corporate governance is a straightforward agency perspective, sometimes referred to as separation of ownership and control.[1]

> Corporate governance can be defined as the way the management of a firm is influenced by many stakeholders. Depending on which stakeholders are involved, we can identify five aspects of corporate governance. Those aspects address the agency problems between (i) shareholders and managers, (ii) creditors and managers, (iii) workers and managers, (iv) suppliers and customers, and (v) government and firms. The mechanisms used to address each of these aspects differentiate various systems of corporate governance. Other institutional features, such as (a) human resource management, (b) managerial labor market, (c) competitive product markets, and (d) corporate laws also influence the system of corporate governance.[2]

At first sight, these definitions appear quite different, strongly influenced by the corporate governance structures prevailing in the home economies of the authors.[3] Hoshi represents one end of the spectrum of available definitions covering a great variety of parties. Shleifer and Vishny, on the other hand—whose definition that includes equity and credit providers is unusually broad by U.S. standards—represent a position near the other end of the spectrum, which regards shareholders as the only relevant stakeholders. But first impressions may be deceiving since both definitions share a vast area of common ground, particularly in taking an agency perspective.

The U.S. discussion focuses on the core agency relation between management and external shareholders,[4] but there are other agency relations involving management as well. These relations have effects on two levels. The first effect is as an agency relation between management and, e.g., employees and suppliers due to a vulnerability of the latter parties toward decisions taken by the manage-

---

[1] Shleifer/Vishny (1997: 737-8).

[2] Hoshi (this volume Ch. 11: Abstract).

[3] On a more general level, Turnbull (1997) elaborates the point of "ethnocentric, contextual, and intellectual contingencies" as a factor shaping the current international discussion of corporate governance.

[4] Common corporate governance research deals with larger corporations whose size usually necessitates a separation of ownership and control, thus creating the core agency relation. More generally, one could shift the attention to the body that decides on the employment of a company's resources regardless of whether or not owners are members of this organ. This slight refinement avoids such theoretical cases as co-determination in owner-managed companies which lack the core relation but should not be excluded from corporate governance analysis.

ment. This might result, for instance, from some kind of specificity, such as employer-specific investments in human capital or customer-specific investments with respect to the location of a plant. On a second level, regardless of whether there is an agency relation between management and other parties, other parties may affect the agency relation between management and owners, such as debt and—consequently—lenders, according to the free cash flow hypothesis[5] as a means of mitigating the core agency problem. Another example is co-determination when it is not granted in exchange for vulnerability.

As noted above, the definition by Shleifer/Vishny (1997) is, for U.S. standards, unusually broad; however, with respect to their argumentation, the group of relevant stakeholders is surprisingly small.[6] They argue that shareholders are exposed to the highest vulnerability toward expropriation by management because their "investments are largely sunk, and further investment in the firm is generally not needed from them." (p. 751) On p. 738 they relate the degree with which something has been sunk to its specificity. In more general terms, of course, this is nothing other than a reasoning based on the availability of the alternatives of exit and voice. Hence, one would have expected a check of a larger group of stakeholders, in particular in a general survey with some concentration on *comparative* corporate governance. A full-fledged corporate governance analysis must go beyond a mere investigation of the core agency conflict. In particular, a comparative analysis does not allow for the omission of parties and mechanisms that are of little importance in one system; instead, this must be marked as an empty category which may have significance and content in other systems. A recent, more abstract definition which is consistent with the thoughts developed above is provided by Schmidt (1997: 2)[7]:

> Corporate governance is the totality of the institutional and organizational mechanisms, and the corresponding decision-making, intervention and control rights, which serve to resolve conflicts of interest between the various groups which have a stake in a firm and which, either in isolation or in their interaction, determine how important decisions are taken in a firm, and ultimately also determine which decisions are taken.[8]

Having formulated such an ambitious agenda for research, it must be admitted that the aim of this report and its parallel articles is comparatively modest: they intend to provide a pool of relevant facts in view of the core agency relation

---

[5] Jensen (1986).

[6] The definition determines the group of relevant stakeholders which, in turn, influences the adequacy of performance measures; for a treatment of the latter relationship, cf. de Jong (1997: 10-3). For example, the dominance of shareholder return as a measure for company performance is partly a result of the dominance of the view that stresses the importance of the core agency relation in corporate governance analysis.

[7] In conformity with the general line of Hart (1995).

[8] Schmidt (1997: 2) refers this definition to profit-oriented, large firms in the legal form of corporations.

between shareholders and managers. The reasoning above will serve to put the following in perspective.

I. The Corporate Sector in Germany

Current U.S.-molded corporate governance discussion concentrates on the problem of how to make the management act in the owners' interest.[9] By definition, this problem only occurs if ownership and control are separated. Consequently, limited companies, and in particular the public limited company (*Aktiengesellschaft, AG*), stand at the center of the analyses, since in other legal forms of business organization, ownership and control are more closely aligned. Because *AG*s are mainly large companies,[10] it might be tempting to overestimate the problem.[11] In 1996, the approximately 3,900 *AG*s contributed about 20% to the total sales of all enterprises.[12,13] Table 1 depicts the weight of the different legal forms of business organization as of 1994.[14]

Considering their economic weight, *AG, GmbH,* and *KG* stand at the center of interest. In addition, they are also the most relevant legal forms of business organization from a corporate governance perspective that concentrates on the separation of ownership and control, which should be of particular importance to larger entities. Note in Table 2 that large *GmbH*s and *KG*s are of similar economic significance.

To narrow the focus even further, the problem of separation of ownership and control is more pronounced in exchange-listed *AG*s, which constituted barely

---

[9] For a broader approach comprising corporate, contractual, and work governance, see recently Gelauff/den Broeder (1997).

[10] In 1994, there were 66 *AG*s among the 100 largest companies (as measured by value added); Monopolkommission (1996: 256).

[11] Although one has to consider that many private limited companies (*Gesellschaft mit beschränkter Haftung, GmbH*) and, to a lesser extent, partnerships, are part of an *AG*-dominated group of companies (*Konzern*); see below Secs. A.II.1. and B.II.2.

[12] Deutsche Bundesbank (1997: 28).

[13] At the end of 1997, 4,548 *AG*s with a statutory capital of DM 221.575 billion were registered; Deutsche Bundesbank (1998: 46). Hansen (1997: 205) estimates for the end of 1996 777,000 *GmbH*s with a statutory capital of DM 302.4 billion. One must rely on estimates because the Federal Statistical Office (*Statistisches Bundesamt*) has suspended its regular counting of limited companies.

[14] The remarkable increase in the number of *AG*s from 1992 to 1997 can, with some justification, at least partially be attributed to the Law on Small Public Companies and Deregulation of Equity Legislation (*Gesetz für kleine Aktiengesellschaften und zur Deregulierung des Aktienrechts*) which became effective on August 10, 1994. This law lessens the regulatory burden and co-determination requirements (cf. Sec C.I.1. below) of small *AG*s and thus increases their attractiveness as compared to *GmbH*s. Maybe this is the turning point that will revert the decline of the *AG* relative to the *GmbH* during the last decades.

Table 1: Number of Firms by Legal Form of Business Organization and Shares in Taxable Deliveries and Performances, 1994

Legal Form of Business Organization	Number of Firms	Percent of Firms	Taxable Deliveries and Performances in Mil. DM	Percent of Taxable Deliveries and Performances
Aktiengesellschaft (AG)	2,253	0.1	1,283,247	19.6
Gesellschaft mit beschränkter Haftung (GmbH)	400,723	14.4	2,114,546	32.3
Kommanditgesellschaft (KG)	88,581	3.2	1,445,507	22.1
Offene Handelsgesell-schaft (OHG)	230,547	8.3	401,584	6.1
Sole Proprietor	2,018,431	72.4	977,639	14.9
Other	46,539	1.7	322,220	5.0
Total	2,787,074	100	6,544,744	100

Note: Included are taxpaying firms with annual sales above DM 25,000; *OHG* including *Gesellschaften des bürgerlichen Rechts* etc.; KG including *GmbH & Co. KG*; *AG* including *Bergrechtliche Gewerkschaften*.

Source: Statistisches Bundesamt (1997: 37).

Table 2: Distribution of Taxable Deliveries and Performances by Firm Size and Legal Form of Business Organization, 1994

	AG*			GmbH			KG			All Legal Tax-payers
Taxable Deliveries and Per-formances (in mil. DM)	Number	Share in Taxable Deliveries and Per-formances of All AGs	Share in Total Taxable Deliver-ies and Per-form-ances	Number	Share in Taxable Deliver-ies and Per-form-ances of All GmbHs	Share in Total Taxable Deliver-ies and Per-form-ances	Number	Share in Taxable Deliveries and Per-formances of All KGs	Share in Total Taxable De-liveries and Perform-ances	Share in Total Taxable De-liveries and Perform-ances
<5	952	0.1%	0%	344,777	19.0%	6.1%	56,157	5.8%	1.3%	21.2%
5-10	142	0.1%	0%	28,144	9.3%	3.0%	11,306	5.6%	1.2%	6.3%
10-25	217	0.3%	0.1%	17,370	12.5%	4.0%	11,093	12.1%	2.7%	8.9%
25-50	165	0.5%	0.1%	5,566	9.1%	2.9%	4,904	11.9%	2.6%	6.9%
50-100	187	1.0%	0.2%	2,575	8.4%	2.7%	2,730	13.1%	2.9%	6.9%
>100	590	98.0%	19.2%	2,291	41.8%	13.5%	2,391	51.5%	11.4%	49.9%
Total	2,253	100%	19.6%	400,723	100%	32.3%	88,581	100%	22.1%	100%

Note: * Including *KGaA* and *Bergrechtliche Gewerkschaften*.

Source: Statistisches Bundesamt (1997: 45).

one-sixth of all *AG*s with an aggregated market capitalization of DM 1,004 billion at the end of 1996.[15]

These numbers were presented to put the scope of the following analysis into perspective. In particular, Section B mainly deals with (listed) *AG*s, which represent an important but by no means dominant part of the German economy.

II. Institutional Setting

This section is intended to provide a rough outline of, first, the legal structure of the most relevant legal forms of business organization including the provisions concerning groups of companies, and, second, of regulation in the financial sector.

1. Legal Forms of Business Organization

The current structure of the German corporate sector with regard to the legal form is the aggregate result of each individual entrepreneur's decision. Determinants of his decision could be criteria such as formal requirements (e.g., provisions governing internal firm structure, accounting, disclosure, co-determination), taxation, liability, and funding (e.g., access to debt and equity, marketability of stakes in equity) of the different legal forms. Only some issues can be treated or touched upon in this survey.[16]

The description of legal structures starts with the *AG*, which has three mandatory organs: the management board, the supervisory board, and the general meeting. Their competences are explained in Table 3.

The current shareholder value debate highlights an interesting feature of German corporate law which cyclically comes under discussion. The management board conducts the business of the *AG* and is supervised by the supervisory board. There is, however, no clear-cut legal obligation that requires both boards to act solely in the interest of shareholders, the 'owners' of the *AG*, to maximize the equity's market value.[17] Instead, among legal scholars[18] as well as among

---

[15] Deutsche Bundesbank (1997: 28) and Deutsches Aktieninstitut (1997: FB_05-1-b). Due to the recent popularity of the *AG* this share has decreased to one seventh as of the end of 1997.

[16] Cf. Drukarczyk (1996: Ch. 6) and Schmidt et al. (1997: 27-33) with further references.

[17] Leaving aside for the moment the important problem that large shareholders, a common type of owner in Germany, may prefer a goal other than market value maximization.

[18] This survey is not an appropriate place to dwell on this subject. Schmidt/Spindler (1997), coming from an economic and legal background respectively, provide a thorough discussion of market value maximization and German company law; cf. also von Werder (1998). For an economic and historical perspective, see Spremann (1994). For recent statements supporting shareholder orientation and delivering references to opposing statements, cf. Wenger (1996b: 420-33), Mülbert (1997), and Schilling (1997).

Table 3: Distribution of Competences at the *AG*

Management Board	Supervisory Board	General Meeting

• leads the company under own responsibility (§ 76 AktG).
• represents the company in and out of court (§ 78 AktG).
• members of the management board are appointed from the supervisory board for a maximum period of 5 years (§ 84 (1) AktG). A repeated appointment is allowed.
• the management board has to report on (§ 90 AktG):
  - intended business strategies;
  - profitability of the company;
  - economic development and situation of the company;
  - business transactions with a major impact;
  - other important cases.
• the management board has specific duties in the case of losses which exceed half of the equity, of overindebtedness (*Überschuldung*), and of inability to pay (*Zahlungsunfähigkeit*) (§ 92 AktG).
• the members of the management board have to respect the due diligence of a businessman (§ 93 (1) AktG).
• in the case of neglecting its duties, the management board is liable for compensation of the damage (§ 93 (2) AktG).
	• in general, the supervisory board consists of representatives of the shareholders and the labor side[*].
	• it includes a minimum of 3 and a maximum of 21 members (§ 95 AktG).
	• the representatives of the shareholders are elected for a maximum period of approximately 5 years (§ 102 (1)AktG). A repeated election is allowed.
	• the functions of the supervisory board consist of the appointment of the management board and its control, i.e., its withdrawal (§ 111 AktG).
	• the supervisory board is not allowed to fulfill the administrative role of the management. The statutes of the company or the supervisory board can mandate that special transactions require its approval (§ 111 (4) AktG).
	• if the supervisory board denies the approval, the management board can require the approval of the shareholder meeting where at least a qualifying majority of 75% is needed (§ 111 (4) AktG).
	• the due diligence of § 93 AktG is also required for the members of the supervisory boards (§ 116 AktG).
	• the supervisory board elects a chairman and a minimum of one vice-chairman (§ 107 (1) AktG). The supervisory board has the right to form subcommittees, to prepare negotiations, and to control the implementation of decisions (§ 107 (3) AktG).
	• the number of seats of one person on supervisory boards is limited to 10, with the additional allowance of 5 mandates in the case of groups of companies (§ 100 (2) AktG).
		• the shareholder meeting decides only if law, the statutes of the company, or the management board require it.
		• it decides especially about (§ 119 (1) AktG):
		  - the appointment of members of the supervisory board representing the shareholders;
		  - the appropriation of profit;
		  - the exoneration of the members of the management and supervisory board;
		  - the appointment of the certified accountant;
		  - changes of the statutes of the company;
		  - measures concerning the increase and decrease of the equity;
		  - the appointment of auditors in order to check events during the foundation of the company or during its management;
		  - the closing-down of the corporation.
		• the decisions at the shareholder meeting are determined with a simple majority; law or the statutes of the company can require larger majorities or additional requirements (§ 133 AktG).
		• the votes are determined by the nominal capital of the presented shares (§ 134 AktG).

Note: [*] Cf. Sec. C.I.1. for additional information on provisions with respect to supervisory board co-determination.

Source: Taken from Schmidt et al. (1997: 75) with slight revisions.

board members[19], there is no small support for a stakeholder approach, i.e., one in which boards are obliged to consider the interests of a variety of constituencies, or, put differently, to ascribe an interest to the corporation itself (*Unternehmensinteresse*). Without going into further detail, this issue is of importance from a corporate governance perspective because the boards' scope increases with the number of constituencies to which the boards are responsible.[20] In short, current shareholder value discussion has increased shareholder orientation in general,[21] but the position of the stakeholder approach is still strong.

The *GmbH* shares many features with the *AG*, but there are also decisive differences. A basic difference is that the relevant act (*GmbHG*) provides a great deal of modifiable law. Two kinds of *GmbH*s can be distinguished. (1) The *GmbH* not subject to supervisory board co-determination has two mandatory actors, at least one executive and the entirety of shareholders[22]. Separation of ownership and control is feasible since an executive need not hold a stake in the company. The position of the shareholders is stronger because, roughly speaking, their power exceeds the unified competences of the general meeting and the supervisory board at the *AG*, consequently making the position of the executive(s) weaker than at the *AG*. The shareholders may establish a supervisory board and decide on its rights. (2) The *GmbH* subject to supervisory board co-determination, i.e., a *GmbH* with more than 500 employees, has a mandatory supervisory board with employees represented in accordance with the relevant co-determination régime.[23] The employees gain their power at the expense of the shareholders, who, nevertheless, still hold a position stronger than at the *AG*.[24]

Large *GmbH*s are an important factor in the corporate sector: 17 of 47 (36%)[25] of the companies subject to full-parity co-determination (more than 1,000 employees) and 329 of 740 (44%)[26] of the companies subject to quasi-parity co-determination (more than 2,000 employees) chose the legal form of the *GmbH*.

---

[19] Cf. Secs. B.I.5. (result of a questionnaire: German management boards feel more obliged to employees than to shareholders) and B.IV. (the attitude Thyssen's CEO revealed with respect to the share price during the takeover attempt by Krupp).

[20] Cf. recently Mülbert (1997: 170).

[21] In the statements of corporate managers (cf. the questionnaires of DAX companies in Börsen-Zeitung (1996) and Zeitschrift für das gesamte Kreditwesen (1996)), and scholars (cf. Mülbert (1997)). Also, mutual funds have recently started to demand stronger shareholder orientation; cf., for instance, the statements by representatives of Union Investment, one of the largest investment companies; Börsen-Zeitung (1996b) and Handelsblatt (1997b).

[22] This notion hints at the fact that a decision of the shareholders does not require a shareholder meeting; Kübler (1994: 330).

[23] Cf. Sec. C.I.1. for additional information.

[24] Bea/Scheurer (1995: 1291-3) provide more details on the differing effects of one-third and quasi-parity co-determination on the control situation at the *GmbH*.

[25] Data as of 1992; Kronenberg/Volkmann/Wendeling-Schröder (1994: 25).

[26] Data most probably as of 1995 or 1996; Tegtmeier (1996: 28).

Moreover, there are 4,866 *GmbH*s (1.2% of all *GmbH*s liable to pay turnover tax) whose annual taxable sales exceed DM 50 million.[27] At these *GmbH*s, the agency problems generated by the separation of ownership and control may begin to become similar to those at the *AG*. Moreover, since stakes in *GmbH*s show a low degree of marketability, the control forces market for corporate control and share market, which provides a benchmark for evaluating the management's quality, are almost completely powerless.[28] On the other hand, the control situation is considerably influenced by the fact that *GmbH*s are the most common legal form in groups of companies.[29] In sum, we know little about the corporate governance at large *GmbH*s; however, there is a high probability that they would be an interesting subject for corporate governance research.

The *KG* represents the bridge between unlimited- and limited-liability companies because there are two classes of partners: at least one full liable general partner, *Komplementär*, and limited partners, *Kommanditisten*, whose liability is confined to their contribution. No boards are required by law, even taking into account supervisory board co-determination.[30] Since only partners are allowed to be in charge of business, the problem of the separation of ownership and control is not particularly pronounced in the ordinary *KG*. This statement may not hold for widely held *KG*s, *Publikums-KG*s, with more than 1,000 limited partners, but since they are often established for tax-saving purposes[31] this type is of little interest for a corporate governance analysis. However, there are many *KG*s with large sales[32] which might be of some interest from a corporate governance perspective, but only little evidence is available.

Konzerne (groups of companies) are a very important element of the German corporate sector.[33] The relevant legal provisions, which are closely related to takeover regulation, are quite complex; therefore, this survey can deliver a rough outline only[34] which is, moreover, confined to the provisions of the *Aktiengesetz* whose conditions apply if the dominated company is an *AG* or *KGaA*.[35] The general characteristic of a *Konzern* is that at least one legally independent

---

[27] As of 1994; Statistisches Bundesamt (1997: 45) and see Table 2.

[28] Bea/Thissen (1997: 788).

[29] Cf. below in this section.

[30] With the exception of the rare forms of *GmbH & Co. KG* and *AG & Co. KG*; Kübler (1994: 557-9).

[31] Kübler (1994: 133).

[32] As of 1994, the annual taxable sales exceed DM 50 million at 5,121 *KG*s, i.e., 5.8% of all *KG*s liable to pay turnover tax; Statistisches Bundesamt (1997: 45) and see Table 2.

[33] Nevertheless, their scientific coverage by economic scholars is weak.

[34] For a more detailed, corporate governance-related introduction, cf. Schmidt et al. (1997: 77-95). Theisen (1991: 65-114), delivers an interdisciplinary (law and economics) introduction.

[35] Cf. Theisen (1991: 96-101) and Kübler (1994: 510-9) for *GmbH*- and partnership-*Konzerne*.

company is under centralized control exerted by the parent company.[36] The law distinguishes between three *Konzern* categories: (1) integration, where the dominating company holds 100% of the integrated dependent company's shares; (2) contractual groups of companies (*Vertragskonzern*), where dominating and dependent companies enter into a contract of domination (*Beherrschungsvertrag*), in most cases in connection with a profit transfer agreement (*Gewinnabführungsvertrag*); and (3) groups of companies based on actual dependence (*Faktischer Konzern*), where the relation between dominating and dependent companies is not subject to one of the types of contracts mentioned above. The *faktische Konzern* is the clearly predominating category,[37] and the *GmbH* is the most common legal form of business organization for dependent companies.[38]

Konzerne raise many interesting questions, such as the protection of minority shareholders in dependent companies, including the squeeze-out during the process of integration; the protection of shareholders of a dominating company because its management may be tempted to enlarge its scope by shifting some action to the dependent company, at which intensity of control may be considerable lower; or, to name a final example, the control situation at a company that is both dominating and dependent. In sum, *Konzerne* seem to be a promising subject of corporate governance research and should be dealt with separately from non-*Konzern* linkage.

2. Regulation in the Financial Sector

Turning to regulation in the financial sector, the appropriate starting point is the relevance with respect to corporate governance. To give structure to the discussion, two sets of partially overlapping regulations will be distinguished from one another: regulations applying to corporate governance actors and regulations

---

[36] Law (§ 17 AktG) provides a definition of dependency: a legally independent company is a dependent (with respect to *Konzernierung*) company if another—the dominating company—can exert dominating influence. If a company controls a majority of equity or voting rights at another company, the latter is regarded as being dependent unless it successfully refutes this supposition.

[37] Pellens (1994: 125) (sample: 108 bilateral *Konzern* relationships, 1989) finds the following shares: *Faktischer Konzern* 78.7%, *Vertragskonzern* 21.3% and integration 0%. They are confirmed by Windolf/Beyer (1995: 14) (sample: 623 largest German companies, 1990-1992). Mellewigt (1995: 208-12) (sample: 151 listed *Konzerne* with 6,368 subsidiaries, 1993) provides additional information.

[38] With a share of 82.4% (*AG/KGaA* 4.6%, partnerships 13.0%), Pellens (1994: 124), and 86.3% (*AG/KGaA* 9.1%, other forms 4.6%), Mellewigt (1995: 208), respectively. Binder (1994: 393) (sample: 2,986 companies with an owner whose stake amounted to 25% or more, 1990) discovers that *GmbHs* as dependent companies are connected with a higher equity stake than *AGs* as dependent companies; this may be partially due to the difference in the balance of power among the organs at both legal forms.

applying to corporate governance markets and actions. Again, only the most important issues can be touched upon.

Banks and investment companies[39] are supervised by the *Bundesaufsichtsamt für das Kreditwesen* (German Federal Banking Supervisory Office)[40], and insurance companies by the *Bundesaufsichtsamt für das Versicherungswesen* (German Federal Insurance Supervisory Office)[41]. Of most importance with respect to corporate governance, the regulations restrict—among other things— the admissible equity and debt holder positions that institutions are allowed to take.[42]

Coming to markets and actions, it seems appropriate to distinguish between the share market and the market for corporate control, although they are partially identical. The regulation of stock exchanges and the trading therein is a complex interaction of different authorities situated in a three-level structure consisting of the *Bundesaufsichtsamt für den Wertpapierhandel* (German Federal Authority for Securities Trading)[43] at the federal level, the authorities of the federal states in which an exchange is existent (*Börsenaufsichtsbehörden der Länder*), and the trading supervisory bodies at the exchanges (*Handelsüberwachungsstellen an den Börsen*). The main fields of activity are insider transactions, ad-hoc disclosure, and, generally, to ensure fair trading in accordance with rules and regulations.[44] Relevant regulation as far as the market for corporate control is concerned includes the obligation to almost immediately report considerable changes in the control of voting rights—beginning with a threshold of 5%[45]— and the introduction of the *Übernahmekodex* (takeover code) on a voluntary basis.[46] Both were introduced in 1995, and the latter was amended on January 1, 1998.[47]

---

[39] Investment companies are, by legal definition, banks and, realiter, mainly bank-associated; cf. Sec. B.II.4. below.

[40] As of 1995 its staff amounts to 490; Bundesaufsichtsamt für das Kreditwesen (1996).

[41] As of 1995 its staff amounts to 351; Bundesaufsichtsamt für das Versicherungswesen (1996).

[42] For banks, see Hopt (1996a: 248-50), for investment companies Kümpel (1995: 945-8), and for insurance companies Hohlfeld (1995: cols. 1908-11).

[43] The authority started its business at the beginning of 1995 as a part of the measures taken by the *Wertpapierhandelsgesetz* (Securities Trading Law) of 1994. As of 1996 its staff amounts to 93; Bundesaufsichtsamt für den Wertpapierhandel (1997).

[44] For the distribution of competences, cf. Bundesaufsichtsamt für den Wertpapierhandel (1996: 30-3) and Claussen (1996a: 289-93).

[45] The *Bundesaufsichtsamt für den Wertpapierhandel* is the competent authority; cf. Sec. B.V.3. below for further details.

[46] Cf. Sec. B.IV. below for further details.

[47] The amendments touch the mandatory offer: its trigger, price, and time period within which it must be made; Die Aktiengesellschaft (1997a). The amended code is documented in Die

It is hard to estimate the intensity of regulation and its impact on corporate governance in Germany in absolute terms. But it seems safe to say that the relative intensity of regulation of the relevant German actors has been satisfying international standards for a long time. That comes as no surprise, since this kind of regulation is mainly the result of international coordination. The intensity of control of markets and actions has recently sharply increased (foundation of the *Bundesaufsichtsamt für den Wertpapierhandel*, stricter rules concerning several fields of disclosure, insider trading, trading supervision, and takeovers) and has made at least one large step toward closing the gap to international standards.

B. Owners

I. Control by the Board[48]

This section discusses the data available on the characteristics of boards in order to assess in whose interest the members of the boards are likely to act. The analysis starts with the supervisory board.[49,50]

1. Structure of the Supervisory Board

The law prescribes a minimum number of board members of three and a maximum number of no more than 21, depending on company size and co-determination rules. Recent empirical analyses calculated an average size of 13.25[51], 9.39,[52] and 11.68[53] members respectively. Although only 17.43% of the

---

Aktiengesellschaft (1998). For first analyses, see Hopt (forthcoming) and Kirchner/Ehricke (1998).

[48] Cf. Ch. 4 of this volume on the board. The contributions of Hopt, Theisen, and Semler refer to Germany.

[49] For a recent treatise of the *Aufsichtsrat,* cf. Hopt (1997a).

[50] This analysis intends to present the findings of recent empirical studies. So it only exceptionally falls back on older, partly well-known studies such as Vogel (1980) (sample: 295 *AGs* with 200 to 2,000 employees, questionnaire in 1975/76), Bleicher (1987) (interviews with 779 supervisory board members in 1985/86) and Gerum/Steinmann/Fees (1988) (sample: 484 *AGs* and *GmbHs,* May 1979).

Unless not indicated otherwise, the following analysis is confined to the capital-side members; cf. Sec. C.I.1. for supervisory board co-determination.

[51] Korn/Ferry International (1996: 10). The German subsample of this international questionnaire (Austria, Belgium, Denmark, Finland, France, Greece, Ireland, Italy, the Netherlands, Portugal, Spain, Switzerland, the U.K.) contains 59 management board and 24 supervisory board respondents, time of questionnaire execution unknown.

[52] Leimkühler (1996: 308) (sample: 562 listed *AGs,* 1992).

[53] Pfannschmidt (1993: 83) (sample: 492 German companies, December 31, 1989).

companies exhaust the maximum number of board members,[54] shareholder representatives unanimously share the opinion[55] prevailing among academics[56] that supervisory board size should be reduced. Trade unions successfully opposed this proposal,[57] which had become part of a draft statute but was abandoned in the course of the legislation process.[58] Length of contract of the shareholder representatives may not exceed approximately five years, but as prolongation is feasible, actual tenure is unlimited by law. Company rules to limit tenures are almost absent, a fact that is criticized by practitioners who fear that a long tenure, in combination with the board members' interest in being re-elected—not to mention their age—may diminish their ability to be critical monitors.[59] There are no current figures that describe the propagation of committees on German supervisory boards, but available data indicate that their spread has been rising until recently. In a mid-seventies sample, 42% of the companies had at least one committee,[60] whereas in a mid-eighties sample only one-quarter was not equipped with any committee.[61] In the latter sample, there were on average 1.5 committees, with the staff committee being the most common and the finance committee being regarded as the most important. Interestingly, only 7% of the boards possessed an audit committee, and this committee reached only position five on the importance ranking.[62] Currently, committees other than the staff and board committee still seem rare, but interviewed board members (shareholder representatives) highly recommend their establishment.[63] It remains to be seen whether this is due to an expected gain in efficacy or intended to circum-

---

[54] Leimkühler (1996: 308).

[55] Result of consultations of more than 100 shareholder representatives on German supervisory boards, time of interviews unknown; Bremeier/Mülder/Schilling (1994: 69-70).

[56] For instance, in the discussions at the 61st *Deutscher Juristentag*, in Karlsruhe, September 17-19, 1996.

[57] The *Deutsche Angestellten Gewerkschaft DAG*; Handelsblatt (1996); and the largest trade union, *IG Metall*; Handelsblatt (1997). An *IG Metall* official termed this proposal an "attack on co-determination"; Börsen-Zeitung (1997j).

[58] See Sec. D below.

[59] Bremeier/Mülder/Schilling (1994: 49-50).

[60] Vogel (1980: 186-7). Vogel's data are confirmed by Gerum/Steinmann/Fees (1988: 100), who find at least one committee in 39% of the *AGs*; for further data on committees as of 1979, see Gerum/Steinmann/Fees (1988: 99-105, 116-7).

[61] Bleicher (1987: 25-8).

[62] Another mid-eighties sample showed a propagation of 16.3%; Söllner (1988: 194) (interviewed 64 auditors, approximately 1985-1987).

[63] Bremeier/Mülder/Schilling (1994: 70-3). The audit committee as seen by the CEOs was subject to an inquiry conducted by Coenenberg/Reinhart/Schmitz (1997) (sample: CEOs of the 100 largest German companies, response rate 48%, August 1995).

vent co-determination requirements,[64] a practice which has come under close scrutiny by the courts.[65]

2. Composition of the Supervisory Board

The two most recent data sources provide the following empirical evidence: 43% of supervisory boards include a former member of the management board. The following numbers were compiled for other categories: retired executive of another company (13%), investor/shareholder (61%), commercial banker (70%), former government official (0%), current government official (13%), workplace representative (96%).[66] The background of supervisory board members as of 1993 can be categorized as follows: non-financial companies (27.4%), banks and insurance companies (9.7%), politicians and civil servants (4.3%), other share-holder representatives (9.9%), external union members (13.5%), and other labor representatives (35.2%).[67] 5% of the members are women,[68] and at least one foreigner serves on 30% of the boards.[69,70]

The figures above do not speak against qualified supervisory board members acting in the interest of the shareholders; on the other hand, they also do not allow more positive conclusions to be drawn. A look at the nomination process of new members might provide further insight. Unfortunately, the only recent source providing "hard" data uses ambiguous terms.[71] So all that can be noted is the widespread impression that there is often too close a connection between the two boards, which can negatively affect the intensity of control exerted by the supervisory board. This connection manifests itself in the often strong influence of CEOs and chairmen of the supervisory board on the selection of new super-

---

[64] In the late seventies, employees were represented in only 35% of all committees in accor-dance with co-determination-régime parity; Gerum/Steinmann/Fees (1988: 102).

[65] Hopt (1995: 482) and Mertens (1996: 497-500).

[66] Korn/Ferry International (1996: 12).

[67] Bundesverband deutscher Banken (1995: Table 2) (sample: the 100 largest companies with 89 supervisory boards, mandates as of 1993).

[68] Almost unchanged percentage since 1985/86; Bleicher (1987: 79).

[69] Korn/Ferry International (1996: 14-5).

[70] For further, though older data see Vogel (1980: 120-31), Bleicher (1987: 79), and Gerum/ Steinmann/Fees (1988: 47-55).

[71] Korn/Ferry International (1996: 20, 24) identifies as most relevant sources of influence on the nomination of supervisory board members institutional investors (this term seems to cover all corporate shareholders) (58%), full board (50%), CEO/chairman (CEO of the management board or chairman of the supervisory board or both?) (42%), and nominating committee (38%). Share-holder nomination (71%) is most important for identifying candidates for supervisory board members, followed by internal appointment (54%) and existing contact of a board member (54%).

visory board members,[72] and in the common practice of the retiring CEO moving to the supervisory board and often becoming its chairman.[73]

Personal links are another phenomenon that casts doubt on supervisory board members' willingness to monitor in the shareholders' interest.[74] Compared to the previous fields, the data situation here is more satisfying.[75] One relevant figure is the number of mandates per person.[76] Table 4 depicts recent figures.

Table 4:　　Distribution of Supervisory Board Mandates, 1989/1992

Mandates per Person	1	2	3	4	5	6	7	8	9	10	11	>11	Sum
Number of Persons	5,191	481	156	83	53	26	19	11	3	5	4	5	6,037
	3,707	320	104	43	37	16	12	3	3	2	3	0	4,250
% of Mandates	66.7	12.4	6.0	4.3	3.4	2.0	1.7	1.1	0.3	0.6	0.6	0.8	100
	51.39	8.87	4.33	2.38	2.56	1.33	1.16	0.33	0.37	0.28	0.46	0.0	100

Sources: Pfannschmidt (1993: 86) (upper lines for 1989), and Leimkühler (1996: 309) (lower lines for 1992).

Interestingly, 14%/12.8% of the persons hold 33.3%/48.61% of the mandates. Whether a person with several mandates is able to fulfill his monitoring duty sufficiently can only be judged on a case-by-case basis.[77] But multiple mandates are a potential source of inadequate monitoring both directly (overstress) and indirectly, as multiple mandates are a presupposition for personal links which may serve to entrench a group of persons and companies apart from the shareholders' interest.

[72] Bremeier/Mülder/Schilling (1994: 30-3) and Püschel/von Specht (1997) (members of a personnel consultancy). The mid-seventies sample of Vogel (1980: 201) supports this conventional wisdom only partially: in 31% of his companies the incumbent supervisory board makes a pre-selection of future board members. The numbers for management and supervisory board in cooperation, management board, and controlling shareholder are 7%, 6%, and 56% respectively.

[73] This practice is controversially discussed among interviewed shareholder representatives on supervisory boards; Bremeier/Mülder/Schilling (1994: 37-9).

[74] The analysis of personal links is complicated by the fact that available data do not treat links within a *Konzern* separately. The same complication holds for capital links.

[75] For this reason the results of older studies on this subject, such as Ziegler (1984) (approximately 300 of the largest German firms, data as of 1976), Biehler/Ortmann (1985) (inquiry of 40 managers and supervisory board members of large companies, inquiry executed about 1982), Pappi/Kappelhoff/Melbeck (1987) (Ziegler's sample), and Biehler/Liepmann (1988) (330 largest companies, data as of 1981), are not reported, but the more recent investigations confirm their basic findings.

[76] Current law limits the number to ten mandates and five additional manadates within a group of companies.

[77] See below Sec. B.I.3.

Personal links among companies are common in Germany,[78] and the simultaneous membership in supervisory and management boards is instrumental. The *Monopolkommission* regularly calculates a degree of personal linkage: it is the number of links among the 100 largest companies (by value added) as a percentage of the theoretical maximum of links. In 1994, the degree of linkage amounted to 7.7% (1992: 7.3%).[79] Pfannschmidt (1993) and Leimkühler (1996) both analyze the linkage created by persons via their membership on both boards: 13%[80]/12.69%[81] of the persons in their samples are responsible for all links.[82] The shares of the boards in the three types of links (supervisory board-supervisory board, supervisory board-management board and vice versa, and management board-management board) are 71.2%/27%/1.8%[83] and 68%/26.6%/5.4%[84] respectively.

Personal links are predominantly established by shareholder representatives.[85] Among this group, banks and insurance companies take an outstanding position: they occupy the top four positions on the list of the companies that are connected with the most other companies.[86] This sector, together with the utility sector, shows the highest degree of linkage[87] and accounts for more than one-half of the links established by management board members on supervisory boards.[88] Management board members of the three *Großbanken* (Deutsche Bank, Dresdner Bank, and Commerzbank) are represented on the boards of 21 of the 24 non-financial DAX companies.[89] More than one in four shareholder representatives on a DAX company supervisory board and eleven supervisory board chairmen come from the banking sector.[90] Regression analysis reveals that there are

---

[78] In Pfannschmidt's (1993: 98) sample only 12.8% of the companies are not connected with another company by a personal link.

[79] Monopolkommission (1996: 290).

[80] Pfannschmidt (1993: 91).

[81] Leimkühler (1996: 310).

[82] 7,962 links among 492 companies (Pfannschmidt (1993: 90)), and 6,062 links among 562 companies (Leimkühler (1996: 310)). Note that in both studies a person who holds mandates in companies A and B creates two links.

[83] Pfannschmidt (1993: 91).

[84] Leimkühler (1996: 310).

[85] 92.1%; Pfannschmidt (1993: 91). Leimkühler (1996: 309) finds that of the 1,952 employee representatives, only 79 hold more than one mandate (2:73; 3:6).

[86] Pfannschmidt (1993: 99).

[87] Leimkühler (1996: 310-1).

[88] Monopolkommission (1996: 283).

[89] André (1996: 1838); he analyzes the shareholder representatives on the supervisory boards of the 30 DAX companies as of 1995. These findings are supported by Seger (1997: 183-5) (data as of 1990).

[90] As of the end of 1996; Hansen (1997b). According to its new CEO, Breuer, Deutsche Bank plans to withdraw members of its management board from the positions of chairmen on

significantly more personal links among banks and non-banks and, though less significantly, among insurance companies and non-insurance companies than among other pairs of companies.[91] These figures underline that banks and insurance companies, in particular the *Großbanken* and Allianz, are an integral part of the personal links, in particular among large companies.[92]

Evaluating these facts from a control perspective results in a preliminary estimation. Control incentives for supervisory board members in general and for members of financial institutions in particular remain to be analyzed, but current structures on the shareholders' bench may contain some disincentives. First, personal links seem to serve other purposes: an empirical test cannot reject the hypothesis that board size is independent of the number of company links.[93] Correlation between credit volume and the number of bank representatives on the borrowers' supervisory boards is significantly positive and potential customer-supplier pairs show significantly more personal (and capital) links than other pairs of companies.[94] Another study indicates that the debt ratio is significantly higher if a bank representative chairs the supervisory board; on the other hand, there is no significant relation between bank liabilities to balance sheet total and bank representatives holding the supervisory board chair, and a significant negative relation between bank liabilities to balance sheet total and bankers holding ordinary supervisory board seats.[95] A broken-tie analysis reveals that supervisory boards are used to establish and to maintain intercompany links.[96] Using the supervisory board this way may be value adding, but it can also be a misuse of the board that might reduce intensity of control.[97]

Second, interlocking directorates and direct and indirect reciprocal personal links create interdependencies among their members that might result in an atmos-

---

supervisory boards at other companies. However, his own chairmanship on the supervisory board at the Deutsche Börse AG may be an exception; Börsen-Zeitung (1997n).

[91] Pfannschmidt (1993: 159-68).

[92] A sub-feature of personal linkage are seats on the boards of competing companies either held by a single individual or several individuals meeting regularly at an institution, e.g., a managment board. Examples of the former case can be found at Pfannschmidt (1993: 232-6) and Wardenbach (1996: 63). Since unions are organized by industry, this problem is also of relevance for union members sitting on supervisory boards.

[93] Leimkühler (1996: 312).

[94] Pfannschmidt (1993: 162-5, 173-82).

[95] Seger (1997: 188-90, 217) (sample: 44 large listed industrial *AG*s which are not dependent in a *Konzern*; data for the sources of potential influence are as of 1990, performance (both accounting and stock market data) and financing figures as of 1991 and 1992).

[96] Schreyögg/Papenheim-Tockhorn (1995) (sample: 56 German limited companies, 1969-1988).

[97] The supervisory board as a platform for separate interests is discussed by Schmidt et al. (1997: 238-9).

phere of mutual consideration at the expense of the shareholders.[98] In addition to the already-mentioned figures, there is further evidence of the existence of a closely interwoven group on the side of the shareholder bench: 60% of the shareholder bench supervisory board members of DAX companies are board members of at least one other DAX company.[99] Windolf and Beyer determine a center of personal linkage that is not only established by Allianz and Deutsche Bank but also by Volkswagen, Thyssen, Hochtief, and MAN.[100] Reciprocal and circular forms of personal interlocking, which can be assumed to be more appropriate for entrenchment and are more common among the largest companies, are dominated by hierarchical forms.[101] This may be due to the widespread propagation of *Konzerne* at which the link-type 'management board parent company-supervisory board subsidiary' is preferred by far.[102] In summary, evidence is difficult to interpret, which is at least partially caused by the fact that intra-*Konzern* and other links are not investigated separately. It would be interesting to know the distribution of types of personal links with intra-*Konzern* links exempt.

3. Supervisory Board at Work

The board must be called for a meeting semi-annually and should be called quarterly.[103] Recent data is mixed: according to interviewed shareholder representatives, there are four meetings per annum in most companies,[104] whereas the union *IG Metall* reports that in two-fifths of the companies only two meetings are held.[105,106] The average meeting lasts 3 hours and 45 minutes.[107] The agenda can

---

[98] Members of a personnel consultancy, Püschel/von Specht (1997), share the impression that personal interlocking reduces the supervisory board's intensity of control.

[99] Hansen (1994: R78); André (1996) presents supporting evidence.

[100] Windolf/Beyer (1995: 20); they analyze two samples: 623 largest German companies and 520 largest companies in the U.K., 1990-1992.

[101] Beyer (1996: 90-1, 97) using network analysis tools (sample: about 700 West German companies, 1992). Beyer's result may be biased towards hierarchical forms since he excludes the very important link-type 'supervisory board-supervisory board' from his sample.

[102] Mellewigt (1995: 218).

[103] The recent amendment of the *AktG* by the *KonTraG* (*Gesetz zur Kontrolle und Transparenz im Unternehmensbereich*; see *BGBl. I* 24/1998, 786-94) which became effective April 27, 1998 increased this requirement as regards listed *AGs* (there should be one meeting in the calendar quarter and the board must be called for two meetings semi-annually). This article bases on the legislation as effective before the *KonTraG* and contrasts it with the changes brought about by the *KonTraG*; see in particular Sec. D.

[104] Bremeier/Mülder/Schilling (1994: 68-9).

[105] Handelsblatt (1995); *IG Metall* conducted an inquiry of 123 companies, presumably in 1995.

[106] Bleicher (1987: 41-4) calculates the following frequencies: complete board 3.8 meetings per annum, board committee 3.5, finance committee 3.12, audit committee 3.07.

be a powerful instrument for controlling the board's work. Unfortunately, no recent statistics seem to be available.[108] According to Sarrazin, ordinary member and chairman on several supervisory boards, it is the management board that sets the agenda, prepares the meeting documents, and sends these documents on behalf of the supervisory board chairman to the board members in accordance with the timetable set in the statute or in the board's internal rules of procedure.[109] Thus, the management is in a good position to control the meeting of and the information flow to its monitors. Rare available empirical evidence on the preparatory information of the board members is mixed: in the mid-eighties, 81% of the interviewed persons considered the information to be adequate;[110] the more recent inquiry of the *IG Metall*, however, reports of 92 companies (75% of the sample) at which items on the agenda were treated on the basis of papers presented in the meeting.[111] An illustrative example is the auditor's report. It is the supervisory board's duty to examine and to comment on this report, and the management board must deliver the report immediately after its receipt. Usually, the supervisory board chairman receives the report, and each supervisory board member is entitled to a copy of his own as long as the supervisory board has not reached an opposing decision. But despite the importance of the duty of inspecting this report and the time and effort that is presumably needed for this task, only in a minority of companies is the auditor's report delivered to the ordinary supervisory board members.[112] To summarize, it seems safe to say that no standards for the information provision of the supervisory board by the management have emerged so far.[113]

On a formal basis, the law explicitly prescribes some obligations of the supervisory board. Looking at the implementation, the supervisory board considers the following as its top priority concerns: meeting financial goals, business strategy, improved productivity, and developing non-domestic business. Top priority objectives and duties are responsibilities to shareholders, selecting the CEO, long-term corporate strategy, financial and operational performance, reviewing the CEO's performance, and responsibilities to employees.[114]

Back offices are a means of enhancing the monitoring capability, in particular of persons who are members on several supervisory boards. Again, hard data are

---

[107] Audit committee 3 hours 20 minutes, investment committee 3 hours, finance committee 2 hours 50 minutes; Bleicher (1987: 45-7).

[108] Cf. Gerum/Steinmann/Fees (1988: 106-10) for data as of 1979.

[109] Sarrazin (1995: 128).

[110] Bleicher (1987: 53).

[111] Handelsblatt (1995).

[112] Forster (1995: 3) and Bremeier/Mülder/Schilling (1994: 84-5).

[113] Bremeier/Mülder/Schilling (1994: 75-8).

[114] Korn/Ferry International (1996: 25-7). Cf. Vogel (1980: 158) for mid-seventies evidence.

lacking. Especially bank managers enjoy support of back offices.[115] But back offices are not without drawbacks: they might get in conflict with the strictly personal nature of a board mandate and the duty to observe strict secrecy.[116] A suspected lack of confidentiality would diminish the information flow. And there is the question of who pays the staff. Currently, staff often seem to be paid by the company that employs the board member. From the perspective of the employing company's shareholders, this is only justified if the board membership contributes to the value of the employing company. To be consistent, this structure requires congruent interests of the receiving company's shareholders—in whose interest the board member is intended to act—and the employing company's shareholders. This short paragraph indicates that the back office is a promising subject for future research.

The chairman occupies a central position, due both to his formal competences and to his actual influence. He is by far the best-informed board member[117] since he holds the closest contact with management[118] as well as with his board colleagues, in particular the committees' chairmen. He can influence structure of and information available to the board. Moreover, if there is any contact between auditor and supervisory board at all, it is primarily established by the chairman.[119] Without any doubt, he is the decisive board member.[120] His deputy seems to play no accentuated role, which is most probably caused by the fact that he is an employee representative, at least in companies that come under the *Mitbestimmungsgesetz*.[121]

Number and type of transactions that need the supervisory board's approval are an indicator of its formal power. In the impression of shareholder bench members, the catalog of these transactions has been shrinking during recent years, a trend which they ascribe to co-determination.[122] Correspondingly, chairman and management have gained power.

Another factor determining intensity of control is how much time a board

---

[115] Bremeier/Mülder/Schilling (1994: 111). An example of a professional supervisory board member is Röller, retired CEO of Dresdner Bank, who, as of summer 1997, still performs nine mandates including three chairs. At Dresdner Bank he has a back office of seven persons at his disposal; Mülbert (1997a: 62).

[116] Lutter/Krieger (1995).

[117] Bleicher (1987: 53).

[118] Bleicher (1987: 54-6) and Bremeier/Mülder/Schilling (1994: 78-82).

[119] Söllner (1988: 171-8, 185-7, 215-8).

[120] Unanimous tenor of the shareholder bench members interviewed by Bremeier/Mülder/ Schilling (1994: 57-60). For the chairman in general, cf. Sarrazin (1995).

[121] This evaluation is supported by Bleicher's finding that vice chairmen regard themselves as being worse informed than ordinary members; Bleicher (1987: 53).

[122] Bremeier/Mülder/Schilling (1994: 73-5). Gerum/Steinmann/Fees (1988: 71-84) provide hard data for the situation in the *AG*s as of 1979.

member spends on duty. Despite all the actual diversity, Bremeier et al. tentatively calculate an expenditure of time for the chairman ranging from 75 to 160 hours and for the ordinary member of 60 hours per annum.[123,124]

4. Incentives of Supervisory Board Members

The basic theme concerning the supervisory board is in whose interest its members are likely to act, in particular if they protect the shareholders' interest. Their potential ability has been analyzed thus far, and now the focus is on their incentives. Asked for their objectives, the supervisory board members consider themselves to be responsible to the shareholders.[125] 100% of the interviewed board members regard their monitoring of the management as being effective.[126] Remuneration is seen as an appropriate incentive.[127] Terms and actual amounts are to some extent publicly available.[128] Board member remuneration ranges from DM 3,000 to DM 107,300, with an average of DM 34,400 per annum.[129] Board members criticize the low level and the loose connection between remuneration and company performance.[130] The latter is partially supported by recently available empirical evidence: Schmid (1997) finds that supervisory board remuneration is positively related to performance, but also to company size,[131] whereas Knoll/Knoesel/Probst (1997)[132] cannot identify significant explanatory power of company performance for remuneration.[133] Moreover,

[123] Assuming four meetings per annum; Bremeier/Mülder/Schilling (1994: 98-107).

[124] Committees are another point under the heading Supervisory Board at Work; available data has already been presented in Sec. B.I.1. above.

[125] As opposed to the management, see Sec. B.I.5. below; Korn/Ferry International (1996: 26).

[126] Korn/Ferry International (1996: 29).

[127] However, recent research by Gedenk (1998) (using questionnaires returned from 66 supervisory organs and 88 executives of majority-owned industrial companies to test agency theory-related hypotheses) concludes that non-financial job characteristics, in particular the degree of independence on the job, also play a role as incentive mechanisms for management and supervisory board members which should not be neglected.

[128] In the company's charter and annual report; Knoll/Knoesel/Probst (1997: 8). Disclosure obligation is confined to the board in its entirety and does not comprise remuneration of individual members.

[129] Schmid (1997: 74) (sample: 110 of the 120 largest listed *AG*s without banks, insurance companies, and others, 1991). The chairman's remuneration usually exceeds the ordinary members' remuneration by 50-100%; Bremeier/Mülder/Schilling (1994: 113).

[130] Bremeier/Mülder/Schilling (1994: 113).

[131] Moreover, Schmid (1997) finds further determinants.

[132] Their sample consists of 125 companies, analysis period from 1988/89 to 1993.

[133] Cf. Theisen (1987: 170-7, Appendix 1) for further data (sample: the 50 largest industry companies and the five largest banks, 1984-1985).

some board members are not allowed to keep compensation for themselves.[134] Share ownership would be another possibility of enhancing the weak pecuniary incentives to thorough monitoring and to monitoring in the shareholders' interest, but unfortunately data are not available.[135] Turning from a personal to an institutional perspective, it can be added that only about one-half of the mandates of the shareholder bench are held by a person or an institution[136], e.g., a company which actually holds an equity stake in the company under consideration.[137] Consequently, on supervisory boards of companies subject to one-half co-determination, this share presumably drops to almost one quarter. In addition, incentives given by personal and corporate equity ownership should not be treated as identical without closer consideration.

Liability is an alternative control mechanism. The law does provide severe liability rules, but the procedure of implementation it prescribes makes them of little actual significance.[138] Moreover, the supervisory boards provide only little information about their monitoring activities,[139] which means adverse conditions for evaluating the board with respect to, among other things, the liability rules. In addition, the law does not require the supervisory board, even when confined to the shareholder bench, to exclusively represent the shareholders' interests. However, turning away from this legal perspective, there is weak evidence that supervisory board turnover rate is negatively related to performance,[140] the core shareholder interest. Studies that analyze the reverse relation—i.e., supervisory board characteristics as explanatory variables for company performance—do not yet exist for Germany.[141]

---

[134] In particular at banks; Bremeier/Mülder/Schilling (1994: 113-5). This could be interpreted as a payment for, among other things, a back office on the payroll of the board member employing firm. For efficiency reasons, more transparancy is to be recommended.

[135] Members of the management and supervisory boards of companies whose shares are traded at the *Neue Markt*, the new stock exchange segment, have to disclose their holdings of shares in the company under consideration; Buhleier/Helmschrott (1997: 778).

[136] Keeping in mind that de jure supervisory board mandates are personal.

[137] Gerum/Steinmann/Fees (1988: 47-51).

[138] Hopt (1996: 914-5).

[139] Theisen (1987: 155-70) and Theisen/Salzberger (1997), analyzing the reporting duties of the supervisory board in the annual report. Interestingly, some improvements, albeit from a very low standard, can be seen in the reports for 1993 and 1994; presumably, this is a response to the fierce critique boards had to stand in recent years.

[140] Franks/Mayer (1997: 12-3) (the sample of this part of their study covers 75 large listed industrial and commercial companies, 1990-1994) find a weak though not significant relation which disappears in their regression analysis (p. 23). Kaplan (1993: 12-3) cannot find a strong relation (he investigates 42 of the largest companies during the eighties). Moreover, Franks and Mayer analyze the relation between supervisory board characteristics and ownership structure; see Sec. B.II.5. below.

[141] With the exception of studies which investigate banks' supervisory board presence as one of their potential sources of influence: Cable (1985) (sample: 48 of the 100 largest companies as

A widely shared impression is that supervisory board co-determination has reduced the board's intensity of control, at least the plenum's. According to interviewed representatives of the capital side, the participation of labor representatives causes a ritualization of the meeting that precludes an open and potentially controversial exchange of views (among the capital side or between capital side and management),[142] thus fostering the problem of undiscussibility.[143] As a consequence, informal contact gains importance, which weakens the position of the ordinary supervisory board member, strengthens the chairman's position,[144] and presumably enlarges the management's scope.

This section has summarized a great deal of evidence on those supervisory board features that are at the root of the current discomfort with supervisory board effectiveness. These have found their way into the general discussion after some recent spectacular company crises and have become the impetus for current legislative initiatives.[145]

5. Management Board[146]

According to recent data, the management board has an average size of 4.2[147], 7.1[148], 3.4[149] and 4.56[150] members respectively; this increases with company size.[151] Compared to the U.S., management board remuneration in Germany is

of 1970, performance data 1968-1972) finds a significant positive relation between bank representatives on supervisory boards and performance; Nibler's (1995) (sample: 158 of the largest 200 companies including non-*AG*s, 1991) findings are inconclusive for banks in general but differ remarkably for single *Großbanken;* and Wenger/Kaserer (1998: 74-7) (sample: 48 large non-financial companies, 1973-1993) discover a negative relation between ordinary board members coming from banks and performance and a positive one for supervisory board chairmen coming from banks, but neither relation is significant. Seger (1997: 195-9) finds a negative, partially significant effect of supervisory board chairmanships on performance but cannot detect a significant explanatory power of bankers being ordinary supervisory board members.

[142] Bremeier/Mülder/Schilling (1994: 60-1).

[143] Lorsch (1996: 210) identified the same problem for German supervisory boards that he had previously found on U.S. boards.

[144] Bremeier/Mülder/Schilling (1994: 58-61).

[145] Cf. Sec. D.

[146] Again, the survey concentrates on more recent data and falls back on older studies such as Vogel (1980: 87-101), Poensgen/Lukas (1982) (sample covers the years from 1961 to 1975), Bleicher/Paul (1986) (data approximately as of 1982), and Bleicher/Leberl/Paul (1989: 93-110) (sample covers the years from 1982 to 1986) only if necessary.

[147] Pfannschmidt (1993: 80).

[148] Krüger/Buchholz/Altrock (1993: 6) (sample: 31 of the largest 100 companies, data were collected in 1992).

[149] Leimkühler (1996: 308).

[150] Korn/Ferry International (1996: 10).

[151] Krüger/Buchholz/Altrock (1993: 6) and Pfannschmidt (1993: 84-5).

moderate:[152] it varies widely around a mean value of DM 730,000.[153] Compensation is positively related to company performance, but there are further determinants that in some cases are more influential, most notably company size.[154] Stock options for the management board have recently become a subject of intense discussion, though they are currently of only negligible importance.[155] Data describing equity ownership of the management board are not available.

Management board turnover increases with inferior company performance.[156] Te Wildt finds that the probability for a CEO change increases with a weakness in relative company performance (accounting measures) as does the probability that a company outsider will become the new CEO. Contrasting his results with available evidence for the U.S., te Wildt concludes that, contrary to common opinion, the relationship between performance and CEO turnover in Germany is closer than in the U.S.[157] It is of particular interest that ownership structure exerts influence on management compensation as well as on management turnover.[158] In summary, the incentives provided by remuneration and the threat of dismissal seem to work in the right direction but, very confusingly, German management

---

[152] Kaplan (1996: 303).

[153] Schmid (1997: 74).

[154] FitzRoy/Schwalbach (1990) (95 German companies, data from 1969 to 1985 or 1982) find a weak relationship between performance and compensation, whereas size, diversification, and compensation are strongly correlated. Kraft/Niederprüm (1996) (two samples: 325 companies, 1988-1991, and 84-91 companies, 1987-1991) compute a significant relation between compensation and performance, but the influence of company size is much stronger. Schwalbach/Graßhoff (1997) (two samples: 220 companies, 1988-1992, and 88 *AG*s, 1968-1990) also discover a much stronger influence of size on compensation as compared to performance. Schmid (1997) finds a positive influence of both performance and size on compensation.

[155] According to the *Deutsches Aktieninstitut* (inquiry carried out in April 1996 with the 100 companies representing the DAX-100 index, response rate 50%), only 6% of the sample companies have already introduced such plans, and another 16% intend to do. 56.4% of the remaining 39 companies have established other forms of performance-related compensation schemes, most notably dividend- and profit-related or individual forms of variable remuneration; Leven (1997). Korn/Ferry International (1996: 34) report a slightly higher figure for stock options which, nevertheless, is the lowest of all covered geographic areas. For the dissemination of performance-related management compensation at the DAX companies as of the end of 1996, see the inquiry of the Börsen-Zeitung (1996). Kohler (1997: 250-3) delivers some details of stock option plans in German companies. Additionally, Wenger/Kaserer (this volume Ch. 6: Sec. C) investigate in a case-study manner recent stock option plans. A first tentative analysis suggests that incentives provided by these plans are more appropriate at companies with influential private shareholders (p. 21).

[156] Franks/Mayer (1997: 12-3, 22-3) and Kaplan (1996: 306-7), the latter stresses that this relation holds similarly in Germany, Japan, and the U.S., although management board turnover in Germany is lower.

[157] Te Wildt (1996) (sample: almost all *AG*s listed at the official or regulated market segment, 1986-1991).

[158] See Sec. B.II.5. below.

boards feel more obliged to the employees than to the shareholders.[159] Regarding liability, the remarks above on the supervisory board also hold for the management board.

II. Control by Shareholders

1. Ownership Structure: General Analysis[160]

From a control perspective, the ownership structure of domestic *AGs* is a key figure. Choosing the right statistics requires careful consideration, since similar but essentially different ones are available. The most recent figures (Table 5) reveal a long-term trend of increasing shareholdings of domestic institutions.

Table 5:   Ownership Structure of Domestic Shares, 1984, 1990, and 1996

Year	Banks	Insurance Companies	Investment Funds	Non-Financial Companies	Private House-holds Incl. Organizations	Public Sector	Foreigners
1984	7.6%	3.1%	2.7%	36.1%	18.8%	10.2%	21.4%
1990	9.4%	3.2%	3.3%	41.4%	18.3%	6.0%	18.6%
1996	9.5%	5.6%	5.8%	37.3%	15.7%	10.9%	15.3%

Notes: Percentage of nominal value; without shares issued by insurance companies with the exception of minor own holdings of banks.[161]
Sources: Deutsche Bundesbank (1996: 32) and Deutsche Bundesbank (1997c: 32).

Statistics based on total shares in circulation in a country are more easily available, but they also include foreign shares possessed by residents (Table 6).[162]

A founded analysis requires more information, in particular about the size of holdings and the voting structure, but some remarks can be made already. Share

[159] Korn/Ferry International (1996: 26). No other board in any of the covered geographic regions ranks this way. A slightly more recent empirical study by Pellens/Rockholtz/Stienemann (1997) (interviews with management boards of 42 parent companies included in the DAX-100 index, most probably conducted in 1996/97) finds that 50% of the management boards regard the shareholders as being the primary stakeholder group, 45.2% give no ranking.

[160] Cf. Becht (1997) for a general treatment of the problems to measure ownership and control accurately.

[161] Note that more than one-third of domestic shares is not deposited at banks and ownership structures in the two deposit sub-samples differ; Deutsche Bundesbank (1997c: 32).

[162] According to preliminary data for 1996, foreigners' holdings of domestic stocks amounted to DM 227.3 billion (market value), that is 11.7% of the aggregate amount foreigners invested in domestic stocks and residents invested in domestic and foreign stocks. Data for the reverse direction show that residents held DM 326.2 billion (16.8%) in foreign stocks; Deutsche Bundesbank (1997b: 88-9).

Table 6:   Ownership Structure of Shares in Circulation, 1990 and 1996

Year	Banks	Insurance Companies	Investment Funds	Non-Financial Companies	Private Households Incl. Organizations	Public Sector	Foreigners
1990	10.3%	11.2%	4.3%	41.6%	16.9%	3.6%	12.1%
1996	11.2%	12.2%	9.1%	37.6%	15.2%	3.0%	11.7%

Notes: Percentage of market value.
         Preliminary data for 1996.
Source: Original data from Deutsche Bundesbank (1997b: 76-7, 88-9).

ownership of private households is traditionally of little significance in Germany,[163] as are shareholdings by institutional investors other than banks, investment funds, and insurance companies. On the other hand, shareholding of financial and non-financial companies is traditionally strong: note in particular the impressive increase in investment funds shareholdings. Insurance companies' holdings increased strongly from DM 15.9 billion (5.6% of invested funds) in 1980 to DM 209.4 billion (15.7%), with an additional DM 55 billion invested in shares via *Spezialfonds*[164]. However, they are far from exhausting legal restriction on investments in shares.[165] The *Bundesbank* estimates that half of each of the banks' shareholdings totalling DM 165 billion are ascribable to participating interests (with cross-links within the banking sector having a share of approximately one-third) and to share portfolios.[166] Shareholdings of non-financial companies have developed steadily at approximately the current level during the

[163] Even if one takes into account indirect shareholdings via investment funds (*Publikumsfonds*) which amounted to DM 40 billion at the end of 1995 (direct holdings: DM 245.6 billion) with DM 30 billion invested in domestic companies; Deutsche Bundesbank (1997: 36).

[164] Generally speaking, investment companies offer two types of investment funds: *Publikumsfonds* for the ordinary investor and *Spezialfonds* whose number and type of investor is confined to a maximum of ten legal persons by law. It seems plausible that the difference in investor structure influences intensity of control; see Sec. B.II.4. below.

[165] Deutsche Bundesbank (1997: 37-8). Note that figures do not distinguish between foreign and domestic shares. For additional data on the shareholdings of insurance companies, cf. Baums/Fraune (1995: 106).

[166] Deutsche Bundesbank (1997: 39). Again, no distinction is made between domestic and foreign shares. A bank-associated source states that 40% of banks' shareholdings are stakes in non-financial companies; Schröder/Schrader (1997: 4).

For detailed analyses of German banks' equity holdings, cf. Böhm (1992) and Roggenbuck (1992), both stating that during recent years the structure of the holdings has changed: the number of participations has increased but the average size has decreased. In particular, the *Großbanken* have reduced the size of their holdings instead of selling them completely. Haas (1994) analyzes in detail the shareholdings of the ten largest private banks, public credit institutions, and cooperative banks as of December 31, 1990. Cf. also the analysis of Mülbert (this volume Ch. 6).

last years; however, a significant decrease occurred in 1996.[167] A very important feature is that about three-quarters consist of cross-holdings.[168] Thus, to get a better impression of the control situation, it is appropriate to take a closer look at the links among the non-financial companies, within the financial sector, and in general.

2. Linkage

Konzerne are a major issue when looking at the linkage within the corporate sector. Despite their widespread dissemination, *Konzerne* are not subject to official statistics, but recent data of other studies are available. 73.61% (by number) and 96.38% (by statutory capital) of all *AG*s are part of a *Konzern*. In the sub-sample of the *Konzern-AG*s, 34.27% (by number) are only dependent, 27.41% are only controlling, and 38.32% are both dependent and controlling *AG*s.[169] Narrowing the focus to listed *AG*s, the situation is as follows: 96.96% (by number) and 98.83% (by statutory capital) of all listed *AG*s are part of a *Konzern*. Of the listed *Konzern-AG*s, 12.18% (by number) are only dependent, 40.96% are only controlling, and 46.86% are both dependent and controlling *AG*s.[170] Another investigation of exchange-listed *AG*s reveals that 92.3% (334 companies) of the *AG*s are part of a *Konzern*, with 78 companies being a parent company and 256 companies being a subsidiary.[171] These figures are confirmed by Mellewigt.[172] In summary, it seems safe to say that ownership structure in Germany is characterized—in international comparison—by an outstanding incidence of hierarchical linkage within the corporate sector.[173]

The significance of corporate shareholdings is illustrated by the relation of net

[167] Percentage dropped from 41.2% in 1995. However, a similar development could be observed from 1992 (42.9%) to 1993 (38.4%), followed by an immediate recovery in 1994 (41.1%); data in Deutsche Bundesbank (1997b: 80-7).

[168] Deutsche Bundesbank (1997: 38-9).

[169] Görling (1993). His sample includes all *AG*s as of 1992; due to Görling's definitions—he only uses (a relatively high percentage of) shareholding as a criterion—his calculations should be interpreted as the lower boundary of *Konzernierung*. Moreover, he estimates that about 50% of the *GmbH*s are part of a *Konzern*.

[170] Görling (1993); in his study, exchange listed means that shares are officially listed or traded at the regulated market segment.

[171] Pellens (1994: 121). Note that Pellens uses the *Konzern* definition of the *Handelsgesetzbuch* (§ 290; Pellens, p. 18) that is much wider than that of Görling; in particular, Pellens goes beyond mere capital links.

[172] Mellewigt (1995: 140).

[173] Résumé by Windolf/Beyer (1995: 9-12). Using network analysis tools they contrast their samples (Germany and the U.K.) and take into account related evidence from the U.S. and Japan.

market capitalization amounting to only 72.9% of gross market capitalization.[174] A further indicator is the degree of capital linkage among the 100 largest German companies (by value added) that amounted to 11.7% in 1994.[175]

The following figures demonstrate the remarkable role of the financial sector: in 1994, insurer Allianz (20), Dresdner Bank (14), insurer Münchener Rück (12), and Deutsche Bank (11) were the companies that possessed the most equity holdings at other companies among the largest 100.[176] The share portfolios of Allianz and Deutsche Bank[177] encompass 4.87% and 3.43% of gross market capitalization.[178] Wenger identifies a group of four companies within the financial sector—Allianz, Bayerische Hypotheken- und Wechselbank, Dresdner Bank, and Münchener Rückversicherung—which hold, on an aggregated basis, participations in each other ranging from 28% to 42%[179] and are the core in a web of links within the financial and non-financial sectors.[180] This corresponds with the findings of Windolf and Beyer, who uncover Deutsche Bank and Allianz as centers of hierarchical control via capital links.[181]

Finally, it is to be emphasized that personal and capital links should not be treated separately since personal links parallel financial links in Germany.[182]

---

[174] Wenger (1996: 11) (sample consists of all 563 *AG*s whose shares were traded either at the official or regulated market at the end of 1994). Net market capitalization is adjusted for direct and indirect shareholdings that companies included in the sample hold at each other. Due to lax disclosure obligations for shareholdings, the figure should be regarded as the upper limit. These obligations have been sharpened since then; cf. Sec. B.V.3. below.

[175] Monopolkommission (1996: 266). The maximum value of 100% would indicate that all companies are linked with each other. Another indicator is the degree of linkage via joint ventures with 4.6% in 1994; Monopolkommission (1996: 281).

[176] Monopolkommission (1996: 264). For additional data as of 1990, cf. Seger (1997: 180-1).

[177] According to recent statements of leading Deutsche Bank members, the bank feels discontented with its insufficiently diversified portfolio, both by country and by sector, but the current tax régime is regarded as an almost insurmountable obstacle to European-wide active portfolio management; cf. Deutsche Bank Research members Schröder/Schrader (1997: 21), referring to statements of Deutsche Bank directors, and the remark of the new Deutsche Bank CEO Breuer in Börsen-Zeitung (1997k).

[178] Wenger (1996: 18-22).

[179] Wenger (1996: 16-7) with more detailed figures.

[180] Cf. Wenger/Kaserer (this volume Ch. 6: Sec. B.I.) for an impressive illustration.

[181] Windolf/Beyer (1995: 12) ascribe this status also to Daimler-Benz, Mannesmann, Siemens, and Veba from the non-financial corporate sector.

[182] In contrast to the situation in the U.K.; Windolf/Beyer (1995: 18).

3. Ownership Structure: Control Analysis[183]

One decisive feature with regard to control is the size of the stake held by the owners. The larger a stake, the larger the potential intensity of control.[184] From this perspective, the ownership structure of German *AG*s provides excellent preconditions since, in an international context,[185] ownership is concentrated and

Table 7: Largest Directly Held Stake in 402 Officially Listed *AG*s, 1996[186]

Size of Largest Directly Held Stake in % of Total Voting Stock	No. of Cases	Size of Largest Directly Held Stake in % of Total Voting Stock	No. of Cases
0-4.99	5	50-54.99	36
5-9.99	7	55-59.99	14
10-14.99	26	60-64.99	19
15-19.99	15	65-69.99	10
20-24.99	19	70-74.99	16
25-29.99	38	75-79.99	37
30-34.99	11	80-84.99	8
35-39.99	14	85-89.99	22
40-44.99	17	90-94.99	21
45-49.99	16	95-100	51

Note: Basis of the calculation is Bundesaufsichtsamt für den Wertpapierhandel (1996a).
Source: Becht/Böhmer (1997: Table 31).

[183] It must be taken into account that control analysis of ownership structures depends on the extent of disclosed information. This has been a severe difficulty for Germany and has only recently been improving due to the disclosure obligations of the *Wertpapierhandelsgesetz*; cf. Sec. B.V.3. below.

[184] A large shareholder (or voting right holder), however, may be inclined to use his power to realize other goals than market value maximization; Shleifer/Vishny (1997: 753-5, 758-61).

[185] However, comparisons have to cope with the difficulty that concentration statistics are affected by the disclosure régime (degree of concentration as publicly known can be expected to be negatively correlated with required disclosure of ownership data); Becht (1997a: 4-7).

[186] To put the German situation in an international perspective, the figures in Dietl (1998: 124) for Germany (550 listed *AG*s and *KGaA*s, as of 1994), Japan (all 1,321 stock corporations listed in the first section of Tokyo, Osaka, and Nagoya stock exchanges, as of 1995), and the U.S. (all U.S. corporations included in the S&P 500, S&P MidCap 400, and S&P SmallCap 600, as of 1994) are reproduced. Dietl distinguishes five size brackets with respect to the percentage of voting rights controlled by the largest shareholder:

0%- 9.99%	3.2% (G)	61.1% (J)	66.0% (U.S.)
10%-24.99%	6.9% (G)	21.3% (J)	17.4% (U.S.)
25%-49.99%	16.7% (G)	12.9% (J)	13.0% (U.S.)
50%-74.99%	31.9% (G)	4.7% (J)	2.1% (U.S.)
75%-100%	41.3% (G)	— (J)	1.5% (U.S.)

large stakes are widespread:[187] as of 1990, in 85% of all *AG*s the major share-holder held at least 25%, in France and the U.K. the figures were 79% and 16% respectively.[188] Ownership is concentrated in Germany, and it is even more concentrated at smaller companies (Table 7).[189]

Moreover, Becht/Böhmer (1997) found out that the largest stake with a medium size of 55.8% is by far the most important factor contributing to concentration; the second largest stakes and others of decreasing size add comparatively less to concentration.[190] In addition, note that stakes are clustered at the legally important thresholds of 25% (blocking minority), 50% (simple majority), and 75% (supermajority).[191]

In relation to a high degree of concentration, the share of dispersed owner-ship[192] is small (Table 8).

Table 8:   Dispersed Ownership, 1994

Share of Dispersed Ownership in %	0 -10	>10 -20	>20 -30	>30 -40	>40 -50	>50 -60	>60 -70	>70 -80	>80 -90	>90	n.a.
Percentage	30.8%	12.7%	20.3%	11.1%	9.7%	2.2%	3.4%	3.9%	0.7%	2.5%	2.7%

Note: Share of dispersed ownership in voting rights and in common stock respectively at 558 *AG*s traded at the official or regulated market as of September 30, 1994. Percentage refers to the number of *AG*s.
Source: Kopp (1996: 139).

Another important feature is, of course, the identity of the owner. Here, a distinction must be made between first- and multi-stage analyses, because the direct owner must not be the ultimate owner as the example of corporate share-holdings shows. The analysis here starts with immediate ownership (first stage). Tables 9 and 10 contain the most recent figures.

Windolf and Beyer provide the most encompassing figures on stake sizes and holders (Table 11). Again, as in the tables above, some characteristics are

[187] Windolf/Beyer (1995: 9-10). The cumulated stakes of the five largest shareholders add up to an average of 41.5% in Germany (1990), 25.4% in the U.S. (1980), 33.1% in Japan (1984), 86.9% in Italy (1993), and 20.9% in the U.K. (1970); OECD (1995: 100).

[188] Franks/Mayer (1995: 176).

[189] Nibler (1995: 5).

[190] The medium size of the three (five) largest stakes is 68.6% (70.7%); Becht/Böhmer (1997: Table 31) (sample: 402 officially listed companies that reported to the *Bundesaufsichtsamt für den Wertpapierhandel* by 1996).

[191] Becht/Böhmer (1997: 36).

[192] Dispersed ownership raises the questions of rational passivity and proxy voting; see Sec. B.II.4. below.

Table 9:   Identity and Stakes of the Largest Shareholder, 1990/91

Largest Shareholder	Widely Spread	Stake of the Largest Shareholder in %					Total
		1<x<10	10<x<25	25<x<50	50<x<75	x>75	
Non-Financial *AG*s	0	0	2	11	26	51	90
Other Legal Forms	0	0	1	12	10	31	54
Banks	0	0	4	12	8	12	36
Insurance Companies	0	1	5	7	6	5	24
Other Inst. Investors	0	1	0	9	11	5	26
Public Sector	0	0	3	4	9	5	21
Families	0	0	3	11	34	25	73
Foreigners	0	1	5	3	12	30	51
Widely Spread	24	0	0	0	0	0	24
Total	24	3	23	69	116	164	399

Note: Sample consists of 399 *AG*s traded at the official market.
Source: Drukarczyk (1993: 437), taken from Schmidt et al. (1997: 69).

Table 10: Stakes of Some Categories of Owners, 1990

Type of Owner	Proportion of Disclosed Stakes in %						Unknown
	0-5	5-15	15-25	25-50	50-75	75-100	
Trusts, Institutional Investors	3.7%	22.2%	18.5%	35.2%	16.7%	3.7%	0%
Banks	2.6%	46.2%	7.7%	38.5%	2.6%	0%	2.6%
Family Groups	6.9%	8.6%	12.1%	19.0%	32.8%	15.5%	5.2%
Other German Companies	2.5%	22.5%	7.5%	21.3%	25%	21.3%	0%

Note: 171 German industrial and commercial quoted companies.
Source: Franks/Mayer (1995: 178).[193]

striking, especially in an international context: the concentration of ownership, with 51% of all stakes constituting a majority in equity (7.3% in the parallel British sample); majority stakes held by non-financial companies and by individuals, families, and family foundations, but hardly ever by the financial sector;[194] and families as major shareholders focused at smaller companies, whereas banks, the state, and foreign companies as major shareholders are most prominent at larger companies.[195]

[193] They conduct a comparison with a sample of French companies.

[194] Windolf/Beyer (1995: 9).

[195] Franks/Mayer (1997: 8-9), comparing three different samples of quoted industrial and commercial companies.

Table 11: Stake Sizes and Holders at the Largest 500 Companies, 1992

Type of Owner	Degree of Concentration of Participation in %						All Stakes in %
	<4.9	5-9.9	10-24.9	25-49.9	50-74.9	>75	
Individuals, Families, Family Foundations	19.2%	17.2%	12.3%	18.4%	22.6%	21.1%	18.9%
Domestic Non-Financial Companies	19.2%	25.0%	30.1%	21.1%	49.2%	46.3%	36.1%
Foreign Non-Financial Companies	6.4%	6.3%	2.7%	5.3%	9.4%	21.4%	11.7%
Banks	20.5%	20.3%	23.3%	18.4%	2.8%	0.6%	10.8%
Insurance Companies	16.7%	26.5%	12.3%	19.3%	3.8%	4.2%	10.6%
Property Management Companies	2.5%	3.1%	8.2%	3.5%	0.9%	0.6%	2.8%
State	15.4%	1.6%	11.0%	14.0%	11.3%	5.8%	9.1%
Total	78	64	146	114	106	313	821
Total in %	9.5%	7.8%	17.8%	13.9%	12.9%	38.1%	100%

Note: 821 Stakeholders were identified.
Source: Windolf/Beyer (1995: 8).[196]

These results are mainly confirmed by the recent analysis of Becht and Böhmer. They find three important groups of stakeholders: industry and trade with a median stake size of about 70%, designated holding companies (about 25%), and individuals and family pools (about 20%).[197] From this perspective the financial sector is not a prominent stakeholder. However, many stakeholders hold only a single block, while the eleven largest multi-stakeholders account for 111 stakes.[198] Taking a closer look at this group, one finds that the top-six group exclusively consists of financial institutes.[199] However, focusing on the financial sector, as is usual in the current German corporate governance debate, has probably resulted in another sector escaping the public attention it deserves: the utility and financial sectors show the highest degrees of personal linkage.[200] Moreover, in the analysis of Becht and Böhmer,[201] among the 20 (23) companies with four or more directly held stakes (voting blocks), there are 10 (10) banks, 4

[196] They conduct a comparison with a sample of British companies.

[197] Becht/Böhmer (1997: 37 and Figure 9).

[198] There are 890 blocks in the analysis of Becht/Böhmer (1997: Table 33), of which 608 are held by persons or entitities holding only a single block (2 blocks/45 holders; 3/15; 4/9).

[199] Deutsche Bank (23 stakes), Allianz (19), Münchener Rück (12), Dresdner Bank (11), Bayerische Vereinsbank (9), and Commerzbank (8). The first non-financial stakeholder, Bayernwerk (7), follows in position 7; Becht/Böhmer (1997: Table 34).

[200] Leimkühler (1996: 310-1) and Sec. B.I.2. above.

[201] Becht/Böhmer (1997: Table 34).

(5) insurance companies, 3 (2) utilities, and 3 (6) other companies.[202] So it might be a worthwhile effort to separate the utility sector from the large 'non-financial sector' category and to analyze it separately. As to the concentrated ownership in Germany, the data provided by Becht and Böhmer enable the formulation of the more differentiated conclusion that there seems to be a significant difference between stakeholders owning only a single block or two blocks and those few stakeholders who own a multitude of blocks.[203]

Turning to multi-stage analysis, the vagueness of the notion "ultimate control" must first of all be considered. Typically, this kind of study tries to identify the ultimately controlling owner if there is a chain of owners, which is the usual situation with legal entities as owners. The search ends at the point of ultimate control according to definition, but a wide range of definitions is applicable. Consequently, comparing studies of this type must be done with great care.

Unfortunately, very recent studies are not available, but the studies at hand cover long periods of time and thus reveal long-term trends.[204] Bayhurst, Fey, and Schreyögg[205] replicate for 1986 a two-stage study that previously had been conducted for 1972[206] and 1979[207] data.[208] See Table 12 for their results for the first stage.

On the second stage (Table 13), only two classes are distinguished: owner control and manager control.[209]

A more detailed analysis reveals, among other things, that the share of manager-controlled companies increases with company size; that the previous trend towards manager control has stopped with the exception of the largest

---

[202] Of course, to become more than a tentative hint, the figures would have to consider sizes of stakes and economic significance of the companies the stakes are held in.

[203] However, a caveat seems approriate: there are still large loopholes in existence even after the disclosure requirements of the *Wertpapierhandelsgesetz* (cf. Sec. B.V.3.) have become effective.

[204] For more recent studies in this field, see Franks/Mayer (1997: 13-6), who investigate the hierarchy level at which several owner types hold ultimate control. And Monopolkommision (1996: 274), which takes into account at least some indirect holdings when it investigates the ownership structure of the 100 largest companies (by value added).

[205] Bayhurst/Fey/Schreyögg (1994).

[206] Schreyögg/Steinmann (1981).

[207] Steinmann/Schreyögg/Dütthorn (1983).

[208] The samples include the 230 largest industrial companies, the 20 largest service companies, the 50 largest trade companies, the 25 largest banks, and the 25 largest insurance companies in each year.

[209] The latter category comprises all companies of the categories I and II if they are ultimately controlled by a widely held company, a cooperative association, or a state-owned company, all companies of category III if the majority of the minority stakes is ultimately manager-controlled, and all companies of category IV; Bayhurst/Fey/Schreyögg (1994: 11-2).

Table 12: Control Situation (First Stage) at 350 Large Companies, 1972, 1979, and 1986

Control Category	Percentage		
	1972	1979	1986
Sole Ownership[a] (I)	52%	50%	51%
Control by One Majority Owner[b] (II)	20%	16%	15%
Control by Several Minority Owners[c] (III)	15%	19%	21%
Widely Dispersed Ownership[d] (IV)	13%	15%	12%

Notes: [a] $x \geq 75\%$; x: stake in equity.
[b] $50\% < x < 75\%$, or $25\% < x < 50\%$ and rest totally dispersed.
[c] precondition: not too large a number of minorities; $\Sigma x_i > 50\%$, or $25\% < \Sigma x_i \leq 50\%$ and rest totally dispersed.
[d] each $x_i \leq 1\%$, or $\Sigma x_i \leq 25\%$ and rest totally dispersed, or $\Sigma x_i > 25\%$ and precondition of category III is not met.
Source: Bayhurst/Fey/Schreyögg (1994: 7, 10).

Table 13: Control Situation (Second Stage) at 350 Large Companies, 1972, 1979, and 1986

Control Category	Percentage		
	1972	1979	1986
Owner Control	44%	38%	39%
Manager Control	56%	62%	61%

Source: Bayhurst/Fey/Schreyögg (1994: 12).

companies; and that manager control is particularly pronounced in the financial sector (banks: 100%; insurance companies: 84%),[210] an interesting fact when seen in connection with their central role in German corporate governance.

The results of a similarly constructed study by Iber are presented in the Tables 14 and 15.[211] To highlight some interpretations of the figures, large stakes are, not surprisingly, more common at smaller companies.[212] In the long run, families and their variations have lost significance as large stakeholders, whereas non-financial companies, banks, and foreigners have gained. The trend toward concentration has not continued in the last period.

[210] Bayhurst/Fey/Schreyögg (1994: 19-27).

[211] Iber (1985); his samples comprise all *AG*s which were traded at the official or regulated market and whose statutory capital exceeded DM 10 million, DM 6 million, and DM 4.75 million in 1983, 1973, and 1963 respectively.

[212] Consider the differences in the percentage figures of companies and of market value; Iber (1985: 1111).

Table 14: Large Stakes at Listed *AG*s, 1963, 1973, and 1983

	Percentage of Companies			Percentage of Market Value		
	1963	1973	1983	1963	1973	1983
Stake of the Largest Shareholder						
x≥75%	22.1%	32.3%	38.9%	13.1%	24.3%	17.9%
75%>x≥50%	33.6%	31.1%	26.6%	22.7%	19.3%	16.9%
50%>x≥25%	29.1%	29.3%	22.9%	24.7%	28.5%	32.2%
25%>x≥1%	3.2%	2.3%	5.0%	11.2%	9.2%	16.5%
x<1%	12.0%	5.0%	6.6%	28.3%	18.7%	16.6%
Aggregate Stake of All Shareholders with a Stake of at Least 1%						
x≥75%	36.3%	56.3%	58.8%	18.9%	42.4%	39.0%
75%>x≥50%	35.7%	26.1%	22.6%	30.3%	19.4%	18.5%
50%>x≥25%	14.1%	10.9%	9.3%	15.8%	12.1%	12.8%
x<25%	13.9%	6.7%	9.3%	35.0%	26.1%	29.7%
Aggregate Stake of All Shareholders with a Stake of at Least 25%						
x≥75%	33.9%	50.1%	54.2%	17.0%	33.0%	26.4%
75%>x≥50%	34.7%	29.6%	22.6%	26.3%	27.1%	26.8%
50%>x≥25%	16.2%	12.9%	11.6%	17.2%	12.0%	13.7%
No Stake	15.2%	7.3%	11.6%	39.5%	27.9%	33.1%

Source: Iber (1985: 1111, 1114).

Table 15: Identity of Majority Owners (Second Stage), 1963, 1973, and 1983

Shareholder Group	Percentage of Companies			Percentage of Market Value		
	1963	1973	1983	1963	1973	1983
Individuals, Families, Family Foundations	26.7%	23.8%	22.6%	10.2%	7.6%	6.4%
Non-Financial Companies	6.9%	11.1%	11.3%	3.0%	7.2%	5.3%
Public Sector	8.0%	8.5%	9.3%	11.4%	8.7%	8.9%
Foreigners	7.7%	9.7%	11.3%	9.1%	14.5%	9.2%
Banks	4.3%	8.5%	8.0%	1.2%	4.5%	3.3%
Insurance Companies	1.6%	0.9%	1.7%	0.4%	0.3%	1.1%
Others	0.5%	0.9%	1.3%	0.5%	0.8%	0.6%
*AG*s Without a Majority Owner	44.3%	36.6%	34.5%	64.2%	56.4%	65.2%

Source: Iber (1985: 1113).

4. Voting Rights and Voting Structure[213]

Several factors concerning voting rights affect ownership, and because voting structure may differ, the latter must be analyzed separately.[214,215] Generally, the rule "one share, one vote" holds, but there are minor exceptions: at a maximum of 30 *AGs*, mainly at utilities, a part of the shares provides multiple voting rights.[216] Preference shares, which usually do not include a voting right, are of more significance: at the end of 1994, 450 *AGs* had quoted only ordinary shares at the official or regulated market, 73 *AGs* had quoted both ordinary and preference shares, and 39 *AGs* had quoted only preference shares; statutory capital of ordinary shares totalled DM 78,305 billion, that of preference shares DM 4,278 billion.[217,218] Even if there are only shares issued with one vote each, maximum voting rights, which often limit the maximal voting power of a shareholder to 5 or 10% of capital, can distort the vote, in particular when the proxy system is taken into consideration.[219] Currently, about 20 *AGs* have maximum voting rights in use,[220] especially companies with widely dispersed ownership.[221] Another categorization divides shares into name and registered shares: name shares make the shareholders' identity more transparent since each shareholder is entitled to inspect the share register. The registered share that is not freely transferable (*vinkulierte Namensaktie*) grants the *AG*—and thus in particular the management—some control over the composition of shareholders. Registered shares are an exception on the German quotations sheet.[222]

---

[213] Cf. also the comparative analysis of shareholder representation in the EU by Baums (this volume Ch. 6), and the report on the development of the connection between ownership and voting rights in an historical perspective delivered by Dunlavy (this volume Ch. 1).

[214] Becht (1997: 11 and elsewhere) provides a four-quadrant matrix as an analytical tool to investigate the situations with dispersed or concentrated ownership and voting power respectively. Cf. Becht/Böhmer (1997: Table 9 and accompanying text) and Becht (1997: 93-7) for a brief overview of the relevant devices.

[215] The following analysis is confined to exchange-listed companies.

[216] Claussen (1996: 492); cf. Küting (1994: 288) for some data as of 1992.

[217] Statistisches Bundesamt (1995: 358); the office has discontinued providing these figures.

[218] At the end of 1995 the price of the ordinary share exceeded that of the preference share of the same company with an average of 18%, but in some cases the preference share was more expensive; Mella/Jähnke (1996). Cf. Kruse/Berg/Weber (1993) for an empirical analysis of the difference in price.

[219] On maximum voting rights, Baums (1990).

[220] Claussen (1996: 491); cf. Küting (1994: 288) for some data as of 1992.

[221] In the sample of Baums/Fraune (1995) (24 largest *AGs* with widely dispersed ownership, data as of 1992) nine companies had maximum voting rights in effect; Fraune (1996: 23-6). One interpretation is that the companies preferred the thereupon increased influence of banks via proxy voting to the influence of other potential larger shareholders.

[222] According to Kerber (1990: 790), as of approximately 1989 (no exact date given) at 64 listed *AGs*, among them 23 insurance companies, at least part of the shares were *Namensaktien*, and among them were 42 *AGs* (14 insurance companies) with *vinkulierten Namensaktien*.

Another feature preventing voting structure from perfectly paralleling ownership structure is attributed stakes, i.e., shares that are not held directly by those who effectively exercise control. In a way, this perspective bears some resemblance to the multi-stage analysis above. Becht and Böhmer conduct their investigation for both voting blocks (directly held and attributed stakes) and directly held stakes; they find similar results as to the distribution of block sizes,[223] dominance of the largest block in comparison with other large blocks,[224] the number of voting blocks held by a single entity or person,[225] and the importance and identity of entities or persons controlling several blocks[226] (Table 16).

Table 16: Largest Voting Block in 402 Officially Listed *AG*s, 1996

Size of Largest Voting Block in % of Total Voting Stock	No. of Cases	Size of Largest Voting Block in % of Total Voting Stock	No. of Cases
0-4.99	2	50-54.99	36
5-9.99	8	55-59.99	13
10-14.99	23	60-64.99	20
15-19.99	14	65-69.99	11
20-24.99	19	70-74.99	19
25-29.99	29	75-79.99	48
30-34.99	11	80-84.99	11
35-39.99	9	85-89.99	20
40-44.99	11	90-94.99	27
45-49.99	13	95-100	58

Note: Basis of the calculation is Bundesaufsichtsamt für den Wertpapierhandel (1996a).
Source: Becht/Böhmer (1997: Table 32).

When it comes to the general meeting, the holder of voting shares possesses the following options: he can attend the meeting himself, he can give his voting

[223] Compare Tables 7 and 16. Note in both cases the clustering at legally important thresholds; cf. Sec. B.II.3. above.

[224] Medium size of the largest voting block is 59.7% (directly held stake: 55.8%), the respective figures of the three and five largest blocks are 68.3% (68.6%) and 70.9% (70.7%) respectively; Becht/Böhmer (1997: Tables 31 and 32) and Sec. B.II.3. above.

[225] There are 739 voting blocks (890 directly held stakes) in the analysis of Becht and Böhmer, of which 423 (608) are held by persons or entitities who only hold a single block (2 blocks: 42 (45) holders; 3: 15 (15); 4: 5(9)); Becht/Böhmer (1997: Table 33) and Sec. B.II.3. above.

[226] Again, there is a dominance of the financial sector, though somewhat less pronounced: Allianz (25 voting blocks, 19 directly-held stakes), Deutsche Bank (24/23), Dresdner Bank (14/11), Münchener Rück (13/12), VIAG (10/n.a., but note that Bayernwerk, of which VIAG holds 97%, was the top non-financial holder of directly held stakes with seven participations), RWE (10/4), Bayerische Vereinsbank (9/9), and Commerzbank (7/8); Becht/Böhmer (1997: Table 34) and Sec. B.II.3. above. However, as to the simultaneous analysis of the number and size of the voting blocks held by different categories of holders, data for voting blocks are not as detailed as for directly held stakes; cf. Sec. B.II.3. above.

rights to a proxy either with or without specified instructions, or he can disclaim exercise of his voting right. For small shareholders it is often rational not to attend the meeting personally. In Germany, banks are the 'natural' proxies. This setting can result in voting structures at the meeting that differ markedly from ownership structures, in particular at widely held companies.

The average percentage of present shares at general meetings of all listed companies amounted to 73% in 1994,[227] but attendance rates vary widely.[228] At DAX companies in 1997, an average of 63.05% of voting rights was present (Table 17).[229]

Table 17: Present Shares at the General Meetings of DAX Companies, 1995-1997

Company	1995	1996	1997	Company	1995	1996	1997
Allianz Holding	78.27	78.03	78.65	Lufthansa	61.40	72.80	69.90
BASF	35.00	46.82	44.00	MAN	70.50	64.02	65.00
Bayer	49.69	47.82	48.31	Mannesmann	39.33	45.88	47.05
BMW	76.86	77.37	74.21	Metro	—	—	79.55
Commerzbank	48.57	44.30	50.48	Münchener Rück	77.80	78.11	77.00
Daimler-Benz	67.84	67.84	65.55	Preussag	70.32	74.07	66.51
Degussa	67.95	66.79	67.84	RWE	74.78	74.35	75.00
Deutsche Bank	46.90	47.30	47.91	SAP	61.58	78.50	77.02
Deutsche Telekom	—	—	86.09	Schering	39.70	43.19	45.64
Dresdner Bank	72.20	68.21	74.06	Siemens	53.16	48.00	46.00
Henkel	77.34	78.87	69.35	Thyssen	67.11	62.70	58.48
Hoechst	70.85	64.24	62.45	Veba	51.35	52.10	48.15
Hypo Bank	68.12	66.62	62.65	Vereinsbank	56.75	60.89	61.92
Karstadt	69.22	72.50	67.74	Viag	77.02	67.66	68.37
Linde	57.20	58.54	59.40	Volkswagen	41.90	42.65	47.15
Average (DAX)	61.74	62.51	63.05				

Note: Present shares in %.
Source: Figures collected by the *Deutsche Schutzvereinigung für Wertpapierbesitz (DSW)*, taken from: Benner-Heinacher (1997: 2522).

When considering voting structures, two main categories of companies can be distinguished: companies with a large share of dispersed ownership and companies with dominating shareholders. At the former group, general meeting attendance is lower[230] and banks dominate present shares due to proxy voting: in a

[227] Handelsblatt (1995a).

[228] E.g., in 1994, average attendance rate for a sample of ten large companies was 52.1% with a minimum of 32.9% and a maximum of 71.5%; Schmidt et al. (1997: 97).

[229] Figures collected by the *Deutsche Schutzvereinigung für Wertpapierbesitz (DSW)*, cited in Benner-Heinacher (1997: 2522).

[230] Cf. the findings of Böhm (1992: 66-74 and accompanying tables) (his voting analysis includes 32 companies as of 1986). The data of Gottschalk (1988) (sample: 32 companies, 1986

1992 sample, an average of 84.09% of present shares were associated with a
bank, consisting of proxy votes (60.95%), dependent investment companies
(10.11%), and bank equity ownership (13.02%).[231] The conclusion that 84.09%
are under bank control may be too far-reaching. First, one can assume with some
certainty that the share of proxies with instructions is not negligible.[232] Second,
turning to investment funds,[233] it is true that domestic investment companies
which are majority-owned by domestic banks manage 87.2% of the funds
managed by investment funds,[234] and that ownership of the large banks at the
largest investment companies often amounts to 100% or little less.[235] But
Spezialfonds held 70% of the domestic shares in the portfolios of domestic
investment funds;[236] in this category of investment fund, it should be harder for
banks to use the voting rights in their interests if they differ from those of their
customers.[237] Nevertheless, the position of a few banks, in particular the three
Großbanken, at the general meetings of widely held companies is impressive.[238]
Other parties are of little importance.[239]

or 1987), Nibler (1995: 3-4), Baums/Fraune (1995: 102), and Seger (1997: 181-2) (65 companies
as of 1990) confirm this fact.

[231] Baums/Fraune (1995: 103).

[232] According to Westermann (1996: 269), the share of 15-month blank proxies has fallen
from 80% to 60%. The Commerzbank answered Nibler (1995: 4) that 50.4% of safe-keeping
clients gave a 15-month blank proxy. One can conclude that 49.6% gave either a proxy with
instructions (presumably medium shareholders) or no proxy at all (presumably the largest and
the smallest shareholders, though with differing motivation). Widespread shareholder passivity is
illustrated by the fact that banks have return rates of 3% to 5% when they ask the shareholders
for instructions as they are obliged to by law; Bundesverband deutscher Banken (1994: 73), von
Rosen (1996: 291), and Westermann (1996: 273-4). Monopolkommission (1998: 93) mentions
return rates of 1% to 3%. Unfortunately, detailed data in this field are lacking. Moreover, the
percentage figures above refer to clients and accounts respectively which cannot, without further
information, be transformed into voting right figures.

[233] Cf. Roggenbuck (1992: 357-85) for a detailed description of the largest investment
companies in Germany, and Baums (1996) for a description of the legal framework.

[234] As of the end of 1995; Baums/König (1997: 5).

[235] As of 1994; Baums/König (1997: 8).

[236] As of May 1997; Deutsche Bundesbank (1998: 55). An encompassing analysis of the
Spezialfonds business is provided annually by Kandlbinder; see most recently Kandlbinder
(1997).

[237] This thought hints at competition as a counterforce towards a use of potential power by
banks at the expense of their customers. Competition can be assumed to be fiercer at the market
for *Spezialfonds* due to the small number, avoiding the collective action problem, and the qualification of the customers. However, there is some competition in the market for *Publikumsfonds* as
well: in an empirical investigation, Krahnen/Schmid/Theissen (1997) (sample: 11 large *Publikumsfonds* investing in German blue chips, 1987-1993) discover that risk-adjusted underperformance results in a loss of market share.

[238] From a control perspective, the small number is of high importance since it makes
coordinated behavior much easier.

[239] Cf. the detailed figures at Baums/Fraune (1995).

In addition to supervisory board mandates, voting rights are the most important building block of the strong position that a few banks hold at companies with dispersed ownership, usually the largest companies, which is the core of the controversially discussed power of the banks. Moreover, as can be seen in Table 18, in these banks themselves, dispersed ownership prevails and thus they have, via proxies,[240] a strong position at their own meetings, nourishing the impression that the banks' managements exert considerable control at other companies but are not subject to owner control themselves.

Table 18: Share in Voting Rights of the Five Largest Private Banks at Their Own General Meetings, 1992

	Deutsche Bank	Dresdner Bank	Commerz bank	Bayr. Vereinsbank	Bayr. Hypo	Total
Deutsche Bank	32.07%	14.14%	3.03%	2.75%	2.83%	54.82%
Dresdner Bank	4.72%	44.19%	4.75%	5.45%	5.04%	64.15%
Commerzbank	13.43%	16.35%	18.49%	3.78%	3.65%	55.70%
Bayr. Vereinsbank	8.80%	10.28%	3.42%	32.19%	3.42%	58.11%
Bayr. Hypo	5.90%	10.19%	5.72%	23.87%	10.74%	56.42%

Note: Percentage of present shares; including majority-controlled bank subsidiaries and investment companies[241].
Source: Baums/Fraune (1995: 106).

5. Effects of Ownership and Voting Structure: The Evidence

Available empirical evidence on the effects of ownership and voting structure shows some well-established trends but also mixed evidence on other features.[242] Starting with ownership and performance, clear trends are that performance increases with ownership concentration[243] and decreases with state ownership.[244]

[240] At its own general meeting, a bank can only exercise proxies with specified instruction. That banks nevertheless represent a large number of shareholders at their own general meetings is compatible with the conclusion that, in this case, they spend much more effort in overcoming shareholder passivity; Monopolkommission (1998: 101).

[241] Empirical analysis does not support the hypothesis that affiliated investment companies buy shares of their parent bank with respect to the bank's general meeting; Baums/König (1997: 12-5) (sample: investment companies of the five banks, 1992).

[242] For a survey of older empirical studies not covered here, see Kaulmann (1987: 96-100) and Lipka (1995: 59-85). See also Sec. B.IV. for the results of Böhmer's (1997) empirical study on the connection between the ownership structure of bidding companies and their cumulated abnormal returns during the period surrounding the first external knowledge of the (intended) bid.

[243] Cable (1985), Nibler (1995), and Gorton/Schmid (1996) for their 1985 (57 *AG*s) but not for their 1974 sample (88 *AG*s). Bühner (1984) (sample: 40 industry *AG*s, 1966-1981) finds that

Evidence on shareholdings of banks shows every possible outcome: these share-holdings are both positively[245] and negatively related[246], as well as unrelated[247] with performance. Lipka (1995)[248] finds that owner-controlled companies (multi-stage analysis) perform better than manager-controlled companies, whereas Kaulmann (1987) (two-stage analysis) cannot find a large difference with the exception of state ownership. Contrary to expectations, Herrmann (1996) discovers that companies which are completely or partially owned by founda-tions do not have an inferior performance as compared with exchange-listed companies.[249] For IPOs, Bessler, Kaen, and Sherman cannot detect hardly any significant connection between ownership structure (stake sizes) and post-IPO stock price performance.[250] The evidence for the effect of voting rights exercised by banks on performance is mixed: Gorton/Schmid (1996) and Seger (1997)[251] find no relation, whereas Nibler's (1995) sample shows a significant negative connection.[252] In addition, the relation between proxy voting rights exercised by banks and their supervisory board representation is weak, whereas it is stronger for bank equity ownership.[253] Supervisory board "representation goes hand in hand with ownership" when the major shareholder is another company or a family.[254] This result is confirmed by a regression which reveals a relation

owner-controlled companies are by far more successful than manager-controlled; since he conducts a first-stage analysis, owner-controlled is equivalent to closely held. Seger's (1997: 197-8) findings, however, indicate a negative, partially significant influence of concentration of non-bank shareholdings on performance.

[244] Kaulmann (1987) (largest industrial companies in France, Germany, and the U.K., 1975-1984) and Nibler (1995).

[245] Nibler (1995) and Gorton/Schmid (1996), 1974 sample. Schmid (1996) (sample: 62 non-financial *AG*s, 1990, accounting measures) finds a relation for return on equity but not for return on assets.

[246] Wenger/Kaserer (this volume Ch. 6); the study investigates effect of ownership of eight banks and two insurance companies.

[247] Gorton/Schmid (1996), 1985 sample, and Seger (1997: 195-9), who finds a significantly positive effect of *Großbanken* shareholdings and a negative, partially significant effect of other banks' shareholdings which, in the aggregate, wipe each other out.

[248] Sample: 72 listed companies, 1982-1988.

[249] Herrmann's (1996) sample consists of 65 'foundation companies', about 300 listed companies, and performance data from a company data base, and covers the period 1990-1992. Moreover, he provides data about the propagation of foundation-owned companies.

[250] Bessler/Kaen/Sherman (this volume Ch. 7: Sec. F.I.) (47 German IPOs, 1987-1992).

[251] Seger (1997: 195-9).

[252] Moreover, the negative relation remains in existence for the combination of voting rights and equity holdings, but turns into a positive one if supervisory board representation of banks is added; Nibler (1995).

[253] Böhm (1992: 199-205, 265-71), Edwards/Fischer (1994: 198-210), Gorton/Schmid (1996: 28-30), and Seger (1997: 186-7, 189-90).

[254] Franks/Mayer (1997: 10).

between supervisory board turnover and sales of large share stakes, but fails to find a connection between the former and proxy voting rights.[255] Manager-controlled companies show a higher degree of personal linkage, in particular via supervisory board, than companies in other control classes.[256] This finding does, at least, not contradict the thesis that personal links serve, among other things, the purpose of managerial entrenchment.

Turning to the management board, data for turnover and remuneration are available. Evidence on turnover is mixed. Schrader and Lüthje find that the CEO more likely leaves the company voluntarily or is dismissed in companies with a large shareholder[257] and in smaller companies.[258] In a more sophisticated analysis, Franks and Mayer discover that management board turnover is higher in lossmaking than in non-lossmaking companies for both closely and widely[259] held companies, but the difference is significant only for closely held companies. Taking a closer look at this group, they could not find significant differences in turnover rates depending on the identity of the large shareholder (family, bank, other company) either in a first- or in a multi-stage analysis. To make things even more complicated, a regression analysis which they also conduct does not confirm the just-mentioned relations between ownership structure and turnover rate.[260] The connection between performance and remuneration is much closer in companies with a large shareholder[261] and, to some extent, in companies completely or partially controlled by foundations.[262] Schmid (1997) discovers the direction of some determinants' effect on remuneration of both management (mb) and supervisory board (sb): shareholder concentration (mb:-/sb:-), bank equity ownership (mb:+/sb: +), majority ownership of a family (mb:0/sb:0), and voting right restrictions (mb:+/sb: 0).

Not surprisingly, available evidence does not offer a clear-cut picture of control by shareholders in Germany. Concentrated shareholdings and voting rights prevail, which is a good precondition for intensive control.[263] The relevant players are families and non-financial companies (equity ownership) and banks

---

[255] Franks/Mayer (1997: 23-4).

[256] One-stage analysis of Pfannschmidt (1993: 252-8).

[257] The finding holds for individuals/families (prevalence of dismissals) and legal entities (prevalence of voluntary leaves) as large shareholders.

[258] Schrader/Lüthje (1995) (sample: 32 *AG*s with sales exceeding DM 1 billion in 1991, 1965-1993). The latter observation is confirmed by te Wildt (1996).

[259] No shareholder owns more than 25%.

[260] Franks/Mayer (1997: 13, 16-7, 22-3). Moreover, they cannot discover a relation between management board turnover and proxy voting rights (p. 24).

[261] Kraft/Niederprüm (1996).

[262] Herrmann (1996).

[263] Bearing in mind the reservations put forward by Shleifer/Vishny (1997), see Sec. B.II.3. above.

(proxy voting rights). The superior performance of closely held companies is compatible with the interpretation that ownership includes the incentive to exercise control with the goal of market value maximization, whereas concentrated proxy voting rights, typical for widely held companies, either do not entail the necessary power or the power is used to pursue other goals.[264] Important features of proxy voting are still a puzzle: Why do banks offer this service without charging an explicit fee? What percentage of proxy voting rights is without instructions and thus at the banks' disposal?[265] Since "active" users of the proxy mechanism (those giving instructions) are likely to be larger shareholders, the recently sharpened disclosure rules on shareholdings may, as a side effect, shed some light on the proxy votes as well. Moreover, these disclosure rules will push empirical research on ownership structures, which until recently has depended on vague data. Capital linkage,[266] an inevitable consequence of extensive corporate ownership, needs more detailed analysis that at least considers hierarchical (*Konzern*) and circular linkage separately. In addition, this research may provide some new insights concerning the motivation of the potential monitors, which currently can be supposed to range from mutual entrenchment, to market-value-maximizing monitoring that enlarges managerial slack at the monitor's disposal, to market-value-maximizing monitoring for the advantage of one's own shareholders, to name but a few options. In particular, the incentives of large banks' managements, who are almost free from owner control themselves and who play a central role in the monitoring of large companies, are far from being known for certain.

III. The Share Market

Table 19 mirrors the general notion that the German share market is underdeveloped. The increase of market capitalization as a percentage of GDP reflects the extraordinarily large IPO of Deutsche Telekom in November 1996 rather than a major change in trend.

In addition, the German stock market is said to be top-heavy. At the end of 1996, 680 *AG*s were listed with a total market capitalization of approximately DM one billion, but the scenery was dominated by a few companies (Table 20).[267]

---

[264] The superior performance of closely held companies is a relative measure and does, of course, not imply that these companies do indeed pursue market value maximization.

[265] Intransparency in this field leaves room for suspicion, such as the following put forward by Adams (1994: 152-3) and Wenger/Kaserer (1998: n. 52), who hypothesize that today's main purpose of proxy voting is to hide ownership of larger holdings.

[266] In connection with paralleling personal linkage.

[267] Cf. also Hansen (1997a).

Table 19: The German Stock Market

Year	Number of *AGs*			Market Value of Listed *AGs*		Turnover in Domestic Stocks[d]	
	All[a] Number	Listed[b] Number	Percentage	Mil. DM	Percentage of GDP	Mil. DM	Percentage of Market Value
1980	2,147	459	21.4%	140,491	9.5%	n.a.	n.a.
1985	2,148	451	21.0%	438,810	24.1%	n.a.	n.a.
1990	2,685	649	24.2%	561,203	23.1%	1,621,155	289%
1994	3,527	666	18.9%	773,882	23.3%	1,870,764	242%
1995	3,780	678	17.9%	826,382	23.9%	1,643,903	199%
1996	4,043	681	16.8%	1,034,073	29.1%	2,312,907	224%

Notes: a Until 1993 only West Germany; from 1994 on Germany.
   b Until 1986 only companies with common stock officially listed or with trading privileges on the former *Geregelter Freiverkehr* (exchange segment second to official market). Since then companies with common or preferred stock traded on any of three exchange segments.
   c Turnover statistics were changed significantly at the beginning of 1987 and are not suitable for comparisons; for details, see Deutsche Bundesbank (1998: 48).

Sources: Deutsche Börse (1995: 112; 1996: 28; 1997: 12), Deutsche Bundesbank (1997: 28; 1997a: 61*; 1998: 46, 48), Deutsches Aktieninstitut (1997: FB_02-2), Federation of European Stock Exchanges (1997: 2), and Statistisches Bundesamt (1996: 641).

Table 20: Concentration at the German Stock Market, 1996/97

No.	Ranked by	
	Market Capitalization; Σ in %	Stock Exchange Turnover; Σ in %
1	6.6%	6.5%
3	16.6%	19.3%
5	24.5%	30.2%
10	41.6%	50.3%
30	71.6%	84.0%
50	80.8%	92.2%
100	87.6%	97.3%

Note: Parent population: Shares that are continuously traded at the Frankfurt Stock Exchange with a free float exceeding 15%. Market capitalization as of June 30, 1997. Stock exchange turnover from July 1, 1996 to June 30, 1997.
Source: Deutsches Aktieninstitut (1997: FB_05-5, FB_06-3).

The strength of the share market as a force in corporate governance increases with its informational efficiency. Available evidence is compatible with the conclusion that the German share market is only weak-form efficient.[268] It seems safe to assume that the coverage with financial analysts is one determinant of a market's efficiency. In particular, if economies of scale and scope exist, the smallness of the German market can be expected to be an impediment to profes-

---

[268] Kopp (1996: 104-6) provides a brief survey.

sional analyses coverage. Due to its top-heaviness, this is even more true for the large majority of companies. From this perspective, the significance of the share market as a force in corporate governance should be low and confined to a small number of companies.

Financing is another channel by which the share market can exert control. However, as the data above have already suggested, the share market, via external equity financing, plays a minor role in financing listed *AG*s;[269] it is most important at the largest *AG*s.[270] The data in Tables 21 and 22 give an idea of the amounts under discussion.

A higher payout ratio could ceteris paribus increase a company's need for external financing and thus intensify control by the market. From this perspective, it is tempting to analyze available evidence on dividends and payout ratios, but the results would be almost meaningless.[271] Since the payout ratio relates dividends and profit, and German accounting rules[272] leave the

Table 21: Share Sales in Germany

Year	Listed[a] Companies; Issue Price in Mil. DM	Unlisted Companies; Issue Price in Mil. DM
1980	3,967	2,979
1985	9,338	1,672
1990	21,970	6,051
1994	25,111[b]	4,051
1995	17,184[b]	6,415
1996	28,860[b]	5,354
1997	18,797	3,442

Notes: [a]   Listed companies include companies whose shares are traded either at the official or at the regulated (since May 1987) market, but not companies whose shares are traded at the unregulated market. Until May 1988, companies are included whose shares were traded in the former *Geregelter Freiverkehr* (exchange segment second to official market).

[b]   All exchange segments: DM 27,532 mil. (1994), DM 25,715 mil. (1995), DM 52,612 mil. (1996); Deutsche Börse (1996: 9; 1997: 12).

Until 1993 only West Germany; from 1994 on Germany. Data include IPOs.

Source: Deutsche Bundesbank (1998: 44).

[269] Deutsche Bundesbank (1997: 31) for the importance of external equity financing via shares in general. Mayer/Alexander (1990: 457-8) calculate the gross sources of finance of the 115 largest quoted *AG*s for the period from 1982 to 1988. They find an overwhelming share of retentions (89.6%) and a small one for new equity (8.2%). Since these kind of data are highly sensitive to definition, they are only intended to illustrate the proportions. Cf. Sec. C.II. for further evidence on the financing of German companies.

[270] The ten largest share issues from 1990 to 1996 accounted for almost 25% of total funds raised at the share market; Deutsche Bundesbank (1997: 32).

[271] Unless the data would have been adjusted for just this purpose, but currently no such study seems to have been published.

[272] Cf. Sec. B.V.2. below.

Table 22: Number and Volume of Going Publics in Germany[273]

Year	Number of Going Publics	Volume of Going Publics; Issue Price in Mil. DM
1980	3	51
1985	13	1,804
1990	34	3,032
1994	15	1,287
1995	20	6,975
1996	14	24,807[a]
1997[b]	16	2,939

Notes: [a] The issue price of the Deutsche Telekom IPO alone amounted to DM 20,141 mil.
[b] Until August. For a complete survey of 1997, cf. Hansen (1998). However, his figures are not reproduced here, because they are not fully compatible with the data set above and a uniform data set seems to be preferable.

Sources: Deutsches Aktieninstitut (1997: FB_03-2, FB_03-6, FB_03-7) and Börsen-Zeitung (1996a).

management plenty of scope in defining profit, analysis would have to start somewhere before, at a point at which management is not able to frame the figures, to result in meaningful findings.[274] Moreover, the law grants management and supervisory board the power to keep a high percentage of the annual net profit in the company, i.e., to actually take away these funds from the payout decision of the general meeting.[275] In addition, with respect to dividend policy, taking the corporate sector as an aggregate, the high degree of capital linkage in Germany has a similar effect as a higher retention rate, increasing the amount of funds under management control.[276] Share repurchases are another means in this respect but, generally speaking, they are not admissible in Germany.[277]

[273] Cf. also Gerke (this volume Ch. 7) on the situation in Germany with respect to venture capital and IPOs.

[274] As to the German dividend regulation, cf. Leuz/Deller/Stubenrath (1997: in particular 22-4) who also provide a comparison with the respective prescriptions in the U.S. and the U.K. Regardless of the corporate governance perspective, it must be stated that "there is only little evidence on the dividend policy pursued by German firms"; Behm/Zimmermann (1993: 227). The reader who is interested in figures (and empirical analyses of the determinants of dividends) is referred to Haegert/Lehleiter (1985), Linnhoff/Pellens (1987), König (1991), and Behm/Zimmermann (1993). Mayer/Alexander (1990: 461-3) (Germany and the U.K), Augustin (1994) (Germany and the U.S.), Amihud/Murgia (1997) (Germany and the U.S.), and de Jong (1997: 17-9) (82 largest European corporations) attempt to relate payout ratios from different countries.

[275] Cf. Drukarczyk (1993: 423-5, 440-51) for an economic analysis of German dividend regulations.

[276] Wenger/Kaserer (this volume Ch. 6: Sec. B.I.).

[277] See Kopp (1996: 17-25) for details. A relaxation of the relevant rules is part of the planned law amendment; Claussen (1996: 489-91).

However, the dissemination of international accounting philosophies has gained momentum recently.[278] Listings at foreign exchanges (Table 23),[279] which may require more shareholder-oriented accounting and disclosure rules, are a driving force, especially listings in the U.S. or, to be more precise, at the NYSE.

Table 23: German Stocks Listed at Foreign Exchanges, 1996

Amsterdam	12	Milan	3	Switzerland	34
Brussels	9	Nasdaq	11[a]	Stockholm	2
London	12	NYSE	5	Tokyo	9
Luxemburg	7	Paris	15	Vienna	23
Madrid	3	Singapore	1		

Note: [a] American Depositary Receipts (ADR).
Source: Deutsche Börse (1997: 69).

The trend towards a listing in the U.S. has continued since then and can be expected to persist.[280] But also at home, Anglo-Saxon-originated (or at least -oriented) accounting rules are gaining importance. The *Neue Markt* (new market), a new stock exchange segment which started on March 10, 1997,[281] requires the quoted companies, among other things,[282] to prepare their accounting in accordance with either IAS, U.S. GAAP, or German accounting rules in connection with reconciliation.[283]

To summarize, from an international perspective, the strength of the German share market as a force in corporate governance seems to be low, but the internationalization of share markets works as a counterforce.

IV. The Market for Corporate Control

M&A activity is not unusual in Germany. According to the evidence presented in Table 24, it seems that the declining tendency which followed the jump in activity in connection with German unification has been broken.[284]

[278] Cf. Secs. B.V.2. and 3. below.

[279] Cf. Schiereck (1997) for a recent treatment of this subject.

[280] As of the end of 1997, seven German companies have their shares quoted at the NYSE: Daimler-Benz, Deutsche Telekom, Fresenius Medical Care, Hoechst, Pfeiffer Vacuum Technology, SGL Carbon, Veba; Börsen-Zeitung (1997m). Moreover, for the first time, German companies carried out their IPOs abroad, in the U.S.; Handelsblatt (1996a) and Börsen-Zeitung (1996a).

[281] As of February 1998, 17 companies, many of them IPOs, are listed at the *Neue Markt*.

[282] Cf. Sec. B.V.2. below.

[283] Francioni (1997: 70).

[284] Cf. Müller-Stewens/Schäfer (1997) for additional data.

Table 24: Purchases of German Companies, 1992-1997

Year	1992	1993	1994	1995	1996	1997
German Buyer	1,044	843	730	889	1,010	933
Foreign Buyer	402	382	293	406	448	647
Total	1,446	1,225	1,023	1,295	1,325	1,580

Source: M + A International GmbH, Königstein; published in: Börsen-Zeitung (1997) and Handelsblatt (1998).

According to Gerke/Garz/Oerke (1995), at the stock market, the shareholders of target companies can earn a cumulated abnormal return (CAR) that reaches its peak at 8.7%, whereas the shares of bidding companies show no abnormal returns in the time period surrounding the publication of takeover plans.[285] Contrary to that, Böhmer/Löffler (1997) find a significant positive CAR of the shares of the bidding companies.[286] Böhmer (1997) focuses on the ownership structure of the bidding companies. His results support the basic trends that were reported in Section B.II.5. on the evidence of the effects of ownership structure: he finds the best CARs for bidders with minority blockholders ($25\% < x \leq 50\%$) and family-owned bidders, whereas companies without some concentration in ownership only achieve inferior CARs. State-controlled bidders showed the lowest, even negative CARs; moreover, shareholdings of banks also were connected with lower CARs.[287]

Takeovers, which at least began as hostile transactions, have been almost negligible until now (Table 25).[288] The reasons for the almost complete absence

[285] Gerke/Garz/Oerke (1995) (sample: 105 listed bidding and 19 listed target companies, in six cases both bidding and target company were listed, 1987-1992). Bühner (1990, 1990a) conducted an extensive analysis (covering mergers executed from 1973 to 1985, using both capital market and accounting data, analyzing a wide range of topics) but the results of his capital market analysis are impaired by methodological deficiencies.

[286] Böhmer/Löffler (1997) (sample: 672 takeovers by listed companies or their subsidiaries, 1980-1993) do not investigate the returns of target companies' shares. In addition to the above-mentioned result, they find that the general economic conditions are an important explanatory factor for CARs. Moreover, they document the sensitivity of the results of takeover studies with respect to the intensity of control prescribed by law and accordingly exerted by the *Bundeskartellamt*. This finding implies serious consequences for the construction of such studies.

[287] Böhmer (1997) (sample: 297 acquisitions conducted by 85 listed bidders, 1984-1988).

[288] For further lists and descriptions respectively of those transactions that may be summarized under the heading hostile takeover, see Peltzer (1989) (Zellstoffabrik Waldhof, Harpener, WMF and a list of voluntary takeover bids 1981-1988), Franks/Mayer (1990: 228-9) (Feldmühle Nobel), Nolte/Leber (1990: 577) (Zellstoffabrik Waldhof, Harpener, WMF, Springer, Feldmühle Nobel, Schering, Bibliographisches Institut und F.A. Brockhaus, Kolb & Schüle), Baums (1993) (case study on Continental), Droste (1995: 259-61) (Springer, Feldmühle Nobel, Continental), Jenkinson/Ljungqvist (1996) (Dywidag, Holzmann), Bästlein (1997: 281-4) (Feldmühle Nobel, Continental, Hoesch, Holzmann), Schmidt et al. (1997: 126-7) (Zellstoffabrik Waldhof,

of hostile takeovers in Germany until now are well known, so that the most important ones only have to be mentioned here:[289] impediments caused by law such as the two-board structure, co-determination, and capital protection rules; by the market structure such as the small number of widely held listed *AGs*, interlocking shareholdings, and the proxy voting system; as well as statutory anti-takeover provisions such as maximum and multiple voting rights and *vinkulierte Namensaktien*.[290,291]

Table 25: Hostile Takeover Attempts in Germany, 1968-1997

Year	Target Company	Bidder/Buyer	Successful?
1968/69	Zellstoffabrik Waldhof	H.D. Krages	yes
1971	WMF AG	Quist KG	yes
1987/88	Harpener AG	Inspectorate AG	yes
1988	Springer AG	Kirch-Gruppe	no
1988	Feldmühle Nobel AG	Flick	no
1988	Schering AG	ICN Pharmaceuticals	no
1988	Bibliographisches Institut und F.A. Brockhaus AG	Maxwell Communications	no
1989	ASS AG	Investor group under the leadership of Bankhaus H. Aufhäuser	yes
Late 1980s/1992	DYWIDAG	Walter Holding GmbH	yes
1990	Continental AG	Pirelli SpA	no
1990/92	AMB (Aachener und Münchener Beteiligungsgesellschaft)	AGF (Assurance Générale de France)	no
1991	Sabo AG	John Deere	yes
1991/92	Hoesch AG	Fried. Krupp GmbH	yes
Since 1994	Holzmann AG	Hochtief AG	—
1997	Thyssen AG	Krupp AG	no

Sources: Table mainly based on Flassak (1995: 218), Jenkinson/Ljungqvist (1996), and Kopp (1996: 142).

Harpener, Feldmühle Nobel, Continental, Hoesch, Holzmann), and Franks/Mayer (this volume Ch. 8) (Feldmühle Nobel, Continental, Hoesch).

[289] Baums (1993a: 154-8), Bästlein (1997: 269-309), and Schmidt et al. (1997: 128-30).

[290] For evidence of the latter category, cf. Sec. B.II.4. above; it would be interesting to analyze the reasons why (and when) companies established provisions that are, at least as a side effect, an impediment to takeovers.

[291] Hopt (1991) and Michalski (1997) analyze the legal admissibility of defense mechanisms against hostile takovers.

Nevertheless, there are substantial sales of large share stakes in Germany[292] which may serve as a substitute for the Anglo-American type of market of corporate control. However, the different turnover rates for supervisory and management board conditional on a sale of a large share stake are more likely to reflect the change in ownership rather than control implications since there is no relation to performance.[293]

In Germany, there are no specific laws regulating takeovers, only soft law: the *Übernahmekodex* (takeover code) which came into force on October 1, 1995, and replaced another voluntary code. The *Übernahmekodex* was developed by an expert commission (*Börsensachverständigenkommission*) appointed by the Federal Ministry of Finance. The code regulates the contents of an offer and the duties of bidding (in particular setting rules for a mandatory bid) and target company, and establishes an *Übernahmekommission* (takeover commission).[294] The provisions have the "character of recommendations,"[295] which are recognized voluntarily by potential bidder and target companies and financial services. The only reaction of the commission to a breach of the *Übernahmekodex* by a subscriber is to make this fact generally known. The current dissemination of the *Übernahmekodex* can be called disappointing.[296] In a recent attempt to foster dissemination, the *Deutsche Börse* announced that, beginning in 1998, recognition of the *Übernahmekodex* will be a precondition for inclusion in the DAX and

---

[292] The turnover of large shareholdings in the sample of German firms amounted to 7.2% of capital stock p.a. compared with takeover activity in the U.K. with a peak of about 4% of the capital stock of the corporate sector; Franks/Mayer (1997: 20).

[293] Franks/Mayer (1997: 20-4).

[294] For details, see Neye (1995), Thoma (1996), International Business Lawyer (1997: 56-8), Hopt (forthcoming), and Kirchner/Ehricke (1998). Weisgerber (1997: 432-3) reports on takeover bids made from October 1995 to the end of 1996; all bids made according to the *Übernahmekodex* until the end of 1997 are documented in Baumann (this volume Ch. 8: Appendix 1).

[295] Neye (1995: 1464).

[296] As of April 30, 1997, only 259 of 678 listed companies recognized the code. 7 of the 30 companies representing the DAX and a majority (37) of the 70 companies representing the MDAX (roughly speaking, this index includes the companies nos. 31 to 100 following the DAX companies) had still refused to recognize the code. With respect to market capitalization, the recognition rates amount to 80% (DAX) and 59% (MDAX). In contrast, all major financial services providers have joined the code; Börsen-Zeitung (1997a, b) and Hopt (1997: 395). As of September 30, 1997, figures had slightly improved: 5 (32) companies representing the DAX (MDAX) had not recognized the code; Börsen-Zeitung (1998). Companies that want their shares quoted at the *Neue Markt* must recognize the code; Francioni (1997: 70). The force of the code is impaired by the fact that companies can join and leave it on very short notice: after being excluded from the DAX, Metallgesellschaft left the code but, on the other hand, was involved, as a bidder, in a kind of takeover at Agiv AG für Industrie und Verkehrswesen which finally failed; Börsen-Zeitung (1997b, c) and Hopt (1997: 396). During the recent spectacular takeover attempt of Thyssen by Krupp it went the other way round: Krupp recognized the code on March 18, 1997 (it had to do so because its advising and financing banks had recognized the code), whereas first rumors concerning the takeover leaked out the evening before and the bid was actually made on March 18, 1997; Handelsblatt (1997a), cf. below for this takeover.

MDAX, and withdrawal—as in the case of Metallgesellschaft—will lead to exclusion from the respective index.[297]

The reason for this state of takeover law is that German legislation follows another path: protection of minority shareholders within a *Konzern* instead of protection at the stage of *Konzernierung*.[298] However, theoretical analyses and empirical evidence suggest that the relevant rules do not offer sufficient protection.[299] An empirical study of lump-sum compensations offered in case of domination and profit transfer agreements reveals that the precontractual share price exceeds the offered compensation by an average of 37.14%.[300] In court, minority shareholders are able to obtain an average increase of little less than 25%.[301] This regulatory environment includes perverse incentives for takeover activities. Ideally, the gain of a bidder in a takeover stems from his more efficient use of resources which increases general allocational efficiency. In the German case, the bidder may realize a gain on the whole by exploiting the minority even when he uses the resources less efficiently.

Until March 1997, one would have made the usual résumé without long reflection: the market for corporate control is a very weak force in German corporate governance. However, since then, two remarkable cases have taken place. The first was the hostile bid of Krupp for Thyssen,[302] which created pressure to induce cooperation negotiations between the two companies. They quickly resulted in a steel joint venture. The hostile bid contributed much to the outcome and to the short period of time needed to achieve it; moreover, finally, a complete merger of Krupp and Thyssen has been agreed upon. The event of the

---

[297] Börsen-Zeitung (1997l).

[298] Neye (1995: 1464).

[299] Schmidt et al. (1997: 77-93) provide an extensive economic analysis of the relevant rules.

[300] Wenger/Hecker (1995: 77) (sample: 42 companies with 46 cases (due to four companies with two categories of shares), 1983-1992).

[301] Wenger/Hecker (1995: 81). The sample differs from the one used to calculate the difference between offered and precontractual share price; it consists of 28 companies, time period starting 1970.

[302] Krupp's bid was effective for less than 24 hours. March 17: First rumors leak out in the evening. March 18: Krupp makes its intentions generally known, recognizes the *Übernahmekodex*, and, in the afternoon, makes a bid of DM 435 per share for all Thyssen shares (last price at the the floor trading on March 17: DM 346.50). March 19: Both companies agree to negotiate, the bid will be suspended during the talks which should produce results by March 27. March 24: Due to good progress in the negotiations, Krupp withdraws its bid. March 26: Thyssen and Krupp sign a memorandum of understanding to join their steel activities; cf., for example, the reports in Börsen-Zeitung and Handelsblatt during the relevant period, a short summary can be found in Börsen-Zeitung (1997o). As of February 1998, both supervisory boards have agreed to merge Krupp and Thyssen in total, i.e., not only the steel activities, and the general meetings will have to decide on the merger—which is intended to become effective on March 1, 1999—later this year; Handelsblatt (1998a, b).

hostile bid served to highlight some corporate governance features of Germany. As Krupp's intentions became known, Thyssen's CEO called the *Montan-mitbestimmung* (co-determination applying to mining and steel companies) in this case "pleasant".[303] Moreover, as a part of his defense instruments, he announced some surprises with respect to the value of the Thyssen share, which he considered to be in excess of DM 550. After the agreement with Krupp had been reached in spring 1997, he saw no necessity to continue efforts in this direction.[304] It would be interesting to know how Thyssen shareholders react to this treatment of their wealth. Moreover, a crucial feature of personal linkage came under discussion: Deutsche Bank (Deutsche Morgan Grenfell) and Dresdner Bank (Dresdner Kleinwort Benson) were—besides Goldman Sachs—Krupp's advisors and financiers. A member of Deutsche Bank's management board sat on Thyssen's supervisory board, and current and retired Dresdner Bank management board members sat on the supervisory boards of both Thyssen and Krupp. A final point to be mentioned is the public reaction which, in addition to its focus on the planned reduction of workforce, concentrated on the presumed power of banks, specifically of the Deutsche Bank. The highly negative attitude of the German public towards this takeover should not be understated as one of the primary impediments to future attempts.

Another case that attracted public attention in the second half of March 1997 was that of the construction companies Hochtief and Holzmann. In 1994, Hochtief started a hostile takeover of Holzmann, but was stopped by the *Bundes-kartellamt*.[305] In the last week of March, Deutsche Bank and Hochtief announced that they intended to pool their voting rights (just exceeding 50%) with the aim of coordinating the activities of both construction companies. Furthermore, a management board member of Deutsche Bank was to become supervisory board chairman at Holzmann. While the latter element has since been put into effect, Hochtief and Deutsche Bank, due to a likely rejection by the *Bundeskartellamt*, have abandoned the plan to pool their voting rights. Nevertheless, the event has borne some fruit: Holzmann has reversed its position and now welcomes the cooperation which it had long opposed.[306] Negotiations about details of the cooperation have succeeded since then.[307] The latest news is that the court sustained Hochtief's motion against the *Bundeskartellamt*'s prohibition decree

---

[303] Börsen-Zeitung (1997d).

[304] Börsen-Zeitung (1997d, e, i).

[305] Cf. Jenkinon/Ljungqvist (1996) for a detailed analysis of this long-lasting affair; see also Schmidt et al. (1997: 127).

[306] Börsen-Zeitung (1997f, g, h), Handelsblatt (1997c, d), and Monopolkommission (1998: 91-2).

[307] Handelsblatt (1997e).

that forbade Hochtief to add an additional stake of 10% in Holzmann to its 24.9% block. However, the judgment is not yet final.[308]

The recent cases may not have been takeover attempts of an Anglo-American style, but they share the common feature that initial hostile action created pressure for negotiations that otherwise possibly would not have been conducted. From this perspective, these two cases show the market for corporate control at work. Is this recent "accumulation" of cases mere coincidence, or is it the starting point of a more active market for corporate control? Put another way: Does the above-mentioned résumé need to be revised?[309] Presumably only slightly. Recent cases may have increased the awareness of the danger of becoming the target in a hostile takeover on German management boards. This is supported by the facts that foreign investment banks (Goldman Sachs) have entered as new players who are not part of the web of mutual dependencies, and that large German banks are willing to take part in a hostile takeover, even of a DAX company. On the other hand, the other legal and structural obstacles listed above remain in effect, beginning with the point that Thyssen is one of the rare widely held companies. However, the example of Deutsche Bank at Holzmann shows that even long-time large shareholders may side with a bidder that the incumbent management regards as hostile.

V. Auditing, Accounting, and Disclosure

1. Auditing

At the *AG* the procedure is as follows: the supervisory board proposes a balance sheet auditor, the general meeting elects the auditor, and the management board appoints him. It is generally criticized that, de facto, it is often the management board that selects the auditor. This contributes further to the critical closeness of this relationship that is already established by the fact that the management negotiates with the auditor—among other things—the auditor's compensation.[310] The management board gives the annual financial statement (comprising annual balance sheet, profit and loss account, and notes to the financial statements) and the status report to the auditor. The auditor's duty is to check, under inclusion of the accountancy, whether the provisions of law and charter are met and that the

---

[308] As of March 1998; cf. Börsen-Zeitung (1998a).

[309] Schmitz (1997), Wenger (1997), Baums (1997) and Drukarczyk/Schmidt (1997) discuss the Krupp-Thyssen case from a corporate governance perspective.

[310] Clemm (1995: 98) and Götz (1995: 341). The auditors' remuneration is not regulated by law; Lenz (1996: 273).

documents do not misrepresent the company's situation.[311] If the auditor does not raise objections, he gives the auditor's certificate to the management board, which passes the documents to the supervisory board immediately.[312]

The auditor's duty to speak up is twofold:[313] first, if he realizes that the company is in danger or that representatives of the company have committed a breach of provisions of law, partnership agreement, or charter; and second, he has to list and explain if adverse changes of the financial and earnings situation have occurred—as compared with the year before—or if losses have considerably affected results for the previous year.

The central and strong position of those to be controlled towards their monitors stands at the center of the current critique.[314] Taking this problem as a given for the moment, the crucial question is if other forces provide incentives to the auditor to conduct a thorough and objective examination.

Liability could be such a force. But it is currently limited to a maximum of DM 500,000, which is regarded as being totally out-of-date.[315] Dependence of the auditor on his client could impair the quality of examination. The law requires, roughly speaking, that the remuneration the auditor receives from one customer must not exceed 50% of his total income.[316] A look at the current structure of the auditing market in Germany shows a high degree of concentration on the supply side that has further increased during the last years.[317] The market is dominated by seven large companies[318] who occupy, irrespective of the measure used, far more than 50% of the market. There is no group of important national second-tier auditors following the international cooperating "Big 7".[319] The dominating auditing companies are so big that the danger of their dependence on particular customers seems to be negligible. A different kind of dependence may emerge if auditors also offer other services that may influence the

---

[311] Kübler (1994: 284, 359). Thus, the main focus of the auditor's activity is whether the reporting, which is foremost a reflection of the past, conforms with legal and other provisions rather than serving as a judgment of the management's quality.

[312] Cf. Secs. B.I.1. and 3. above for the information of the supervisory board in praxis and for the dissemination of audit committees.

[313] § 321 Handelsgesetzbuch.

[314] It is addressed by a recent draft statute; cf. Sec. D below.

[315] Hopt (1996: 918).

[316] § 319 Handelsgesetzbuch.

[317] Helmenstein (1996); he analyzes the market structure in 1987 and 1991. This observation is confirmed by Gloßner (1998); she analyzes the market structure (auditing of companies quoted in the official market) in 1987 and 1995, and by Marten/Schultze (1998) (250 non-financial *AGs*, 1990-1994; they also take a comparative European perspective).

[318] KPMG, C&L, BDO, Schitag, Wollert-Elmendorff, Arthur Andersen, Price Waterhouse; Lenz (1996).

[319] Lenz (1996: 279); he investigates the auditors at all German *AGs* in 1990, provided data were available.

economic position of the company when the company is audited by the same auditor that has provided these services.[320] The Big 7 offer a wide range of services, e.g., auditing, tax consulting, corporate finance, business consulting, and legal consulting. To give a particular illustrative example: the corporate finance advice turns out to be wrong and adversely influences the company's earnings. The advising service provider is also the auditor. In this setting, the management of the company and the auditor may share the common interest not to disclose the unfavorable situation, at least not completely.[321]

Auditor rotation, either of the auditing company or of the responsible auditor within one auditing company, is another means of avoiding dependence, but it is not without drawbacks. Currently, neither form is mandatory in Germany, but empirical evidence on the changes of auditing companies is available:[322] Coenenberg and Marten confirm the trend towards large international auditors. No influence on the auditor change was exerted by, among other things, a (refused or qualified) certificate, divergence of opinions, and the financial situation of the audited company. Among the influential factors were a change in the top management or ownership structure of the audited company, its earnings situation, the auditor's remuneration, and his reputation. Moreover, as far as groups of companies are concerned, there is a significant trend towards a single auditor for all group companies.

2. Accounting[323]

What is the function of accounting from a corporate governance perspective? If one regards corporate governance first and foremost as an agency problem with the management being the agent, accounting should have the highest possible information content, revealing the true position of the company and the actions already taken by the management as well as existing latitude for future decisions. These requirements hold for all actual and potential parties connected with the company, such as shareholders (including the market for corporate control), lenders, employees, customers, and suppliers, despite their conflicting interests in some respects. Transparency would be the key demand, not allowing (hidden)

---

[320] With a warning regarding this situation, see Clemm (1996: 277).

[321] Another critical case is when auditors audit financial statements that they have also, at least partially, prepared. Although, not surprisingly, law prohibits this situation, it actually does occur; Dörner/Oser (1995: 1092).

[322] Coenenberg/Marten (1993) (sample: 234 companies and auditors respectively who were at least one side of an auditor change, 1989-1991). For a more detailed version of the study, see the dissertation of Marten (1994).

[323] The corporate governance relevance of accounting is closely connected with its disclosure. For the sake of a more convenient structure of the discussion, disclosure is dealt with below in Sec. B.V.3.

scope of the management.[324] In its orientation such accounting is neutral; any orientation can be achieved by rules that refer to the result of accounting, e.g., rules to ensure a certain amount of liable capital.

It is a generally accepted view that German accounting rules are lender-oriented. This orientation is attained by the interplay of the management's rights concerning accounting— which, roughly speaking, tend to undervalue assets and overvalue liabilities—with withdrawal limitations which refer to the low net wealth and profits resulting from this way of accounting. Thus, lender orientation and protection is not achieved by adequate information, which would also serve the other interested parties, but by the high probability that there is enough liable capital available, whether it is shown in the balance sheet or not.[325]

The decisive point from a corporate governance perspective is that the German form of lender-orientation also serves the interests of the agents, who prefer the largest scope possible.[326] Moreover, because of the close connection between accounting and taxation in Germany, even the shareholders have some interest in the disguise of a company's wealth and earnings. In a nutshell, German accounting is not only lender- but also management-oriented.[327]

Nevertheless, despite this negative evaluation, German accounting data do contain useful information as empirical studies have discovered: they are appropriate to prognosticate company crises and their disclosure causes some reaction at the stock market.[328] However, with the management's latitude concerning accounting, the information value stock market participants ascribe to accounting data drops.[329] More expressive is a comparison of the stock market relevance of

---

[324] Of course, this analysis is partial, since also competitors will welcome transparency, in particular if they are not subject to such a regulation themselves.

[325] Wenger (1996a) is very critical in this respect, in particular p. 3. Küting (1997) is along the same lines in his conclusion (p. 91) of case studies of the accounting in several large German companies.

[326] The size of this scope is impressively revealed by a case study that asked domestic practicing accountants from different European countries to prepare the profit and loss account for identical business data using three régimes: usual practice (used as standard=100), profit minimizing accounting rules, and profit maximizing rules. The difference between maximum and minimum was highest for Germany (85) and lowest for the U.K. (12). In addition, German rules allowed by far the lowest minimum profit (20) followed by the Netherlands (54); the figure for the U.K. is 89; Touche Ross *Accounting for Europe* (London 1989), taken from: CEPS (1995: 18-9).

[327] This passage is far from being an extensive analysis of German accounting. For a tour d'horizon through the most prominent features of German accounting, cf. Ballwieser (1996). Kübler (1995) provides an instructive comparison of the different accounting philosophies in Germany and the U.S.

[328] Cf. Coenenberg/Haller (1993) for a comprehensive survey.

[329] Keller/Möller (1992) (sample: 153 listed non-financial *AGs* and 25 listed bank *AGs*, 1974-1986) find that the information value of accounting data of banks, who enjoy an even broader scope with respect to accounting, is lower than that of non-bank companies.

U.S. and German accounting data. Contrary to the conventionally held belief, Harris, Lang, and Möller find that German accounting figures are significantly associated with stock market data. In particular, earnings show nearly the same explanatory power for stock returns in both countries.[330] In addition, for Germany, in a case of a parent company of a group of companies, a distinction must be made between the accounting of the individual firm and that on a consolidated basis. Available evidence on their information value for stock market participants is mixed.[331] Finally, Baetge and Thiele demonstrate for large German companies that profit, cash flow, and equity figures calculated according to German accounting rules may indeed differ largely from those calculated according to U.S. GAAP; however, these differences disappear to a great extent when the accounting data are analyzed with sophisticated artificial neuronal networks.[332]

The globalization of capital markets seems to be a powerful counterforce to the above-assumed preference of managers for intransparency, since there is a tendency towards accounting according to international and foreign standards (IAS, U.S. GAAP) at German companies.[333] Two channels seem to be at work, the first of which is listing abroad,[334] which demands the observance of the accounting regulations required by the supervisory authority and the exchange in the respective country. However, taking a closer look, it seems that among the major international exchanges, only a listing at U.S. exchanges involves such requirements to make a modification of domestic accounting as expensive as a separate accounting that follows the standards abroad from its outset.[335] This is the main reason why so few German companies are listed at a U.S. exchange.

Second, but even without the requirement of a listing abroad, the pressure from international investors,[336] who prefer more homogeneous and transparent accounting rules for the sake of a better comparability and thus analyzability of

---

[330] Harris/Lang/Möller (1994) (sample: 230 listed German and 230 listed U.S. companies, 1981-1992). Cf. Harris/Lang/Möller (1995) for a German version of the study.

[331] Pellens (1994: 156-61) (sample: 18 *Konzern* parent *AG*s and 18, to a certain extent comparable *AG*s which are not part of a *Konzern*, 1988-1990) finds a higher information value of consolidated data, whereas Schulte's (1996: 225, 258-9) (sample: 40 large listed parent companies, 1989-1991) findings are mixed.

[332] Baetge/Thiele (this volume Ch. 9: Sec. B.IV.).

[333] Budde/Steuber (1996) and Schulte (1996: 58-63).

[334] Cf. Sec. B.III. above for the evidence.

[335] Gidlewitz (1996: 38-46) and Glaum/Mandler (1996: 62). The high relevance of this issue for the SEC is documented by a recent statement of its former chairman Ruder (1996: 2): ". . . an extremely important current problem: the difficulty of reconciling U.S. accounting and disclosure standards with international accounting and disclosure standards."

[336] For an impressive example of such pressure, cf. von Werder (1998: 80-1) (quoting a newspaper report describing the presentation of Schering at a major U.S. investor on the occasion of a 'roadshow').

investment opportunities, appears to be strong enough a force to induce large German companies either to prepare an additional balance sheet using internationally accepted standards or to use the scope granted by German accounting rules in this direction.[337,338] Another example of the influence of this force is that the new German exchange segment, the *Neue Markt*, requires of its listed companies accounting according to IAS, U.S. GAAP, or German standards with reconciliation.[339] As far as accounting is concerned, the requirements for a listing in this segment are stricter than those for the blue chips.

The resulting increase in transparency has to be welcomed from a corporate governance perspective. Nevertheless, one must bear in mind that this development affects almost exclusively the small group of large, internationally acting *Konzerne*,[340,341] while leaving listed, domestically oriented companies unaffected, not to mention the vast amount of corporations without listing that are not part of a *Konzern*. Another point that deserves some attention is the structure of the driving forces behind this evolution affecting corporate governance.[342]

---

[337] Cf. Budde/Steuber (1996: 546), Buhleier/Helmschrott (1997: 776), and Thiele/Tschesche (1997) for examples. As of spring 1997, only 13 of the approximately 600 companies whose shares are traded at the official or regulated market publish quarterly accounting data prepared in accordance with international standards; Gutschlag (1997). Besides, this note highlights the close connection between accounting and disclosure.

[338] Another indication of this development is delivered by the regular analysis of the published annual reports of the 500 largest listed companies: judging the reports from their information value for shareholders quality is still moderate (42.49% of the maximum result for the 1995 reports) and has increased only slightly during the last years in general and even decreased in some company sectors. However, especially annual reporting by large companies, e.g., the companies representing the DAX, has improved during recent years, but it still leaves much room for further improvement; Baetge/Armeloh/Schulte (1997, 1997a) and Baetge/Thiele (this volume Ch. 9: Sec. B.V.).

[339] Francioni (1997: 70).

[340] A recent inquiry among 256 large German companies conducted by the auditing company BDO Deutsche Warentreuhand revealed the wide gap with respect to the realized or intended internationalization of accounting between companies of different size and, closely related, international orientation: only 18% of the companies with 2,000 employees or less plan to prepare a year-end financial statement in accordance with international principles, as opposed to almost 70% of the companies with annual sales exceeding DM 10 billion; Blick durch die Wirtschaft (1997).

[341] Cf. Sec. D for a recent draft statute dealing with this subject.

[342] I.e., the interplay between investors, exchanges, regulators, and—often—non-state standard setters which play an important role in the field of accounting; cf. Gidlewitz (1996: 95-182) (International Accounting Standards Committee (IASC) and other actors), and Siebert (1996: 43-73) (U.S. standard setters, in particular the Financial Accounting Standards Board, (FASB)), for the relevant standard setters.

3. Disclosure[343]

Legal and other provisions dealing with disclosure are numerous and can be found in a wide range of references. To keep things simple, for the purpose of this survey only two rough categories are delineated: disclosure of business conditions and disclosure of equity ownership. The strictest disclosure requirements regarding year-end financial statements hold for corporations[344] with demands increasing with size.[345] *Konzerne* with a corporation as parent company have to prepare an additional year-end financial statement, to which the disclosure requirements for large corporations apply, covering the whole group.[346] Corporations whose shares are traded at the official or regulated market have to meet the strictest demands regardless of their size. Moreover, companies who have their shares traded at the official market are obliged to publish a semi-annual report. Empirically, the information value investors ascribe to this report is not large in absolute terms, but in a relative perspective resembles that of the annual report.[347] These findings are supported by the fact that the information value of annual reports is lower for companies who publish a semi-annual report.[348] Companies quoted at the recently established *Neue Markt* are required to deliver quarterly reports;[349] about 35 companies whose shares are traded at the

---

[343] Cf. Lowenstein (1996: 1335-6, 1345) for a forceful pleading of disclosure and transparency as a force in corporate governance: ". . . good disclosure has been a most efficient and effective mechanism for inducing managers to manage better. . . . Almost unnoticed, good financial disclosure has become a corporate governance tool of the first order. . . . A free press stands guard in the political arena. Think of accountants and security analysts as the guardians of industry. . . .."

Cf. also Fox (this volume Ch. 9) for a general treatment of the connection between disclosure and corporate governance.

[344] Very large economic units of other legal forms of business organization (exceeding in three consecutive years two of the following criteria: balance sheet total: DM 125 million, sales: DM 250 million, number of employees: 5,000) must also disclose their year-end financial statements.

[345] Size is measured by balance sheet total, sales, and number of employees, and the corporations are divided into three categories. Häger (1993) analyzes the year-end financial statements disclosed by 116 and 14 corporations (111 *AG*s and 19 *GmbH*s) belonging to the medium size bracket for the business years 1987-1989 and 1988-1989 respectively. He finds many cases of overfulfillment of disclosure requirements, supporting the conclusion that disclosure requirements are not such a heavy burden as they are usually considered to be. Moreover, the statements of *AG*s contain more information than those of *GmbH*s. On the other hand, in particular for small and medium corporations, legally required and actually realized disclosure diverge markedly; for some figures and further references, cf. Baetge/Apelt (1992: 402-5).

[346] Kübler (1994: 357-8, 360).

[347] Coenenberg/Henes (1995) (sample: 167 companies, 1988-1993). Interestingly, only 72.5% of the semi-annual reports were published within the time period provided by law (two months); Coenenberg/Henes (1995: 977).

[348] Keller/Möller (1993) (sample: 153 companies, 1974-1986).

[349] Francioni (1997: 70).

official or regulated market report quarterly on a voluntary basis.[350] The intuitively plausible assertion that equity investors appreciate the disclosure of expressive information on business conditions meeting international standards as a means to limit the management's latitude finds empirical support by Kaserer (1996). He finds a highly significant negative effect of disclosing such information exceeding mandatory obligations on the extent of the underpricing of German IPOs.[351]

Besides the periodic disclosure, there is the obligation for companies whose shares are traded at the official or regulated market to immediately disclose facts that may have a considerable effect on the share price. Since January 1995, this duty has increased because ad hoc disclosure is supervised by the newly established *Bundesaufsichtsamt für den Wertpapierhandel* (*BAWe*) and has become subject to a stronger threat of punishment. In 1996, German firms sent 1,024 ad hoc news items to the *BAWe*.[352] The most frequent contents in 1996 concerned the year-end financial statement and dividends (29.7%/1995: 35.8%), semi-annual report (11.6%/20.7%), changes in stakeholdings (10.4%/7.9%), and changes in statutory capital (7.8%/7.9%).[353] Since 95% of the news is disseminated electronically via systems such as Reuters, vwd, Bloomberg, etc.,[354] it can be assumed that the news becomes public quickly. Correspondingly, the number of trading halts in individual stocks has decreased considerably.[355] At the majority of companies, the new disclosure rules did not cause a change in information policy, but those companies that altered their policy now inform earlier.[356] Empirical studies on the information value of ad hoc disclosure have not been published yet, but they can most probably be expected soon.

Turning to disclosure of equity ownership, it must be noted again that legal provisions are widely spread across several laws.[357] The strictest provisions refer to the direct and indirect disposal of voting rights and have been in force since

---

[350] As of spring 1997; Gutschlag (1997).

[351] Kaserer (1996) (sample: all 165 German IPOs of non-financial companies, 1983-1993).

[352] Bundesaufsichtsamt für den Wertpapierhandel (1997: 21).

[353] Data for 1996 from Bundesaufsichtsamt für den Wertpapierhandel (1997: 22), data for 1995 calculated from a graph in Bundesaufsichtsamt für den Wertpapierhandel (1996: 23). The quality of these figures as an indicator for the future structure of ad hoc news may be impaired, since during the first months companies delivered a great deal of irrelevant news because of difficulties in separating relevant from irrelevant facts; Bundesaufsichtsamt für den Wertpapier-handel (1996: 21).

[354] Bundesaufsichtsamt für den Wertpapierhandel (1997: 22); the flow of the news is described by Wölk (1997: 73-6).

[355] 1993: 86, 1994: 62 and 1995: 25; Gerke/Bank/Lucht (1996: 616).

[356] Inquiry by Gerke/Bank/Lucht (1996) (sample: 62 listed companies).

[357] Neye (1996), Becht/Böhmer (1997: 6-13 and accompanying tables), and Veit/Tönnies (1997) provide surveys; the latter in connection with evidence for 190 of the 500 largest German corporations.

the beginning of 1995. The relevant rules of the *Wertpapierhandelsgesetz (WpHG)* demand disclosure if the voting rights at the disposal of one natural or legal person obtain, exceed, or fall below one of the thresholds of 5%, 10%, 25%, 50%, and 75%.[358] Note that this requirement concerns companies whose shares are traded at the official market only. Other provisions refer to a wider range of companies, but, on the other hand, are far less severe because they are restricted to ownership and voting rights respectively of domestic corporations, use higher thresholds, etc.

From a theoretical perspective, it seems safe to say that the earlier facts are disclosed the better. But considering this statement in light of foreign/ international disclosure provisions as driving forces for domestic required or voluntary disclosure, it must be considered that the very requirements for *which* facts are to be disclosed are a result of the corporate governance system they originated in. Ideally, these requirements assure the publication of those facts that contain information value for company outsiders. It would be a surprise if this set of facts were the same for all countries.[359] For the case of Germany, one may conclude that the advance of disclosure standards from abroad means an improvement, albeit in probably too mechanized a way to be achieved.

C. Other Stakeholders

I. Employees in Particular Co-Determination[360]

1. Supervisory Board Co-Determination

There are two kinds of co-determination in Germany:[361] via supervisory boards and via works councils. This section starts with supervisory board co-determination, for which three régimes can be distinguished: (1) full-parity co-determination (*Montanmitbestimmungsgesetz* 1951); (2) quasi-parity co-determination

---

[358] This regulation was supplemented by the requirement to disclose all voting rights which refer to the thresholds as of the beginning of 1995. The *BAWe* (1996a) published a report on the voting rights at the companies under consideration as of September 30, 1996, and now provides a regularly updated downloadable version of this database on its WWW site. On the one hand, the data in this report represent a degree of transparency that had never been reached before; on the other hand, due to the consideration of both direct and indirect voting rights, the data are hard to interpret. For example, the aggregated voting rights at SAP, a company included in the DAX, exceed 600%. Cf. Becht/Böhmer (1997: 22-35 and accompanying tables) for a rigorous analysis of the relevant rules of the *WpHG* which reveals substantial deficiencies.

[359] Cf. Fanto (1996) for an instructive elaboration of this train of thought.

[360] Cf. Ch. 5 of this volume on co-determination. The contributions of Gerum/Wagner and Roe refer to Germany.

[361] Neglecting the *Arbeitsdirektor* (personnel director) according to *Montanmitbestimmungsgesetz* and *Mitbestimmungsgesetz*.

(*Mitbestimmungsgesetz* 1976);[362] and (3) one-third co-determination (*Betriebsverfassungsgesetz* 1952).[363]

(1) Full-parity co-determination: The oldest régime applies to *AG*s and *GmbH*s in the coal, steel, and mining industry with more than 1,000 employees.[364] Depending on statutory capital, 11, 15, or 21 members sit on the board. There are two equally large benches of shareholder and employee representatives. The former are elected by the general meeting, the latter—which include at least one worker and one non-manual employee each coming from the company under consideration—by the employees. The chairman is supposed to be a neutral person whose neutrality is ensured by the following procedure: the other 10, 14, or 20 members propose a candidate for election by the general meeting and the proposition must be supported by a majority of each bench.

(2) Quasi-parity co-determination:[365] The latest régime applies to all *AG*s, *KGaA*s, and *GmbH*s with more than 2,000 employees that are not subject to full-parity co-determination.[366] Depending on the number of employees, the board consists of 12, 16, or 20 members. Again, the shareholder and the employee benches can be differentiated. Compared with full-parity co-determination, the electing bodies do not change, but the composition of the employee bench does: two seats (three if the board comprises 20 members) are reserved for union representatives. Moreover, at least one worker, one non-manual employee, and one managerial employee, all of whom must be on the company's payroll, have to sit on the board. The remaining seats on this bench are to be distributed among these three groups in accordance with their proportion in the company. The chairman is not neutral. The board members elect one of their fellow members with a majority of two-thirds. If this requirement cannot be met, the shareholder representatives elect the chairman and the employee representatives elect his deputy. The chairman occupies a powerful position since his vote breaks a tie.

(3) One-third co-determination: This law applies to all *AG*s and *KGaA*s with less than 500 employees which were registered before August 10, 1994,[367] and are not family dominated. Moreover, it also applies to all *AG*s and *KGaA*s with

---

[362] To gain an impression of the discussions before its introduction, cf. the final report of the commission of experts entrusted by the government; Sachverständigenkommission (1970).

[363] The following passages deliver only a rough outline of the legal setting.

[364] 47 companies as of December 31, 1992; Kronenberg/Volkmann/Wendeling-Schröder (1994: 25).

[365] Theisen (1998) provides a recent survey of court decisions relating to this régime.

[366] 740 companies, data most probably as of 1995 or 1996; Tegtmeier (1996: 28). As of 1994, the distribution of the companies subject to quasi-parity co-determination among the legal forms of business organization was as follows: *AG*s (406), *GmbH*s (280), *KGaA*s (4), *GmbH & Co. KG*s (13), cooperative associations (10); Theisen (1998: 154).

[367] This distinction is a consequence of the *Gesetz für kleine Aktiengesellschaften und zur Deregulierung des Aktienrechts* of August 2, 1994, and aims at increasing the attractiveness of the *AG* relative to the *GmbH*.

more than 499 and *GmbHs* with more than 500 but less than 2,001 employees which are not family dominated and are not subject to full-parity co-determination.[368] The number of board seats ranges from 3 to 21, depending on statutory capital, and must be divisible by three. The bench of the shareholder representatives holds two-thirds of the seats, the employee bench the final third. For the election of both benches the procedure described above holds. Again, there are particular provisions concerning the makeup of the employee bench: if there is only one employee representative, he must be on the company's payroll; if there are two or more, at least two must be on the company's payroll, among them at least one worker and one non-manual employee each. The chairman and his deputy need a simple majority for election.

(4) Major exemptions: Regardless of their size, the following companies are exempt from co-determination: sole proprietorships, mere partnerships, and organizations concerned with propagating attitudes (media-, church-, union-, politics-related companies).

Co-determination has not been at the center of research during recent years.[369] Consequently, little current empirical evidence is at hand. The composition of the employee bench (Tables 26 and 27) seems to be an appropriate starting point.

The data are about 20 years old, but they nevertheless do apply to the current régimes. Note that one-half régimes result in a much stronger involvement of external members on the employee bench; they are almost without exception trade union representatives. The dominance of internal—in particular works

Table 26: Composition of Employee Benches in *AGs* Subject to One-Third Co-Determination, 1975/76

Type of Employee Representative	Percentage on Employee Bench
Chairman or Deputy of Company or Central Works Council	39%
Ordinary Member of Works Council	35%
Company Worker	7%
Company Non-Manual Employee	14%
Company Managerial Employee	1%
External Trade Union Representative	3%
Other	1%

Source: Vogel (1980: 133).

[368] Only rough estimations of their number are feasible; according to them there were 400 to 700 companies subject to this régime as of August 1994; Seibert/Köster/Kiem (1996: 132).

[369] Cf. Hamel (1993) and Sadowski/Junkes/Lent (1997) for surveys of empirical research on both supervisory board and works council co-determination and Müller (1986: Appendix) for a survey in tabular form of older studies on supervisory board co-determination.

Table 27:　Composition of Employee Benches in *AG*s Subject to Full- or Quasi-Parity Co-Determination, 1979

Type of Employee Representative	Percentage on Employee Bench with 6 Members	Percentage on Employee Bench with 8 Members	Percentage on Employee Bench with 10 Members	Percentage on Employee Bench in General
Member of Company Works Council	42.3%	50.9%	48.1%	46.0%
Chairman of *Konzern* Works Council	1.6%	2.7%	1.6%	1.8%
Member of Subsidiary Works Council	3.3%	5.7%	8.1%	5.4%
Non-Member of Works Council Employee	3.1%	3.0%	2.5%	2.9%
Managerial Employee	16.7%	12.7%	10.3%	13.7%
External Trade Union Representative	31.5%	23.6%	29.0%	29.0%
Internal Trade Union Representative	1.6%	1.4%	0.4%	1.2%

Source:　Gerum/Steinmann/Fees (1988: 58).

council members[370]—as opposed to external employee representatives is confirmed by the fact that about two-thirds of deputy chairmen in the case of one-half régimes come from this group.[371]

Turning to supervisory board committees, there seems to be a clear distinction between one-half and one-third régimes (Table 28).[372]

The only extensive empirical study on supervisory board co-determination was conducted by Gerum, Steinmann, et al.[373] To highlight some of their findings, one can point to their estimations of co-determination potentials which are a compressed form of presentation of their large pool of facts. They discover that co-determination potential is related to the dependency status of a company

[370] This statement still holds: as of 1993, external trade union representatives held 211 (28%) employee seats on the supervisory boards of the 100 largest companies (by sales), whereas other employee representatives, most probably insiders, held 549 (72%); Bundesverband deutscher Banken (1995: Table 2). This facet points to the close connection between supervisory board and works council co-determination; for the latter, see Sec. C.I.2. below.

[371] Gerum/Steinmann/Fees (1988: 61).

[372] Note that the following data come from mid- and late-seventies samples respectively.

[373] Its results can be found in one major publication, Gerum/Steinmann/Fees (1988), and several articles which focus on particular issues, such as Steinmann/Gerum (1980) (transactions that need the board's approval), Gerum/Richter/Steinmann (1981) (co-determination in *Konzern-AG*s) and Steinmann/Fees/Gerum (1985) (ownership structure and co-determination).

Table 28: Employee Representatives in *AG* Supervisory Board Committees, 1975/76
and 1979

Employee Representation	One-Half Régimes Percentage of All Committees	One-Third Régimes Percentage of All Committees
Share According to Régime	35%	15%
Share Lower than Régime Standard	42%	37%
None	4%	48%
Not Attributable to a Category Above	20%	—

Note: Due to rounding percentages may not add to 100.
Sources: Vogel (1980: 191) (one-third régime), and Gerum/Steinmann/Fees (1988: 102) (one-half régime).

(being highest in dependent companies in the iron and steel sector, followed by dependent *Konzern* companies, and being lowest at *Konzern* parent companies and independent companies), ownership structure (co-determination potential higher in companies of the public sector, in manager-controlled companies, and in companies that depend on a domestic parent company), company size (co-determination potential increases with size), and responsible trade union.

The enumeration reveals the interdependence between co-determination via supervisory boards and some of those company features which were dealt with in previous sections. Nevertheless, the approach to co-determination appropriate for this survey is its effect on the intensity of control exerted by the supervisory board with respect to the management. Any empirical or theoretical foundation we can refer to is weak. From a theoretical perspective, examples of relevant issues are qualification, motivation, and incentives (including the election procedure) of employee representatives, and the question of whether they have uniform or heterogeneous interests. Does the addition of at least one further player (assuming homogeneous interests) affect the dynamics of board interaction? Many kinds of cooperation can easily be substantiated: a coalition of management and employee representatives to save their company-specific human capital, of both benches (assuming their homogeneity) to fight management entrenchment, or of capital bench and management, e.g., due to personal links.[374] Moreover, the effects on other control forces such as the market for corporate control have to be taken into account.[375]

---

[374] Cf., e.g., Ganske (1996) and Pistor (1997) for some tentative thoughts.

[375] Kübler (1994a: 571) hypothesizes that the effect of co-determination on the market for corporate control "may be one of the reasons why management today tends to have a more favorable view of co-determination than 15 years ago." Along the same lines, see Hopt (1994: 210). This point was impressively confirmed by the statement of Thyssen's CEO during the takeover attack by Krupp; cf. Sec. B.IV. above. A recent questionnaire by Förschle/Glaum/Mandler (1998: 894-5) (top managers from 66 large, quoted non-financial *AG*s, fall 1997) confirms that

Objective, "hard" facts with respect to the board's intensity of control are, of course, difficult to collect, but there is even a lack of scientifically conducted interrogations.[376] At best, we depend on interrogations with almost unknown specifications; otherwise we must turn to anecdotal "evidence" that may put disproportionate weight on non-representative peculiarities, or that may be instrumentalized to create a picture that serves the interests of its originator rather than delivering an unbiased impression of reality. This leads to the general rule that interpretations require utmost caution.

Having made these reservations, what picture does emerge? Not surprisingly, members of the shareholder bench pass a negative judgment on supervisory board co-determination. It is said to weaken the position of ordinary members since controversial discussions among members of the shareholder bench are not welcomed, to devalue board meetings as a forum of open discussions, and to strengthen the chairman, in particular due to his central position in the information flow.[377] The fear that employee representatives do not strictly observe the principle of board secrecy, which has been nourished by actual cases, leads to efforts to keep information from the supervisory board.[378] According to interviews with a wide range of participants, the board meeting degenerates into a ritual and fractionalizes. Separate meetings of each bench before a board meeting are common practice. The CEO is invited by each bench to provide information. The decision-making process takes place in these bench meetings. In sum, co-determination is said to weaken the supervisory board as a force in corporate governance.[379]

The employee representatives should not be regarded as a homogeneous group. The instructive contributions by internal employee representatives are appreciated by shareholder representatives as opposed to effects of external

---

managment board members indeed evaluate co-determination suprisingly positive: 53% opposed and 18% strongly opposed the abolishment of supervisory board co-determination.

[376] Surprisingly, there also seems to be a lack of encompassing studies that investigate the changes in companies' by-laws, etc., in the years surrounding the implementation of the quasi-parity régime in 1976. The early analysis of Ulmer (1977) is one of the rare exceptions. His analysis of 58 changes in statutes of *AG*s subject to the quasi-parity régime in the first eight months of 1977 does not, among other things, support the hypothesis that companies try to cut the catalog of transactions that need the supervisory board's approval (p. 515). However, the interviewees of a recent interrogation reported an opposing development; Bremeier/ Mülder/Schilling (1994: 73).

[377] Bremeier/Mülder/Schilling (1994: 20-1, 58-9, 61-5).

[378] Hopt (1994: 206). However, the danger is also valid for the shareholder bench: think, for instance, of the staff of a back office, in particular of a member on several boards (which should be the regular case for a person having a back office at his disposal), of members sitting on the boards of competing companies, or of the regular contact, for example on a management board, between members sitting on the boards of competing companies.

[379] Pistor (1997: 47); she presents results of interviews with representatives of trade unions, political parties, and legislators (no further specifications given).

members coming from unions.[380] The interest of the former group are said to be focused on the company, whereas the latter are thought to have a broader, at least sectoral, perspective and to pursue union interests.[381] These conflicts, however, are settled during the bench meetings; in the board meetings the employee representatives act with one voice.[382] Puzzling—though older—evidence is delivered by Vogel, who reports that unanimous votes in one-third régime supervisory boards are common;[383] this finding contradicts, at least partially, the impression of antagonism provided by other references. Employee representatives specialize in employee-related subjects such as workplace, social aspects, wages, and benefits, but they do not contribute much to issues like business strategy.[384] Union officials concede a lack of knowledge among employee representatives in the fields of accounting and finance. For this reason, the *Deutsche Gewerkschaftsbund* (*DGB*, German Trade Union Federation) offers training courses.[385]

Taking a short look at pecuniary effects, Schmid, in his analysis of remuneration determinants, finds that the one-half régimes exert a significantly negative influence on management board remuneration, but the influence is not significant for supervisory board compensation.[386] The latter comes as no surprise, since employee representatives who are members of a *DGB* union are expected to and indeed do give their remuneration exceeding DM 6,000 per annum to the *Hans-Böckler-Stiftung* (trade union foundation).[387] Thus it can be concluded that remuneration is an even weaker incentive for employee representatives to achieve market value maximizing by the management than for the shareholder representatives.[388]

In summary, keeping in mind the reservations outlined above, the sparse empirical evidence suggests that supervisory board co-determination weakens intensity of supervisory board control. Empirical studies whose starting point is not the supervisory board, but which instead compare features of companies that are subject to different co-determination provisions, could be an alternative way

---

[380] Bremeier/Mülder/Schilling (1994: 61-5). This impression is confirmed by the interviewees of Vitols et al. (1997: 20) (comparative study of Germany and the U.K., interviews with company members and related persons in four sectors, 1995-1997).

[381] Hopt (1994: 208) and Pistor (1997: 48).

[382] Pistor (1997: 45).

[383] Vogel (1980: 260-3).

[384] Pistor (1997: 45-6). Her findings are confirmed by Vogel (1980: 252), who analyzes to which subjects employee representatives have brought forward a motion.

[385] Pistor (1997: 46) and Vitols et al. (1997: 20).

[386] Schmid (1997: 78-9).

[387] Kronenberg/Volkmann/Wendeling-Schröder (1994: 27) and Knoll/Knoesel/Probst (1997: 241-2).

[388] At some sending banks, the sent supervisory board members must also cede their supervisory board remuneration, at least partially; Bremeier/Mülder/Schilling (1994: 114).

to yield more conclusive results. Unfortunately, this kind of study shares a basic problem. Ideally, studies like these contrast at least two groups of companies which differ only by one major characteristic, so that discovered differences can be attributed, with some justification, to the distinguishing characteristic. Due to the criteria co-determination laws use to allocate companies to the different co-determination régimes, the few available studies have great difficulties in defining a meaningful control group[389].[390] Using an innovative design, Baums and Frick overcome this problem by investigating whether judicial decisions on company-specific, supervisory board co-determination issues caused an abnormal performance of the shares of the company under consideration.[391] Regardless of the court's decision, they could not find significant abnormal returns. A single study of this kind must be interpreted with particular caution. Several explanations are straightforward, e.g., co-determination does not affect supervisory board work; it does affect supervisory board work but the board is out of power as a force in corporate governance; regardless of the influence of co-determination on the supervisory board's corporate governance efficacy, corporate governance and company performance are unrelated. In a nutshell, this innovative study provides "hard" data, but is nevertheless compatible with interpretations in many directions.

2. Works Council Co-Determination

Works council co-determination is the second kind of co-determination in Germany. A works council is mandatory for all businesses and plants with five or more permanent employees, regardless of their legal form of business organization. Works councillors are elected by all employees for a term of four years.[392] The number of members depends on the size of the workforce. Basically, works council co-determination refers to the individual plant, but the law provides for an aggregate works council for firms with several plants and for a group works council for groups of companies.

Works council participation rights (Table 29) are particularly pronounced in

---

[389] E.g., because size is the main criterion used by co-determination laws, it is almost impossible to define a control group of domestic companies of equal size not subject to co-determination laws. Consequently, one is forced to compare companies that are distinguished by more than one major feature.

[390] Cf. Frick/Sadowski (1995: 48-9, 79-80) and Baums/Frick (1997: 5-8) for a survey. The surveyed studies analyze factor productivities, factor intensities, and many other variables; they find at best a weak effect of supervisory board co-determination. See also Raiser (1997) for a general assessment.

[391] Baums/Frick (1997) (sample: 23 judicial decisions, 1974-1995).

[392] Neither the right to stand as a candidate nor the right to vote is confined to union members; nevertheless, unions hold a strong position in works councils: about three-quarters of works councillors are union members; Müller-Jentsch (1995: 56-7).

social matters, less strong in personnel matters, and weak in financial and economic issues.[393] The latter needs some modification as far as companies with more than 100 permanent employees are concerned: they have to establish a business and finance committee (*Wirtschaftsausschuß*) consisting of three to seven members. The committee meets monthly, and on that occasion the employer is obliged to inform the committee thoroughly and in good time of the company's financial situation and its implications for the workforce.[394]

The task here is not to give a comprehensive analysis of works council co-determination,[395] but to investigate its relevance for corporate governance, understood as the agency problem of how to monitor the management. Direct relevance is hard to judge, but it probably tends to be low due to its focus on the plant level and the concentration of participation rights on other than financial and economic matters.[396]

Turning to indirect relevance, an interesting interaction between both types of co-determination becomes evident: works councillors supply more than one half of employee representatives on supervisory boards. Moreover, at least as members of a *Wirtschaftsausschuß*, works councillors can collect both a wide range of basic plant-level information as well as information on the business and financial situation. Conditions seem to be such that a works councillor sitting on the supervisory board has a solid information base at his disposal[397] and, equally important, his information base most likely is highly complementary to the information the shareholder representatives have at hand. Thus, from a mere informational perspective[398] the makeup of the supervisory board prescribed by co-determination is a good starting point for management board monitoring.

To recap, the analysis of co-determination, a highly political issue, is dominated by opinions, not by facts. The judgment of co-determination in

---

[393] Müller-Jentsch (1995: 59-60).

[394] Schmidt et al. (1997: 45).

[395] Managers give works council co-determination good marks; Müller-Jentsch (1995: 67). For a more detailed analysis of works council co-determination, see, for instance, Müller-Jentsch (1995) and Schmidt et al. (1997: 222-30, 253). As for the empirical evidence, the same statement holds that was given with respect to supervisory board co-determination: studies are rare and do not lead to conclusive results; surveys are delivered by Hamel (1993), Sadowski/Frick (1995), Sadowski/Junkes/Lent (1997), and Baums/Frick (1997: 9, Appendices A1 and A2).

[396] The latter is confirmed by empirical evidence on the actual main tasks of works councils: they are principally occupied with personnel matters, technical change, health and safety, classification of wage groups, working hours, etc.; results of a questionnaire of the *Hans-Böckler-Stiftung* presented by Müller-Jentsch (1995: 65-6).

[397] This may be one main reason why internal employee representatives are generally highly appreciated supervisory board members of the capital side.

[398] I.e., leaving aside all other factors, as, for instance, the incentive to monitor.

Table 29:   Rights of the Works Council According to the Works Constitution Law of 1988

	Co-Decision (cd), Consultation (cons), and Information (inform) Rights of the Council
Social Matters	
Conduct of Employees	cd
Working Hours	cd
Wage Payment Procedures	cd
Holiday Planning	cd
Installation of Electronic Surveillance Equipment	cd
Regulations Regarding Accident Prevention	cd
Social Services and Amenities	cd
Employee Housing	cd
Wage Scales	cd
Piece Rates	cd
Suggestion Schemes	cd
Personnel Matters	
Planning of the Structuring of Jobs, Operations, and Working Environment	cons
Alterations in Jobs, Operations, or Working Environment Contradictory to Ergonomics	cd
Personnel Planning	cons
Personnel Questionnaires*	cd
Written Employment Contracts*	cd
Recruiting and Selection Standards*	cd
Establishment of In-Plant Vocational Training Facilities	cons
Introduction of Vocational Training Programs	cons
Implementation of Vocational Training	cd
Hiring, Classification, Transfer, Redeployment[a]	cd
Dismissals[b]	cd
Economic Matters	
Economic Conditions of the Company, Production Situation, Production Program, Financial Situation, Marketing Situation, Investment Program, Rationalization Plans, New Work Methods[c], Reduction or Close-Down of the Company, Transfer of the Plant, Mergers, Changes in the Organization and the Business Purposes	inform
Mass Layoff	cons
Social Consequences of Operational Changes and Mass Layoff	cd

Notes:
    *   Right to veto.
    a   These rights hold only for firms with at least 20 employees. Only in specific cases is the works council entitled to object to hiring, classification, transfer, and redeployment.
    b   Only in specific cases is the works council entitled to object to a dismissal.
    c   Consultation rights regarding the social, personnel, and economic consequences of new work methods on employees.

Source: Schmidt et al. (1997: 224); adjusted version of a table taken from: Adams, R.J. and C.H. Rummel 'Workers' Participation in Management in West Germany: Impact on the Worker, the Enterprise and the Trade Union' *Industrial Relations* 8/1 (1977) 4-22.

general is positive,[399] whereas its positive effect on corporate governance is doubted. The latter, however, should by no means be interpreted to mean that under current regulation the supervisory board would be a perfect monitoring device once supervisory board co-determination was abolished. The market for corporate control could be expected to gain power as a force in corporate governance, but the above analysis has pointed to several weaknesses of the shareholder bench that would remain valid.

II. Lenders[400]

1. Lenders and Corporate Governance

The role of lenders as a force in corporate governance has not yet been extensively analyzed. Lenders are interested in the repayment of a credit in accordance with the credit contract. Since—among other things—the management's actions are one of the factors determining repayment, lenders may be motivated to carry out monitoring. Thus, in a manner similar to that of the workforce, they become another party in the corporate governance game and, consequently, increase the degree of complexity even further.

For illustration, some very tentative thoughts will be developed. In this survey, corporate governance is understood as the agency problem between management and owners. Shareholders and debtholders share the same subject—the management—but cannot generally be expected to pursue the same goal. In particular, it is well known from the option interpretation of equity and debt[401] as well as from agency theory itself[402] that shareholders' gains can stem from either a more efficient use of resources or from the exploitation of other stakeholders, such as lenders. On the other hand, it is widely hypothesized that too strong an influence of lenders might cause an allocationally inefficient degree of risk aversion.[403] Moreover, the intensity of lender control, regardless of its aim, may run in a different cycle than intensity of shareholder control: if there is a huge cushion of equity, the need for lender control is small, whereas the need for shareholder control may be large.[404] Accordingly, intensity of lender control can be assumed to be highest in situations of financial distress and, a step further, in cases of bankruptcy. This leads to another very important determinant of

---

[399] Cf., for instance, the general tendency of the interviewees of Pistor (1997: 44).

[400] Cf. Ch. 10 of this volume on lenders' role in corporate governance.

[401] Cf., for example, Ross/Westerfield/Jaffe (1993: 636-9).

[402] Jensen/Meckling (1976: 333-43).

[403] Cf., for instance, Macey/Miller (1995/96).

[404] For an elaboration of corporate governance dependent on the company's health, cf. Rao/Sokolow/White (1996).

intensity of lender control: the legal framework. Lenders' liability, bankruptcy provisions, and the strength of the position of lenders in general—including enforceability, etc., of negotiated provisions in credit contracts—are of decisive significance to the intensity of control and, more generally, the credit supply. Thus, any encompassing analysis of lenders' role in corporate governance, for a single country as well as comparatively, requires an economic analysis of the legal setting.[405]

To describe lenders' role in corporate governance, another approach is also suitable. So far, the remarks have dealt with the direct involvement of lenders. Jensen's free cash flow hypothesis[406] is the most prominent example of an indirect involvement: additional debt with its fixed payment obligations is used to take away free cash flow from the management's disposal. Debt is used to mitigate the agency problem between management and shareholders, i.e., to produce positive "governance externalities." This view of "interdependent governance" could be extended to a "theory of interactive governance." Different parties acting in the governance process produce—as a side effect—signals. The interactive element arises when these parties act on these signals—like voice and exit—produced by another party while pursuing self-interested maximizing behavior.[407] This approach points out the important feature that the corporate governance analysis of debt, labor, and other non-shareholder stakeholders, who can be assumed to be interested in the management's behavior but do not necessarily pursue the goal of market value maximization (either of equity or of total wealth), must go beyond a partial analysis of debt, etc., and must end up in an analysis of corporate governance as a multi-party game. Of course, any partial analysis of the management-shareholder relation is necessarily incomplete, too.

Having outlined this ambitious research map, one must contrast it with the small basis of empirical and theoretical work done so far, internationally[408] as well as for Germany. This can be mainly traced back to the only recently awakened interest in the role of lending in corporate governance, as well as to the problem of obtaining data that go beyond aggregate sectoral figures, not to speak of details of credit contracts.

---

[405] As in the comparative analysis of the bankruptcy laws of France, Germany, and the U.S. in Drukarczyk/Schmidt (this volume Ch. 10: Sec. C.). For a recent investigation of covenants, see Thießen (1996).

[406] Jensen (1986).

[407] Triantis/Daniels (1995) work out a tentative concept of interactive governance.

[408] Short (1994: 228-40) provides a survey of theoretical approaches and executed (U.S.) empirical research from an international perspective.

2. Empirical Evidence for Germany

Before turning to some highly aggregated German data on financing,[409] some more qualifying remarks are needed. These kind of data are highly sensitive to definition, a fact that has to be kept in mind, in particular if international comparison is intended. In a flow-of-funds analysis, fractions are usually calculated relating funding sources with investment figures. In the denominator, gross or net investment may be used. The latter excludes replacement investments, which cause the same funding needs as net investments since depreciations are no means of payment. In the nominator, the cussedness of aggregation has to be taken into account. First, at the single company, it must be doubted if, for example, bank deposits and bank loans can be netted without losing valuable information.[410] The insufficiency of the net sources approach is evident if, on the occasion of sectoral aggregation, bank deposits of one company are netted with the bank loans of another company from this sector. This surely leads to an underestimation of the significance of bank financing. The description of financing structures is biased, too, if intra-sectoral credits and deposits are netted away.[411]

One important feature of both equity and debt financing, from a corporate governance perspective, is whether the funds are collected from outside or are generated internally. The former is assumed to be connected with a higher intensity of control. Prowse (Table 30) and Corbett and Jenkinson (Table 31) provide international comparative data.

Table 30: Gross Funding of Non-Financial Corporations, 1970-1990

	Germany		U.K.		Japan	
	1970-1985	1986-1990	1970-1985	1986-1990	1970-1985	1986-1990
Retentions	76%	78%	68%	50%	52%	54%
External Finance	24%	22%	32%	50%	48%	46%
Intermediated Debt	21%	18%	19%	35%	41%	32%
Securities	3%	4%	13%	15%	7%	14%

Note: As percentage of total gross financing.
Source: Prowse (1995: 24).

[409] For a far more extensive analysis of lenders as a force in corporate governance, cf. Schmidt et al. (1997: 141-63).

[410] For instance, the payouts to beneficiaries of intra-company pension schemes may cause c.p. a higher amount of bank deposits; however, these deposits are not held voluntarily but are needed for payouts within the near future, and, consequently, are connected with a funding need.

[411] There are problems with the stock approach as well, e.g., the just-mentioned problems of aggregation or the scope provided by accounting rules which was demonstrated in Sec. B.V.2. above. Methodological issues are discussed by Edwards/Fischer (1994: Ch. 3), Corbett/Jenkinson (1997: 71-4), and Schmidt et al. (1997: 142-55).

Table 31: Gross Sources of Finance of the Non-Financial Enterprise Sector, 1970-1989

	Germany	Japan	U.K.	U.S.
Internal	62.4%	40.0%	60.4%	62.7%
Bank Finance	18.0%	34.5%	23.3%	14.7%
Bonds	0.9%	3.9%	2.3%	12.8%
New Equity	2.3%	3.9%	7.0%	−4.9%[a]
Trade Credit	1.8%	15.6%	1.9%	8.8%
Capital Transfer	6.6%	—	2.3%	—
Other	8.0%	2.1%	2.9%	5.9%

Notes: As percentage of total gross financing.
   [a] The U.S. data on a gross basis nonetheless net out intra-sector purchases and sales of equity and are, thus, impossible to compare with the respective data for the other countries.
Source: Corbett/Jenkinson (1994: 9).

The data demonstrate the pronounced importance of internal financing in Germany that has increased significantly during the course of time.[412] Moreover, they reveal the great similarity of financing structures of Germany on the one hand and the U.K. and the U.S. on the other hand, which are usually described as having rather different patterns, whereas the structures of Germany and Japan, which are often thought to share many common features, differ markedly.

Turning to debt, the equity ratio is a good starting point to put things into perspective. The equity ratio of West German companies for 1995 is estimated to amount to 18%.[413] Table 32 provides some details of the capital structure, in particular liability structure.

Liabilities are mainly given on a long-term basis. Because (re-)negotiating financial contracts can be assumed as an occasion at which a particularly intense control could be exerted, choice of original maturities seems not to contribute much to intensity of control. Consequently, the control situation during the lifetime of a contract gains importance. As was the case with equity, identity and concentration of lenders are important determinants of intensity of control. Since funding via open markets (bonds) is of little importance, the holding of liabilities

---

[412] Corbett/Jenkinson (1997: 77) calculate the respective rates for five-year periods from 1970-1994 for net sources of finance: it is lowest for 1970-1974 (68.6%) and highest for 1985-1989 (89.3%).

[413] Deutsche Bundesbank (1996a: 44). The figure is the result of the *Bundesbank*'s balance sheet statistics of about 60,000 German companies, which does not include firms from the financial sector, agriculture, and professional services firms. The estimation is based on one-quarter of the complete sample; the figure for 1994 (full sample) is 17.9%. Comparing equity ratios in four EU countries, Deutsche Bundesbank (1994) demonstrates impressively that balance sheet figures should not be compared without thorough adjustment.

Table 32: Selected Financial Ratios of Business Undertakings Engaged in the
Production of Goods and Services, 1990-1996

Ratio	1990	1991	1992	1993	1994	1995	1996
Long-Term Funds as Percentage of Total Liabilities and Equity	73.9%	73.1%	74.2%	77.1%	76.8%	77.2%	77.4%
Short-Term Funds as Percentage of Total Liabilities and Equity	26.1%	26.9%	25.8%	22.9%	23.2%	22.8%	22.6%
Long-Term Liabilities as Percentage of Total Liabilities	66.2%	65.4%	67.5%	70.2%	69.1%	68.9%	68.3%
Short-Term Liabilities as Percentage of Total Liabilities	33.8%	34.6%	32.5%	29.8%	30.9%	31.1%	31.7%
Liabilities to Banks as Percentage of Total Liabilities	58.6%	59.7%	60.5%	61.5%	63.5%	63.1%	63.6%
Long-Term Liabilities[a] to Banks as Percentage of Total Liabilities to Banks	60.2%	60.9%	64.2%	68.1%	68.0%	67.0%	67.1%
Short-Term Liabilities to Banks as Percentage of Total Liabilities to Banks	39.8%	39.1%	35.8%	31.9%	32.0%	33.0%	32.9%
(Long-Term) Liabilities to Insurance Companies and Loan Associations as Percentage of Total Liabilities	4.3%	3.5%	3.3%	3.2%	3.4%	3.7%	3.9%
(Long-Term) Bonds as Percentage of Total Liabilities[b]	3.2%	2.9%	4.2%	8.3%	10.2%	3.9%	3.4%
(Long-Term) Pension Liabilities as Percentage of Total Liabilities	9.8%	9.4%	9.4%	9.4%	9.8%	9.6%	9.4%

Notes: a   Long-term liabilities to banks have an original maturity exceeding one year. Original
as opposed to remaining maturity seems to be the appropriate measure from a
corporate governance perspective.
   b   The temporary increase in bond financing can be attributed to the *Treuhandanstalt*.
The recent decline to the usual size is consistent with the interpretation that the role
of bond financing has not changed in the private sector, narrowly defined. This
assessment was recently supported by the Deutsche Bundesbank (1998a: 57-9).
Source: Original data from Deutsche Bundesbank (1997b: 56-7).

can be assumed to be quite concentrated, a good precondition for control. Banks,
by far the most important lenders, should possess an enormous expertise in the
lending business, which is one of their core businesses. Besides a lack of expertise, other factors may weaken their willingness or ability to control:[414] with the

---

[414] Bearing in mind that control in this section means control of the management by lenders
for the purpose of saving their loans which might, but need not, coincide with control of the
management as intended by shareholders.

dissemination of collateralization, the intensity of lender control can be thought to decrease.[415] Competitiveness in the loan business is regarded to be strong;[416] moreover, (very) large borrowers can alternatively turn to the open market for financing.[417] Thus, lenders may find it difficult to achieve the desired control rights. This analysis can only scratch the surface, for what is missing is empirical evidence on the contractual and actual relation between lender and borrower.[418]

Pension liabilities are another prominent part of liabilities.[419] Contrary to other countries, pension commitments of a company need not to be managed in a separate pool but can and often do become an integrated part of the company's balance sheet. The intensity of control attached to them is hard to estimate. On the one hand, these funds finally have to be paid out to meet an obligation, and intertemporal calculations have to use an interest rate of 6%. These features resemble usual debt. On the other hand, the "lender", the employee, cannot exert any influence as to the investment of these funds. In sum, these funds are surely not at the completely free disposal of the company's management, but it is no hard exercise to think of pension schemes which are connected with tighter control.[420]

---

[415] According to a questionnaire executed in 1983/84, two-thirds of short- and medium-term bank loans are collateralized; Drukarczyk/Duttle/Rieger (1985: 112-3). For long-term loans the share is estimated to be higher; Drukarczyk (1993: 338).

[416] Edwards/Fischer (1994: 109-11).

[417] In addition, the number of bank connections increases markedly with company size; Edwards/Fischer (1994: 141), quoting late-seventies empirical evidence by Braun, P.A. 'Das Firmenkundengeschäft der Banken im Wandel' (Dissertation University of Augsburg 1981). Empirical evidence presented by Fischer (1990) points in the same direction: contrary to public opinion, the importance of close relationships between banks and companies at the credit market (*Hausbankbeziehung*) is comparatively low and is expected to decrease further. However, recent empirical research revealed that, in some respects, *Hausbanken* and other banks (still) differ significantly in their behavior; Krahnen/Elsas (1998) (newspaper article describing their ongoing research).

[418] For some evidence on contractual clauses in *DM-Auslandsanleihen* (foreign DM bonds), cf. Hopt (1990: 356-61). In this context, the significance of the *Allgemeine Geschäftsbedingungen* (General Standard Terms and Conditions) in lending relations and, if there is any significance, their economic analysis from a corporate governance perspective would be interesting. The former point is addressed by a recent study by Leuz/Deller/Stubenrath (1997). In an empirical comparison of accounting-based payout restrictions in the U.S., U.K., and Germany, they find a complementary relationship between legal and contractual payout restrictions for all three countries with a particularly high importance of legal constraints for Germany. Moreover, they contribute additional empirical evidence on covenants in corporate DM-bonds issued by German companies or their foreign subsidiaries and in bank debt contracts; Leuz/Deller/Stubenrath (1997: 24-30).

[419] The *Deutsche Bundesbank* (1997: 32) calls them a substitute for equity.

[420] A thorough analysis also has to include the pension insurance scheme; cf. Edwards/Fischer (1994: 55-8) and Schmidt et al. (1997: 144-5, 152-5, 161-3) for further treatment of this subject.

So far the presented data of financial structures and, in particular, liability structures have dealt with varying but in any case very large and encompassing samples of the non-financial business sector. However, it is well known that each category of company size possesses its typical characteristics. To mention the most important, the significance of bank liabilities decreases as firm size increases, whereas pension liabilities are most important at large companies.[421]

The *AG* stands at the center of this survey. Recent data on the financing structure of smaller and larger *AG*s demonstrate that these size-related differences even hold for the small class of *AG*s (Table 33).[422]

Table 33: Financial Structure of Smaller and Larger *AG*s, 1987 and 1994

	Smaller *AG*s		Larger *AG*s	
	1987	1994	1987	1994
Own Funds[a,b]	30.9%	28.8%	33.4%	33.6%
Subscribed Capital	16.3%	15.6%	10.8%	9.3%
Share Premiums	2.4%	4.2%	7.8%	11.9%
Reserves[b]	12.2%	9.0%	14.8%	12.3%
Outside Funds, Total[b,c]	69.1%	71.2%	66.6%	66.4%
Amounts Owed to Credit Institutions	17.8%	21.6%	4.0%	4.3%
Provisions for Pensions	14.6%	12.9%	16.7%	17.5%
Other Outside Funds[b,c]	36.7%	36.8%	45.9%	44.7%
Balance Sheet Total	100%	100%	100%	100%

Notes: As percentage of balance sheet total.
           Sample consists of 114 smaller *AG*s, whose 1994 sales do not exceed DM 79 mil., and 295 larger *AG*s from the manufacturing, construction, and distribution sectors.
           [a] Gross, i.e., without deduction of adjustments and before appropriation of net income.
           [b] Including special reserves.
           [c] Including deferred income.
Source: Deutsche Bundesbank (1997: 32).

3. German Banks and Corporate Governance: A Synopsis of Empirical Evidence

Banks are the most important group of lenders; moreover, they are central players in German corporate governance due to the many corporate governance-related functions they occupy:[423] lenders, shareholders, proxies, members on

---

[421] More details can be found in Kaen/Sherman (1994: Chs. 7-8) and Schmidt et al. (1997: 150-4).

[422] Cf. also Seger (1997: 185-6); for his sample of 144 *AG*s bank liabilities to balance sheet total increases with decreasing company size.

[423] For a comprehensive survey, cf. Edwards/Fischer (1994). In the discussion of the German banking system, the fact often is neglected that approximately 50% (by balance sheet total) of the German banking sector is state-owned and -guaranteed respectively; Sinn (1997: 15-6). The largest *Landesbanken*, in particular the WestLB, are possibly already or will possibly

supervisory boards, running of investment companies, major (potential) advisors for and financiers of (yet very few) takeovers, and major players in the shaping of the German exchange structure[424].[425] In addition, more indirectly, it can be hypothesized with some justice that they are one of the pressure groups who is able to exert some influence on legislators, government, supervisory offices, science, and media.[426] For this wealth of potential channels of influence, it seems appropriate to provide a synopsis of the respective evidence as we approach the end of this survey.[427]

First, there are studies analyzing the effect of potential bank influence coming from a variety of sources without separating single sources. The findings are quite mixed: Perlitz/Seger (1994)[428] calculate a negative effect of bank influence on the performance of the companies possibly influenced, whereas Chirinko/

become a group that should not be neglected in the bank-related corporate governance discussion that is currently focused on the private *Großbanken*. Cf. Sinn (1997) for a recent treatise on this part of the German banking sector.

[424] Banks own 81% of the shares of the Deutsche Börse AG. Breuer, its supervisory board chairman, is CEO of Deutsche Bank, 12 of 21 supervisory board members are bank representatives, and bankers have a strong position in other exchange bodies as well; Monopolkommission (1998: 87, 89). Moreover, the banks exercise a significant influence on the smaller exchanges (*Regionalbörsen*); Schmidt/Oesterhelweg/Treske (1997: 406). Taking a venture capital perspective, the dominating role of the banks in German stock exchanges is criticized by the Wissenschaftlicher Beirat beim Bundesministerium für Wirtschaft (1997: 14, 16).

[425] Mülbert (1996) delivers a recent extensive overview from both an economic and legal perspective.

[426] Wenger (1996b).

[427] A more detailed synopsis is given by Schmidt/Prigge (forthcoming). Moreover, some theoretical reasoning why banks are so difficult an object of research and the severe consequences for designing and interpreting empirical studies are elaborated. To give a short hint: one main impediment to a clearer understanding is the varying and usually unobservable connection between the factor that may provide the bank with a source of influence, e.g., proxy votes, its own shareholdings, etc., and the goals pursued by the banks, e.g., maximizing value of the equity stake held, enlarging business with the influenced company, etc., when using the influence. For instance, if some power is attached to a supervisory board seat, it may be used for very different purposes. Empirical research that starts at a single source of potential influence and tries to investigate its effects at the company under influence faces the difficulty that the measures used to detect an effect may mirror a variety of goals that may possibly offset each other. Of course, this problem is even worse using more than one potential source of influence inseparably, like the first type of studies described below. A better way would be to start research at a certain goal pursued by banks and not at a potential source of influence. This way, however, is, at least currently, out of reach. Cf. also Sherman/Kaen (1997), Monopolkommission (1998: 78-107), and Seger (1997: 141-68); the latter provides a thorough review of most of the cited studies and also addresses methodological aspects in some detail.

[428] Using three criteria (total voting power at the general meeting, chairmanship on the supervisory board, and liabilities owed to banks, all as of 1990), Perlitz and Seger divide a sample of 110 listed industry companies into one group at which banks have a great potential influence (58 companies) and one group at which banks only have a small potential influence (52 companies). They find a significant difference between both categories: companies of the first group show a significantly lower profitability and growth (data from 1990 to 1992).

Elston (1996)[429], using the same criterion for potential bank influence, do not find a relation. Cable (1985)[430] and Nibler (1995)[431] discover a positive relation.

Second, there are studies which investigate the effect of single potential sources of influence on performance. With respect to bank loans, Nibler (1995), Chirinko/Elston (1996),[432] and Seger (1997)[433] find a negative effect. However, as always, causation is unclear: it is evident that companies with inferior or even weak performance may have a larger funding need and are more likely to demand intermediated instead of open-market financing.[434] Turning to share ownership of banks, the results are inconclusive again:[435] Nibler (1995) and Schmid (1996) find a positive relation; Chirinko/Elston (1996) and Seger (1997)[436] cannot discover a relation; Gorton/Schmid (1996) calculate a positive connection for their 1974 sample but are unable to detect one for their 1985 sample; and, finally, Wenger/Kaserer (this volume Ch. 6) find a negative relation between equity ownership of the financial sector, mainly banks, and company performance. Böhmer (1997) reports substantially lower CARs for bidders with direct bank ownership as compared with bidders without any shareholdings by banks. For proxy voting, Nibler's (1995) study reveals a negative relation, whereas Gorton/Schmid (1996) and Seger (1997) cannot find such a connection. Cable (1985) finds out a positive relation between bankers' supervisory board membership and company performance. Nibler's (1995) results are inconclusive, as are those by Wenger/Kaserer (1998), who discover a negative relation for ordinary board seats but a positive one for the chairmanship, both of which, however, are not significant. And Seger (1997) finds that ordinary board seats do not show a significant relation, whereas supervisory board chairmanship is significantly negatively connected with performance.[437]

---

[429] Sample of the sub-analysis using the Perlitz-Seger measure: 64 listed industrial corporations, 1965-1990.

[430] Criteria: voting rights, supervisory board seats, and loans.

[431] Criteria: voting rights and supervisory board seats.

[432] Sample of this part of the analysis: 270 listed industrial corporations, 1965-1990.

[433] Seger (1997: 195-9). Moreover, Seger (1997: 188-91) finds a significant negative relation between supervisory board memberships of bank representatives and bank liabilities to balance sheet total, whereas he cannot discover significant relations of bank liabilities to balance sheet total, either with bankers occupying the supervisory board chair or with banks' shareholdings.

[434] In addition, Kaserer (1996) is unable to detect a significant effect of the importance of bank loans as a means of funding on the extent of the underpricing of German IPOs.

[435] Neuberger (1997) analyzes theoretical and empirical evidence of the welfare effects of banks shareholdings.

[436] But he discovers significant reciprocally offsetting effects for particular groups of banks.

[437] With respect to IPOs, Kaserer (1996) finds a weakly significant underpricing reducing effect of banks' supervisory board chairmanships.

In addition, there are studies which investigate the effect of bank ties on the financing of companies. Elston/Albach (1995)[438] observe that companies with closer ties to banks, measured with the Cable criterion, exhibited investment functions with less sensitivity to liquidity constraints than companies with more distance to banks for the period 1983-1992, but not for the periods 1967-1972 and 1973-1982. The evidence for the latest period allows not only the interpretation that bank affiliation improves liquidity, but others as well, as Elston and Albach demonstrate: banks might prefer well-performing companies, bank affiliation might serve as a signal for other lenders, or bank-associated companies might have been able to expand their internal financing potential.[439] Schwiete/ Weigand (1997)[440] cannot find an effect of bank shareholdings on the debt-equity ratios of companies. On the contrary, Seger (1997) finds that some sources of potential bank influence do affect the financial structure of companies. Debt ratio in particular increases, in a non-linear manner, with banks' shareholdings and is higher if a bank representative is supervisory board chairman.[441] Bank equity ownership possesses no explanatory power for companies' debt funding. Schmid (1996) cannot detect an effect of bank equity ownership on return on assets, but observes a u-shaped return-on-equity-curve as a function of the amount of bank shareholdings.[442] These findings are compatible with the view that banks do execute corporate control activity and get paid for it: to internalize compensation payment for small bank shareholdings, compensation is integrated in a higher debt interest rate at the expense of the return on equity, with increasing bank shareholdings compensation more and more is becoming part of the return on equity.

Finally, Chirinko and Elston have tried to evaluate the importance of bank influence, stemming from various sources, as a control mechanism for German *AG*s as compared with three other mechanisms: concentrated ownership, payout ratios for dividends, and significance of interest payments[443].[444] They find a highly significant substitution relation between ownership concentration and bank influence, suggesting that banks fill the control gap at companies with dispersed ownership.[445] As this interpretation conforms with the prominent representation of bankers on the supervisory boards of the (mainly widely held)

---

[438] Sample: 121 companies, 1967-1992, bank affiliation as of 1991.

[439] Elston/Albach (1995: 10).

[440] Sample: 230 *AG*s of the producing sector, 1965-1986.

[441] Seger (1997: 214-7).

[442] Seger (1997: 200-2) also finds a non-linear, though reversely shaped connection.

[443] Dividend and interest payments as control device are both based on the free cash flow hypothesis of Jensen (1986).

[444] The threat of a takeover is another control mechanism, but due to its insignificance in Germany, Chirinko/Elston (1996: 10) decided not to include it.

[445] Chirinko/Elston (1996: 28-30).

DAX companies[446] and the increase in importance of proxy voting with declining ownership concentration,[447] the question as to the bank's control motivation and goals remains unsolved.

The synopsis reveals that empirical research is gaining momentum but is still far away from enabling a full understanding. As it is a defining characteristic of universal banking, the wide range of junctions between banking and corporate sector comes as no surprise. Different functions may overlap, so it can be hypothesized that bank representation on supervisory boards is part of the loan control technology used by banks.[448] Possibly due to the environment, such as lenders' liability, the supervisory board may have proved to be an adequate platform for lender control, thereby possibly impairing it as an instrument of owner control.[449]

D. Conclusion

The presented pool of facts conforms with the résumé drawn by Franks and Mayer[450] at the end of their comparative study: "How well do the theories of ownership and the market for corporate control square with these observations? The answer is not well at all; they leave a large number of unresolved issues." This statement holds for a theory of German corporate governance as a compact unit, as well as for comparative research on corporate governance in different countries.

Focusing, in accordance with the international discussion, on the *AG* and, consequently, on big business governance, one must keep in mind that these companies represent a significant but not dominant part of the German economy. The main feature of German corporate governance is that open markets[451]—i.e., the share market and the market for corporate control, and in connection with them, disclosure and accounting as informational preconditions for efficient open markets[452]—are only weak forces in German corporate governance. Instead, concentrated ownership is a common feature, with families and corporations as

---

[446] Cf. Sec. B.I.2. above.

[447] Cf. Sec. B.II.4. above.

[448] Pfannschmidt (1993: 158-65) finds a positive relation between the debt ratios of companies and the number of bank representatives sitting on their supervisory boards.

[449] The same point can be put forward with respect to supervisory board co-determination; for an elaboration, cf. Wiendieck (1992: 164-72, 179-80), lenders only, and Schmidt et al. (1997: 160-1, 238-9).

[450] Franks/Mayer (1995: 189).

[451] As opposed to intermediated markets.

[452] Leaving aside competitive product markets as an almost unrenounceable precondition for an efficient use of resources.

the most important owners. Whereas theory suggests that the former group has great though not unambiguous incentives to use resources efficiently, the latter points at a distinctive characteristic in Germany—the high degree of linkage, both personal and financial. Linkage is suspected of being misused as a shield to weaken the power of ultimate residual claimants. This development is fostered by the high importance of some kind of stakeholder approach, which is characteristic for Germany and, when used as a shield against control by residual claimants, can both directly and indirectly lower intensity of control of the agents, at least of that control which aims at directing them to pursue the owner's goals. The representation of employees and other constituencies on supervisory boards as well as the low importance managers attach to the maximization of equity market value highlight this general attitude. Banks, in particular a few large banks, play a central role in German corporate governance by running a great variety of businesses. Their shares are widely held, and consequently their management can be assumed to be exposed to a comparably low level of owner control. *Konzerne* are a feature that causes a great deal of personal and financial linkage. They seem to deserve a closer examination in future corporate governance research. Looking at the relative importance of open and non-open markets and at the significance of linkage, the characterization of German corporate governance as an insider system[453] seems to have a good fit.[454]

---

[453] Franks/Mayer (1995: 184). In Berglöf's (1997) terminology, the German system could be described as control-oriented as opposed to an arm's-length system.

[454] Since most of the paired characterizations concentrate on corporate *finance* they do not go beyond the financial sphere and consequently fail to appropriately describe a corporate *governance* structure with its focus on *control*. (Berglöf (1997: 157-9) discusses several of the paired characterizations of corporate governance systems.) They miss the role played by other stakeholders, particularly employees as well as other basic features such as the legal system; for a more pronounced treatment of legal aspects, see Wymeersch (1994), and recently the pioneering empirical studies by La Porta et al. (1996, 1997, 1997a).

On a more general level, the benefit of *paired* characterizations must be considered. At an early stage of research they were doubtlessly useful for a first, very tentative understanding of rather complex structures, but it seems that corporate governance research should try to leave this stage behind. Obviously, a limitation to *two* categories—even taking into account that simplification is the purpose and defining attribute of categorization—is too narrow in a medium-term perspective. (See de Jong (1997: 6-10) for a recent categorization of European corporations differentiating between *three* categories (Anglo-Saxon, Germanic, and Latinic).) Proof, or at least circumstantial evidence, can be found in the fact that categories are usually tailored so that Germany and Japan are grouped under a common heading. Prowse's (1996: 5) remarks are revealing: "Although there are some differences, methods of finance and governance in Japan and Germany share a number of important characteristics. In particular, they both look different from those of the United States." This may be true, but it does not justify the placement of Germany and Japan in the same category in an even only slightly refined categorization. The future of such categorizations will more probably be to serve as a source of relevant characteristics of corporate governance systems containing those features mentioned in a more abstract way by Schmidt (1997); see Sec. A above. If categories are created, their number should be small while exceeding two. Used in this way, categorization will most likely remain a useful instru-

Spurred by some spectacular company crises during recent years and the general discussion of the condition of the German economy, corporate governance has become a field of legislative initiatives. It could not be expected that basic structures which have developed during decades would be peremptorily dismantled. Instead, two recent corporate governance-related reform laws suggest minor changes of details and not of complete structures. The following paragraphs summarize some highlights of the law for a reform of German stock corporation law (*KonTraG*)[455].

The relation between supervisory board and auditor is to become closer. The supervisory board hires the balance sheet auditor, and his participation at the balance sheet meeting of the supervisory board or the respective committee becomes mandatory, as well as the delivery of his report to the supervisory board. Moreover, the reform is intended to increase auditors' liability, reduce the maximum sales coming from a single customer, and implement an auditor rotation within the auditing firm.

As to the position of banks in general meetings at other companies, it is planned that in case of a bank equity ownership exceeding 5%, the bank can either make use of the voting rights of its own shares or of the proxy voting rights without specified instructions given to it by its customers, but not of both.

Several measures aim at increasing supervisory board efficiency. Candidates for supervisory boards of quoted companies must disclose their offices and mandates before the election. In addition, each board of a quoted company has to deliver these data of its members annually. As a side effect, this transparency makes personal linkage more obvious. While the original intention was for companies subject to quasi-parity co-determination to have the option of reducing the number of board members to 12, severe attacks, especially from the unions' side, have caused this measure to be abandoned.

In February and March 1998, as a reaction to the accounting and disclosure requirements at international capital markets, the legislative bodies passed a law to facilitate capital raising.[456] According to this law, quoted parent companies of a *Konzern* which prepare a consolidated year-end financial statement in accordance with internationally accepted standards such as IAS rules or U.S. GAAP

---

ment in comparative corporate governance analysis.

[455] Cf. Seibert (1997) for details of the first draft, Die Aktiengesellschaft (1997) for a comprehensive collection of expert opinions, and Monopolkommission (1998: 74-7) for critical comments. Cf. Federal Ministry of Justice (1997) for the guidelines of the draft as adopted by the federal cabinet on November 6, 1997. The principal parts of this version are documented in Zeitschrift für Wirtschaftsrecht (1997a). The bill (cf. *BGBl I* 24/1998, 786-94) passed the legislative bodies and became effective in April 1998. Cf. Lingemann/Wasmann (1998) for a first description of the final version and Förschle/Glaum/Mandler (1998) for a recent questionnaire investigating the attitude of German top managers as towards the *KonTraG* and related issues. See Hopt (this volume Ch. 4: Sec. C) for an assessment of the *KonTraG*.

[456] *Kapitalaufnahmeerleichterungsgesetz*; see *BGBl I* 22/1998, 707-9.

need not deliver an additional statement according to German rules.[457] Note that the *Konzernabschluß* is neither the basis for taxation nor for payout restrictions (lender protection).

The fact that corporate governance issues have even reached legislative initiatives[458] is a clear indication that corporate governance has become an important point on the agenda. The subject can be put in even a broader perspective: in Germany, a top issue is the increasing competition among economies (*Standortwettbewerb*). In its latest annual expert opinion, the German Council of Economic Experts[459] dealt in some detail with the *Standortwettbewerb,* which it defines as the competition of the immobile factors of an economy tied to the *Standort*—mainly employees—for the internationally mobile factors—mainly capital and entrepreneurial initiative—by making the *Standort* as attractive as possible.[460] Corporate governance as a whole as well as the corporate governance-related options it supplies clearly are part of the offer with which the *Standort Deutschland* and its contenders join the international competition for mobile factors.[461] Consequently, a better understanding of corporate governance would

---

[457] Funke (1998). Cf. Zeitschrift für Wirtschaftsrecht (1997) for details of the draft statute which originally proposed a smaller group of eligible companies encompassing those companies that raise funds in foreign markets. The law is valid for six years. During this time span the legislators intend to substantially reform the German *Konzern* accounting law and to catch up with international development in this field. For this purpose a private German standard-setting body is to be set up; Funke (1998). In March 1998, the *Deutsche Rechnungslegungs Standards Committee* was actually founded; Börsen-Zeitung (1998b).

[458] And also official commissions: in February 1998, the *Monopolkommission* (1998) published a special expert opinion on corporate finance and control in Germany.

[459] Among other things, the *Sachverständigenrat zur Begutachtung der gesamtwirtschaftlichen Entwicklung* annually delivers an expert opinion on the state of the German economy to the federal government.

[460] Sachverständigenrat (1997: 178-84).

[461] The *Sachverständigenrat* (1997: 178) does not mention corporate governance explicitly, but lists the legal system as one relevant issue. Surely, the notion of corporate governance covers far too many different issues and actors to be able to ascribe to it a uniform degree of strength in relation to the *Standort,* which is the decisive category in this respect. For example, a bad design of the available legal structures of business organization (in comparison with other legal systems) is a more serious disadvantage than a bad environment for going publics due to underdeveloped share markets. This is because an entrepreneur cannot use a foreign legal form of business organization for his German business, whereas a candidate for a going public can turn to a foreign share market, which, of course, is a worse situation than a setting with adequate domestic markets. However, the important point here is not to weigh the importance of different characteristics of a *Standort* for its attractiveness (quality of available legal forms of business organization vs. quality of share markets), but to investigate in a partial analysis the strength of the link between characteristic and *Standort,* and, relatedly, the importance this characteristic has, due to this connection, for an economy and its success in attracting value-added capacity. This argument holds for the usual case that place of value-added creation and real head of administration are situated in the same *Standort.*

A look at U.S. corporate law helps to clarify the distinction made above. In the U.S., 50 states

be useful. However, as noted above in the short discussion of comparative analysis of corporate governance systems, our knowledge of the complex inter-relations characterizing corporate governance is still in its infancy, and needs substantial improvement in the future.

and the District of Columbia compete for the incorporation of companies. Since within the U.S. there is no mandatory connection between the state of corporation and the state(s) where the actual process of value-added creation take(s) place, state corporate law is—at best—of minor importance for the attractiveness of a state as *Standort* for the value creation process.

References

Adams, Michael 'Die Usurpation von Aktionärsbefugnissen mittels Ringverflechtung in der "Deutschland AG". Vorschläge für Reformen im Wettbewerbs-, Steuer- und Unternehmensrecht' *Die Aktiengesellschaft* 39 (1994) 148-58.

Die Aktiengesellschaft *Die Aktienrechtsreform 1997 nach den Vorschlägen des Referentenentwurfs eines Gesetzes zur Kontrolle und Transparenz im Unternehmensbereich (KonTraG)* (with contributions by Adams, Assmann, Baums, Claussen, Gelhausen, Götz, Hopt, Kübler, Lutter, Martens, Mertens, Peltzer, Seibert, Wenger) *Die Aktiengesellschaft* (Special Edition, August 1997).

Die Aktiengesellschaft 'Überarbeitung des freiwilligen Übernahmekodex' *Die Aktiengesellschaft* 42 (1997a) R487-R488.

Die Aktiengesellschaft 'Übernahmekodex mit den Änderungen durch Bekanntmachung vom 28.11.1997. Börsensachverständigenkommission beim Bundesministerium der Finanzen' *Die Aktiengesellschaft* 43 (1998) 133-7.

Amihud, Yakov and Maurizio Murgia 'Dividends, Taxes, and Signaling: Evidence from Germany' *Journal of Finance* 52 (1997) 397-408.

André, Thomas J. 'Some Reflections on Corporate Governance: A Glimpse at German Supervisory Boards' 70 *Tul. L. Rev.* 1819-79 (1996).

Augustin, Reinhard R. 'Ausschüttungspolitik deutscher und amerikanischer börsennotierter Unternehmen' *Recht der internationalen Wirtschaft* 40 (1994) 659-62.

Baetge, Jörg and Bernd Apelt 'Publizität kleiner und mittelständischer Kapitalgesellschaften und Harmonisierung der Rechnungslegung' *Betriebswirtschaftliche Forschung und Praxis* 44 (1992) 393-411.

Baetge, Jörg, Karl-Heinz Armeloh, and Dennis Schulte 'Empirische Befunde über die Qualität der Geschäftsberichterstattung börsennotierter deutscher Kapitalgesellschaften' *Deutsches Steuerrecht* 35 (1997) 212-9.

Baetge, Jörg, Karl-Heinz Armeloh, and Dennis Schulte 'Qualität der Geschäftsberichte insgesamt nur ausreichend' *Handelsblatt* no. 71, 14.4.1997a, 22.

Ballwieser, Wolfgang 'Zum Nutzen handelsrechtlicher Rechnungslegung' in: Ballwieser, Wolfgang, Adolf Moxter, and Rolf Nonnenmacher (eds.) *Festschrift für Hermann Clemm zum 70. Geburtstag* 1-25 (Munich 1996).

Bästlein, Hanno M. *Zur Feindlichkeit öffentlicher Übernahmeangebote. Eine ökonomische Betrachtung von Ursachen und Auswirkungen unter besonderer Berücksichtigung der deutschen Situation* (Dissertation University of Freiburg) (Frankfurt am Main et al. 1997).

Baums, Theodor 'Höchststimmrechte' *Die Aktiengesellschaft* 35 (1990) 221-42.

Baums, Theodor 'Hostile Takeovers in Germany. A Case Study on Pirelli vs. Continental AG' (Working Paper of the Institut für Handels- und Wirtschaftsrecht, University of Osnabrück, no. 3/1993).

Baums, Theodor 'Takeovers vs. Institutions in Corporate Governance in Germany' in: Prentice, David D. and Peter R.J. Holland (eds.) *Contemporary Issues in Corporate Governance* 151-83 (Oxford 1993a).

Baums, Theodor 'Universal Banks and Investment Companies in Germany' in: Saunders, Anthony and Ingo Walter (eds.) *Universal Banking: Financial System Design Reconsidered* 124-60 (Chicago et al. 1996).

Baums, Theodor 'Lehren aus dem Fall Krupp-Thyssen' *Wirtschaftsdienst* 77 (1997) 259-60.

Baums, Theodor and Christian Fraune 'Institutionelle Anleger und Publikumsgesellschaft: eine empirische Untersuchung' *Die Aktiengesellschaft* 40 (1995) 97-112.

Baums, Theodor and Bernd Frick 'Co-Determination in Germany: The Impact on the Market Value of the Firm' (Working Paper of the Institut für Handels- und Wirtschaftsrecht, University of Osnabrück, no. 1/1997).

Baums, Theodor and Markus König 'Investmentfonds im Universalbankkonzern: Rechtstatsachen und aktuelle Reformfragen' in: Forster, Karl-Heinz, Barbara Grunewald, Marcus Lutter, and Johannes Semler (eds.) *Aktien- und Bilanzrecht* (Festschrift Kropff) 3-36 (Düsseldorf 1997).

Bayhurst, Andrée, Andreas Fey, and Georg Schreyögg 'Wer kontrolliert die Geschäftspolitik deutscher Großunternehmen? Empirische Ergebnisse zur Kontrollsituation der 350 größten deutschen Unternehmen der Jahre 1972, 1979 und 1986 im Vergleich' (Fernuniversität Hagen, Faculty of Economics, Discussion Paper no. 213, 1994).

Bea, Franz Xaver and Steffen Scheurer 'Die Kontrolle bei der GmbH' *Der Betrieb* 48 (1995) 1289-96.

Bea, Franz Xaver and Susanne Thissen 'Institutionalisierung des Shareholder-Value-Konzepts bei der GmbH' *Der Betrieb* 50 (1997) 787-92.

Becht, Marco 'The Separation of Ownership and Control: A Survey of 7 European Countries' (Preliminary Report to the European Commission submitted on October 27, 1997 by the European Corporate Governance Network, vol. 1. This version: October 25, 1997; http://www.ecgn.ulb.ac.be/).

Becht, Marco 'Beneficial Ownership of Listed Companies in the United States' part of: European Corporate Governance Network (ed.) 'The Separation of Ownership and Control: A Survey of 7 European Countries' (Preliminary Report to the European Commission submitted on October 27, 1997, vol. 1. This version: January 23, 1997a; http://www.ecgn.ulb.ac.be/).

Becht, Marco and Ekkehart Böhmer 'Transparency of Ownership and Control in Germany' part of: European Corporate Governance Network (ed.) 'The Separation of Ownership and Control: A Survey of 7 European Countries' (Preliminary Report to the European Commission submitted on October 27, 1997, vol. 1. This version: October 29, 1997; http://www.ecgn.ulb.ac.be/).

Behm, Ulrich and Heinz Zimmermann 'The Empirical Relationship Between Dividends and Earnings in Germany' *Zeitschrift für Wirtschafts- und Sozialwissenschaften* 113 (1993) 225-54.

Benner-Heinacher, Jella S. 'Mindeststandards für Übernahmeregeln in Deutschland' *Der Betrieb* 50 (1997) 2521-4.

Berglöf, Erik 'A Note on the Typology of Financial Systems' in: Hopt, Klaus J. and Eddy Wymeersch (eds.) *Comparative Corporate Governance: Essays and Materials* 151-64 (Berlin and New York 1997).

Beyer, Jürgen 'Governance Structures. Unternehmensverflechtungen und Unternehmenserfolg in Deutschland' in: Albach, Horst (ed.) *Governance Structures* 79-101 (*Zeitschrift für Betriebswirtschaft* Supplementary Issue 3/1996).

Biehler, Hermann and Peter Liepmann 'Personelle Verbindungen und intersektorale Finanzbeziehungen zwischen den größten deutschen Unternehmen' *Jahrbuch für Nationalökonomie und Statistik* 204 (1988) 48-68.

Biehler, Hermann and Rolf Ortmann 'Personelle Verbindungen zwischen Unternehmen. Ergebnisse einer Interviewserie bei Vorstands- und Aufsichtsratsmitgliedern großer deutscher Unternehmen' *Die Betriebswirtschaft* 45 (1985) 4-18.

Binder, Christof 'Beteiligungsstrategien in der Konzernpraxis. Eine empirische Untersuchung der Beteiligungshöhen in deutschen Konzernen' *Die Aktiengesellschaft* 39 (1994) 391-6.

Bleicher, Knut *Der Aufsichtsrat im Wandel. Eine repräsentative Studie über Aufsichtsräte in bundesdeutschen Aktiengesellschaften* (Gütersloh 1987).

Bleicher, Knut, Diethard Leberl, and Herbert Paul *Unternehmungsverfassung und Spitzenorganisation. Führung und Überwachung von Aktiengesellschaften im internationalen Vergleich* (Wiesbaden 1989).

Bleicher, Knut and Herbert Paul 'Das amerikanische Board-Modell im Vergleich zur deutschen Vorstands-/Aufsichtsratsverfassung—Stand und Entwicklungstendenzen' *Die Betriebswirtschaft* 46 (1986) 263-88.

Blick durch die Wirtschaft (1997) 'Jedes dritte Unternehmen will internationale Bilanz. Kleine und mittlere Betriebe haben starke Vorbehalte gegen neue Rechnungslegungsvorschriften' *Blick durch die Wirtschaft* no. 95, 21.5.97, 1.

Böhm, Jürgen *Der Einfluß der Banken auf Großunternehmen* (Dissertation University of Duisburg) (Hamburg 1992).

Böhmer, Ekkehart 'Industry Groups, Bank Control, and Large Shareholders: An Analysis of German Takeovers' (Working Paper, Preliminary Version, Humboldt University Berlin, 14.3.1997).

Böhmer, Ekkehart and Yvonne Löffler 'Kursrelevante Ereignisse bei Unternehmensübernahmen: Eine empirische Analyse des deutschen Kapitalmarktes' (Working Paper, Humboldt University Berlin, 22.8.1997).

Börsen-Zeitung (1996) 'BZ-Umfrage per Ultimo' *Börsen-Zeitung* no. 250, 31.12.96, 17-20.

Börsen-Zeitung (1996a) 'Telekom hat der Börse einen Dienst erwiesen' *Börsen-Zeitung* no. 250, 31.12.96, 49.

Börsen-Zeitung (1996b) 'Engagement für Aktionärsinteressen' *Börsen-Zeitung* no. 217, 9.11.96, 31.

Börsen-Zeitung (1997) 'Großes Interesse an Frankreichs Unternehmen' *Börsen-Zeitung* no. 5, 9.1.97, 3.

Börsen-Zeitung (1997a) 'Übernahmekodex von 259 Unternehmen anerkannt' *Börsen-Zeitung* no. 38, 25.2.97, 1.

Börsen-Zeitung (1997b) 'Übernahmekodex braucht Gesetz' *Börsen-Zeitung* no. 46, 7.3.97, 1.

Börsen-Zeitung (1997c) 'DSW kritisiert Übernahmekodex' *Börsen-Zeitung* no. 17, 25.1.97, 9.

Börsen-Zeitung (1997d) 'Krupp bietet 435 DM je Thyssen-Aktie. Thyssen wehrt sich mit aller Kraft' *Börsen-Zeitung* no. 54, 19.3.97, 1.

Börsen-Zeitung (1997e) 'Der Charme der Stahlfusion' *Börsen-Zeitung* no. 59, 26.3.97, 1.

Börsen-Zeitung (1997f) 'Kartellamt: Mit Holzmann-Pool soll die Fusionskontrolle umgangen werden' *Börsen-Zeitung* no. 59, 26.3.97, 1.

Börsen-Zeitung (1997g) 'Kartellamt hat schwere Bedenken' *Börsen-Zeitung* no. 59, 26.3.97, 5.

Börsen-Zeitung (1997h) 'Fusion Holzmann/Hochtief wird es nicht geben' *Börsen-Zeitung* no. 59, 26.3.97, 5.

Börsen-Zeitung (1997i) 'Krupp leistet bis 1,3 Mrd. DM Ausgleich. 300 Mill. DM Vorabgewinn für Thyssen' *Börsen-Zeitung* no. 61, 28./29.3.97, 1.

Börsen-Zeitung (1997j) 'Geringe Aussicht auf verkleinerte Aufsichtsräte' *Börsen-Zeitung* no. 114, 19.6.97, 7.

Börsen-Zeitung (1997k) '"Nicht der Karstadt des Finanzgewerbes"' *Börsen-Zeitung* no. 111, 14.6.97, 5.

Börsen-Zeitung (1997l) 'Übernahmekodex wird für Dax Pflicht' *Börsen-Zeitung* no. 158, 20.8.97, 3.

Börsen-Zeitung (1997m) 'Sechs deutsche Aktien an der NYSE' *Börsen-Zeitung* no. 184, 25.9.97, 9.

Börsen-Zeitung (1997n) 'Breuer favorisiert Gewinn je Aktie als Meßlatte. Deutsche Bank will Vergütung in Aktien steigern—Mittelfristig kein Vorsitz im Aufsichtsrat mehr' *Börsen-Zeitung* no. 222, 19.11.97, 6.

Börsen-Zeitung (1997o) 'Drehbuch und Regie im Fall Krupp/Thyssen' *Börsen-Zeitung* no. 249, 31.12.97, 17.

Börsen-Zeitung (1998) 'Aktien nach DAX-Kriterien' *Börsen-Zeitung* no. 6, 10.1.98, 11.

Börsen-Zeitung (1998a) 'Hochtief darf bei Philip Holzmann aufstocken' *Börsen-Zeitung* no. 54, 19.3.98, 7.

Börsen-Zeitung (1998b) 'Rechnungslegungskomitee gegründet' *Börsen-Zeitung* no. 62, 31.3.98, 10.

Bremeier, Eberhard, Jürgen B. Mülder, and Florian Schilling 'Praxis der Aufsichtsratstätigkeit in Deutschland—Chancen zur Professionalisierung' (AMROP International, Düsseldorf 1994).

Budde, Wolfgang Dieter, and Elgin Steuber 'Rechnungslegung im Spannungsfeld zwischen Gläubigerschutz und Information der Gesellschafter' *Die Aktiengesellschaft* 41 (1996) 542-50.

Buhleier, Claus and Harald Helmschrott 'Auf dem Weg zu den Weltstandards bei der Konzernrechnungslegung? Zur Anwendbarkeit der IAS und US-GAAP' *Betriebs-Berater* 52 (1997) 775-9.

Bühner, Rolf 'Rendite-Risiko-Effekte der Trennung von Eigentum und Leitung im diversifizierten Großunternehmen' *Zeitschrift für betriebswirtschaftliche Forschung* 36 (1984) 812-24.

Bühner, Rolf *Erfolg von Unternehmenszusammenschlüssen in der Bundesrepublik Deutschland* (Stuttgart 1990).

Bühner, Rolf 'Reaktion des Kapitalmarktes auf Unternehmenszusammenschlüsse. Eine empirische Untersuchung' *Zeitschrift für betriebswirtschaftliche Forschung* 42 (1990a) 294-316.

Bundesaufsichtsamt für das Kreditwesen 'Geschäftsbericht 1995. Teil A' (Berlin 1996).

Bundesaufsichtsamt für das Versicherungswesen 'Jahresbericht 1995' (Berlin 1996).

Bundesaufsichtsamt für den Wertpapierhandel 'Jahresbericht 1995' (Frankfurt am Main 1996).

Bundesaufsichtsamt für den Wertpapierhandel 'Bedeutende Stimmrechtsanteile an amtlich notierten Aktiengesellschaften zum 30. September 1996' (Frankfurt am Main 1996a).

Bundesaufsichtsamt für den Wertpapierhandel 'Jahresbericht 1996' (Frankfurt am Main 1997).

Bundesverband deutscher Banken 'Die Macht der Banken—Anhörung im Bundestag. Stellungnahme des Bundesverbandes deutscher Banken' *Zeitschrift für Bankrecht und Bankwirtschaft* 6 (1994), 70-7.

Bundesverband deutscher Banken 'Erhebungen zu Anteilsbesitz und Aufsichtsratsmandaten. Methodik und Ergebnisse' (Cologne 1995).

Cable, John 'Capital Market Information and Industrial Performance: The Role of West German Banks' *Economic Journal* 95 (1985) 118-32.

CEPS 'Corporate Governance in Europe' (Centre for European Policy Studies Working Party Report no. 12, Rapporteur Karel Lannoo, Brussels 1995).

Chirinko, Robert S. and Julie Ann Elston 'Banking Relationships in Germany: Empirical Results and Policy Implications' (Working Paper, Emory University, May 1996).

Claussen, Carsten P. 'Aktienrechtsreform 1997' *Die Aktiengesellschaft* 41 (1996) 481-94.

Claussen, Carsten P. *Bank- und Börsenrecht. Handbuch für Lehre und Praxis* (Munich 1996a).

Clemm, Hermann 'Der Abschlußprüfer als Krisenwarner und der Aufsichtsrat—Anmerkungen zu einem—wieder einmal—aktuellen Thema' in: Lanfermann, Josef (ed.) *Internationale Wirtschaftsprüfung* (Festschrift Havermann) 83-107 (Düsseldorf 1995).

Clemm, Hermann 'Reform des Aufsichtsrats? Bemerkungen und Wünsche aus der Wirtschaftsprüfer-Sicht' *Betriebswirtschaftliche Forschung und Praxis* 48 (1996) 269-84.

Coenenberg, Adolf Gerhard and Axel Haller 'Externe Rechnungslegung' in: Hauschildt, Jürgen and Oskar Grün (eds.) *Ergebnisse empirischer betriebswirtschaftlicher Forschung. Zur Realtheorie der Unternehmung* (Festschrift Witte) 557-99 (Stuttgart 1993).

Coenenberg, Adolf Gerhard and Frank Henes 'Der Informationsgehalt der Zwischenberichtspublizität nach §44b Börsengesetz' *Zeitschrift für betriebswirtschaftliche Forschung* 47 (1995) 969-95.

Coenenberg, Adolf Gerhard and Kai-Uwe Marten 'Der Wechsel des Abschlußprüfers' *Der Betrieb* 46 (1993) 101-10.

Coenenberg, Adolf Gerhard, Alexander Reinhart, and Jochen Schmitz 'Audit Committees—Ein Instrument der Unternehmensüberwachung? Reformdiskussion im Spiegel einer Befragung der Vorstände deutscher Unternehmen' *Der Betrieb* 50 (1997) 989-97.

Corbett, Jenny and Tim Jenkinson 'The Financing of Industry, 1970-1989: An International Comparison' (Centre for Economic Policy Research, Discussion Paper no. 948, May 1994).

Corbett, Jenny and Tim Jenkinson 'How Is Investment Financed? A Study of Germany, Japan, the United Kingdom and the United States' *Manchester School of Economic and Social Studies* 65 (1997) Supplement 69-93.

Deutsche Börse 'Jahresbericht der Deutschen Börsen 1994' (Frankfurt am Main 1995).

Deutsche Börse 'Fact Book 1995. Zahlen zur Deutschen Börse' (Frankfurt am Main 1996).

Deutsche Börse 'Fact Book 1996' (Frankfurt am Main 1997).

Deutsche Bundesbank 'Eigenmittelausstattung der Unternehmen ausgewählter EG-Länder im Vergleich' *Monatsbericht* 46/10 (1994) 73-88.

Deutsche Bundesbank 'Wertpapierdepots' (Statistische Sonderveröffentlichung no. 9, August 1996).

Deutsche Bundesbank 'Ertragslage und Finanzierungsverhältnisse westdeutscher Unternehmen im Jahre 1995' *Monatsbericht* 48/11 (1996a) 33-57.

Deutsche Bundesbank 'Shares as Financing and Investment Instruments' *Monthly Report* 49/1 (1997) 27-40.

Deutsche Bundesbank *Monthly Report* 49/3 (1997a).

Deutsche Bundesbank 'Ergebnisse der gesamtwirtschaftlichen Finanzierungsrechnung für Deutschland 1990 bis 1996' (Statistische Sonderveröffentlichung no. 4, June 1997b).

Deutsche Bundesbank 'Wertpapierdepots' (Statistische Sonderveröffentlichung no. 9, August 1997c).

Deutsche Bundesbank 'Kapitalmarktstatistik' (Statistisches Beiheft zum Monatsbericht 2, February 1998).

Deutsche Bundesbank 'Strukturveränderungen am deutschen Kapitalmarkt im Vorfeld der Europäischen Währungsunion' *Monatsbericht* 50/4 (1998a) 55-70.

Deutsches Aktieninstitut 'DAI-Factbook 1997. Statistiken, Analysen und Grafiken zu Aktionären, Aktiengesellschaften und Börsen' (Frankfurt am Main 1997).

Dietl, Helmut M. *Capital Markets and Corporate Governance in Japan, Germany and the United States. Organizational Responses to Market Inefficiencies* (London and New York 1998).

Dörner, Dietrich and Peter Oser 'Erfüllen Aufsichtsrat und Wirtschaftsprüfer ihre Aufgaben? Zugleich ein Plädoyer für eine bessere Zusammenarbeit von Aufsichtsrat und Wirtschaftsprüfern' *Der Betrieb* 48 (1995) 1085-93.

Droste (ed.) *Mergers & Acquisitions in Germany* (Bicester 1995).

Drukarczyk, Jochen *Theorie und Politik der Finanzierung* 2nd edn. (Munich 1993).

Drukarczyk, Jochen *Finanzierung. Eine Einführung* 7th edn. (Stuttgart 1996).

Drukarczyk, Jochen, Josef Duttle, and Reinhard Rieger *Mobiliarsicherheiten. Arten, Verbreitung, Wirksamkeit* (Cologne 1985).

Drukarczyk, Jochen and Hartmut Schmidt 'Permanente Unternehmenskontrolle statt gelegentlicher Schreckschüsse' *Wirtschaftsdienst* 77 (1997) 261-3.

Edwards, Jeremy S.S. and Klaus Fischer *Banks, Finance and Investment in Germany* (Cambridge 1994).

Elston, Julie Ann and Horst Albach 'Bank Affiliation and Firm Capital Investment in Germany' *ifo Studien—Zeitschrift für empirische Wirtschaftsforschung* 41 (1995) 3-16.

Fanto, James A. 'The Absence of Cross-Cultural Communication: SEC Mandatory Disclosure and Foreign Corporate Governance' 17 *Nw. J. Int'l L. & Bus.* 119-206 (1996).

Federal Ministry of Justice 'KonTraG: Zusammenfassung der Entwurfsregelungen' (Internet Release, http://www.bmj.bund.de/misc/m_56z_97.html, Bonn 1997).

Federation of European Stock Exchanges 'European Stock Exchanges Statistics' (Brussels, January 1997).

Fischer, Klaus 'Hausbankbeziehungen als Instrument der Bindung zwischen Banken und Unternehmen. Eine theoretische Untersuchung' (Dissertation University of Bonn 1990).

FitzRoy, Felix R. and Joachim Schwalbach 'Managerial Compensation and Firm Performance. Some Evidence from West Germany' (Wissenschaftszentrum Berlin für Sozialforschung, Discussion Paper no. FS IV 90-20, December 1990).

Flassak, Hansjörg *Der Markt für Unternehmenskontrolle. Eine ökonomische Analyse vor dem Hintergrund des deutschen Gesellschaftsrechts* (Dissertation University of Hohenheim) (Bergisch Gladbach et al. 1995).

Förschle, Gerhart, Martin Glaum, and Udo Mandler 'Gesetz zur Kontrolle und Transparenz im Unternehmensbereich: Umfrage unter Führungskräften börsennotierter Unternehmen' *Der Betrieb* 51 (1998) 889-95.

Forster, Karl-Heinz 'MG, Schneider, Balsam und die Folgen—was können Aufsichtsräte und Abschlußprüfer gemeinsam tun?' *Die Aktiengesellschaft* 40 (1995) 1-7.

Francioni, Reto 'Der Betreuer im Neuen Markt' *Die Bank* (1997) 68-71.

Franks, Julian and Colin Mayer 'Capital Markets and Corporate Control: A Study of France, Germany and the U.K.' *Economic Policy* 10 (1990) 191-231.

Franks, Julian and Colin Mayer 'Ownership and Control' in: Siebert, Horst (ed.) *Trends in Business Organizations: Do Participation and Cooperation Increase Competitiveness?* 171-95 (Tübingen 1995).

Franks, Julian and Colin Mayer 'Ownership, Control and the Performance of German Corporations' (Working Paper, London Business School and University of Oxford, 14.10.1996, revised 25.1.1997).

Fraune, Christian *Der Einfluß institutioneller Anleger in der Hauptversammlung* (Dissertation University of Osnabrück 1995) (Cologne et al. 1996).

Frick, Bernd and Dieter Sadowski 'Works Councils, Unions, and Firm Performance' in: Buttler, Friedrich, Wolfgang Franz, Roland Schettkat, and David Soskice (eds.) *Institutional Frameworks and Labor Market Performance: Comparative Views on the U.S. and German Economies* 46-81 (London and New York 1995).

Funke, Rainer 'Öffnung des deutschen Konzernbilanzrechts' *Zeitschrift für das gesamte Kreditwesen* 51 (1998) 150.

Ganske, Torsten *Mitbestimmung, Property-Rights-Ansatz und Transaktionskostentheorie* (Diss. University of Frankfurt am Main 1995) (Frankfurt am Main et al. 1996).

Gedenk, Karen 'Agency-Theorie und die Steuerung von Geschäftsführern' *Die Betriebswirtschaft* 58 (1998) 22-37.

Gelauff, George M.M. and Corina den Broeder 'Governance of Stakeholder Relationships. The German and Dutch Experience' (SUERF [Société Universitaire Européene de Recherches Financières] Studies no. 1, Amsterdam 1997).

Gerke, Wolfgang, Matthias Bank, and Georg Lucht 'Die Wirkungen des WpHG auf die Informationspolitik der Unternehmen' *Die Bank* (1996) 612-6.

Gerke, Wolfgang, Hendrik Garz, and Marc Oerke 'Die Bewertung von Unternehmensübernahmen auf dem deutschen Aktienmarkt' *Zeitschrift für betriebswirtschaftliche Forschung* 47 (1995) 805-20.

Gerum, Elmar, Bernd Richter, and Horst Steinmann 'Unternehmenspolitik im mitbestimmten Konzern. Empirische Befunde zur Ausgestaltung von Einflußstrukturen im mitbestimmten konzernverbundenen Aktiengesellschaften' *Die Betriebswirtschaft* 41 (1981) 345-60.

Gerum, Elmar, Horst Steinmann, and Werner Fees *Der mitbestimmte Aufsichtsrat. Eine empirische Untersuchung* (Stuttgart 1988).

Gidlewitz, Hans-Jörg *Internationale Harmonisierung der Konzernrechnungslegung unter besonderer Berücksichtigung der Bestimmungen des IASC und des HGB* (Dissertation University of Duisburg) (Frankfurt am Main et al. 1996).

Glaum, Martin and Udo Mandler *Rechnungslegung auf globalen Kapitalmärkten. HGB, IAS und US-GAAP* (Wiesbaden 1996).

Gloßner, Veronika 'Eine Konzentrationsmessung von Pflichtprüfungsmandaten börsennotierter Aktiengesellschaften' *Die Wirtschaftsprüfung* 51 (1998) 216-24.

Görling, Helmut 'Die Verbreitung zwei- und mehrstufiger Unternehmensverbindungen. Ergebnisse einer empirischen Untersuchung' *Die Aktiengesellschaft* 38 (1993) 538-47.

Gorton, Gary and Frank A. Schmid 'Universal Banking and the Performance of German Firms' (NBER Working Paper no. 5453, February 1996).

Gottschalk, Arno 'Der Stimmrechtseinfluß der Banken in den Aktionärsversammlungen von Großunternehmen' *WSI-Mitteilungen* 41 (1988) 294-304.

Götz, Heinrich 'Die Überwachung der Aktiengesellschaft im Lichte jüngerer Unternehmenskrisen' *Die Aktiengesellschaft* 40 (1995) 337-53.

Gutschlag, Thomas 'Der Neue Markt: Eine erste Zwischenbilanz' *Börsen-Zeitung* no. 75, 19.4.97, B12.

Haas, Jochen 'Der Anteilsbesitz der Kreditwirtschaft an Nichtbanken' (Dissertation University of Saarbrücken 1994).

Haegert, Lutz and Peter Lehleiter 'Das Ausschüttungsverhalten deutscher Aktiengesellschaften unter dem Einfluß der Körperschaftsteuerreform' *Zeitschrift für betriebswirtschaftliche Forschung* 37 (1985) 912-23.

Häger, Ralf *Das Publizitätsverhalten mittelgroßer Kapitalgesellschaften* (Dissertation University of Hanover 1993) (Frankfurt am Main et al. 1993).

Hamel, Winfried 'Mitbestimmung' in: Hauschildt, Jürgen and Oskar Grün (eds.) *Ergebnisse empirischer betriebswirtschaftlicher Forschung. Zur Realtheorie der Unternehmung* (Festschrift Witte) 25-53 (Stuttgart 1993).

Handelsblatt (1995) 'Mehr Einflußmöglichkeiten für Aufsichtsräte gefordert' *Handelsblatt* no. 192, 5.10.95, 3.

Handelsblatt (1995a) 'Kopper fordert mehr Rückhalt für Banken' *Handelsblatt* no. 201, 18.10.95, 37.

Handelsblatt (1996) 'DAG gegen den kleinen Aufsichtsrat' *Handelsblatt* no. 240, 11.12.96, 6.

Handelsblatt (1996a) 'Keine Angst vor doppelter Buchführung' *Handelsblatt* no. 232, 2.12.96, 30.

Handelsblatt (1997) 'IG Metall kritisiert Konzept der Koalition zur Aktienrechtsreform' *Handelsblatt* no. 27, 7./8.2.97, 4.

Handelsblatt (1997a) 'Krupp hat den Übernahmekodex erst am Dienstag anerkannt' *Handelsblatt* no. 55, 19.3.97, 12.

Handelsblatt (1997b) 'Anleger-Rechte sollen gestärkt werden' *Handelsblatt* no. 34, 18.2.97, 44.

Handelsblatt (1997c) 'Holzmann-Poolvertrag geplatzt' *Handelsblatt* no. 103, 3.6.97, 1.

Handelsblatt (1997d) 'Hochtief und Holzmann suchen neue Wege' *Handelsblatt* no. 104, 4.6.97, 14.

Handelsblatt (1997e) 'Hochtief und Holzmann kommen sich näher' *Handelsblatt* no. 224, 20.11.97, 14.

Handelsblatt (1998) 'Europa holt bei Firmenkäufen gegenüber den USA auf' *Handelsblatt* no. 13, 20.1.98, 13.

Handelsblatt (1998a) 'Mittelfristig Umsatz von 100 Mrd. DM angepeilt' *Handelsblatt* no. 27, 9.2.98, 16.

Handelsblatt (1998b) 'Thyssen-Krupp. Fusion wird am 1.3.1999 eingetragen' *Handelsblatt* no. 64, 1.4.98, 13.

Hansen, Herbert 'Das Gewicht der Banken in den Aufsichtsräten deutscher Aktiengesellschaften' *Die Aktiengesellschaft* 39 (1994) R76, R78-79.

Hansen, Herbert 'Der GmbH-Bestand stieg auf 777 000 Gesellschaften an. Gleichzeitig Anmerkung zu der Einstellung der statistischen Erhebung bei den Kapitalgesellschaften' *GmbH-Rundschau* 88 (1997) 204-7.

Hansen, Herbert 'Die Kopflastigkeit des deutschen Kurszettels' *Die Aktiengesellschaft* 42 (1997a) R78, R80-82.

Hansen, Herbert 'Die Zusammensetzung der Aufsichtsräte bei den DAX-Gesellschaften' *Die Aktiengesellschaft* 42 (1997b) R123-R124.

Hansen, Herbert 'Ende 1997: 4548 AG mit 222 Mrd. Grundkapital' *Die Aktiengesellschaft* 43 (1998) R112, R114, and R116.

Harris, Trevor S., Mark Lang, and Hans Peter Möller 'The Value Relevance of German Accounting Measures: An Empirical Analysis' *Journal of Accounting Research* 32/2 (1994) 187-209.

Harris, Trevor S., Mark Lang, and Hans Peter Möller 'Zur Relevanz der Jahresabschlußgrößen Erfolg und Eigenkapital für die Aktienbewertung in Deutschland und den USA' *Zeitschrift für betriebswirtschaftliche Forschung* 47 (1995) 996-1028.

Hart, Oliver 'Corporate Governance: Some Theory and Implications' *Economic Journal* 105 (1995) 678-89.

Helmenstein, Christian 'Anbieterkonzentration auf dem Markt für Jahresabschlußprüfungen' *Die Betriebswirtschaft* 56 (1996) 41-8.

Herrmann, Markus *Unternehmenskontrolle durch Stiftungen. Untersuchung der Performancewirkungen* (Dissertation University of Konstanz) (Wiesbaden 1996).

Hohlfeld, Knut 'Versicherungswirtschaft, Anlagevorschriften der Versicherungen' in: Gerke, Wolfgang and Manfred Steiner (eds.) *Handwörterbuch des Bank- und Finanzwesen* cols. 1906-14 2nd edn. (Stuttgart 1995).

Hopt, Klaus J. 'Änderungen von Anleihebedingungen: Schuldverschreibungsgesetz, § 796 BGB und AGBG' in: Baur, Jürgen F., Klaus J. Hopt, and K. Peter Mailänder (eds.) *Festschrift für Ernst Steindorff zum 70. Geburtstag am 13. März 1990* 341-82 (Berlin et al. 1990).

Hopt, Klaus J. 'Präventivmaßnahmen zur Abwehr von Übernahme- und Beteiligungsversuchen' in: 'WM-Festgabe für Heinsius' 22-30 (*Wertpapier-Mitteilungen* Special Issue 1991).

Hopt, Klaus J. 'Labor Board Representation on Corporate Boards: Impacts and Problems for Corporate Governance and Economic Integration in Europe' *International Review of Law and Economics* 14 (1994) 203-14.

Hopt, Klaus J. 'Arbeitnehmervertretung im Aufsichtsrat. Auswirkungen der Mitbestimmung auf corporate governance und wirtschaftliche Integration in Europa' in: Duel, Ole, Marcus Lutter, and Jürgen Schwarze (eds.) *Festschrift für Ulrich Everling* 475-92 (Baden-Baden 1995).

Hopt, Klaus J. 'Die Haftung von Vorstand und Aufsichtsrat. Zugleich ein Beitrag zur corporate governance-Debatte' in: Immenga, Ulrich, Wernhard Möschel, and Dieter Reuter (eds.) *Festschrift für Ernst-Joachim Mestmäcker zum siebzigsten Geburtstag* 909-31 (Baden-Baden 1996).

Hopt, Klaus J. 'Corporate Governance und deutsche Universalbanken' in: Feddersen, Dieter, Peter Hommelhoff, and Uwe H. Schneider (eds.) *Corporate Governance. Optimierung der Unternehmensführung und der Unternehmenskontrolle im deutschen und amerikanischen Aktienrecht* 243-63 (Cologne 1996a).

Hopt, Klaus J. 'Europäisches und deutsches Übernahmerecht' *Zeitschrift für das gesamte Handelsrecht und Wirtschaftsrecht* 161 (1997) 368-420.

Hopt, Klaus J. 'The German Two-Tier Board (Aufsichtsrat): A German View on Corporate Governance' in: Hopt, Klaus J. and Eddy Wymeersch (eds.) *Comparative Corporate Governance: Essays and Materials* 3-20 (Berlin and New York 1997a).

Hopt, Klaus J. 'Auf dem Weg zum deutschen Übernahmegesetz—Überlegungen zum Richtlinienentwurf 1997, zum Übernahmekodex (1997) und zum SPD-Entwurf 1997' in: Lieb, Manfred, Ulrich Noack, and Harm Peter Westermann (eds.) *Das Arbeits- und Wirtschaftsrecht am Ende des 20. Jahrhunderts* (Festschrift Zöllner) (Cologne, forthcoming 1998).

Iber, Bernhard 'Zur Entwicklung der Aktionärsstruktur in der Bundesrepublik Deutschland (1963-1983)' *Zeitschrift für Betriebswirtschaft* 55 (1985) 1101-19.

International Business Lawyer 'Takeover! A Power Play' 25 *Int'l Bus. Law.* 52-66 (1997).

Jenkinson, Tim and Alexander Ljungqvist 'Hostile Stakes and the Role of Banks in German Corporate Governance' (Working Paper, University of Oxford, 4.11.1996).

Jensen, Michael C. 'The Agency Costs of Free Cash Flow, Corporate Finance, and Takeovers' *American Economic Review Papers and Proceedings* 76 (1986) 323-9.

Jensen, Michael C. and William H. Meckling 'Theory of the Firm: Managerial Behavior, Agency Costs and Ownership Structure' *Journal of Financial Economics* 3 (1976) 305-60.

de Jong, Henk Wouter 'The Governance Structure and Performance of Large European Corporations' *Journal of Management and Governance* 1 (1997) 5-27.

Kaen, Fred R. and Heidemarie C. Sherman 'German Banking and German Corporate Governance' *Tokyo Club Papers* 7 (1994) 229-68.

Kandlbinder, Hans Karl 'Der Boom der Spezialfonds' *Zeitschrift für das gesamte Kreditwesen* 50 (1997) 754-66, 771.

Kaplan, Steven N. 'Top Executives, Turnover and Firm Performance in Germany' (NBER Working Paper no. 4416, August 1993).

Kaplan, Steven N. 'Corporate Governance und Unternehmenserfolg: Ein Vergleich zwischen Deutschland, Japan und den USA' in: Feddersen, Dieter, Peter Hommelhoff, and Uwe H. Schneider (eds.) *Corporate Governance. Optimierung der Unternehmensführung und der Unternehmenskontrolle im deutschen und amerikanischen Aktienrecht* 301-15 (Cologne 1996).

Kaserer, Christoph 'Underpricing, Unternehmenskontrolle und die Rolle der Banken' (Preliminary Working Paper, University of Würzburg, 1996).

Kaulmann, Thomas *Property rights und Unternehmungstheorie. Stand und Weiterentwicklung der empirischen Forschung* (Dissertation TU Munich 1986) (Munich 1987).

Keller, Erich and Hans Peter Möller 'Einstufung der Bankbilanzen am Kapitalmarkt infolge von § 26a KWG. Konzeption und Ergebnisse einer kapitalmarktorientierten empirischen Untersuchung zum Informationsgehalt der Jahresabschlüsse deutscher Aktiengesellschaften' *Zeitschrift für Bankrecht und Bankwirtschaft* 4 (1992) 169-83.

Keller, Erich and Hans Peter Möller 'Die Auswirkungen der Zwischenberichterstattung auf den Informationswert von Jahresabschlüssen am Kapitalmarkt. Konzeption und Ergebnisse einer kapitalmarktorientierten empirischen Untersuchung zum Informationsgehalt der Jahresabschlüsse deutscher Aktiengesellschaften' in: *Empirische Kapitalmarktforschung* 35-60 *Zeitschrift für betriebswirtschaftliche Forschung* (Special Issue no. 31, Düsseldorf 1993).

Kerber, Markus 'Dürfen vinkulierte Namensaktien zum Börsenhandel zugelassen werden? Ein Beitrag zum Spannungsverhältnis von Vinkulierung und Fungibilität' *Wertpapier-Mitteilungen* 44 (1990) 789-93.

Kirchner, Christian and Ulrich Ehricke 'Funktionsdefizite des Übernahmekodex der Börsensachverständigenkommission' *Die Aktiengesellschaft* 43 (1998) 105-16.

Knoll, Leonhard, Jochen Knoesel, and Uwe Probst 'Aufsichtsratsvergütungen in Deutschland: Empirische Befunde' *Zeitschrift für betriebswirtschaftliche Forschung* 49 (1997) 236-54.

Kohler, Klaus 'Stock Options für Führungskräfte aus Sicht der Praxis' *Zeitschrift für das gesamte Handelsrecht und Wirtschaftsrecht* 161 (1997) 246-68.

König, Rolf Jürgen 'Dividende und Jahresüberschuß' *Zeitschrift für Betriebswirtschaft* 61 (1991) 1149-55.

Kopp, Hans Joachim *Erwerb eigener Aktien. Ökonomische Analyse vor dem Hintergrund von Unternehmensverfassung und Informationseffizienz des Kapitalmarktes* (Dissertation Wiss. Hochschule Koblenz) (Wiesbaden 1996).

Korn/Ferry International 'Board Meeting in Session. European Board of Directors Study' (1996).

Kraft, Kornelius and Antonia Niederprüm 'Management Incentives in Theory and Practice' (Working Paper, University of Essen, February 1996).

Krahnen, Jan P. and Ralf Elsas 'Relationship Banking. Wandel im Kreditgeschäft' *Frankfurter Allgemeine Zeitung* no. 52, 3.3.1998, B7.

Krahnen, Jan P., Frank A. Schmid, and Erik Theissen 'Performance and Market Share: Evidence from the German Mutual Fund Industry' (Center for Financial Studies, Working Paper no. 1/97, Frankfurt am Main, September 1997).

Kronenberg, Brigitte, Gert Volkmann, and Ulrike Wendeling-Schröder 'WSI-Mitbestimmungsbericht 1992' *WSI-Mitteilungen* 47 (1994) 24-9.

Krüger, Wilfried, Wolfgang Buchholz, and Frank Altrock 'Führungsorganisation deutscher Großunternehmungen—Gestaltungsalternativen und ihre empirische Relevanz' (Justus-Liebig-Universität Gießen, Fachbereich Wirtschaftswissenschaften, Professur für Betriebswirtschaftslehre II, Working Paper no. 1/1993).

Kruse, Hermann, Erik Berg, and Martin Weber 'Erklären unternehmensspezifische Faktoren den Kursunterschied von Stamm- und Vorzugsaktien?' *Zeitschrift für Bankrecht und Bankwirtschaft* 5 (1993) 23-31.

Kübler, Friedrich *Gesellschaftsrecht. Die privatrechtlichen Ordnungsstrukturen und Regelungsprobleme von Verbänden und Unternehmen* 4th edn. (Heidelberg 1994).

Kübler, Friedrich 'Institutional Investors and Corporate Governance: A German Perspective' in: Baums, Theodor, Richard M. Buxbaum, and Klaus J. Hopt (eds.) *Institutional Investors and Corporate Governance* 565-79 (Berlin and New York 1994a).

Kübler, Friedrich 'Vorsichtsprinzip versus Kapitalmarktinformation. Bilanzprobleme aus der Perspektive der Gesellschaftsrechtsvergleichung' in: Förschle, Gerhart, Klaus Kaiser, and Adolf Moxter (eds.) *Rechenschaftslegung im Wandel* (Festschrift Budde) 361-75 (Munich 1995).

Kümpel, Siegfried *Bank- und Kapitalmarktrecht* (Cologne 1995).

Küting, Karlheinz 'Stimmrechtsmehrheit versus Anteilsmehrheit' *Wirtschaftswissenschaftliches Studium* 23 (1994) 285-9.

Küting, Karlheinz 'Der Wahrheitsgehalt deutscher Bilanzen' *Deutsches Steuerrecht* 35 (1997) 84-91.

La Porta, Rafael, Florencio Lopez-de-Silanes, Andrei Shleifer, and Robert W. Vishny 'Law and Finance' (NBER Working Paper no. 5661, July 1996).

La Porta, Rafael, Florencio Lopez-de-Silanes, Andrei Shleifer, and Robert W. Vishny 'Legal Determinants of External Finance' *Journal of Finance* 52 (1997) 1131-50.

La Porta, Rafael, Florencio Lopez-de-Silanes, Andrei Shleifer, and Robert W. Vishny 'Agency Problems and Dividend Policies Around the World' (Working Paper, 2nd Draft, November 1997a).

Leimkühler, Claudia 'Ist die öffentliche Kritik am deutschen Aufsichtsratssystem gerechtfertigt? Empirische Untersuchung über die personellen Verflechtungen zwischen den Vorständen und Aufsichtsräten der in Deutschland börsennotierten Aktiengesellschaften' *Die Wirtschaftsprüfung* 49 (1996) 305-13.

Lenz, Hansrudi 'Die Struktur des Marktes für Abschlußprüfungsmandate bei deutschen Aktiengesellschaften' *Die Wirtschaftsprüfung* 49 (1996) 269-79 (part I) and 313-8 (part II).

Leuz, Christian, Dominic Deller, and Michael Stubenrath 'An International Comparison of Accounting-Based Payout Restrictions in the United States, United Kingdom and Germany' (Working Paper, Department of Business and Economics, University of Frankfurt am Main, 1997)

Leven, Franz-Josef 'Aktienoptionspläne für Führungskräfte in Deutschland. Ergebnisse einer Umfrage des Deutschen Aktieninstituts' *Aktienkultur & BVH-News* 4/1 (1997) 50-3.

Lingemann, Stefan and Dirk Wasmann 'Mehr Kontrolle und Transparenz im Aktienrecht: Das KonTraG tritt in Kraft' *Betriebs-Berater* 53 (1998) 853-62

Linnhoff, Ulrich and Bernhard Pellens 'Ausschüttungspolitik deutscher Konzerne. Eine empirische Untersuchung zum Ausschüttungsverhalten deutscher Konzernobergesellschaften' *Zeitschrift für betriebswirtschaftliche Forschung* 39 (1987) 987-1006.

Lipka, Sabine *Managementeffizienz und Kapitalmarktkontrolle. Empirische Tests neuerer Ansätze der Theorie der Firma* (Dissertation University of Cologne) (Frankfurt am Main 1995).

Lorsch, Jay W. 'German Corporate Governance and Management: An American's Perspective' in: von Werder, Axel (ed.) *Grundsätze ordnungsmäßiger Unternehmungsführung (GoF) für die Unternehmungsleitung (GoU), Überwachung (GoÜ) und Abschlußprüfung (GoA)* 199-225 (Düsseldorf 1996).

Lowenstein, Louis 'Financial Transparency and Corporate Governance: You Manage What You Measure' 96 *Colum. L. Rev.* 1335-62 (1996).

Lutter, Marcus and Gerd Krieger 'Hilfspersonen von Aufsichtsratsmitgliedern' *Der Betrieb* 48 (1995) 257-60.

Macey, Jonathan R. and Geoffrey P. Miller 'Corporate Governance and Commercial Banking: A Comparative Examination of Germany, Japan, and the United States' 48 *Stan. L. Rev.* 73-112 (1995/96).

Marten, Kai-Uwe *Der Wechsel des Abschlußprüfers* (Dissertation University of Augsburg 1993) (Düsseldorf 1994).

Marten, Kai-Uwe and Wolfgang Schultze 'Konzentrationsentwicklungen auf dem deutschen und europäischen Prüfungsmarkt' *Zeitschrift für betriebswirtschaftliche Forschung* 50 (1998) 360-86.

Mayer, Colin and Ian Alexander 'Banks and Securities Markets: Corporate Financing in Germany and the United Kingdom' *Journal of the Japanese and International Economies* 4 (1990) 450-75.

Mella, Frank and René Jähnke 'Die Hälfte des Kapitals liegt in festen Händen' *Börsen-Zeitung* no. 12, 18.1.96, 6.

Mellewigt, Thomas *Konzernorganisation und Konzernführung. Eine empirische Untersuchung börsennotierter Konzerne* (Dissertation University of Mainz) (Frankfurt am Main et al. 1995).

Mertens, Hans-Joachim in: Zöllner, Wolfgang (ed.) *Kölner Kommentar zum Aktiengesetz* (Cologne et al. 1996).

Michalski, Lutz 'Abwehrmechanismen gegen unfreundliche Übernahmeangebote ("unfriendly takeovers") nach deutschem Aktienrecht' *Die Aktiengesellschaft* 42 (1997) 152-63.

Monopolkommission *Wettbewerbspolitik in Zeiten des Umbruchs* (Elftes Hauptgutachten der Monopolkommission 1994/95) (Baden-Baden 1996).

Monopolkommission 'Ordnungspolitische Leitlinien für ein funktionsfähiges Finanzsystem' (Special Expert Opinion of the Monopolkommission, Cologne 1998).

Mülbert, Peter O. *Empfehlen sich gesetzliche Regelungen zur Einschränkung des Einflusses der Kreditinstitute auf Aktiengesellschaften?* (Expert Opinion for the 61st Deutscher Juristentag 1996) (Munich 1996).

Mülbert, Peter O. 'Shareholder Value aus rechtlicher Sicht' *Zeitschrift für Unternehmens- und Gesellschaftsrecht* 26 (1997) 129-72.

Mülbert, Peter O. 'Begrenzung der Bankenmacht—Sind die Vorschläge der Bundesregierung zur Reform des Aktienrechts ausreichend?' in: Bundestagsfraktion Bündnis 90/Die Grünen (ed.) 'Das deutsche Bankensystem. Innovationsbremse oder Erfolgsgarant?' 61-8 (Dokumentation der Veranstaltung am 5. März 1997 in Bonn, 1997a).

Müller, Helmut *Mitbestimmung im Aufsichtsrat und Kontrolle der Unternehmenspolitik. Eine empirische Untersuchung zur Handhabung repräsentativer Mitbestimmung in einem Mitarbeiterunternehmen* (Dissertation University of Erlangen-Nuremberg 1984) (Frankfurt am Main et al. 1986).

Müller-Jentsch, Walther 'Germany: From Collective Voice to Co-Management' in: Rogers, Joel and Wolfgang Streeck (eds.) *Works Councils, Consultation, Representation, and Cooperation in Industrial Relations* 53-78 (Chicago and London 1995).

Müller-Stewens, Günter and Michael Schäfer 'Stahlcoup wirft Fragen auf' *Handelsblatt* no. 79, 24.4.97, B1-B2.

Neuberger, Doris 'Anteilsbesitz von Banken: Wohlfahrtsverlust oder Wohlfahrtsgewinn?' *ifo Studien— Zeitschrift für empirische Wirtschaftsforschung* 43 (1997) 15-34.

Neye, Hans-Werner 'Der neue Übernahmekodex der Börsensachverständigenkommission' *Zeitschrift für Wirtschaftsrecht* 16 (1995) 1464-70.

Neye, Hans-Werner 'Harmonisierung der Mitteilungspflichten zum Beteiligungsbesitz von börsennotierten Aktiengesellschaften' *Zeitschrift für Wirtschaftsrecht* 17 (1996) 1853-8.

Nibler, Marcus 'Bank Control and Corporate Performance in Germany: The Evidence' (Working Paper no. 48, St. John's College Cambridge, June 1995).

Nolte, Cornelius and Hendrik Leber 'Feindliche Unternehmensübernahmen—eine Gefahr für deutsche Unternehmen?' *Die Betriebswirtschaft* 50 (1990) 573-85.

OECD 'Eigentumsverhältnisse, Kontrolle und Entscheidungsprozesse in deutschen Unternehmen' in: 'OECD Wirtschaftsberichte: Deutschland 1995' 94-145 (Paris 1995).

Pappi, Franz Urban, Peter Kappelhoff, and Christian Melbeck 'Die Struktur der Unternehmensverflechtungen in der Bundesrepublik. Eine Blockmodellanalyse der Personal- und Kapitalverflechtungen zwischen den größten Unternehmen' *Kölner Zeitschrift für Soziologie und Sozialpsychologie* 39 (1987) 693-717.

Pellens, Bernhard *Aktionärsschutz im Konzern. Empirische und theoretische Analyse der Reformvorschläge der Konzernverfassung* (Habil.-Schrift University of Bochum 1993) (Wiesbaden 1994).

Pellens, Bernhard, Carsten Rockholtz, and Marc Stienemann 'Marktwertorientiertes Konzerncontrolling in Deutschland. Eine empirische Untersuchung' *Der Betrieb* 50 (1997) 1933-9.

Peltzer, Martin 'Hostile Takeovers in der Bundesrepublik Deutschland? Möglichkeiten und Hindernisse' *Zeitschrift für Wirtschaftsrecht* 10 (1989) 69-79.

Perlitz, Manfred and Frank Seger 'The Role of Universal Banks in German Corporate Governance' *Business & the Contemporary World* 6/4 (1994) 49-67.

Pfannschmidt, Arno *Personelle Verflechtungen über Aufsichtsräte. Mehrfachmandate in deutschen Unternehmen* (Dissertation University of Bonn) (Wiesbaden 1993).

Pistor, Katharina 'Co-Determination in Germany: A Socio-Political Model with Governance Externalities' (Paper, Harvard 1997).

Poensgen, Otto H. and Andreas Lukas 'Fluktuation, Amtszeit und weitere Karriere von Vorstandsmitgliedern. Eine Untersuchung zu Aktiengesellschaften des Verarbeitenden Gewerbes' *Die Betriebswirtschaft* 42 (1982) 177-95.

Prowse, Stephen 'Corporate Governance in an International Perspective: A Survey of Corporate Control Mechanisms Among Large Firms in the U.S., U.K., Japan and Germany' *Financial Markets, Institutions & Instruments* 4/1 (1995).

Prowse, Stephen 'Corporate Finance in International Perspective: Legal and Regulatory Influences on Financial System Development' *Economic Review Federal Reserve Bank of Dallas* 1996/3 2-15.

Püschel, Ulf R. and Andreas von Specht 'Verflechtungen verpflichten' *Blick durch die Wirtschaft* no. 215, 7.11.97, 3.

Raiser, Thomas 'Bewährung des Mitbestimmungsgesetzes nach zwanzig Jahren?' in: Assmann, Heinz-Dieter, Tomas Brinkmann, Georgios Gounalakis, Helmut Kohl, and Rainer Walz (eds.) *Wirtschafts- und Medienrecht in der offenen Demokratie* (Freundesgabe Kübler) 479-92 (Heidelberg 1997).

Rao, Ramesh K.S., David Simon Sokolow, and Derek White 'Fiduciary Duty à la Lyonnais: an Economic Perspective on Corporate Governance in a Financially-Distressed Firm' 22 *J. Corp. L.* 53-78 (1996).

Roggenbuck, Harald E. *Begrenzung des Anteilsbesitzes von Kreditinstituten an Nichtbanken— Gesetzliche Regelungen, empirischer Befund sowie anlage- und geschäftspolitische Bedeutung* (Dissertation University of Hamburg 1991) (Frankfurt am Main et al. 1992).

von Rosen, Rüdiger 'Die Repräsentanz der Streubesitzaktionäre in der Hauptversammlung deutscher Aktiengesellschaften' in: Feddersen, Dieter, Peter Hommelhoff, and Uwe H. Schneider (eds.) *Corporate Governance. Optimierung der Unternehmensführung und der Unternehmenskontrolle im deutschen und amerikanischen Aktienrecht* 289-300 (Cologne 1996).

Ross, Stephen A., Randolph W. Westerfield, and Jeffrey F. Jaffe *Corporate Finance* 3rd edn. (Burr Ridge et al. 1993).

Ruder, David S. 'Reconciling U.S. Disclosure Policy with International Accounting and Disclosure Standards' 17 *Nw. J. Int'l L. & Bus.* 1-14 (1996).

Sachverständigenkommission 'Mitbestimmung im Unternehmen' (Bericht der Sachverständigenkommission zur Auswertung der bisherigen Erfahrungen bei der Mitbestimmung) (Bundestagsdrucksache VI/334, Bonn 1970).

Sachverständigenrat 'Wachstum, Beschäftigung Währungsunion—Orientierungen für die Zukunft' (Jahresgutachten 1997/98 des Sachverständigenrates zur Begutachtung der gesamtwirtschaftlichen Entwicklung) (Bonn 1997).

Sadowski, Dieter, Joachim Junkes, and Cornelia Lent 'Mitbestimmung—Gewinne und Investitionen' (Expertise für das Projekt 'Mitbestimmung und neue Unternehmenskulturen' der Bertelsmann Stiftung und der Hans-Böckler-Stiftung) (Gütersloh 1997).

Sarrazin, Jürgen 'Die besonderen Aufgaben des Aufsichtsratsvorsitzenden' in: Scheffler, Eberhard (ed.) *Corporate Governance* 125-46 (Wiesbaden 1995).

Schiereck, Dirk 'Entwicklungstendenzen bei den Börsennotierungen deutscher Gesellschaften im Ausland' *Die Aktiengesellschaft* 42 (1997) 362-7.

Schilling, Wolf Ulrich 'Shareholder Value und Aktiengesetz' *Betriebs-Berater* 52 (1997) 373-81.

Schmid, Frank A. 'Beteiligungen deutscher Geschäftsbanken und Corporate Performance' *Zeitschrift für Wirtschafts- und Sozialwissenschaften* 116 (1996) 273-310.

Schmid, Frank A. 'Vorstandsbezüge, Aufsichtsratsvergütung und Aktionärsstruktur' *Zeitschrift für Betriebswirtschaft* 67 (1997) 67-83.

Schmidt, Hartmut, Olaf Oesterhelweg, and Kai Treske 'Der Strukturwandel im Börsenwesen: Wettbewerbstheoretische Überlegungen und Trends im Ausland als Leitbilder für den Finanzplatz Deutschland' *Kredit und Kapital* 30 (1997) 369-411.

Schmidt, Hartmut and Stefan Prigge 'Macht der Banken' in: Thießen, Friedrich (ed.), *Enzyklopädisches Lexikon für das Geld-, Bank- und Börsenwesen* 4th edn. (Frankfurt am Main, forthcoming 1998).

Schmidt, Hartmut, Jochen Drukarczyk, Dirk Honold, Stefan Prigge, Andreas Schüler, and Gönke Tetens *Corporate Governance in Germany* (Baden-Baden 1997).

Schmidt, Reinhard H. 'Corporate Governance: The Role of Other Constituencies' (University of Frankfurt am Main, Working Paper no. 3, 1997).

Schmidt, Reinhard H. and Gerald Spindler 'Shareholder-Value zwischen Ökonomie und Recht' in: Assmann, Heinz-Dieter, Tomas Brinkmann, Georgios Gounalakis, Helmut Kohl, and Rainer Walz (eds.) *Wirtschafts- und Medienrecht in der offenen Demokratie* (Freundesgabe Kübler) 515-55 (Heidelberg 1997).

Schmitz, Ronaldo 'Zur Rolle der Banken bei feindlichen Übernahmen' *Wirtschaftsdienst* 77 (1997) 251-3.

Schrader, Stephan and Christian Lüthje 'Das Ausscheiden der Spitzenführungskraft aus dem Unternehmen' *Zeitschrift für Betriebswirtschaft* 65 (1995) 467-93.

Schreyögg, Georg and Heike Papenheim-Tockhorn 'Dient der Aufsichtsrat dem Aufbau zwischenbetrieblicher Kooperationsbeziehungen? Eine Längsschnittstudie zur Rekonstitution "gebrochener Verflechtungen" zwischen deutschen Kapitalgesellschaften' *Zeitschrift für Betriebswirtschaft* 65 (1995) 205-30.

Schreyögg, Georg and Horst Steinmann 'Zur Trennung von Eigentum und Verfügungsgewalt— Eine empirische Analyse der Beteiligungsverhältnisse in deutschen Großunternehmen' *Zeitschrift für Betriebswirtschaft* 51 (1981) 533-58.

Schröder, Ulrich and Alexander Schrader 'The Changing Role of Banks and Corporate Governance in Germany: Evolution Towards the Market?' (The Johns Hopkins University, American Institute for Contemporary German Studies, Economic Studies Working Paper Series no. 13, January 1997).

Schulte, Jörn *Rechnungslegung und Aktienkursentwicklung. Erklärung und Prognosen von Aktienrenditen durch Einzel- und Konzernabschlußdaten* (Dissertation University of Bochum 1995) (Wiesbaden 1996).

Schwalbach, Joachim and Ulrike Graßhoff 'Managervergütung und Unternehmenserfolg' *Zeitschrift für Betriebswirtschaft* 67 (1997) 203-17.

Schwiete, Mark and Jürgen Weigand 'Bankbeteiligungen und das Verschuldungsverhalten deutscher Unternehmen' *Kredit und Kapital* 30 (1997) 1-34.

Seger, Frank *Banken, Erfolg und Finanzierung. Eine Analyse für deutsche Unternehmen* (Dissertation University of Mannheim 1996) (Wiesbaden 1997).

Seibert, Ulrich 'Kontrolle und Transparenz im Unternehmensbereich (KonTraG). Der Referenten-Entwurf zur Aktienrechtsnovelle' *Wertpapier-Mitteilungen* 51 (1997) 1-9.

Seibert, Ulrich, Beate-Katrin Köster, and Roger Kiem *Die kleine AG. Gesellschaftsrechtliche, umwandlungsrechtliche und steuerrechtliche Aspekte* 3rd edn. (Cologne 1996).

Sherman, Heidemarie C. and Fred R. Kaen 'Die deutschen Banken und ihr Einfluß auf Unternehmensentscheidungen' *ifo Schnelldienst* 50/23 (1997) 3-20.

Shleifer, Andrei and Robert W. Vishny 'A Survey of Corporate Governance' *Journal of Finance* 52 (1997) 737-83.

Short, Helen 'Ownership, Control, Financial Structure and the Performance of Firms' *Journal of Economic Surveys* 8 (1994) 203-49.

Siebert, Henning *Grundlagen der US-amerikanischen Rechnungslegung. Ziele und Inhalte der Verlautbarungen der SEC und des FASB sowie ihre Unterschiede zum deutschen Bilanzrecht* (Dissertation University of Bonn) (Cologne 1996).

Sinn, Hans-Werner *Der Staat im Bankwesen. Zur Rolle der Landesbanken in Deutschland* (Munich 1997).

Söllner, Helmut (1988) *Informationsprozesse zwischen Abschlußprüfer und Aufsichtsrat in deutschen Aktiengesellschaften. Eine empirische Untersuchung* (Dissertation University of Erlangen-Nuremberg 1987) (Frankfurt am Main et al. 1988).

Spremann, Klaus 'Wertsteigerung als Managementprinzip in Europa?' in: Höfner, Klaus and Andreas Pohl (eds.) *Wertsteigerungs-Management. Das Shareholder Value-Konzept: Methoden und erfolgreiche Beispiele* 303-19 (Frankfurt am Main and New York 1994).

Statistisches Bundesamt 'Statistisches Jahrbuch 1995' (Wiesbaden 1995).

Statistisches Bundesamt 'Statistisches Jahrbuch 1996' (Wiesbaden 1996).

Statistisches Bundesamt 'Fachserie 14: Finanzen und Steuern, Reihe 8: Umsatzsteuer 1994' (Wiesbaden 1997).

Steinmann, Horst, Werner Fees, and Elmar Gerum 'Managerkontrolle und Mitbestimmung. Empirische Befunde zur Eigentümerstruktur als Determinante des Mitbestimmungspotentials' *Zeitschrift für Betriebswirtschaft* 55 (1985) 992-1011.

Steinmann, Horst and Elmar Gerum 'Unternehmenspolitik in der Mitbestimmten Unternehmung. Empirische Befunde zum Einfluß des Aufsichtsrates von Aktiengesellschaften' *Die Aktiengesellschaft* 25 (1980) 1-10.

Steinmann, Horst, Georg Schreyögg, and Carola Dütthorn 'Managerkontrolle in deutschen Großunternehmen—1972 und 1979 im Vergleich' *Zeitschrift für Betriebswirtschaft* 53 (1983) 4-25.

Tegtmeier, Werner 'Sachgerechte Dynamik' *Mitbestimmung* 42 (1996) 28-31.

Theisen, Manuel René *Die Überwachung der Unternehmungsführung: betriebswirtschaftliche Ansätze zur Entwicklung erster Grundsätze ordnungsmäßiger Überwachung* (Habil.-Schrift University of Regensburg 1985/86) (Stuttgart 1987).

Theisen, Manuel René *Der Konzern. Betriebswirtschaftliche und rechtliche Grundlagen der Konzernunternehmung* (Stuttgart 1991).

Theisen, Manuel René 'Die Rechtsprechung zum Mitbestimmungsgesetz 1976—eine vierte Zwischenbilanz' *Die Aktiengesellschaft* 43 (1998) 153-70.

Theisen, Manuel René and Wolfgang Salzberger 'Die Berichterstattung des Aufsichtsrats. Eine empirische Analyse der Überwachungsberichte von 1984-1994' *Der Betrieb* 50 (1997) 105-15.

Thiele, Stefan and Frank Tschesche 'Zur Bilanzierungspraxis der DAX-Unternehmen im Geschäftsjahr 1996. Mehr "Einblick" durch internationale Rechnungslegungsnormen?' *Der Betrieb* 50 (1997) 2497-502.

Thießen, Friedrich 'Covenants in Kreditverträgen: Alternative oder Ergänzung zum Insolvenzrecht?' *Zeitschrift für Bankrecht und Bankwirtschaft* 8 (1996) 19-37.

Thoma, Georg F. 'Der neue Übernahmekodex der Börsensachverständigenkommission' *Zeitschrift für Wirtschaftsrecht* 17 (1996) 1725-34.

Triantis, George G. and Ronald J. Daniels 'The Role of Debt in Interactive Corporate Governance' 83 *Cal. L. Rev.* 1073-113 (1995).

Turnbull, Shann 'Corporate Governance: Its Scope, Concerns and Theories' *Corporate Governance* 5 (1997) 180-205.

Ulmer, Peter 'Die Anpassung von AG-Satzungen an das Mitbestimmungsgesetz—eine Zwischenbilanz' *Zeitschrift für das gesamte Handelsrecht und Wirtschaftsrecht* 141 (1977) 490-519.

Veit, Klaus-Rüdiger and Michael Tönnies 'Ausmaß und Transparenz von Unternehmenszusammenschlüssen bei großen Kapitalgesellschaften. Ergebnisse einer empirischen Untersuchung' *Der Betrieb* 50 (1997) 1829-32.

Vitols, Sigurt, Steven Casper, David Soskice, and Stephen Woolcock 'Corporate Governance in Large British and German Companies: Comparative Institutional Advantage or Competing for Best Practice' (Anglo-German Foundation for the Study of Industrial Society, Working Paper, 1997).

Vogel, C. Wolfgang *Aktienrecht und Aktienwirklichkeit. Organisationsrecht und Aufgabenteilung von Vorstand und Aufsichtsrat. Eine empirische Untersuchung deutscher Aktiengesellschaften* (Dissertation University of Giessen 1978/79) (Baden-Baden 1980).

Wardenbach, Frank *Interessenkonflikte und mangelnde Sachkunde als Bestellungshindernisse zum Aufsichtsrat der AG* (Dissertation University of Bonn) (Cologne 1996).

Weisgerber, Thomas. 'Der Übernahmekodex in der Praxis' *Zeitschrift für das gesamte Handelsrecht und Wirtschaftsrecht* 161 (1997) 421-34.

Wenger, Ekkehard 'Expert Opinion for the Monopolkommission. Part III: Überkreuzverflechtungen und die Blockade des Marktes für Unternehmenskontrolle' (1996).

Wenger, Ekkehard 'Expert Opinion for the Monopolkommission. Part VI: Die Beeinträchtigung der Informationsverarbeitung am Kapitalmarkt durch unzureichende Rechnungslegungs- und Publizitätsvorschriften' (1996a).

Wenger, Ekkehard 'Kapitalmarkttrecht als Resultat deformierter Anreizstrukturen' in: Sadowski, Dieter, Hans Czap, and Hartmut Wächter (eds.) *Regulierung und Unternehmenspolitik. Methode und Ergebnisse der betriebswirtschaftlichen Rechtsanalyse* 419-58 (Wiesbaden 1996b).

Wenger, Ekkehard 'Im Selbstbedienungsladen des Konzernmanagements wird der Privatanleger noch immer verhöhnt' *Wirtschaftsdienst* 77 (1997) 254-8.

Wenger, Ekkehard and Renate Hecker 'Übernahme- und Abfindungsregeln am deutschen Aktienmarkt' *ifo Studien—Zeitschrift für empirische Wirtschaftsforschung* 41 (1995) 51-87.

Wenger, Ekkehard and Christoph Kaserer 'The German System of Corporate Governance: A Model Which Should Not Be Imitated' in: Black, Stanley and Matthias Moersch (eds.) *Competition and Convergence: The German and Anglo-American Models* 40-81 (Washington, D.C. 1998).

von Werder, Axel 'Shareholder Value-Ansatz als (einzige) Richtschnur des Vorstandshandelns?' *Zeitschrift für Unternehmens- und Gesellschaftsrecht* 27 (1998) 69-91.

Westermann, Harm Peter 'Vollmachtstimmrecht und Streubesitzaktionäre in der Hauptversammlung deutscher Aktiengesellschaften' in: Feddersen, Dieter, Peter Hommelhoff, and Uwe H. Schneider (eds.) *Corporate Governance. Optimierung der Unternehmensführung und der Unternehmenskontrolle im deutschen und amerikanischen Aktienrecht* 264-86 (Cologne 1996).

Wiendieck, Markus *Unternehmensfinanzierung und Kontrolle durch Banken: Deutschland—Japan—USA* (Dissertation University of Cologne) (Wiesbaden 1992).

te Wildt, Claus *CEO Turnover and Corporate Performance: The German Case* (Dissertation University of Kiel) (Kiel 1996).

Windolf, Paul and Jürgen Beyer 'Kooperativer Kapitalismus. Unternehmensverflechtungen im internationalen Vergleich' *Kölner Zeitschrift für Soziologie und Sozialpsychologie* 47 (1995) 1-36.

Wissenschaftlicher Beirat beim Bundesministerium für Wirtschaft 'Wagniskapital' (Gutachten des Wissenschaftlichen Beirats beim Bundesministerium für Wirtschaft, BMWi Studienreihe no. 95, Bonn 1997).

Wölk, Armin 'Ad hoc-Publizität—Erfahrungen aus der Sicht des Bundesaufsichtsamtes für den Wertpapierhandel' *Die Aktiengesellschaft* 42 (1997) 73-80.

Wymeersch, Eddy 'Elements of Comparative Corporate Governance in Western Europe' in: Isaksson, Mats and Rolf Skog (eds.) *Aspects of Corporate Governance* 83-116 (Stockholm 1994).

Zeitschrift für das gesamte Kreditwesen 'Shareholder Value und Aktienkultur—eine Umfrage bei den DAX-Werten' *Zeitschrift für das gesamte Kreditwesen* 49 (1996) 481-95.

Zeitschrift für Wirtschaftsrecht 'ZIP-Dokumentation: Regierungsentwurf Kapitalaufnahmeerleichterungsgesetz' *Zeitschrift für Wirtschaftsrecht* 18 (1997) 706-10.

Zeitschrift für Wirtschaftsrecht 'ZIP-Dokumentation: Regierungsentwurf zur Änderung des Aktiengesetzes ("KonTraG")' *Zeitschrift für Wirtschaftsrecht* 18 (1997a) 2059-68 and 2100-4.

Ziegler, Rolf 'Das Netz der Personen- und Kapitalverflechtungen deutscher und österreichischer Wirtschaftsunternehmen' *Kölner Zeitschrift für Soziologie und Sozialpsychologie* 36 (1984) 585-614.

A Status Report on Corporate Governance Rules and Practices in Some Continental European States

EDDY WYMEERSCH, Ghent

The purpose of this contribution is to outline elements of the structure of large business corporations in Europe, mainly on the European continent. The first part deals with the overall characteristics of the factual structure of the corporate world in Western Europe. Differences in legal form are striking, while the use of the public securities markets points to fundamental differences in ownership. In the second part, the legal structure of the board of directors is analyzed. The analysis concentrates on the unitary board as the most frequently found model. The two-tier board is described, both with and without employee participation. The third part focuses on the differences in ownership structure. On the basis of the author's research, the concentration of ownership in the different systems within Europe has been mapped. Further investigation is aimed at identifying the different classes of shareholders: institutionals do not play a predominant role, shares being mainly owned by other companies, by individuals, or by foreign investors. The role of the equity markets is a direct function of the differences in the use of the markets as a financing source. A final point of comparison relates to the market for corporate control, both in its private segment and in the public takeover market.

Contents

Figure

Tables

A. Introduction

I. Economic Aspects: Structure of Companies in Europe

1. In most European legal systems, companies may be formed either as public or as private companies limited by shares. These will be referred to as the *SA-AG* or the *SARL-GmbH* type of company. These are the most-used company types as far as the larger business entities are concerned. In addition, some legal systems spawn other types that are chosen especially for tax reasons. This is the case of the limited partnership, or *société en commandite simple*, known in most continental European systems. Especially in Germany, the specific hybrid of the *GmbH & Co. KG*, combining the advantages of the non-incorporated *Kommanditgesellschaft* and the limited liability of the *GmbH*, is frequently used as an alternative to the company limited. As other jurisdictions do not offer the same tax advantages, this company type will be less frequently found there.

Table 1 gives an overview of the main business firm types that have been used in some selected European states. These figures—especially in the residual category "other"—include the individual firms run by one physical person.

A few comments can be made with respect to the figures in Tables 1 and 2:

1. In Germany, Austria, Italy, and in the Netherlands, the *AG* or *NV* represents a minor fraction of the overall number of companies. Of these, only a small proportion is listed on the stock exchange. These company types are framed to house the largest business firms.

2. In France[1], Belgium, Spain, and Switzerland, the *SA* form is almost a full alternative to the *SARL*, the private company limited. The listing of *SA*s on exchanges is rare, and occurs only for the largest companies.

3. In the U.K., the number of public companies limited is relatively high, and listing is relatively frequent. Many smaller companies are listed.

4. In relation to GDP and population, both Belgium and Switzerland have the highest proportion of companies per 1,000 inhabitants. However, as the relation to GDP would indicate, some of these (U.K., Sweden, Belgium) are smaller entities. The opposite phenomenon is visible in Germany and Italy, in both cases due to the high number of other types of companies (Table 1).

5. As a consequence of the 1997 market rise, there will be a significant increase in the number of listed companies for 1997. See further Table 8.

6. For comparative purposes, the above list illustrates that it is very difficult, without further comments, to put the *SA* types as used in each of the compared states on the same footing. In Germany, for example, the *SA* is

---

[1] The relatively high number of *SA* is linked to the favorable tax and social security status of the *président directeur-général* in the *SA*, not available to directors of *SARL*, Guyon, Yves *Droit des Affaires* vol. 1, no. 341, 350, 489, 511 8ᵗʰ edn. (Paris 1994).

Table 1: Company Types

	SA	SARL	SNC-OHG	SCS-KG	S.Coop.	Other
Belgium[a]	146,797	197,686	4,207	2,673	53,960	n.a.
France[b]	169,269	591,102	30,285	1,485	20,761	1,097,398
Italy[c]	31,583	224,567	367,731	133,315	35,646	116,278
Germany[d]	2,164	359,358	210,167	87,317	45,818	1,926,988
Netherlands[e]	2,042	156,170	87,072	n.a.	n.a.	419,510
U.K.[f]	11,500	1,024,700	n.a.	n.a.	n.a.	n.a.
Spain[g]	116,888	326,644		85	16,494	1,092,799
Switzerland[h]	170,703	10,705	16,775	3,533	14,167	164,019
Sweden[i]	210,418	0	76,550	0	15,111	260,686
Austria[j]	833	n.a.	n.a.	n.a.	n.a.	n.a.

Note: Number of firms.
Sources:
[a]   Rijksregister.
[b]   1993; Cozian and Viandier, infra n. 2, 3.
[c]   Source ISTAT—Censimento sul 1991. See Bianchi, Bianco, and Enriques, infra n. 85.
[d]   1994 figures; Statistisches Bundesamt 'Fachserie 14: Finanzen und Steuern, Reihe 8: Umsatzsteuer 1992' 30 (Wiesbaden 1995).
[e]   1995 figures; CBS 'Statistisch jaarboek' (1996).
[f]   DTI 'Companies in 1995-1996' 25 (HMSO, London).
[g]   'Annuario El Pais' (1997).
[h]   BFS 'Statistisches Jahrbuch der Schweiz' 166, T. 6.3 (1997).
[i]   'Statistik Årsbook' 275, Tab. 292 (1997).
[j]   'Statistisches Jahrbuch für die Republik Österreich' 371 (1995).

aimed at the largest business firms, while in other states it is the usual business form. Hence, harmonization of company law may have a radically different impact according to the state considered. Several states have therefore declared the rules adopted for the implementation of the directives equally applicable to the *SA* and to the *SARL* forms.

7. Some of the figures reproduced may be overstating the number of effectively existing companies.[2,3]

---

[2] A comment should be made on the reliability of these figures. In France and Belgium the figures are based on a count of the new formations minus dissolutions of companies. This figure stands for a higher number than the overall number of active companies (See for France, Cozian, Maurice and Alain Viandier *Droits des Sociétés* 5, n. 2 9th edn. (Paris 1996)). The same applies to Belgium: out of 688,183 firms subject to VAT, only 260,708 were legal persons (end of 1996). The number of companies that filed annual accounts is even much lower (79,499 *NV-SAs* and 77,651 *SPRL-BVBAs* for 1995).

[3] "Other firms" in Table 2 includes sole traders and other different types of enterprises.

Table 2:   Companies Related to Population and GDP

	SA	Population (1,000 Inhabitants)	Number of Companies per 1,000 Inhabitants	SA + SARL	Population (1,000 Inhabitants)	Number of Companies per 1,000 Inhabitants
Belgium	146,797	10,137	14.48	344,483	10,137	33.98
France	169,269	58,414	2.90	760,371	58,414	13.02
Italy	31,583	57,283	0.55	256,150	57,283	4.47
Germany	2,164	81,662	0.03	361,522	81,662	4.43
Netherlands	2,042	15,457	0.13	158,212	15,457	10.24
U.K.	11,500	58,260	0.20	1,036,200	58,260	17.79
Spain	116,888	39,210	2.98	443,532	39,210	11.31
Switzerland	170,703	7,081	24.11	181,408	7,081	25.62
Sweden	210,418	8,827	23.84	210,418	8,827	23.84
Austria	833	8,047	0.10	833	8,047	0.10

	SA	GDP (Bil. ECU)	Number Companies per GDP Bil. ECU	SA + SARL	GDP (Bil. ECU)	Number Companies per GDP Bil. ECU
Belgium	146,797	269.2	545.31	344,483	269.2	1,279.65
France	169,269	1,537.6	110.09	760,371	1,537.6	494.52
Italy	31,583	1,087.2	29.05	256,150	1,087.2	235.61
Germany	2,164	2,412.5	0.90	361,522	2,412.5	149.85
Netherlands	2,042	395.5	5.16	158,212	395.5	400.03
U.K.	11,500	1,010.8	11.38	1,036,200	1,010.8	1,025.13
Spain	116,888	559.6	208.88	443,532	559.6	792.59
Switzerland	170,703	306.1	557.67	181,408	306.1	592.64
Sweden	210,418	230.6	912.48	210,418	230.6	912.48
Austria	833	233.3	3.57	833		

Sources: Own calculations; 'Statistique' *Bulletin de la Banque de France* (August 1997) 200.

II. Listed and Publicly Traded Companies

2. In all the jurisdictions compared, companies can be formed freely, i.e., without government intervention. Only in the Netherlands has some form of supervision been maintained, with the Ministry of Justice being entitled to declare whether it raises "objections" to a company's charter. As a consequence, model instructions were developed to which all companies are expected to conform. These "departmental guidelines" have a considerable influence on company charters and structure.[4] For example, though the use of bearer shares is legally permissible, it is de facto not allowed for smaller Dutch companies. In the past, the use of anti-takeover devices does not seem to have raised objections from the Ministry.

3. Company law has been subject to considerable re-regulation during the last thirty years.[5] This re-regulation is due on the one hand to endogenous factors, such as the overall reform of the private law code,[6] and the need to remodel specific parts of the statute or to recast the company law provisions scattered over different acts into one single statute. Although these reforms have modified a substantial number of rules, one can analyze them as essentially a re-enactment of previously existing rules. However, in addition, more fundamental changes were introduced, mainly as a consequence of the implementation of the European directives, but also as a result of exogenous factors such as the need to adapt to the requirements of the financial markets whose role had become more significant. Political pressure, whether for economic democracy or for other objectives, has led to the introduction of co-determination in the companies acts of some states, or of rules on groups of companies. The more recent company law reforms have taken place along with or driven by substantial changes in the financial markets, among other things by the formation of a more integrated and more competitive European capital market. This explains why more recent changes are found not in the companies acts but in the "securities regulation", often a scattered set of rules enacted by government, by government agencies, or even by self-regulatory bodies.

4. Apart from piecemeal changes, company laws have been overhauled in several states. The German reform of the *AG* in 1965 was probably the most thorough of the reforms, building on the 1937 *Aktiengesetz* but introducing a fundamental chapter on groups of companies. The French Companies Act of 1966 is mainly a re-enactment of the previously disparate company law provisions. It has been amended several times since then. The U.K. restated its legislation in 1985, adding further changes in 1989. The Dutch introduced company law as part of the new Dutch Civil Code, dealing with "legal persons"[7] and adapting many rules to the new economic and legal environment. Similar re-enactments are found in Portugal and Spain, while the Italian and Swiss laws

---

[4] For the text of these guidelines, see Van der Heijden, Egidius J.J. and Willem C.L. Van der Grinten *Handboek van de naamloze en de besloten vennootschap* 742 12th edn. (Zwolle 1992).

[5] For a fundamental analysis, see Buxbaum, Richard M. and Klaus J. Hopt *Legal Harmonization and the Business Enterprise: Corporate and Capital Market Law Harmonization Policy in Europe and the USA* (Berlin and New York 1988).

[6] E.g., the new Dutch Civil Code (NBW), dealing in its Book 2 with the *SA* and *SARL* type of companies (called *NV* and *BV*).

[7] Book 1 dealing with physical persons, Book 2 with legal persons.

have been subject to more specific, sometimes repeated changes. In Belgium, an overhaul of the entire subject was proposed in the late 1970s but was never discussed in Parliament.[8] The same happened in Italy.[9] The Nordic Codes introduced companies acts that are largely similar (Sweden, Finland) or contain common features (Denmark).[10]

5. As part of these company law reforms, the national company statutes have been almost continuously modified in order to implement the European directives, especially the specific company law directives. Securities directives should also be mentioned, as these have imposed the framework for rules on disclosure, ownership reporting, insider trading, and other related subjects. These directives have led to a considerable degree of harmonization, primarily in "external" company life, such as the rules on capital, accounting, representation, mergers, and demergers.

However, the central part of internal company life and structure has largely been left outside the harmonization, mainly as a consequence of member states' reluctance to modify the internal company structure that is often based on delicate balances of influence and power. These matters deal with core rules in the governance debate, such as the "one share, one vote rule"; the structure of the board; the corporate control market, especially the regulation of takeovers and the protections against them; the rules on groups of companies; and the protection of minority shareholders. Mostly as part of the regulation of the securities markets, member states have been dealing with some of the following issues: rules on listing on stock exchanges, on listing requirements with respect to the use of anti-takeover devices, on disclosure of significant holdings of shares, on mandatory takeover bids, or on voting rights exercised by investment funds. Each of these plays a significant role in the governance debate. However, these only concern the listed companies, not the vast majority of—sometimes very large—unlisted firms.

6. In addition to securities markets regulation, reference should also be made to sector-specific requirements—mainly dealing with banks, investment firms, insurance companies, investment funds, etc.—that have an impact on governance issues. Many of these originate in European directives.

By way of example, one could refer to the four eye principle, made mandatory by the Second Banking Directive,[11] two-tier boards, de facto mandatory in the

---

[8] See Bill no. 387 (Belgian Chamber of representatives, 1979-1980, no. 1, 5 December 1979).

[9] See the 1965 *progetto De Gregorio*.

[10] Danish Companies Act 1969; Swedish Companies Act 1975; Finnish Companies Act as amended 14 February 1997.

[11] Art. 3 (2) First Banking Directive of 12 December 1977 *OJEC* L 322/30, 17.12.1977.

Belgian banking sector,[12] the obligation for financial institutions to have an "adequate internal organization", "sound administrative and accounting procedures", and "adequate internal control mechanisms",[13] further the requirement to have the firm's head office in the state of its registered office (limiting emigration of firms),[14] while the license for commercial banks to hold shares in non-banking firms has been extended all over the EU.[15] One could also mention the voting right restrictions applicable to investment funds, which are not allowed to exercise control.[16] Many of the more recently discussed topics affecting governance of publicly traded companies are therefore dealt with outside the traditional companies acts, as these are applicable to all companies, whether listed or not.

7. The role of securities commissions and supervisory bodies should not remain unmentioned. These bodies play a role, not only in imposing additional formal requirements applicable to issuers of securities traded on the "regulated markets", but as driving forces behind the supervision and enforcement of these rules. Their influence is variable and difficult to measure, not least because not all member states have comparable securities commissions. In the sixties and seventies, their influence was more visible because they recommended many of the rules that have since been introduced by statute, often after having been made mandatory by way of European directive. The rules on preferential subscription rights on new share issues, the rules on the repurchase of own shares, and also the obligation to draw up consolidated accounts were imposed long before the directives came into force. Apart from formal regulation, several of these bodies made use of instruments of self-regulation, e.g., in the field of insider trading.[17]

In a longer-term perspective, one could state that their influence is gradually being eroded due to the introduction of more formal regulation and the increasing internationalization of the markets.

8. As a consequence of this rather pragmatic approach to company regulation, several European states have a two- or even a three-tier company legislation.

The first tier is composed of the companies whose shares are traded on the public markets. These are predominantly the stock exchange-listed firms. They

---

[12] Art. 26 Belgian Banking Act 22 March 1993.

[13] Art. 10 Investment Services Directive of 10 May 1993 *OJEC* L 141/27, 11.6.1993.

[14] E.g., art. 3 (2) ISD, supra n. 13.

[15] Art. 12 Second Banking Directive of 15 December 1989 *OJEC* L 386/1, 30.12.1989.

[16] See art. 25 (1) 1985 Directive on Ucits of 20 December 1985 *OJEC* L 375/3, 31.12.1985.

[17] See Hopt, Klaus J. and Michael R. Will *Europäisches Insiderrecht* (Stuttgart 1975) containing a collection of the main instruments applicable to insider trading in the early '70s. See Timmerman, Levinus 'Zelfregulering in de sfeer van het vennootschapsrecht' *De Naamlooze Vennootschap* 77 (1997) 69. On the subject in general, see Wymeersch, Eddy 'L'auto-régulation dans le domaine financier' in: *L'autorégulation* (colloque organisé à Bruxelles le 16 décembre 1992 par l'A.D.Br. et le Centre de Droit Privé de l'Université Libre de Bruxelles) 169-92 (Brussels 1995).

are subject to general company law, to specific public regulations applicable to listed companies, and finally to rules of soft law imposed by the market authorities.

Some companies have issued shares to the public in the past and are held to similar rules as the fully listed ones. These are sometimes called the "issuers that have called on the public savings markets."[18] Their securities may be traded on an over-the-counter market, or on the newly created market segments like Easdaq or *Nouveau Marché*[19]. Each regulation must be checked as to whether it will be applicable to this set of companies. Publicly traded but not officially listed companies still constitute a small number.

A second segment relates to the companies that have been formed according to the *SA* rules, but are closely held. Here only company law applies. They are the vast majority of *SA*-type companies.

Finally, mention should also be made of the *SARL* type or closely held companies, which in some jurisdictions (e.g., Netherlands, Belgium, or to some extent France) are subject to rules that are largely identical or very similar to the ones applicable to the *SA*.

III. Stock Exchanges and Regulated Markets

9. All European states have their own stock exchanges—usually one per country, although some states have maintained several, albeit increasingly integrated, exchanges. In addition, regulated markets[20] function alongside the official markets. The importance of these markets varies considerably both in absolute terms and in terms of relative importance to their respective economic systems. In order to measure the significance of the stock exchange phenomenon and, more particularly, the significance of securities financing on turnover figures in the different economies of Europe, several yardsticks are being used. The traditional yardstick is the relationship between market capitalization and GDP (Table 5). However, other measures could be used, such as the absolute ranking of the capitalization of each of the markets (Table 3) or the population (Table 4).

The following tables give an overview of the importance of the different stock exchanges in Europe in terms of capitalization, turnover, and turnover velocity of domestic shares. The figures are in million ECU (= 1.2 million US$) and have been sorted in Table 3 in ascending order.

---

[18] This is the French and Belgian expression of "sociétés faisant ou ayant fait appel public à l'épargne"; see, e.g., art. 26 Belgian Companies Act; also art. 72 French Companies Act 1966.

[19] A common venture of the French, Belgian, Dutch, and German exchanges.

[20] The term regulated market is here used in the meaning of art. 1 (13) ISD, supra n. 13.

Table 3 indicates that the French, German, and U.K. markets concentrate 61% of overall European capitalization, although only 52% of the European population lives in these states.

Table 4 classifies the states in terms of population. Here three to four states appear to be most heavily bent on securities financing.

Table 3: Market Capitalization of Domestic Shares, 1995

	Market Capitalization Mil. ECU	Share in %
Athens	18,988	0.49
Lisbon	19,706	0.51
Luxembourg	25,909	0.66
Ireland	27,658	0.71
Vienna	28,719	0.74
Oslo	45,792	1.18
Helsinki	49,444	1.27
Copenhagen	57,281	1.47
Brussels	95,751	2.46
Stockholm	194,045	4.98
Madrid	194,681	5.00
Italian Exchange	206,997	5.31
Amsterdam	223,452	5.73
Swiss	322,354	8.27
Paris	471,426	12.10
Germany	531,533	13.64
London	1,382,809	35.49
Total	3,896,545	100

Source: Based on figures published by the European Federation of Stock Exchanges.

10. One could presume that market capitalization would be related to both GDP and population, because a larger economy, being based on a larger population, would normally produce larger firms and hence a higher capitalization. In case of disparity between the two ratios, other factors must be taken into account. In fact, some economies, although relatively small in terms of population, have maintained large international firms. Also, some economies tend to be more securities market-oriented than others: this factor can be measured by comparing the relative size of the economies to the overall capitalization (last column of

Table 4:   Market Capitalization Related to Population, 1995

	Market Capitalization Mil. ECU	Share in %	Population (1,000 Inhabitants)	Share in %	Mil. ECU Capitalization per 1,000 Inhabitants
Athens	18,988	0.49	10,459	2.73	1.82
Lisbon	19,706	0.51	9,921	2.59	1.99
Vienna	28,719	0.74	8,047	2.10	3.57
Italian Exchange	206,997	5.31	57,283	14.95	3.61
Madrid	194,681	5.00	39,210	10.23	4.97
Germany	531,533	13.64	81,662	21.31	6.51
Ireland	27,658	0.71	3,580	0.93	7.73
Paris	471,426	12.10	58,141	15.17	8.11
Brussels	95,751	2.46	10,137	2.65	9.45
Helsinki	49,444	1.27	5,108	1.33	9.68
Oslo	45,792	1.18	4,360	1.14	10.50
Copenhagen	57,281	1.47	5,228	1.36	10.96
Amsterdam	223,452	5.73	15,457	4.03	14.46
Stockholm	194,045	4.98	8,827	2.30	21.98
London	1,382,809	35.49	58,260	15.20	23.74
Swiss	322,354	8.27	7,081	1.85	45.52
Luxembourg	25,909	0.66	413	0.11	62.73
Total/Average	3,896,545	100	383,174	100	10.17

Source: Based on figures published by the European Federation of Stock Exchanges.

Table 5). Measured in terms of population, an imbalance would indicate the presence of major international firms that are productive outside the national boundaries: Switzerland and the U.K., and to a lesser extent Sweden and the Netherlands, illustrate this phenomenon.

Table 5 attempts to rate the fifteen EU member states, Switzerland, and Norway according to their relative involvement in securities business. It proceeds to a classification according to the intensity of use of securities markets, distinguishing three classes: high, middle, and low intensity users (Table 6, col. e).

In the hypothesis that there should be a linear relationship between market capitalization, GDP, and population, it is apparent that five states show a higher than average intensity in the use of securities markets. The U.K., with 11.2% of EU GDP, holds a concentration of 35.49% of the capitalization of the entire

Table 5: Markets Classified per % of GDP, 1996

	Market Capitalization Mil. ECU	GDP Bil. ECU	Market Capitalization in % of GDP
Vienna	28,719	233.3	12.31
Italian Exchange	206,997	1,087.2	19.04
Lisbon	19,706	99.8	19.75
Germany	531,533	2,412.5	22.03
Athens	18,988	77.8	24.41
Paris	471,426	1,537.6	30.66
Copenhagen	57,281	173.3	33.05
Madrid	194,681	559.6	34.79
Brussels	95,751	269.2	35.57
Helsinki	49,444	125.0	39.56
Ireland	27,658	64.3	43.01
Oslo	45,792	103.4	44.29
Amsterdam	223,452	395.5	56.50
Stockholm	194,045	230.6	84.15
Swiss	322,354	306.1	105.31
London	1,382,809	1,010.8	136.80
Luxembourg	25,909	10.6	244.42

Source: Based on figures published by the European Federation of Stock Exchanges.

Union.[21] Similar disparities can be shown for Switzerland, Sweden, the Netherlands, and Luxembourg. All of these are states in which the securities business has experienced the strongest development. These states will pay the highest attention to market organization, and to regulation of the securities business and financing in general.

At the opposite end of the spectrum, Spain, Austria, Italy, France, and Germany are the states where securities matters play a relatively less important role in comparison to their relative economic weight. The figures are particularly striking for Germany and for Italy, two states that stand for 40% of EU GDP and for 36% of EU population but only for 18.95% of capitalization. It also means that industry in these five states—or 67% of the European economy—is mainly supported by financing means other than securities financing, and that securities

[21] Including Switzerland and Norway.

Table 6:   Market Capitalization Related to GDP, 1996

	Cap.		GDP			GDP per capita (10,000 ECU)
	Mil. ECU	%	Bil. ECU	%		
	a	b=% T	c	d=% T	e=b-d	f
London	1,382,809	35.49	1,010.8	11.62	23.87	1.73
Swiss	322,354	8.27	306.1	3.52	4.75	4.32
Stockholm	194,045	4.98	230.6	2.65	2.33	2.61
Amsterdam	223,452	5.73	395.5	4.55	1.19	2.56
Luxembourg	25,909	0.66	10.6	0.12	0.54	2.57
Oslo	45,792	1.18	103.4	1.19	-0.01	2.37
Ireland	27,658	0.71	64.3	0.74	-0.03	1.80
Helsinki	49,444	1.27	125	1.44	-0.17	2.45
Athens	18,988	0.49	77.8	0.89	-0.41	0.74
Copenhagen	57,281	1.47	173.3	1.99	-0.52	3.31
Brussels	95,751	2.46	269.2	3.10	-0.64	2.66
Lisbon	19,706	0.51	99.8	1.15	-0.64	1.01
Madrid	194,681	5.00	559.6	6.43	-1.44	1.43
Vienna	28,719	0.74	233.3	2.68	-1.95	2.90
Paris	471,426	12.10	1,537.6	17.68	-5.58	2.64
Italian Exchange	206,997	5.31	1,087.2	12.50	-7.19	1.90
Germany	531,533	13.64	2,412.5	27.74	-14.10	2.95
Total (T)	3,896,545	100	8,696.6	100		2.27

Source: Based on figures published by the European Federation of Stock Exchanges.

financing has not been widely practiced in two-thirds of Europe. The latter figures are the more striking as these states contain some of the larger European firms.

In between are the smaller European states, where, although negative, the ratio would indicate that the securities capitalization is more or less in balance with their economic weight.

As could be expected, there is no direct relationship between market development and wealth, measured in terms of GDP per capita (Table 6, col. f: GDP/population).

The findings from this comparison are relatively simple and have been formulated by many writers before: the relative importance of securities markets shows significant differences among the European states. Some are more, others are less market-oriented. The vast majority—both in terms of numbers and of relative economic weight—belong to the latter category. The dividing line that appears from these data will also show up in many other fields of corporate organization and regulation.

11. A further analysis and classification in terms of turnover and turnover velocity gives a different view. However, a warning statement must first be made about the significance of these figures. According to the methodology followed by the European Federation of Stock Exchanges, two methods are used for calculating turnover: the first is based on the figures of trading within a given stock exchange;[22] the second (* in Table 8) includes trading in domestic shares outside the home exchange, and therefore includes trading over-the-counter

Table 7: Turnover and Turnover Velocity, 1995

	Turnover Mil. ECU	Share in %	Velocity	Capitalization % of Total
Luxembourg	373	0.02	1.61	0.74
Ireland*	5,445	0.26	19.69	0.88
Lisbon	3,237	0.15	22.61	0.46
Madrid	39,887	1.87	24.37	5.21
Copenhagen	21,757	1.02	27.50	2.52
Helsinki	14,685	0.69	33.51	1.39
Athens	4,678	0.22	36.36	0.41
Brussels	14,263	0.67	41.04	1.11
Paris	163,463	7.68	41.98	12.40
Vienna	10,188	0.48	42.59	0.76
Amsterdam*	96,434	4.53	43.09	7.12
Italian Exchange	66,885	3.14	49.83	4.27
Stockholm*	78,032	3.67	52.48	4.73
Oslo*	19,147	0.90	56.09	1.09
Swiss*	245,605	11.54	79.03	9.89
London*	878,044	41.27	84.56	33.05
Germany*	465,654	21.88	106.16	13.96
Total	2,127,777	100		100

Note:* Turnover calculated according to Regulated Environment View; see supra n. 22 and infra n. 23.

Source: Based on figures published by the European Federation of Stock Exchanges.

[22] This is the Trading System View (TSV), counting only trades that have passed through the exchange's trading system, and not including securities business transactions by members away from the exchange system.

and abroad.[23] Also, most exchanges would include trading in investment funds and similar securities which are not included in capitalization figures.

As Table 7 shows, turnover velocity is not only linked to investors' interest for the market, but is also due to the scarcity of shares on the market. This explains the very high figures for Germany. We will later attempt to quantify the volume of shares effectively available on the markets, based on a rough calculation of the difference of total amount of shares issued and shares held by the principal shareholder ("free float").[24]

Table 8:   Number of Domestic Listed Shares and New Listings, 1995-1997

Listed Shares	New 1995 a	Total b	% c = a/b	New 1996 a	Total b	% c = a/b	New 1997 a	Total b	% c = a/b
Amsterdam	7	217	3.23	6	217	2.76	24	201	11.94
Athens	18	197	9.14	20	217	9.22	12	220	5.45
Brussels	1	143	0.70	8	146	5.48	16	136	11.76
Copenhagen	11	213	5.16	6	237	2.53	5	237	2.11
Germany	20	678	2.95	11	681	2.79	29	699	8.87
Helsinki	10	73	13.70	3	71	4.23	13	124*	10.48
Ireland	0	62	0.00	1	61	1.64	10	77*	12.99
Italian Exchange	14	250	5.60	15	244	6.15	13	235	5.53
Lisbon	8	169	4.73	3	158	1.90	7	148	4.73
London	184	1,745	10.54	345	2,339*	14.75	236	2,465	9.58
Luxembourg	1	362	0.28	1	54	1.85	3	56	5.35
Madrid	7	362	1.93	11	357	3.08	40	384	10.42
Oslo	26	151	17.22	20	158	12.66	46	196	23.47
Paris	23	710	3.24	39	686	5.69	47	683	6.88
Stockholm	16	212	7.55	15	217	6.91	50	245	20.41
Swiss	7	216	3.24	11	213	5.16	13	216	6.02
Vienna	7	95	7.37	2	94	2.13	4	101*	3.96

Note: Figures with * refer to more substantial structural changes.
Sources: Federation of the European Stock Exchanges 'Annual Report' (1995), 'Annual Report' (1996), 'Monthly Statistics' (1997); Hansen, Herbert 'Ende 1997: 4548 AG mit 222 Mrd. Grundkapital' *Die Aktiengesellschaft* 43 (1998) R112.

[23] This is called the Regulated Environment View (REV), in which all trades are counted over which the exchange has a regulatory oversight, therefore encompassing almost all trades made by members in other European or foreign markets. The second view will result in turnover figures being higher than if the TSV were adopted. For Copenhagen and Madrid both figures are available, leading to considerable differences: for Copenhagen, 3.4 vs. 21.7 billion ECU, and for Madrid 39.8 vs. 125.3 billion ECU.

[24] See infra no. 113 et seq.

The number of shares available on a market also illustrates its importance. During recent years there have been many new listings on most European markets. The growth has been unevenly spread, with traditional leaders growing at a lower percentage than markets that had previously stayed behind. As mentioned before, the increase of new listings in 1997 will probably be the highest for many years all over Europe (Table 8).

In comparison to other world securities markets, European markets are still relatively minor, as emerges from Table 9.

Table 9: European Markets in Comparison With the Main Markets in the World, 1996

	Cap. Mil. ECU	GDP Bil. ECU	Cap. GDP %	Number of Securities	Domestic Turnover Mil. ECU
France	471,426	1,538	30.66	686	220,608
Germany	531,553	2,413	22.03	681	621,454
U.K.	1,382,809	1,011	136.80	2,339	452,019
U.S.	6,702,115	5,967	112.32	7,740	5,525,408
Japan	2,398,523	3,626	66.15	1,766	703,127

Sources: Federation of European Stock Exchanges 'Annual Report' (1996); own calculations.

B. Legal structure

I. Description of Different Company Types

12. The "public company limited by shares"[25] is the main company type for the larger business firm. In addition, it is important to mention the "limited partnership by shares", or the *société en commandite par actions,* a company type that has recently been regaining favor for reasons explained below. The "public company limited" is—if not the only—at least the usual type of company whose shares are traded on the public markets. The main reason for this is that only its shares are freely negotiable. However, their transfer may be subject to certain restrictions within the limits allowed by the market regulators.[26]

---

[25] Referred to as the *SA* or *société anonyme,* to which the *Aktiengesellschaft (AG),* the *naamloze vennootschap (NV),* and the *Società per Azioni (Spa)* are equivalent. The private company is referred to as the *société à responsabilité limitée (SARL), de besloten vennootschap (BV),* or the *Gesellschaft mit beschränkter Haftung (GmbH).* For the U.K., public and private company limited could be classified along the same lines, although the distinction seems to be different.

[26] According to the 1979 directive, listing is conditional upon the shares being freely transferable. However, if shares may be acquired only subject to approval, a derogation may be

The "private company limited" is considered suitable for the smaller business firm with closely held shares and usually a more limited governance structure. Family businesses are often organized by way of "private company limited", although some larger firms, including subsidiaries—especially in Germany— have also adopted this form.

There is difference of opinion as to what extent the public and private company are to be considered comparable company forms. In some jurisdictions, e.g., the Netherlands, Belgium, and France, they would be regarded as largely equivalent in the sense that rules applicable to one type are also applicable to the other.[27] Therefore, the main differences relate to the transferability of their shares and their management structure. The German opinion is different in its consideration of the *GmbH* as closer to the (contractual) company than the *AG,* which is qualified as a legal entity (*Körperschaft*). Flexibility of charter rules vary substantially.[28]

13. Generally speaking, in the other states both *SA* and *SARL* are by and large structured along the same lines: these entities have full legal personality and are composed of a general meeting of shareholders and of a management organ, the latter being either a board or one or several persons, acting more or less individually. In both types, the surveillance of the management's activities may be entrusted to an auditor as an external professional. The auditor is appointed by the shareholders in the general meeting.[29] The appointment of an auditor is imposed by the Fourth Directive, although the conditions for his appointment have not yet been harmonized.[30]

---

granted "if the use of the approval clause does not disturb the market". See schedule A (II) (2) annexed to the Listing Conditions Directive of 5 March 1979 *OJEC* L 66/21, 16.3.1979.

[27] This is particularly striking in the Dutch Civil Code, which repeats many of the rules applicable to the *NV* verbatim to the *BV*. Both are "capital" corporations, as opposed to the "companies" based on personal relations. More recent specific regulations have increased the differences between the two forms.

[28] Especially the German *AktG* contain obligatory rules for the *AG*: § 23 (5) AktG. In the other states, parties enjoy a certain flexibility as to the framing of the charter. For a comparative overview, see Lutter, Marcus and Herbert Wiedemann (eds.) *Gestaltungsfreiheit im Gesellschaftsrecht: Deutschland, Europa und USA* (*Zeitschrift für Unternehmens- und Gesellschaftsrecht* Special Volume no. 13) (Berlin 1998).

[29] Art. 393 (2) NBW; however, if the general meeting has not appointed the auditors, the supervisory board may do so. § 119 (4) AktG; s. 385 Companies Act 1985; art. 223 French Companies Act 1966; art. 64 Belgian Companies Act.

[30] The requirement to have the annual accounts audited was imposed by the Fourth Directive (art. 51 Directive of 25 July 1978 *OJEC* L 222/11, 14.8.1978). The conditions of appointment and legal status within the company were planned to be harmonized by the directive still pending (art. 54 to 62 Amended Proposal of 20 November 1991); the Eighth Directive of 10 April 1984 *OJEC* L 126/20, 12.5.1984 spells out the conditions to which auditors have to comply with in order to qualify for the audit function.

14. The substantial differences in the use of the different corporate forms, as documented above, are difficult to attribute to single explanations.[31] Regulations dealing with labor matters or taxes would be equally applicable whatever the form chosen. In jurisdictions in which the *SA* form is more frequently used, this may be due to its greater flexibility, its potential for unlimited growth, and the greater prestige attached to that corporate form. More specific elements are difficult to identify.

According to the laws of most continental jurisdictions, if bearer shares are allowed, these may not be issued except by public companies limited. Access to the status of public company limited is highly appreciated as these shares are more easily transferable, an important characteristic for tax purposes. Therefore, access to this company type has been restricted by different means: the imposition of heavier requirements in terms of disclosure,[32] accounting, supervision, and so on would frighten many users. The Dutch technique is a remnant of the former state authorization requirement: the Justice Department has to give its "approval"—in fact, a declaration of no objection—of the company charter, checking whether the charter conforms to the law.[33] The use of shares as collateral for security purposes may also be more difficult for the shares subject to transfer restrictions.

15. Stock exchange-listed companies on the continent frequently issue bearer shares.[34] Nominative shares are issued to important shareholders, especially to controlling shareholders, as often listing of these shares is not applied for. These shares can be transferred to private parties, and do not have to be sold on the markets.[35] Bearer securities can circulate in bearer form. Individual investors may still require bearer shares to be delivered. Increasingly, shares are deposited

---

[31] For a broad analysis, see Hopt, Klaus J. 'Gestaltungsfreiheit im Gesellschaftsrecht in Europa—Generalbericht' in: Lutter and Wiedemann (eds.), supra n. 28, 123.

[32] The *BV* was introduced in the Netherlands in 1971 in order to limit the impact of the then new annual account disclosure requirements. See Sanders, Pieter and W. Westbroek *BV en NV* 6 5th edn. (Deventer 1988).

[33] The department also requires the identity of the final beneficiary of the shares to be known, in order to prevent the company being used for illegal purposes, especially to avoid fraudulent liquidations and bankruptcies.

[34] For listed shares, the bearer form is usual in Belgium and Germany; it is also available for Dutch and French shares circulating abroad. In France, bearer shares were de facto eliminated after *dématérialisation* became compulsory (L. 30 December 1981), all shares being registered in the central repository's name. However, the identity of shareholders is not known to the issuer. See Cozian and Viandier, supra n. 2, no. 914, p. 3293; Frison-Koche, Marie-Anne and Michel Jockey 'Pourquoi existe-t-il encore des titres au porteur?' *JCP* (1994) Ed. E., I, 344; Causse, Heré 'Principe, nature et logique de la "dématérialisation"' *JCP* (1992) Ed E, I, 194.

[35] Another technique with identical effects is to lodge the controlling block in an intermediate holding company. In case of a transfer of the shares of that company, this would result in an indirect transfer of control that might trigger the same rules (i.a., mandatory bid rules) as if the shares were directly sold; see infra no. 140 et seq.

with central depositories and transferred by book entry. Most securities markets have one single central depository and transfer system. The different national systems have mutual links for exchange of transfers. There is no Europe-wide bookkeeping transfer system. This considerably burdens cross-border share trading.[36] Recently, several states have introduced "dematerialized" securities, which are mostly bonds but also include shares. No physical certificate is issued: the securities exist and circulate by mere book entry. In several systems these securities are part of the larger category of nominative securities, while in others they form a separate legal category.[37]

16. The southern European states admit quite freely the use of the *société anonyme*, also for smaller business firms in Belgium. This would include the use of bearer shares even for small companies. In France, Italy, or Spain, only nominative shares would be allowed. Other differences relate to minimum capital requirements—according to the Second Company Law Directive, 25,000 ECU for the *SA* but none for the *SARL*—or the need to organize a board of directors in contrast to a system where one person can manage the company. It should be noted that in most states, these differences have become less significant: minimum capital requirements are relatively similar, and accounting and auditing rules often apply based on the size of the enterprise rather than the company type. Some of the European directives have substantially underpinned this latter development, being applicable according to the size of the enterprise whether the latter is run by an *SA* or an *SARL*.[38]

II. Groups of Companies

17. Larger European companies are usually structured as groups composed of numerous subsidiaries. These subsidiaries may be integrated in the group's functioning and then will normally be fully owned. Their legal form will often be the *SA*, although the *SARL* or even other forms—including limited and unlimited

[36] See European Directive on Settlement Finality in Payment and Securities Settlement Systems, Amended Proposal, Com (97), 345-def *OJEC* C 259/6, 26.8.1997.

[37] On the legal status of dematerialized securities in Belgium, see Tison, Michel 'De uitgifte van gedematerialiseerde vennootschapseffecten. Bemerkingen bij de Wet van 7 april 1995' in: Braeckmans, Herman and Eddy Wymeersch (eds.) *Het gewijzigde vennootschapsrecht 1995* 227-62 (Antwerpen 1996).

[38] The First (9 March 1968 *OJEC* L 65/8, 14.3.1968), Fourth (supra n. 30), Seventh (13 June 1983 *OJEC* L 193/1, 18.7.1983), and Eleventh (21 December 1989 *OJEC* L 395/36, 30.12.1989) Directives are applicable to both the public (*SA*) and private (*SARL*) company limited, dealing mainly with disclosure. The directives on capital, mergers, and division are applicable to the public company only. However, some member states have declared their national laws applicable to both types: Netherlands, Belgium, Denmark, and Italy. Fear of evasion of the *SARL* lies at the basis of this extension. For details, see Schutte-Veenstra, Johanna M. *Harmonisatie van het kapitaalbeschermingsrecht in de EEG* 230 et seq. (Deventer 1991).

partnerships—may also be found. The use of partially owned subsidiaries is widespread, in 50/50 relationships as well as any other proportion. Also, many listed companies are subsidiaries of either other listed companies or of closely held parent companies, leading to the typical pyramidal structure that is characteristic of many of the European economies. As a rule, these subsidiaries are still active in the same line of business as the parent. The phenomenon will be further documented in the chapter dealing with the analysis of share ownership, where corporate ownership of listed companies will be separately mentioned in the statistical data.[39]

Some of the largest and most powerful business firms are composed of widely diversified conglomerate types of portfolios, holding controlling or significant minority positions (these are sometimes called "reference shareholders") in a certain number of companies. These diversified holding companies are more frequently found in the Latin European states. Their economic function cannot be described in uniform terms: some are closer to diversified investment companies; others are more akin to investment banks. They constitute important centers of economic power.[40]

The phenomenon of group law presents itself in very diversified ways: both in large groups and in small—even one-man—firms, issues of protection of creditors and of minority shareholders are regularly met. Also, the group influence is usually taken into account in today's rulemaking.

18. The prevalence of the phenomenon of groups of companies has led to the development of sometimes elaborate systems of group law—in most cases in terms of case law, and increasingly also in terms of statutory rules. In the 1965 revision of the *Aktiengesetz,* Germany introduced a comprehensive system of group law based on the distinction between contractual group relations and de facto group relations. The former only exist in Germany, primarily because of tax considerations. Portugal has partly copied the German rules. Although all states are familiar with de facto groups, they have not developed structured schemes of group law. In fact, the central issues of group law have been dealt with in national case law. Regulations often contain references to the group concept in order to determine the factual data to be taken into account or to establish the ambit of the regulation.

19. Matters of group law have a considerable impact on corporate governance issues.[41] On the European continent, most governance issues arise in a context of

---

[39] See further Chapter D.

[40] See Wymeersch, Eddy 'Holding Companies in Belgium' in: Hopt, Klaus J. and Eddy Wymeersch (eds.) *Comparative Corporate Governance. Essays and Materials* 67-118 (Berlin and New York 1997).

[41] There have been numerous studies published on groups of companies in Europe: among the comparative overviews, see Lutter, Marcus (ed.) *Konzernrecht in Ausland (Zeitschrift für Unternehmens- und Gesellschaftsrecht* Special Volume no. 11) (Berlin and New York 1994);

groups of companies, whereby parent companies leave limited freedom to subsidiaries, or refuse to assume liability for the subsidiary's fate after having diverted its assets or its opportunities to other group entities. The presence of minority shareholders, especially in listed subsidiaries, is likely to exacerbate these issues, while market supervisors tend to intervene, often by mandating adequate disclosure, or sometimes by recommending conduct likely to protect the minority. One of the usual protective techniques is mandating the controlling shareholder to take over the minority shareholders: this device, especially in its form of a "mandatory takeover bid", is therefore more an instrument of group law[42] and minority protection than a market equality rule.

There is a quite substantial difference between German law rules on groups of companies and the case law rules developed in the other states. German law on de facto groups—the rules on contractual groups aim at allowing greater freedom to the parent—starts from the presumption that a parent may not harm the subsidiary, and if it does, it should fully indemnify on a case-by-case basis within the next accounting period. In the other jurisdictions, as far as case law is available, the parent company can avail itself of the synergies created within the group to impose certain burdens on its subsidiaries, provided these burdens do not exceed the subsidiary's capacity to support these,[43] and in the longer term are offset by benefits flowing to the subsidiary. Whether this exchange of profits and charges should take place between economically interdependent group entities, or whether the intragroup dealings should have been the subject of a comprehensive "master plan", is the subject of discussion.[44] The rules imposed by securities supervisors may call for a stricter standard of fairness. This standard was applied by the Belgian supervisor who stated in the 1970s that parent companies should ensure that in parent-subsidiary group dealings a "reasonable balance" be struck between benefits and charges.[45] The judiciary does not intervene unless gross imbalance has been proved.[46]

Wymeersch, Eddy (ed.) *Groups of Companies in the EEC* (Berlin and New York 1993); I Gruppi di Società *Rivista delle società* 3 vols. (Milan 1996). On the policy issues: Hopt, Klaus J. 'Legal Issues and Questions of Policy in the Comparative Regulation of Groups of Companies' in: I Gruppi di Società, supra, vol.1, 45.

[42] See Hommelhoff, Peter and Detlef Kleindiek 'Takeover-Richtlinie und europäisches Konzernrecht *Die Aktiengesellschaft* 35 (1990) 106.

[43] E.g., cash advances at very unfavorable conditions. Also loans to insolvent group entities would not be admissible.

[44] The latter is the standard adopted in the leading French case of *Rozenblum*, Cour de cassation, Cass. crim. fr., 4 February 1985, D., 1985, 478, note Ohl; *JCP* (1986) II, 20585, note Jeandidier; *Revue des sociétés* (1985) 648, note B. Bouloc. A similar opinion is found in the Belgian case law, see *Wiskeman* case, Brussels, 15 September 1992 *J.T.* (1993) 312.

[45] See Banking Commission 'Annual Report' 1985-86' 72 et seq.; for further details, see Wymeersch, Eddy 'The Groups of Companies in Belgian Law' in: Wymeersch (ed.), supra n. 41,

Solutions to group issues have been sought in disclosure, especially by imposing publication of consolidated accounts.[47] More recently, governance mechanisms have been increasingly used in attempting to deal with specific group problems. The presence of parent company representatives on the subsidiary's board without outside board members is often discussed. Special reports on intragroup dealings are required.[48] Some legislators submit intragroup transactions to special scrutiny procedures, effectuated by "independent directors".[49] Parent company influence may be especially investigated by an audit committee composed of independent directors.

III. Securities Regulation

20. Starting from the mid-1960s, European regulators have paid increasing attention to the regulation of their securities markets. The increased financing needs, especially for the restructuring of the industry after the earlier post-World War II period, called for a more active role for securities financing.[50] This phenomenon of heavier regulatory involvement was particularly visible in France (1967), and to some extent in Italy (1974). The evolution was quite diverse in the different states: although Belgium had the oldest securities regulatory system (1935), it took until 1990-1995 to thoroughly reform its market. Germany did not pay attention to its markets until the mid-1990s (1994). In the meantime, compe-

---

1-83, esp. 54 et seq.; also in 'Le droit belge des groupes de sociétés' *Liber Amoricum Commission Droit et Vie des Affaires* 615 (Brussels 1998).

[46] For the Belgian cases, see Cour d'appel de Bruxelles, 16 June 1981 *Revue pratique des sociétés* (1981) n° 6139, 145; Tribunal correctionnel de Bruxelles, 27 April 1978 *Revue pratique des sociétés* (1978) n° 6000, 276 - *S.A. Etablissements d'Aoust Frères*; Cour d'appel de Bruxelles, 9 October 1984 *Revue pratique des sociétés* (1986) n° 6371, 50 - *S.A. SOCFIN c. S.A. COGEFON* see: Tribunal de Commerce de Bruxelles, 23 November 1981 *Jurisprudence commerciale de Belgique* (1982) 533; Cour d'appel de Bruxelles, 24 June 1987 *Revue pratique des sociétés* (1987) n° 6452, 250; Tribunal correctionnel de Bruxelles, 20 February 1987 *Revue pratique des sociétés* (1987) n° 6442, 158 - *faillite S.A. Galeries Anspach c/ Jean-Pierre Willot*; Cour d'appel de Bruxelles (4e Ch.), 15 September 1992 *Journal des tribunaux* (1993) 312, *Tijdschrift voor Rechtspersoon en Vennootschap* (1994) 275 *Wiskeman* note A. François.

[47] These have been rendered obligatory in the EU for all larger groups by the Seventh Company Law Directive, supra n. 38. Parent companies exceeding more than two of the following criteria are subject to consolidation: 10,000,000 ECU balance sheet total, 20,000,000 ECU turnover, average number of employees: 250 (art. 27 Fourth Directive, supra n. 30).

[48] § 311 AktG.

[49] This is the case of art. 60 bis Belgian Companies Act. Other company laws deal with the subject under the general heading of "conflict of interests", see art. 101 et seq. French Companies Act 1966. For comments, see Guyon, supra n. 1, 419, 428.

[50] This reasoning was particularly striking for the French regulation, aimed at increasing confidence in the French market to allow the transition from France's rural economy to an industrial economic pattern.

tition between market centers had considerably increased, with London playing an increasingly leading role in continental European share dealing. The need to implement the Investment Services Directive, the full liberalization of securities trading under the Maastricht Treaty,[51] the cross-border establishment of securities firms in the EU,[52] and finally the introduction of a common currency have offered a renewed occasion for regulators in most states to overhaul their regulatory system. Substantial changes have already been announced, especially in the U.K., where policy is heading towards the integration of the supervision of banks, investment firms, and insurance companies under one supervisory body.[53]

Table 10: Securities Markets Supervisors

		Regulator	Other Authorities
1935	Belgium	CBF	Comité direction
1965	Luxembourg	IML	Commissariat aux bourses
1967	France	COB	
1974	Italy	Consob	
1985	United Kingdom	SIB	
1991	Spain	Cnmv	
1991	Netherlands	STE	
1991	Portugal	CMVM	
1994	Germany	BAWe	

In the meantime, due to the abolition of capital restrictions, competition between markets has risen dramatically. Table 11 sheds some light on the market share in domestic equity which—at a certain moment in the early 1990s—continental European stock exchanges lost to London. It would appear that as the markets have adapted to competition they have been able to stem this evolution during the mid-1990s. No more recent figures were available.

21. These efforts to re-regulate the securities markets also affected rules relating to the governance of listed companies. Securities regulation traditionally

---

[51] See art. 73 A to H of the treaty; in fact the 1988 directive 88/361/EEC of 24 June 1988 *OJEC* L 178/5, 8.7.1988, had already achieved the same liberalisation.

[52] Due to the Investment Services Directive, Supra n. 13.

[53] See the U.K.'s FSA, Financial Services Authority 'An Outline' (October 1997), and the Consultation Papers on Consumer Involvement, Practitioner Involvement and Paying for Bank Supervision; Blair, William 'The Reform of Financial Regulation in the U.K.' *Journal of International Banking Law* 13 (1998) 43-9.

Table 11: SEAQ International Trading in Continental European Shares

	1990/Q1	1990/Q2	1990/Q3	1990/Q4	1991/Q1	1992
German	12.5	12.2	11.3	12.8	10.3	10.9
French	26.9	26.6	25.3	26.3	29.5	27.1
Italian	23.1	18.1	19.1	27.1	24.7	28.4
Spanish	14.3	15.9	25.5	18.4	18.7	20.1
Dutch	38.3	49.8	63.0	54.2	52.9	29.8
Swiss	—	29.2	25.5	33.5	35.5	30.3
Swedish	39.5	64.9	62.4	50.0	45.0	33.4

Note: Trading of continental European stocks effected by members of the LSE, as a % of stock trading on "home country" exchange.

Sources: Worthington, P.M. 'Global Equity Turnover: Market Comparison' *Bank of England Quaterly Bulletin* (May 1991) 246-9; for further analysis, see Pagano, Marco and Benn Steil 'Equity Trading: The Evolution of European Trading Systems' in: Steil, Benn (ed.) *The European Equity Markets* 1-58 (London 1996). For the 1992 figure: 'London's Share of Global Equity Turnover' *Bank of England Quarterly Bulletin* 33 (1993) 355 ("Financial Market Developments"). There is, however, considerable controversy as to the way transactions are registered; see the study presented by Bertrand Jacquillat, Carole Gresse, and Roland Gillet in February 1998, *Financieel Economische Tijd* 12 February 1998.

has played a relatively important role in company life, at least as far as listed companies are concerned. Very often, the regulatory bodies have recommended—and increasingly imposed—requirements that, in addition to the requirement of the law, exercised a significant influence on their corporate life. As a consequence, a kind of informal or parallel company law has developed. In many cases, these rules were later incorporated in the statute and made applicable to all companies. This phenomenon of "juridification" has often transited through the European harmonization process, with national soft law rules being adopted at the EU level and later extended all over Europe. These developments have mostly concerned the status of the minority shareholders, although indirectly the governance systems were affected.

In the *United Kingdom*, securities regulation largely remained self-regulatory, as imposed by the London Stock Exchange. This pattern was changed by the Financial Services Act of 1986, which provided for a comprehensive set of regulation for all types of financial services on a functional basis. Some parts of the regulatory system, affecting more specifically company life, were untouched and continue to be based on self-regulatory instruments: this is especially the case for the rules on takeovers, administered by the Panel on Takeovers and Mergers, and the rules on listing of securities on the stock exchange. The most significant of these rules include mandating takeover bids on acquisition of a

30% share stake in a listed company, rules relating to the position of a controlling shareholder in relation to the listed company (essentially: arm's-length dealings), and rules relating to the waiver of preference rights.[54] However, the Exchange does not formally require compliance with the "one share, one vote rule", or any similar rule declaring voting rights proportional to capital contribution. In 1997, the government announced a substantial overhaul of the regulatory apparatus, reducing if not eliminating the role of self-regulation; whether there will be any substantial role left for soft law is doubtful. The position of the Takeover Panel is not discussed, but may have to be reviewed if the draft directive on takeovers were to be adopted.[55]

22. Among the prominent quasi-regulatory sources of governance rules, one could mention the recommendations of the *Belgian* Banking Commission, dating back to the mid-thirties. These recommendations concerned a wide range of company law issues, such as the recognition of preferential subscription rights, the repurchase of own shares, and the conditions of dealing with intragroup transactions. With respect to specific governance matters, mention must be made of the—already old—recommendation stating that the remuneration of the directors should be decided by the general meeting rather than settled by an internal committee of the board.[56]

Similar actions have been developed by the *French* Commission des opérations de bourse (COB). However, the COB's action is more frequently based on explicit regulatory provisions. In its 1995 annual report, the COB declared that it largely approved of the recommendations of the Viénot Report, including its use of non-binding instruments such as recommendations and disclosure. It recommended disclosures relating to boards monitoring their own performance and procedures.[57] In an unrelated field, the COB introduced the practice of "fairness opinions" for restructuration transactions involving listed

---

[54] Atkinson, Nigel *A Practitioner's Guide to the Stock Exchange Yellow Book* 33 and 76 (Surrey 1995). The exchange does not formally impose the "one share, one vote rule": the 'Listing Rules' App. 1 to Ch. 13, r. 2 and r. 3 merely require that the words 'non-voting', 'limited voting', or 'restricted voting' appear in the designation of non-voting shares. See further Boros, Elizabeth Jane *Minority Shareholders' Remedies* 40-1 (Oxford 1995); Stapledon, Geof P. *Institutional Shareholders and Corporate Governance* 58-9 (Oxford 1996)

[55] Vaughan, David and David Lloyd-Jones 'The Proposed European Directive: Failure to Satisfy the Principle of Subsidiarity' (Joint Opinion and Working Paper, published by the Panel of Takeovers and Mergers, London 1997).

[56] This recommendation, which is at odds with today's recommended practices, dealt with specific circumstances whereby the board was not informed about the remuneration paid to each of the directors. See Banking Commission 'Annual Report 1956-1957' 117 et seq.; 'Annual Report 1961' 124.

[57] See COB 'Annual Report 1995' 46.

companies, especially when conflicts of interest arise, whether between the parties (e.g. parent - subsidiary) or between different classes of shareholders.[58]

In *Finland, Sweden,* and *Denmark,* the supervision of securities markets has been put directly in the hands of the Ministry. In the *Netherlands* and in Germany, some form of self-regulation was maintained, but supervision by a government agency is increasingly dominating the scene. As a consequence, the impact of securities regulation on corporate law developments has become less visible.[59] Nevertheless, self-regulatory instruments such as stock exchange listing conditions continue to contain important rules on governance issues: for example, in the Netherlands, the present limitation on anti-takeover protections is governed by the Dutch listing conditions.[60] One could also mention self-regulatory codes on takeovers in *Germany,*[61] and previous ones on insider trading. Recently proposed self-regulatory codes in governance matters also favor stock exchange-linked enforcement mechanisms.[62]

In the longer term, the regulatory interventions of stock exchanges and market organizers are likely to become increasingly hollowed out as their regulatory functions are cut down. There is a clear tendency, after implementation of the ISD, to change their definition to mere competitive service providers, reducing their regulatory and supervisory tasks to the functioning of the markets.[63] However, as mentioned in the next paragraph, new self-regulatory instruments will be proposed by associations of listed companies, company directors, etc., stating codes of conduct and good practice. Enforcement issues may therefore become more prominent.

---

[58] COB 'Annual Report 1995' 42.

[59] Without a clear statutory basis, it would seem that a government agency would be loath to interfere in company law matters.

[60] This is so-called Regulation X, the result of a provisional agreement between the Association of Listed Companies, the stock exchange, and the Ministry. The listed companies applying for a new listing were invited by the Amsterdam Stock Exchange not to use more than two of the protective techniques listed in annex to the listing agreement (art. 13 of Regulation X). However, the subject of anti-takeover protections is planned to be governed by a judicial procedure, see the proposal referred to in n. 73.

[61] For the text of the code, see 'Übernahmekodex der Börsensachverständigenkommission' *Die Aktiengesellschaft* 40 (1995) 572-5 and the comments by Assmann, Heinz-Dieter 'Verhaltensregeln für freiwillige öffentliche Übernahmeangebote' *Die Aktiengesellschaft* 40 (1995) 563-72. The amended version is documented in *Die Aktiengesellschaft* 43 (1998) 133-7.

[62] See further no. 23 et seq. This is the case for the numerous instruments on corporate governance.

[63] For details of this development, see Wymeersch, Eddy 'The Implementation of the ISD and CAD in the National Legal Systems' in: Ferrarini, Guido (ed.) *European Securities Markets. The Investment Services Directive and Beyond* 3 (London 1998); also in *Rivista delle società* 42 (1997) 400-49. See the decision of the Italian Stock Exchanges to have the shares in the *Borsa Italiana* offered to the public: *Financial Times* August 11, 1997.

IV. Legislative and Self-Regulatory Reforms

23. The recent pressure on company structures and on their management—caused in part by some major collapses but also as a consequence of the integration of the European markets—has raised a large public debate about corporate governance issues. In several European states, proposals for new regulations of different kinds have been tabled while companies pay ample attention to governance matters, in their structures as well as in their nomination policies and in their disclosures. The climate has changed considerably over the last two to three years. A short overview of the most recent initiatives and trends is therefore appropriate. This overview will also deal with the most important self-regulatory initiatives.

In the *United Kingdom*, the 1991 Cadbury Report on "The Financial Aspects of Corporate Governance", containing the "Code of Best Practice", gave a response to the credibility crisis caused by a few important collapses. The committee that drafted the code was set up by the Financial Reporting Council, the stock exchange, and the accounting profession. It drew on existing expertise and further took on contributions from a wide audience. The code is applicable to all listed companies and is enforced by a disclosure mechanism: listed companies must report about their implementation of the code's recommendation. The stock exchange and public opinion exercise pressure to ensure optimal follow-up on the code rules. In May of 1995, a first implementation report was published, indicating a considerable degree of compliance, especially by the larger corporations.[64] Later reports have complained about the administrative and other burdens resulting from the code, especially for the smaller companies.[65] Another committee published a special report on directors' pay called the Greenbury Report.[66] The Hampel Committee will further evaluate developments originating in the Cadbury Code; its report has been published in March 1998.[67]

24. In *France*, a comparable initiative was launched that resulted in the Viénot Report "le Conseil d'administration des sociétés cotées", published in the summer of 1995. In contrast to the British report, this was mainly the product of

---

[64] 'The Financial Aspects of Corporate Governance, Compliance with the Code of Best Practice' (24 May 1995).

[65] See the Arthur Andersen Report: 'Corporate Governance, Too Great a Burden?' (1996).

[66] Greenbury, Richard (chairman) 'Directors Remuneration' (Report of a Study Group chaired by Sir Richard Greenbury, July 1995). Differently from the Cadbury Report, the Greenbury Report did not receive ample attention in the other member states of the EU.

[67] Recent press reports would indicate that the Hampel Report will not take an activist stand, but may rather soften some of the Cadbury Report's requirements: Kelly, J. 'Boardroom Rules Report May Take Softy Approach' *Financial Times* 23 July 1997, 9; Hampel Report (Committee on Corporate Governance, Final Report, London, January 1998).

discussions within the French employers' associations.[68] The report has no binding force, but it has attracted wide attention and was commented on in the press at large. However, although the report did not propose substantial changes in present practices, it would seem that the implementation of its recommendations has lagged behind. There has been no official follow-up in terms of a compliance report. Although the report warned of legislative interventions, the French Senate, especially at the instigation of Senator Marini, has launched an investigation of French governance rules.[69] This resulted in the Marini Report: proposals for legislative change prepared for Parliament dealing with a very broad range of topics, several of which are directly linked to governance matters. However, due to a change of government, it would not seem that legislative changes will occur in the near future.

In *Spain*, the CNMV, the securities supervisor, recently instituted a commission to draw up guidelines that would be enforced through disclosure mechanisms. It was announced that Spanish boards would be composed of three types of directors, those representing the management, those representing the core shareholders, and those representing the independent directors, charged with protecting the investors.[70]

25. In the *Netherlands*, there has been a long-standing debate about governance issues. In the 1960s, the discussion focused on structural changes in the *NV* and the compulsory introduction of co-determination, leading to what is sometimes called the "miracle from The Hague", i.e., the typically Dutch co-determination system.[71] During the 1980s it focused on the typically Dutch anti-takeover techniques that protect most Dutch listed companies from an unfriendly takeover.[72] In 1994, an agreement was reached between the Ministry of Finance, the stock exchange, and the association of listed companies, whereby protective devices would be limited.[73] In the mid-1990s, attention shifted to governance

---

[68] The *Association Française des Entreprises privées* and the *Conseil National du Patronat Français*. No outside members took part in the preparation of the Viénot Report.

[69] Marini, Philippe 'La modernisation du droit des sociétés' (Report, Documentation française, Paris 1996).

[70] See Maliniak, Th. 'Madrid se met à l'heure du "gouvernement d'entreprise"' *La Tribune* 11 April 1997.

[71] For a historical overview, see Maeijer, Jozef M.M. *De naamloze en de besloten vennootschap* 477 (Deventer 1994). For more details, see infra no. 100.

[72] For an impressive overview of these techniques, see Voogd, Rudolf Paul *Statutaire beschermingsmiddelen bij beursvennootschappen* (Deventer 1989).

[73] On November 7, 1997, a bill was introduced in Parliament (Tweede Kamer, 1997-1998, 25732) submitting takeover to a one-year waiting period, after which the company will have to convince the court that it has good reasons to withstand the lifting of the protection mechanisms. For the proposed system, see 'Rechter kan bescherming opheffen, Zalm kan akkoord met overtuiging brengen' *Financieele Dagblad* 29 February 1996. Previously the VEB had urged the

issues, as in several companies complaints about inefficiencies at the level of the supervisory board had been formulated. A wide public debate resulted. A series of proposals were formulated by a commission, composed of representatives of the listed companies, the stock exchange, institutional investors, accounting firms, and associations for the protection of investors, and headed by J. Peters, a prominent retired business leader. The final report, "Corporate Governance in the Netherlands, the Forty Recommendations", was released on June 25, 1997.[74] It does not substantially challenge Dutch corporate practices, but it does propose a series of specific changes to board activities, procedures, and disclosures.[75] Enforcement would mainly be based on disclosure in the annual report,[76] under the surveillance of the auditors.

In *Germany*, the debate gained momentum after the collapse of some major German firms and the difficulties experienced in other leading firms, such as Daimler. A wide discussion resulted, also relating to the effects of the introduction of the Euro on shares with nominal value. Proposals have been submitted to Parliament.[77] At present the government has approved a proposal "zur Kontrolle und Transparenz im Unternehmensbereich" called *KonTraG*.[78] The following elements are of interest for the present overview:

- repurchase of own shares will be allowed under strict conditions (previously forbidden);
- shares with multiple voting rights (inclusive Höchststimmrecht) will no longer be allowed;
- there will not be a mandatory reduction of the number of members of the supervisory board, while members may continue to sit on ten boards;
- minority claims against directors will be made more accessible by reducing the threshold to 5% or 2 million marks (previously 10%);
- auditors will be appointed by the supervisory board, not by the management board;

abolition of preference shares: 'VEB wil uitschakeling prefs' *Financieele Dagblad* 2 February 1996.

[74] 'Corporate Governance in Nederland—De veertig aanbevelingen' (25 June 1997).

[75] The report has been the subject of wide criticism, e.g., by Vinken, P.J. 'Meer invloed voor de aandeelhouders?' *De Naamloze Vennootschap* 74 (1996) 301 and de Koning, C. 'De voorstellen van de Commissie Peters: Ferme vlag, milde lading' *De Naamloze Vennootschap* 74 (1996) 305.

[76] On the subject, see Timmerman, supra n. 17, 69.

[77] For the original proposals, see Seibert, Ulrich 'Kontrolle und Transparenz im Unternehmensbereich (KonTraG), der Referentenentwurf zur Aktienrechtsnovelle' *Wertpapier-Mitteilungen* 51 (1997) 1-9; Claussen, Carsten P. 'Wie ändert das KonTraG das Aktiengesetz?' *Der Betrieb* 51 (1998) 177-86. For an update, see Hansen, Herbert 'Kabinett stimmt Reform des Aktienrechts zu' *Die Aktiengesellschaft* 42 (1997) R487.

[78] See also Hopt (Ch. 4: Sec. C.I.) and Prigge (Ch. 12: Sec. D) in this volume.

- the influence of the banks will be somewhat curbed: banks may not vote as proxy holders if voting in their own name for more than 5% of the shares.

26. The discussion on corporate governance has been particularly active in *Belgium*. Due to specific circumstances, especially the change in control in one of the larger Belgian companies,[79] the discussion took a somewhat different, and possibly more radical, turn. As a consequence of the merger between the French parent company of a major Belgian holding company with a competitor of its Belgian subsidiary, the government insisted on putting controls on the power of intervention by the French parent in the competing Belgian sub-subsidiary. After lengthy discussions, it was agreed that a charter amendment would be adopted whereby a certain number of independent directors would be appointed in the Belgian subsidiary; in case of a conflict of interest, the representatives of the French parent would not take part in the procedure. Simultaneously, a draft amendment of the Companies Act was circulated, whereby the so-called "autonomous company limited" would have been introduced for all listed companies, initially on a voluntary basis. The draft mainly provided for the institution of independent directors and proposed to reduce the influence of major shareholders to 10% of the votes. Against heavy opposition from the business world, the draft seems to have been dropped.[80] It should be pointed out that most of the reform proposals could be introduced on a voluntary basis under the present statute.

At the level of soft regulation, several initiatives were undertaken to identify fields in which the present practices could be improved. At the ethical level, a commission ("Santens Commission") of the Association of Catholic Employers published a series of "interim recommendations" of a non-binding nature, taking account of the governance situation in both listed and unlisted firms.

Three highly publicized codes were released in early 1998. The "Association of Belgian Enterprise" (FEB-VBO)[81] recommended to its members the rules laid down in its code of conduct. The rules are largely based on a—slimmed down—version of the Cadbury Code. Applicable to all firms, they have a non-binding status. The "Banking and Finance Commission", the government supervisory

---

[79] More specifically, as a consequence of the merger between French Compagnie de Suez and French Lyonnaise des Eaux, Tractebel—formerly 66%, now 50.6% subsidiary of Société générale de Belgique, which in its turn was a 63% subsidiary of Suez—would have come under direct control of the merged board. As the merged entity was in part active on the same markets as Tractebel (engineering, power supply, waste processing; Tractebel also controls the electric power supply in Belgium) it was deemed necessary to avoid the French parent imposing decisions that could run contrary to the interests of Tractebel.

[80] See also Van Ommeslaghe, Pierre 'Vers une société anonyme autonome?' *Liber Amoricum Commission Droit et Vie des Affaires* 389 (Brussels 1998).

[81] VBO-FEB 'Recommandations pour le bon fonctionnement du conseil d'administration d'une société' (Brussels, December 1996) The same organization also instituted an *observatoire*, aimed at monitoring development and practices in the governance field.

body of the banking and securities sectors, released guidelines aimed at listed companies and companies that have issued securities publicly. These guidelines call for disclosure on the specified list of items. They are not legally binding but would have some moral force. The stock exchange also issued recommendations addressed to listed companies only. These recommendations would be binding as far as the obligation to report on present governance practices go. They refer to a list of recommendations presented as a "benchmark" for good corporate conduct.[82]

27. It is striking that many of these efforts for better governance were undertaken on the basis of rather general or anecdotal evidence about corporate relations and actual practices. Very few reliable investigations have been undertaken about the effective structure of share ownership and the significance on board structure, composition, and practices. Event studies are rare and are often related to traditional financial disclosures or to insider trading.

In the U.K. and in Germany, however, there has been more ample information available on the actual position of the corporate world and its structure. Recent reports and studies will amplify this information.[83] In the other European states, information has been piecemeal. Meritorious efforts have been undertaken, especially in the Korn/Ferry International Reports.[84] Particularly in France, there are almost no factual data available about the structure of share ownership, the interrelations between major corporate groups, or the functioning composition of the boards.

At the initiative of Barca, Berglöf, and others, a "European Corporate Governance Network" was formed of groups of researchers from the different European states invited to research data according to a uniform scheme. Some of the draft national reports have already been presented.[85] In at least two other European states, major official investigations have been undertaken to identify the main lines of power in the business world. The first one was undertaken in the 1980s in Sweden, where a major report was drafted under the title "The

---

[82] The three documents have been reprinted in *Revue de la banque—Bank- en Financiewezen* 62 (1998) 100 et seq.

[83] Esp. Schmidt, Hartmut, Jochen Drucarczyk, Dirk Honold, Stefan Prigge, Andreas Schüler, and Gönke Tetens *Corporate Governance in Germany* (Baden-Baden 1997).

[84] Especially Korn/Ferry International 'Board Meeting in Session. European Boards of Director Study' (1996).

[85] Especially the Italian report already contains a considerable contribution to the factual data. Bianchi, Marcello, Magda Bianco, and Luca Enriques 'Ownership, Pyramidal Groups and Separation Between Ownership and Control in Italy' part of: European Corporate Governance Network (ed.) 'The Separation of Ownership and Control: A Survey of 7 European Countries' (Preliminary Report to the European Commission submitted on October 27, 1997, vol. 1; http://www.ecgn.ulb.ac.be/).

Structure of Ownership in Swedish Industry".[86] Recently, the Swedish Company Law Committee published its report on "The Structure of the Corporation", leading to new provisions in the Swedish Companies Act.[87] In Italy, the Banca d'Italia undertook a comprehensive investigation of the Italian corporate world, and a series of reports and studies was published.[88] Further implementation action is under consideration.[89]

28. At the European level, corporate governance issues have been on the agenda since the sixties. As mentioned before, these are the fields in which the harmonization has been the least successful. In 1996, the European Commission undertook an investigation about the present state of corporate matters, including governance issues, in a report called "The Simplification of the Operating Regulations for Public Limited Companies in the European Union"—"La simplification de la réglementation sur le fonctionnement des sociétés anonymes dans l'Union Européenne". On the basis of this report, the commission launched an investigation to identify the main points in which present legal structures should be adapted and possibly harmonized. The results are expected for later in 1998. The Centre for European Policy Studies published a code of conduct on corporate governance.[90]

Apart from these more or less official activities, reports, investigations, and studies have been undertaken in several member states. Many of these are not based on extensive empirical evidence. These reports and studies can be regarded as declarations of opinions of the bodies or organizations supporting them rather than policy documents. This lack of structured information, as well as difficulties in accessing the information—in part because of language reasons—will explain the fragmented nature of the developments that follow.

---

[86] A report prepared by The Stock Ownership and Efficiency Commission, Swedish Ministry of Industry, 1988.

[87] See Skog, Rolf 'The Structure of the Corporation: Proposal for New Provisions to the Swedish Companies Act' *International Company and Commercial Law Review* 5 (1995) 269.

[88] Barca, Fabricio, Magda Bianco, Luigi Cannari, Riccardo Cesari, Carlo Gola, G. Manitta, Giorgio Salvo, and Luigi Federico Signorini *Proprietà, modelli di controllo et riallocazione nelle imprese industriale italiane, vol. 1: Assetti proprietari e mercato delle imprese* (Bologna 1994); Barca, Fabricio, Marcello Bianchi, Francesco Brioschi, Luigi Buzzacchi, Paola Casavola, L. Filippa, and Marcello Pagnini *Gruppo, Proprietà et controllo nelle imprese italiane medio-grandi, vol. 2: Assetti proprietari e mercato delle imprese* (Bologna 1994).

[89] This is the "Draghi" Report, dealing with the reform of the Italian securities market and containing a section on governance rules; see 'Italian Takeover Reforms Take Shape' *Financial Times* 12 February 1998; See further Marchetti, Piergaetano 'Le raccommandazioni Consob in materia di controlli societari: un contributo alla riforma' *Rivista delle società* 42 (1997) 193 with the text of Commissione Nazionale per le Società e la Borsa 'Raccomandazioni in materia di controlli societari' 200 et seq.

[90] Guidelines for good practice; CEPS 'Corporate Governance in Europe' 3-4 (Brussels 1995).

C. The Board of Directors[91]

29. The purpose of the present chapter is to give an overview of the structure and functioning of the governing bodies, mainly in listed companies. It will contain legal developments and, as far as available, factual data. However, data are still relatively rare and often not very reliable, and the descriptions by state will therefore be very unequal.

In most EU member states, public companies limited by shares are obliged by statute to organize a board of directors, usually composed of three directors. In the United Kingdom, company law merely imposes the appointment of at least two directors; whether these form a board is left to the charter or to practice. In private companies, the management may be taken care of by one single person, a board structure being optional.

Most European companies laws have adopted the unitary board structure.[92] Some have made the two-tier board optional, while a few have imposed two-tier boards in order to organize workers' direct or indirect participation.[93] The latter issue is directly linked to the two-tier structure, although the opposite is not true.

Although many of the same issues are met in both unitary and two tier-structures, the answers are fundamentally influenced by the structure of the board; therefore, these subjects will be dealt with separately.

I. Unitary Boards

30. Unitary boards are the prevalent board structure in most European states. They are the exclusive board structure in Belgium,[94] Denmark, Greece, Ireland, Luxembourg, the United Kingdom, Spain, Italy, Sweden, and Switzerland. In some of these jurisdictions, representation of labor representatives or other stakeholders at the board level has been introduced.[95]

1. The Role of the Board of Directors

31. It may seem striking, but in most jurisdictions the role of the board of directors has not been described in the law, nor has it sometimes even been alluded to. Often its role will appear, negatively, from liability rules, or from the

---

[91] The board is also subject of Ch. 4 in this volume.

[92] This is the case in all EU states except Austria and Portugal, where no co-determination system applies, and Germany and the Netherlands.

[93] Especially Germany, the Netherlands, and Austria; see infra no. 87 et seq.

[94] Except for banks; see infra no. 91.

[95] See infra no. 95 et seq.

court cases in which directors' duties have been spelled out. But a positive description or analysis of the duties of the directors, and what it means to "direct" a company, is generally lacking in the legislative instruments, or has been described in terms of vague standards of care.[96]

According to French law, for example, the "board of directors is entrusted with extensive powers to act in all circumstances on behalf of the company; it exercises the powers within the limits of the social purpose, and the competencies expressly attributed to the general meeting of shareholders."[97] Similar vague descriptions appear in the Belgian law and in the Netherlands code. These definitions do not confer a useful description of the role of the board within the functioning of the company, except by making clear that all competencies belong to the board that have not expressly—by law or by charter—been attributed to the general meeting.[98] In larger companies the center of power has shifted to the board, while the role of the shareholders is limited to the appointment or dismissal of the board and charter amendments, including the ultimate decisions about the company's future (e.g., in cases of share issues, loss of capital, mergers, dissolution, etc.).

32. There is a wide diversity of opinion concerning in whose interest the board should act: as the agents of the company, the directors are accountable to their principal, the legal person.[99] In most if not all legal systems compared, there is agreement that the board should act in "the interest of the company". The rule means that directors may not act in the interest of one shareholder, whatever the importance of his stake, but should instead serve the interests of all shareholders.[100] Also, one shareholder individually cannot enforce the agency relationship; in principle, only the company, i.e., a majority of shareholders, can act.[101] It

---

[96] E.g., art. 127 Spanish Corporation Act: "... directors shall exercise the same degree of diligence as an orderly businessman and a faithful representative".

[97] Art. 98 French Companies Act 1966.

[98] See, e.g., art. 129 Spanish Corporation Act: "... except as otherwise stipulated, the board of directors is in charge of directing the company". See also art. 54 Belgian Companies Act.

[99] Under U.K. law, in principle, directors can only be sued by the general meeting, known as the "rule in *Foss v. Harbottle*"; for details, see Gower, Laurence C.B. and Paul Davies *Principles of Modern Company Law* 659 et seq. (London 1996). The same principle is followed, e.g., in French law, art. 244 French Companies Act 1966; or in Belgian law, art. 62 Belgian Companies Act. But later legislation or judicial developments have granted increasing rights to minority shareholders to sue on behalf and for the account of the company.

[100] The idea is sometimes expressly mentioned in the statute.

[101] See as to the possibility to exercise class actions or derivative actions in the different jurisdictions: art. 66 Belgian Companies Act; for France: Merle, Philippe *Droit Commercial, Droit des Sociétés* 409 et seq. 5th edn. (Paris 1996); for the U.K.: Gower and Davies, supra n. 99, 665 et seq.; for Switzerland: Forstmoser, Peter, Arthur Meier-Hayoz, and Peter Nobel *Schweizerisches Aktienrecht* 421 et seq. (Bern 1996); for Italy: Jaeger, Pier G. and Francesco Denozza *Appunti di diritto commerciale* 111 et seq. (Milan 1994); in the Netherlands, derivative actions are not allowed, see Van Schilfgaarde, Peter *Van de BV en de NV* 151 (Deventer 1995).

further raises the question of the extent to which the board can take into account the categorical interests that come under the umbrella of the "company interest": Is the company interest identical to that of the shareholders only, or does it include the interest of other stakeholders? The legal systems have given divergent answers to this question.

Between these two extremes, there are several intermediate opinions. Acting in the interest of the company does not mean that the other constituents can be merely sacrificed to shareholders' interests; it means that these interests can be taken into account as they also serve the interest of these shareholders. However, ultimately, responsibility runs towards providers of capital as the bearers of the firms' ultimate risks.

Another often-discussed opinion states that the board is supposed to act in the interests of the company as such, being the independent entity separate from its shareholders. This criterion implies that the board would act for the continuity of the company as a separate economic entity. Some will reject this analysis by stating that it would mean the board embodying the continuity would be acting in its own interest. This question would create serious difficulties if the board were confronted with the proposal of giving up its existence as the head of a separate legal entity (e.g., in case of a merger). Therefore, it would be more precise to state that the board should act in the interests of the firm, or of the "enterprise as such".

A further point of discussion relates to whether the same rule would be applied to decisions of the general meeting: Could a decision of the general meeting be reviewed on the basis that it is contrary to the interest of the company? It boils down to the question of who is entitled to decide, the shareholders or the judge? The question seems based on a circular reasoning: only the shareholders are entitled to decide what is the ultimate interest of the company. The legal order can only ensure adequate decision-making procedures and good faith in the relations among shareholders deciding on the issue.

33. In the *United Kingdom*, the law does not specify what directors should do nor to whom they are accountable. Only s. 309 (1) states that

> "the matters to which the directors are to have regard in the performance of their functions include the interest of the company's employees in general, as well as the interest of its members."

Although this subsection would seem to indicate double accountability, the section further states that

> "accordingly, the duty imposed by this section on the directors is owed by them to the company (and the company alone) and is enforceable in the same way as any other fiduciary duty owed to a company by its directors."

34. Directors, acting as agents for the company, should act in good faith, taking account of the interests of the shareholders both in the short and in the long term and striking a reasonable balance between them. It is for the directors, not for the courts, to identify what would be in the interests of the company; the test is a subjective one. The directors' duties are of a fiduciary nature and are held in relation to the company; this is to all its shareholders, present and future, but not to individual shareholders.[102] Directors have no specific duties towards creditors unless the company is close to insolvency, when it is dealing on the creditors' risks. In this case, provisions may be made to protect employees' interest.[103] But outside the insolvency hypothesis, the duties owed the employees would be considered part of the general duties owed the company, and in case of conflict would be left to the directors' business judgment.[104] It seems that s. 309 above would reduce directors accountability to shareholders rather than strengthen their accountability to employees.[105] U.K. law would allow directors to take into account the interests of the group as long as it does not run against the interests of their own company.[106]

The Cadbury Report is more explicit on the duties of directors and states among the code principles that "boards are accountable to their shareholders". The board's functions are summarized as follows:

"The responsibilities of the board include setting up the company's strategic aims, providing the leadership to put them into effect, supervising the management of the business and reporting to shareholders on their stewardship". As to the financial aspects of corporate governance, the report mentions the "way in which boards set financial policy and oversee its implementation, including the use of financial controls, and the process whereby they report on the activities and progress of the company to the shareholders".

35. The *Dutch* law states that "except as otherwise stated in the company's charter, the board of directors is in charge of directing the company",[107] while in terms of liability " . . . the director is liable towards the company for the proper fulfilling of his task".[108] The board should act "in the interest of the company and of the enterprise which it supports".[109] It is especially the latter rule which is at

---

[102] In some cases, directors may be acting in a way that implies fiduciary duties, e.g., on advising shareholders on a takeover bid or other share transactions.

[103] On the basis of s. 719 Companies Act 1985 and s. 187 Insolvency Act 1986; see Gower and Davies, supra n. 99, 219.

[104] Palmer, Francis B. and Clive Maximilian Schmitthoff *Palmer's Company Law* § 8.507 (London).

[105] Gower and Davies, supra n. 99, 603 and n. 40.

[106] Palmer and Schmitthoff, supra n. 104, § 8.509. See: *Charterbridge Corp v. Lloyds Bank Ltd* [1970] Ch 62 *Pergamon Press Ltd. v. Maxwell* [1970] 1.W.L.R., 1167.

[107] Art. 129 NBW: "het bestuur is belast met het bestuur van de vennootschap". A more detailed list of duties is stipulated for the supervisory board, esp. art. 164 NBW.

[108] Art. 8 NBW.

[109] See art. 140 (2) NBW: "bij de vervulling van hun taak richten de commissarissen zich naar het belang van de vennootschap en de met haar verbonden onderneming". For a critique, see Honée, Harry J.M.N. 'Commissarissen, gezanten uit Niemandsland?' *De Naamlooze Vennootschap* 74 (1996) 276 et seq.

the basis of an intensive debate. This debate turns on whether the duties of the board tend towards the company, i.e., the shareholders, or towards the "enterprise." In particular, it concerns whether—and to what extent—these duties include the interests of the employees, the corporate group interest, and the interests of other stakeholders such as the creditors or even the general interest. Several tendencies have appeared in legal writing.

There is agreement that the clause refers to the obligation of the board to take account of the several interests involved, and not only to serve the interest of the shareholders. According to some, the interest of the "enterprise" refers to the firm's long-term continuity, its healthy continuation, and expansion.[110] Others consider the notion to refer instead to the balancing of interests affected.[111] In this respect, attention should be drawn to the rule in the Act on Enterprise Councils, according to which decisions by a firm's management are reviewable before court if the "entrepreneur in balancing the interests involved, could reasonably not have come to his decision".[112] The procedure is brought before the specialized Enterprise Chamber of the Amsterdam Court of Appeal. On the merits, this type of review of board decisions would, however, be limited to cases in which the board has manifestly neglected said duty ("review on a marginal basis"), while the normal leeway for exercising business judgment would be left untouched.[113] Most decisions have been taken on procedural grounds, not on the merits. Therefore, boards generally retain a large freedom to decide about the overall long-term interest of the company, but may give precedence to categorical interests over the interests of the shareholders.

Measures of judicial redress have been imposed for not taking into account the employee interests.[114] In one court case, it was held that on closing down a division, the board should have balanced the interests of the different groups of employees in the firm.[115] In another case involving the closing down of a profitable Dutch subsidiary of a German group, the board's decision was held as unjustified, especially as not all interests involved had been duly taken into account.[116]

---

[110] See Maeijer, supra n. 71, no. 293, p. 366 et seq.

[111] See Van der Heijden and Van der Grinten, supra n. 4, 23; see Maeijer, supra n. 71, no. 293, p. 367.

[112] Art. 26 (4) Act on Enterprise Councils 1971.

[113] Maeijer, supra n. 71, no. 485, p. 684.

[114] Art. 26 (5) Act on Enterprise Councils provides for, i.a., withdrawal of the firm's decision or injunction forbidding implementation of a decision taken. These measure can only be imposed if the Enterprise Council has applied for them.

[115] HR 7 July 1982, *NJ* (1983) 35 (*Enka*).

[116] See OK 7 July 1988, *NJ* (1989) 845 (*Fluke* case) note Maeijer, where the decision was held manifestly unreasonable to close down a division in the interest of the group that was in

Apart from these employee-related cases, on the basis of the general principles of law, decisions taken in the interest of one single party, e.g., one shareholder, the board itself, or one of its members, would be open to challenge as a "diversion of competencies",[117] which comes very close to a violation of a fiduciary duty. Similar remedies would apply to decisions whereby one of the categorical interests affected would unduly and beyond proportion be damaged by the firm's decision. Here interests of creditors would rank lower than those of employees. The general interest would, as a rule, not be considered an objective to be pursued by a private business firm.

As to taking into account the group interest as a whole, it was held[118] in the decision relating to the Dutch subsidiary of an international group that the interest of the entire group, its continuous existence, and the interest of the employees' activities in other divisions of the group could be taken into consideration as prevailing over the interest of an individual subsidiary.[119]

The Peters Report dealt in great detail with the relations between the board and the shareholders, significantly called "capital suppliers". There is a marked difference between the proposed report and the final document in the latter's increased shareholder orientation. In the report, continuity of the firm is an essential goal. A reasonable balance should be aimed at between the interests of the capital suppliers and the other interests affected by company decision. In the long term there should be no conflicting interests.[120] The report calls for more attention to the position of the shareholders, especially the institutional investors. The report stated that the decision-making power of the capital suppliers mainly refers to the dialogue within the general meeting, calling for disclosure and response by the board. The "one share, one vote" rule should be considered a guiding principle, to be set aside in specific cases, e.g., if too small a number of shareholders attends the meeting or if a hostile bid has been threatened.[121]

36. According to *French* law, for example, the "board of directors is entrusted with extensive powers to act in all circumstances on behalf of the company; it exercises the powers within the limits of the social purpose, and the competencies expressly attributed to the general meeting of shareholders."[122] French law contains no further description of the role of the board. Its members are elected by the general meeting of shareholders by a simple majority. The board is

---

itself profitable if it had not been shown whether or to what extent the group interest had been balanced against the interest of the employees of the division.

[117] Called *Détournement de pouvoir*.

[118] HR 7 July 1982 (*Enka*) *NJ* (1983) 35, ann. Ma.

[119] HR 7 July 1982 (*Enka*) *NJ* (1983) 35, ann. Ma.

[120] See Peters Report, supra n. 74, § 1.1

[121] See Peters Report, supra n. 74, § 5.1

[122] Art. 98 French Companies Act 1966.

chaired by the *président*, who is elected by the board members. He is the key figure in French company life. The independence of the *président-directeur général* (*PDG*), as the central figure within the board,[123] is seen as the expression of the idea that the directors should act in the interest of the enterprise. There seem to be two ways to analyze this notion, namely that directors should act in the interest of the shareholders, or that they should act in the interest of the business entity as such in an attempt to ensure its survival.

The French Viénot Report has described the conception of the French business leaders as to how the directors should view their task: "In all circumstances, directors should act in the interest of the enterprise. The interest of the enterprise can be defined as the supreme interest of the legal person itself, namely the enterprise considered as autonomous economic agent, acting in pursuit of its own objectives, separate from the interest of its shareholders, its employees, and its creditors (including the tax authorities, its suppliers, and its clients), but corresponding to their common general interest, which is to ensure prosperity and continuity of the firm".[124]

37. The *German* situation is to a certain extent comparable to the Dutch one in that the interest of the shareholder and the maximization of his wealth is not the only nor ultimate touchstone for the company's conduct. In German law, too, there has been a long-standing discussion over which interests the board is supposed to serve. The law itself contains some references to the "interest of the company" or, as is often mentioned in case law and is more clearly underlined in the co-determined firms, to the "interest of the enterprise" (*Unternehmensinteresse*). The reference to the "enterprise interest" does not imply that it is to be considered as the central touchstone to which all other interests involved are subordinated. This idea—that the independent enterprise interest, the *Unternehmen an sich,* could be considered as the all-overriding interest—was developed early in the century, but has been abandoned today.

Company law is instead considered to be based on a series of conflicting interests, among which those of the shareholders are important but not dominant, their role being instrumental to the realization of other interests involved, such as those of the employees, the creditors, and even of the general welfare. In co-determined firms, the conjunction of capital and labor has a tendency to relegate all other interests to a minor role. The question is increasingly analyzed from the procedural angle: all interests involved should adequately be taken into consideration, but no review of the decision on its substantive merits will take place;

---

[123] See about the *PDG*, infra no. 63.

[124] Viénot Report, supra n. 68, 9. Also on p. 6: "whatever the composition or the conditions of organization of the board, the latter has and remains the collegiate body representing collectively all of the shareholders and feels bound to act in all circumstances in the enterprise's own interest".

the rule primarily obligates the parties to engage in an adequate and fair decision-making process, cooperation, conflict-solving, and cooperative exercise of direction powers.[125] At least from the legal point of view, it would seem that this flexible formulation of the position of the parties involved does not prevent the board from duly taking account of the long-term shareholders' wealth.

The *Austrian* Companies Act states that the management board should act on its own responsibility in the interests of the enterprise, taking into account the interests of shareholders, the employees, and the general interest.[126]

38. In *Switzerland,* too, the subject of balancing the different interests affected by the company's conduct is receiving ample attention.[127] According to the present legislation, company law only considers the relationship between the company and its management with the shareholders, the relations among shareholders, and the relationship of the company to the creditors. The board, elected exclusively by shareholders, should "take care in good faith of the interests of the company".[128] Relations with the other external factors—such as employees, consumers, suppliers, the markets, or the general interest—are left to specific regulations (e.g., labor law, competition law) but are not considered part of company law nor company decision making. This partial approach does not prevent the company from taking these interests into account, as its decision may be likely to affect them. However, it is widely accepted—albeit controversial—that the company should be managed in its own long-term interest, in the interest of the "enterprise as such" (*an sich*), whereby short-term shareholder interests should yield to the long-term enterprise interest. In practice, a majority decision is deemed to express the company interest, and the courts reluctantly check whether the decisions would be contrary to that long-term perspective. However, recent changes in the law have introduced a wider protection for the minority interest. Co-determination has been proposed for larger firms (more than 500 employees), but it was turned down in a 1976 referendum. There is no obligation to act in furtherance of the public or general interest.[129]

39. The situation under *Belgian* law is not very different from the Swiss approach, including the fact that only creditors enjoy specific protection as part of the company organization. Company law ignores other outside interests such as employees, suppliers, consumers, and the general interest. These matters are

---

[125] See Kübler, Friedrich *Gesellschaftsrecht. Die privatrechtlichen Ordnungsstrukturen und Regelungsprobleme von Verbänden und Unternehmen* § 14 III and § 32 III 4th edn. (Heidelberg 1994). Mülbert, Peter O. 'Shareholder Value aus rechtlicher Sicht' *Zeitschrift für Unternehmens- und Gesellschaftsrecht* 26 (1997) 129-72.

[126] § 70 (1) ÖAktG.

[127] For an overview, Forstmoser, Meier-Hayoz, and Nobel, supra n. 101, § 3.

[128] Art. 717 (1) Swiss OR.

[129] As was mentioned in the German AktG 1937.

left to specific regulations which must be respected. In company decision making, the board must serve the interests of the company as such, which includes taking into account the long-term relations with employees, the markets, or the public authorities. Ultimately, with the board's accountability to the shareholders, decisions should be driven by the shareholders' interest. This is understood as referring to the views of the majority—whether or not they were expressed at a general meeting— provided no oppression takes place. Courts are rather loath to interfere with shareholder decisions and do not review decisions on the basis of the balancing of interests. Remedies have been provided for the protection of minority interests, both on the basis of general rules of *abus de droit*—meaning that a shareholder manifestly oppresses other shareholders—or on the basis of specific regulations in the companies act.[130] These concern only the relations between the shareholders, and therefore are limited to internal company life. There has been a doctrinal opinion urging the courts also to take into account the wider enterprise interest and review company decisions for their violation.[131] Case law has remained hostile to this current, limiting its review to violations of the applicable regulation or to the internal company relations.

The *Danish* Act contains a list of matters to which boards of listed companies should pay special attention. These relate to matters such as quorum, frequency of meetings, attribution of competences to managing directors or other bodies, ways and means of supervision, and so on.[132]

40. To limit this overview, one could conclude that with respect to the question of to what extent boards of European companies are considered to serve the interests of the shareholders, the European legal systems offer a variety of answers. The most shareholder-minded systems are the British, the Swiss, and Belgian, which limit attention for non-shareholder interests to long-term strategies aimed at ultimately protecting the wealth of the shareholders. In the other systems, there are different tendencies: some opt for a balancing of interests,

---

[130] Art. 190 ter and quater Belgian Companies Act provides for an individual shareholder's right to sue an annulment of decisions of the general meeting on the basis of "abusive use of the competencies of the general meeting" and "diversion of competencies" (*détournement de pouvoir*). These remedies would include cases in which minority interests have been oppressed. Interference with the competencies of the board would be included (art. 190bis Belgian Companies Act). In addition, art. 190ter and quater Belgian Companies Act provide for withdrawal procedures, whereby shareholders owning 30% or more of the shares are entitled to acquire, by court order, the shares of the other shareholders, if "serious grounds" have been proved. This remedy would be a useful instrument for solving oppression cases. It does not apply to listed companies.

[131] See: Geens, Koen 'De jurisprudentiële bescherming van de minderheidsaandeelhouders tegen door de meerderheid opgezette beschermingsconstructies' *Tijdschrift voor Privaatrecht* 26 (1989) 35. Van Gerven, Walter 'Bedrijfsbezetting en verkoop in eigen beheer door werknemers van de onderneming' *Rechtskundig Weekblad* 40 (1976-1977) 65.

[132] Art. 56 (5) Danish Companies Act.

primarily of capital and labor; some extend it to other stakeholders; and others see the ultimate continuity of the firm as the primary assignment of the board, an opinion which comes close to defending the interests of the firm "as such". The practical effects of this analysis also differ: although judges everywhere are very loath to interfere—in fact they almost never do—with the business decisions, remedies are granted on the basis of violations of procedural rules, informational unbalances, or the refusal to take into consideration one of the classes of stakeholders. Review on the merits seems to be extremely rare.

2. Appointment and Dismissal of Board Members

41. In most systems with unitary boards, the U.K. excepted,[133] members are formally elected by the general meeting of shareholders, which also determines the number of seats on the board. A committee of shareholders may sometimes exercise the right to elect board members.[134] At the general meeting, the majority elects all members of the board[135] and representation of minority shareholders is rarely organized.[136] Charter rules providing for minority protection are rare, at least in the larger companies.[137] Swiss law contains a provision whereby, if the company has issued different classes of shares, each class is entitled to at least one representative on the board.[138] Swedish law provides that the charter may

---

[133] In the U.K., the articles may give power to the directors to appoint additional directors, and the general meeting will not intervene. See Palmer and Schmitthoff, supra n. 104, § 8.006; also there is no requirement that directors be appointed by the general meeting of shareholders: Gower and Davies, supra n. 99, 180. It is, however, the normal practice for directors to be appointed by an ordinary resolution.

[134] See, e.g., art. 59 Danish Companies Act, in which the committee has competencies usually pertaining to the supervisory board.

[135] Cumulative voting is considered admissible in Belgian law: De Bie, Erik 'Het cumulatief stemrecht en de evenredige vertegenwoordiging van aandeelhouders in de raad van bestuur van een N.V.' *Tijdschrift voor Rechtspersoon en Vennootschap* (1995) 69. Cumulative voting is not a usual practice in the U.K.: see Gower and Davies, supra n. 99, 181.

[136] In many systems, the appointment of directors cannot be placed in the hands of any other body than the general meeting. So, e.g., in Italian law: Jaeger and Denozza, supra n. 101, 1, 381; also in Swiss law: Forstmoser, Meier-Hayoz, and Nobel, supra n. 101, § 27, no. 21. Presentation or veto rights would be invalid. In the U.K., however, an outsider, e.g., a vendor of a business to the company, may be given power to appoint one or more directors: Palmer and Schmitthoff, supra n. 104, § 8.006.

[137] Proportional representation in Belgian companies: Van Gerven, Dirk 'De evenredige en onevenredige vertegenwoordiging van aandeelhouders in de raad van bestuur van een N.V.' *Tijdschrift voor Belgisch Handelsrecht—Revue de droit commercial belge* 24 (1991) 850. One should also mention the Spanish law (art. 137 Spanish Corporation Act) and the Irish Act providing for minority shareholders to be represented. So also the Italian law: Jaeger and Denozza, supra n. 101, 381. Also in Danish law: art. 49 (2) Danish Companies Act.

[138] With different rights attached, not merely different nominal value: art. 709 (1) Swiss OR; see Forstmoser, Meier-Hayoz, and Nobel, supra n. 101, § 29, no. 289.

provide for one or more board members to be appointed "in another way", i.e., without election at the general meeting.[139]

In some cases the general meeting is restricted in its choice, especially by nomination rights exercised by the holders of preference shares or of a certain minimum number of shares, or of third parties. The Dutch expressly recognize this practice: holders of preference shares, especially a foundation closely linked to the board, may propose to each seat at least two candidates for election by the shareholders. However, the nomination may be overruled, and the election is free if the general meeting votes with a two-thirds majority.[140]

Systems of representation of different classes of shares are allowed in some legal systems[141] on a proportional basis, and sometimes even on a disproportional one.[142] Election would invariably be subject to a majority decision of the general meeting without quorum requirement, although some national laws may be more stringent. As in most continental European companies with concentrated share ownership, board appointment takes place with the approval of controlling shareholders.

Appointments also often take place by co-optation, i.e., the board elects a new director to fill a vacancy during the year and submits it for approval at the next general meeting.[143] In some cases, this procedure follows on the recommendation of a nomination committee constituted from within the board.[144] The presence of controlling shareholders explains that these normally would have to agree with the appointment of all board members.[145]

42. On the European continent, factual practices ensure the appointment of directors who express the position of the main shareholders. Agreements

---

[139] Ch. 8 § 1 Swedish Companies Act; also Ch. 8 § 1 Finnish Companies Act. In Denmark, nomination of board members may be conferred not only on "shareholders committees" but also on "public authorities or others" (art. 49 (2) Danish Companies Act).

[140] See art. 133 and 243 NBW. For further analysis of these and many other protective techniques, see Voogd, supra n. 72; Maeijer, supra n. 71, 533 et. seq. Similar techniques are reportedly admitted under Luxembourg law.

[141] E.g., in Belgian law, Heenen, Jacques 'Le choix des administrateurs' *Revue pratique des sociétés* (1956) 65, no. 4558; Van Gerven, supra n. 137; Tilleman, Bernard *Bestuur van vennootschappen* 139 (Kalmthout 1996). But the general meeting should keep a minimal freedom of choice between the candidates; for a case where no such freedom existed, see Trib. Brussels, 13 December 1984 *Revue pratique des sociétés* (1985) 122, no. 6333 (*Rossel*); Brussels, 31 August 1983 *Revue pratique des sociétés* (1983) 294, no. 6245.

[142] See Guyon, supra n. 1, no. 319, 322; also in Italian law, Jaeger and Denozza, supra n. 101, 381.

[143] In France, see art. 94 French Companies Act 1966, in Belgium art. 55 (5) Belgian Companies Act. For criticism of this procedure, see Vincke, François 'The Corporate Governance Debate in Belgium' in: Hopt and Wymeersch (eds.), supra n. 40, 130.

[144] Art. 49 (2) Danish Companies Act.

[145] There are exceptions: the Spanish law provides for proportional representation (art. 137 Spanish Corporation Act).

between shareholders may provide for representation of each of the partners on the board. Also, there is a widespread practice that important shareholders obtain at least one seat on the board, even if they only hold a minority block, as part of building good relations between shareholders. Although no definite percentage could be put forward, one could say that in Belgian companies a 10% stake confers the right to at least one seat; in France, a 5% stake has been mentioned in the largest holding companies.

In *Belgium*, board membership depends on election by the general meeting. In practice, however, board members often are co-opted by the present board, and the appointment is later ratified by the general meeting. This feature is in line with the ownership structure: board members normally are not appointed except with the consent of the dominant or reference shareholder. Therefore, appointment by co-optation could, de facto, be considered equal to election by the shareholders in the general meeting. Formal procedures for the selection of board members have recently been introduced on a voluntary basis by some companies: nomination committees have been introduced; others have organized a systematic search for board members according to the profile designed by the nomination committee. Also, the general meeting is increasingly better informed about the professional profile of candidates for election to the board. In the absence of structured proxy material, this type of disclosure is sometimes found in the annual reports.[146]

In *British* practice, where in most companies no significant shareholders have to approve nominations, nomination committees normally play a larger role. Although the setting up of nomination committees was not part of the Cadbury Code of Best Practice, a majority of 70% of the largest companies mentioned the organization of said committees.[147]

Noteworthy is the *Dutch* rule, requiring disclosure of significant information in case board members are appointed based on the nomination or recommendation of certain parties, especially the holders of preference shares: this information relates to age, profession, and ownership of shares in the company, but also includes other occupations, including other board memberships. These recommendations or nominations have to be grounded.[148]

The issue of minority shareholder representation has been discussed in the *French* Viénot Report. Both with respect to the larger minority shareholder and

---

[146] For the Belgian practice, see Petrofina, Cobepa, General Bank. Some information about the directors can be found in the annual reports of Solvay. No information in the annual report of, e.g., GBL, Soc. Gén., NPM, Almanij, Royale Belge, Tractebel, U.M., Kredietbank, Bekaert, CBR, CMB, Delhaize, Electrabel.

[147] 'Compliance with the Code of Best Practice', supra n. 64, 19, Table 6, according to which 49% of the 100 largest, and 60% of the following 250 largest U.K. companies had introduced a nomination committee, a substantial increase over a 1991 census (9% and 7%).

[148] Art. 142 (2) NBW, see infra no. 88 for supervisory board members.

with respect to the investors at large, it was considered that no separate representation should be introduced; rather, it was thought to be more efficient to appoint independent directors, even in companies that were fully controlled by one or a few shareholders. Independent directors should be selected among persons having the "sensitivity "of these market investors.[149]

43. The former description is confirmed by the findings made by Korn/Ferry in their 1995 study. In all compared systems, results show that the main source of influence on the appointment of directors comes from the chairman or CEO, often supported by the full board. It is only in Germany, France, and Belgium that shareholders have a stronger (in Germany because of the *Aufsichtsrat*) or weaker (France and Belgium) influence on appointments. For France and Belgium, institutional investors are mentioned also as having a significant influence on board nomination: one can probably identify these "institutional investors" as "holding companies", in which case the finding would be comparable to the one made for Germany. In each case, the larger or largest shareholder has a significant influence on the nomination of board members. Anecdotal evidence supports this finding.

This study further reveals some other interesting features of board selection procedures. A distinction is made between the appointment of inside and outside directors.[150]

Outside directors in Belgium and France are mostly identified by either an existing contact of a board member (46%) or by shareholder nomination (60%), it being understood that the latter case refers to the dominant shareholder. Internal appointments account for 17% and executive search for only 3%. Minority shareholder nomination is unknown. In the southern European states, executive search stands for 14%, while existing contacts represent not more than 31%, and shareholder nomination 41%. Where state representatives have to be classified is unclear: 17% of directors have been identified "by other means". These figures contrast heavily with the ones reproduced for the U.K., where executive search accounts for 55% and existing contacts for 52%. Shareholder nomination stands for only 14%, a figure in line with the structure of ownership of U.K. companies. One can presume that in some cases, institutional investors have been included in the figures standing for shareholder nomination. Striking also is the large proportion of nominations brought about on the basis of existing contacts.

With respect to inside directors, in all systems compared, appointments from within the organization are most likely to have been effectuated or influenced by the CEO or chairman, or by the full board. This was the case for 89% in the U.K., where the nomination committee also was active in 45% of cases. Institutional investors account for only 8%, while unions and government played

---

[149] Viénot Report, supra n. 68, 17.

[150] Korn/Ferry International, supra n. 84, Table 11.

almost no role in this type of appointment. For France and Belgium, although the same factors presented the highest weight in the internal procedure for inside directors, institutional investors were identified as influential in the appointment of members of the board. There might have been the same confusion about the definition of institutional investors, as these seem to refer to the holding companies.

Whatever the method of appointment, directors are in charge of directing the company in the interest of all shareholders, and not only of those who nominated them. Directors are not the representatives of one but of all shareholders. This idea is the common idea in all systems compared.[151] However, there seems to be a tendency for certain directors to be identified with a specific shareholder. The Belgian Banking and Finance Commission recommended that the annual report identify the shareholder which the director is supposed to represent.[152]

The Dutch system is essentially based on co-optation.[153] The Peters Code recommends that boards establish a publicly disclosed profile of their composition, number of members, tasks, and procedures, taking into account, e.g., internationalization, nature of the business, the firm's specific risks, and so on. The supervisory board should be composed in such a way that its members can function independently and with a sense of critique towards each other and towards the management board. The organization of a nomination and remuneration committee is recommended.[154]

It is striking that appointment procedures—including the call for comparable safeguards such as the formation of a nomination committee—though they reflect different underlying objectives, all strive towards more objective, balanced appointments.

44. The codes of conduct that have been published in several European states contain some recommendations dealing with the appointment of directors. A common recommendation concerns the institution of a nomination committee as an internal committee within the board. According to the Cadbury Code, this committee should be composed of a majority of non-executive directors and chaired by the chairman of the board.[155] The French Viénot Report contains a similar recommendation: the committee should be composed of directors and officers, and at least one independent director. It should be chaired by the chair-

---

[151] E.g., Viénot Report, supra n. 68, 14: "quelles que soient sa composition et l'origine de ses membres, le conseil d'administration représente collectivement l'ensemble des actionnaires".

[152] Banking and Finance Commission, mentioned no. 26.

[153] At least as far as the co-determined companies are concerned. In the other ones, the general meeting keeps its privileges.

[154] § 2.2 of the Report (supra n. 74) and Rec. 15.

[155] 4.30 Cadbury Report, see no. 23; in the same sense: § 14 of the Hampel Committee recommendations, supra n. 67.

man of the board.[156] The Belgian recommendations are less explicit.[157] One body of rules underlines that the role of the nomination committee would be "to limit somewhat the absolute appointment and dismissal privileges of the general meeting".[158] The committee would urge the board to act more independently in relation to the shareholders.

The recommendations are less explicit as to the criteria to be followed in the selection of future directors: the French recommendation stresses that it is useful to pursue an "equilibrium in the board composition, taking into account composition and evolution of the ownership of the company", especially with a view to "appointing independent directors, representation of specific interests, desirability of renewal of certain appointments, and continuity of the members' expertise".[159] As far as the supervisory board is concerned, similar ideas have been developed in the Dutch system.[160]

45. The removal of directors is subject to different legal regimes. In most legal systems, directors could be dismissed at will (*ad nutum*).[161] In at least French and Belgian law, this rule has been considered to be a rule of "public order", not allowing any contract nor technique that would obviate the general meeting's right to dismiss at will.[162] Any technique, such as a notice, indemnity, or other aimed at alleviating the results of the rule, would be considered void.[163] The principle is related to the strong influence exercised by controlling shareholders in many of the continental European states. It plays a significant

---

[156] Viénot, supra n. 68, 18.

[157] Belgian Stock Exchange, see no. 26.

[158] See Santens Report, supra no. 26, Recommendation no. 9.

[159] Viénot, supra n. 68, 18.

[160] See infra no. 102; as to the elements contained in the Peters Report, supra n. 74.

[161] See also in the Spanish Act, art. 131 Spanish Corporation Act. The same applies in Belgian, British (s. 303 Companies Act 1985), Danish (art. 50 (1) Danish Companies Act), French (art. 90 French Companies Act 1966); Finnish (Ch 8 § 2 Finnish Companies Act), Irish, Luxembourg (art. 51 Companies Act), Greek, and Swedish (Ch 8 § 2 Swedish Companies Act), law; but Italian law would admit an indemnity of the revocation was without "just cause"; art. 2383 c.c.

[162] For Belgium, see 13 April 1989 *Revue critique de jurisprudence belge* (1991) 205, note Nelissen Grade; Pas., 1989, I, 825; French law: Cozian and Viandier, supra n. 2, no. 685, p. 247; Guyon, supra n. 1, 328, 336. The Marini Report, supra n. 69, proposed to validate clauses allowing for damages on dismissal of board members: no. 32, p. 121.

[163] For the French situation allowing reasonable indemnities albeit in indirect ways, see Cozian and Viandier, supra n. 2, 249 et seq. Belgian law would allow for certain directors to be treated as employees: Cass., 28 May 1984, Pas., 1984, I, 1172; Cass., 30 May 1988, Pas., 1988, I, 1169; cf. art. 93 French Companies Act 1966 prohibiting that directors also qualify as employees, invoking labor law protection.

role in the case of a takeover bid.[164] It also is a strong element in the context of groups of companies: the parent usually has no legally enforceable right to enjoin the subsidiary to engage in certain action, but it can exercise significant leverage over the directives of the subsidiary.

The prohibition of any indemnification would also limit the value of golden parachutes.[165] In practice, however, indemnities are often paid: these may be due in exchange for the shares which the dismissed director holds,[166] or in exchange for a promise not to compete with the dismissing company.

In other systems directors may be dismissed at will, although an indemnity may be stipulated. Dutch law, for example, allows the dismissal of management board members at will by the general meeting. Indemnities are due if the dismissal is contrary to the rules of labor law or to contractual rules. Also, the charter could provide the general meeting to decide with a two-thirds quorum.[167] The same rules apply in private companies limited, except that it may be stipulated that dismissal may not take place except under very strenuous circumstances. A similar approach is followed in Swiss law.[168]

U.K. law also allows directors to be dismissed at will by the general meeting.[169] However, managing and executive directors may claim compensation if provided for in their service contract. These contracts may provide for service for not more than five years.[170] In practice they are shorter, with a one-year term recommended.[171] Institutional investors often insist on an even shorter term. The

---

[164] There have been some well-publicized cases of the dismissal of an entire board after takeovers or similar transactions: in France see Navigation mixte, or in Belgium after the takeover of Société générale de Belgique in 1988.

[165] Golden parachutes promised by a third party would be valid: Cass. com. fr., 7 February 1989 *Revue pratique des sociétés* (1989) 643, note Chartier.

[166] For the discussion in French law, see Cozian and Viandier, supra n. 2, no. 690, p. 251 and Marini Report, supra n. 69, Recommandation no. 32 pleading for allowing a certain indemnity.

[167] Art. 134 NBW, at least if the directors were appointed by the general meeting. Cf. art. 161 NBW for supervisory board members and art. 244 NBW for the *BV*.

[168] The charter may impose a quorum requirement, and that indemnification is allowed (art. 705 Swiss OR).

[169] S. 303 Companies Act 1985, by "ordinary resolution", i.e., simple majority.

[170] S. 319 Companies Act 1985; beyond a five-year duration, the approval of the general meeting is required. The service contracts are open to inspection of any member of the company (s. 318 (7) Companies Act 1985).

[171] See Greenbury Report, supra n. 66, rule D2: "There is a strong case for setting notice or contract periods at, or reducing them to, one year or less." This statement has been substantially diluted in the Hampel Committee's draft report, supra n. 67, where it reads: "There should be no fixed rules for the length of service or age of non-executive directors; but there is a risk of becoming less efficient and objective with length of service and advancing age, and boards should be vigilant against this" (Rec. 16). Maintained in the final report, supra n. 67, Rec. 19.

outright removal of directors, except in cases of a change of control, is rather rare; often directors will resign voluntarily, or their mandate will not be renewed.

In France, as in Belgium, directors can be removed at will. The rule also applies to the *président directeur-général* in French companies.[172] However, he enjoys certain privileges attached to employee status, especially under tax and social security regulations.[173] For comparative purposes, it can be mentioned that members of the managing board in the Netherlands are also considered employees.[174]

3. Relationship with the General Meeting

46. The question arises as to what influence controlling or significant shareholders are legally entitled to exercise on the board. In most jurisdictions, the board should act on its own authority, and therefore the general meeting is not entitled to give binding instructions to the board.[175] In systems with widely dispersed ownership, the rule will flow from the facts. However, in many continental European companies where ownership is concentrated the rule is widely admitted, although the factual practice often will be different. The dominant shareholder's influence mainly is based on the power of the general meeting to dismiss the directors at will. The shareholder—primarily the dominant shareholder—experiences no great difficulties in imposing his views on the company's board. There is a wide range of countervailing measures, few of which are very efficient: definition of the role of the board as a body acting in the interest of all shareholders,[176] appointment of independent directors,[177] and regulation of transactions in which the controlling shareholder may have a substantial interest.[178]

In the United Kingdom, the issue is controversial:[179] although the factual situation in large companies prevents shareholders from intervening in matters normally subject to board decision, the Companies Act and the stock exchange require an increasing number of major decisions to be submitted to the general meeting. The stock exchange listing conditions require that transactions take place at arm's length in case the listed company has a dominant shareholder.

---

[172] Art. 110 French Companies Act 1966.

[173] Guyon, supra n. 1, no. 341, 350; Cozian and Viandier, supra n. 2, no. 677, p. 244.

[174] See infra no. 88.

[175] See Netherlands: HR 21 January 1955 *NJ* (1959) 43 HB (*Forumbank*). For France: Cass. civ., 4 June 1946, S. 1947, I, 153; *JCP* (1947) II, 3518, note Bastian; Cass. com., 22 January 1991 *Revue pratique des sociétés* (1992) 61, note Legros.

[176] See supra no. 31 et seq.

[177] See infra no. 49 et seq.

[178] See infra no. 72.

[179] See Gower and Davies, supra n. 99, 184-7.

In the group of companies context, parent companies usually are not entitled by law to direct their subsidiary under threat of the parent's liability. In some states, this even entails the threat of criminal prosecutions against the subsidiary's directors for misappropriating the subsidiary's assets.[180] In the Netherlands, it is accepted that the charter may provide for the parent to give binding "injunctions" to the subsidiary.[181] A similar but even stronger "injunctive power" lies at the basis of the German "contractual group" covenant. In practice, the subsidiary will follow up the parent's directives. In case of a severe crisis, the dilemma for the subsidiary directors will become very poignant: acting in the interest of the parent, they will be liable and may be criminally prosecuted. In the other case, the parent will dismiss them. Examples of resistance by subsidiary directors are rare.

4. Managing and Supervising Directors

a. General

47. The concept of the unitary structure implies that all directors are considered to be in the same position: they direct the company and supervise its activities. In practice, however, not all directors are actively involved in managing the company. There is a gliding scale of functions of a board of directors varying mostly according to the size of the company, although tradition and historical factors may play an important role.

In smaller, especially family companies, most if not all members are in charge of effectively managing the company. A structure often found in smaller companies is that of the single managing director in charge of effective management, with the other board members acting in a more or less supervisory function. This single director is also often in charge of representation of the company, and may or may not sign with one of the company's officers.

In larger companies a distinction must be made between the functions of managing the company and that of its "direction", consisting mainly of the supervision of the management's activities, deciding on the company's policies, and major issues, such as major investment, divestments, etc. Three levels can be distinguished: effective management, supervision, and representation of the

---

[180] E.g., under the French section on *abus de biens sociaux* art. 425 and 437 French Companies Act 1966, and Cass. crim., 4 February 1985 *JCP* D. (1985) 478, note Ohl. Similarly in Belgian law: art. 492bis Criminal Code; providing the director has a personal interest in the transaction.

[181] See Timmermans, Christian W.A. and Levinus Timmerman 'The Law on Groups of Companies in the Netherlands' in: Wymeersch (ed.), supra n. 41, 231-77, at no. 34, 264; also at 248, 261.

company in relation to third parties.[182] Especially the latter element has received wide attention in the companies acts, also as a consequence of the EU "First Company Law Directive". This directive introduced a system of harmonized external representation aimed at protecting third parties.

The unitary structure does not imply that each of the directors should be involved in each of these duties: in practice, management and representation are often exercised by one and the same person(s), in larger companies by internal committees or their members. Directors not effectively involved in managing the company's business, it would seem, tend to assume a supervisory role. However, the exact nature of this supervisory role is not clearly described, and all decision making takes place with all directors involved. Major investments, long-term policy decisions, and also items involving strictly defined legal matters would normally be considered part of the board's functions, including "supervision".[183] Supervision of the managing directors, often members of the board, would in practice be included. The law does not distinguish between managing duties and supervisory functions: the rules on director's liability do not recognize this differentiation, and all directors are held to the same duties of care.[184]

One sometimes finds the—misleading—distinction between "active" and "passive" directors; a better differentiation would be "executive" and "non-executive" directors. In larger companies, the actual functioning of the board of directors may—depending on its composition—not be very different from the way the two-tier boards functions, except that in terms of legal duties and responsibilities the tasks have not been differentiated.[185]

b. What is Managing or Directing the Company?

48. In smaller companies, the board and its members may be directly involved in the actual running of the business of the company; in larger entities, however, the board's tasks are clearly differentiated from those of the actual management. This distinction is rarely expressed in the legal instruments, except for a series of matters that by law have expressly to be submitted to the board.

---

[182] For a comparative analysis, see 'EEC Report on the Simplification of Operating Regulations for Public Limited Companies in the European Union' no. 123 et. seq. (1996).

[183] For a list, see Guyon, supra n. 1, no 338, 345.

[184] See, however, the Australian case: *AWA Ltd v. Daniels (Deloitte Haskins and Sells)* (1992) 7 ACSR 759; 10 ACCL 933, recognizing the limited management functions of boards of large corporations, and the different roles of executives and non-executives; see Ford, Harold A.J. and Robert P. Austin *Principles of Corporations Law* at A § 7060 (Sydney 1995). The Hampel Report, supra n. 67, Rec. 5, states that "executive and non-executive directors should continue to have the same duties under the law".

[185] For this train of thought, cf. also the contributions of Bhagat and Black, and Hopt (Sec. B.IV.1.) in Ch. 4 of this volume.

Belgian law describes the role of the board as the "administration of the company", adding that the board has all powers to decide and represent the company. The definition of the functions of the management and of the board may flow from the charter. The U.K. Companies Act is totally silent as to the tasks of the director. The scope of his activities largely depends on the size of the firm and the nature of the business. French or Spanish law are not more explicit: "la Société anonyme est administrée par un conseil d'administration composé. . . ."[186] However, French law is ambiguous as it grants the same powers to the board and to the *PDG*, its chairman and CEO.[187] Danish law states that the board shall supervise the management of the company's affairs ". . . and arrange for an appropriate organization of the company's activities."[188]

Further information as to the role of the board can be read in the codes of conduct. According to the Cadbury Report: "Every company should be headed by an effective board which can both lead and control the business."[189]

The Viénot Report has defined the tasks of the board in four items:

- defining the firm's strategies;
- appointing the managers in charge of implementing the strategy;
- controlling the management; and
- ensuring the quality of disclosure to shareholders and to the markets, whether in the accounts or upon the occurrence of specific significant transactions.[190]

A similar description is found in one of the Belgian recommendations.[191] The board should not get involved in actual management except in cases of crisis, fundamental divergence of opinion between the shareholders, or manifest error by the management. The duties of the directors, therefore, are often stated in general terms of their duty of care, without detailing the precise scope of their task. In systems with a two-tier structure, the competencies of each of the bodies have been more clearly defined.[192]

---

[186] Art. 89 French Companies Act 1966; cf. art. 127 Spanish Corporation Act.

[187] Art. 98 and 113 French Companies Act 1966 describe their competencies in almost identical broad terms. The Viénot Report, supra n. 68, considered that this opaque situation allowed boards to better organize themselves. The Marini Report, supra n. 69, 42, agreed with this assessment.

[188] Art. 54 Danish Companies Act.

[189] Cadbury Report, supra no. 23, 20.

[190] See Viénot Report, supra n. 68, 6.

[191] See VBO, supra n. 81, no. 1: "defining strategies, approval of budgets for investments, research and development, appointment of the management and supervision of their activities." See also Santens Report, supra no. 26, 14.

[192] See infra no. 87 et seq.

c. The Independent or Non-Executive Directors

49. One of the central themes in the present governance debate concerns the designation of independent, non-executive, or outside directors. The subject is still very controversial in most continental European states, while the practice seems to be increasingly widespread following the example set in the United Kingdom. In most other continental states, the directors are elected by the majority of shareholders, but de facto appointed by the controlling or reference shareholders. The question of the appointment of independent directors may be moot, both in legal terms and in practice.[193] However, the degree of independence should in practice vary as some directors may take a more independent stand, especially in relation to the management. To act against the will of the major shareholder on fundamental policy issues would be very difficult.

The subject has a different meaning against the background of the existing governance systems. Independent directors are seen as a countervailing power against the dominant influence on the board, whether of the management or of the shareholders. Therefore, in states where the shareholders have limited impact on decision making, independent directors will be seen as a check on the overwhelming influence of the management. This is the case in the U.K. and in the U.S., where due to the wide distribution of share ownership, management was able to exercise a dominant influence. Hence, the appointment of independent directors is a favorite instrument for the institutional investors to bend the company's policies without assuming responsibility for the actual management decision.

In the systems where shareholders have an overwhelming influence, independent directors are seen as instrumental in balancing these shareholders' influence in favor of other shareholders, mainly small investors. Independence has therefore to be defined in different terms both in relation to the management and to the dominant shareholders. Also, independent directors in this hypothesis can only exercise "balancing" power, keeping in check the overwhelming influence of the dominant shareholder without being able to actively orient the firm's policy. The dominant shareholder will not easily surrender his influence—except on a de facto basis—especially as this would reduce the value of his shares. Therefore, it has been more difficult to impose independent directors on the continental European schemes than in a system with wide share ownership. The situation in Germany and in the Netherlands is different. In Germany, where boards are composed of representatives of either capital or labor, the issue of independent directors seems to be pointless. Under the Dutch system of co-

---

[193] In its May 1995 compliance report, the Cadbury Committee (see supra no. 23) found that almost all of the 100 largest U.K. companies had three or more independent directors.

determination, all directors are supposed to represent the interest of the company, and in that sense all are independent.[194]

50. There is also a question of semantics: in the United Kingdom, reference is made to non-executive directors as opposed to the "executives"; while in France, the *directeurs indépendants* are called to stand aloof from the influence of the management, the shareholders, and all interest groups. In some documents one finds reference to "outside" directors, or even "unrelated" directors.[195] There clearly are gradations of independence implied.

The issue of independence of directors presents itself in quite different terms if the directors are appointed by the board itself, e.g., if there are no significant shareholders, or if the election of directors is a matter which is only formally submitted to the shareholders. The issue of independent directors will come up in relation to the person who has nominated them, often the chairman of the board. As the chairman normally is not in a position to remove the director from office—which is the case with a dominant shareholder—this type of director might be supposed to enjoy a greater freedom of action.[196] Moreover, independence is not only a question of regulation and legal status. At the end of the day, it is a matter of the strength of the director, of his personal stamina and willpower.

In regulated sectors, especially in banks, securities firms, financial institutions, or insurance companies, the regulators have recommended the appointment of independent directors as an instrument for internalizing some of the control functions they considered necessary.[197]

51. The 1995 amendments to the Belgian Companies Act have introduced the intervention of an "independent director" as a general requirement with respect to the valuation of transactions implying a conflict of interest between the company and its controlling or significant shareholder. The rule is only applicable to transactions between stock exchange-listed companies and their controlling or significant shareholder: the ambit of the rule, therefore, clearly refers to the shareholding structure of Belgian listed companies.[198] In order to avoid financial substance being siphoned off to these shareholders, the rule provides that said intragroup transactions must be submitted to a procedure aimed at verifying whether the

---

[194] About the specific characteristics of the Dutch system, see infra no. 100.

[195] As required by the Canadian Code, mainly referring to whether directors should (as is required by French law: art. 95 French Companies Act 1966, see infra no. 76) or may hold shares in the company (as is recommended practice in Canada and Australia that directors should not be substantial shareholders of the company).

[196] See Cadbury, Adrian 'The Governance Debate' *Egon Zehnder International* (1997) 20.

[197] For a comparative and critical overview of the subject, see Baums, Theodor 'Should Banks Own Industrial Firms? Remarks From the German Perspective' *Revue de la banque— Bank- en Financiewezen* 56 (1992) 249-55. See further no. 90.

[198] See supra n. 79. This applies especially as directors can always be dismissed at will by the general meeting. It is in that sense that directors cannot be factually very independent.

transaction has taken place under objective conditions. Directors who are "independent vis-à-vis the transaction" will be designated "ad hoc" by the board and charged with drawing up a report analyzing the transaction and its conditions. "Independent" in this case means directors who have not previously been involved in the transaction. The report is then submitted to the board for decision. The conclusion of the report is published in the company's annual report. Although these directors cannot be considered "independent" in the usual sense, it means that their report will not be biased by their possible allegiance to the controlling shareholder: their reputation as a director might be at stake.[199] Similar procedures exist in French law, but do not call on "independent" directors.[200]

A more recent Belgian development relates to the consequences of the merger of French Compagnie de Suez with Lyonnaise des Eaux, and its effects on a Belgian sub-subsidiary.[201] The governance problem was solved by urging the French dominant shareholder to agree to a change of the charter of its Belgian sub-subsidiary, in order to ensure the appointment of a minority of independent directors and to a number of other safeguards for the company's independence. The changes were the result of negotiations with the Belgian government. It is striking that the presence of dominant shareholders has raised important governance issues, and in specific cases solutions have been sought by appointing persons who are more independent towards the dominant shareholder. Simultaneously, disclosure and expert valuation practices have been imposed to avoid controlling shareholders taking advantage of their position.[202] That these practices have been developed in Belgium is due to the presence of dominant shareholders in most listed companies.

52. The debate about the designation of independent directors is still in its infancy in many European states. Codes of conduct are increasingly recommending their appointment. Some larger companies seem to be following the recommendation and have publicly announced the appointment of independent directors. Their role in decision making, their internal position, and their actual practices, however, are still undefined or poorly documented. Also, there is some theoretical debate about their role and about their responsibilities. The following overview of the codes of conduct can help to situate the present debate in Europe, although the actual practice lags behind in most cases.

---

[199] See Vincke, supra n. 143, 19. For an extensive analysis of the new regulation, see Wymeersch, Eddy *De Belangenconflicten in vennootschappen* (Antwerpen 1996), Ernst, Philippe *Belangenconflicten in naamloze vennootschappen* (Antwerpen 1997).

[200] See art. 101 French Companies Act 1966.

[201] See supra no. 26 for the factual analysis.

[202] Similar expert valuation procedure had previously been imposed or recommended by the Belgian Banking Commission.

The *United Kingdom* has a long tradition of promoting the appointment of "non-executive directors" or "Neds"[203] The Cadbury Code on "Financial Aspects of Corporate Governance" strongly supports the idea and recommends that

"the board should include non-executive directors of sufficient calibre and number for their views to carry significant weight in the board's decisions."[204]

In addition, although there is no recommendation as to how many board members should be non-executive, a majority of the non-executives should be "independent from management and free from any business or other relationship which could materially interfere with the exercise of their independent judgment."[205] The majority of companies of all sizes have boards on which all or the majority of non-executive directors are independent. The larger the company, the more likely it is to have three or more independent non-executives on the board.[206] In the 100 largest U.K. companies, almost all had three non-executives; in the 100 to 250 bracket, 90% still met the requirements. Only very few had no non-executives, and a majority, especially smaller companies, had only one. Another survey measured the attitude of smaller companies towards the phenomenon: smaller companies considered two non-executives sufficient, while few agreed with the requirement that the majority of the board should be composed of non-executives.[207] The Hampel Committee maintained the recommendation and further reinforced it by requiring on the one hand that at least one-third of the board must be non-executive directors, while the majority of non-executive directors should be independent.[208]

In a system in which the majority of the board is composed of non-executive directors, one could argue that the system comes close to a two-tier system.[209] Some hold the view that in the U.K. an overwhelming number of listed companies in effect function under a system which comes quite close to the two-tier

---

[203] Non-executive directors would, under U.K. law be held to the same standards of care and diligence: Palmer and Schmitthoff, supra n. 104, § 8.050. For the Australian opinion, see supra n. 184 (*AWA* case).

[204] Point 1.3 of the Code of Best Practice, supra no. 23.

[205] Apart from their fees and shareholding, however. Point 2.2 of the Code, supra no. 23.

[206] See Compliance Report, supra n. 64, §17 and Table 4.

[207] In fact, only 6% of 523 companies outside the FTSE 350, see Arthur Andersen, supra n. 65, 11, reflecting an investigation with companies outside the FTSE 350 calling for reconsideration by the Hampel Committee, supra n. 67. This also reflects the City Group for Smaller Companies' opinion. Cf. Bhagat and Black (this volume Ch. 4) for U.S. evidence.

[208] Recommendations 8 and 11, Hampel (preliminary) Report, supra n. 67.

[209] This is still very much opposed in the U.K.: 21% of the respondents in the Arthur Andersen enquiry, supra n. 65, among non FTSE 350 listed companies agreed that the two-tier board should be included in the brief of the Hampel Committee, supra n. 67. The latter concluded that there is "overwhelming support in the U.K. for the unitary board".

board regime, without giving in to the symbolism of the two-tier system, considered akin to co-determination.

53. In *France*, the Rapport Viénot commented on the institution of the "independent director", defined as "the director who is free from any direct or indirect link to the company or to other companies of the group and can be considered to take part in board proceeding in a fully objective manner." Starting from the idea that the board incorporates the common interest of all shareholders, it concludes that it should be composed, in a balanced way, of representatives of the shareholders, of the "technostructure", and of independent directors. The independent directors were situated as against the inside director: the latter's influence, especially also the *PDG's*,[210] should remain limited. French law contains an express provision limiting the number of inside directors on the board.[211] As to the necessity to appoint directors independent from other influences such as the shareholders, the suppliers, or the clients, it was considered that many French companies already have numerous directors chosen exclusively for their technical expertise. The participation of independent directors corresponds to an expectation of the markets, and is likely to reinforce the quality of decision making. As to whether this practice should be generalized, the report considered that, within the framework of a balanced board composition as determined by the board, at least two independent directors should be appointed.[212]

This recommendation was not supported by the later Marini Report, which objected on several counts to the institution of independent directors, at least as a legal requirement. It also feared, for example, that the *PDG* would easily be able to influence the independent director, e.g., on his reappointment.[213] Also, it was mentioned that the function of independent directors was not clearly defined: Should they act as agents for the minority, or act in the interest of the company as different from its members?[214] The COB has supported the Viénot recommendation. It seems, however, that some prefer a more reserved attitude, especially pointing to the differences in the economic context[215] while underlining the risks of stakeholder decision making.

---

[210] See Marini Report, supra n. 69, 43.

[211] See art. 93 French Companies Act 1966, stating that only one-third of the board's members can be employees; the rules do not apply to employee representatives.

[212] Rapport Viénot, supra n. 68, 15.

[213] Marini Report, supra n. 69, 44.

[214] Questions raised by Le Cannu, Paul 'Légitimité du pouvoir et efficacité du contrôle dans les sociétés par actions' *Bulletin joly* (1995) 637.

[215] See Fleuriot, Pierre 'L'évolution du gouvernement d'entreprise en France et ses conséquences pour les sociétés cotées' *COB, Bulletin* no. 296 (November 1995) 34, attributing the need for independent directors to the predominance of inside directors on the boards of U.S. or U.K. companies.

Some French companies have reported the appointment of independent board members, e.g., Pechiney,[216] Paribas,[217] Usinor-Sacilor,[218] and Crédit Lyonnais.[219] A 1996 survey identified 93 out of 541 directors of CAC 40 companies as being independent. These are composed either of CEOs or directors of other companies that have no business links with the company, or of directors who have been selected for their competence (former CEOs or business leaders, former civil servants or high judges, representatives of employers organizations, of shareholder associations, or even university professors). It should be mentioned that no practicing lawyer was a member of a French CAC 40 board of directors.[220]

54. The first *Belgian* reports on corporate governance mentioned the issue of proposing relatively timid solutions. According to the Santens Report, the non-executive director should be opposed to the inside director, who as manager of the firm acts as its officer and normally as its employee. The latter type of director should not form the majority of the board. In addition, a sufficient number of "independent" directors—directors able to act objectively and independently and not linked to the management, the firm, nor to significant shareholders—should be added to the board to ensure that its majority is not dominated by the officers. These directors should act in board committees and render objective opinions.[221]

A more timid attitude was taken by the VBO code: in some cases, directors not linked to shareholders could make a significant contribution to deliberations in the board. All directors should decide in full independence.[222]

The Stock Exchange Recommendations[223] clearly distinguished "inside" or executive directors, and "outside directors". Among the latter it was considered

---

[216] Pechiney (3 to 4 members: Ridding, J. 'Rodier Set on Loosening Bonds of French Capitalism' *Financial Times* 15 November 1995, 21). For Paribas: Lévy-Lang, A. 'Corporate Governance et capitalisme français' *Centre d'information sur l'épargne et le Crédit* no. 183-4 (1995).

[217] Colette Neuville, founder of the Association des actionnaires minoritaires, a known shareholder activist organization, was called to the supervisory board of Paribas. Henisse, P. 'Tentatives diverses dans les entreprises françaises' *Les Échos* 30 January 1996.

[218] Its board of 18 members was composed of eight outsiders, four of whom were non-industrialists: Le Masson, Thomas 'Usinor Sacilor ouvre son conseil d'administration' *Les Échos* 5 October 1995.

[219] See the declaration of Mr. Peyrelevade, reportedly a "strong believer in corporate governance Anglo-Saxon style", who intended to reduce the *PDG*'s power and introduce independent directors, in Jack, Andrew 'Peyrelevade Exerts Anglo-Saxon Influence. The Crédit Lyonnais Chairman Plans Big Changes in Corporate Governance' *Financial Times* 3 October 1995.

[220] Conflicts of interests or adverse commercial impressions for their law offices are mentioned as a possible explanation.

[221] See Santens Report, supra no. 26, 15.

[222] Supra n. 81.

[223] Supra n. 82.

useful to appoint at least two "independent" board members. It is striking that the Stock Exchange Recommendations contain an elaborate definition of criteria for measuring independence. These criteria are based in part on the Toronto Stock Exchange Code, and are somewhat adapted to the Belgian factual situation. As the outside directors may continue to be linked to the company—e.g., as former executives or related to substantial shareholders—a more visible balancing of influences was pursued.

The definition of "independence of a director" might be reproduced here:

"A director is considered independent who

- is not part of management, nor of the management of any other related firm (subsidiaries, etc.); also an independent director should not have been in any management function during the last year preceding his appointment;
- has no family ties with one of the managing directors that could materially influence his independent judgment;
- does not take part in the board of directors nor in the management of one of the significant shareholders. He should not be elected on nomination of one of these shareholders, nor entertain any business, financial, or other relationship with said shareholders;
- is not a supplier of goods or services in a way that this may influence his judgment; the same applies to the partnership or to the associates of which the adviser or consultant is a member;
- is not engaged in any other relationship to the company in a way that, in the opinion of the board, may interfere with the independence of his judgment; the mere remuneration of the director nor his limited "ownership of shares will not be deemed to lead to said interference."

In Belgium, non-executive directors are frequently found. However, whether these would qualify as "independent" directors is difficult to determine.[224] Recently a certain number of companies[225] have formally appointed—and sometimes identified in their annual report—directors who are considered "independent", in the sense of not being related to the management or to the shareholders.

55. According to the *Dutch* scheme of the co-determined company, the members of the supervisory council are the bearers of the confidence of all parties involved and are selected on the basis of a delicate balancing, taking into account different types of expertise, including international, social, and financial.[226] In that sense they could be considered independent. Also, management board members may not be part of the supervisory board, and a corresponding

---

[224] E.g., former inside directors, directors of related companies, directors of holding companies, or significant shareholders.

[225] See the following Belgian companies: Société générale, Ackermans en Van Haaren, NPM.

[226] See Rinnooy Kan, Alexander H.G. 'Wijziging structuurregime niet aan de orde' in: Wildenberg, Ivo W. and F.J.M. Zwetsloot (eds.) *Naar een nieuwe machtsdeling in de Nederlandse vennootschap* 54 (Deventer 1994).

rule is extended to subsidiaries.[227] The Peters Report assumed that all directors should act independently of each other and in relation to stakeholders, and would not act as agents for the parties by whom they were nominated.[228] Not more than one former management member should be appointed to the supervisory board.[229] In smaller companies, the party appointing a director may also dismiss.[230] This rule does not apply to the supervisory board of the large co-determined boards. A reservation is made for representatives of the state, especially in formerly state-owned firms.[231] With respect to companies not subject to co-determination schemes, there is no information available as to the presence of independent directors. The Peters Report stressed the need to secure independence; members of the supervisory board do not act with a mandate for those who have nominated them, nor for any specific interest group. It recommended not appointing more than one former member of the management board to the supervisory board.[232]

5. Board's Size

56. In larger *SA*-type companies, the company should be directed by at least three members, acting as a board.[233] Some jurisdictions—e.g., U.K. law[234]—impose or allow two directors,[235] and there is a tendency to require only one, at least for wholly owned subsidiaries.[236] In private companies limited, the law may allow the appointment of one director only, sometimes for the entire period of the company's life span.

In most jurisdictions, the number of board members is left to the charter or to the general meeting. There is a widespread practice in several continental systems to constitute relatively large boards. Although the average board counts

---

[227] See Peters Report, supra n. 74, Recommendation 10, applicable to all relationships that could hamper the supervisory board member in independently exercising his functions.

[228] Recommendation 5, Peters Report, supra n. 74, adding that their action should be "independent from all partial interest involved in the firm".

[229] Peters Report, supra n. 74, Recommendation 4.

[230] Art. 143 NBW.

[231] Art. 161 (4) NBW.

[232] § 2.5 and 2.6 of the Peters Report, supra n. 74.

[233] See, e.g., Belgian law, art. 55 Belgian Companies Act; Danish law, art. 49 (1) Danish Companies Act; French law, art. 89 French Companies Act 1966 (3 to 12; or 15 if listed)

[234] At least for companies founded after 1929: s. 282 Companies Act 1985. But a company with one director and one secretary is also permissible. Swiss law also merely requires a president and a secretary: art. 712 (1) Swiss OR.

[235] E.g., art. 55 (1) Belgian Companies Act, in case the company has only two shareholders.

[236] See e.g. Guyon, supra n. 1, no. 350, 358; Rapport Marini, supra n. 69, 35. Spanish law requires at least one director: art. 123 Spanish Corporation Act.

around 12 to 14 members, some are much larger. The laws almost never contain limitations on the number of board seats, at least in the unitary board system. No limitations apply in Belgian, Danish, Dutch, English, Greek, Irish, Italian, Luxembourg, Spanish, and Swedish law. French law did contain an express limitation but has recently become more lax: before 1994, the number was restricted to 12, but it has now been increased to a maximum of 24, which can be extended to 30 in case of a merger.[237] The Marini Report proposed to abolish the rule and leave it to the charter.[238]

57. There is some empirical data with respect to board size and composition. In the *United Kingdom*, the average board size was 10.07, more than 50% of the boards being composed of 6 to 10 members, and 38% of more. In a more recent study,[239] the minimum and maximum were reported to be 4 and 16, with a mean of 9. The number of non-executive directors varied between 0 and 10, with a mean of 3.9.

The French and Belgian boards are reported to be quite large. According to a Korn/Ferry study, the average board amounted to 12.05, with 55% of the companies having boards with over 10 members.[240] For *Belgium*, the following detailed figures were found (Tables 12 and 13). Belgian holding companies obviously had larger boards than industrial companies.

It is interesting to note that board composition in Belgium is not necessarily related to the presence of several groups of minority shareholders; companies with a majority controlling shareholder (those with an * in Table 13) nevertheless have plethoric boards. This would indicate that board membership serves wider purposes than mere decision making, and constitutes the basis for networking and representation of smaller share owners, to name a few alternatives. There is a tendency to reduce the number of board seats.

In *France*, the average number of board members of the largest French companies, represented in the market index CAC 40, was 13 in 1996, down from

---

[237] Art. 89 French Companies Act as increased by L. 11 February 1994. It seems that certain mergers were hampered by the former limitations of the number of seats. Employee directors are not to be included in the maximum (art. 97-1 French Companies Act) However, the merger exemption applies only for three years. The same applies to non-listed companies: max. 12 members. Viandier and Cozian, supra n. 2, 228, report that some mergers are arranged for that purpose.

[238] Propositions of the Marini Report, supra n. 69, no. 29, p. 121.

[239] Ezzamel, Mahmoud and Robert Watson 'Executive Remuneration and Corporate Performance' in: Keasey, Kevin and Mike Wright (eds.) *Corporate Governance: Responsibilities, Risks and Remunerations* 77 (Chichester et al. 1997).

[240] Korn/Ferry International, supra n. 84, 10.

Table 12: Board Size in Belgian Listed Companies

	Portfolio Holding Companies	Share in %	Other Companies	Share in %	Total	Share in %
3-10 Members	59	63	34	89	93	70
11-16 Members	21	22	1	3	22	17
More Than 16	14	15	3	8	17	13
Total	94	100	38	100	132	100
Average	10.44		6.84		9.4	

Note: Portfolio holding companies as defined in Royal Decree No. 64 of November 10, 1967. In addition, 6 companies were in liquidation, and have not been included in the calculation. Moreover, the Central Bank as a listed company is subject to specific rules on board composition.
Source: Own research.

Table 13: The 14 Belgian Listed Companies with the Largest Boards, 1996

Company	Board Size	Company	Board Size
Gevaert	35	GBL	20
Bank BBL	27	Distrigaz	20
General Bank	26	Ibel	20
Tractebel*	26	Soc. Generale*	20
Cobepa*	25	Royale Belge.	19
Electrabel	23	Petrofina	19
Almanij	22	Kredietbank	19

Note: * indicates companies with a majority controlling shareholder.
Source: Own research.

the figures previously mentioned by Charkham.[241] The three largest board consisted of 23 to 22 members.[242]

58. The same Korn/Ferry source found that *southern European states* have smaller boards composed on average of only 8.98 members.[243] These figures are

[241] Charkham, Jonathan P. *Keeping Good Company. A Study of Corporate Governance in Five Countries* 132 (Oxford 1994), mentions that the average board counts between 11 and 19 members, with an exceptional 28 members in BSN.

[242] Relating to Danone (23), Axa-UAP (22), Suez-Lyonnaise des Eaux (22); Vuchot Ward Howell 'Gouvernement d'entreprise, 1997: Annee de l'élan' (Paris, September 1997).

[243] Korn/Ferry International, supra n. 84, 10.

not confirmed for *Italy*, where, according to Consob figures,[244] boards were composed on average of 12 members, of whom 1.3 are executives (Table 14).

Table 14: Board Size in Italian Companies

	1985	1990	1995
Number of Board Members	12.0	12.7	11.5
Number of Executives on Board	1.3	1.3	1.3

Sources: Consob and study by Bianchi, Bianco, and Enriques, supra n. 85.

In *Switzerland*, boards seem to be larger, and mainly vary according to the number of investors. In 75% of the widely owned firms, the board was composed of more than 10 members, 22 being the maximum. Companies with dominant shareholders or even a single shareholder had boards of at least eight members.[245]

The size of boards in Europe seems to correspond by and large to the usual or recommended size in the United States or Canada. A few points of reference: General Motors stated that its board has 14 members, it considers a board of 15 members to be optimal. The Toronto Stock Exchange declared to have received submissions for boards of between 10 and 16 directors. Canadian banks have boards exceeding 30 members.

The British, French, and Dutch codes of conduct contain no specific recommendations on this point.[246]

Belgium has obviously recommended a more activist stand: the stock exchange's benchmark recommended a board of between 7 and 12 members, two of whom should be "independent" directors.[247] The Banking and Finance Commission[248] added that the directors should be identified according to the shareholders which they are supposed to represent. Due to the presence of dominant shareholders and the distribution of influence in the company's board, directors often are elected on the basis of an agreement between shareholders whereby each is apportioned representative influence according to his ownership

---

[244] Sources: Consob and study by Bianchi, Bianco, and Enriques, supra n. 85.

[245] Spencer Stuart 'Enquête sur les conseils d'administration' 8 (by F. Dysli, June 1996).

[246] The former Belgian recommendations were along the same lines: between 7 and 12 in the Santens Report, supra no. 26, a limited number in order to encourage teamwork according to the VBO code, supra n. 81.

[247] Supra n. 82; this recommendation serves as a benchmark but has no legally binding value.

[248] Supra n. 82.

position. Therefore, directors are in practice often identified as representing one of the shareholders. This type of disclosure undoubtedly runs against the concepts of Belgian company law, according to which the board of directors and its members represent the company and should act in the interests of all shareholders. The identification of a director to one of the shareholders creates the misleading impression that these directors may lawfully defend their principal's interest in the company.

6. Limitations on the Number of Seats

59. It is widely accepted that effective board membership does not allow directors to occupy more than a handful of seats. Five to six directorships of major companies is often cited as a practical figure. The present situation, though quite diverse in the different continental European states, might point towards a need for expressly limiting the number of seats. The present situation could be documented as follows:

In the *Netherlands*,[249] the overall number of directors—members of the supervisory board—in listed and unlisted companies was 6,542. If one counts only the stock exchange-listed companies, exclusive of the listed investment funds, the concentration of seats seems relatively low: only 20 directors out of 593 sat on four or more boards of listed companies.

Table 15: Concentration of Supervisory Board Seats in Dutch Listed Companies

Mandates per Person	1	2	3	4+	Total
Number of Persons	472	69	32	20	593

Source: Peters Report, supra n. 74, 36.

However, these figures only relate to listed companies, and do not include similar functions in closely held companies. Results from another inquiry showed that half the supervisory board members held at least one other directorship.[250] The Peters Report recommended limiting the number of directorships—without stating a specific figure—so as to allow directors to effectively discharge their duties. It further considered that in order to safeguard directors' independ-

---

[249] Peters Report, supra n. 74, 36.

[250] Deloitte & Touche 'Corporate governance en het toezicht door de commissaris, Hoe houdt de Raad van Commissarissen greep op het bestuur van de onderneming?' (Rotterdam 1995).

ence of judgment, members of the supervisory board of the parent should not be directors of its subsidiaries.[251]

60. The *French* situation is specific in two respects. French law contains an express limitation with respect the number of boards on which directors may serve. The rule has recently become more flexible: before 1994 the number was restricted to 12, but it has now been increased to a maximum of 24.[252] In order to ensure effective board membership, one person may not occupy more than eight seats. The law contains some important escape routes: it applies only to companies located in France[253] and not to foreign companies; it does not apply to legal persons appointed as board members, nor to the representatives these may appoint; furthermore, subsidiaries are excluded from the calculation to a certain extent.[254]

The Viénot Report subscribed to the present state of the French law, but added among the main items on the directors' charter:

"the director should devote to the affairs of the company the time and the attention necessary. When he exercises functions as chairman or as director general, he should, in principle, not accept more than five directorships in French or foreign listed companies outside his group."[255]

The Marini Report was stricter, proposing on the one hand a formal tightening of the existing rules and forcing the consideration of the relative importance of the different functions. On the other hand, it advocated abolishing restrictions within the same group.

The second issue relates to the prevalence of cross ownership in French listed companies, leading to interlocking directorships. According to the Viénot Report, these cross holdings are transitional because of "the relative weakness of French capitalism". Also, it was pointed out that the French state itself lies at the root of many of these cross ownership structures by creating the *noyaux durs*, control devices based on reciprocal holdings that were aimed at keeping control after the mass privatizations. With the development of the markets, the increased foreign interest for French shares, and the surge of the institutional investors, these cross ownership links are expected to be unwound. Therefore, the Viénot Report recommended that boards should avoid the number of interlocking

---

[251] Peters Report, supra n. 74, Rec. 9 and 10. In addition to art. 160 NBW, according to which members of the supervisory board should not be employed by the company or its subsidiary. The Peters Report stated the principle in more general terms and extended it to any form of lack of independence, whether as a consequence of group relationships or of other relationships.

[252] Art. 89 French Companies Act as increased by L. 11 February 1994. The same applies to non-listed companies: max. 12 members.

[253] Art. 92 French Companies Act 1966.

[254] Provided the director is also a director of the direct parent.

[255] Supra n. 68, 23; the Marini Report, supra n. 69, 46, did not recommend action on this issue.

directorships being "excessive". In addition, it recommended the avoidance of interlocking directors sitting on each other's remuneration or audit committees.[256] 1997 figures relating to the CAC 40 companies indicated that concentration continued to be high: 14% of board members in that group sat on 34% of the board seats. Certain boards have issued policy statements limiting the number of seats to be held by their directors: Société générale aims at a maximum of five seats.

A typical French phenomenon is the prevalence of company directors originating from one of the top schools, among which the *Ecole Nationale de l'Administration* is the best known. In the early 1990s, 46% of the top business leaders of 200 large French firms had been educated at the *ENA* or at the *Ecole polytechnique*, or were related to official state functions (esp. *inspection des finances*), creating permeability between top business and top state functions.[257] In 1997, 45% of the CAC 40 companies were managed by Frenchmen originating from one of these *grands corps*.[258] According to a survey, there is a feeling among French directors that participation in several boards may create conflicts of interests, especially also because the companies are linked at the equity level.[259]

Most legal systems do not contain limitations on the number of seats directors may sit on. This is the case in *Belgian* law, where some anecdotal figures are available as to the highest concentration of board membership. For example, it has been reported that one person occupied 122[260] seats in Belgian firms, mostly smaller businesses. Leading businessmen regularly sit on 8 to 15 boards. In France, several board members hold seats in 7 to 8 boards in addition to several committee memberships.[261]

61. In some jurisdictions, sector regulations may limit board members' ability to occupy seats in other companies. This is the case in the banking field in Spain. In Belgium, an elaborate regulation limits the number of board seats a managing

---

[256] See the Viénot Report, supra n. 68, 17.

[257] See OECD 'Etudes Economiques de L'OCDE: France' 131 (Paris 1997), referring to Bauer, M. and B. Bertin-Mourot 'Comment les entreprises françaises et allemandes sélectionnent-elles leurs dirigeants?' (cadres CFDT, January 1993). In 1997, this figure was reduced to 40% for the CAC 40 companies: Vuchot Ward Howell, supra n. 242.

[258] Vuchot Ward Howell Study, supra n. 242. In Générale des Eaux, this proportion reached 100%. This report contains detailed information on this point.

[259] This was the opinion expressed by numerous French directors: see Jack, A. 'French directors under fire' *Financial Times* 13 October 1995. See also Goldstein, Andrea 'Privatisations et contrôle des entreprises en France' *Revue économique* 47 (1996) 1309, 1325.

[260] Hermans, R. and G. Muelenaer 'Groep Wauters: uitgebeend' *Trends* 16 May 1996, 35.

[261] Vuchot Ward Howell, supra n. 242, mentions five well-known names with between 6 and 8 seats of large CAC 40 companies.

director of a bank can occupy.[262] Bank managers should abstain from being involved in the management of other companies. Exceptions apply to the management of the bank's subsidiaries and to membership of boards of companies in which the bank holds shares, and in financial companies.[263] These restrictions do not apply to members of the supervisory board of the bank: here the rule is that these members are not restricted in taking up other board seats, except in companies in which the bank participates. In this case the prohibition applies unless the director is acting as the representative of a shareholder other than the bank.

7. Chairman of the Board

62. The question of whether the CEO should also be allowed to chair the board is the subject of intensive debate in several jurisdictions. Traditionally, in the unitary structure, the functions were not separated: the person effectively in charge of running the business was also chairing the board. Gradually, a further refinement of the two functions developed. The present state of affairs in systems with a one-tier board could be summarized as follows. Generally, there are no legal rules relating to this issue. It is governed by practice and is affected by codes of conduct or similar recommendations.

The Cadbury Committee considered that, in principle, the chair should be separate from that of the chief executive's office.[264] However, it did not recommend the full separation but stated that "there should be a clearly accepted division of responsibilities at the head of the company, which will ensure a balance of power and authority, such that no one individual has unfettered powers of decision. Where the chairman is also the chief executive, it is essential that there should be a strong and independent element on the board."[265] The Hampel Committee took a stronger stand, declaring that separation is preferred.[266] It added, however, that whether or not the two functions are separated,

---

[262] There is a relationship with the issue of banks' liability as a consequence of being involved in the management of other companies, see infra n. 372.

[263] See art. 27 Banking Act 22 March 1993. For further details, see the bank protocol, infra no. 91.

[264] The May 1995 Compliance Report of the Cadbury Committee (see supra n. 64) found that in 82 of the 500 largest U.K. companies, both functions were clearly separate.

[265] Code of Best Practice, 1.2; compare with the § 4.9 in the report itself. In the Compliance Report (Table 3) it was found that the vast majority of companies had split the two functions, with the few remaining other cases having introduced an independent director (about 14%;) only 5% did not have two non-executive directors.

[266] § 14, Hampel Committee, supra n. 67: "...and companies should justify a decision to combine the roles".

there should be a clearly identified "lead non-executive director."[267] This director is seen as an equilibrating factor in relation to the management.

The present situation in the *U.K.* was described in the Cadbury Compliance Report. It linked the issue of separation to the presence of "an independent element of non-executive directors", which could compensate for the non-separation of both functions. The separation was clearly more prevalent in the largest companies, with about 82% in the third largest class of listed companies that had separated the functions of chairman and CEO. Another 15% had an "independent element of NEDs". In the lowest third class, only 72% had intro-duced the separation, while an additional 5% had the said "independent element". The appointment of a separate chairman is favorably regarded by the market.[268] The smaller companies were less convinced about the usefulness of a separation of both functions: a survey among the 350 non-FTSE companies indicated that only 21% believed that the chairman should always be a non-executive.[269] From the Korn/Ferry study, it appears that in 1995 the chairman was a non-executive in 84% of the cases considered, while in 12% the two functions were inter-twined.[270]

63. The *French* situation is more complex as far as the unitary board is concerned. Normally, the board is chaired by its president, a board member elected by the board. However, the *Président* is also the highest officer[271] of the company, and by virtue of the law acts as its *directeur-général*. In his double capacity of *président directeur-general* (or *PDG*), he disposes of "the largest powers to act in all circumstances on behalf of the company."[272] As a conse-quence, the *PDG* has an extremely powerful position, leading to the "effacement" of the role of the board.[273] He represents the company in all its dealings with third parties: if he would exceed the limits of his powers or even act ultra vires, bona fide third parties would not have to worry and the company would nevertheless be bound. Although the position is that of a director elected by the board and not by the general meeting, the *PDG* is not subservient to the

---

[267] § 15, Hampel Report, supra n. 67.

[268] See the research by Dahya, J., A.A. Loonie, and D.M. Power 'The Case for Separating the Roles of Chairman and CEO. An Analysis of Stock Market and Accounting Data' (Univ. Dundee), cited in: Arthur Andersen, supra n. 65, showing abnormal positive returns the year after separation of the functions.

[269] Arthur Andersen, supra n. 65, 11.

[270] Korn/Ferry International, supra n. 84.

[271] Cozian and Viandier, supra n. 2, no. 677, p. 244, who write that he is a "salarié de l'entreprise".

[272] Art. 98 French Companies Act 1966 for the board and art. 113 (2) French Companies Act 1966 for the *PDG*. "Le président est investi des pouvoirs les plus étendus pour agir en toute circonstance au nom de la société".

[273] Also: Guyon, supra n. 1, 343, 351.

board—in fact, it is rather the opposite. Normally, the *PDG* picks his fellow board members and submits his choice to the dominant shareholders.

This strong personal leadership has been repeatedly criticized as leading to hollowing out the role of the board.[274] According to the Viénot Report, this could be counterbalanced by limiting the presence of executive directors on the board, which, as mentioned above, should not exceed one-third of the board's members.[275] It was pointed out that companies that would like to more clearly differentiate both functions should either organize the separation in their internal ordinance, or resort to the two-tier system, which, however, is rarely used in France. Moreover, taking into account its broadly defined role,[276] the board should examine and decide on transactions that are of real strategic impor tance.[277] For all these reasons, the Viénot Report found that the present state of affairs in France did not need to be reformed in this respect, but confirmed the idea that the president "works out and proposes the strategy of the company, which is decided upon by the board."[278] The Marini Report confirmed the opinions expressed in the Viénot committee, but proposed that companies could voluntarily split the two functions by appointing even within the unitary board a *directeur general* distinct from the chairman.[279]

Many French companies have maintained the structure of the CEO as chairman of the board. No precise data are available; according to Korn/Ferry, in the case of unitary boards, 45% would have voted for separate functions, while in 45% of the cases the CEO would also be chairman.[280] However, these figures do not differentiate between France and Belgium. Recently it was reported that an increasing number of French companies are changing to the two-tier structure: from 12.5% in 1995 to 20% in 1996 for the CAC 40 listed companies. This reflects a better division of competencies. It would also avoid the chairman of the supervisory board being involved in actual management of the company.[281]

---

[274] "Le rôle des autres membres du conseil ... est souvent discret" writes the OECD Report on France, supra n. 257, 127. For different viewpoints, see Cozian and Viandier, supra n. 2, no. 650, p. 237: Les administrateurs servent-ils à quelque chose?

[275] See supra no. 60.

[276] The board's role was defined as follows in the Viénot Report, supra n. 68, 6: "to define the enterprise's—and not the company's [EW's comment]—strategy, to appoint the managers in charge of the actual operation of the company within the defined strategy, to supervise the management and insure the quality of the information distributed to the shareholders and to the markets".

[277] Viénot Report, supra n. 68, 12.

[278] Viénot Report, supra n. 68, 12.

[279] Marini Report, supra n. 69, 35.

[280] Korn/Ferry International, supra n. 84, Table 6.

[281] No member of the supervisory board may take part in the *directoire*: art. 133 French Companies Act 1966.

64. The *Belgian* situation is somewhat ambiguous: boards are of a unitary type, and two-tier boards are not provided for by the law.[282] In smaller companies, the board structure would be as follows: one or several members, mostly also owners of a substantial number of shares, would be actively involved in daily management of the company. These would be called "delegated directors" and would normally also be entitled to represent the company in relation to third parties. In addition, a certain number of non-executive directors would be called to the board. The board would be chaired either by a senior managing director, by a representative of one of the principal shareholders, or more rarely by a third party.

In larger companies, the day-to-day management often will be delegated to a committee of "delegated directors". These may form a *comité de direction*,[283] to which the powers of the board can in part be delegated if the charter has so provided. This committee is chaired by the CEO who may also be chairing the board, although in some cases he will merely be a member of the board. The other members of this *comité* may be directors or officers. Some of these committee members will be named "delegated directors", and they will normally be entitled to represent the company. The organization of this management committee does not amount to making the Belgian board of the two-tier type, at least by law. Companies decide freely on the applicable regime, and one often finds either no management committee or the same person chairing the two bodies.

The following table gives an overview of the situation in 64 Belgian listed companies in which a *comité de direction* has been constituted. In the other companies, one or two of the directors had power to represent the company without forming a board. In a minority of companies, the board was chaired by a director who was not involved in the actual management of the company. In the other cases the situation was relatively complex and offered a wide spectrum, ranging from the chairman who actually presided at the management committee, to his participation in the committee as a member, to being a delegate of the company in charge of its day-to-day management. The latter is called "delegated director".[284] For comparative purposes, one could classify the delegated director among the cases in which the chairman is effectively involved in managing the company. Therefore, a distinction will be made between cases in which the chairman of the board actually takes no part in the management of the company

---

[282] Art. 54 Belgian Companies Act. The voluntary organization of a two-tier board would not be compatible to present company law. A two-tier regime is optional in the banking sector: see infra no. 91.

[283] The powers of this committee are defined in the charter of the company. It would be contrary to the law to delegate all powers.

[284] This is the *administrateur délégué* or *gedelegeerd bestuurder*, entitled to represent —mostly jointly with another director or officer—the company in regard to third parties.

and cases in which he does take part; in the latter subdivision, one should distinguish whether he also chairs the management committee or acts in another capacity (e.g., as delegate of the board).

Table 16: Belgian Listed Companies: Chairman—CEO, 1994

A.	Chairman of the Board Acting as			%
		1. Only Chairman of the Board	17	26.56
		2. Chairman of the Management Committee	8	12.50
		3. Chairman of the Management Committee and Delegated Board Member	1	1.56
		4. Member of the Management committee	11	17.19
		5. Member of the Management Committee and Delegated Board Member	12	18.75
		6. Delegated Board Member	15	23.44
		Total Sample Companies	64	100
B.	Chairman of the Management Committee Acting as			
		Member of the Board	6	

Source: Own research.

One could conclude that in a significant minority of Belgian listed companies (26.6%), the function of chairman is separated from daily management of the company. In 14% of the cases, the CEO was also chairing the board. In another 36% of the sample, the chairman of the board was a member of the management committee, while some other person, mostly another director, was heading the management committee. This would seem to indicate that the chairman became more actively involved in effective management.

In practice there is increasing pressure to clearly separate both functions: this was recommended in the Employers' Association Recommendation[285] and in the stock exchange benchmark. In the banking field, banking protocol has imposed a clear separation of functions, also to enable a smooth transition in case one of

[285] See VBO, supra n. 81, § 9: "La fonction du Président du conseil d'administration, avec son rôle de surveillance, et la fonction de Chef de l'exécutif, avec son rôle d'exécutif, sont des fonctions différentes qui sont normalement confiées à des personnes différentes."

both functions becomes vacant. The special regime applicable to credit institutions will be dealt with under the two-tier boards.[286]

Paragraph 8 of Chapter 8 of the *Swedish* Companies Act expressly states that the managing director of a larger company shall not be chairman of the board.[287] A similar rule has been introduced in the *Finnish* Act: here it is provided that a managing director may be the chairman of the board of directors if there is a supervisory board.[288] No comparable rule is found in *Danish* law.

65. In the other European states, there is no specific rule applicable to this issue. The practice as documented in the Korn/Ferry study[289] indicates that in southern European states, 57% of the companies analyzed had both functions separated, another 7% was considering the introduction of such a separation, while the remaining 36% was not considering such a change.

For France and Belgium, the aggregate figures were:
- separation: 45%;
- considering separation: 9%;
- not considering: 45%.

Although there is a tendency to introduce separate functions, there continues to be resistance in several of the European states.

8. Nationality of Board Members

66. As European companies are gradually becoming more international in terms of ownership, product markets covered, financing, and business culture, one could expect boards also to reflect these broader constituencies. Very few explicit rules exist.

Within the European Union, rules discriminating against nationals of other member states would be contrary to EU policy, and probably would be void.[290] Switzerland has maintained nationality requirements, providing that the majority of board members are Swiss nationals and have their place of residence within Switzerland.[291] Indirectly, similar rules may apply to EU companies; for

---

[286] See further infra no. 91.

[287] I.e., with more than one million kronor.

[288] Ch. 8 § 18 Finnish Companies Act.

[289] Korn/Ferry International, supra n. 84, 17.

[290] There may be doubt as to the validity of these rules. The Dutch Ministry of Justice would object to clauses excluding EU citizens: Sanders and Westbroek, supra n. 32, at 6.2. but there would be no objections to requiring supervisory board members to be residents of the Netherlands (see Sanders and Westbroek, at 7.2.).

[291] Art. 708 Swiss OR. However, the federal council could waive the requirement for Swiss-based holding companies whose activity essentially consists of holding participations abroad. Forstmoser et al. are critical of this provision, and indicate escape mechanisms: see Forstmoser, Mayer-Hayoz, and Nobel, supra n. 101, § 29, no. 288. Art. 708 (2) Swiss OR imposes the

example, an EU-based airline can maintain its status as an EU carrier and be entitled to the treaty-based freedoms of transport only on the condition that the majority of its shares are owned by EU nationals and that the majority of the board members are EU nationals.[292] Compulsory residence requirements are found in the Danish Companies Act: half of the members of the board of directors and the managers should reside in the EU. However, the minister may grant an exemption.[293]

Some figures are available with respect to the international composition of boards and the credentials of non-national board members. Apart from nationality, language skill and life experiences in foreign countries are reported to be relevant.[294] The Korn/Ferry study contained some figures for the EU states showing that in France and Belgium, two-thirds of the management board are foreign nationals.[295] These figures differ considerably for France: according to another source, only 14% of the CAC 40 board members were foreign nationals. This weak foreign presence contrasts with the estimated 30% foreign ownership of French listed shares.[296] The southern European companies surveyed by Korn/Ferry count 50% of foreign nationals on their boards, while only one-third are foreigners in British, northern European, and German companies. There is no marked difference between management board and supervisory board in this respect. Countries with the smallest domestic markets tend to have boards with the greatest international character. With respect to language skill, northern European companies score much higher than southern Europeans companies (89% v. 50%).

The study concluded that

> "the findings show a relative lack of international credentials among supervisory board directors when compared with those of the management boards reporting to them. This is offset, perhaps, by the greater presence of management of foreign nationals on supervisory boards. These differences may of course be a source of tension when companies face decisions concerning international strategy, although possibly providing a positive system of 'checks and balances'."[297]

---

appointment of at least one Swiss resident with power to represent the company. Less than 20% of Swiss firms have non-Swiss nationals on their boards. See Spencer Stuart, supra n. 245, 21.

[292] See art. 2 e) Council Regulation 2343/90 of 24 July 1990 on access for air carriers to scheduled intra-Community air service routes and on the sharing of passenger capacity between air carriers on scheduled air services between member states, *OJEC* L 217/8, 11.8.1990.

[293] Art. 52 (2) Danish Companies Act. The rule has been amended to extend the requirement to residence in other EU states. In the same sense: Ch. 8 §4 Finnish Companies Act; Ch. 8 § 4 Swedish Companies Act limits the same requirement to the managing director and "at least half the number of board members".

[294] See Korn/Ferry International, supra n. 84.

[295] Korn/Ferry International, supra n. 84.

[296] Vuchot Ward Howell study, supra n. 242.

[297] Korn/Ferry International, supra n. 84, 16.

Another study relating to Switzerland indicated that internationalization of board composition of major Swiss companies is less developed: 43% of the 100 largest Swiss firms that realize an average of 70% of their turnover outside Switzerland had no non-Swiss member on their board. As to the other companies, the following table illustrates that only 6 out of 100 had truly international boards. One could add that most of these non-Swiss members were German (43%), Dutch (14%), or American (14%), reflecting in many cases the foreign commercial involvement of these companies.[298]

Table 17: Non-Swiss Members on Swiss Companies' Boards

Number of Non-Swiss Members on Swiss Boards	0	1	2	3	9
Share in %	43%	34%	14%	3%	6%

Source: Egon Zehnder International, supra n. 298.

9. Duration of Contract

67. Board members usually are elected for a certain period of time ranging from three years (Italy), through four (Denmark, Finland, Portugal), five (Spain), or six (Belgium, France, Greece, Luxembourg).[299] However, in most jurisdictions their appointment may be revoked without notice or even indemnity. The harshness of this rule may be mitigated by stipulating an employment contract. The Cadbury Committee recommended a three-year term, and the Greenbury Committee recommended one year. According to these, reelection should not be automatic. In France, the law provides for a maximum of six years for the members of a board of directors.[300] Members of the *directoire* are better protected: their mandate lasts between two and six years, depending on the charter. They can be dismissed by the general meeting on proposition of the supervisory council. Damages will be due if the dismissal takes place without just cause.[301]

10. Age Limitation

68. A delicate issue is the existence of a compulsory retirement age. The issue is not of trivial importance in terms of governance, as former executives

---

[298] See Egon Zehnder International 'Nicht Schweizer in Schweizer Verwaltungsräten' (1997).

[299] See EEC Report, supra no. 28, at no. 128.

[300] Art. 90 French Companies Act 1966.

[301] Art. 121 French Companies Act 1966.

often become "non-executive" directors and are sometimes qualified as independent.

Once again French law is quite formal: the company's charter should provide for a retirement age, but there is no limitation on the charter's freedom. If the charter contains no provisions, at least two-thirds of the board should not be older than seventy.[302] The average age is 61.[303] Belgian law contains no retirement age for board members. However, in the banking field, retirement of the members of the management board usually is fixed at 65.[304] No similar rules apply to the supervisory board in banks. Some companies have rules on retirement in their charter.[305] Dutch law imposes supervisory board members an age limit of 72.[306] There is no information available as to the effective age classes of board members in other states.

11. Gender Composition

69. In contrast to state bodies, where regulations often impose a certain minimum presence of women in the governing bodies, there are no company law rules known on this issue.

Some figures are available with respect to the composition of boards according to gender: In the U.K. and in southern Europe, women represent 5% and 4% of all board members, in France they represent 3% (of whom 1% are employee representatives), and in Belgium about 5%. This figure is increased to 9% if one looks only at the supervisory boards. These percentages are not very different from the ones found in the northern European States: 6% in management and 5% in supervisory boards. In Switzerland, 17% of the boards had one female member.[307] In Germany, only 1% of the *Vorstand* and 5% of the *Aufsichtsrat* are women. Women usually have a non-executive function, explaining their low representation in the German *Vorstand*. From our own research, it appears that most women in the *Aufsichtsrat* are employee representatives.

---

[302] See art. 90-1 French Companies Act 1966. Also French directors are required to own shares in the company managed: art. 95 French Companies Act 1966.

[303] Vuchot Ward Howell study, supra n. 242, based on the 40 CAC 40 listed companies.

[304] See § 1 (e) of the protocol, BFC 'Annual Report 1991-1992' 254.

[305] See Cobepa 'Annual Report 1994' 18.

[306] See art. 142 (4) NBW for the details. The charter may provide for a lower figure.

[307] Spencer Stuart, supra n. 245. However, the overall figures would not be very different from the other European states.

12. Conflicts of Interest and Interlocking Directorships

70. The issue of conflicts of interest arises in two factual settings. On the one hand, there is the traditional personal conflict of interest between a director and the company. This would also include indirect conflicts with companies in which a director holds a significant personal interest.

The other issue relates to conflicts arising from the fact that directors are taking part in the boards of two companies, thus causing them to serve two masters without direct personal interests. This issue usually comes up in Europe within the framework of groups of companies where directors serve on the boards of related companies. But it also relates to directors of unrelated companies sitting on each other's boards, where they tend to reciprocate favorable treatment. It also arises outside the presence of common directors, i.e., when the general meeting of the subsidiary decides in favor of the parent company, disregarding the interests of the subsidiary.

71. Several pieces of legislation contain provisions on directors dealing with the company they have been appointed to. These provisions usually consist of disclosure rules,[308] rules imposing abstention from voting[309], or rules submitting the transaction to the approval of the shareholders[310] or to the supervisory board.[311]

French law is applicable to all transactions between a director and the company, whether he has a personal or merely an indirect interest. Some specifically dangerous transactions would be void without more safeguards: loans or guarantees.[312] Transactions with a company in which the director has an interest or of which he is director or manager would be subject to the conflicts procedure. According to French law, their content is disclosed as these contracts are submitted for approval to the general meeting of shareholders;[313] even then, the contract can be voided if it has been prejudicial to the company. The whole procedure is reported to be frequently used in the group context. According to French law, the general prohibition—except the rule on loans and guarantees— would be applicable to transactions between companies with common directors. However, transactions with significant shareholders, especially within the group,

---

[308] E.g., in Belgium, art. 60 Belgium Companies Act; in Italy, art. 2391 c.c.; art. 59 Luxembourg Companies Act.

[309] E.g., Italian law, art. 2391 c.c.; French law: art. 103 French Companies Act 1966; Belgian law has abolished this abstention, except for listed companies: see art. 60 Belgian Companies Act.

[310] See, e.g., in France, art. 101 French Companies Act 1966. Belgian and Italian law contains no reference to approval by the general meeting.

[311] In Italy, art. 2391 c.c.

[312] Art. 106 French Companies Act 1966.

[313] Art. 103 French Companies Act 1966.

would only be subject to the rule—or to other specific safeguards—to the extent that there is a common director, or that the director has a direct or indirect interest in the company or firm with which the contract is entered into. These rules do not establish a real group supervision instrument.[314]

Italian law[315] states a general rule on conflicts of interest, also applicable to transactions between companies with common directors. Violation leads to liability, but also to criminal sanctions.[316] The rule is reported to create difficult issues in the group context. As to the wider issue of conflicts of interest at the shareholder level, Italian law prohibits shareholders from voting on matters in which they have a conflicting interest either for themselves or for third parties.[317] There is controversy as to the effects of the rule.

72. The *Belgian* law belongs to the same tradition. It has paid detailed attention to the wider issue of group relationships, as many Belgian listed companies are dominated by major, often foreign shareholders. In Belgium, the mere fact of serving on the board of related companies would not be qualified as a conflict of interest triggering the special procedures aimed at safeguarding the financial interest of the company. These procedures would only be applicable if the interlocking director had a significant personal interest in one of the companies involved, e.g., by being a major shareholder. The transaction would then be considered an "indirect" conflict of interest.

With respect to transactions between a parent and a listed subsidiary, the Belgian law contains a different approach: it submits transactions between a listed subsidiary and its parent or other significant shareholder to a special procedure, calling for objective assessment of the transaction's conditions by "independent" directors and for general disclosure.[318] The board remains free as to the conditions of the transaction, but disclosure is supposed to be a sufficient deterrent. The rule was aimed at avoiding transactions whereby the parent would appropriate the assets of the subsidiary at undervalued prices. It does not cover corporate opportunities.[319]

73. According to *U.K.* law, directors, as common law trustees, may not contract with the company. The company charter may waive this general prohibition. The U.K. Companies Act contains on the one hand a number of specific prohibitions on transactions between the company and its directors, or its holding

---

[314] See Guyon, supra n. 1, no. 420, p. 430 and no. 620, p. 640.

[315] Art. 2391 c.c.; Jaeger and Denozza, supra n. 101, 388.

[316] Art. 2631 c.c.

[317] Art. 2373 c.c.; for further details, see Ernst, supra n. 199, and the numerous references.

[318] Art. 60 bis Belgian Companies Act. The directors are not considered independent in general, but only "as to the transaction involved."

[319] For further details, see Wymeersch, supra n. 199.

company. These rules relate to "substantial property transactions",[320] to transactions exceeding an amount stated in the charter,[321] or loans and guarantees.[322]
In addition, it restricts the freedom of charter provisions that are exempt from the
general principle by requiring that the directly or indirectly conflicting interest be
disclosed to the board, although not to the general meeting. It is unclear to what
extent this procedure is exempt from the application of the common law prohibition.[323] In general, however, other issues dealing with conflicting interests would
be dealt with under the general rules on fiduciary duties. The question of whether
the interest of the group can be taken into account is controversial.[324]

74. *Dutch* law, being based on a two-tier management structure, solves the
issue of conflicting interests by attributing the power to decide to the supervisory
board with respect to all issues of conflicting interests with managing board
members.[325] As the supervisory board has no power to decide on company
affairs, conflicts of interest normally do not arise at the supervisory board level.
In case even at that level a conflict would exist, the board could lawfully decide.
However, the general meeting could appoint other persons as empowered to
decide on conflict issues, also to avoid collusion between supervisory and
management boards.[326] Only personal interests of directors are taken into
account: these may be direct or indirect, but have to be personal. The mere
presence of an interlocking director would not trigger the application of the rule.
A specific rule forbids supervisory board members from sitting on the management board of a subsidiary.[327] There are no rules relating to conflicting interests
at the shareholder level.

The *Nordic states* have enacted more elaborate rules on conflicts of interest.
These relate both to conflicts at the level of the director and of the shareholder.
Swedish law forbids board members and managing directors "from dealing with
matters relating to agreements between [themselves] and the company", including matters in which they have an indirect interest.[328] The other members of the
board will then act. Swedish law further contains the general rule according to
which the board may not enter into contracts or take any other measure "likely to

---

[320] S. 320 Companies Act 1985.

[321] S. 322 A Companies Act 1985.

[322] S. 330 et seq. Companies Act 1985.

[323] See Palmer and Schmitthoff, supra n. 104, § 8.519, for the discussion.

[324] See Palmer and Schmitthoff, supra n. 104, § 8.508.

[325] Art. 146 and 256 NBW.

[326] Van der Heijden and Van der Grinten, supra n. 4, no. 278, 486.

[327] Art. 160 NBW.

[328] Ch. 8 § 10 Swedish Companies Act; cf. Ch. 8 § 10 Finnish Companies Act and art. 58
Danish Companies Act.

give an undue advantage to a shareholder or a third party to the detriment of the company or of the other shareholders."[329]

According to *German* law, conflicts of interest are an inherent ingredient of decision making at the supervisory board level. Labor representatives have duties not only to the company, but also to the employees of the firm, or to the union of which they often are employees. Representatives of shareholders often belong to the boards of other sometimes competing companies. It is the prevailing opinion that the existence of such conflicting interests does not disqualify a board member from taking part in the vote, but also does not exempt him from taking care of the interest of the firm.[330] Loans to members of the supervisory board are subject to additional safeguards.[331]

The conflicts of interest issue does not appear prominently in the codes of conduct that have been published: it seems to have been assumed that present law suffices to deal with the matter. The Cadbury Code does not mention the issue, while the Viénot recommendations refer to the legal position.[332]

The *Belgian* documents only obliquely touch the problem by obliging disclosure about the fact that directors represent significant shareholders, or by calling for disclosure of information about agreements between significant shareholders.[333] Conflicting interests at the level of the auditors is referred to in the Stock Exchange benchmark:[334] the board should ensure that the auditors have no—direct or indirect—relations with the company that might influence their judgment. Although a replica of the auditor's professional obligation of independence, this recommendation extends the rule to the board of directors.

The *Dutch* Peters Report is more elaborate on the issue of conflicting interests. For both the supervisory board and the managing board, the general principle is stated that "any appearance of mingling the firms' interests and those of the board members should be avoided."[335] At the level of the supervisory board, independence of judgment is the cornerstone of the Dutch co-determination system. Therefore, a board member should leave if his position would be "incompatible" with the company's interests. The chairman should, if necessary,

---

[329] Ch. 8 § 13 Swedish Companies Act; cf. Ch. 8 § 14 Finnish Companies Act, there seems to be no similar rule in Danish law.

[330] Lutter, Marcus and Gerd Krieger *Rechte und Pflichten des Aufsichtsrats* no. 304 et. seq. 3rd edn. (Freiburg 1993). For empirical evidence of interlocking directorships, cf. Prigge (this volume Ch. 12: Sec. B.I.2.).

[331] §115 AktG.

[332] Viénot Report, supra n. 68, stating that board members should declare any conflict of interest, even if only potential, and abstain from voting, 'Charte de l'administrateur', at p. 73.

[333] Banking and Finance Commission Recommendations, mentioned no. 26.

[334] Supra n. 82.

[335] § 13 and 35, Peters Report Recommendations, supra n. 74. "Good faith must not only be done, but must manifestly be seen to be done", write Gower and Davies, supra n. 99, 610.

play an "active and decisive role" in these cases.[336] The same principle is further detailed by forbidding board members to sit on boards of subsidiaries, to receive performance-related fees, and on other issues. Functional conflicts due to the mere presence on several boards are not expressly addressed.

It is striking that while most—although not all—legal systems have elaborate rules dealing with conflicts of interests at the level of the board, few have introduced any rules at the level of transactions with shareholders.

13. The Director as Shareholder

75. Should directors also be shareholders of the company on whose boards they serve? In order to align interests of directors and of shareholders, it has often been recommended that directors have a personal pecuniary interest in the welfare of the company they manage, either by holding a certain amount of equity, by being remunerated in part by way of options, or through other equity-linked instruments. However, the question may be different according to the status of the directors: non-executive directors may be less independent if their decisions have an impact on their personal financial situation.

76. The legal situation is quite different from state to state. Earlier in the century, company laws contained a requirement for directors to own a minimum number of shares. This was considered a guarantee for the dutiful performance of their tasks, and a pledge in case a liability claim would have arisen. These requirements have been abolished in most states. Some states maintained voluntary requirements, often leaving the decision to the charter.[337] The French law maintained a formal legal obligation for directors to be owners of the number of shares of the company, as determined by the charter, or of at least one share.[338] As a consequence, the Viénot Report recommended that directors be owners of a significant number of shares of the company, if necessary investing their remuneration to acquire shares.[339] Without forcing directors to own shares, Swedish law requires directors to notify their shareholding to the company for

---

[336] Peters Report, supra n. 74, § 2.8.

[337] See Swiss law, art. 707 (1) Swiss OR. However violation of the rule has no significant consequences, Forstmoser, Meier-Hayoz, and Nobel, supra n. 101, § 27, no. 2. The rule was abrogated in Belgian (former art. 57 Belgian Companies Act) and Italian law (art. 2387 c.c., abrogated L. 4 June 1985, n. 281). Some companies may still have the requirement in their charter.

[338] Art. 95 French Companies Act 1966. The directors who do not comply are considered *démissionnaire*.

[339] Viénot Report, supra n. 68, 22.

entry into the share register. Insider trading rules impose additional obligations.[340]

14. Remuneration and Remuneration Systems

77. The remuneration of the directors is a subject which has raised considerable debate, not only in the United Kingdom but increasingly in several continental states as well. In most member states little reliable information is available, and therefore empirical studies have to be read with great caution. It is one of the fields in which law and practice tend to diverge notably.

78. Several issues might be dealt with. A first series of issues relates to the legal rules applicable to the granting of remunerations, either for directors or for managing directors. Whether the restrictions on conflicts of interest apply calls for special attention. The second issue concerns the different types of remuneration, as practiced or as recommended by the conduct rules. Here, performance-linked remunerations will be looked at. Another item is the practice of determination of the remuneration by internal committees of the board. Disclosure of remuneration also deserves some attention. Finally, an attempt will be made to identify levels of remuneration in some European states.

79. It is part of the agency relationship between shareholders and directors that the latter's remuneration should be decided upon by the shareholders. This is the rule in most of the legal systems as far as the directors are concerned. It follows that no remuneration is due unless decided by the general meeting.[341]

a. The Legal Framework

French law contains strict rules on the remuneration of directors and managing directors. The principle is that the board of directors is entitled to a fixed annual sum determined by the general meeting.[342] This sum is divided among the directors on the board, taking into account their presence at the meeting (*jetons de présence*) or at specialized committees. It is usual to divide the lump sum, half per person, half per meeting. Additional remuneration may be granted to individual directors for specific assignments. However, these would be subject to the

---

[340] Ch. 8 § 5 Swedish Companies Act, Ch. 8 § 5 Finnish Companies Act; cf. art. 53 Danish Companies Act.

[341] For the French case law, see Le Cannu, Paul 'Les rémunérations des dirigeants de sociétés commerciales' *Association européenne pour le droit bancaire et financier* (1997) 253. On the Belgian law: Cass. 6 March 1980, Pas., 1980, I, 832.

[342] Art. 108 French Companies Act 1966; no remuneration is due except as decided by the general meeting.

disclosure and voting rules on conflicts of interest.[343] Executive directors, including the *PDG*, are paid by "contractual" arrangement as determined by the board. The same applies to the *directeurs généraux*.[344] The retirement and pension benefits are considered a complement to the remuneration itself. Direc- tors who pay themselves higher salaries than allowed by the general meeting risk criminal prosecution if the remuneration is proven to be excessive.[345] It has been mentioned that within groups of companies, directors are often employees of the parent, and receive no salary if they are appointed directors of a subsidiary.[346]

80. *Italian* law follows a comparable pattern: the directors' remuneration is fixed by charter or by the general meeting.[347] Directors have a right to be paid and to receive an amount which corresponds to their efforts: if not, their claim would be enforceable in court.[348] Directors may, however, also be employees and receive a salary: to that effect, they would have to be subordinates of the board.

Belgian law closely follows the French model, except that the Companies Act contains no provisions on the subject.[349] It is generally accepted that directors cannot fix their remuneration themselves. Often, the general meeting allows for an overall remuneration to be further implemented by the board. The same applies to *tantièmes* granted by the general meeting as part of the distribution of the profits. Service contracts with managing directors are matters that are acted upon by the board of directors. However, the rules on conflicts of interest may apply if entered into with someone who is already director. The same applies to early termination compensation.[350]

Swiss law states that directors are entitled to receive a just compensation. *Tantièmes* may be granted, but they are less attractive because they have to be paid out of taxed profits. Therefore, companies usually pay salaries. These can be decided upon by the general meeting, but they are usually granted by the board and are often composed in part of a fixed salary and in part of a performance-linked element. The board is expected to act thereby in a just and reasonable way (*angemessen*). Delegated members of the board are often paid on an employment basis.[351]

---

[343] Art. 109 French Companies Act 1966.

[344] Art. 110 and 115 French Companies Act 1966; French law limits the number of officers of the highest rank that a company can appoint: companies with a capital of less than 500,000 French francs can have only two directors-general.

[345] On the basis of the criminal provision on *abus de biens sociaux*, Art., L., See Picard-l'Amézec 'L'autorémunération du président du conseil d'administration' *Bulletin joly* (1988) 319.

[346] Le Cannu, supra n. 341, 253.

[347] Art. 2389 c.c.; Jaeger and Denozza, supra n. 101, 383.

[348] Jaeger and Denozza, supra n. 101, 383.

[349] Art. 53 Belgian Companies Act merely states that directors are "paid or unpaid" agents.

[350] See Wymeersch, supra n. 199, 38.

[351] Forstmoser, Meier-Hayoz, and Nobel, supra n. 101, § 28, no. 133.

In the *U.K.*, remuneration is only due if it has been provided for. Usually the charter will call for a shareholder vote, but if all members approve this would be considered equivalent. Extra remuneration due for extra services is subject to rules on conflict of interest: in these cases, the articles of incorporation must be followed. This type of remuneration is subject to equitable review, which is not the case for the remuneration decided by the general meeting.

The members of the supervisory board in the *Netherlands* are not under an employment contract. They receive a remuneration decided upon by the share-holders.[352] Here, too, this remuneration can be a flat fee, as seems to be usual, or a share in the profits (*tantième*).[353] Under Dutch law, the directors are usually bound to the company under an employment contract[354] by virtue of which they receive a "salary". This salary is determined by the general meeting.[355]

b. The Codes of Conduct

81. Several codes of conduct relating to corporate governance issues contain more or less elaborate recommendations with respect to remuneration issues.

By far the most developed document was drafted by the British "Study Group on Directors' Remuneration", set up in 1995 in response to public concern over directors' pay (*Greenbury Committee*). The committee issued a series of Best Practice Recommendations, dealing in great detail with issues like "the remuneration committee", "disclosure and approval provisions", "remuneration policy", and "service contracts".

The following are among the more substantive guidelines:
- remuneration packages should attract, retain, and motivate directors . . . but avoid paying more than is necessary;
- assessment of the relative position of the company and relative performance are to be taken into account;
- performance-related elements should be designed to align interests of directors and shareholders;
- service contracts should preferably be concluded for periods of one year or less;

---

[352] Art. 145 NBW; but it seems acceptable that the charter empowers the board to decide for itself, or that the remuneration is fixed by a third party, e.g., the holder of the preference shares; Van der Heijden and Van der Grinten, supra n. 4, no. 292, 514.

[353] See Sanders and Westbroek, supra n. 32, § 7.3, 167; Van der Heijden and Van der Grinten, supra n. 4, no. 292, 515, drawing attention to the conflicting interests at stake.

[354] See, e.g., Van der Heijden and Van der Grinten, supra n. 4, no. 245, 435; Van Schilfgaarde, supra n. 101, no. 45, p. 143.

[355] Art. 245 NBW, unless the charter provides otherwise. Unsalaried directors seem to be rare in the Netherlands.

- a robust line is to be taken on payment of compensation where performance has been unsatisfactory;
- the remuneration committee should make a yearly report to the shareholders on behalf of the board, giving information on share options for each director in accordance with the applicable accounting rules.

The *Hampel Committee's* report by and large followed the ideas set forth in the *Cadbury* Report. However, it warned about remunerating non-executive directors in shares of the company, as this is not considered "universal practice".[356]

82. The issue of directors' remuneration has attracted much less interest in the other states. There is some discussion about introducing performance-related fees and about disclosure of individual remunerations, with most states calling only for aggregate figures.

The *Viénot* Report[357] contained no recommendations with respect to remuneration; it only mentioned that remuneration committees should not be composed of directors sitting on each other's boards. However, one rarely sees any detailed information on remuneration: annual accounts only publish aggregate amounts, including salaries paid to former directors, etc. The remunerations paid to French CEOs are not disclosed on an individual basis. From time to time, however, figures published in the press create a public outcry.[358]

The *Belgian* codes[359] are less discreet: the principle of performance-related remuneration is put forward as a rule of good governance for managing directors, not for non-executives. Remunerations are to be fixed by a remuneration committee, if such a committee has been instituted. The rules by which the remuneration has been calculated should be set forth in the annual report without disclosing individual fees or advantages. The Banking and Finance Commission calls for similar aggregate disclosure, but includes all remunerations (including options, perks, loans to directors, etc.).

Finally the Dutch *Peters* Report stated that the supervisory board members' remuneration should not be a function of the results of the company. Therefore, it is considered objectionable to grant options or to pay fees for separate functions (e.g., counseling). The annual account should disclose the existence of any business relationship between said member and the company in its notes. Any other remuneration or advantage is considered objectionable.[360] Ownership of

---

[356] § 23 Hampel Committee, supra n. 67. But caution was urged "in the use of inter-company comparisons and remuneration surveys". Disclosure of individual directors' remuneration, including for foreign nationals, was recommended (§§ 29 and 30).

[357] Supra n. 68.

[358] For further details, see Cozian and Viandier, supra n. 2, 242. The French Cour de Cassation has decided that publication of salary figures is not a violation of the director's privacy; Cass., 28 May 1991, D., 1991, 213, note Kaiser, *JCP* (1992) II, 21845, note F. Ringel.

[359] Supra n. 82.

[360] Peters Report, supra n. 74, § 2.13 and 14.

shares and options on shares should be disclosed on an aggregate basis. Management board members receive a salary: here the annual report should disclose, on an aggregate basis, salaries paid to present and former members.[361]

Disclosure of directors' remuneration has been rendered mandatory by the Fourth Company Law Directive: ". . . emoluments . . . granted to the members of the administration, managerial and supervising bodies . . . and any commitments arising or entered into in respect of retirement pensions for former members of those bodies, with an indication of the total for each category."[362]

This disclosure only gives information as to the overall management charge, but gives no insight as to the remuneration paid to the directors effectively in charge. Therefore, in all EU states—the U.K. excepted— the annual reports give no useful information as to the management remuneration. Among the many factors contributing to the opaqueness of the figure, one could point to the pooling of executive and non-executive directors, of pensions paid to former directors, and of remuneration of officers; the inclusion—or non-inclusion—of remuneration from subsidiaries; and the inclusion or exclusion of fringe benefits.

c. Levels of Remuneration

83. In some European states there is some information available as to remunerations actually paid.

In France, non-executive directors are paid per meeting attended. An annual average 137,000 French francs (about $22,000) with a maximum of 385,000 francs (about $62,500) and a minimum of nil has been noted in French exchange-listed companies.[363] For the U.K., a figure of 350,000 French francs ($57,000) was cited in a French source.[364] In Germany, members of the supervising council usually obtain 34,400 marks (figures from 1991).[365] Labor representatives are obliged to pay any fee above 6,000 marks to the union they belong to. Fees are considered too low for effective exercise of the supervisory functions. In Belgium, some research shows an average remuneration of about 2.820 million Belgian francs ($95,145), with a low of 1.686 million francs ($57,250) and a high of 4.045 million francs ($137,351).[366] There is some evidence that pay was

---

[361] Peters Report, supra n. 74, § 4.4.

[362] Art. 43 (1), (12) Fourth Directive, supra n. 30.

[363] Vuchot Ward Howell, supra n. 242, 27. Based on average figures, i.e., total remuneration divided by the number of directors.

[364] Vuchot Ward Howell, supra n. 242, 26.

[365] Schmid, Frank A. 'Vorstandsbezüge, Aufsichtsratsvergütung und Aktionärsstruktur' *Zeitschrift für Betriebswirtschaft* 67 (1997) 67-83, 74.

[366] Only Bel-20 companies; figures 1995.

related to turnover more than to any other variable.[367] In Switzerland, a salary of between 50,000 and 1,000,000 Swiss francs is mentioned ($34,000 to $67,000).[368]

These figures must be read with great caution. Older figures indicate that overall remuneration—after taxes—of company leaders in general is substantially lower than American salaries, the latter being heavily influenced by stock options and similar techniques of participation. The considerable impact of social security contributions and the absence of performance-related participation in several European states also explain the difference in after-tax remuneration. Average remuneration of directors or CEOs was more than double that of remuneration paid to officers.

Table 18: Salaries: An International Comparison

	Salary + Bonus	Social Charges	Addit. Salary	Perks	Partici- pation	Total	Index 100	After Tax	Index 100
Netherlands	234	5	36	21	0	296	71	103	69
Sweden	194	126	0	16	0	336	80.6	104	69
Germany	292	10	42	21	0	365	87.5	152	101
Spain	284	6	45	45	0	380	91.1	160	107
Belgium	251	84	37	26	0	398	95.4	101	67
U.K.	221	21	74	21	63	400	95.9	140	93
Italy	283	75	32	16	16	422	101	157	105
France	279	88	5	11	66	449	108	147	98
Japan	250	5	48	69	0	372	89.2	137	91
Canada	281	5	42	16	64	408	97.8	163	109
Switzerland	329	21	48	11	16	425	102	172	115
U.S.	445	5	48	16	233	747	179	260	173
Average	279	38	38	24	38	417	100	150	100

Source: Charlety, Patricia 'Les développements récents de la littérature' in: Revue d'économie financière *Corporate Governance, Le gouvernement d'entreprise Revue d'économie financière* (Special Edition, Winter 1994, no. 31) 47, based on 1990 Hay and Towers-Perin data.

84. The Korn/Ferry investigation indicates that granting stock options is not the usual practice in Europe, the U.K. excepted. However, as no figures are disclosed, these statistics may underestimate the frequency of use of these

---

[367] Van der Elst, Christoph 'De remuneratie van de Raad van Bestuur van de Bel-20 vennootschappen' (Working Paper, Ghent 1997).

[368] Vuchot Ward Howell, supra n. 242, 26.

remuneration techniques. In the U.K., 61% of the executive board members received stock options, compared with 11% in Germany, 28% in northern European states, 15% in France and Belgium, and 33% in the other European states. Non-executive members were less well served: 12% in the U.K. and 22% in northern Europe, but 0% in southern Europe.[369] The latter figure is confirmed by another investigation: in Switzerland, only 2 out of 100 companies granted a share in the results, while none had a stock option plan.[370]

15. Non-Shareholder Interests in the Unitary Board

85. Compulsory representation of non-shareholder interests is rather rare in the unitary board. There is no usual practice of electing creditors or other stakeholders to the board. Employee representation will be dealt with separately.[371] However, in cases of reorganizations, creditors may insist on having some supervision rights with respect to the functioning of the company. At least in the French, Belgian, and Luxembourg legal systems, banks are reluctant to be formally a part of the board as this may increase their risk of liability in case of a later collapse of the company. Indeed, banks that intervene too strongly in the affairs of a company may be qualified as "de facto directors" and be liable for careless management.[372]

In Denmark, the charter may mandate that one or more board members will be nominated by the state or by others. Similar rules apply in Swedish and Finnish law.[373] It is unlawful to have non-shareholder interests represented on a Swiss board.[374]

A different though related question considers whether directors may represent specific groups of shareholders, either majority, significant, or minority shareholders. The prevailing opinion is that by law, the directors as a whole represent the company and all its shareholders rather than one specific shareholder. In directing the company, they should act in the interest of all shareholders. The usual expression is that directors should defend the interests of the company. The

---

[369] Korn/Ferry International, supra n. 84, 34.

[370] Spencer Stuart study, supra n. 245, 15.

[371] Infra no. 95 et seq.

[372] For an overview of this subject, see Simont, Lucien and André Bruyneel *La responsabilité extra-contractuelle du donneur de crédit en droit comparé* (Paris 1984); Travaux de l'Association H. Capitant vol. XXXV *La responsabilité du banquier. Aspects nouveaux* (Paris 1986); Wymeersch, Eddy 'Bank Liability for Improper Credit Decisions, Experience in Continental Europe' in: Cranston, Ross (ed.) *Banks, Liability and Risk* 179 2nd edn. (London 1995).

[373] Art. 49 (2) Danish Companies Act; Ch. 8 § 1 Swedish Companies Act; Ch. 8 § 4 Finnish Companies Act.

[374] See Forstmoser, Meier-Hayoz, and Nobel, supra n. 101, § 27, no. 292.

opinion is sometimes seen as a further illustration of the equal treatment rule.[375] Also, directors have no specific obligation to any specific shareholder and do not escape liability on the basis of having acted on the instruction of one shareholder.

The principle that a director does not stand for the interests of a specific shareholder has traditionally been formulated in Belgian[376] and French law, where de facto directors often are appointed by the mere will of the majority shareholder. The Swiss law expresses the same idea by stating that the "board members and the management have to treat the shareholders under similar conditions on an equal basis."[377]

86. A different issue is whether minority shareholders may be especially represented on the board. Several legal systems allow such representation, e.g., Danish law allows the charter to stipulate that board members may be nominated by third parties.[378] It is admitted that in Belgian law such minority representation would be lawful.[379] But even these directors are supposed to take the interest of the company as a whole to heart, not that of their principal.

Several codes of conduct and prominent writers are adamant on this point: "[W]hatever its composition or the origin of its members, the board represents collectively and jointly the shareholders. . . . Directors are solely there to serve the company and they should neither be selected to represent a particular interest nor, once appointed, should they seek to do so."[380]

The Viénot Report is equally clear: "[W]hatever an individual member's qualities and specific competencies, each board member should consider himself as the representative of all the shareholders and should act and take up personal responsibility accordingly."[381]

The Dutch code also stresses that directors—members of the supervising board—must decide and act without mandate from those by whom they were nominated for election to the board. They should act "independently from the partial interests that are present in the firm's decision making."[382] This rule is particularly important as it illustrates the Dutch concept of co-determination that is based not on representation but on objective decision making and due balancing of interests.

---

[375] In that sense but with further refinements, see Forstmoser, Meier-Hayoz, and Nobel, supra n. 101, § 39, no. 11 et seq.

[376] E.g., Banking Commission 'Annual Report 1967' 169; 'Annual Report 1974-1975' 166.

[377] See art. 707 (2) Swiss OR; for commentary, see Forstmoser, Meier-Hayoz and Nobel, supra n. 101, § 30, no. 18 and § 39, no. 17 et seq.

[378] Art. 49 (2) Danish Companies Act.

[379] See Heenen, supra n. 141, and Van Gerven, supra n. 137.

[380] Cadbury, Adrian 'The U.K. Code of Best Practice and Issues Common to Other Codes on Corporate Governance' *Revue de la banque—Bank- en Financiewezen* 61 (1997) 479.

[381] Viénot Report, supra n. 68, 14.

[382] Recommendation 5 of the Peters Code, supra n. 74.

The Belgian approach is different and heavily tributary to the situation by which directors de facto represent specific shareholders. A limited but significant example could be found in the 1989 takeover regulation. The members of the target's board are obliged to give their opinion on the bid. However, directors who represent certain shareholders—necessarily on a de facto basis—should state whether their "principals" will tender their shares.[383] This line of reasoning appears again in the Companies Act's section on conflicts of interests; here, transactions with shareholders who have a dominant or significant influence on the appointment of directors are subject to stricter disclosure and reporting requirements.[384] A further step in this identification technique was set in the Banking and Finance Commission Recommendations on Corporate Governance. According to these, listed companies should indicate "which directors de facto represent the dominant shareholder."[385]

II. Two-Tier Boards Without Employee Representation

87. In several jurisdictions the companies are headed by a two-tier board, mostly called a "supervisory" board and a "managing" board. In some jurisdictions this two-tier system is optional; in others it is compulsory. Membership of employees—here called "co-determination"—is usually placed at the level of the supervisory board, although in some legal systems it has been introduced in the managing board.

Systems with an optional two-tier board system that is not necessarily linked to co-determination are found in Finland, in France, and with smaller firms in the Netherlands;[386] however, the two-tier structure seems to be used infrequently in some of these jurisdictions.[387]

Two-tier boards without worker representation is the compulsory regime for Austrian and Portuguese companies. This structure is also found in Italy, where the managing board is headed by a *collegio sindacale* whose powers and influence, however, are considerably less than the traditional supervisory board.

There is some confusion in statistical data classifying Belgium among the systems with a two-tier board: this feature is a consequence of banking law, and

---

[383] Art. 15 § 2 al. 3 *R.D.* 8 November 1989.

[384] Art. 60 bis Belgian Companies Act, supra no. 72

[385] Point 1,1 of the recommendation of the Banking and Finance Commission, mentioned no. 26.

[386] See art. 140 e.d. NBW. It applies only to the large *NV*: art. 153 and 158 NBW.

[387] According to some sources, in France, where the regime was introduced in 1966, not more than 1% of the companies have introduced a *directoire*. Larger companies are making a more intensive use of the two-tier system.

therefore is legally restricted to credit institutions. No other companies may technically introduce a two-tier board.

88. In the *Netherlands*, the two-tier structure is compulsory for companies—both *NV* and *BV*—subject to the co-determination regime, analyzed infra. If this is not applicable these companies may introduce a two-tier board, but they must provide for it in their charter. Some large companies do not have a two-tier board because they are exempt from the co-determination rules. Companies that have opted for a two-tier board determine the number of members of the supervisory board in their charter: one person could suffice, but their number may be fixed by the general meeting.

The Dutch supervisory board is in charge of supervising the management and "the general functioning of the affairs of the company and of the enterprise that it carries on." This rule was introduced to underline the board's duties towards the firm's employees to act as a "diligent employer", even in the absence of broader co-determination.[388] The board is seen not as the representative of the shareholders, but as a body in charge of the overriding interests of the "enterprise".

The functions of the board are determined by the charter. Usually the board supervises the management on behalf of the shareholders: this is the historical task of the supervisory board. It further advises the management and is involved in major decision making. By law, few management decisions are subject to the board's approval. In the absence of approval, management would be acting without authority; however, this defect could not be invoked against third parties. The approval by the board does not include a power of substitution: the board can merely approve or disapprove. Often the charter will confer decision powers—e.g., if the directors do not agree among themselves—or may provide for action on recourse of a management board member. The board will represent the company in case of conflict of interest between the company and one of its managers.[389] If provided for, it may also appoint or dismiss the management.[390] The board approves the annual accounts, but is not in charge of supervision of the financial management or of the accounting by the company.[391] According to Dutch law, these are the auditor's duties; he is appointed by the general meeting.[392]

---

[388] "Een goed werkgever" ("a good employer"); Van der Heijden and Van der Grinten, supra n. 4, no. 273, 475.

[389] Art. 133 and art. 134 NBW.

[390] Art. 146 NBW.

[391] Van der Heijden and Van der Grinten, supra n. 4, no. 274, 477.

[392] Art. 393 (2) NBW. If the general meeting does not act, the supervisory board will provide for his appointment; if not, it is the management board's responsibility.

In principle, the supervisory board members are appointed by the general meeting.[393] The law contains two restrictions. On the one hand, the charter can determine that not more than one-third of the members of the supervisory board will be appointed by another body than the general meeting;[394] this privilege is often attributed to the state or local communities, but may also entitle bondholders, banks, holders of insurance policies, or even employees to exercise influence on the board.[395] More important is the right to limit the election to candidates nominated by another body: this might be a foundation or a body holding a specific class of shares. It is one of the most-used anti-takeover instruments.

In small Dutch companies, supervisory board members may be elected without time limitation. In larger companies a four-year limitation applies.[396] Dutch law provides an express age limit for supervisory board members.[397] Upon appointment of a supervisory board member, the law requires that certain information be disclosed, such as his professional occupation, his age, the number of shares he owns in the company, and the other functions he occupies or has occupied in other companies. His other mandates on supervisory boards in other companies should also be mentioned.

Managing directors are appointed—or dismissed—by the general meeting.[398] The charter can provide for them to be appointed by the supervisory board. Directors are usually qualified as "employees" of the companies, indicating that their relationship is a contractual one. The contract will therefore determine the duration and salary. Dismissal will also be governed by labor law: rules on indemnities, etc., will apply. However, the managing director can always be removed without notice.

89. In *France,* too, a two-tier system may be introduced by charter provision in the public company limited by shares (*SA*) The members of the management board, called *directoire*, are appointed by the supervisory board. The number of its members varies from one (in companies with less than 1 million French francs

---

[393] Art. 143 NBW; see Sanders and Westbroek, supra n. 32, 7.2, and the critique at p. 165. The stock exchange introduced a requirement in its listing regulation that the foundation holding the preference shares that form the basis for the nomination should not, by virtue of having a majority of the same directors, have a board composition identical to the company's board.

[394] Art. 143 NBW.

[395] However, the rule does not apply to companies subject to the Dutch co-determination regime. Nomination may be exercised by the joint committee of the members of the supervisory board and the management board, provided the latter are not in a majority, Van der Heijden and Van der Grinten, supra n. 4, no. 290, 511.

[396] See art. 133 NBW, Van der Heijden and Van der Grinten, supra n. 4, no. 250, 249.

[397] Put at 72 years: art. 142 (a) NBW.

[398] Art. 132 NBW. But the charter may provide for compulsory presentation rights, e.g., by holders of preference shares: art. 133 NBW and Van der Heijden and Van der Grinten, supra n. 4, no. 250, 249. This presentation cannot be overruled by the general meeting except with a two-thirds majority.

in capital) to five, or seven if the company is listed.[399] The president also is appointed by the supervisory board. Unless otherwise mentioned in the charter, members are appointed for a four-year term. Members of the supervisory council cannot be members of the *directoire*. Also, the same person may not be part of the *directoire* of more than two companies.[400] The supervisory council is appointed by the shareholders and is in charge of permanently supervising the company. Certain transactions (real estate, guarantees, transfer of stakes in other companies) must be authorized by the supervisory council. It is composed of 3 to 12 members, to be increased to 24 in case of a merger. Members are appointed for six years and may not sit on more than eight supervisory boards.

90. *Austria* has maintained the former German approach dating back to the 1937 German law. A two-tier board is compulsory, with at least one person at the management level (*Vorstand*) acting on his own responsibility.[401] At the supervisory level, there should be at least three members. Members are elected by the general meeting, but one-third may be appointed—or revoked—by specific shareholders, such as the holders of a class of shares. The number varies according to the size of the capital.[402] Members cannot act in more than ten supervisory boards, or sit on more than twenty if acting as a representative of public bodies or of banks. Members may not be revoked except by a three-fourths majority.

91. *Belgian* law recognizes the two-tier board, but only in the field of credit institutions. In Belgium, banks may—in practice, they are urged to—introduce a two-tier board.[403] In major Belgian banks, the board of directors acts as a supervisory board; it deals with general policy issues and is in charge of oversight of the management board's actual banking activities. The rules governing the composition of the board are laid down in a "protocol" entered into by the banking supervisor, the bank, and its principal shareholders, and it is aimed at ensuring the "autonomy of the bank". This arrangement serves to isolate the bank's actual management from the influence of the controlling shareholders with the aim of ensuring that the bank is run in its own interest, rather than that of its controlling or reference shareholders.[404] These rules were developed over time and laid down in several successive protocols, one of whose covenants deals with the composition of the board. According to the 1973 protocol,[405] the bank's

---

[399] Art. 129 French Companies Act 1966.

[400] See art. 127 French Companies Act 1966, for other restrictions.

[401] § 70 ÖAktG.

[402] § 86 (1) ÖAktG: up to 7 million schilling capital, 7 members; between 5 and 50 million, 12 members; and above 50 million, 20 members.

[403] Art. 26 Banking Act 22 March 1993.

[404] About the subject, see Le Brun, Jean *La protection de l'épargne public et la commission bancaire* 104-17 (Brussels 1979) and De Mûelenaere, Philippe 'L'autonomie de la fonction bancaire' *Revue de la banque—Bank- en Financiewezen* 56 (1992) 545.

[405] For the text, see Banking Commission 'Annual Report 1973-1974' 238.

board should show a diversified and equilibrated composition. A sufficient but not dominant representation of the important shareholders must be provided for. On the basis of this philosophy, the banks' boards were in part composed of persons who, without representing specific interests, came very close to the idea of the independent director.

This approach was scaled down in the early 1990s when shareholders more clearly took over the reins of power. The objective is no longer to reduce the influence of the dominant shareholder nor to avoid the bank functioning in the exclusive interest of this shareholder;[406] instead, the rule is aimed at excluding the undesirable shareholder.[407] The board serves to establish a "positive and constructive" dialogue with the shareholders. Therefore, the specific reference to the board composition has been modified: the majority of the board can be composed of members who represent the shareholders. Independent third parties are still welcome. In practice, it is difficult to determine which members of the board are to be considered "independent".

92. Technically, the *Italian società per azioni* also is characterized by the presence of two levels of "boards". The larger companies are managed by a board of directors—the *consiglio di amministrazione*—composed of inside and outside directors. This board often elects an internal managing board, the *comitato esecutivo*. In addition, Italian law provides for a surveillance body, the *collegio sindacale*, composed of members elected by the general meeting and in charge of supervising the activities of all company organs, including the general meeting. The Italian legal writers do not consider this board to be comparable to the German supervisory board, however; instead, they classify the Italian system as belonging to the unitary board system.[408]

93. According to *German* law, a public company limited by shares, or *Aktiengesellschaft*, is required to have a two-tier board even if it is not subject to the co-determination rules: the supervisory board or *Aufsichtsrat* and the managing board or *Vorstand* have been expressly provided for in the *Aktiengesetz*.[409] No similar rules apply to the *Gesellschaft mit beschränkter Haftung* or *GmbH*.[410] The supervisory board is mainly in charge of the selection, appointment, or dismissal and the supervision of the *Vorstand*. Its task is mainly that of supervising the functioning of the company; it is called upon to decide in only a

---

[406] As was mentioned in the 1973 protocol, Banking Commission 'Annual Report 1973-1974' 239.

[407] See Banking and Finance Commission 'Annual Report 1991-1992' 251.

[408] See Jaeger and Denozza, supra n. 101, 378.

[409] See Lutter and Krieger, supra n. 330, 320; Kübler, supra n. 125, 182 et seq.

[410] But also in cooperative societies. The rules on co-determination may require the organization of a supervisory board, e.g., under the steel and coal co-determination.

limited number of matters. In the smaller companies, the supervisory board is the representative of the shareholders.

The number of members of a supervisory board has been determined by law[411] so as to secure a sufficient density of discussion: there should be at least three members, with a maximum according to the company's capital. Members are elected by the shareholders. Some members may also be appointed by designated shareholders, or by the owner of special classes of shares. This rule was introduced to allow the state to be represented on boards, but it can also be used to ensure representation of minority shareholders. Not more than one-third of the members can be so appointed in order to safeguard power to be exercised by the majority of the shareholders. To secure their independence of judgment, supervisory board members may not be members of the *Vorstand*, nor may they take part in the management of a subsidiary. In order to avoid cross agreements, a supervisory board member of one company may not be the manager of another company at which a member of the former company's *Vorstand* serves on the supervisory board.[412] It is, however, common for members of the enterprise council (*Betriebsrat*) to also take part in the supervisory board.[413] The number of mandates that supervisory board members may exercise has been the subject of discussion: according to the present law, members may not sit on more than ten boards of other commercial companies with obligatory supervisory boards. However, five seats within the group are not included.[414] Reduction of this maximum is being considered.

Dismissal by the general meeting requires a three-fourths majority. But it is lawful to fix a lower degree, such as a simple majority, or to require additional safeguards (e.g., serious reasons for dismissal). Labor representatives are protected: only a three-fourths majority can oblige them to quit. Terms of office last for a maximum of five years.[415] Remuneration is determined in the charter or by a decision of the general meeting.[416] In practice, members are subject to strict secrecy rules that are organized by the Companies Act.[417]

The tasks of the *Aufsichtsrat* can be described as follows:

- the appointment or dismissal of the *Vorstand* members;

---

[411] § 95 AktG, 9 members for companies with up to 3 million marks; 15 members for companies with more than 3 million, except that 21 members are allowed if the company disposes of more than 20 million marks capital.

[412] This is called the *Verbot der Überkreuzverflechtung*; §100 (2) no. 2 AktG.

[413] Lutter and Krieger, supra n. 330, 28.

[414] § 100 (2) no. 1 AktG.

[415] § 102 (1) AktG.

[416] § 113 AktG.

[417] §§ 93 (1) and 116 AktG. The subject has been intensively discussed in legal literature.

- the supervision of the general management of the company. This extends to the business aspects of the decision and not only the merely formal legal validity. The board cannot give instructions to the *Vorstand*; however, it also cannot take over the management duties itself.
- specific tasks imposed by law, such as the representation of the company in the case of a conflict of interest by a member of the *Vorstand*, the calling of a general meeting, or the approval of the annual accounts;
- further tasks introduced by the internal ordinance of the board:
  - · the election of the chairman of the board;
  - · the formation of committees that act as advisers to the board but may also enjoy limited decision competencies;
  - · rules on decision making: no proxies are admitted.

One meeting per trimester is advised, with at least one per six months. Usually the supervisory board meets four times a year.

94. In general, the *Vorstand* or managing board is in charge of managing and representing the company. The number of members is fixed by the charter, but larger companies have at least two members (above 3 million marks capital).[418] They cannot be members of the supervisory board. The members of the *Vorstand* are appointed by the *Aufsichtsrat* for a term not exceeding five years. Dismissal by the *Aufsichtsrat* must be based on "serious grounds" (*wichtigen Grund*), such as gross misconduct, incapacity to run the firm in an orderly way, or loss of confidence from the shareholders.[419] The contractual relationship with the company is governed by the rules of a service contract (*Dienstvertrag*), which would render certain rules on indemnification applicable in case of dismissal. The *Vorstand* acts on all matters relating to the company, and its competencies cannot be limited by charter. However, the charter or the supervisory board can determine that certain matters must be subject to the latter's agreement. Clauses subjecting certain decisions to the approval of the general meeting are not effective.

III. Boards With Employee Representation[420]

95. Boards with employee representation are first and foremost a German-Dutch phenomenon. However, the comparative overview indicates that in several other European states, employee representation has been introduced, mainly in the seventies, either as part of the unitary board's functioning or, more usually, in the two-tier structure. Apart from mandated co-determination, most states have

---

[418] § 76 (3) AktG.

[419] § 84 (3) AktG.

[420] Co-determination is also the subject of Ch. 5 of this volume.

voluntary systems of co-decision making at board level, based either on employer-organized co-decision making or on collective labor agreements. These evolutions are not very well documented and have not been investigated in detail.

1. Voluntary Co-Determination in the Two-Tier Board Structure

96. *Finland* has introduced an optional regime: companies opting for a one-tier board should provide for the designation of a board of three members to be elected by the general meeting of shareholders.[421] However, the charter can stipulate for a minority of board members to be appointed differently, i.e., by the employees. Also, larger companies with a capital exceeding 0.5 million markkas must appoint a "managing director" to act within the limits of his assignment by the board of directors. Larger companies, defined by the criterion above, may provide for a two-tier system: the supervisory board must be composed of at least five members, elected by the general meeting or in a different way, therefore allowing for employee representation.[422] The supervisory boards, according to the law, "supervise the management of the company." The charter may include in its mission decisions of particular importance, such as "the considerable extension or reduction of the operations or an essential change in the organization of the company." The supervisory board reports to the general meeting. Although there is no compulsory system of employee representation, there is a widespread practice of organizing voluntary representation: 300 companies are reported to have voluntarily introduced this type of industrial democracy.

2. Mandatory Co-Determination in the Two-Tier Board Structure

97. Two-tier boards with employee representation are compulsory in Germany; the obligation also applies to larger firms in the Netherlands.[423] Conceptually, the two systems are quite different in structure and in composition. Also, several of the questions that have been met in the analysis of the unitary boards will not show up here, as, for example, with the issue of the separation of functions between chairman and CEO, or with the matter of conflicts of interest.

---

[421] In smaller companies with less than 500,000 markkas of capital (about $13,500) the board can be composed of less than three members (Ch. 8 §1 Finnish Companies Act).

[422] Ch. 8 §§ 11 and 11 (a) Finnish Companies Act, introduced by L. 14 February 1997.

[423] It applies only to the large *NV*: art. 153 and 158 NBW.

98. The *German* system[424] is based on compulsory representation of both shareholders and employees on the supervisory board. There are three systems of co-determination:

a) in the steel and coal sector (*Montanmitbestimmung*), in which the supervisory board is composed of ten members—five of whom represent capital and five of whom represent labor—while an eleventh member is added in a neutral position, elected by the general meeting on proposition of the majority of the members of each section of the supervisory board. In addition, an *Arbeitsdirektor* is appointed as a member of the managing board; he is elected on the proposition of the majority of the board as well as by the majority of the representatives of the employees. This rule applies to all *AG*s and *GmbH*s in the steel and coal sector with more than 1,000 employees.

b) in the other sectors of the economy, co-determination is mandatory, either according to the scheme applicable to smaller firms in accordance with a 1952 law (*Betriebsverfassungsgesetz*), or to larger firms according to the 1976 *Mitbestimmungsgesetz*. According to the 1952 law, one-third of the members of the supervisory board must be employees of the firm. This applies to all firms with more than 500 employees, except firms belonging to a single physical person or to a partnership of physical persons.

c) The 1976 system is based on a modified system of equal representation and is applicable to all larger companies with 2,000 or more employees in the group, regardless of their legal form. This is the most frequently applied system, and will be analyzed here.

The German system of labor participation is based on a complex system of direct or indirect representation on the supervisory board. In the largest companies, counting 20,000 or more employees, the board is composed of ten members elected by the shareholders and ten members elected by the employees. The majority of the employee representatives are direct employees of the enterprise—numbering seven in the largest enterprises and elected by the employee delegates[425]—and the remaining three are representatives of the unions represented in the group.[426] The chairman of the board is elected by the representatives of the shareholders: he has a casting vote in case of a tie, but this is seldom used.[427]

---

[424] On German co-determination, see also Gerum and Wagner (Ch. 5), Roe (Ch. 5), and Prigge (Ch. 5: Sec. C.I.) in this volume.

[425] See § 9 MitbestG. Direct election is optional for the larger enterprises.

[426] For details, see § 7 (2) to (4) MitbestG.

[427] See Hopt, Klaus J. 'The German Two-Tier Board (*Aufsichtsrat*): A German View on Corporate Governance' in: Hopt and Wymeersch (eds.), supra n. 40, 3, indicating that "it would alienate good relations with labor and well beyond."

Representatives of the shareholders are elected for a period of four years[428] by the general meeting, in which the banks play a leading role. These members cannot be revoked except with a three-fourths majority. Supervisory board members are appointed for a five-year term. They can be members of not more than ten other supervisory boards, except within groups, where they can take up an additional five seats. Members of this board cannot be managers of subsidiaries of the same company, nor can they be managers of the company at which they have been elected to serve on the supervisory board.[429]

The managing board is usually composed of five members, one of whom is the labor director. Under German law, the members of the managing board are appointed by the supervisory board for a definite period of time[430] and cannot be dismissed except on serious grounds.[431] Independence of office results. These guarantees for independence are not present under Dutch law.[432] According to this dual structure, members of the management board are not part of the supervisory board: as a consequence both bodies have different chairpersons.

99. A 1994 census[433] of bank and other representation on the supervisory board in the 30 largest DAX companies indicated that:

- out of 292 seats, banks filled 98 (33.6%); in 16 cases the chairman of the board was a banker
- the other board members were:
  - board members of affiliated companies: 73 (24.6%)
  - members of a management board and former members of the company's management board: 74 (25%)
  - others 49 (16.8%).

The appointment of members of the *Vorstand* was reported to be effectuated essentially by the chairman of the board, while the nomination committee played a limited role (20%). This role was more marked for members of the supervisory board (38%), while institutional investors (probably the banks) accounted for 58% of the influence.

From our observations based on 566 companies listed on German exchanges, it appears that the number of members on German boards essentially varies with the size of the firm. The management board—whether co-determined or not—is on average composed of 3.48 persons, while the supervisory board on average

---

[428] § 102 AktG. This rule results in practice in a four- to five-year term: Hopt, supra n. 427.

[429] § 100 (2) no. 3 AktG. Both rules serve to avoid the supervised being supervisors.

[430] Five years in Germany, § 84 (1) phrase 1 AktG. Cf. art. 272 NBW.

[431] See § 84 (3) AktG.

[432] Cf. art. 272 NBW.

[433] Hansen, Herbert 'Die Zusammensetzung von Aufsichtsräten der DAX-Gesellschaften und die Aufwirkungen auf ihre Effizienz' *Die Aktiengesellschaft* 39 (1994) R403. The census only relates to non-employee representative members.

counts 10.09 members. In total, there were 5,175 supervisory board members, of whom 1,966 were employee representatives. German boards are mainly a men's business: in the management boards of 566 companies there were 8 women, mostly in smaller enterprises. At the supervisory board level, female presence is somewhat more evident: out of 5,175 members, 279 were women (5.39%). Of these, however, 221 were employee representatives. Capital was represented by 58 women, which amounts to 1.12% of the total number of members of the supervisory board. Obviously German businessmen do not like to be supervised by their female colleagues.

The exclusion of banks and insurance companies, which are known for relatively large boards, reveals a somewhat different picture of German boards. The average management board counts 2.9 members, while the supervisory board is reduced to 8.7. Female presence is equally rare: 14 out of 1,457 managing directors and 219 out of 4,368 members of the supervisory board were female, in percentage terms substantially in line with the overall figures for the entire business world in Germany.[434]

100. The *Dutch* system is quite different from the German one. Instead of being based on the proportional—according to some, "adversarial"—representation of both components of the enterprise, it is founded on the consensus between the two traditional production factors, capital and labor.[435]

The system, known as the *structuurvennootschap,* is based on the mandatory structure of the supervisory board, with the law imposing a number of statutory requirements and fixing competencies. Labor representation at the level of the supervisory board is indirect and based on co-optation of members of the board who, without being labor representatives, enjoy the confidence of the employees. Therefore, members of the supervisory board are in a specific position of independence: they do not represent labor interests but have to take care of "the interest of the company and its related enterprise" as a whole. The *structuur* regime is applicable to all larger companies, both of the *NV* and of the *BV* type. Companies are considered "large" if they have own funds exceeding 25 million guilder, have an "enterprise council", and employ more than 100 persons within the Netherlands.

There are important exceptions to the rule that are especially designed to take the international group structure of some of the major Dutch firms into account: Dutch parent companies of international groups such as Royal Dutch, Unilever, Philips, Akzo, and Heineken are fully exempted as mere holding companies of

---

[434] On the German board, cf. also Hopt, Theisen, and Semler in Ch. 4, and Prigge (Sec. B.I.) in Ch. 12 of this volume.

[435] This difference of approach has been underlined by Unilever's chairman Tabaksblat, M. 'Corporate Governance in internationaal perspectief' *De Naamloze Vennootschap* 73 (1995) 243, 245.

groups because the majority of their employees are located outside the Netherlands.[436] Further full exemptions relate to subsidiaries—including joint ventures—of groups that are subject to the co-determination rules at the parent company level. Besides, there is also a "scaled down" regime, according to which two essential competencies of the board would not apply: these are the rules on appointment or dismissal of managing directors and the rules on approval of the annual accounts, both of which privileges are exercised at the parent company level. But the rules on co-optation of members of the supervisory board and their supervisory powers on the management board remain fully applicable. This regime has been provided for certain group entities that are subject to the *structuur* regime, but because they are dominated by Dutch or foreign parents that are not subject to the co-determination rules, these parents would otherwise not be able to effectively exercise control over their Dutch subsidiaries. This regime can be invoked by parents if the majority of its employees are active outside Holland, or by joint ventures that have no participants that are Dutch parents subject to the co-determination rules.[437] Upon acquisition of Dutch subsidiaries, foreign parents sometimes maintain the co-determination regime. Finally, there have been some cases in which the Minister of Justice has granted exemption to the *structuur* regime.[438]

101. According to the Dutch *structuur* regime, the companies subject to its rules must introduce a two-tier board.[439] The typical *structuur* regime implies that the members of the supervisory board—at least three—are co-opted by this board, acting on proposals submitted by the general meeting, by the enterprise council, or by the management board. For that purpose the shareholders may institute shareholder committees. The appointment by the board may be opposed by the general meeting or by the enterprise council, i.e., by capital or by labor. Objections may be based on the grounds mentioned in the law, especially "the expectation that the nominee will be unfit for the function as board member or that the board will not be correctly composed."[440] If the board maintains its appointment notwithstanding the objections, the matter may be brought by the "enterprise council"—i.e., mainly the employees of the firm—before the "Enterprise Chamber", a specialized chamber of the Amsterdam Court of Appeal.

---

[436] This criterion leads to distortions, as many Dutch firms would qualify under the exemption. See Van den Hoek, Paul C. 'Dient het structuurregime te worden aangepast aan gewijzigde omstandigheden of inzichten' in: Van Schilfgaarde, Peter (eds.) *Knelpunten in de vennootschapswetgeving* 42 (Deventer 1995).

[437] Art. 155 NBW.

[438] 27 cases had been published in 1992: see Van der Heijden and Van der Grinten, supra n. 4, 65. These were reported as not significant.

[439] See art. 150 NBW; cf. art. 158 NBW, and Van der Heijden and Van der Grinten, supra n. 4, no. 272, 473.

[440] As this is stated in art. 158 (6) NBW.

In practice, conflicting views are settled either by the candidate's refusal of the nomination or by the board preferring to propose a new candidate. In about 25 years, only 11 cases have been brought before the court.

There is some case law dealing with objections against the appointment of board members, mostly based on the third ground, i.e., the board has not been composed in a balanced way. Among the cases that have been commented on, the objection was upheld based on the finding that the board would be exclusively composed of persons with economic-financial and technical expertise, without anyone having knowledge and experience in the field of social relations.[441] In another case, objections were upheld because two out of three members were group officers who had no experience of the Netherlands, having never lived nor worked there.[442] It has been suggested that a board which is composed exclusively of officers of the parent company is not composed in a balanced way. In another case it was considered that the supervisory board should be composed of members that are sufficiently independent in relation to the parent company. The mere fact that officers of the parent were appointed to the board would not exclude the board from acting independently. As three out of five would have been officers of the parent, their nomination was considered not justified on that ground.[443] In practice, however, most conflicts are settled in accordance with the underlying purpose of the legislature, i.e., to promote harmonious relations between labor and capital.[444]

The number of members of this board is determined by the charter; if it is not provided for in the charter, it is determined by the board itself. The same rules apply as to the age limit in non-co-determined companies. In principle, the supervisory board has the same competencies as in the common "non-structure" system; however, the law contains a list of subject matters which must be submitted to the supervisory board, either for decision or for advice, before being submitted to the general meeting.[445]

As has been made clear from the preceding description, the Dutch system is not based on employee representation but on the presence of board members who enjoy the confidence of both shareholders and personnel and adhere to a large vision of the business's purpose, incorporating the "interest of the firm" rather than that of the shareholders or the employees. The role of the supervisory

---

[441] *Nederlandse Standard Electric Maatschappij* Decision of 16 March 1979 *De Naamloze Vennootschap* 57 (1979) 94, note Van Schilfgaarde.

[442] In the case of *Cyanamid*: *De Naamloze Vennootschap* 61 (1983) 233, note Van Schilfgaarde; for an overview of these cases, see Van Schilfgaarde, note 362, 370 et seq.; also: Slagter, Wicher Jan *Compendium van het ondernemingsrecht* 262 7th edn. (Deventer 1996).

[443] *Kodak Nederland*, OK 2 February 1989, *NJ* (1989) 86, note Maeijer; *De Naamloze Vennootschap* 67 (1989) 20, note Van Schilfgaarde.

[444] In this sense, see Sanders and Westbroek, supra n. 32, 326; Slagter, supra n. 442, 262.

[445] Art. 164 NBW, providing for a right of approval of the management board's decision.

council has therefore been defined by the law as the "surveillance of the policies pursued by the management board and of the general state of affairs of the companies, and of its related enterprise."[446]

In the *structuur* regime, the appointment of the management board members must be decided by the supervisory board; the charter cannot provide nomination rights for any other body. However, the supervisory board informs the general meeting or the shareholders commission of its intended nomination. The enterprise council is entitled to give its opinion on the intended appointment. Unless otherwise provided for in the charter, the supervisory board determines the duration of the directors employment contract.

102. The Dutch *structuur* regime has been criticized in legal and other writings. Some have argued that, as presently organized, the regime results in insufficient external scrutiny on management, the supervisory board members being all too dependent on the management board. Cronyism is considered one of the main causes for the collapse (DAF, OGEM) or endangerment (Philips) of some long-established Dutch companies. Increased shareholder influence is argued.[447]

The thesis has been the subject of criticism, with some pleading for a more moderate reform. Finally, a committee was set up under the chairmanship of J. Peters (the *Peters Report*) composed of representatives of the Association of Listed Companies, the stock exchange, institutional investors, the association for the protection of investors in securities, and others. Some of these recommendations can be summarized as follows:

• the board should act independently: its members should be able to operate independently against each other and in relation to the management; all members, even those proposed by certain constituencies, should act in the interest of the company and without mandate of these constituencies;

• not more than one former management board member should be a member of the supervisory board. Officers should instead be invited to take up functions on other companies' boards;

• as a rule, board membership should be limited in time: re-appointment should be carefully considered and is not automatic;

• members should participate in board meetings: in case of frequent absenteeism, the member will be approached;

• any appearance of mixing of interests between the firm and a board member should be avoided; conflicting interests should be immediately reported to the chairman;

---

[446] Art. 140 (2) NBW.

[447] See, e.g., Wildenberg and Zwetsloot (eds.), supra n. 226; for a more balanced opinion: Van den Hoek, supra n. 436.

- although there is no express rule limiting the number of board seats a member can occupy, it is recommended that members should not take up mandates in other companies so as not to jeopardize the full implementation of their duties;
- independence of supervision should not be hampered by members sitting on boards of subsidiaries, on cross board participation, or on any other ground;
- board committees are recommended; they should be mentioned in the annual report;
- investor relations should be actively pursued.

103. *Austria* has introduced employee representation more or less along the lines of the original German pattern: at the level of the supervisory board in large companies,[448] one-third of the members should be employee representatives. These are appointed for an indefinite time period by the works council or, in larger firms, by the central works council, and chosen from among their members. They can be revoked by these at any time. Union influence is reported to be strong. Liability, according to the statute, is the same as for any other member of the supervisory board.

3. Mandatory Co-Determination in the One-Tier Board Structure

Employee representation exists in the one-board system in several states: it is obligatory in Denmark, Sweden, Luxembourg, and France, and optional in Finland. The conditions of application and functioning are quite diverse. There is no statistical data available as to the significance of this phenomenon.

104. *Luxembourg* company law provides for a one-tier board. Labor representation was introduced by law in 1974 with respect to public companies limited established in Luxembourg with more than 1,000 employees in the *grand duchy*.[449] It also applied to firms with a 25% state participation or with a state "concession" or franchise. In fact, it mainly viewed Arbed, CLT-RTL, and a few other companies.[450]

These companies must have a board composed of at least nine members: one-third should be elected by the employees. Employee directors are in the same legal position as any other director, especially as far as liabilities are con-

---

[448] I.e., capital exceeding 1 million schilling and more than 50 shareholders or employing more than 300 employees. See Kolvenbach, Walter and Peter Hanau 'Austria' in: Kolvenbach, Walter and Peter Hanau (eds.) *Handbook on Employee Co-Management* 16 (Deventer 1987); art. 110 Labor Code.

[449] See Chapter II L. 6 May 1974 "instituant des comités mixtes dans les entreprises du secteur privé et organisant la représentation des salariés dans les sociétés anonymes."

[450] Cegedel (power supply) and Luxair (airline) are also submitted.

cerned.[451] Election is indirect: the members are elected by the representatives of the employees. In the steel sector, union representatives can be designated. Employee-elected directors enjoy special protections against dismissal from their employment: only the tribunal can dismiss, but the company management can suspend in the event of "gross violation" of duties. Revocation of this board member can only take place by decision of the representatives who have elected the board member.

105. In *France*, there is a threefold system of voluntary co-determination within the unitary board. Co-determination had long been opposed both by employers and employees, the unions refusing to be involved with running the firm.[452] Gradually the idea gained momentum, and in 1982 a form of obligatory representation in the public sector firms was introduced, followed in 1986 by an optional minority co-determination system in the private sector.[453] A 1994 law rendered the system compulsory for privatized state enterprises.[454] The system of co-determination[455] was introduced in all firms with an enterprise council: two representatives of this council take part in the board, as observers and without votes. In fact, their influence is very limited; decisions are made by the directors in a preliminary meeting. This type of co-determination decision making has been referred to as "a mockery".

Another system of co-determination is based on a voluntary scheme: it can be introduced by the general meeting by way of a charter amendment.[456] Representatives of employees of the firm—numbering between two and four, and occupying a maximum of one-third of the board seats—are elected by their peers, not by the general meeting. They take part in the meetings of the board in the same position as the other directors. Revocation is not *ad nutum* as for the other directors, but only by judicial decision for fault. In practice there are reports that the system is not very effective, especially because of the fear that information might be divulged by the representatives.[457] Also, the directors fear that co-decision will increase the union's power. Often board meetings are split in

---

[451] Art. 29 L. 6 May 1974.

[452] For a short overview, see Guyon, supra n. 1, no. 393, p. 402. For a more general perspective: Hopt, Klaus J. 'Problèmes fondamentaux de la participation en Europe' *Revue trimestrielle de droit commercial et de droit économique* 34 (1981) 401.

[453] Ordonnance no. 86-1135 of 2 October 1986; see Le Fèvre, Alain 'La participation de salariés aux conseils d'administration ou de surveillance des sociétés anonymes' *Revue des sociétés* 105 (1987) 189.

[454] L. 25 July 1994.

[455] See ordonnance n° 86-1135 of 2 October 1986.

[456] See art. 97-1 French Companies Act 1966. Large companies like Saint-Gobain, Compagnie générale d'électricité, and CCF are reported to have introduced this type of co-determination.

[457] See OECD, supra n. 257, 127.

two parts, with the representatives invited to the formal part. The number of companies that have opted for this regime is unknown, but would seem rather small.

France introduced a more elaborate system of co-determination for its privatized public sector enterprises, including firms that are majority-owned by the French state or by its organizations.[458] Apart from representatives of the state and expert members (both one-third), one-third of the members of the supervisory board or of the management board are representatives of the employees.

The appointment of stakeholder representatives is not favored by the Viénot Report as it would transform the board into a battlefield for specific interests. This has not prevented some companies from inviting individual shareholders to their boards.[459] Further involvement of employee representatives obviously is not a priority in France.[460]

Employee representatives on French boards are relatively rare: in only 14 out of the 40 CAC 40 companies were there employee representatives. These stood for only 7% of the overall number of employees. It was stated that the often-heard objections that for secrecy reasons the board could not meet in front of employee representatives was not considered convincing due to their small number.[461]

106. In the 1977 Co-Determination Act, *Sweden* introduced a system of compulsory co-determination with respect to all companies—of *SA* or of cooperative types—that employ more than 25 persons: two labor representatives must be appointed to the board. If there are more than 1,000 employees, three members of the board are to be so designated. These board members have the same rights and duties as all other board members. This type of participation is mainly regarded as serving informational purposes because representatives usually are reportedly loath to intervene in the board's decision making.

107. In *Denmark*, the Companies Act provides that half the number of the members of the board elected by the shareholders or by the other parties entitled to appoint directors[462] will be elected by the employees, with a minimum of two. Companies and groups (parents and subsidiaries) with at least 35 employees are subject to this regime, applicable to the parent companies. Only companies located in Denmark qualify.[463]

---

[458] See L. 83-675 of 26 July 1983. See Cozian and Viandier, supra n. 2, no. 1886, p. 587.

[459] 'Eurotunnel's new train of thought for shareholders' *Financial Times* November 25, 1995.

[460] Also no reference is made to these issues in the Marini Report, supra n. 69.

[461] Vuchot Ward Howell, supra n. 242, 19.

[462] See about these, supra no. 85.

[463] Art. 49 Danish Companies Act.

4. Voluntary and Other Schemes

108. In *Switzerland*, although the law does not mandate employee participation at the board level, some companies have voluntarily organized this type of decision making. On a voluntary basis some firms have introduced co-determination; for example, shareholders at Nestle elected two employees from a list proposed by the chairman of the personnel delegation. Other examples are the retail distributors Migros and Co-op.

109. In *Ireland*, the Worker Participation (State Enterprises) Act of 1977 introduced board-level employee participation at a selected number of state-owned enterprises employing 43,700 employees.[464] Members are appointed by the minister competent for the state firm in question, and are nominated either by the union or by a percentage of the employees (a minimum of 15%). Also, only employees of the firm may be appointed. The system has not been extended to the private sector, although proposals have been made to that purpose.

110. In *Italian* business firms, employees are not represented at the board level. The Italian union tradition is based on confrontation, not on *co-gestione*. In *Belgium*, there is no labor representation at the boards. In some state-owned firms there may be limited representation of labor, e.g., in the national railway company, where three members are presented by the unions and elected by the employees. In *Portugal* and *Spain*, there is no legally imposed system of co-determination. Spain abolished its system which was introduced in 1962-1965, but it can be continued on a voluntary basis. The latter is the case in state-owned enterprises.

In addition to representation at the board level, employees may be able to influence decision making through their participation in other bodies, most frequently the "enterprise council." These are parallel bodies that are mandatory for all larger organizations whether they are engaged in business or not. These bodies are mostly not involved in corporate decision making but restricted to employment conditions, including lay-off and plant closures. At the European level, a "European Works Council" has become compulsory for all larger undertakings or groups of undertakings with at least 1,000 employees within the EU, of which there are at least 150 employees in two or more member states.[465]

---

[464] See Kolvenbach, Walter 'Ireland' in: Kolvenbach and Hanau (eds.), supra n. 448, 9 et seq.

[465] See Council Directive of 22 September 1994 on the establishment of a European Works Council (EWC) or a procedure in community-scale undertakings and community-scale groups of undertakings for the purposes of informing and consulting employees, *OJEC* L 254/64, 30.9.1994. The directive does not create compulsory structures as to the scope, composition, competence, and mode of operation of the EWC: these must primarily be determined by means of an agreement between the central management and a negotiating body representing the employees (art. 5).

D. The Share Markets

111. The patterns of share ownership in listed companies found in the different continental European states present significant differences. In order to document this aspect of the corporate governance relationship, one can rely on the disclosures required of important shareholders with respect to their holdings, acquisitions, or disposals of shares. These disclosures have been mandated in accordance with the European directive of 1988 and have now been implemented in all EU members states. The states, however, have introduced lower thresholds than the ones mandated by the directive, typically starting from a 5% threshold. Some states have imposed even lower percentages, such as the U.K. and Italy, in the latter case in order to enable identification of Mafia or Mafia-linked ownership.[466] Small holdings linked through agreements or where shareholders were acting in concert should normally be reported.[467]

The analysis of these filings presents some difficulties, as in some states interpretation of the figures is difficult because of the separation of direct and indirect ownership, leading to risks of double counting, for example. Furthermore, control structures based on elements other than share ownership are not always documented. Finally, one would expect these filings to be reliable as criminal sanctions have been provided for shareholders who did not file. In practice, however, there might be cases in which beneficial ownership has not been reported or where subsequent changes were reported without canceling a previous entry, and so on.

On the basis of these data, research can be directed in several ways. An attempt can be made to determine the volume of shares that are effectively available for trading on the markets: this free float would be determined as the total number of issued shares minus the shares that have been reported by significant shareholders. The figure should be qualified: significant non-reporting shareholders—other than institutional investors—may be not willing to sell their block.

A second line of research could relate to the control structures. Several approaches can be followed. The number of listed companies that have one majority shareholder could be identified. These companies are firmly controlled. As will be documented later, this pattern in which one shareholder holds a majority block is prevalent in all continental European systems, at least if measured in terms of number of listed companies.

Another approach consists of measuring concentration of ownership, in which case several important shareholders are identified. The underlying hypothesis is that these important shareholders de facto—if not de jure—act in common

---

[466] See L. 216/1974 as amended in 1992, art. 1/5.

[467] See art. 7 Directive 12 December 1988 *OJEC* L 348/62, 17.12.1988.

understanding and control the company. However, in some cases, significant shareholders may not always agree on a common policy. Linked to this type of research, one could further attempt to identify the mechanisms which have been put into place to fend off takeover attempts.

A third approach is much more ambitious: it consists of identifying the ultimate control through the pyramids of holding companies that are especially frequent in Europe. This method is being applied and its results investigated by the European Corporate Governance Network.[468]

The identification of the controlling parties at the upstream levels in the ownership structure often stops at the doorstep of privately held companies that may be located in states with strict secrecy laws. Therefore, a precise picture of these structures will sometimes be impossible to achieve. From our observation, it would not seem that significant amounts of shares have been placed in offshore vehicles, especially not in the larger companies.

A different method of research uses macro figures: it will yield information on the amount of shares held by the different classes of securities holders, such as physical persons, institutional investors, etc. The figures must be supplemented by statistical censuses of ownership or by the overall figures published by the different supervisory bodies of institutional investors. This type of research gives insight into the overall significance of public ownership of companies, and may help to identify policy issues with respect to governance in general.

I. The Distribution of Share Ownership

112. Since the implementation of the 1988 EU directive on major holdings of shares in listed companies, a more precise picture of the most significant holdings in listed companies may be drawn. These figures are partly based on official publications and partly on private publications based on the official data. In some of the member states, especially the United Kingdom, the Netherlands, and Germany, the reporting of indirect and nominee holdings and of different classes of shares makes the situation less transparent than in the more southern European states. Therefore, some of these data may still need further study and refinement. However, we think that the following figures give a fair view of ownership in European listed companies.

---

[468] Mentioned above no. 27. A survey of first results is provided in: Becht, Marco 'The Separation of Ownership and Control: A Survey of 7 European Countries' (Preliminary Report to the European Commission submitted on October 27, 1997 by the European Corporate Governance Network, vol. 1; http://www.ecgn.ulb.ac.be/).

1. Belgian Companies

113. The structure of ownership of shares in Belgium and France is often considered to be largely identical. From analysis based on the official reports, it appears that ownership in Belgium is considerably more concentrated than in France (Table 19): companies with widely distributed shares are less frequent, while a larger number of issuers have the majority of their shares effectively

Table 19: Ownership Concentration in Belgian Listed Companies, 1997

	Share in All Listed Companies in %
Majority Controlled (+ 50%)	68.38
Controlled Between 45% and 50%	2.94
Controlled Between 40%and 45%	8.09
Between 30% and 40%	7.35
Less Than 30%	12.50

Source: Own research.

Table 20: Ownership Concentration in Belgian Listed Companies by Size of the Company, 1997

Classes of Market Capitalization in BEF	Number	Total Listed	%
0-100 Mil.	9	10	90.00
100-500 Mil.	4	6	66.67
500-1,000 Mil.	4	10	40.00
1-2 Bil.	15	21	71.43
2-5 Bil.	21	24	87.50
5-10 Bil.	6	12	50.00
10-25 Bil.	14	17	82.35
25-50 Bil.	5	8	62.50
50-100 Bil.	7	12	58.33
> 100 Bil.	8	16	50.00
Total	93	136	68.38

Source: Own research.

controlled by one shareholder, or by a few shareholders acting jointly. The figures relate to all listed companies as of January 1997.

If these figures are further detailed according to the size of the company measured in terms of market capitalization, one obtains the following table, illustrating the prevalence of concentrated ownership in the smaller companies and wider ownership in the largest ones (Table 20).

Table 20 shows that only in a handful of listed companies are the majority of the shares in the hands of public investors, making them prone to public takeover bids. The majority of listed companies have one single shareholder. However, as this may be a holding company, decision making may be less concentrated because several parties may be involved in the holding company.

A third classification gives the three largest shareholders by classes of issuers and further highlights the strong concentration of ownership. In only 15 out of 136 listed companies did the three reporting shareholders hold less than 35%. At the 50%+ level, 69.1% were effectively owned by the three largest shareholders. Even in the largest companies, control was firmly held (Table 21).

Table 21: Holdings by the Three Most Important Shareholders in Belgian Listed Companies, 1997

Classes of Market Capitalization in BEF	>90%	50%-90%	45%-50%	35%-45%	25%-35%	10%-25%	5%-10%	<5%	Total
0-100 Mil.	2	7				1			10
100-500 Mil.	1	3		1		1			6
500-1,000 Mil.		6		2	2				10
1-2 Bil.	2	14	1	2	2				21
2-5 Bil.	1	17	2	3	1				24
5-10 Bil.	1	6		2	1	2			12
10-25 Bil.	1	14	1			1			17
25-50 Bil.		5		1	1			1	8
50-100 Bil.		6		4		1		1	12
> 100 Bil.		8		6	2				16
Total	8	86	4	21	9	6	0	2	136
	5.9%	63.2%	2.9%	15.4%	6.6%	4.4%	0.0%	1.5%	100.0%

Source: Own research.

This high concentration of ownership has adverse effects on the market liquidity: the free float enables the measurement of the volume of shares available for investment (Table 22).

Table 22: Free Float in Belgian Listed Shares, June 1997

Classes of Market Capitalization in BEF	Capitalization in Mil. BEF	Free Float in Mil. BEF	%
0-100 Mil.	363.01	94.62	26.07
100-500 Mil.	1,086.15	428.63	39.46
500-1,000 Mil.	6,277.65	2,620.91	41.75
1-2 Bil.	32,295.54	10,910.61	33.78
2-5 Bil.	81,197.76	28,299.97	34.85
5-10 Bil.	78,861.47	33,600.28	42.61
10-25 Bil.	253,479.98	82,216.28	32.44
25-50 Bil.	292,577.47	139,480.41	47.67
50-100 Bil.	855,768.02	454,347.47	53.09
> 100 Bil.	3,286,436.29	1,544,929.24	47.01
Total	4,888,343.33	2,296,928.42	46.99
BEL-20	3,330,499.99	1,702,206.43	51.11

Source: Own research.

114. In all classes but one, less than 50% of the shares were not in firm hands. Typically, in the group with the highest capitalization, control was firmly held, a phenomenon also found in other states. If one only considers shares that are included in the market index of the most active shares (BEL-20 index), 51% would be freely available.

One could conclude that ownership of listed companies is still very concentrated in Belgium, while the free float is relatively limited. According to one source, only 31% of the listed shares were owned by investors other than known large investors and institutions.[469] We have come to somewhat less dramatic results (46%). This characteristic contributes to the lack of depth of the Belgian markets.

It is also apparent that Belgian groups have protected themselves against unfriendly bidders by concentrating ownership. The evolution should be illustrated by a historical reconstruction over the last ten to fifteen years. However, there are no reliable figures for the years before 1990. Anecdotal evidence

---

[469] Van Waterschoot, Jerry 'Corporate governance de aandeelhouders achter de beursgenoteerde bedrijven' *Revue de la banque—Bank- en Financiewezen* 61 (1997) 429.

indicates that major groups have attempted to reinforce their position by acquiring a majority stake, or by taking advantage of the legal instruments according to which a virtual majority could be held by holders of very large blocks (45%+).[470] The turning point was the takeover of Société Générale de Belgique, which sent a shock wave through the Belgian business world and incited many companies to protect themselves. A striking element is that Belgian control relations are based on ownership—effective or virtual—while other protective instruments and anti-takeover devices are not compatible with the law. In this respect the Belgian situation is quite different from the Dutch one, but also from the German and even the French.

In normal circumstances, non-controlling shareholders have little impact on company decision making. An analysis of attendance of general meetings of Belgian listed companies indicates that in most general meetings the majority of the shares were represented, but that small shareholders, including institutional investors, rarely took part in the meeting.[471] Except for the controlling shareholders, the use of proxies is still very rare—proxies usually being given to the chairman of the board—and only a couple public proxy solicitations have taken place. Voting by mail is allowed by law[472] but very rarely used due to the uncertainty of the identity of the shareholder, as most shares are issued in bearer form.

2. French Companies

115. The French stock market is composed of two segments: the first market, or formerly the official market at the Paris Bourse, and the *Second Marché*, dealing in less seasoned stocks. In both market segments, 387 shares are listed, representing a capitalization of 2,355 billion French francs.

116. The structure of ownership of French companies presents a different picture depending on the market segment on which the shares are traded. The first or main market lists the major French shares, many issued by companies with widely owned shares. On France's main market one sees a percentage of not

---

[470] In practice, a 45% owner could, in case of a takeover, increase his holding to over 50% by empowering the board to issue additional shares. These issues could be placed in friendly hands, provided the full market price is paid. The placing of shares warrants in friendly hands also is used to defend against takeovers. These techniques offer only a temporary protection up to five years, after which they have to be submitted to the general meeting. For an overview, see Geens, Koen 'The Post Société générale de Belgique era: public offers regulated anew and defence measures curbed' in: Maeijer, Jozef M.M. and Koen Geens (eds.) *Defensive Measures Against Hostile Takeover in the Common Market* 55 (1990).

[471] See Wymeersch, Eddy and Christoph Van der Elst 'De werking van de algemene vergadering in de Belgische beursgenoteerde vennootschappen. Een empirisch onderzoek' *Tijdschrift voor Belgisch Handelsrecht—Revue de droit commercial belge* 30 (1997) 72.

[472] See art. 74 (4) Belgian Companies Act.

majority controlled companies (about 64% at the 50%+ level) that is higher than in several other European states, such as Belgium, Switzerland, Italy, or Spain.

On the *Second Marché* and other markets for smaller companies, ownership concentration is striking: 67.5% are fully controlled by the main reporting shareholder. One can presume that several of these companies have rather recently opened themselves up for investors, and/or that former owners continue to hold substantial amounts of shares.

Table 23: Ownership Concentration in French Listed Companies, 1995

	First Market		*Second Marché*		Total
	Companies	%	Companies	%	
Over 90%	3	1.63	7	3.45	
Over 50%	65	35.33	130	64.04	
Fully Controlled	68	36.96	137	67.49	52.97
45% to 50%	11	5.98	14	6.90	6.46
35% to 45%	25	13.59	15	7.39	10.34
25% to 35%	22	11.96	20	9.85	10.85
10% to 25%	38	20.65	13	6.40	13.18
Less Than 10%	20	10.87	4	1.97	6.20
Total	184	100.00	203	100.00	100.00

Source: Own calculations based on: Les Actions Françaises, 1996.

117. As shown from Table 24, France has a relatively high number of large to very large listed companies, while numerous smaller companies with a low capitalization are still part of exchange trading (including the *Second Marché*).

If one looks into the more detailed data relating to ownership of the three most important shareholders in companies listed on the first market, it appears that the three most important shareholders dominate 53.8% of listed companies, while only in another 17.4% do these three shareholders hold less than 25%. In only 5 out of 184 listed companies would one have found a concentration of less than 10% for the three largest holders of shares. However, these do not range in the class of the largest companies: in these very large companies, some controlling shareholders have maintained a central network of power, resulting in concentration in the range of 25% to 35%. These are the so-called *noyaux durs*, in part put into place after the privatization of the formerly state-owned French firms (Table 25).

Table 24: Market Capitalization of French Listed Companies, September 1995

Capitalization in FRF	Number	%	Capitalization in Mil. FRF	%
0-100 Mil.	15	3.88	991	0.04
100-200 Mil.	29	7.49	4,306	0.18
200-300 Mil.	32	8.27	7,822	0.33
300-500 Mil.	36	9.30	14,663	0.62
500-1,000 Mil.	57	14.73	41,289	1.75
1-2 Bil.	51	13.18	73,115	3.10
2-5 Bil.	66	17.05	203,188	8.63
5-10 Bil.	42	10.85	291,659	12.38
10-25 Bil.	36	9.30	565,895	24.02
25-50 Bil.	13	3.36	453,675	19.26
50-75 Bil.	6	1.55	368,114	15.63
>75 Bil.	4	1.03	330,983	14.05
Total	387	100.00	2,355,700	100.00

Source: Own calculations.

Table 25: Ownership Concentration: Holding of the Three Most Important Shareholders in the Companies Listed on the First French Market

Capitalization in FRF	>90%	50%-90%	45%-50%	35%-45%	25%-35%	10%-25%	<10%	Total
0-100 Mil.		1					1	2
100-500 Mil.		8			1	2		11
500-1,000 Mil.		8		2	2			12.
1-2 Bil.		9	2	1	3	3		18
2-5 Bil.	3	29	3	7	4	2		48
5-10 Bil.	1	22	3	3	2	5		36
10-25 Bil.		15	6	6	1	4	2	34
25-50 Bil.		2	1		2	6	2	13
50-75 Bil.					2	4		6
>75 Bil.		1		1	1	1		4
Total	4	95	15	20	18	27	5	184
%	2.17	51.63	8.15	10.87	9.78	14.67	2.72	100

Source: Own calculations.

A different picture is obtained by adding up the figures for the first and the second markets (Table 26).

Table 26: Ownership Concentration: Holding of the Three Most Important Shareholders in the Companies Listed on the First and Second French Markets

Capitalization in FRF	>90%	50%-90%	45%-50%	35%-45%	25%-35%	10%-25%	<10%	Total
0-100 Mil.		10	1	1	2		1	15
100-200 Mil.		27		1	1			29
200-300 Mil.	3	23	1	1	1	1	2	32
300-500 Mil.	2	25		3	3	3		36
500-1,000 Mil.	2	49	1	2	3			57
1-2 Bil.	3	37	2	2	4	3		51
2-5 Bil.	7	42	3	8	4	2		66
5-10 Bil.	1	27	3	3	3	5		42
10-25 Bil.		16	7	6	1	4	2	36
25-50 Bil.		2	1		2	6	2	13
50-75 Bil.					2	4		6
>75 Bil.		1		1	1	1		4
Total	18	259	19	28	27	29	7	387
%	4.65	66.93	4.91	7.24	6.98	7.49	1.81	100

Source: Own calculations.

On the *Second Marché* ownership is more concentrated, as became apparent from Table 23. The aggregate figures about ownership by the three principal reporting shareholders would therefore indicate a higher concentration of ownership than appeared from the figures relating solely to the first market. Analyzing concentration in the overall French share market, in 71.58% of the listed companies, the three most important shareholders held 50% or more of the shares. At the other end of the spectrum, there were only 9.3% of the listed companies in which the public investors held 75% or more of the shares, the three most prominent investors holding 25% or less.

118. If the percentages owned by the controlling shareholders and other shareholders who have reported their holdings is deducted from the total market capitalization, a more precise picture about the volume of shares made available for investment might emerge. For the overall market, the free float amounts to 57% of total market capitalization, amounting to 60% for the first market and a mere 28% for the other market.

On the official market, in the range of the largest French companies, the majority of shares is effectively available for investment. This applies only for the last four classes of capitalization. 15% (59 companies out of 387) of the French listed companies stood for 73% of capitalization, meaning that shares of most other companies are effectively held by one or more significant shareholders. These 59 companies had distributed more than 50% of their shares to the investing public. If the limit of the free float is set at 65% of the shares issued, only 23 companies qualified, with 49% of total market capitalization (Table 27).

Table 27: Free Float of French Stock Exchange-Listed Companies

Capitalization in FRF	First Market			Second Market		
	Capitalization in Million FRF	Free Float in Million FRF	%	Capitalization in Million FRF	Free Float in Million FRF	%
0-100 Mil.	156	81.90	52.50	835	339.86	40.70
100-500 Mil.	3,511	1,553.06	44.23	23,280	8,138.74	34.96
500-1,000 Mil.	9,903	4,559.11	46.04	31,386	9,282.74	29.58
1-2 Bil.	27,651	15,174.35	54.88	45,464	13,120.54	28.86
2-5 Bil.	153,414	64,685.03	42.16	49,774	12,143.58	24.40
5-10 Bil.	253,713	106,156.30	41.84	37,946	10,441.81	27.52
10-25 Bil.	542,036	284,375.74	52.46	23,859	7,441.78	31.19
25-50 Bil.	453,675	318,053.78	70.11			
50-75 Bil.	368,114	279,058.39	75.81			
>75 Bil.	330,983	215,643.10	65.15			
Total*	2,143,156	1,289,340.76	60.16	212,544	60,909.05	28.66

Note: * Some important companies have classified their shareholders in classes without further identification; in this table they are dealt with as free float.

Source: Own calculations.

119. French companies are predominantly controlled by ownership of shares, whether a majority is owned by one single party (Table 23) or by several parties (Tables 25 and 26). However, control may be enhanced through other devices, such as double voting rights granted to shareholders who have held their shares for more than two years. This is a measure particularly advantageous to the public authorities and their holding entities, stable shareholders by definition. In addition, holding companies are frequently used as instruments to enhance power. Auto control constructions have been largely forbidden: between parent and subsidiary, no voting rights may be exercised by the subsidiary.[473] Between independent companies with one holding ten percent or more of the other, cross shareholdings are unlawful and the smallest holding would have to be sold.[474]

Takeovers, particularly of the recently privatized former state enterprises, are prevented by the formation of *noyaux durs* or *GAS* (*groupes d'actionnaires stables*), particularly in the privatized enterprises. These consist of a series of—often triangular—holdings by financial institutions, banks, insurance companies, and investment funds, constituting a significant part of the "stabilization" of the French industrial structure. These holdings, averaging about 13%, form the specific factor of French enterprise culture even after the privatizations, but they are considered at odds with general principles of corporate governance.[475] They sometimes form the point of entry for the general supervision of the state, the *haute surveillance publique*.

Participation of shareholders in the general meeting has been the subject of constant preoccupation of the French *Commission des opérations de bourse*. Shareholders may either vote in person or by proxy. Proxies cannot be given to non-shareholders, and the president of the meeting votes in favor of the proposals with respect to all proxies given without indication of a proxy holder. Mail voting is allowed in all companies.[476] However, it seems that shareholders continue to abstain from attending, while institutional investors also traditionally do not frequently take part in general meetings. The COB has proposed requiring institutional investors to vote at general meetings and report on their votes exercised. Minority shareholder associations have also become more active and have been granted the status of consumer associations,[477] entitling them to sue directors for liability. Stable shareholders owning 5% of the voting rights (0.5% in listed companies) can also sue for liability.[478]

---

[473] Art. 359-1 French Companies Act 1966.

[474] Art. 358 French Companies Act 1966.

[475] Goldstein, supra n. 259, 1328.

[476] Art. 161 French Companies Act 1966. Mail voting is recognized with respect to shares that remain deposited with a bank or broker for up to five days before the meeting (art. 136 Décret). However, it has been rarely used as the formula is said to be too complex: Guyon, supra n. 1, 301-1, 299.

[477] See, for examples, OECD, supra n. 257, 63 and n. 63.

[478] Individual shareholders can sue directors for liability if they hold, either separately or jointly, 5% of the share capital (art. 245 French Companies Act 1966, art. 200 Décret). These thresholds are reduced for larger companies, down to 1% for those with a capital of between 50 and 100 million francs and to 0.5% above the 100 million francs. However, in 1994, shareholder associations were given the right to sue, provided they have been shareholders for at least two years and own a percentage of shares that would be at least 1% for the class of the largest companies (art. 172-1 French Companies Act 1966, introduced by L. 8 August 1994).

3. Swiss Companies

120. The Swiss figures illustrate a strong concentration in terms of voting rights of ownership of most Swiss listed companies. In the largest Swiss firms, concentration is much lower: 17% of the firms have no shareholder with more than 10% (Table 28).

Table 28: Ownership Concentration in Swiss Listed Companies

	Companies	%
Over 90%	10	5.92
Between 50% and 90%	83	49.11
Subtotal	93	55.03
Between 45% and 50%	10	5.92
Between 35% and 45%	6	3.55
Between 25% and 35%	9	5.33
Between 10% and 25%	18	10.65
Less Than 10%	29	17.16
Unknown	4	2.37
Total	169	100

Source: Own calculations based on: Bank Vontobel 'Swiss Stock Market: Ratio Screening and Free Float' (Zurich 1995).

The data in Table 28 need further analysis to take into account the size of the firms. As could be expected, concentrated ownership characterizes smaller firms, while the wide share ownership feature is found in the larger firms. Strikingly, however, a substantial number is also found in the smaller company classes. At the level of 25% or less, there are 47 out of 169 firms (or 27%) that have no reference shareholder (Table 29).

The Swiss situation presents the characteristics of an intermediate case: more than half the listed companies are majority controlled, but a substantial percentage of the listed companies have no controlling shareholder. Both small and larger companies are involved.

Swiss companies are not only controlled by ownership of shares. Swiss company law and legal praxis have several devices for establishing control: the issue of *Partizipationsscheine*, or non-voting shares leading to a non-capital contribution, is an often-used technique, even for listed companies.[479] It is further

---

[479] See Forstmoser, Meier-Hayoz, and Nobel, supra n. 101, § 46, no. 11 et seq.

Table 29: Ownership Concentration in Swiss Listed Companies Related to Company Size

Market Capitalization in CHF	>90%	50%-90%	45%-50%	35%-45%	25%-35%	10%-25%	<10%	Not Known	Total
0-100 Mil.		14	2			1	5	1	23
100-500 Mil.	2	42	6	3	2	6	6	2	69
500-1,000 Mil.	4	12	1		5	7	4	1	34
1-2 Bil.		6		3	1		2		12
2-5 Bil.	3	5	1		1	2	3		15
5-10 Bil.	1	3				1	2		7
10-25 Bil.						1	3		4
> 25 Bil.		1					4		5
Total	10	83	10	6	9	18	29	4	169

Source: Bank Vontobel, supra Table 28.

legal to limit voting rights, e.g., at a certain percentage of capital (*Höchststimmrecht*), making aggressive takeovers more difficult.[480] In smaller companies the issue of "voting shares"[481] with preferred voting rights is allowed: the privilege is limited to ten times the normal voting franchise for the same capital contribution.[482] Indirectly, partly paid shares may have the same voting rights as fully paid shares.[483] It would be useful to complement the figures above with a further analysis of other control techniques including conventional relations. However, there was no information available on these issues.

4. Italian Companies

121. Italy is characterized by one of the highest concentrations of share ownership in Europe: 65.8% of all exchange-listed companies are majority owned by one single shareholder.[484] Majority control extends over the entire size

[480] Forstmoser, Meier-Hayoz, and Nobel, supra n. 101, § 24, no. 60 et seq.; for the German comparable rule, see Baums, Theodor 'Höchststimmrechte' *Die Aktiengesellschaft* 35 (1990) 221.

[481] *Stimmrechtsaktien*, see Forstmoser, Meier-Hayoz, and Nobel, supra n. 101, § 24, no. 95 and 105.

[482] Forstmoser, Meier-Hayoz, and Nobel, supra n. 101, § 46, no. 56.

[483] Forstmoser, Meier-Hayoz, and Nobel, supra n. 101, § 24, no. 102.

[484] These figures are confirmed by research undertaken by the Banca d'Italia. The largest shareholder owns at least a majority of the capital in 88% of the companies with 500 employees or more, and 79% of the companies with between 200 and 499 employees (Bianco, Magda, Carlo

range: even among the largest, some companies are still majority owned, in this case by the state or its specialized institutions. With respect to the not fully controlled companies, in only 15% would there be no shareholder with more than 25% (Tables 30 and 31).

Table 30: Holding of the Most Important Shareholder in Italian Listed Companies

Capitalization in Bil. ITL	>90%	50%-90%	45%-50%	35%-45%	25%-35%	10%-25%	5%-10%	<5%	Total
0-20		5				1			6
20-50		16	1	2	3	3	1		26
50-100	1	17			1	2			21
100-200		19	3	2	3	3			30
200-500	1	29	1	2	2	5		1	41
500-1,000		20	1	1	2	3			27
1,000-2,000	1	8	2	1	1	3	1	1	18
2,000-5,000		6	1	3	3	1		1	15
5,000-10,000		4			2		2	1	9
>10,000		4			1	1			6
Total	3	128	9	11	18	22	4	4	199
%	1.5	64.3	4.5	5.5	9.0	11.1	2.0	2.0	100

Sources: Consob 'Compagine Azionare Delle Società Quotate in Borsa o Ammese Alle Negoziazioni'; 'Nel Mercato Ristretto Al 31-12-1995' *Bollettino Edizione Speciale* (1996/5); *La Borsa Valori* (Gennaio and Febbraio 1996); own calculations.

Table 31: Ownership Concentration in Italian Listed Companies

	Companies	%
Over 90%	3	1.5
Over 50%	128	64.3
Fully Controlled	131	65.8
45%-50%	9	4.5
35%-45%	11	5.5
25%-35%	18	9.0
10%-25%	22	11.1
Less Than 10%	8	4.0
Total	199	100

Source: Consob, supra Table 30.

Gola, and Luigi Federico Signorini 'Dealing with Separation Between Ownership and Control: State, Family, Coalitions and Pyramidical Groups in Italian Corporate Governance' 8 (Working Paper, presented at the Workshop Corporate Governance and Property Rights, February 1996).

122. According to 1990 Consob figures, in 23 companies the largest share-holder held 75% or more of the shares.[485]

Classifying the companies according to size, majority control would prevail in the lowest quartile (25% of market capitalization). In the highest range, concentration of ownership in the hands of the largest shareholder went down in the top 10% class, except for the very largest, where concentration stayed slightly under majority level. This figure is partly because of the presence of large, recently privatized companies (Stet, Eni, Telecom) and is due to be further reduced. According to this analysis, 32 companies have widely dispersed ownership with no shareholder holding more than 20%. The ownership concentration of the three most important shareholders reached on average 62% (Table 32).

Table 32: Ownership Concentration in Italian Listed Companies: 1 to 10 Largest Stakes

Size Classes by Market Capitalization	Largest Stake	2nd Largest Stake	3rd Largest Stake	4th to 10th Largest Stakes
5%	50.54	14.18	4.19	4.20
10%	51.40	11.07	6.24	5.86
25%	53.27	8.90	4.92	10.87
50%	47.56	11.95	5.17	7.01
75%	49.11	10.11	3.50	6.32
90%	42.42	9.36	2.95	3.54
95%	37.02	7.00	3.17	2.23
Over 95%	48.63	2.55	2.03	2.31
Total	48.02	10.13	4.12	6.13

Source: Bianchi, Bianco, and Enriques, supra n. 85.

5. Dutch Companies

123. The published figures for Dutch companies are very hard to interpret because not all shares carry voting rights and, apart from actual rights, potential rights have to been taken into account. Also, published figures seem to lead to—still unsolved—inconsistencies. These figures relate to 151 out of 217 (69.59%) of the total number of listed companies (listed investment companies included).

However, 6 of these 54 companies in the less than 25% class were presumably controlled by a foundation or other body holding "potential" voting rights to be

[485] As reproduced by Bianchi, Bianco, and Enriques, supra n. 85, Table C.

exercised, for example, in case of unfriendly takeover. This also applies to companies where one shareholder holds more than 25%.

Table 33: Concentration of Voting Power in Dutch Listed Companies

	Companies	%
Majority Controlled	67	44.37
45%-50%	13	8.61
35%-45%	9	5.96
25%-35%	6	3.97
Less Than 25%	54	35.76
Not Known	2	1.32
Total	151	100

Source: ABN-AMRO 'Kerngetallen Nederlandse Beursfondsen' (Amsterdam, February 1997); own calculations.

According to an inquiry undertaken at the Nijmegen University,[486] almost all responding listed companies have introduced protection techniques against takeovers, especially by the use of preference shares or by issuing certificates of deposit standing for shares. In both cases the shareholder has limited—if any—voting rights. Protection against aggressive bids was mentioned as the most important reason for introducing these techniques, although protecting the long-term interest and the interest of other stakeholders was also mentioned. The Dutch co-determination system, leading to co-optation of the board members, was also referred to a somewhat milder—albeit unintended—protection instrument.

The extensive use of protecting devices leads to Dutch companies denying voting rights to shareholders. The above-mentioned inquiry also researched whether shareholders should be given the right to vote, or even to recommend on company matters: the answer was largely negative, most companies deeming that information to shareholders was clearly sufficient. Only in mergers and acquisitions would 25% of the respondents grant shareholders a decisive vote.

---

[486] See Scholten, I.M. and R.J. Schreur 'Corporate Governance: resultaten van een onder-nemungenquête' (Unpublished, Nijmegen University, 1996).

6. German Companies

124. For the sake of comparison, some figures about ownership concentration for German listed companies are also included.[487] The German figures point to a high degree of overall concentration of ownership, with more than two-thirds of all listed companies in firm hands. At the less than 25% level there remains a fairly high percentage of firms representing 11% of all listed companies, with substantially more in the banking sector and substantially less in the insurance field.

Table 34: Stake Size of Principal Shareholders in German Listed Companies

A. All Listed Companies		
	Number	%
1. Majority Control		
>90%	138	24.38
50%-90%	246	43.46
	384	**67.84**
2. Between 45%-50%	18	3.18
3. Between 35%-45%	41	7.24
4. Between 25%-35%	55	9.72
5. Less Than 25%	65	11.48
6. Not Known	3	0.53
Total	**566**	**100.00**

B. All Companies Other Than Banks and Insurance Companies		
	Number	%
1. Majority Control		
>90%	119	23.71
50%-90%	221	44.02
	340	**67.73**
2. Between 45%-50%	18	3.59
3. Between 35%-45%	36	7.17
4. Between 25%-35%	49	9.76
5. Less Than 25%	56	11.16
6. Not Known	3	0.60
Total	**502**	**100.00**

---

[487] Additional figures will be found in Prigge (this volume Ch. 12: Sec. B.II.) and in Schmidt et al., supra n. 83, 53 et seq.

C. Listed Banks

	Number	%
1. Majority Control		
>90%	10	28.57
50%-90%	13	37.14
	23	**65.71**
2. Between 45%-50%	0	0.00
3. Between 35%-45%	4	11.43
4. Between 25%-35%	1	2.86
5. Less Than 25%	7	20.00
6. Not Known	0	0.00
Total	**35**	**34.29**

D. Listed Insurance Companies

	Number	%
1. Majority Control		
>90%	9	31.03
50%-90%	12	41.38
	21	**72.41**
2. Between 45%-50%	0	0.00
3. Between 35%-45%	1	3.45
4. Between 25%-35%	5	17.24
5. Less Than 25%	2	6.90
6. Not Known	0	0.00
Total	**29**	**100.00**

Source: Based on *Hoppenstedt-Aktienführer* (Darmstadt et al. 1996).

7. Swedish Companies

125. The investigation of the structure of ownership in Swedish firms, undertaken in 1985 by the Swedish Ministry of Industry, indicated that out of 107 listed companies, in 45 cases (42%) the voting power was concentrated in the hands of the largest shareholder. Often power was based on multiple voting rights. Compared with the previous survey of 1978, the 1985 figures showed a clear increase in concentration of voting power: the class over 50% increased by twenty percentage points while all other classes declined, with the most significant decline in the class under 10% concentration. We have no information as to how this situation has further developed since 1985.

Table 35: Ownership Concentration in Swedish Companies

	1978		1985	
	Companies	%	Companies	%
Over 50%	19	21.11	45	42.06
Between 40% and 50 %	15	16.67	15	14.02
Between 30% and 40%	10	11.11	18	16.82
Between 20% and 30%	16	17.78	13	12.15
Between 10% and 20%	15	16.67	12	11.21
Under 10%	15	16.67	4	3.74
Total	90	100.00	107	100.00

Source:　Swedish Ministry of Industry 'The Structure of Ownership in Swedish Industry' Table 4.27 (Stockholm 1988).

8. British Companies

126. Comparable figures have been researched for U.K. listed companies. However, it appears difficult to identify the real or beneficial owners of the shares, as these often are registered in the name of trustees or nominees, or managed by portfolio managers that also act for several institutional investors. Not all U.K. listed companies were analyzed: apart from the 100 largest, an additional 325 smaller companies were considered.[488] The sample is therefore biased towards the larger companies. The analysis revealed that, as was expected, full majority control is rare (7%) in U.K. listed companies but not nonexistent, even in the 100 largest companies (five cases). In another 10% of the population, the presence of significant minority blocks was found. As could be expected, the vast majority of U.K. listed companies had no reference shareholder holding 25% or more: these stood for 81% of the population and were found not only in the class of the largest U.K. companies, but all across the sample. In 13% of the sample, no significant block of shares was reported. Even in the classes of the smallest companies, the most frequently encountered model was that of the widely owned company.

[488] Among these 100 largest companies, there were two investment trusts that have not been included in the data. In addition to the 325 smaller listed companies, there were 75 investment trusts, bringing the total sample to 500.

Table 36: U.K. Listed Companies Market Capitalization per Classes, 1994

Capitalization	Companies	%	Capitalization in Bil. £	%
> 5 Bil. £	33	7.76	312.627	49.02
2.5-5 Bil. £	26	6.12	86.459	13.56
1.6-2.5 Bil. £	39	9.18	77.612	12.17
100 Largest Companies*	98	23.06	476.699	74.75
1-1.6 Bil. £	43	10.12	55.164	8.65
0.5-1 Bil. £	67	15.76	50.386	7.90
250-500 Mil. £	94	22.12	32.932	5.16
140-250 Mil. £	123	28.94	22.585	3.54
Total	425	100.00	637.766	100.00

Note: * See n. 488.
Source: 'Crawford's Directory of City Connections' (1995); own calculations.

Table 37: Free Float in U.K. Listed Companies, 1994

Capitalization	Capitalization in Bil. £	Free Float in Bil. £	%	Holdings of Known Holders in Bil. £	%
> 5 Bil. £	312.627	285.077	91.19	27.55	8.81
2.5-5 Bil. £	86.459	75.550	87.38	10.91	12.62
1.6-2.5 Bil. £	77.612	65.380	84.24	12.23	15.76
100 Largest Companies*	476.699	426.007	89.37	50.69	10.63
1-1.6 Bil. £	55.164	47.351	85.84	7.81	14.16
0.5-1 Bil. £	50.386	41.936	83.23	8.45	16.77
250-500 Mil. £	32.932	23.963	72.76	8.97	27.24
140-250 Mil. £	22.585	15.305	67.76	7.28	32.24
Total	637.766	554.561	86.95	83.20	13.05

Note: * See n. 488.
Source: 'Crawford's Directory of City Connections' (1995); own calculations.

Table 38: Holding of the Most Important Shareholder in U.K. Listed Companies

Capitalization	>90%	50%-90%	45%-50%	35%-45%	25%-35%	10%-25%	5%-10%
> 5 Bil. £				2	2	5	6
2.5-5 Bil. £		1		2		8	2
1.6-2.5 Bil. £	1	4		1	1	6	7
100 Largest Companies**	1	5	0	5	3	19	15
1-1.6 Bil. £		2			1	10	13
0.5-1 Bil. £		2		1	5	23	21
250-500 Mil. £		9	2	3	7	43	20
140-250 Mil. £		11	2	5	15	54	29
Total	1	29	4	14	31	149	98
%	0.24	6.82	0.94	3.29	7.29	35.06	23.06

Capitalization	4%-5%	3%-4%	2%-3%	1%-2%	0%-1%	Of Which Board/ Employees	No Reporting Owner*	Total
> 5 Bil. £				1	3	5	14	33
2.5-5 Bil. £	1				5	6	7	26
1.6-2.5 Bil. £		1			6	7	12	39
100 Largest Companies**	1	1	0	1	14	18	33	98
1-1.6 Bil. £				2	4	8	11	43
0.5-1 Bil. £	1		1	2	7	8	4	67
250-500 Mil. £		1			5	31	4	94
140-250 Mil. £	1		1	1	1	41	3	123
Total	3	2	2	6	31	106	55	425
%	0.71	0.47	0.47	1.41	7.29	24.94	12.94	100

Notes: * Employees or board holding less than 0.1%.
        ** See n. 488.
Source: 'Crawford's Directory of City Connections' (1995); own calculations.

Table 39: Stake Size of Principal Shareholder in U.K. Listed Companies, 1994

	Companies	%
>90%	1	0.24
50%-90%	29	6.82
Full Majority Control	30	7.06
Between 45%-50%	4	0.94
Between 35%-45%	14	3.29
Between 25%-35%	31	7.29
Between 10%-25%	149	35.06
Between 5%-10%	98	23.06
Between 4%-5%	3	0.71
Between 3%-4%	2	0.47
Between 2%-3%	2	0.47
Between 1%-2%	6	1.41
Less Than 1%	31	7.29
No Reporting Shareholders	55	12.94
Total	425	100,00
Largest Shareholders is Board and/or Employees	106	24.95

Source: 'Crawford's Directory of City Connections' (1995); own calculations.

9. Summary

127. Table 40 and Figure 1 summarize the ownership concentration in the compared European states in descending order. Almost all listed companies were included except for those in the U.K. The reverse figures would relate to the free float: 47% in Belgium, 60% in France, and 87% for the U.K.

The differences in ownership between the different European states point to substantial differences in approach to company law and securities market regulation. While in Germany, Belgium, and Italy, companies do not heavily rely on financing in the markets, a more intensive use of securities financing is expected in Sweden, France, and the U.K. Therefore, market regulation and surveillance will be more developed in the latter systems. The position of institutional investors could also be linked to the foregoing classification: institutional investors play a leading role in the U.K., in Sweden, and in the Netherlands.

Table 40: Ownership Concentration in Europe

	D	B	I	CH	SW[a]	N	F	U.K.[b]
Over 50%	68	68	66	55	45	44	37	7
25% to 50%	21	26	19	17	39	20	32	12
Under 25%	11	6	15	28	16	36	31	81

Notes: Figures in %.
         [a] At 20% level.
         [b] Based on a sample of 425 companies of the 500 largest companies.
Source: Own calculations.

Figure 1: Ownership Concentration in Europe

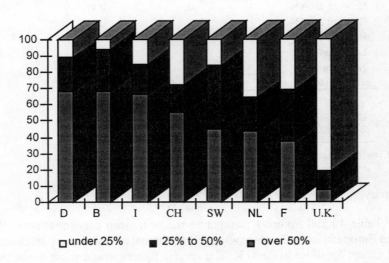

Source: Own calculations.

However, these figures should be compared with caution, as many additional factors may play a substantial role. As will be documented later, they are a useful guideline for the study of the market for corporate control, at least as evidenced by the figures on public takeover bids, although there is no full parallelism between the two series of data. Along with control based on ownership, additional elements are used in most states to firmly establish control. The actual level of control would be much higher than appears from the foregoing ownership figures.

At the other end of the spectrum, one sees that the number of companies with widely dispersed ownership is relatively rare, except in the U.K. These are the largest firms. Here the situation is more diverse among the states. The presence of control mechanisms not based on ownership might play an even more significant role as far as these companies are concerned.

Attempting to streamline the governance systems in the European states, one could distinguish between four types of companies. Most of these are met in all the national systems. Some are prevalent in the country indicated:

a) high ownership concentration: majority control, limited float: Belgium, Germany, Italy;

b) minority ownership concentration: minority control, relatively large float: France, Sweden;

c) low ownership concentration with firm control: large float: Netherlands;

d) wide ownership distribution without firm control: large float: United Kingdom.

II. The Structure of Ownership of Shares of Listed Companies

128. Apart from the data on concentration of ownership that are essential for the understanding of governance structures, an attempt should also be made to collect data on the different classes of owners of shares. The following table, published in 1995, attempts to give an overview of the different classes of shareholders. The figures should be read with caution as these diverge in several respects from other more detailed investigations. They could only be used as an indication for the relative importance of the classes mentioned. No more comprehensive recent information is available.

As in several European states shares are mainly held in bearer form,[489] statistical differences may be attributed to this factor. However, institutional investors and corporate bodies are increasingly holding securities in paperless forms (whether or not the issuer still has made up share certificates),[490] so that for an increasing portion of the overall stock market the identity of the holders should be relatively accurate.

By way of comparison, in the *U.K.*, the Statistical Office has published figures about the different classes of share owners over a period of more than 30 years. Table 41 depicts the last official figures. The lower panel regroups holdings in

---

[489] This would be the case in Germany, the Netherlands, Belgium, and Luxembourg, and also for foreign shares traded on these markets.

[490] Issuers are increasingly taking advantage of issuing shares without issuing certificates: "dematerialized securities". Government bonds are frequently issued in paperless form and shares will soon follow, see supra n. 37.

the hands of institutional investors, illustrating their predominant role in the U.K. securities markets.

Table 41: Classes of Shareholders in U.K. Listed Companies

	1963	1969	1975	1983	1989	1994
Individuals	54.0	47.4	37.5	28.2	20.6	20.3
Charities	2.1	2.1	2.3	2.2	2.3	1.3
Public	1.5	2.6	3.6	3.0	2.0	0.8
Banks	1.3	1.7	0.7	0.3	0.7	0.4
Insurance	10.0	12.2	15.9	20.5	18.6	21.9
Pension Funds	6.4	9.1	16.8	26.7	30.6	27.8
Unit Trusts	1.3	2.9	4.1	3.6	5.9	6.8
Investment Trusts	11.3	10.1	10.5	6.8	1.6	2.0
Other Financial Institutions					1.1	1.3
Industrial-Commercial Companies	5.1	5.4	3.0	5.1	3.8	1.1
Overseas	7.0	6.6	5.6	3.6	12.8	16.3
Total	100	100	100	100	100	100
Institutional Investors	29.0	34.3	47.3	57.6	57.8	59.8
Other Investors	71.0	65.8	52.7	42.4	42.2	40.2

Note: Figures in %.
Source: Central Statistical Office 'Share Ownership: A Report on the Ownership of Shares at 31st December 1994' 8 (London 1995).

129. A partly contemporaneous picture of ownership of *German* shares

Table 42: Share Ownership in German Listed Companies

	1960	1970	1980	1985	1990	1993	1995
Private Households	27	28	19	18	17	16.6	14.6
Enterprises	44	41	45	43	42	38.8	42.1
State	14	11	10	9	5	3.4	4.3
Foreign	6	8	11	13	14	12.2	8.7
Banks	6	7	9	8	10	14.3	10.3
Insurance	3	4	6	9	12	7.1	12.4
Investment Funds							7.6

Note: Figures in %.
Sources: 'Zur Bedeutung der Aktie als Finanzierungsinstrument' *Die Aktiengesellschaft* 35 (1990) R36 et seq.; for 1993 Schmidt et al., supra n. 83, 63; for 1995 Deutsche Bundesbank 'Shares as Financing and Investment Instruments' *Monthly Report* 49/1 (1997) 27-40, 29.

appears from Table 42, illustrating the overwhelming position of the enterprise sector, being ownership of shares in hands of the German groups or *Konzerne*. The relative role of the insurance companies has increased, while that of the banks has remained relatively stable. The state has been retreating from industry while an increasing proportion of German shares is being taken up by foreign investors, including institutions. As to private individuals, in Germany, too, there is a general trend towards their less active direct participation in share markets.[491]

Table 43: Share Ownership in Swedish Listed Companies, Swedish Ministry of Industry

	1979	1983	1985
Physical Persons	36	22	21
Foreign Owners	4	7	8
Mutual Funds	2	5	1
Payroll Investment-National Investment Funds			5
Listed Investment and Holding Companies	14	16	16
Insurance Companies	13	14	11
Listed Non-Financial Companies	5	9	9
Unlisted Non-Financial Companies	8		5
Foundations-Special Interest Organizations	16	24	9
National Pension Insurance	2	3	3
Employee Investment Funds			1
National-Local Governments			2
Other Legal Persons			2
Undistributed			7
Total	100	100	100

Note: Figures in %.
Source: Swedish Ministry of Industry, supra Table 35, Table 4.27.

Different and more recent figures for Sweden have been published by OECD (Table 44).

130. With respect to the overall European situation as documented in the presented figures, a few general comments can be made. In all European states one sees that the relative percentage of shares held by individual investors tends to diminish. Some states have taken measures to combat this tendency, but these seem to have failed. Even in France, where this action was most vigorously carried out, individual ownership is declining in favor of indirect ownership through investment companies.

[491] Cf. also Prigge (this volume Ch. 12: Sec. B.II.).

Table 44: Share Ownership Structure in Swedish Listed Companies, OECD

	1983	1986	1989	1992	1995
Insurance Companies	11	14	15	15	13
Investment Funds	5	6	10	9	9
Charity Funds	2	5	5	6	4
Investment Companies	16	13	8	10	7
Non-Financial Companies	16	17	20	20	9
Individuals	30	25	20	16	15
Other	12	13	15	12	12
Abroad	8	8	7	12	30
Total	100	100	100	100	100

Note: Figures in %.
Source: OECD 'Etudes Economiques de L'OCDE: Suède' 185 (Paris 1997).

Table 45: Share Ownership in Other European Countries

	Belgium[a] 1997	France[b] 1995	Italy[c] 1993	Norway[d] 1992	Netherlands[e] 1996
Households	8.1	19.4	32.2	11.1	} 36.5
Enterprises	48.1	58.0	21.6	21.0	}
Public Sector	3.3	3.4	28.0	21.7	–
Banks	1.0	4.0	10.9	0.7	0.8
Insurance Enterprises	8.2	1.9	0.8	9.4	}
Pension Funds	1.2	–		2.1	} 20.4
Investment Funds	7.4	2.0	2.2	3.9	1.1
Others	–	–	–	1.2	6.5
Rest of the World	22.7	11.2	4.3	28.9	41.2
Total	100	100	100	100	100

Note: Figures in %.
Sources: [a] Own calculations.
      [b] Deutsche Bundesbank, supra Table 42, 29.
      [c] Barca, Fabricio 'On Corporate Governance in Italy: Issues, Facts and Agenda' Table 1 (Paper presented to the OECD Conference on 'The Influence of Corporate Governance and Financing Structures on Economic Performance' Paris, 23-24 February 1995).
      [d] Van Hulle, Cynthia 'Corporate Governance: een overzicht van disciplinerings-mechanismen en empirische evidentie' *Tijdschrift voor Economie en Management* 41 (1996) 81-129, 117.
      [e] Commissie Corporate Governance, supra n. 74, 42.

The increasing share taken up by institutional investors[492] differs considerably over Europe. This trend is overwhelmingly apparent in the U.K., with about 60% according to the comparative table and even more according to some other sources; the U.K. scheme is necessarily market-oriented. In Sweden, too, institutions account for 45% of the total market. In comparison, institutional investors play a more modest role in France and Germany: about 20% of total market capitalization, after having deducted the shares owned by banks. The comparable percentages for Belgium (16%) and for Italy (3%) are even lower (Table 46).

Ownership by public sector bodies is striking for Italy (28%) and for France (5%), decreasing as a consequence of privatizations. In the other states the public sector has reduced its already small holding of listed shares.

Ownership by other companies, i.e., the group phenomenon, is particularly striking in Germany (40.2%) and in Belgium (48.4%). These figures should be related to the high degree of concentration of ownership, in both cases about 68%. It also is significant in Italy (21.6%), France (15%), and—although less— in the Netherlands (11%).[493]

Foreign ownership is the highest in the Netherlands, a finding that could be put in the context of the extensive anti-takeover protective mechanisms in Dutch firms. In the other states it is relatively low, except in Belgium (23%), which can be explained by the strong direct French presence in listed companies. France shows a 30% foreign ownership of listed shares.

III. Institutional Investors as Shareholders

131. A further breakdown of these figures will be necessary to further document institutional ownership in European companies. The definition of "institutional investor" has been widely framed and—apart from the usual pension funds—includes insurance companies, investment funds and companies, and credit institutions or banks that have been allowed to hold shares either in their trading or in their investment portfolio.[494] These would probably be limited to very small amounts.[495]

---

[492] For the present purposes being defined as the insurance companies, the pension funds, the unit trusts, and the investment trusts. For a further analysis of the role played by institutional investors, see Davies, Paul 'Institutional Shareholders in the U.K.' in: Prentice, Daniel D. and Peter R.J. Holland (eds.) *Contemporary Issues in Corporate Governance* 69-96 (Oxford 1993).

[493] Differences in classification explain these lower figures for ownership by other firms as related to share concentration.

[494] The contributions in Ch. 6 of this volume deal with German financial intermediaries.

[495] In several member states, banks have only recently been allowed to hold shares for their own account as part of the implementation of the Investment Services Directive. They are increasingly taking advantage of this possibility.

Institutional investors belong to the most significant owners of shares in the U.S. and in the U.K., where they play a major role in governance develop‑ments.[496] On the continent, the situation is quite different. In part this is due to the different forms of pension funding, which in most countries—the Nether‑lands being a notable exception—is based on a pay-as-you-go system.

Although increasingly significant in terms of volume, the role of institutional investors in the governance mechanisms of listed companies is still quite low. Their investment preferences generally go to bonds—mostly government bonds—to real estate, and more recently to investment funds. In several member states, institutional investors have not invested up to the prudential limits appli‑cable to their overall portfolio, as would be allowed pursuant to the applicable regulations. Moreover, in some states, one finds that institutionals have preferred to invest in foreign shares rather than in domestic ones.[497]

The recognition of the role of institutional investors in the corporate govern‑ance debate is still relatively recent on the European continent. This is not only a question of information or of trend setting, but it is also due to structural factors.[498] In many European states, institutional investors are very much part of banking groups or wider financial groups and therefore do not necessarily enjoy the freedom allowed the independent investment managers in the U.S. or in the U.K. As a consequence, their room for independent action and decision is less clearly traced.

Also, as ownership in most companies is closely held, institutionals have but limited impact on the company's action. Recently, however, even on the European continent, institutional investors have been willing to more actively intervene in company life, either by announcing their willingness to vote at general meeting[499] or by taking legal action against deficient management practices or more clearly against predatory conduct by controlling share‑holders.[500] Also, companies have become more sensitive to investor relations and communication, e.g., by introducing voluntary schemes for proxy solicitation.

---

[496] See Black, Bernard and John C. Coffee 'Hail Britannia? Institutional Investors Behaviour under Limited Regulation' 92 *Mich. L. Rev.* 1997 (1993-1994).

[497] The EU is attempting to lift regulatory barriers on cross-border investment by institu‑tional investors. Its efforts have not been successful.

[498] For a general overview of the issues involved, see Baums, Theodor, Richard M. Buxbaum, and Klaus J. Hopt (eds.) *Institutional Investors and Corporate Governance* 289 (Berlin and New York 1994).

[499] Art. 25 of the 1985 directive on ucits, supra n. 16, prevents investment funds and investment managers from "exercis[ing] significant influence over the management of the company" by acquiring shares to carry voting rights. Some member states have implemented this prohibition by forbidding "any influence". The question arises as to whether this strict prohibition would still allow for any activist stand on their part.

[500] Conspicuously in the mandatory bid cases: see, e.g., in the *Wagon Lits* decision: Cass. 10 May 1994, *Tijdschrift voor Belgisch Handelsrecht—Revue de droit commercial belge* 28 (1995)

Table 46: Shareholdings of Institutional Investors as % of Total Market Capitalization

	Italy[a]	Norway[b]	Belgium[c]	Netherlands[d]	Sweden[e]
Insurance Companies	0.8	9.4	8.2		
Private Pension Funds		2.1			
Public Pension Funds			1.1		
Subtotal	0.8	11.5	9.3	20.4	13
Investment Funds	2.2	3.9	6.6	1.1	9
Banks	10.9	0.7	1.2	0.8	
Other Financial Firms	0	0.2	0	0	7
Total	13.9	16.3	17.1	22.3	29

	France[f]	Germany[g]	U.S.[h]	U.K.[i]
Insurance Companies			6.1	21.9
Private Pension Funds			14.0	
Public Pension Funds			8.2	27.8
Subtotal	9.7	12.4	28.3	49.7
Investment Funds	12.7	7.6	13.1	6.8
Banks	6.5	10.3	2.7	0.4
Other Financial Firms	0	0	0	3.3
Total	28.9	30.3	44.1	60.2

Note: Figures in %.
Sources: [a]   December 1993; Barca, supra Table 45, Table 1.
   [b]   1992; Isaksson, Mats and Rolf Skog 'Corporate Governance in Swedish Listed Companies' in: Baums, Buxbaum, and Hopt (eds.), supra n. 498, 287-310, 289.
   [c]   April 1996; own calculations.
   [d]   1996; Commissie Corporate Governance, supra n. 74, 42.
   [e]   OECD, supra Table 44, 185.
   [f]   December 1994; Own calculations, based on Chocron, Monique and Lydie Marchand 'La clientèle des principaux établissements dépositaires de titres' *Bulletin de la Banque de France* (supplément études) (1er Trimestre 1995) 123-47; Chocron, Monique and Lydie Marchand 'La clientèle des principaux établissement dépositaires de titres aux troisième et quatrième trimestres de 1994 et sur l'ensemble de l'année 1994' *Bulletin de la Banque de France* (June 1995) 107-48. These figures differ considerably from the ones mentioned in Table 45.
   [g]   1995; Deutsche Bundesbank, supra Table 42, 29.
   [h]   1995; Commissie Corporate Governance, supra n. 74, 37.
   [i]   1994; Davies, supra n. 492, 51.

15, note Fr. Glansdorff aff'ing Brussels, 6 August 1992, *Revue pratique des sociétés* (1992) 248; more recently: Comm. Trib. Mechelen 23 January 1998, unreported (*Superclub-Philips*).

IV. The Stock Markets

132. The markets for shares still present a very diverse panorama in Europe. Although their role seems to be changing, it has remained relatively limited on the continent as opposed to the United Kingdom.

Each of the states has its own securities market, often with one or more submarkets on which shares are traded. Most of these national markets have several segments for share trading, usually on the basis of the depth of the market.[501] Major shares are listed on several European markets,[502] where they are usually dealt with in the local currency of dealing.[503] This dual or multiple listing has not prevented the home market from remaining the dominant one. Transparency has been enhanced, recently by the intensive use of electronic data transmission. The linkage between the markets takes place through personal contacts, traders executing transactions on other markets, and often being members of several markets. Linkage by technical devices, especially by electronic links, are still relatively rare as far as trading is concerned. The same applies to linkage at the level of clearing and settlement where bilateral arrangements exist, multilateral arrangements still being at the level of discussion.

This diversity at the level of organization corresponds to an equally diverse panorama at the level of regulation and supervision. Each of the markets has its own regulatory system and its own supervisory bodies. Minimum standards have been introduced by the EU directives. Linkage between the supervisors takes place by cooperation, incorporation in MOU, and by concentration. At the European level, common issues such as interpretation of the directives are discussed in a "contact" committee, aimed at advising the EU commission and at facilitating consultation between the supervisory bodies.[504]

133. It has been illustrated above[505] that the role of the securities markets, especially of the share markets, presents considerable differences within Europe. Three groups of countries were identified, whereby the largest European economies had the least-used securities markets.

These differences in market structure are related to many factors. One of the aspects is the availability of alternative financing mechanisms for listed companies. The relationship of company capital to total assets is an indication of the

---

[501] For a broad overview of the structures, see Hopt, Klaus J., Bernd Rudolph, and Harald Baum (eds.) *Börsenreform, Eine ökonomische, rechtsvergleichende und rechtspolitische Untersuchung* (Stuttgart 1997).

[502] For figures about German shares, see Schmidt et al., supra n. 83, 60.

[503] There are a few exceptions: Luxembourg deals in the national currency of the issuer, as does Amsterdam for American shares.

[504] See art. 20 Directive of 5 March 1979 *OJEC* L 66/21, 16.3.1979 and Directive of 17 April 1989 *OJEC* L 124/8, 5.5.1989.

[505] See supra no. 10.

relative importance of share financing in an economic system. It should be supplemented by the relation between external and internal financing. By way of example only a few facts will be reproduced here. In systems where securities financing plays a less important role, one sees an under-weighing of own funds, leading to an increased call on external financing, mainly through bank loans.[506] Internal savings also point to the same direction. The relative importance played by the firm's own funds can be illustrated by the following data relating to the equity ratio of all firms in a number of selected states:

Table 47: Equity Ratios in Major Industrialized Countries

	Early '80s (Of Which: Industry)	End of '80s (Of Which: Industry)	Change
Japan	13.60 (29.90)	18.70 (30.70)	5.1
Germany	22.50 (26.40)	19.10 (26.00)	-3.4
United Kingdom	26.30 (19.80)	30.10 (25.10)	3.8
France	48.00 (41.50)	49.50 (36.20)	1.5
U.S.	58.00 (42.00)	56.90 (40.10)	-1.1

Note: Figures in % and percentage points respectively.
Source: Deutsches Aktieninstitut 'DAI-Factbook 1996. Statistiken, Analysen und Graphiken zu Aktionären, Aktiengesellschaften und Börsen' p. FB_04-2 (Frankfurt am Main 1996).

The lower equity ratios for the Japanese and German firms are striking if compared to the U.S. and French sample. If one calculates the same ratio for the listed companies only, the comparison becomes somewhat less dramatic: for Germany, listed companies had an equity ratio of 38.6%, double the overall average figure, with the holding companies standing for a maximum of 42.2%. The large difference between the overall figure and the industry is due to the low capitalization of the financial sector (banks, mortgage credit institutions, insurance companies).

However, as can be derived from the figures in Table 48, these differences have narrowed in at least the two noticeably "undercapitalized" states in the period from the mid-1980s through the mid-1990s. One will notice that developments in market structure and market regulation are keeping pace with these changes, with a time lag of about five to ten years. The important provisions in Germany are due to the internalization of pension liabilities.

---

[506] The contributions in Ch. 10 of this volume analyze lenders as a force in corporate governance.

Table 48: Capital Ratios in Major Industrialized Countries

	Own Funds			Debts			Provisions		
	1985	1990	1994	1985	1990	1994	1985	1990	1994
France	20.5	33.0	36.2	73.6	61.8	57.5	4.9	4.6	5.6
Germany	30.3	26.6	31.6	39.3	38.6	34.3	32.0	31.6	33.9
Italy	26.8	28.3	26.5	63.6	62.5	64.5	7.3	7.1	8.0
U.K.	47.8	37.1	36.8	47.8	50.9	46.1	4.4	12.1	17.0
Europe=10	31.6	32.6	33.3	60.8	51.7	49.5	5.8	16.6	17.1
U.S.	45.8	39.8	37.4	50.3	55.5	54.9	—	—	—
Japan	26.4	31.1	32.7	67.8	63.7	62.1	4.8	4.1	4.0

Note: All figures as % of total capital.
Source: OECD, supra n. 257, Table 23; referring to: 'Situation financière des entreprises' *Economie européenne* no. 4, suppl. A.

The analysis of the French situation has pointed to an equally clear trend towards convergence for the largest business firms: for 23 non-financial firms (16 included in the CAC 40) the own funds ratio went from 29.8% in 1985 to 35.4% in 1990 and 41.7% in 1994.[507] This significant evolution was attributed to a change in overall policy, based on less government steering of business firms in favor of more liberalized financial structures. High real interest rates in the 1980s, less debt-favorable tax policies, and the liberalizing of capital movements from 1988 on were also mentioned as part of the explanation of this change.

The relatively small capital basis of German firms raises the question as to their sources of financing. Here also there are some interesting figures available; however, they relate only to Germany. From these it appears that German firms in general—and therefore not only listed firms—have financed themselves mainly from amortization and from credit; equity issues have played a subordinate role, and reserved profits have been negative in many years. This feature should not be surprising taking into account the structure of ownership in German industry and the role played by the German universal banks (Table 49).[508]

These figures call for further detailed comparative study. However, at the present stage of investigation they suggest that the role played by the stock

[507] OECD, supra n. 257, 138.

[508] On these issues, cf. also the contributions in Ch. 6 of this volume on German financial intermediaries and Prigge (Ch. 12: Sec. C.II.).

Table 49: Financing of German Listed Companies

	Reserved Profits	Amortization	Equity Issues	Credit	Total
1960	25.16	22.23	3.16	28.56	79.11
1965	19.62	40.88	0.92	59.04	120.46
1971	9.63	73.31	4.30	104.95	192.19
1975	-20.49	109.74	4.11	94.23	187.59
1980	-41.59	162.53	5.26	202.68	328.88
1985	-40.67	217.79	6.76	177.45	361.33
1988	17.33	243.20	5.28	174.01	439.82
1990	27.11	280.19	21.99	266.55	595.84
1992	-44.28	332.62	11.79	315.81	615.94

Note: Figures in billion DM.
Source: Deutsches Aktieninstitut, supra Table 47, p. FB_04-3.

markets in Europe is relatively different according to the states compared: it is predominant in the U.K. where securities financing is very active, followed by Sweden through to the intermediate cases (France, Belgium, Italy), and down to the lowest users of shares as a financing mechanism (Germany). The Dutch and the Swiss cases call for a separate explanation, related to the role of Switzerland as a financial center and to the presence of large multinational companies in the Netherlands. The use of shares without effective voting rights has probably contributed to the more frequent use of share financing by Dutch firms.

134. In most European states, developments in the stock markets are pointing at quite substantial changes towards a more securities-oriented approach, both by issuers and investors. As a consequence of the process of economic integration within Europe, to be reinforced after the formation of the European Monetary Union, competition between the market centers has considerably increased, leading to a greater openness, better communication through electronic linkages, and the leveling of the playing field both between the European markets and at the international level. These developments started in the early nineties and are still gaining momentum. The effects on the governance scene are inevitable: a greater awareness of each other's practices is evidenced by the considerable attention the Cadbury Code of Conduct has received in all states, and the inevitable references to "good governance" and "shareholder value" in speeches by business leaders all over Europe.[509] It is still too early to predict the effective consequences of this integration process at the level of company laws and

---

[509] See for further details, Wymeersch, Eddy 'Corporate Governance After the Investment Services Directive' *European Financial Services Law* 3 (1996) 98-102 and 130-41.

practices, but it seems likely that these developments will constitute a factor of integration that cannot be denied.

135. The organization and regulation of the securities business has been substantially modified in the 1990s. In an increasingly competitive environment, continental European exchanges fought for market share—not so much among themselves, but mainly against the active London market (SEAQ International). More recently competition from the American markets has been increasingly felt as some large European issuers, hoping to free themselves from the restrictions of the European markets, have applied for listing on the NYSE (Daimler, but also several French companies, or Belgian Petrofina), while new issuers, especially in technological branches, are feeling attracted by Nasdaq.

Several initiatives were taken at the European level. A certain number of markets merged, leading to schemes whereby only one market organizer exists today. This happened in Italy, it is still going on in Germany, and it was achieved in the Netherlands and in Belgium where only one body will be in charge of organizing the different stock market segments (merging stock and derivative markets).

A second reaction leads to the organization of markets for unseasoned shares: Easdaq, a market modeled on and linked with the American Nasdaq, and the NTS (New Trading System), a new market involving the Paris, Brussels, Amsterdam, and German Exchanges, are planned to attract trading in small caps. These "supra-national" initiatives have been reinforced by continued trading on national markets of shares listed on other national markets. However, one has rarely seen issuers applying for a first—or main—listing outside their own state.

A significant structural change is due to the more intensive use of electronic devices in share trading. Several markets have changed to fully electronic— although only partially automated—trading systems. These systems are increasingly order driven, leading sometimes to a type of hybrid between the quote and order-driven price formation systems. Linkage at a Europe-wide level remains largely undeveloped, except at the level of pre-trading information. Each market organizer is striving to keep the order flow in the locally listed shares while offering electronic access to non-resident banks or brokers. Linkages between some of the markets have been established with respect to settlement of securities, but this remains largely bilateral rather than an all-encompassing multilateral network. However, great progress is being pursued in the derivative side of the markets where cooperation between the German, French, and Swiss systems is leading to a fully integrated approach.

Markets in securities have become more active this last decade. Not only has the number of shares offered for investment increased in all European states (in some more rapidly than in others, see Table 8), the volume of investment has also swollen considerably. This movement is due to several factors: the low interest rates, the graying of the population, and the larger needs for pension provisions, but also the increasing popularity of share investments and the offering of attractive new issues on the markets. The role of the institutional investors is likely to become decisive: not only does one see increasing volumes being invested in shares, but overseas investors are also showing a greater interest for European stocks. In the wake of these developments, shareholder activism has increased in several European states. This development has taken several forms, and is in part driven by the higher visibility of company conduct and the related governance questions.

136. Traders on the securities markets are increasingly banks: according to the Second Banking Directive, previously existing restrictions for banks to deal in shares have been removed. Also, banks were allowed to take part in securities firms or brokers. Both banks and brokers compete for order execution and investment advisory services, and are subject to more or less equal regulations. However, additional regulatory requirements, especially those dealing with own funds, tend to drive the smaller and less capitalized brokerage houses out of the market by being taken over, in whole or in parts, by the larger—especially international—banks. As a consequence, states that mainly relied on brokers for their securities trading have seen most of the brokerage firms being bought up by banks. This phenomenon is visible in France and Italy, but also in Belgium and Holland, where takeovers of brokers by banks have been numerous. Even in Germany, where brokers had a more limited role, their position is coming under increasing pressure.

The role of the stock exchanges as market organizers and regulators has come under scrutiny. In several European states, the self-regulatory system, whereby members of the exchanges largely supervised and regulated themselves, has been threatened over the last fifteen years. Some highly visible deficiencies—especially relating to insider dealing cases—have further supported the claim for removing the supervisory role from the exchanges and for further abandoning the self-regulatory approach. Government regulation has, as a consequence, increased substantially in all European states.

137. Several patterns are visible in the reorganization of the regulatory and supervisory framework. As a consequence of the regulation due to the implementation of the Investment Services Directive,[510] many states have substantially revised their regulatory apparatus. On the one hand, prudential matters in most states have been concentrated in the hand of the prudential supervisor, acting for banks, securities firms, and even investment managers and advisers. The central bank as banking supervisor or a specialized agency or ministerial department take care of integrated prudential supervision, often on a consolidated basis.

---

[510] See ISD, supra n. 13; for an overview of these issues, see Wymeersch, supra n. 63; Schwark, Eberhard 'Börsen und Wertpapierhandelsmärkte in der EG' *Wertpapier-Mitteilungen* 51 (1997) 293-307.

Except in the United Kingdom, insurance supervision has been kept separate in most of the states.

Regulation and supervision of markets has been put in the hand of a market authority, often a securities commission. As a consequence, the former stock exchanges have lost their supervisory and regulatory powers, becoming commercial service providers to the financial community and competing with similar bodies in other states. In the wake of these developments, self-regulation has largely been eliminated from the regulatory toolbox, while the volume of governmental regulation has considerably increased. Enforcement also is becoming more legalistic.

138. Competition between regulators and between supervisors will in all likelihood follow competition between markets. Present procedures for cooperation between supervisors are relatively weak, leaving ample room for issuers to choose the market of least regulation. The organization of a Europe-wide securities regulator seems far away, a network of regulators and supervisors being a more likely set-up.

However, this competition takes place within the framework of the minimum guarantees built in by the European directives.[511] In the fields of disclosure, market access, and regulation of market structure, these directives have triggered developments that tend towards liberalization within the Union and with third countries. New challenges are appearing on the horizon, especially the integration of European standards and practices with American ones. Disclosure and accounting standards represent two examples of these developments.

139. The rules on financial disclosure have largely been harmonized by the European Union in a series of directives going back to the late 1970s.[512] The rules introduce a set of minimum safeguards, which, along with mutual recognition, in fact avoid duplication of disclosure requirements without allowing for downward competition. There remain numerous points of difference, however, both in the fields of financial disclosure and of annual accounts.

The fourth and seventh directives on annual accounts and consolidated annual accounts have left national regulators and hence issuers with a number of options that result in financial statements being less than fully comparable. Therefore, large international companies increasingly adhere to IAS, or if they envisage a full listing on an American market, even to U.S. GAAP. Negotiations are going on with the ultimate aim of ensuring mutual recognition of accounting rules and financial statement on both sides of the Atlantic.

---

[511] Cf. also the extensive treatment of competition in securities regulation by Romano (this volume Ch. 3).

[512] For an overview of the disclosure policy, see Wymeersch, Eddy 'The EU Directives on Financial Disclosure' *European Financial Services Law* 3 (1996) 34-45.

V. Takeovers and the Market for Corporate Control[513]

140. The structure of ownership is a determinant factor for the way the corporate control market is organized and functions. In all states there is an active "private" market for corporate assets and corporate control. In terms of number of transactions, about half the number of transactions taking place worldwide involve European companies, whether at the buying or at the selling side. This would be even more true in terms of funds involved.

This market is quite effective and runs through the communication channels of the large accounting firms and investment banks that operate across Europe. The transactions mostly—if not exclusively—relate to privately owned firms, including subsidiaries and divisions of listed companies. Both in terms of number of transactions and of turnover, it largely exceeds the more visible markets for public takeover bids (Tables 50 and 51).

Table 50: Mergers and Acquisitions in Value of Transactions

	1990	1991	1992	1993	1994	1995
France	18.9	26.8	21.7	29.8	21.2	20.9
Germany	15.1	20.3	21.4	11.4	10.1	16.5
Italy	20.0	7.5	23.3	16.5	9.0	9.2
U.K.	77.4	56.6	45.5	42.3	36.4	124.2
Belgium	5.9	3.1	1.0	4.9	1.4	1.6
The Netherlands	13.9	5.9	15.5	8.3	5.2	8.5
Spain	8.5	15.5	10.6	9.0	7.3	4.1
Sweden	6.9	11.5	6.9	12.5	7.7	8.8
Switzerland	5.8	0.7	2.2	3.4	2.7	8.2
Rest of Europe	13.3	12.1	12.0	12.2	10.0	24.3
Europe	185.7	160.0	160.1	150.3	111.0	226.3
U.S.	108.2	71.2	96.7	176.4	226.7	356.0

Note: Figures in bil. $.
Source: OECD, supra n. 257, 133; OECD 'Etudes Economiques de L'OCDE: Etats-Unis' 165 (Paris 1995-96).

141. More directly of interest for the present study is the public control market, especially by way of public takeovers and comparable transactions. Here a relatively wide diversity of factual situations can be found, largely attributable

---

[513] The contributions in Ch. 8 of this volume deal with the market for corporate control.

Table 51: Mergers and Acquisitions in Number of Transactions

	Acquisitions		Selling Transactions	
	1995	1996	1995	1996
Belgium	49	55	55	89
France	378	343	350	332
Germany	444	450	362	322
Italy	109	130	170	162
Netherlands	273	319	145	136
Spain	32	46	160	107
U.K.	664	664	449	468
Sweden	93	152	72	120
Switzerland	186	192	76	74
Rest of Europe	365	463	645	754
Europe	2,593	2,814	2,484	2,564
Canada	298	323	180	250
U.S.	1,228	1,553	699	849
Japan	351	445	89	69
Rest of World	842	817	1,890	2,220
Total	2,719	3,138	2,858	3,388

Note: Figures include minority investments and joint ventures.
Source: KPMG 'Deal Watch 1996' (no. 1 and 2) 26 et seq.

to diverging features of share ownership and related regulations. The following tables attempt to give data about the frequency of public takeovers in some jurisdictions. However, a warning is in order about the confusing terminology: due to regulatory definitions, several European states do not define "takeovers" but rather public "offers to acquire", thereby including transactions as freeze-outs that are effectuated by a public bid for the shares, bids by issuers to acquire their own shares, and other similar transactions.

142. From the following table, one can deduct that a quite substantial number of takeovers takes place in the *United Kingdom*. These takeovers obviously are mostly non-aggressive bids, although the number of unfriendly bids is not negligible: 15% of the bids are unsuccessful or withdrawn.[514] Seventy percent are successful. Also noteworthy are the mandatory bids, i.e., bids that have to be

---

[514] Or 40% if one adds the "initially unrecommended" and the "unrecommended at the end of the offer period" to the unsuccessful proposals, and those proposals that are withdrawn before the documents are issued.

brought after a shareholder acquires more than 30% of the shares. Rule of the City Code on Takeovers and Mergers requires any person—including persons acting in concert—who acquires 30% of the shares carrying voting rights to extend offers to all holders of any class of equity shares (voting or non-voting). One can presume that most of these bids are unfriendly, for in the case of a friendly bid the bidder would prefer to make a public offer without first building up an important toehold and being exposed to the need of having to bid for all the remaining shares.

Table 52: Takeovers in the United Kingdom

	1988 -89	1989 -90	1990 -91	1991 -92	1992 -93	1993 -94	1994 -95	1995 -96	1996 -97
1. Successful Proposals	184	163	102	99	62	57	75	123	137
2. Unsuccessful Proposals	40	36	11	22	13	11	11	16	14
3. Proposals Withdrawn Before Issue of Documents	7	6	1	3	1	0	2	5	5
4. Proposals Involving Minorities	22	25	18	18	12	13	20	12	15
5. Total 1-4	253	230	132	142	88	81	108	156	171
Of Which									
6.1. Number of Companies Involved	224	211	130	130	85	79	100	145	156
6.2. Mandatory Bids				13	13	10	12	7	9
6.3. Initially Unrecommended				39	28	24	33	37	37
6.4. Unrecommended at End of Offer Period			34	17	9	8	24	32	30
7. Other Cases Under Consideration	195	142	142	116	141	340	201	241	223

Source: Takeover Panel 'Annual Reports'.

The above figures illustrate the frequency of takeovers in the U.K.: over the years, about 8% to 10% of the listed companies have been involved as targets of a takeover that was effectively published. If one adds the number of transactions that were taken into consideration, even those that have not materialized or were not published, then the relationship to all listed companies increases to about 15% to 20%. The threat of a takeover is not to be disregarded in the U.K. Equally striking is the number of "unrecommended bids", i.e., bids that were opposed by the incumbent management: in about one-third of these cases the management resisted the bid. We have no data as to whether or not this resistance failed. Mandatory bids under Rule 9 of the Takeover Code are also noteworthy: these represented on average 11% of all bids. This would indicate that markets have largely assimilated the rule whereby crossing the 30% threshold leads to a mandatory bid. Often investors buy up to 29.9%. It also points to acquisitions against the management's recommendation.

143. The *French* situation is also well documented. The officially published statistics indicate that there are many "public offers to acquire", whether for cash or in exchange for securities. If one analyzes the figures, there appear to be several types of transactions to be classified under the heading of control transactions or *offre publique d'acquisition* (or *OPA*).

Table 53: Public Bids for Shares in France

Public Bids for Shares in France	1989	1990	1991	1992	1993	1994	1995
A. Cash Takeovers (*OPA*)							
1. Number of Targets	23	13	23	9	6	7	13
2.1. Increased Bid	8	8	0	2		3	12
2.2. Number of Targets	4	2		2	0	1	2
3.1. Competing Bids	1	2	0	2	2	2	7
3.2. Number of Targets	1	1		2	0	2	5
4. Total *OPA*	32	23	18	13	8	12	24
B. Exchange Offers (*OPE*)		2	5	4	3	3	8
1. Competing Bids							1
C. Total Bids	32	25	23	17	11	15	32
D. Freeze-Out (*OPR*)	n.a.	27	20	41	33	30	70
E. Bloc Transactions	48	81	67	40	24	14	18
F. Total Control Transactions (C+E)	80	106	90	57	41	29	50

Source: Own calculations based on: Commission des operations de bourse 'Annual Reports' (Paris 1989-1995).

Related to the number of companies listed, one could state that about 2% to 3% of all listed companies have been involved in a takeover situation. These bids are mostly friendly, at least as far as one can see from the figures published.[515] There were one or a few contested bids in most of these years, resulting in competing bids and then later in increased bids. There seems to be a tendency for having fewer takeover bids in general but more competing bids once a fight has been triggered. Although no figures have been published about their frequency,

---

[515] If only a minority was tendered, then bids could also be analyzed as being unfriendly bids, at least bids to which the incumbent management has not agreed.

the mandatory bid rule (at a one-third threshold in France) also has influenced the structure of the takeover market, for the bidder might prefer to publicly bid for the shares without first acquiring a one-third block as was usual before the rule's modification. Also, bidders now must bid for all the shares rather than for two-thirds as the previous rule required.

144. The French statistics classify under the same heading the bids that are mandated after a shareholder has acquired full legal control as a consequence of his purchase of a controlling block from another shareholder. The number of these transactions was quite substantial due to the structure of share ownership, as mentioned above. The number of transactions is also showing a downward trend, probably because the more obvious controlling blocks have been transferred as restructuration of the business sector has been achieved. To further identify this type of transaction, one also finds an overview, for a typical year, of the shares held by the acquirer before his acquiring a controlling block, his block acquisition, and the final outcome of his holding after the public bid. Most of these transactions take the technical form of a limit order, placed on the stock market, for all shares offered.[516] This procedure is less expensive than a public bid, as the latter calls for extensive disclosure and marketing efforts. The frequency of these bloc transactions confirms that, according to French tradition, company restructuring takes place by voluntary measures rather than on the markets. This factor is also illustrated by the frequency and importance of mergers and acquisitions in France, which is the second highest in the EU (Table 54).[517]

145. In *Belgium*, public offers to acquire are also frequently found and are motivated by a variety of reasons. Published data give the following picture (Table 55). Here again, not all transactions relate to takeovers: control transactions are relatively rare and most of the time have been agreed to by the partners before the public takeover is announced. Belgium also has introduced the mandatory bid rule, which is relatively frequently applied, both with respect to companies that are exchange listed and companies whose shares are widely distributed in the public at large. The rule is triggered by the acquisition of control as a consequence of a share acquisition at a price above market (item 3 in Table 55). In other cases, the public offers related to the repurchase of own shares or to freeze-out transactions (item 1).

146. In the other European states, takeovers are relatively rare: there have been a few attempts in *Germany,* all of which failed or ended in a "voluntary"

---

[516] This is the so-called *maintien de cours.* Most transactions have resulted in a delisting of the shares.

[517] See Figures in OECD, supra n. 257, Table 21.

Table 54: *Bloc de Contrôle* Transactions in France, 1993

Company	Pre-acquisition %	Block Acquired %	Bid Outcome %
Jod Electr	0	80.10	80.10
Lyon Gerland	45.23	32.67	79.38
Fin atlantique	1.45	64.61	96.90
Stef	Indirect 80%		99.53
CGEF	21.17	51.43	97.75
Verdome	0	98.85	98.82
Optorg	0	50.28	87.58
SFM	16.88	50.66	98.27
Sicma	35.63	50.07	98.65
Catteau	0	56.84	98.78
Forinter	0	89.40	98.78
Ferm Vichy	0	94.40	94.54
Eaux Vichy	0	87.21	97.12
Atlantis	0	72.28	96.79
IGF	0	91.47	91.47
Albert	0	37.66	95.86
Fnac	0	50.01	98.15
BIMP	62.71	12.62	94.07
Barphone	0	71.14	98.60
MJ Develop	2.19	51.27	61.70
CGP Packag	0	89.51	99.59
Batibail	38.33	12.55	53.85
Maneurop	0	53.63	98.28
Axime-Sgin		13.21	62.89

Source: Own calculations based on: Commission des operations de bourse 'Annual Report' (Paris 1993).

Table 55: Takeovers in Belgium

	1988	1989	1990	1991	1992	1993-94 n.a.	1995	1996
1. Bid by Majority Shareholder	5	15	13	15	11		8	14
of Which "Exchange Order"	1	6	5	3	2		2	
2. Repurchase Bid for own Shares	2	0	1	0	5		3	4
3. Other Bids	2	5	9	2	1		2	3
of Which Aggressive Bids	6	0	0	0	1		2	0
4. Bids for Foreign Shares	2	0	6	1	1		0	n.a.
5. Total Bids for Shares	17	20	29	18	18		14	21
6. Bids for Real Estate Funds	0	8	14	15	2		1	0
7. Total Number of Bids	17	28	43	33	21	n.a.	15	23

Source: Banking and Finance Commission 'Statistical Bulletin'.

merger. The Continental-Pirelli case[518] and the more recent Krupp-Hoesch case have been well documented. A few have been attempted in the *Netherlands*, but failed.

There were also some attempts in *Italy*.[519] Moreover, Consob reports frequent freeze-out transactions that take the form of a public offer to acquire.

Table 56: Takeovers in Italy

	1992	1993	1994	1995	1996	1997/1
1974 Law	0	2	4	8	15	6
1992 Law						
voluntaria	2		2	3	8	3
concorrente		1		1		
rilancio				1		
obbligatoria						
preventiva		2				1
successiva	2	3	11	9	9	4
incrementale					1	
residuale		5	6	9	10	3
Total	4	11	19	23	28	11

Note: Offers to acquire (1974 law) and takeover bids (1992 law).
Source: Consob 'Bolletino' (Ed. Speziale, 5/97).

Italy has two regimes applicable to takeovers. According to the 216/1974 law, all public offers to acquire or exchange are subject to regulation. Since 1992, offers aimed at the acquisition of shares listed on the stock exchange or on assimilated markets are subject to the law 149/92 of February 18, 1992. The latter introduces a complex regime classifying takeovers in specific classes. The main classes mentioned are *obbligatoria* or mandated—as opposed to *voluntaria*—when someone acquires or intends to acquire control of a listed company: in this case the offer can be *preventiva*, when he intends to acquire said control, or *successiva*, when he has already acquired control in a private transaction but is legally obliged to bring a public bid. The number of shares to be acquired should be such as to secure control and at least 10%. *Incrementale* is the additional bid to be brought by the shareholder who has already acquired half

---

[518] For an analysis, see Baums, Theodor 'Hostile Takeovers in Germany. A Case Study on Pirelli vs. Continental AG' (Working Paper of the Institut für Handels- und Wirtschaftsrecht, University of Osnabrück, no. 3/1993). See also Franks and Mayer (Ch. 8) in this volume.

[519] See *Romagnolo* case, Rigotto, Marco 'l'OPA Credito Romagnolo' *Rivista delle società* 41 (1996) 158 et seq., in general: Cusmai, Mauro and Raffaele D'Ambrosio 'Riflessioni sull'Istituto dell'OPA obbligatoria' *Rivista di diritto commerciale* (1995) 407-50.

of the controlling block of shares, but within 12 months acquires 2% in a manner other than within a public bid. Compulsory squeeze-outs, at the 10% level, are classified as *residuale*.

Switzerland has a quite important practice of both friendly and unfriendly takeovers.[520] In 1994, 18 takeovers were submitted to the Commission for the Regulation of the Swiss Stock Exchange, none of which was aggressive. In 1995, eight cases were submitted, including the first aggressive bid (*Holvis*).[521]

Several European states have introduced some form of regulation of takeover bids. At the EU, a proposal for a thirteenth company law directive was published in 1989,[522] and three revisions have since been released.[523]

At the level of the states, several jurisdictions have introduced rules of conduct relating to takeover that have actually been published: U.K., France, Belgium, Italy, and Spain have enacted elaborate instruments. Most of the regulations impose bidding for all (U.K., France, and Belgium) or for at least the majority of the shares (Italy). Also, the target's management would usually be required to stand off and not undertake any defensive action. Germany has introduced a voluntary code of conduct relating to tender offers.[524]

The most controversial section of the proposed directive relates to the mandatory bid rule. This rule is already in effect in several EU states (U.K., France, Belgium, Italy, Spain) while some are considering its introduction (Austria). There remain some significant differences as to the events triggering the obligation to bid: whether crossing a specific threshold (as is the case in the U.K. (30%), in France (one-third), in Spain (different levels), or in Switzerland (33 1/3%))[525] or acquiring control (to be defined in light of the specific elements

---

[520] See 'Schweizerischer Übernahme-Kodex der Vereinigung der Schweizer Börsen' *Wertpapier-Mitteilungen* 46 (1992) 1090-2; Meier-Schatz, Christian 'Besprechung des Entscheides der Regulierungskommission' *Schweizerische Juristenzeitung* 91 (1995) 190.

[521] See *Schweizerische Zeitschrift für Wirtschafsrecht* 68 (1996) 180-96; 69 (1997) 109; see further Schwarz, Jörg 'Das neue Schweizerische Aktienrecht und der Übernahmekodex' *Wertpapier-Mitteilungen* 46 (1992) 1052-8, 1053. For the *Holvis* case, see *Schweizerische Zeitschrift für Wirtschafsrecht* 67 (1995) 186.

[522] Com (88) 823 final, published in *OJEC* C 64/8, 14.3.1989; see Centre d'études juridiques européennes de Genève *Les prises de participations: l'exemple des offres publiques d'achat* (Lausanne 1990).

[523] For the other proposals, see Com (95), 655-fin *OJEC* C 162/5, 6.6.1996; for a comment: Schuster, Gunnar 'Der neue Vorschlag für eine EG Takeover-Richtlinie und seine Auswirkungen auf den Übernahmekodex' *Europäische Zeitschrift für Wirtschaftsrecht* 8 (1997) 237-41. The latest proposal is dated 11 November 1997 *OJEC* C 378/10, 13.12.1997.

[524] For a broad study of the issues involved, see Hopt, Klaus J. 'Europäisches und deutsches Übernahmerecht' *Zeitschrift für das gesamte Handelsrecht und Wirtschaftsrecht* 161 (1997) 368-420.

[525] Hertig, Gérard (ed.) *L'avant-projet de loi fédérale sur les bourses et le commerce des valeurs mobilières* (Zurich 1992). For an overview of the present regulation: Hansen, Herbert 'Der Schweizer Aktienmarkt' *Die Aktiengesellschaft* 42 (1997) R490.

of the case at hand (Belgium, Italy), in one case on showing that a control premium has been paid (Belgium)), the rules remain quite diverse. In Austria, opposition obviously has given in to a mandatory requirement, while in Germany the situation is still undecided. Opposition against the rule is strong in the Netherlands and in Sweden[526].

E. Conclusion

147. The purpose of this contribution is to outline elements of the structure of large business corporations in Europe, mainly on the European continent. The present research dealing with corporate governance is characterized by a significant lack of reliable data. Therefore, it seemed necessary to first explore factual situations underlying the European corporate world, and thus research data dealing mainly with the listed companies in several of the major European states. These data were not always available or easily accessible. Consequently, the resulting picture gives an incomplete overview of the corporate scene: only listed companies have been included, thereby excluding the majority of even larger corporate entities in most states. Also, not all states have been included, especially for lack of accessible information. The overall picture nevertheless yields a sufficient typology of the large corporation in Western Europe.

The first part deals with the overall characteristics of the factual structure of the corporate world in Western Europe. Differences in legal form are striking, while the use of the public securities markets points to fundamental differences in ownership, and therefore in governance structure. While in the U.K. securities financing is a predominant characteristic of companies, the reverse is true in the largest continental economies.

The legal environment is the expression of the foregoing factual elements: company law has received more attention in systems with less securities financing, the rules on groups of companies serving some of the objectives pursued by the markets. However, as in all economic systems, securities financing is increasingly called upon, and regulation and government supervision develop alongside. The formation of a Europe-wide securities market, faced with an accelerated move towards integration after the introduction of the common currency, leads to an overhaul of the securities regulatory structures. Issues of corporate governance are receiving attention in most states, leading sometimes to changes in the law and more frequently to the adoption of self-regulatory codes of best practice. These new instruments are the vectors of a new wave of de facto harmonization within the European Union.

---

[526] Skog, Rolf 'Does Sweden Need a Mandatory Bid Rule? A Critical Analysis' (Corporate Governance Forum, Stockholm 1995).

In the second part, the legal structure of the board of directors is analyzed, referring to the sparse empirical evidence that was available. The descriptive analysis deals with different aspects of the boards' composition and functioning on a comparative basis. The analysis focuses on the unitary board as the most frequently found model. In separate sections the two-tier board is described, in the hypothesis both that employees are involved or that no such involvement is necessary or practiced.

With respect to different items of analysis, the present legal situation is described, confronted with empirical evidence (if available), and further documented with reference to the recently issued codes of conduct. From this comparison, it will become evident that on the one hand substantial convergence is taking place within Europe's systems of governance. The U.K. Cadbury Code of Best Practice is often used as the benchmark, while systems with a two-tier board are framed on a substantially different model. At the apex of the comparison, one will find an analysis of the differences as to the objectives that companies in the different structures are supposed to pursue, i.e., whether shareholder wealth will be the sole and ultimate goal or whether the interest of the "enterprise" will be the yardstick of corporate conduct. These differences exist equally at the level of the conduct rules.

The third part of the status report focuses on the differences in ownership structure. On the basis of the author's research, the concentration of ownership in the different systems within Europe has been mapped, leading to the overall picture, in Table 40 and Chart 1, evidencing that in most European systems, stock exchange-listed companies are largely—if not majority—owned by one single party. As a consequence, the volume of shares available for investment is rather limited, leading to—though less visible the last two years—an anemic status of the equity markets.

Further investigation is aimed at identifying the different classes of shareholders in the listed companies: while individuals have reduced their direct holdings to about 20% in most states, institutionals do not play a predominant role. Except in the U.K. and to a lesser extent in Sweden, institutionals—other than banks—hold about 20% of the shares. The remainder is often owned by other companies—this is the group phenomenon—or by foreign investors.

The role of the equity markets, mainly concentrated around the traditional stock exchanges, is a direct function of the differences in the use of the markets as a financing source. Systems with concentrated ownership of shares tend to call less frequently on the public capital markets. There is some evidence that this phenomenon may lead to underweighing these companies' equity basis. The system of regulation traditionally was a function of the intensity of use of the equity markets. However, with the formation of the internal market within the E.U. leading to the stronger competition between the markets, new patterns of organization of the markets and of their regulation and supervision appear. The

European harmonization process, especially the Investment Services Directive, is both a product and a key to further market integration.

A final point of comparison between market structures relates to the market for corporate control, both in its private segment and in the public takeover market. The structure of ownership determines the way this market functions: public takeovers are the vector for the market for corporate control in the U.K., but much less so in France, Belgium, or Switzerland, where control often changes hands as a consequence of a private control transaction, followed by a —often mandatory—public bid. The latter then serves purposes of minority protection rather than being an instrument of the control market.

Selected Bibliography

Part I: Roots and Perspectives of Corporate Governance

Aoki, Masahiko and Hugh Patrick (eds.) *The Japanese Main Bank System: Its Relevance for Developing and Transforming Economies* (Oxford 1994).

Bebchuk, Lucian Arye (ed.) *Corporate Law and Economic Analysis* (Cambridge 1990).

Berle, Adolf A. and Gardiner C. Means *The Modern Corporation and Private Property* (New York 1932).

Buxbaum, Richard M., Gérard Hertig, Alain Hirsch, and Klaus J. Hopt (eds.) *European Economic and Business Law. Legal and Economic Analyses on Integration and Harmonization* (Berlin and New York 1996).

Coase, Ronald H. 'The Nature of the Firm' *Economica* N.F. 4 (1937) 386-405.

Dorresteijn, Adriaan, Ina Kuiper, and Geoffrey Morse *European Corporate Law* (Deventer 1994).

Fama, Eugene F. and Michael C. Jensen 'Separation of Ownership and Control' *Journal of Law and Economics* 26 (1983) 301-25.

Fama, Eugene F. and Michael C. Jensen 'Agency Problems and Residual Claims' *Journal of Law and Economics* 26 (1983) 327-49.

Garvey, Gerald T. and Peter L. Swan 'The Economics of Corporate Governance: Beyond the Marshallian Firm' *Journal of Corporate Finance* 1 (1994) 139-74.

Gilson, Ronald J. 'Corporate Governance and Economic Efficiency. When Do Institutions Matter?' 74 *Wash. U. L.Q.* 327-45 (1996).

Hart, Oliver 'Corporate Governance: Some Theory and Implications' *Economic Journal* 105 (1995) 678-89.

Hopt, Klaus J. 'Ideelle und wirtschaftliche Grundlagen der Aktien-, Bank- und Börsenrechtsentwicklung im 19. Jahrhundert' in: Coing, Helmut and Walter Wilhelm (eds.) *Wissenschaft und Kodifikation des Privatrechts im 19. Jahrhundert* vol. v *Geld und Banken* 128-68 (Frankfurt am Main 1980).

Hopt, Klaus J. and Gunther Teubner (eds.) *Corporate Governance and Directors' Liabilities— Legal, Economic and Sociological Analyses on Corporate Social Responsibility* (Berlin and New York 1985); cf. *Governo dell'impresa e responsibilità dell'alta direzione. Analisi giuridica, economica e sociologica della responsibilità sociale dell'impresa (documenti Isvet)* (Milano 1986).

Horn, Norbert and Jürgen Kocka (eds.) *Recht und Entwicklung der Großunternehmen im 19. und frühen 20. Jahrhundert/Law and the Formation of the Big Enterprises in the 19th and Early 20th Centuries* (Göttingen 1979).

Jensen, Michael C. 'Eclipse of the Public Corporation' *Harvard Business Review* 67/5 (1989) 61-74.

Jensen, Michael C. 'The Modern Industrial Revolution, Exit, and the Failure of Internal Control Systems' *Journal of Finance* 48 (1993) 831-80.

Jensen, Michael C. and William H. Meckling 'Theory of the Firm: Managerial Behavior, Agency Costs and Ownership Structure' *Journal of Financial Economics* 3 (1976) 305-60.

Jensen, Michael C. and William H. Meckling 'Rights and Production Functions: An Application to Labor-Managed Firms and Co-Determination' *Journal of Business* 52 (1979) 469-506.

McCahery, Joseph, Sol Picciotto, and Colin Scott (eds.) *Corporate Control and Accountability. Changing Structures and the Dynamics of Regulation* (Oxford 1994).

Roe, Mark J. *Strong Managers, Weak Owners. The Political Roots of American Corporate Finance* (Princeton 1994).

Roe, Mark J. 'Chaos and Evolution in Law and Economics' 109 *Harv. L. Rev.* 641-68 (1995/96).

Romano, Roberta *The Genius of American Corporate Law* (Washington 1993).

Williamson, Oliver E. 'The Modern Corporation: Origins, Evolution, Attributes' *Journal of Economic Literature* 19 (1981) 1537-68.
Williamson, Oliver E. 'Corporate Finance and Corporate Governance' *Journal of Finance* 43 (1988) 567-91.

Part II: Building Blocks of Corporate Governance Systems

American Law Institute 'Principles of Corporate Governance: Analysis and Recommendations' 2 vols. (St. Paul 1994).
André, Thomas J. 'Some Reflections on Corporate Governance: A Glimpse at German Supervisory Boards' 70 *Tul. L. Rev.* 1819-79 (1996).
Bacon, Jeremy 'Corporate Boards and Corporate Governance' (Conference Board Report 1036, New York 1993).
Baum, Harald and Ulrike Schaede 'Institutional Investors and Corporate Governance in Japanese Perspective' in: Baums, Theodor, Richard M. Buxbaum, and Klaus J. Hopt (eds.) *Institutional Investors and Corporate Governance* 609-64 (Berlin and New York 1994).
Baums, Theodor 'The German Banking System and its Impact on Corporate Finance and Governance' in: Aoki, Masahiko and Hugh Patrick (eds.) *The Japanese Main Bank System. Its Relevance for Developing and Transforming Economies* 409-49 (New York 1994).
Baums, Theodor 'Vollmachtstimmrecht der Banken—Ja oder Nein?' *Die Aktiengesellschaft* 41 (1996) 11-26.
Baums, Theodor, Richard M. Buxbaum, and Klaus J. Hopt (eds.) *Institutional Investors and Corporate Governance* (Berlin and New York 1994).
Baums, Theodor and Christian Fraune 'Institutionelle Anleger und Publikumsgesellschaft: eine empirische Untersuchung' *Die Aktiengesellschaft* 40 (1995) 97-112.
Baums, Theodor and Bernd Frick 'Co-Determination in Germany: The Impact on the Market Value of the Firm' (Working Paper of the Institut für Handels- und Wirtschaftsrecht, University of Osnabrück, no. 1/1997).
Baums, Theodor and Markus König 'Investmentfonds im Universalbankkonzern: Rechtstatsachen und aktuelle Reformfragen' in: Forster, Karl-Heinz, Barbara Grunewald, Marcus Lutter, and Johannes Semler (eds.) *Aktien- und Bilanzrecht* (Festschrift Kropff) 3-36 (Düsseldorf 1997).
Becht, Marco 'Beneficial Ownership of Listed Companies in the United States' part of: European Corporate Governance Network (ed.) 'The Separation of Ownership and Control: A Survey of 7 European Countries' (Preliminary Report to the European Commission submitted on October 27, 1997, vol. 1; http://www.ecgn.ulb.ac.be/).
Becht, Marco and Ekkehart Böhmer 'Transparency of Ownership and Control in Germany' part of: European Corporate Governance Network (ed.) 'The Separation of Ownership and Control: A Survey of 7 European Countries' (Preliminary Report to the European Commission submitted on October 27, 1997, vol. 1; http://www.ecgn.ulb.ac.be/).
Becht, Marco and Ariane Chapelle 'Ownership and Control in Belgium' part of: European Corporate Governance Network (ed.) 'The Separation of Ownership and Control: A Survey of 7 European Countries' (Preliminary Report to the European Commission submitted on October 27, 1997, vol. 1; http://www.ecgn.ulb.ac.be/).
Beyer, Jürgen 'Governance Structures. Unternehmensverflechtungen und Unternehmenserfolg in Deutschland' in: Albach, Horst (ed.) *Governance Structures* 79-101 (*Zeitschrift für Betriebswirtschaft* Supplementary Issue 3/1996).
Bianchi, Marcello, Magda Bianco, and Luca Enriques 'Ownership, Pyramidal Groups and Separation Between Ownership and Control in Italy' part of: European Corporate Governance Network (ed.) 'The Separation of Ownership and Control: A Survey of 7 European Countries' (Preliminary Report to the European Commission submitted on October 27, 1997, vol. 1; http://www.ecgn.ulb.ac.be/).

Black, Bernard S. 'Shareholder Activism and Corporate Governance in the United States' in: Newman, Peter (ed.) *The New Palgrave Dictionary of Economics and the Law* (London, forthcoming 1998).

Bleicher, Knut *Der Aufsichtsrat im Wandel. Eine repräsentative Studie über Aufsichtsräte in bundesdeutschen Aktiengesellschaften* (Gütersloh 1987).

Bloch, Laurence and Elizabeth Kremp 'Ownership and Control in France' part of: European Corporate Governance Network (ed.) 'The Separation of Ownership and Control: A Survey of 7 European Countries' (Preliminary Report to the European Commission submitted on October 27, 1997, vol. 1; http://www.ecgn.ulb.ac.be/).

Böckli, Peter 'Corporate Governance: The "Cadbury Report" and the Swiss Board Concept of 1991' *Schweizerische Zeitschrift für Wirtschaftsrecht* 68 (1996) 149-63.

Böhm, Jürgen *Der Einfluß der Banken auf Großunternehmen* (Dissertation University of Duisburg) (Hamburg 1992).

Böhmer, Ekkehart 'Industry Groups, Bank Control, and Large Shareholders: An Analysis of German Takeovers' (Working Paper, Preliminary Version, Humboldt University Berlin, 14.3.1997).

Bremeier, Eberhard, Jürgen B. Mülder, and Florian Schilling 'Praxis der Aufsichtsratstätigkeit in Deutschland—Chancen zur Professionalisierung' (AMROP International, Düsseldorf 1994).

Cable, John 'Capital Market Information and Industrial Performance: The Role of West German Banks' *Economic Journal* 95 (1985) 118-32.

Chirinko, Robert S. and Julie Ann Elston 'Banking Relationships in Germany: Empirical Results and Policy Implications' (Working Paper, Emory University, May 1996).

Coffee, John C. 'Liquidity versus Control: The Institutional Investor as Corporate Monitor' 91 *Colum. L. Rev.* 1277-368 (1991).

Council of Institutional Investors (ed.) 'Does Ownership Add Value? A Collection of 100 Empirical Studies' (Washington 1994).

Demsetz, Harold and Kenneth Lehn 'The Structure of Corporate Ownership: Causes and Consequences' *Journal of Political Economy* 93 (1985) 1155-77.

Deutscher Juristentag (ed.) 'Empfehlen sich gesetzliche Regelungen zur Einschränkung des Einflusses der Kreditinstitute auf Aktiengesellschaften? Sitzungsberichte' in: *Verhandlungen des 61. Deutschen Juristentages* vol. II/2, part N (Munich 1996).

Edwards, Jeremy S.S. and Klaus Fischer *Banks, Finance and Investment in Germany* (Cambridge 1994).

Fanto, James A. 'The Absence of Cross-Cultural Communication: SEC Mandatory Disclosure and Foreign Corporate Governance' 17 *Nw. J. Int'l L. & Bus.* 119-206 (1996).

Fox, Merritt B. 'Securities Disclosure in a Globalizing Market: Who Should Regulate Whom' 95 *Mich. L. Rev.* 2498-632 (1997).

Franks, Julian and Colin Mayer 'Hostile Takeovers and the Correction of Managerial Failure' *Journal of Financial Economics* 40 (1996) 163-81.

Franks, Julian and Colin Mayer 'Ownership, Control and the Performance of German Corporations' (Working Paper, London Business School and University of Oxford, 1997).

Frick, Bernd and Dieter Sadowski 'Works Councils, Unions, and Firm Performance' in: Buttler, Friedrich, Wolfgang Franz, Roland Schettkat, and David Soskice (eds.) *Institutional Frameworks and Labor Market Performance: Comparative Views on the U.S. and German Economies* 46-81 (London and New York 1996).

Gerke, Wolfgang, Hendrik Garz, and Marc Oerke 'Die Bewertung von Unternehmensübernahmen auf dem deutschen Aktienmarkt' *Zeitschrift für betriebswirtschaftliche Forschung* 47 (1995) 805-20.

Gerum, Elmar, Horst Steinmann, and Werner Fees *Der mitbestimmte Aufsichtsrat. Eine empirische Untersuchung* (Stuttgart 1988).

Gordon, Jeffrey N. 'Corporation, Markets, and Courts ' 91 *Colum. L. Rev.* 1931-88 (1991).

Gordon, Jeffrey N. 'Institutions as Relational Investors: A New Look at Cumulative Voting' 94 *Colum. L. Rev.* 124-92 (1994).

Gordon, Jeffrey N. 'Employees, Pensions, and the New Economic Order' 97 *Colum. L. Rev.* 1519-66 (1997).

Gorton, Gary and Frank A. Schmid 'Universal Banking and the Performance of German Firms' (NBER Working Paper no. 5453, February 1996).

Gugler, Klaus, Susanne Kalss, Alex Stomper, and Josef Zechner 'The Separation of Ownership and Control: An Austrian Perspective' part of: European Corporate Governance Network (ed.) 'The Separation of Ownership and Control: A Survey of 7 European Countries' (Preliminary Report to the European Commission submitted on October 27, 1997, vol. 1; http://www.ecgn.ulb.ac.be/).

Hamel, Winfried 'Mitbestimmung' in: Hauschildt, Jürgen and Oskar Grün (eds.) *Ergebnisse empirischer betriebswirtschaftlicher Forschung. Zur Realtheorie der Unternehmung* (Festschrift Witte) 25-53 (Stuttgart 1993).

Harris, Trevor S., Mark Lang, and Hans Peter Möller 'The Value Relevance of German Accounting Measures: An Empirical Analysis' *Journal of Accounting Research* 32/2 (1994) 187-209.

Herrmann, Markus *Unternehmenskontrolle durch Stiftungen. Untersuchung der Performancewirkungen* (Dissertation University of Konstanz) (Wiesbaden 1996).

Hopt, Klaus J. 'Zur Funktion des Aufsichtsrats im Verhältnis von Industrie und Bankensystem/Functions of the Supervisory Board in the Bank-Industry Relationship' in: Horn, Norbert and Jürgen Kocka (eds.) *Recht und Entwicklung der Großunternehmen im 19. und frühen 20. Jahrhundert/Law and the Formation of the Big Enterprises in the 19th and Early 20th Centuries* 227-42 (Göttingen 1979).

Hopt, Klaus J. 'Die Haftung von Vorstand und Aufsichtsrat. Zugleich ein Beitrag zur corporate governance-Debatte' in: Immenga, Ulrich, Wernhard Möschel, and Dieter Reuter (eds.) *Festschrift für Ernst-Joachim Mestmäcker zum siebzigsten Geburtstag* 909-31 (Baden-Baden 1996).

Hopt, Klaus J. 'Corporate Governance und deutsche Universalbanken' in: Feddersen, Dieter, Peter Hommelhoff, and Uwe H. Schneider (eds.) *Corporate Governance. Optimierung der Unternehmensführung und der Unternehmenskontrolle im deutschen und amerikanischen Aktienrecht* 243-63 (Cologne 1996).

Jensen, Michael C. 'The Agency Costs of Free Cash Flow, Corporate Finance, and Takeovers' *American Economic Review Papers and Proceedings* 76 (1986) 323-9.

de Jong, Abe, Rezault Kabir, Teye Marra, and Ailsa Roell 'Ownership and Control in The Netherlands' part of: European Corporate Governance Network (ed.) 'The Separation of Ownership and Control: A Survey of 7 European Countries' (Preliminary Report to the European Commission submitted on October 27, 1997, vol. 1; http://www.ecgn.ulb.ac.be/).

Kaplan, Steven N. 'Top Executives, Turnover, and Firm Performance in Germany' *Journal of Law, Economics & Organization* 10 (1994) 142-59.

Knoll, Leonhard, Jochen Knoesel, and Uwe Probst 'Aufsichtsratsvergütungen in Deutschland: Empirische Befunde' *Zeitschrift für betriebswirtschaftliche Forschung* 49 (1997) 236-54.

Kole, Stacey and Kenneth Lehn 'Deregulation, the Evolution of Corporate Governance Structure, and Survival' *American Economic Review Papers and Proceedings* 87 (1997) 421-5.

Leimkühler, Claudia 'Ist die öffentliche Kritik am deutschen Aufsichtsratssystem gerechtfertigt? Empirische Untersuchung über die personellen Verflechtungen zwischen den Vorständen und Aufsichtsräten der in Deutschland börsennotierten Aktiengesellschaften' *Die Wirtschaftsprüfung* 49 (1996) 305-13.

Lin, Laura 'The Effectiveness of Outside Directors as a Corporate Governance Mechanism—Theories and Evidence' 90 *Nw. U.L. Rev.* 898-976 (1996).

Lipka, Sabine *Managementeffizienz und Kapitalmarktkontrolle. Empirische Tests neuerer Ansätze der Theorie der Firma* (Dissertation University of Cologne) (Frankfurt am Main 1995).

Lorsch, Jay W. with Elizabeth MacIver *Pawns or Potentates. The Reality of America's Corporate Boards* (Harvard 1989).

Lowenstein, Louis 'Financial Transparency and Corporate Governance: You Manage What You Measure' 96 *Colum. L. Rev.* 1335-62 (1996).

Manne, Henry G. 'Mergers and the Market for Corporate Control' *Journal of Political Economy* 73 (1965) 110-20.

Marini, Philippe 'La modernisation du droit des sociétés' (Rapport au Premier ministre, Paris 1996).

McDaniel, Morey W. 'Bondholders and Corporate Governance' 41 *Bus. Lawyer* 413-60 (1986).

Morck, Randall, Andrei Shleifer, and Robert W. Vishny 'Management Ownership and Market Valuation. An Empirical Analysis' *Journal of Financial Economics* 20 (1988) 293-315.

Mülbert, Peter O. *Empfehlen sich gesetzliche Regelungen zur Einschränkung des Einflusses der Kreditinstitute auf Aktiengesellschaften?* (Expert Opinion for the 61st Deutscher Juristentag 1996, Munich 1996).

Nibler, Marcus 'Bank Control and Corporate Performance in Germany: The Evidence' (University of Cambridge, Faculty of Economics and Politics, Research Paper Series no. 48, 1995).

Van Ommeslaghe, Pierre 'Vers une société anonyme "autonome"' *Liber Amoricum Commission Droit et Vie des Affaires* 389-406 (Brussels 1998).

Parkinson, John E. *Corporate Power and Responsibility* (Oxford 1994).

Perlitz, Manfred and Frank Seger 'The Role of Universal Banks in German Corporate Governance' *Business & the Contemporary World* 6/4 (1994) 49-67.

Pezard, Alice 'La responsabilité civile des dirigeants sociaux' in: Ploix, Hélène (ed.) *Gouvernement d'entreprise, corporate governance: dimension juridique, méthode, responsabilités* 97-153 (Paris 1997).

Pfannschmidt, Arno *Personelle Verflechtungen über Aufsichtsräte. Mehrfachmandate in deutschen Unternehmen* (Dissertation University of Bonn) (Wiesbaden 1993).

Renneboog, Luc 'Concentration of Ownership and Pyramidal Shareholding Structures in Belgian Listed Companies' part of: European Corporate Governance Network (ed.) 'The Separation of Ownership and Control: A Survey of 7 European Countries' (Preliminary Report to the European Commission submitted on October 27, 1997, vol. 1; http://www.ecgn.ulb.ac.be/).

Romano, Roberta 'A Guide to Takeovers: Theory, Evidence, and Regulation' 9 *Yale J. on. Reg.* 119-180 (1992).

Romano, Roberta 'Public Pension Fund Activism in Corporate Governance Reconsidered' 93 *Colum. L. Rev.* 795-853 (1993).

Sadowski, Dieter, Joachim Junkes, and Cornelia Lent 'Mitbestimmung—Gewinne und Investitionen' (Expertise für das Projekt 'Mitbestimmung und neue Unternehmenskulturen' der Bertelsmann Stiftung und der Hans-Böckler-Stiftung) (Gütersloh 1997).

Schmid, Frank A. 'Banken, Aktionärsstruktur und Unternehmenssteuerung' *Kredit und Kapital* 29 (1996) 402-27 (part I) and 545-64 (part II).

Schmid, Frank A. 'Beteiligungen deutscher Geschäftsbanken und Corporate Performance' *Zeitschrift für Wirtschafts- und Sozialforschung* 116 (1996) 273-310.

Schmid, Frank A. 'Vorstandsbezüge, Aufsichtsratsvergütung und Aktionärsstruktur' *Zeitschrift für Betriebswirtschaft* 67 (1997) 67-83.

Schmidt, Hartmut and Stefan Prigge 'Macht der Banken' in: Thießen, Friedrich (ed.) *Enzyklopädisches Lexikon für das Geld-, Bank- und Börsenwesen* 4th edn. (Frankfurt am Main, forthcoming 1998).

Schmidt, Reinhard H. and Gerald Spindler 'Shareholder-Value zwischen Ökonomie und Recht' in: Assmann, Heinz-Dieter, Tomas Brinkmann, Georgios Gounalakis, Helmut Kohl, and Rainer Walz (eds.) *Wirtschafts- und Medienrecht in der offenen Demokratie* (Festschrift Kübler) 515-55 (Heidelberg 1997).

Schrader, Stephan and Christian Lüthje 'Das Ausscheiden der Spitzenführungskraft aus dem Unternehmen' *Zeitschrift für Betriebswirtschaft* 65 (1995) 467-93.

Schreyögg, Georg and Heike Papenheim-Tockhorn 'Dient der Aufsichtsrat dem Aufbau zwischenbetrieblicher Kooperationsbeziehungen? Eine Längsschnittstudie zur Rekonstitution "gebrochener Verflechtungen" zwischen deutschen Kapitalgesellschaften' *Zeitschrift für Betriebswirtschaft* 65 (1995) 205-30.

Schulte, Jörn *Rechnungslegung und Aktienkursentwicklung. Erklärung und Prognosen von Aktienrenditen durch Einzel- und Konzernabschlußdaten* (Dissertation University of Bochum 1995) (Wiesbaden 1996).

Schwalbach, Joachim and Ulrike Graßhoff 'Managervergütung und Unternehmenserfolg' *Zeitschrift für Betriebswirtschaft* 67 (1997) 203-17.

Schwiete, Mark and Jürgen Weigand 'Bankbeteiligungen und das Verschuldungsverhalten deutscher Unternehmen' *Kredit und Kapital* 30 (1997) 1-34.

Seger, Frank *Banken, Erfolg und Finanzierung. Eine Analyse für deutsche Unternehmen* (Dissertation University of Mannheim 1996) (Wiesbaden 1997).

Shleifer, Andrei and Robert W. Vishny 'Large Shareholders and Corporate Control' *Journal of Political Economy* 94 (1988) 461-88.

Stapledon, Geof P. *Institutional Shareholders and Corporate Governance* (Oxford 1996).

Theisen, Manuel René *Die Überwachung der Unternehmungsführung: betriebswirtschaftliche Ansätze zur Entwicklung erster Grundsätze ordnungsmäßiger Überwachung* (Stuttgart 1987).

Theisen, Manuel René and Wolfgang Salzberger 'Die Berichterstattung des Aufsichtsrats. Eine empirische Analyse der Überwachungsberichte von 1984-1994' *Der Betrieb* 50 (1997) 105-15.

Triantis, George G. and Ronald J. Daniels 'The Role of Debt in Interactive Corporate Governance' 83 *Cal. L. Rev.* 1073-113 (1995).

Viénot 'Le conseil d'administration des sociétés côtées' (Paris 1995).

Wenger, Ekkehard 'Expert Opinion for the Monopolkommission' (Unpublished, available from the author. Würzburg 1996).

Wenger, Ekkehard and Renate Hecker 'Übernahme- und Abfindungsregeln am deutschen Aktienmarkt' *ifo Studien—Zeitschrift für empirische Wirtschaftsforschung* 41 (1995) 51-87.

von Werder, Axel (ed.) *Grundsätze ordnungsmäßiger Unternehmungsführung (GoF) für die Unternehmungsleitung (GoU), Überwachung (GoÜ) und Abschlußprüfung (GoA)* (Düsseldorf 1996).

te Wildt, Claus *CEO Turnover and Corporate Performance: The German Case* (Dissertation University of Kiel) (Kiel 1996).

Part III: Analyses of Corporate Governance Systems and Comparative Corporate Governance

Agrawal, Anup and Charles R. Knoeber 'Firm Performance and Mechanisms to Control Agency Problems Between Managers and Shareholders' *Journal of Financial and Quantitative Analysis* 31 (1996) 377-97.

Albach, Horst (ed.) *Governance Structures* (Zeitschrift für Betriebswirtschaft Supplementary Issue 3/1996).

Allen, Franklin and Douglas Gale 'A Welfare Comparison of Intermediaries and Financial Markets in Germany and the U.S.' *European Economic Review* 39 (1995) 179-209.

Aoki, Masahiko and Ronald Dore (eds.) *The Japanese Firm: Sources of Competitive Strength* (Oxford 1994).

Aoki, Masahiko and Kim Hyung-Ki (eds.) *Corporate Governance in Transitional Economies. Insider Control and the Role of Banks* (Washington 1995).

Becht, Marco 'The Separation of Ownership and Control: A Survey of 7 European Countries' (Preliminary Report to the European Commission submitted on October 27, 1997 by the European Corporate Governance Network, vol. 1; http://www.ecgn.ulb.ac.be/).

Berglöf, Erik 'Corporate Governance' in: Steil, Benn (ed.) *The European Equity Markets* 147-84 (Copenhagen 1996).

Black, Bernard S. and Ronald J. Gilson 'Venture Capital and the Structure of Capital Markets: Banks versus Stock Markets' *Journal of Financial Economics* 47 (1998) 243-77.

Blair, Margaret M. *Ownership and Control. Rethinking Corporate Governance for the Twenty-First Century* (Washington 1995).

Bleicher, Knut, Diethard Leberl, and Herbert Paul *Unternehmungsverfassung und Spitzenorganisation. Führung und Überwachung von Aktiengesellschaften im internationalen Vergleich* (Wiesbaden 1989).

Blommestein, Hans 'The Impact of Institutional Investors on OECD Financial Markets' *Financial Markets Trends* (OECD) no. 68 (November 1997) 15-54.

Cadbury, Adrian (Chairman) 'Report of the Committee on the Financial Aspects of Corporate Governance' (London 1992).

CEPS 'Corporate Governance in Europe' (Centre for European Policy Studies Working Party Report no. 12, Rapporteur Karel Lannoo, Brussels 1995).

Charkham, Jonathan P. *Keeping Good Company. A Study of Corporate Governance in Five Countries* (Oxford 1994).

Cheffins, Brian R. 'Corporate Governance in the United Kingdom: Lessons for Canada' *Canadian Business Law Journal* 28 (1997) 69-106.

Chew, Donald H. (ed.) *Studies in International Corporate Finance and Governance Systems. A Comparison of the U.S., Japan, & Europe* (New York and Oxford 1997).

Corbett, Jenny and Tim Jenkinson 'The Financing of Industry, 1970-1989: An International Comparison' *Journal of the Japanese and International Economies* 10 (1996) 71-96.

'Cross-Border Views of Corporate Governance' 1998/1 *Colum. Bus. L. Rev.* (Special Symposium Issue).

Dietl, Helmut M. *Capital Markets and Corporate Governance in Japan, Germany and the United States. Organizational Responses to Market Inefficiencies* (London and New York 1998).

Dimsdale, Nicholas and Martha Prevezer (eds.) *Capital Markets and Corporate Governance* (Oxford 1994).

Feddersen, Dieter, Peter Hommelhoff, and Uwe H. Schneider (eds.) *Corporate Governance. Optimierung der Unternehmensführung und der Unternehmenskontrolle im deutschen und amerikanischen Aktienrecht* (Cologne 1996).

Franks, Julian and Colin Mayer 'Capital Markets and Corporate Control: A Study of France, Germany and the U.K.' *Economic Policy* 10 (1990) 191-231.

Franks, Julian and Colin Mayer 'Corporate Ownership and Control in the U.K., Germany and France' *Journal of Applied Corporate Finance* 9/4 (1996/97) 30-45.

Frydman, Roman, Cheryl W. Gray, and Andrej Rapaczynski (eds.) *Corporate Governance in Central Europe and Russia* (2 vols., Budapest et al. 1996).

Fukao, Mitsuhiro *Financial Integration, Corporate Governance, and the Performance of Multinational Companies* (Washington 1995).

Gelauff, George M.M. and Corina den Broeder 'Governance of Stakeholder Relationships. The German and Dutch Experience' (SUERF [Société Universitaire Européene de Recherches Financières] Studies no. 1, Amsterdam 1997).

Gilson, Ronald J. and Mark J. Roe 'Understanding the Japanese Keiretsu: Overlaps Between Corporate Governance and Industrial Organization' 102 *Yale L.J.* 871-906 (1993).

Greenbury, Richard (chairman) 'Directors Remuneration' (Report of a Study Group chaired by Sir Richard Greenbury, London, July 1995).

Hampel Report (Committee on Corporate Governance, Final Report, London, January 1998).

Hopt, Klaus J. 'New Ways in Corporate Governance: European Experiments with Labor Representation on Corporate Boards' 82 *Mich. L. Rev.* 1338-63 (1984).

Hopt, Klaus J. 'Labor Board Representation on Corporate Boards: Impacts and Problems for Corporate Governance and Economic Integration in Europe' *International Review of Law and Economics* 14 (1994) 203-14.

Hopt, Klaus J. 'Europäisches und deutsches Übernahmerecht' *Zeitschrift für das gesamte Handelsrecht und Wirtschaftsrecht* 161 (1997) 368-420.

Hopt, Klaus J. 'Shareholder Rights and Remedies: A View From Germany and the Continent' *Company Financial and Insolvency Law Review* 2 (1997) 261-83.

Hopt, Klaus J. and Eddy Wymeersch (eds.) *European Takeovers—Law and Practice* (London et al. 1992).

Hopt, Klaus J. and Eddy Wymeersch (eds.) *Comparative Corporate Governance: Essays and Materials* (Berlin and New York 1997).

International Task Force on Corporate Governance 'International Corporate Governance. Who Holds the Reins?' (London 1995).

Isaksson, Mats and Rolf Skog (eds.) *Aspects of Corporate Governance* (Stockholm 1994).

de Jong, Henk Wouter 'The Governance Structure and Performance of Large European Corporations' *Journal of Management and Governance* 1 (1997) 5-27.

Kaplan, Steven N. 'Top Executive Rewards and Firm Performance: a Comparison of Japan and the United States' *Journal of Political Economy* 102 (1994) 510-46.

Kester, W. Carl 'Industrial Groups as Systems of Corporate Governance' *Oxford Review of Economic Policy* 8 (1992) 24-44.

Kojima, Kenji 'Corporate Governance in Germany, Japan, and the United States: a Comparative Study' *Kobe Economic & Business Review* 38 (1993) 171-243.

Korn/Ferry International 'Board Meeting in Session. European Board of Directors Study' (1996).

La Porta, Rafael, Florencio Lopez-de-Silanes, Andrei Shleifer, and Robert W. Vishny 'Law and Finance' (NBER Working Paper no. 5661, July 1996).

La Porta, Rafael, Florencio Lopez-de-Silanes, Andrei Shleifer, and Robert W. Vishny 'Legal Determinants of External Finance' *Journal of Finance* 52 (1997) 1131-50.

La Porta, Rafael, Florencio Lopez-de-Silanes, Andrei Shleifer, and Robert W. Vishny 'Agency Problems and Dividend Policies Around the World' (Working Paper, 2nd Draft, November 1997).

Lorsch, Jay W. 'German Corporate Governance and Management: An American's Perspective' in: von Werder, Axel (ed.) *Grundsätze ordnungsmäßiger Unternehmungsführung (GoF) für die Unternehmungsleitung (GoU), Überwachung (GoÜ) und Abschlußprüfung (GoA)* 199-225 (Düsseldorf 1996).

Macey, Jonathan R. and Geoffrey P. Miller 'Corporate Governance and Commercial Banking: A Comparative Examination of Germany, Japan, and the United States' 48 *Stan. L. Rev.* 73-112 (1995/96).

Mayer, Colin 'Corporate Governance, Competition and Performance' (OECD Working Paper no. 164, Paris 1996).

Meier-Schatz, Christian 'Corporate Governance and Legal Rules: A Transnational Look at Concepts and Problems of Internal Management Control' *Journal of Corporation Law* 13 (1988) 431-80.

Milhaupt, Curtis J. 'A Relational Theory of Japanese Corporate Governance: Contract, Culture, and the Rule of Law' 37 *Harv. Int'l L.J.* 3-64 (1996).

Milhaupt, Curtis J. 'The Markets for Innovation in the United States and Japan: Venture Capital and the Comparative Corporate Governance Debate' 91 *Nw. U.L. Rev.* 865-98 (1997).

Miwa, Yoshiro *Firms and Industrial Organization in Japan* (London 1996).

Monks, Robert A.G. and Nell Minow *Corporate Governance* (Cambridge and Oxford 1995).

Monks, Robert A.G. and Nell Minow *Watching the Watchers: Corporate Governance for the 21st Century* (Cambridge and Oxford 1996).

Monopolkommission 'Ordnungspolitische Leitlinien für ein funktionsfähiges Finanzsystem' (Special Expert Opinion of the Monopolkommission, Cologne 1998).

OECD 'Eigentumsverhältnisse, Kontrolle und Entscheidungsprozesse in deutschen Unternehmen' in: 'OECD Wirtschaftsberichte: Deutschland 1995' 94-145 (Paris 1995).

OECD 'Corporate Governance. Improving Competitiveness and Access to Capital in Global Markets' (A report to the OECD by the Business Sector Advisory Group on Corporate Governance) (Paris 1998).

OECD 'Institutional Investors in the New Financial Landscape' (Paris, forthcoming 1998).

Picot, Arnold (ed.) *Corporate Governance. Unternehmensüberwachung auf dem Prüfstand* (Stuttgart 1995).

Ploix, Hélène (ed.) *Gouvernement d'entreprise, corporate governance: dimension juridique, méthode, responsabilités* (Paris 1997).

Pound, John 'The Rise of the Political Model of Corporate Governance and Corporate Control' 68 *N.Y.U. L. Rev.* 1003-71 (1993).

Prentice, David D. and Peter R.J. Holland (eds.) *Contemporary Issues in Corporate Governance* (Oxford 1993).

Prevezer, Martha and Martin Ricketts 'Corporate Governance: the UK Compared with Germany and Japan' in: Dimsdale, Nicholas and Martha Prevezer (eds.) *Capital Markets and Corporate Governance* 237-56 (Oxford 1994).

Prowse, Stephen 'Corporate Governance in an International Perspective: A Survey of Corporate Control Mechanisms Among Large Firms in the U. S., U. K., Japan and Germany' *Financial Markets, Institutions & Instruments* 4/1 (1995).

Raaijmakers, Matheus J.G.C. 'Corporate Governance. Some Comparative Notes on the Governance of (Large) Public Corporations' in: Raaijmakers, M.J.G.C., R. van Rooij, and A.J.S.M. Tervoort (eds.) *Ondernemingsrecht in international perspectief* 179-205 (Deventer 1995).

Raaijmakers Matheus J.G.C. and Willem J. de Ridder *"Corporate Governance" in Nederland, besluitvorming en verantwoording in beursondernemingen* (Den Haag 1996).

Revue d'économie financière 'Corporate Governance, Le gouvernement d'entreprise' (Special Edition, Winter 1994, no. 31).

Rock, Edward B. 'America's Fascination with German Corporate Governance' 74 *Wash. U. L.Q.* 367-91 (1996).

Roe, Mark J. 'Some Differences in Corporate Structure in Germany, Japan, and the United States' 102 Yale L.J. 1927-2003 (1993).

Roe, Mark J. 'Comparative Corporate Governance' in: Newman, Peter (ed.) *The New Palgrave Dictionary of Economics and the Law* (London, forthcoming 1998).

Saunders, Anthony and Ingo Walter (eds.) *Universal Banking: Financial System Design Reconsidered* (Chicago et al. 1996).

Scheffler, Eberhard (ed.) *Corporate Governance* (Wiesbaden 1995).

Schmidt, Hartmut, Jochen Drukarczyk, Dirk Honold, Stefan Prigge, Andreas Schüler, and Gönke Tetens *Corporate Governance in Germany* (Baden-Baden 1997).

Scholtens, Bert 'Bank- and Market-Oriented Financial Systems: Fact or Fiction?' *Banca Nazionale del Lavoro* 50 (1997) 301-23.

Sheard, Paul (ed.) *Japanese Firms, Finance and Markets* (Melbourne 1996).

Sheikh, Saleem and William Rees (eds.) *Corporate Governance & Corporate Control* (London 1995).

Shleifer, Andrei and Robert W. Vishny 'A Survey of Corporate Governance' *Journal of Finance* 52 (1997) 737-83.

Short, Helen 'Ownership, Control, Financial Structure and the Performance of Firms' *Journal of Economic Surveys* 8 (1994) 203-49.

Tricker, Robert I. *International Corporate Governance: Text, Readings, and Cases* (New York 1994).

Wiendieck, Markus *Unternehmensfinanzierung und Kontrolle durch Banken: Deutschland—Japan—USA* (Dissertation University of Cologne) (Wiesbaden 1992).

Windolf, Paul and Jürgen Beyer 'Kooperativer Kapitalismus. Unternehmensverflechtungen im internationalen Vergleich' *Kölner Zeitschrift für Soziologie und Sozialpsychologie* 47 (1995) 1-36.

Wirtschaftsprüferkammer-Mitteilungen 'Special Issue: Rechnungslegung und Abschlußprüfung in globalen Kapitalmärkten/Financial Accounting and Auditing in Global Capital Markets' (1997).

Wymeersch, Eddy 'Elements of Comparative Corporate Governance in Western Europe' in: Isaksson, Mats and Rolf Skog (eds.) *Aspects of Corporate Governance* 83-116 (Stockholm 1994).

Country Index*

---

* See also separate Subject Index.

Subject Index*

accounting 544 *see also* FASB; IAS; IPOs: and accounting standards; *Konzerne*: accounting of; lenders: and accounting; U.S. GAAP; Germany: 988-9; Japan: 937; Switzerland: 821-3
  basic assumptions FASB: 745; Germany: 745-7, 999; IAS: 745; Japan: 937
  and corporate governance 723-6, 998-9
  driving forces of internationalization Germany: 990, 1000-1
  empirical evidence Germany: 999-1000; U.S.: 999-1000
  EU 754-5
  IAS vs. German standards 732
  legislatory reform Germany: 744 n. 2, 747-9, 1026-7
  management report Germany: 747
  regulation of 1188
  tax accounting Germany: 745-7
  U.S. vs. German standards 730-2, 1000
agency problems 850-1, 907, 945-7
  creditors and managers 853-4
  customer/supplier relation 855-6, 867
  government and company 856-7; Japan: 862-3, 863-4, 867, 868, 871
  shareholders and managers 851-2, 886-7, 945-7
  workers and managers 854-5, 857-8, 867 *see also* co-determination: and agency theory; employees: role in corporate governance
amakudari (Japan) 862, 863-4
auditing *see also* management board: and auditor; supervisory board: and auditor
  accounting auditor Japan: 936-7
  appointment of auditors Germany: 749-50, 996
  and corporate governance 736
  duties of auditors Germany: 737-9, 749-51, 997; Japan: 924-5; U.S.: 737-9
  incentives of auditors 736-7, 997-8
  legislatory reform (Germany) 751-2; *see also* KonTraG

auditing continued
  statutory auditors Japan: 924-5, 926-8, 936-7
  U.S. Generally Accepted Auditing Standards 737-8
bankruptcy 864, 867
bankruptcy law 867, 1015 *see also* lenders: lender liability; France: 770-3, 777; Germany: 776-7, 778; U.S.: 773-5, 778
  and contractual lending arrangements 776, 780
  costs of 769-70; France: 776, 779; Germany: 776, 779; U.S.: 776, 779
banks
  and corporate monitoring 458-60, 461-3, 472-9, 523; Japan: 940-1
  and financial linkage *see also* banks: as shareholders; Germany: 457, 971, 975
  general meetings of Germany: 983
  German banks and corporate governance 482-4, 523-4, 1020-4
  Hauptbank (Switzerland) *see* banks: main banks
  Hausbank (Germany) *see* banks: main banks
  hidden reserves in equity holdings Germany: 460, 467, 467-70, 471-2, 476
  house banks 789; Switzerland: 821 *see also* banks: main banks
  information Germany: 453
  as lenders 458-9, 461-3, 617-20 *see also* lenders; Germany: 454, 465-6, 480-1, 1017, 1018-9, 1020, 1020-4; Japan: 938-40, 1017; U.K.: 1017; U.S.: 1017
  main banks 791-3; Germany: 793, 1019 n. 417; Japan: 793, 860-1, 886, 892, 893-4, 897, 940; Sweden: 789-90, 797-8, 799-804, 804-6; Switzerland: 821, 825
  and managment board turnover Germany: 480, 1020-4
  and proxy voting Austria: 550; Germany: 539-40, 556, 565, 644, 981-3, 984, 986, 1020-4; Nether-

---

* See also separate Country Index.